Baseball Weekly
1997 Almanac

Everything the baseball fan needs — all in one book

Edited by
Paul White
Editor, *Baseball Weekly*

With contributions from
the staffs of *Baseball Weekly*
and USA TODAY Sports

Project Editor, John M. Shostrom

A Balliett & Fitzgerald Book

An Owl Book
Henry Holt and Company
New York

Henry Holt and Company, Inc.
Publishers since 1866
115 West 18th Street
New York, New York 10011

Henry Holt® is a registered trademark
of Henry Holt and Company, Inc.

Published in Canada by Fitzhenry & Whiteside Ltd.,
195 Allstate Parkway, Markham, Ontario L3R 4T8.

ISSN: 1091-7071

ISBN 0-8050-5147-3

Henry Holt books are available for special promotions and premiums.
For details contact: Director, Special Markets.

First Edition—1997

Printed in the United States of America
All first editions are printed on acid-free paper. ∞

10 9 8 7 6 5 4 3 2 1

Balliett & Fitzgerald, Inc.
Managing editor: Duncan Bock
Production editor: Sue Canavan
Assistant editor: Maria Fernandez
Project coordinator: Michelle Mattox
Copyeditor: Roger Mooney
Proofreader: Kevin Kerr
Editorial assistant: Manena Frazier
Fact checking: Ed H. Foley

Acknowledgments
We would like to thank Keith Cutler for making this possible, as well as
Kevin Ohe, Susan Mayoralgo, Russell Beeker, Greg Frazier, Steve Borell
and Mary Kay Linge.

Major league statistics provided by Elias Sports Bureau.
Minor league statistics provided by Howe SportsData International.
Record book and historical statistics provided by Pete Palmer.
Disabled list information provided by The Baseball Workshop.
Photographs of Major League Baseball are used with the permission of
Major League Baseball.

Contents

Leading off
Introduction. 5

Around the leagues
Issues, news, opinions, obituaries. 7

NL/AL beat
1996 league wrap-ups, All-Star Game, league leaders 29

Postseason
1996 NL and AL Division Series, Championship Series,
World Series, box scores, statistics. 39

For the record
Historical records. 57

Major league report
Every team's 1996 player statistics, disabled list,
directory, 1997 preview, and more. 77
American League East 78
American League Central. 118
American League West. 158
National League East. 190
National League Central 230
National League West 270
1996 Final team statistics. 302

League forecasts
1997 preview 303

Final player statistics
Listed alphabetically by position 311

Minor league report
League wrap-ups, final player statistics, leaders. 335

Youth leagues
Little League, features, championship results, listings 379

High school/college/Olympics
The best teams, the hottest prospects. 385

Nostalgia
Features, profiles 393

Leading off

▶*Baseball Weekly*
editor Paul White:
Now it's my turn to
ask the questions

USA SNAPSHOTS®

A look at statistics that shape the sports world

New age for baseball fans

Breakdown, by age, of adults attending major league baseball games this year and expected audience by 2005:

18-24: 14% (1996), 15% (2005)
25-34: 23% (1996), 20% (2005), 28% (2005)
35-44: 25%
45-54: 18%, 21%
55-64: 8%, 10%
65 and older: 9%, 9%

☐ 1996
▧ 2005

Note: Might exceed 100% due to rounding

Source: Mediamark Research

By Cindy Hall and Kevin Rechin, USA TODAY

Now it's my turn to ask the questions

It was somehow appropriate that the importance of what had happened in baseball finally hit home on Thanksgiving. A labor agreement had been in place for a whole two days after what had seemed an eternity of waiting for common sense and responsibility to prevail. Thanksgiving—it was the first day I had spent with my wife's family in four years that not once did my mother-in-law ask either "Are they ever going to settle that baseball mess?" or "Do you think they could have another strike?"

The sudden change began to sink in. No questions about labor contracts. About strikes. About owners. Not from talk-show hosts, fans or in-laws. Not a single soul asked. Ahhhhh, so wonderful.

And though nobody has asked me, I have a few questions of my own. Not about labor. About baseball. About this coming full 1997 season:

How many teams will borrow Mark Whiten this year?

Will the White Sox's Jerry Reinsdorf or the Marlins' Wayne Huizenga be more disappointed by his team's attendance?

Would anyone really be shocked if the Disneyland Angels hired Mickey Hatcher and Minnie Minoso as coaches?

Will the Twins promote catcher Jose Valentin, brother of the Brewers' Jose Valentin, to really confuse us? And would they dare trade for John Valentin?

Is Rocky Coppinger this year's Andy Pettitte?

Who's going to play the practical jokes in the White Sox clubhouse?

Will Pirates outfielder Al Martin know anybody at spring training?

Is Terry Francona's best qualification for managing this year's Phillies his having spent last year coaching the Tigers?

Will new Marlins manager Jim Leyland ask Bobby Bonilla to DH in games at American League parks?

Is 1997's Opening Day being played on Tuesday to avoid its conflicting with the Final Four?

Who really thinks a little thing like a rotator cuff can keep the Padres' Ken Caminiti off the field?

Got your tickets yet for the Royals-Pirates series?

Has Pat Gillick met all of Peter Angelos's relatives, or will more magically appear in the Orioles' offices?

Where in the *world* can they put expansion teams in 2002?

Exactly what will Bob Watson do to get fired by George Steinbrenner?

Oh yeah, Paul Molitor, can you get 225 hits and steal 18 bases again at age 41?

Can we realign? Or does Tampa Bay just get stuck in the AL West?

Will those "fan-friendly" White Sox continue to chip away at the ballpark time for organist and Chicago icon Nancy Faust?

How many more years will Cardinals reliever T.J. Mathews have to wait for Dennis Eckersley to get old?

Would the commissioner-searchers consider Philadelphia mayor Ed Rendell, a no-nonsense guy who knows the game inside-out and loves it even more?

If the improving Brewers get into the wild-card race, can we put a moratorium on the word "overachievers" and just give them credit?

Does new Royals DH Chili Davis realize that all of the 17 DHs used by Kansas City last year also played the field, 13 of them played at least two positions, five played three positions and four played four positions?

Will Carlos Baerga bring his usual bodyguard-driver entourage to Mets training camp?

More important, will Baerga bring a body that doesn't need two guards?

Will all the little people who were laid off during the strike ever find jobs in baseball again?

Do they want to?

Will Players Association executive director Don Fehr stick around for the next march toward Armageddon? (Sorry, I couldn't go cold turkey. Purging the mind of labor stuff isn't easy.)

—*by Paul White, editor*

Around the leagues

▶**1996 highlights and lowlights**

▶**AL and NL award winners**

▶**Hall of Fame inductees**

▶**Obituaries**

▶*and more ...*

USA SNAPSHOTS®

A look at statistics that shape the sports world

'Juiced' balls or 'lite' pitching?

More than one in three baseball fans think this year's scoring barrage is due to pitching talent spread thinner by expansion. Fans' top theories[1]:

Expansion diluting pitching	38%
Umps shrinking strike zone	21%
Owner conspiracy[2]	17%
Hitters bigger, stronger	11%
More new, smaller stadiums	6%
Ball wound tighter	5%
Having team in Colorado	2%

1 – Survey of 1,336 fans on the Internet
2 – Game being tinkered with to raise scoring, draw fans

Source: ESPNET SportsZone

By Scott Boeck and Marcia Staimer, USA TODAY

Labor peace! Owners change their minds

It took baseball owners more than four years to come up with a five-year plan. But despite acting commissioner Bud Selig's hopeful insistence that the game was on the verge of a "very powerful recovery," the timetable for a turnaround from a labor war that included the longest and costliest work stoppage in pro sports history is still unclear.

In ratifying the labor agreement they had voted down just three weeks before, owners agreed to give up the fight—both with the players' union and among themselves. "We just took a hard look at it and agreed it was in everyone's best interest to get this over with," said Baltimore Orioles owner Peter Angelos.

Not that it was a defeat. The conciliatory remarks by both owners and union officials indicated this truly was a compromise. By getting the players to agree to a luxury tax on salaries, the owners obtained a concession that would have been unthinkable four years ago. Even Marvin Miller, who retired undefeated and untied as union chief in 1982, had expressed reservations about the deal in recent months. At the same time, the players did not give in to a salary cap or any other severe drag on salaries, and they successfully held out to receive service time from the strike. Other partial winners included low-revenue teams such as the Pittsburgh Pirates, the Montreal Expos and the Kansas City Royals, who will receive at least some help in the revenue-sharing department even if they still will not be on equal footing with their high-revenue counterparts.

And then there are the fans, who will be able to look forward to uninterrupted baseball at least through the year 2000, and possibly through 2001. They will also be able to look forward to interleague play, beginning next year, and perhaps to a new commissioner.

Even Selig and Chicago White Sox owner Jerry Reinsdorf—the owners most responsible for the work stoppage—emerged on a positive note after rallying enough votes to pass the agreement by an overwhelming 26-4 margin. "The hero is Bud Selig," said management negotiator Randy Levine, who hammered out the deal with Players Association executive director Donald Fehr. "I thought his job of leadership was one of the most extraordinary I have ever seen."

Selig had rallied owners against the labor deal during a vote in Chicago on Nov. 6. The deal, which required approval by three-quarters of baseball's owners, failed by an 18-12 margin. But Reinsdorf's subsequent signing of Albert Belle to a five-year, $55 million deal outraged many owners. And although Reinsdorf insists that the Belle signing had little to do with the result of the re-vote, many teams clearly were troubled by the eye-popping salaries given in recent weeks to Belle, John Smoltz (four years, $31 million by the Atlanta Braves) and Bobby Bonilla (four years, $23.3 million by the Florida Marlins). After the first vote, Selig met with Fehr, who would not budge on the deal he had crafted with Levine. Owners had projected losses, on average, of at least $100 million a year over the course of the proposed deal. But Levine told them during the Nov. 6 meeting that the alternative of not accepting the deal could result in heavier losses.

In weeks before the agreement, baseball seemed on the verge of another nuclear winter. In August, owners considered asking federal district court judge Sonia Sotomayor to lift the injunction of March 1995 that restored the terms of baseball's expired collective bargaining agreement and led the players to end their 232-day strike. That, in turn, would have allowed the owners to make another attempt to declare an impasse in bargaining and impose their own labor system, perhaps after this season. All of which might have led to another strike by the players. Instead, Selig got enough votes to pass the labor agreement. "When you look at all the alternatives, whether you like all the parts or not, it was the right thing to do," said Jerry Colangelo, owner of the expansion Arizona Diamondbacks, who are scheduled to begin play in 1998.

If future historians look at the events in Chicago as the beginning of the sport's recovery, they might look further back to Sept. 6, 1995, when Cal Ripken Jr. broke Lou Gehrig's record for consecutive games played. A memorable 1995 postseason that included expanded playoffs and wild-card teams led to a lucrative new televison contract with NBC and Fox. In some places, attendance began to head upward this season, but overall it has yet to reach the pre-strike levels of 1994.

The labor agreement rescued interleague play and assured that teams would play at least 15 games against opponents in corresponding divisions in '97—16 games in the case of the American League West and National League West divisions. The Arizona Diamondbacks and the Tampa Bay Devil Rays will be assigned to different leagues, with Arizona joining the NL. Interleague play will be necessary with an odd number of teams in each league, a first in this century. The owners have the authority to add two more expansion franchises by 1999, in time for the 2002 season. Likely candidates include Charlotte, N.C.; Northern Virginia; and either Mexico City or Monterrey.

With the restoration of service time, the approval of the deal added 14 free agents to the marketplace, including White Sox right-hander Alex Fernandez, outfielder Moises Alou of the Montreal Expos and Oakland A's shortstop Mike Bordick.

The owners hope expansion, interleague play and baseball's business relationships with youth marketers like Fox will help transform the game from a stodgy, middle-aged "pastime" into a hip, youth-oriented league like the NFL or NBA. That won't be easy. Baseball went nearly two years without a marketing chief and owners have yet to embrace the efforts of Greg Murphy, who earlier this year became CEO of the reorganized MLB Enterprises. Murphy has said that he has $500 million of potential sponsorship deals that could be consummated with a labor agreement. One, a Nike/Reebok deal worth $325 million over 10 years, blew up in November when owners turned it down.

Even though sponsors now are assured of labor peace at least through the year 2000, most marketing plans include long lead times that might make implementation for the '97 season difficult. "Unless somebody had developed a promotion for '97 and literally is ready to push the button to make it roll, it would be highly unlikely they'd jump on the bandwagon immediately," said Rick White, former head of MLB Properties, who now runs Strategic Merchandising Associates. "The clubs I talk to are unaware of impending deals."

One hang-up among clubs is a reluctance to sacrifice their local marketing ties for the good of a group effort. There's also talk of joint business projects with the Players Association, with the cooperative efforts of the NBA and NFL as the model. As with the labor battle, the marketing and growth of the game hinges on revenue sharing and joint operations. Those are words not usually associated with baseball people. But the new agreement might be a sign that baseball is ready to move forward in a united front.

—by Pete Williams

Alomar-Hirschbeck incident spotlights player-umpire tensions

Emotions were high as Baltimore visited Toronto on the final weekend of the regular season. The Orioles' magic number for clinching the American League wild-card berth was down to two after they won the opener of the four-game series. According to several sources, this is what happened in the first inning of the Sept. 27 game:

Orioles second baseman Roberto Alomar was called out on a third strike that replays showed was several inches outside. He turned to umpire John Hirschbeck and said, "You can't call that a strike."

Hirschbeck: "It was a strike."

Alomar: "It was outside."

Hirschbeck: "Do your job. Swing the bat."

Alomar: "I'll do my job. You do yours."

Hirschbeck, 42, an American League umpire since 1984, warned Alomar, 28, not to say anything more or risk an ejection. Alomar returned to the dugout, but when Hirschbeck heard more complaining, he ejected Alomar. The second baseman stormed back out, with Orioles manager Davey Johnson in pursuit. Alomar and Hirschbeck exchanged profanities, a not-uncommon occurrence in the heat of a baseball argument. Johnson asked Hirschbeck why he tossed Alomar. Hirschbeck, who is reputed to be among the more confrontational umpires, reportedly replied, "He's a f— a—."

An enraged Alomar spat into the umpire's face before he was hauled away. After the game, Alomar said Hirschbeck had gotten "real bitter" since the death of his seven-year-old son, John, in 1993 from a disease called adrenoleukodystrophy (ALD). Another of Hirschbeck's four children suffers from ALD as well.

Also after the game, Hirschbeck insisted he did not call Alomar a name. "Of course, [Alomar]'s going to say that I called him a name. Let's say I did. There's still no excuse for him."

Hirschbeck, upon hearing the next day of Alomar's remarks about his son, stormed into the visitors' clubhouse and said he would "kill" Alomar. He had to be restrained before he reached the player's locker.

After initially denying that he had anything to apologize for, Alomar issued a statement of apology on Sept. 30. In his two-page statement Alomar called his conduct "indefensible" and said he would never repeat it. "I wish to take this opportunity to apologize to John Hirschbeck and his family for any pain and embarrassment that my comments and actions may have caused them," Alomar said. "I deeply regret my disrespectful conduct towards a man that I know always gives his utmost as an umpire." Alomar and the Orioles pledged to contribute $50,000 each toward the research of ALD at Johns Hopkins University and the Kennedy Kreiger Institute.

"While I understand that this gesture in no way excuses or mitigates my conduct, I do hope that it demonstrates my honest concern and complete remorse for what has happened," Alomar said in the statement. He said he would apologize in person at Hirschbeck's convenience. On Oct. 5, Hirschbeck forgave Alomar, noting his apology and saying it was time to bring closure to the matter.

But Alomar's statement wasn't enough for Hirschbeck's peers. "What Alomar did was reprehensible," said umpires union president Jerry Crawford, an NL umpire. "They think the apology ends it. But that doesn't make up for it." The umpires voted on the night of Sept. 30 to boycott the Division Series if Alomar were to take the field for Baltimore, but Major League Baseball got a federal court order to force the umpires to work; the umpires had agreed to a five-year deal in May 1995 that included a no-strike clause.

Even though U.S. District Judge Edmund Ludwig was legally bound to force the umpires to return to work, he offered strong comments indicating that he was on their side philosophically. He called Alomar's actions "assaultive and outrageous behavior."

American League president Gene Budig had given Alomar a five-game regular-season suspension (the last two games of 1996 and the first three in 1997), but Alomar appealed. He was allowed to play on Sept. 28 and hit the 10th-inning home run that clinched Baltimore's wild-card spot. Alomar later hit a 12th-inning home run in Game 4 to clinch the O's Division Series win over the Indians, but he hit only .217 and committed a crucial error in Baltimore's ALCS loss to the Yankees. In both road stadiums he was booed incessantly.

Alomar eventually dropped the appeal and accepted the suspension for 1997, but the umpires were infuriated that it did not take effect during the playoffs, and they are afraid of what they've seen in other sports. "If you've watched professional sports through the years, if you've watched what happened in the NBA last year with the official [Ron Garretson] being attacked [by the Lakers' Nick Van Exel], then this [Roberto Alomar] situation here, pretty soon we're going to be like English soccer," AL umpire Ken Kaiser said, "where if you don't like the game, you shoot the official."

American League crew chief Jim Evans, who is in his 26th season in the league, agreed. "There are certain safety factors that come into play in our jobs," he said. "I've seen what happens in soccer when fans stampede the field. Fans reflect the behavior of the players. Some of these things have to be addressed."

The sport's powers listened. A meeting was planned that was to include representatives of the players' and umpires' associations, as well as the two league presidents and acting commissioner Bud Selig. They will attempt to draw up a formal code of on-field conduct and explore ways to improve player-umpire relations. "This will give us the opportunity to alleviate certain tensions among on-field participants," Selig said in October.

The Alomar incident has galvanized the

Johnson held back Alomar after the ejection.

umpires' resolve and helped them raise the sport's consciousness of their stressful situation. "We are one fraternity. We are a very proud fraternity," Evans said. "There's a lot of integrity in this business, and we are very upset at what has happened to one of our brothers as an umpire."

Though stymied in their legal battle, the men in blue won a nearly unanimous verdict in the court of public opinion. When the six-man crew took the field for Game 3 of the Baltimore-Cleveland series, they received a standing ovation from 44,000 fans at Jacobs Field.

Many longtime baseball people say there is a widening gulf between players and umpires. "I don't think there is as much respect either way as there was 10 years ago," said former AL Cy Young Award winner Mike Flanagan, now an Orioles broadcaster. "The players seem more demanding of the umpires, and there's less patience on the side of the umpires."

—*by Bill Koenig*

Bidding adieu to Dodger blue

By Anne Ryan, USA TODAY

Tommy Lasorda retired after 20 years as manager of the Dodgers.

He brought Hollywood to Chavez Ravine and claimed to bleed Dodger blue. He served as baseball's head cheerleader and unofficial ambassador, but in retiring from baseball because of health concerns and a desire to spend more time with his family, Tommy Lasorda left behind a career sometimes criticized as more style than substance.

No one can deny the bottom line: After 20 seasons as Dodgers manager, Lasorda exited the game with 1,613 wins, seven division titles, four National League pennants and two World Series championships.

Lasorda, 69, underwent an angioplasty procedure on June 26, two days after he had suffered a heart attack. He said on July 29 that he was medically cleared to return but realized it made sense to retire. "For me to get into a uniform again—as excitable as I am—I could not continue," said Lasorda, who was made a Dodgers vice president of development in Arizona, Florida and the Dominican Republic. "I decided it's best for me and the organization to step down."

Since Lasorda took over for Walter Alston in 1976, the Dodgers have become one of Tinseltown's longest-running hits; in 1996 they drew more than 3 million fans for a record 11th time. Along the way, Lasorda became a Hollywood figure. His clubhouse office became a haven for singers, musicians and movie-industry people. On the field, Lasorda's energy level was unparalleled. He was still pitching batting practice when he was hospitalized in June.

His Dodgers won the World Series over the New York Yankees in the strike-interrupted 1981 season, and he engineered one of baseball's biggest post-season upsets in 1988, leading L.A. to a five-game World Series victory against the heavily favored Oakland A's. In recent years, critics charged that the game had passed him by and wondered if his reliance on motivation rather than strategy worked with Generation X players. But the team's executive vice president, Fred Claire, summed up the skipper's legacy, saying, "You cannot say 'Dodgers' without thinking of Tommy."

—by Pete Williams

Curtain falls on the Kirby era

Kirby Puckett's absence hung like a cloud over the All-Star Game in Philadelphia. Cal Ripken, Ken Griffey Jr. and others in the American League All-Star clubhouse commented that it didn't seem the same without "Puck" around.

In 1992, in San Diego, when Griffey was making his third All-Star appearance and Puckett his seventh, the Mariners' superstar reluctantly asked who was going to play center field, he or Puckett? After all, both of them had been voted to the starting outfield. It was Puckett who made the decision easy for Griffey and the Twins' Tom Kelly, that year's All-Star manager. "You take center," Puckett told Griffey during the workout day. "You're younger than me. You still like to run. Remember, anything in the gap is yours."

With that, what could have been a troublesome issue was settled. That's how Puckett did things: with a minimum of ego and a dash of self-effacing humor. Even though he was worth millions when vision problems forced him to retire in mid-July, he still played the game as if he was just happy to be in the majors.

At 5-foot-9 and 223 pounds, with an expressive, pie-shaped face, Puckett did not have a superstar's build. Still, he ranked among the most feared hitters and best defensive center fielders. Puckett retired with a .318 average in 12 seasons, all with the Twins. He is Minnesota's career leader in hits (2,304), doubles (414), total bases (3,453), at-bats (7,244) and runs (1,071). He hit 207 career home runs and had 1,085 RBI, with 10 All-Star Game appearances. A mainstay of the Twins' world championship teams of 1987 and 1991, Puckett could dominate big games like few players dare dream about. In Game 6 of the '91 World Series, he made a game-saving catch in center field. Then, in the 11th inning, he won the game with a dramatic home run.

Puckett, 35, awoke on March 28, 1996, with a large black dot at the center of the field of vision in his right eye. First, doctors attempted to treat him with blood-thinning medication to lower the pressure in the eye. That was followed up with three laser surgeries. On July 12, specialist Bert Glaser of the Retina Institute in Baltimore wanted to remove bloody fluid from Puckett's eye. But the damage to the retina was too severe to proceed, and glaucoma was also found in Puckett's left eye, though his vision in that eye still was 20/20.

After the examination in Baltimore, Puckett, whose vision was now 20/400 in his right eye, flew back to Minneapolis to give his teammates and Twin Cities fans the bad news. "The world is not over," said Puckett, with a bandage over his eye. "Baseball has been a great part of my life. Now I have to close this chapter and go on with part two of my life."

The dismay over Puckett's retirement was not confined to Minnesota. "He had that happy spirit and enthusiasm he brought to the park every day," said first baseman Cecil Fielder, then with the Tigers. "To lose a champion like that is not good." Added veteran teammate Paul Molitor, "There are few players I've seen who always receive a positive response at visiting ballparks," he said. "Nolan Ryan, Cal Ripken and Kirby."

Through the titles and the last-place finishes, the Twins' stocky center fielder never carried himself higher than the game. A smile rarely disappeared from his face. He is sorely missed.

—by Tim Wendel

Wizard of Oz bows out in Atlanta

By Robert Hanashiro, USA TODAY

Ozzie Smith had his farewell in the NLCS.

Ozzie Smith's favorite play of his 19 seasons came against the Atlanta Braves. So did the unhappy ending to one of baseball's feel-good careers. "Anybody who has any competitive bone in their body doesn't want it to end that way," Smith said after what was most likely his final major league appearance.

In the decisive game of the National League Championship Series, Smith, 41, lifted a fly ball into foul territory at Atlanta Fulton County Stadium that Braves right fielder Jermaine Dye caught easily. The pinch-hitting appearance was hardly significant, coming as it did in the fifth inning of an Atlanta rout that was already 10-0, except that the twig-like magician known as The Wizard received standing ovations before and after the at-bat. After the game, Smith said, "That's how it's been for me around baseball the last two months."

The Braves had eliminated the Cardinals in an excruciating seven-game series. Ozzie was in his trademark *GQ*-level street clothes, a small suitcase zipped tight next to his clubhouse stall, uniform No. 1 in a trunk for the return flight to St. Louis. Smith's next baseball reservations, though, should be for Cooperstown. He'll be up for Hall of Fame election in 2002, assuming that this really was his final game. He left his glove in the door. "If I choose to [come back], that's my right," Smith said.

Smith was as eager to get out the clubhouse door as he was reluctant to rule out playing again. But Cardinals owners were working their way through the room, thanking players for an exciting season. When they finally found Ozzie coming from a room off the clubhouse, the emotional embrace attracted camera crews and reporters. By the time Smith was able to work his way back to his locker, National League president Leonard Coleman appeared to offer his own private words and a hug.

Smith had dealt with the attention for much of the season, since confirming his expected retirement plans in a press conference on June 19. From the emotional ovation at the All-Star Game in Philadelphia, through stops at virtually every stadium in the NL, and to the crowning moment of Ozzie Smith Day, on Sept. 28 in St. Louis, he's been the center of attention.

The major league record holder for career double plays and assists by a shortstop, Smith won 13 consecutive Gold Gloves from 1980 to '92. Twice he tied the NL record for fielding percentage in a season (.987). At the plate, one of his 29 career home runs even won a crucial 1985 playoff game against the Dodgers.

Through those 2,573 regular season and 14 All-Star games, he became The Wizard not so much for his consistent defensive excellence as for his often spectacular plays. In Smith's view, defensive gem No. 1 came just a few games into his career. It was April 20, 1978, Smith's rookie season with the Padres, four years before the Cardinals acquired him from San Diego for shortstop Garry Templeton. In the fourth inning, the Braves' Jeff Burroughs grounded a ball through the middle. As Smith dived to his left, the ball caromed unexpectedly into the air. Ozzie reached up, grabbed the ball barehanded and threw out Burroughs at first base.

Because Ozzie has played in the age of replays and highlight reels, most fans can cite their own favorites. As Smith said with understatement before walking out the clubhouse door, "It's been a great 19 years."

—*by Paul White*

1997 BASEBALL WEEKLY ALMANAC

Mexico passes the litmus test

The San Diego Padres, forced to leave San Diego during the Republican National Convention, won two of three games from the New York Mets in their home away from home in Monterrey, Mexico, on the weekend of Aug. 16-18—but the real winner was Mexico. The series, the first regular-season games ever played outside of the United States and Canada, was a historic first step in the eventual expansion of Major League Baseball to Mexico.

"There's got to be a first, and this is it," says Padres owner John Moores. "I'm not sure this is a test for Monterrey, but if it is, a lot of things look very good. The ballpark is OK. The fans are very knowledgeable. Monterrey didn't fail." The pregame atmosphere at El Estadio Monterrey was much like that at a playoff. There were more than 200 accredited reporters, and the games were televised throughout Mexico and Central and South America.

While none of the three games was sold out, there were very few empty seats visible at Friday's opener. Fans delighted at the opportunity to see major league baseball were, nonetheless, somewhat subdued. "It was more like a World Series crowd with a lot of people who don't normally go to the ballpark and are not quite sure how to act," noted Roland Hemond, senior executive vice president of baseball operations for the Arizona Diamondbacks.

They did, however, cheer returning national hero Fernando Valenzuela. In Friday's game, the Padres' Valenzuela pitched six shutout innings before leaving with a 15-1 lead in the seventh. A standing crowd showered him with chants of "Toro" as he tipped his cap.

While the Padres and Monterrey officials had made more than $100,000 in changes to the stadium, including additional lighting, fielders on both teams were having problems seeing the ball. Other players complained about the field being too hard, the grass too short or the temperature too hot. But most appreciated the enthusiasm of the fans and focused on what they came to do. "I think everybody on the team was just trying to get down and play baseball," says Padres outfielder Steve Finley. "We just had to put all the hoopla aside."

Some players and coaches got out into the community: The Padres' Archi Cianfrocco signed autographs at the mall, several Padres players and coaches visited an orphanage, and Mets coaches and infielders Carlos Baerga and Alvaro Espinoza put on a clinic for 1,200 Little Leaguers on Sunday morning. And for the Latin American players—three from the Padres and five from the Mets—it was like being back at home. "I am very happy to be here," says Venezuelan Roberto Petagine of the Mets. "It has been a very good experience. The hotel is nice, the park is fine and the fans are great. And it's good to be in Spanish-speaking country."

Jose "Pepe" Maiz, the popular owner of the stadium and the Mexican League champion Monterrey Sultanes, believes the Mexican economy is slowly growing and will be able to support an expansion club in a few years. Maiz is being joined in his efforts by another important figure in Mexican baseball, Juan Manuel Ley. He owns current Caribbean Series champion Culiacan of the Mexican Pacific League. "I'm talking with Pepe about a joint venture to make an application for a team here in Monterrey," says Ley. "We are thinking of having a team here in three to five years."

The Mexicans' timetable seems perfectly acceptable to National League president Leonard Coleman. "I'm not talking about tomorrow, or the next day, or within a year," he said. "But soon Monterrey will have a major league ballclub."

—by Milton Jamail, professor of Latin American politics at the University of Texas

Baseball maps a global strategy

As pitching coach for the Los Angeles Dodgers, Dave Wallace is finding out that linguistic skills are just as important as the ability to teach a breaking ball or to judge when it's time for a pitcher to come out of the game. On the first day of spring training, Wallace greeted his pitchers in four languages by saying "Good morning" in English, Spanish, Japanese and Korean. "And in case you think pitching coaches have it easy," Wallace told the group, "repeat it back to me."

It is no secret that the Dodgers clubhouse long has seemed like a gate area at an international airport, a room full of players from far-flung places. But with the addition of Japanese star Hideo Nomo in 1995, and with the permanent arrival of Korean right-hander Chan Ho Park this year, the Los Angeles clubhouse has become a virtual Tower of Babel.

When Ramon Martinez, a native of the Dominican Republic, suffered a torn groin muscle on April 6 and was replaced in the rotation by Park, the Dodgers had a true "United Nations" rotation of Nomo, Pedro Astacio (Dominican Republic), Tom Candiotti (USA), Park and Ismael Valdes (Mexico). Of the 294 players in the Dodgers organization, 133 (45%) hail from outside the USA.

Even though Major League Baseball remains a strictly North American affair, scouting is quickly becoming a high-stakes international competition. "I don't know if anyone has a leg up anymore," says Atlanta Braves general manager John Schuerholz, whose staff has signed such international players as World Series star Andruw Jones (Netherlands Antilles) and Glenn Williams (Australia). "The fact is that the entire industry is looking to the far corners of the globe for international players."

The major leagues had four Latin American players in 1950, but by '95 that number had increased to 160. "It's a reflection on how big the game has got-ten around the world," says Fred Claire, the Dodgers' executive vice president and general manager.

The San Diego Padres, who have aggressively targeted the Mexican fan base under their new ownership, hosted three games in August against the New York Mets in Monterrey. The Seattle Mariners hope to begin the 1997 season in Japan, and the Florida Marlins have explored the possibility of playing regular-season games in Puerto Rico. The Boston Red Sox worked out a deal with the Hiroshima Carp of the Japanese League in which Boston will give cash or a player to be named later in exchange for pitcher Robinson Perez Checo—a Dominican.

Even the expansion Arizona Diamondbacks and Tampa Bay Devil Rays, who don't begin play until 1998, have combined to sign more than 50 Latin players, including Cuban-defectors-turned-Diamondbacks Vladimir Nunez and Larry Rodriguez. Why the internationalization now? One reason is that with baseball having become an official medal sport at the Olympics in Barcelona in 1992, foreign programs have pumped money into the sport, which has jump-started the development of talent.

The Dominican Republic, which contributed 75 major leaguers—including Moises Alou, Raul Mondesi and Sammy Sosa—to '95 rosters, continues to pump out prospects. But many personnel people are turning their attention to Venezuela, which has produced major leaguers such as Andres Galarraga, Ozzie Guillen and Omar Vizquel but is still relatively untapped. When the Houston Astros opened a baseball academy just outside of Valencia, Venezuela, in 1989, they were seen as pioneers. Now, the Astros have 20 legitimate prospects in their system as a result of the academy, with outfielders Bob Abreu and Richard Hidalgo and right-hander Oscar Henriquez likely to make it to the majors by 1998.

"We should be in position over the

next few years to add two or three guys a year," says David Rawnsley, the Astros' director of international development. "For us, it's like getting an additional first-round pick each year for significantly less risk."

"You see [foreign] players with bat speed and arm strength developed far beyond the level of U.S. teenagers," says Tommy Jones, the Arizona Diamondbacks' director of field operations. "They don't have TV and all the distractions that American kids do."

Nomo's arrival in 1995 gave hope that more players would be forthcoming from Japan. New York Mets manager Bobby Valentine, who managed in Japan in 1995, suggested there were at least 10 Japanese pitchers as good as or better than Nomo. "The pitchers are throwing faster, and the hitters are starting to show more power," said former big leaguer Jim Marshall, who has played and managed in Japan. "That will be a big plus if they get a chance to play here."

That remains a big if. Normally, a Japanese player cannot become a free agent until after his 10th season in the majors in Japan. Nomo had completed just five years with the Kintetsu Buffaloes, but the club did not put up much resistance when Nomo and his agent, Don Nomura, began negotiating with major league clubs.

Other players might encounter bigger stumbling blocks. The next Japanese player to enter the majors might be Hideki Irabu, 27, the hardest thrower in the Japanese League. The Padres have shown interest in Irabu, who can become a free agent after the 1997 season.

The signings of Cuban pitchers Livan Hernandez ($4.5 million, from Florida) and Osvaldo Fernandez ($3.2 million, from San Francisco) have led to further support of a worldwide draft, which would include all amateur players in the June draft and effectively prevent a repetition of what happened in the winter of 1996, when agent Joe Cubas shopped the pair around to the highest bidders. During the January 1996 owners meetings in Los Angeles, general managers agreed in principle to a worldwide draft

Hideo Nomo is the first Asian major league star.

and a plan that would place a cap on money spent on player development and scouting, which, like payrolls, varies widely by team.

Baseball's final frontier? Perhaps it's Europe, which experienced a huge boom in basketball following the 1992 Olympics and the popularity of the NBA's Dream Team. Surveys indicate increased European participation in baseball, and Brewers manager Phil Garner said the sport soon will benefit from the end of the Cold War. "I really think the next major impact will be [former] Eastern bloc countries," he said.

"I think we're just in the early stages of the internationalization of the game," Oakland GM Sandy Alderson said. "And I think the game will change significantly as we get players from Eastern Europe, Russia, China. I think eventually we'll end up with teams located outside North America."

—*by Pete Williams*

17

Players rate the fans: yea or nay

During each game, the Baltimore Orioles salute their patrons at Camden Yards with a scoreboard message proclaiming them "baseball's best fans." Apparently that is more than a marketing ploy. Orioles fans were also rated No. 1 in a *Baseball Weekly* survey of 249 major league players, as every one of the 131 American League players polled rated Orioles fans as either "very good" or "good." Cleveland and Colorado fans were right behind in player approval.

On the other hand, players said Pittsburgh and Montreal had the worst fans. Pirates fans were given a 32 percent "terrible" rating, while Expos fans were close at 31 percent. A group of players called Pittsburghers "a bunch of no-shows," although one loyal Pirates player said his city's fans were the best in sportsmanship.

Pittsburgh resident Thomas Perka, who attends 15 to 20 games a year at Three Rivers Stadium, says if 32 percent of the players think Pittsburgh fans are terrible, it can only be a reflection on the athletes. "As in anything in life, what you get out of something is only as good as what you put into it." People view the players as money-hungry, he said.

As for Montreal, players said Expos fans were clueless: "No hockey puck on the field," said one. "They don't know when to cheer," according to another. But a season-ticket-holder since the Expos came to Montreal in 1969 stepped up in defense of Olympic Stadium fans. "We're a hell of a lot noisier than fans in Toronto," said Jerry Price of Montreal.

Players have a love-hate relationship with New York Yankees fans. Bronx fans were rated very good by 26 percent of the players, but also terrible by 23 percent of the players. "Not only do they rag on opposing players, they rag on everybody else," said St. Louis infielder Luis Alicea, who spent 1995 with the Red Sox. "They even rag on your family."

American League players tended to be less critical of fans than were their NL counterparts. Fans of all but four AL teams—Detroit, Milwaukee, Oakland and California—received at least a 60 percent favorable rating (combining good with very good), but only seven NL teams scored that high.

A whopping 81 percent of American League players polled rated Orioles fans as very good. "They're very aware of not only the home team, but the visitors' statistics and history," said Kansas City Royals closer Jeff Montgomery.

It was a sentiment echoed over and over. Players continually used words such as "classy"and "knowledgeable" to describe spectators at Camden Yards. "They cheer a great play, even if the visiting team makes it," Boston Red Sox pitcher Aaron Sele said.

Colorado Rockies fans ranked first in the National League. Eighty-five percent of 118 National League players rated Rockies fans as very good. Only 2 percent rated them as "poor," and they received nary a terrible vote. "When there are two outs in the ninth inning, and all those people stand up, you can feel the mound shaking," Rockies pitcher Curtis Leskanic said. "It's so loud, you wouldn't believe it. You're right in the middle of everything, and people are standing up and cheering," he said. "It's the most awesome feeling in the world. You feel like a rock star, because everybody is there to watch you."

Players see a dramatic improvement in Cleveland fans now that the club has moved from Cleveland Stadium to Jacobs Field. Cleveland fans are now rated 72 percent very good, 26 percent good and 2 percent poor. "Everyone is into the ballgame," Seattle pitcher Rusty Meacham said. "They just go crazy there. They're into every pitch, every hit. I would have said they were the worst three years ago."

Milwaukee fans, who received a 64 percent negative rating, were called "brutal" and "rude." Several Angels players recalled a particularly rough weekend series in 1995 when a "crazy guy jumped into the bullpen and challenged relievers

Red Sox fan Tim Donovan yelled at Cleveland's Albert Belle during a Fenway Park game.

to a fight." During that same series, Angels designated hitter Chili Davis poked a fan he thought was heckling him. It turned out to be the wrong fan, and Davis was fined $5,000 by the American League.

Boston had a 77 percent positive rating, but Fenway fans were low on some players' lists because fans have thrown things at them in the past. One Chicago Cubs pitcher says he had small vodka bottles—the type served on airlines—thrown at him in Boston when he was in the American League.

Who has the least enthusiastic fans? "Kansas City," stated former Royals pitcher Tom Gordon, now with the Red Sox. "They don't say [bleep] either way."

In the National League, Chicago Cubs fans are right up there among the best, with a 95 percent positive response from players. Former Cubs star Andre Dawson, now with the Florida Marlins, explained why. "I think with Harry Caray being the Pied Piper, and Chicago being a major tourist center, the tourists and everybody else want to visit Wrigley Field and experience the excitement," he said. "The Bleacher Bums, they're the ones who create that excitement there. It makes that ballpark sort of overwhelming for players."

Rangers pitcher John Burkett agreed. "They are knowledgeable, and they're having fun, whether the Cubs are winning or not," he said. "They get there so early, too.

They get thousands of fans for batting practice." Several San Diego players said they were impressed by Cubs fans when they gave Tony Gwynn a rousing ovation for going 5-for-5 one day at Wrigley Field.

The Atlanta Braves also ranked high—95 percent positive comments and just 5 percent negative responses—but several Chicago Cubs players said Atlanta fans were "front-runners."

The notorious Philadelphia boo birds of unhappiness did not go unnoticed. "They'd boo their mothers," a Pittsburgh player said. "In Philadelphia they booed Miss Pennsylvania all during the national anthem. She barely got out 'Oh say can you see' before they started booing."

Occasionally, players have problems with their own hometown fans. Florida Marlins outfielder Jeff Conine recalled his first career home run at then Joe Robbie Stadium. "The guy who caught it gave me the home run ball," Conine recalled. "But then he said he wanted the bat that I hit it with. I said, 'No, that's mine.' So he said, 'Then give me the ball back.' Then he got belligerent. He was hammered [drunk]. They escorted him out."

Los Angeles Dodgers second baseman Nelson Liriano could work for Major League Baseball's marketing department. He rated every city as good. Why? "Every fan who comes to the park is a good fan," he said.

—*by Bill Koenig*

A painful portrait

It was so quiet in the Toronto Blue Jays' clubhouse, you could have heard a resin bag drop. The players were mesmerized by a guest whose talk had nothing to do with scouting reports or news from the labor front.

He was former major league outfielder Bill Tuttle. His face was slightly discolored. His right cheekbone seemed curiously higher than normal. His jaw slacked a bit—but he wasn't complaining. Tuttle, 66, has had five major operations and has gone through two years of therapy in his fight against oral cancer. He says he brought on the disease himself by four decades of chewing tobacco.

It cost him his cheekbone, his appearance, his teeth, his taste buds, his appetite and part of his hearing, but not his dignity or his desire to help others. He has become a crusader for the National Spit Tobacco Education Program (NSTEP), making the rounds to warn current players of the consequences of using chewing tobacco. He is usually accompanied by his wife, Gloria, and longtime friend Joe Garagiola, the NSTEP chairman. Last year, Tuttle received the U.S. surgeon general's highest award, the Exemplary Service Medallion, for his work.

"I chewed for 40 years, and I didn't know anything about what could happen," he said. "I'm blessed. I just saw the doctor, and he told me I'm clean. This is the best I've looked and felt in two years."

Tuttle used to chew 10 to 12 hours a day. "It's a powerful addiction," he said. "If they assured me I had a 100 percent chance of not getting cancer again, I'd have some chew in my mouth tomorrow."

In the fall of 1993, he developed a sore in his mouth. His doctor took a biopsy, and it came back positive. Surgeons at the University of Minnesota Medical Center, near Tuttle's hometown of Anoka, told him the operation probably would take 2½ hours to cut out "a little piece" of his mouth. "That little piece turned into the biggest tumor the doctor said he ever took out of someone's mouth," Tuttle said.

The reconstructive surgery, done on Nov. 11, 1993, lasted 13½ hours. Skin from his neck was used to replace his cancer-riddled cheek. Then two slabs of skin were transplanted from his chest up to his neck. Arm nerves had to be severed, and today Tuttle can't raise his right arm straight up or open a bottle of ketchup. That operation was just a warmup. Within six weeks, the cancer returned. In an operation a year later, surgeons rotated part of his skull 180 degrees, creating an ersatz cheekbone. Then they transplanted muscles from his leg to hold the thing up like a rubber band.

Last year they found more cancer in the back of Tuttle's mouth. More radiation. More chemotherapy. For four months, he couldn't swallow. A tubelike siphon had to be inserted into his nose. And, Tuttle said, "I had to sleep in a chair because I couldn't breathe if I lay down flat." One night he tried it anyway. An hour later, he awoke gasping for breath. He pounded on a wall, to awaken his wife who was sleeping in another room. She called 911 and help came—with not a minute to spare.

The scared straight approach of Tuttle's Blue Jays visit seems to be working. "It was a very powerful message," said center fielder Otis Nixon, who chewed for years until he stopped cold turkey in 1991.

Garagiola said that baseball has to eliminate tobacco use, but it can't be legislated or ordered out. It must be each player's personal choice. He said that chewing and dipping is either a macho thing or peer pressure. "People have made tobacco a part of baseball, but tobacco isn't a baseball tradition. Cancer isn't a baseball tradition."

—by Bill Koenig

Tragedy and redemption

April 1: McSherry's death raises medical issue

Umpire John McSherry's death from a heart attack during the Opening Day Reds-Expos game raised serious questions about umpires' overall health—and to what extent Major League Baseball should regulate its rules keepers' physical condition.

McSherry, 51, was one of the game's most popular arbiters. But in recent years, coworkers grew concerned about the 25-year veteran's weight—328 pounds on a 6-foot-2½ frame. He collapsed near home plate at Cincinnati's Riverfront Stadium about two minutes into the game. Doctors said McSherry had sudden cardiac death, a condition in which the heart beats out of control. He had experienced a series of health problems dating to a 1991 game in which he collapsed because of dehydration. The National League said McSherry underwent his annual medical checkup in February. "[Umpires] have to be in good health and be able to stand the rigors of the job," said Richie Phillips, head of the umpires' union, when questioned about umpires' physical requirements after McSherry's death. "I don't know if any kind of [weight] prohibitions do any good."

Just seven pitches into the April 1 game, McSherry backed away from the plate, waved to the other umpires, took a few labored steps and collapsed. Although the other umpires were willing to continue the game because they thought McSherry would have wanted them to, it was canceled by the league and replayed the next day.

McSherry loved his job. "A good umpire has to like the life," McSherry said in 1990. "He has to work hard at it and be able to handle situations, which is probably the most difficult thing in the whole ball of wax."

—by Deron Snyder

Gooden was carried off the field by teammates.

May 14: Gooden goes from no hope to no-hitter

Dwight Gooden's no-hitter epitomized a rebirth in which he went from drug-suspension exile to a member of the Yankees rotation. Gooden hadn't pitched in the majors in almost two years, and he was only 1-3 with a 5.67 ERA before the May 14 gem against Seattle. Gooden went 11-2 in the middle of the season before fading in New York's championship run because of a tired arm.

Gooden pitched his 2-0 masterpiece against the powerful Mariners despite giving up six walks. Not far into the game, Yankees catcher Joe Girardi was thinking no-hitter. "I started looking early, right after the fifth. I knew we'd have [Ken] Griffey, [Edgar] Martinez and maybe Jay Buhner coming up in the sixth, and we'd have to face them again in the ninth," Girardi said.

Gooden put men on second and third in the ninth with one out, but he struck out Buhner and then got Paul Sorrento for the final out.

Gooden dedicated the game to his father, Dan, who had successful double-bypass surgery the day after the no-hitter.

—by Peter Pascarelli and Ernie Palladino

Murray and Molitor reach milestones

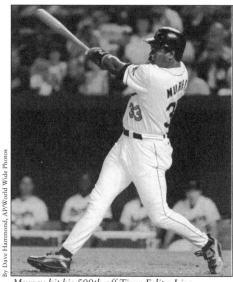

Murray hit his 500th off Tiger Felipe Lira.

By Dave Hammond, AP/World Wide Photos

Sept. 6: O's Murray joins a Fortune 500/3,000 firm

Eddie Murray of the Orioles, having only recently returned to Baltimore from Cleveland in a trade, made home run news when he blasted a milestone dinger off the Tigers' Felipe Lira on Sept. 6. When the ball landed in the right-center-field bleachers at Camden Yards, Murray, 40, joined Hank Aaron and Willie Mays as the only players in baseball history to have at least 3,000 hits and 500 homers. Appropriately, it came on the first anniversary of fellow Oriole Cal Ripken's record-breaking 2,131st consecutive game, which also happened at Camden Yards.

"Wow. It's a neighborhood you don't know if you belong in yet," Murray said in a postgame interview. "It's hard to see yourself being mentioned in the same voice with those guys. They're people everybody knows. You say baseball, and you say those guys."

Five years after he retires, Murray will join a club with many more members and even more significance. "This puts him in the Hall of Fame as far as I'm concerned," Orioles manager Davey Johnson said. "Five hundred homers and 3,000 hits, that's a great achievement."

Hitting the first 498 home runs took Murray, who was the American League Rookie of the Year in 1977, the better part of 20 seasons. The next two, however, seemingly took forever. Murray hit No. 498 on Aug. 16. He then went two weeks without another homer, including nine consecutive games at home. After hitting No. 499 in Seattle, he played five more games before clubbing the big one.

In his march to becoming the 15th major leaguer to reach 500 dingers, Murray hit 241 in home games and 259 on the road, with 392 in the American League with the O's and the Indians, and 108 in the National League during stints with the Dodgers and the Mets. A rock of consistency and durability, he is the only man to reach the mark without having a 40-homer year. His season high was 33 in 1983, during his first tour with Baltimore.

—by Tim Wendel and David Hughes

Sept. 16: Molitor hits 3,000 with triple

A day after missing the chance to get his 3,000th hit at home, Minnesota's Paul Molitor finally reached his milestone in Kansas City on Sept. 16, in the process becoming the 21st major leaguer to achieve the mark and the first to do it with a triple. With one out in the fifth inning, Molitor hit an opposite-field fly ball to the alley off Kansas City rookie Jose Rosado. Center fielder Rod Myers and right fielder Jon Nunnally both tried to run it down but slowed up as they came together, and the ball dropped behind them.

"I think the only time I took my eye off the ball was to make sure I touched first base," said Molitor, who went 0-for-3 the day before against Seattle at the Metrodome. "I didn't hit the ball particularly well."

For the 40-year-old Molitor it was his 211th hit of the season, and he is the first player to have 200 hits in the same season he got his 3,000th hit. He finished the year with a career-high 225, breaking his mark of 216 in 1991, the second-to-last of his 15 years with the Milwaukee Brewers. This year he also became the oldest man to lead his league in hits since Pete Rose topped the National League in 1981.

After the 3,000th hit, Molitor's teammates ran onto the field to congratulate him, as did Twins manager Tom Kelly, who rarely leaves the dugout to join celebrations. The crowd gave Molitor a standing ovation, as the Royals played a highlight tribute to Molitor on the video scoreboard along with taped congratulatory remarks from 3,000-hit men George Brett, Rod Carew and Robin Yount, the last a longtime teammate of Molitor's with the Brewers.

Afterward, Yount and Royals executive Brett visited Molitor in the Twins' clubhouse. "I joked a little about respecting my elders," Molitor said.

Molitor, the Twins' designated hitter, played 161 games this year, a career high. That feat, considering how much he'd been hurt in the past, once seemed as unlikely as 3,000 hits. "It must have been about five years ago I was reading some publication, and it had listed in there the odds of the current players to get to 3,000," Molitor said. "Robin [Yount] was like 4-to-1 and [George] Brett was like 8-to-1. I think I was like 1,000-to-1—just because of injuries and I was older."

He didn't get to 2,000 hits until he singled off Bret Saberhagen on July 30, 1991. But Molitor has had three of his four 200-hit seasons since then. A likely Hall of Famer, he will be remembered as one of the game's greatest hitters no matter where his hit total stands when he retires, probably after the 1998 season.

Molitor actually considered retiring last year. After 45 games of the 1995 season, he was batting .227. "I was on a West Coast trip in June and early July, and I remember thinking, 'This isn't any fun,'"

Molitor waved to the K.C. crowd after his triple.

By Orlin Wagner, AP/World Wide Photos

Molitor said. "I had to force myself to go to the park every day. That's the opposite of everything I've ever tried to do, in terms of respecting the game and having fun playing it."

"I had a couple of good series before the break, and the rest of the season unfolded in a much more positive manner. [He ended the 1995 season with a .270 batting average, 15 home runs and 60 RBI.] I had enough fun that I said I'd like to try to do this again. The clarity in your thinking comes when you put down the bats for a couple of weeks, and I felt like I still had more to give."

—by Alan Eskew and Pete Williams

1996 Hall of Fame inductees

Bunning and Weaver went into the Hall together.

Weaver's election can't be argued

Even before he was chosen, Earl Weaver just walked into the Hall of Fame as if he belonged. "The guy at the door thought I was already in the Hall of Fame," Weaver said, recalling how he once got into a reception for those already enshrined. "He let me right in. Well, I got some free beer."

Weaver was one of four men chosen in 1996 by the Veterans Committee, after the Baseball Writers Association of America failed to vote anyone in. Already enshrined from his 17 seasons with the Orioles are masters of Weaver's recipe for success: pitching (Jim Palmer), defense (Brooks Robinson) and three-run homers (Frank Robinson).

This year, it was Weaver who was on the dais, with scores of his players and fans on hand to honor him. He got a lot of laughs during his acceptance speech when he said of umpires, "Now it's time to recognize a group of men who seldom receive credit for a job well done." He added, "My biggest fault [with umpires] was trying to get in the last word."

Though the Earl of Baltimore is remembered for his animated run-ins with, and record 91 ejections by, umpires, it's his trademark index cards that former players and coaches emphasized. "All of the sudden, he'd run back to the clubhouse," Brooks Robinson remembered. "He was going to check the stats" he kept on the index cards.

Weaver's pitching coach Ray Miller said, "He did it long before everybody had computers. He was absolutely the best at getting the right guy up to bat at the right time." That all translated into a 1480-1060 record, a .583 winning percentage that ranks seventh among managers in this century. Weaver is 13th on the post-1900 victory list, and he won six AL East titles, four pennants and a World Series after he took over the Orioles on July 11, 1968.

"The players—Palmer, [Andy] Etchebarren—all had their run-ins with him," Brooks Robinson said. "We respect him more now than ever." It's true of Palmer—he conducted a letter-writing campaign to get his old skipper into Cooperstown.

Weaver, a manager who was never fired, gives as much credit to the fans as to the players. "The fans are the people who keep you in town," Weaver said. "The owner and the general manager don't do it. If the fans stop coming. . . ."

—by Paul White

Bunning is still not giving any ground

New Hall of Famer Jim Bunning was the hardest-working player I knew. He was a smart one, and it was no surprise that he went on to a political career that's landed him in Congress, where he's a Republican member of the House of Representatives.

On Aug. 4 he used the Cooperstown induction ceremony to make another kind of political statement, as he chastised baseball for its greed, aloofness and then lack of a labor agreement. "To the owners, I would like to say, Get your house in order," said Bunning. "To the owners and players alike, I say, Get a commissioner—a *real* commissioner." To the players he advised, "Realize that the fans are the reason you're paid the salary you make. Treat them with respect and dignity."

Bunning, a 12-year union player rep while a pitcher, and the author of a House bill to repeal baseball's antitrust exemption, insisted afterward at a press conference that his concern was genuine, citing the canceled 1994 postseason as a disaster that could have recurred.

As a player, he was not the most talented pitcher in the game. He had to seek every edge for himself, and he was willing to work for it. He played for Detroit from 1955 to 1963, and frugal Tigers GM Jim Campbell hated to see him come into his office to talk contract. When Bunning sat on the other side of his desk, Campbell knew he would be outmaneuvered and outnegotiated. Bunning came in much better prepared than Campbell, and eventually the right-hander would leave with a few more thousand bucks than Campbell wanted to pay. "The Lizard" (so-called because of his thin, narrow eyes and bony cheeks marked with freckles) was an agent before there were agents.

Bunning was a terrific competitor. He won 100 games in each league. He pitched a no-hitter for the Tigers and a perfect game for the Philadelphia Phillies. He was always in shape, and he was the first player I knew who kept a book on the batters. He'd study it on buses, planes and trains. I would kid him about it, and he would laugh, but he never showed it to me. He'd never give away that edge.

Do I think Bunning should be in the Hall of Fame? It's a tough call. I put him on my ballot at least a dozen times, and I'm glad the veterans committee is honoring him. I had great respect for The Lizard. Still do, in fact.

—by Joe Falls, who writes for
The Detroit News

Negro leagues' winningest pitcher wins Hall backing

Bill Foster won more games in the Negro leagues than anyone, including Satchel Paige, who's credited with 129. Foster had 137 wins in 15 seasons (1923-37) and would have won more except for the Depression. He was 29 years old in 1933, his last full season, when he was 8-4 for the Chicago American Giants. Thereafter he was forced to barnstorm and take other jobs to make a living; he managed the Harlem Globetrotters and coached at Alcorn State, his alma mater, from 1960 until shortly before his death in 1978.

Foster, a half brother of his first manager, 1981 Hall of Fame inductee Rube Foster, was 21-3 in 1927 for the American Giants as they won a second consecutive pennant. Foster also claimed to have beaten Paige twice in one day—with two shutouts.

—by John B. Holway, a baseball historian from Springfield, Va.

25

Hanlon's savvy brought teams pennants

Ned Hanlon joined Earl Weaver as the first pair of managers to be elected in the same year since Connie Mack and John McGraw were enshrined in 1937. Like Weaver, Hanlon achieved his greatest success in Baltimore. He won five pennants, had a career 1,315-1,164 record from 1889 to 1907 and was credited with bringing future Hall of Famers Wee Willie Keeler, Dan Brouthers and McGraw to the old Orioles.

Hanlon, who was born in 1857, finished his playing career with 1,317 career hits and a .260 batting average.

Hanlon was notorious for manufacturing a home field advantage, by sloping foul lines for bunts and keeping the ground hard to make it easy for batters to hit "Baltimore chops."

Hanlon retired to Baltimore and died in 1937.

—by Pat Coleman

1996 award winners

AL Most Valuable Player: Juan Gonzalez

The Rangers' Juan Gonzalez scored an upset in winning the American League MVP voting, edging the favorite, 21-year-old Seattle Mariners shortstop Alex Rodriguez, by three points. "I'm surprised, myself," said Gonzalez, who, after the MVP votes were in, clubbed five homers against the Yankees in Texas's losing Division Series. During the regular season, he hit .314 and set team records with 47 homers and 144 RBI to lead the Rangers to their first AL West title. Gonzalez received 11 of the 28 first-place votes in the balloting by the Baseball Writers Association of America; Rodriguez, who led the league in batting with a .358 average, got 10, but both Seattle writers put teammate Ken Griffey Jr. first.

Caminiti sparkled at bat and in the field.

NL Most Valuable Player: Ken Caminiti

Ken Caminiti became the first San Diego Padre to win the National League MVP and only the fourth from that league to be a unanimous pick. His 40 home runs, 130 RBI and .621 slugging average all set club marks. Caminiti also won his second straight NL Gold Glove at third base and hit .326, a career high. He was tremendous during the Padres' drive to the NL West crown, leading the league in all three Triple Crown cate-

gories after the All-Star break. He hit three home runs in the Padres' first-round playoff loss to the Cardinals.

Hentgen won 20 and led the AL in innings.

AL Cy Young Award: Pat Hentgen

In another surprising vote, Toronto's Pat Hentgen beat New York left-hander Andy Pettitte in the American League Cy Young vote. The Blue Jays right-hander led Pettitte in all major categories except wins, in which he was one shy of Pettitte's league-leading 21, and received 16 first-place votes to the Yankee's 11. Hentgen led the AL in complete games, with 10, and was tied for the lead in shutouts, with three. His 3.22 ERA was second to teammate Juan Guzman's 2.93.

NL Cy Young Award: John Smoltz

Right-hander John Smoltz of the Braves had the dominating season that had long been forecast for him. The 24-8 Smoltz, who was first on 26 of 28 Cy Young ballots, led the league in wins and strikeouts (276) before adding four more victories for Atlanta in a brilliant postseason, his only loss coming on an unearned run in Game 5 of the World Series. He was fourth in the NL in ERA, with a 2.94 mark. Kevin Brown of the Marlins, at 1.89 the major leagues' ERA leader, was the first-place choice of the other two voters.

1997 BASEBALL WEEKLY ALMANAC

By Robert Hanashiro, USA TODAY

By Ann Heisenfelt, AP/World Wide Photos

AL Managers of the Year:
Joe Torre and Johnny Oates

The Yankees' Joe Torre and the Rangers' Johnny Oates, whose teams met in the first round of the playoffs, were voted co–Managers of the Year in the American League. Torre led New York past Texas in four games on its way to a World Series victory and became only the third man to win an MVP and a Manager of the Year award. Oates's Rangers fought off a stiff challenge from the Mariners and won their first AL West title, with a 90-72 record. The season was vindication for Oates, who was fired by Baltimore after the '94 season despite having a 237-199 record there.

NL Manager of the Year:
Bruce Bochy

The Padres' Bruce Bochy, 41, is the youngest manager in the major leagues, and in '96 he became the first San Diego skipper to be named the National League Manager of the Year. In just his second season at the helm, he led the club to a 91-71 record and the Padres' second NL West championship.

AL Rookie of the Year:
Derek Jeter

In Derek Jeter's junior high yearbook is this prediction: "Derek Jeter, most likely to play shortstop for the New York Yankees." Nostradamus was never so accurate, as Jeter capped his first season by being unanimously chosen the American League Rookie of the Year. He stunned everyone by hitting .314 with 10 homers, 78 RBI, 102 runs scored and 14 steals in the regular season before going 22-for-61 (.361) in the postseason. On defense, he made just 22 errors at one of the game's most demanding positions.

NL Rookie of the Year:
Todd Hollandsworth

The Dodgers continued what is now a five-year streak when left fielder Todd Hollandsworth was named the National League's top rookie. He won the award in a close vote over Marlins shortstop Edgar Renteria and Pirates catcher Jason Kendall. Hollandsworth batted .291 while leading all NL rookies in hits, doubles, homers, RBI and steals.

1996 Gold Glove winners

AMERICAN LEAGUE

P	Mike Mussina	Baltimore
C	Ivan Rodriguez	Texas
1B	J.T. Snow	California
2B	R. Alomar	Baltimore
3B	Robin Ventura	Chicago
SS	Omar Vizquel	Cleveland
OF	Jay Buhner	Seattle
OF	Kenny Lofton	Cleveland
OF	Ken Griffey Jr.	Seattle

NATIONAL LEAGUE

P	Greg Maddux	Atlanta
C	C. Johnson	Florida
1B	Mark Grace	Chicago
2B	Craig Biggio	Houston
3B	Ken Caminiti	San Diego
SS	Barry Larkin	Cincinnati
OF	M. Grissom	Atlanta
OF	Barry Bonds	SF
OF	Steve Finley	San Diego

1996 Silver Slugger winners

AMERICAN LEAGUE

C	Ivan Rodriguez	Texas
1B	Mark McGwire	Oakland
2B	R. Alomar	Baltimore
SS	A. Rodriguez	Seattle
3B	Jim Thome	Cleveland
OF	Ken Griffey Jr.	Seattle
OF	Albert Belle	Cleveland
OF	Juan Gonzalez	Texas
DH	Paul Molitor	Minn.

NATIONAL LEAGUE

P	Tom Glavine	Atlanta
C	Mike Piazza	LA
1B	A. Galarraga	Colorado
2B	Eric Young	Colorado
SS	Barry Larkin	Cincinnati
3B	Ken Caminiti	San Diego
OF	Ellis Burks	Colorado
OF	Barry Bonds	SF
OF	Gary Sheffield	Florida

Obituaries: selected major leaguers

Johnny Berardino: May 19, Los Angeles; 1939-52 Browns, Indians, Pirates.

Ewell Blackwell: Oct. 29, Hendersonville, N.C.; 1942-55 Reds, Yankees, Athletics.

Don Bollweg: May 26, Wheaton, Ill.; 1950-55 Cardinals, Yankees, Athletics.

Johnny Bucha: April 28, Bethlehem, Pa.; 1948-53 Cardinals, Tigers.

Jim Busby: July 8, Augusta, Ga.; 1950-62 White Sox, Senators, Indians, Orioles, Red Sox, Colt .45s.

Hank Camelli: July 14, Wellesley, Mass.; 1943-47 Pirates, Braves.

Babe Dahlgren: Sept. 4, Arcadia, Calif.; 1935-46 Red Sox, Yankees, Braves, Cubs, Browns, Dodgers, Phillies.

Red Embree: Sept. 24, Eugene, Ore.; 1941-49 Indians, Yankees, Browns.

Gil English: Aug. 31, Trinity, N.C.; 1931-44 Giants, Tigers, Braves, Dodgers.

Del Ennis: Feb. 8, Huntingdon Valley, Pa.; 1946-59 Phillies, Cardinals, Reds, White Sox.

Nanny Fernandez: Sept. 19, Lomita, Calif.; 1942-50 Braves, Pirates.

Tom Ferrick: Oct. 15, Lima, Pa.; 1941-52 Athletics, Indians, Browns, Senators, Yankees.

Roger Freed: Jan. 9, Chino, Calif.; 1970-79 Orioles, Phillies, Reds, Expos, Cardinals.

Milt Gaston: April 26, Hyannis, Mass.; 1924-34 Yankees, Browns, Senators, Red Sox, White Sox.

Gary Geiger: April 24, Murphysboro, Ill.; 1958-70 Indians, Red Sox, Braves, Astros.

Jim Gleeson: May 1, Kansas City, Mo.; 1936-42 Indians, Cubs, Reds.

Gordon Goldsberry: Feb. 23, Lake Forest, Calif.; 1949-52 White Sox, Browns.

Hank Gornicki: Feb. 16, Riviera Beach, Fla.; 1941-46 Cardinals, Cubs, Pirates.

Bob Grim: Oct. 23, Shawnee, Kan.; 1954-62 Yankees, Athletics, Indians, Reds, Cardinals.

Tom Hafey: Oct. 2, El Cerrito, Calif.; 1939-44 Giants, Browns.

Harry Hanebrink: Sept. 9, Bridgeton, Mo.; 1953-59 Braves, Phillies.

Lum Harris: Nov. 11, Pell City, Ala.; 1941-47 Athletics, Senators.

Joe Hoerner: Oct. 4, Hermann, Mo.; 1963-77 Colt .45s, Cardinals, Phillies, Braves, Athletics, Rangers, Reds.

Joe Holden: May 10, St. Clair, Pa.; 1934-36 Phillies.

Al Hollingsworth: April 28, Austin, Texas; 1935-46 Reds, Phillies, Dodgers, Senators, Browns, White Sox.

Alex Kellner: May 3, Tucson, Ariz.; 1948-59 Athletics, Reds, Cardinals.

Gus Keriazakos: May 4, Hilton Head, S.C.; 1950-55 White Sox, Senators, Athletics.

Elmer Klumpp: Oct. 18, Menominee Falls, Wis.; 1934-37 Senators, Dodgers.

Bruce Konopka: Sept. 27, Denver; 1942-46 Athletics.

Jerry May: June 30, Swoope, Va; 1964-73 Pirates, Royals, Mets.

Barney McCosky: Sept. 6, Venice, Fla.; 1939-53 Tigers, Athletics, Reds, Indians.

Willie Miranda: Sept. 7, Baltimore; 1951-59 Senators, White Sox, Browns, Yankees, Orioles.

Walt Moryn: July 21, Winfield, Ill.; 1954-61 Dodgers, Cubs, Cardinals, Pirates.

Bob Muncrief: Feb. 6, Duncanville, Texas; 1937-51 Browns, Indians, Pirates, Cubs, Yankees.

Red Munger: July 23, Houston; 1943-56 Cardinals, Pirates.

Charlie Neal: Nov. 18, Dallas; 1956-63 Dodgers, Mets, Reds.

Bill Nicholson: March 8, Chestertown, Md.; 1936-53 Athletics, Cubs, Phillies.

Jim Pendleton: March 20, Houston; 1953-62 Braves, Pirates, Reds, Colt .45s.

Ray Pepper: March 24, Belle Mina, Ala.; 1932-36 Cardinals, Browns.

Johnny Pramesa: Sept. 9, Los Angeles; 1949-52 Reds, Cubs.

Jerry Robertson: March 24, Burlington, Kan.; 1969-70 Expos, Tigers.

Don Ross: April 4, Arcadia, Calif.; 1938-46 Tigers, Dodgers, Indians.

Connie Ryan: Jan. 3, Metairie, La.; 1942-54 Giants, Braves, Reds, Phillies, White Sox.

Joe Schultz: Jan. 10, St. Louis; 1939-48 Pirates, Browns.

Bill Serena: April 17, Hayward, Calif.; 1949-54 Cubs.

Mike Sharperson: May 26, Las Vegas; 1987-93 Blue Jays, Dodgers

Ray Shore: Aug. 13, St. Louis; 1946-49 Browns.

Harry Shuman: Oct. 25, Philadelphia; 1942-44 Pirates, Phillies.

Elmer Singleton: Jan. 5, Ogden, Utah; 1945-59 Braves, Pirates, Senators, Cubs.

Les Tietje: Oct. 2, Rochester, Minn.; 1933-38 White Sox, Browns.

Dick West: March 13, Fort Wayne, Ind.; 1938-43 Reds.

Pete Whisenant: March 22, Port Charlotte, Fla.; 1952-61 Braves, Cardinals, Reds, Senators, Twins.

Al Zarilla: Sept. 4, Honolulu; 1943-53 Browns, Red Sox, White Sox.

—compiled by Bill Carle (through Nov. 18)

NL/AL beat

▶**1996 division-by-division wrap-ups**

▶**1996 All-Star Game wrap-up and box score**

▶**League batting and pitching leaders**

USA SNAPSHOTS®

A look at statistics that shape the sports world

Diamonds in the rough

Playoff managers Bobby Cox (Braves) and Tony La Russa (Cardinals) are fifth and sixth, respectively, among managers with the most ejections from a game since 1991:

Manager	Ejections
Cito Gaston	18
Lou Piniella	18
Mike Hargrove	16
Jim Leyland	17
Bobby Cox	**15**
Tony La Russa	**14**
Hal McRae	13

Note: Joe Torre (Yankees) is tied with several others at 12.

Source: Society of American Baseball Research   By Scott Boeck and Bob Laird, USA TODAY

AL East: Yanks hung on to beat Birds

The American League East was predicted to be baseball's toughest division in 1996, with the Orioles, Yankees and Red Sox all expected to contend. With a new Baltimore management team in place (manager Davey Johnson and GM Pat Gillick) and several prominent new players (Roberto Alomar, Bobby Bonilla, Randy Myers, B.J. Surhoff, David Wells), it seemed that owner Peter Angelos would win his off-season duel with Yankees boss George Steinbrenner. Like Baltimore, New York was home to plenty of new faces as the season began, including Joe Girardi, Dwight Gooden, Tino Martinez and Tim Raines. The staff ace was David Cone, Steinbrenner's spoils of an intense bidding war with Angelos.

In the end, New York and Baltimore held up their parts of the bargain by advancing to the ALCS, and the Yankees went all the way for their first World Series title since 1978. Boston, the 1995 division champ, stumbled in losing 19 of its first 25 games but re-entered the postseason race in September. New York moved into the lead for good on April 30 and swept four at Camden Yards after the All-Star break to leave the Orioles 10 games behind.

STANDINGS AT ALL-STAR BREAK				
	W	L	Pct.	GB
New York	52	33	.612	—
Baltimore	46	39	.541	6
Boston	38	49	.437	15
Toronto	36	49	.424	16
Detroit	27	61	.307	26½

Baltimore had lost 51 of 91 games during one stretch. Along the way, they replaced the Bronx Zoo as baseball's zaniest soap opera. In the subplot with the most impact, Angelos vetoed Gillick's proposed trades of Bonilla and starter Wells, which would have effectively ended Baltimore's chances. Angelos said Oriole fans deserved a contending team, and his faith was rewarded when Baltimore won 37 of its last 58 games.

The race grew tighter thanks to New York's free fall. The Yankees, whose lead stood at a dozen games on July 29, clung to a four-game advantage after going 13-17 in August. But the Orioles dropped two of three in mid-September against the Yankees, who won the division the following week. Baltimore clinched the wild card on Sept. 28.

The Red Sox finished only three games behind Baltimore in the wild-card race, which was remarkable in that they trailed the Yankees by 17 games on Aug. 1. In that month, they won 22 of 31 to be 1½ games off the wild-card pace and 5½ behind the Yankees. But the stress of playing catch-up proved too much for the Red Sox, who finished seven back despite first baseman Mo Vaughn's 143 RBI.

No lineup looked forward to facing the Blue Jays' staff, led by Pat Hentgen, who won the Cy Young Award, and Juan Guzman, who led the league with a 2.93 ERA. Toronto compiled the league's fourth-best ERA (4.57), and its 4.02 mark in the second half was tops. But the Jays, suffering from the free-agency defections of Roberto Alomar, Al Leiter, Paul Molitor and Devon White, were never in the race. Toronto simply didn't have enough offense.

Only Detroit's was worse. And as everyone found out over the course of the season, being better than the Tigers wasn't hard. Under rookie manager Buddy Bell, Detroit lost 109 games in one of the worst seasons in major league history. They set the AL mark for worst ERA (6.38), along with major league records for striking out (1,268) and most homers allowed (241).

FINAL STANDINGS				
	W	L	Pct.	GB
New York	92	70	.568	—
Baltimore	88	74	.543	4
Boston	85	77	.525	7
Toronto	74	88	.457	18
Detroit	53	109	.327	39

AL Central: Cleveland was still on top

The Cleveland Indians won the division by a mere 14½ games instead of the outrageous 30-game bulge they enjoyed in their magical 1995 season. They led the majors with 99 victories and—for the first time in franchise history—qualified for postseason play in consecutive seasons. But they proved to be human, struggling through an 18-21 slump between May 27 and July 6 and being plagued by dissension and controversy throughout the year. General manager John Hart made unpopular trades, dealing DH Eddie Murray and overweight second baseman Carlos Baerga. Left fielder Albert Belle earned his fifth suspension in six years after smashing into Milwaukee infielder Fernando Vina on a baserunning play. There were also many injuries, including ones to first baseman Julio Franco, newcomer Jack McDowell and unhappy starter Dennis Martinez, who went on the DL three times with a sore elbow. Finally, the Indians' postseason was ended by Baltimore in a four-game Division Series. There were many highlights, though: Belle's 148 RBI were the most in the AL since 1949. Third baseman Jim Thome (38 HR, 116 RBI) and outfielder Manny Ramirez (33 HR, 112 RBI) had career highs in both categories. Pitcher Charles Nagy went 17-5 with a 3.41 ERA and started the All-Star Game.

STANDINGS AT ALL-STAR BREAK			
	W	L	Pct.	GB
Cleveland	52	35	.598	—
Chicago	50	37	.575	2
Milwaukee	43	43	.500	8½
Minnesota	41	45	.477	10½
Kansas City	38	50	.432	14½

The White Sox (85-77) led the wildcard race for 51 days after the All-Star break before they folded. Starters Wilson Alvarez, Kevin Tapani and rookie James Baldwin were a combined 2-7 with an earned run average over 7.00 in September, and the team's No. 5 starters were 3-12 for the season. The club did have three 100-RBI men for the first time: first

baseman Frank Thomas (134), third baseman Robin Ventura (105) and right fielder Danny Tartabull (101).

The Milwaukee Brewers finished under .500 but showed promise even after unloading outfielder Greg Vaughn, infielders Kevin Seitzer and Pat Listach, and left-hander Graeme Lloyd. John Jaha (34 HR, 118 RBI) and Dave Nilsson (.331, 84 RBI), who shared first base and DH; shortstop Jose Valentin (24 HR, 95 RBI); and third baseman Jeff Cirillo (.325, 83 RBI) all had career years at the plate. On the mound, Scott Karl and Ben McDonald won 13 and 12 games, respectively.

The Minnesota Twins' year will be remembered for saying hello to Paul Molitor and goodbye to Kirby Puckett. Molitor hit an amazing .341 and got his 3,000th hit on Sept. 16. The joyous Puckett woke up one day in spring training unable to see out of one eye, and he had to retire. Pitchers Rick Aguilera, Dan Naulty and Dave Stevens also were injured, and in this season of offense, the Twins were the only team in the American League without a 20-homer man.

For the first time in their 28-year history, the Kansas City Royals finished last. With an $18.4 million payroll, expectations were low—and they were met. Craig Paquette led the Royals with 22 home runs and 67 RBI. Jose Offerman hit .303 while playing three infield positions. The pitching was strong. Tim Belcher and Kevin Appier won 15 and 14 games, respectively, and left-hander Chris Haney, who had back surgery in 1995, turned into a workhorse with 228 innings pitched.

FINAL STANDINGS			
	W	L	Pct.	GB
Cleveland	99	62	.615	—
Chicago	85	77	.525	14½
Milwaukee	80	82	.494	19½
Minnesota	78	84	.481	21½
Kansas City	75	86	.466	24

AL West: Texas won yearlong slugfest

If you love the long ball, the American League West was the place to be in '96. Despite missing 18 games with a torn right arch, the A's Mark McGwire led the majors with 52 home runs. He was complemented in the power barrage by Geronimo Berroa's 36 dingers and Terry Steinbach's 35 as Oakland blasted 243 home runs, the third-highest total in the majors. Only in the AL West could an attack like that of the A's be overshadowed.

The most feared offense in the division was actually 750 miles north, in Seattle. The Mariners were the modern-day version of Murderers' Row, with Ken Griffey Jr., Edgar Martinez, Jay Buhner and Alex Rodriguez, who became the third-youngest player in AL history to win a batting title (.358). Griffey hit 49 home runs and Buhner 44. The Mariners won a team-record 85 games and scored 993 runs; only six teams have scored 1,000 runs in a season. Still, it wasn't enough to beat Texas in the division or Baltimore in the wild-card race. Injuries derailed the Seattle juggernaut: Griffey missed 21 games, and Martinez, usually the team's DH, cracked four ribs in an accident during a rare appearance playing third base. Ace Randy Johnson missed much of the season with a bulging disk in his back. With Johnson out, the Mariners' pitching betrayed them, as the team ERA soared to 5.21 and Mariners manager Lou Piniella had to use 25 pitchers

STANDINGS AT ALL-STAR BREAK

	W	L	Pct.	GB
Texas	51	36	.586	—
Seattle	46	39	.541	4
California	43	45	.489	8½
Oakland	43	45	.489	8½

In '96, the Rangers won their first division championship and made their postseason debut. With Juan Gonzalez, Dean Palmer and Rusty Greer, Texas had enough power to hold their own against the A's and the Mariners. Gonzalez set club records with 47 homers and 144 RBI. He averaged 1.08 RBI per game

played, the best in the majors since 1938.

Even though Texas slumped coming down the stretch, it captured the division because of its pitching and defense. Shortstop Kevin Elster (who also chipped in with an amazing 99 RBI) and center fielder Darryl Hamilton combined with All-Star catcher Ivan Rodriguez and second baseman Mark McLemore to make the Rangers very strong up the middle. The defense made an improved, balanced pitching staff better. Ken Hill and Bobby Witt led the staff with 16 victories each, followed by Roger Pavlik's 15 and Darren Oliver's 14. In one of the best trades for the stretch run, Rangers GM Doug Melvin picked up John Burkett, who was 5-2 in the final two months. The bullpen will be the riddle to solve next season, as manager Johnny Oates tried a number of closers and setup arrangements without success.

The Anaheim Angels don't have much to remember from the '96 season. Besides injuries to center fielder Jim Edmonds and pitchers Mark Langston and Steve Ontiveros, the club was overwhelmed by uncertainty. The Disney Co. bought the club and fired most of the front office early in the season. The Angels used a major-league-record 29 pitchers and also established team marks for players used (52), most home runs allowed (219) and most wild pitches (80). Jim Abbott was symbolic of how far the Angels have sunk. In 1995, Abbott was 11-8 with a 3.70 ERA; in 1996, he fell to 2-18 with a 7.48 ERA.

FINAL STANDINGS

	W	L	Pct.	GB
Texas	90	72	.556	—
Seattle	85	76	.528	4½
Oakland	78	84	.481	12
California	70	91	.435	19½

NL East: Braves arms ruled again

The Atlanta Braves have become a National League dynasty in the '90s. Despite having an inconsistent bullpen, they finished with a league-best 96-66, won another division title, by eight games, and had their fourth National League pennant in six seasons. Right-hander John Smoltz won a franchise-record 14 straight and went 24-8 with 276 strikeouts. The Braves went 19-10 in August, built their lead to 12½ games and held on through a sleepy 12-15 September to become the first NL team to win its division five consecutive times. Atlanta's pitching staff set a major league record with 1,245 strikeouts and allowed the fewest walks in the majors (451). The offense clubbed 197 home runs, its third-highest total since moving to Atlanta in 1966.

STANDINGS AT ALL-STAR BREAK				
	W	L	Pct.	GB
Atlanta	54	33	.621	—
Montreal	49	38	.563	5
New York	41	46	.471	13
Florida	40	47	.460	14
Philadelphia	37	49	.430	16½

Manager Felipe Alou performed his annual miracle in Montreal. Whereas .500 seemed like a reasonable goal, the second-place Expos led the Braves early, finished 88-74 and remained in the wild-card race until the final weekend. They did it even with injuries to center fielder Rondell White (68 games missed) and first baseman David Segui (41 games). Shortstop Mark Grudzielanek had 201 hits, and outfielder Henry Rodriguez set a club record with 36 home runs. Mel Rojas finished with 36 saves, and Jeff Fassero and Pedro Martinez each had 222 strikeouts.

The Florida Marlins underachieved much of the season but finished third, 16 games behind Atlanta. The Marlins were 40-47 before firing manager Rene Lachemann; under John Boles they improved to 40-35. Right fielder Gary Sheffield correctly said he had a "monster year," hitting .314 with 42 home runs and 120 RBI. Right-hander Kevin Brown had a major-league-leading 1.89 ERA and went 17-11 despite the worst run support in the majors. Left-hander Al Leiter added 16 victories, including the team's first no-hitter. Shortstop Edgar Renteria and second baseman Luis Castillo will be the Marlins' middle infield of the future.

The Mets finished a disappointing 71-91, and manager Dallas Green was replaced by Bobby Valentine. Two of the team's prized young pitchers, Jason Isringhausen and Bill Pulsipher, had major surgery, and Paul Wilson (5-12) had a disappointing rookie season. The Mets finished 10th in the league in runs but first in errors. Center fielder Lance Johnson hit .333 with 227 hits to become the first player in history to lead both leagues in hits. Todd Hundley broke Roy Campanella's major league record for catchers with 41 home runs. Left fielder Bernard Gilkey hit .317 with 30 home runs and 117 RBI, and closer John Franco became the first left-hander in history to save 300 games.

The Philadelphia Phillies suited up 54 players to tie the National League record. They were a league-worst 67-95, and manager Jim Fregosi lost his power struggle with GM Lee Thomas and was fired. Catcher Benito Santiago hit 30 homers and drove in 85 runs. Right-hander Curt Schilling (9-10) came all the way back from shoulder surgery to lead the NL with eight complete games and average nearly a strikeout per inning. Ricky Bottalico converted 34 of 38 saves. Injuries hampered veterans Darren Daulton, Len Dykstra, Sid Fernandez and Gregg Jefferies, as well as rookie pitcher Mike Grace, who started 7-2 but didn't pitch after June.

FINAL STANDINGS				
	W	L	Pct.	GB
Atlanta	96	66	.593	—
Montreal	88	74	.543	8
Florida	80	82	.494	16
New York	71	91	.438	25
Philadelphia	67	95	.414	29

NL Central: Cards flew past the Astros

For the second consecutive season, the National League Central was decided the way it should be: head-to-head. And if the Houston Astros are going to return to the postseason one of these years, they'll have to handle those showdowns. The Astros jumped past St. Louis and into first place on Aug. 24 with the first of two consecutive victories against the Cardinals in the Astrodome. But those would be Houston's only wins against the eventual division champs in 13 meetings. A year earlier, the Astros beat Cincinnati just once in 13 tries in losing the crown to the Reds. The Cardinals got one more crack at the Astros just over a week later, and that three-game series proved crucial. The Redbirds won the opener in 10 innings and cruised 12-3 the next day to take over first place for good. That began a 17-9 September for the Cards, who won the division by six games as the Astros lost 13 of their last 21 games.

STANDINGS AT ALL-STAR BREAK				
	W	L	Pct.	GB
St. Louis	46	41	.529	—
Houston	47	42	.528	—
Cincinnati	39	43	.476	4½
Chicago	41	46	.471	5
Pittsburgh	39	48	.448	7

Cardinals manager Tony La Russa and his coaching staff were new to the league in '96, and St. Louis was only .500 on June 28 but tied for first place. Then starter Andy Benes, 3-8 on June 18, caught fire, finishing 18-10 and taking third place in the Cy Young Award voting. Many of St. Louis's newcomers helped win the division title. Left fielder Ron Gant led the club with 30 home runs, and third baseman Gary Gaetti was next with 23. Todd Stottlemyre's 14 wins trailed only Benes, and Dennis Eckersley saved 30 games at age 41.

Meanwhile, the Astros struggled to find consistent offense behind their big three of Craig Biggio, Jeff Bagwell and Derek Bell; to find pitching depth after starters

Mike Hampton and Shane Reynolds; and to find healthy, dependable arms in the bullpen. The Astros spent 102 days in or tied for first place, and a 14-6 stretch from July 19 to Aug. 11 got Houston 10 games over .500.

The season was even more frustrating for the Cincinnati Reds. It began with pitcher Pete Schourek, who was 3-0 (after winning 18 games the previous season) but then came down with elbow problems. Right fielder Reggie Sanders, the one Reds slugger after Gant left for St. Louis, had three stints on the disabled list and played only half the team's games. Second baseman Bret Boone never got untracked, batting just .233.

Chicago Cubs right fielder Sammy Sosa was leading the league in home runs with 40 on Aug. 20. He got his 100th RBI that day, but it came when he was hit on the hand by a pitch with the bases loaded. That ended his season and doomed the Cubs, who had inconsistent pitching (4.36 ERA) and finished last in the league in batting average and next-to-last in on-base average.

The Pittsburgh Pirates were just plain last in the division, but even they were within 1½ games of the lead on June 23. The Pirates went 24-46 the rest of the way, even with a major-league-high 11-game winning streak in September. Struggling financially, the Pirates traded Denny Neagle to Atlanta. Manager Jim Leyland resigned at the end of the season, and the rest of the club's veterans just waited to learn where they would be dealt in the offseason.

FINAL STANDINGS				
	W	L	Pct.	GB
St. Louis	88	74	.543	—
Houston	82	80	.506	6
Cincinnati	81	81	.500	7
Chicago	76	86	.469	12
Pittsburgh	73	89	.451	15

NL West: Padres dodged defeat at end

By sweeping a season-ending series in Los Angeles, San Diego won the West by a game and headed to the postseason for the first time since 1984. By the final day, though, both teams knew they were headed for the playoffs, robbing the decisive game of much of its drama. The Padres were in or tied for first place for 142 days, but they were two games out going into the final three-game showdown. League batting champ Tony Gwynn got the winning hit on the next-to-last day to clinch a playoff spot, and his brother Chris got the division winner in the 11th inning of the finale. Still, the tandem that drove the club most of the season was third baseman Ken Caminiti and center fielder Steve Finley. Caminiti led the NL in batting average, RBI and home runs after the All-Star break on his way to the MVP award. He and Finley combined to hit more home runs (70) and drive in more runs (225) than any duo in Padres history. Catcher John Flaherty was acquired from Detroit in June, went hitless in his first two games and then had a 27-game hitting streak.

STANDINGS AT ALL-STAR BREAK

	W	L	Pct.	GB
San Diego	48	41	.539	—
Los Angeles	47	42	.528	1
Colorado	42	44	.488	4½
San Francisco	38	48	.442	8½

The Dodgers had to overcome a slow start and two traumatic developments to keep pace with the Padres. Cancer was discovered in Brett Butler's tonsils in May, and on June 25 manager Tom Lasorda took a leave of absence because of heart problems. On July 29, he officially retired and Bill Russell took over the club and led it to a 35-21 mark. Pitching carried Los Angeles—Hideo Nomo won 16 games to lead the team, and Ramon Martinez won his last seven as the team's 3.46 ERA led the majors. Catcher Mike Piazza broke his own Los Angeles record for a catcher with 36 homers and finished with a .336 average,

and right fielder Raul Mondesi overcame a dreadful start to finish at .297. First baseman Eric Karros had 34 home runs and 111 RBI, but Butler was missed in center field and at the top of the lineup. Todd Hollandsworth took over left field in August and won the fifth straight NL Rookie of the Year award for the Dodgers.

The Colorado Rockies' road futility was too much for them to overcome. Because of Coors Field, the Rockies scored 961 runs; no other NL team reached 800. But Colorado finished eight games out because of a 28-53 record on the road. First baseman Andres Galarraga led the league with 47 home runs and became the first man to reach 150 RBI in 34 years, but outfielder Ellis Burks put together the most impressive season, hitting .344 and finishing in the top 10 in 11 offensive categories.

San Francisco had only one man with any numbers—Barry Bonds. What made his 40 home run-40 stolen base season, only the second one in major league history, all the more amazing is that he had little support and drew a league-record 151 walks. After the first week of the season, the Giants were never again able to put their planned starting lineup on the field, and slugger Matt Williams missed 57 games. The attrition wore down Dusty Baker's mostly untried troops during the second half; behind by 8½ games at the All-Star break, the team finished 23 out.

FINAL STANDINGS

	W	W	Pct.	GB
San Diego	91	71	.562	—
Los Angeles	90	72	.556	1
Colorado	83	79	.512	8
San Francisco	68	94	.420	23

Piazza's HR paces NL win; Cal breaks nose in photo op

National 6, American 0

```
American  0 0 0 0 0 0 0 0 0—0  7 0
National  1 2 1 0 0 2 0 0 x—6 12 1
```

American	AB	R	H	BI	BB	SO	AVG.
Lofton cf	3	0	2	0	0	0	.667
Carter cf	1	0	1	0	0	0	1.000
Boggs 3b	3	0	0	0	0	0	.000
e-Fryman ph-3b	1	0	0	0	0	1	.000
RAlomar 2b	3	0	1	0	0	0	.333
Knoblauch 2b	1	0	1	0	0	0	1.000
Belle lf	4	0	0	0	0	3	.000
MVaughn 1b	3	0	1	0	0	0	.333
McGwire 1b	1	0	1	0	0	0	1.000
IRodriguez c	2	0	0	0	0	1	.000
c-SAlomar ph-c	2	0	0	0	0	0	.000
CRipken ss	3	0	0	0	0	0	.000
Percival p	0	0	0	0	0	0	—
RHernandez p	0	0	0	0	0	0	—
f-DWilson ph	1	0	0	0	0	0	.000
ByAnderson rf	2	0	0	0	0	0	.000
Pavlik p	0	0	0	0	0	0	—
d-ARodriguez ph-ss	1	0	0	0	0	0	.000
Nagy p	0	0	0	0	0	0	—
a-EMartinez ph	1	0	0	0	0	0	.000
Finley p	0	0	0	0	0	0	—
b-Buhner ph-rf	2	0	0	0	0	0	.000
Totals	34	0	7	0	0	5	

a-grounded out for Nagy in the 2nd; b-lined out for Finley in the 5th; c-flied out for IRodriguez in the 6th; d-fouled out for Pavlik in the 7th; e-struck out for Boggs in the 8th; f-flied out for Hernandez in the 9th. BATTING—2B: MVaughn. GIDP: SAlomar. LOB: 7. BASERUNNING—SB: Lofton 2. FIELDING—DP: 1.

National	AB	R	H	BI	BB	SO	AVG.
LJohnson cf	4	1	3	0	0	0	.750
Larkin ss	3	1	1	0	0	0	.333
OSmith ss	1	0	0	0	0	0	.000
Bonds lf	3	0	1	1	0	0	.333
PJMartinez p	0	0	0	0	0	0	—
Sheffield rf	1	0	0	0	0	0	.000
McGriff 1b	2	0	0	0	0	2	.000
Glavine p	0	0	0	0	0	0	—
Caminiti 3b	2	1	1	1	0	1	.500
TdWorrell p	0	0	0	0	0	0	—
Kendall c	0	0	0	0	0	0	—
Piazza c	3	1	2	2	0	1	.667
Hundley c	1	0	0	0	0	0	.000
Wohlers p	0	0	0	0	0	0	—
ALeiter p	0	0	0	0	0	0	—
Bichette rf	3	1	1	0	0	1	.333
Trachsel p	0	0	0	0	0	0	—
Grudzielanek 3b	1	0	0	0	0	0	.000
CpJones 3b	2	1	1	0	0	0	.500
Bottalico p	0	0	0	0	0	0	—
Burks lf	2	0	1	0	0	1	.500
Biggio 2b	3	0	0	1	0	1	.000
EYoung pr-2b	1	0	0	0	0	0	.000
Smoltz p	0	0	0	0	0	0	—
a-HRodriguez ph	1	0	1	1	0	0	1.000
KBrown p	0	0	0	0	0	0	—
Bagwell 1b	2	0	0	0	0	1	.000
Totals	35	6	12	6	0	8	

a-singled for Smoltz in the 2nd. BATTING—2B: LJohnson, Piazza, Bichette. 3B: Burks. HR: Piazza off Nagy; Caminiti off Pavlik. RBI: Bonds, Caminiti, Piazza 2, Biggio, HRodriguez. LOB: 5. BASERUNNING—SB: LJohnson. CS: LJohnson, Bonds. FIELDING—E: Caminiti. DP: 1.

American	IP	H	R	ER	BB	SO	ERA
Nagy L, 0-1	2	4	3	3	0	1	13.50
Finley	2	3	1	1	0	4	4.50
Pavlik	2	3	2	2	0	2	9.00
Percival	1	1	0	0	0	1	0.00
RHernandez	1	1	0	0	0	0	0.00

National	IP	H	R	ER	BB	SO	ERA
Smoltz W, 1-0	2	2	0	0	0	1	0.00
KBrown	1	0	0	0	0	0	0.00
Glavine	1	0	0	0	0	1	0.00
Bottalico	1	0	0	0	0	1	0.00
PJMartinez	1	2	0	0	0	1	0.00
Trachsel	1	0	0	0	0	0	0.00
TdWorrell	1	2	0	0	0	1	0.00
Wohlers	.2	0	0	0	0	0	0.00
Leiter	.1	0	0	0	0	0	0.00

Wild pitch: Pavlik. Time: 2:35. Attendance: 62,670.

Eight years ago Mike Piazza was a 62nd-round draft pick of the Los Angeles Dodgers. On July 9 in Philadelphia, he shot to the top of the baseball world. Piazza, who's from nearby Phoenixville Area High School, hit a 445-foot home run into the upper deck of Veterans Stadium in the second inning of the All-Star Game, then added an RBI double in the third. The National League went on to shut out the American League 6-0, and the Dodgers catcher was picked as the game's Most Valuable Player. The Braves' John Smoltz started for the NL, and Charles Nagy of the Indians got the nod for the American League.

The NL got on the board right away, as the Mets' Lance Johnson, a replacement starter for injured Padre Tony Gwynn, led off the game with a double and came around on groundouts by the two Barrys, Larkin of the Reds and Bonds of the Giants. In the second inning, after Piazza's dinger, Expo Henry Rodriguez singled in Chipper Jones of the Braves for the third run. The Piazza double for the fourth run came off the Angels' Chuck Finley. The NL finished the scoring with two runs in the sixth off Roger Pavlik of the Rangers, highlighted by a homer off the bat of the Padres' Ken Caminiti.

This year's game, the first in which no player drew a walk, was the American League's most lopsided loss since 1976. The National League shutout was its first since 1987, and it extended the league's winning streak to three.

Cal Ripken had almost stolen the show before the game when he suffered a broken nose during, of all things, the pregame American League team photo. While dismounting a three-tiered platform in center field, Ripken accidentally caught a forearm from White Sox reliever Roberto Hernandez. After his nose was reset, Ripken was cleared to start his 13th consecutive All-Star Game. "I didn't want it to go down in the history of the All-Star Game as the only injury sustained during the team picture," said a visibly embarrassed Ripken, whose consecutive-games-played streak continued when the season resumed. Before his bad break, Veterans Stadium had been a special place for Ripken. In 1983, only Ripken's second year in the big leagues, the Orioles won the World Series there, with Ripken catching the last out—a soft, humpback liner.

As part of the festivities, Phillies Hall of Famers Richie Ashburn, Jim Bunning, Steve Carlton, Robin Roberts and Mike Schmidt threw out the ceremonial first pitches. Piazza caught the pitch from Schmidt, 20 years after the third baseman hit two home runs at Veterans Stadium in the first pro ball game Piazza ever saw.

American League leaders

Batting

BATTING AVERAGE

	G	AB	R	H	PCT
Rodriguez, Sea	146	601	141	215	.358
F. Thomas, Chi	141	527	110	184	.349
Molitor, Minn	161	660	99	225	.341
Knoblauch, Minn	153	578	140	197	.341
Greer, Tex	139	542	96	180	.332
Nilsson, Mil	123	453	81	150	.331
Alomar, Balt	153	588	132	193	.328
E. Martinez, Sea	139	499	121	163	.327
Seitzer, Mil-Clev	154	573	85	187	.326
Vaughn, Bos	161	635	118	207	.326

HOME RUNS

McGwire, Oak	52
Anderson, Balt	50
Griffey, Sea	49
Belle, Clev	48
Gonzalez, Tex	47
Buhner, Sea	44
Vaughn, Bos	44
F. Thomas, Chi	40
Fielder, Det-NY	39
Palmeiro, Balt	39

TRIPLES

Knoblauch, Minn	14
Vina, Mil	10
Guillen, Chi	8
Martinez, Chi	8
Molitor, Minn	8
Offerman, KC	8
Carter, Tor	7
Meares, Minn	7
Valentin, Mil	7
B. Williams, NY	7

DOUBLES

Rodriguez, Sea	54
E. Martinez, Sea	52
Rodriguez, Tex	47
Cirillo, Mil	46
Cordova, Minn	46
Ramirez, Clev	45
Alomar, Balt	43
Greer, Tex	41
Molitor, Minn	41
3 tied	40

RUNS BATTED IN

Belle, Clev	148
Gonzalez, Tex	144
Vaughn, Bos	143
Palmeiro, Balt	142
Griffey, Sea	140
Buhner, Sea	138
F. Thomas, Chi	134
Rodriguez, Sea	123
Jaha, Mil	118
2 tied	117

RUNS SCORED

Rodriguez, Sea	141
Knoblauch, Minn	140
Alomar, Balt	132
Lofton, Clev	132
Griffey, Sea	125
Belle, Clev	124
Thome, Clev	122
E. Martinez, Sea	121

HITS

Phillips, Chi	119
Vaughn, Bos	118
Molitor, Minn	225
Rodriguez, Sea	215
Lofton, Clev	210
Vaughn, Bos	207
Knoblauch, Minn	197
Alomar, Balt	193
Rodriguez, Tex	192
Belle, Clev	187
Seitzer, Mil-Clev	187
3 tied	184

BASES ON BALLS

Phillips, Chi	125
E. Martinez, Sea	123
Thome, Clev	123
McGwire, Oak	116
F. Thomas, Chi	109
O'Neill, NY	102
Belle, Clev	99
Knoblauch, Minn	98
3 tied	95

STOLEN BASES

Lofton, Clev	75
Goodwin, KC	66
Nixon, Tor	54
Knoblauch, Minn	45
Vizquel, Clev	35
Durham, Chi	30
McLemore, Tex	27
Amaral, Sea	25
Damon, KC	25
Listach, Mil-NY	25

SLUGGING AVG.

McGwire, Oak	.730
Gonzalez, Tex	.643
Anderson, Balt	.637
Rodriguez, Sea	.631
Griffey, Sea	.628
F. Thomas, Chi	.626
Belle, Clev	.623
Thome, Clev	.612
E. Martinez, Sea	.595
Vaughn, Bos	.583

ON-BASE AVG.

McGwire, Oak	.467
E. Martinez, Sea	.464
F. Thomas, Chi	.459
Thome, Clev	.450
Knoblauch, Minn	.448
Vaughn, Bos	.420
Seitzer, Mil-Clev	.416
Rodriguez, Sea	.414
Alomar, Balt	.411
O'Neill, NY	.411

TOTAL BASES

Rodriguez, Sea	379
Belle, Clev	375
Vaughn, Bos	370
Anderson, Balt	369
Gonzalez, Tex	348
Griffey, Sea	342
Palmeiro, Balt	342
F. Thomas, Chi	330
Ramirez, Clev	320
Buhner, Sea	314

Pitching

WON-LOST

Pettitte, NY	21	8
Hentgen, Tor	20	10
Mussina, Balt	19	11
Nagy, Clev	17	5
Fernandez, Chi	16	10
Hill, Tex	16	10
Witt, Tex	16	12
5 tied	15	

ERA

Guzman, Tor	2.93
Hentgen, Tor	3.22
Nagy, Clev	3.41
Fernandez, Chi	3.45
Appier, KC	3.62
Hill, Tex	3.63
Clemens, Bos	3.63
Pettitte, NY	3.87
McDonald, Mil	3.90
Belcher, KC	3.92

STRIKEOUTS

Clemens, Bos	257
Finley, Cal	215
Appier, KC	207
Mussina, Balt	204
Fernandez, Chi	200
Alvarez, Chi	181
Hentgen, Tor	177
Gordon, Bos	171
Hill, Tex	170
Nagy, Clev	167

COMPLETE GAMES

Hentgen, Tor	10
Hill, Tex	7
Pavlik, Tex	7
Clemens, Bos	6
Erickson, Balt	6
Fernandez, Chi	6
Wakefield, Bos	6
4 tied	5

SHUTOUTS

Hentgen, Tor	3
Hill, Tex	3
Robertson, Minn	3
Clemens, Bos	2
Lira, Det	2
28 tied	1

INNINGS PITCHED

Hentgen, Tor	265.2
Fernandez, Chi	258.0
Hill, Tex	250.2
Mussina, Balt	243.1
Clemens, Bos	242.2
Belcher, KC	238.2
Finley, Cal	238.0
Radke, Minn	232.0
Haney, KC	228.0
Tapani, Chi	225.1

GAMES PITCHED

Guardado, Minn	83
Myers, Det	83
Stanton, Bos-Tex	81
Slocumb, Bos	75
Jackson, Sea	73
Nelson, NY	73
Groom, Oak	72
Hernandez, Chi	72
R. Lewis, Det	72
Mohler, Oak	72

SAVES

Wetteland, NY	43
Mesa, Clev	39
Hernandez, Chi	38
Percival, Cal	36
Fetters, Mil	32
Henneman, Tex	31
R. Myers, Balt	31
Slocumb, Bos	31
Timlin, Tor	31
Montgomery, KC	24

National League leaders

Batting

BATTING AVERAGE	G	AB	R	H	PCT
Gwynn, SD	116	451	67	159	.353
Burks, Col	156	613	142	211	.344
Piazza, LA	148	547	87	184	.336
Johnson, NY	160	682	117	227	.333
Grace, Chi	142	547	88	181	.331
Caminiti, SD	146	546	109	178	.326
Young, Col	141	568	113	184	.324
Gilkey, NY	153	571	108	181	.317
Bagwell, Hou	162	568	111	179	.315
Sheffield, Fla	161	519	118	163	.314

HOME RUNS
Galarraga, Col	47
Bonds, SF	42
Sheffield, Fla	42
Hundley, NY	41
Burks, Col	40
Caminiti, SD	40
Castilla, Col	40
Sosa, Chi	40
Piazza, LA	36
Rodriguez, Mtl	36

TRIPLES
Johnson, NY	21
Grissom, Atl	10
Howard, Cin	10
Finley, SD	9
Burks, Col	8
DeShields, LA	8
Lankford, StL	8
Abbott, Fla	7
Mondesi, LA	7
Otero, Phil	7

DOUBLES
Bagwell, Hou	48
Burks, Col	45
Finley, SD	45
Gilkey, NY	44
Rodriguez, Mtl	42
Bell, Hou	40
Lansing, Mtl	40
Martin, Pitt	40
Mondesi, LA	40
3 tied	39

RUNS BATTED IN
Galarraga, Col	150
Bichette, Col	141
Caminiti, SD	130
Bonds, SF	129
Burks, Col	128
Bagwell, Hou	120
Sheffield, Fla	120
Gilkey, NY	117
Bell, Hou	113
Castilla, Col	113

RUNS SCORED
Burks, Col	142
Finley, SD	126
Bonds, SF	122
Galarraga, Col	119
Sheffield, Fla	118
Johnson, NY	117
Larkin, Cin	117
Bichette, Col	114

C. Jones, Atl	114
2 tied	113

HITS
Johnson, NY	227
Burks, Col	211
Grissom, Atl	207
Grudzielanek, Mtl	201
Bichette, Col	198
Finley, SD	195
Castilla, Col	191
Galarraga, Col	190
Martin, Pitt	189
Mondesi, LA	188

BASES ON BALLS
Bonds, SF	151
Sheffield, Fla	142
Bagwell, Hou	135
Henderson, SD	125
Larkin, Cin	96
C. Jones, Atl	87
Piazza, LA	81
Weiss, Col	80
Hundley, NY	79
Lankford, StL	79

STOLEN BASES
Young, Col	53
Johnson, NY	50
DeShields, LA	48
Bonds, SF	40
Martin, Pitt	38
Henderson, SD	37
McRae, Chi	37
Larkin, Cin	36
Hunter, Hou	35
Lankford, StL	35

SLUGGING AVG.
Burks, Col	.639
Sheffield, Fla	.624
Caminiti, SD	.621
Bonds, SF	.615
Galarraga, Col	.601
Bagwell, Hou	.570
Larkin, Cin	.567
Sosa, Chi	.564
Piazza, LA	.563
Gilkey, NY	.562

ON-BASE AVG.
Sheffield, Fla	.465
Bonds, SF	.461
Bagwell, Hou	.451
Piazza, LA	.422
Henderson, SD	.410
Larkin, Cin	.410
Burks, Col	.408
Caminiti, SD	.408
Grace, Chi	.396
Gilkey, NY	.393

TOTAL BASES
Burks, Col	392
Galarraga, Col	376
Finley, SD	348
Castilla, Col	345
Caminiti, SD	339
Bichette, Col	336
Grissom, Atl	328
Johnson, NY	327
Bagwell, Hou	324
Sheffield, Fla	324

Pitching

WON-LOST
Smoltz, Atl	24	8
Andy Benes, StL	18	10
Brown, Fla	17	11
Ritz, Col	17	11
Neagle, Pitt-Atl	16	9
Reynolds, Hou	16	10
Nomo, LA	16	11
Leiter, Fla	16	12
7 tied	15	

ERA
Brown, Fla	1.89
Maddux, Atl	2.72
Leiter, Fla	2.93
Smoltz, Atl	2.94
Glavine, Atl	2.98
Trachsel, Chi	3.03
Schilling, Phil	3.19
Nomo, LA	3.19
Fassero, Mtl	3.30
Valdes, LA	3.32

STRIKEOUTS
Smoltz, Atl	276
Nomo, LA	234
Fassero, Mtl	222
Martinez, Mtl	222
Kile, Hou	219
Reynolds, Hou	204
Leiter, Fla	200
Stottlemyre, StL	194
Hamilton, SD	184
Schilling, Phil	182

COMPLETE GAMES
Schilling, Phil	8
Smoltz, Atl	6
Brown, Fla	5
Fassero, Mtl	5
Maddux, Atl	5
Stottlemyre, StL	5
5 tied	4

SHUTOUTS
Brown, Fla	3
R. Martinez, LA	2
Nomo, LA	2
Schilling, Phil	2
Smiley, Cin	2
Smoltz, Atl	2
Stottlemyre, StL	2
Trachsel, Chi	2
26 tied	1

INNINGS PITCHED
Smoltz, Atl	253.2
Maddux, Atl	245.0
Reynolds, Hou	239.0
Navarro, Chi	236.2
Glavine, Atl	235.1
Brown, Fla	233.0
Fassero, Mtl	231.2
Andy Benes, StL	230.1
Nomo, LA	228.1
Valdes, LA	225.0

GAMES PITCHED
Clontz, Atl	81
Patterson, Chi	79
Dewey, SF	78
Shaw, Cin	78
Wohlers, Atl	77
Nen, Fla	75
Rojas, Mtl	74
McMichael, Atl	73
Osuna, LA	73
Plesac, Pitt	73

SAVES
Brantley, Cin	44
Worrell, LA	44
Hoffman, SD	42
Wohlers, Atl	39
Rojas, Mtl	36
Beck, SF	35
Nen, Fla	35
Bottalico, Phil	34
Eckersley, StL	30
J. Franco, NY	28

1997 BASEBALL WEEKLY ALMANAC

Postseason

▶**AL and NL Division Series**

▶**NLCS and ALCS game descriptions and composite box scores**

▶**World Series game-by-game wrapups, box scores and player statistics**

▶*and more ...*

USA SNAPSHOTS®

A look at statistics that shape the sports world

Start spreading the news ...

The Yankees' 1996 World Series title gives New York its 50th championship in professional baseball, football, basketball and hockey since 1901.

31

7

4

8

Baseball	Football	Basketball	Hockey
▶Yankees 23	▶Giants 4 NFL/ 2 Super Bowls	▶Knicks 2 NBA	▶Rangers 4 Stanley Cups
▶Giants 5		▶Nets 2 ABA	
▶Mets 2	▶Jets 1 Super Bowl		▶Islanders 4 Stanley Cups
▶Dodgers 1			

Source: USA TODAY research

Bob Laird, USA TODAY

AL Division Series: Player statistics

Baltimore 3, Cleveland 1

SERIES BATTING / BALTIMORE

	G	AB	R	H	2B	3B	HR	RBI	SO	BB	AVG
CRipken ss	4	18	2	8	3	0	0	2	0	3	.444
Murray dh	4	15	1	6	1	0	0	1	3	4	.400
Surhoff lf	4	13	3	5	0	0	3	5	0	1	.385
Anderson cf	4	17	3	5	0	0	2	4	2	3	.294
RAlomar 2b	4	17	2	5	0	0	1	4	2	3	.294
Zeile 3b	4	19	2	5	1	0	0	0	2	5	.263
Bonilla rf	4	15	4	3	0	0	2	5	4	6	.200
Parent c	4	5	0	1	0	0	0	0	0	2	.200
Incaviglia lf	2	5	1	1	0	0	0	0	0	4	.200
Palmeiro 1b	4	17	4	3	1	0	1	2	1	6	.176
Hoiles c	4	8	1	1	0	0	0	0	3	3	.143
Dvereaux rf-lf	4	1	0	0	0	0	0	0	0	0	.000
Alxnder pr-dh	3	0	2	0	0	0	0	0	0	0	---
Totals	4	150	25	43	6	0	9	23	17	40	.289

SERIES PITCHING / BALTIMORE

	G	CG	IP	H	R	ER	BB	SO	HB	WP	W	L	S	ERA
RMyers	3	0	3	0	0	0	0	3	0	0	0	0	2	0.00
TeMthws	3	0	2.2	3	0	0	1	2	0	1	0	0	0	0.00
Benitez	3	0	4	1	1	1	2	6	0	0	2	0	0	2.25
Erickson	1	0	6.2	6	3	3	2	6	0	0	0	0	0	4.05
Mussina	1	0	6	7	4	3	2	6	0	0	0	0	0	4.50
DWells	2	0	13.2	15	7	7	4	6	0	0	1	0	0	4.61
ARhodes	2	0	1	1	1	1	1	1	0	0	0	0	0	9.00
Orosco	4	0	1	2	4	4	3	2	1	0	0	1	0	36.00
Totals	4	0	38	35	20	19	15	32	1	0	3	1	2	4.50

SERIES BATTING / CLEVELAND

	G	AB	R	H	2B	3B	HR	RBI	SO	BB	AVG
Vizquel ss	4	14	4	6	1	0	0	2	3	4	.429
MRamirez rf	4	16	4	6	2	0	2	2	1	4	.375
Vizcaino 2b	3	12	1	4	2	0	0	1	1	1	.333
Thome 3b	4	10	1	3	0	0	0	0	1	5	.300
Seitzer dh-1b	4	17	1	5	1	0	0	4	2	4	.294
Belle lf	4	15	2	3	0	0	2	6	3	2	.200
Lofton cf	4	18	3	3	0	0	0	1	2	3	.167
Franco 1b-dh	4	15	1	2	0	0	0	1	1	6	.133
SAlomar c	4	16	0	2	0	0	0	3	0	2	.125
Knt 2b-1b-3b	4	8	2	1	1	0	0	0	0	0	.125
Giles ph	1	1	0	0	0	0	0	0	0	1	.000
Wilson ph	1	1	0	0	0	0	0	0	0	0	.000
Cndle ph-dh	2	0	1	0	0	0	0	0	1	0	---
Pena c	1	0	0	0	0	0	0	0	0	0	---
Totals	4	143	20	35	7	0	4	20	15	32	.245

SERIES PITCHING / CLEVELAND

	G	CG	IP	H	R	ER	BB	SO	HB	WP	W	L	S	ERA
Asnmchr	3	0	1.2	0	0	0	1	2	0	0	1	0	0	0.00
Tavarez	2	0	1.1	1	0	0	2	1	0	0	0	0	0	0.00
Ogea	1	0	0.1	0	0	0	1	0	0	0	0	0	0	0.00
Mesa	3	0	4.2	8	2	2	0	7	0	0	0	1	0	3.86
Hershiser	1	0	5	7	4	3	3	3	1	0	0	0	0	5.40
JMcDwell	1	0	5.2	6	4	4	1	5	1	0	0	0	0	6.35
Plunk	3	0	4	1	3	3	2	6	0	0	1	0	0	6.75
Nagy	2	0	11.1	15	9	9	5	13	1	0	0	1	0	7.15
Embree	3	0	1	0	1	1	0	1	1	0	0	0	0	9.00
Shuey	3	0	2	5	2	2	2	2	0	0	0	0	0	9.00
Totals	4	0	37	43	25	24	17	40	4	0	1	3	0	5.84

Albert Belle hit a grand slam in Cleveland's only victory.

Baltimore burst Indians' bubble

How does a team that goes into a funk, striking out a record 23 times in one game, end up popping corks afterward? "You don't hit 257 home runs by not putting the ball in play," Baltimore's Bobby Bonilla said with a laugh. "It takes some hacks to do that. We're gonna swing the bats." So swing, and miss, they did. Yet despite being down to their last strike in Game 4, the Orioles outlasted Cleveland 4-3 in 12 innings to clinch the Division Series.

The 23 K's in that game topped the old postseason mark of 17, set by Detroit in Game 1 of the 1968 World Series. There was a good reason for the strikeouts. The fall evening's conditions were terrible; Oriole Eddie Murray said: "Outfielders can't get a jump. Hitters can't see the ball." And the Tribe disappeared despite leading the majors with 99 victories and spending 170 straight days in first place. The Indians had set franchise records with 952 runs and 218 home runs.

Bonilla led the way in the 10-4 opening-game romp. He became the first Oriole non-pitcher to hit a postseason grand slam. (Oddly, both Mike Cuellar, in the 1970 ALCS, and Dave McNally, in that year's World Series, had done it.) B.J. Surhoff hit two dingers, and Brady Anderson added another.

The Indians were playing so tight in Game 2, they had an impromptu meeting in the dugout. It didn't help, as the Orioles won 7-4, snapping an eighth-inning tie on a controversial play in which the Indians claimed Surhoff was running out of the baseline on a potential double play.

Back home in Game 3, Cleveland won 9-4. Albert Belle led the way with a seventh-inning grand slam. In Game 4, Baltimore clinched when Roberto Alomar singled in the tying run in the ninth, then homered to lead off the 12th.

—by Bill Koenig

Yanks penned in Texas sluggers

Grim faces and dead silence greeted the media horde upon its entrance into the Texas Rangers' clubhouse following New York's 6-4 clincher in Game 4 of the Division Series. Players slumped in chairs and sofas in the middle of the room. Some tried to wash away the bitter defeat with cold drinks. Others simply stared into space, thinking of what might have been.

Texas had a fearsome lineup all season, with a top-four ranking in runs, total bases, homers and RBI. But the team slumped toward the end and, except for cleanup hitter Juan Gonzalez, didn't regain its stroke against the Yankees. "We had our chances in every game," Mickey Tettleton said. "That's all we can ask for."

Texas led in every game of the series and scored first in the last three. But the Rangers couldn't touch the Yankees' pen, which yielded just one run in 19⅔ innings of work. The Rangers failed to score past the sixth inning in the series and twice were shut down after the third. Texas batted .218 overall—compared with .284 in the regular season.

Everyone knew what the Yankees' dynamic duo—closer John Wetteland and setup man Mariano Rivera—could do. But this series was the shining moment for lesser-known relievers Jeff Nelson and David Weathers, who were each 1-0 with a 0.00 ERA.

The Rangers' vaunted defense, which committed a major-league-low 87 errors, failed them at the most inopportune time. After beating the Yankees and David Cone 6-2 in the opener behind John Burkett's complete-game gem and homers from Gonzalez and Dean Palmer, the Rangers were locked into extra innings in Game 2. But Palmer, who one night earlier made a sparkling defensive play at third base to prevent a big inning, threw away Charlie Hayes's sacrifice bunt in the 12th, allowing Derek Jeter to score for a 5-4 victory.

When the series relocated to The Ballpark in Arlington, the disparity between the bullpens was highlighted. Rangers manager Johnny Oates, exhibiting zero faith in his shaky pen, sent starter Darren Oliver to the mound for the ninth inning of Game 3 to nurse a 2-1 lead. Oliver exited after yielding singles to Jeter and Tim Raines, who eventually scored the tying and winning runs.

Oates had no choice but to use his relief corps in Game 4 after starter Bobby Witt lasted just 3⅓ innings. Seven Texas relievers entered the game, but they couldn't hold on as the Yankees came from behind for a 6-4 victory.

Nevertheless, the 1996 Texas Rangers will live in history for winning the franchise's first postseason berth. "I've never been on a team that put their butts on the line every day like this one did," Ranger Mark McLemore said. "We just didn't get the hits."

—by Deron Snyder

AL Division Series: Player statistics

New York 3, Texas 1

SERIES BATTING / NEW YORK

	G	AB	R	H	2B	3B	HR	RBI	SO	BB	AVG
Williams cf	4	15	5	7	0	0	3	5	2	1	.467
Jeter ss	4	17	2	7	1	0	0	1	0	2	.412
Fielder dh	3	11	2	4	0	0	1	4	1	2	.364
Duncan 2b	4	16	0	5	0	0	0	3	0	4	.313
Martinez 1b	4	15	3	4	2	0	0	0	3	1	.267
Raines lf	4	16	3	4	0	0	0	0	3	1	.250
Girardi c	4	9	1	2	0	0	0	1	4	1	.222
Hayes ph-3b	3	5	0	1	0	0	0	1	0	0	.200
O'Neill rf	4	15	0	2	0	0	0	0	0	2	.133
Boggs 3b	3	12	0	1	1	0	0	0	0	2	.083
Strawberry dh2	5	0	0	0	0	0	0	0	0	2	.000
Leyritz c-ph	2	3	0	0	0	0	0	0	0	1	.000
RRivera ph-rf	2	1	0	0	0	0	0	0	0	1	.000
Fox pr-dh	2	0	0	0	0	0	0	0	0	0	---
Sojo 2b	2	0	0	0	0	0	0	0	0	0	---
Totals	4	140	16	37	4	0	4	15	13	20	.264

SERIES PITCHING / NEW YORK

	G	CG	IP	H	R	ER	BB	SO	HB	WP	W	L	S	ERA
Wthers	2	0	5	1	0	0	0	5	0	0	1	0	0	0.00
MRivera	2	0	4.2	0	0	0	1	1	0	0	0	0	0	0.00
Wtteland	3	0	4	2	0	0	4	4	0	0	0	0	2	0.00
Nelson	2	0	3.2	2	0	0	2	5	0	0	1	0	0	0.00
Lloyd	2	0	1	1	0	0	0	0	0	0	0	0	0	0.00
Key	1	0	5	5	2	2	1	3	0	0	0	0	0	3.60
Pettitte	1	0	6.1	4	4	4	6	3	0	1	0	0	0	5.68
Bhringer	2	0	1.1	3	2	1	2	0	0	0	1	0	0	6.75
Cone	1	0	6	8	6	6	2	8	0	0	0	1	0	9.00
Rogers	2	0	2	5	2	2	1	0	0	0	0	0	0	9.00
Totals	4	0	39	31	16	15	20	30	0	1	3	1	1	3.46

SERIES BATTING / TEXAS

	G	AB	R	H	2B	3B	HR	RBI	SO	BB	AVG
Gonzalez rf	4	16	5	7	0	0	5	9	3	2	.438
Rodriguez c	4	16	1	6	1	0	0	2	2	3	.375
Elster ss	4	12	2	4	2	0	0		3	2	.333
Palmer 3b	4	19	3	4	1	0	1	2	0	5	.211
Hamilton cf	4	19	0	3	0	0	0	0	0	2	.158
McLemore 2b	4	15	1	2	0	0	0	2	0	4	.133
Clark 1b	4	16	1	2	0	0	0	0	3	2	.125
Greer lf	4	16	2	2	0	0	0	0	3	3	.125
Tettleton dh	4	12	1	1	0	0	0	1	5	7	.083
Newson ph	3	1	0	0	0	0	0	0	1	0	.000
Buford pr	3	0	0	0	0	0	0	0	0	0	---
Totals	4	142	16	31	4	0	6	16	20	30	.218

SERIES PITCHING / TEXAS

	G	CG	IP	H	R	ER	BB	SO	HB	WP	W	L	S	ERA
Cook	2	0	1.1	0	0	0	1	0	0	0	0	0	0	0.00
Hennmn	3	0	1	1	0	0	1	1	0	0	0	0	0	0.00
Patterson	1	0	0.1	1	0	0	0	0	0	0	0	0	0	0.00
Burkett	1	1	9	10	2	2	1	7	0	0	1	0	0	2.00
Stanton	3	0	3.1	2	1	1	3	3	0	0	0	1	0	2.70
Russell	2	0	3	3	1	1	0	1	0	0	0	0	0	3.00
Oliver	1	0	8	6	3	3	2	3	1	0	0	1	0	3.38
Hill	1	0	6	5	3	3	3	1	1	0	0	0	0	4.50
Pavlik	1	0	2.2	4	2	2	0	1	0	0	0	1	0	6.75
Witt	1	0	3.1	4	3	3	2	3	0	1	0	0	0	8.10
Vosberg	1	0	0	1	0	0	0	0	0	0	0	0	0	---
Totals	4	1	38	37	16	15	13	20	2	1	1	3	0	3.55

NL Division Series: Player statistics

St. Louis 3, San Diego 0

SERIES BATTING / ST. LOUIS

	G	AB	R	H	2B	3B	HR	RBI	SO	BB	AVG
Sweeney ph	1	1	0	1	0	0	0	0	0	0	1.000
Lankford cf	1	2	1	1	0	0	0	0	1	0	.500
AnBenes p	1	2	1	1	0	0	0	0	0	1	.500
Gant lf	3	10	3	4	1	0	1	4	2	0	.400
Jordan rf	3	12	4	4	0	0	1	3	1	3	.333
Clayton ss	2	6	1	2	0	0	0	0	3	1	.333
Smith ss	2	3	1	1	0	0	0	0	2	0	.333
Mabry 1b	3	10	1	3	0	1	0	1	1	1	.300
Pagnozzi c	3	11	0	3	0	0	0	2	1	3	.273
Alicea 2b	3	11	1	2	2	0	0	0	1	4	.182
McGee cf	3	10	1	1	0	0	0	1	1	3	.100
Gaetti 3b	3	11	1	1	0	0	1	3	0	0	.091
Honeycutt p	3	1	0	0	0	0	0	0	0	1	.000
Gallego 2b	2	1	0	0	0	0	0	0	0	1	.000
Osborne p	1	1	0	0	0	0	0	0	0	0	.000
Stottlemyre p	1	2	0	0	0	0	0	0	0	2	.000
Eckersley p	3	0	0	0	0	0	0	0	0	0	---
Petkovsek p	1	0	0	0	0	0	0	0	0	0	---
Mathews p	1	0	0	0	0	0	0	0	0	0	---
Mejia pr	1	0	0	0	0	0	0	0	0	0	---
Totals	3	94	15	24	3	1	3	14	13	23	.255

SERIES PITCHING / ST. LOUIS

	G	CG	IP	H	R	ER	BB	SO	HB	WP	W	L	S	ERA
Eckersley	3	0	3.2	3	0	0	0	2	0	0	0	0	3	0.00
Petkvsek	1	0	2	0	0	0	1	0	0	0	1	0	0	0.00
Mathews	1	0	1	1	0	0	0	2	0	0	1	0	0	0.00
Stottlmyre	1	0	6.2	5	1	1	2	7	1	0	1	0	0	1.35
Hneycutt	3	0	2.2	3	1	1	2	0	0	1	0	0	0	3.38
AnBenes	1	0	7	6	4	4	1	9	0	0	0	0	0	5.14
Osborne	1	0	4	7	4	4	0	5	0	0	0	0	0	9.00
Totals	3	0	27	25	10	10	4	28	1	0	3	0	3	3.33

SERIES BATTING / SAN DIEGO

	G	AB	R	H	2B	3B	HR	RBI	SO	BB	AVG
CGwynn ph	2	2	1	2	0	0	0	0	0	0	1.000
Lvngstne ph	2	1	1	0	0	0	0	0	0	0	.500
Johnson c	2	8	2	3	1	0	0	0	0	1	.375
Henderson lf	3	12	2	4	0	0	0	1	2	3	.333
Cianfrcco 1b	3	3	1	1	0	0	0	0	0	1	.333
TGwynn rf	3	13	0	4	1	0	0	1	0	2	.308
Caminiti 3b	3	10	3	3	0	0	3	3	2	5	.300
Reed 2b	3	11	0	3	1	0	0	2	0	1	.273
Gomez ss	3	12	0	2	0	0	0	1	0	4	.167
Joyner 1b	3	9	0	1	0	0	0	0	0	2	.111
Finley cf	3	12	0	1	0	0	0	1	0	4	.083
Ashby p	1	1	0	0	0	0	0	0	0	1	.000
Sanders p	1	1	0	0	0	0	0	0	0	0	.000
Hamilton p	1	2	0	0	0	0	0	0	0	2	.000
Vaughn lf-ph	3	3	0	0	0	0	0	0	0	1	.000
Flaherty c	2	4	0	0	0	0	0	0	0	1	.000
Hoffman p	2	0	0	0	0	0	0	0	0	0	---
Veras p	2	0	0	0	0	0	0	0	0	0	---
Worrell p	2	0	0	0	0	0	0	0	0	0	---
Bochtler p	1	0	0	0	0	0	0	0	0	0	---
Blair p	1	0	0	0	0	0	0	0	0	0	---
Valenzuela p	1	0	0	0	0	0	0	0	0	0	---
Lopez pr	1	0	0	0	0	0	0	0	0	0	---
Totals	3	105	10	25	3	0	3	9	4	28	.238

SERIES PITCHING / SAN DIEGO

	G	CG	IP	H	R	ER	BB	SO	HB	WP	W	L	S	ERA
Blair	1	0	2	1	0	0	2	3	0	0	0	0	0	0.00
Veras	2	0	1	1	0	0	1	0	0	0	0	0	0	0.00
Vinzuela	1	0	.2	0	0	0	2	0	0	0	0	0	0	0.00
Worrell	2	0	3.2	4	1	1	1	2	0	0	0	0	0	2.45
Hamilton	1	0	3	3	3	0	6	1	0	0	1	0		4.50
Ashby	1	0	5.1	7	4	4	1	5	0	1	0	0	0	6.75
Sanders	1	0	4.1	3	4	4	4	0	0	0	0	0	0	8.31
Hoffman	2	0	1.2	3	2	2	1	2	0	0	0	1	0	10.00
Bochtler	1	0	.1	0	1	1	2	0	0	1	0	1	0	27.00
Totals	3	0	25	24	15	15	13	23	1	2	0	3	0	5.40

Rickey Henderson scored a rare Padres run in Game 2.

St. Louis winged onward

With all the talk of Padres and Cardinals, this Division Series had the overtones of a holy war, and many of the St. Louis players felt a sense of redemption after their three-game sweep of San Diego. Outfielder Brian Jordan, criticized for having given up a promising NFL career, hit the clinching home run in the 7-5 Game 3 win. Andy Benes, labeled an underachiever during his seven seasons in San Diego, pitched seven strong innings against his former teammates in Game 2. Todd Stottlemyre, who entered 1996 with a 7.50 career postseason ERA, shut down the Padres 3-1 in Game 1. And Dennis Eckersley, whose career has been marred by giving up historic postseason home runs to Kirk Gibson and Roberto Alomar, saved all three games in his first playoff series since 1992.

Only three Cardinals—Willie McGee, Tom Pagnozzi and Ozzie Smith—were members of the last Cardinals playoff team, the 1987 club that lost in the World Series to the Minnesota Twins. But the 1996 team had many playoff veterans, including manager Tony La Russa and GM Walt Jocketty, who were together for Oakland's 1988-90 World Series appearances. La Russa and Jocketty overhauled the Cards roster for '96, and the new-old players had key roles against San Diego. In addition to Benes, Stottlemyre and Eckersley, 41-year-old ex-A's setup man Rick Honeycutt got the win in Game 2. Third baseman Gary Gaetti, a member of the '87 Twins, slammed the decisive three-run homer in Game 1. And Ron Gant, 31, the left fielder for the 1991-93 Atlanta Braves, contributed a home run and four RBI.

By contrast, the Padres showed signs of postseason inexperience. Third baseman Ken Caminiti, who has won Gold Gloves the last two seasons, committed three errors. Padres pitchers surrendered 13 walks, nine more than the Cardinals. "It's a tough loss," said outfielder Tony Gwynn. "But you have to keep everything in perspective. You learn your lessons and hopefully you get better."

—by Pete Williams

There was no Dodging the blame

The Los Angeles Dodgers know the kind of team they could be if all the pieces came together. They would have deep pitching, timely hitting, an effective blend of veterans and youth. In other words, they would look a lot like the team that thrashed them in this year's Division Series—the Atlanta Braves. Before the series, the Braves were understandably worried about L.A. In the National League, only the Dodgers had as many quality arms as Atlanta.

But once the games began, Atlanta had an answer for everything the Dodgers threw at them. Until the Braves busted out for a four-run fourth inning in Game 3, they were winning an intriguing contest of "Anything You Can Do, I Can Do Better." "We both had good pitching," said Dodgers manager Bill Russell. "They came across with more runs. Why? They're big-game guys."

Game 1 in Los Angeles came down to two big flies by the respective catchers: Atlanta's Javy Lopez's went out for the decisive 10th-inning home run, while Dodger Mike Piazza's blow barely stayed in the yard.

This year the Dodgers picked the worst possible time to fall on their faces. First they fumbled away the NL West title by losing a three-game series at home to the San Diego Padres, then followed that up by being swept by the Braves. They didn't win much sympathy from their fans, either. L.A. was the only team not to sell out a playoff game this season. For Game 1, there were 12,000 empty seats at Chavez Ravine. By Game 2, which the Braves won 3-2 behind Greg Maddux and three solo homers, "Make Some Noise" became the public-service announcement on the scoreboard.

While the Dodgers battled through much this season—from Tommy Lasorda's farewell to Brett Butler's courageous fight against cancer—they went out on a bad note. Down the stretch, the Dodgers' stars failed them. The team was homerless in the series, and the heart of the order—Mike Piazza, Eric Karros and Raul Mondesi—went 5-for-30 with three RBI.

By Game 3, ace Hideo Nomo was L.A.'s last hope, but he lasted only 3⅔ innings in his worst performance of the season, giving up five hits, five earned runs and five walks in the 5-2 clincher. "I could not throw strikes," he said afterward. "I made mistakes. Piazza wanted balls outside, but I made the pitch down the middle."

In the Dodgers' clubhouse, attempts were made to put a positive spin on the last two weeks—how it didn't matter when compared with how much the ball club had accomplished and endured this season. But Piazza said, "It's embarrassing that you don't go out there and give them a little more fight."

—by Tim Wendel

NL Division Series: Player statistics

Atlanta 3, Los Angeles 0

SERIES BATTING / ATLANTA

	G	AB	R	H	2B	3B	HR	RBI	SO	BB	AVG
Glavine p	1	2	1	1	1	0	0	0	0	0	.500
McGriff 1b	3	9	1	3	1	0	1	3	2	1	.333
Perez c	1	3	0	1	0	0	0	0	0	0	.333
Lopez c	2	7	1	2	0	0	1	1	1	0	.286
CJones 3b	3	9	2	2	0	0	1	2	3	4	.222
Dye rf	3	11	1	2	0	0	1	1	0	6	.182
Lemke 2b	3	12	1	2	1	0	0	2	0	1	.167
Klesko lf	3	8	1	1	0	0	1	1	3	4	.125
Blauser ss	3	9	0	1	0	0	0	0	1	3	.111
Grissom cf	3	12	2	1	0	0	0	0	1	2	.083
Pendleton ph	1	1	0	0	0	0	0	0	0	1	.000
Maddux p	1	2	0	0	0	0	0	0	0	1	.000
Polonia ph	2	2	0	0	0	0	0	0	0	1	.000
Smoltz p	1	2	0	0	0	0	0	0	0	0	.000
Wohlers p	3	0	0	0	0	0	0	0	0	0	---
Belliard ss	3	0	0	0	0	0	0	0	0	0	---
McMichael p	2	0	0	0	0	0	0	0	0	0	---
Bielecki p	1	0	0	0	0	0	0	0	0	0	---
AJones lf-ph	3	0	0	0	0	0	0	0	1	0	---
Totals	3	89	10	16	3	0	4	10	12	24	.180

SERIES PITCHING / ATLANTA

	G	CG	IP	H	R	ER	BB	SO	HB	WP	W	L	S	ERA
Maddux	1	0	7	3	2	0	0	7	0	0	1	0	0	0.00
Wohlers	3	0	3.1	1	0	0	4	0	0	0	0	0	2	0.00
Bielecki	1	0	.2	0	0	0	1	1	0	0	0	0	0	0.00
Smoltz	1	0	9	4	1	1	2	7	0	0	1	0	0	1.00
Glavine	1	0	6.2	5	1	1	3	7	0	0	1	0	0	1.35
McMichl	2	0	1.1	1	1	1	1	3	0	0	0	0	0	6.75
Totals	3	0	28	14	5	3	7	29	0	0	3	0	2	0.96

SERIES BATTING / LOS ANGELES

	G	AB	R	H	2B	3B	HR	RBI	SO	BB	AVG
Hllndsworth lf	3	12	1	4	3	0	0	1	0	3	.333
Piazza c	3	10	1	3	0	0	0	2	1	2	.300
Gagne ss	3	11	2	3	1	0	0	0	0	5	.273
Castro 2b	2	5	0	1	1	0	0	1	1	1	.200
Mondesi rf	3	11	0	2	2	0	0	1	0	4	.182
Kirby cf	3	8	1	1	0	0	0	0	2	1	.125
Nomo p	1	1	0	0	0	0	0	0	0	1	.000
Clark ph	2	2	0	0	0	0	0	0	0	2	.000
Ashley ph	2	2	0	0	0	0	0	0	0	2	.000
Hansen ph	2	2	0	0	0	0	0	0	0	0	.000
Curtis cf	1	2	0	0	0	0	0	0	1	1	.000
Valdes p	1	2	0	0	0	0	0	0	0	0	.000
RMartinez p	1	3	0	0	0	0	0	0	0	2	.000
DeShields 2b	2	4	0	0	0	0	0	0	0	1	.000
Karros 1b	3	9	0	0	0	0	0	0	2	3	.000
Wallach 3b	3	11	0	0	0	0	0	0	0	1	.000
Candiotti p	1	0	0	0	0	0	0	0	0	0	---
Osuna p	2	0	0	0	0	0	0	0	0	0	---
Dreifort p	1	0	0	0	0	0	0	0	0	0	---
Guthrie p	1	0	0	0	0	0	0	0	0	0	---
Radinsky p	2	0	0	0	0	0	0	0	0	0	---
Astacio p	1	0	0	0	0	0	0	0	0	0	---
Worrell p	1	0	0	0	0	0	0	0	0	0	---
Totals	3	95	5	14	7	0	0	5	7	29	.147

SERIES PITCHING / LOS ANGELES

	G	CG	IP	H	R	ER	BB	SO	HB	WP	W	L	S	ERA
Candiotti	1	0	2	0	0	0	0	1	0	0	0	0	0	0.00
Astacio	1	0	1.2	0	0	0	0	1	0	0	0	0	0	0.00
Radinsky	2	0	1.1	0	0	0	1	2	0	0	0	0	0	0.00
Worrell	1	0	1	0	0	0	0	1	0	0	0	0	0	0.00
Dreifort	1	0	.2	0	0	0	0	0	0	0	0	0	0	0.00
Guthrie	1	0	.1	0	0	0	1	1	0	0	0	0	0	0.00
RMartinez	1	0	8	3	1	1	3	6	0	0	0	0	0	1.12
Valdes	1	0	6.1	5	3	3	0	5	0	0	0	1	0	4.26
Osuna	2	0	2	3	1	1	1	4	1	0	0	1	0	4.50
Nomo	1	0	3.2	5	5	5	5	3	0	0	0	1	0	12.27
Totals	3	0	27	16	10	10	12	24	1	0	0	3	0	3.33

ALCS:
Player Statistics

New York 4, Baltimore 1

SERIES BATTING / NEW YORK

	G	AB	R	H	2B	3B	HR	RBI	BB	SO	AVG
Williams cf	5	19	6	9	3	0	2	6	5	4	.474
Jeter ss	5	24	5	10	2	0	1	1	0	5	.417
Strwbrry rf-lf	4	12	4	5	0	0	3	5	2	2	.417
O'Neill rf	4	11	1	3	0	0	1	2	3	2	.273
Raines lf	5	15	2	4	1	0	0	0	1	1	.267
Girardi c	4	12	1	3	0	1	0	0	1	3	.250
Lyritz c-ph-rf	3	8	1	2	0	0	1	2	1	4	.250
Duncan 2b	4	15	0	3	2	0	0	0	0	3	.200
Sojo 2b	3	5	0	1	0	0	0	0	0	1	.200
Martinez 1b	5	22	3	4	1	0	0	0	0	2	.182
Fielder dh	5	18	3	3	0	0	2	8	4	5	.167
Hayes ph-3b	4	7	0	1	0	0	0	0	2	2	.143
Boggs 3b	3	15	1	2	0	0	0	0	1	3	.133
Fox dh	2	0	0	0	0	0	0	0	0	0	.—
Aldrete ph	1	0	0	0	0	0	0	0	0	0	.—
Totals	5	183	27	50	9	1	10	24	20	37	.273

SERIES PITCHING / NEW YORK

	G	CG	IP	H	R	ER	BB	SO	HB	WP	W	L	SV	ERA
Rivera	2	0	4	6	0	0	1	5	0	0	1	0	0	0.00
Lloyd	2	0	1.2	0	0	0	1	0	0	0	0	0	0	0.00
Weathers	2	0	3	3	0	0	0	0	0	0	1	0	0	0.00
Key	1	0	8	3	2	2	1	5	0	0	1	0	0	2.25
Cone	1	0	6	5	2	2	5	5	0	1	0	0	0	3.00
Pettitte	2	0	15	10	6	6	5	7	0	0	1	0	0	3.60
Wettelnd	4	0	4	2	2	2	1	5	0	0	0	0	1	4.50
Nelson	2	0	2.1	5	3	3	0	2	0	0	0	1	0	11.57
Rogers	1	0	3	5	4	4	2	3	0	1	0	0	0	12.00
Totals	5	0	47	39	19	19	15	33	0	2	4	1	1	3.64

SERIES BATTING / BALTIMORE

	G	AB	R	H	2B	3B	HR	RBI	BB	SO	AVG
Incaviglia dh	1	2	1	1	0	0	0	0	0	0	.500
Zeile 3b	5	22	3	8	0	0	3	5	2	1	.364
Murray dh-ph	5	15	1	4	0	0	1	2	2	2	.267
Surhoff lf-ph	5	15	0	4	0	0	0	2	1	2	.267
CRipken ss	5	20	1	5	1	0	0	1	0	4	.250
Palmeiro 1b	5	17	4	4	0	0	2	4	4	4	.235
Alomar 2b	5	23	2	5	2	0	0	1	0	4	.217
Anderson cf	5	21	5	4	1	0	1	1	3	5	.190
Hoiles c	4	12	1	2	0	0	1	2	1	3	.167
Parent c	2	6	0	1	0	0	0	0	0	2	.167
Bonilla rf	5	20	1	1	0	0	1	2	1	4	.050
Tarasco rf	2	1	0	0	0	0	0	0	0	1	.000
Devereaux lf	3	2	0	0	0	0	0	0	0	1	.000
Totals	5	176	19	39	4	0	9	19	15	33	.222

SERIES PITCHING / BALTIMORE

	G	CG	IP	H	R	ER	BB	SO	HB	WP	W	L	SV	ERA
Mathews	3	0	2.1	0	0	0	2	3	1	0	0	0	0	0.00
Rhodes	3	0	2	2	0	0	2	0	1	0	0	0	0	0.00
Myers	3	0	4	4	1	1	3	2	0	0	0	1	0	2.25
Erickson	2	0	11.1	14	9	3	4	8	0	0	1	0	0	2.38
Mills	3	0	2.1	3	1	1	1	3	0	0	0	0	0	3.86
Wells	1	0	6.2	8	3	3	6	1	0	1	0	0	0	4.05
Orosco	4	0	2	2	1	1	2	0	0	0	0			4.50
Mussina	1	0	7.2	8	5	5	2	6	0	0	0	1	0	5.87
Benitez	3	0	2.1	3	2	2	3	2	0	0	0	0	1	7.71
Coppingr	1	0	5.1	6	5	5	1	3	0	0	0	1	0	8.44
Totals	5	0	46	50	27	21	20	37	2	1	1	4	1	4.11

Darryl Strawberry hit three home runs against Baltimore.

By Nell Seiler, USA TODAY

Yanks "made things happen"

The Kid didn't let the ball roll between his legs like Roberto Alomar, the Gold Glove second baseman. The Kid didn't leave 34 runners on base, or hit 5-for-31 with men in scoring position. The Kid didn't go 1-for-20 like Bobby Bonilla, the $4.3 million right fielder. Heck, Jeffrey Maier wasn't anywhere *near* Baltimore when the Orioles became the second team ever to be swept at home in a League Championship Series.

Perhaps the Orioles did have Game 1 of the American League Championship Series stolen from them on the controversial eighth-inning home run by New York Yankees rookie shortstop Derek Jeter, a play in which Maier, the 12-year-old New Jersey schoolboy (when he's not playing hooky) reached over the wall and deflected a fly ball into the seats, whereupon right-field umpire Rich Garcia ruled it a game-tying home run. The Yanks went on to win the game 5-4 in 11 innings on a home run off Baltimore closer Randy Myers by center fielder Bernie Williams.

The Orioles, however, have no one to blame but themselves after that. How could a team that played so well and got every conceivable break in upsetting the Cleveland Indians look so wretched against New York? How could the magic carpet they rode back to respectability from their late-July abyss crash so abruptly?

"They certainly played a lot better than we did, and they deserve to be American League champions," Orioles manager Davey Johnson said. "They played solid baseball. They made things happen. They didn't let us make things happen. That's an attribute of a great team."

The Orioles, who hit a major-league-record 257 home runs this season, were entirely too reliant on the long ball during the series. They never did figure out how to advance runners, and their reliance on the three-run homer left visions of Earl Weaver puffing a cigarette butt in the dugout tunnel. They hit nine home runs in the five ALCS games, and 13 of their 19 runs in the series came on the long ball. Five other runs scored on sacrifice flies or groundouts. "We were kind of a one-dimensional team," Johnson said. "A guy makes a mistake and we whack it. It helps if you have a little more speed, a few more contact hitters. You will be able to manufacture some more runs."

Even more puzzling was the unraveling of the Orioles infield, which committed four errors—two by Alomar, one each by shortstop Cal Ripken and third baseman Todd Zeile—and failed to turn several key double plays. "We played a little jittery at times," Johnson said. "We usually don't make very many mistakes defensively, certainly not in our infield."

Most costly was Bernie Williams' ground ball that rolled through Alomar's legs in the third inning of Game 5. It led to five unearned runs, including four on home runs by Cecil Fielder and by Darryl Strawberry, who went deep three times in the series. "That ball kind of tricked me," said Alomar, a six-time Gold Glove Award winner with a .985 fielding percentage this season. "I thought it was going to take a hop and come up, and it just stayed down. Hey, I'm a human being. I'm not going to catch every ball. I wish I could."

Then there was Zeile's bizarre play in the eighth inning of Game 3. Faking a throw to second base, Zeile had the ball slip out of his hand and trickle several feet away. An alert Williams raced home from third with the tie-breaking run in the 5-2 game. And how about Scott Erickson's giving up three home runs in the third inning of the clincher? He had surrendered just one home run in 385 lifetime at-bats to players in the Yankees' Game 5 lineup.

The Yankees went 9-0 at Camden Yards this season, and the Orioles joined the 1991 Toronto Blue Jays, who lost three consecutive games to Minnesota at SkyDome, as the only teams to be swept at home in a League Championship Series. The Orioles seemed flat at the plate. Outfielder Brady Anderson was 4-for-21 with one RBI. Bonilla—bothered by a sore shoulder after crashing into the wall in the first game—was 1-for-20 in the ALCS and 4-for-35 in the postseason, although three of his hits were homers.

As the Orioles waited till next year, the Yankees and manager Joe Torre waited to go to the World Series. The Braves-Cardinals series was still to be decided, with St. Louis leading 2-1 at the time the Yanks clinched. Now that Torre had finally reached the Fall Classic after a record 4,272 Series-less games as a player or manager, he knew he would find himself face-to-face with a familiar foe. Torre managed the Braves for three seasons, winning a divisional title and the NL Manager of the Year award with them in 1982, and from 1990 to '95, he was at the helm in St. Louis, where he went 351-354 but is still remembered fondly. When the last out in the Orioles-Yankees game was shown on the video board in St. Louis as fans awaited Game 4 of the NLCS, the crowd cheered. The ovation grew louder when Torre appeared on the screen. Organist Ernie Hayes played "New York, New York" before the national anthem.

New York, New York is again excited about baseball since Torre came to the Bronx. As the Yankees came off the field in Baltimore, streaming toward the champagne celebration in the clubhouse, Torre, 56, hugged them individually. "I wanted the players to celebrate in the middle of the field like I've done in every other series victory," he said. "I just wanted to watch them and as they came back, grab them and hug them. I started crying." Torre also said he harbored no resentment against his old employers. But anyone could see that the prospect of defeating either of them in the Fall Classic would be sweet.

Ex–National Leaguer Todd Zeile liked New York's chances in a Braves-Yankees showdown. "Atlanta goes through spurts offensively," he said. "They have the pitching, but their offense can go up and down. Good pitching can shut them down, and the Yankees have that."

—by Bill Koenig and Tim Wendel

NLCS: Player Statistics

Atlanta 4, St. Louis 3

SERIES BATTING / ATLANTA

	G	AB	R	H	2B	3B	HR	RBI	SO	BB	AVG
Belliard ss	4	6	0	4	0	0	0	2	0	0	.667
Lopez c	7	24	8	13	5	0	2	6	3	1	.542
Neagle p	2	2	0	1	0	0	0	0	0	0	.500
Lemke 2b	7	27	4	12	2	0	1	5	3	2	.444
CJones 3b	7	25	6	11	2	0	0	4	4	1	.440
Grissom cf	7	35	7	10	1	0	1	3	0	8	.286
Smoltz p	2	7	1	2	0	0	0	1	0	3	.286
Klesko lf	6	16	1	4	0	0	1	3	2	6	.250
Mordecai 3b	4	4	1	1	0	0	0	0	0	1	.250
McGriff 1b	7	28	6	7	0	1	2	7	3	5	.250
AJones lf	5	9	3	2	0	0	1	3	3	2	.222
Dye rf	7	28	2	6	1	0	0	4	1	7	.214
Blauser ss	7	17	5	3	0	1	0	2	4	6	.176
Glavine p	2	6	0	1	0	1	0	3	0	3	.167
Perez c	4	1	0	0	0	0	0	0	1	0	.000
Wohlers p	3	1	0	0	0	0	0	0	0	1	.000
Polonia ph	3	3	0	0	0	0	0	0	0	0	.000
Maddux p	2	4	0	0	0	0	0	0	0	2	.000
Pendletn ph	6	6	0	0	0	0	0	0	1	3	.000
Bielecki p	3	0	0	0	0	0	0	0	0	0	---
Avery p	2	0	0	0	0	0	0	0	0	0	---
McMichael p	3	0	0	0	0	0	0	0	0	0	---
Wade p	1	0	0	0	0	0	0	0	0	0	---
Clontz p	1	0	0	0	0	0	0	0	0	0	---
Totals	7	249	44	77	11	3	8	43	25	51	.309

SERIES PITCHING / ATLANTA

	G	CG	IP	H	R	ER	BB	SO	HB	WP	W	L	S	ERA
Wohlers	3	0	3	0	0	0	0	4	0	1	0	0	2	0.00
Bielecki	3	0	3	0	0	0	1	5	0	0	0	0	0	0.00
Avery	2	0	2	2	0	0	1	1	0	0	0	0	0	0.00
Clontz	1	0	.2	0	0	0	0	0	0	0	0	0	0	0.00
Wade	1	0	.1	0	0	0	0	1	0	0	0	0	0	0.00
Smoltz	2	0	15	12	2	2	3	12	0	2	2	0	0	1.20
Glavine	2	0	13	10	3	3	0	9	1	0	1	1	0	2.08
Neagle	2	0	7.2	2	2	2	3	8	0	0	0	0	0	2.35
Maddux	2	0	14.1	15	9	4	2	10	0	1	1	1	0	2.51
McMichl	3	0	2	4	2	2	1	3	0	0	0	1	0	9.00
Totals	6	0	61	45	18	13	11	53	1	4	4	3	2	1.92

SERIES BATTING / ST. LOUIS

	G	AB	R	H	2B	3B	HR	RBI	BB	SO	AVG
Clayton ss	5	20	4	7	0	0	0	1	1	4	.350
McGee cf	6	15	0	5	0	0	0	0	0	3	.333
Gaetti 3b	7	24	1	7	0	0	1	4	1	5	.292
Young ph-1b	4	7	1	2	0	1	0	2	0	2	.286
Mabry 1b	7	23	1	6	0	0	0	0	0	6	.261
AnBenes p	3	4	0	1	1	0	0	0	1	2	.250
Gant lf	7	25	3	6	1	0	2	4	2	6	.240
Jordan rf	7	25	3	6	1	1	1	2	1	3	.240
Pagnozzi c	7	19	1	3	1	0	0	1	1	4	.158
Gallego 3b	7	14	1	2	0	0	0	0	1	3	.143
Mejia cf	3	1	1	0	0	0	0	0	0	1	.000
AlBenes p	2	1	0	0	0	0	0	0	0	1	.000
Jackson p	1	1	0	0	0	0	0	0	0	1	.000
Stottlemyr p	2	2	0	0	0	0	0	0	0	0	.000
Osborne p	2	3	0	0	0	0	0	0	0	3	.000
Sheaffer c	2	3	0	0	0	0	0	0	0	1	.000
Sweeney rf	5	4	1	0	0	0	0	0	0	2	.000
Alicea 2b	5	8	0	0	0	0	0	0	2	1	.000
Smith ss	3	9	0	0	0	0	0	0	0	1	.000
Lankford cf	5	13	1	0	0	0	0	1	1	4	.000
Petkovsek p	6	0	0	0	0	0	0	0	0	0	---
Honeycutt p	5	0	0	0	0	0	0	0	0	0	---
Fossas p	5	0	0	0	0	0	0	0	0	0	---
Eckersley p	3	0	0	0	0	0	0	0	0	0	---
Mathews p	2	0	0	0	0	0	0	0	0	0	---
Totals	7	221	18	45	4	2	4	15	11	53	.204

SERIES PITCHING / ST. LOUIS

	G	CG	IP	H	R	ER	BB	SO	HB	WP	W	L	S	ERA
Eckersley	3	0	3.1	2	0	0	0	4	0	0	1	0	1	0.00
Mathews	2	0	.2	2	0	0	1	2	0	0	0	0	0	0.00
Fossas	5	0	4.1	1	1	1	3	1	0	0	0	0	0	2.08
AlBenes	2	0	6.1	3	2	2	2	5	1	0	0	1	0	2.84
AnBenes	3	0	15.1	19	9	9	3	9	0	0	0	1	0	5.28
Petkvsek	6	0	7.1	11	6	6	3	7	0	1	0	1	0	7.36
Hneycutt	5	0	4	5	4	4	3	3	0	0	0	0	0	9.00
Jackson	1	0	3	7	3	3	3	3	0	0	0	0	0	9.00
Osborne	2	0	7.2	12	8	8	4	6	1	1	1	1	0	9.39
Stottlmyr	3	0	8	15	11	11	3	11	0	1	1	0	1	12.38
Totals	7	0	60	77	44	44	25	51	3	2	3	4	1	6.60

The Braves celebrated their 14-0 win in Game 5 of the NLCS.

By Mary Butkus, AP/World Wide Photos

Atlanta gunned down St Louis' lead, season

The St. Louis Cardinals, whose magical run through the postseason ended with a third consecutive loss to the Atlanta Braves in the deciding seventh game, were left to ponder what might have been—and to contemplate the greatness of Atlanta's rotation. The Braves in the '90s are about pitching, about a seemingly endless parade of Cy Young Award winners who kept Atlanta in the series even after the Cardinals went up three games to one.

In Game 5, seven shutout innings from this year's Cy Young winner, John Smoltz, and the first Atlanta offensive outburst of October considerably shrunk the Cards' comfort zone. That 14-0 reality check got the Braves out of the Busch Stadium bedlam and back to Atlanta, where four-time Cy Young winner Greg Maddux and 1991 winner Tom Glavine completed the first comeback from 3-1 in NLCS history by allowing only one run between them in the final two games. The record-setting 15-0 finale was the biggest slaughter in almost a century of postseason play. The clincher broke two of the Braves' just-set Game 5 marks, for most runs in an NLCS game and for the biggest margin of victory in any postseason contest.

Before the simultaneous Atlanta hitting explosion and pitching dominance, Cardinals manager Tony La Russa had discovered that DH-less National League baseball provided new and sterner tactical challenges. He said that you "do some little things right and that can be the difference in the game." He had been up to all those challenges early in the series, as the little things went right for him time after time during the three consecutive victories that transformed the Cardinals from being a team NBC didn't want to be stuck with on prime time TV during the Division Series to being the improbable underdogs that America yearns for in October.

By winning Games 2, 3 and 4, the Cardinals made themselves this year's version of the Seattle Mariners, the compelling surprise that baseball seems to need every year to redeem itself. But like the Mariners' 1995 fairy tale, this came up short of a happy ending.

Even trailing three games to one, the Braves kept the edge in pitching matchups. A strong—though losing—effort from their only non-Cy starter, Denny Neagle (he won *only* 16 games in '96), in Game 4 allowed Atlanta manager Bobby Cox to line up his terrific trio to pitch with their normal rest.

La Russa returned to Atlanta with Andy Benes and Donovan Osborne set to pitch on just three days' rest, and it cost him. Benes pitched well in Game 6, allowing only three hits and two runs in his five-inning stint, but Maddux was masterful, giving up one run and walking nobody before handing the ball to closer Mark Wohlers with two out in the eighth. Benes has yet to win a game in his postseason career, which includes 1995's Mariners run.

The Braves were thought to have been a bit more vulnerable to Osborne's left-handedness with slugging first baseman Fred McGriff struggling a bit, but the first baseman, who had broken out of his slump in Game 5 with a homer and three RBI, went 3-for-5 with another home run and four RBI as Atlanta pounded Osborne for six runs in the first inning of Game 7. The Braves then ganged up on three relievers for nine more runs by the seventh inning.

The most poignant moment of the one-sided anticlimax came in the fifth inning, when the Cardinals' future Hall of Fame shortstop Ozzie Smith, retiring at age 41 after 19 seasons and innumerable spectacular plays, came up to pinch-hit against Glavine. The game was already 10-0, and Smith's final at-bat was unsuitably undramatic except for the fans' response. After receiving a standing ovation from the Atlanta–Fulton County Stadium crowd, he lifted a foul fly that was easily caught by Braves right fielder Jermaine Dye. Smith then got another standing O to end what he afterward called a "storybook career."

Cox and the Braves had spent the previous weekend wondering if they were facing something more magical than a please-make-my-wish-come-true Cinderella. From the Braves' dugout, this had stopped being cute several games ago. "It's frustrating," Cox said after the most galling of the three losses, St. Louis's four-run comeback in Game 4, in which Neagle took a 3-0 lead into the seventh inning.

"We knew somewhere along the line somebody was going to [win a game from] us," Braves third baseman Chipper Jones had said after the first loss. It happened again in the next game. But Cox wrote off the Game 3 loss more to those "little things" than to the Braves' .220 postseason batting average to that point. "I would take exactly what we did today, with a little bit of luck on our side," he said. "Jermaine Dye hit two bullets that both were caught. The one in the first inning changes the entire game; it's 3-0 in a heartbeat," instead of the 1-0 edge that ex-Brave left fielder Ron Gant wiped out in the Cards' next at-bat with a two-run homer. Gant hit another dinger off Tom Glavine later in the game, both shots coming off what Cox called "horrible changeups."

Cox said of the balls Dye hit, "You can't make them fall in," but the Braves did it in Game 5 so frequently that every Braves starter had a hit by the fourth inning. Before that 22-hit attack, Atlanta had averaged only 3½ runs over their previous 24 games.

In contrast to the consistency of the vaunted pitching, who knew which offense would show up in the World Series? In the NLCS, it was in the doldrums one day, dominant the next.

—*by Paul White*

By Robert Deutsch, USA TODAY

The exultant New York Yankees piled into an heap after their comeback World Series victory.

1996 World Series

▸**Game 1:** Oct. 20
Atlanta 12, New York 1

▸**Game 2:** Oct. 21
Atlanta 4, New York 0

▸**Game 3:** Oct. 22
New York 5, Atlanta 2

▸**Game 4:** Oct. 23
New York 8, Atlanta 6

▸**Game 5:** Oct. 24
New York 1, Atlanta 0

▸**Game 6:** Oct. 26
New York 3, Atlanta 2

New York wins series 4-2

Yanks' triumph of the heart

All across New York City, this World Series was an affair of the heart. From the Washington Heights section of Upper Manhattan, where Frank Torre waited 72 days at Columbia-Presbyterian Medical Center for a second chance at life, to the manager's office at Yankee Stadium, where his brother Joe put a human face on the games with his dignity and his devotion to family. And from Jimmy Key's apartment, where he proposed to his girlfriend on a sunny fall afternoon, six hours before going out to pitch the clinching victory, to the millions of born-again Yankees fans who fell in love with this eclectic mix of selfless stars and humble heroes, willing a comeback against a seemingly invincible foe.

When third baseman Charlie Hayes squeezed Mark Lemke's foul pop for the final out on Oct. 26, stranding the tying run in scoring position and clinching a 3-2 victory, the Yankees had their 23rd world championship. "Now, I know how Neil Armstrong felt when he walked on the moon," third baseman Wade Boggs said.

"We have a better appreciation of it now, how dominant this franchise has been to win all those championships," backup catcher Jim Leyritz said. Leyritz hit one of the biggest World Series home runs in Yankees history in Game 4, tying the score in the eighth inning with a three-run blast. Afterward, he said it wouldn't mean a thing if the Yankees didn't go on to win the Series. But they did. "When Charlie caught that last out, I said, 'Now it's time to celebrate. Now it's time to enjoy that home run,'" Leyritz said.

The Yankees became the first team in history to win four

consecutive games and the Series after dropping the first two contests at home. "This team and this coaching staff typify New York," Yankees owner George Steinbrenner said. "It's a city of battlers."

The Yankees almost blew a 12-game lead over Baltimore in the American League East but held on to win. Then they dropped their playoff opener to Texas, but came back to win. They had six come-from-behind victories in the postseason. Outfielder Paul O'Neill said, "This team was built around guys who would rather go 0-for-4 and win than go 5-for-5 and lose. That's how you get to the World Series."

Boggs agreed. "This team's got guts," he said. "The players here leave their egos at the door. There's not a selfish bone in anyone's body on this team." It's all a reflection of the manager, of course.

"Often today, when you talk about players, the first thing that comes to mind is how much money they make," said Torre, "or that they can really put some numbers up. The only number this team was concerned with was the one in the win column. That's a refreshing change. Everybody has a piece of it. We went through a series [in which] every player on our roster helped us win a game."

The Yankees won despite batting just .216 in the World Series, the lowest mark for a winner since Baltimore hit .213 against Philadelphia in 1983. They were outscored by the Braves 26-18. Cecil Fielder, in his first World Series, was the hottest hitter, going 9-for-23. "People say that players who make a lot of money should be satisfied, but I really wasn't," Fielder said. "Individual accomplishments are nice, but being in the World Series is what it's all about."

The real stars were the Yankees pitchers. In Games 3, 5 and 6, starters David Cone, Andy Pettitte and Key held their own against Atlanta aces Tom Glavine, John Smoltz and Greg Maddux, respectively. The Braves hit just .205 and scored two runs over the final 23 innings of the Series after taking a 6-0 lead in Game 4. The Yankees bullpen posted a 6-1 record in the postseason with seven saves and a 1.81 ERA, and closer John Wetteland, who saved all four wins, was named the Series MVP.

"The year has been a blessing," catcher Joe Girardi said. "How could you dream up a better script?" This script, starring good guy Joe Torre, the kid from Brooklyn, would have been rejected by Hollywood as being too hokey, too contrived. Yet the perfect slogan provided by Frank Torre—This Team Has Heart!—was all too real. After suffering three heart attacks, he had been waiting for a new heart since Aug. 8. It arrived on Oct. 24, some 72 days later.

Joe Torre returned from Atlanta after Game 5, reaching his Brooklyn home at 5:15 on Oct. 25. Thirty minutes later, the phone rang. "I thought it was my wife because she was

Game 1

Atlanta 12, New York 1

Atlanta	026 013 000	-	12
New York	000 010 000	-	1

BATTING

ATLANTA	AB	R	H	BI	BB	SO	LO	AVG
Grissom cf	5	2	2	1	0	0	0	.400
Lemke 2b	4	0	2	1	0	0	0	.500
CJones 3b	4	1	1	3	0	0	2	.250
McGriff 1b	5	2	2	2	0	2	1	.400
Lopez c	4	2	1	0	1	1	0	.250
Perez c	0	0	0	0	0	0	0	.000
Dye rf	5	0	1	0	0	1	3	.200
AJones lf	4	3	3	5	0	0	1	.750
Klesko dh	4	1	0	0	0	1	2	.000
Blauser ss	3	1	1	0	1	1	0	.333
a-Polonia ph	1	0	0	0	0	1	0	.000
Belliard ss	0	0	0	0	0	0	0	.000
Totals	39	12	13	12	1	6	10	

a-struck out for Blauser in the 8th.

►**BATTING - HR:** AJones (2, 2nd inning off Pettitte, 1 on, 2 out; 3rd inning off Boehringer, 2 on, 2 out); McGriff (1, 5th inning off Boehringer, 0 on, 1 out). **S:** Lemke. **SF:** CJones. **2- out RBI:** AJones 5. **LOB:** 3.
►**BASERUNNING - SB:** CJones (1, 3rd base off Pettitte/Leyritz).

NEW YORK	AB	R	H	BI	BB	SO	LO	AVG
Jeter ss	3	1	0	0	1	1	3	.000
Boggs 3b	4	0	2	1	0	0	0	.500
Williams cf	3	0	0	0	1	1	3	.000
Martinez 1b	3	0	1	0	1	0	3	.333
Fielder dh	4	0	0	0	0	1	3	.000
Strawberry lf	3	0	0	0	0	0	1	.000
Raines lf	1	0	0	0	0	0	0	.000
O'Neill rf	2	0	0	0	1	0	1	.000
Aldrete rf	0	0	0	0	0	0	0	.000
a-Hayes ph	1	0	0	0	0	0	0	.000
Duncan 2b	3	0	0	0	0	0	1	.000
Fox 2b	0	0	0	0	0	0	0	.000
b-Sojo ph	1	0	0	0	0	0	0	.000
Leyritz c	3	0	1	0	1	1	0	.333
Totals	31	1	4	1	5	5	12	

a-flied to right for Aldrete in the 9th; b-grounded to shortstop for Fox in the 9th.

►**BATTING - 2B:** Boggs (1, Smoltz). **2-out RBI:** Boggs. **Runners left in scoring position, 2 out:** Fielder 1, Jeter 1, Williams 2. **LOB:** 8.
►**FIELDING - E:** Duncan (1, ground ball).

PITCHING

ATLANTA	IP	H	R	ER	BB	SO	BF	ERA
Smoltz (W, 1-0)	6	2	1	1	5	4	25	1.50
McMichael	1	2	0	0	0	1	5	0.00
Neagle	1	0	0	0	0	3	0.00
Wade	.2	0	0	0	0	0	2	0.00
Clontz	.1	0	0	0	0	0	1	0.00

NEW YORK	IP	H	R	ER	BB	SO	BF	ERA
Pettitte (L, 0-1)	2.1	6	7	7	1	1	14	27.00
Boehringer	3	5	5	3	0	2	15	9.00
Weathers	1.2	1	0	0	0	0	6	0.00
Nelson	1	1	0	0	0	1	4	0.00
Wetteland	1	0	0	0	2	3	0.00

►**UMPIRES - HP:** Jim Evans. **1B:** Terry Tata. **2B:** Tim Welke. **3B:** Steve Rippley. **LF:** Larry Young. **RF:** Gerry Davis.
►**GAME DATA - T:** 3:02. **Att:** 56,365. **Weather:** 53 degrees, overcast. **Wind:** 5 mph, in from left center.

Game 2

Atlanta 4, New York 0

Atlanta	1 0 1 0 1 1 0 0 0 -	4
New York	0 0 0 0 0 0 0 0 0 -	0

BATTING

ATLANTA	AB	R	H	BI	BB	SO	LO	AVG
Grissom cf	5	1	2	1	0	1	2	.400
Lemke 2b	4	2	2	0	0	0	1	.500
CJones 3b	3	0	1	0	1	1	1	.286
McGriff 1b	3	0	2	3	0	1	0	.500
Lopez c	4	0	1	0	0	0	2	.250
Dye rf	4	0	1	0	0	0	3	.222
AJones lf	3	0	0	0	0	1	1	.429
Pendleton dh	4	1	1	0	0	1	0	.250
Blauser ss	2	0	0	0	1	0	1	.200
a-Polonia ph	1	0	0	0	0	0	0	.000
Belliard ss	0	0	0	0	0	0	0	.000
Totals	33	4	10	4	2	5	12	

a-grounded to second for Blauser in the 9th.
▶BATTING - 2B: Lemke (1, Key); Grissom (1, Key); CJones (1, Key); Pendleton (1, Key). S: Lemke. SF: McGriff. 2-out RBI: McGriff, Grissom. Runners left in scoring position, 2 out: Dye 2, Grissom 1. GIDP: Blauser, Lopez. LOB: 7.
▶FIELDING - DP: 1 (Lemke-Blauser-McGriff).

NEW YORK	AB	R	H	BI	BB	SO	LO	AVG
Raines lf	4	0	2	0	0	0	1	.400
Boggs 3b	4	0	1	0	0	0	2	.375
Williams cf	4	0	0	0	0	1	2	.000
Martinez 1b	4	0	0	0	0	2	1	.143
Fielder dh	4	0	2	0	0	0	0	.250
Fox pr	0	0	0	0	0	0	0	.000
O'Neill rf	4	0	1	0	0	1	2	.167
Duncan 2b	3	0	0	0	0	1	1	.000
Girardi c	3	0	0	0	0	0	1	.000
Jeter ss	2	0	1	0	0	0	0	.200
Totals	32	0	7	0	0	5	10	

▶BATTING - 2B: O'Neill (1, Maddux). Runners left in scoring position, 2 out: Girardi 1, Williams 1, O'Neill 1. GIDP: Boggs. LOB: 6.
▶BASERUNNING - CS: Raines (1, 2nd base by Maddux/Lopez).
▶FIELDING - E: Raines (1, bobble). DP: 2 (Duncan-Jeter-Martinez, Key-Duncan-Martinez).

PITCHING

ATLANTA	IP	H	R	ER	BB	SO	BF	ERA
Maddux (W, 1-0)	8	6	0	0	0	2	29	0.00
Wohlers	1	1	0	0	0	3	4	0.00

NEW YORK	IP	H	R	ER	BB	SO	BF	ERA
Key (L, 0-1)	6	10	4	4	2	0	29	6.00
Lloyd	.2	0	0	0	0	2	2	0.00
Nelson	1.1	0	0	0	0	2	4	0.00
MRivera	1	0	0	0	0	1	3	0.00

HBP: AJones (by Key); Jeter (by Maddux).
▶UMPIRES - HP: Terry Tata. 1B: Tim Welke. 2B: Steve Rippley. 3B: Larry Young. LF: Gerry Davis. RF: Jim Evans.
▶GAME DATA - T: 2:44. Att: 56,340. Weather: 55 degrees, cloudy. Wind: 5 mph, left to right.

still in Atlanta. She was gonna fly back the next day," Torre said. "It was the hospital, telling me that they were taking Frank down to prep him for [transplant] surgery."

Joe had planned to give Frank the game ball from his first World Series victory, in Game 3. He brought it to the hospital but had to leave it outside his brother's room because it wasn't sterilized. Frank watched Game 6 on a small TV in his room in the intensive-care unit. "His blood pressure was going up 30 points between commercials," said Dr. Mehmet Oz, one of the surgeons who performed the transplant. "That game was the perfect stress test for him."

"This is a dreamland for me," Joe Torre said after the surgery. "Everything that has happened to me the last 48 hours has been unbelievable. I thought about Frank, but I think I ran out of tears in the Baltimore series. This was more exhilaration. I think the thing with my brother [Rocco], who passed away [in June], and my brother Frank has taken the game and put it more on a personal playing field. I think maybe this has humanized the game."

The baseball world was indeed moved by the Torres' travails. Even Bobby Cox, the Braves manager, said, "If somebody had to beat us, and Joe Torre was the guy, it wouldn't bother me one bit. He's a class guy. I'm glad things worked out for his family."

Before the Series' last pitch, Yankees bench coach Don Zimmer turned to Torre and said, "This is it, this one's for Frank."

An inauspicious start

It wasn't easy getting there. The Yanks were outscored 16-1 in dropping the first two games. The mastery by the Braves was total and varied: In Game 1, Atlanta hit three homers in a 12-1 laugher, with John Smoltz getting the win. Then, in Game 2, Greg Maddux pitched an eight-inning, six-hit, 82-pitch masterpiece, saying afterward, "[It] was one I'll probably take to my grave."

When the Yanks got to Atlanta, they were greeted with headlines that served as perfect bulletin board fodder: Why Bother to Play It Out? asked one. "Another story said the '27 Yankees couldn't beat the Braves," Yankees shortstop Derek Jeter said, "but they forgot about the '96 Yankees."

This year's team limped south a red-faced bunch. "We were a little embarrassed by what happened in New York," Cone said. "We never let our crowd get into either game." Cone, the Yankees' starter in Game 3, was to go ahead of his teammates to get his proper rest but he couldn't get out of New York the day of Game 2. "I was supposed to leave on Delta at four o'clock," he said. "But we taxied out the runway and were sitting there for half

Rookie shortstop Derek Jeter scored five runs in the Series.

an hour. We had some kind of computer problem and they said it might take three hours to get it fixed."

The pilot did not recognize Cone when the pitcher asked to get off the plane so he could return to Yankee Stadium to see the game. But he allowed Cone to get off. The pitcher flew down on the charter with the rest of the club. "It wasn't the first time I've been up until three o'clock in the morning," he said with a smile. Cone, who bounced back from an aneurysm to go 7-2 with a 2.88 ERA in the regular season, won 5-2 to keep the Yanks alive. He allowed just four hits and one run in six innings in shutting down an offense that had outscored the opposition 48-2 the previous five games.

"One thing you never question is David Cone's insides," Yanks pitching coach Mel Stottlemyre said. "He's gonna spill his guts for you and give you everything he has." Cone showed that courage in the sixth, when, after forcing in a run with a bases-loaded walk, he got Javy Lopez on a foul pop to end the inning. On offense, Yankees center fielder Bernie Williams had an RBI single in the first and a two-run home run against Greg McMichael in the eighth. It was his sixth homer of the postseason, tying the major league record shared by Pittsburgh's Bob Robertson (1971), Philadelphia's Len Dykstra (1993) and Seattle's Ken Griffey Jr. (1995).

"Everybody was talking about the Braves, how great they are, figuring out their place in history," Cone said after the victory. "We get one more win, we're going back to New York, and it gets interesting."

The turning point

The Yankees' euphoria appeared short-lived when the Braves took a 6-0 lead in Game 4. It was still 6-3 in the eighth inning when Atlanta closer Mark Wohlers took

Game 3

New York 5, Atlanta 2

New York	1 0 0	1 0 0	0 3 0	- 5
Atlanta	0 0 0	0 0 1	0 1 0	- 2

BATTING

NEW YORK	AB	R	H	BI	BB	SO	LO	AVG
Raines lf	4	1	1	0	1	0	1	.333
Jeter ss	3	1	1	0	1	1	1	.250
Williams cf	5	2	2	3	0	1	3	.167
Fielder 1b	3	0	1	0	1	0	0	.273
Fox pr	0	1	0	0	0	0	0	.000
Martinez 1b	0	0	0	0	1	0	0	.143
Hayes 3b	5	0	0	0	0	3	4	.000
Strawberry rf	3	0	1	1	1	2	0	.167
Duncan 2b	3	0	1	0	0	1	2	.111
Sojo 2b	1	0	1	1	0	0	0	.500
Girardi c	2	0	0	0	1	2	2	.000
Cone p	2	0	0	0	0	1	3	.000
a-Leyritz ph	1	0	0	0	0	0	0	.250
Rivera p	1	0	0	0	0	0	2	.000
Lloyd p	0	0	0	0	0	0	0	.000
Wetteland p	0	0	0	0	0	0	0	.000
Totals	**33**	**5**	**8**	**5**	**6**	**11**	**18**	

a-grounded to shortstop for Cone in the 7th.

▶**BATTING - 2B:** Fielder (1, McMichael). **HR:** Williams (1, 8th inning off McMichael, 1 on, 0 out). **S:** Jeter, Girardi. **Runners left in scoring position, 2 out:** Hayes 2, Cone 2, Raines 1, Rivera 1. **LOB:** 9.

▶**FIELDING - E:** Jeter (1, bobbled ground ball in 9th). **DP:** 1 (Fielder-Jeter-Fielder).

ATLANTA	AB	R	H	BI	BB	SO	LO	AVG
Grissom cf	4	1	3	0	0	0	0	.500
Lemke 2b	4	0	1	1	0	0	3	.417
CJones 3b	3	0	1	0	1	1	1	.300
McGriff 1b	3	0	0	0	1	0	5	.364
Klesko lf	3	0	1	1	1	2	2	.000
Lopez c	4	0	1	0	0	0	4	.250
AJones rf	4	0	0	0	0	2	2	.273
Blauser ss	4	0	0	0	0	2	1	.111
Glavine p	1	1	0	0	1	0	0	.000
a-Polonia ph	0	0	0	0	1	0	0	.000
McMichael p	0	0	0	0	0	0	0	.000
Clontz p	0	0	0	0	0	0	0	.000
Bielecki p	0	0	0	0	0	0	0	.000
b-Pendleton ph	1	0	0	0	0	0	1	.200
Totals	**31**	**2**	**6**	**2**	**5**	**7**	**19**	

a-walked for Glavine in the 7th; b-grounded to second for Bielecki in the 9th.

▶**BATTING - 3B:** Grissom (1, Rivera). **2-out RBI:** Klesko. **Runners left in scoring position, 2 out:** Lopez 2. **GIDP:** Lemke. **LOB:** 7.

▶**BASERUNNING - CS:** AJones (1, 2nd base by Cone/Girardi); Polonia (1, 2nd base by Rivera/Girardi).

▶**FIELDING - E:** Blauser (1, ground ball in 4th). **Outfield assists:** AJones (Raines at 1st base). **DP:** 1 (AJones-McGriff).

PITCHING

NEW YORK	IP	H	R	ER	BB	SO	BF	ERA
Cone (W, 1-0)	6	4	1	1	4	3	24	1.50
Rivera (H, 1)	1.1	2	1	1	1	1	6	3.86
Lloyd (H, 1)	.2	0	0	0	0	1	2	0.00
Wetteland (S, 1)	1	0	0	0	0	2	4	0.00

ATLANTA	IP	H	R	ER	BB	SO	BF	ERA
Glavine (L, 0-1)	7	4	2	1	3	8	28	1.29
McMichael	0	3	3	3	0	0	3	27.00
Clontz	1	1	0	0	1	1	5	0.00
Bielecki	1	0	0	0	2	2	5	0.00

McMichael pitched to 3 batters in the 8th.

IBB: Strawberry (by Clontz).

▶**UMPIRES - HP:** Tim Welke. **1B:** Steve Rippley. **2B:** Larry Young. **3B:** Gerry Davis. **LF:** Jim Evans. **RF:** Terry Tata.

▶**GAME DATA - T:** 3:22. **Att:** 51,843. **Weather:** 70 degrees, clear. **Wind:** 10 mph, left to right.

Game 4

New York 8, Atlanta 6

```
New York   000 003 030 2 - 8
Atlanta    041 010 000 0 - 6
```

BATTING

NEW YORK	AB	R	H	BI	BB	SO	LO	AVG
Raines lf	5	1	0	0	1	1	2	.214
Jeter ss	4	2	2	0	2	2	0	.333
Williams cf	4	1	0	0	2	1	2	.125
Fielder 1b	4	1	2	1	1	0	1	.333
Fox pr-3b	0	0	0	0	0	0	0	.000
e-Boggs ph-3b	0	0	0	1	1	0	0	.375
Hayes 3b-1b	5	1	3	1	1	0	3	.273
Strawberry rf	5	0	2	0	1	2	5	.273
Duncan 2b	5	1	0	0	0	1	7	.071
Girardi c	2	0	0	0	0	0	0	.000
b-O'Neill ph	1	0	0	0	0	1	2	.143
Leyritz c	2	1	1	3	0	0	0	.000
Rogers p	1	0	1	0	0	0	0	1.000
Boehringer p	0	0	0	0	0	0	0	.000
a-Sojo ph	1	0	1	0	0	0	0	.667
Weathers p	0	0	0	0	0	0	0	.000
c-Martinez ph	1	0	0	0	0	1	2	.125
Nelson p	0	0	0	0	0	0	0	.000
d-Aldrete ph	1	0	0	0	0	0	0	.000
Rivera p	0	0	0	0	0	0	0	.000
Lloyd p	1	0	0	0	0	0	0	.000
Wetteland p	0	0	0	0	0	0	0	.000
Totals	42	8	12	6	9	9	24	

a-singled for Boehringer in the 5th; b-struck out for Girardi in the 6th; c-struck out for Weathers in the 6th; d-grounded to short for Nelson in the 8th; e-walked for Fox in the 10th.
▶**BATTING - HR:** Leyritz (1, 8th inning off Wohlers, 2 on, 1 out). **2-out RBI:** Boggs. **GIDP:** Williams. **LOB:** 13.
▶**FIELDING - DP:** 1 (Jeter-Duncan-Hayes).

ATLANTA	AB	R	H	BI	BB	SO	LO	AVG
Grissom cf	5	0	1	2	0	0	0	.421
Lemke 2b	5	0	1	0	0	1	1	.353
CJones 3b-ss	3	2	1	0	2	0	0	.308
McGriff 1b	3	1	2	1	2	0	2	.429
Clontz p	0	0	0	0	0	0	0	.000
Lopez c	2	1	0	1	1	1	3	.214
Wohlers p	0	0	0	0	0	0	0	.000
Avery p	0	0	0	0	0	0	0	.000
Klesko 1b	1	0	0	0	0	1	0	.000
AJones lf	4	1	3	1	1	1	1	.400
Dye rf	4	0	0	0	0	0	5	.154
Blauser ss	3	1	1	1	0	2	0	.167
Belliard ss	0	0	0	0	0	0	0	.000
a-Polonia ph	1	0	0	0	0	1	1	.000
Pendleton 3b	1	0	0	0	0	0	1	.167
Neagle p	1	0	0	0	0	1	0	.000
Wade p	0	0	0	0	0	0	0	.000
Bielecki p	1	0	0	0	0	1	0	.000
Perez c	1	0	0	0	0	0	1	.000
Totals	35	6	9	6	6	9	15	

a-struck out for Belliard in the 8th.
▶**BATTING - 2B:** Grissom (2, Rogers); AJones (1, Weathers). **HR:** McGriff (2, 2nd inning off Rogers, 0 on, 0 out). **S:** Neagle, Dye. **SF:** Lopez. **2-out RBI:** Grissom 2, AJones. **GIDP:** McGriff. **LOB:** 8.
▶**FIELDING - E:** Dye, Klesko. **DP:** 1 (Blauser-Lemke-McGriff).

PITCHING

NEW YORK	IP	H	R	ER	BB	SO	BF	ERA
Rogers	2	5	5	5	2	0	13	22.50
Boehringer	2	0	0	0	0	3	6	5.40
Weathers	1	1	1	1	2	2	6	3.37
Nelson	2	0	0	0	1	2	7	0.00
Rivera	1.1	2	0	0	1	1	7	2.45
Lloyd (W, 1-0)	1	0	0	0	0	1	2	0.00
Wetteland (S, 2)	.2	1	0	0	0	0	3	0.00

ATLANTA	IP	H	R	ER	BB	SO	BF	ERA
Neagle	5	5	3	2	4	3	23	3.00
Wade	0	0	0	0	1	0	1	0.00
Bielecki	2	0	0	0	1	4	7	0.00
Wohlers (BS, 1)	2	6	3	3	0	1	12	9.00
Avery (L, 0-1)	.2	1	2	1	3	0	6	13.50
Clontz	.1	0	0	0	1	0	2	0.00

Rogers pitched to 2 batters in the 3rd; Neagle pitched to 4 in the 6th; Wade pitched to 1 in the 6th.
IBB: McGriff (by Weathers); Williams (by Avery). **Balk:** Weathers.
▶**UMPIRES - HP:** Steve Rippley. **1B:** Larry Young. **2B:** Gerry Davis. **3B:** Jim Evans. **LF:** Terry Tata. **RF:** Tim Welke.
▶**GAME DATA - T:** 4:17. **Att:** 51,881. **Weather:** 60 degrees, clear. **Wind:** 7 mph, out to center.

the mound. Wohlers was working on a streak of 7⅓ scoreless innings when he gave up consecutive singles to Hayes and Darryl Strawberry. Suddenly, you could hear a tomahawk drop as the crowd sensed the danger of the moment. The fans got a momentary sense of relief when Mariano Duncan hit into a fielder's choice. Meanwhile, in the Yankees dugout, Leyritz—who had entered the game as a defensive replacement in the sixth—rustled through the bat rack. Leyritz eschewed his own bat because he hadn't been swinging very well. He had been using Strawberry's bat that night during batting practice. "Darryl's bats have a thinner handle," he said. "Wohlers throws so hard, I can get around a little quicker." Leyritz worked the count to 2-and-2, then blasted a hanging slider over the left-field fence. Suddenly—improbably—the game was tied and the Yankees were breathing. "If he throws a good slider there, I never touch it," Leyritz said later. "When I hit it, I knew it had a chance, especially the way the ball was carrying."

When Leyritz hit first base, he flashed back to his dramatic 15th-inning home run that beat Seattle in Game 2 of the 1995 Division Series. Just as he did that night, he clapped his hands as he rounded the bag. "I couldn't get too flamboyant this time," he said. "It wasn't a game-winning home run. But I never thought I'd top that Seattle home run." Someone compared this homer to the one Boston's Bernie Carbo hit in Game 6 of the '75 World Series, the one that brought the Red Sox back from exactly the same deficit. But Leyritz, who grew up in Cincinnati, wanted to hear nothing of it. "I was a big Reds fan," he said.

Ironically, Leyritz probably was going to be drafted by the Braves out of high school. But three days before the draft, he broke his leg and didn't sign with anyone. He wound up attending Middle Georgia Junior College for two years, then the University of Kentucky for one more before signing with the Yankees as a free agent in 1985. He was the senior Yankee in service time, with five years, 126 days on the major league roster. "I've been through it all in New York," he said. "When I first got here, we were trying to get out of last place. I've been here for the entire ride."

The ride wasn't yet over in Game 4. The Yankees stranded three runners in the ninth inning before going ahead in the 10th when Boggs drew a bases-loaded walk from Steve Avery. "[It was] probably the biggest base on balls I ever got in my career," said Boggs, who has 1,280 walks to go with his 2,697 hits. "Surprisingly, I was relaxed. I cleared everything out of my mind as I walked up to the plate. I was fortunate enough to lay off some pretty nasty sliders and work the count to 3-and-2." Boggs was pinch-hitting for Andy Fox. The Yanks had runners on first and second with two out when the Braves intentionally walked Williams to load the bases for Fox. After the walk, New York added an insurance run on an error for an 8-6 victory.

"It's getting melodramatic," Boggs said after the win. "It's all getting spooky." The rally matched the second-largest come-from-behind victory in World Series history. The Philadelphia A's overcame an eight-run deficit to beat the Chicago Cubs 10-8 in Game 4 in 1929, and the Brooklyn Dodgers also rallied from a 6-0 hole to beat the Yankees 13-8 in Game 2 in 1956. At four hours, 17 minutes, the game was the longest in Series history, eclipsing Game 4 in 1993 between Toronto and Philadelphia (4:14).

Pettitte put Yanks ahead

In Game 5, Pettitte, later the runner-up in the AL Cy Young Award voting, was rematched against the NL Cy Young winner, John Smoltz. "I never compare myself to their starters," Pettitte said modestly. "I'll never do what they accomplished." Tsk, tsk. Pettitte, who got bombed 12-1 in the Series opener, proceeded to anesthetize the Braves 1-0 on five hits over 8⅓ innings. "I'm glad I got to make up for my pathetic outing in New York," said Pettitte after his 96-pitch outing. "I was glad to get another opportunity to pitch. I didn't want to finish the year like that."

What had Pettitte learned from his first outing against the Braves? "I didn't learn anything," he jokingly said. "I wasn't out there long enough." Pettitte cut up the Braves with a game plan unlike that used in any of his other 38 starts this season. Instead of busting hitters inside, he worked the outside corner like a street cop. "It was a totally different style," he said. "I only threw three or four balls inside the whole night. I was throwing sinkers away. My ball was running away like crazy. We stayed out there all night. They never adjusted."

Pitching on just three days' rest helped Pettitte. "I felt tired, and the ball was sinking a little bit more," he said. "They kept hitting ground balls." Pettitte recorded 14 ground-ball outs, none bigger than the two plays he started himself in the sixth. With two men on and nobody out, he barehanded Lemke's bunt and fired to third for the force. Then he started a 1-4-3 double play on Chipper Jones's tapper back to the box. Pettitte, who led the majors with 11 pickoffs this season, also had time to nail 19-year-old Andruw Jones in the fifth inning. Jones had hit one of his two Game 1 homers off Pettitte.

The victory wasn't assured until O'Neill hauled in pinch-hitter Luis Polonia's fly on the run in right-center for the final out. Two pitches earlier, Yankees outfield coach Jose Cardenal had wisely positioned O'Neill seven or eight feet toward center, enabling him to make the catch. "I moved everyone around to the left," Cardenal

Game 5

New York 1, Atlanta 0

New York	000	100 000	- 1
Atlanta	000	000 000	- 0

BATTING

NEW YORK	AB	R	H	BI	BB	SO	LO	AVG
Jeter ss	4	0	0	0	0	1	2	.250
Hayes 3b	4	1	0	0	0	2	2	.200
Williams cf	4	0	0	0	0	2	0	.100
Fielder 1b	4	0	3	1	0	1	0	.421
Martinez 1b	0	0	0	0	0	0	0	.125
Strawberry lf	3	0	0	0	1	1	2	.214
O'Neill rf	2	0	0	0	2	0	1	.111
Duncan 2b	4	0	0	0	0	1	6	.056
Sojo 2b	0	0	0	0	0	0	0	.667
Leyritz c	2	0	1	0	2	1	0	.375
Pettitte p	4	0	0	0	0	1	4	.000
Wetteland p	0	0	0	0	0	0	0	.000
Totals	31	1	4	1	5	10	17	

▶BATTING - **2B:** Fielder (2, Smoltz). **Runners left in scoring position, 2 out:** Duncan 3, Pettitte 1. **LOB:** 8.
▶BASERUNNING - **SB:** Leyritz (1, 2nd base off Smoltz/Lopez); Duncan (1, 2nd base off Wohlers/Lopez).
▶FIELDING - **E:** Jeter (2, bobbled ground ball). **DP:** 2 (Duncan-Jeter-Fielder; Pettitte-Duncan-Fielder).

ATLANTA	AB	R	H	BI	BB	SO	LO	AVG
Grissom cf	3	0	2	0	1	1	0	.455
Lemke 2b	4	0	0	0	0	2	4	.286
CJones 3b	4	0	1	0	0	0	2	.294
McGriff 1b	3	0	0	0	1	1	1	.353
Lopez c	4	0	0	0	0	0	3	.167
AJones lf	2	0	1	0	1	0	1	.412
b-Klesko ph	0	0	0	0	1	0	0	.000
Dye rf	3	0	0	0	0	0	2	.125
c-Polonia ph	1	0	0	0	0	0	2	.000
Blauser ss	3	0	0	0	0	0	0	.133
Smoltz p	2	0	1	0	0	0	0	.500
a-Mordecai ph	1	0	0	0	0	0	0	.000
Wohlers p	0	0	0	0	0	0	0	.000
Totals	30	0	5	0	4	4	15	

a-grounded to shortstop for Smoltz in the 8th; b-intentionally walked for AJones in the 9th; c-flied to right for Dye in the 9th.
▶BATTING - **2B:** CJones (2, Pettitte). **Runners left in scoring position, 2 out:** Dye 1, Lemke 1, Polonia 1. **GIDP:** Lopez, Jones. **LOB:** 7.
▶BASERUNNING - **SB:** AJones (1, 2nd base off Pettitte/Leyritz); Grissom (1, 2nd base off Pettitte/Leyritz). **CS:** AJones (2, 2nd base by Pettitte).
▶FIELDING - **E:** Grissom (1, dropped fly ball in right-center in 4th). **DP:** 1 (McGriff).

PITCHING

NEW YORK	IP	H	R	ER	BB	SO	BF	ERA
Pettitte (W, 1-1)	8.1	5	0	0	3	4	31	5.91
Wetteland (S, 3)	.2	0	0	0	1	0	3	0.00

ATLANTA	IP	H	R	ER	BB	SO	BF	ERA
Smoltz (L, 1-1)	8	4	1	0	3	10	31	0.64
Wohlers	1	0	0	0	2	0	5	6.75

WP: Wohlers. **IBB:** Leyritz (by Wohlers); Klesko (by Wetteland).
▶UMPIRES - **HP:** Larry Young. **1B:** Gerry Davis. **2B:** Jim Evans. **3B:** Terry Tata. **LF:** Tim Welke. **RF:** Steve Rippley.
▶GAME DATA - **T:** 2:54. **Att:** 51,881. **Weather:** 65 degrees, clear. **Wind:** 6 mph, left to right.

Game 6

New York 3, Atlanta 2

Atlanta	000	100	001 - 2	
New York	003	000	00x - 3	

BATTING

ATLANTA	AB	R	H	BI	BB	SO	LO	AVG
Grissom cf	5	0	2	1	0	0	2	.444
Lemke 2b	5	0	0	0	0	0	4	.231
CJones 3b	4	0	1	0	0	0	0	.286
McGriff 1b	3	1	0	0	1	0	0	.300
Lopez c	3	0	1	0	1	2	1	.190
AJones lf-rf	3	0	1	0	1	2	1	.400
Dye rf	1	0	0	1	1	0	1	.118
a-Klesko ph-lf	2	1	1	0	0	0	2	.100
Pendleton dh	3	0	1	0	1	0	4	.222
Belliard pr	0	0	0	0	0	0	0	.000
Blauser ss	3	0	1	0	0	0	1	.167
b-Polonia ph	1	0	0	0	0	1	2	.000
Totals	33	2	8	2	5	5	18	

a-popped to second for Dye in the 6th; b-struck out for Blauser in the 9th.

▸BATTING - 2B: Blauser (1, Key); CJones (3, Key). 2-out RBI: Grissom. Runners left in scoring position, 2 out: Lemke 2, Klesko 1. GIDP: Pendleton. LOB: 9.

▸BASERUNNING - CS: Pendleton (1, 2nd base by Key/Girardi).

▸FIELDING - DP: 2 (Blauser-Lemke-McGriff; McGriff-Blauser-McGriff).

NEW YORK	AB	R	H	BI	BB	SO	LO	AVG
Jeter ss	4	1	1	1	0	1	1	.250
Boggs 3b	3	0	0	0	0	0	1	.273
Hayes 3b	1	0	0	0	0	0	0	.188
Williams cf	4	0	2	1	0	0	0	.167
Fielder dh	4	0	1	0	0	0	2	.391
Martinez 1b	3	0	0	0	0	1	1	.091
Strawberry lf	2	0	0	0	1	1	0	.188
O'Neill rf	3	1	1	0	0	0	1	.167
Duncan 2b	1	0	0	0	0	0	0	.053
Sojo 2b	2	0	1	0	0	0	0	.600
Girardi c	3	1	2	1	0	0	1	.200
Totals	30	3	8	3	1	3	7	

▸BATTING - 2B: O'Neill (2, Maddux); Sojo (1, Maddux). 3B: Girardi (1, Maddux). 2-out RBI: Williams. Runners left in scoring position, 2 out: Fielder 2, Girardi 1. GIDP: Jeter, O'Neill. LOB: 4.

▸BASERUNNING - SB: Jeter (1, 2nd base off Maddux/Lopez); Williams (1, 2nd base off Wohlers/Lopez).

▸FIELDING - E: Duncan (2, ground ball bounced out of glove in 3rd). DP: 1 (Jeter-Martinez).

PITCHING

ATLANTA	IP	H	R	ER	BB	SO	BF	ERA
Maddux (L, 1-1)	7.2	8	3	3	1	3	30	1.72
Wohlers	.1	0	0	0	0	0	1	6.23

NEW YORK	IP	H	R	ER	BB	SO	BF	ERA
Key (W, 1-1)	5.1	5	1	1	3	1	22	3.97
Weathers	.1	0	0	0	1	1	2	3.00
Lloyd	.1	0	0	0	0	0	1	0.00
Rivera	2	0	0	0	1	1	7	1.59
Wetteland (S, 2)	1	3	1	1	0	2	6	2.08

▸UMPIRES - HP: Gerry Davis. 1B: Jim Evans. 2B: Terry Tata. 3B: Tim Welke. LF: Steve Rippley. RF: Larry Young. Ejections: Atlanta manager Cox by Welke (5th).

▸GAME DATA - T: 2:52. Att: 56,375. Weather: 57 degrees, partly cloudy. Wind: 5 mph, out to left.

said. "Luis was struggling to get around [on Wetteland]. We were playing him to the opposite field."

After fouling off four pitches, Polonia sent one over O'Neill's head. Playing with a pulled hamstring, O'Neill just caught up to it with his outstretched right hand. "I wish he had moved me out farther so I would have had an easier play," O'Neill quipped. "The ball carried and carried."

The Yankees got their lone run on Marquis Grissom's error. It was the fourth time in Series history—and the first since an error by Mets second baseman Tim Teufel in Game 1 of the 1986 Series—that an unearned run decided a 1-0 game. And the last 1-0 World Series victory by the Yankees? Game 7 in 1962, when Ralph Terry shut out the Giants. It also was the first time since 1906 that the visiting team won the first five games of the Series. "We have a special thing going on here," Pettitte said before boarding the charter back to New York. "I think we're destined to win this thing."

The Yankees' victory gave them an 8-0 postseason road record. No other team had won more than five road games in any one postseason. Why do the Yankees play so well on the road? Torre had one theory. "I think maybe distraction-wise . . . families coming in who need tickets," he said. "Plus the fact you feel you should win because of the home crowd. A lot of those things make you maybe try too hard and lose your focus. We come on the road and just seem more relaxed."

Back to the Bronx

There were distractions aplenty when the Series returned to the Apple, with celebrities and politicians scrambling to hop back onto the Yankees bandwagon. Yankee Stadium had more stars on the evening of Game 6 than there are on a clear night on Georgia's Stone Mountain. Billy Crystal, Matthew Broderick, Matt Dillon, Mel Gibson, Eddie Murphy, Julia Roberts, Susan Sarandon and Tim Robbins, Jimmy Smits, Nick Turturro and Elisabeth Shue all found their way to the D Train—OK, maybe their stretch limos. Spike Lee got on the bus, hung around the pregame batting cage and took pictures with a small camera. Then vice-presidential candidate Jack Kemp, New York governor George Pataki, New Jersey governor Christine Whitman and New York City mayor Rudy Giuliani held their own Republican caucus.

And how did Key, the Yankees' starter, kill time leading up to the game? He asked his girlfriend, Karin Kane, to marry him. "We decided today was a good day," Key said. "We'd been living together for a while, so it was sort of an assumed thing." Kane was working in a real estate office when Key came to town in 1992

as a free agent, needing a place to live.

"I was on the phone when he walked into the sales office," she said. "Someone else took him around." Everyone knows pitching and real estate have so much in common—location, location, location—but Kane wasn't familiar with Key's line of work. "I didn't know the first thing about baseball. I asked my brother, John, 'Who is Jimmy Key? Is he any good?'"

Having received her ring a day before Key earned his, Kane said she was "a wreck" during the game. But Key dispatched the Braves on five hits before leaving in the sixth inning with a 3-1 lead. It was Key who had beaten the Braves in relief in the clinching Game 6 of the 1992 World Series when he was with Toronto. Key is the ninth pitcher to win two decid-

ing games in World Series play and just the second to do it with two different clubs. Catfish Hunter won the clincher for Oakland in 1972 and for the Yankees in 1978. Key bounced back with 12 victories this year after missing most of last season with rotator cuff surgery.

And so the Yanks had their first world championship since 1978, setting off an impromptu 56,000-voice chorus of "New York, New York." The Yankees had proven their mettle. "Sometimes, it looks like we're sleepwalking out there," Joe Torre said. "But once we get it in gear, we have a lot of heart."

Two miles away, a beaming Frank Torre couldn't have said it any better.
—*by Bill Koenig*

POSTSEASON

World Series: Composite player statistics

New York 4, Atlanta 2

ATLANTA BRAVES

Batting	G	AB	R	H	2B	3B	HR	RBI	SO	BB	AVG
Smoltz p	2	2	0	1	0	0	0	0	0	0	.500
Grissom cf	6	27	4	12	2	1	0	5	1	2	.444
AJones lf	6	20	4	8	1	0	2	6	3	6	.400
McGriff 1b	6	20	4	6	0	0	2	6	5	4	.300
CJones 3b-ss	6	21	3	6	3	0	0	3	4	2	.286
Lemke 2b	6	26	2	6	1	0	0	2	0	3	.231
Pndltn dh-3b	4	9	1	2	1	0	0	0	1	1	.222
Lopez c	6	21	3	4	0	0	0	1	3	4	.190
Blauser ss	6	18	2	3	1	0	0	1	1	4	.167
Dye rf	5	17	0	2	0	0	0	1	1	1	.118
Klesko dh-lf-1b	5	10	2	1	0	0	0	1	2	4	.100
Mordecai ph	1	1	0	0	0	0	0	0	0	0	.000
Bielecki p	2	1	0	0	0	0	0	0	0	1	.000
Glavine p	1	1	1	0	0	0	0	0	1	1	.000
Neagle p	2	1	0	0	0	0	0	0	0	1	.000
Perez c	2	1	0	0	0	0	0	0	0	0	.000
Polonia ph	6	5	0	0	0	0	0	0	1	2	.000
Wohlers p	3	0	0	0	0	0	0	0	0	0	—
Belliard ss	4	0	0	0	0	0	0	0	0	0	—
McMichael p	2	0	0	0	0	0	0	0	0	0	—
Clontz p	3	0	0	0	0	0	0	0	0	0	—
Avery p	1	0	0	0	0	0	0	0	0	0	—
Maddux p	1	0	0	0	0	0	0	0	0	0	—
Wade p	2	0	0	0	0	0	0	0	0	0	—
Totals	6	201	26	51	9	1	4	26	23	36	.254

Pitching	G	CG	IP	H	R	BB	SO	HB	WP	W	L	S	ER	ERA
Bielecki	2	0	3	0	0	3	6	0	0	0	0	0	0	0.00
Clontz	3	0	1.2	1	0	1	2	0	0	0	0	0	0	0.00
Wade	2	0	.2	0	0	1	0	0	0	0	0	0	0	0.00
Smoltz	2	0	14	6	2	8	14	0	0	1	1	0	1	0.64
Glavine	1	0	7	4	2	3	8	0	0	0	1	0	1	1.29
Maddux	2	0	15.2	14	3	1	5	1	0	1	1	0	3	1.72
Neagle	2	0	6	5	3	4	3	0	0	0	0	0	2	3.00
Wohlers	4	0	4.1	7	3	2	4	0	1	0	0	0	3	6.23
Avery	1	0	.2	1	2	3	0	0	0	0	1	0	1	13.50
McMichael	2	0	1	5	3	0	1	0	0	0	0	0	3	27.00
Totals	6	0	54	43	18	26	43	1	1	2	4	0	14	2.33

SCORE BY INNINGS

Atlanta	168	135	011	0	-	26
New York	103	213	060	2	-	18

NEW YORK YANKEES

Batting	G	AB	R	H	2B	3B	HR	RBI	SO	BB	AVG
Rogers p	1	1	0	1	0	0	0	0	0	0	1.000
Sojo 2b	5	5	0	3	1	0	0	1	0	0	.600
Fielder dh-1b	6	23	1	9	2	0	0	2	2	2	.391
Leyritz c	4	8	1	3	0	0	1	3	3	2	.375
Boggs 3b	4	11	0	3	1	0	0	2	1	0	.273
Jeter ss	6	20	5	5	0	0	0	1	4	6	.250
Raines lf	4	14	2	3	0	0	0	0	2	1	.214
Girardi c	4	10	1	2	0	1	0	1	1	2	.200
Strawberry lf-rf	5	16	0	3	0	0	0	1	4	6	.188
Hayes 3b-1b	5	16	2	3	0	0	0	1	1	5	.188
O'Neill rf	5	12	1	2	2	0	0	0	3	2	.167
Williams cf	6	24	3	4	0	0	1	4	3	6	.167
Martinez 1b	6	11	0	1	0	0	0	0	2	5	.091
Duncan 2b	6	19	1	1	0	0	0	0	0	4	.053
Aldrete rf	2	1	0	0	0	0	0	0	0	0	.000
Lloyd p	3	1	0	0	0	0	0	0	0	0	.000
Rivera p	3	1	0	0	0	0	0	0	0	0	.000
Cone p	1	2	0	0	0	0	0	0	0	1	.000
Pettitte p	2	4	0	0	0	0	0	0	0	1	.000
Wetteland p	4	0	0	0	0	0	0	0	0	0	—
Fox 2b-3b	4	0	1	0	0	0	0	0	0	0	—
Boehringer p	2	0	0	0	0	0	0	0	0	0	—
Weathers p	2	0	0	0	0	0	0	0	0	0	—
Nelson p	3	0	0	0	0	0	0	0	0	0	—
Key p	1	0	0	0	0	0	0	0	0	0	—
Totals	6	199	18	43	6	1	2	16	26	43	.216

Pitching	G	CG	IP	H	R	BB	SO	HB	WP	W	L	S	ER	ERA
Nelson	3	0	4.1	1	0	1	5	0	0	0	0	0	0	0.00
Lloyd	4	0	2.2	0	0	4	0	1	0	0	0	0	0	0.00
Cone	1	0	6	4	1	4	3	0	0	1	0	0	1	1.50
Rivera	4	0	5.2	4	1	3	4	0	0	0	0	0	1	1.59
Wetteland	5	0	4.1	4	1	1	6	0	0	0	0	4	1	2.08
Weathers	3	0	3	2	1	3	3	0	0	0	0	0	1	3.00
Key	2	0	11.1	15	5	5	1	1	0	1	1	0	5	3.97
Boehringer	2	0	5	5	5	0	5	0	0	0	0	0	3	5.40
Pettitte	2	0	10.2	11	7	4	5	0	0	1	1	0	7	5.91
Rogers	1	0	2	5	5	2	0	0	0	0	0	0	5	22.50
Totals	6	0	55	51	26	23	36	1	0	4	2	4	24	3.93

E: Jeter 2, Duncan 2, Blauser, Dye, Grissom, Klesko, Raines. **DP:** Atlanta 6, New York 7. **LOB:** Atlanta 41, New York 48. **SB:** CJones, Duncan, Leyritz, Grissom, AJones, Jeter, Williams. **CS:** AJones 2, Polonia, Raines, Pendleton. **S:** Lemke 2, Dye, Girardi, Jeter, Neagle. **SF:** CJones, Lopez, McGriff. **BB:** off Weathers (McGriff), off Avery (Williams), off Wetteland (Klesko), off Wohlers (Leyritz). **HBP:** by Maddux (Jeter), by Key (AJones). **Balk:** Weathers. **Umpires:** Evans, Tata, Welke, Rippley, Young, Davis

World Series notes

John Wetteland got a victory lift from Joe Girardi.

▶New York won—hands down, hands up, hands in cuffs notwithstanding—the battle of the fans. Their behavior bordered on exemplary during Game 6 after the more common moron-on-the-field interruptions of the first two games. The New Yorkers simply out-yelled their Atlanta counterparts, creating a far more electric atmosphere at Yankee Stadium.

▶Bobby Cox's ejection from Game 6 was the exclamation point on a dismal postseason performance by umpires. The missed call (Marquis Grissom out at second) by Terry Tata led to Cox's getting the thumb from Tim Welke at third base. Welke erred from three different spots in six games. Both teams found his Game 3 strike zone unfathomable. He stood like a statue on the right-field line in Game 4, costing Jermaine Dye a shot at a foul fly. Derek Jeter then singled to start a three-run sixth inning for the Yankees. The umps blew a great opportunity, going from standing ovations in the wake of the Roberto Alomar incident to standing around and missing calls with everybody watching.

▶How do you know the baseball season is long? It outlasted football season in baseball's final four cities. The NFL teams in New York, Atlanta, Baltimore and St. Louis were a combined 9-32 at the end of the postseason.

▶The fans cleared away as Charlie Hayes cozied up to the stands to catch Mark Lemke's foul pop for the final out. No Jeffrey Maiers in sight this night. "They got away from me," said Hayes, smiling. "They understand the game here."

▶The Yankees ground crew is a treat with their end-of-the-fifth version of "YMCA," but how many spots do they miss dragging the infield as they dance, then put down their screens to form the song's letters?

▶Jim Leyritz and Tino Martinez stood with their wives in the Yankees clubhouse, waiting to go on Fox's postgame show. Said Karri Leyritz, "Thanks, Tino. I was cursing you last year." Despite husband Jim's winning homer in Game 2, Martinez and the Seattle Mariners eliminated the Yankees in 1995's Division Series.

▶John Wetteland had a season's worth of assorted sweat stains and dirt on his cap, the closer's trademark. Most players got new caps for the World Series, but he was adamant about keeping his old one. (He did agree to get the Series logo sewed on.) He insists he's not superstitious. "I get a hat in spring training," Wetteland said. "I keep it. It has all the work in it. It has character."

▶Atlanta third baseman Terry Pendleton has now been with World Series losers five times: the Cardinals in 1985 and 1987, and the Braves in 1991, 1992 and 1996.

▶Actress Jane Fonda said after Game 1 that Fox was keeping her and hubby Ted Turner, the Braves' owner, off the TV celebrity sightings because Turner and Fox's Rupert Murdoch are in a cable-TV fight. For the record: Ted and Jane got their first TV face time in Game 4.

—by Paul White and Timothy McQuay

For the record

1997 Baseball Weekly Almanac

▶All-time single-
  season, league
  and club records
▶Career records

▶Top fielding marks
▶Active player and
  individual records
▶All no-hitters

Record qualifications

All-time records:
1000 games played minimum for BA, OBA and SA.
1500 innings pitched minimum for ERA.
100 wins minimum for winning percentage.

Active-player records:
One-half of above all-time minimum requirements.

Club records:
Same as active-player records, except pitchers
winning percentage (40 wins minimum).

Season records:
3.1 plate appearances per game for BA, OBA
and SA.
1 inning pitched per game for ERA.
15 victories for winning percentage.

Active-player records

Players listed through 1996 season.

Hitters

Games played: Most, career

2971	Eddie Murray, 1977-1996
2627	Andre Dawson, 1976-1996
2573	Ozzie Smith, 1978-1996
2422	Paul Molitor, 1978-1996
2381	Cal Ripken, 1981-1996
2340	Rickey Henderson, 1979-1996
2326	Harold Baines, 1980-1996
2293	Alan Trammell, 1977-1996
2212	Tim Wallach, 1980-1996
2123	Wade Boggs, 1982-1996

At-bats: Most, career

11,169	Eddie Murray, 1977-1996
9927	Andre Dawson, 1976-1996
9795	Paul Molitor, 1978-1996
9396	Ozzie Smith, 1978-1996
9217	Cal Ripken, 1981-1996
8528	Rickey Henderson, 1979-1996
8366	Harold Baines, 1980-1996
8288	Alan Trammell, 1977-1996
8100	Wade Boggs, 1982-1996
8099	Tim Wallach, 1980-1996

Runs: Most, career

1829	Rickey Henderson, 1979-1996
1644	Paul Molitor, 1978-1996
1614	Eddie Murray, 1977-1996
1419	Tim Raines, 1979-1996
1373	Andre Dawson, 1976-1996
1367	Wade Boggs, 1982-1996
1366	Cal Ripken, 1981-1996
1307	Brett Butler, 1981-1996
1264	Ryne Sandberg, 1981-1996
1257	Ozzie Smith, 1978-1996

Hits: Most, career

3218	Eddie Murray, 1977-1996
3014	Paul Molitor, 1978-1996
2774	Andre Dawson, 1976-1996
2697	Wade Boggs, 1982-1996
2560	Tony Gwynn, 1982-1996
2549	Cal Ripken, 1981-1996
2460	Ozzie Smith, 1978-1996
2450	Rickey Henderson, 1979-1996
2425	Harold Baines, 1980-1996
2365	Alan Trammell, 1977-1996

Total bases: Most, career

5344	Eddie Murray, 1977-1996
4787	Andre Dawson, 1976-1996
4428	Paul Molitor, 1978-1996
4181	Cal Ripken, 1981-1996
3906	Harold Baines, 1980-1996
3712	Rickey Henderson, 1979-1996

3640	Wade Boggs, 1982-1996
3607	Ryne Sandberg, 1981-1996
3487	Joe Carter, 1983-1996
3442	Alan Trammell, 1977-1996

2B: Most, career

553	Eddie Murray, 1977-1996
544	Paul Molitor, 1978-1996
518	Wade Boggs, 1982-1996
503	Andre Dawson, 1976-1996
487	Cal Ripken, 1981-1996
432	Tim Wallach, 1980-1996
416	Harold Baines, 1980-1996
412	Rickey Henderson, 1979-1996
412	Alan Trammell, 1977-1996
411	Tony Gwynn, 1982-1996

3B: Most, career

128	Brett Butler, 1981-1996
109	Tim Raines, 1979-1996
105	Paul Molitor, 1978-1996
99	Lance Johnson, 1987-1996
98	Andre Dawson, 1976-1996
98	Juan Samuel, 1983-1996
89	Vince Coleman, 1985-1996
89	Willie McGee, 1982-1996
82	Tony Gwynn, 1982-1996
76	Ryne Sandberg, 1981-1996

HR: Most, career

501	Eddie Murray, 1977-1996
438	Andre Dawson, 1976-1996
357	Joe Carter, 1983-1996
353	Cal Ripken, 1981-1996
334	Barry Bonds, 1986-1996
329	Mark McGwire, 1986-1996
328	Jose Canseco, 1985-1996
323	Harold Baines, 1980-1996
317	Fred McGriff, 1986-1996
315	Gary Gaetti, 1981-1996

RBI: Most, career

1899	Eddie Murray, 1977-1996
1591	Andre Dawson, 1976-1996
1369	Cal Ripken, 1981-1996
1356	Harold Baines, 1980-1996
1280	Joe Carter, 1983-1996
1195	Chili Davis, 1981-1996
1155	Gary Gaetti, 1981-1996
1149	Paul Molitor, 1978-1996
1125	Tim Wallach, 1980-1996
1033	Jose Canseco, 1985-1996

SB: Most, career

1186	Rickey Henderson, 1979-1996
787	Tim Raines, 1979-1996
752	Vince Coleman, 1985-1996
580	Ozzie Smith, 1978-1996
543	Brett Butler, 1981-1996
498	Otis Nixon, 1983-1996
484	Paul Molitor, 1978-1996
380	Barry Bonds, 1986-1996
378	Juan Samuel, 1983-1996
337	Ryne Sandberg, 1981-1996

BB: Most, career

1675	Rickey Henderson, 1979-1996

1318	Eddie Murray, 1977-1996
1280	Wade Boggs, 1982-1996
1168	Tim Raines, 1979-1996
1099	Tony Phillips, 1982-1996
1087	Brett Butler, 1981-1996
1082	Barry Bonds, 1986-1996
1072	Ozzie Smith, 1978-1996
1022	Chili Davis, 1981-1996
1004	Paul Molitor, 1978-1996

HBP: Most, career

111	Andre Dawson, 1976-1996
95	Andres Galarraga, 1985-1996
86	Mike Macfarlane, 1987-1996
85	Craig Biggio, 1988-1996
81	Joe Carter, 1983-1996
78	Brady Anderson, 1988-1996
78	Gary Gaetti, 1981-1996
77	Tim Wallach, 1980-1996
73	Rickey Henderson, 1979-1996
71	Juan Samuel, 1983-1996

GIDP: Most, career

305	Eddie Murray, 1977-1996
283	Cal Ripken, 1981-1996
245	Harold Baines, 1980-1996
238	Julio Franco, 1982-1996
231	Tony Pena, 1980-1996
217	Andre Dawson, 1976-1996
213	Tony Gwynn, 1982-1996
206	Wade Boggs, 1982-1996
199	Chili Davis, 1981-1996
199	Gary Gaetti, 1981-1996

BA: Highest, career

.337	Tony Gwynn, 1982-1996
.333	Wade Boggs, 1982-1996
.327	Frank Thomas, 1990-1996
.326	Mike Piazza, 1992-1996
.315	Edgar Martinez, 1987-1996
.313	Kenny Lofton, 1991-1996
.309	Mark Grace, 1988-1996
.309	Hal Morris, 1988-1996
.308	Paul Molitor, 1978-1996
.307	Jeff Bagwell, 1991-1996

Slug avg: Highest, career

.599	Frank Thomas, 1990-1996
.580	Albert Belle, 1989-1996
.559	Mike Piazza, 1992-1996
.552	Juan Gonzalez, 1989-1996
.549	Ken Griffey, 1989-1996
.548	Barry Bonds, 1986-1996
.544	Mark McGwire, 1986-1996
.530	Fred McGriff, 1986-1996
.530	Jim Thome, 1991-1996
.530	Tim Salmon, 1992-1996

On-base avg: Highest, career

.452	Frank Thomas, 1990-1996
.422	Wade Boggs, 1982-1996
.417	Edgar Martinez, 1987-1996
.406	Rickey Henderson, 1979-1996
.406	Jeff Bagwell, 1991-1996
.404	Barry Bonds, 1986-1996
.404	Jim Thome, 1991-1996

.395	John Olerud, 1989-1996
.392	Tim Salmon, 1992-1996
.391	Chuck Knoblauch, 1991-1996
.391	Dave Magadan, 1986-1996

Extra-base hits: Most, career

1089	Eddie Murray, 1977-1996
1039	Andre Dawson, 1976-1996
883	Cal Ripken, 1981-1996
869	Paul Molitor, 1978-1996
787	Harold Baines, 1980-1996
785	Joe Carter, 1983-1996
728	Tim Wallach, 1980-1996
727	Gary Gaetti, 1981-1996
723	Ryne Sandberg, 1981-1996
718	Barry Bonds, 1986-1996

Pitchers

Games: Most, career

997	Lee Smith, 1980-1996
964	Dennis Eckersley, 1975-1996
885	Jesse Orosco, 1979-1996
795	Rick Honeycutt, 1977-1996
723	Roger McDowell, 1985-1996
712	John Franco, 1984-1996
685	Paul Assenmacher, 1986-1996
652	Danny Darwin, 1978-1996
630	Dennis Martinez, 1976-1996
623	Mike Jackson, 1986-1996

Complete games: Most, career

121	Dennis Martinez, 1976-1996
112	Fernando Valenzuela, 1980-1996
100	Roger Clemens, 1984-1996
100	Dennis Eckersley, 1975-1996
81	Mark Langston, 1984-1996
75	Greg Maddux, 1986-1996
74	Frank Viola, 1982-1996
68	Dwight Gooden, 1984-1996
67	Orel Hershiser, 1983-1996
65	Tom Candiotti, 1983-1996

Saves: Most, career

473	Lee Smith, 1980-1996
353	Dennis Eckersley, 1975-1996
323	John Franco, 1984-1996
274	Randy Myers, 1985-1996
242	Doug Jones, 1982-1996
242	Jeff Montgomery, 1987-1996
221	Todd Worrell, 1985-1996
211	Rick Aguilera, 1985-1996
193	Mike Henneman, 1987-1996
186	Jeff Russell, 1983-1996

Shutouts: Most, career

38	Roger Clemens, 1984-1996
31	Fernando Valenzuela, 1980-1996
29	Dennis Martinez, 1976-1996
25	Orel Hershiser, 1983-1996
24	Dwight Gooden, 1984-1996
21	David Cone, 1986-1996
21	Doug Drabek, 1986-1996
21	Greg Maddux, 1986-1996

| 20 | Dennis Eckersley, 1975-1996 |
| 20 | Ramon Martinez, 1988-1996 |

Wins: Most, career

240	Dennis Martinez, 1976-1996
192	Roger Clemens, 1984-1996
192	Dennis Eckersley, 1975-1996
176	Frank Viola, 1982-1996
172	Mark Langston, 1984-1996
171	Fernando Valenzuela, 1980-1996
168	Dwight Gooden, 1984-1996
165	Orel Hershiser, 1983-1996
165	Greg Maddux, 1986-1996
164	Jimmy Key, 1984-1996

Losses: Most, career

182	Dennis Martinez, 1976-1996
165	Dennis Eckersley, 1975-1996
161	Danny Darwin, 1978-1996
157	Kevin Gross, 1983-1996
155	Mike Morgan, 1978-1996
150	Frank Viola, 1982-1996
146	Mark Langston, 1984-1996
143	Rick Honeycutt, 1977-1996
143	Scott Sanderson, 1978-1996
141	Fernando Valenzuela, 1980-1996

HR allowed: Most, career

356	Dennis Martinez, 1976-1996
332	Dennis Eckersley, 1975-1996
297	Scott Sanderson, 1978-1996
294	Frank Viola, 1982-1996
283	Mark Langston, 1984-1996
272	Danny Darwin, 1978-1996
226	Kevin Gross, 1983-1996
225	Jimmy Key, 1984-1996
214	Fernando Valenzuela, 1980-1996
201	Greg Swindell, 1986-1996

BB: Most, career

1190	Mark Langston, 1984-1996
1121	Bobby Witt, 1986-1996
1117	Dennis Martinez, 1976-1996
1105	Fernando Valenzuela, 1980-1996
966	Kevin Gross, 1983-1996
864	Frank Viola, 1982-1996
856	Roger Clemens, 1984-1996
850	Chuck Finley, 1986-1996
788	Danny Jackson, 1983-1996
783	Mark Gubicza, 1984-1996

K: Most, career

2590	Roger Clemens, 1984-1996
2335	Mark Langston, 1984-1996
2334	Dennis Eckersley, 1975-1996
2070	Dennis Martinez, 1976-1996
2013	Fernando Valenzuela, 1980-1996
2001	Dwight Gooden, 1984-1996
1844	Frank Viola, 1982-1996
1812	David Cone, 1986-1996
1769	Danny Darwin, 1978-1996
1740	Sid Fernandez, 1983-1996

Wild pitches: Most, career

115	Fernando Valenzuela, 1980-1996
107	Mark Gubicza, 1984-1996
105	Bobby Witt, 1986-1996
104	John Smoltz, 1988-1996
102	David Cone, 1986-1996
90	Orel Hershiser, 1983-1996
89	Tom Candiotti, 1983-1996
89	Mike Morgan, 1978-1996
86	Frank Viola, 1982-1996
84	Chuck Finley, 1986-1996

Win pct: Highest, career

.687	Mike Mussina, 1991-1996
.646	Dwight Gooden, 1984-1996
.634	Roger Clemens, 1984-1996
.630	David Cone, 1986-1996
.619	Randy Johnson, 1988-1996
.613	Greg Maddux, 1986-1996
.612	Jimmy Key, 1984-1996
.609	Pat Hentgen, 1991-1996
.607	Jack McDowell, 1987-1996
.606	Ramon Martinez, 1988-1996

ERA: Lowest, career

2.57	John Franco, 1984-1996
2.86	Greg Maddux, 1986-1996
2.98	Lee Smith, 1980-1996
2.98	Jesse Orosco, 1979-1996
3.00	Mark Eichhorn, 1982-1996
3.06	Roger Clemens, 1984-1996
3.11	Alejandro Pena, 1981-1996
3.16	Orel Hershiser, 1983-1996
3.16	David Cone, 1986-1996
3.20	Jeff Fassero, 1991-1996

Innings: Most, career

3859.2	Dennis Martinez, 1976-1996
3193.0	Dennis Eckersley, 1975-1996
2841.0	Fernando Valenzuela, 1980-1996
2836.1	Frank Viola, 1982-1996
2776.0	Roger Clemens, 1984-1996
2772.0	Mark Langston, 1984-1996
2710.2	Danny Darwin, 1978-1996
2561.2	Scott Sanderson, 1978-1996
2529.1	Orel Hershiser, 1983-1996
2462.1	Kevin Gross, 1983-1996

AL single-season records

ACTIVE PLAYERS in caps.

Hitters

At-bats: Most

705	Willie Wilson, KC-1980
692	Bobby Richardson, NY-1962
691	Kirby Puckett, Min-1985
689	Sandy Alomar, Cal-1971
687	TONY FERNANDEZ, Tor-1986
686	Horace Clarke, NY-1970
680	Kirby Puckett, Min-1986
679	Harvey Kuenn, Det-1953
679	Bobby Richardson, NY-1964

677	Don Mattingly, NY-1986				
677	Jim Rice, Bos-1978				

Runs: Most

177	Babe Ruth, NY-1921
167	Lou Gehrig, NY-1936
163	Lou Gehrig, NY-1931
163	Babe Ruth, NY-1928
158	Babe Ruth, NY-1920
158	Babe Ruth, NY-1927
152	Al Simmons, Phi-1930
151	Joe DiMaggio, NY-1937
151	Jimmie Foxx, Phi-1932
151	Babe Ruth, NY-1923

Hits: Most

257	George Sisler, StL-1920
253	Al Simmons, Phi-1925
248	Ty Cobb, Det-1911
246	George Sisler, StL-1922
241	Heinie Manush, StL-1928
240	WADE BOGGS, Bos-1985
239	Rod Carew, Min-1977
238	Don Mattingly, NY-1986
237	Harry Heilmann, Det-1921
236	Jack Tobin, StL-1921

Total bases: Most

457	Babe Ruth, NY-1921
447	Lou Gehrig, NY-1927
438	Jimmie Foxx, Phi-1932
419	Lou Gehrig, NY-1930
418	Joe DiMaggio, NY-1937
417	Babe Ruth, NY-1927
410	Lou Gehrig, NY-1931
409	Lou Gehrig, NY-1934
406	Jim Rice, Bos-1978
405	Hal Trosky, Cle-1936

2B: Most

67	Earl Webb, Bos-1931
64	George Burns, Cle-1926
63	Hank Greenberg, Det-1934
60	Charlie Gehringer, Det-1936
59	Tris Speaker, Cle-1923
56	George Kell, Det-1950
55	Gee Walker, Det-1936
54	Hal McRae, KC-1977
54	JOHN OLERUD, Tor-1993
54	ALEX RODRIGUEZ, Sea-1996

3B: Most

26	Sam Crawford, Det-1914
26	Joe Jackson, Cle-1912
25	Sam Crawford, Det-1903
24	Ty Cobb, Det-1911
24	Ty Cobb, Det-1917
23	Ty Cobb, Det-1912
23	Earle Combs, NY-1927
23	Sam Crawford, Det-1913
23	Dale Mitchell, Cle-1949
22	Bill Bradley, Cle-1903
22	Earle Combs, NY-1930
22	Birdie Cree, NY-1911
22	Elmer Flick, Cle-1906
22	Tris Speaker, Bos-1913
22	Snuffy Stirnweiss, NY-1945

HR: Most

61	Roger Maris, NY-1961
60	Babe Ruth, NY-1927
59	Babe Ruth, NY-1921
58	Jimmie Foxx, Phi-1932
58	Hank Greenberg, Det-1938
54	Mickey Mantle, NY-1961
54	Babe Ruth, NY-1920
54	Babe Ruth, NY-1928
52	Mickey Mantle, NY-1956
52	MARK McGWIRE, Oak-1996

RBI: Most

184	Lou Gehrig, NY-1931
183	Hank Greenberg, Det-1937
175	Jimmie Foxx, Bos-1938
175	Lou Gehrig, NY-1927
174	Lou Gehrig, NY-1930
171	Babe Ruth, NY-1921
170	Hank Greenberg, Det-1935
169	Jimmie Foxx, Phi-1932
167	Joe DiMaggio, NY-1937
165	Lou Gehrig, NY-1934
165	Al Simmons, Phi-1930

SB: Most

130	RICKEY HENDERSON, Oak-1982
108	RICKEY HENDERSON, Oak-1983
100	RICKEY HENDERSON, Oak-1980
96	Ty Cobb, Det-1915
93	RICKEY HENDERSON, NY-1988
88	Clyde Milan, Was-1912
87	RICKEY HENDERSON, NY-1986
83	Ty Cobb, Det-1911
83	Willie Wilson, KC-1979
81	Eddie Collins, Phi-1910

BB: Most

170	Babe Ruth, NY-1923
162	Ted Williams, Bos-1947
162	Ted Williams, Bos-1949
156	Ted Williams, Bos-1946
151	Eddie Yost, Was-1956
149	Eddie Joost, Phi-1949
148	Babe Ruth, NY-1920
146	Mickey Mantle, NY-1957
145	Harmon Killebrew, Min-1969
145	Ted Williams, Bos-1941
145	Ted Williams, Bos-1942

K: Most

186	ROB DEER, Mil-1987
185	PETE INCAVIGLIA, Tex-1986
182	CECIL FIELDER, Det-1990
179	ROB DEER, Mil-1986
175	JOSE CANSECO, Oak-1986
175	ROB DEER, Det-1991
175	Dave Nicholson, Chi-1963
175	Gorman Thomas, Mil-1979
172	Bo Jackson, KC-1989
172	Jim Presley, Sea-1986

GIDP: Most

36	Jim Rice, Bos-1984
35	Jim Rice, Bos-1985
32	Jackie Jensen, Bos-1954
32	CAL RIPKEN, Bal-1985
31	Tony Armas, Bos-1983
31	Bobby Doerr, Bos-1949
31	Jim Rice, Bos-1983
30	Billy Hitchcock, Phi-1950
30	Dave Winfield, NY-1983
30	Carl Yastrzemski, Bos-1964

BA: Highest

.426	Nap Lajoie, Phi-1901
.420	George Sisler, StL-1922
.420	Ty Cobb, Det-1911
.409	Ty Cobb, Det-1912
.408	Joe Jackson, Cle-1911
.407	George Sisler, StL-1920
.406	Ted Williams, Bos-1941
.403	Harry Heilmann, Det-1923
.401	Ty Cobb, Det-1922
.398	Harry Heilmann, Det-1927

Slug avg: Highest

.847	Babe Ruth, NY-1920
.846	Babe Ruth, NY-1921
.772	Babe Ruth, NY-1927
.765	Lou Gehrig, NY-1927
.764	Babe Ruth, NY-1923
.749	Jimmie Foxx, Phi-1932
.739	Babe Ruth, NY-1924
.737	Babe Ruth, NY-1926
.735	Ted Williams, Bos-1941
.732	Babe Ruth, NY-1930

On-base avg: Highest

.551	Ted Williams, Bos-1941
.545	Babe Ruth, NY-1923
.530	Babe Ruth, NY-1920
.526	Ted Williams, Bos-1957
.516	Babe Ruth, NY-1926
.513	Ted Williams, Bos-1954
.513	Babe Ruth, NY-1924
.512	Mickey Mantle, NY-1957
.512	Babe Ruth, NY-1921
.499	Ted Williams, Bos-1942

Extra-base hits: Most

119	Babe Ruth, NY-1921
117	Lou Gehrig, NY-1927
103	ALBERT BELLE, Cle-1995
103	Hank Greenberg, Det-1937
100	Jimmie Foxx, Phi-1932
100	Lou Gehrig, NY-1930
99	Hank Greenberg, Det-1940
99	Babe Ruth, NY-1920
99	Babe Ruth, NY-1923
98	Hank Greenberg, Det-1935

Pitchers

Games: Most

90	Mike Marshall, Min-1979
89	MARK EICHHORN, Tor-1987
88	Wilbur Wood, Chi-1968
85	Mitch Williams, Tex-1987

84	Dan Quisenberry, KC-1985	26	Bob Groom, Was-1909	1.27	Walter Johnson, Was-1918
83	EDDIE GUARDADO, Min-1996	26	Happy Townsend, Was-1904	1.30	Jack Coombs, Phi-1910
83	MIKE MYERS, Det-1996	25	Patsy Flaherty, Chi-1903	1.36	Walter Johnson, Was-1910
83	Ken Sanders, Mil-1971	25	Fred Glade, StL-1905	1.39	Walter Johnson, Was-1912
82	Eddie Fisher, Chi-1965	25	Walter Johnson, Was-1909	1.39	Harry Krause, Phi-1909
81	KENNY ROGERS, Tex-1992	25	Scott Perry, Phi-1920		
81	MIKE STANTON, Bos-Tex-1996	25	Red Ruffing, Bos-1928		

Innings: Most

81	Duane Ward, Tor-1991	24	Joe Bush, Phi-1916	464.0	Ed Walsh, Chi-1908
81	John Wyatt, KC-1964	24	Pat Caraway, Chi-1931	454.2	Jack Chesbro, NY-1904
		24	Sam Gray, StL-1931	422.1	Ed Walsh, Chi-1907

Complete games: Most

		24	Tom Hughes, NY-Was-1904	393.0	Ed Walsh, Chi-1912
48	Jack Chesbro, NY-1904			390.1	Jack Powell, NY-1904
42	George Mullin, Det-1904			384.2	Cy Young, Bos-1902

HR allowed: Most

42	Ed Walsh, Chi-1908	50	Bert Blyleven, Min-1986	383.0	Rube Waddell, Phi-1904
41	Cy Young, Bos-1902	46	Bert Blyleven, Min-1987	382.1	George Mullin, Det-1904
40	Cy Young, Bos-1904	43	Pedro Ramos, Was-1957	382.0	Joe McGinnity, Bal-1901
39	Bill Dinneen, Bos-1902	42	Denny McLain, Det-1966	360.0	Cy Young, Bos-1904
39	Joe McGinnity, Bal-1901	40	SHAWN BOSKIE, Cal-1996		

AL club records

39	Rube Waddell, Phi-1904	40	Fergie Jenkins, Tex-1979		
38	Walter Johnson, Was-1910	40	Jack Morris, Det-1986		

BA: Highest, season

38	Jack Powell, NY-1904	40	Orlando Pena, KC-1964	.316	Detroit, 1921
38	Cy Young, Bos-1901	40	BRAD RADKE, Min-1996	.313	St. Louis, 1922
		40	Ralph Terry, NY-1962	.309	New York, 1930

Saves: Most

				.308	St. Louis, 1920
57	Bobby Thigpen, Chi-1990			.308	Cleveland, 1921

BB: Most

51	DENNIS ECKERSLEY, Oak-1992	208	Bob Feller, Cle-1938		
		204	Nolan Ryan, Cal-1977		

BA: Lowest, season

48	DENNIS ECKERSLEY, Oak-1990	202	Nolan Ryan, Cal-1974	.211	Chicago, 1910
		194	Bob Feller, Cle-1941	.214	New York, 1968
46	BRYAN HARVEY, Cal-1991	192	Bobo Newsom, StL-1938	.217	Texas, 1972
46	JOSE MESA, Cle-1995	183	Nolan Ryan, Cal-1976	.218	St. Louis, 1910
46	Dave Righetti, NY-1986	181	Bob Turley, Bal-1954	.221	Chicago, 1909
45	DENNIS ECKERSLEY, Oak-1988	179	Tommy Byrne, NY-1949		
		177	Bob Turley, NY-1955		

Slug avg: Highest, season

45	JEFF MONTGOMERY, KC-1993	171	Bump Hadley, Chi-StL-1932	.489	New York, 1927
				.488	New York, 1930
45	Dan Quisenberry, KC-1983			.484	Cleveland, 1994

K: Most

45	Duane Ward, Tor-1993	383	Nolan Ryan, Cal-1973	.484	Seattle, 1996
		367	Nolan Ryan, Cal-1974	.483	New York, 1936

Shutouts: Most

		349	Rube Waddell, Phi-1904		

On-base avg: Highest, season

13	Jack Coombs, Phi-1910	348	Bob Feller, Cle-1946	.385	Boston, 1950
11	Dean Chance, LA-1964	341	Nolan Ryan, Cal-1977	.385	Detroit, 1921
11	Walter Johnson, Was-1913	329	Nolan Ryan, Cal-1972	.384	New York, 1930
11	Ed Walsh, Chi-1908	327	Nolan Ryan, Cal-1976	.383	Cleveland, 1921
10	Bob Feller, Cle-1946	325	Sam McDowell, Cle-1965	.383	New York, 1927
10	Bob Lemon, Cle-1948	313	Walter Johnson, Was-1910		
10	Jim Palmer, Bal-1975	308	RANDY JOHNSON, Sea-1993		

Runs: Most, season

10	Ed Walsh, Chi-1906	308	Mickey Lolich, Det-1971	1067	New York, 1931
10	Joe Wood, Bos-1912			1065	New York, 1936

Win pct: Highest

10	Cy Young, Bos-1904	.938	Johnny Allen, Cle-1937	1062	New York, 1930
		.900	RANDY JOHNSON, Sea-1995	1027	Boston, 1950

Wins: Most

		.893	Ron Guidry, NY-1978	1002	New York, 1932
41	Jack Chesbro, NY-1904	.886	Lefty Grove, Phi-1931		
40	Ed Walsh, Chi-1908	.882	Bob Stanley, Bos-1978		

HR: Most, season

36	Walter Johnson, Was-1913	.872	Joe Wood, Bos-1912	257	Baltimore, 1996
34	Joe Wood, Bos-1912	.862	Bill Donovan, Det-1907	245	Seattle, 1996
33	Walter Johnson, Was-1912	.862	Whitey Ford, NY-1961	243	Oakland, 1996
33	Cy Young, Bos-1901	.857	ROGER CLEMENS, Bos-1986	240	New York, 1961
32	Cy Young, Bos-1902	.850	Chief Bender, Phi-1914	225	Minnesota, 1963
31	Jim Bagby, Cle-1920			225	Detroit, 1987
31	Jack Coombs, Phi-1910				

ERA: Lowest

31	Lefty Grove, Phi-1931	0.96	Dutch Leonard, Bos-1914		

SB: Most, season

31	Denny McLain, Det-1968	1.14	Walter Johnson, Was-1913	341	Oakland, 1976
		1.16	Addie Joss, Cle-1908	288	New York, 1910

Losses: Most

		1.26	Cy Young, Bos-1908	287	Washington, 1913
26	Pete Dowling, Mil-Cle-1901	1.27	Ed Walsh, Chi-1910		

| 280 | Chicago, 1901 |
| 280 | Detroit, 1909 |

GIDP: Most, season

174	Boston, 1990
172	Minnesota, 1996
171	Boston, 1982
171	Boston, 1983
170	Philadelphia, 1950

Fielding avg: Highest, season

.986	Baltimore, 1995
.986	Baltimore, 1994
.986	New York, 1995
.986	Toronto, 1990
.986	Baltimore, 1989

Errors: Most, season

410	Detroit, 1901
401	Baltimore, 1901
393	Milwaukee, 1901
385	St. Louis, 1910
382	New York, 1912

Errors: Fewest, season

84	Minnesota, 1988
86	Toronto, 1990
87	Texas, 1996
87	Oakland, 1990
87	Baltimore, 1989

Double plays: Most, season

217	Philadelphia, 1949
214	New York, 1956
208	Philadelphia, 1950
207	Boston, 1949
206	Boston, 1980
206	Toronto, 1980

ERA: Lowest, season

1.78	Philadelphia, 1910
1.93	Philadelphia, 1909
1.99	Chicago, 1905
2.02	Cleveland, 1908
2.03	Chicago, 1910

ERA: Highest, season

6.38	Detroit, 1996
6.24	St. Louis, 1936
6.08	Philadelphia, 1936
6.01	St. Louis, 1939
6.00	St. Louis, 1937

Shutouts: Most, season

32	Chicago, 1906
28	Los Angeles, 1964
27	Cleveland, 1906
27	Philadelphia, 1907
27	Philadelphia, 1909

HR allowed: Most, season

241	Detroit, 1996
233	Minnesota, 1996
226	Baltimore, 1987
220	Kansas City, 1964
219	Cleveland, 1987
219	California, 1996

HR allowed: Fewest, season

6	Boston, 1913
7	St. Louis, 1908
8	Philadelphia, 1910
8	Chicago, 1909
8	Detroit, 1907
8	Cleveland, 1907

Walks allowed: Most, season

827	Philadelphia, 1915
812	New York, 1949
801	St. Louis, 1951
784	Detroit, 1996
779	Washington, 1949

NL single-season records

Hitters

At-bats: Most

701	JUAN SAMUEL, Phi-1984
699	Dave Cash, Phi-1975
698	Matty Alou, Pit-1969
696	Woody Jensen, Pit-1936
695	Omar Moreno, Pit-1979
695	Maury Wills, LA-1962
689	Lou Brock, StL-1967
687	Dave Cash, Phi-1974
682	LANCE JOHNSON, NY-1996
681	Jo-Jo Moore, NY-1935
681	Lloyd Waner, Pit-1931

Runs: Most

192	Billy Hamilton, Phi-1894
166	Billy Hamilton, Phi-1895
165	Willie Keeler, Bal-1894
165	Joe Kelley, Bal-1894
162	Willie Keeler, Bal-1895
160	Jesse Burkett, Cle-1896
160	Hugh Duffy, Bos-1894
159	Hughie Jennings, Bal-1895
158	Chuck Klein, Phi-1930
158	Bobby Lowe, Bos-1894

Hits: Most

254	Lefty O'Doul, Phi-1929
254	Bill Terry, NY-1930
250	Rogers Hornsby, StL-1922
250	Chuck Klein, Phi-1930
241	Babe Herman, Bro-1930
240	Jesse Burkett, Cle-1896
239	Willie Keeler, Bal-1897
238	Ed Delahanty, Phi-1899
237	Hugh Duffy, Bos-1894
237	Joe Medwick, StL-1937
237	Paul Waner, Pit-1927

Total bases: Most

450	Rogers Hornsby, StL-1922
445	Chuck Klein, Phi-1930
429	Stan Musial, StL-1948
423	Hack Wilson, Chi-1930
420	Chuck Klein, Phi-1932
416	Babe Herman, Bro-1930

409	Rogers Hornsby, Chi-1929
406	Joe Medwick, StL-1937
405	Chuck Klein, Phi-1929
400	Hank Aaron, Mil-1959

2B: Most

64	Joe Medwick, StL-1936
62	Paul Waner, Pit-1932
59	Chuck Klein, Phi-1930
57	Billy Herman, Chi-1935
57	Billy Herman, Chi-1936
56	Joe Medwick, StL-1937
55	Ed Delahanty, Phi-1899
53	Stan Musial, StL-1953
53	Paul Waner, Pit-1936
52	Johnny Frederick, Bro-1929
52	Enos Slaughter, StL-1939

3B: Most

36	Chief Wilson, Pit-1912
31	Heinie Reitz, Bal-1894
29	Perry Werden, StL-1893
28	Harry Davis, Pit-1897
27	George Davis, NY-1893
27	Sam Thompson, Phi-1894
27	Jimmy Williams, Pit-1899
26	Kiki Cuyler, Pit-1925
26	John Reilly, Cin-1890
26	George Treadway, Bro-1894

HR: Most

56	Hack Wilson, Chi-1930
54	Ralph Kiner, Pit-1949
52	George Foster, Cin-1977
52	Willie Mays, SF-1965
51	Ralph Kiner, Pit-1947
51	Willie Mays, NY-1955
51	Johnny Mize, NY-1947
49	ANDRE DAWSON, Chi-1987
49	Ted Kluszewski, Cin-1954
49	Willie Mays, SF-1962

RBI: Most

190	Hack Wilson, Chi-1930
170	Chuck Klein, Phi-1930
166	Sam Thompson, Det-1887
165	Sam Thompson, Phi-1895
159	Hack Wilson, Chi-1929
154	Joe Medwick, StL-1937
153	Tommy Davis, LA-1962
152	Rogers Hornsby, StL-1922
151	Mel Ott, NY-1929
150	ANDRES GALARRAGA, Col-1996

SB: Most

118	Lou Brock, StL-1974
111	Billy Hamilton, Phi-1891
111	John Ward, NY-1887
110	VINCE COLEMAN, StL-1985
109	VINCE COLEMAN, StL-1987
107	VINCE COLEMAN, StL-1986
104	Maury Wills, LA-1962
102	Jim Fogarty, Phi-1887
102	Billy Hamilton, Phi-1890
99	Jim Fogarty, Phi-1889

BB: Most

151	BARRY BONDS, SF-1996
148	Eddie Stanky, Bro-1945
148	Jim Wynn, Hou-1969
147	Jimmy Sheckard, Chi-1911
144	Eddie Stanky, NY-1950
142	GARY SHEFFIELD, Fla-1996
137	Ralph Kiner, Pit-1951
137	Willie McCovey, SF-1970
137	Eddie Stanky, Bro-1946
136	Jack Clark, StL-1987
136	Jack Crooks, StL-1892

K: Most

189	Bobby Bonds, SF-1970
187	Bobby Bonds, SF-1969
180	Mike Schmidt, Phi-1975
169	ANDRES GALARRAGA, Mon-1990
168	JUAN SAMUEL, Phi-1984
163	Donn Clendenon, Pit-1968
162	JUAN SAMUEL, Phi-1987
161	Dick Allen, Phi-1968
160	HENRY RODRIGUEZ, Mon-1996
158	ANDRES GALARRAGA, Mon-1989

GIDP: Most

30	Ernie Lombardi, Cin-1938
29	Ted Simmons, StL-1973
28	Sid Gordon, Bos-1951
27	John Bateman, Mon-1971
27	Carl Furillo, Bro-1956
27	ERIC KARROS, LA-1996
27	Ron Santo, Chi-1973
27	Ken Singleton, Mon-1973
26	Sid Gordon, NY-1943
26	Cleon Jones, NY-1970
26	Billy Jurges, NY-1939
26	Ernie Lombardi, Cin-1933
26	Willie Montanez, Phi-SF-1975
26	Willie Montanez, SF-Atl-1976
26	Dave Parker, Cin-1985
26	Joe Torre, Mil-1964

BA: Highest

.440	Hugh Duffy, Bos-1894
.424	Willie Keeler, Bal-1897
.424	Rogers Hornsby, StL-1924
.410	Ed Delahanty, Phi-1899
.410	Jesse Burkett, Cle-1896
.409	Jesse Burkett, Cle-1895
.407	Ed Delahanty, Phi-1894
.404	Billy Hamilton, Phi-1894
.404	Ed Delahanty, Phi-1895
.403	Rogers Hornsby, StL-1925

Slug avg: Highest

.756	Rogers Hornsby, StL-1925
.750	JEFF BAGWELL, Hou-1994
.723	Hack Wilson, Chi-1930
.722	Rogers Hornsby, StL-1922
.702	Stan Musial, StL-1948
.696	Rogers Hornsby, StL-1924
.694	Hugh Duffy, Bos-1894

.687	Chuck Klein, Phi-1930
.679	Rogers Hornsby, Chi-1929
.678	Babe Herman, Bro-1930

On-base avg: Highest

.548	John McGraw, Bal-1899
.523	Billy Hamilton, Phi-1894
.507	Rogers Hornsby, StL-1924
.502	Joe Kelley, Bal-1894
.502	Hugh Duffy, Bos-1894
.500	Ed Delahanty, Phi-1895
.498	Rogers Hornsby, Bos-1928
.491	Arky Vaughan, Pit-1935
.490	Billy Hamilton, Phi-1895
.489	Rogers Hornsby, StL-1925

Extra-base hits: Most

107	Chuck Klein, Phi-1930
103	Chuck Klein, Phi-1932
103	Stan Musial, StL-1948
102	Rogers Hornsby, StL-1922
97	Joe Medwick, StL-1937
97	Hack Wilson, Chi-1930
95	Joe Medwick, StL-1936
94	Babe Herman, Bro-1930
94	Rogers Hornsby, Chi-1929
94	Chuck Klein, Phi-1929

Pitchers

Games: Most

106	Mike Marshall, LA-1974
94	Kent Tekulve, Pit-1979
92	Mike Marshall, Mon-1973
91	Kent Tekulve, Pit-1978
90	Wayne Granger, Cin-1969
90	Kent Tekulve, Phi-1987
87	Rob Murphy, Cin-1987
85	Kent Tekulve, Pit-1982
85	Frank Williams, Cin-1987
84	Ted Abernathy, Chi-1965
84	Enrique Romo, Pit-1979
84	Dick Tidrow, Chi-1980

Complete games: Most

75	Will White, Cin-1879
73	Charley Radbourn, Pro-1884
72	Pud Galvin, Buf-1883
72	Jim McCormick, Cle-1880
71	Pud Galvin, Buf-1884
68	John Clarkson, Chi-1885
68	John Clarkson, Bos-1889
67	Bill Hutchison, Chi-1892
66	Jim Devlin, Lou-1876
66	Charley Radbourn, Pro-1883

Saves: Most

53	RANDY MYERS, Chi-1993
48	ROD BECK, SF-1993
47	LEE SMITH, StL-1991
45	BRYAN HARVEY, Fla-1993
45	Bruce Sutter, StL-1984
44	JEFF BRANTLEY, Cin-1996
44	Mark Davis, SD-1989
44	TODD WORRELL, LA-1996
43	LEE SMITH, StL-1992
43	LEE SMITH, StL-1993

43	JOHN WETTELAND, Mon-1993
43	Mitch Williams, Phi-1993

Shutouts: Most

16	Pete Alexander, Phi-1916
16	George Bradley, StL-1876
13	Bob Gibson, StL-1968
12	Pete Alexander, Phi-1915
12	Pud Galvin, Buf-1884
11	Tommy Bond, Bos-1879
11	Sandy Koufax, LA-1963
11	Christy Mathewson, NY-1908
11	Charley Radbourn, Pro-1884
10	John Clarkson, Chi-1885
10	Mort Cooper, StL-1942
10	Carl Hubbell, NY-1933
10	Juan Marichal, SF-1965
10	John Tudor, StL-1985

Wins: Most

59	Charley Radbourn, Pro-1884
53	John Clarkson, Chi-1885
49	John Clarkson, Bos-1889
48	Charlie Buffinton, Bos-1884
48	Charley Radbourn, Pro-1883
47	Al Spalding, Chi-1876
47	John Ward, Pro-1879
46	Pud Galvin, Buf-1883
46	Pud Galvin, Buf-1884
45	George Bradley, StL-1876
45	Jim McCormick, Cle-1880

Losses: Most

48	John Coleman, Phi-1883
42	Will White, Cin-1880
40	George Bradley, Tro-1879
40	Jim McCormick, Cle-1879
37	George Cobb, Bal-1892
36	Bill Hutchison, Chi-1892
36	Stump Wiedman, KC-1886
35	Jim Devlin, Lou-1876
35	Red Donahue, StL-1897
35	Pud Galvin, Buf-1880

HR allowed: Most

46	Robin Roberts, Phi-1956
41	Phil Niekro, Atl-1979
41	Robin Roberts, Phi-1955
40	Phil Niekro, Atl-1970
40	Robin Roberts, Phi-1957
39	Murry Dickson, StL-1948
38	Lew Burdette, Mil-1959
38	Warren Hacker, Chi-1955
38	Don Sutton, LA-1970
37	MARK LEITER, SF-Mon-1996

BB: Most

289	Amos Rusie, NY-1890
270	Amos Rusie, NY-1892
262	Amos Rusie, NY-1891
227	Mark Baldwin, Pit-1891
218	Amos Rusie, NY-1893
213	Cy Seymour, NY-1898
203	John Clarkson, Bos-1889
200	Amos Rusie, NY-1894

199	Bill Hutchison, Chi-1890
194	Mark Baldwin, Pit-1892

K: Most
441	Charley Radbourn, Pro-1884
417	Charlie Buffinton, Bos-1884
382	Sandy Koufax, LA-1965
369	Pud Galvin, Buf-1884
345	Mickey Welch, NY-1884
345	Jim Whitney, Bos-1883
341	Amos Rusie, NY-1890
337	Amos Rusie, NY-1891
335	Tim Keefe, NY-1888
323	Lady Baldwin, Det-1886

Win pct: Highest
.947	Roy Face, Pit-1959
.941	Rick Sutcliffe, Chi-1984
.905	GREG MADDUX, Atl-1995
.889	Freddie Fitzsimmons, Bro-1940
.880	Preacher Roe, Bro-1951
.875	Fred Goldsmith, Chi-1880
.870	DAVID CONE, NY-1988
.864	OREL HERSHISER, LA-1985
.857	DWIGHT GOODEN, NY-1985
.842	Tom Hughes, Bos-1916
.842	Ron Perranoski, LA-1963
.842	Emil Yde, Pit-1924

ERA: Lowest
1.04	Mordecai Brown, Chi-1906
1.12	Bob Gibson, StL-1968
1.14	C. Mathewson, NY-1909
1.15	Jack Pfiester, Chi-1907
1.17	Carl Lundgren, Chi-1907
1.22	Pete Alexander, Phi-1915
1.23	George Bradley, StL-1876
1.28	C. Mathewson, NY-1905
1.31	Mordecai Brown, Chi-1909
1.33	Jack Taylor, Chi-1902

Innings: Most
680.0	Will White, Cin-1879
678.2	Charley Radbourn, Pro-1884
657.2	Jim McCormick, Cle-1880
656.1	Pud Galvin, Buf-1883
636.1	Pud Galvin, Buf-1884
632.1	Charley Radbourn, Pro-1883
623.0	John Clarkson, Chi-1885
622.0	Jim Devlin, Lou-1876
622.0	Bill Hutchison, Chi-1892
620.0	John Clarkson, Bos-1889

NL club records

BA: Highest, season
.349	Philadelphia, 1894
.343	Baltimore, 1894
.337	Chicago, 1876
.331	Boston, 1894
.330	Philadelphia, 1895

BA: Lowest, season
.208	Washington, 1888
.208	Detroit, 1884

.210	Washington, 1886
.213	Brooklyn, 1908
.219	New York, 1963

Slug pct: Highest, season
.484	Boston, 1894
.483	Baltimore, 1894
.481	Chicago, 1930
.476	Philadelphia, 1894
.474	Brooklyn, 1953

On-base avg: Highest, season
.418	Baltimore, 1894
.414	Philadelphia, 1894
.401	Boston, 1894
.394	Philadelphia, 1895
.394	Baltimore, 1897

Runs: Most, season
1220	Boston, 1894
1171	Baltimore, 1894
1143	Philadelphia, 1894
1068	Philadelphia, 1895
1041	Chicago, 1894

HR: Most, season
221	New York, 1947
221	Cincinnati, 1956
221	Colorado, 1996
209	Chicago, 1987
208	Brooklyn, 1953

SB: Most, season
441	Baltimore, 1896
415	New York, 1887
409	Brooklyn, 1892
401	Baltimore, 1897
382	Chicago, 1887

GIDP: Most, season
166	St. Louis, 1958
161	Chicago, 1933
161	Cincinnati, 1933
157	Chicago, 1938
154	Atlanta, 1985

Fielding avg: Highest, season
.986	Cincinnati, 1995
.985	St. Louis, 1992
.985	San Francisco, 1994
.984	Pittsburgh, 1992
.984	Cincinnati, 1977

Errors: Most, season
639	Philadelphia, 1883
607	Pittsburgh, 1890
595	Chicago, 1884
584	Baltimore, 1892
565	New York, 1892

Errors: Fewest, season
94	St. Louis, 1992
95	Cincinnati, 1977
96	Cincinnati, 1992
100	Cincinnati, 1958
101	Pittsburgh, 1992
101	San Francisco, 1993

Double plays: Most, season
215	Pittsburgh, 1966
198	Los Angeles, 1958
197	Atlanta, 1985
195	Pittsburgh, 1963
195	Pittsburgh, 1970

ERA: Lowest, season
1.22	St. Louis, 1876
1.61	Providence, 1884
1.64	Providence, 1880
1.67	Hartford, 1876
1.69	Louisville, 1876

ERA: Highest, season
6.71	Philadelphia, 1930
6.37	Cleveland, 1899
6.21	St. Louis, 1897
6.13	Philadelphia, 1929
5.99	Cincinnati, 1894

Shutouts: Most, season
32	Chicago, 1907
32	Chicago, 1909
30	Chicago, 1906
30	St. Louis, 1968
29	Chicago, 1908

HR allowed: Most, season
198	Colorado, 1996
194	San Francisco, 1996
192	New York, 1962
185	St. Louis, 1955
185	Atlanta, 1970

HR allowed: Fewest, season
5	Cincinnati, 1909
6	Chicago, 1909
8	Philadelphia, 1908
11	Chicago, 1907
12	Pittsburgh, 1905
12	Chicago, 1906
12	Pittsburgh, 1907
12	Pittsburgh, 1909

Walks allowed: Most, season
716	Montreal, 1970
715	San Diego, 1974
702	Montreal, 1969
701	St. Louis, 1911
701	Atlanta, 1977

Career records

Hitters

Games played: Most
3562	Pete Rose, 1963-1986
3308	Carl Yastrzemski, 1961-1983
3298	Hank Aaron, 1954-1976
3035	Ty Cobb, 1905-1928
3026	Stan Musial, 1941-1963
2992	Willie Mays, 1951-1973
2973	Dave Winfield, 1973-1995
2971	EDDIE MURRAY, 1977-1996
2951	Rusty Staub, 1963-1985
2896	Brooks Robinson, 1955-1977

2856	Robin Yount, 1974-1993	
2834	Al Kaline, 1953-1974	
2826	Eddie Collins, 1906-1930	
2820	Reggie Jackson, 1967-1987	
2808	Frank Robinson, 1956-1976	
2792	Honus Wagner, 1897-1917	
2789	Tris Speaker, 1907-1928	
2777	Tony Perez, 1964-1986	
2730	Mel Ott, 1926-1947	
2707	George Brett, 1973-1993	

At-bats: Most

14,053	Pete Rose, 1963-1986
12,364	Hank Aaron, 1954-1976
11,988	Carl Yastrzemski, 1961-1983
11,434	Ty Cobb, 1905-1928
11,169	EDDIE MURRAY, 1977-1996
11,008	Robin Yount, 1974-1993
11,003	Dave Winfield, 1973-1995
10,972	Stan Musial, 1941-1963
10,881	Willie Mays, 1951-1973
10,654	Brooks Robinson, 1955-1977
10,430	Honus Wagner, 1897-1917
10,349	George Brett, 1973-1993
10,332	Lou Brock, 1961-1979
10,277	Cap Anson, 1871-1897
10,230	Luis Aparicio, 1956-1973
10,195	Tris Speaker, 1907-1928
10,116	Al Kaline, 1953-1974
10,078	Rabbit Maranville, 1912-1935
10,006	Frank Robinson, 1956-1976
9949	Eddie Collins, 1906-1930

Runs: Most

2246	Ty Cobb, 1905-1928
2174	Hank Aaron, 1954-1976
2174	Babe Ruth, 1914-1935
2165	Pete Rose, 1963-1986
2062	Willie Mays, 1951-1973
1996	Cap Anson, 1871-1897
1949	Stan Musial, 1941-1963
1888	Lou Gehrig, 1923-1939
1882	Tris Speaker, 1907-1928
1859	Mel Ott, 1926-1947
1829	RICKEY HENDERSON, 1979-1996
1829	Frank Robinson, 1956-1976
1821	Eddie Collins, 1906-1930
1816	Carl Yastrzemski, 1961-1983
1798	Ted Williams, 1939-1960
1774	Charlie Gehringer, 1924-1942
1751	Jimmie Foxx, 1925-1945
1736	Honus Wagner, 1897-1917
1729	Jim O'Rourke, 1872-1904
1720	Jesse Burkett, 1890-1905

Hits: Most

4256	Pete Rose, 1963-1986
4189	Ty Cobb, 1905-1928
3771	Hank Aaron, 1954-1976
3630	Stan Musial, 1941-1963
3514	Tris Speaker, 1907-1928
3419	Carl Yastrzemski, 1961-1983
3418	Cap Anson, 1871-1897
3415	Honus Wagner, 1897-1917
3315	Eddie Collins, 1906-1930
3283	Willie Mays, 1951-1973
3242	Nap Lajoie, 1896-1916
3218	EDDIE MURRAY, 1977-1996
3154	George Brett, 1973-1993
3152	Paul Waner, 1926-1945
3142	Robin Yount, 1974-1993
3110	Dave Winfield, 1973-1995
3053	Rod Carew, 1967-1985
3023	Lou Brock, 1961-1979
3014	PAUL MOLITOR, 1978-1996
3007	Al Kaline, 1953-1974

Total bases: Most

6856	Hank Aaron, 1954-1976
6134	Stan Musial, 1941-1963
6066	Willie Mays, 1951-1973
5854	Ty Cobb, 1905-1928
5793	Babe Ruth, 1914-1935
5752	Pete Rose, 1963-1986
5539	Carl Yastrzemski, 1961-1983
5373	Frank Robinson, 1956-1976
5344	EDDIE MURRAY, 1977-1996
5221	Dave Winfield, 1973-1995
5101	Tris Speaker, 1907-1928
5060	Lou Gehrig, 1923-1939
5044	George Brett, 1973-1993
5041	Mel Ott, 1926-1947
4956	Jimmie Foxx, 1925-1945
4884	Ted Williams, 1939-1960
4862	Honus Wagner, 1897-1917
4852	Al Kaline, 1953-1974
4834	Reggie Jackson, 1967-1987
4787	ANDRE DAWSON, 1976-1996

2B: Most

792	Tris Speaker, 1907-1928
746	Pete Rose, 1963-1986
725	Stan Musial, 1941-1963
724	Ty Cobb, 1905-1928
665	George Brett, 1973-1993
657	Nap Lajoie, 1896-1916
646	Carl Yastrzemski, 1961-1983
640	Honus Wagner, 1897-1917
624	Hank Aaron, 1954-1976
605	Paul Waner, 1926-1945
583	Robin Yount, 1974-1993
581	Cap Anson, 1871-1897
574	Charlie Gehringer, 1924-1942
553	EDDIE MURRAY, 1977-1996
544	PAUL MOLITOR, 1978-1996
542	Harry Heilmann, 1914-1932
541	Rogers Hornsby, 1915-1937
540	Joe Medwick, 1932-1948
540	Dave Winfield, 1973-1995
539	Al Simmons, 1924-1944

3B: Most

309	Sam Crawford, 1899-1917
295	Ty Cobb, 1905-1928
252	Honus Wagner, 1897-1917
243	Jake Beckley, 1888-1907
233	Roger Connor, 1880-1897
222	Tris Speaker, 1907-1928
220	Fred Clarke, 1894-1915
205	Dan Brouthers, 1879-1904
194	Joe Kelley, 1891-1908

191	Paul Waner, 1926-1945
188	Bid McPhee, 1882-1899
187	Eddie Collins, 1906-1930
185	Ed Delahanty, 1888-1903
184	Sam Rice, 1915-1934
182	Jesse Burkett, 1890-1905
182	Edd Roush, 1913-1931
181	Ed Konetchy, 1907-1921
178	Buck Ewing, 1880-1897
177	Rabbit Maranville, 1912-1935
177	Stan Musial, 1941-1963

HR: Most

755	Hank Aaron, 1954-1976
714	Babe Ruth, 1914-1935
660	Willie Mays, 1951-1973
586	Frank Robinson, 1956-1976
573	Harmon Killebrew, 1954-1975
563	Reggie Jackson, 1967-1987
548	Mike Schmidt, 1972-1989
536	Mickey Mantle, 1951-1968
534	Jimmie Foxx, 1925-1945
521	Willie McCovey, 1959-1980
521	Ted Williams, 1939-1960
512	Ernie Banks, 1953-1971
512	Eddie Mathews, 1952-1968
511	Mel Ott, 1926-1947
501	EDDIE MURRAY, 1977-1996
493	Lou Gehrig, 1923-1939
475	Stan Musial, 1941-1963
475	Willie Stargell, 1962-1982
465	Dave Winfield, 1973-1995
452	Carl Yastrzemski, 1961-1983

RBI: Most

2297	Hank Aaron, 1954-1976
2213	Babe Ruth, 1914-1935
2076	Cap Anson, 1871-1897
1995	Lou Gehrig, 1923-1939
1951	Stan Musial, 1941-1963
1937	Ty Cobb, 1905-1928
1922	Jimmie Foxx, 1925-1945
1903	Willie Mays, 1951-1973
1899	EDDIE MURRAY, 1977-1996
1860	Mel Ott, 1926-1947
1844	Carl Yastrzemski, 1961-1983
1839	Ted Williams, 1939-1960
1833	Dave Winfield, 1973-1995
1827	Al Simmons, 1924-1944
1812	Frank Robinson, 1956-1976
1732	Honus Wagner, 1897-1917
1702	Reggie Jackson, 1967-1987
1652	Tony Perez, 1964-1986
1636	Ernie Banks, 1953-1971
1609	Goose Goslin, 1921-1938

SB: Most

1186	RICKEY HENDERSON, 1979-1996
938	Lou Brock, 1961-1979
912	Billy Hamilton, 1888-1901
892	Ty Cobb, 1905-1928
787	TIM RAINES, 1979-1996
752	VINCE COLEMAN, 1985-1996

66

744 Eddie Collins, 1906-1930
739 Arlie Latham, 1880-1909
738 Max Carey, 1910-1929
722 Honus Wagner, 1897-1917
689 Joe Morgan, 1963-1984
668 Willie Wilson, 1976-1994
657 Tom Brown, 1882-1898
649 Bert Campaneris, 1964-1983
616 George Davis, 1890-1909
594 Dummy Hoy, 1888-1902
586 Maury Wills, 1959-1972
583 George Vanhaltren, 1887-1903
580 OZZIE SMITH, 1978-1996
574 Hugh Duffy, 1888-1906

BB: Most
2056 Babe Ruth, 1914-1935
2019 Ted Williams, 1939-1960
1865 Joe Morgan, 1963-1984
1845 Carl Yastrzemski, 1961-1983
1733 Mickey Mantle, 1951-1968
1708 Mel Ott, 1926-1947
1675 RICKEY HENDERSON, 1979-1996
1614 Eddie Yost, 1944-1962
1605 Darrell Evans, 1969-1989
1599 Stan Musial, 1941-1963
1566 Pete Rose, 1963-1986
1559 Harmon Killebrew, 1954-1975
1508 Lou Gehrig, 1923-1939
1507 Mike Schmidt, 1972-1989
1499 Eddie Collins, 1906-1930
1464 Willie Mays, 1951-1973
1452 Jimmie Foxx, 1925-1945
1444 Eddie Mathews, 1952-1968
1420 Frank Robinson, 1956-1976
1402 Hank Aaron, 1954-1976

HBP: Most
287 Hughie Jennings, 1891-1918
272 Tommy Tucker, 1887-1899
267 Don Baylor, 1970-1988
243 Ron Hunt, 1963-1974
230 Dan McGann, 1896-1908
198 Frank Robinson, 1956-1976
192 Minnie Minoso, 1949-1980
183 Jake Beckley, 1888-1907
173 Curt Welch, 1884-1893
165 Kid Elberfeld, 1898-1914
153 Fred Clarke, 1894-1915
151 Chet Lemon, 1975-1990
143 Carlton Fisk, 1969-1993
142 Nellie Fox, 1947-1965
141 Art Fletcher, 1909-1922
140 Bill Dahlen, 1891-1911
137 Frank Chance, 1898-1914
134 Dummy Hoy, 1888-1902
134 Nap Lajoie, 1896-1916
134 John McGraw, 1891-1906

K: Most
2597 Reggie Jackson, 1967-1987
1936 Willie Stargell, 1962-1982
1883 Mike Schmidt, 1972-1989

1867 Tony Perez, 1964-1986
1816 Dave Kingman, 1971-1986
1757 Bobby Bonds, 1968-1981
1748 Dale Murphy, 1976-1993
1730 Lou Brock, 1961-1979
1710 Mickey Mantle, 1951-1968
1699 Harmon Killebrew, 1954-1975
1697 Dwight Evans, 1972-1991
1686 Dave Winfield, 1973-1995
1570 Lee May, 1965-1982
1556 Dick Allen, 1963-1977
1550 Willie McCovey, 1959-1980
1537 Dave Parker, 1973-1991
1532 Frank Robinson, 1956-1976
1527 Lance Parrish, 1977-1995
1526 Willie Mays, 1951-1973
1513 Rick Monday, 1966-1984

GIDP: Most
328 Hank Aaron, 1954-1976
323 Carl Yastrzemski, 1961-1983
319 Dave Winfield, 1973-1995
315 Jim Rice, 1974-1989
305 EDDIE MURRAY, 1977-1996
297 Brooks Robinson, 1955-1977
297 Rusty Staub, 1963-1985
287 Ted Simmons, 1968-1988
284 Joe Torre, 1960-1977
283 CAL RIPKEN, 1981-1996
277 George Scott, 1966-1979
275 Roberto Clemente, 1955-1972
271 Al Kaline, 1953-1974
270 Frank Robinson, 1956-1976
268 Tony Perez, 1964-1986
266 Dave Concepcion, 1970-1988
261 Ernie Lombardi, 1931-1947
256 Ron Santo, 1960-1974
255 Buddy Bell, 1972-1989
254 Al Oliver, 1968-1985

BA: Highest
.366 Ty Cobb, 1905-1928
.359 Rogers Hornsby, 1915-1937
.356 Joe Jackson, 1908-1920
.346 Ed Delahanty, 1888-1903
.345 Tris Speaker, 1907-1928
.344 Ted Williams, 1939-1960
.344 Billy Hamilton, 1888-1901
.342 Dan Brouthers, 1879-1904
.342 Babe Ruth, 1914-1935
.342 Harry Heilmann, 1914-1932
.342 Pete Browning, 1882-1894
.341 Willie Keeler, 1892-1910
.341 Bill Terry, 1923-1936
.340 George Sisler, 1915-1930
.340 Lou Gehrig, 1923-1939
.338 Jesse Burkett, 1890-1905
.338 Nap Lajoie, 1896-1916
.337 TONY GWYNN, 1982-1996
.336 Riggs Stephenson, 1921-1934
.334 Al Simmons, 1924-1944

Slug avg: Highest
.690 Babe Ruth, 1914-1935

.634 Ted Williams, 1939-1960
.632 Lou Gehrig, 1923-1939
.609 Jimmie Foxx, 1925-1945
.605 Hank Greenberg, 1930-1947
.579 Joe DiMaggio, 1936-1951
.577 Rogers Hornsby, 1915-1937
.562 Johnny Mize, 1936-1953
.559 Stan Musial, 1941-1963
.558 Willie Mays, 1951-1973
.557 Mickey Mantle, 1951-1968
.554 Hank Aaron, 1954-1976
.549 KEN GRIFFEY, 1989-1996
.548 Ralph Kiner, 1946-1955
.548 BARRY BONDS, 1986-1996
.545 Hack Wilson, 1923-1934
.544 MARK McGWIRE, 1986-1996
.543 Chuck Klein, 1928-1944
.540 Duke Snider, 1947-1964
.537 Frank Robinson, 1956-1976

On-base avg: Highest
.482 Ted Williams, 1939-1960
.474 Babe Ruth, 1914-1935
.466 John McGraw, 1891-1906
.455 Billy Hamilton, 1888-1901
.447 Lou Gehrig, 1923-1939
.434 Rogers Hornsby, 1915-1937
.433 Ty Cobb, 1905-1928
.428 Jimmie Foxx, 1925-1945
.428 Tris Speaker, 1907-1928
.424 Eddie Collins, 1906-1930
.424 Ferris Fain, 1947-1955
.423 Dan Brouthers, 1879-1904
.423 Joe Jackson, 1908-1920
.423 Max Bishop, 1924-1935
.422 WADE BOGGS, 1982-1996
.421 Mickey Mantle, 1951-1968
.419 Mickey Cochrane, 1925-1937
.417 Stan Musial, 1941-1963
.416 Cupid Childs, 1888-1901
.415 Jesse Burkett, 1890-1905

Extra-base hits: Most
1477 Hank Aaron, 1954-1976
1377 Stan Musial, 1941-1963
1356 Babe Ruth, 1914-1935
1323 Willie Mays, 1951-1973
1190 Lou Gehrig, 1923-1939
1186 Frank Robinson, 1956-1976
1157 Carl Yastrzemski, 1961-1983
1136 Ty Cobb, 1905-1928
1131 Tris Speaker, 1907-1928
1119 George Brett, 1973-1993
1117 Jimmie Foxx, 1925-1945
1117 Ted Williams, 1939-1960
1093 Dave Winfield, 1973-1995
1089 EDDIE MURRAY, 1977-1996
1075 Reggie Jackson, 1967-1987
1071 Mel Ott, 1926-1947
1041 Pete Rose, 1963-1986
1039 ANDRE DAWSON, 1976-1996
1015 Mike Schmidt, 1972-1989
1011 Rogers Hornsby, 1915-1937

Pitchers

Games: Most

1070	Hoyt Wilhelm, 1952-1972
1050	Kent Tekulve, 1974-1989
1002	Rich Gossage, 1972-1994
997	LEE SMITH, 1980-1996
987	Lindy McDaniel, 1955-1975
964	DENNIS ECKERSLEY, 1975-1996
944	Rollie Fingers, 1968-1985
931	Gene Garber, 1969-1988
906	Cy Young, 1890-1911
899	Sparky Lyle, 1967-1982
898	Jim Kaat, 1959-1983
885	JESSE OROSCO, 1979-1996
880	Jeff Reardon, 1979-1994
874	Don McMahon, 1957-1974
864	Phil Niekro, 1964-1987
858	Charlie Hough, 1970-1994
848	Roy Face, 1953-1969
824	Tug McGraw, 1965-1984
807	Nolan Ryan, 1966-1993
802	Walter Johnson, 1907-1927

Complete games: Most

749	Cy Young, 1890-1911
646	Pud Galvin, 1875-1892
554	Tim Keefe, 1880-1893
531	Walter Johnson, 1907-1927
531	Kid Nichols, 1890-1906
525	Bobby Mathews, 1871-1887
525	Mickey Welch, 1880-1892
489	Charley Radbourn, 1880-1891
485	John Clarkson, 1882-1894
468	Tony Mullane, 1881-1894
466	Jim McCormick, 1878-1887
448	Gus Weyhing, 1887-1901
437	Pete Alexander, 1911-1930
434	Christy Mathewson, 1900-1916
422	Jack Powell, 1897-1912
410	Eddie Plank, 1901-1917
394	Will White, 1877-1886
393	Amos Rusie, 1889-1901
388	Vic Willis, 1898-1910
386	Tommy Bond, 1874-1884

Saves: Most

473	LEE SMITH, 1980-1996
367	Jeff Reardon, 1979-1994
353	DENNIS ECKERSLEY, 1975-1996
341	Rollie Fingers, 1968-1985
323	JOHN FRANCO, 1984-1996
311	Tom Henke, 1982-1995
310	Rich Gossage, 1972-1994
300	Bruce Sutter, 1976-1988
274	RANDY MYERS, 1985-1996
252	Dave Righetti, 1979-1995
244	Dan Quisenberry, 1979-1990
242	DOUG JONES, 1982-1996
242	JEFF MONTGOMERY, 1987-1996
238	Sparky Lyle, 1967-1982

227	Hoyt Wilhelm, 1952-1972
221	TODD WORRELL, 1985-1996
218	Gene Garber, 1969-1988
216	Dave Smith, 1980-1992
211	RICK AGUILERA, 1985-1996
201	Bobby Thigpen, 1986-1994
193	Roy Face, 1953-1969
193	MIKE HENNEMAN, 1987-1996
192	Mitch Williams, 1986-1995
188	Mike Marshall, 1967-1981
186	JEFF RUSSELL, 1983-1996
184	Steve Bedrosian, 1981-1995
184	Kent Tekulve, 1974-1989
180	Tug McGraw, 1965-1984
180	JOHN WETTELAND, 1989-1996
179	Ron Perranoski, 1961-1973

Shutouts: Most

110	Walter Johnson, 1907-1927
90	Pete Alexander, 1911-1930
79	Christy Mathewson, 1900-1916
76	Cy Young, 1890-1911
69	Eddie Plank, 1901-1917
63	Warren Spahn, 1942-1965
61	Nolan Ryan, 1966-1993
61	Tom Seaver, 1967-1986
60	Bert Blyleven, 1970-1992
58	Don Sutton, 1966-1988
57	Pud Galvin, 1875-1892
57	Ed Walsh, 1904-1917
56	Bob Gibson, 1959-1975
55	Mordecai Brown, 1903-1916
55	Steve Carlton, 1965-1988
53	Jim Palmer, 1965-1984
53	Gaylord Perry, 1962-1983
52	Juan Marichal, 1960-1975
50	Rube Waddell, 1897-1910
50	Vic Willis, 1898-1910

Wins: Most

511	Cy Young, 1890-1911
417	Walter Johnson, 1907-1927
373	Pete Alexander, 1911-1930
373	Christy Mathewson, 1900-1916
364	Pud Galvin, 1875-1892
363	Warren Spahn, 1942-1965
361	Kid Nichols, 1890-1906
342	Tim Keefe, 1880-1893
329	Steve Carlton, 1965-1988
328	John Clarkson, 1882-1894
326	Eddie Plank, 1901-1917
324	Nolan Ryan, 1966-1993
324	Don Sutton, 1966-1988
318	Phil Niekro, 1964-1987
314	Gaylord Perry, 1962-1983
311	Tom Seaver, 1967-1986
309	Charley Radbourn, 1880-1891
307	Mickey Welch, 1880-1892
300	Lefty Grove, 1925-1941
300	Early Wynn, 1939-1963

Losses: Most

316	Cy Young, 1890-1911
310	Pud Galvin, 1875-1892
292	Nolan Ryan, 1966-1993
279	Walter Johnson, 1907-1927
274	Phil Niekro, 1964-1987
265	Gaylord Perry, 1962-1983
256	Don Sutton, 1966-1988
254	Jack Powell, 1897-1912
251	Eppa Rixey, 1912-1933
250	Bert Blyleven, 1970-1992
248	Bobby Mathews, 1871-1887
245	Robin Roberts, 1948-1966
245	Warren Spahn, 1942-1965
244	Steve Carlton, 1965-1988
244	Early Wynn, 1939-1963
237	Jim Kaat, 1959-1983
236	Frank Tanana, 1973-1993
232	Gus Weyhing, 1887-1901
231	Tommy John, 1963-1989
230	Bob Friend, 1951-1966
230	Ted Lyons, 1923-1946

HR allowed: Most

505	Robin Roberts, 1948-1966
484	Fergie Jenkins, 1965-1983
482	Phil Niekro, 1964-1987
472	Don Sutton, 1966-1988
448	Frank Tanana, 1973-1993
434	Warren Spahn, 1942-1965
430	Bert Blyleven, 1970-1992
414	Steve Carlton, 1965-1988
399	Gaylord Perry, 1962-1983
395	Jim Kaat, 1959-1983
389	Jack Morris, 1977-1994
383	Charlie Hough, 1970-1994
380	Tom Seaver, 1967-1986
374	Catfish Hunter, 1965-1979
372	Jim Bunning, 1955-1971
356	DENNIS MARTINEZ, 1976-1996
347	Mickey Lolich, 1963-1979
346	Luis Tiant, 1964-1982
338	Early Wynn, 1939-1963
332	DENNIS ECKERSLEY, 1975-1996

BB: Most career

2795	Nolan Ryan, 1966-1993
1833	Steve Carlton, 1965-1988
1809	Phil Niekro, 1964-1987
1775	Early Wynn, 1939-1963
1764	Bob Feller, 1936-1956
1732	Bobo Newsom, 1929-1953
1707	Amos Rusie, 1889-1901
1665	Charlie Hough, 1970-1994
1566	Gus Weyhing, 1887-1901
1541	Red Ruffing, 1924-1947
1442	Bump Hadley, 1926-1941
1434	Warren Spahn, 1942-1965
1431	Earl Whitehill, 1923-1939
1408	Tony Mullane, 1881-1894
1396	Sam Jones, 1914-1935
1390	Jack Morris, 1977-1994
1390	Tom Seaver, 1967-1986

1379	Gaylord Perry, 1962-1983
1371	Mike Torrez, 1967-1984
1363	Walter Johnson, 1907-1927

Hit batsmen: Most

277	Gus Weyhing, 1887-1901
219	Chick Fraser, 1896-1909
210	Pink Hawley, 1892-1901
205	Walter Johnson, 1907-1927
190	Eddie Plank, 1901-1917
185	Tony Mullane, 1881-1894
179	Joe McGinnity, 1899-1908
174	Charlie Hough, 1970-1994
171	Clark Griffith, 1891-1914
163	Cy Young, 1890-1911
160	Jim Bunning, 1955-1971
158	Nolan Ryan, 1966-1993
156	Vic Willis, 1898-1910
155	Bert Blyleven, 1970-1992
154	Don Drysdale, 1956-1969
148	Adonis Terry, 1884-1897
147	Bert Cunningham, 1887-1901
146	Silver King, 1886-1897
144	Win Mercer, 1894-1902
142	Frank Foreman, 1884-1902

K: Most

5714	Nolan Ryan, 1966-1993
4136	Steve Carlton, 1965-1988
3701	Bert Blyleven, 1970-1992
3640	Tom Seaver, 1967-1986
3574	Don Sutton, 1966-1988
3534	Gaylord Perry, 1962-1983
3509	Walter Johnson, 1907-1927
3342	Phil Niekro, 1964-1987
3192	Fergie Jenkins, 1965-1983
3117	Bob Gibson, 1959-1975
2855	Jim Bunning, 1955-1971
2832	Mickey Lolich, 1963-1979
2803	Cy Young, 1890-1911
2773	Frank Tanana, 1973-1993
2590	ROGER CLEMENS, 1984-1996
2583	Warren Spahn, 1942-1965
2581	Bob Feller, 1936-1956
2560	Tim Keefe, 1880-1893
2556	Jerry Koosman, 1967-1985
2502	Christy Mathewson, 1900-1916

Wild pitches: Most

343	Tony Mullane, 1881-1894
277	Nolan Ryan, 1966-1993
274	Mickey Welch, 1880-1892
252	Bobby Mathews, 1871-1887
240	Tim Keefe, 1880-1893
240	Gus Weyhing, 1887-1901
226	Phil Niekro, 1964-1987
221	Mark Baldwin, 1887-1893
221	Pud Galvin, 1875-1892
221	Will White, 1877-1886
214	Charley Radbourn, 1880-1891
214	Jim Whitney, 1881-1890
206	Jack Morris, 1977-1994
206	Adonis Terry, 1884-1897
203	Matt Kilroy, 1886-1898

189	George Bradley, 1875-1888
187	Tommy John, 1963-1989
183	Steve Carlton, 1965-1988
182	John Clarkson, 1882-1894
179	Charlie Hough, 1970-1994
179	Toad Ramsey, 1885-1890

Win pct: Highest

.795	Al Spalding, 1871-1878
.717	Spud Chandler, 1937-1947
.690	Dave Foutz, 1884-1896
.690	Whitey Ford, 1950-1967
.688	Bob Caruthers, 1884-1893
.686	Don Gullett, 1970-1978
.680	Lefty Grove, 1925-1941
.671	Joe Wood, 1908-1922
.667	Vic Raschi, 1946-1955
.665	Larry Corcoran, 1880-1887
.665	Christy Mathewson, 1900-1916
.660	Sam Leever, 1898-1910
.657	Sal Maglie, 1945-1958
.656	Dick McBride, 1871-1876
.655	Sandy Koufax, 1955-1966
.654	Johnny Allen, 1932-1944
.651	Ron Guidry, 1975-1988
.650	Lefty Gomez, 1930-1943
.648	John Clarkson, 1882-1894
.648	Mordecai Brown, 1903-1916

ERA: Lowest

1.82	Ed Walsh, 1904-1917
1.89	Addie Joss, 1902-1910
2.04	Al Spalding, 1871-1878
2.06	Mordecai Brown, 1903-1916
2.10	John Ward, 1878-1894
2.13	Christy Mathewson, 1900-1916
2.14	Tommy Bond, 1874-1884
2.16	Rube Waddell, 1897-1910
2.17	Walter Johnson, 1907-1927
2.23	Orval Overall, 1905-1913
2.28	Will White, 1877-1886
2.28	Ed Reulbach, 1905-1917
2.30	Jim Scott, 1909-1917
2.35	Eddie Plank, 1901-1917
2.35	Larry Corcoran, 1880-1887
2.38	George McQuillan, 1907-1918
2.38	Ed Killian, 1903-1910
2.38	Eddie Cicotte, 1905-1920
2.39	Candy Cummings, 1872-1877
2.39	Doc White, 1901-1913

Innings: Most

7356.0	Cy Young, 1890-1911
6003.1	Pud Galvin, 1875-1892
5914.2	Walter Johnson, 1907-1927
5404.1	Phil Niekro, 1964-1987
5386.0	Nolan Ryan, 1966-1993
5350.1	Gaylord Perry, 1962-1983
5282.1	Don Sutton, 1966-1988
5243.2	Warren Spahn, 1942-1965
5217.1	Steve Carlton, 1965-1988
5190.0	Pete Alexander, 1911-1930
5056.1	Kid Nichols, 1890-1906
5047.2	Tim Keefe, 1880-1893

4970.0	Bert Blyleven, 1970-1992
4956.0	Bobby Mathews, 1871-1887
4802.0	Mickey Welch, 1880-1892
4782.2	Tom Seaver, 1967-1986
4780.2	Christy Mathewson, 1900-1916
4710.1	Tommy John, 1963-1989
4688.2	Robin Roberts, 1948-1966
4564.0	Early Wynn, 1939-1963

General club records

Highest percentage for league champion

.832	St. Louis, UA-1884
.798	Chicago, NL-1880
.788	Chicago, NL-1876
.777	Chicago, NL-1885
.763	Chicago, NL-1906

Lowest percentage for league champion

.509	New York, NL-1973
.525	Minnesota, AL-1987
.551	New York, AL-1981
.556	Philadelphia, NL-1983
.556	Oakland, AL-1974

Most wins

116	Chicago, NL-1906
111	Cleveland, AL-1954
110	Pittsburgh, AL-1909
110	New York, AL-1927
109	New York, AL-1961
109	Baltimore, AL-1969

Fewest Wins

36	Philadelphia, AL-1916
38	Washington, AL-1904
38	Boston, NL-1935
40	New York, NL-1962
42	Washington, AL-1909
42	Philadelphia, NL-1942
42	Pittsburgh, NL-1952

Most league championships

34	New York, AL
21	Brooklyn-Los Angeles, NL
19	New York-San Francisco, NL
16	Chicago, NL
15	St. Louis, NL
15	Philadelphia-Oakland, AL

Individual fielding records

Gold Gloves: Most, pitcher

16	Jim Kaat
9	Bob Gibson
8	Bobby Shantz
7	MARK LANGSTON
7	GREG MADDUX

5	Ron Guidry
5	Phil Niekro
4	Jim Palmer
3	Harvey Haddix
2	Andy Messersmith
2	Mike Norris
2	Rick Reuschel

Gold Gloves: Most, catcher

10	Johnny Bench
7	Bob Boone
6	Jim Sundberg
5	Bill Freehan
5	IVAN RODRIGUEZ
4	Del Crandall
4	TONY PENA
3	Earl Battey
3	Gary Carter
3	Sherm Lollar
3	Thurman Munson
3	TOM PAGNOZZI
3	Lance Parrish
3	BENITO SANTIAGO

Gold Gloves: Most, first base

11	Keith Hernandez
9	Don Mattingly
8	George Scott
7	Vic Power
7	Bill White
6	Wes Parker
4	Steve Garvey
4	MARK GRACE
3	Gil Hodges
3	EDDIE MURRAY
3	Joe Pepitone

Gold Gloves: Most, second base

9	RYNE SANDBERG
8	Bill Mazeroski
8	Frank White
6	ROBERTO ALOMAR
5	Joe Morgan
5	Bobby Richardson
4	Bobby Grich
3	CRAIG BIGGIO
3	Nellie Fox
3	Davey Johnson
3	Bobby Knoop
3	Harold Reynolds
3	Manny Trillo
3	Lou Whitaker

Gold Gloves: Most, third base

16	Brooks Robinson
10	Mike Schmidt
6	Buddy Bell
5	Ken Boyer
5	Doug Rader
5	Ron Santo
4	GARY GAETTI
4	ROBIN VENTURA
3	Frank Malzone
3	TERRY PENDLETON
3	TIM WALLACH
3	MATT WILLIAMS

Gold Gloves: Most, shortstop

13	OZZIE SMITH
9	Luis Aparicio
8	Mark Belanger
5	Dave Concepcion
4	TONY FERNANDEZ
4	ALAN TRAMMELL
4	OMAR VIZQUEL
3	BARRY LARKIN
3	Roy McMillan
2	Gene Alley
2	Larry Bowa
2	Don Kessinger
2	CAL RIPKEN
2	Maury Wills
2	Zoilo Versalles

Gold Gloves: Most, outfield

12	Roberto Clemente
12	Willie Mays
10	Al Kaline
8	Paul Blair
8	ANDRE DAWSON
8	Dwight Evans
8	Garry Maddox
7	Curt Flood
7	KEN GRIFFEY JR.
7	Dave Winfield
7	DEVON WHITE
7	Carl Yastrzemski

Assists: Most, pitcher

227	Ed Walsh, Chi/A-1907
223	Will White, Cin/A-1882
190	Ed Walsh, Chi/A-1908
178	Harry Howell, StL/A-1905
177	Tony Mullane, Lou/A-1882
174	John Clarkson, Chi/N-1885
172	John Clarkson, Bos/N-1889
166	Jack Chesbro, NY/A-1904
163	George Mullin, Det/A-1904
160	Ed Walsh, Chi/A-1911

Assists: Most, catcher

238	Bill Rariden, New/F-1915
215	Bill Rariden, Ind/F-1914
214	Pat Moran, Bos/N-1903
212	Oscar Stanage, Det/A-1911
212	Art Wilson, Chi/F-1914
210	Gabby Street, Was/A-1909
204	Frank Snyder, StL/N-1915
203	George Gibson, Pit/N-1910
202	Bill Bergen, Bro/N-1909
202	Claude Berry, Pit/F-1914

Assists: Most, first base

184	Bill Buckner, Bos/A-1985
180	MARK GRACE, Chi/N-1990
167	MARK GRACE, Chi/N-1991
166	Sid Bream, Pit/N-1986
161	Bill Buckner, Chi/N-1983
159	Bill Buckner, Chi/N-1982
157	Bill Buckner, Bos/A-1986
155	Mickey Vernon, Cle/A-1949
152	EDDIE MURRAY, Bal/A-1985
152	Fred Tenney, Bos/N-1905

Assists: Most, second base

641	Frankie Frisch, StL/N-1927
588	Hughie Critz, Cin/N-1926
582	Rogers Hornsby, NY/N-1927
572	Ski Melillo, StL/A-1930
571	RYNE SANDBERG, Chi/N-1983
568	Rabbit Maranville, Pit/N-1924
562	Frank Parkinson, Phi/N-1922
559	Tony Cuccinello, Bos/N-1936
557	Johnny Hodapp, Cle/A-1930
555	Lou Bierbauer, Pit/N-1892

Assists: Most, shortstop

621	OZZIE SMITH, SD/N-1980
601	Glenn Wright, Pit/N-1924
598	Dave Bancroft, Phi-NY/N-1920
597	Tommy Thevenow, StL/N-1926
595	Ivan DeJesus, Chi/N-1977
583	CAL RIPKEN, Bal/A-1984
581	Whitey Wietelmann, Bos/N-1943
579	Dave Bancroft, NY/N-1922
574	Rabbit Maranville, Bos/N-1914
573	Don Kessinger, Chi/N-1968

Assists: Most, third base

412	Graig Nettles, Cle/A-1971
410	Graig Nettles, NY/A-1973
410	Brooks Robinson, Bal/A-1974
405	Harlond Clift, StL/A-1937
405	Brooks Robinson, Bal/A-1967
404	Mike Schmidt, Phi/N-1974
399	Doug DeCinces, Cal/A-1982
396	Buddy Bell, Tex/A-1982
396	Clete Boyer, NY/N-1962
396	Mike Schmidt, Phi/N-1977

Assists: Most, outfield

50	Orator Shaffer, Chi/N-1879
48	Hugh Nicol, StL/A-1884
45	Hardy Richardson, Buf/N-1881
44	Chuck Klein, Phi/N-1930
44	Tommy McCarthy, StL/A-1888
43	Jimmy Bannon, Bos/N-1894
43	Charlie Duffee, StL/A-1889
42	Jim Fogarty, Phi/N-1889
41	Jim Lillie, Buf/N-1884
41	Orator Shaffer, Buf/N-1883

Assists: Most, pitcher, active players

71	Greg Maddux, Atl/N-1996
64	Greg Maddux, Chi/N-1992
64	Fernando Valenzuela, LA/N-1982
60	Orel Hershiser, LA/N-1988
59	Greg Maddux, Atl/N-1993
59	Dennis Martinez, Bal/A-1979

Assists: Most, catcher, active players

100	Tony Pena, Pit/N-1985
100	Benito Santiago, SD/N-1991
99	Tony Pena, Pit/N-1986
99	Mike Piazza, LA/N-1993
95	Tony Pena, Pit/N-1984

Assists: Most, first base, active players

180	Mark Grace, Chi/N-1990
167	Mark Grace, Chi/N-1991
152	Eddie Murray, Bal/A-1985
147	Eric Karros, LA/N-1993
147	Rafael Palmeiro, Tex/A-1993

Assists: Most, second base, active players

571	Ryne Sandberg, Chi/N-1983
550	Ryne Sandberg, Chi/N-1984
539	Ryne Sandberg, Chi/N-1992
522	Ryne Sandberg, Chi/N-1988
515	Ryne Sandberg, Chi/N-1991

Assists: Most, shortstop, active players

621	Ozzie Smith, SD/N-1980
583	Cal Ripken, Bal/A-1984
570	Ozzie Guillen, Chi/A-1988
555	Ozzie Smith, SD/N-1979
549	Ozzie Smith, StL/N-1985

Assists: Most, third base, active players

392	Terry Pendleton, StL/N-1989
389	Vinny Castilla, Col/N-1996
383	Tim Wallach, Mon/N-1985
372	Robin Ventura, Chi/A-1992
371	Terry Pendleton, StL/N-1986

Assists: Most, outfield, active players

22	Joe Orsulak, Bal/N-1991
21	Tim Raines, Mon/N-1983
19	Brett Butler, Cle/A-1985
19	Bernard Gilkey, StL/N-1993
19	Tony Gwynn, SD/N-1986
19	Wayne Kirby, Cle/N-1993
19	Manny Ramirez, Cle/A-1996

Putouts: Most, pitcher

57	Dave Foutz, StL/N-1886
54	Tony Mullane, Lou/A-1882
50	George Bradley, StL/N-1876
50	Guy Hecker, Lou/A-1884
49	Mike Boddicker, Bal/A-1984
47	Larry Corcoran, Chi/N-1884
45	Ted Breitenstein, StL/N-1895
45	Al Spalding, Chi/N-1876
44	Jim Devlin, Lou/N-1876
44	Dave Foutz, StL/N-1887
44	Bill Hutchison, Chi/N-1890

Putouts: Most, catcher

1135	Johnny Edwards, Hou/N-1969
1056	MIKE PIAZZA, LA/N-1996

1008	Johnny Edwards, Cin/N-1963
994	JAVY LOPEZ, Atl/N-1996
981	DARREN DAULTON, Phi/N-1993
978	Randy Hundley, Chi/N-1969
976	TONY PENA, Pit/N-1983
971	Bill Freehan, Det/A-1968
956	Gary Carter, NY/N-1985
954	Gary Carter, Mon/N-1982

Putouts: Most, first base

1846	Jiggs Donahue, Chi/A-1907
1759	George Kelly, NY/N-1920
1755	Phil Todt, Bos/A-1926
1710	Wally Pipp, Cin/N-1926
1697	Jiggs Donahue, Chi/A-1906
1691	Candy LaChance, Bos/A-1904
1687	Tom Jones, StL/A-1907
1682	Ernie Banks, Chi/N-1965
1667	Wally Pipp, NY/A-1922
1662	Lou Gehrig, NY/A-1927

Putouts: Most, second base

529	Bid McPhee, Cin/N-1886
484	Bobby Grich, Bal/A-1974
483	Bucky Harris, Was/A-1922
478	Nellie Fox, Chi/A-1956
472	Lou Bierbauer, Phi/A-1889
466	Billy Herman, Chi/N-1933
463	Bill Wambsganss, Bos/A-1924
461	Cub Stricker, Cle/A-1887
460	Buddy Myer, Was/A-1935
459	Bill Sweeney, Bos/N-1912

Putouts: Most, shortstop

425	Hughie Jennings, Bal/N-1895
425	Donie Bush, Det/A-1914
408	Joe Cassidy, Was/A-1905
407	Rabbit Maranville, Bos/N-1914
405	Dave Bancroft, NY/N-1922
405	Eddie Miller, Bos/N-1940
404	Monte Cross, Phi/A-1898
396	Dave Bancroft, NY/N-1921
395	Mickey Doolan, Phi/N-1906
392	Buck Weaver, Chi/A-1913

Putouts: Most, third base

255	Denny Lyons, Phi/A-1887
251	Jimmy Williams, Pit/N-1899
251	Jimmy Collins, Bos/N-1900
243	Jimmy Collins, Bos/N-1898
243	Willie Kamm, Chi/A-1928
236	Willie Kamm, Chi/A-1927
233	Frank Baker, Phi/A-1913
232	Bill Coughlin, Was/A-1901
229	Ernie Courtney, Phi/N-1905
228	Jimmy Austin, StL/A-1911

Putouts: Most, outfield

547	Taylor Douthit, StL/N-1928
538	Richie Ashburn, Phi/N-1951
514	Richie Ashburn, Phi/N-1949
512	Chet Lemon, Chi/A-1977
507	Dwayne Murphy, Oak/A-1980
503	Dom DiMaggio, Bos/A-1948

503	Richie Ashburn, Phi/N-1956
502	Richie Ashburn, Phi/N-1957
496	Richie Ashburn, Phi/N-1953
495	Richie Ashburn, Phi/N-1958

Putouts: Most, pitcher, active players

40	Kevin Brown, Bal/A-1995
39	Greg Maddux, Chi/N-1990
39	Greg Maddux, Chi/N-1991
39	Greg Maddux, Atl/N-1993
37	Kevin Brown, Tex/A-1992
37	Orel Hershiser, LA/N-1987
37	Greg Maddux, Atl/N-1996

Putouts: Most, catcher, active players

1056	Mike Piazza, LA/N-1996
994	Javy Lopez, Atl/N-1996
981	Darren Daulton, Phi/N-1993
976	Tony Pena, Pit/N-1983
925	Joe Oliver, Cin/N-1992

Putouts: Most, first base, active players

1580	Mark Grace, Chi/N-1992
1538	Eddie Murray, Bal/A-1984
1527	Andres Galarraga, Col/N-1996
1520	Mark Grace, Chi/N-1991
1504	Eddie Murray, Bal/A-1978

Putouts: Most, second base, active players

400	Carlos Baerga, Cle/A-1992
389	Juan Samuel, Phi/N-1985
388	Juan Samuel, Phi/N-1984
374	Juan Samuel, Phi/N-1987
361	Craig Biggio, Hou/N-1996

Putouts: Most, shortstop, active players

320	Shawon Dunston, Chi/N-1986
304	Ozzie Smith, StL/N-1983
297	Cal Ripken, Bal/A-1984
288	Ozzie Smith, SD/N-1980
287	Cal Ripken, Bal/A-1992

Putouts: Most, third base, active players

162	Tim Wallach, Mon/N-1984
151	Tim Wallach, Mon/N-1983
148	Tim Wallach, Mon/N-1985
146	Gary Gaetti, Min/A-1985
142	Gary Gaetti, Min/A-1984

Putouts: Most, outfield, active players

469	Lenny Dykstra, Phi/N-1993
448	Brett Butler, Cle/A-1984
444	Joe Carter, Cle/A-1988
443	Devon White, Tor/A-1992
439	Lenny Dykstra, Phi/N-1990
439	Rickey Henderson, NY/-1985
439	Devon White, Tor/A-1991

Individual records

Hitters

Most consecutive games played, career

2316	CAL RIPKEN, 1982-1996
2130	Lou Gehrig, 1925-1939
1307	Everett Scott, 1916-1925
1207	Steve Garvey, 1975-1983
1117	Billy Williams, 1963-1970
1103	Joe Sewell, 1922-1930
895	Stan Musial, 1951-1957
829	Eddie Yost, 1949-1955
822	Gus Suhr, 1931-1937
798	Nellie Fox, 1955-1960

Longest hitting streak, season

56	Joe DiMaggio, NY/A-1941
44	Willie Keeler, Bal/N-1897
44	Pete Rose, Cin/N-1978
42	Bill Dahlen, Chi/N-1894
41	George Sisler, StL/A-1922
40	Ty Cobb, Det/A-1911
39	PAUL MOLITOR, Mil/A-1987
37	Tommy Holmes, Bos/N-1945
36	Billy Hamilton, Phi/N-1894
35	Fred Clarke, Lou/N-1895
35	Ty Cobb, Det/A-1917
34	Dom DiMaggio, Bos/A-1949
34	George McQuinn, StL/A-1938
34	BENITO SANTIAGO, SD/N-1987
34	George Sisler, StL/A-1925
33	George Davis, NY/N-1893
33	Hal Chase, NY/A-1907
33	Rogers Hornsby, StL/N-1922
33	Heinie Manush, Was/A-1933
31	Rico Carty, Atl/N-1970
31	Willie Davis, LA/N-1969
31	Ed Delahanty, Phi/N-1899
31	Nap Lajoie, Cle/A-1906
31	Ken Landreaux, Min/A-1980
31	Sam Rice, Was/A-1924
30	George Brett, KC/A-1980
30	Goose Goslin, Det/A-1934
30	Ron LeFlore, Det/A-1976
30	Stan Musial, StL/N-1950
30	Elmer Smith, Cin/N-1898
30	Tris Speaker, Bos/A-1912
30	JEROME WALTON, Chi/N-1989

Longest hitting streak, season, active players

39	Paul Molitor, Mil/A-1987
34	Benito Santiago, SD/N-1987
30	Jerome Walton, Chi/N-1989
29	Hal Morris, Cin/N-1996
28	Wade Boggs, Bos/A-1985
28	Marquis Grissom, Atl/N-1996
27	John Flaherty, SD/N-1996
26	John Olerud, Tor/A-1993
25	Wade Boggs, Bos/A-1987
25	Tony Gwynn, SD/N-1983
25	Lance Johnson, Chi/A-1992

Most pinch hits, career

150	Manny Mota, 1962-1982
145	Smoky Burgess, 1949-1967
143	Greg Gross, 1973-1989
123	Jose Morales, 1973-1984
116	Jerry Lynch, 1954-1966
114	Red Lucas, 1923-1938
113	Steve Braun, 1971-1985
108	Terry Crowley, 1969-1983
108	Denny Walling, 1975-1992
107	Gates Brown, 1963-1975
103	Mike Lum, 1967-1981
102	Jim Dwyer, 1973-1990
100	Rusty Staub, 1963-1985
95	Larry Biittner, 1970-1983
95	Vic Davalillo, 1963-1980
95	Gerald Perry, 1983-1995
94	Jerry Hairston, 1973-1989
93	Dave Philley, 1941-1962
93	Joel Youngblood, 1976-1989
92	Jay Johnstone, 1966-1985

Most pinch hits, career, active players

87	Dwight Smith, 1989-1996
81	Milt Thompson, 1984-1996
72	John Vander Wal, 1991-1996
68	Chris Gwynn, 1987-1996
68	Lenny Harris, 1988-1996
65	Mike Aldrete, 1986-1996
63	Dave Hansen, 1990-1996
59	Dave Clark, 1986-1996
59	Joe Orsulak, 1983-1996
58	John Cangelosi, 1985-1996

Most pinch-hit home runs, career

20	Cliff Johnson, 1972-1986
18	Jerry Lynch, 1954-1966
16	Gates Brown, 1963-1975
16	Smoky Burgess, 1949-1967
16	Willie McCovey, 1959-1980
14	George Crowe, 1952-1961
12	Joe Adcock, 1950-1966
12	Bob Cerv, 1951-1962
12	Jose Morales, 1973-1984
12	Graig Nettles, 1967-1988
11	Jeff Burroughs, 1970-1985
11	Jay Johnstone, 1966-1985
11	C. Maldonado, 1981-1995
11	Fred Whitfield, 1962-1970
11	Cy Williams, 1912-1930
10	MARK CARREON, 1987-1996
10	Jim Dwyer, 1973-1990
10	Mike Lum, 1967-1981
10	Ken McMullen, 1962-1977
10	Don Mincher, 1960-1972
10	Wally Post, 1949-1964
10	Champ Summers, 1974-1984
10	Jerry Turner, 1974-1983
10	Gus Zernial, 1949-1959

Most pinch hit home runs, career, active players

10	Mark Carreon, 1987-1996
9	Mike Aldrete, 1986-1996
9	John Vander Wal, 1991-1996
8	Dwight Smith, 1989-1996
7	Dave Clark, 1986-1996
7	Jack Howell, 1985-1996
7	Kevin Roberson, 1993-1996
6	Chris Gwynn, 1987-1996
6	Rex Hudler, 1984-1996
5	Eric Anthony, 1989-1996
5	Billy Ashley, 1992-1996
5	Chili Davis, 1981-1996
5	Andre Dawson, 1976-1996
5	Thomas Howard, 1990-1996
5	Mark Johnson, 1995-1996
5	Paul Sorrento, 1989-1996
5	Terry Steinbach, 1986-1996
5	Milt Thompson, 1984-1996
5	Rick Wilkins, 1991-1996

Pitchers

Most consecutive scoreless innings, season

59	OREL HERSHISER, LA/N-Aug. 30 to Sept. 28, 1988 (end of season; allowed a run in first inning of next start, April 5, 1989)
58	Don Drysdale, LA/N-May 14 to June 8, 1968
55.2	Walter Johnson, Was/A-Apr. 10 to May 14, 1913
53	Jack Coombs, Phi/A-Sept. 5 to 25, 1910
47	Bob Gibson, StL/N-June 2 to 26, 1968
45.1	Carl Hubbell, NY/N-July 13 to Aug. 1, 1933 (allowed a run charged to starter in a relief appearance on July 19, after 12 scoreless innings, had a 33-inning string afterwards)
45	Sal Maglie, NY/N-Aug. 16 to Sept. 13, 1950
45	Doc White, Chi/A-Sept. 12 to 30, 1904
45	Cy Young, Bos/A-Apr. 25 to May 17, 1904
44	Ed Reulbach, Chi/N-Sept. 17 to Oct. 3, 1908 (end of season; added 6 more innings on Apr. 17, 1909 for a total of 50 over 2 years)
43.2	Rube Waddell, Phi/A-Aug. 22 to Sept. 5, 1905
42	George "Rube" Foster, Bos/A-May 1 to 26, 1914
41	Jack Chesbro, Pit/N-June 26 to July 16, 1902
41	Grover Cleveland Alexander, Phi/N-Sept. 7 to 24, 1911
41	Art Nehf, Bos/N-Sept. 13 to Oct. 4, 1917
41	Luis Tiant, Cle/A-Apr. 28 to May 17, 1968
40	Walter Johnson, Was/A-May 7 to 26, 1918

40 Gaylord Perry, SF/N-Aug. 28 to Sept. 10, 1967

40 Luis Tiant, Bos/A-Aug. 19 to Sept. 8, 1972

39.2 Mordecai Brown, Chi/N-June 8 to July 8, 1908

39.2 Billy Pierce, Chi/A-Aug. 3 to 19, 1953

39 Ed Walsh, Chi/A-Aug. 10 to 22, 1906

39 Christy Mathewson, NY/N-May 3 to 21, 1901

39 Don Newcombe, Bro/N-July 25 to Aug. 11, 1956

39 Ray Culp, Bos/A-Sept. 7 to 25, 1968

39 Gaylord Perry, SF/N-Sept. 1 to 23, 1970

38.1 Bill Lee, Chi/N-Sept. 5 to 26, 1938

38 Jim Galvin, Buf/N-Aug. 2 to 8, 1884

38 John Clarkson, Chi/N-May 18 to 27, 1885

38 Jim Bagby, Cle/A-June 30 to July 16, 1917

38 Ray Herbert, Chi/A-May 1 to 14, 1963

37 George Bradley, StL/N-July 8 to 18, 1876

37 Cy Young, Bos/A-June 13 to July 1, 1903

37 Walter Johnson, Was/A-June 27 to July 13, 1913

37 Ed Walsh, Chi/A-July 31 to Aug.14, 1910

37 Joel Horlen, Chi/A-May 11 to 29, 1968

37 Mike Torrez, Oak/A-Aug. 29 to Sept. 15, 1976

36 Ed Morris, Pit/N-Sept. 5 to 17, 1888

36 Hal Brown, Bal/A-July 7 to Aug. 8, 1961 (allowed 4 runs on July 17 in a rained-out game)

36 Jim McGlothlin, Cal/A-May 22 to June 11, 1967

36 Charlie Hough, Tex/A-Aug. 23 to Sept. 14, 1983 (GREGG OLSON, Bal/AL had a streak of 41 scoreless innings over two seasons from Aug. 4, 1989, to May 4, 1990, 26 in 1989 and 15 in 1990)

Most strikeouts, game

21 Tom Cheney, Was/A-Sept. 12, 1962 (16 innings)

20 ROGER CLEMENS, Bos/A-Apr. 29, 1986

20 ROGER CLEMENS, Bos/A-Sept. 18, 1996

19 Charlie Sweeney, Pro/N-June 7, 1884

19 Hugh (One Arm) Daily, Chi/UA-July 7, 1884

19 Luis Tiant, Cle/A-July 3, 1968 (10 innings)

19 Steve Carlton, StL/N-Sept.15, 1969

19 Tom Seaver, NY/N-Apr. 22, 1970

19 Nolan Ryan, Cal/A-June 14, 1974 (12 innings)

19 Nolan Ryan, Cal/A-Aug. 12, 1974

19 Nolan Ryan, Cal/A-Aug. 20, 1974 (11 innings)

19 Nolan Ryan, Cal/A-June 8, 1977 (10 innings)

19 DAVID CONE, NY/N-Oct. 6, 1991

18 Jim Whitney, Bos/N-June 14, 1884 (15 innings)

18 Dupee Shaw, Bos/UA-July 19, 1884

18 Henry Porter, Mil/UA-Oct. 3, 1884

18 Jack Coombs, Phi/A-Sept. 1, 1906 (24 innings)

18 Bob Feller, Cle/A-Oct. 2, 1938 (1st game)

18 Warren Spahn, Bos/N-June 14, 1952 (15 innings)

18 Sandy Koufax, LA/N-Aug. 31, 1959

18 Sandy Koufax, LA/N-Apr. 24, 1962

18 Jim Maloney, Cin/N-June 14, 1965 (11 innings)

18 Chris Short, Phi/N-Oct. 2, 1965 (15 innings in an 18-inning game)

18 Don Wilson, Hou/N-July 14, 1968

18 Nolan Ryan, Cal/A-Sept. 10, 1976

18 Ron Guidry, NY/A-June 17, 1978

18 Bill Gullickson, Mon/N-Sept. 10, 1980

18 RAMON MARTINEZ, LA/N-June 4, 1990

18 RANDY JOHNSON, Sea/A-Sept. 27, 1992

Most bases on balls, game

16 Bill George, NY/N-May 30, 1887 (1st game)

16 George Van Haltren, Chi/N-June 27, 1887

16 Henry Gruber, Cle/PL-Apr. 19, 1890

16 Bruno Haas, Phi/A-June 23, 1915

16 Tommy Byrne, NY/A-Aug. 22, 1951 (13 innings)

15 Carroll Brown, Phi/A-July 12, 1913

14 Ed Crane, Was/N-Sept. 1, 1886

14 Charlie Hickman, Bos/N-Aug. 16, 1899 (2nd game)

14 Henry Mathewson, NY/N-Oct. 5, 1906

14 Skipper Friday, Was/A-June 17, 1923

13 Bill George, NY/N-May 17, 1887

13 John Kirby, Ind/N-June 9, 1887

13 Cy Seymour, NY/N-May 24, 1899 (10 innings)

13 Mal Eason, Bos/N-Sept. 3, 1902

13 Pete Schneider, Cin/N-July 6, 1918

13 George Turbeville, Phi/A-Aug. 24, 1935 (15 innings)

13 Tommy Byrne, NY/A-June 8, 1949

13 Dick Weik, Was/A-Sept. 1, 1949

13 Bud Podbielan, Cin/N-May 18, 1953 (11 innings)

No-hit games, nine or more innings (number to left is career total to that date, if greater than 1)

Joe Borden, Phi vs Chi NA, 4-0; July 28, 1875.

George Bradley, StL vs Har NL, 2-0; July 15, 1876.

Lee Richmond, Wor vs Cle NL, 1-0; June 12, 1880 (perfect game).

Monte Ward, Pro vs Buf NL, 5-0; June 17, 1880 (perfect game).

Larry Corcoran, Chi vs Bos NL, 6-0; Aug. 19, 1880.

Jim Galvin, Buf at Wor NL, 1-0; Aug. 20, 1880.

Tony Mullane, Lou at Cin AA, 2-0; Sept. 11, 1882.

Guy Hecker, Lou at Pit AA, 3-1; Sept. 19, 1882.

2 Larry Corcoran, Chi vs Wor NL, 5-0; Sept. 20, 1882.

Charley Radbourn, Pro at Cle NL, 8-0; July 25, 1883.

Hugh (One Arm) Daily, Cle at Phi NL; 1-0; Sept. 13, 1883.

Al Atkisson, Phi vs Pit AA, 10-1; May 24, 1884.

Ed Morris, Col at Pit AA, 5-0; May 29, 1884.

Frank Mountain, Col at Was AA, 12-0; June 5, 1884.

3 Larry Corcoran, Chi vs Pro NL, 6-0; June 27, 1884.

2 Jim Galvin, Buf at Det NL, 18-0; Aug. 4, 1884.

Dick Burns, Cin at KC UA, 3-1; Aug. 26, 1884.

Ed Cushman, Mil vs Was UA, 5-0; Sept. 28, 1884.

Sam Kimber, Bro vs Tol AA, 0-0; Oct. 4, 1884 (10 innings, darkness).

John Clarkson, Chi at Pro NL, 4-0; July 27, 1885.

Charlie Ferguson, Phi vs Pro NL, 1-0; Aug. 29, 1885.

2 Al Atkisson, Phi vs NY AA, 3-2; May 1, 1886.

Adonis Terry, Bro vs StL AA, 1-0; July 24, 1886.

Matt Kilroy, Bal at Pit AA, 6-0; Oct. 6, 1886.

2 Adonis Terry, Bro vs Lou AA, 4-0; May 27, 1888.

Henry Porter, KC at Bal AA, 4-0; June 6, 1888.

Ed Seward, Phi vs Cin AA, 12-2; July 26, 1888.

Gus Weyhing, Phi vs KC AA, 4-0; July 31, 1888.

Silver King, Chi vs Bro PL, 0-1; June 21, 1890, (8 innings, lost the game; bottom of 9th not played).

Cannonball Titcomb, Roch vs Syr AA, 7-0; Sept. 15, 1890.

Tom Lovett, Bro vs NY NL, 4-0; June 22, 1891.

Amos Rusie, NY vs Bro NL, 6-0; July 31, 1891.

Ted Breitenstein, StL vs Lou AA, 8-0; Oct. 4, 1891 (1st game, first start in the major leagues).

Jack Stivetts, Bos vs Bro NL, 11-0; Aug. 6, 1892.

Ben Sanders, Lou vs Bal NL, 6-2; Aug. 22, 1892.

Bumpus Jones, Cin vs Pit NL, 7-1; Oct. 15, 1892 (1st game in the major leagues).

Bill Hawke, Bal vs Was NL, 5-0; Aug. 16, 1893.

Cy Young, Cle vs Cin NL, 6-0; Sept. 18, 1897 (1st game).

2 Ted Breitenstein, Cin vs Pit NL, 11-0; Apr. 22, 1898.

Jim Hughes, Bal vs Bos NL, 8-0; Apr. 22, 1898.

Red Donahue, Phi vs Bos NL, 5-0; July 8, 1898.

Walter Thornton, Chi vs Bro NL, 2-0; Aug. 21, 1898 (2nd game).

Deacon Phillippe, Lou vs NY NL, 7-0; May 25, 1899.

Noodles Hahn, Cin vs Phi NL, 4-0; July 12, 1900.

Earl Moore, Cle vs Chi AL, 2-4; May 9, 1901 (lost on two hits in the 10th).

Christy Mathewson, NY vs StL NL, 5-0; July 15, 1901.

Nixey Callahan, Chi vs Det AL, 3-0; Sept. 20, 1902 (1st game).

Chick Fraser, Phi at Chi NL; 10-0; Sept. 18, 1903 (2nd game).

2 Cy Young, Bos vs Phi AL, 3-0; May 5, 1904 (perfect game).

Bob Wicker, Chi at NY NL, 1-0; June 11, 1904 (won in 12 innings after allowing one hit in the 10th).

Jesse Tannehill, Bos at Chi AL, 6-0; Aug. 17, 1904.

2 Christy Mathewson, NY at Chi NL, 1-0; June 13, 1905.

Weldon Henley, Phi at StL AL, 6-0; July 22, 1905 (1st game).

Frank Smith, Chi at Det AL, 15-0; Sept. 6, 1905 (2nd game).

Bill Dinneen, Bos vs Chi AL, 2-0; Sept. 27, 1905 (1st game).

Johnny Lush, Phi at Bro NL, 6-0; May 1, 1906.

Mal Eason, Bro at StL NL, 2-0; July 20, 1906.

Harry McIntyre, Bro vs Pit NL, 0-1; Aug. 1, 1906 (lost on four hits in 13 innings after allowing the first hit in the 11th).

Frank (Jeff) Pfeffer, Bos vs Cin NL, 6-0; May 8, 1907.

Nick Maddox, Pit vs Bro NL, 2-1; Sept. 20, 1907.

3 Cy Young, Bos at NY AL, 8-0; June 30, 1908.

Hooks Wiltse, NY vs Phi NL, 1-0; July 4, 1908 (1st game, 10 innings).

Nap Rucker, Bro vs Bos NL, 6-0; Sept. 5, 1908 (2nd game).

Dusty Rhoades, Cle vs Bos AL, 2-1; Sept. 18, 1908.

2 Frank Smith, Chi vs Phi AL, 1-0; Sept. 20, 1908.

Addie Joss, Cle vs Chi AL, 1-0; Oct. 2, 1908 (perfect game).

Red Ames, NY vs Bro NL. 0-3; Apr. 15, 1909 (lost on seven hits in 13 innings after allowing the first hit in the 10th).

2 Addie Joss, Cle at Chi AL, 1-0; Apr. 20, 1910.

Chief Bender, Phi vs Cle AL, 4-0; May 12, 1910.

Tom L. Hughes, NY vs Cle AL, 0-5; Aug. 30, 1910 (2nd game; lost on seven hits in 11 innings after allowing the first hit in the 10th).

Joe Wood, Bos vs StL AL, 5-0; July 29, 1911 (1st game).

Ed Walsh, Chi vs Bos AL, 5-0; Aug. 27, 1911.

George Mullin, Det vs StL AL, 7-0; July 4, 1912 (2nd game).

Earl Hamilton, StL at Det AL, 5-1; Aug. 30, 1912.

Jeff Tesreau, NY at Phi NL, 3-0; Sept. 6, 1912 (1st game).

Jim Scott, Chi at Was AL, 0-1; May 14, 1914 (lost on two hits in the 10th).

Joe Benz, Chi vs Cle AL, 6-1; May 31, 1914.

George Davis, Bos vs Phi NL, 7-0; Sept. 9, 1914 (2nd game).

Ed Lafitte, Bro vs KC FL, 6-2; Sept. 19, 1914.

Rube Marquard, NY vs Bro NL, 2-0; Apr. 15, 1915.

Frank Allen, Pit at StL FL, 2-0; Apr. 24, 1915.

Claude Hendrix, Chi at Pit FL, 10-0; May 15, 1915.

Alex Main, KC at Buf FL, 5-0; Aug. 16, 1915.

Jimmy Lavender, Chi at NY NL, 2-0; Aug. 31, 1915 (1st game).

Dave Davenport, StL vs Chi FL, 3-0; Sept. 7, 1915.

2 Tom L. Hughes, Bos vs Pit NL, 2-0; June 16, 1916.

Rube Foster, Bos vs NY AL, 2-0; June 21, 1916.

Joe Bush, Phi vs Cle AL, 5-0; Aug. 26, 1916.

Hubert (Dutch) Leonard, Bos vs StL AL, 4-0; Aug. 30, 1916.

Eddie Cicotte, Chi at StL AL, 11-0; Apr. 14, 1917.

George Mogridge, NY at Bos AL, 2-1; Apr. 24, 1917.

Fred Toney, Cin at Chi NL, 1-0; May 2, 1917 (10 innings).

Hippo Vaughn, Chi vs Cin NL, 0-1; May 2, 1917 (lost on two hits in the 10th, Toney pitched a no-hitter in this game).

Ernie Koob, StL vs Chi AL, 1-0; May 5, 1917.

Bob Groom, StL vs Chi AL, 3-0; May 6, 1917 (2nd game).

Ernie Shore, Bos vs Was AL, 4-0; June 23, 1917. (1st game, perfect game. Shore relieved Babe Ruth in first inning after Ruth had been thrown out of the game for protesting a walk to the first batter. The runner was caught stealing and Shore retired the remaining 26 batters in order.)

2 Hubert (Dutch) Leonard, Bos at Det AL, 5-0; June 3, 1918.

Hod Eller, Cin vs StL NL, 6-0; May 11, 1919.

Ray Caldwell, Cle at NY AL, 3-0; Sept. 10, 1919 (1st game).

Walter Johnson, Was at Bos AL, 1-0; July 1, 1920.

Charlie Robertson, Chi at Det AL, 2-0; Apr. 30, 1922 (perfect game).

Jesse Barnes, NY vs Phi NL, 6-0; May 7, 1922.

Sam Jones, NY at Phi AL, 2-0; Sept. 4, 1923.

Howard Ehmke, Bos at Phi AL, 4-0; Sept. 7, 1923.

Jesse Haines, StL vs Bos NL, 5-0; July 17, 1924.

Dazzy Vance, Bro vs Phi NL, 10-1; Sept. 13, 1925 (1st game).

Ted Lyons, Chi at Bos AL, 6-0; Aug. 21, 1926.

Carl Hubbell, NY vs Pit NL, 11-0;
May 8, 1929.

Wes Ferrell, Cle vs StL AL, 9-0;
April 29, 1931.

Bobby Burke, Was vs Bos AL, 5-0;
Aug. 8, 1931.

Bobo Newsom, StL vs Bos AL, 1-2;
Sept. 18, 1934 (lost on one hit in
the 10th).

Paul Dean, StL at Bro NL, 3-0;
Sept. 21, 1934 (2nd game).

Vern Kennedy, Chi vs Cle AL, 5-0;
Aug. 31, 1935.

Bill Dietrich, Chi vs StL AL, 8-0;
June 1, 1937.

Johnny Vander Meer, Cin vs Bos NL,
3-0; June 11, 1938

2 Johnny Vander Meer, Cin at Bro
NL, 6-0; June 15, 1938 (next start
after June 11)

Monte Pearson, NY vs Cle AL, 13-0;
Aug. 27, 1938 (2nd game).

Bob Feller, Cle at Chi AL, 1-0;
Apr. 16, 1940 (opening day).

Tex Carleton, Bro at Cin NL, 3-0;
Apr. 30, 1940.

Lon Warneke, StL at Cin NL, 2-0;
Aug. 30, 1941.

Jim Tobin, Bos vs Bro NL, 2-0;
Apr. 27, 1944.

Clyde Shoun, Cin vs Bos NL, 1-0;
May 15, 1944.

Dick Fowler, Phi vs StL AL, 1-0;
Sept. 9, 1945 (2nd game).

Ed Head, Bro vs Bos NL, 5-0;
Apr. 23, 1946.

2 Bob Feller, Cle at NY AL, 1-0;
Apr. 30, 1946.

Ewell Blackwell, Cin vs Bos NL, 6-0;
June 18, 1947.

Don Black, Cle vs Phi AL, 3-0;
July 10, 1947 (1st game).

Bill McCahan, Phi vs Was AL, 3-0;
Sept. 3, 1947.

Bob Lemon, Cle at Det AL, 2-0;
June 30, 1948.

Rex Barney, Bro at NY NL, 2-0;
Sept. 9, 1948.

Vern Bickford, Bos vs Bro NL, 7-0;
Aug. 11, 1950.

Cliff Chambers, Pit at Bos NL, 3-0;
May 6, 1951 (2nd game).

3 Bob Feller, Cle vs Det AL, 2-1;
July 1, 1951 (1st game).

Allie Reynolds, NY at Cle AL, 1-0;
July 12, 1951.

2 Allie Reynolds, NY vs Bos AL, 8-0;
Sept. 28, 1951 (1st game).

Virgil Trucks, Det vs Was AL, 1-0;
May 15, 1952.

Carl Erskine, Bro vs Chi NL, 5-0;
June 19, 1952.

2 Virgil Trucks, Det at NY AL, 1-0;
Aug. 25, 1952.

Bobo Holloman, StL vs Phi AL, 6-0;

May 6, 1953 (1st start in the major
leagues).

Jim Wilson, Mil vs Phi NL, 2-0;
June 12, 1954.

Sam Jones, Chi vs Pit NL, 4-0;
May 12, 1955.

2 Carl Erskine, Bro vs NY NL, 3-0;
May 12, 1956.

Johnny Klippstein (7 innings), Hershell
Freeman (1 inning) and Joe Black
(3 innings), Cin at
Mil NL, 1-2; May 26, 1956
(lost on three hits in 11 innings
after allowing the first hit in the
10th).

Mel Parnell, Bos vs Chi AL, 4-0;
July 14, 1956.

Sal Maglie, Bro vs Phi NL, 5-0;
Sept. 25, 1956.

Don Larsen, NY AL vs Bro NL, 2-0;
Oct. 8, 1956 (World Series, perfect
game).

Bob Keegan, Chi vs Was AL, 6-0;
Aug. 20, 1957 (2nd game).

Jim Bunning, Det at Bos AL, 3-0;
July 20, 1958 (1st game).

Hoyt Wilhelm, Bal vs NY AL, 1-0;
Sept. 20, 1958

Harvey Haddix, Pit at Mil NL, 0-1; May
26, 1959 (lost on one hit in 13
innings after pitching 12 perfect
innings).

Don Cardwell, Chi vs StL NL, 4-0;
May 15, 1960 (2nd game).

Lew Burdette, Mil vs Phi NL, 1-0;
Aug.18, 1960.

Warren Spahn, Mil vs Phi NL, 4-0;
Sept. 16, 1960.

2 Warren Spahn, Mil vs SF NL, 1-0;
Apr. 28, 1961.

Bo Belinsky, LA vs Bal AL, 2-0;
May 5, 1962.

Earl Wilson, Bos vs LA AL, 2-0;
June 26, 1962.

Sandy Koufax, LA vs NY NL, 5-0;
June 30, 1962.

Bill Monbouquette, Bos at Chi AL,
1-0; Aug. 1, 1962.

Jack Kralick, Min vs KC AL, 1-0;
Aug. 26, 1962.

2 Sandy Koufax, LA vs SF NL, 8-0;
May 11, 1963.

Don Nottebart, Hou vs Phi NL, 4-1;
May 17, 1963.

Juan Marichal, SF vs Hou NL, 1-0;
June 15, 1963.

Ken T. Johnson, Hou vs Cin NL, 0-1;
Apr. 23, 1964 (lost the game).

3 Sandy Koufax, LA at Phi NL, 3-0;
June 4, 1964.

2 Jim Bunning, Phi at NY NL, 6-0;
June 21, 1964 (1st game, perfect
game).

Jim Maloney, Cin vs NY NL, 0-1;
June 14, 1965 (lost on two hits in

11 innings after pitching 10 hitless
innings).

2 Jim Maloney, Cin at Chi NL, 1-0;
Aug. 19, 1965 (1st game,
10 innings).

4 Sandy Koufax, LA vs Chi NL, 1-0;
Sept. 9, 1965 (perfect game).

Dave Morehead, Bos vs Cle AL, 2-0;
Sept. 16, 1965.

Sonny Siebert, Cle vs Was AL, 2-0;
June 10, 1966.

Steve D. Barber (8⅔ innings) and Stu
Miller (⅓ inning) Bal vs Det AL, 1-
2; April 30, 1967 (1st game, lost
the game)

Don Wilson, Hou vs Atl NL, 2-0;
June 18, 1967.

Dean Chance, Min at Cle AL, 2-1;
Aug. 25, 1967 (2nd game).

Joe Horlen, Chi vs Det AL, 6-0;
Sept. 10, 1967 (1st game).

Tom Phoebus, Bal vs Bos AL, 6-0;
Apr. 27, 1968.

Catfish Hunter, Oak vs Min AL, 4-0;
May 8, 1968 (perfect game).

George Culver, Cin at Phi NL, 6-1;
July 29, 1968 (2nd game).

Gaylord Perry, SF vs StL NL, 1-0;
Sept. 17, 1968.

Ray Washburn, StL at SF NL, 2-0;
Sept. 18, 1968.

Bill Stoneman, Mon at Phi NL, 7-0;
Apr. 17, 1969.

3 Jim Maloney, Cin vs Hou NL, 10-0;
Apr. 30, 1969.

2 Don Wilson, Hou at Cin NL, 4-0;
May 1, 1969.

Jim Palmer, Bal vs Oak AL, 8-0;
Aug. 13, 1969.

Ken Holtzman, Chi vs Atl NL, 3-0;
Aug. 19, 1969.

Bob Moose, Pit at NY NL, 4-0;
Sept. 20, 1969.

Dock Ellis, Pit at SD NL, 2-0; June 12,
1970 (1st game).

Clyde Wright, Cal vs Oak AL, 4-0;
July 3, 1970.

Bill Singer, LA vs Phi NL, 5-0; July 20,
1970.

Vida Blue, Oak vs Min AL, 6-0;
Sept. 21, 1970.

2 Ken Holtzman, Chi at Cin NL, 1-0;
June 3, 1971.

Rick Wise, Phi at Cin NL, 4-0;
June 23, 1971.

Bob Gibson, StL at Pit NL, 11-0;
Aug. 14, 1971.

Burt Hooton, Chi vs Phi NL, 4-0;
April 16, 1972.

Milt Pappas, Chi vs SD NL, 8-0;
Sept. 2, 1972.

2 Bill Stoneman, Mon vs NY NL, 7-0;
Oct. 2, 1972 (1st game).

Steve Busby, KC at Det AL, 3-0;
Apr. 16, 1973.

Nolan Ryan, Cal at KC AL, 3-0; May 15, 1973.

2 Nolan Ryan, Cal at Det AL, 6-0; July 15, 1973.

Jim Bibby, Tex at Oak AL, 6-0; July 20, 1973.

Phil Niekro, Atl vs SD NL, 9-0; Aug. 5, 1973.

2 Steve Busby, KC at Mil AL, 2-0; June 19, 1974.

Dick Bosman, Cle vs Oak AL, 4-0; July 19, 1974.

3 Nolan Ryan, Cal vs Min AL, 4-0; Sept. 28, 1974.

4 Nolan Ryan, Cal vs Bal AL, 1-0; June 1, 1975.

Ed Halicki, SF vs NY NL, 6-0; Aug. 24, 1975 (2nd game).

Vida Blue (5 innings), Glenn Abbott (1 inning), Paul Lindblad (1 inning) and Rollie Fingers (2 innings), Oak vs Cal AL, 5-0; Sept. 28, 1975.

Larry Dierker, Hou vs Mon NL, 6-0; July 9, 1976.

Blue Moon Odom (5 innings) and Francisco Barrios (4 innings), Chi at Oak AL, 2-1; July 28, 1976.

John Candelaria, Pit vs LA NL, 2-0; Aug. 9, 1976.

John Montefusco, SF at Atl NL, 9-0; Sept. 29, 1976.

Jim Colborn, KC vs Tex AL, 6-0; May 14, 1977.

DENNIS ECKERSLEY, Cle vs Cal AL, 1-0; May 30, 1977.

Bert Blyleven, Tex at Cal AL, 6-0; Sept. 22, 1977.

Bob Forsch, StL vs Phi NL, 5-0; Apr. 16, 1978.

Tom Seaver, Cin vs StL NL, 4-0; June 16, 1978.

Ken Forsch, Hou vs Atl NL, 6-0; Apr. 7, 1979.

Jerry Reuss, LA at SF NL, 8-0; June 27, 1980.

Charlie Lea, Mon vs SF NL, 4-0; May 10, 1981 (2nd game).

Len Barker, Cle vs Tor AL, 3-0; May 15, 1981 (perfect game).

5 Nolan Ryan, Hou vs LA NL, 5-0; Sept. 26, 1981.

Dave Righetti, NY vs Bos AL, 4-0; July 4, 1983.

2 Bob Forsch, StL vs Mon NL, 3-0; Sept. 26, 1983.

Mike Warren, Oak vs Chi AL, 3-0; Sept. 29, 1983.

Jack Morris, Det at Chi AL, 4-0; Apr. 7, 1984.

Mike Witt, Cal at Tex AL, 1-0; Sept. 30, 1984 (perfect game).

Joe Cowley, Chi at Cal AL, 7-1; Sept. 19, 1986.

Mike Scott, Hou vs SF NL, 2-0; Sept. 25, 1986.

Juan Nieves, Mil at Bal AL, 7-0; Apr. 15, 1987.

Tom Browning, Cin vs LA NL, 1-0; Sept. 16, 1988 (perfect game).

MARK LANGSTON (7 innings) and Mike Witt (2 innings), Cal vs Sea AL, 1-0; Apr. 11, 1990.

RANDY JOHNSON, Sea vs Det AL, 2-0; June 2, 1990.

6 Nolan Ryan, Tex at Oak AL, 5-0; June 11, 1990.

Dave Stewart, Oak at Tor AL, 5-0; June 29, 1990.

FERNANDO VALENZUELA, LA vs StL NL, 6-0; June 29, 1990.

Andy Hawkins, NY at Chi AL, 0-4; July 1, 1990 (8 innings, lost the game; bottom of 9th not played).

TERRY MULHOLLAND, Phi vs SF NL, 6-0; Aug. 15, 1990.

Dave Stieb, Tor at Cle AL, 3-0; Sept. 2, 1990.

7 Nolan Ryan, Tex vs Tor AL, 3-0; May 1, 1991.

Tommy Greene, Phi at Mon NL, 2-0; May 23, 1991.

Bob Milacki (6 innings), Mike Flanagan (1 inning), Mark Williamson, (1 inning) and GREGG OLSON (1 inning), Bal at Oak AL, 2-0; July 13, 1991.

MARK GARDNER, Mon at LA NL, 0-1; July 26, 1991 (9 innings, lost on two hits in 10th, relieved by JEFF FASSERO, who allowed one more hit).

DENNIS MARTINEZ, Mon at LA NL, 2-0; July 28, 1991 (perfect game).

WILSON ALVAREZ, Chi at Bal AL, 7-0; Aug. 11, 1991.

BRET SABERHAGEN, KC vs Chi AL, 7-0; Aug. 26, 1991.

KENT MERCKER (6 innings), MARK WOHLERS (2 innings) and ALEJANDRO PENA (1 inning), Atl at SD NL, 1-0; Sept. 11, 1991.

Matt Young, Bos at Cle AL, 1-2; April 12, 1992 (1st game) (8 innings, lost the game, bottom of 9th not played).

KEVIN GROSS, LA vs SF NL, 2-0; Aug. 17, 1992.

CHRIS BOSIO, Sea vs Bos AL, 7-0; Apr. 22, 1993.

JIM ABBOTT, NY vs Cle AL, 4-0; Sept. 4, 1993.

DARRYL KILE, Hou vs NY NL, 7-1; Sept. 8, 1993.

KENT MERCKER, Atl at LA NL, 6-0; Apr. 8, 1994.

SCOTT ERICKSON, Min vs Mil AL, 6-0; Apr. 27, 1994.

KENNY ROGERS, Tex vs Cal AL, 4-0; July 28, 1994 (perfect game).

RAMON MARTINEZ, LA vs Fla NL, 7-0; July 14, 1995.

AL LEITER, Fla vs Col NL, 11-0; May 11, 1996.

DWIGHT GOODEN, NY vs Sea AL, 2-0; May 14, 1996.

HIDEO NOMO, LA at Col NL, 9-0; Sept. 17, 1996.

No-hit games, less than 9 innings

Larry McKeon, 6 innings, rain, Ind at Cin AA, 0-0; May 6, 1884.

Charlie Gagus, 8 innings, darkness, Was vs Wil UA, 12-1; Aug. 21, 1884.

Charlie Getzien, 6 innings, rain, Det vs Phi NL, 1-0; Oct. 1, 1884.

Charlie Sweeney (2 innings) and Henry Boyle (3 innings), 5 innings, rain, StL vs StP UA, 0-1; Oct. 5,1884.

Dupee Shaw, 5 innings, agreement, Pro at Buf NL, 4-0; Oct. 7, 1885 (1st game).

George Van Haltren, 6 innings, rain, Chi vs Pit NL, 1-0; June 21,1888.

Ed Crane, 7 innings, darkness, NY vs Was NL, 3-0; Sept. 27, 1888.

Matt Kilroy, 7 innings, darkness, Bal vs StL AA, 0-0; July 29, 1889 (2nd game).

George Nicol, 7 innings, darkness, StL vs Phi AA, 21-2; Sept. 23, 1890.

Hank Gastright, 8 innings, darkness, Col vs Tol AA, 6-0; Oct. 12, 1890.

Jack Stivetts, 5 innings, called so Boston could catch train to Cleveland for Temple Cub playoffs, Bos at Was NL, 6-0; Oct. 15, 1892 (2nd game).

Elton Chamberlain, 7 innings, darkness, Cin vs Bos NL, 6-0; Sept. 23, 1893 (2nd game).

Ed Stein, 6 innings, rain, Bro vs Chi NL, 6-0; June 2, 1894.

Red Ames, 5 innings, darkness, NY at StL NL, 5-0; Sept. 14, 1903 (2nd game, first game in the major leagues).

Rube Waddell, 5 innings, rain, Phi vs StL AL, 2-0; Aug. 15, 1905.

Jake Weimer, 7 innings, agreement, Cin vs Bro NL, 1-0; Aug. 24, 1906 (2nd game).

Jimmy Dygert (3 innings) and Rube Waddell (2 innings), 5 innings, rain, Phi vs Chi AL, 4-3; Aug. 29, 1906. (Waddell allowed hit and two runs in 6th, but rain caused game to revert to 5 innings).

Stoney McGlynn, 7 innings, agreement, StL at Bro NL, 1-1; Sept. 24, 1906 (2nd game).

Lefty Leifield, 6 innings, darkness, Pit
at Phi NL, 8-0; Sept. 26, 1906
(2nd game).

Ed Walsh, 5 innings, rain, Chi vs NY
AL, 8-1; May 26, 1907.

Ed Karger, 7 perfect innings, agreement, StL vs Bos NL, 4-0;
Aug. 11, 1907 (2nd game).

Howie Camnitz, 5 innings, agreement, Pit at NY NL, 1-0; Aug. 23,
1907 (2nd game).

Rube Vickers, 5 perfect innings, darkness, Phi at Was AL, 4-0; Oct. 5,
1907 (2nd game).

Johnny Lush, 6 innings, rain, StL at
Bro NL, 2-0; Aug. 6, 1908.

King Cole, 7 innings, called so
Chicago could catch train, Chi at
StL NL,
4-0; July 31, 1910 (2nd game).

Jay Cashion, 6 innings, called so
Cleveland could catch train, Was
vs Cle AL, 2-0; Aug. 20, 1912
(2nd game).

Walter Johnson, 7 innings, rain, Was
vs StL AL, 2-0; Aug. 25, 1924.

Fred Frankhouse, 7⅔ innings, rain,
Bro vs Cin NL, 5-0; Aug. 27,
1937.

John Whitehead, 6 innings, rain, StL
vs Det AL, 4-0; Aug. 5, 1940 (2nd
game).

Jim Tobin, 5 innings, darkness, Bos
vs Phi NL, 7-0; June 22, 1944
(2nd game).

Mike McCormick, 5 innings, rain, SF
at Phi NL, 3-0; June 12, 1959
(allowed hit in 6th, but rain
caused game to revert to 5
innings).

Sam Jones, 7 innings, rain, SF at StL
NL, 4-0; Sept. 26, 1959.

Dean Chance, 5 perfect innings, rain,
Min vs Bos AL, 2-0; Aug. 6, 1967.

David Palmer, 5 perfect innings, rain,
Mon at StL NL, 4-0; Apr. 21,
1984 (2nd game).

Pascual Perez, 5 innings, rain, Mon at
Phi NL, 1-0; Sept. 24, 1988.

MELIDO PEREZ, 6 innings, rain, Chi
at NY AL, 8-0; July 12, 1990.

Major league report

▶1996 season
 wrap-up
▶1996 team MVPs
▶Week-by-week
 season notes

▶What to watch for
 in 1997
▶Team rosters and
 statistics
▶Franchise records

AL East
Yankees 78
Orioles.............86
Red Sox 94
Blue Jays 102
TIgers 110

AL Central
Indians 118
White Sox 126
Brewers.........134
Twins.............142
Royals 150

AL West
Rangers.........158
Mariners........166
Athletics 174
Angels 182

NL East
Braves...........190
Expos.............198
Marlins 206
Mets..............214
Phillies...........222

NL Central
Cardinals.......230
Astros.............238
Reds..............246
Cubs 254
Pirates...........262

NL West
Padres...........270
Dodgers 278
Rockies 286
Giants............294

New York Yankees

By Robert Deutsch, USA TODAY

Mariano Rivera allowed only one home run in 1996, as batters had a .228 slugging percentage against him.

1996 Yankees: That championship season

The Yankees won it all last season despite going through a major transition—they had a new manager, a new GM and a host of new players. It was a year of high expectations sparked by remarkable early success and a payroll that ended up at more than $60 million. It all fell together when the Yankees came from behind in three consecutive postseason series, including a 2-0 deficit to the defending champion Atlanta Braves, to win the World Series for the first time since 1978. "I don't know if it's destiny, because we certainly worked our rear ends off all year," center fielder Bernie Williams said. "We're proud to be the ones to give [New York] a championship."

After a late-summer swoon that saw them lose 9½ games of their once 12-game lead, the Yankees righted their ship in September and won their first full-season division title since 1980. As Williams grabbed a fly ball for the final out in the clincher, the Yankees poured from their dugout and into a group embrace near second base. And that was nothing compared with the bedlam that broke out when Charlie Hayes caught Mark Lemke's pop foul to clinch the World Series win over Atlanta.

The Yanks had many key players, but they became the first World Series winners not to place a man in the top 10 in MVP voting. Cy Young Award runner-up Andy Pettitte topped the AL victory list and led the staff after David Cone went down with a throwing-arm aneurysm in May. Dwight Gooden went from suspended drug abuser to no-hit pitcher. Jimmy Key returned sooner than expected from rotator-cuff surgery and won the final game of the World Series.

After slow starts, catcher Joe Girardi and first baseman Tino Martinez emerged as leaders. Mariano Duncan went from being a backup infielder to leading the Yanks in batting average. Shortstop Derek Jeter was the unanimous choice for AL Rookie of the Year. Williams established himself as the Yanks' quiet leader. Darryl Strawberry

provided a spark after his July 4 return to the Yanks. Wade Boggs helped his Hall of Fame chances with a championship ring. Setup man Mariano Rivera finished third in the AL Cy Young voting and was the Yanks' top MVP vote-getter (he was 12th), and World Series MVP John Wetteland led the AL in saves for nearly five months but then missed time with a groin injury.

The disappointments were few. Paul O'Neill struggled with hard luck and a harsh temper. Tim Raines missed more than three months with a chronic hamstring problem but returned strong down the stretch. Ruben Sierra slumped and sulked until he was dealt to Detroit for Cecil Fielder, who had a fine postseason. Kenny Rogers battled shoulder problems all season and failed in the playoffs. Jeff Nelson endured a roller-coaster season in the setup role to Rivera.

But the biggest story in the end, and one with many coincidences, was that of Joe Torre, the Yankees skipper. He had managed Atlanta in the 1980s and finally got to the World Series against the Braves after 4,272 major league games as a player and a manager—no one has waited longer—the same week his brother Frank, a former World Series player as a Milwaukee Braves first baseman in the 1950s, underwent a successful heart transplant.

1996 Yankees: Week-by-week notes

These notes were excerpted from the following issues of Baseball Weekly.

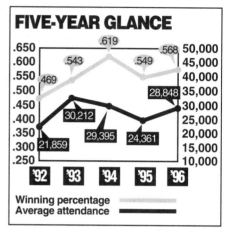

FIVE-YEAR GLANCE

Winning percentage
Average attendance

▶**April 10:** Dwight Gooden went 653 days between major league starts, but the wait was hardly worth it. Gooden allowed five runs and five hits on April 7, including two homers, in five innings as the Yankees dropped a 7-2 decision to the Texas Rangers. It was Gooden's first appearance in the majors since June 24, 1994.

▶**April 24:** Kenny Rogers made the most of his first chance to pitch for the Yankees, holding Minnesota hitless on April 21 until the sixth inning, as the Yanks won 9-5. He had been sent to Florida to work out because bad weather kept him out of the rotation.

▶**May 15:** Right-hander David Cone had successful surgery to remove an aneurysm from his right shoulder. "You don't make up for David, you just do the best you can," said manager Joe Torre, who isn't planning for Cone to return until next season.

▶**May 22:** Dwight Gooden threw a storybook no-hitter against the powerful Seattle Mariners on May 14. The question for Joe Torre was how long to leave in Gooden, who walked six and threw 131 pitches in the game. "The mindset was, if the first guy [in the ninth] gets a hit, [left-hander Steve] Howe comes in," Torre said.

▶**June 12:** On June 4, owner George Steinbrenner ordered the dismissal of 40 low-level employees, mostly in stadium operations. Included was 74-year-old clubhouse doorman Charlie Zabransky, whose job was restored a day later after players took up a collection to pay his salary.

▶**June 19:** For the second time in a month, left-hander Jimmy Key found himself on the DL, after he strained his left calf muscle while jogging to the mound on June 10 to start an inning.

▶**July 17:** George Steinbrenner gave himself a 66th birthday present and exploded a Fourth of July blockbuster, signing slugger Darryl Strawberry. Strawberry was expected to join the Yanks in time to begin the second half of the season against the Orioles. But manager Joe Torre summoned Strawberry to Yankee Stadium on July 7. Strawberry went 0-for-4 against the Brewers but received a 25-second standing ovation in the second inning when he made his first appearance as New York's DH.

▶**July 24:** After two days of negotiations and one subpar outing in a semi-pro playoff game, 41-year-old right-hander Jack Morris had his offer by the Yankees rescinded. The Yanks had sent fifth starter Ramiro Mendoza back to the minor leagues after he struggled through his third consecutive subpar outing on July 15, against the Red Sox.

▶**Aug. 7:** Less than one hour after acquiring Cecil Fielder and 30 minutes before the trade deadline, the Yankees obtained right-hander David Weathers from the Marlins for righty Mark Hutton. Weathers, 26, was 2-2 with a 4.54 ERA in 31 games (eight starts) in Florida. Hutton, 26, was 0-2 with a 5.04 ERA in 12 games, including two starts.

▶**Aug. 14:** David Cone threw 15 minutes of batting practice Monday, another step in his comeback from aneurysm surgery in his right shoulder. "I think I'm ready to take the next step and throw in a game," Cone said after his 70-pitch session.

▶**Aug. 21:** Even though manager Joe Torre has insisted all season that team meetings only spotlight and worsen potential problems, he gathered his beleaguered troops on Aug. 17 in the face of a suddenly hot AL East race. On Aug. 13, one day after he surrendered a 10th-inning home run to Harold Baines in a 3-2 loss to the White Sox, closer John Wetteland hobbled off the field during warmups with a strained right groin muscle. On Aug. 16, Wetteland—who leads the majors with 38 saves—was placed on the 15-day DL.

▶**Aug. 28:** General manager Bob Watson's search for a lefty middle reliever reaped dividends on Aug. 23 when the Yankees acquired southpaw Graeme Lloyd and infielder/outfielder Pat Listach from the Brewers. The Yanks sent struggling reliever Bob Wickman and outfielder Gerald Williams to Milwaukee.

▶**Sept. 4:** The arrival of Charlie Hayes from the Pirates for minor league righty Chris Corn didn't sit well with 38-year-old third baseman Wade Boggs. Hayes will platoon with Boggs, a lifetime .333 hitter who's batting .226 this year against lefties. "It's not for me to ask questions about my future," said Boggs. "I'll get 3,000 hits somewhere."

▶**Sept. 11:** David Cone's triumphant seven-inning no-hit performance in his comeback start was bad news for Kenny Rogers last week, as the enigmatic lefty was skipped in the rotation after surrendering 25 runs in his last 19⅓ innings.

▶**Sept. 18:** Bob Watson says that he and Joe Torre deserve to be released if the Yankees don't win. Watson went so far as to say he believed that Steinbrenner would bring out the ax if the Yanks don't win the division, even if they qualify for the playoffs as a wild card and then win the World Series.

▶**Sept. 25:** Kenny Rogers received a clean bill of health—sort of—with the diagnosis last week that he suffers from an inflamed left shoulder. It was feared that he had problems with the rotator cuff or the tendons in his left shoulder. Said Rogers: "It makes me feel mentally comfortable that I can put this thing on the back burner and not be so tentative." Rogers pitched 5⅔ shutout innings in a victory against the Orioles despite the injury.

▶**Oct. 2:** It was a season of drastic change

sparked by a new general manager, a new manager and a host of new players replacing several popular figures, but in the end the Yankees won their first full-season division title since 1980, with the clincher coming on Sept. 25 at Yankee Stadium with a 19-2 thrashing of the Brewers. The heroes in this Yankee surge were many. Cy Young contender Andy Pettitte led the AL with 21 wins. After slow starts, catcher Joe Girardi and first baseman Tino Martinez emerged as leaders. Shortstop Derek Jeter will be the AL Rookie of the Year. Center fielder Bernie Williams established himself as a superstar-in-waiting. Mariano Rivera redefined the setup role, while John Wetteland led the AL in saves for nearly five months before being slowed by a groin injury.

Team directory

▶**Owner:** George Steinbrenner
▶**General manager:** Bob Watson
▶**Ballpark:**
Yankee Stadium
East 161st Street and River Avenue
Bronx, N.Y.
718-293-4300
Capacity 57,545
Parking (independently owned); $6
Public transportation available
Family and wheelchair sections, ramps, senior citizen discount ($2 tickets day of game), group discounts, monument park behind left center field with plaques honoring famous Yankees
▶**Team publications:**
Yankees Magazine, media guide, scorecard, yearbook
718-293-4300
▶**TV, radio broadcast stations:**
WABC 770 AM, WPIX Channel 11, MSG Network
▶**Spring training:**
Legends Field
3802 Martin Luther King Blvd.
Tampa, Fla.
813-879-2244
Capacity: 10,000

NEW YORK YANKEES 1996 final stats

BATTERS	BA	SLG	OB	G	AB	R	H	TB	2B	3B	HR	RBI	BB	SO	SB	CS	E
Duncan	.340	.500	.352	109	400	62	136	200	34	3	8	56	9	77	4	3	12
Jeter	.314	.430	.370	157	582	104	183	250	25	6	10	78	48	102	14	7	22
Boggs	.311	.389	.389	132	501	80	156	195	29	2	2	41	67	32	1	2	7
B. Williams	.305	.535	.391	143	551	108	168	295	26	7	29	102	82	72	17	4	5
O'Neill	.302	.474	.411	150	546	89	165	259	35	1	19	91	102	76	0	1	0
Girardi	.294	.374	.346	124	422	55	124	158	22	3	2	45	30	55	13	4	3
Martinez	.292	.466	.364	155	595	82	174	277	28	0	25	117	68	85	2	1	5
R. Rivera	.284	.443	.381	46	88	17	25	39	6	1	2	16	13	26	6	2	0
Hayes	.284	.418	.294	20	67	7	19	28	3	0	2	13	1	12	0	0	0
Raines	.284	.468	.383	59	201	45	57	94	10	0	9	33	34	29	10	1	1
Leyritz	.264	.381	.355	88	265	23	70	101	10	0	7	40	30	68	2	0	6
Strawberry	.262	.490	.359	63	202	35	53	99	13	0	11	36	31	55	6	5	0
Fielder	.252	.484	.350	160	591	85	149	286	20	0	39	117	87	139	2	0	7
Listach	.240	.312	.317	87	317	51	76	99	16	2	1	33	36	51	25	5	5
Sojo	.220	.272	.250	95	287	23	63	78	10	1	1	21	11	17	2	2	8
Aldrete	.213	.435	.301	63	108	16	23	47	6	0	6	20	14	19	0	1	1
Howard	.204	.278	.228	35	54	9	11	15	1	0	1	9	2	8	1	0	1
Fox	.196	.265	.276	113	189	26	37	50	4	0	3	13	20	28	11	3	12
James	.167	.167	.231	6	12	1	2	2	0	0	0	0	1	2	1	0	0
Kelly	.143	.143	.217	13	21	4	3	3	0	0	0	2	2	9	0	1	1
Posada	.071	.071	.133	8	14	1	1	1	0	0	0	0	1	6	0	0	0
McIntosh	.000	.000	.000	3	3	0	0	0	0	0	0	0	0	0	0	0	0
Luke	---	---	---	1	0	1	0	0	0	0	0	0	0	0	0	0	0

PITCHERS	W-L	ERA	G	GS	CG	GF	Sho	SV	IP	H	R	ER	HR	BB	SO
Aldrete	0-0	0.00	1	0	0	1	0	0	1.0	1	0	0	0	0	0
M. Rivera	8-3	2.09	61	0	0	14	0	5	107.2	73	25	25	1	34	130
Pavlas	0-0	2.35	16	0	0	8	0	1	23.0	23	7	6	0	7	18
Wetteland	2-3	2.83	62	0	0	58	0	43	63.2	54	23	20	9	21	69
Cone	7-2	2.88	11	11	1	0	0	0	72.0	50	25	23	3	34	71
Pettitte	21-8	3.87	35	34	2	1	0	0	221.0	229	105	95	23	72	162
Lloyd	2-6	4.29	65	0	0	15	0	0	56.2	61	30	27	4	22	30
Nelson	4-4	4.36	73	0	0	27	0	2	74.1	75	38	36	6	36	91
Rogers	12-8	4.68	30	30	2	0	1	0	179.0	179	97	93	16	83	92
Key	12-11	4.68	30	30	0	0	0	0	169.1	171	93	88	21	58	116
Gooden	11-7	5.01	29	29	1	0	1	0	170.2	169	101	95	19	88	126
Hutton	0-2	5.04	12	2	0	5	0	0	30.1	32	19	17	3	18	25
Mecir	1-1	5.13	26	0	0	10	0	0	40.1	42	24	23	6	23	38
Boehringer	2-4	5.44	15	3	0	1	0	0	46.1	46	28	28	6	21	37
Bones	7-14	6.22	36	24	0	2	0	0	152.0	184	115	105	30	68	63
Gibson	0-0	6.23	4	0	0	2	0	0	4.1	6	3	3	1	0	3
Howe	0-1	6.35	25	0	0	4	0	1	17.0	19	12	12	1	6	5
Whitehurst	1-1	6.75	2	2	0	0	0	0	8.0	11	6	6	1	2	1
Mendoza	4-5	6.79	12	11	0	0	0	0	53.0	80	43	40	5	10	34
Polley	1-3	7.89	32	0	0	9	0	0	21.2	23	20	19	5	11	14
Weathers	0-2	9.35	11	4	0	1	0	0	17.1	23	19	18	1	14	13
Brewer	1-0	9.53	4	0	0	1	0	0	5.2	7	6	6	0	8	8
Kamieniecki	1-2	11.12	7	5	0	0	0	0	22.2	36	30	28	6	19	15

1997 preliminary roster

PITCHERS (18)
Brian Boehringer
David Cone
Chris Cumberland
Dwight Gooden
Graeme Lloyd
Jim Mecir
Rafael Medina
Ramiro Mendoza
Jeff Nelson
Andy Pettitte
Dan Rios
Mariano Rivera
Kenny Rogers
Tim Rumer
Mike Stanton
Julian Vazquez
David Weathers
David Wells

CATCHERS (3)
Mike Figga
Joe Girardi
Jorge Posada

INFIELDERS (9)
Wade Boggs
Mariano Duncan
Cecil Fielder
Andy Fox
Charlie Hayes
Derek Jeter
Pat Kelly
Gabby Martinez
Tino Martinez

OUTFIELDERS (8)
Ricky Ledee
Matt Luke
Paul O'Neill
Tim Raines
Ruben Rivera
Shane Spencer
Darryl Strawberry
Bernie Williams

Games played by position

PLAYER	G	C	1B	2B	3B	SS	OF	DH
Aldrete	63	0	9	0	0	0	15	15
Boggs	132	0	0	0	123	0	0	4
Duncan	109	0	0	104	3	0	3	2
Fielder	160	0	80	0	0	0	0	79
Fox	113	0	0	72	31	9	1	3
Girardi	124	120	0	0	0	0	0	2
Hayes	20	0	0	0	19	0	0	0
Howard	35	0	0	30	6	0	0	0
James	6	0	0	0	0	0	4	1
Jeter	157	0	0	0	0	157	0	0
Kelly	13	0	0	10	0	0	0	3
Leyritz	88	55	5	2	13	0	3	13
Listach	87	0	0	12	0	7	68	1
Luke	1	0	0	0	0	0	0	1
Martinez	155	0	151	0	0	0	0	3
McIntosh	3	1	1	0	1	0	0	0
O'Neill	150	0	1	0	0	0	146	3
Posada	8	4	0	0	0	0	0	3
Raines	59	0	0	0	0	0	50	2
R. Rivera	46	0	0	0	0	0	45	0
Sojo	95	0	0	41	34	23	0	0
Strawberry	63	0	0	0	0	0	34	26
B. Williams	143	0	0	0	0	0	140	2

Minor Leagues

Tops in the organization

BATTER	CLUB	AVG.	G	AB	R	H	HR	RBI
Ricky Ledee	Col	.305	135	495	106	151	29	101
Kurt Bierek	Tam	.303	88	320	48	97	11	55
Kraig Hawkins	Tam	.299	75	268	41	80	1	21
Kevin Riggs	Nrw	.290	118	403	75	117	2	37
T. Woodson	Col	.288	114	420	53	121	21	81

HOME RUNS

Shane Spencer	Col	32
Ricky Ledee	Col	29
Ivan Cruz	Col	28
Tracy Woodson	Col	21
Several Players Tied At		19

WINS

Tam Corn		Chris		12
K. Henthorne		Tam		12
Bob St. Pierre		Tam		12
Jay Tessmer		Tam		12
Several Players Tied At				11

RBI

Ricky Ledee	Col	101
Ivan Cruz	Col	96
Shane Spencer	Col	95
Cody Samuel	GBo	86
Tracy Woodson	Col	81

SAVES

Jay Tessmer	Tam	35
Dave Pavlas	Col	26
Dan Rios	Col	17
Craig Dingman	One	9
Several Players Tied At		8

STOLEN BASES

Rod Smith	GBo	57
D. McDonald	One	29
Garrett Butler	One	29
D. Shumpert	GBo	28
Tim Barker	Col	24

STRIKEOUTS

B. Boehringer	Col	132
K. Henthorne	Tam	129
M. Jerzembeck	Tam	125
Rafael Medina	Nrw	112
S. Randolph	GBo	111

PITCHER	CLUB	W-L	ERA	IP	H	BB	SO
Jay Tessmer	Tam	12-4	1.48	97	68	19	104
Matt Dunbar	Col	7-3	1.80	105	77	45	94
Tim Rumer	Col	6-2	2.30	98	72	34	94
K. Henthorne	Tam	12-7	2.47	153	138	34	129
R. Mendoza	Col	6-2	2.51	97	96	19	61

Sick call: 1996 DL report

PLAYER	Days on the DL
Mike Aldrete	28
David Cone	122
Mariano Duncan	18
Tony Fernandez	182
Mike Figga	30
Mark Hutton	44
Scott Kamieniecki	84*
Pat Kelly	147**
Jimmy Key	30*
Pat Listach	38
Melido Perez	182
Tim Raines	96*
John Wetteland	24
Bernie Williams	15

* Indicates two separate terms on Disabled List.
** Indicates three separate terms on Disabled List.

1996 salaries

	Bonuses	Total earned salary
Cecil Fielder, dh		$9,237,500
Paul O'Neill, of		$5,300,000
Kenny Rogers, p		$5,000,000
David Cone, p		$4,666,666
Melido Perez, p		$4,650,000
John Wetteland, p		$4,000,000
Bernie Williams, of		$3,000,000
Joe Girardi, c	$75,000	$2,325,000
Tino Martinez, 1b		$2,300,000
Pat Listach, ss		$2,200,000
Wade Boggs, 3b	$50,000	$2,050,000
Charlie Hayes, 3b	$250,000	$1,750,000
Jimmy Key, p		$1,750,000
Tony Fernandez, ss		$1,500,000
Tim Raines, of		$1,450,000
Ricky Bones, p	$75,000	$1,425,000
Jim Leyritz, c	$70,000	$1,400,579
Scott Kamieniecki, p		$1,100,000
Dwight Gooden, p	$100,000	$950,000
Pat Kelly, 2b		$900,000
Jeff Nelson, p		$860,000
Marlano Duncan, 2b	$120,000	$845,000
Luis Sojo, ss	$75,000	$625,000
Darryl Strawberry, of		$560,000
Mike Aldrete, 1b		$250,000
David Weathers, p		$225,000
Graeme Lloyd, p	$25,000	$205,000
Andy Pettitte, p	$45,000	$195,000
Mariano Rivera, p		$131,125
Derek Jeter, ss	$10,000	$130,000
Wally Whitehurst, p		$125,000
Dave Pavlas, p		$120,000
Michael Figga, c		$109,000
Dale Polley, p		$109,000
Ruben Rivera, of		$109,000

Average 1996 salary: $1,803,760
Total 1996 team payroll: $61,327,870

New York (1903-1996)

84

Runs: Most, career

1959	Babe Ruth, 1920-1934
1888	Lou Gehrig, 1923-1939
1677	Mickey Mantle, 1951-1968
1390	Joe DiMaggio, 1936-1951
1186	Earle Combs, 1924-1935

Hits: Most, career

2721	Lou Gehrig, 1923-1939
2518	Babe Ruth, 1920-1934
2415	Mickey Mantle, 1951-1968
2214	Joe DiMaggio, 1936-1951
2153	Don Mattingly, 1982-1995

2B: Most, career

534	Lou Gehrig, 1923-1939
442	Don Mattingly, 1982-1995
424	Babe Ruth, 1920-1934
389	Joe DiMaggio, 1936-1951
344	Mickey Mantle, 1951-1968

3B: Most, career

163	Lou Gehrig, 1923-1939
154	Earle Combs, 1924-1935
131	Joe DiMaggio, 1936-1951
121	Wally Pipp, 1915-1925
115	Tony Lazzeri, 1926-1937

HR: Most, career

659	Babe Ruth, 1920-1934
536	Mickey Mantle, 1951-1968
493	Lou Gehrig, 1923-1939
361	Joe DiMaggio, 1936-1951
358	Yogi Berra, 1946-1963

RBI: Most, career

1995	Lou Gehrig, 1923-1939
1971	Babe Ruth, 1920-1934
1537	Joe DiMaggio, 1936-1951
1509	Mickey Mantle, 1951-1968
1430	Yogi Berra, 1946-1963

SB: Most, career

326	R. HENDERSON, 1985-1989
251	Willie Randolph, 1976-1988
248	Hal Chase, 1905-1913
233	Roy White, 1965-1979
184	Ben Chapman, 1930-1936
184	Wid Conroy, 1903-1908

BB: Most, career

1847	Babe Ruth, 1920-1934
1733	Mickey Mantle, 1951-1968
1508	Lou Gehrig, 1923-1939
1005	Willie Randolph, 1976-1988
934	Roy White, 1965-1979

BA: Highest, career

.349	Babe Ruth, 1920-1934
.340	Lou Gehrig, 1923-1939
.325	Earle Combs, 1924-1935
.325	Joe DiMaggio, 1936-1951
.315	PAUL O'NEILL, 1993-1996

Slug avg: Highest, career

.711	Babe Ruth, 1920-1934
.632	Lou Gehrig, 1923-1939
.579	Joe DiMaggio, 1936-1951
.557	Mickey Mantle, 1951-1968
.526	Reggie Jackson, 1977-1981

On-base avg: Highest, career

.484	Babe Ruth, 1920-1934
.447	Lou Gehrig, 1923-1939
.421	Mickey Mantle, 1951-1968
.410	Charlie Keller, 1939-1952
.404	PAUL O'NEILL, 1993-1996

Complete games: Most, career

261	Red Ruffing, 1930-1946
173	Lefty Gomez, 1930-1942
168	Jack Chesbro, 1903-1909
164	Herb Pennock, 1923-1933
164	Bob Shawkey, 1915-1927

Saves: Most, career

224	Dave Righetti, 1979-1990
151	Rich Gossage, 1978-1989
141	Sparky Lyle, 1972-1978
104	Johnny Murphy, 1932-1946
78	Steve Farr, 1991-1993

Shutouts: Most, career

45	Whitey Ford, 1950-1967
40	Red Ruffing, 1930-1946
40	Mel Stottlemyre, 1964-1974
28	Lefty Gomez, 1930-1942
27	Allie Reynolds, 1947-1954

Wins: Most, career

236	Whitey Ford, 1950-1967
231	Red Ruffing, 1930-1946
189	Lefty Gomez, 1930-1942
170	Ron Guidry, 1975-1988
168	Bob Shawkey, 1915-1927

K: Most, career

1956	Whitey Ford, 1950-1967
1778	Ron Guidry, 1975-1988
1526	Red Ruffing, 1930-1946
1468	Lefty Gomez, 1930-1942
1257	Mel Stottlemyre, 1964-1974

Win pct: Highest, career

.725	Johnny Allen, 1932-1935
.717	Spud Chandler, 1937-1947
.706	Vic Raschi, 1946-1953
.700	Monte Pearson, 1936-1940
.690	Whitey Ford, 1950-1967

ERA: Lowest, career

2.54	Russ Ford, 1909-1913
2.58	Jack Chesbro, 1903-1909
2.72	Al Orth, 1904-1909
2.73	Tiny Bonham, 1940-1946
2.73	George Mogridge, 1915-1920

Runs: Most, season

177	Babe Ruth, 1921
167	Lou Gehrig, 1936
163	Lou Gehrig, 1931
163	Babe Ruth, 1928
158	Babe Ruth, 1920
158	Babe Ruth, 1927

Hits: Most, season

238	Don Mattingly, 1986
231	Earle Combs, 1927
220	Lou Gehrig, 1930
218	Lou Gehrig, 1927
215	Joe DiMaggio, 1937

2B: Most, season

53	Don Mattingly, 1986
52	Lou Gehrig, 1927
48	Don Mattingly, 1985
47	Lou Gehrig, 1926
47	Lou Gehrig, 1928
47	Bob Meusel, 1927

3B: Most, season

23	Earle Combs, 1927
22	Earle Combs, 1930
22	Birdie Cree, 1911
22	Snuffy Stirnweiss, 1945
21	Earle Combs, 1928

HR: Most, season

61	Roger Maris, 1961
60	Babe Ruth, 1927
59	Babe Ruth, 1921
54	Mickey Mantle, 1961
54	Babe Ruth, 1920
54	Babe Ruth, 1928

RBI: Most, season

184	Lou Gehrig, 1931
175	Lou Gehrig, 1927
174	Lou Gehrig, 1930

171 Babe Ruth, 1921
167 Joe DiMaggio, 1937

SB: Most, season

93 RICKEY HENDERSON, 1988
87 RICKEY HENDERSON, 1986
80 RICKEY HENDERSON, 1985
74 Fritz Maisel, 1914
61 Ben Chapman, 1931

BB: Most, season

170 Babe Ruth, 1923
148 Babe Ruth, 1920
146 Mickey Mantle, 1957
144 Babe Ruth, 1921
144 Babe Ruth, 1926

BA: Highest, season

.393 Babe Ruth, 1923
.381 Joe DiMaggio, 1939
.379 Lou Gehrig, 1930
.378 Babe Ruth, 1924
.378 Babe Ruth, 1921

Slug avg: Highest, season

.847 Babe Ruth, 1920
.846 Babe Ruth, 1921
.772 Babe Ruth, 1927
.765 Lou Gehrig, 1927
.764 Babe Ruth, 1923

On-base avg: Highest, season

.545 Babe Ruth, 1923
.530 Babe Ruth, 1920
.516 Babe Ruth, 1926
.513 Babe Ruth, 1924
.512 Mickey Mantle, 1957

Complete games: Most, season

48 Jack Chesbro, 1904
38 Jack Powell, 1904
36 Al Orth, 1906
33 Jack Chesbro, 1903
31 Ray Caldwell, 1915

Saves: Most, season

46 Dave Righetti, 1986
43 JOHN WETTELAND, 1996
36 Dave Righetti, 1990
35 Sparky Lyle, 1972
33 Rich Gossage, 1980

Shutouts: Most, season

9 Ron Guidry, 1978
8 Whitey Ford, 1964
8 Russ Ford, 1910
7 Whitey Ford, 1958
7 Catfish Hunter, 1975
7 Allie Reynolds, 1951
7 Mel Stottlemyre, 1971
7 Mel Stottlemyre, 1972

Wins: Most, season

41 Jack Chesbro, 1904
27 Carl Mays, 1921
27 Al Orth, 1906
26 Joe Bush, 1922
26 Russ Ford, 1910
26 Lefty Gomez, 1934
26 Carl Mays, 1920

K: Most, season

248 Ron Guidry, 1978
239 Jack Chesbro, 1904
218 Melido Perez, 1992
217 Al Downing, 1964
210 Bob Turley, 1955

Win pct: Highest, season

.893 Ron Guidry, 1978
.862 Whitey Ford, 1961
.842 Ralph Terry, 1961
.839 Lefty Gomez, 1934
.833 Spud Chandler, 1943

ERA: Lowest, season

1.64 Spud Chandler, 1943
1.65 Russ Ford, 1910
1.74 Ron Guidry, 1978
1.82 Jack Chesbro, 1904
1.83 Hippo Vaughn, 1910

Most pinch-hit homers, season

4 Johnny Blanchard, 1961

Most pinch-hit homers, career

9 Yogi Berra, 1946-1963
8 Bob Cerv, 1951-1962

Longest hitting streak

56 Joe DiMaggio, 1941
33 Hal Chase, 1907
29 Roger Peckinpaugh, 1919
29 Earle Combs, 1931
29 Joe Gordon, 1942

Most consecutive scoreless innings

33 Jack Aker, 1969

No-hit games

Tom L. Hughes, NY vs Cle AL, 0-5; Aug. 30, 1910 (2nd game; lost on 7 hits in 11 innings after allowing the first hit in the 10th)
George Mogridge, NY at Bos AL, 2-1; Apr. 24, 1917.
Sam Jones, NY at Phi AL, 2-0; Sept. 4, 1923.
Monte Pearson, NY vs Cle AL, 13-0; Aug. 27, 1938 (2nd game).
Allie Reynolds, NY at Cle AL, 1-0; July 12, 1951.

Allie Reynolds, NY vs Bos AL, 8-0; Sept. 28, 1951 (1st game).
Don Larsen, NY AL vs Bro NL, 2-0; Oct. 8, 1956 (World Series, perfect game).
Dave Righetti, NY vs Bos AL, 4-0; July 4, 1983.
Andy Hawkins, NY at Chi AL, 0-4; July 1, 1990 (8 innings, lost the game; bottom of 9th not played).
JIM ABBOTT, NY vs Cle AL, 4-0; Sept. 4, 1993.
DWIGHT GOODEN, NY vs Sea AL, 2-0; May 14, 1996.

ACTIVE PLAYERS in caps.

Players' years of service are listed by the first and last years with this team and are not necessarily consecutive; all statistics record performances for this team only.

Rafael Palmeiro set an Orioles record for RBI and tied his career high in homers.

1996 Orioles: O's went long at the Yards

The Orioles set the major league home run record and secured their first post-season appearance in 13 years. They did it despite Bobby Bonilla's griping over the DH role, Cal Ripken's moving temporarily to third base and Roberto Alomar's getting into an ugly dispute with an umpire on the final weekend. Then, with the Alomar–John Hirschbeck controversy still swirling, the second baseman led the Orioles to an upset of the Cleveland Indians in the Division Series. The wild ride finally ended with a defeat at the hands of the eventual World Series champion Yankees in the ALCS.

It was a season of change, as the Orioles got themselves a new manager, a new general manager and a revamped roster that had one of the game's highest payrolls. But it was an old hand, owner Peter Angelos, who played the most crucial role in the team's march to the playoffs. The Orioles fell 12 games behind the Yankees on July 28, and GM Pat Gillick wanted to trade veterans Bonilla and David Wells for prospects. But Angelos vetoed the deals, believing the team could still win the wild card, and he was proved right when the Orioles won 37 of their last 58 games and clinched the final AL playoff spot on the season's last weekend.

The Orioles had a tremendous stable of talent; in some postseason games every man in their lineup had slugged at least 20 homers, most likely a major league first. They broke the Yankees' 1961 homer mark by hitting 257 and became only the 16th team in history with four 100-RBI men.

Many Orioles had notable seasons: Outfielder Brady Anderson hit a club-record 50 homers, breaking Frank Robinson's mark of 49, and first baseman Rafael Palmeiro broke Jim Gentile's all-time team record of 141 RBI by knocking in 142. Alomar, signed as a free agent from Toronto, started hot, flirted with .400 well into May and finished with a .328 average to go with his usual sparkling defense. Ripken, in a

brief demonstration of possible things to come, moved to third base for a while and, of course, didn't miss a game. He put up a .278, 26-homer, 102-RBI year but showed hints of slowing in the field.

Bonilla finally settled into right field and, despite going 4-for-35 in the playoffs, put up the regular-season offensive numbers (28 HR, 116 RBI) expected of him. Catcher Chris Hoiles, under fire for his defensive shortcomings, had 25 homers and became one of the few players to hit a two-out, ninth-inning grand slam with his team down three runs. He did it on May 17 against Seattle for a 14-13 victory.

The pitching was disappointing, as the staff finished with a 5.14 ERA and couldn't hold leads against the Yankees in the ALCS. An inconsistent and thin starting rotation gave manager Davy Johnson headaches all year. Ace Mike Mussina finished 19-11 but pitched poorly down the stretch, Scott Erickson and David Wells were erratic, and Johnson had to rush rookie Rocky Coppinger to the majors to be the fourth starter. Though mostly a veteran staff, the Orioles got significant contributions from Coppinger (10 wins) and from second-year reliever Armando Benitez (20 strikeouts in $14\frac{1}{3}$ innings), who pitched very well in September and could become the closer in the future.

1996 Orioles: Week-by-week notes

These notes were excerpted from the following issues of Baseball Weekly.

▶**April 3:** The Opening Day lineup featured a mild surprise, with manager Davey Johnson listing Bobby Bonilla at designated hitter and not third base or right field. "I'm a little disappointed," Bonilla said.

▶**April 10:** The Orioles began the season 4-0 for the first time since 1985, getting quality starts from each of their top four pitchers—Mike Mussina, David Wells, Scott Erickson and Kent Mercker.

▶**April 24:** The Orioles were outscored 44-17 in three losses to Boston and Texas. The 16 runs the Orioles allowed in the eighth inning of their 26-7 April 20 loss to Texas was the second most in this century.

▶**May 1:** Center fielder Brady Anderson continued his torrid batting, hitting his 11th homer on April 28 to tie the major league April record.

▶**May 15:** Davey Johnson returned unhappy DH Bobby Bonilla to right field. Bonilla had struggled as a DH, batting only .202 in the first 30 games.

▶**May 22:** In a span of 29 days, the Orioles played the three longest nine-inning night games in major league history—four hours and 15 minutes against Texas, 4:21 against New York and 4:20 against Seattle. The 14-13 marathon on May 17 against the Mariners ended when catcher Chris Hoiles hit a two-out grand slam in the ninth.

▶**May 29:** Second baseman Roberto Alomar was batting .401 after 47 games. He was particularly effective after Davey Johnson dropped him a notch to the No. 3 spot in the lineup, batting .491 (28-for-57) with four home runs and 19 RBI.

▶**June 5:** The Orioles' pitching continued to struggle, with the team ERA at 5.42 after an 8-3 loss to California on June 1.

▶**June 19:** Shortstop Cal Ripken broke the world consecutive-games record when he played in No. 2,216 in Kansas City on June 14, breaking the mark set by Sachio Kinugasa of the Hiroshima

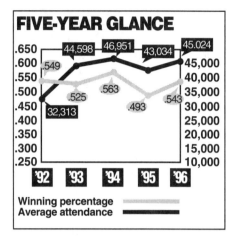

FIVE-YEAR GLANCE

Winning percentage
Average attendance

Carp in Japan's Central League.

▶**July 3:** "Some people think leadership is standing on the dugout and waving a towel. I personally don't believe that." Thus spoke Cal Ripken after owner Peter Angelos suggested the All-Star shortstop provide team leadership as the Orioles struggle to figure out why they are playing so far below expectations. Davey Johnson shuffled the top of his batting order on June 28, moving Roberto Alomar to the leadoff spot after hitting him second or third all season. Brady Anderson, leading the majors in home runs at the time, dropped to the No. 2 spot, with Ripken rising to the third slot.

▶**July 17:** The Orioles fell 10 games out after being swept in four games by the Yankees at Camden Yards, raising the possibility they might start trading veterans for young players. After the Yankees series, the Orioles were a dismal 11-27 against teams with winning records.

▶**July 24:** Cal Ripken was back at shortstop on July 21 after six games at third base so the Orioles could test 25-year-old Manny Alexander at short. Alexander was 1-for-18 during the experiment, managing only a broken-bat single. Ripken's longtime teammate, DH Eddie Murray, returned to the flock in a trade that sent pitcher Kent Mercker to Cleveland. The deal allows Murray to come back to Baltimore to hit the nine homers that he needs to reach 500.

▶July 31: Davey Johnson's proposal to switch to a four-man rotation triggered another clubhouse controversy, with Mike Mussina privately expressing reluctance to pitch on shorter rest. "I don't see how anyone could go against it, because of where we're at and how we're doing," closer Randy Myers said.

▶Aug. 7: Owner Peter Angelos says the club has an obligation to its fans to make every effort to reach the postseason and is reported to have blocked trades of Bobby Bonilla and David Wells arranged by general manager Pat Gillick.

▶Aug. 14: The Orioles climbed back into the wild-card race by going 9-4 on their longest road trip of the season, then began a stretch in which they played 12 of 16 games at home The starting pitching improved after Davey Johnson switched to a four-man rotation of Mike Mussina, David Wells, Scott Erickson and Rocky Coppinger.

▶Sept. 4: Shut out in their attempt to acquire left-hander Denny Neagle, the Orioles on Aug. 29 resolved another need by acquiring right-handed sluggers Todd Zeile and Pete Incaviglia from Philadelphia. Two days later, the Orioles broke the club record for home runs in a season—with 28 games remaining. Their previous record had been 214 in 1985.

▶Sept. 11: Mike Mussina pitched the Orioles' first shutout of the season in the team's 141st game, beating the Tigers 6-0 on Sept. 7. The victory was Mussina's eighth in his past nine starts, giving him 19 for the season.

▶Sept. 25: The Orioles renewed their bickering down the stretch, with Randy Myers questioning Davey Johnson after being pulled with one out in the ninth inning of a pivotal game in New York. Alan Mills replaced him with a 2-1 lead, and the Yankees rallied to win 3-2 in 10 innings.

▶Oct. 2: It was a tumultuous season featuring a new manager, a new general manager and a nasty incident in which Roberto Alomar spit in the face of an umpire. In the end, the owner earned a save by vetoing trades of David Wells and Bobby Bonilla. The Orioles set the major league home run

record (and at times fielded a lineup with nine players who would finish with 20 or more homers) and secured the wild card, their first postseason appearance in 13 years. Brady Anderson broke Frank Robinson's team record with 50 homers, and Rafael Palmeiro broke Jim Gentile's Orioles record with 142 RBI. The offensive talent was unmistakable, but the pitchers finished with a 5.14 ERA and Mike Mussina failed four times to win his 20th game.

Team directory

▶**Owner:** Peter Angelos
▶**General manager:** Pat Gillick
▶**Ballpark:**
Oriole Park at Camden Yards
Baltimore, Md.
410-685-9800
Capacity 48,262
Public transportation available
Disability seating, ramps, elevators, sound-amplification devices for the hearing-impaired, special menu selection board for the speaking-impaired
▶**Team publications:**
Orioles Magazine, media guide, yearbook
410-685-9800
▶**TV, radio broadcast stations:**
WBAL 1090 AM, WJZ Channel 13, Home Team, Sports Cable
▶**Camps and/or clinics:**
Fantasy Camp (ages 30-plus), February, 410-799-0005
Cal Ripken Sr. Baseball School (ages 8-18), Mount St. Mary's, Emmitsburg, Md., late June and early July, 301-791-3512
Elrod Hendricks Camp, Reistertown, Md., July, 410-685-9800
Summer clinics, the Orioles region, during the season, 410-685-9800
▶**Spring training:**
Al Lang Stadium
St. Petersburg, Fla.
Capacity 6,500
813-893-7490

BALTIMORE ORIOLES 1996 final stats

BATTERS	BA	SLG	OB	G	AB	R	H	TB	2B	3B	HR	RBI	BB	SO	SB	CS	E
Alomar	.328	.527	.411	153	588	132	193	310	43	4	22	94	90	65	17	6	11
Huson	.321	.357	.333	17	28	5	9	10	1	0	0	2	1	3	0	0	1
Bowers	.308	.359	.308	21	39	6	12	14	2	0	0	3	0	7	0	0	0
Incaviglia	.303	.545	.314	12	33	4	10	18	2	0	2	8	0	7	0	0	0
Anderson	.297	.637	.396	149	579	117	172	369	37	5	50	110	76	106	21	8	3
Surhoff	.292	.482	.352	143	537	74	157	259	27	6	21	82	47	79	0	1	15
Palmeiro	.289	.546	.381	162	626	110	181	342	40	2	39	142	95	96	8	0	8
Bonilla	.287	.491	.363	159	595	107	171	292	27	5	28	116	75	85	1	3	6
C. Ripken	.278	.466	.341	163	640	94	178	298	40	1	26	102	59	78	1	2	14
Murray	.260	.417	.327	152	566	69	147	236	21	1	22	79	61	87	4	0	0
Hoiles	.258	.474	.356	127	407	64	105	193	13	0	25	73	57	97	0	1	7
Smith	.244	.423	.298	27	78	9	19	33	2	0	4	10	3	20	0	2	1
Polonia	.240	.309	.285	58	175	25	42	54	4	1	2	14	10	20	8	6	1
Zeile	.239	.436	.326	29	117	17	28	51	8	0	5	19	15	16	0	0	3
Tarasco	.238	.310	.297	31	84	14	20	26	3	0	1	9	7	15	5	3	0
Zaun	.231	.352	.309	50	108	16	25	38	8	1	1	13	11	15	0	0	3
B. Ripken	.230	.333	.281	57	135	19	31	45	8	0	2	12	9	18	0	0	3
Devereaux	.229	.350	.305	127	323	49	74	113	11	2	8	34	34	53	8	2	3
Parent	.226	.474	.252	56	137	17	31	65	7	0	9	23	5	37	0	0	2
Hammonds	.226	.383	.301	71	248	38	56	95	10	1	9	27	23	53	3	3	3
Devarez	.111	.222	.158	10	18	3	2	4	0	1	0	0	1	3	0	0	0
Alexander	.103	.103	.141	54	68	6	7	7	0	0	0	4	3	27	3	3	5
Kingsale	---	---	---	3	0	0	0	0	0	0	0	0	0	0	0	0	0

PITCHERS	W-L	ERA	G	GS	CG	GF	Sho	SV	IP	H	R	ER	HR	BB	SO
Corbin	2-0	2.30	18	0	0	5	0	0	27.1	22	7	7	2	22	20
Mathews	2-2	3.38	14	0	0	5	0	0	18.2	20	7	7	3	7	13
Orosco	3-1	3.40	66	0	0	10	0	0	55.2	42	22	21	5	28	52
R. Myers	4-4	3.53	62	0	0	50	0	31	58.2	60	24	23	7	29	74
Benitez	1-0	3.77	18	0	0	8	0	4	14.1	7	6	6	2	6	20
Sackinsky	0-0	3.86	3	0	0	2	0	0	4.2	6	2	2	1	3	2
Rhodes	9-1	4.08	28	2	0	5	0	1	53.0	48	28	24	6	23	62
McDowell	1-1	4.25	41	0	0	11	0	4	59.1	69	32	28	7	23	20
Mills	3-2	4.28	49	0	0	23	0	3	54.2	40	26	26	10	35	50
Rodriguez	0-1	4.32	8	1	0	2	0	0	16.2	18	11	8	2	7	12
Mussina	19-11	4.81	36	36	4	0	1	0	243.1	264	137	130	31	69	204
Krivda	3-5	4.96	22	11	0	4	0	0	81.2	89	48	45	14	39	54
Erickson	13-12	5.02	34	34	6	0	0	0	222.1	262	137	124	21	66	100
Wells	11-14	5.14	34	34	3	0	0	0	224.1	247	132	128	32	51	130
Coppinger	10-6	5.18	23	22	0	1	0	0	125.0	126	76	72	25	60	104
Yan	0-0	5.79	4	0	0	2	0	0	9.1	13	7	6	3	3	7
J. Myers	0-0	7.07	11	0	0	5	0	0	14.0	18	13	11	4	3	6
Milchin	3-1	7.44	39	0	0	7	0	0	32.2	44	28	27	6	17	29
Haynes	3-6	8.29	26	11	0	8	0	1	89.0	122	84	82	14	58	65
Shepherd	0-1	8.71	13	0	0	6	0	0	20.2	31	27	20	6	18	17
Stephenson	0-1	12.79	3	0	0	2	0	0	6.1	13	9	9	1	3	3
Alexander	0-0	67.50	1	0	0	1	0	0	0.2	1	5	5	1	4	0

1997 preliminary roster

PITCHERS (20)
Armando Benitez
Shawn Boskie
Rocky Coppinger
Archie Corbin
Tom Davey
Scott Erickson
Jimmy Haynes
Mike Johnson
Jimmy Key
Rick Krivda
Terry Mathews
Alan Mills
Julio Moreno
Mike Mussina
Randy Myers
Jesse Orosco
Arthur Rhodes
Nerio Rodriguez
Francisco Saneaux
Esteban Yan

CATCHERS (3)
Cesar Devarez
Chris Hoiles
B.J. Waszgis

INFIELDERS (11)
Manny Alexander
Roberto Alomar
Juan Bautista
Mike Bordick
Danny Magee
Domingo Martinez
Scott McClain
Willis Otanez
Rafael Palmeiro
Cal Ripken
B.J. Surhoff

OUTFIELDERS (8)
Wady Almonte
Brady Anderson
Danny Clyburn
Eric Davis
Jeffrey Hammonds
Pete Incaviglia
Eugene Kingsale
Tony Tarasco

Games played by position

PLAYER	G	C	1B	2B	3B	SS	OF	DH
Alexander	54	0	0	7	7	21	3	1
Alomar	153	0	0	141	0	0	0	10
Anderson	149	0	0	0	0	0	143	2
Bonilla	159	0	9	0	4	0	108	44
Bowers	21	0	0	0	0	0	21	0
Devarez	10	10	0	0	0	0	0	0
Devereaux	127	0	0	0	0	0	112	10
Hammonds	71	0	0	0	0	0	70	1
Hoiles	127	126	1	0	0	0	0	0
Huson	17	0	0	12	3	0	1	0
Incaviglia	12	0	0	0	0	0	7	4
Kingsale	3	0	0	0	0	0	2	0
Murray	152	0	1	0	0	0	0	149
Palmeiro	162	0	159	0	0	0	0	3
Parent	56	51	1	0	0	0	0	0
Polonia	58	0	0	0	0	0	34	18
B. Ripken	57	0	1	30	25	0	0	0
C. Ripken	163	0	0	0	6	158	0	0
Smith	27	0	0	0	0	0	20	6
Surhoff	143	0	2	0	106	0	27	10
Tarasco	31	0	0	0	0	0	23	6
Zaun	50	49	0	0	0	0	0	0
Zeile	29	0	0	0	29	0	0	0

Minor Leagues

Tops in the organization

BATTER	CLUB	AVG.	G	AB	R	H	HR	RBI
Mike Berry	Hd	.354	126	478	112	169	14	116
Brent Bowers	Roc	.318	107	434	77	138	13	44
Bryan Bogle	Hd	.317	126	495	86	157	22	92
D. Newstrom	Hd	.313	122	403	84	126	11	75
Rick Short	Fre	.312	126	474	68	148	3	54

HOME RUNS

Chris Kirgan	Hd	35
Brent Cookson	Roc	25
Willis Otanez	Bow	24
Bryan Bogle	Hd	22
Joe Hall	Roc	19

WINS

Calvin Maduro	Roc	12
Greg Dean	Hd	10
Matt Marenghi	Hd	9
Julio Moreno	Fre	9
Nerio Rodriguez	Roc	9

RBI

Chris Kirgan	Hd	131
Mike Berry	Hd	116
Johnny Isom	Fre	104
Joe Hall	Roc	95
Bryan Bogle	Hd	92

SAVES

Matt Snyder	Hd	20
F. Hernandez	Fre	12
Jimmy Myers	Roc	12
Alvie Shepherd	Fre	10
Keith Shepherd	Roc	9

STOLEN BASES

Curtis Charles	Blu	31
Darrell Dent	Blu	30
Eddy Martinez	Blu	28
Several Players Tied at		25

STRIKEOUTS

Julio Moreno	Fre	147
Calvin Maduro	Roc	127
Nerio Rodriguez	Roc	120
Matt Marenghi	Hd	114
S. Ponson	Fre	110

PITCHER	CLUB	W-L	ERA	IP	H	BB	SO
N. Rodriguez	Roc	9-7	2.21	126	93	42	120
S. Ponson	Fre	7-6	3.45	107	98	28	110
Julio Moreno	Fre	9-10	3.50	162	167	38	147
C. Maduro	Roc	12-12	3.64	168	165	54	127
K. Shepherd	Roc	4-7	4.01	94	91	37	98

Sick call: 1996 DL report

PLAYER	Days on the DL
Armando Benitez	128
Jeffrey Hammonds	37
Jeff Huson	58
Aaron Lane	40
Roger McDowell	67*
Alan Mills	40
Billy Percibal	157
Arthur Rhodes	71*
Mark Smith	69
B.J. Surhoff	15
Tony Tarasco	19

Indicates two separate terms on Disabled List.

1996 salaries

	Bonuses	Total earned salary
Cal Ripken, ss	$50,000	$6,650,000
Rafael Palmeiro, 1b		$5,268,506
Roberto Alomar, 2b	$275,000	$4,518,901
Bobby Bonilla, of		$4,319,426
Mike Mussina, p		$4,000,000
Brady Anderson, of	$30,000	$3,613,333
Chris Hoiles, c		$3,350,000
David Wells, p	$200,000	$3,200,000
Scott Erickson, p	$100,000	$2,900,000
Todd Zeile, 3b	$200,000	$2,700,000
Randy Myers, p		$2,600,000
B.J. Surhoff, 3b	$350,000	$2,016,666
Eddie Murray, 1b		$2,000,000
Mike Devereaux, of	$200,000	$900,000
Roger McDowell, p		$750,000
Jesse Orosco, p	$250,000	$750,000
Alan Mills, p	$60,000	$600,000
Pete Incaviglia, of	$250,000	$550,000
Jeffrey Hammonds, of	$15,000	$300,000
Arthur Rhodes, p		$300,000
Tony Tarasco, of		$300,000
Terry Mathews, p		$292,500
Bill Ripken, 2b		$250,000
Manny Alexander, ss		$190,000
Armando Benitez, p		$155,000
Mark Smith, of		$130,000
Archie Corbin, p		$115,000
Rocky Coppinger, p		$109,000
Aaron Lane, p		$109,000
Mike Milchin, p		$109,000
Mark Parent, c		$109,000
Billy Percibal, p		$109,000

Average 1996 salary: $1,622,323
Total 1996 team payroll: $53,194,332
Termination pay: $1,933,523

Baltimore (1954-1996), includes St. Louis Browns (1902-1953)

Runs: Most, career

1366	CAL RIPKEN, 1981-1996
1232	Brooks Robinson, 1955-1977
1091	George Sisler, 1915-1927
1084	EDDIE MURRAY, 1977-1996
1013	Harlond Clift, 1934-1943

Hits: Most, career

2848	Brooks Robinson, 1955-1977
2549	CAL RIPKEN, 1981-1996
2295	George Sisler, 1915-1927
2080	EDDIE MURRAY, 1977-1996
1574	Boog Powell, 1961-1974

2B: Most, career

487	CAL RIPKEN, 1981-1996
482	Brooks Robinson, 1955-1977
363	EDDIE MURRAY, 1977-1996
343	George Sisler, 1915-1927
294	Harlond Clift, 1934-1943

3B: Most, career

145	George Sisler, 1915-1927
88	Baby Doll Jacobson, 1915-1926
72	Del Pratt, 1912-1917
72	Jack Tobin, 1916-1925
70	Ken Williams, 1918-1927
68	Brooks Robinson, 1955-1977 (6)

HR: Most, career

353	CAL RIPKEN, 1981-1996
343	EDDIE MURRAY, 1977-1996
303	Boog Powell, 1961-1974
268	Brooks Robinson, 1955-1977
185	Ken Williams, 1918-1927

RBI: Most, career

1369	CAL RIPKEN, 1981-1996
1357	Brooks Robinson, 1955-1977
1224	EDDIE MURRAY, 1977-1996
1063	Boog Powell, 1961-1974
959	George Sisler, 1915-1927

SB: Most, career, all-time

351	George Sisler, 1915-1927
252	Al Bumbry, 1972-1984
247	Burt Shotton, 1909-1917
204	BRADY ANDERSON, 1988-1996
192	Jimmy Austin, 1911-1929

BB: Most, career

986	Harlond Clift, 1934-1943
960	CAL RIPKEN, 1981-1996
889	Boog Powell, 1961-1974
886	Ken Singleton, 1975-1984
884	EDDIE MURRAY, 1977-1996

BA: Highest, career

.344	George Sisler, 1915-1927
.326	Ken Williams, 1918-1927
.318	Jack Tobin, 1916-1925
.317	Baby Doll Jacobson, 1915-1926
.309	Bob Dillinger, 1946-1949
.301	Bob Boyd, 1956-1960 (8)

Slug avg: Highest, career

.558	Ken Williams, 1918-1927
.543	Frank Robinson, 1966-1971
.512	Jim Gentile, 1960-1963
.498	EDDIE MURRAY, 1977-1996
.486	Bob Nieman, 1951-1959

On-base avg: Highest, career

.403	Ken Williams, 1918-1927
.401	Frank Robinson, 1966-1971
.394	Harlond Clift, 1934-1943
.388	Randy Milligan, 1989-1992
.388	Ken Singleton, 1975-1984

Complete games: Most, career

211	Jim Palmer, 1965-1984
210	Jack Powell, 1902-1912
174	Barney Pelty, 1903-1912
150	Harry Howell, 1904-1910
143	Urban Shocker, 1918-1924

Saves: Most, career

160	GREGG OLSON, 1988-1993
105	Tippy Martinez, 1976-1986
100	Stu Miller, 1963-1967
74	Eddie Watt, 1966-1973
58	Dick Hall, 1961-1971

Shutouts: Most, career

53	Jim Palmer, 1965-1984
33	Dave McNally, 1962-1974
30	Mike Cuellar, 1969-1976
27	Jack Powell, 1902-1912
26	Milt Pappas, 1957-1965

Wins: Most, career

268	Jim Palmer, 1965-1984
181	Dave McNally, 1962-1974
143	Mike Cuellar, 1969-1976
141	Mike Flanagan, 1975-1992
138	Scott McGregor, 1976-1988

K: Most, career

2212	Jim Palmer, 1965-1984
1476	Dave McNally, 1962-1974
1297	Mike Flanagan, 1975-1992
1011	Mike Cuellar, 1969-1976
944	Milt Pappas, 1957-1965

Win pct: Highest, career

.687	MIKE MUSSINA, 1991-1996
.638	Jim Palmer, 1965-1984
.620	Wally Bunker, 1963-1968
.619	Dick Hall, 1961-1971
.619	Mike Cuellar, 1969-1976

ERA: Lowest, career

2.06	Harry Howell, 1904-1910
2.52	Fred Glade, 1904-1907
2.62	Barney Pelty, 1903-1912
2.63	Jack Powell, 1902-1912
2.67	Carl Weilman, 1912-1920
2.86	Jim Palmer, 1965-1984 (6)

Runs: Most, season

145	Harlond Clift, 1936
137	George Sisler, 1920
134	George Sisler, 1922
132	ROBERTO ALOMAR, 1996
132	Jack Tobin, 1921

Hits: Most, season

257	George Sisler, 1920
246	George Sisler, 1922
241	Heinie Manush, 1928
236	Jack Tobin, 1921
224	George Sisler, 1925
211	CAL RIPKEN, 1983 (10)

2B: Most, season

51	Beau Bell, 1937
49	George Sisler, 1920
47	Heinie Manush, 1928
47	CAL RIPKEN, 1983
47	Joe Vosmik, 1937

3B: Most, season

20	Heinie Manush, 1928
20	George Stone, 1906
18	George Sisler, 1920
18	George Sisler, 1921
18	George Sisler, 1922
18	Jack Tobin, 1921
12	Paul Blair, 1967 (24)

HR: Most, season

50	BRADY ANDERSON, 1996	
49	Frank Robinson, 1966	
46	Jim Gentile, 1961	
39	RAFAEL PALMEIRO, 1995	
39	RAFAEL PALMEIRO, 1996	
39	Boog Powell, 1964	
39	Ken Williams, 1922	

RBI: Most, season

155	Ken Williams, 1922
142	RAFAEL PALMEIRO, 1996
141	Jim Gentile, 1961
134	Moose Solters, 1936
124	EDDIE MURRAY, 1985

SB: Most, season

57	Luis Aparicio, 1964
53	BRADY ANDERSON, 1992
51	George Sisler, 1922
46	Armando Marsans, 1916
45	George Sisler, 1918

BB: Most, season

126	Lu Blue, 1929
121	Roy Cullenbine, 1941
118	Harlond Clift, 1938
118	Burt Shotton, 1915
118	Ken Singleton, 1975

BA: Highest, season

.420	George Sisler, 1922
.407	George Sisler, 1920
.378	Heinie Manush, 1928
.371	George Sisler, 1921
.358	George Stone, 1906
.328	Ken Singleton, 1977(*)
.328	ROBERTO ALOMAR, 1996(*)

Slug avg: Highest, season

.646	Jim Gentile, 1961
.637	BRADY ANDERSON, 1996
.637	Frank Robinson, 1966
.632	George Sisler, 1920
.627	Ken Williams, 1922

On-base avg: Highest, season

.467	George Sisler, 1922
.452	Roy Cullenbine, 1941
.449	George Sisler, 1920
.442	Bob Nieman, 1956
.439	Ken Williams, 1923

Complete games: Most, season

36	Jack Powell, 1902
35	Harry Howell, 1905
33	Red Donahue, 1902
33	Jack Powell, 1903
32	Harry Howell, 1904
25	Jim Palmer, 1975 (20)

Saves: Most, season

37	GREGG OLSON, 1990
36	GREGG OLSON, 1992
34	Don Aase, 1986
33	LEE SMITH, 1994
31	RANDY MYERS, 1996
31	GREGG OLSON, 1991

Shutouts: Most, season

10	Jim Palmer, 1975
8	Steve Barber, 1961
7	Milt Pappas, 1964
6	Fred Glade, 1904
6	Harry Howell, 1906
6	Dave McNally, 1972
6	Jim Palmer, 1969
6	Jim Palmer, 1973
6	Jim Palmer, 1976
6	Jim Palmer, 1978

Wins: Most, season

27	Urban Shocker, 1921
25	Steve Stone, 1980
24	Mike Cuellar, 1970
24	Dave McNally, 1970
24	Urban Shocker, 1922

K: Most, season

232	Rube Waddell, 1908
226	Bobo Newsom, 1938
204	MIKE MUSSINA, 1996
202	Dave McNally, 1968
199	Jim Palmer, 1970

Win pct: Highest, season

.808	Alvin Crowder, 1928
.808	Dave McNally, 1971
.800	Jim Palmer, 1969
.792	Wally Bunker, 1964
.783	MIKE MUSSINA, 1992

ERA: Lowest, season

1.59	Barney Pelty, 1906
1.77	Jack Powell, 1906
1.89	Harry Howell, 1908
1.89	Rube Waddell, 1908
1.93	Harry Howell, 1907
1.95	Dave McNally, 1968 (7)

Most pinch-hit homers, season

3	Sam Bowens, 1967
3	Jim Dwyer, 1986
3	Whitey Herzog, 1962
3	Sam Horn, 1991
3	Pat Kelly, 1979

Most pinch-hit homers, career

9	Jim Dwyer, 1980-1988
7	Benny Ayala, 1979-1984

Longest hitting streak

41	George Sisler, 1922
34	George McQuinn, 1938
34	George Sisler, 1925
29	Mel Almada, 1938
28	Ken Williams, 1922
24	RAFAEL PALMEIRO, 1994

Most consecutive scoreless innings

41	GREGG OLSON, 1989-1990
36	Hal Brown, 1961

No-hit games

Earl Hamilton, StL at Det AL, 5-1; Aug. 30, 1912.

Ernie Koob, StL vs Chi AL, 1-0; May 5, 1917.

Bob Groom, StL vs Chi AL, 3-0; May 6, 1917 (2nd game).

Bobo Newsom, StL vs Bos AL, 1-2; Sept. 18, 1934 (lost on 1 hit in the 10th).

Bobo Holloman, StL vs Phi AL, 6-0; May 6, 1953 (first start in the major leagues).

Hoyt Wilhelm, Bal vs NY AL, 1-0; Sept. 20, 1958

Steve D. Barber (8.2 innings) and Stu Miller (0.1 inning), Bal vs Det AL, 1-2; Apr. 30, 1967 (1st game, lost the game)

Tom Phoebus, Bal vs Bos AL, 6-0; Apr. 27, 1968.

Jim Palmer, Bal vs Oak AL, 8-0; Aug. 13, 1969.

Bob Milacki (6 innings), Mike Flanagan (1 inning), Mark Williamson, (1 inning) and GREGG OLSON (1 inning), Bal at Oak AL, 2-0; July 13, 1991.

John Whitehead, six innings, rain, StL vs Det AL, 4-0; Aug. 5, 1940 (2nd game).

ACTIVE PLAYERS in caps.

Leader from the franchise's current location is included. If not in the top five, leader's rank is listed in parenthesis; asterisk (*) indicates player is not in top 25.

Players' years of service are listed by the first and last years with this team and are not necessarily consecutive; all statistics record performances for this team only.

Boston Red Sox

By Russell Becker, Baseball Weekly

Mo Vaughn didn't look back, topping his '95 marks in batting average, homers and RBI.

1996 Red Sox: Too far down to come back

The 1996 Red Sox started the year with 19 losses in the first 25 games and ended it with players holding impromptu press conferences about their futures. In between, the patched-together Sox somehow made another run at the postseason, but it fell short and the franchise remains without a world championship since 1918.

The Sox started by hoping that overweight slugger Kevin Mitchell would get into the lineup for more than two straight games, but by the end of the season, Mitchell and many others were long gone. The Sox broke the team record for players used for a second straight year, and questions about the 1997 season only started with "Who will be the manager?" Skipper Kevin Kennedy was replaced by Jimy Williams, and the future of many players was uncertain.

The biggest asset by far for Boston last year was Mo Vaughn, who bettered his '95 numbers with another huge year despite playing most of the time with a nagging finger injury. Vaughn, who signed a multiyear contract after his league MVP year, had promised not to rest on his laurels, and then went out and produced. He doesn't like some of the things the front office has done, and his words to that effect appeared almost weekly. But he is the team leader on the field and in the clubhouse.

Other standouts were Reggie Jefferson and new additions Darren Bragg and Jeff Frye, who were both picked up in midstream and proceeded to form the 1-2 catalyst at the top of the order.

Jose Canseco, Wil Cordero and Mike Greenwell were gone for huge chunks of the season as the lineup battled injuries all year. The bullpen, which was supposed to again be a bright spot, was torn apart by injuries and inconsistency (don't underestimate what the loss of reliever Stan Belinda meant to this team), and closer Heathcliff Slocumb had only one stretch of consistency—but that was enough to help Boston roar back into the wild-card picture.

Team MVP

Mo Vaughn: At the All-Star break, Mo Vaughn said he didn't see how the Red Sox could turn around their season. They did, nearly making the playoffs, and the big first baseman provided much of the impetus. With numbers bettering his AL MVP performance of the previous year, Vaughn finished in the top 10 in batting (.326), home runs (44) and RBI (143), as well as in hits, runs and total bases.

Roger Clemens, one of the more outspoken critics of management, went 10-13 and would have been better if the Red Sox had scored a few more runs and held some leads for him. In September he tied his major league record with a 20-strikeout game in Detroit. In the rest of the rotation, Tim Wakefield had a terrible start but finished over .500, the Sox are still waiting for Aaron Sele to develop, and Tom Gordon had a winning record that should have been better because he had the majors' best run support.

By the time the Sox turned to face the off-season, the team was in turmoil: Greenwell turned down a new deal to be a role player for next season and packed to leave; Clemens departed for Toronto; John Valentin wondered about his future, with Nomar Garciaparra on board to be the team's shortstop of the future; and third baseman Tim Naehring, hurt again at the end of the year, didn't know where he would fit in, since Valentin would either have to move to third or be traded. Uncertainty was the only thing Boston could count on as it looked toward 1997.

1996 Red Sox: Week-by-week notes

These notes were excerpted from the following issues of Baseball Weekly.

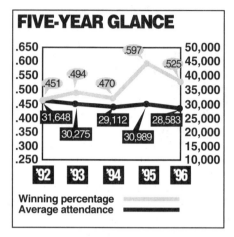

FIVE-YEAR GLANCE

Winning percentage
Average attendance

▶**April 17:** The franchise's worst start in 69 years was a total team effort, with all parts of the Red Sox's game contributing to leaving the team 7½ games out of first after only 12 games. "If you've got any pride, you ought to be embarrassed, frustrated or sick," 1995 MVP first baseman Mo Vaughn said after a 14-2 loss to the Indians—the Sox's third in a row at Fenway Park after winning the home opener.

▶**April 24:** Manager Kevin Kennedy hit the ceiling after a pitching performance he called disgraceful: Three pitchers threw 13 balls in a row on April 21. "You have to question big league guys that can't even get the ball in the vicinity of home plate," Kennedy said.

▶**May 1:** A three-game sweep by the Kansas City Royals, who had been baseball's second-worst team, left Boston at 6-19.

▶**May 8:** Red Sox fans/Yankee haters who laugh at the hirings and firings of George Steinbrenner felt a touch of Boss fever last week as Sammy Ellis, a past victim of Steinbrenner's moves, became manager Kevin Kennedy's fourth pitching coach in a little more than a season.

▶**May 15:** Jose Canseco came off the DL and became the left fielder for the Sox's weekend series in Toronto. Then he threw Domingo Cedeno out trying to stretch a single into a double with two out in the ninth inning of a tie game that the Red Sox won in the 11th. Canseco said he hadn't played left since 1986 with Oakland.

▶**May 22:** On May 18 the bullpen torched Roger Clemens's superb effort in another tough loss. Clemens left with a 4-2 lead with one out in the eighth inning—after the 64th 10-strikeout game of his career. After that game, the bullpen was 0-4 with a 10.42 ERA in Clemens's starts, blowing four saves and leaving the Rocket 2-4 despite a 3.69 ERA.

▶**June 19:** Jose Canseco has a ruptured disc and a hip flexor. Despite his pain, though, Canseco was on an incredible power pace—17 home runs in a span of 123 at-bats.

▶**June 26:** The Red Sox dropped 14 games out of first with five consecutive losses in Cleveland and Texas through June 22.

▶**July 3:** The Sox entered a two-game home series against the Indians last week determined to show they could beat a team that had defeated them 13 times in a row dating back to last year's playoffs. They lost the first game, then rallied to win the finale, avoiding the first season series shutout in franchise history.

▶**July 11:** Left fielder–DH Reggie Jefferson continued to stake his claim for playing time by posting huge numbers. He's hitting .376 and slugged his ninth homer of the year on July 6.

▶**July 17:** After a four-game sweep of Detroit, the Sox were 9-1 against the woeful Tigers and 31-48 against the rest of the league. Roger Clemens is 2-0 against Detroit and 2-8 against other AL squads.

▶**Aug. 7:** The Red Sox seemed to cash in their 1996 season as five veterans left via trade or the disabled list. Kevin Mitchell went to Cincinnati for two minor leaguers; Jamie Moyer, to Seattle for outfielder Darren Bragg; Mike Stanton, to Texas for two pitchers, Mark Brandenburg and Kerry Lacy; Jose Canseco, to the DL for back surgery; and shortstop John

Valentin, to the DL for his left shoulder. Other clubs weren't interested in left fielder Mike Greenwell, who has a $3.7 million contract and is not likely to return next year. Wil Cordero, expected back from a broken leg soon, is projected as the 1997 left fielder.

▶**Aug. 14:** Last year, the Red Sox rode a 14-1 start by late arrival Tim Wakefield to the AL East title. Recently, the Sox, left for dead in what had been a lost season, were rolling—and Wakefield was again at the front. The knuckleballer reeled off five wins in six starts to raise his record to 10-10 and bring the club within five games of .500.

▶**Aug. 21:** The Red Sox won 13 of 18 games through Aug. 18, bursting back into long-shot contention for the AL wild-card spot. At the front of all the excitement was Roger Clemens, whose 19 consecutive scoreless innings came at the perfect time. Clemens is just 6-11, but his ERA was down to 3.98.

▶**Aug. 28:** The Red Sox crawled to the .500 mark for the first time all year behind Roger Clemens on Aug. 22. Clemens beat Oakland 2-1 last week and almost ran his shutout streak to 28 innings.

▶**Sept. 4:** When the Oakland series began, on Aug. 30, the Sox were a mere 1½ games off the wild-card pace and only 5½ behind the Yankees for the AL East lead. Oakland, however, shut down Boston for two games and ended a run of 15 consecutive Red Sox games with at least one homer.

▶**Sept. 11:** Mike Greenwell was a one-man wrecking crew at Seattle on Sept. 2, driving in all nine of the Sox's runs in a 9-8 win over the Mariners. Greenwell's assault left him one shy of the club record for a game but was a record for a player driving in all of his team's runs in a game.

▶**Sept. 18:** Two losses in Chicago and a 3-3 homestand all but buried the Red Sox. Through Sept. 16 the Red Sox were six games behind Baltimore for the wild card.

▶**Sept. 25:** One day after Roger Clemens tied his own strikeout record by whiffing 20 in Detroit on Sept. 18, general manager Dan Duquette restated the club's wish for Clemens to pitch the rest of his career in Boston. "Clemens has indicated to us he wants to stay here, and we have indicated to him we want him," Duquette said.

▶**Oct. 2:** The Red Sox started the year with 19 losses in 25 games, and they ended it with Kevin Kennedy's being fired as manager and with players holding impromptu press conferences about their futures. In between, the Sox made another run at the postseason—and finished another year without bringing a championship to Boston. Mo Vaughn topped his '95 MVP numbers with another monster year. Roger Clemens was 10-13 with very little support. Tim Wakefield started miserably but finished well. With the future uncertain for Clemens, Mike Greenwell, Tim Naehring and John Valentin, the clubhouse was a ball of confusion, with much of it occurring before the Sox were officially eliminated.

Team directory

▶**Owners:** JRY Corporation and John Harrington
▶**General manager:** Dan Duquette
▶**Ballpark:**
Fenway Park
4 Yawkey Way
Boston, Mass.
617-267-9440
Capacity 33,871
Public transportation available
Family, wheelchair, and vision-impaired sections, ramps, sound amplification and TDD ticket information for hearing-impaired
▶**Team publications:**
Media guide, official scorebook, yearbook
617-267-9440
▶**TV, radio broadcast stations:**
WEEI 850 AM, WABU Channel 68, New England Sports Network Cable TV
▶**Spring training:**
City of Palms Park
Fort Myers, Fla.
Capacity 6,850
813-334-4700

BOSTON RED SOX 1996 final stats

BATTERS	BA	SLG	OB	G	AB	R	H	TB	2B	3B	HR	RBI	BB	SO	SB	CS	E
Pemberton	.512	.780	.556	13	41	11	21	32	8	0	1	10	2	4	3	1	0
Nixon	.500	.750	.500	2	4	2	2	3	1	0	0	0	0	1	1	0	0
Jefferson	.347	.593	.388	122	386	67	134	229	30	4	19	74	25	89	0	0	3
Vaughn	.326	.583	.420	161	635	118	207	370	29	1	44	143	95	154	2	0	15
Mitchell	.304	.413	.385	27	92	9	28	38	4	0	2	13	11	14	0	0	2
Valentin	.296	.436	.374	131	527	84	156	230	29	3	13	59	63	59	9	10	17
Greenwell	.295	.441	.336	77	295	35	87	130	20	1	7	44	18	27	4	0	4
Canseco	.289	.589	.400	96	360	68	104	212	22	1	28	82	63	82	3	1	0
Naehring	.288	.444	.363	116	430	77	124	191	16	0	17	65	49	63	2	1	11
Cordero	.288	.404	.330	59	198	29	57	80	14	0	3	37	11	31	2	1	10
Frye	.286	.389	.372	105	419	74	120	163	27	2	4	41	54	57	18	4	9
Haselman	.274	.439	.331	77	237	33	65	104	13	1	8	34	19	52	4	2	3
Selby	.274	.411	.337	40	95	12	26	39	4	0	3	6	9	11	1	1	4
Stanley	.270	.506	.383	121	397	73	107	201	20	1	24	69	69	62	2	0	10
Bragg	.261	.405	.366	127	417	74	109	169	26	2	10	47	69	74	14	9	3
O'Leary	.260	.427	.327	149	497	68	129	212	28	5	15	81	47	80	3	2	7
Beltre	.258	.290	.299	27	62	6	16	18	2	0	0	6	4	14	1	0	1
Delgado	.250	.250	.348	26	20	5	5	5	0	0	0	1	3	3	0	0	2
Tinsley	.245	.333	.298	92	192	28	47	64	6	1	3	14	13	56	6	8	1
Garciaparra	.241	.471	.272	24	87	11	21	41	2	3	4	16	4	14	5	0	1
Rodriguez	.239	.299	.292	27	67	7	16	20	1	0	1	9	4	8	0	0	3
Malave	.235	.382	.257	41	102	12	24	39	3	0	4	17	2	25	0	0	1
Cole	.222	.319	.296	24	72	13	16	23	5	1	0	7	8	11	5	3	1
Hosey	.218	.333	.282	28	78	13	17	26	2	2	1	3	7	17	6	3	1
Cuyler	.200	.300	.299	50	110	19	22	33	1	2	2	12	13	19	7	3	3
Manto	.196	.363	.317	43	102	15	20	37	6	1	3	10	17	24	0	1	5
Hatteberg	.182	.273	.357	10	11	3	2	3	1	0	0	0	3	2	0	0	0
Pirkl	.174	.348	.174	9	23	2	4	8	1	0	1	1	0	4	0	0	0
Pozo	.172	.310	.210	21	58	4	10	18	3	1	1	11	2	10	1	0	4
Tatum	.125	.125	.125	2	8	1	1	1	0	0	0	0	0	2	0	0	0
Clark	.000	.000	.000	3	3	0	0	0	0	0	0	0	0	1	0	0	0
McKeel	---	---	---	1	0	0	0	0	0	0	0	0	0	0	0	0	0

PITCHERS	W-L	ERA	G	GS	CG	GF	Sho	SV	IP	H	R	ER	HR	BB	SO
Slocumb	5-5	3.02	75	0	0	60	0	31	83.1	68	31	28	2	55	88
Lacy	2-0	3.38	11	0	0	3	0	0	10.2	15	5	4	2	8	9
Brandenburg	5-5	3.43	55	0	0	13	0	0	76.0	76	35	29	8	33	66
Clemens	10-13	3.63	34	34	6	0	2	0	242.2	216	106	98	19	106	257
Maddux	3-2	4.48	23	7	0	2	0	0	64.1	76	37	32	12	27	32
Garces	3-2	4.91	37	0	0	9	0	0	44.0	42	26	24	5	33	55
Wakefield	14-13	5.14	32	32	6	0	0	0	211.2	238	151	121	38	90	140
Sele	7-11	5.32	29	29	1	0	0	0	157.1	192	110	93	14	67	137
Hudson	3-5	5.40	36	0	0	16	0	1	45.0	57	35	27	4	32	19
Gordon	12-9	5.59	34	34	4	0	1	0	215.2	249	143	134	28	105	171
Doherty	0-0	5.68	3	0	0	1	0	0	6.1	8	10	4	1	4	3
Belinda	2-1	6.59	31	0	0	10	0	2	28.2	31	22	21	3	20	18
Mahomes	3-4	6.91	31	5	0	10	0	2	57.1	72	46	44	13	33	36
Eshelman	6-3	7.08	39	10	0	1	0	0	87.2	112	79	69	13	58	59
Suppan	1-1	7.54	8	4	0	2	0	0	22.2	29	19	19	3	13	13
Gunderson	0-1	8.31	28	0	0	2	0	0	17.1	21	17	16	5	8	7
Knackert	0-1	9.00	8	0	0	2	0	0	10.0	16	12	10	1	7	5
Harris	0-0	12.46	4	0	0	1	0	0	4.1	7	6	6	2	5	4
Minchey	0-2	15.00	2	2	0	0	0	0	6.0	16	11	10	1	5	4
Grundt	0-0	27.00	1	0	0	0	0	0	0.1	1	1	1	0	0	0

1997 preliminary roster

PITCHERS (18)		CATCHERS (4)	INFIELDERS (11)	OUTFIELDERS (11)
M. Brandenburg	Ron Mahay	Bill Haselman	Wil Cordero	Darren Bragg
Robinson Checo	Rafael Orellano	Scott Hatteberg	Bo Dodson	Jose Canseco
Vaughn Eshelman	Aaron Sele	Walt McKeel	Chris Donnels	Adam Hyzdu
Rich Garces	H.Slocumb	Mike Stanley	Jeff Frye	Reggie Jefferson
Tom Gordon	Jeff Suppan		N. Garciaparra	Shane Mack
Chris Hammond	Rick Trlicek		Roberto Mejia	Jose Malave
Butch Henry	Tim Wakefield		Tim Naehring	Trot Nixon
Joe Hudson			Archimedez Pozo	Troy O'Leary
Kerry Lacy			Tony Rodriguez	Roy Padilla
Mike Maddux			John Valentin	Rudy Pemberton
Pat Mahomes			Mo Vaughn	Jesus Tavarez

Games played by position

PLAYER	G	C	1B	2B	3B	SS	OF	DH
Beltre	27	0	0	8	13	6	0	1
Bragg	127	0	0	0	0	0	121	0
Canseco	96	0	0	0	0	0	11	84
Clark	3	0	1	0	1	0	0	1
Cole	24	0	0	0	0	0	24	0
Cordero	59	0	1	37	0	0	0	13
Cuyler	50	0	0	0	0	0	45	2
Delgado	26	14	1	1	4	0	6	0
Frye	105	0	0	100	0	3	5	1
Garciaparra	24	0	0	1	0	22	0	1
Greenwell	77	0	0	0	0	0	76	0
Haselman	77	69	2	0	0	0	0	2
Hatteberg	10	10	0	0	0	0	0	0
Hosey	28	0	0	0	0	0	26	2
Jefferson	122	0	16	0	0	0	45	49
Malave	41	0	0	0	0	0	38	0
Manto	43	0	1	4	26	4	1	2
McKeel	1	1	0	0	0	0	0	0
Mitchell	27	0	0	0	0	0	21	4
Naehring	116	0	0	1	116	0	0	0
Nixon	2	0	0	0	0	0	2	0
O'Leary	149	0	0	0	0	0	146	0
Pemberton	13	0	0	0	0	0	13	0
Pirkl	9	0	2	0	0	0	0	3
Pozo	21	0	0	10	10	0	0	1
Rodriguez	27	0	0	0	5	21	0	1
Selby	40	0	0	14	14	0	6	1
Stanley	121	105	0	0	0	0	0	10
Tatum	2	0	0	0	2	0	0	0
Tinsley	92	0	0	0	0	0	83	1
Valentin	131	0	0	0	12	118	0	1
Vaughn	161	0	146	0	0	0	0	15

Minor Leagues
Tops in the organization

BATTER	CLUB	AVG.	G	AB	R	H	HR	RBI
Adam Hyzdu	Tre	.337	109	374	71	126	25	80
R. Pemberton	Paw	.326	102	396	77	129	27	92
Phil Clark	Paw	.325	97	369	57	120	12	69
Damian Sapp	Mch	.322	90	335	55	108	18	52
T.R. Lewis	Paw	.314	79	274	55	86	14	52

HOME RUNS
R. Pemberton	Paw	27
Alan Zinter	Paw	26
Adam Hyzdu	Tre	25
Tyrone Woods	Tre	25
Todd Carey	Tre	20

WINS
Carl Pavano	Tre	16
Jim Farrell	Sar	15
Juan Pena	Mch	12
Brian Rose	Tre	12
Several Players Tied at		11

RBI
R. Pemberton	Paw	92
Andy Abad	Tre	80
Adam Hyzdu	Tre	80
Todd Carey	Tre	78
Walt Mckeel	Tre	78

SAVES
Scott Jones	Mch	18
Harris Reggie	Tre	17
Chuck Beale	Low	16
Chuck Ricci	Paw	13
Brent Knackert	Paw	12

STOLEN BASES
Rick Holifield	Tre	36
Donnie Sadler	Tre	34
Aaron Fuller	Paw	33
Roy Padilla	Sar	25
Several Players Tied at		24

STRIKEOUTS
Juan Pena	Mch	156
Carl Pavano	Tre	146
Jeff Suppan	Paw	142
Jim Farrell	Sar	124
Jay Yennaco	Mch	117

PITCHER	CLUB	W-L	ERA	IP	H	BB	SO
Carl Pavano	Tre	16-5	2.63	185	154	47	146
Nate Minchey	Paw	7-4	2.96	97	89	21	61
Juan Pena	Mch	12-10	2.97	188	149	34	156
Jeff Suppan	Paw	10-6	3.22	145	130	25	142
Jim Farrell	Sar	15-9	3.25	177	155	51	124

Sick call: 1996 DL report

PLAYER	Days on the DL
Stan Belinda	113**
Jose Canseco	68*
Wil Cordero	83
Milt Cuyler	109
Vaughn Eshelman	24
Rich Garces	63*
Mike Greenwell	82
Butch Henry	182
Mike Maddux	88
Jose Malave	19
Jeff Manto	32
Nate Minchey	94
Kevin Mitchell	63*
Tim Naehring	18
Aaron Sele	18
Jeff Suppan	36
John Valentin	15

* Indicates two separate terms on Disabled List.
** Indicates three separate terms on Disabled List.

1996 salaries

	Bonuses	Total earned salary
Roger Clemens, p		$5,500,000
Mo Vaughn, 1b	$50,000	$5,400,000
Jose Canseco, of	$225,000	$4,725,000
Mike Greenwell, of		$3,700,000
Tom Gordon, p	$150,000	$3,050,000
John Valentin, ss		$2,672,500
Mike Stanley, c		$2,300,000
Wil Cordero, 2b		$1,850,000
Heathcliff Slocumb, p	$25,000	$1,425,000
Stan Belinda, p		$1,275,000
Tim Naehring, 3b		$1,200,000
Reggie Jefferson, 1b	$125,000	$695,000
Mike Maddux, p		$600,000
Tim Wakefield, p		$450,000
Butch Henry, p		$400,000
Aaron Sele, p	$65,000	$380,000
Bill Haselman, c	$10,000	$310,000
Milt Cuyler, of	$40,000	$242,500
Troy O'Leary, of		$240,000
Lee Tinsley, of		$225,000
Pat Mahomes, p		$202,500
Jeff Manto, 3b		$200,000
Vaughn Eshelman, p		$140,000
Rich Garces, p		$132,500
Darren Bragg, of	$15,000	$130,000
Nate Minchey, p		$130,000
Jeff Frye, 2b		$125,000
Mark Brandenburg, p	$5,000	$123,500
Jeff Suppan, p		$117,000
Reggie Harris, p		$112,000
Nomar Garciaparra, ss		$109,000
Kerry Lacy, p		$109,000

Average 1996 salary: $1,195,953
Total 1996 team payroll: $38,270,500
Termination pay: $245,902

Boston (1901-1996)

Runs: Most, career

1816	Carl Yastrzemski, 1961-1983
1798	Ted Williams, 1939-1960
1435	Dwight Evans, 1972-1990
1249	Jim Rice, 1974-1989
1094	Bobby Doerr, 1937-1951

Hits: Most, career

3419	Carl Yastrzemski, 1961-1983
2654	Ted Williams, 1939-1960
2452	Jim Rice, 1974-1989
2373	Dwight Evans, 1972-1990
2098	WADE BOGGS, 1982-1992

2B: Most, career

646	Carl Yastrzemski, 1961-1983
525	Ted Williams, 1939-1960
474	Dwight Evans, 1972-1990
422	WADE BOGGS, 1982-1992
381	Bobby Doerr, 1937-1951

3B: Most, career

130	Harry Hooper, 1909-1920
106	Tris Speaker, 1907-1915
90	Buck Freeman, 1901-1907
89	Bobby Doerr, 1937-1951
87	Larry Gardner, 1908-1917

HR: Most, career

521	Ted Williams, 1939-1960
452	Carl Yastrzemski, 1961-1983
382	Jim Rice, 1974-1989
379	Dwight Evans, 1972-1990
223	Bobby Doerr, 1937-1951

RBI: Most, career

1844	Carl Yastrzemski, 1961-1983
1839	Ted Williams, 1939-1960
1451	Jim Rice, 1974-1989
1346	Dwight Evans, 1972-1990
1247	Bobby Doerr, 1937-1951

SB: Most, career

300	Harry Hooper, 1909-1920
267	Tris Speaker, 1907-1915
168	Carl Yastrzemski, 1961-1983
141	Heinie Wagner, 1906-1918
134	Larry Gardner, 1908-1917

BB: Most, career

2019	Ted Williams, 1939-1960
1845	Carl Yastrzemski, 1961-1983
1337	Dwight Evans, 1972-1990
1004	WADE BOGGS, 1982-1992
826	Harry Hooper, 1909-1920

BA: Highest, career

.344	Ted Williams, 1939-1960
.338	WADE BOGGS, 1982-1992
.337	Tris Speaker, 1907-1915
.320	Pete Runnels, 1958-1962
.320	Jimmie Foxx, 1936-1942

Slug avg: Highest, career, all-time

.634	Ted Williams, 1939-1960
.605	Jimmie Foxx, 1936-1942
.527	MO VAUGHN, 1991-1996
.520	Fred Lynn, 1974-1980
.502	Jim Rice, 1974-1989

On-base avg: Highest, career

.482	Ted Williams, 1939-1960
.429	Jimmie Foxx, 1936-1942
.428	WADE BOGGS, 1982-1992
.414	Tris Speaker, 1907-1915
.408	Pete Runnels, 1958-1962

Complete games: Most

275	Cy Young, 1901-1908
156	Bill Dinneen, 1902-1907
141	George Winter, 1901-1908
121	Joe Wood, 1908-1915
119	Lefty Grove, 1934-1941

Saves: Most, career

132	Bob Stanley, 1977-1989
104	Dick Radatz, 1962-1966
91	Ellis Kinder, 1948-1955
88	Jeff Reardon, 1990-1992
69	Sparky Lyle, 1967-1971

Shutouts: Most, career

38	ROGER CLEMENS, 1984-1996
38	Cy Young, 1901-1908
28	Joe Wood, 1908-1915
26	Luis Tiant, 1971-1978
25	Dutch Leonard, 1913-1918

Wins: Most, career

192	R. CLEMENS, 1984-1996
192	Cy Young, 1901-1908
123	Mel Parnell, 1947-1956
122	Luis Tiant, 1971-1978
116	Joe Wood, 1908-1915

K: Most, career

2590	R. CLEMENS, 1984-1996
1341	Cy Young, 1901-1908
1075	Luis Tiant, 1971-1978
1043	Bruce Hurst, 1980-1988
986	Joe Wood, 1908-1915

Win pct: Highest, career,

.695	Roger Moret, 1970-1975
.684	Dave Ferriss, 1945-1950
.674	Joe Wood, 1908-1915
.659	Babe Ruth, 1914-1919
.640	Tex Hughson, 1941-1949

ERA: Lowest, career

1.99	Joe Wood, 1908-1915
2.00	Cy Young, 1901-1908
2.12	Ernie Shore, 1914-1917
2.13	Dutch Leonard, 1913-1918
2.19	Babe Ruth, 1914-1919

Runs: Most, season

150	Ted Williams, 1949
142	Ted Williams, 1946
141	Ted Williams, 1942
139	Jimmie Foxx, 1938
136	Tris Speaker, 1912

Hits: Most, season

240	WADE BOGGS, 1985
222	Tris Speaker, 1912
214	WADE BOGGS, 1988
213	Jim Rice, 1978
210	WADE BOGGS, 1983

2B: Most, season

67	Earl Webb, 1931
53	Tris Speaker, 1912
51	WADE BOGGS, 1989
51	Joe Cronin, 1938
47	WADE BOGGS, 1986
47	George Burns, 1923
47	Fred Lynn, 1975

3B: Most, season

22	Tris Speaker, 1913
20	Buck Freeman, 1903
19	Buck Freeman, 1902
19	Buck Freeman, 1904
19	Larry Gardner, 1914
19	Chick Stahl, 1904

HR: Most, season

50	Jimmie Foxx, 1938
46	Jim Rice, 1978
44	MO VAUGHN, 1996
44	Carl Yastrzemski, 1967
43	Tony Armas, 1984
43	Ted Williams, 1949

RBI: Most, season

175	Jimmie Foxx, 1938
159	Vern Stephens, 1949
159	Ted Williams, 1949

145 Ted Williams, 1939
144 Walt Dropo, 1950
144 Vern Stephens, 1950

SB: Most, season

54 Tommy Harper, 1973
52 Tris Speaker, 1912
46 Tris Speaker, 1913
42 OTIS NIXON, 1994
42 Tris Speaker, 1914

BB: Most, season

162 Ted Williams, 1947
162 Ted Williams, 1949
156 Ted Williams, 1946
145 Ted Williams, 1941
145 Ted Williams, 1942

BA: Highest, season

.406 Ted Williams, 1941
.388 Ted Williams, 1957
.383 Tris Speaker, 1912
.369 Ted Williams, 1948
.368 WADE BOGGS, 1985

Slug avg: Highest, season

.735 Ted Williams, 1941
.731 Ted Williams, 1957
.704 Jimmie Foxx, 1938
.694 Jimmie Foxx, 1939
.667 Ted Williams, 1946

On-base avg: Highest, season

.551 Ted Williams, 1941
.526 Ted Williams, 1957
.513 Ted Williams, 1954
.499 Ted Williams, 1942
.499 Ted Williams, 1947

Complete games: Most, season

41 Cy Young, 1902
40 Cy Young, 1904
39 Bill Dinneen, 1902
38 Cy Young, 1901
37 Bill Dinneen, 1904

Saves: Most, season

40 Jeff Reardon, 1991
33 JEFF RUSSELL, 1993
33 Bob Stanley, 1983
31 Bill Campbell, 1977
31 HEATHCLIFF SLOCUMB, 1996

Shutouts: Most, season

10 Joe Wood, 1912
10 Cy Young, 1904
9 Babe Ruth, 1916
8 ROGER CLEMENS, 1988
8 Carl Mays, 1918

Wins: Most, season

34 Joe Wood, 1912
33 Cy Young, 1901
32 Cy Young, 1902
28 Cy Young, 1903
26 Cy Young, 1904

K: Most, season

291 ROGER CLEMENS, 1988
258 Joe Wood, 1912
257 ROGER CLEMENS, 1996
256 ROGER CLEMENS, 1987
246 Jim Lonborg, 1967

Win pct: Highest, season

.882 Bob Stanley, 1978
.872 Joe Wood, 1912
.857 ROGER CLEMENS, 1986
.806 Dave Ferriss, 1946
.793 Ellis Kinder, 1949

ERA: Lowest, season

0.96 Dutch Leonard, 1914
1.26 Cy Young, 1908
1.49 Joe Wood, 1915
1.62 Ray Collins, 1910
1.62 Cy Young, 1901

Most pinch-hit homers, season

5 Joe Cronin, 1943
4 Del Wilber, 1953

Most pinch-hit homers, career

7 Ted Williams, 1939-1960
5 Joe Cronin, 1935-1945

Longest hitting streak

34 Dom DiMaggio, 1949
30 Tris Speaker, 1912
28 WADE BOGGS, 1985
27 Dom DiMaggio, 1951
26 Buck Freeman, 1902
26 Johnny Pesky, 1947

Most consecutive scoreless innings

45 Cy Young, 1904
42 Rube Foster, 1914
40 Luis Tiant, 1972
39 Ray Culp, 1968
37 Cy Young, 1903

No-hit games

Cy Young, Bos vs Phi AL, 3-0; May 5, 1904 (perfect game).
Jesse Tannehill, Bos at Chi AL, 6-0; Aug. 17, 1904.
Bill Dinneen, Bos vs Chi AL, 2-0; Sept. 27, 1905 (1st game).
Cy Young, Bos at NY AL, 8-0; June 30, 1908.

Joe Wood, Bos vs StL AL, 5-0; July 29, 1911 (1st game).
Rube Foster, Bos vs NY AL, 2-0; June 21, 1916.
Hubert (Dutch) Leonard, Bos vs StL AL, 4-0; Aug. 30, 1916.
Ernie Shore, Bos vs Was AL, 4-0; June 23, 1917. (1st game, perfect game. Shore relieved Babe Ruth in the first inning after Ruth had been thrown out of the game for protesting a walk to the first batter. The runner was caught stealing and Shore retired the remaining 26 batters in order.)
Hubert (Dutch) Leonard, Bos at Det AL, 5-0; June 3, 1918.
Howard Ehmke, Bos at Phi AL, 4-0; Sept. 7, 1923.
Mel Parnell, Bos vs Chi AL, 4-0; July 14, 1956.
Earl Wilson, Bos vs LA AL, 2-0; June 26, 1962.
Bill Monbouquette, Bos at Chi AL, 1-0; Aug. 1, 1962.
Dave Morehead, Bos vs Cle AL, 2-0; Sept. 16, 1965.
Matt Young, Bos at Cle AL, 1-2; Apr. 12, 1992 (1st game; 8 innings, lost the game, bottom of 9th not played).

ACTIVE PLAYERS in caps.

Players' years of service are listed by the first and last years with this team and are not necessarily consecutive; all statistics record performances for this team only.

Toronto Blue Jays

Pat Hentgen became the first Toronto pitcher to win the Cy Young Award.

By Russell Beeker, USA TODAY

1996 Blue Jays: Good arms not enough

The Blue Jays' 1996 season, after a .389 winning percentage and dead-last finish the year before, could be summed up in one word: improvement. Toronto got better despite losing Paul Molitor, Al Leiter, Devon White and Robbie Alomar to free agency. Still, the group that finished 74-88 (.457) had almost as many unanswered questions at the end of the season as it had at the start.

The Jays began the season with serious concerns about their pitching but ended with the best second-half ERA in the league. In '95, Pat Hengten had stumbled (10-14, 5.14 ERA) while Juan Guzman downright fell down (4-14, 6.32). But in '96, Guzman won the ERA title (2.93) and Hengten got the Cy Young Award. The latter won 20 games with a 3.22 ERA, led the league with 265⅔ innings pitched and 10 complete games, and was tied for first with three shutouts.

In the bullpen Tim Crabtree arrived as a setup man, with a team-low 2.54 ERA, and Mike Timlin converted 31 of 38 save opportunities. Timlin's season was a drastic improvement on the closer situation in '95, when Jays relievers converted 22 of 40 saves. Lefty Paul Spoljaric showed he belongs, with a 3.08 ERA. Looking ahead, Crabtree said, "Guys are going to have to show they can do the job or they'll be replaced by someone who can."

He could have been referring to some of the Jays' pitchers from last season. Right-hander Marty Janzen started off 4-0, wound up at Class AAA Syracuse and was roughed up in his only September start. Jeff Ware started in the rotation but didn't last; ditto Paul Quantrill. The Blue Jays' best pitching prospects, Chris Carpenter and Jose Pett, remain a year away.

But the Jays had most of their trouble when they were at the plate. Toronto was 13th in the AL in runs scored per game, ahead of only Detroit. The biggest disappointment was first baseman John Olerud, the 1993 batting champion. He

finished at .273 with 18 homers and 61 RBI, the latter only the fifth-highest total on the team behind Joe Carter, Ed Sprague, Carlos Delgado and Alex Gonzalez. Olerud went from cleanup hitter to $6.5 million part-time player and did not hit a home run in his final 23 games. He had only 398 at-bats, though aside from a back problem that cost him a few games, he wasn't out with any injuries.

Shawn Green had a second straight poor first half but rebounded after the All-Star break. Second baseman Tomas Perez, who finally won the job over a cast of five, can make great plays like Robbie Alomar. It's the routine ones that give the youngster trouble, and he's light-years away from having a bat like Alomar's.

Third baseman Sprague had his best year (36 HR, 101 RBI), Carter added 30 homers and led the team with 107 RBI, Delgado hit the ball well enough to avoid being sent down to Syracuse, and shortstop Gonzalez won over manager Cito Gaston with his defense and his bat, but last season's Jays had a better record than only the Tigers and the Angels in the AL.

1996 Blue Jays: Week-by-week notes

These notes were excerpted from the following issues of Baseball Weekly.

▸**April 10:** Manager Cito Gaston hit the 1,000-game mark in Cleveland as Juan Guzman resembled the Juan Guzman of old, handcuffing the Indians in a lopsided victory, Gaston's 538th.

▸**April 17:** SkyDome sign: "No Alomar, No Molitor, No Fans." The Jays had their smallest crowd ever at SkyDome for their second game of the season against the Angels: 25,446, barely above their season-ticket base of 22,000.

▸**April 24:** With two out in the eighth and a 3-1 lead, Cito Gaston went to the mound on April 20 to take out Juan Guzman. "I said 'I feel fine, let me finish it,'" Guzman said. He then got Ken Griffey Jr., who had homered in the first, to ground out.

▸**May 8:** Designated hitter Carlos Delgado was moved into the No. 3 spot, taking over for sputtering first baseman John Olerud. Delgado, 23, responded by batting .333 (23-for-69) with five homers and 19 RBI. In 24 starts last season, Juan Guzman had four wins. This season, a healthy Guzman won four of his first six starts. He had a 1.88 ERA while pitching a pair of complete games. In his first six starts, his shortest outing was eight innings.

▸**May 15:** Cito Gaston had seen plenty of strange plays in his years in baseball, but none stranger than on May 8 in Arlington. Shortstop Alex Gonzalez was on first. Center fielder Otis Nixon was the hitter. Gonzalez was off and running. Catching ball four, Ivan Rodriguez threw out Gonzalez at second. Hold on! Gonzalez is entitled to the base. Problem was, he bounced off the back end and second base ump Durwood Merrill called him out a second time when Mark McLemore alertly applied the tag.

▸**May 29:** The Jays were 3-6 on their road trip despite having a 2.55 ERA. They hit a combined .221 and scored 25 runs in the nine games.

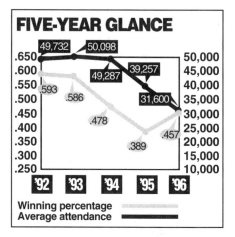

FIVE-YEAR GLANCE

Winning percentage
Average attendance

▸**June 12:** It was a rough week for left-hander Frank Viola, who knocked Cito Gaston in print for being "too laid-back to manage a young team," then was released. In six starts, Viola, 36, was 1-3 and had a 7.71 ERA.

▸**June 19:** The sun might always shine in California, but not for the Blue Jays. They blew sizable leads in losing the first three games of their series against California.

▸**July 3:** Second baseman Domingo Cedeno is no replacement for Roberto Alomar. Here's an example: Otis Nixon was on second and Cedeno was at first when Nixon took off for third. Nixon was safe, but Cedeno was thrown out on the back end of the attempted double steal. "He's supposed to follow if I don't have a hold on him," Cito Gaston said, but "if you don't have a good jump, you're not supposed to steal."

▸**July 11:** Left fielder Joe Carter, whose home run won the World Series for the Blue Jays three years ago, reached a milestone on July 6 with his 20th homer of 1996, the 11th consecutive season in which he reached that mark.

▸**July 17:** The Jays began the second half of the schedule with a 38-49 record, one less win than after the same number of games last season. It's not that big a difference for a team that's minus Paul Molitor, Roberto Alomar, Al Leiter and Devon White.

▶**July 24:** Juan Guzman's complete-game shutout on July 16 in Baltimore was only the second of his major league career. The AL ERA leader, who is bidding for Comeback Player of the Year honors after going 4-14 last season, allowed the Orioles only five hits.

▶**July 31:** The Jays granted Joe Carter and Cito Gaston one-year extensions. Carter will earn the same amount he earns this season: $6.5 million.

▶**Aug. 14:** The Blue Jays dropped six of seven and were swept by their season-long nemesis, Texas, on Aug. 9-11. The Rangers are 8-1 against Toronto this year. In getting shut out by John Burkett, the Rangers' newest pitcher, on Aug. 11, the Jays' first five strikeout victims were all caught looking.

▶**Aug. 28:** Otis Nixon had seen plenty of slumping teams during his 12-year career, so he called a team meeting in Minnesota. The Jays then won the final game of the Twins series, swept three in Kansas City for the first time since 1986 and won the first three in Chicago for a seven-game winning streak.

▶**Sept. 11:** Juan Guzman's successful comeback season ended in an emergency trip to the operating room in New York on the morning of Sept. 7. He underwent an appendectomy and will miss the rest of the season. Guzman went 11-8 and leads the AL with a 2.93 ERA. He pitched 187⅔ innings, enough to make him eligible for ERA honors.

▶**Sept. 18:** Third baseman Ed Sprague has 34 homers. Only three Jays have hit more: George Bell, 47, in 1987; Jesse Barfield, 40, in 1986; and Fred McGriff, 36, in 1989.

▶**Sept. 25:** On Sept. 21, Woody Williams pitched five hitless innings against the Orioles before Chris Hoiles led off the sixth with a slow roller to third. Ed Sprague fielded the ball but had trouble hauling it from his glove, allowing Hoiles to beat the throw. It was ruled a hit, and after that, the strike zone was only a memory for Jays pitchers. With the bases loaded, two out and a 2-0 count on Bobby Bonilla, Cito Gaston went to reliever Scott Brow, who walked Bonilla

and Cal Ripken to tie the score. He then served up a grand slam to Eddie Murray. Two hits. Six runs.

▶**Oct. 2:** The Blue Jays had nowhere to go but up, after last year's dead-last finish with 56 wins and a .389 win percentage. They passed California and Detroit in the wins column, with a 74-88 (.457) record. Not exactly a giant leap for mankind, but the improvements came despite the loss of four key players to free agency. When the curtain came down, Juan Guzman had won the ERA title and Pat Hentgen was worthy of the Cy Young, leading the Yankees' Andy Pettitte in every category but wins. Joe Carter was his old self and Ed Sprague had a career year, but the pitching, catching and offense remain problematical. Next season the Jays must reach a more competitive stage before they can think of contending.

Team directory

▶**Owners:** Inter-Brew S.A. (Canadian Imperial Bank of Commerce owns 10%)

▶**General manager:** Gord Ash

▶**Ballpark:**
SkyDome
Toronto, Ontario
416-341-1000
Capacity 51,000
Public transportation available
Family and wheelchair sections, no-alcohol sections, ramps, Playland

▶**Team publications:**
Scorebook Magazine (Buzz Communications), 416-961-3319

▶**TV, radio broadcast stations:**
TSN and Baton Broadcasting,
FAN 590, CBCTV

▶**Spring training:**
Dunedin Stadium at Grant Field
311 Douglas Ave.
Dunedin, Fla.
Capacity 6,218
813-733-9302

TORONTO BLUE JAYS 1996 final stats

BATTERS	BA	SLG	OB	G	AB	R	H	TB	2B	3B	HR	RBI	BB	SO	SB	CS	E
R. Perez	.327	.406	.354	86	202	30	66	82	10	0	2	21	8	17	3	0	2
Nixon	.286	.327	.377	125	496	87	142	162	15	1	1	29	71	68	54	13	2
Green	.280	.448	.342	132	422	52	118	189	32	3	11	45	33	75	5	1	2
Olerud	.274	.472	.382	125	398	59	109	188	25	0	18	61	60	37	1	0	2
Delgado	.270	.490	.353	138	488	68	132	239	28	2	25	92	58	139	0	0	4
Brumfield	.256	.448	.316	90	308	52	79	138	19	2	12	52	24	58	12	3	3
Samuel	.255	.457	.319	69	188	34	48	86	8	3	8	26	15	65	9	1	2
Carter	.253	.475	.306	157	625	84	158	297	35	7	30	107	44	106	7	6	9
T. Perez	.251	.332	.311	91	295	24	74	98	13	4	1	19	25	29	1	2	15
Sprague	.247	.496	.325	159	591	88	146	293	35	2	36	101	60	146	0	0	15
O'Brien	.238	.410	.331	109	324	33	77	133	17	0	13	44	29	68	0	1	3
Brito	.238	.363	.344	26	80	10	19	29	7	0	1	7	10	18	1	1	4
Gonzalez	.235	.391	.300	147	527	64	124	206	30	5	14	64	45	127	16	6	21
Mosquera	.227	.318	.261	8	22	2	5	7	2	0	0	2	0	3	0	1	0
Martinez	.227	.332	.288	76	229	17	52	76	9	3	3	18	16	58	0	0	3
Cairo	.222	.296	.300	9	27	5	6	8	2	0	0	1	2	9	0	0	0
Crespo	.184	.265	.375	22	49	6	9	13	4	0	0	4	12	13	1	0	1
Stewart	.176	.235	.222	7	17	2	3	4	1	0	0	2	1	4	1	0	1
Huff	.172	.241	.200	11	29	5	5	7	0	1	0	0	1	5	0	0	0

PITCHERS	W-L	ERA	G	GS	CG	GF	Sho	SV	IP	H	R	ER	HR	BB	SO
Crabtree	5-3	2.54	53	0	0	21	0	1	67.1	59	26	19	4	22	57
Guzman	11-8	2.93	27	27	4	0	1	0	187.2	158	68	61	20	53	165
Johnson	0-0	3.00	10	0	0	2	0	0	9.0	5	3	3	0	5	7
Spoljaric	2-2	3.08	28	0	0	12	0	1	38.0	30	17	13	6	19	38
Hentgen	20-10	3.22	35	35	10	0	3	0	265.2	238	105	95	20	94	177
Timlin	1-6	3.65	59	0	0	56	0	31	56.2	47	25	23	4	18	52
Risley	0-1	3.89	25	0	0	11	0	0	41.2	33	20	18	7	25	29
Flener	3-2	4.58	15	11	0	0	0	0	70.2	68	40	36	9	33	44
Williams	4-5	4.73	12	10	1	0	0	0	59.0	64	33	31	8	21	43
Hanson	13-17	5.41	35	35	4	0	1	0	214.2	243	143	129	26	102	156
Quantrill	5-14	5.43	38	20	0	7	0	0	134.1	172	90	81	27	51	86
Brow	1-0	5.59	18	1	0	9	0	0	38.2	45	25	24	5	25	23
Andujar	1-3	6.99	8	7	0	0	0	0	37.1	46	30	29	8	16	11
Janzen	4-6	7.33	15	11	0	3	0	0	73.2	95	65	60	16	38	47
Viola	1-3	7.71	6	6	0	0	0	0	30.1	43	28	26	6	21	18
Bohanon	0-1	7.77	20	0	0	6	0	1	22.0	27	19	19	4	19	17
Ware	1-5	9.09	13	4	0	6	0	0	32.2	35	34	33	6	31	11
Carrara	0-1	11.40	11	0	0	3	0	0	15.0	23	19	19	5	12	10
Silva	0-0	13.50	2	0	0	0	0	0	2.0	5	3	3	1	0	0

1997 preliminary roster

PITCHERS (18)
Luis Andujar
Roger Clemens
Tim Crabtree
Kelvim Escobar
Huck Flener
Juan Guzman
Erik Hanson
Pat Hentgen
Marty Janzen
Robert Person
Dan Plesac
Paul Quantrill
Bill Risley
Mark Sievert
Paul Spoljaric
Mike Timlin
Woody Williams
Joe Young

CATCHERS (4)
Sandy Martinez
Julio Mosquera
Charlie O'Brien
Benito Santiago

INFIELDERS (10)
Tilson Brito
Felipe Crespo
Carlos Delgado
Tom Evans
Carlos Garcia
Alex Gonzalez
Ryan Jones
Jeff Patzke
Tomas Perez
Ed Sprague

OUTFIELDERS (8)
Jacob Brumfield
Joe Carter
Shawn Green
Orlando Merced
Otis Nixon
Robert Perez
Anthony Sanders
Shannon Stewart

Games played by position

PLAYER	G	C	1B	2B	3B	SS	OF	DH
Brito	26	0	0	18	0	5	0	2
Brumfield	90	0	0	0	0	0	83	5
Cairo	9	0	0	9	0	0	0	0
Carter	157	0	41	0	0	0	115	15
Crespo	22	0	2	10	6	0	0	0
Delgado	138	0	27	0	0	0	0	108
Gonzalez	147	0	0	0	0	147	0	0
Green	132	0	0	0	0	0	127	1
Huff	11	0	0	0	3	0	9	0
Martinez	76	75	0	0	0	0	0	0
Mosquera	8	8	0	0	0	0	0	0
Nixon	125	0	0	0	0	0	125	0
O'Brien	109	105	0	0	0	0	0	0
Olerud	125	0	101	0	0	0	0	15
R. Perez	86	0	0	0	0	0	79	2
T. Perez	91	0	0	75	11	5	0	0
Samuel	69	0	17	0	0	0	24	24
Sprague	159	0	0	0	148	0	0	10
Stewart	7	0	0	0	0	0	6	0

Minor Leagues

Tops in the organization

BATTER	CLUB	AVG.	G	AB	R	H	HR	RBI
Jeff Patzke	Knx	.303	124	429	70	130	4	66
S. Stewart	Syr	.298	112	420	77	125	6	42
Felipe Crespo	Syr	.285	107	389	56	111	10	64
Craig Stone	Dun	.285	117	428	62	122	14	57
A. Thompson	Dun	.282	129	425	64	120	11	50

HOME RUNS

Rickey Cradle	Syr	20
Mike Whitlock	Hag	20
Ryan Jones	Knx	20
Several Players Tied At		18

WINS

Roy Halladay	Dun	15
Mike Halperin	Knx	13
Kelvim Escobar	Knx	12
Mike Johnson	Hag	11
Mark Sievert	Syr	11

RBI

Ryan Jones	Knx	97
Mike Whitlock	Hag	91
L. Delacruz	Knx	79
Chris Weinke	Syr	73
Vic Davila	Dun	72

SAVES

Dane Johnson	Syr	22
James Mann	Stc	17
Brian Smith	Knx	16
David Bleazard	Mht	10
John Crowther	Hag	10

STOLEN BASES

Abraham Nunez	Stc	37
Fausto Solano	Hag	35
S. Stewart	Syr	35
Randy Albaral	Mht	33
Scott Pose	Syr	30

STRIKEOUTS

Joe Young	Dun	193
Kelvim Escobar	Knx	157
Mike Johnson	Hag	155
Chris Carpenter	Knx	150
Roberto Duran	Knx	128

PITCHER	CLUB	W-L	ERA	IP	H	BB	SO
Chris McBride	Hag	8-3	2.04	102	79	16	62
Clint Lawrence	Hag	7-2	2.30	94	79	21	52
Roy Halladay	Dun	15-7	2.73	165	158	46	109
Mike Johnson	Hag	11-8	3.15	163	157	39	155
Mike Gordon	Dun	3-12	3.44	133	127	64	102

Sick call: 1996 DL report

PLAYER	Days on the DL
Tim Crabtree	21
Felipe Crespo	22
Juan Guzman	15
Sandy Martinez	15
Otis Nixon	15
Bill Risley	67*
Juan Samuel	15
Paul Spoljaric	24
Woody Williams	109*

Indicates two separate terms on Disabled List.

1996 salaries

	Bonuses	Total earned salary
Joe Carter, of	$25,000	$6,525,000
John Olerud, 1b		$6,500,000
Pat Hentgen, p	$100,000	$2,350,000
Erik Hanson, p		$2,333,333
Juan Guzman, p		$2,240,000
Otis Nixon, of		$1,900,000
Ed Sprague, 3b		$1,450,000
Paul Quantrill, p		$775,000
Michael Timlin, p		$635,000
Charlie O'Brien, c		$500,000
Jacob Brumfield, of		$350,000
Juan Samuel, 2b		$325,000
Shawn Green, of		$287,500
Bill Risley, p		$235,000
Alex Gonzalez, ss		$232,875
Woody Williams, p		$225,000
Carlos Delgado, 1b		$165,000
Sandy Martinez, c		$165,000
Tomas Perez, ss		$140,000
Tim Crabtree, p		$133,000
Dane Johnson, p		$125,000
Scott Brow, p		$115,000
Robert Perez, of		$114,500
Paul Spoljaric, p		$112,500
Tilson Brito, ss		$109,000
Huck Flener, p		$109,000
Julio Mosquera, c		$109,000

Average 1996 salary: $1,046,693
Total 1996 team payroll: $28,260,708
Termination pay: $517,869

Toronto (1977-1996)

Runs: Most, career

768	Lloyd Moseby, 1980-1989
641	George Bell, 1981-1990
555	Tony Fernandez, 1983-1993
538	Willie Upshaw, 1978-1987
530	Jesse Barfield, 1981-1989

Hits: Most, career

1319	Lloyd Moseby, 1980-1989
1294	George Bell, 1981-1990
1250	Tony Fernandez, 1983-1993
1028	Damaso Garcia, 1980-1986
982	Willie Upshaw, 1978-1987

2B: Most, career

242	Lloyd Moseby, 1980-1989
237	George Bell, 1981-1990
213	JOHN OLERUD, 1989-1996
210	Tony Fernandez, 1983-1993
204	Rance Mulliniks, 1982-1992

3B: Most, career

70	Tony Fernandez, 1983-1993
60	Lloyd Moseby, 1980-1989
50	Alfredo Griffin, 1979-1993
42	Willie Upshaw, 1978-1987
36	ROBERTO ALOMAR, 1991-1995

HR: Most, career

202	George Bell, 1981-1990
182	JOE CARTER, 1991-1996
179	Jesse Barfield, 1981-1989
149	Lloyd Moseby, 1980-1989
131	Ernie Whitt, 1977-1989

RBI: Most, career

740	George Bell, 1981-1990
651	Lloyd Moseby, 1980-1989
634	JOE CARTER, 1991-1996
527	Jesse Barfield, 1981-1989
518	Ernie Whitt, 1977-1989

SB: Most, career

255	Lloyd Moseby, 1980-1989
206	ROBERTO ALOMAR, 1991-1995
194	Damaso Garcia, 1980-1986
153	Tony Fernandez, 1983-1993
126	DEVON WHITE, 1991-1995

BB: Most, career

547	Lloyd Moseby, 1980-1989
514	JOHN OLERUD, 1989-1996
416	Rance Mulliniks, 1982-1992
403	Ernie Whitt, 1977-1989
390	Willie Upshaw, 1978-1987

BA: Highest, career

.307	ROBERTO ALOMAR, 1991-1995
.293	JOHN OLERUD, 1989-1996
.290	Tony Fernandez, 1983-1993
.288	Damaso Garcia, 1980-1986
.286	George Bell, 1981-1990

Slug avg: Highest, career

.530	FRED McGRIFF, 1986-1990
.486	George Bell, 1981-1990
.486	JOE CARTER, 1991-1996
.483	Jesse Barfield, 1981-1989
.471	JOHN OLERUD, 1989-1996

On-base avg: Highest, career

.395	JOHN OLERUD, 1989-1996
.389	FRED McGRIFF, 1986-1990
.382	ROBERTO ALOMAR, 1991-1995
.372	Otto Velez, 1977-1982
.365	Rance Mulliniks, 1982-1992

Complete games: Most, career

103	Dave Stieb, 1979-1992
73	Jim Clancy, 1977-1988
28	JIMMY KEY, 1984-1992
27	Luis Leal, 1980-1985
25	Doyle Alexander, 1983-1986
25	Dave Lemanczyk, 1977-1980

Saves: Most, career

217	Tom Henke, 1985-1992
121	Duane Ward, 1986-1995
43	MIKE TIMLIN, 1991-1996
31	Joey McLaughlin, 1980-1984
30	Roy Lee Jackson, 1981-1984

Shutouts: Most, career

30	Dave Stieb, 1979-1992
11	Jim Clancy, 1977-1988
10	JIMMY KEY, 1984-1992
6	PAT HENTGEN, 1991-1996
4	Jesse Jefferson, 1977-1980
4	TODD STOTTLEMYRE, 1988-1994

Wins: Most, career

174	Dave Stieb, 1979-1992
128	Jim Clancy, 1977-1988
116	JIMMY KEY, 1984-1992
69	TODD STOTTLEMYRE, 1988-1994
67	JUAN GUZMAN, 1991-1996
67	PAT HENTGEN, 1991-1996

K: Most, career

1631	Dave Stieb, 1979-1992
1237	Jim Clancy, 1977-1988
944	JIMMY KEY, 1984-1992
865	JUAN GUZMAN, 1991-1996
671	Duane Ward, 1986-1995

Win pct: Highest, career

.639	Doyle Alexander, 1983-1986
.609	PAT HENTGEN, 1991-1996
.604	JUAN GUZMAN, 1991-1996
.589	JIMMY KEY, 1984-1992
.569	Dave Stieb, 1979-1992

ERA: Lowest, career

3.39	Dave Stieb, 1979-1992
3.42	JIMMY KEY, 1984-1992
3.56	Doyle Alexander, 1983-1986
3.87	John Cerutti, 1985-1990
3.93	PAT HENTGEN, 1991-1996

Runs: Most, season

121	PAUL MOLITOR, 1993
116	DEVON WHITE, 1993
111	George Bell, 1987
110	DEVON WHITE, 1991
109	ROBERTO ALOMAR, 1993
109	JOHN OLERUD, 1993

Hits: Most, season

213	Tony Fernandez, 1986
211	PAUL MOLITOR, 1993
200	JOHN OLERUD, 1993
198	George Bell, 1986
192	ROBERTO ALOMAR, 1993

2B: Most, season

54	JOHN OLERUD, 1993
42	JOE CARTER, 1991
42	DEVON WHITE, 1993
41	ROBERTO ALOMAR, 1991
41	George Bell, 1989
41	Tony Fernandez, 1988

3B: Most, season

17	Tony Fernandez, 1990
15	Dave Collins, 1984
15	Alfredo Griffin, 1980
15	Lloyd Moseby, 1984
11	ROBERTO ALOMAR, 1991

HR: Most, season

47	George Bell, 1987
40	Jesse Barfield, 1986
36	FRED McGRIFF, 1989
36	ED SPRAGUE, 1996
35	FRED McGRIFF, 1990

RBI: Most, season

134	George Bell, 1987
121	JOE CARTER, 1993
119	JOE CARTER, 1992
118	Kelly Gruber, 1990
111	PAUL MOLITOR, 1993

SB: Most, season

60	Dave Collins, 1984
55	ROBERTO ALOMAR, 1993
54	Damaso Garcia, 1982
54	OTIS NIXON, 1996
53	ROBERTO ALOMAR, 1991

BB: Most, season

119	FRED McGRIFF, 1989
114	JOHN OLERUD, 1993
94	FRED McGRIFF, 1990
87	ROBERTO ALOMAR, 1992
84	JOHN OLERUD, 1995

BA: Highest, season

.363	JOHN OLERUD, 1993
.341	PAUL MOLITOR, 1994
.332	PAUL MOLITOR, 1993
.326	ROBERTO ALOMAR, 1993
.322	Tony Fernandez, 1987

Slug avg: Highest, season

.605	George Bell, 1987
.599	JOHN OLERUD, 1993
.559	Jesse Barfield, 1986
.552	FRED McGRIFF, 1988
.536	Jesse Barfield, 1985

On-base avg: Highest, season

.473	JOHN OLERUD, 1993
.410	PAUL MOLITOR, 1994
.408	ROBERTO ALOMAR, 1993
.405	ROBERTO ALOMAR, 1992
.402	PAUL MOLITOR, 1993

Complete games: Most, season

19	Dave Stieb, 1982
15	Jim Clancy, 1980
14	Dave Stieb, 1980
14	Dave Stieb, 1983
12	Jerry Garvin, 1977
12	Tom Underwood, 1979

Saves: Most, season

45	Duane Ward, 1993
34	Tom Henke, 1987
34	Tom Henke, 1992
32	Tom Henke, 1990
32	Tom Henke, 1991

Shutouts: Most, season

5	Dave Stieb, 1982
4	Dave Stieb, 1980
4	Dave Stieb, 1983
4	Dave Stieb, 1988
3	Jim Clancy, 1982
3	Jim Clancy, 1986
3	PAT HENTGEN, 1994
3	PAT HENTGEN, 1996
3	Dave Lemanczyk, 1979

Wins: Most, season

21	Jack Morris, 1992
20	PAT HENTGEN, 1996
19	PAT HENTGEN, 1993
18	Dave Stieb, 1990
17	Doyle Alexander, 1984
17	Doyle Alexander, 1985
17	JIMMY KEY, 1987
17	Dave Stieb, 1982
17	Dave Stieb, 1983
17	Dave Stieb, 1989

K: Most, season

198	Dave Stieb, 1984
194	JUAN GUZMAN, 1993
187	Dave Stieb, 1983
180	Jim Clancy, 1987
177	PAT HENTGEN, 1996

Win pct: Highest, season

.778	Jack Morris, 1992
.762	JUAN GUZMAN, 1992
.750	Dave Stieb, 1990
.739	Doyle Alexander, 1984
.680	JIMMY KEY, 1987
.680	Dave Stieb, 1989

ERA: Lowest, season

2.48	Dave Stieb, 1985
2.64	JUAN GUZMAN, 1992
2.76	JIMMY KEY, 1987
2.83	Dave Stieb, 1984
2.93	JUAN GUZMAN, 1996

Most pinch-hit homers, season

2	Jeff Burroughs, 1985
2	Rico Carty, 1979
2	Otto Velez, 1979
2	Ernie Whitt, 1982
2	Al Woods, 1977

Most pinch-hit homers, career

4	Jesse Barfield, 1981-1989
4	Ernie Whitt, 1977-1989

Longest hitting streak

26	JOHN OLERUD, 1993
22	George Bell, 1989
21	Damaso Garcia, 1983
21	Lloyd Moseby, 1983
20	Damaso Garcia, 1980

Most consecutive scoreless innings

31	Dave Stieb, 1988

No-hit game

Dave Stieb, Tor at Cle AL, 3-0;
    Sept. 2, 1990.

ACTIVE PLAYERS in caps.

Players' years of service are listed by the first and last years with this team and are not necessarily consecutive; all statistics record performances for this team only.

Detroit Tigers

By Duane Burleson, AP/World Wide Photo

Bobby Higginson was a big success in just his second season with Detroit.

1996 Tigers: Can it get any worse?

Rookie manager Buddy Bell had a nearly impossible task last year, and the Tigers ended up having one of the worst seasons in baseball history. "Every organization goes through this at some point," Bell said. "We're not unique. You prepare yourself for it, but if you're driven at all or have any respect for the game, this is hard."

The Tigers' pitching staff set major league records for the most home runs and grand slams allowed in a season, and the American League mark for highest ERA. The 109 losses were the most ever by one of baseball's most-storied franchises. The Tigers started the season 8-7 before losing 39 of their next 45 games. Then they played nearly .500 baseball for more than two months before collapsing in September with a 4-22 record.

On the bright side, a couple of Detroit's younger players, first baseman Tony Clark and outfielder Bobby Higginson, made great strides this season and will likely be regulars for years to come. Clark hit 27 home runs and drove in 72 in only 100 games to finish third in the American League Rookie of the Year voting. Higginson became a full-time player, batting .320 with 26 home runs and 81 RBI.

The pitching staff was a season-long nightmare, as its 6.38 ERA was exceeded only by the 1930 Phillies' 6.71—although there are great hopes for rookie left-hander Justin Thompson, who went only 1-6 but showed good stuff in his 11 starts. "We have some guys in our starting rotation who aren't ready for the big leagues yet," Bell said, diplomatically not naming names, "but I don't think all our problems are related to pitching. We've got a long way to go offensively and defensively, too."

The veterans started leaving, as Alan Trammell, a 20-year Tiger, announced his retirement and Cecil Fielder, Detroit's marquee player for more than six seasons, was dealt to New York to save money. Ruben Sierra, part of the package in the Fielder trade, was such a negative influence that he was dealt to Cincinnati shortly after the season despite the fact that the Tigers will pick up the majority of his hefty contract. By the end of the year, the only full-time veteran player left was Travis Fryman, who moved from third base to shortstop out of necessity after the Tigers had been through just about anyone else they could find to try at short. Fryman hit 22 homers and led the club with 100 RBI.

Most of the rest of the roster looked like open tryouts, as Bell and general manager Randy Smith tried to assess youngsters such as outfielder Kimera Bartee and pitcher Trever Miller and gave second chances to players like third baseman Phil Nevin and pitcher Todd Van Poppel. "There are some good things that are happening for us," Bell said. "But I don't think anyone could be happy with where we are and where we've been this year. But I believe if we stay the course, we'll turn this thing around."

Team MVP

Bobby Higginson: Outfielder Bobby Higginson made huge progress in a season that played out just about as expected in Detroit—long and disappointing. But Higginson emerged as more than just a regular in the lineup. He moved to the verge of joining the game's elite. In fact, he was one of only 17 major leaguers in 1996 to bat over .300 with an on-base average better than .400 and a slugging average above .500. His .320 average led the club, and his 26 homers and 81 RBI were second among the Tigers.

1996 Tigers: Week-by-week notes

These notes were excerpted from the following issues of Baseball Weekly.

▶**April 10:** Manager Buddy Bell is considering adding a 12th pitcher because his starters took such a beating during the first week of the season.

▶**April 17:** Led by first baseman Cecil Fielder's six homers and 14 RBI, Tigers hitters kept the team over .500 despite the pitching staff's ERA of 6.49, the worst in the AL.

▶**May 1:** Even with his team suffering through an eight-game losing streak, general manager Randy Smith refused to hit the panic button by recalling left-handers Justin Thompson, C.J. Nitkowski or Trever Miller, the top three pitching prospects at Toledo. "There is no way we're going to rush some of our kids ahead of schedule just so we can win a couple more games," Smith said.

▶**May 15:** Pitching problems continue to ail the Tigers, as they threaten the 1930 Phillies' all-time worst ERA of 6.71.

▶**May 22:** A 16-4 loss to Chicago on May 18 was Detroit's fifth straight and 25th in 29 games. Even with a 12-32 start, Buddy Bell's job is secure. "It'd be safe even if he went 0-162 this season," Randy Smith said. "Our future is with Buddy."

▶**May 29:** As the losses piled up, Randy Smith shook up the deck. Pitchers Jose Lima, Scott Aldred and John Farrell (a combined 0-10) were sent to the minors. As replacements, Detroit called up catcher Raul Casanova, relievers Mike Walker and Bob Scanlan, and left-hander Justin Thompson.

▶**June 12:** Justin Thompson was put on the 15-day DL on June 7 because of a sore shoulder after only two big league starts, during which he was 0-1 with a 2.03 ERA, allowing just nine hits while striking out 13 in 13⅓ innings.

▶**June 26:** When right-handers Felipe Lira and Brian Williams posted back-to-back four-hit shutouts on June 21-22 against Minnesota, it representated a dramatic departure for the staff. For both

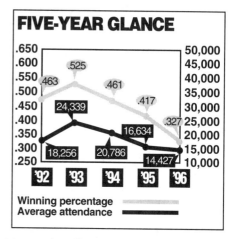

FIVE-YEAR GLANCE

Winning percentage
Average attendance

Lira and Williams it was the first complete game of their careers, to say nothing about being shutouts.

▶**July 3:** The Tigers now are concentrating on winning games, and not on keeping their heads above water. Fueling the optimism has been the performance of several younger players, particularly first baseman Tony Clark and outfielders Bobby Higginson and Kimera Bartee.

▶**July 11:** Left-handed reliever Mike Myers is threatening the AL record for most appearances in a season. The record of 90 was set by Minnesota's Mike Marshall in 1979, and Myers entered the All-Star break slightly ahead of that pace.

▶**July 31:** It was revealed that outfielder Melvin Nieves broke shortstop Andujar Cedeno's nose with a punch when the club was on a recent road trip to Milwaukee. Buddy Bell said the incident doesn't bother him that much as long as the two players don't carry on some kind of grudge. "They've resolved it, and we've talked to them about it," Bell said.

▶**Aug. 7:** Randy Smith's three trades just before the July 31 deadline ran the number of deals he's made in nine months as general manager to 12. The biggest deal was unloading Cecil Fielder and his salary ($9.6 million for the rest of '96 and all of '97) to the Yankees for outfielder-DH Ruben Sierra, pitching prospect Matt Drews and $1 million. Detroit also traded center fielder Chad Curtis to Los Angeles for left-handers Joey Eischen and John Cummings, and right-hander Greg Gohr to California for infielder Damion Easley. The moves free up $5.4 million. Much of the money will go into pay raises for third baseman Travis Fryman and second baseman Mark Lewis, and for free-agent signings during the off-season.

▶**Aug. 14:** The Tigers beat New York 13-7 on Aug. 10 for their ninth win in 11 games. One of the keys to the Tigers' surge has been improved starting pitching, particularly from right-hander Omar Olivares, who had four complete games in his first 17 starts and is averaging seven innings per outing.

▶**Aug. 21:** The Michigan Supreme Court refused to hear an appeal from the Tiger Stadium Fan Club and its efforts to stop the release of $55 million in state funds to help build a new stadium in downtown Detroit. It was the final legal hurdle for the team in its efforts to build a $245 million, 37,000-to 40,000-seat stadium.

▶**Sept. 4:** The club picked up a one-year option on Buddy Bell's contract, extending it through the 1998 season. The Tigers have struggled in Bell's first season, but it wasn't unexpected as the franchise rebuilds. On Aug. 28, Bell moved Travis Fryman from third base to short-stop, a position he last played in the 1993 All-Star Game. With Andujar Cedeno struggling and Damion Easley hurt, Bell felt he had to make the move.

▶**Sept. 11:** Buddy Bell likes what he's seen from Phil Nevin, the No. 1 overall pick in the 1992 draft by Houston, acquired in a trade with the Astros for closer Mike Henneman last season. Nevin spent most of this season learning to be a catcher at Class AA Jacksonville. But since he's been recalled, he's played mostly at third base.

▶**Sept. 18:** The pitching continues to break futility records. By Sept. 15, Detroit had allowed 234 home runs to smash the previous record of 226, by the '87 Orioles. The 11 grand slams allowed by Detroit's pitchers established another major league record. The Tigers also were on pace for all-time AL worsts in ERA and runs allowed, in addition to getting close to league marks for hit batters and wild pitches.

▶**Sept. 25:** In the Tigers' 13-6 loss in Milwaukee on Sept. 21—their 13th in 14 games—Melvin Nieves took a called third strike in the sixth inning for the Tigers' 1,204th strikeout of the year, a major league record. The previous mark was set by the Mets in 1968.

▶**Oct. 2:** Buddy Bell knew what he faced in his first year on the job. That didn't make it any easier, however, as the Tigers went through one of the worst seasons of all time. The pitching staff set an AL mark for highest ERA, and the 109 losses are the most in the franchise's 96-year history. All ties to the powerhouse teams of the 1980s were cut when shortstop Alan Trammell announced his retirement. Cecil Fielder, Detroit's marquee player for more than six seasons, had already been dealt to New York to free money for a more youthful, streamlined team. Second-year man Bobby Higginson showed great promise, hitting .320 with 26 homers.

Team directory

▶**Owner:** Michael and Marion Ilitch
▶**General manager:** Randy Smith
▶**Ballpark:**
Tiger Stadium
2121 Trumbull Ave.
Detroit, Mich.
313-962-4000
Capacity 47,051
Pay parking lot (independently owned)
Public transportation available
Wheelchair section, ramps, group sales department
▶**Team publications:**
Scorebook/program
▶**TV, radio broadcast stations:**
WJR 760 AM, WKBD Channel 50, PASS Cable
▶**Camps and/or clinics:**
Tigers' Fantasy Camp
▶**Spring training:**
Marchant Stadium
Lakeland, Fla.
Capacity 7,027
941-686-8075

DETROIT TIGERS 1996 final stats

BATTERS	BA	SLG	OB	G	AB	R	H	TB	2B	3B	HR	RBI	BB	SO	SB	CS	E
Higginson	.320	.577	.404	130	440	75	141	254	35	0	26	81	65	66	6	3	9
Pride	.300	.513	.372	95	267	52	80	137	17	5	10	31	31	63	11	6	3
Nevin	.292	.533	.338	38	120	15	35	64	5	0	8	19	8	39	1	0	5
M. Lewis	.270	.396	.326	145	545	69	147	216	30	3	11	55	42	109	6	1	9
Easley	.268	.393	.331	49	112	14	30	44	2	0	4	17	10	25	3	1	6
Fryman	.268	.437	.329	157	616	90	165	269	32	3	22	100	57	118	4	3	10
Curtis	.263	.393	.346	104	400	65	105	157	20	1	10	37	53	73	16	10	9
Bartee	.253	.304	.308	110	217	32	55	66	6	1	1	14	17	77	20	10	2
Bautista	.250	.375	.342	25	64	12	16	24	2	0	2	8	9	15	1	2	1
Clark	.250	.503	.299	100	376	56	94	189	14	0	27	72	29	127	0	1	6
Flaherty	.250	.408	.290	47	152	18	38	62	12	0	4	23	8	25	1	0	5
Ausmus	.248	.354	.328	75	226	30	56	80	12	0	4	22	26	45	3	4	4
Sierra	.247	.375	.320	142	518	61	128	194	26	2	12	72	60	83	4	4	6
Nieves	.246	.485	.322	120	431	71	106	209	23	4	24	60	44	158	1	2	13
Gomez	.242	.305	.340	48	128	21	31	39	5	0	1	16	18	20	1	1	6
Cruz	.237	.289	.256	14	38	5	9	11	2	0	0	0	1	11	0	0	6
Trammell	.233	.259	.267	66	193	16	45	50	2	0	1	16	10	27	6	0	6
E. Williams	.200	.307	.267	77	215	22	43	66	5	0	6	26	18	50	0	2	0
Cedeno	.196	.358	.213	52	179	19	35	64	4	2	7	20	4	37	2	1	12
Hiatt	.190	.286	.261	7	21	3	4	6	0	1	0	1	2	11	0	0	0
Casanova	.188	.341	.242	25	85	6	16	29	1	0	4	9	6	18	0	0	3
Singleton	.161	.179	.230	18	56	5	9	10	1	0	0	3	4	15	0	2	0
Hyers	.077	.115	.200	17	26	1	2	3	1	0	0	0	4	5	0	0	0
Penn	.071	.071	.071	6	14	0	1	1	0	0	0	1	0	3	0	0	0

PITCHERS	W-L	ERA	G	GS	CG	GF	Sho	SV	IP	H	R	ER	HR	BB	SO
Eischen	1-1	3.24	24	0	0	3	0	0	25.0	27	11	9	3	14	15
R. Lewis	4-6	4.18	72	0	0	19	0	2	90.1	78	45	42	9	65	78
Moehler	0-1	4.35	2	2	0	0	0	0	10.1	11	10	5	1	8	2
Thompson	1-6	4.58	11	11	0	0	0	0	59.0	62	35	30	7	31	44
Olivares	7-11	4.89	25	25	4	0	0	0	160.0	169	90	87	16	75	81
Myers	1-5	5.01	83	0	0	25	0	6	64.2	70	41	36	6	34	69
Sager	4-5	5.01	22	9	0	1	0	0	79.0	91	46	44	10	29	52
Olson	3-0	5.02	43	0	0	28	0	8	43.0	43	25	24	6	28	29
Cummings	3-3	5.12	21	0	0	7	0	0	31.2	36	20	18	3	20	24
Lira	6-14	5.22	32	32	3	0	2	0	194.2	204	123	113	30	66	113
Lima	5-6	5.70	39	4	0	15	0	3	72.2	87	48	46	13	22	59
B. Williams	3-10	6.77	40	17	2	17	1	2	121.0	145	107	91	21	85	72
Keagle	3-6	7.39	26	6	0	5	0	0	87.2	104	76	72	13	68	70
Nitkowski	2-3	8.08	11	8	0	0	0	0	45.2	62	44	41	7	38	36
Veres	0-4	8.31	25	0	0	11	0	0	30.1	38	29	28	6	23	28
Urbani	2-2	8.37	16	2	0	3	0	0	23.2	31	22	22	8	14	20
Walker	0-0	8.46	20	0	0	12	0	1	27.2	40	26	26	10	17	13
Van Poppel	3-9	9.06	37	15	1	8	1	1	99.1	139	107	100	24	62	53
Miller	0-4	9.18	5	4	0	0	0	0	16.2	28	17	17	3	9	8
Christopher	1-1	9.30	13	0	0	3	0	0	30.0	47	36	31	12	11	19
Sodowsky	1-3	11.84	7	7	0	0	0	0	24.1	40	34	32	5	20	9
Maxcy	0-0	13.50	2	0	0	0	0	0	3.1	8	5	5	2	2	1
Farrell	0-2	14.21	2	2	0	0	0	0	6.1	11	10	10	2	5	5
McCurry	0-0	24.30	2	0	0	1	0	0	3.1	9	9	9	3	2	0

1997 preliminary roster

PITCHERS (20)
Willie Blair
Doug Brocail
Bryan Corey
John Cummings
Glenn Dishman
Roberto Duran
Ramon Fermin
Fernando Harris
Todd Jones
Greg Keagle
Felipe Lira
Dan Miceli
Brian Moehler
Mike Myers
Omar Olivares
Willis Roberts
John Rosengren
A.J. Sager
Justin Thompson
Greg Whiteman

CATCHERS (3)
Raul Casanova

Brian Johnson
Matt Walbeck

INFIELDERS (9)
Richard Almanzar
Tony Clark
Deivi Cruz
Damion Easley
Travis Fryman
Luis Garcia
Dave Hajek
Orlando Miller
Phil Nevin

OUTFIELDERS (8)
Kimera Bartee
Decomba Conner
Juan Encarnacion
Bobby Higginson
Brian Hunter
Melvin Nieves
Curtis Pride
Bubba Trammell

Games played by position

PLAYER	G	C	1B	2B	3B	SS	OF	DH
Ausmus	75	73	0	0	0	0	0	0
Bartee	110	0	0	0	0	0	99	2
Bautista	25	0	0	0	0	0	22	1
Casanova	25	22	0	0	0	0	0	3
Cedeno	52	0	0	0	1	51	0	0
Clark	100	0	86	0	0	0	0	12
Cruz	14	0	0	8	0	4	0	1
Curtis	104	0	0	0	0	0	104	0
Easley	49	0	0	17	5	21	2	3
Flaherty	47	46	0	0	0	0	0	0
Fryman	157	0	0	0	128	29	0	0
Gomez	48	0	0	0	0	47	0	0
Hiatt	7	0	0	0	3	0	2	1
Higginson	130	0	0	0	0	0	123	4
Hyers	17	0	9	0	0	0	1	2
M. Lewis	145	0	0	144	0	0	0	1
Nevin	38	4	0	0	24	0	9	1
Nieves	120	0	0	0	0	0	105	11
Penn	6	0	0	0	0	0	1	4
Pride	95	0	0	0	0	0	48	31
Sierra	142	0	0	0	0	0	56	81
Singleton	18	0	0	0	0	0	15	1
Trammell	66	0	0	11	8	43	1	0
E. Williams	77	0	7	0	3	0	2	52

Minor Leagues

Tops in the organization

BATTER	CLUB	AVG.	G	AB	R	H	HR	RBI
B. Trammell	Tol	.316	134	491	95	155	33	99
R. Almanzar	Lak	.306	124	471	81	144	1	36
Gabriel Kapler	Fay	.300	138	524	81	157	26	99
F. Catalanotto	Jax	.298	132	497	105	148	17	67
Phil Nevin	Jax	.294	98	344	77	101	24	69

HOME RUNS

Phil Hiatt	Tol	42
B. Trammell	Tol	33
Terrel Hansen	Jax	26
Gabriel Kapler	Fay	26
Sean Freeman	Jax	25

WINS

Brian Moehler	Jax	15
Clayton Bruner	Fay	14
Trever Miller	Tol	13
David Melendez	Fay	11
Greg Whiteman	Lak	11

RBI

Phil Hiatt	Tol	119
Gabriel Kapler	Fay	99
B. Trammell	Tol	99
Tony Mitchell	Tol	84
Chris Lemonis	Vis	82

SAVES

Bryan Corey	Fay	34
Rick Greene	Jax	30
Eric Dinyar	Lak	27
M. Christopher	Tol	22
Dave Tuttle	Vis	21

STOLEN BASES

David Roberts	Jax	65
R. Almanzar	Lak	53
Scott Sollman	Jam	35
Malvin DeJesus	Vis	34
Several Players Tied At		32

STRIKEOUTS

Clayton Bruner	Fay	152
J. Bettencourt	Fay	148
Brian Barnes	Tol	144
Greg Whiteman	Lak	122
David Melendez	Fay	121

PITCHER	CLUB	W-L	ERA	IP	H	BB	SO
C. Bruner	Fay	14-5	2.59	157	124	77	152
D. Melendez	Fay	11-4	2.62	131	114	40	121
Willis Roberts	Lak	9-7	2.89	149	133	69	105
J. Bettencourt	Fay	7-11	3.24	153	127	58	148
D. Borkowski	Fay	10-10	3.33	178	158	54	117

Sick call: 1996 DL report

PLAYER	Days on the DL
Raul Casanova	55
Greg Gohr	25
Bob Higginson	27
Greg Keagle	45
Richie Lewis	20
Melvin Nieves	32*
C.J. Nitkowski	18
Omar Olivares	44
Curtis Pride	27
Justin Thompson	75
Alan Trammell	55*

Indicates two separate terms on Disabled List.

1996 salaries

	Bonuses	Total earned salary
Ruben Sierra, of		$6,200,000
Travis Fryman, 3b	$25,000	$5,175,000
Mark Lewis, 2b		$670,000
Alan Trammell, ss		$600,000
Omar Olivares, p	$280,000	$505,000
Andujar Cedeno, ss		$500,000
Brad Ausmus, c		$350,000
Eddie Williams, 3b	$25,000	$350,000
Todd Van Poppel, p		$318,000
Damion Easley, 2b		$305,000
John Cummings, p		$170,000
Bobby Higginson, of		$170,000
Richie Lewis, p		$170,000
Felipe Lira, p		$170,000
Melvin Nieves, of		$170,000
A.J. Sager, p		$160,000
Curtis Pride, of		$150,000
Jose Lima, p		$145,000
Joey Eischen, p		$135,000
Mike Myers, p		$127,500
Phil Nevin, 3b		$120,000
Kim Bartee, of		$109,000
Tony Clark, 3b		$109,000
Greg Keagle, p		$109,000
Trever Miller, p		$109,000
Justin Thompson, p		$109,000

Average 1996 salary: $661,750
Total 1996 team payroll: $17,205,500
Termination pay: $750,000

Detroit (1901-1996)

Runs: Most, career

2088 Ty Cobb, 1905-1926
1774 Charlie Gehringer, 1924-1942
1622 Al Kaline, 1953-1974
1386 Lou Whitaker, 1977-1995
1242 Donie Bush, 1908-1921

Hits: Most, career

3900 Ty Cobb, 1905-1926
3007 Al Kaline, 1953-1974
2839 Charlie Gehringer, 1924-1942
2499 Harry Heilmann, 1914-1929
2466 Sam Crawford, 1903-1917

2B: Most, career

665 Ty Cobb, 1905-1926
574 Charlie Gehringer, 1924-1942
498 Al Kaline, 1953-1974
497 Harry Heilmann, 1914-1929
420 Lou Whitaker, 1977-1995

3B: Most, career

284 Ty Cobb, 1905-1926
249 Sam Crawford, 1903-1917
146 Charlie Gehringer, 1924-1942
145 Harry Heilmann, 1914-1929
136 Bobby Veach, 1912-1923

HR: Most, career

399 Al Kaline, 1953-1974
373 Norm Cash, 1960-1974
306 Hank Greenberg, 1930-1946
262 Willie Horton, 1963-1977
245 CECIL FIELDER, 1990-1996

RBI: Most, career

1804 Ty Cobb, 1905-1926
1583 Al Kaline, 1953-1974
1442 Harry Heilmann, 1914-1929
1427 Charlie Gehringer, 1924-1942
1264 Sam Crawford, 1903-1917

SB: Most, career

865 Ty Cobb, 1905-1926
400 Donie Bush, 1908-1921
317 Sam Crawford, 1903-1917
294 Ron LeFlore, 1974-1979
236 ALAN TRAMMELL,
    1977-1996

BB: Most, career

1277 Al Kaline, 1953-1974
1197 Lou Whitaker, 1977-1995
1186 Charlie Gehringer, 1924-1942
1148 Ty Cobb, 1905-1926
1125 Donie Bush, 1908-1921

BA: Highest, career

.368 Ty Cobb, 1905-1926
.342 Harry Heilmann, 1914-1929
.337 Bob Fothergill, 1922-1930
.325 George Kell, 1946-1952
.321 Heinie Manush, 1923-1927

Slug avg: Highest, career

.616 Hank Greenberg, 1930-1946
.518 Harry Heilmann, 1914-1929
.516 Ty Cobb, 1905-1926
.503 Rudy York, 1934-1945
.501 Rocky Colavito, 1960-1963

On-base avg: Highest, career

.434 Ty Cobb, 1905-1926
.420 Johnny Bassler, 1921-1927
.412 Hank Greenberg, 1930-1946
.412 Roy Cullenbine, 1938-1947
.410 Harry Heilmann, 1914-1929

Complete games: Most, career

336 George Mullin, 1902-1913
245 Hooks Dauss, 1912-1926
213 Bill Donovan, 1903-1918
212 Hal Newhouser, 1939-1953
200 Tommy Bridges, 1930-1946

Saves: Most, career

154 MIKE HENNEMAN,
    1987-1995
125 John Hiller, 1965-1980
120 Willie Hernandez, 1984-1989
85 Aurelio Lopez, 1979-1985
55 Terry Fox, 1961-1966

Shutouts: Most, career

39 Mickey Lolich, 1963-1975
34 George Mullin, 1902-1913
33 Tommy Bridges, 1930-1946
33 Hal Newhouser, 1939-1953
29 Bill Donovan, 1903-1918

Wins: Most, career

222 Hooks Dauss, 1912-1926
209 George Mullin, 1902-1913
207 Mickey Lolich, 1963-1975
200 Hal Newhouser, 1939-1953
198 Jack Morris, 1977-1990

K: Most, career

2679 Mickey Lolich, 1963-1975
1980 Jack Morris, 1977-1990
1770 Hal Newhouser, 1939-1953
1674 Tommy Bridges, 1930-1946
1406 Jim Bunning, 1955-1963

Win pct: Highest, career

.654 Denny McLain, 1963-1970
.639 Aurelio Lopez, 1979-1985
.629 Schoolboy Rowe, 1933-1942
.626 MIKE HENNEMAN,
     1987-1995
.616 Harry Coveleski, 1914-1918

ERA: Lowest, career

2.34 Harry Coveleski, 1914-1918
2.38 Ed Killian, 1904-1910
2.42 Ed Summers, 1908-1912
2.49 Bill Donovan, 1903-1918
2.61 Ed Siever, 1901-1908

Runs: Most, season

147 Ty Cobb, 1911
144 Ty Cobb, 1915
144 Charlie Gehringer, 1930
144 Charlie Gehringer, 1936
144 Hank Greenberg, 1938

Hits: Most, season

248 Ty Cobb, 1911
237 Harry Heilmann, 1921
227 Charlie Gehringer, 1936
226 Ty Cobb, 1912
225 Ty Cobb, 1917
225 Harry Heilmann, 1925

2B: Most, season

63 Hank Greenberg, 1934
60 Charlie Gehringer, 1936
56 George Kell, 1950
55 Gee Walker, 1936
50 Charlie Gehringer, 1934
50 Hank Greenberg, 1940
50 Harry Heilmann, 1927

3B: Most, season

26 Sam Crawford, 1914
25 Sam Crawford, 1903
24 Ty Cobb, 1911
24 Ty Cobb, 1917
23 Ty Cobb, 1912
23 Sam Crawford, 1913

HR: Most, season

58 Hank Greenberg, 1938
51 CECIL FIELDER, 1990
45 Rocky Colavito, 1961
44 CECIL FIELDER, 1991
44 Hank Greenberg, 1946

RBI: Most, season

183 Hank Greenberg, 1937

170 Hank Greenberg, 1935
150 Hank Greenberg, 1940
146 Hank Greenberg, 1938
140 Rocky Colavito, 1961

SB: Most, season

96 Ty Cobb, 1915
83 Ty Cobb, 1911
78 Ron LeFlore, 1979
76 Ty Cobb, 1909
68 Ty Cobb, 1916
68 Ron LeFlore, 1978

BB: Most, season

137 Roy Cullenbine, 1947
135 Eddie Yost, 1959
132 TONY PHILLIPS, 1993
125 Eddie Yost, 1960
124 Norm Cash, 1961

BA: Highest, season

.420 Ty Cobb, 1911
.409 Ty Cobb, 1912
.403 Harry Heilmann, 1923
.401 Ty Cobb, 1922
.398 Harry Heilmann, 1927

Slug avg: Highest, season

.683 Hank Greenberg, 1938
.670 Hank Greenberg, 1940
.668 Hank Greenberg, 1937
.662 Norm Cash, 1961
.632 Harry Heilmann, 1923

On-base avg: Highest, season

.487 Norm Cash, 1961
.486 Ty Cobb, 1915
.481 Harry Heilmann, 1923
.475 Harry Heilmann, 1927
.468 Ty Cobb, 1925

Complete games: Most, season

42 George Mullin, 1904
35 Roscoe Miller, 1901
35 George Mullin, 1905
35 George Mullin, 1906
35 George Mullin, 1907

Saves: Most, season

38 John Hiller, 1973
32 Willie Hernandez, 1984
31 Willie Hernandez, 1985
27 Tom Timmermann, 1970
24 MIKE HENNEMAN, 1992
24 MIKE HENNEMAN, 1993
24 Willie Hernandez, 1986

Shutouts: Most, season

9 Denny McLain, 1969
8 Ed Killian, 1905
8 Hal Newhouser, 1945
7 Billy Hoeft, 1955
7 George Mullin, 1904
7 Dizzy Trout, 1944

Wins: Most, season

31 Denny McLain, 1968
29 George Mullin, 1909
29 Hal Newhouser, 1944
27 Dizzy Trout, 1944
26 Hal Newhouser, 1946

K: Most, season

308 Mickey Lolich, 1971
280 Denny McLain, 1968
275 Hal Newhouser, 1946
271 Mickey Lolich, 1969
250 Mickey Lolich, 1972

Win pct: Highest, season

.862 Bill Donovan, 1907
.842 Schoolboy Rowe, 1940
.838 Denny McLain, 1968
.808 Bobo Newsom, 1940
.784 George Mullin, 1909

ERA: Lowest, season

1.64 Ed Summers, 1908
1.71 Ed Killian, 1909
1.78 Ed Killian, 1907
1.81 Hal Newhouser, 1945
1.91 Ed Siever, 1902

Most pinch-hit homers, season

3 Gates Brown, 1968
3 Norm Cash, 1960
3 John Grubb, 1984
3 Larry Herndon, 1986
3 Frank Howard, 1963
3 Charlie Maxwell, 1961
3 Ben Oglivie, 1976
3 Dick Wakefield, 1948
3 Vic Wertz, 1962
3 Gus Zernial, 1958

Most pinch-hit homers, career

16 Gates Brown, 1963-1975
8 Norm Cash, 1960-1974

Longest hitting streak

40 Ty Cobb, 1911
35 Ty Cobb, 1917
30 Goose Goslin, 1934
30 Ron LeFlore, 1976
29 Dale Alexander, 1930
29 Pete Fox, 1935

Most consecutive scoreless innings

33 Harry Coveleskie, 1914

No-hit games

George Mullin, Det vs StL AL, 7-0;
July 4, 1912 (2nd game).
Virgil Trucks, Det vs Was AL, 1-0;
May 15, 1952.
Virgil Trucks, Det at NY AL, 1-0;
Aug. 25, 1952.
Jim Bunning, Det at Bos AL, 3-0;
July 20, 1958 (1st game).
Jack Morris, Det at Chi AL, 4-0;
Apr. 7, 1984.

ACTIVE PLAYERS in caps.

Players' years of service are listed by the first and last years with this team and are not necessarily consecutive; all statistics record performances for this team only.

117

Cleveland Indians

Jim Thome bettered his career highs in homers (38), RBI (116) and runs scored (122).

1996 Indians: An incomplete success

It was a long, strange trip for the Indians this season, but no one complained until the end. For the first time in franchise history, Cleveland qualified for the postseason for the second straight year, clinching the American League Central division title on Sept. 17. In 1995 the Indians had hammered people as they won 100 games in a 144-game season. It was harder this year, and it was difficult to take when they were surprisingly dispatched from the playoffs by Baltimore in the first round. After their World Series loss to Atlanta in 1995, nothing short of the ultimate title was going to satisfy the team or its fans. "People got up to play us every day," said shortstop Omar Vizquel. "It showed us we weren't invincible."

While 1995 was a breeze—they set a record by winning the AL Central by 30 games—the 1996 Indians had to deal with slumps, clubhouse turmoil, controversial trades and disputes with fans, opposing players and the league president. "We hit a few more bumps in the road this year," said manager Mike Hargrove. "Last year we didn't hit one bump." General manager John Hart caused some of the bumps when he traded popular Eddie Murray and Carlos Baerga in late July. Murray was sent to Baltimore for pitcher Kent Mercker, and Baerga was shipped to the Mets for infielders Jose Vizcaino and Jeff Kent. "That shook the club up," said Hart.

Jack McDowell and Julio Franco, the big free agents signed over the winter, had injury problems. McDowell went on the disabled list for the first time in his career on July 26 with a strained right forearm. Franco missed about two months of action with a strained right hamstring but played well when he regained his health. McDowell continued to struggle when he came off the DL, but he won his last three decisions.

Albert Belle was the top Indians hitter, in more ways than one. First he threw a ball at a photographer, injuring him

> ## Team MVP
>
> **Albert Belle:** Albert Belle played through another year of controversy to lead the AL in RBI with 148, slug 48 home runs and hit .311. He also came out as the major leagues' top player in the statistical evaluation that determines free-agent compensation. The controversial slugger finished in the top 10 in home runs, total bases, runs, hits, walks, multi-hit games, extra-base hits, slugging average and outfield assists.

slightly. Then Belle refused to trade his autograph to a fan who had caught his 21st homer in a game at The Ballpark in Arlington. Three days later, while breaking up a double play between first and second, he nearly turned Milwaukee second baseman Fernando Vina into a pile of dust, with a forearm. From that point on he was booed every time he came to the plate on the road. Amid all of this, he ended up with 48 homers, 148 RBI and at least one smashed Jacobs Field clubhouse thermostat. In November he signed a record $55 million contract with the White Sox.

Jim Thome and Manny Ramirez backed Belle with outstanding seasons. Thome hit 38 home runs and had 116 RBI, while Ramirez hit 33 homers and drove in 112 runs.

Charles Nagy emerged as the No. 1 starter. He went 17-5 with a 3.41 ERA. Orel Hershiser had 15 victories, McDowell was 13-9, and Chad Ogea went 10-5. Dennis Martinez, like Murray signed as a free agent after the 1993 season to help teach the Indians how to win, made three trips to the DL and won't return in 1997. Closer Jose Mesa, who converted 46 of 48 save chances in 1995, was still effective, but his ERA rose from 1.13 to 3.73 as he went 38 for 43 in saves.

1996 Indians: Week-by-week notes

These notes were excerpted from the following issues of Baseball Weekly.

▶**April 10:** The Indians, who led the major leagues in runs, home runs and batting average last year, were limited to an AL-worst eight runs in their first four games.

▶**May 15:** Closer Jose Mesa said he's just now started to throw as hard as he did last year. "I don't know why it's taken me this long to come around," he said.

▶**May 22:** AL president Gene Budig, saying that another fine or suspension would not address the problem, ordered left fielder Albert Belle to undergo immediate counseling for hitting *Sports Illustrated* photographer Tony Tomsic with a baseball on April 6. If Belle does not follow Budig's ruling, he will be suspended. He was also ordered to do community service.

▶**May 29:** All-Star second baseman Carlos Baerga, a lifetime .305 hitter, is in a major slump. He's hitting .216 (19-for-88) in May, and since July 1 of last year, he has just eight home runs. Baerga came to camp at close to 230 pounds, at least 15 pounds overweight. He hasn't lost it, and the front office has ordered him to start doing postgame workouts.

▶**June 5:** The Indians were swept in a three-game series last week for the first time since Chicago did it on June 23-25, 1995. This time, Texas pulled off the sweep in The Ballpark in Arlington.

▶**June 19:** Wherever Albert Belle goes, boos follow. Over the weekend in Yankee Stadium, he heard the loudest jeers of the season. Belle also spent parts of two days in New York appealing his five-game suspension for his May 31 collision with Milwaukee second baseman Fernando Vina. Manager Mike Hargrove briefly pulled the team off the field in the seventh inning on June 14 after the crowd threw balls at Belle and center fielder Kenny Lofton. At least one souvenir bat was thrown, and the Yankees responded by putting security personnel in left field and behind the Indians' dugout. "This is the most vicious reaction to Albert that I've seen this

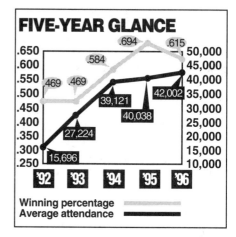

FIVE-YEAR GLANCE

Winning percentage
Average attendance

season," Hargrove said after the game.

▶**June 26:** Albert Belle was paid during his two-day (reduced from five) suspension, but general manager John Hart said the club would not pay his $25,000 fine. The fine went to Cleveland's RBI (Reviving Baseball in the Inner City) Program.

▶**July 3:** Dennis Martinez left his start against Chicago in the fourth inning with a strained ligament in his right elbow and will be sidelined until after the All-Star break. Martinez, 8-4, has not won since May 31.

▶**July 11:** The Indians were 33-14 on May 26. They've gone 19-21 since and have lost 11 of their last 17. A players-only meeting was held before the July 6 game, but the Tribe still lost 3-2. "Right now we're dead," utility infielder Alvaro Espinoza said.

▶**July 17:** With Julio Franco on the DL, Herbert Perry sidelined after knee surgery and DH Eddie Murray unable to play first base because of a left-shoulder injury, the Indians acquired Mark Carreon from San Francisco on July 9 for lefty Jim Poole. Carreon was 9-for-15 with the Tribe through July 14.

▶**July 31:** Albert Belle became the Indians' all-time home run leader on July 25 in Camden Yards when he clubbed his 227th with the Indians, one more than Earl Averill hit from 1929 to 1939. Belle added a solo home run in his next at-bat.

▶**Aug. 7:** Dennis Martinez has a low

opinion of the trades that sent Carlos Baerga and Alvaro Espinoza to the Mets and Eddie Murray to Baltimore. "Everyone is on their tiptoes around here," said Martinez. "They don't know what's going on. They're in limbo." The Indians sent Baerga and Espinoza to the Mets for infielders Jose Vizcaino and Jeff Kent, and Murray to the O's for left-hander Kent Mercker, since sent down to Buffalo.

▶**Aug. 21:** Jack McDowell came off the DL on Aug. 9 after missing time with a strained muscle in his right forearm. He's been unable to throw his curveball, and in his last start, on Aug. 14, McDowell couldn't hold a 6-0 lead against the Angels. When Mike Hargrove removed him in the third—with the Tribe leading 6-5—he was not happy. "I didn't get a chance to know how my arm felt," said McDowell after the 8-7 loss.

▶**Aug. 28:** Charles Nagy started for the AL All-Star team after going 11-2 with a 3.53 ERA in the first half. In eight starts since then, he's gone 1-2 with five no-decisions. He has not won since July 25.

▶**Sept. 4:** The Indians became the fifth AL team to sweep a season series from a club in a non-strike year when they beat Detroit 9-3 on Aug. 28 to give them a 12-0 record against the Tigers. Orel Hershiser pitched seven innings for the win.

▶**Sept. 11:** The Indians feel they have three solid starters for the postseason— Orel Hershiser, Charles Nagy and Chad Ogea. The struggling Jack McDowell remains a question mark, as do the injured and unhappy Dennis Martinez and the inexperienced Albie Lopez.

▶**Sept. 18:** Albert Belle likes the clubhouse meat-locker cold. Some of his teammates don't. Between innings on Sept. 11, Belle kept turning the thermostat down, but his teammates kept turning it up. Belle finally took his bat and drove one thermostat through the wall and knocked another clear off.

▶**Sept. 25:** The Tribe clinched its second consecutive division title on Sept. 17 in Comiskey Park.

▶**Oct. 2:** After going 100-44 in 1995, this year the Indians experienced things that other teams go through—slumps; club-house turmoil; disputes with fans, opposing players and AL President Gene Budig; and controversial trades. But the Indians still got to postseason play in consecutive years for the first time. Despite suspensions and fines, Albert Belle set the franchise record for career homers, and his 148 RBI were the second most in Tribe history. Jim Thome (38 homers, 116 RBI) and right fielder Manny Ramirez (33 homers, 112 RBI) also supplied career-high power numbers. But Jose Mesa, who had a 1.13 ERA and converted 46 of 48 save chances last year, was less effective: 38 saves in 43 chances, with a 3.73 ERA.

Team directory

▶**Owner:** Richard E. Jacobs
▶**General manager:** John Hart
▶**Ballpark:**
Jacobs Field
2401 Ontario St.
Cleveland, Ohio
216-420-4200
Capacity 42,865
Downtown parking available; public transportation; handicapped seating; extremely accessible with escalators, elevators and ramps; all 38 bathrooms have diaper-changing areas; two unisex bathrooms for the physically challenged and kids.
▶**Team publications:**
Game Face Magazine, Tribe Talk
216-420-4200
▶**TV, radio broadcast stations:**
WKNR 1220 AM, WUAB Channel 43, SportsChannel Ohio
▶**Camps and/or clinics:**
Cleveland Indians Baseball Heaven (fantasy camp), January, 800-75-TRIBE
▶**Spring training:**
Chain O'Lakes Park
Winter Haven, Fla.
Capacity 4,520
813-291-5803

CLEVELAND INDIANS 1996 final stats

BATTERS	BA	SLG	OB	G	AB	R	H	TB	2B	3B	HR	RBI	BB	SO	SB	CS	E
Giles	.355	.612	.434	51	121	26	43	74	14	1	5	27	19	13	3	0	0
Seitzer	.326	.466	.416	154	573	85	187	267	35	3	13	78	87	79	6	1	5
Carreon	.324	.451	.385	142	142	16	46	64	12	0	2	14	11	9	1	1	2
Franco	.322	.470	.407	112	432	72	139	203	20	1	14	76	61	82	8	8	9
Thompson	.318	.455	.348	8	22	2	7	10	0	0	1	5	1	6	0	0	0
Lofton	.317	.446	.372	154	662	132	210	295	35	4	14	67	61	82	75	17	10
Thome	.311	.612	.450	151	505	122	157	309	28	5	38	116	123	141	2	2	17
Belle	.311	.623	.410	158	602	124	187	375	38	3	48	148	99	87	11	0	10
Ramirez	.309	.582	.399	152	550	94	170	320	45	3	33	112	85	104	8	5	9
Jackson	.300	.500	.364	5	10	2	3	5	2	0	0	1	1	4	0	0	0
Vizquel	.297	.417	.362	151	542	98	161	226	36	1	9	64	56	42	35	9	20
Vizcaino	.285	.335	.310	48	179	23	51	60	5	2	0	13	7	24	6	2	4
Baerga	.267	.396	.302	100	424	54	113	168	25	0	10	55	16	25	1	1	15
Kent	.265	.422	.328	39	102	16	27	43	7	0	3	16	10	22	2	1	1
Alomar	.263	.397	.299	127	418	53	110	166	23	0	11	50	19	42	1	0	9
Candaele	.250	.364	.267	24	44	8	11	16	2	0	1	4	1	9	0	0	0
Kirby	.250	.313	.333	27	16	3	4	5	1	0	0	1	2	2	0	1	0
Wilson	.250	.750	.308	10	12	2	3	9	0	0	2	5	1	6	0	0	0
Espinoza	.223	.402	.279	59	112	12	25	45	4	2	4	11	6	18	1	1	3
T. Pena	.195	.236	.255	67	174	14	34	41	4	0	1	27	15	25	0	1	3
Leius	.140	.302	.178	27	43	3	6	13	4	0	1	3	2	8	0	0	1
G. Pena	.111	.444	.200	5	9	1	1	4	0	0	1	2	1	4	0	0	0
Perry	.083	.167	.154	7	12	1	1	2	1	0	0	0	1	2	1	0	0
Diaz	.000	.000	.000	4	1	0	0	0	0	0	0	0	0	0	0	0	0

PITCHERS	W-L	ERA	G	GS	CG	GF	Sho	SV	IP	H	R	ER	HR	BB	SO
Plunk	3-2	2.43	56	0	0	12	0	2	77.2	56	21	21	6	34	85
Shuey	5-2	2.85	42	0	0	18	0	4	53.2	45	19	17	6	26	44
Poole	4-0	3.04	32	0	0	8	0	0	26.2	29	15	9	3	14	19
Assenmacher	4-2	3.09	63	0	0	25	0	1	46.2	46	18	16	1	14	44
Nagy	17-5	3.41	32	32	5	0	0	0	222.0	217	89	84	21	61	167
Mesa	2-7	3.73	69	0	0	60	0	39	72.1	69	32	30	6	28	64
Hershiser	15-9	4.24	33	33	1	0	0	0	206.0	238	115	97	21	58	125
Martinez	9-6	4.50	20	20	1	0	1	0	112.0	122	63	56	12	37	48
Graves	2-0	4.55	15	0	0	5	0	0	29.2	29	18	15	2	10	22
Ogea	10-6	4.79	29	21	1	2	1	0	146.2	151	82	78	22	42	101
Anderson	3-1	4.91	10	9	0	0	0	0	51.1	58	29	28	9	14	21
McDowell	13-9	5.11	30	30	5	0	1	0	192.0	214	119	109	22	67	141
Tavarez	4-7	5.36	51	4	0	13	0	0	80.2	101	49	48	9	22	46
Embree	1-1	6.39	24	0	0	2	0	0	31.0	30	26	22	10	21	33
Lopez	5-4	6.39	13	10	0	0	0	0	62.0	80	47	44	14	22	45
Swindell	1-1	6.59	13	2	0	1	0	0	28.2	31	21	21	8	8	21
Mercker	4-6	6.98	24	12	0	2	0	0	69.2	83	60	54	13	38	29
Roa	0-0	10.80	1	0	0	0	0	0	1.2	4	2	2	0	3	0

1997 preliminary roster

PITCHERS (21)
Brian Anderson
Paul Assenmacher
Bartolo Colon
Maximo DelaRosa
Travis Driskill
Alan Embree
Mike Gordon
Danny Graves
Orel Hershiser
Mike Jackson
Steve Kline
Albie Lopez

Mike Matthews
Jack McDowell
Jose Mesa
Charles Nagy
Chad Ogea
Eric Plunk
Paul Shuey
Teddy Warrecker
Casey Whitten

CATCHERS (2)
Sandy Alomar
Einar Diaz

INFIELDERS (10)
Tony Fernandez
Julio Franco
Damian Jackson
Herbert Perry
Kevin Seitzer
Richie Sexson
Jim Thome
Omar Vizquel
Matt Williams
Enrique Wilson

OUTFIELDERS (7)
Bruce Aven
Chad Curtis
Brian Giles
Trenidad Hubbard
Kenny Lofton
Alex Ramirez
Manny Ramirez

Games played by position

PLAYER	G	C	1B	2B	3B	SS	OF	DH
Alomar	127	124	1	0	0	0	0	0
Baerga	100	0	0	100	0	0	0	0
Belle	158	0	0	0	0	0	152	6
Candaele	24	0	0	11	3	1	0	0
Carreon	38	0	34	0	0	0	5	2
Diaz	4	4	0	0	0	0	0	0
Espinoza	59	0	18	5	20	16	0	1
Franco	112	0	97	0	0	0	0	13
Giles	51	0	0	0	0	0	16	21
Jackson	5	0	0	0	0	5	0	0
Kent	39	0	20	9	6	0	0	5
Kirby	27	0	0	0	0	0	18	3
Leius	27	0	7	6	8	0	0	1
Lofton	154	0	0	0	0	0	152	0
T. Pena	67	67	0	0	0	0	0	0
G. Pena	5	0	0	1	3	0	0	0
Perry	7	0	5	0	1	0	0	0
Ramirez	152	0	0	0	0	0	149	3
Seitzer	154	0	70	0	12	0	0	73
Thome	151	0	0	0	150	0	0	1
Thompson	8	0	0	0	0	0	8	0
Vizcaino	48	0	0	45	0	4	0	1
Vizquel	151	0	0	0	0	150	0	0
Wilson	10	0	0	0	0	0	1	3

Minor Leagues

Tops in the organization

BATTER	CLUB	AVG.	G	AB	R	H	HR	RBI
Sean Casey	Kin	.331	92	344	62	114	12	57
Alex Ramirez	Can	.329	131	513	79	169	14	85
Brian Giles	Buf	.314	83	318	65	100	20	64
Scott Morgan	Clm	.311	87	305	62	95	22	80
C. Candaele	Buf	.311	94	392	66	122	6	37

HOME RUNS

R. Branyan	Clm	40
Nigel Wilson	Buf	30
Rod Mccall	Can	27
Bruce Aven	Buf	24
Several Players Tied At		22

WINS

David Caldwell	Kin	13
Travis Driskill	Can	13
Jimmy Williams	Buf	12
Noe Najera	Kin	12
Several Players Tied At		11

RBI

R. Branyan	Clm	106
Nigel Wilson	Buf	95
D. Stumberger	Clm	89
Rod McCall	Can	85
Alex Ramirez	Can	85

SAVES

S. Winchester	Clm	26
Wilmer Montoya	Can	25
Danny Graves	Buf	19
Rafael Mesa	Kin	15
Tony Dougherty	Kin	10

STOLEN BASES

Patricio Claudio	Kin	36
Milt Anderson	Clm	29
Damian Jackson	Buf	24
Enrique Wilson	Buf	23
Bruce Aven	Buf	22

STRIKEOUTS

Travis Driskill	Can	148
R. Delamaza	Can	132
Noe Najera	Kin	131
Dannon Atkins	Clm	129
Igor Oropeza	Bak	114

PITCHER	CLUB	W-L	ERA	IP	H	BB	SO
Jared Camp	Wtn	10-2	1.69	96	68	30	99
Jaret Wright	Kin	7-4	2.50	101	65	55	109
F. Sanders	Clm	9-3	2.52	121	103	37	109
Noe Najera	Kin	12-2	2.70	140	124	62	131
Joe Roa	Buf	11-8	3.27	165	161	36	82

Sick call: 1996 DL report

PLAYER	Days on the DL
Mark Carreon	37
Alan Embree	37
Julio Franco	44*
Daron Kirkreit	182
Scott Leius	20
Dennis Martinez	52**
Jack McDowell	18
Chad Ogea	30
Herb Perry	19
Jeff Sexton	93
Greg Swindell	17

Indicates two separate terms on Disabled List.
**Indicates three separate terms on Disabled List.*

1996 salaries

	Bonuses	Total earned salary
Albert Belle, of	$150,000	$5,650,000
Jack McDowell, p		$4,800,000
Dennis Martinez, p		$3,789,456
Kenny Lofton, of	$50,000	$3,575,000
Charles Nagy, p	$150,000	$3,487,500
Omar Vizquel, ss	$50,000	$3,050,000
Kent Mercker, p		$2,825,000
Sandy Alomar Jr., c	$25,000	$2,575,000
Julio Franco, 1b		$2,379,458
Jose Vizcaino, ss		$2,200,000
Jeff Kent, 3b		$1,960,000
Orel Hershiser, p	$200,000	$1,750,000
Jim Thome, 3b	$75,000	$1,600,000
Jose Mesa, p	$400,000	$1,325,000
Kevin Seitzer, 3b	$150,000	$1,150,000
Manny Ramirez, of		$1,100,000
Mark Carreon, of	$100,000	$1,000,000
Paul Assenmacher, p		$871,400
Eric Plunk, p		$750,000
Tony Pena, c	$33,333	$558,333
Julian Tavarez, p		$408,333
Alan Embree, p		$155,000
Casey Candaele, 2b		$150,000
Chad Ogea, p		$145,000
Paul Shuey, p		$138,000
Albie Lopez, p		$132,000
Nigel Wilson, of		$125,000
Brian Giles, of		$110,000
Daron Kirkreit, p		$109,000
Jeffrey Sexton, p		$109,000

Average 1996 salary: $1,599,249
Total 1996 team payroll: $47,977,480
Termination pay: $315,573

Cleveland (1901-1996)

Runs: Most, career

1154	Earl Averill, 1929-1939
1079	Tris Speaker, 1916-1926
942	Charlie Jamieson, 1919-1932
865	Nap Lajoie, 1902-1914
857	Joe Sewell, 1920-1930

Hits: Most, career

2046	Nap Lajoie, 1902-1914
1965	Tris Speaker, 1916-1926
1903	Earl Averill, 1929-1939
1800	Joe Sewell, 1920-1930
1753	Charlie Jamieson, 1919-1932

2B: Most, career

486	Tris Speaker, 1916-1926
424	Nap Lajoie, 1902-1914
377	Earl Averill, 1929-1939
375	Joe Sewell, 1920-1930
367	Lou Boudreau, 1938-1950

3B: Most, career

121	Earl Averill, 1929-1939
108	Tris Speaker, 1916-1926
106	Elmer Flick, 1902-1910
89	Joe Jackson, 1910-1915
83	Jeff Heath, 1936-1945

HR: Most, career

242	ALBERT BELLE, 1989-1996
226	Earl Averill, 1929-1939
216	Hal Trosky, 1933-1941
215	Larry Doby, 1947-1958
214	Andy Thornton, 1977-1987

RBI: Most, career

1084	Earl Averill, 1929-1939
919	Nap Lajoie, 1902-1914
911	Hal Trosky, 1933-1941
884	Tris Speaker, 1916-1926
869	Joe Sewell, 1920-1930

SB: Most, career

325	KENNY LOFTON, 1992-1996
254	Terry Turner, 1904-1918
240	Nap Lajoie, 1902-1914
233	Ray Chapman, 1912-1920
207	Elmer Flick, 1902-1910

BB: Most, career

857	Tris Speaker, 1916-1926
766	Lou Boudreau, 1938-1950
725	Earl Averill, 1929-1939
712	Jack Graney, 1908-1922
703	Larry Doby, 1947-1958

BA: Highest, career

.375	Joe Jackson, 1910-1915
.354	Tris Speaker, 1916-1926
.339	Nap Lajoie, 1902-1914
.327	George Burns, 1920-1928
.323	Ed Morgan, 1928-1933

Slug avg: Highest, career

.580	ALBERT BELLE, 1989-1996
.551	Hal Trosky, 1933-1941
.542	Joe Jackson, 1910-1915
.542	Earl Averill, 1929-1939
.530	JIM THOME, 1991-1996

On-base avg: Highest, career

.444	Tris Speaker, 1916-1926
.441	Joe Jackson, 1910-1915
.405	Ed Morgan, 1928-1933
.404	JIM THOME, 1991-1996
.399	Earl Averill, 1929-1939

Complete games: Most, career

279	Bob Feller, 1936-1956
234	Addie Joss, 1902-1910
194	Stan Coveleski, 1916-1924
188	Bob Lemon, 1941-1958
181	Mel Harder, 1928-1947

Saves: Most, career

128	DOUG JONES, 1986-1991
87	JOSE MESA, 1992-1996
53	Ray Narleski, 1954-1958
48	Steve Olin, 1989-1992
46	Jim Kern, 1974-1986
46	Sid Monge, 1977-1981

Shutouts: Most, career

45	Addie Joss, 1902-1910
44	Bob Feller, 1936-1956
31	Stan Coveleski, 1916-1924
31	Bob Lemon, 1941-1958
27	Mike Garcia, 1948-1959

Wins: Most, career

266	Bob Feller, 1936-1956
223	Mel Harder, 1928-1947
207	Bob Lemon, 1941-1958
172	Stan Coveleski, 1916-1924
164	Early Wynn, 1949-1963

K: Most, career

2581	Bob Feller, 1936-1956
2159	Sam McDowell, 1961-1971
1277	Bob Lemon, 1941-1958
1277	Early Wynn, 1949-1963
1161	Mel Harder, 1928-1947

Win pct: Highest, career

.667	Vean Gregg, 1911-1914
.663	Johnny Allen, 1936-1940
.630	Cal McLish, 1956-1959
.623	Addie Joss, 1902-1910
.622	Wes Ferrell, 1927-1933

ERA: Lowest, career

1.89	Addie Joss, 1902-1910
2.31	Vean Gregg, 1911-1914
2.39	Bob Rhoads, 1903-1909
2.45	Bill Bernhard, 1902-1907
2.50	Otto Hess, 1902-1908

Runs: Most, season

140	Earl Averill, 1931
137	Tris Speaker, 1920
136	Earl Averill, 1936
133	Tris Speaker, 1923
132	KENNY LOFTON, 1996

Hits: Most, season

233	Joe Jackson, 1911
232	Earl Averill, 1936
227	Nap Lajoie, 1910
226	Joe Jackson, 1912
225	Johnny Hodapp, 1930

2B: Most, season

64	George Burns, 1926
59	Tris Speaker, 1923
52	ALBERT BELLE, 1995
52	Tris Speaker, 1921
52	Tris Speaker, 1926

3B: Most, season

26	Joe Jackson, 1912
23	Dale Mitchell, 1949
22	Bill Bradley, 1903
22	Elmer Flick, 1906
20	Jeff Heath, 1941
20	Joe Vosmik, 1935

HR: Most, season

50	ALBERT BELLE, 1995
48	ALBERT BELLE, 1996
43	Al Rosen, 1953
42	Rocky Colavito, 1959
42	Hal Trosky, 1936

RBI: Most, season

162	Hal Trosky, 1936

148 ALBERT BELLE, 1996
145 Al Rosen, 1953
143 Earl Averill, 1931
142 Hal Trosky, 1934

SB: Most, season

75 KENNY LOFTON, 1996
70 KENNY LOFTON, 1993
66 KENNY LOFTON, 1992
61 Miguel Dilone, 1980
60 KENNY LOFTON, 1994

BB: Most, season

123 JIM THOME, 1996
111 Mike Hargrove, 1980
109 Andy Thornton, 1982
106 Les Fleming, 1942
105 Jack Graney, 1919

BA: Highest, season

.408 Joe Jackson, 1911
.395 Joe Jackson, 1912
.389 Tris Speaker, 1925
.388 Tris Speaker, 1920
.386 Tris Speaker, 1916

Slug avg: Highest, season

.714 ALBERT BELLE, 1994
.690 ALBERT BELLE, 1995
.644 Hal Trosky, 1936
.627 Earl Averill, 1936
.623 ALBERT BELLE, 1996

On-base avg: Highest, season

.483 Tris Speaker, 1920
.479 Tris Speaker, 1925
.474 Tris Speaker, 1922
.470 Tris Speaker, 1916
.469 Tris Speaker, 1923

Complete games: Most, season

36 Bob Feller, 1946
35 Bill Bernhard, 1904
34 Addie Joss, 1907
33 Otto Hess, 1906
32 George Uhle, 1926

Saves: Most, season

46 JOSE MESA, 1995
43 DOUG JONES, 1990
39 JOSE MESA, 1996
37 DOUG JONES, 1988
32 DOUG JONES, 1989

Shutouts: Most, season

10 Bob Feller, 1946
10 Bob Lemon, 1948
 9 Stan Coveleski, 1917
 9 Addie Joss, 1906

9 Addie Joss, 1908
9 Luis Tiant, 1968

Wins: Most, season

31 Jim Bagby, 1920
27 Bob Feller, 1940
27 Addie Joss, 1907
27 George Uhle, 1926
26 Bob Feller, 1946
26 George Uhle, 1923

K: Most, season

348 Bob Feller, 1946
325 Sam McDowell, 1965
304 Sam McDowell, 1970
283 Sam McDowell, 1968
279 Sam McDowell, 1969

Win pct: Highest, season

.938 Johnny Allen, 1937
.773 Bill Bernhard, 1902
.773 CHARLES NAGY, 1996
.767 Vean Gregg, 1911
.767 Bob Lemon, 1954

ERA: Lowest, season

1.16 Addie Joss, 1908
1.59 Addie Joss, 1904
1.60 Luis Tiant, 1968
1.71 Addie Joss, 1909
1.72 Addie Joss, 1906

Most pinch-hit homers, season

3 Gene Green, 1962
3 Ron Kittle, 1988
3 Ted Ulaender, 1970
3 Fred Whitfield, 1965

Most pinch-hit homers, career

8 Fred Whitfield, 1963-1967
5 Chuck Hinton, 1965-1971

Longest hitting streak

31 Nap Lajoie, 1906
29 Bill Bradley, 1902
28 Joe Jackson, 1911
28 Hal Trosky, 1936
27 Bruce Campbell, 1938

Most consecutive scoreless innings

41 Luis Tiant, 1968
38 Jim Bagby, 1917

No-hit games

Earl Moore, Cle vs Chi AL, 2-4;
    May 9, 1901 (lost on two hits in
    the 10th).

Dusty Rhoades, Cle vs Bos AL, 2-1;
    Sept. 18, 1908.
Addie Joss, Cle vs Chi AL, 1-0;
    Oct. 2, 1908 (perfect game).
Addie Joss, Cle at Chi AL, 1-0;
    Apr. 20, 1910.
Ray Caldwell, Cle at NY AL, 3-0;
    Sept. 10, 1919 (1st game).
Wes Ferrell, Cle vs StL AL, 9-0;
    Apr. 29, 1931.
Bob Feller, Cle at Chi AL, 1-0;
    Apr. 16, 1940 (opening day).
Bob Feller, Cle at NY AL, 1-0;
    Apr. 30, 1946.
Don Black, Cle vs Phi AL, 3-0;
    July 10, 1947 (1st game).
Bob Lemon, Cle at Det AL, 2-0;
    June 30, 1948.
Bob Feller, Cle vs Det AL, 2-1;
    July 1, 1951 (1st game).
Sonny Siebert, Cle vs Was AL, 2-0;
    June 10, 1966.
Dick Bosman, Cle vs Oak AL, 4-0;
    July 19, 1974.
DENNIS ECKERSLEY, Cle vs Cal
    AL, 1-0; May 30, 1977.
Len Barker, Cle vs Tor AL, 3-0;
    May 15, 1981 (perfect game).

ACTIVE PLAYERS in caps.

*Players' years of service are listed by
the first and last years with this team
and are not necessarily consecutive;
all statistics record performances for
this team only.*

125

Chicago White Sox

Chicago
White Sox

Frank Thomas led the White Sox in almost every offensive category.

By Russell Beeker, Baseball Weekly

1996 White Sox: Ruined by September fade

The White Sox wrecked a decent comeback season by playing under .500 during the last month. In 1995 they had finished 32 games behind Cleveland, but in '96 they lost the wild card to Baltimore only in the season's last weekend after leading that race for most of the second half. "We were better than we were portrayed, but not as good as we wanted," said manager Terry Bevington.

The starting pitching failed in the stretch. Wilson Alvarez, Kevin Tapani and rookie James Baldwin went a combined 2-7 in September, and the middle relief was awful from late June to the finish. Sox GM Ron Schueler took heat for making only a few patchwork moves in the last two months while other contenders were stockpiling name players, but as he put it, "I wasn't going to mortgage the future by giving away our best prospects."

"We just didn't get it done," concluded the team's superstar, first baseman Frank Thomas. "There are no excuses on our part. We played hard all year long. It's easy to lay the blame on everyone, but it's not easy to lay the blame on anything."

It was a memorable season offensively, with team records in home runs, runs, RBI and slugging average. The club had three 100-RBI men for the first time: Frank Thomas (134), Robin Ventura (105) and Danny Tartabull (101). The 1977 South Side Hitmen's team record of 192 homers fell on the last weekend, and eight players reached double digits in dingers: Thomas had 40, Ventura 34, Tartabull 27, Harold Baines 22, Tony Phillips 12, and Dave Martinez, Ray Durham and Ron Karkovice 10 each. Thomas extended his streak of hitting .300 with 100 runs, 100 RBI, 100 walks and 20 home runs to six consecutive seasons. The club's outfield was completely revamped, with Phillips filling the leadoff spot with 119 runs, Martinez sharing center field with Darren Lewis, and Tartabull holding down right.

Alex Fernandez had a career year with 200 strikeouts, 257 innings pitched and

six complete games. His final game, a 4-2 decision at Minnesota, was emotional because of the possibility that he would leave. In December, he signed with Miami, his hometown team. The myriad fifth starters were a dismal 3-12 on the year.

Some critics say the Sox's bullpen was overworked early, and thus young relievers such as Matt Karchner and Bill Simas, setup men for closer Roberto Hernandez, were burned out by the second half. Hernandez finished with 38 saves and an outstanding 1.91 ERA, but he blew eight saves, tied for second-most in the league. The bullpen failures were reflected in Chicago's 40-46 record in one- and two-run games.

Interest in the White Sox faded last season, which may have occurred because the team went 23-32 over the last four months at Comiskey Park after a hot start there. In November, though, the signing of free-agent slugger Albert Belle, who has hit 98 homers in the last two years, prompted a surge in ticket sales. The team drew just 1,676,416 at Comiskey Park in 1996, an average of 21,220, but owner Jerry Reinsdorf had said that the poor showing at the gate didn't necessarily mean that the team would spend less in 1997. He obviously was telling the truth, because Belle is costing Reinsdorf $55 million (not counting the new luxury tax) for the next five years.

1996 White Sox: Week-by-week notes

These notes were excerpted from the following issues of Baseball Weekly.

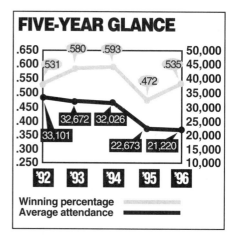

FIVE-YEAR GLANCE

Winning percentage
Average attendance

▶**April 10:** Catcher Ron Karkovice redeemed himself for five strikeouts in five at-bats in the season opener in Seattle by hitting .333 for the rest of the week. A Seattle newspaper had quipped, "We didn't know Ron Karkovice had five Ks in his name."

▶**April 17:** Before Oakland beat right-hander Alex Fernandez 7-2 on April 12, he had gone 8-0 in 13 starts since Aug. 5, 1995.

▶**May 1:** Jason Bere's elbow tendinitis left the door wide open for rookie James Baldwin, who finished 1995 with a 12.89 ERA in six appearances. Baldwin won his first start, barely making it through five innings in a 6-5 victory at Texas.

▶**May 8:** The White Sox were 1-4 on a trip against opposing starters who had a combined .606 career winning percentage, a group that included Dennis Martinez, Jack McDowell, David Cone and Dwight Gooden. The Sox went from a half game behind Cleveland to 4½ away before winning a game started by the Yankees' Jimmy Key, 11-5. First baseman Frank Thomas was named the AL Player of the Month for April. He had a .379 average, nine home runs, 25 RBI and 20 runs scored for the month.

▶**May 29:** Sox starters hadn't completed a game until Kevin Tapani beat Milwaukee 12-1 on May 26, but the staff is second to Boston in AL strikeouts with 7.1 a game.

▶**June 5:** Right fielder Danny Tartabull is the last of general manager Ron Schueler's 1996 acquisitions to begin to produce, but the right fielder is showing signs of recovery. He had five RBI last week, although he was still hitting under .230.

▶**June 19:** Kevin Tapani is keeping the White Sox in contention with a 7-3 record after a combined 10-13 tally last year with the Twins and the Dodgers. His 3.11 ERA ranks among the league leaders.

▶**June 26:** Ray Durham's standout second-base defense goes beyond his nearly errorless play (two on the year). His range is wide, he's particularly adept at going back on popups, and he doesn't hurry himself on throws. Double-play partner Ozzie Guillen said, "He remembers everything you tell him, and he's starting to position himself now."

▶**July 3:** In 1995, Frank Thomas tied Frank Howard's 1970 AL record for intentional walks by a right-handed batter, with 29. This year he already has 17.

▶**July 11:** Designated hitter Harold Baines's two home runs on July 6 keyed Chicago's 3-2 win against Cleveland—the third win in a row at Jacobs Field against the Indians. But the Indians salvaged the last game of the series the next day, dropping the White Sox two games behind.

▶**July 17:** The fracture in Frank Thomas's left foot is a stress test for the White Sox, who won't have their MVP candidate until at least August.

▶**July 24:** The first four starters could cram into the league's Top 10 in ERA when James Baldwin gets enough innings. Kevin Tapani, Wilson Alvarez and Alex Fernandez are under 4.00, and Baldwin is at 3.77.

▶**July 31:** Ron Schueler sounded like Douglas MacArthur returning to the Philippines when, after trading with California for backup catcher Pat Borders, he vowed, "I'm not finished."

▶**Aug. 7:** Frank Thomas was 7-for-14 with six RBI in his first four games back from a foot stress fracture. The White

Sox had slipped in all offensive categories but steals without Thomas. They hit .253 compared to .281 with him, averaged 4.6 runs a game after 5.7, had 8.5 hits a contest to 9.9 and walked 3.5 times to 4.7. Worse yet, their 8-11 record after going 50-37 dropped them from two games behind Cleveland to six out.

▶**Aug. 14:** The White Sox will not go down without a fight. They fought among themselves in New York when Frank Thomas, frustrated over umpiring calls in two consecutive games, had to be restrained by third baseman Robin Ventura. The result: Thomas pushed Ventura in the chest, and half the team had to run to the rescue.

▶**Aug. 28:** The White Sox's five fifth starters are a combined 2-12. The club was searching for still another after Scott Ruffcorn failed as a sub for Jason Bere, whose return from an April elbow muscle tear was delayed by a stiff shoulder. Alex Fernandez was the only consistent starter going into the last week of August. That's not unusual. His career second-half record is 39-26.

▶**Sept. 4:** The White Sox didn't make big-name acquisitions at the 25-man postseason roster deadline. Their moves were patchwork—catcher Don Slaught from the Angels for a player to be named in case Ron Karkovice's ailing right knee gives out, and free-agent right-hander Marvin Freeman from Colorado as insurance against other injuries.

▶**Sept. 11:** Closer Roberto Hernandez went a full year without giving up a home run to a right-handed batter until Detroit's Travis Fryman beat him with a three-run drive on Sept. 2. Knee arthroscopy ended Matt Karchner's season. He had a 7-4 record, but his 5.76 ERA, up from 1.63 in late May, typified the failure of the Sox's middle relievers.

▶**Sept. 18:** Two important defenders have gone down: Ozzie Guillen's strained side muscle prevents him from swinging a bat, and Ron Karkovice's knees are ready for arthroscopy.

▶**Sept. 25:** Despite being in the thick of the wild-card race, the club might not make 1.7 million in home attendance, its lowest since new Comiskey Park opened in 1991.

▶**Oct. 2:** The end was hard to take, as the White Sox led the wild-card race for 51 days after the All-Star break, until losing it to the Orioles in the last two days. The buck stopped on the mound: Starters Wilson Alvarez, Kevin Tapani and James Baldwin were a combined 2-7 in September with an ERA over 7.00; the many fifth starters were 3-12; and middle relief was deplorable from late June on. Three telling statistics: an eight-game losing streak in June, a 40-46 mark in one- and two-run decisions, and a 44-37 home record after a 21-5 start there. Frank Thomas rolled along, having his sixth consecutive season with a .300 average, 20 home runs, 100 runs, 100 RBI and 100 walks.

Team directory

▶**Owner:** Jerry Reinsdorf (chairman), Eddie Einhorn (vice-chairman) and a board of directors
▶**General manager:** Ron Schueler
▶**Ballpark:**
Comiskey Park
333 W. 35th St.
Chicago, Ill.
312-924-1000
Capacity 44,321
Parking for 7,000 vehicles; $10
Public transportation available
Kids Corner (with photo booth and uniforms for imitation baseball cards), elevators and seating for the handicapped, escalators, ramps, cash station, Hall of Fame
▶**Team publications:**
Program, yearbook, media guide, calendar, team photos and player photos, 312-451-5300
▶**TV, radio broadcast stations:**
WMVP 1000 AM, WGN TV-9, Sports Channel Chicago
▶**Camps and/or clinics:**
Chicago White Sox Training Centers
708-752-9225
▶**Spring training:**
Ed Smith Stadium
Sarasota, Fla.
Capacity 7,500
813-953-3388

CHICAGO WHITE SOX 1996 final stats

BATTERS	BA	SLG	OB	G	AB	R	H	TB	2B	3B	HR	RBI	BB	SO	SB	CS	E
Machado	.667	.833	.667	4	6	1	4	5	1	0	0	2	0	0	0	0	0
Martin	.350	.421	.374	70	140	30	49	59	7	0	1	14	6	17	10	2	6
F. Thomas	.349	.626	.459	141	527	110	184	330	26	0	40	134	109	70	1	1	9
Martinez	.318	.468	.393	146	440	85	140	206	20	8	10	53	52	52	15	7	6
Slaught	.313	.428	.355	76	243	25	76	104	10	0	6	36	15	22	0	0	4
Baines	.311	.503	.399	143	495	80	154	249	29	0	22	95	73	62	3	1	0
Mouton	.294	.439	.361	87	214	25	63	94	8	1	7	39	22	50	3	0	2
Ventura	.287	.520	.368	158	586	96	168	305	31	2	34	105	78	81	1	3	11
Phillips	.277	.399	.404	153	581	119	161	232	29	3	12	63	125	132	13	8	7
Durham	.275	.406	.350	156	557	79	153	226	33	5	10	65	58	95	30	4	11
Cedeno	.272	.346	.308	89	301	46	82	104	12	2	2	20	15	64	6	3	10
Guillen	.263	.367	.273	150	499	62	131	183	24	8	4	45	10	27	6	5	11
Snopek	.260	.510	.304	46	104	18	27	53	6	1	6	18	6	16	0	1	5
Munoz	.259	.259	.355	17	27	7	7	7	0	0	0	1	4	1	0	0	2
Borders	.258	.384	.296	50	151	12	39	58	4	0	5	14	8	29	0	1	5
Tartabull	.254	.487	.340	132	472	58	120	230	23	3	27	101	64	128	1	2	7
Lewis	.228	.312	.321	141	337	55	77	105	12	2	4	53	45	40	21	5	3
Karkovice	.220	.366	.270	111	355	44	78	130	22	0	10	38	24	93	0	0	5
Kreuter	.219	.368	.308	46	114	14	25	42	8	0	3	18	13	29	0	0	2
Norton	.217	.478	.333	11	23	4	5	11	0	0	2	3	4	6	0	1	2
Robertson	.143	.286	.143	6	7	0	1	2	1	0	0	0	0	1	0	0	0
Cameron	.091	.091	.167	11	11	1	1	1	0	0	0	0	1	3	0	1	0

PITCHERS	W-L	ERA	G	GS	CG	GF	Sho	SV	IP	H	R	ER	HR	BB	SO
Jones	0-0	0.00	2	0	0	1	0	0	2.0	0	0	0	0	1	1
Hernandez	6-5	1.91	72	0	0	61	0	38	84.2	65	21	18	2	38	85
Darwin	0-1	2.93	22	0	0	9	0	0	30.2	26	10	10	5	9	15
L. Thomas	2-3	3.23	57	0	0	11	0	0	30.2	32	11	11	1	14	20
Fernandez	16-10	3.45	35	35	6	0	1	0	258.0	248	110	99	34	72	200
Castillo	5-4	3.60	55	0	0	13	0	2	95.0	95	45	38	10	24	57
Alvarez	15-10	4.22	35	35	0	0	0	0	217.1	216	106	102	21	97	181
Baldwin	11-6	4.42	28	28	0	0	0	0	169.0	168	88	83	24	57	127
Simas	2-8	4.58	64	0	0	16	0	2	72.2	75	39	37	5	39	65
Tapani	13-10	4.59	34	34	1	0	0	0	225.1	236	123	115	34	76	150
Keyser	1-2	4.98	28	0	0	10	0	1	59.2	78	35	33	3	28	19
Bertotti	2-0	5.14	15	2	0	4	0	0	28.0	28	18	16	5	20	19
Levine	0-1	5.40	16	0	0	5	0	0	18.1	22	14	11	1	7	12
Karchner	7-4	5.76	50	0	0	13	0	1	59.1	61	42	38	10	41	46
Magrane	1-5	6.88	19	8	0	3	0	0	53.2	70	45	41	10	25	21
McCaskill	5-5	6.97	29	4	0	13	0	0	51.2	72	41	40	6	31	28
Sirotka	1-2	7.18	15	4	0	2	0	0	26.1	34	27	21	3	12	11
Bere	0-1	10.26	5	5	0	0	0	0	16.2	26	19	19	3	18	19
Ruffcorn	0-1	11.37	3	1	0	1	0	0	6.1	10	8	8	1	6	3
Freeman	0-0	13.50	1	1	0	0	0	0	2.0	4	3	3	0	1	1
Sauveur	0-0	15.00	3	0	0	0	0	0	3.0	3	5	5	1	5	1

1997 preliminary roster

PITCHERS (21)
Wilson Alvarez
James Baldwin
Jason Bere
Mike Bertotti
Carlos Castillo
Tony Castillo
Chris Clemons
Nelson Cruz
Jeff Darwin
Jayson Durocher
Scott Eyre
Tom Fordham
Roberto Hernandez
Matt Karchner
Alan Levine
Jamie Navarro
Scott Ruffcorn
Bill Simas
Mike Sirotka
Larry Thomas
Brian Woods

CATCHERS (2)
Ron Karkovice
Robert Machado

INFIELDERS (8)
Ray Durham
Ozzie Guillen
Paco Martin
Greg Norton
Olmedo Saenz
Chris Snopek
Frank Thomas
Robin Ventura

OUTFIELDERS (8)
Jeff Abbott
Albert Belle
Mike Cameron
Jimmy Hurst
Darren Lewis
Dave Martinez
Lyle Mouton
Tony Phillips

Games played by position

PLAYER	G	C	1B	2B	3B	SS	OF	DH
Baines	143	0	0	0	0	0	0	141
Borders	50	49	0	0	0	0	0	1
Cameron	11	0	0	0	0	0	8	2
Cedeno	89	0	0	64	6	7	0	1
Durham	156	0	0	150	0	0	0	3
Guillen	150	0	0	0	0	146	2	0
Karkovice	111	111	0	0	0	0	0	0
Kreuter	46	38	2	0	0	0	0	1
Lewis	141	0	0	0	0	0	138	0
Machado	4	4	0	0	0	0	0	0
Martin	70	0	0	10	3	24	0	22
Martinez	146	0	23	0	0	0	121	0
Mouton	87	0	0	0	0	0	47	28
Munoz	17	0	0	7	1	2	1	2
Norton	11	0	0	0	2	6	0	1
Phillips	153	0	1	2	0	0	150	0
Robertson	6	0	2	0	0	0	0	2
Slaught	76	71	0	0	0	0	0	2
Snopek	46	0	0	0	27	12	0	3
Tartabull	132	0	0	0	0	0	122	10
F. Thomas	141	0	139	0	0	0	0	0
Ventura	158	0	14	0	150	0	0	0

Minor Leagues

Tops in the organization

BATTER	CLUB	AVG.	G	AB	R	H	HR	RBI
Mario Valdez	Bir	.330	111	370	68	122	13	71
Jeff Abbott	Nvl	.325	113	440	64	143	14	60
Carlos Lee	Hck	.313	119	480	65	150	8	70
Mike Cameron	Bir	.300	123	473	120	142	28	77
Juan Thomas	Prw	.299	134	495	88	148	20	71

HOME RUNS

Mike Cameron	Bir	28
Mike Robertson	Nvl	21
Brian Simmons	Prw	21
Juan Thomas	Prw	20
Jimmy Hurst	Nvl	19

WINS

Rich Pratt	Bir	13
Scott Ruffcorn	Nvl	13
Scott Eyre	Bir	12
Tom Fordham	Nvl	12
Jason Olsen	Prw	12

RBI

Jimmy Hurst	Nvl	90
Mike Cameron	Bir	77
Mike Robertson	Nvl	74
Brian Simmons	Prw	72
Several Players Tied At		71

SAVES

Stacy Jones	Bir	26
Chad Bradford	Hck	18
Alan Levine	Nvl	12
D. Hasselhoff	Prw	11
Todd Rizzo	Bir	10

STOLEN BASES

Ramon Gomez	Hck	57
Mike Cameron	Bir	39
Rashad Albert	Brs	34
Doug Brady	Nvl	20
S. McKinnon	Prw	20

STRIKEOUTS

Carlos Castillo	Prw	158
Tom Fordham	Nvl	155
Russ Herbert	Prw	148
Nelson Cruz	Bir	142
Jason Olsen	Prw	142

PITCHER	CLUB	W-L	ERA	IP	H	BB	SO
Barry Johnson	Nvl	7-2	2.53	114	95	40	83
Jason Olsen	Prw	12-6	2.72	162	132	50	142
Chris Clemons	Bir	6-6	2.90	130	127	48	95
Nelson Cruz	Bir	6-6	3.20	149	150	41	142
Tom Fordham	Nvl	12-9	3.29	178	143	83	155

Sick call: 1996 DL report

PLAYER	Days on the DL
Jason Bere	150*
Matt Karchner	50
Chad Kreuter	72
Norberto Martin	60
Frank Thomas	22
Larry Thomas	20

* Indicates two separate terms on Disabled List.

1996 salaries

	Bonuses	Total earned salary
Frank Thomas, 1b		$7,150,000
Robin Ventura, 3b	$25,000	$6,000,000
Danny Tartabull, of		$5,300,000
Alex Fernandez, p		$4,500,000
Ozzie Guillen, ss		$4,000,000
Wilson Alvarez, p	$125,000	$2,825,000
Roberto Hernandez, p	$205,000	$2,105,000
Tony Phillips, of	$300,000	$2,100,000
Harold Baines, of	$725,000	$1,875,000
Darren Lewis, of	$125,000	$1,625,000
Ron Karkovice, c	$100,000	$1,600,000
Kevin Tapani, p	$400,000	$1,500,000
Dave Martinez, of	$230,000	$930,000
Tony Castillo, p		$660,000
Pat Borders, c	$25,000	$375,000
Chad Kreuter, c		$350,000
Don Slaught, c	$100,000	$350,000
Jason Bere, p		$230,000
Domingo Cedeno, ss		$230,000
Ray Durham, 2b	$20,000	$170,000
Norberto Martin, 2b	$5,000	$165,000
Matt Karchner, p		$135,000
Lyle Mouton, of		$135,000
Bill Simas, p		$130,000
Larry Thomas, p		$130,000
James Baldwin, p		$115,000
Mike Cameron, of		$115,000
Jeff Darwin, p		$110,000
Mike Bertotti, p		$109,500

Average 1996 salary: $1,552,396
Total 1996 team payroll: $45,019,500
Termination pay: $191,667

Chicago (1901-1996)

Runs: Most, career

1319	Luke Appling,	1930-1950
1187	Nellie Fox,	1950-1963
1065	Eddie Collins,	1915-1926
893	Minnie Minoso,	1951-1980
791	Luis Aparicio,	1956-1970

Hits: Most, career

2749	Luke Appling,	1930-1950
2470	Nellie Fox,	1950-1963
2007	Eddie Collins,	1915-1926
1652	HAROLD BAINES,	1980-1996
1576	Luis Aparicio,	1956-1970

2B: Most, career

440	Luke Appling,	1930-1950
335	Nellie Fox,	1950-1963
296	HAROLD BAINES,	1980-1996
266	Eddie Collins,	1915-1926
260	Minnie Minoso,	1951-1980

3B: Most, career

104	Shano Collins,	1910-1920
104	Nellie Fox,	1950-1963
102	Luke Appling,	1930-1950
102	Eddie Collins,	1915-1926
82	Johnny Mostil,	1918-1929

HR: Most, career

222	FRANK THOMAS,	1990-1996
214	Carlton Fisk,	1981-1993
208	HAROLD BAINES,	1980-1996
154	Bill Melton,	1968-1975
144	R. VENTURA,	1989-1996

RBI: Most, career

1116	Luke Appling,	1930-1950
914	HAROLD BAINES,	1980-1996
808	Minnie Minoso,	1951-1980
804	Eddie Collins,	1915-1926
762	Carlton Fisk,	1981-1993

SB: Most, career

368	Eddie Collins,	1915-1926
318	Luis Aparicio,	1956-1970
250	Frank Isbell,	1901-1909
226	L. JOHNSON,	1988-1995
206	Fielder Jones,	1901-1908

BB: Most, career

1302	Luke Appling,	1930-1950
965	Eddie Collins,	1915-1926
770	FRANK THOMAS,	1990-1996
658	Nellie Fox,	1950-1963
658	Minnie Minoso,	1951-1980

BA: Highest, career

.340	Joe Jackson,	1915-1920
.331	Eddie Collins,	1915-1926
.327	FRANK THOMAS,	1990-1996
.317	Zeke Bonura,	1934-1937
.315	Bibb Falk,	1920-1928

Slug avg: Highest, career

.599	FRANK THOMAS,	1990-1996
.518	Zeke Bonura,	1934-1937
.499	Joe Jackson,	1915-1920
.470	Ron Kittle,	1982-1991
.468	Minnie Minoso,	1951-1980

On-base avg: Highest, career

.452	FRANK THOMAS,	1990-1996
.426	Eddie Collins,	1915-1926
.407	Joe Jackson,	1915-1920
.399	Luke Appling,	1930-1950
.397	Minnie Minoso,	1951-1980

Complete games: Most, career

356	Ted Lyons,	1923-1946
273	Red Faber,	1914-1933
249	Ed Walsh,	1904-1916
206	Doc White,	1903-1913
183	Eddie Cicotte,	1912-1920
183	Billy Pierce,	1949-1961

Saves: Most, career

201	Bobby Thigpen,	1986-1993
134	ROBERTO HERNANDEZ, 1991-1996	
98	Hoyt Wilhelm,	1963-1968
75	Terry Forster,	1971-1976
57	Wilbur Wood,	1967-1978

Shutouts: Most, career

57	Ed Walsh,	1904-1916
42	Doc White,	1903-1913
35	Billy Pierce,	1949-1961
29	Red Faber,	1914-1933
28	Eddie Cicotte,	1912-1920

Wins: Most, career

260	Ted Lyons,	1923-1946
254	Red Faber,	1914-1933
195	Ed Walsh,	1904-1916
186	Billy Pierce,	1949-1961
163	Wilbur Wood,	1967-1978

K: Most, career

1796	Billy Pierce,	1949-1961
1732	Ed Walsh,	1904-1916
1471	Red Faber,	1914-1933
1332	Wilbur Wood,	1967-1978
1098	Gary Peters,	1959-1969

Win pct: Highest, career

.648	Lefty Williams,	1916-1920
.644	Virgil Trucks,	1953-1955
.616	Jim Kaat,	1973-1975
.615	Juan Pizarro,	1961-1966
.611	J. McDOWELL,	1987-1994

ERA: Lowest, career

1.81	Ed Walsh,	1904-1916
2.18	Frank Smith,	1904-1910
2.25	Eddie Cicotte,	1912-1920
2.30	Jim Scott,	1909-1917
2.30	Doc White,	1903-1913

Runs: Most, season

135	Johnny Mostil,	1925
120	Zeke Bonura,	1936
120	Fielder Jones,	1901
120	Johnny Mostil,	1926
120	Rip Radcliff,	1936

Hits: Most, season

224	Eddie Collins,	1920
218	Joe Jackson,	1920
208	Buck Weaver,	1920
207	Rip Radcliff,	1936
204	Luke Appling,	1936

2B: Most, season

46	FRANK THOMAS,	1992
45	Floyd Robinson,	1962
44	Ivan Calderon,	1990
44	Chet Lemon,	1979
43	Bibb Falk,	1926
43	Earl Sheely,	1925

3B: Most, season

21	Joe Jackson,	1916
20	Joe Jackson,	1920
18	Jack Fournier,	1915
18	Harry Lord,	1911
18	Minnie Minoso,	1954
18	Carl Reynolds,	1930

HR: Most, season

41	FRANK THOMAS,	1993
40	FRANK THOMAS,	1995
40	FRANK THOMAS,	1996
38	FRANK THOMAS,	1994
37	Dick Allen,	1972
37	Carlton Fisk,	1985

RBI: Most, season

138	Zeke Bonura,	1936
134	FRANK THOMAS,	1996
128	Luke Appling,	1936
128	FRANK THOMAS,	1993
121	Joe Jackson,	1920

SB: Most, season

77	Rudy Law	1983
56	Luis Aparicio	1959
56	Wally Moses	1943
53	Luis Aparicio	1961
53	Eddie Collins	1917

BB: Most, season

138	FRANK THOMAS	1991
136	FRANK THOMAS	1995
127	Lu Blue	1931
125	TONY PHILLIPS	1996
122	Luke Appling	1935
122	FRANK THOMAS	1992

BA: Highest, season

.388	Luke Appling	1936
.382	Joe Jackson	1920
.372	Eddie Collins	1920
.360	Eddie Collins	1923
.359	Carl Reynolds	1930

Slug avg: Highest, season

.729	FRANK THOMAS	1994
.626	FRANK THOMAS	1996
.607	FRANK THOMAS	1993
.607	FRANK THOMAS	1995
.603	Dick Allen	1972

On-base avg: Highest, season

.487	FRANK THOMAS	1994
.474	Luke Appling	1936
.461	Eddie Collins	1925
.460	Eddie Collins	1915
.459	FRANK THOMAS	1996

Complete games: Most, season

42	Ed Walsh	1908
37	Frank Smith	1909
37	Ed Walsh	1907
34	Frank Owen	1904
33	Ed Walsh	1910
33	Ed Walsh	1911

Saves: Most, season

57	Bobby Thigpen	1990
38	ROBERTO HERNANDEZ, 1993	
38	ROBERTO HERNANDEZ, 1996	
34	Bobby Thigpen	1988
34	Bobby Thigpen	1989

Shutouts: Most, season

11	Ed Walsh	1908
10	Ed Walsh	1906
8	Reb Russell	1913
8	Ed Walsh	1909
8	Wilbur Wood	1972

Wins: Most, season

40	Ed Walsh	1908
29	Eddie Cicotte	1919
28	Eddie Cicotte	1917
27	Ed Walsh	1911
27	Ed Walsh	1912
27	Doc White	1907

K: Most, season

269	Ed Walsh	1908
258	Ed Walsh	1910
255	Ed Walsh	1911
254	Ed Walsh	1912
215	Gary Peters	1967

Win pct: Highest, season

.842	Sandy Consuegra	1954
.806	Eddie Cicotte	1919
.774	Clark Griffith	1901
.759	Richard Dotson	1983
.750	Reb Russell	1917
.750	Bob Shaw	1959
.750	Monty Stratton	1937
.750	Doc White	1906

ERA: Lowest, season

1.27	Ed Walsh	1910
1.41	Ed Walsh	1909
1.42	Ed Walsh	1908
1.52	Doc White	1906
1.53	Eddie Cicotte	1917

Most pinch-hit homers, season

3	Ron Northey	1956
3	John Romano	1959
3	Oscar Gamble	1977

Most pinch-hit homers, career

7	Jerry Hairston	1973-1989
5	Smoky Burgess	1964-1967

Longest hitting streak

27	Luke Appling	1936
26	Guy Curtwright	1943
25	LANCE JOHNSON	1992
23	Minnie Minoso	1955
22	Eddie Collins	1920
22	Sam Mele	1953

Most consecutive scoreless innings

45	Doc White	1904
39	Billy Pierce	1953
39	Ed Walsh	1906
38	Ray Herbert	1963
37	Ed Walsh	1910
37	Joel Horlen	1968

No-hit games

Nixey Callahan, Chi vs Det AL, 3-0; Sept. 20, 1902 (1st game).

Frank Smith, Chi at Det AL, 15-0; Sept. 6, 1905 (2nd game).

Frank Smith, Chi vs Phi AL, 1-0; Sept. 20, 1908.

Ed Walsh, Chi vs Bos AL, 5-0; Aug. 27, 1911.

Jim Scott, Chi at Was AL, 0-1; May 14, 1914 (lost on 2 hits in the tenth).

Joe Benz, Chi vs Cle AL, 6-1; May 31, 1914.

Eddie Cicotte, Chi at StL AL, 11-0; Apr. 14, 1917.

Charlie Robertson, Chi at Det AL, 2-0; Apr. 30, 1922 (perfect game).

Ted Lyons, Chi at Bos AL, 6-0; Aug. 21, 1926.

Vern Kennedy, Chi vs Cle AL, 5-0; Aug. 31, 1935.

Bill Dietrich, Chi vs StL AL, 8-0; June 1, 1937.

Bob Keegan, Chi vs Was AL, 6-0; Aug. 20, 1957 (2nd game).

Joe Horlen, Chi vs Det AL, 6-0; Sept. 10, 1967 (1st game).

Blue Moon Odom (5 innings) and Francisco Barrios (4 innings), Chi at Oak AL, 2-1; July 28, 1976.

Joe Cowley, Chi at Cal AL, 7-1; Sept. 19, 1986.

WILSON ALVAREZ, Chi at Bal AL, 7-0; Aug. 11, 1991.

Ed Walsh, five innings, rain, Chi vs NY AL, 8-1; May 26, 1907.

MELIDO PEREZ, six innings, rain, Chi at NY AL, 8-0; July 12, 1990.

ACTIVE PLAYERS in caps.

Players' years of service are listed by the first and last years with this team and are not necessarily consecutive; all statistics record performances for this team only.

133

Milwaukee Brewers

John Jaha took over as the Brewers' top power hitter and was ninth in the AL in RBI.

1996 Brewers: Not bad; help arrived too

The Brewers fell short of having a winning season, but there's hope for the future after some trades. A nine-game losing streak in August deprived the team of any wild-card hopes, but if you take that streak out, the Brewers played exciting, competitive ball for most of the season despite some major changes in late July and August. General manager Sal Bando dealt several high-salaried players to contenders for younger players. The Brewers were not likely to re-sign Greg Vaughn, Kevin Seitzer, Pat Listach and Graeme Lloyd, so they used them for trade bait.

Outfielder Marc Newfield and pitchers Ron Villone and Bruce Florie, acquired for Vaughn, showed signs they could contribute in the future. So did pitcher Bob Wickman and outfielder Gerald Williams, acquired for Listach and Lloyd in a deal with the Yankees. Jeromy Burnitz, who came from Cleveland for Seitzer, should be in the outfield mix next spring.

Of those who played the whole season in Milwaukee, first basemen–DHs John Jaha and Dave Nilsson, shortstop Jose Valentin and third baseman Jeff Cirillo all had outstanding offensive seasons. Jaha eclipsed the 30 homer and 100 RBI marks for the first time. Nilsson stayed healthy most of the season and hit more than 60 points over his lifetime average. Valentin hit 24 homers and drove in 95 runs. Cirillo's .325 average missed the league's top 10 by a point, and only Paul Molitor has had as impressive totals as Cirillo has in his first two seasons as a Brewer.

On the mound, right-hander Ben McDonald (12-10) turned out to be a good acquisition. Cal Eldred made a solid comeback from elbow surgery, ending the season 4-4 in 15 starts. Scott Karl (13-9) showed he's a quality starter, and 20-year-old Jeff D'Amico made the big jump from Class AA to the majors and went 6-6. The rotation looks pretty good for the future, but the bullpen was disappointing. Mike Fetters got 32 saves but blew seven others. The middle relief was dreadful until Villone, Florie and Wickman arrived, and

> ## Team MVP
>
> **John Jaha:** Several members of the Milwaukee Brewers had career years in 1996, and first baseman John Jaha led the way, topping the 30-home-run and 100-RBI marks for the first time to lead the team in both categories. Jaha also batted .300, led the Brewers in runs scored and took over as the team's big gun after Greg Vaughn was traded.

Florie and Wickman had some tenderness in their arms by the end of the season.

Defense also was a disappointment. While Valentin had his best year at the plate, he had his worst in the field, with 37 errors. Nilsson struggled when he played in the outfield and at first base. Others committed fundamental physical and mental errors at times. Catcher Mike Matheny played well defensively but left some questions as to whether he can hit in the majors.

Newfield, the brightest of the newcomers, was arrested for marijuana possession in Detroit on Sept. 27. The 23-year-old outfielder said he learned his lesson, but he will have to establish himself as a solid citizen with the fans next season in addition to proving that he should be the starting left fielder. Bando made the late-season deals so he could free up some money for several players who are eligible for arbitration, though the club's aim is to wrap up the core players for the long term. Outfielders Todd Dunn and Brian Banks and utilityman Tim Unroe, all of whom came up in September, could get long looks for 1997, along with outfielder Geoff Jenkins and infielder Antone Williamson.

"Progress was made in some areas this season," manager Phil Garner said. "Offensively, we showed improvement. We still have work to do in other areas. We have to get to the point where .500 is considered minimal if we are to take the next step."

1996 Brewers: Week-by-week notes

These notes were excerpted from the following issues of Baseball Weekly.

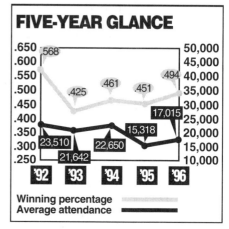

FIVE-YEAR GLANCE

Winning percentage
Average attendance

▶**April 3:** Brewers president Bud Selig said for the first time that the club most likely would have to move if the proposed $250 million stadium is not built. The stadium is to be financed with $90 million put up by the Brewers and $160 million raised by an ongoing sales tax.

▶**April 10:** Greg Vaughn had four homers in the first four games. Vaughn is trying to return to left field after double shoulder surgery restricted him to DH last season.

▶**April 17:** The Southeast Wisconsin Professional Baseball District board voted on April 15 to retain the sales-tax portion of the financing for the new stadium, as the Brewers seem close to finalizing their portion of funding.

▶**April 24:** The Brewers tied a club record by scoring eight or more runs in four consecutive games on April 17-20. Infielder-DH Kevin Seitzer continued to lead the offense with a .370 average, five homers and 17 RBI, and Greg Vaughn had seven homers and 18 RBI. The Brewers, who were not expected to hit many home runs, had 23 in their first 15 games.

▶**May 8:** The Brewers continued to have problems holding leads. Through a stretch in which the team lost eight of 10, it blew leads in seven games. "We haven't gotten the consistency you'd like from our relief pitching," manager Phil Garner said. "We're still looking for guys to fill certain roles out there."

▶**May 15:** Jose Valentin, who started the season as a no-hit, good-field shortstop, was moved to third in the lineup because he's hitting over .300 with some power.

▶**May 22:** Right-hander Ben McDonald made the longest start by any Brewer this season when he went 7⅓ innings against the White Sox on May 16.

▶**May 29:** A 10-game road trip that began like a pleasant Sunday drive turned into a roller-coaster ride. A four-game sweep in Minnesota on May 17-20 gave the Brewers five consecutive wins, in which the team hit .331 and the staff ERA was 1.80. After Cleveland snapped the streak with a 6-5 win on May 21, the Brewers seemed to be back on track the next night when they jumped off to a 10-3 lead, but a five-run Cleveland rally cut the lead to 10-8 going into the ninth. With two on and two out, closer Mike Fetters struck out Albert Belle to end the game. But the Brewers then lost three in a row in Cleveland and Chicago.

▶**June 12:** Right-hander Cal Eldred, trying to come back from elbow surgery, started a rehab assignment at New Orleans and could be ready to join the Brewers by the All-Star break.

▶**June 19:** Jeff Cirillo and Kevin Seitzer, who were supposed to share playing time, are two of the hottest hitters in the AL. Cirillo was hitting .341 and Seitzer .357 through June 16. Cirillo reached base in 37 of his last 41 games, and Seitzer hit safely in 23 of his last 24 games. Phil Garner did a juggling act to keep both players in the lineup, using Seitzer mainly at first and DH, while Cirillo played third.

▶**June 26:** Greg Vaughn had 69 RBI as of June 23 and was on a pace to eclipse the club record of 126 set in 1983 by Cecil Cooper.

▶**July 3:** The Brewers set a club record by homering in 18 consecutive games, eclipsing the old mark of 15 set by the 1982 Harvey's Wallbangers team that won the AL pennant. Greg Vaughn tied a mark set by Gorman Thomas in 1979 when he hit his 12th home run in June.

▶**July 11:** Right-hander Jeff D'Amico, who had an outstanding June 28 debut, ran into reality when he gave up five runs on six hits in 3⅔ innings in his second start, on July 3. At 20, D'Amico is the youngest player in the majors.

▶**July 17:** Cal Eldred will be on a 90-pitch limit for a while after making his seven-inning season debut on July 14 against the Blue Jays. Eldred missed 14 months after undergoing radical surgery on his right elbow. He allowed three runs and five hits on 95 pitches.

▶**July 24:** The Brewers were averaging nine runs a game with a .322 team average for the first nine games after the All-Star break. Greg Vaughn took over the major league RBI lead during the stretch, with 92.

▶**July 31:** The Brewers' bullpen continues to be the club's weak spot. In the first four games of a West Coast road trip, the bullpen blew three games after nice performances by starting pitchers. The one exception in the struggling bullpen has been closer Mike Fetters, who had 18 saves as of July 25.

▶**Aug. 14:** The Brewers virtually fell out of the wild-card race with a six-game losing streak at home on Aug. 6-10. They started the week with bad pitching and ended it with untimely hitting.

▶**Aug. 28:** Right-hander Bob Wickman's trade to the Brewers represented a homecoming for the reliever. Wickman, 27, is from Abrams, Wis., and played ball at the University of Wisconsin–Whitewater before turning pro. He and outfielder Gerald Williams were obtained in an Aug. 23 trade that sent infielder-outfielder Pat Listach and pitcher Graeme Lloyd to the Yankees. Wickman wasted no time paying dividends, with 1⅓ scoreless innings against the Indians on Aug. 24 to get the win.

▶**Sept. 11:** It could be a free-for-all next spring for the three outfield positions. Among the candidates are Marc Newfield, Gerald Williams, Chuckie Carr, Todd Dunn, Jeromy Burnitz, Matt Mieske

and No. 1 1995 draft pick Geoff Jenkins.

▶**Sept. 18:** Right-hander Ben McDonald finally got his 11th win in the 15-4 game. McDonald had gotten little run support in seven losses and four no-decisions while he was stuck on 10 wins.

▶**Oct. 2:** The Brewers fell just short of their .500 goal, but they showed promise. John Jaha and Dave Nilsson, who shared first base and DH; Jose Valentin; and Jeff Cirillo all had career years at the plate. Ben McDonald was a good acquisition. Cal Eldred came back from Tommy John surgery, ending with a two-hit, six-inning performance in a 7-2 win on Sept. 28 against the Tigers. The bullpen was the most disappointing area. Mike Fetters recorded 32 saves but was inconsistent. The middle relief was horrible until Ron Villone and Bob Wickman arrived.

Team directory

▶**Owner:** Allan H. (Bud) Selig
▶**General manager:** Sal Bando
▶**Ballpark:**
Milwaukee County Stadium
201 South 46th St.
Milwaukee, Wis.
414-933-4114
Capacity 53,192
Parking for approximately 11,000 cars; $5 or $7
Public transportation available
Family and wheelchair sections, ramps, Designated Driver Program including free taxi transportation for single ticket holders participating in the DDP
▶**Team publications:**
Media guide, *Lead Off Magazine*
▶**TV, radio broadcast stations:**
WTMJ 620 AM, WVTV-TV 18
▶**Camps and/or clinics:**
Gatorade Youth Camp, during the season, 414-933-4114
Fantasy Camp, winter, 414-933-4114, 800-336-CAMP
▶**Spring training:**
Compadre Stadium
Chandler, Ariz.
Capacity 5,000 (10,000 including lawn)
602-895-1200

MILWAUKEE BREWERS 1996 final stats

BATTERS	BA	SLG	OB	G	AB	R	H	TB	2B	3B	HR	RBI	BB	SO	SB	CS	E
Banks	.571	1.286	.625	4	7	2	4	9	2	0	1	2	1	2	0	0	0
Nilsson	.331	.525	.407	123	453	81	150	238	33	2	17	84	57	68	2	3	7
Cirillo	.325	.504	.391	158	566	101	184	285	46	5	15	83	58	69	4	9	18
Newfield	.307	.508	.354	49	179	21	55	91	15	0	7	31	11	26	0	1	1
Jaha	.300	.543	.398	148	543	108	163	295	28	1	34	118	85	118	3	1	6
Dunn	.300	.400	.300	6	10	2	3	4	1	0	0	1	0	3	0	0	0
Vina	.283	.392	.342	140	554	94	157	217	19	10	7	46	38	35	16	7	16
Vaughn	.280	.571	.378	102	375	78	105	214	16	0	31	95	58	99	5	2	4
Loretta	.279	.318	.339	73	154	20	43	49	3	0	1	13	14	15	2	1	2
Mieske	.278	.471	.324	127	374	46	104	176	24	3	14	64	26	76	1	5	1
Carr	.274	.377	.310	27	106	18	29	40	6	1	1	11	6	21	5	4	0
Burnitz	.265	.470	.377	94	200	38	53	94	14	0	9	40	33	47	4	1	1
Valentin	.259	.475	.336	154	552	90	143	262	33	7	24	95	66	145	17	4	37
Williams	.252	.382	.299	125	325	43	82	124	19	4	5	34	19	57	10	9	4
Levis	.236	.283	.348	104	233	27	55	66	6	1	1	21	38	15	0	0	1
Hulse	.222	.248	.272	81	117	18	26	29	3	0	0	6	8	16	4	1	1
Koslofski	.214	.381	.298	25	42	5	9	16	3	2	0	6	4	12	0	0	1
Matheny	.204	.342	.243	106	313	31	64	107	15	2	8	46	14	80	3	2	8
Unroe	.188	.188	.350	14	16	5	3	3	0	0	0	0	4	5	0	1	1
Ward	.179	.328	.309	43	67	7	12	22	2	1	2	10	13	17	3	0	0
Stinnett	.077	.077	.172	14	26	1	2	2	0	0	0	0	2	11	0	0	2
Perez	.000	.000	.000	4	4	0	0	0	0	0	0	0	0	0	0	0	0

PITCHERS	W-L	ERA	G	GS	CG	GF	Sho	SV	IP	H	R	ER	HR	BB	SO
Burrows	2-0	2.84	8	0	0	4	0	0	12.2	12	4	4	2	10	5
Villone	0-0	3.28	23	0	0	10	0	2	24.2	14	9	9	4	18	19
Fetters	3-3	3.38	61	0	0	55	0	32	61.1	65	28	23	4	26	53
Jones	5-0	3.41	24	0	0	8	0	1	31.2	31	13	12	3	13	34
McDonald	12-10	3.90	35	35	2	0	0	0	221.1	228	104	96	25	67	146
Wickman	7-1	4.42	70	0	0	18	0	0	95.2	106	50	47	10	44	75
Eldred	4-4	4.46	15	15	0	0	0	0	84.2	82	43	42	8	38	50
Karl	13-9	4.86	32	32	3	0	1	0	207.1	220	124	112	29	72	121
Miranda	7-6	4.94	46	12	0	5	0	1	109.1	116	68	60	12	69	78
Wickander	2-0	4.97	21	0	0	6	0	0	25.1	26	16	14	2	17	19
VanEgmond	3-5	5.27	12	9	0	1	0	0	54.2	58	35	32	6	23	33
D'Amico	6-6	5.44	17	17	0	0	0	0	86.0	88	53	52	21	31	53
Sparks	4-7	6.60	20	13	1	2	0	0	88.2	103	66	65	19	52	21
Florie	0-1	6.63	15	0	0	5	0	0	19.0	20	16	14	3	13	12
Garcia	4-4	6.66	37	2	0	14	0	4	75.2	84	58	56	17	21	40
Potts	1-2	7.15	24	0	0	7	0	1	45.1	58	39	36	7	30	21
Carpenter	0-0	7.56	8	0	0	2	0	0	8.1	12	8	7	1	2	2
Boze	0-2	7.79	25	0	0	8	0	1	32.1	47	29	28	5	25	19
Reyes	1-0	7.94	5	0	0	2	0	0	5.2	8	5	5	1	2	2
Kiefer	0-0	8.10	7	0	0	2	0	0	10.0	15	9	9	1	5	5
Mercedes	0-2	9.18	11	0	0	4	0	0	16.2	20	18	17	6	5	6
Givens	1-3	12.86	4	4	0	0	0	0	14.0	32	22	20	3	7	10

1997 preliminary roster

PITCHERS (19)
Joel Adamson
Peter Benny
Jeff D'Amico
Valerio de los Santos
Cal Eldred
Mike Fetters
Bryce Florie
Scott Karl
Sean Maloney
Ben McDonald
Jose Mercedes
Angel Miranda

Al Reyes
Henry Santos
Steve Sparks
Tim VanEgmond
Ron Villone
Jeff Ware
Bob Wickman

CATCHERS (4)
Bobby Hughes
Jesse Levis
Mike Matheny
Kelly Stinnett

INFIELDERS (9)
Ronnie Belliard
Jeff Cirillo
John Jaha
Mark Loretta
Dave Nilsson
Tim Unroe
Jose Valentin
Fernando Vina
Antone Williamson

OUTFIELDERS (8)
Brian Banks
Jeromy Burnitz
Chuck Carr
Todd Dunn
Kenny Felder
Matt Mieske
Mark Newfield
Gerald Williams

Games played by position

PLAYER	G	C	1B	2B	3B	SS	OF	DH
Banks	4	0	1	0	0	0	3	0
Burnitz	94	0	0	0	0	0	52	15
Carr	27	0	0	0	0	0	27	0
Cirillo	158	0	2	1	154	0	0	3
Dunn	6	0	0	0	0	0	6	0
Hulse	81	0	0	0	0	0	68	4
Jaha	148	0	85	0	0	0	0	63
Koslofski	25	0	0	0	0	0	22	1
Levis	104	90	0	0	0	0	0	6
Loretta	73	0	0	28	23	21	0	0
Matheny	106	104	0	0	0	0	0	1
Mieske	127	0	0	0	0	0	122	0
Newfield	49	0	0	0	0	0	49	0
Nilsson	123	2	24	0	0	0	61	40
Perez	4	0	0	0	0	0	3	1
Stinnett	14	14	0	0	0	0	0	1
Unroe	14	0	11	0	3	0	1	1
Valentin	154	0	0	0	0	151	0	0
Vaughn	102	0	0	0	0	0	100	1
Vina	140	0	0	137	0	0	0	0
Ward	43	0	0	0	0	0	32	1
Williams	125	0	0	0	0	0	119	2

Minor Leagues

Tops in the organization

BATTER	CLUB	AVG.	G	AB	R	H	HR	RBI
Todd Dunn	Elp	.340	98	359	72	122	19	78
Gerald Parent	Ogd	.332	102	313	54	104	6	54
Josh Tyler	Stk	.322	75	273	42	88	2	33
M. Rennhack	Stk	.320	121	456	67	146	17	103
Brad Seitzer	Elp	.319	115	433	78	138	17	87

HOME RUNS

Kelly Stinnett	No	27
Tim Unroe	No	25
Drew Williams	Stk	24
Scott Krause	Stk	22
Jonas Hamlin	Elp	21

WINS

Travis Smith	Elp	13
Joshua Bishop	Blt	12
Steve Woodard	Stk	12
Joe Wagner	Stk	12
Several Players Tied At		11

RBI

Mike Rennhack	Stk	103
Mike Kinkade	Blt	100
Jonas Hamlin	Elp	94
Scott Krause	Stk	94
Brad Seitzer	Elp	87

SAVES

Sean Maloney	Elp	38
Scott Huntsman	Stk	12
Alfredo Gutierrez	Ogd	9
Cris Carpenter	No	8
Aldren Sadler	Elp	8

STOLEN BASES

Greg Martinez	Elp	44
Scott Krause	Stk	27
Ronnie Belliard	Elp	26
Anthony Iapoce	Blt	23
Mike Kinkade	Blt	23

STRIKEOUTS

Peter Benny	Blt	150
Scott Gardner	Stk	148
Steve Woodard	Stk	142
V. de los Santos	Blt	137
Jason Dawsey	Blt	119

PITCHER	CLUB	W-L	ERA	IP	H	BB	SO
Jason Dawsey	Blt	6-4	1.51	101	71	42	119
Brian Givens	No	10-9	3.02	137	124	57	117
Jeff D'Amico	Elp	5-4	3.19	96	89	13	76
Travis Smith	Elp	13-5	3.36	166	175	60	116
V. de los Santos	Blt	10-8	3.55	165	164	59	137

Sick call: 1996 DL report

PLAYER	Days on the DL
Chuck Carr	141*
Cal Eldred	104
Brian Givens	32
David Hulse	33
Pat Listach	15
Jamie McAndrew	182
Dave Nilsson	34
Turner Ward	99
Kevin Wickander	45

Indicates two separate terms on Disabled List.

1996 salaries

	Bonuses	Total earned salary
Ben McDonald, p		$2,000,000
Mike Fetters, p		$1,700,000
John Jaha, 1b	$50,000	$1,100,000
Dave Nilsson, c		$1,075,000
Bob Wickman, p	$50,000	$850,000
Cal Eldred, p	$152,000	$712,000
Turner Ward, of	$25,000	$400,000
Chuck Carr, of		$325,000
Jose Valentin, ss	$20,000	$300,000
David Hulse, of		$270,000
Matt Mieske, of		$200,000
Gerald Williams, of		$200,000
Jeromy Burnitz, of		$190,000
Fernando Vina, 2b		$190,000
Jeff Cirillo, 3b		$187,500
Bryce Florie, p		$172,500
Scott Karl, p		$155,000
Jesse Levis, c		$150,000
Kelly Stinnett, c		$147,500
Marc Newfield, of		$142,500
Angel Miranda, p	$15,000	$135,000
Ron Villone, p		$130,000
Jamie McAndrew, p		$128,000
Tim VanEgmond, p		$115,000
Jeff D'Amico, p		$109,000
Ramon Garcia, p		$109,000
Doug Jones, p		$109,000
Mark Loretta, ss		$109,000

Average 1996 salary: $407,535
Total 1996 team payroll: $11,411,000
Termination pay: $290,000

139

Milwaukee (1970-1996), including Seattle Pilots (1969)

Runs: Most, career

1632	Robin Yount, 1974-1993
1275	PAUL MOLITOR, 1978-1992
821	Cecil Cooper, 1977-1987
726	Jim Gantner, 1976-1992
596	Don Money, 1973-1983

Hits: Most, career

3142	Robin Yount, 1974-1993
2281	PAUL MOLITOR, 1978-1992
1815	Cecil Cooper, 1977-1987
1696	Jim Gantner, 1976-1992
1168	Don Money, 1973-1983

2B: Most, career

583	Robin Yount, 1974-1993
405	PAUL MOLITOR, 1978-1992
345	Cecil Cooper, 1977-1987
262	Jim Gantner, 1976-1992
215	Don Money, 1973-1983

3B: Most, career

126	Robin Yount, 1974-1993
86	PAUL MOLITOR, 1978-1992
42	Charlie Moore, 1973-1986
38	Jim Gantner, 1976-1992
33	Cecil Cooper, 1977-1987

HR: Most, career

251	Robin Yount, 1974-1993
208	Gorman Thomas, 1973-1986
201	Cecil Cooper, 1977-1987
176	Ben Oglivie, 1978-1986
169	GREG VAUGHN, 1989-1996

RBI: Most, career

1406	Robin Yount, 1974-1993
944	Cecil Cooper, 1977-1987
790	PAUL MOLITOR, 1978-1992
685	Ben Oglivie, 1978-1986
605	Gorman Thomas, 1973-1986

SB: Most, career

412	PAUL MOLITOR, 1978-1992
271	Robin Yount, 1974-1993
137	Jim Gantner, 1976-1992
136	Tommy Harper, 1969-1971
112	PAT LISTACH, 1992-1996

BB: Most, career

966	Robin Yount, 1974-1993
755	PAUL MOLITOR, 1978-1992
501	Gorman Thomas, 1973-1986
440	Don Money, 1973-1983
432	Ben Oglivie, 1978-1986

BA: Highest, career

.303	PAUL MOLITOR, 1978-1992
.302	Cecil Cooper, 1977-1987
.300	KEVIN SEITZER, 1992-1996
.290	DARRYL HAMILTON, 1988-1995
.285	Robin Yount, 1974-1993

Slug avg: Highest, career

.474	JOHN JAHA, 1992-1996
.470	Cecil Cooper, 1977-1987
.461	Gorman Thomas, 1973-1986
.461	Ben Oglivie, 1978-1986
.459	GREG VAUGHN, 1989-1996

On-base avg: Highest, career

.376	KEVIN SEITZER, 1992-1996
.367	PAUL MOLITOR, 1978-1992
.361	JOHN JAHA, 1992-1996
.358	Johnny Briggs, 1971-1975
.355	Mike Hegan, 1970-1977

Complete games: Most, career

81	Mike Caldwell, 1977-1984
69	Jim Slaton, 1971-1983
55	Moose Haas, 1976-1985
51	Jim Colborn, 1972-1976
50	Teddy Higuera, 1985-1994
50	Lary Sorensen, 1977-1980

Saves: Most, career

133	DAN PLESAC, 1986-1992
97	Rollie Fingers, 1981-1985
73	MIKE FETTERS, 1992-1996
61	DOUG HENRY, 1991-1994
61	Ken Sanders, 1970-1972

Shutouts: Most, career

19	Jim Slaton, 1971-1983
18	Mike Caldwell, 1977-1984
12	Teddy Higuera, 1985-1994
10	Bill Travers, 1974-1980
8	CHRIS BOSIO, 1986-1992
8	Moose Haas, 1976-1985

Wins: Most, career

117	Jim Slaton, 1971-1983
102	Mike Caldwell, 1977-1984
94	Teddy Higuera, 1985-1994
91	Moose Haas, 1976-1985
81	Bill Wegman, 1985-1995

K: Most, career

1081	Teddy Higuera, 1985-1994
929	Jim Slaton, 1971-1983

800	Moose Haas, 1976-1985
749	CHRIS BOSIO, 1986-1992
696	Bill Wegman, 1985-1995

Win pct: Highest, career

.606	Pete Vuckovich, 1981-1986
.595	Teddy Higuera, 1985-1994
.570	CAL ELDRED, 1991-1996
.560	Mike Caldwell, 1977-1984
.535	Moose Haas, 1976-1985

ERA: Lowest, career

3.61	Teddy Higuera, 1985-1994
3.65	Jim Colborn, 1972-1976
3.72	Lary Sorensen, 1977-1980
3.74	Mike Caldwell, 1977-1984
3.76	CHRIS BOSIO, 1986-1992

Runs: Most, season

136	PAUL MOLITOR, 1982
133	PAUL MOLITOR, 1991
129	Robin Yount, 1982
121	Robin Yount, 1980
115	PAUL MOLITOR, 1988

Hits: Most, season

219	Cecil Cooper, 1980
216	PAUL MOLITOR, 1991
210	Robin Yount, 1982
205	Cecil Cooper, 1982
203	Cecil Cooper, 1983

2B: Most, season

49	Robin Yount, 1980
46	JEFF CIRILLO, 1996
46	Robin Yount, 1982
44	Cecil Cooper, 1979
42	Robin Yount, 1983

3B: Most, season

16	PAUL MOLITOR, 1979
13	PAUL MOLITOR, 1991
12	Robin Yount, 1982
11	Robin Yount, 1988
10	FERNANDO VINA, 1996
10	Robin Yount, 1980
10	Robin Yount, 1983

HR: Most, season

45	Gorman Thomas, 1979
41	Ben Oglivie, 1980
39	Gorman Thomas, 1982
38	Gorman Thomas, 1980
36	George Scott, 1975

RBI: Most, season

126	Cecil Cooper, 1983
123	Gorman Thomas, 1979
122	Cecil Cooper, 1980
121	Cecil Cooper, 1982
118	JOHN JAHA, 1996
118	Ben Oglivie, 1980

SB: Most, season

73	Tommy Harper, 1969
54	PAT LISTACH, 1992
45	PAUL MOLITOR, 1987
41	DARRYL HAMILTON, 1992
41	PAUL MOLITOR, 1982
41	PAUL MOLITOR, 1983
41	PAUL MOLITOR, 1988

BB: Most, season

98	Gorman Thomas, 1979
95	Tommy Harper, 1969
89	Darrell Porter, 1975
89	GREG VAUGHN, 1993
87	Johnny Briggs, 1973

BA: Highest, season

.353	PAUL MOLITOR, 1987
.352	Cecil Cooper, 1980
.331	DAVE NILSSON, 1996
.331	Robin Yount, 1982
.327	Willie Randolph, 1991

Slug avg: Highest, season

.578	Robin Yount, 1982
.573	Sixto Lezcano, 1979
.566	PAUL MOLITOR, 1987
.563	Ben Oglivie, 1980
.543	JOHN JAHA, 1996

On-base avg: Highest, season

.438	PAUL MOLITOR, 1987
.424	Willie Randolph, 1991
.414	Sixto Lezcano, 1979
.407	DAVE NILSSON, 1996
.406	KEVIN SEITZER, 1996

Complete games: Most, season

23	Mike Caldwell, 1978
22	Jim Colborn, 1973
17	Lary Sorensen, 1978
16	Mike Caldwell, 1979
16	Lary Sorensen, 1979

Saves: Most, season

33	DAN PLESAC, 1989
32	MIKE FETTERS, 1996
31	Ken Sanders, 1971
30	DAN PLESAC, 1988
29	Rollie Fingers, 1982
29	DOUG HENRY, 1992

Shutouts: Most, season

6	Mike Caldwell, 1978
5	Marty Pattin, 1971
4	Mike Caldwell, 1979
4	Jim Colborn, 1973
4	Teddy Higuera, 1986
4	Bill Parsons, 1971
4	Jim Slaton, 1971

Wins: Most, season

22	Mike Caldwell, 1978
20	Jim Colborn, 1973
20	Teddy Higuera, 1986
18	Teddy Higuera, 1987
18	Lary Sorensen, 1978
18	Pete Vuckovich, 1982

K: Most, season

240	Teddy Higuera, 1987
207	Teddy Higuera, 1986
192	Teddy Higuera, 1988
180	CAL ELDRED, 1993
173	CHRIS BOSIO, 1989

Win pct: Highest, season

.750	Pete Vuckovich, 1982
.727	Mike Caldwell, 1979
.727	CHRIS BOSIO, 1992
.710	Mike Caldwell, 1978
.682	Bill Wegman, 1991

ERA: Lowest, season

2.36	Mike Caldwell, 1978
2.45	Teddy Higuera, 1988
2.79	Teddy Higuera, 1986
2.81	Bill Travers, 1976
2.83	Jim Lonborg, 1972

Most pinch-hit homers, season

2	Max Alvis, 1970
2	Bobby Darwin, 1975
2	Bob Hansen, 1974
2	Andy Kosco, 1971
2	Ken McMullen, 1977
2	MATT MIESKE, 1995

Most pinch-hit homers, career

3	MATT MIESKE, 1993-1996
2	Max Alvis, 1970
2	Bobby Darwin, 1975-1976
2	Bob Hansen, 1974-1976
2	Mike Hegan, Sea-1969, 1970-1977
2	Andy Kosco, 1971
2	Ken McMullen, 1977

Longest hitting streak

39	PAUL MOLITOR, 1987
24	Dave May, 1973
22	Cecil Cooper, 1980
19	DARRYL HAMILTON, 1991
19	PAUL MOLITOR, 1989
19	PAUL MOLITOR, 1990
19	Robin Yount, 1989

Most consecutive scoreless innings

32	Teddy Higuera, 1987

No-hit games

Juan Nieves, Mil at Bal AL, 7-0; Apr. 15, 1987.

ACTIVE PLAYERS in caps.

Players' years of service are listed by the first and last years with this team and are not necessarily consecutive; all statistics record performances for this team only.

Minnesota Twins

Minnesota Twins

Paul Molitor was an inspiring leader for the Twins and topped the AL with 225 hits.

By Russell Beeker, Baseball Weekly

1996 Twins: No pitching, no power, no Puck

There is a statistical category that has defined the Twins' last few losing seasons. It is called ERA. In 1996, it was joined by a second significant acronym, DL, and together they consigned the Twins to a 78-84 record. Even that, however, was much better their 56-88 of '95, which was tied for worst in the league.

The Twins began the spring feeling that if their key players stayed healthy and their young players improved, they could finish with a winning record. Then, in order, Rick Aguilera strained his wrist while picking up a suitcase, Kirby Puckett woke up almost blind in one eye, Dan Naulty developed a circulatory problem in his shoulder, Dave Stevens punched a phone box and Aguilera had a hamstring strain end his season.

In a three-month span, Puckett retired, second baseman Chuck Knoblauch signed a deal of $30 million for five years, Puckett was honored at the Dome, and DH Paul Molitor got his 3,000th hit. "I remember thinking that we've had an awful lot of press conferences for a team that was around .500," GM Terry Ryan said. "That's not a good sign. Sometimes it makes you wonder what's next."

Whether it's Ryan, manager Tom Kelly or Molitor, someone deserves credit for this team's overachieving. What are the most obvious components of a winning team? Power in the cleanup spot, dominance in the closer's role and experience in the rotation. The Twins had none of these. They had no established cleanup hitter. Rookie Todd Walker hit cleanup in his second big-league game. Stevens began the season as their closer, then was demoted, then hurt himself on a dugout phone box and finally finished the season in middle relief. He was replaced by Naulty, whose season was ended by a circulatory problem, and then a combination of Mike Trombley and Eddie Guardado. The former spent half the season in the minors; the latter was a struggling starter until '95. The Twins' rotation was made of sophomores Frank Rodriguez and Brad Radke, journeymen Scott Aldred and Rich

Team MVP

Paul Molitor: In the season he would turn 40, Paul Molitor was supposed to be going home to his native Minnesota to play out his career. Instead he had one of his greatest years. With a league-high 225 hits, Molitor passed 3,000 for his career, finished third in the league in batting at .341 and was tied for third in triples (hit No. 3,000 was a triple). He also stole 18 bases.

Robertson, and rookie Travis Miller. Even Aguilera doesn't qualify as an experienced starter—he had pitched in relief since 1989.

Consider that Minnesota was burdened by such inexperience yet easily outplayed the California Angels, who have a dominant closer, experienced starters and lots of power. Of their final 31-man roster, only six Twins had ever played a 162-game major league season. The players and coaches credited two people for the Twins' improving this much, Molitor and Kelly. "I think a lot of the learning I did myself can be attributed to Molly—just watching him around the ballpark and on the field, and watching the way he approaches the game and runs the bases and hits in certain situations," first baseman Scott Stahoviak said.

The Twins were the only team in the American League without a 20-home-run hitter, finishing last in the majors in that department. They manufactured runs and victories until their youngsters ran out of gas. This team went 49-18 when its pitchers achieved quality starts (six innings or more, allowing three earned runs or fewer). "We've gotten back into respectability, which was our goal," Ryan said. "We've got a good, young nucleus, and we know who's going to be here—we're not in jeopardy of losing any of our key players."

1996 Twins: Week-by-week notes

These notes were excerpted from the following issues of Baseball Weekly.

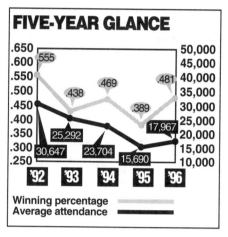

FIVE-YEAR GLANCE

Winning percentage
Average attendance

▶**April 3:** The Twins entered the season without the services of either outfielder Kirby Puckett or closer-turned-starter Rick Aguilera. Puckett was placed on the DL on March 30 with blurred vision. Aguilera has tendinitis in his right wrist and was placed on the 15-day DL, retroactive to March 24.

▶**April 17:** Kirby Puckett's blurred vision appears to stem from an early form of glaucoma, his retinal specialist, Dr. Bert Glaser, said.

▶**May 1:** If the Twins' fortunes and Kirby Puckett's health fail to improve, the team could be without designated hitter Paul Molitor and second baseman Chuck Knoblauch in the near future. Molitor said that Puckett's ability to play next season could influence his decision to stay with the Twins. And Knoblauch said the Twins will have to show an ability to win for him to sign a long-term deal or re-sign with Minnesota if he becomes a free agent.

▶**May 8:** The Twins set what is believed to be an AL record for most runs in the month of April, with 175. That output gave them a record of 14-12 in April, culminated by a three-game sweep of the Royals at the Metrodome that featured three comeback wins.

▶**May 22:** The Twins have been out-homered 62-31 this season, through May 18. They are on pace to allow 251. The team record (set in '87 and matched in '95) is 210, and the major league record is 226, set by Baltimore in '87.

▶**May 29:** How inexperienced is the pitching staff? Four of the Twins pitchers have earned their first major league victories this season; another four earned their first victories last season. One of the latter, Rich Robertson, improved to 1-7 on May 24 by pitching the Twins' first complete-game shutout since last August. For all of his struggles, he has three of the Twins' four complete games this season.

▶**June 5:** The Twins reshuffled their rotation with Rick Aguilera out because of soreness in his right wrist. Scott Aldred, claimed off waivers from the pitching-poor Tigers on May 28, pitched 4⅔ scoreless innings on May 31.

▶**June 19:** Right-hander Frank Rodriguez has had trouble with the third inning against the Tigers. This season, he has allowed 12 hits and 11 runs, 10 earned, while recording four outs. Rodriguez is 0-3 against the last-place Tigers, 5-4 against the rest of the league.

▶**June 26:** Rick Aguilera, having made two successful starts in his conversion effort, said he has much more to prove. Aguilera won as a starter for the first time in seven years on June 15 at the Metrodome, beating the Tigers 4-1. In his next start, he allowed two runs in eight innings, losing 2-0 to the Tigers.

▶**July 3:** Paul Molitor is the oldest player on the roster by seven years, yet he is the only Twin who has started every game. His durability and ability have put Molitor in position to chase his 3,000th hit this season. He began needing 211 and enters the All-Star break lacking 96.

▶**July 17:** The face of the franchise changed dramatically on July 12 when Kirby Puckett announced his retirement because of continuing eye problems. In addition to the effect on the team's play, some officials are concerned that without the beloved Puckett, the popularity of the team could wane, which could hinder the quest for a new stadium.

▶**July 24:** Reliever Dave Stevens gave up a game-losing 11th-inning home run to Alvaro Espinoza on July 20 for his second decisive home run allowed in three batters in three days against Cleveland. He had given up a total of four homers and five walks to 13 batters in his last four appearances. On his way to the clubhouse, he punched a metal phone box in the dugout. The resulting two gashes on his right hand required six stitches.

▶**Aug. 7:** Plenty of young Twins pitchers have privately questioned the way they've been handled in the past. LaTroy Hawkins took his complaints public recently. After pitching a complete-game shutout for Class AAA Salt Lake, Hawkins, once the Twins' top pitching prospect, complained about manager Tom Kelly and pitching coach Dick Such, adding that he expects to be traded. "They try to change everything when I get to the big leagues," Hawkins said.

▶**Aug. 14:** Think the Twins are happy with their decision to sign Paul Molitor as their DH, rather than stick with Pedro Munoz? Molitor has been phenomenal, and Munoz, who signed with the A's, has been hurt. He underwent knee surgery on June 5 and is not expected to play again this season. Molitor had 92 RBI through Aug. 11.

▶**Aug. 28:** Last week was a mixed bag for the Twins. They signed their best player, Chuck Knoblauch, to a five-year deal worth $30 million, making him the highest-paid second baseman in baseball and tying him with Kirby Puckett as the highest-paid Twin ever. But they also had their rights to top draft pick Travis Lee endangered. The Twins did not tender Lee a formal offer within 15 days of the draft, as the rules require.

▶**Sept. 4:** Paul Molitor could become the first player 40 or older to lead his league in hits since 1981, when Pete Rose did it.

▶**Sept. 11:** Chuck Knoblauch was hit in the helmet by a pitch from the Rangers' Roger Pavlik in his second at-bat on Sept. 4. Chance? Well, consider that Knoblauch's single in his first at-bat gave him a .909 season average against Pavlik.

▶**Sept. 18:** The Twins have all but shelved starter Rick Aguilera for the rest of the year, and the current five-man rotation—Brad Radke, Frank Rodriguez, Rich Robertson, Travis Miller and Scott Aldred—has a combined career record of 61-86.

▶**Oct. 2:** ERA and ER visits relegated the Twins to mediocrity in 1996, but it was an improvement over their aimless flailings of '95. The starting pitching suffered because Rick Aguilera strained his wrist while picking up a suitcase and then had a hamstring strain end his season early. The offense was wounded by the absence of longtime team leader Kirby Puckett, who retired after retinal damage and a glaucoma diagnosis. Chuck Knoblauch, left fielder Marty Cordova and Paul Molitor, who got his 3,000th hit while leading the league in that department, led the offense, which desperately lacked a cleanup man. The Twins were last in the league in home runs, while the pitching staff was near the top in homers allowed.

Team directory

▶**Owner:** Carl R. Pohlad
▶**General manager:** Terry Ryan
▶**Ballpark:**
Hubert H. Humphrey Metrodome
501 Chicago Ave. S.
Minneapolis, Minn.
612-375-1366
Capacity 48,678
Public transportation available
Family and wheelchair sections, elevators
▶**Team publications:**
Twins Magazine
612-375-7458
▶**TV, radio broadcast stations:**
WCCO 830 AM, WCCO-TV
Channel 4, Midwest Sports Channel
▶**Camps and/or clinics:**
Twins Clinics, weekends throughout the summer, 612-375-7498
▶**Spring training:**
Lee County Sports Complex
Fort Myers, Fla.
Capacity 7,500
813-768-4200

MINNESOTA TWINS 1996 final stats

BATTERS	BA	SLG	OB	G	AB	R	H	TB	2B	3B	HR	RBI	BB	SO	SB	CS	E
Molitor	.341	.468	.390	161	660	99	225	309	41	8	9	113	56	72	18	6	1
Knoblauch	.341	.517	.448	153	578	140	197	299	35	14	13	72	98	74	45	14	8
Kelly	.323	.457	.375	98	322	41	104	147	17	4	6	47	23	53	10	2	2
Cordova	.309	.478	.371	145	569	97	176	272	46	1	16	111	53	96	11	5	3
Brede	.300	.400	.333	10	20	2	6	8	0	1	0	2	1	5	0	0	0
Coomer	.296	.511	.340	95	233	34	69	119	12	1	12	41	17	24	3	0	4
Becker	.291	.434	.372	148	525	92	153	228	31	4	12	71	68	118	19	5	3
Myers	.286	.426	.320	97	329	37	94	140	22	3	6	47	19	52	0	0	3
Stahoviak	.284	.469	.376	130	405	72	115	190	30	3	13	61	59	114	3	3	5
Hale	.276	.368	.347	85	87	18	24	32	5	0	1	16	10	6	0	0	0
Meares	.267	.391	.298	152	517	66	138	202	26	7	8	67	17	90	9	4	22
Lawton	.258	.365	.339	79	252	34	65	92	7	1	6	42	28	28	4	4	3
Walker	.256	.329	.281	25	82	8	21	27	6	0	0	6	4	13	2	0	2
Walbeck	.223	.298	.252	63	215	25	48	64	10	0	2	24	9	34	3	1	2
Raabe	.222	.222	.200	7	9	0	2	2	0	0	0	1	0	1	0	0	1
Reboulet	.222	.261	.298	107	234	20	52	61	9	0	0	23	25	34	4	2	2
Durant	.210	.247	.293	40	81	15	17	20	3	0	0	5	10	15	3	0	5
Hocking	.197	.268	.243	49	127	16	25	34	6	0	1	10	8	24	3	3	1
Quinlan	.000	.000	.000	4	6	0	0	0	0	0	0	0	0	3	0	0	1

PITCHERS	W-L	ERA	G	GS	CG	GF	Sho	SV	IP	H	R	ER	HR	BB	SO
Trombley	5-1	3.01	43	0	0	19	0	6	68.2	61	24	23	2	25	57
Naulty	3-2	3.79	49	0	0	15	0	4	57.0	43	26	24	5	35	56
Radke	11-16	4.46	35	35	3	0	0	0	232.0	231	125	115	40	57	148
Stevens	3-3	4.66	49	0	0	38	0	11	58.0	58	31	30	12	25	29
Rodriguez	13-14	5.05	38	33	3	4	0	2	206.2	218	129	116	27	78	110
Robertson	7-17	5.12	36	31	5	1	3	0	186.1	197	113	106	22	116	114
Guardado	6-5	5.25	83	0	0	17	0	4	73.2	61	45	43	12	33	74
Aguilera	8-6	5.42	19	19	2	0	0	0	111.1	124	69	67	20	27	83
Hansell	3-0	5.69	50	0	0	23	0	3	74.1	83	48	47	14	31	46
Parra	5-5	6.04	27	5	0	7	0	0	70.0	88	48	47	15	27	50
Aldred	6-9	6.21	36	25	0	0	0	0	165.1	194	125	114	29	68	111
Klingenbeck	1-1	7.85	10	3	0	2	0	0	28.2	42	28	25	5	10	15
Bennett	2-0	7.90	24	0	0	10	0	1	27.1	33	24	24	7	16	13
Hawkins	1-1	8.20	7	6	0	1	0	0	26.1	42	24	24	8	9	24
Miller	1-2	9.23	7	7	0	0	0	0	26.1	45	29	27	7	9	15
Serafini	0-1	10.38	1	1	0	0	0	0	4.1	7	5	5	1	2	1

1997 preliminary roster

PITCHERS (17)
Rick Aguilera
Scott Aldred
Eddie Guardado
Latroy Hawkins
Scott Klingenbeck
Travis Miller
Dan Naulty
Jose Parra
Dan Perkins
Brad Radke
Todd Ritchie
Rich Robertson
Frankie Rodriguez
Dan Serafini
Dave Stevens
Bob Tewksbury
Mike Trombley

CATCHERS (3)
Greg Myers
Terry Steinbach
Jose Valentin

INFIELDERS (11)
David Arias
Ron Coomer
Denny Hocking
Chuck Knoblauch
Corey Koskie
Ryan Lane
Pat Meares
Paul Molitor
Jamie Ogden
Scott Stahoviak
Todd Walker

OUTFIELDERS (9)
Rich Becker
Brent Brede
Marty Cordova
Torii Hunter
J.J. Johnson
Roberto Kelly
Chris Latham
Matt Lawton
Ryan Radmanovich

Games played by position

PLAYER	G	C	1B	2B	3B	SS	OF	DH
Becker	148	0	0	0	0	0	146	0
Brede	10	0	0	0	0	0	7	0
Coomer	95	0	57	0	9	0	23	3
Cordova	145	0	0	0	0	0	145	0
Durant	40	37	0	0	0	0	0	0
Hale	85	0	6	14	3	0	3	10
Hocking	49	0	1	2	0	6	33	1
Kelly	98	0	0	0	0	0	93	2
Knoblauch	153	0	0	151	0	0	0	2
Lawton	79	0	0	0	0	0	75	1
Meares	152	0	0	0	0	150	1	0
Molitor	161	0	17	0	0	0	0	143
Myers	97	90	0	0	0	0	0	0
Quinlan	4	0	0	0	4	0	0	0
Raabe	7	0	0	1	6	0	0	0
Reboulet	107	0	13	22	36	37	7	3
Stahoviak	130	0	114	0	0	0	0	9
Walbeck	63	61	0	0	0	0	0	0
Walker	25	0	0	4	20	0	0	1

Minor Leagues

Tops in the organization

BATTER	CLUB	AVG.	G	AB	R	H	HR	RBI
Brian Raabe	Slk	.351	116	482	103	169	18	69
Brent Brede	Slk	.348	132	483	102	168	11	86
Todd Walker	Slk	.339	135	551	94	187	28	111
Adrian Gordon	Ftw	.297	110	343	58	102	1	47
Rafael Alvarez	Ftw	.295	125	495	62	146	4	59

HOME RUNS

Todd Walker	Slk	28
R. Radmanovich	Nbr	25
Anthony Lewis	Nbr	24
Several Players Tied At		18

WINS

Dan Perkins	Ftm	13
Will Rushing	Ftm	13
Benj Sampson	Nbr	12
Phil Stidham	Slk	11
Mark Redman	Slk	10

RBI

Todd Walker	Slk	111
Anthony Lewis	Nbr	95
Brent Brede	Slk	86
R. Radmanovich	Nbr	86
Tom Quinlan	Slk	81

SAVES

Fred Rath	Ftm	18
Tom Gourdin	Ftm	16
Paul Morse	Nbr	13
Mike Trombley	Slk	10
Jose Parra	Slk	8

STOLEN BASES

Armann Brown	Ftm	36
Luis Rivas	Twi	35
Mitch Simons	Slk	35
Cesar Bolivar	Twi	26
Chris Latham	Slk	26

STRIKEOUTS

Jason Bell	Nbr	177
Mark Redman	Slk	175
Travis Miller	Slk	143
Robert Boggs	Ftw	134
R. McBride	Elz	127

PITCHER	CLUB	W-L	ERA	IP	H	BB	SO
Trevor Cobb	Ftm	7-3	2.64	126	101	43	98
Dan Perkins	Ftm	13-7	2.96	137	125	37	111
Jason Bell	Nbr	8-9	3.08	184	154	60	177
Mark Redman	Slk	10-11	3.08	193	171	86	175
S. Klingenbeck	Slk	9-3	3.11	151	159	41	100

Sick call: 1996 DL report

PLAYER	Days on the DL
Rick Aguilera	71*
Denny Hocking	98**
Roberto Kelly	15
Greg Myers	19
Dan Naulty	56
Kirby Puckett	182
Dave Stevens	41*
Matt Walbeck	77

Indicates two separate terms on Disabled List.
**Indicates three separate terms on Disabled List.*

1996 salaries

	Bonuses	Total earned salary
Kirby Puckett, of		$6,200,000
Chuck Knoblauch, 2b		$4,670,000
Rick Aguilera, p		$3,500,000
Paul Molitor, 1b	$25,000	$2,025,000
Roberto Kelly, of	$25,000	$550,000
Marty Cordova, of		$500,000
Greg Myers, c		$475,000
Jeff Reboulet, ss	$25,000	$350,000
Pat Meares, ss		$275,000
Matt Walbeck, c		$225,000
Chip Hale, 2b		$175,000
Brad Radke, p		$175,000
Dave Stevens, p		$172,000
Mike Trombley, p		$162,500
Eddie Guardado, p		$155,000
Rich Becker, of		$152,500
Scott Aldred, p		$150,000
Rich Robertson, p		$140,000
Scott Stahoviak, 3b		$140,000
Frankie Rodriguez, p		$137,500
Jose Parra, p		$125,000
Ron Coomer, 3b		$122,500
Greg Hansell, p		$117,500
Dennis Hocking, ss		$117,500
Matt Lawton, of		$115,000
Travis Miller, p		$109,000
Dan Naulty, p		$109,000
Todd Walker, 3b		$109,000

Average 1996 salary: $759,071
Total 1996 team payroll: $21,254,000
Termination pay: None

Minnesota (1961-1996), including Washington Senators (1901-1960)

Runs: Most, career

1466	Sam Rice, 1915-1933
1258	Harmon Killebrew, 1954-1974
1154	Joe Judge, 1915-1932
1071	Kirby Puckett, 1984-1995
1037	Buddy Myer, 1925-1941

Hits: Most, career

2889	Sam Rice, 1915-1933
2304	Kirby Puckett, 1984-1995
2291	Joe Judge, 1915-1932
2100	Clyde Milan, 1907-1922
2085	Rod Carew, 1967-1978

2B: Most, career

479	Sam Rice, 1915-1933
421	Joe Judge, 1915-1932
414	Kirby Puckett, 1984-1995
391	Mickey Vernon, 1939-1955
329	Tony Oliva, 1962-1976

3B: Most, career

183	Sam Rice, 1915-1933
157	Joe Judge, 1915-1932
125	Goose Goslin, 1921-1938
113	Buddy Myer, 1925-1941
108	Mickey Vernon, 1939-1955
90	Rod Carew, 1967-1978 (8)

HR: Most, career

559	Harmon Killebrew, 1954-1974
293	Kent Hrbek, 1981-1994
256	Bob Allison, 1958-1970
220	Tony Oliva, 1962-1976
207	Kirby Puckett, 1984-1995

RBI: Most, career

1540	Harmon Killebrew, 1954-1974
1086	Kent Hrbek, 1981-1994
1085	Kirby Puckett, 1984-1995
1045	Sam Rice, 1915-1933
1026	Mickey Vernon, 1939-1955

SB: Most, career

495	Clyde Milan, 1907-1922
346	Sam Rice, 1915-1933
321	George Case, 1937-1947
271	Rod Carew, 1967-1978
214	CHUCK KNOBLAUCH, 1991-1996

BB: Most, career

1505	Harmon Killebrew, 1954-1974
1274	Eddie Yost, 1944-1958
943	Joe Judge, 1915-1932

864	Buddy Myer, 1925-1941
838	Kent Hrbek, 1981-1994

BA: Highest, career

.334	Rod Carew, 1967-1978
.328	Heinie Manush, 1930-1935
.323	Sam Rice, 1915-1933
.323	Goose Goslin, 1921-1938
.318	Kirby Puckett, 1984-1995

Slug avg: Highest, career

.514	Harmon Killebrew, 1954-1974
.502	Goose Goslin, 1921-1938
.500	Roy Sievers, 1954-1959
.481	Jimmie Hall, 1963-1966
.481	Kent Hrbek, 1981-1994

On-base avg: Highest, career

.393	Rod Carew, 1967-1978
.393	Buddy Myer, 1925-1941
.392	John Stone, 1934-1938
.391	CHUCK KNOBLAUCH, 1991-1996
.389	Eddie Yost, 1944-1958

Complete games: Most, career

531	Walter Johnson, 1907-1927
206	Case Patten, 1901-1908
141	Bert Blyleven, 1970-1988
139	Tom Hughes, 1904-1913
133	Jim Kaat, 1959-1973

Saves: Most, career

184	RICK AGUILERA, 1989-1996
108	Ron Davis, 1982-1986
104	Jeff Reardon, 1987-1989
96	Firpo Marberry, 1923-1936
88	Al Worthington, 1964-1969

Shutouts: Most, career

110	Walter Johnson, 1907-1927
31	Camilo Pascual, 1954-1966
29	Bert Blyleven, 1970-1988
23	Jim Kaat, 1959-1973
23	Dutch Leonard, 1938-1946

Wins: Most, career

417	Walter Johnson, 1907-1927
190	Jim Kaat, 1959-1973
149	Bert Blyleven, 1970-1988
145	Camilo Pascual, 1954-1966
128	Jim Perry, 1963-1972

K: Most, career

3509	Walter Johnson, 1907-1927
2035	Bert Blyleven, 1970-1988
1885	Camilo Pascual, 1954-1966
1851	Jim Kaat, 1959-1973
1214	FRANK VIOLA, 1982-1989

Win pct: Highest, career

.622	Firpo Marberry, 1923-1936
.602	Sam Jones, 1928-1931
.599	Walter Johnson, 1907-1927
.598	Earl Whitehill, 1933-1936
.588	Mudcat Grant, 1964-1967

ERA: Lowest, career

2.17	Walter Johnson, 1907-1927
2.64	Doc Ayers, 1913-1919
2.75	Harry Harper, 1913-1919
2.77	Charlie Smith, 1906-1909
2.83	Bert Gallia, 1912-1917
3.15	Jim Perry, 1963-1972 (10)

Runs: Most, season

140	CHUCK KNOBLAUCH, 1996
128	Rod Carew, 1977
127	Joe Cronin, 1930
126	Zoilo Versalles, 1965
122	Buddy Lewis, 1938

Hits: Most, season

239	Rod Carew, 1977
234	Kirby Puckett, 1988
227	Sam Rice, 1925
225	PAUL MOLITOR, 1996
223	Kirby Puckett, 1986

2B: Most, season

51	Mickey Vernon, 1946
50	Stan Spence, 1946
46	MARTY CORDOVA, 1996
45	Joe Cronin, 1933
45	CHUCK KNOBLAUCH, 1994
45	Kirby Puckett, 1989
45	Zoilo Versalles, 1965

3B: Most, season

20	Goose Goslin, 1925
19	Joe Cassidy, 1904
19	Cecil Travis, 1941
18	Joe Cronin, 1932
18	Goose Goslin, 1923
18	Sam Rice, 1923
18	Howie Shanks, 1921
18	John Stone, 1935
16	Rod Carew, 1977 (11)

HR: Most, season

49	Harmon Killebrew, 1964
49	Harmon Killebrew, 1969
48	Harmon Killebrew, 1962
46	Harmon Killebrew, 1961
45	Harmon Killebrew, 1963

RBI: Most, season

140	Harmon Killebrew, 1969
129	Goose Goslin, 1924
126	Joe Cronin, 1930
126	Joe Cronin, 1931
126	Harmon Killebrew, 1962

SB: Most, season

88	Clyde Milan, 1912
75	Clyde Milan, 1913
63	Sam Rice, 1920
62	Danny Moeller, 1913
61	George Case, 1943
49	Rod Carew, 1976 (8)

BB: Most, season

151	Eddie Yost, 1956
145	Harmon Killebrew, 1969
141	Eddie Yost, 1950
131	Harmon Killebrew, 1967
131	Eddie Yost, 1954

BA: Highest, season

.388	Rod Carew, 1977
.379	Goose Goslin, 1928
.376	Ed Delahanty, 1902
.364	Rod Carew, 1974
.359	Rod Carew, 1975

Slug avg: Highest, season

.614	Goose Goslin, 1928
.606	Harmon Killebrew, 1961
.590	Ed Delahanty, 1902
.584	Harmon Killebrew, 1969
.579	Roy Sievers, 1957

On-base avg: Highest, season

.454	Buddy Myer, 1938
.453	Ed Delahanty, 1902
.449	Rod Carew, 1977
.448	CHUCK KNOBLAUCH, 1996
.442	Goose Goslin, 1928

Complete games: Most, season

38	Walter Johnson, 1910
37	Case Patten, 1904
36	Walter Johnson, 1911
36	Walter Johnson, 1916
36	Al Orth, 1902
25	Bert Blyleven, 1973 (*)

Saves: Most, season

42	RICK AGUILERA, 1991
42	Jeff Reardon, 1988
41	RICK AGUILERA, 1992
34	RICK AGUILERA, 1993
34	Ron Perranoski, 1970

Shutouts: Most, season

11	Walter Johnson, 1913
9	Bert Blyleven, 1973
9	Walter Johnson, 1914
9	Bob Porterfield, 1953
8	Walter Johnson, 1910
8	Walter Johnson, 1917
8	Walter Johnson, 1918
8	Camilo Pascual, 1961

Wins: Most, season

36	Walter Johnson, 1913
33	Walter Johnson, 1912
28	Walter Johnson, 1914
27	Walter Johnson, 1915
26	Alvin Crowder, 1932
25	Jim Kaat, 1966 (6)

K: Most, season

313	Walter Johnson, 1910
303	Walter Johnson, 1912
258	Bert Blyleven, 1973
249	Bert Blyleven, 1974
243	Walter Johnson, 1913

Win pct: Highest, season

.837	Walter Johnson, 1913
.800	Stan Coveleski, 1925
.800	Firpo Marberry, 1931
.774	FRANK VIOLA, 1988
.773	Bill Campbell, 1976

ERA: Lowest, season

1.14	Walter Johnson, 1913
1.27	Walter Johnson, 1918
1.36	Walter Johnson, 1910
1.39	Walter Johnson, 1912
1.49	Walter Johnson, 1919
2.49	Dave Goltz, 1978 (*)

Most pinch-hit homers, season

4	Don Mincher, 1964

Most pinch-hit homers, career

8	Bob Allison, 1961-1970
7	Don Mincher, 1961-1966

Longest hitting streak

33	Heine Manush, 1933
31	Sam Rice, 1924
31	Ken Landreaux, 1980
29	Sam Rice, 1920
28	Sam Rice, 1930

Most consecutive scoreless innings

55	Walter Johnson, 1913
40	Walter Johnson, 1918
37	Walter Johnson, 1913

No-hit games

Walter Johnson, Was at Bos AL, 1-0; July 1, 1920.

Bobby Burke, Was vs Bos AL, 5-0; Aug. 8, 1931.

Jack Kralick, Min vs KC AL, 1-0; Aug. 26, 1962.

Dean Chance, Min at Cle AL, 2-1; Aug. 25, 1967 (2nd game).

SCOTT ERICKSON, Min vs Mil AL, 6-0; Apr. 27, 1994.

Jay Cashion, six innings, called so Cleveland could catch train, Was vs Cle AL, 2-0; Aug. 20, 1912 (2nd game).

Walter Johnson, seven innings, rain, Was vs StL AL, 2-0; Aug. 25, 1924.

Dean Chance, five perfect innings, rain, Min vs Bos AL, 2-0; Aug. 6, 1967.

ACTIVE PLAYERS in caps.

Leader from the franchise's current location is included. If not in the top five, leader's rank is listed in parenthesis; asterisk (*) indicates player is not in top 25.

Players' years of service are listed by the first and last years with this team and are not necessarily consecutive; all statistics record performances for this team only.

By Russell Beeker, Baseball Weekly

Kevin Appier finished in the league's top five in ERA, strikeouts and batting-average-against.

1996 Royals: Last, for the first time

For the first time in their 28-year history, the Kansas City Royals finished last. "We're the first team to finish last in Royals history," pitcher Chris Haney said. "I'm not happy to say I'm part of that. It's not where we wanted to be at the start of the season." The Royals, who were 75-86, have had worse records, but had always managed to avoid the cellar. Not in 1996.

The Royals' payroll had been cut from $42 million to $18.4 million over three years, so expectations were not high for last season. During the winter they had lost free agents Tom Gordon, Gary Gaetti and Greg Gagne and traded Wally Joyner to save money.

"It's not so much we're a young team, but an inexperienced team," manager Bob Boone said at one point in the season. They will enter 1997 with more experience. In the off-season they turned to veteran Chili Davis to fill a power-hitter void. Craig Paquette, who was released by Oakland in spring training and spent most of April with Class AAA Omaha, led the Royals with 22 home runs and 67 RBI. "I'm excited about this team," Boone said. "We need a little help. It's going to be up to the front office to help us, to work diligently."

In 1996, the starting pitching was strong, with veterans Kevin Appier, Tim Belcher and Mark Gubicza, but Gubicza missed the second half with a broken leg and was traded to the Angels for Davis. The staff's 4.55 ERA ranked third in the league. Left-hander Haney, who had back surgery in 1995, turned into a workhorse with 228 innings and won a career-high 11 games.

A pleasant surprise was the play of Jose Offerman, who batted over .300 and played solid defense at second and first after starting the season at shortstop. Offerman led the team in average, hits, runs and total bases. Disappointments included DHs Bob Hamelin and Joe Vitiello. Hamelin, the 1994 American League Rookie of the Year, was seldom

Team MVP

Kevin Appier: During an early-season losing streak by the Royals, right-hander Appier questioned management's commitment to winning. Part of the answer was to not trade Appier, as had been rumored, but to extend his contract and make him a cornerstone of the rebuilding process. He earned that respect with another strong season on a weak team, producing a 3.62 ERA (fifth in the league) and a 14-11 record. His 207 strikeouts trailed only Roger Clemens and Chuck Finley.

used in September. He finished with a .255 batting average, nine home runs and 40 RBI in 239 at-bats. Vitiello, a first-round pick in 1991 and the American Association's top hitter with a .344 average in 1994, was sent back to Omaha in July to regain his stroke and was recalled in August. He had 257 at-bats, hitting .241 with eight home runs and 40 RBI.

Weakness in the No. 3 and No. 4 slots in the batting order separated the Royals from the wild-card contenders. Bip Roberts once batted cleanup for the Royals though he went the whole year without homering. He hit well when healthy but had two stints on the DL. Johnny Damon, a possible No. 3 hitter, faded in August and September; he wound up hitting .272 but did steal 25 bases. Outfielder Michael Tucker went the other way—he raised his average 41 points after July 1, but an injury ended his season on Aug. 27. Boone was often criticized for using too many different lineups, and only Damon, outfielder Tom Goodwin and Offerman had more than 500 at-bats. But for the manager, 1996 was a season dedicated to learning which Royals will be able to help in the future.

1996 Royals: Week-by-week notes

These notes were excerpted from the following issues of Baseball Weekly.

▶**April 24:** "The Limbo," a song with the lyric "How low can you go?" is blared out every game at Kauffman Stadium. The Royals' answer: lower than a blade of grass. They lost five in a row and seven of eight to fall into the AL Central basement.

▶**May 1:** To shore up the infield defense, manager Bob Boone made David Howard the starting shortstop and moved Jose Offerman from short to first base. The Royals, who made 22 errors in their first 18 games, went six games without an error after the switch.

▶**May 22:** Outfielder–third baseman Craig Paquette was mired in a 1-for-20 slump before his May 18 home run, which ended a 55-inning homerless drought by the Royals.

▶**May 29:** Right-hander Mark Gubicza went from his worst to his best in 10 days. On May 14 at Texas, Gubicza surrendered a career-high nine earned runs on a dozen hits in four innings in a 10-0 loss. But in the May 24 rematch, Gubicza blanked the Rangers 8-0 on four hits. It was the Royals' fifth straight win, but the streak came to an end the next day with a 2-1 loss to Texas.

▶**June 12:** Kevin Young was cut as a sophomore and freshman while trying out for the Washington High baseball team in Kansas City, Kansas, but a decade later he is playing for the Royals. Young debuted on June 9, going 1-for-2 while playing right field and third base against Seattle.

▶**June 19:** Craig Paquette belted three-run homers in back-to-back games on June 12 and 13. The Royals had not had a three-run homer since May 9. In an 11-game stretch, Paquette hit .333 (14-for-42) with two doubles, four home runs, 11 runs and 10 RBI.

▶**July 3:** Righty ace Kevin Appier knew his agent, Jeff Borris, was in Kansas City on June 28 for contract negotiations with Royals general manager Herk Robinson. He didn't know how the talks had gone when he pitched against Minnesota, but

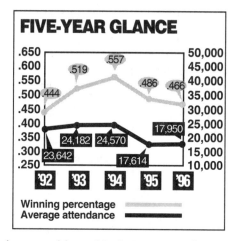

FIVE-YEAR GLANCE

Winning percentage
Average attendance

he was able to block it out, pitching a complete-game victory. Appier's pitching went better than the talks, which stalled over the Royals' failure to include a blanket no-trade clause. Appier has agreed to a three-year contract for just less than $15 million to remain with the Royals.

▶**July 11:** The Royals have a big vacancy in their rotation with Mark Gubicza probably out for the season with a fractured left tibia caused by a Paul Molitor line drive on July 5 at Minnesota. The earliest he could pitch would be eight weeks after the injury. Closer Jeff Montgomery's blown save that day was the fourth in five opportunities. He had given up 14 runs on 17 hits, including seven home runs, in his last 13 innings.

▶**July 17:** Left-hander Chris Haney has won his last four starts, with a 3.27 ERA in 33 innings, including a complete-game, eight-hit, no-walk gem on July 11 against the White Sox. In six April starts, he went 0-4 with a 6.68 ERA.

▶**July 24:** Jeff Montgomery passed Dan Quisenberry as the Royals' all-time saves leader, with 239, on July 20 against Chicago. His record-tying save the night before was dramatic, as he wriggled out of a bases-loaded, one-out situation to preserve Kansas City's 3-2 triumph against Cleveland.

▶**July 31:** Kevin Appier was signed: He secured a one-year no-trade clause from the Royals and also can name six clubs he will not be traded to after the year is up. If Appier is traded, his salary escalates by $400,000.

▶**Aug. 7:** Second baseman Bip Roberts, with zero home runs entering August, has been batting cleanup for the Royals lately. Roberts, ordinarily a leadoff man, may lack power, but he leads Kansas City with a career-high 46 RBI. Craig Paquette, who did not join the Royals until April 28, leads the club with 14 home runs, also a career high.

▶**Aug. 14:** Rookie outfielder Johnny Damon tied a Royals record when he drove in seven runs in an 18-3 rout on Aug. 10 at California. The Royals had been the only team in the American League without a grand slam, but Damon took care of that by driving a Jim Abbott pitch over the right-field wall. The Royals may have found a leadoff hitter in Jose Offerman, who has hit safely in 10 of his past 13 games. In his last 36 plate appearances, Offerman has reached base 18 times—seven singles, three doubles, three triples, one home run and four walks. His 55 walks top the club.

▶**Aug. 21:** Right-hander Tim Belcher has been one of the premier starters in the AL. He's 12-7, and only seven pitchers in the league have won more games. His 3.88 ERA is tied for seventh in the AL, and he is sixth in the league with 181 innings pitched.

▶**Aug. 28:** Craig Paquette went from being released in spring training by Oakland, to starting the season in the minors, to having a career year for the Royals. Despite missing the first 24 games, Paquette leads the Royals with 18 home runs and 55 RBI, both career highs.

▶**Sept. 11:** Jeff Montgomery, the club's lone All-Star in 1996, had season-ending shoulder surgery on Sept. 4. With Montgomery out, manager Bob Boone said he would use rookie Jaime Bluma, Hipolito Pichardo and left-hander Jason Jacome in save situations.

▶**Sept. 18:** Jose Offerman and Tim Belcher signed two-year contract extensions last week. Offerman leads the Royals with a .289 average, a .376 on-base average, 32 doubles and 207 total bases.

Belcher, who turns 35 next month, said, "This is the first multiyear deal I've ever signed."

▶**Oct. 2:** For the first time in their 28-year history, the rebuilding Royals, 75-86, finished last. In three years, the payroll was pared from $42 million to $18.4 million, and over the winter the Royals lost free agents Tom Gordon, Gary Gaetti and Greg Gagne and traded Wally Joyner. Craig Paquette, was a pleasant surprise, leading the Royals with 22 home runs and 67 RBI, but the highly touted Johnny Damon fizzled the last two months, winding up with a .272 average and 25 stolen bases. The pitching was good: The team 4.57 ERA ranked third in the league, and veteran starters Kevin Appier, Tim Belcher and Mark Gubicza are signed for 1997. Jose Offerman batted above .300 and played surprisingly solid defense at second and first after starting at shortstop.

Team directory

▶**Owner:** Greater Kansas Community Foundation, Board of Directors; David Glass, Chairman of the Board; Michael Hennan, President

▶**General manager:** Herk Robinson

▶**Ballpark:**
Ewing Kauffman Stadium
1 Royal Way
Kansas City, Mo.
816-921-2200
Capacity 40,625
Pay parking lot; $5
Public transportation available
Wheelchair section and ramps, handicapped accessible

▶**Team publications:**
Yearbook, scorecard, media guide

▶**TV, radio broadcast stations:**
KMBZ 980 AM, KMBC Channel 62, KCWB Channel 29, Fox Sports Rocky Mountain

▶**Spring training:**
Baseball City Stadium
Baseball City, Fla.
Capacity 7,000 (1,000 on grass)
813-424-7211

KANSAS CITY ROYALS 1996 final stats

BATTERS	BA	SLG	OB	G	AB	R	H	TB	2B	3B	HR	RBI	BB	SO	SB	CS	E
Offerman	.303	.417	.384	151	561	85	170	234	33	8	5	47	74	98	24	10	16
Randa	.303	.433	.351	110	337	36	102	146	24	1	6	47	26	47	13	4	10
Stynes	.293	.359	.309	36	92	8	27	33	6	0	0	6	2	5	5	2	3
Myers	.286	.444	.357	22	63	9	18	28	7	0	1	11	7	16	3	2	0
Roberts	.283	.357	.331	90	339	39	96	121	21	2	0	52	25	38	12	9	4
Goodwin	.282	.330	.334	143	524	80	148	173	14	4	1	35	39	79	66	22	5
Sweeney	.279	.412	.358	50	165	23	46	68	10	0	4	24	18	21	1	2	1
Macfarlane	.274	.499	.339	112	379	58	104	189	24	2	19	54	31	57	3	3	4
Lockhart	.273	.411	.319	138	433	49	118	178	33	3	7	55	30	40	11	6	13
Damon	.271	.368	.313	145	517	61	140	190	22	5	6	50	31	64	25	5	6
Tucker	.260	.442	.346	108	339	55	88	150	18	4	12	53	40	69	10	4	2
Paquette	.259	.452	.296	118	429	61	111	194	15	1	22	67	23	101	5	3	14
Hamelin	.255	.435	.391	89	239	31	61	104	14	1	9	40	54	58	5	2	4
Mercedes	.250	.250	.250	4	4	1	1	1	0	0	0	0	0	1	0	0	0
Young	.242	.470	.301	55	132	20	32	62	6	0	8	23	11	32	3	3	1
Vitiello	.241	.401	.342	85	257	29	62	103	15	1	8	40	38	69	2	0	0
Lennon	.233	.333	.378	14	30	5	7	10	3	0	0	1	7	10	0	0	1
Howard	.219	.305	.291	143	420	51	92	128	14	5	4	48	40	74	5	6	11
Nunnally	.211	.456	.308	35	90	16	19	41	5	1	5	17	13	25	0	0	2
Fasano	.203	.343	.283	51	143	20	29	49	2	0	6	19	14	25	1	1	5
Norman	.122	.122	.232	54	49	9	6	6	0	0	0	0	6	14	1	1	0

PITCHERS	W-L	ERA	G	GS	CG	GF	Sho	SV	IP	H	R	ER	HR	BB	SO
Rosado	8-6	3.21	16	16	2	0	1	0	106.2	101	39	38	7	26	64
Bluma	0-0	3.60	17	0	0	10	0	5	20.0	18	9	8	2	4	14
Appier	14-11	3.62	32	32	5	0	1	0	211.1	192	87	85	17	75	207
Belcher	15-11	3.92	35	35	4	0	1	0	238.2	262	117	104	28	68	113
Montgomery	4-6	4.26	48	0	0	41	0	24	63.1	59	31	30	14	19	45
Huisman	2-1	4.60	22	0	0	5	0	1	29.1	25	15	15	4	18	23
Haney	10-14	4.70	35	35	4	0	1	0	228.0	267	136	119	29	51	115
Jacome	0-4	4.72	49	2	0	21	0	1	47.2	67	27	25	5	22	32
Linton	7-9	5.02	21	18	0	0	0	0	104.0	111	65	58	13	26	87
Gubicza	4-12	5.13	19	19	2	0	1	0	119.1	132	70	68	22	34	55
Pichardo	3-5	5.43	57	0	0	28	0	3	68.0	74	41	41	5	26	43
Pugh	0-1	5.45	19	1	0	8	0	0	36.1	42	24	22	9	12	27
Magnante	2-2	5.67	38	0	0	9	0	0	54.0	58	38	34	5	24	32
Bevil	1-0	5.73	3	1	0	1	0	0	11.0	9	7	7	2	5	7
Robinson	1-0	6.00	5	0	0	2	0	0	6.0	9	4	4	0	3	5
Valera	3-2	6.46	31	2	0	7	0	1	61.1	75	44	44	7	27	31
Granger	0-0	6.61	15	0	0	5	0	0	16.1	21	13	12	3	10	11
Scanlan	0-1	6.85	17	0	0	4	0	0	22.1	29	19	17	2	12	6
Clark	1-1	7.79	12	0	0	5	0	0	17.1	28	15	15	3	7	12

1997 preliminary roster

PITCHERS (17)
Kevin Appier
Tim Belcher
Brian Bevil
Jaime Bluma
Jamie Brewington
Melvin Bunch
Chris Haney
Rick Huisman
Jason Jacome
Doug Linton
Jeff Montgomery

Hipolito Pichardo
Jim Pittsley
Ken Ray
Jose Rosado
Glendon Rusch
Bob Scanlan

CATCHERS (3)
Sal Fasano
Mike Macfarlane
Mike Sweeney

INFIELDERS (14)
Jay Bell
Bob Hamelin
Jed Hansen
David Howard
Jeff King
Keith Lockhart
Mendy Lopez
Felix Martinez
Sergio Nunez
Jose Offerman
Craig Paquette

Bip Roberts
Chris Stynes
Joe Vitiello

OUTFIELDERS (6)
Johnny Damon
Chili Davis
Tom Goodwin
Roderick Myers
Jon Nunnally
Michael Tucker

Games played by position

PLAYER	G	C	1B	2B	3B	SS	OF	DH
Damon	145	0	0	0	0	0	144	1
Fasano	51	51	0	0	0	0	0	0
Goodwin	143	0	0	0	0	0	136	5
Hamelin	89	0	33	0	0	0	0	47
Howard	143	0	2	3	0	135	1	1
Lennon	14	0	0	0	0	0	11	1
Lockhart	138	0	0	84	55	0	0	1
Macfarlane	112	99	0	0	0	0	0	9
Mercedes	4	4	0	0	0	0	0	0
Myers	22	0	0	0	0	0	19	0
Norman	54	0	0	0	0	0	38	7
Nunnally	35	0	0	0	0	0	29	4
Offerman	151	0	96	38	0	36	1	0
Paquette	118	0	19	0	51	11	47	6
Randa	110	0	7	15	92	0	0	1
Roberts	90	0	0	63	0	0	11	16
Stynes	36	0	0	5	2	0	19	3
Sweeney	50	26	0	0	0	0	0	22
Tucker	108	0	9	0	0	0	98	5
Vitiello	85	0	9	0	0	0	1	70
Young	55	0	27	0	7	0	17	3

Minor Leagues

Tops in the organization

BATTER	CLUB	AVG.	G	AB	R	H	HR	RBI
Jose Amado	Lan	.318	118	444	82	141	10	83
B. Berger	Spo	.307	71	283	46	87	13	58
Mark Quinn	Lan	.302	113	437	63	132	9	71
Mike Sweeney	Oma	.301	91	336	59	101	17	67
Steve Sisco	Wch	.297	122	462	80	137	13	74

HOME RUNS

Jon Nunnally	Oma	25
Larry Sutton	Wch	22
Ryan Long	Wch	20
Kit Pellow	Spo	18
Several Players Tied At		17

WINS

Brian Bevil	Oma	16
Blaine Mull	Lan	15
Steve Olsen	Oma	13
Eric Anderson	Wil	12
Several Players Tied At		11

RBI

Larry Sutton	Wch	84
Jose Amado	Lan	83
Juan Rocha	Lan	83
Jose Cepeda	Lan	81
Ryan Long	Wch	78

SAVES

Jaime Bluma	Oma	25
S. Prihoda	Wil	25
Jose Santiago	Lan	19
Allen McDill	Wch	11
Toby Smith	Wch	8

STOLEN BASES

Sergio Nunez	Wil	44
Jeremy Carr	Wch	41
Rod Myers	Oma	37
Patrick Hallmark	Lan	33
Carlos Febles	Lan	30

STRIKEOUTS

Brian Bevil	Oma	147
Matthew Saier	Wil	129
Phillip Grundy	Wil	117
Glendon Rusch	Oma	117
Blaine Mull	Lan	114

PITCHER	CLUB	W-L	ERA	IP	H	BB	SO
Jim Telgheder	Wch	8-5	2.64	95	83	20	61
Jose Rosado	Oma	10-3	2.79	110	90	39	94
Brian Bevil	Oma	16-7	3.02	143	118	45	147
Todd Thorn	Lan	11-5	3.11	171	161	34	107
Blaine Mull	Lan	15-8	3.25	175	186	40	114

Sick call: 1996 DL report

PLAYER	Days on the DL
Jim Converse	182
Mark Gubicza	86
Bob Hamelin	28
Mike Magnante	25
Les Norman	57
Jim Pittsley	96
Kris Ralston	110
Joe Randa	22
Bip Roberts	64*
Michael Tucker	50*

Indicates two separate terms on Disabled List.

1996 salaries

	Bonuses	Total earned salary
Kevin Appier, p		$5,051,250
Bip Roberts, 2b		$2,500,000
Jeff Montgomery, p	$50,000	$2,150,000
Mark Gubicza, p		$1,600,000
Tim Belcher, p	$425,000	$1,400,000
Jose Offerman, 1b	$200,000	$1,100,000
Mike Macfarlane, c	$100,000	$850,000
Hipolito Pichardo, p	$50,000	$625,000
David Howard, ss	$100,000	$600,000
Chris Haney, p	$75,000	$575,000
Bob Hamelin, 1b		$375,000
Tom Goodwin, of		$312,500
Mike Magnante, p		$250,000
Keith Lockhart, 3b		$207,500
Jon Nunnally, of		$190,000
Doug Linton, p	$30,000	$189,000
Johnny Damon, of	$20,000	$180,000
Michael Tucker, of	$20,000	$160,000
Jason Jacome, p		$150,000
Craig Paquette, 3b		$150,000
Joe Vitiello, 1b	$10,000	$150,000
Kevin Young, 1b		$150,000
Jim Converse, p		$148,000
Joe Randa, 3b		$120,000
Rick Huisman, p		$118,000
Les Norman, of		$118,000
Mike Sweeney, c		$114,000
Jamie Bluma, p		$109,000
Kris Ralston, p		$109,000
Jose Rosado, p		$109,000

Average 1996 salary: $662,008
Total 1996 team payroll: $19,860,250
Termination pay: $120,000

Kansas City (1969-1996)

Runs: Most, career

1583	George Brett, 1973-1993
1074	Amos Otis, 1970-1983
1060	Willie Wilson, 1976-1990
912	Frank White, 1973-1990
873	Hal McRae, 1973-1987

Hits: Most, career

3154	George Brett, 1973-1993
2006	Frank White, 1973-1990
1977	Amos Otis, 1970-1983
1968	Willie Wilson, 1976-1990
1924	Hal McRae, 1973-1987

2B: Most, career

665	George Brett, 1973-1993
449	Hal McRae, 1973-1987
407	Frank White, 1973-1990
365	Amos Otis, 1970-1983
241	Willie Wilson, 1976-1990

3B: Most, career

137	George Brett, 1973-1993
133	Willie Wilson, 1976-1990
65	Amos Otis, 1970-1983
63	Hal McRae, 1973-1987
58	Frank White, 1973-1990

HR: Most, career

317	George Brett, 1973-1993
193	Amos Otis, 1970-1983
169	Hal McRae, 1973-1987
160	Frank White, 1973-1990
143	John Mayberry, 1972-1977

RBI: Most, career

1595	George Brett, 1973-1993
1012	Hal McRae, 1973-1987
992	Amos Otis, 1970-1983
886	Frank White, 1973-1990
552	John Mayberry, 1972-1977

SB: Most, career

612	Willie Wilson, 1976-1990
340	Amos Otis, 1970-1983
336	Freddie Patek, 1971-1979
201	George Brett, 1973-1993
178	Frank White, 1973-1990

BB: Most, career

1096	George Brett, 1973-1993
739	Amos Otis, 1970-1983
616	Hal McRae, 1973-1987
561	John Mayberry, 1972-1977
413	Freddie Patek, 1971-1979

BA: Highest, career

.305	George Brett, 1973-1993
.294	KEVIN SEITZER, 1986-1991
.293	WALLY JOYNER, 1992-1995
.293	Hal McRae, 1973-1987
.290	DANNY TARTABULL, 1987-1991

Slug avg: Highest, career

.518	DANNY TARTABULL, 1987-1991
.487	George Brett, 1973-1993
.480	Bo Jackson, 1986-1990
.469	Willie Aikens, 1980-1983
.459	Steve Balboni, 1984-1988

On-base avg: Highest, career

.380	KEVIN SEITZER, 1986-1991
.376	DANNY TARTABULL, 1987-1991
.375	Darrell Porter, 1977-1980
.374	John Mayberry, 1972-1977
.371	WALLY JOYNER, 1992-1995

Complete games: Most, career

103	Dennis Leonard, 1974-1986
88	Paul Splittorff, 1970-1984
64	BRET SABERHAGEN, 1984-1991
61	Larry Gura, 1976-1985
53	Steve Busby, 1972-1980
53	Dick Drago, 1969-1973

Saves: Most, career

242	JEFF MONTGOMERY, 1988-1996
238	Dan Quisenberry, 1979-1988
58	Doug Bird, 1973-1978
49	Steve Farr, 1985-1990
40	Ted Abernathy, 1970-1972

Shutouts: Most, career

23	Dennis Leonard, 1974-1986
17	Paul Splittorff, 1970-1984
16	MARK GUBICZA, 1984-1996
14	Larry Gura, 1976-1985
14	BRET SABERHAGEN, 1984-1991

Wins: Most, career

166	Paul Splittorff, 1970-1984
144	Dennis Leonard, 1974-1986
132	MARK GUBICZA, 1984-1996
111	Larry Gura, 1976-1985
110	BRET SABERHAGEN, 1984-1991

K: Most, career

1366	MARK GUBICZA, 1984-1996
1323	Dennis Leonard, 1974-1986
1168	KEVIN APPIER, 1989-1996
1093	BRET SABERHAGEN, 1984-1991
1057	Paul Splittorff, 1970-1984

Win pct: Highest, career

.594	KEVIN APPIER, 1989-1996
.593	Al Fitzmorris, 1969-1976
.587	Larry Gura, 1976-1985
.585	BRET SABERHAGEN, 1984-1991
.576	Doug Bird, 1973-1978

ERA: Lowest, career

2.55	Dan Quisenberry, 1979-1988
3.21	BRET SABERHAGEN, 1984-1991
3.28	KEVIN APPIER, 1989-1996
3.46	Al Fitzmorris, 1969-1976
3.48	Marty Pattin, 1974-1980

Runs: Most, season

133	Willie Wilson, 1980
119	George Brett, 1979
113	Willie Wilson, 1979
108	George Brett, 1985
105	George Brett, 1977
105	KEVIN SEITZER, 1987

Hits: Most, season

230	Willie Wilson, 1980
215	George Brett, 1976
212	George Brett, 1979
207	KEVIN SEITZER, 1987
195	George Brett, 1975

2B: Most, season

54	Hal McRae, 1977
46	Hal McRae, 1982
45	George Brett, 1978
45	George Brett, 1990
45	Frank White, 1982

3B: Most, season

21	Willie Wilson, 1985
20	George Brett, 1979
15	Willie Wilson, 1980
15	Willie Wilson, 1982
15	Willie Wilson, 1987

HR: Most, season

36	Steve Balboni, 1985
35	GARY GAETTI, 1995
34	John Mayberry, 1975

34   DANNY TARTABULL, 1987
32   Bo Jackson, 1989

RBI: Most, season

133   Hal McRae, 1982
118   George Brett, 1980
112   George Brett, 1985
112   Al Cowens, 1977
112   Darrell Porter, 1979

SB: Most, season

83   Willie Wilson, 1979
79   Willie Wilson, 1980
66   TOM GOODWIN, 1996
59   Willie Wilson, 1983
59   Willie Wilson, 1987

BB: Most, season

122   John Mayberry, 1973
121   Darrell Porter, 1979
119   John Mayberry, 1975
103   George Brett, 1985
103   Paul Schaal, 1971

BA: Highest, season

.390   George Brett, 1980
.335   George Brett, 1985
.333   George Brett, 1976
.332   Hal McRae, 1976
.332   Willie Wilson, 1982

Slug avg: Highest, season

.664   George Brett, 1980
.599   BOB HAMELIN, 1994
.593   DANNY TARTABULL, 1991
.585   George Brett, 1985
.563   George Brett, 1979

On-base avg: Highest, season

.454   George Brett, 1980
.436   George Brett, 1985
.421   Darrell Porter, 1979
.417   John Mayberry, 1973
.416   John Mayberry, 1975

Complete games: Most, season

21   Dennis Leonard, 1977
20   Steve Busby, 1974
20   Dennis Leonard, 1978
18   Steve Busby, 1975
16   Larry Gura, 1980
16   Dennis Leonard, 1976

Saves: Most, season

45   JEFF MONTGOMERY, 1993
45   Dan Quisenberry, 1983
44   Dan Quisenberry, 1984
39   JEFF MONTGOMERY, 1992
37   Dan Quisenberry, 1985

Shutouts: Most, season

6   Roger Nelson, 1972
5   Dennis Leonard, 1977
5   Dennis Leonard, 1979
4   Bill Butler, 1969
4   Dick Drago, 1971
4   Al Fitzmorris, 1974
4   MARK GUBICZA, 1988
4   Larry Gura, 1980
4   Dennis Leonard, 1978
4   BRET SABERHAGEN, 1987
4   BRET SABERHAGEN, 1989

Wins: Most, season

23   BRET SABERHAGEN, 1989
22   Steve Busby, 1974
21   Dennis Leonard, 1978
20   MARK GUBICZA, 1988
20   Dennis Leonard, 1977
20   Dennis Leonard, 1980
20   BRET SABERHAGEN, 1985
20   Paul Splittorff, 1973

K: Most, season

244   Dennis Leonard, 1977
207   KEVIN APPIER, 1996
206   Bob Johnson, 1970
198   Steve Busby, 1974
193   BRET SABERHAGEN, 1989

Win pct: Highest, season

.800   Larry Gura, 1978
.793   BRET SABERHAGEN, 1989
.769   BRET SABERHAGEN, 1985
.762   DAVID CONE, 1994
.727   Paul Splittorff, 1977

ERA: Lowest, season

2.08   Roger Nelson, 1972
2.16   BRET SABERHAGEN, 1989
2.46   KEVIN APPIER, 1992
2.56   KEVIN APPIER, 1993
2.69   Charlie Leibrandt, 1985

Most pinch-hit homers, season

2   Carmelo Martinez, 1991
2   Hal McRae, 1986

Most pinch-hit homers, career

2   Steve Balboni, 1984-1988
2   JIM EISENREICH, 1987-1991
2   Chuck Harrison, 1969-1971
2   Carmelo Martinez, 1991
2   Hal McRae, 1973-1987
2   Bob Oliver, 1969-1972
2   Amos Otis, 1970-1983

Longest hitting streak

30   George Brett, 1980
22   BRIAN McRAE, 1991
19   Amos Otis, 1974
19   George Brett, 1983
18   GREGG JEFFERIES, 1992
18   Ed Kirkpatrick, 1973
18   Lou Piniella, 1971
18   Willie Wilson, 1984

Most consecutive scoreless innings

31   BRET SABERHAGEN, 1989

No-hit games

Steve Busby, KC at Det AL, 3-0;
    Apr. 16, 1973.
Steve Busby, KC at Mil AL, 2-0;
    June 19, 1974.
Jim Colborn, KC vs Tex AL, 6-0;
    May 14, 1977.
BRET SABERHAGEN, KC vs Chi
AL, 7-0; Aug. 26, 1991.

ACTIVE PLAYERS in caps.

Players' years of service are listed by the first and last years with this team and are not necessarily consecutive; all statistics record performances for this team only.

KANSAS CITY ROYALS / AL CENTRAL

Texas Rangers

By Chet Gordon, Gannett

Juan Gonzalez was the first Rangers MVP since Jeff Burroughs in 1974.

1996 Rangers: Texas takes it to the top

Just as they had in the first 24 years of their existence, the Rangers busied themselves after the final game of the regular season by packing to leave the clubhouse. But this time it was different. While the first 24 Rangers teams were getting ready to go home, the 25th edition was packing to go to New York for the first round of the playoffs.

The Rangers won their first division title by showing a little grit down the stretch. They lost all but one game off a nine-game lead, but refused to fold. After losing five straight during a nine-game West Coast road trip, including four in a row against second-place Seattle, they won five of their next seven. "I don't think these guys were looking at Seattle over their shoulders as much as they were looking at Texas Rangers history over their shoulders," manager Johnny Oates said. "That was something they faced since spring training. That's something that's over with."

The only blemish on the title was that they won it on a night they lost. They were about four hours into a five-hour-plus, 15-inning loss to the Angels when they learned that the Mariners had lost to the Athletics, clinching the division for Texas. After a moment's hesitation, the Rangers began to congratulate each other. "When the Seattle score went up, it was like the weight of the world went off our shoulders," center fielder Darryl Hamilton said. "The guys in the dugout weren't sure what to do, so we talked it over and decided nobody could take it away from us now. So we decided to start hugging and feeling good." The postgame celebration lasted until 4 a.m.

"It was great because I remember back in spring training how people were picking us to finish third," third baseman Dean Palmer said. "This feels so good. We proved a lot of people wrong." The Rangers reversed their slide in large part because of the combined efforts of starting pitchers John Burkett and Ken Hill. Burkett snapped the five-game losing

Team MVP

Juan Gonzalez: Rangers right fielder Juan Gonzalez returned to his status as one of the game's premier sluggers, even before he almost single-handedly kept Texas in its playoff series with the New York Yankees. Hampered by injuries for two seasons, Gonzalez was the league MVP and set Rangers records with 47 home runs and 144 RBI, finishing second in the AL to Albert Belle in the latter category.

streak by allowing just one run in eight innings of a 7-1 victory on Sept. 21 against the Angels, and Hill pitched a complete game the next day in a 4-1 victory over California. The Rangers pitching staff had had a 6.20 ERA in the 10 games before that. Burkett later got Texas's only victory in the Division Series loss to the Yankees, winning the opener 6-2 with a complete game. Hill tied his previous best with 16 victories on the season. The bullpen, though, was weak. While closer Mike Henneman had a career-high 31 saves, he struggled much of the time (0-7, 5.79 ERA, six blown saves) and was let go after the season. Overall the Texas relievers lost 25 of 40 decisions.

The offense was outstanding, as the Rangers broke or tied team records for runs scored (928), batting average (.284), home runs (221) and RBI (890) in winning the title. Right fielder Juan Gonzalez set individual Rangers marks with 47 homers and 144 RBI, and then single-handedly kept the Division Series close by slugging five home runs in the four games. He averaged 1.08 RBI per game played during the regular season, the best ratio in the majors since 1938. Shortstop Kevin Elster, Palmer, catcher Ivan Rodriguez and left fielder Rusty Greer all set career highs in home runs and RBI.

1996 Rangers: Week-by-week notes

These notes were excerpted from the following issues of Baseball Weekly.

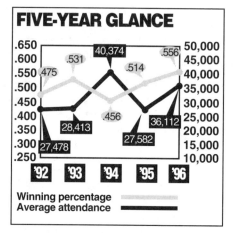

FIVE-YEAR GLANCE

Winning percentage
Average attendance

▶**April 3:** Kevin Elster, who has played just 40 games in the majors over the last four years, became the starting shortstop when Benji Gil went out for up to eight weeks after surgery on a herniated disc.

▶**April 10:** The starting pitching, thought by many to be a weakness, was a strength in a season-opening sweep of the Red Sox. The starters held Boston to six runs in 21⅔ innings.

▶**April 17:** The Rangers ran their season-opening winning streak to seven games, the best start in club history, before finally losing 8-5 to the White Sox. Starting pitchers were 7-0 (Ken Hill, Roger Pavlik and Kevin Gross 2-0, Bobby Witt 1-0) with a 2.49 ERA. Relievers had four saves (two by Mike Henneman, two by Ed Vosberg) and a 0.56 ERA.

▶**April 24:** The Rangers went into the eighth inning on April 19 clinging to a three-run lead against the Orioles. They exited it with a team-record 16 runs off three Orioles pitchers, including utility infielder Manny Alexander, en route to a 26-7 victory.

▶**May 8:** The Rangers accomplished something not done in the AL in 79 years when Ken Hill and Roger Pavlik threw back-to-back one-hitters against the Tigers on May 3-4.

▶**May 15:** Manager Johnny Oates is reconsidering his original plan to have Benji Gil return to the starting lineup. Kevin Elster was hitting .269 and leading AL shortstops with seven homers and 28 RBI though the first 35 games. He was also steady in the field, having made only two errors.

▶**May 22:** The Rangers had the best first quarter in franchise history at 26-14. Their 4½-game lead was the largest of any team in the majors, but they were without right fielder Juan Gonzalez, on the DL with a partially torn left quadriceps muscle, and left fielder Rusty Greer, out with a mild separation of his left shoulder.

▶**June 5:** The Rangers were 18-9 in May,

tying the club record for wins and winning percentage in any month. It was the third-best record in the majors, behind the Braves (19-6) and Indians (19-9). Texas led the AL with a 3.64 ERA and were fourth with a .291 batting average.

▶**June 19:** Roger Pavlik's 9-1 start was the best for a Rangers pitcher ever after 10 decisions. He did it despite a 5.01 ERA, as the offense averaged 7.86 runs per nine innings for him.

▶**June 26:** A strained muscle was diagnosed in closer Mike Henneman's right shoulder, explaining why he blew three of his first six save opportunities in June after setting a club record for saves in a month with 10 in May.

▶**July 3:** Ken Hill, who looked after May like a candidate to start the All-Star Game, struggled in June. He was 1-2 with a 9.00 ERA in five starts for the month.

▶**July 11:** The Rangers lost a chunk of their lead just before the All-Star break, dropping three out of four against second-place Seattle to narrow their margin to four games. The series continued the Rangers' struggles against the Mariners. They are 3-6 against Seattle this year and 7-28 since Sept. 21, 1993.

▶**July 17:** The bullpen seems to hold the key to the Rangers' chances of winning their first division title. Relievers converted 20 of 23 save opportunities and had a 3.95 ERA in the first two months. From June 1 up to the All-Star break, they blew eight of 15 save chances and had a 6.25 ERA.

▶July 31: Juan Gonzalez is having the best season of his life despite missing 25 games because of injuries. His .326 is the best batting average of his career, and his 29 homers and 89 RBI placed him among the league leaders.

▶Aug. 7: Juan Gonzalez tied Hank Greenberg, Joe DiMaggio and Joe Adcock for the most homers ever hit in July. He finished the month with a .407 average, 15 homers and 38 RBI in 27 games, leading the majors in all three categories.

▶Aug. 14: For the second consecutive year, general manager Doug Melvin was able to make a waiver-driven deal after the trading deadline. Melvin acquired right-hander John Burkett from the Florida Marlins on Aug. 8, exactly one year after getting Bobby Witt from the same team. Burkett pitched a six-hit shutout in his AL debut on Aug. 10, blanking Toronto 6-0 as the Rangers completed their first road sweep this season.

▶Aug. 21: The Rangers put some distance between themselves and the Mariners by winning seven consecutive games, and first baseman Will Clark's stroke is coming back. He was 10-for-25 in a six-game stretch through Aug. 18.

▶Aug. 28: The Rangers set a league record with 15 consecutive errorless games, one more than the '91 Angels. The streak lasted for 575 chances and 141⅓ innings before Kevin Elster dropped a routine throw from second baseman Mark McLemore in the fourth inning against the Indians on Aug. 20. Two days later, Ivan Rodriguez set a major league record for doubles by a catcher when he hit his 43rd.

▶Sept. 4: Kevin Elster continued his magical mystery season. Through August he had 23 homers and 94 RBI, club records for a shortstop in both categories. Elster had career highs of 10 homers and 55 RBI before this year.

▶Sept. 25: With their once seemingly safe lead in the West all but evaporated, the Rangers now had to hold on to avoid going down in history with one of the biggest collapses ever. They held a nine-game lead with 17 to play on Sept. 11 but lost eight of their next nine. That included a four-game sweep at the hands of the second-place Mariners, and the lead was down to one.

▶Oct. 2: The Rangers showed grit down the stretch. After losing five in a row on a nine-game West Coast swing, they won five of their next seven and clinched on Sept. 27 on a Seattle loss to Oakland. The Rangers reversed their slide partly because of the clutch pitching of John Burkett and Ken Hill. During the season, Juan Gonzalez set Rangers records with 47 homers and 144 RBI, and Kevin Elster, Dean Palmer, Ivan Rodriguez and Rusty Greer all set career highs in home runs and RBI. The bullpen was a disappointment, going 15-25 for the year.

Team directory

▶**Owners:** J. Thomas Schieffer and Edward W. Rose, managing general partners
▶**General manager:** Doug Melvin
▶**Ballpark:**
The Ballpark in Arlington
1000 Ballpark Way
Arlington, Texas
817-273-5222
Capacity 49,178
Parking for 12,500 cars; $5
No public transportation
Approximately 480 wheelchair seats with additional handicapped seating; restrooms with diaper-changing areas; ramps, escalators and elevators to serve all areas
▶**Team publications:**
On Deck Newsletter, yearbook, *Program Magazine*
817-273-5222
▶**TV, radio broadcast stations:**
KRLD-AM 1080, KXEB 910 AM (Spanish), KTVT-TV 11, Prime Sports Entertainment
▶**Camps and/or clinics:**
Texas Ranger Coaches Clinic, June, 817-273-5222
▶**Spring training:**
Charlotte County Stadium
Port Charlotte, Fla.
Capacity 6,026
813-625-9500

TEXAS RANGERS 1996 final stats

BATTERS	BA	SLG	OB	G	AB	R	H	TB	2B	3B	HR	RBI	BB	SO	SB	CS	E
Gil	.400	.400	.500	5	5	0	2	2	0	0	0	1	1	1	0	1	1
Greer	.332	.530	.397	139	542	96	180	287	41	6	18	100	62	86	9	0	5
Gonzalez	.314	.643	.368	134	541	89	170	348	33	2	47	144	45	82	2	0	2
Valle	.302	.500	.368	42	86	14	26	43	6	1	3	17	9	17	0	0	1
Rodriguez	.300	.473	.342	153	639	116	192	302	47	3	19	86	38	55	5	0	10
Hamilton	.293	.381	.348	148	627	94	184	239	29	4	6	51	54	66	15	5	0
McLemore	.290	.379	.389	147	517	84	150	196	23	4	5	46	87	69	27	10	12
Ortiz	.286	1.000	.286	3	7	1	2	7	0	1	1	1	0	1	0	0	0
Clark	.284	.436	.377	117	436	69	124	190	25	1	13	72	64	67	2	1	4
Buford	.283	.469	.348	90	145	30	41	68	9	0	6	20	15	34	8	5	0
Palmer	.280	.527	.348	154	582	98	163	307	26	2	38	107	59	145	2	0	16
Stillwell	.273	.364	.364	46	77	12	21	28	4	0	1	4	10	11	0	0	3
Frazier	.260	.340	.373	30	50	5	13	17	2	1	0	5	8	10	4	2	2
Newson	.255	.451	.355	91	235	34	60	106	14	1	10	31	37	82	3	0	1
Elster	.252	.462	.317	157	515	79	130	238	32	2	24	99	52	138	4	1	14
Tettleton	.246	.450	.366	143	491	78	121	221	26	1	24	83	95	137	2	1	4
Stevens	.231	.449	.291	27	78	6	18	35	2	3	3	12	6	22	0	0	1
Gonzales	.217	.326	.288	51	92	19	20	30	4	0	2	5	10	11	0	0	2
Faneyte	.200	.200	.200	8	5	0	1	1	0	0	0	1	0	0	0	0	0
Worthington	.158	.316	.333	13	19	2	3	6	0	0	1	4	6	3	0	0	1
Voigt	.111	.111	.111	5	9	1	1	1	0	0	0	0	0	2	0	0	0
Brown	.000	.000	.375	3	4	1	0	0	0	0	0	1	2	2	0	0	0

PITCHERS	W-L	ERA	G	GS	CG	GF	Sho	SV	IP	H	R	ER	HR	BB	SO
Patterson	0-0	0.00	7	0	0	5	0	0	8.2	10	4	0	0	3	5
Vosberg	1-1	3.27	52	0	0	21	0	8	44.0	51	17	16	4	21	32
Russell	3-3	3.38	55	0	0	11	0	3	56.0	58	22	21	5	22	23
Hill	16-10	3.63	35	35	7	0	3	0	250.2	250	110	101	19	95	170
Stanton	4-4	3.66	81	0	0	28	0	1	78.2	78	32	32	11	27	60
Burkett	5-2	4.06	10	10	1	0	1	0	68.2	75	33	31	4	16	47
Cook	5-2	4.09	60	0	0	9	0	0	70.1	53	34	32	2	35	64
Oliver	14-6	4.66	30	30	1	0	1	0	173.2	190	97	90	20	76	112
Pavlik	15-8	5.19	34	34	7	0	0	0	201.0	216	120	116	28	81	127
Gross	11-8	5.22	28	19	1	4	0	0	129.1	151	78	75	19	50	78
Witt	16-12	5.41	33	32	2	1	0	0	199.2	235	129	120	28	96	157
Alberro	0-1	5.79	5	1	0	1	0	0	9.1	14	6	6	1	7	2
Henneman	0-7	5.79	49	0	0	45	0	31	42.0	41	28	27	6	17	34
Heredia	2-5	5.89	44	0	0	21	0	1	73.1	91	50	48	12	14	43
Whiteside	0-1	6.68	14	0	0	7	0	0	32.1	43	24	24	8	11	15
Helling	1-2	7.52	6	2	0	2	0	0	20.1	23	17	17	7	9	16

1997 preliminary roster

PITCHERS (16)
Jose Alberro
Cory Bailey
John Burkett
Wilson Heredia
Xavier Hernandez
Ken Hill
Eric Moody
Darren Oliver
Danny Patterson
Roger Pavlik
Julio Santana
Tanyon Sturtze
Ed Vosberg
John Wetteland
Matt Whiteside
Bobby Witt

CATCHERS (4)
Kevin Brown
Henry Mercedes
Ivan Rodriguez
Mickey Tettleton

INFIELDERS (10)
Mike Bell
Will Clark
Edwin Diaz
Hanley Frias
Benji Gil
Mark McLemore
Dean Palmer
Billy Ripken
Lee Stevens
Fernando Tatis

OUTFIELDERS (8)
Damon Buford
Juan Gonzalez
Rusty Greer
Mark Little
Warren Newson
Lonell Roberts
Marc Sagmoen
Andrew Vessel

Games played by position

PLAYER	G	C	1B	2B	3B	SS	OF	DH
Brown	3	2	0	0	0	0	0	1
Buford	90	0	0	0	0	0	80	3
Clark	117	0	117	0	0	0	0	0
Elster	157	0	0	0	0	157	0	0
Faneyte	8	0	0	0	0	0	6	2
Frazier	30	0	0	1	0	0	15	13
Gil	5	0	0	0	0	5	0	0
Gonzales	51	0	23	5	15	10	1	0
Gonzalez	134	0	0	0	0	0	102	32
Greer	139	0	1	0	0	0	137	1
Hamilton	148	0	0	0	0	0	147	0
McLemore	147	0	0	147	0	0	1	0
Newson	91	0	0	0	0	0	66	9
Ortiz	3	0	0	0	0	0	0	1
Palmer	154	0	0	0	154	0	0	1
Rodriguez	153	146	0	0	0	0	0	6
Stevens	27	0	18	0	0	0	5	0
Stillwell	46	0	1	21	6	9	0	1
Tettleton	143	0	23	0	0	0	0	115
Valle	42	35	5	0	0	0	0	1
Voigt	5	0	0	0	1	0	3	0
Worthington	13	0	6	0	7	0	0	0

Minor Leagues

Tops in the organization

BATTER	CLUB	AVG.	G	AB	R	H	HR	RBI
Lee Stevens	Okc	.325	117	431	84	140	32	94
Luis Ortiz	Okc	.317	124	501	70	159	14	73
Mike Murphy	Tul	.307	121	479	95	147	11	68
Jack Voigt	Okc	.303	134	472	84	143	22	88
Derek Lee	Okc	.301	120	409	59	123	13	62

HOME RUNS			WINS		
Bubba Smith	Tul	32	Ted Silva	Tul	17
Lee Stevens	Okc	32	J. Johnson	Tul	14
Kevin Brown	Tul	26	Jim Brower	Tul	12
Jack Voigt	Okc	22	Rick Helling	Okc	12
Mike Coolbaugh	Tul	17	Scott Mudd	Csc	12

RBI			SAVES		
Bubba Smith	Tul	94	Mike Venafro	Csc	19
Lee Stevens	Okc	94	Eric Moody	Tul	16
Jack Voigt	Okc	88	Bobby Styles	Rng	13
Kevin Brown	Tul	86	Clint Davis	Tul	10
Mike Coolbaugh	Tul	84	Danny Patterson	Okc	10

STOLEN BASES			STRIKEOUTS		
Juan Nunez	Csc	53	Rob Kell	Tul	164
Ruben Mateo	Csc	30	Danny Kolb	Tul	162
Craig Monroe	Hdv	23	Rick Helling	Okc	157
Mike Murphy	Tul	23	Ryan Dempster	Csc	141
Mark Little	Tul	22	Jose Alberro	Okc	140

PITCHER	CLUB	W-L	ERA	IP	H	BB	SO
Danny Kolb	Tul	11-8	2.82	176	123	82	162
Ted Silva	Tul	17-4	2.91	189	170	43	122
Rick Helling	Okc	12-4	2.96	140	124	38	157
R. Dempster	Csc	7-11	3.30	144	120	58	141
J. Johnson	Tul	14-10	3.39	183	178	42	103

Sick call: 1996 DL report

PLAYER	Days on the DL
Will Clark	49**
Benji Gil	51
Juan Gonzalez	24
Kevin Gross	36*
Chris Howard	182
Chris Nichting	155
Lee Stevens	28
Kurt Stillwell	28

Indicates two separate terms on Disabled List.
**Indicates three separate terms on Disabled List.*

1996 salaries

	Bonuses	Total earned salary
Juan Gonzalez, of	$75,000	$6,175,000
Will Clark, 1b		$5,657,365
Ivan Rodriguez, c		$4,000,000
John Burkett, p		$3,550,000
Kevin Gross, p		$3,300,000
Ken Hill, p	$100,000	$3,100,000
Dean Palmer, 3b	$75,000	$2,000,000
Mike Stanton, p		$1,750,000
Mickey Tettleton, c		$1,461,649
Mike Henneman, p		$1,419,681
Bobby Witt, p		$1,350,000
Darryl Hamilton, of	$250,000	$1,300,000
Roger Pavlik, p	$150,000	$1,250,000
Mark McLemore, 2b	$350,000	$1,225,000
David Valle, c	$125,000	$725,000
Jeff Russell, p	$175,000	$445,000
Dennis Cook, p	$65,000	$330,000
Kevin Elster, ss	$90,000	$270,000
Rusty Greer, of		$258,333
Warren Newson, of	$50,000	$250,000
Darren Oliver, p	$40,000	$220,000
Ed Vosberg, p	$20,000	$198,000
Rene Gonzales, 3b		$175,000
Damon Buford, of	$5,000	$165,000
Kurt Stillwell, 2b		$150,000
Chris Howard, p		$130,000
Chris Nichting, p		$116,000
Lee Stevens, 1b		$109,000

Average 1996 salary: $1,467,143
Total 1996 team payroll: $41,080,028
Termination pay: None

Texas (1972-1996), includes Washington Senators (1961-1971)

Runs: Most, career

631	Toby Harrah, 1969-1986
571	RUBEN SIERRA, 1986-1992
544	Frank Howard, 1965-1972
482	Jim Sundberg, 1974-1989
480	JUAN GONZALEZ, 1989-1996

Hits: Most, career

1180	Jim Sundberg, 1974-1989
1174	Toby Harrah, 1969-1986
1141	Frank Howard, 1965-1972
1132	RUBEN SIERRA, 1986-1992
1060	Buddy Bell, 1979-1989

2B: Most, career

226	RUBEN SIERRA, 1986-1992
200	Jim Sundberg, 1974-1989
197	Buddy Bell, 1979-1989
187	Toby Harrah, 1969-1986
174	RAFAEL PALMEIRO, 1989-1993

3B: Most, career

43	RUBEN SIERRA, 1986-1992
30	Chuck Hinton, 1961-1964
27	Ed Brinkman, 1961-1975
27	Jim Sundberg, 1974-1989
24	Ed Stroud, 1967-1970

HR: Most, career

246	Frank Howard, 1965-1972
214	J. GONZALEZ, 1989-1996
153	RUBEN SIERRA, 1986-1992
149	Larry Parrish, 1982-1988
140	DEAN PALMER, 1989-1996

RBI: Most, career

701	Frank Howard, 1965-1972
659	J. GONZALEZ, 1989-1996
656	RUBEN SIERRA, 1986-1992
568	Toby Harrah, 1969-1986
522	Larry Parrish, 1982-1988

SB: Most, career

161	Bump Wills, 1977-1981
153	Toby Harrah, 1969-1986
144	Dave Nelson, 1970-1975
129	Oddibe McDowell, 1985-1994
98	JULIO FRANCO, 1989-1993

BB: Most, career

708	Toby Harrah, 1969-1986
575	Frank Howard, 1965-1972
544	Jim Sundberg, 1974-1989

435	Mike Hargrove, 1974-1978
404	Pete O'Brien, 1982-1988

BA: Highest, career

.319	Al Oliver, 1978-1981
.307	JULIO FRANCO, 1989-1993
.303	Mickey Rivers, 1979-1984
.296	R. PALMEIRO, 1989-1993
.293	Mike Hargrove, 1974-1978

Slug avg: Highest, career

.552	J. GONZALEZ, 1989-1996
.503	Frank Howard, 1965-1972
.477	DEAN PALMER, 1989-1996
.474	R. PALMEIRO, 1989-1993
.471	RUBEN SIERRA, 1986-1992

On-base avg: Highest, career

.399	Mike Hargrove, 1974-1978
.382	JULIO FRANCO, 1989-1993
.367	Frank Howard, 1965-1972
.366	RAFAEL PALMEIRO, 1989-1993
.365	Mike Epstein, 1967-1973

Complete games: Most, career

98	Charlie Hough, 1980-1990
90	Fergie Jenkins, 1974-1981
55	Gaylord Perry, 1975-1980
40	KEVIN BROWN, 1986-1994
36	Joe Coleman, 1965-1970

Saves: Most, career

134	JEFF RUSSELL, 1985-1996
83	Ron Kline, 1963-1966
64	Darold Knowles, 1967-1977
58	Tom Henke, 1982-1994
37	Jim Kern, 1979-1981

Shutouts: Most, career

17	Fergie Jenkins, 1974-1981
12	Gaylord Perry, 1975-1980
11	Charlie Hough, 1980-1990
9	Dick Bosman, 1966-1973
8	Jim Bibby, 1973-1984

Wins: Most, career

139	Charlie Hough, 1980-1990
93	Fergie Jenkins, 1974-1981
87	BOBBY WITT, 1986-1996
78	KEVIN BROWN, 1986-1994
70	KENNY ROGERS, 1989-1995

K: Most, career

1452	Charlie Hough, 1980-1990

1254	BOBBY WITT, 1986-1996
939	Nolan Ryan, 1989-1993
895	Fergie Jenkins, 1974-1981
742	KEVIN BROWN, 1986-1994

Win pct: Highest, career

.578	KENNY ROGERS, 1989-1995
.567	Nolan Ryan, 1989-1993
.566	ROGER PAVLIK, 1992-1996
.564	Fergie Jenkins, 1974-1981
.549	KEVIN BROWN, 1986-1994

ERA: Lowest, career

3.26	Gaylord Perry, 1975-1980
3.35	Dick Bosman, 1966-1973
3.41	Jon Matlack, 1978-1983
3.43	Nolan Ryan, 1989-1993
3.51	Joe Coleman, 1965-1970

Runs: Most, season

124	RAFAEL PALMEIRO, 1993
116	IVAN RODRIGUEZ, 1996
115	RAFAEL PALMEIRO, 1991
111	Frank Howard, 1969
110	RUBEN SIERRA, 1991

Hits: Most, season

210	Mickey Rivers, 1980
209	Al Oliver, 1980
203	RAFAEL PALMEIRO, 1991
203	RUBEN SIERRA, 1991
201	JULIO FRANCO, 1991

2B: Most, season

49	RAFAEL PALMEIRO, 1991
47	IVAN RODRIGUEZ, 1996
44	RUBEN SIERRA, 1991
43	Al Oliver, 1980
42	Buddy Bell, 1979
42	Larry Parrish, 1984

3B: Most, season

14	RUBEN SIERRA, 1989
12	Chuck Hinton, 1963
10	DAVID HULSE, 1993
10	RUBEN SIERRA, 1986
10	Ed Stroud, 1968

HR: Most, season

48	Frank Howard, 1969
47	JUAN GONZALEZ, 1996
46	JUAN GONZALEZ, 1993
44	Frank Howard, 1968
44	Frank Howard, 1970

RBI: Most, season

144	JUAN GONZALEZ, 1996
126	Frank Howard, 1970
119	RUBEN SIERRA, 1989
118	Jeff Burroughs, 1974
118	JUAN GONZALEZ, 1993

SB: Most, season

52	Bump Wills, 1978
51	Dave Nelson, 1972
50	OTIS NIXON, 1995
45	Cecil Espy, 1989
44	Bill Sample, 1983

BB: Most, season

132	Frank Howard, 1970
113	Toby Harrah, 1985
109	Toby Harrah, 1977
107	Mike Hargrove, 1978
107	MICKEY TETTLETON, 1995

BA: Highest, season

.341	JULIO FRANCO, 1991
.333	Mickey Rivers, 1980
.332	RUSTY GREER, 1996
.329	WILL CLARK, 1994
.329	Buddy Bell, 1980

Slug avg: Highest, season

.643	JUAN GONZALEZ, 1996
.632	JUAN GONZALEZ, 1993
.574	Frank Howard, 1969
.554	RAFAEL PALMEIRO, 1993
.552	JOSE CANSECO, 1994

On-base avg: Highest, season

.432	Toby Harrah, 1985
.431	WILL CLARK, 1994
.420	Mike Hargrove, 1977
.416	Frank Howard, 1970
.408	JULIO FRANCO, 1991

Complete games: Most, season

29	Fergie Jenkins, 1974
22	Fergie Jenkins, 1975
21	Gaylord Perry, 1976
18	Jon Matlack, 1978
17	Charlie Hough, 1984

Saves: Most, season

40	Tom Henke, 1993
38	JEFF RUSSELL, 1989
31	MIKE HENNEMAN, 1996
30	JEFF RUSSELL, 1991
29	Jim Kern, 1979
29	Ron Kline, 1965

Shutouts: Most, season

6	Bert Blyleven, 1976
6	Fergie Jenkins, 1974
5	Jim Bibby, 1974
5	Bert Blyleven, 1977
4	Tom Cheney, 1963
4	Joe Coleman, 1969
4	Fergie Jenkins, 1975
4	Fergie Jenkins, 1978
4	Doc Medich, 1981
4	Camilo Pascual, 1968
4	Gaylord Perry, 1975
4	Gaylord Perry, 1977

Wins: Most, season

25	Fergie Jenkins, 1974
21	KEVIN BROWN, 1992
19	Jim Bibby, 1974
18	Charlie Hough, 1987
18	Fergie Jenkins, 1978

K: Most, season

301	Nolan Ryan, 1989
232	Nolan Ryan, 1990
225	Fergie Jenkins, 1974
223	Charlie Hough, 1987
221	BOBBY WITT, 1990

Win pct: Highest, season

.708	KENNY ROGERS, 1995
.692	Fergie Jenkins, 1978
.676	Fergie Jenkins, 1974
.656	KEVIN BROWN, 1992
.652	ROGER PAVLIK, 1996

ERA: Lowest, season

2.19	Dick Bosman, 1969
2.27	Jon Matlack, 1978
2.40	Dick Donovan, 1961
2.42	RICK HONEYCUTT, 1983
2.60	Pete Richert, 1965

Most pinch-hit homers, season

3	Brant Alyea, 1969
3	Don Lock, 1966
3	Tom McCraw, 1971
3	Darrell Porter, 1987
3	Rick Reichardt, 1970
3	Rusty Staub, 1980

Most pinch-hit homers, career

6	Brant Alyea, 1965-1969
6	Geno Petralli, 1985-1993

Longest hitting streak

24	Mickey Rivers, 1980
22	Jim Sundberg, 1978
21	Buddy Bell, 1980
21	JUAN GONZALEZ, 1996
21	Johnny Grubb, 1979
21	Al Oliver, 1980

Most consecutive scoreless innings

36	Charlie Hough, 1983

No-hit games

Jim Bibby, Tex at Oak AL, 6-0; July 20, 1973.

Bert Blyleven, Tex at Cal AL, 6-0; Sept. 22, 1977.

Nolan Ryan, Tex at Oak AL, 5-0; June 11, 1990.

Nolan Ryan, Tex vs Tor AL, 3-0; May 1, 1991.

KENNY ROGERS, Tex vs Cal AL, 4-0; July 28, 1994 (perfect game).

ACTIVE PLAYERS in caps.

Players' years of service are listed by the first and last years with this team and are not necessarily consecutive; all statistics record performances for this team only.

165

By Nell Seiler, USA TODAY

Alex Rodriguez had perhaps the finest offensive season ever turned in by a shortstop.

1996 Mariners: Slugging Seattle fell short

The Seattle Mariners had a good year. They remained in contention until the last weekend of the season, set a franchise record for games won and broke most of the team's offensive records. In the end, though, these accomplishments were dimmed by Seattle's losing the American League West title and falling short in the attempt to get the wild-card berth. "We have nothing to be ashamed of," catcher Dan Wilson said. "We're all disappointed, but our accomplishment was to overcome so many things and take the season so far. We got close."

Defending their first division title, the Mariners lost 1995 Cy Young Award winner Randy Johnson in May with a bulging disk, and though he pitched in relief for a few weeks in August, he never started again and underwent back surgery in September. Designated hitter Edgar Martinez, a two-time AL batting champion, fractured four ribs in July and missed 21 games. In those games, the Mariners were 9-12—and when Martinez returned to the lineup, it was without his usual power. Center fielder Ken Griffey Jr. threw together an MVP-type season despite breaking a bone in his right hand that required surgery. He missed 20 games and had problems with that hand for the rest of the year. "Edgar played in pain the final two months," manager Lou Piniella said as the season ended. "He'd wince whenever he swung and missed. Junior's hand bothered him the last three months. [Right fielder] Jay Buhner had a great season, and the week it ends, he'll have surgery to clean up an ankle that kept locking up on him."

And then there was Alex Rodriguez. Playing his first full big-league season, Rodriguez turned 21 during an unprecedented year. He scored more runs, had more hits, more doubles, more extra-base hits and a higher slugging average than any shortstop in major league history—despite missing two weeks early on with a strained hamstring muscle. His .358 batting average was the highest ever by a player under the age of 22. "Alex is

the best young hitter in baseball," Hall of Fame shortstop Ernie Banks said when the two met during the final week of the season. "He may be the best young player in baseball. Who's better? He's going to break all my records."

Without Johnson, and with injuries that sidelined Greg Hibbard all year and Chris Bosio much of the season, Seattle used 22 pitchers, with 15 of them starting games. Newcomer Sterling Hitchcock led the team with 13 victories—no other starting pitcher had more than seven—and Norm Charlton saved 20 games. Terry Mulholland, acquired late in July, said that the team won't have trouble recruiting pitchers. "You'd have to be a fool not to want to pitch for this team, and a bigger fool to want to pitch against it," Mulholland said. Free-agent left-hander Jeff Fassero, 15-11 with Montreal, was the first to sign with Seattle in the off-season.

A team that shattered its previous records for home runs, RBI, runs, doubles and extra-base hits, the 1996 Mariners had only four complete games and a 5.21 ERA that was the highest in team history. "What we did this season shows the character of this team and the leadership of Lou Piniella," Hitchcock said. "Everybody in here pushed to the point of exhaustion, mentally and physically. Nobody has much left, but it got us close."

1996 Mariners: Week-by-week notes

These notes were excerpted from the following issues of Baseball Weekly.

▶**April 17:** Dan Wilson earned his reputation as a strong defensive catcher in his first two years with Seattle. Now, after a three-homer game against Detroit last week and a second-deck shot a few days later in Toronto, Wilson had four home runs and 10 RBI in his first 10 games.

▶**April 24:** Center fielder Ken Griffey Jr. was batting .215 after 17 games. "I've never seen him struggle like this at the plate—and I doubt anybody has," manager Lou Piniella said.

▶**May 15:** The education of a shortstop continues in Seattle, where 20-year-old Alex Rodriguez has been assigned a new course—batting second in the lineup. Despite missing more than two weeks to injury, he has four home runs and 18 RBI in his first 21 games.

▶**May 22:** Closer Norm Charlton's streak of 17 consecutive saves spread over two seasons came to an end in Baltimore last week when he inherited a 13-10 lead in the ninth against the Orioles and lost on a two-out, 3-2 count grand slam by Chris Hoiles.

▶**May 29:** The Mariners will pay Randy Johnson, Chris Bosio and Greg Hibbard a combined $13 million this season, and Bosio and Hibbard might never pitch again. All three are on the disabled list, and none figures to be back soon.

▶**June 5:** Designated hitter Edgar Martinez may be on the way to shattering the major league record for doubles. With 29 in 53 games, he is on pace to get 90 doubles—23 more than Earl Webb's record of 67 in 1931.

▶**June 12:** Seattle fans are having trouble keeping track of the pitching staff. So is the manager. "If you look at our 11-man staff this season, there's one guy—Bob Wells—who was with us all of 1995," Lou Piniella said. In an odd medical twist, third baseman Russ Davis broke his left fibula when his spikes caught on the tartan surface of Kauffman Stadium last week—virtually the exact injury suffered 10 days earlier by

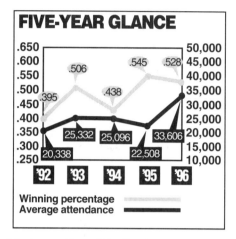

FIVE-YEAR GLANCE

Winning percentage
Average attendance

Mariners reliever *Tim* Davis.

▶**June 26:** Not quite midway through the season, the Mariners already have used 21 pitchers—and produced only six with winning records. Two of those winning pitchers, Randy Johnson and Chris Bosio, are on the DL.

▶**July 11:** Russ Davis will miss the rest of the season with a broken leg, but the Mariners plan to make another Paul Sorrento out of him in the off-season. Davis's problems at the plate are similar to those of first baseman Sorrento, who batted .235 last season in Cleveland but is hitting .320 this year. "Davis basically has the same approach Sorrento had this spring—he's not getting to the pitch out in front, he's back on his back foot and spinning on the ball, not shifting his weight into it," Lou Piniella said.

▶**July 17:** Without Ken Griffey Jr., Randy Johnson and Norm Charlton, the Mariners won back-to-back extra-inning games from California to pull within three games of the AL West lead. In 51 games without Johnson, the team has gone 29-22.

▶**July 24:** On July 20 the Mariners gave cleanup hitter Edgar Martinez his first start of the season at third base—and a second-inning collision with reserve catcher John Marzano left both men injured. Marzano needed 30 stitches to close a gash in his left eyebrow, and Martinez suffered badly bruised ribs. X-rays taken of Martinez the next day were normal, and he will be evaluated on a day-to-day basis.

▶July 31: Through July 28, Alex Rodriguez was second in the league in batting average (.354), second in runs (91), second in doubles (37) and seventh in hits (128). He also had 21 home runs and 79 RBI, already club season records for a shortstop. On his 21st birthday, July 27, the All-Star was rewarded with a four-year, $10.6 million contract extension.

▶Aug. 7: Heading into the final two months of the pennant race, the Mariners used a pair of deals to retool their rotation. Seattle traded for veteran left-handers Terry Mulholland and Jamie Moyer, who soon became the 13th and 14th starters used in 1996.

▶Aug. 14: Randy Johnson is off the DL and in the Mariners' bullpen. In his first two appearances since a bulging disk sidelined him on May 12, he pitched five shutout innings.

▶Aug. 21: When outfielder Mark Whiten, acquired from Atlanta, homered in a pinch-hit at-bat against New York, he became the 45th Mariner used this season, three short of the Seattle record.

▶Aug. 28: Alex Rodriguez keeps piling up great numbers. Last week he became the fifth shortstop in big league history to hit as many as 30 home runs in a season—joining Ernie Banks, Rico Petrocelli, Vern Stephens and Cal Ripken Jr.

▶Sept. 4: For the third time in a month, the Mariners have named an every-day third baseman—the latest being 30-year-old switch-hitter Dave Hollins. Thirty days earlier, it had been Jeff Manto, acquired from Boston. Two weeks later, Manto was benched and the job went to rookie Andy Sheets, one of 28 players recalled from Class AAA Tacoma this year.

▶Sept. 18: Much-traveled free agent Mark Whiten has been a portrait of consistency, hitting over .310 with nine home runs and 25 RBI in his first 25 games.

▶Sept. 25: Ken Griffey Jr. seems happiest dodging the media spotlight, which is now focused on Alex Rodriguez and the Mariners' comeback. Griffey is batting .303 with a career-best 47 home runs and 135 RBI, and the team swept four games

from Texas to close the gap to one game on Sept. 20.

▶Oct. 2: The Mariners won more games than in any other season in their history, stayed in contention until the final two days and shattered nearly every major team offensive record. But the accomplishments were offset by the disappointment of losing the AL West title, then the wild-card race. Many injuries hurt the Mariners, including ones to Randy Johnson, Ken Griffey Jr. and Edgar Martinez. But led by the astounding performance of Alex Rodriguez, who turned 21 during a season in which he hit a major-league-best .358 and had the highest slugging average for a shortstop in major league history, Seattle finished only 4½ games behind Texas. "We fell short, but we gave it a good fight," Lou Piniella said. "It was a successful year in many ways. It was a fun team to manage, a fun team for fans to watch."

Team directory

▶**Owner:** Baseball Club of Seattle
▶**General manager:** Woody Woodward
▶**Ballpark:**
The Kingdome
201 South King St.
Seattle, Wash.
206-628-3555
Capacity 59,856
Public transportation available
Parking for 2,400 cars,
30,000 within a mile.
Family and wheelchair sections,
birthday package, anniversary
package
▶**Team publications:**
Mariners Magazine, Mariners Newsletter, scorecard, media guide
206-296-3663
▶**TV, radio broadcast stations:**
KIRO 710 AM, KSTW Channel 11,
Fox Sports Northwest Cable
▶**Spring training:**
Peoria Sports Complex
Peoria, Ariz.
Capacity 10,000 (3,000 on grass)
602-412-9000

SEATTLE MARINERS 1996 final stats

BATTERS	BA	SLG	OB	G	AB	R	H	TB	2B	3B	HR	RBI	BB	SO	SB	CS	E
Rodriguez	.358	.631	.414	146	601	141	215	379	54	1	36	123	59	104	15	4	15
E. Martinez	.327	.595	.464	139	499	121	163	297	52	2	26	103	123	84	3	3	1
Griffey	.303	.628	.392	140	545	125	165	342	26	2	49	140	78	104	16	1	4
Whiten	.300	.607	.399	40	140	31	42	85	7	0	12	33	21	40	2	1	3
Amaral	.292	.356	.392	118	312	69	91	111	11	3	1	29	47	55	25	6	0
Cora	.291	.417	.340	144	530	90	154	221	37	6	6	45	35	32	5	5	13
Sorrento	.289	.507	.370	143	471	67	136	239	32	1	23	93	57	103	0	2	11
Wilson	.285	.444	.330	138	491	51	140	218	24	0	18	83	32	88	1	2	4
Buhner	.271	.557	.369	150	564	107	153	314	29	0	44	138	84	159	0	1	3
Hunter	.268	.424	.327	75	198	21	53	84	10	0	7	28	15	43	0	1	5
Hollins	.262	.411	.377	149	516	88	135	212	29	0	16	78	84	117	6	6	18
Jordan	.250	.357	.290	15	28	4	7	10	0	0	1	4	1	6	0	0	0
Marzano	.245	.302	.316	41	106	8	26	32	6	0	0	6	7	15	0	0	3
Diaz	.241	.304	.274	38	79	11	19	24	2	0	1	5	2	8	6	3	1
M. Martinez	.235	.471	.350	9	17	3	4	8	2	1	0	3	3	5	2	0	0
Strange	.235	.333	.290	88	183	19	43	61	7	1	3	23	14	31	1	0	2
R. Davis	.234	.377	.312	51	167	24	39	63	9	0	5	18	17	50	2	0	7
Sheets	.191	.264	.262	47	110	18	21	29	8	0	0	9	10	41	2	0	5
Widger	.182	.182	.250	8	11	1	2	2	0	0	0	0	0	5	0	0	2
Ibanez	.000	.000	.167	4	5	0	0	0	0	0	0	0	0	1	0	0	0

PITCHERS	W-L	ERA	G	GS	CG	GF	Sho	SV	IP	H	R	ER	HR	BB	SO
McCarthy	0-0	1.86	10	0	0	1	0	0	9.2	8	2	2	0	4	7
Jackson	1-1	3.63	73	0	0	23	0	6	72.0	61	32	29	11	24	70
Johnson	5-0	3.67	14	8	0	2	0	1	61.1	48	27	25	8	25	85
Klink	0-0	3.86	3	0	0	1	0	0	2.1	3	1	1	1	1	2
Moyer	13-3	3.98	34	21	0	1	0	0	160.2	177	86	71	23	46	79
T. Davis	2-2	4.01	40	0	0	4	0	0	42.2	43	21	19	4	17	34
Charlton	4-7	4.04	70	0	0	50	0	20	75.2	68	37	34	7	38	73
Guetterman	0-2	4.09	17	0	0	1	0	0	11.0	11	8	5	0	10	6
Carmona	8-3	4.28	53	1	0	15	0	1	90.1	95	47	43	11	55	62
Torres	3-3	4.59	10	7	1	1	1	0	49.0	44	27	25	5	23	36
Mulholland	5-4	4.67	12	12	0	0	0	0	69.1	75	38	36	5	28	34
Minor	0-1	4.97	11	0	0	6	0	0	25.1	27	14	14	6	11	14
Wells	12-7	5.30	36	16	1	6	1	0	130.2	141	78	77	25	46	94
Hitchcock	13-9	5.35	35	35	0	0	0	0	196.2	245	131	117	27	73	132
Wolcott	7-10	5.73	30	28	1	0	0	0	149.1	179	101	95	26	54	78
Meacham	1-1	5.74	15	5	0	3	0	1	42.1	57	28	27	9	13	25
Ayala	6-3	5.88	50	0	0	26	0	3	67.1	65	45	44	10	25	61
Bosio	4-4	5.93	18	9	0	4	0	0	60.2	72	44	40	8	24	39
Milacki	1-4	6.86	7	4	0	1	0	0	21.0	30	20	16	3	15	13
Wagner	3-5	6.86	15	14	1	0	0	0	80.0	91	62	61	15	38	41
Menhart	2-2	7.29	11	6	0	4	0	0	42.0	55	36	34	9	25	18
Hurtado	2-5	7.74	16	4	0	6	0	2	47.2	61	42	41	10	30	36
Davison	0-0	9.00	5	0	0	3	0	0	9.0	11	9	9	6	3	9
Harikkala	0-1	12.46	1	1	0	0	0	0	4.1	4	6	6	1	2	1
Suzuki	0-0	20.25	1	0	0	0	0	0	1.1	2	3	3	0	2	1

1997 preliminary roster

PITCHERS (21)
Bobby Ayala
Rafael Carmona
Norm Charlton
Dean Crow
Tim Davis
Jeff Fassero
Tim Harikkala
Edwin Hurtado
Randy Johnson
Derek Lowe
Damaso Marte
Greg McCarthy
Paul Menhart

Ivan Montane
Jamie Moyer
Alex Pacheco
Scott Sanders
Mac Suzuki
Salomon Torres
Bob Wells
Bob Wolcott

CATCHERS (3)
Raul Ibanez
John Marzano
Dan Wilson

INFIELDERS (8)
Joey Cora
Russ Davis
Gio Guevara
Edgar Martinez
Alex Rodriguez
Andy Sheets
Dave Silvestri
Paul Sorrento

OUTFIELDERS (6)
Rich Amaral
Jay Buhner
Lou Frazier
Ken Griffey Jr.
Marcus Sturdivant
Lee Tinsley

Games played by position

PLAYER	G	C	1B	2B	3B	SS	OF	DH
Amaral	118	0	10	15	1	0	91	6
Buhner	150	0	0	0	0	0	142	8
Cora	144	0	0	140	1	0	0	0
R. Davis	51	0	0	0	51	0	0	0
Diaz	38	0	0	0	0	0	28	1
Griffey	140	0	0	0	0	0	137	5
Hollins	149	0	1	0	144	1	0	3
Hunter	75	0	41	0	0	0	29	2
Ibanez	4	0	0	0	0	0	0	2
Jordan	15	0	9	0	0	0	0	2
E. Martinez	139	0	4	0	2	0	0	134
M. Martinez	9	0	0	0	0	0	8	0
Marzano	41	39	0	0	0	0	0	0
Rodriguez	146	0	0	0	0	146	0	0
Sheets	47	0	0	18	25	7	0	0
Sorrento	143	0	138	0	0	0	0	0
Strange	88	0	3	3	39	0	11	10
Whiten	40	0	0	0	0	0	39	0
Widger	8	7	0	0	0	0	0	0
Wilson	138	135	0	0	0	0	0	0

Sick call: 1996 DL report

PLAYER	Days on the DL
Bobby Ayala	58
Chris Bosio	80*
Russ Davis	114
Tim Davis	45
Scott Davison	27
Alex Diaz	81*
Ken Griffey Jr.	23
Greg Hibbard	183
Edwin Hurtado	29
Randy Johnson	119*
Ricky Jordan	121
Edgar Martinez	22
Paul Menhart	47
Alex Rodriguez	15

* Indicates two separate terms on Disabled List.

Minor Leagues

Tops in the organization

BATTER	CLUB	AVG.	G	AB	R	H	HR	RBI
David Arias	Wsc	.322	129	485	89	156	18	93
Scott Smith	Wsc	.314	128	493	95	155	20	101
Luis Tinoco	Wsc	.313	120	431	71	135	12	71
Chris Widger	Tac	.304	97	352	42	107	13	48
Greg Pirkl	Tac	.302	88	348	50	105	21	75

HOME RUNS

James Bonnici	Tac	26
Greg Pirkl	Tac	21
Jim Clifford	Lnc	20
Jesus Marquez	Lnc	20
Scott Smith	Wsc	20

WINS

Ken Cloude	Lnc	15
Greg Wooten	Lnc	15
Bob Milacki	Tac	13
Several Players Tied At		11

RBI

Jesus Marquez	Lnc	106
Scott Smith	Wsc	101
Shane Monahan	Lnc	97
David Arias	Wsc	93
Jose Cruz	Tac	89

SAVES

Dean Crow	Pcy	26
Aaron Scheffer	Wsc	14
J. Thompson	Lnc	14
Brent Iddon	Wsc	11
Several Players Tied At		9

STOLEN BASES

Kyle Towner	Bak	53
M. Sturdivant	Pcy	36
Charles Gipson	Pcy	26
Giomar Guevara	Pcy	21
Several Players Tied At		20

STRIKEOUTS

Marino Santana	Lnc	167
Ken Cloude	Lnc	161
Brett Hinchliffe	Lnc	146
Greg Wooten	Lnc	139
Ivan Montane	Pcy	135

PITCHER	CLUB	W-L	ERA	IP	H	BB	SO
Matt Wagner	Tac	9-2	2.41	93	89	30	82
Bob Milacki	Tac	13-3	2.74	164	131	39	117
Brent Iddon	Wsc	11-4	2.78	97	82	41	114
Robert Worley	Pcy	5-5	2.91	93	86	44	57
Ryan Smith	Pcy	6-9	3.13	98	92	37	65

1996 salaries

	Bonuses	Total earned salary
Ken Griffey Jr., of	$150,000	$7,650,000
Randy Johnson, p		$6,025,000
Jay Buhner, of	$75,000	$5,641,667
Chris Bosio, p		$4,250,000
Edgar Martinez, 3b	$25,000	$3,525,000
Greg Hibbard, p		$2,850,000
Norm Charlton, p		$2,075,000
Dave Hollins, 3b	$600,000	$1,350,000
Mike Jackson, p	$400,000	$1,200,000
Paul Sorrento, 1b	$25,000	$1,025,000
Joey Cora, 2b	$250,000	$850,000
Jamie Moyer, p	$225,000	$825,000
Terry Mulholland, p	$350,000	$700,000
Rich Amaral, of	$50,000	$450,000
Alex Rodriguez, ss		$442,334
Dan Wilson, c	$25,000	$400,000
Doug Strange, 2b	$30,000	$380,000
Alex Diaz, of		$350,000
Bobby Ayala, p		$325,000
Brian Hunter, 1b	$25,000	$300,000
Ricky Jordan, 1b		$250,000
Sterling Hitchcock, p		$235,000
John Marzano, c		$175,000
Bob Wells, p	$10,000	$155,000
Tim Davis, p	$15,000	$140,000
Paul Menhart, p		$140,000
Rafael Carmona, p	$10,000	$125,000
Russ Davis, 3b		$120,000
Greg McCarthy, p		$109,000
Andy Sheets, ss		$109,000
Mark Whiten, of		$109,000

Average 1996 salary: $1,363,903
Total 1996 team payroll: $42,281,001
Termination Pay: $850,000

Seattle (1977-1995)

Runs: Most, career

695	KEN GRIFFEY, 1989-1996
604	E. MARTINEZ, 1987-1996
563	Alvin Davis, 1984-1991
562	JAY BUHNER, 1988-1996
543	Harold Reynolds, 1983-1992

Hits: Most, career

1204	KEN GRIFFEY, 1989-1996
1163	Alvin Davis, 1984-1991
1063	Harold Reynolds, 1983-1992
1031	E. MARTINEZ, 1987-1996
904	JAY BUHNER, 1988-1996

2B: Most, career

256	E. MARTINEZ, 1987-1996
227	KEN GRIFFEY, 1989-1996
212	Alvin Davis, 1984-1991
200	Harold Reynolds, 1983-1992
173	JAY BUHNER, 1988-1996

3B: Most, career

48	Harold Reynolds, 1983-1992
26	Phil Bradley, 1983-1987
23	Spike Owen, 1983-1986
21	KEN GRIFFEY, 1989-1996
20	Ruppert Jones, 1977-1979

HR: Most, career

238	KEN GRIFFEY, 1989-1996
210	JAY BUHNER, 1988-1996
160	Alvin Davis, 1984-1991
117	E. MARTINEZ, 1987-1996
115	Jim Presley, 1984-1989

RBI: Most, career

725	KEN GRIFFEY, 1989-1996
672	JAY BUHNER, 1988-1996
667	Alvin Davis, 1984-1991
484	E. MARTINEZ, 1987-1996
418	Jim Presley, 1984-1989

SB: Most, career

290	Julio Cruz, 1977-1983
228	Harold Reynolds, 1983-1992
108	KEN GRIFFEY, 1989-1996
107	Phil Bradley, 1983-1987
102	Henry Cotto, 1988-1993

BB: Most, career

672	Alvin Davis, 1984-1991
555	E. MARTINEZ, 1987-1996
504	KEN GRIFFEY, 1989-1996
495	JAY BUHNER, 1988-1996
391	Harold Reynolds, 1983-1992

BA: Highest, career

.315	E. MARTINEZ,1987-1996
.302	KEN GRIFFEY, 1989-1996
.301	Phil Bradley, 1983-1987
.290	Bruce Bochte, 1978-1982
.281	Alvin Davis, 1984-1991

Slug avg: Highest, career

.549	KEN GRIFFEY, 1989-1996
.521	Ken Phelps, 1983-1988
.507	EDGAR MARTINEZ, 1987-1996
.502	JAY BUHNER, 1988-1996
.466	TINO MARTINEZ, 1990-1995

On-base avg: Highest, career

.417	E. MARTINEZ, 1987-1996
.392	Ken Phelps, 1983-1988
.382	Phil Bradley, 1983-1987
.381	Alvin Davis, 1984-1991
.381	KEN GRIFFEY, 1989-1996

Complete games: Most, career

56	Mike Moore, 1982-1988
41	MARK LANGSTON, 1984-1989
40	RANDY JOHNSON, 1989-1996
30	Jim Beattie, 1980-1986
28	Glenn Abbott, 1977-1983

Saves: Most, career

98	Mike Schooler, 1988-1992
52	Bill Caudill, 1982-1983
52	NORM CHARLTON, 1993-1996
40	BOBBY AYALA, 1994-1996
36	Shane Rawley, 1978-1981

Shutouts: Most, career

15	RANDY JOHNSON, 1989-1996
9	M. LANGSTON, 1984-1989
9	Mike Moore, 1982-1988
7	Floyd Bannister, 1979-1982
6	Jim Beattie, 1980-1986

Wins: Most, career

101	RANDY JOHNSON, 1989-1996
74	MARK LANGSTON, 1984-1989
66	Mike Moore, 1982-1988
56	ERIK HANSON, 1988-1993
45	Matt Young, 1983-1990

K: Most, career

1658	RANDY JOHNSON, 1989-1996
1078	M. LANGSTON, 1984-1989
937	Mike Moore, 1982-1988
740	ERIK HANSON, 1988-1993
597	Matt Young, 1983-1990

Win pct: Highest, career

.627	RANDY JOHNSON, 1989-1996
.525	M. LANGSTON, 1984-1989
.509	ERIK HANSON, 1988-1993
.444	Floyd Bannister, 1979-1982
.415	Glenn Abbott, 1977-1983

ERA: Lowest, career

3.48	RANDY JOHNSON, 1989-1996
3.69	ERIK HANSON, 1988-1993
3.75	Floyd Bannister, 1979-1982
4.01	M. LANGSTON, 1984-1989
4.04	BILL SWIFT, 1985-1991

Runs: Most, season

141	ALEX RODRIGUEZ, 1996
125	KEN GRIFFEY, 1996
121	EDGAR MARTINEZ, 1995
121	EDGAR MARTINEZ, 1996
113	KEN GRIFFEY, 1993

Hits: Most, season

215	ALEX RODRIGUEZ, 1996
192	Phil Bradley, 1985
184	Harold Reynolds, 1989
182	EDGAR MARTINEZ, 1995
181	EDGAR MARTINEZ, 1992

2B: Most, season

54	ALEX RODRIGUEZ, 1996
52	EDGAR MARTINEZ, 1995
52	EDGAR MARTINEZ, 1996
46	EDGAR MARTINEZ, 1992
42	KEN GRIFFEY, 1991

3B: Most, season

11	Harold Reynolds, 1988
10	Phil Bradley, 1987
9	Ruppert Jones, 1979
9	Harold Reynolds, 1989
8	Phil Bradley, 1985
8	Al Cowens, 1982
8	Ruppert Jones, 1977
8	Spike Owen, 1984
8	Harold Reynolds, 1987

HR: Most, season

49	KEN GRIFFEY, 1996
45	KEN GRIFFEY, 1993
44	JAY BUHNER, 1996
40	JAY BUHNER, 1995
40	KEN GRIFFEY, 1994

RBI: Most, season

140	KEN GRIFFEY, 1996
138	JAY BUHNER, 1996
123	ALEX RODRIGUEZ, 1996
121	JAY BUHNER, 1995
116	Alvin Davis, 1984

SB: Most, season

60	Harold Reynolds, 1987
59	Julio Cruz, 1978
49	Julio Cruz, 1979
46	Julio Cruz, 1982
45	Julio Cruz, 1980

BB: Most, season

123	EDGAR MARTINEZ, 1996
116	EDGAR MARTINEZ, 1995
101	Alvin Davis, 1989
100	JAY BUHNER, 1993
97	Alvin Davis, 1984

BA: Highest, season

.358	ALEX RODRIGUEZ, 1996
.356	EDGAR MARTINEZ, 1995
.343	EDGAR MARTINEZ, 1992
.327	EDGAR MARTINEZ, 1996
.327	KEN GRIFFEY, 1991

Slug avg: Highest, season

.674	KEN GRIFFEY, 1994
.631	ALEX RODRIGUEZ, 1996
.628	EDGAR MARTINEZ, 1995
.628	KEN GRIFFEY, 1996
.617	KEN GRIFFEY, 1993

On-base avg: Highest, season

.479	EDGAR MARTINEZ, 1995
.464	EDGAR MARTINEZ, 1996
.424	Alvin Davis, 1989
.414	ALEX RODRIGUEZ, 1996
.412	Alvin Davis, 1988

Complete games: Most, season

14	MARK LANGSTON, 1987
14	Mike Moore, 1985
13	Mike Parrott, 1979
12	Jim Beattie, 1984
12	Mike Moore, 1987

Saves: Most, season

33	Mike Schooler, 1989
30	Mike Schooler, 1990
26	Bill Caudill, 1982
26	Bill Caudill, 1983
20	NORM CHARLTON, 1996

Shutouts: Most, season

4	Dave Fleming, 1992
4	RANDY JOHNSON, 1994
3	Floyd Bannister, 1982
3	Brian Holman, 1991
3	RANDY JOHNSON, 1993
3	RANDY JOHNSON, 1995
3	MARK LANGSTON, 1987
3	MARK LANGSTON, 1988
3	Mike Moore, 1988

Wins: Most, season

19	RANDY JOHNSON, 1993
19	MARK LANGSTON, 1987
18	ERIK HANSON, 1990
18	RANDY JOHNSON, 1995
17	Dave Fleming, 1992
17	MARK LANGSTON, 1984
17	Mike Moore, 1985

K: Most, season

308	RANDY JOHNSON, 1993
294	RANDY JOHNSON, 1995
262	MARK LANGSTON, 1987
245	MARK LANGSTON, 1986
241	RANDY JOHNSON, 1992

Win pct: Highest, season

.900	RANDY JOHNSON, 1995
.704	RANDY JOHNSON, 1993
.667	ERIK HANSON, 1990
.630	Dave Fleming, 1992
.630	MARK LANGSTON, 1984
.630	Mike Moore, 1985

ERA: Lowest, season

2.48	RANDY JOHNSON, 1995
3.19	RANDY JOHNSON, 1994
3.24	ERIK HANSON, 1990
3.24	RANDY JOHNSON, 1993
3.27	Matt Young, 1983

Most pinch-hit homers, season

2	Leon Roberts, 1978
2	Gary Gray, 1981
2	Ken Phelps, 1986
2	Greg Briley, 1992

Most pinch-hit homers, career

4	Ken Phelps, 1983-1988

Longest hitting streak

21	Dan Meyer, 1979
21	Richie Zisk, 1982
20	ALEX RODRIGUEZ, 1996
19	Phil Bradley, 1986
18	Joey Cora, 1996

Most consecutive scoreless innings

34	MARK LANGSTON, 1988

No-hit games

RANDY JOHNSON, Sea vs Det AL, 2-0; June 2, 1990.
CHRIS BOSIO, Sea vs Bos AL, 7-0; Apr. 22, 1993.

ACTIVE PLAYERS in caps.

Players' years of service are listed by the first and last years with this team and are not necessarily consecutive; all statistics record performances for this team only.

SEATTLE MARINERS / AL WEST

Oakland Athletics

Mark McGwire battled through injuries to lead the majors in homers.

1996 Athletics: The bashers were back

Although they finished with a 78-84 record, the Oakland A's in many ways are able to look back on 1996 with good feelings. Oakland was picked to finish last, as the franchise faced a multitude of changes and problems—new ownership, the reconstruction of Oakland Coliseum, a new manager, a young lineup and almost no experienced pitching—but the team broke a fistful of its offensive records, including those for runs, home runs, hits, on-base average, total bases, doubles and strikeouts. "I never thought we would be as bad as some people thought we would be," A's manager Art Howe said at the end of the season. "We've exceeded many of my expectations, especially offensively."

The other side of the coin was that the A's set about as many negative pitching records: runs allowed, home runs allowed, hits allowed. The staff's 5.20 ERA was the worst in Oakland history, but the manager sees hope. "We came into the season without any idea what our pitching would be like," Howe said. "Our starting rotation underwent a whole turnover, but we come out of the season with a good idea of what our starters can do."

The focal point of the A's 1996 success was first baseman Mark McGwire, who set a new Oakland and personal record with 52 home runs. McGwire was supposed to have to miss as much as the first three months of the season after tearing muscle tissue in his right foot in spring training. Instead, he was back in the lineup after 18 games and led the majors in homers, slugging average (.730) and on-base average (.467), to become the ninth player to accomplish that feat in the same season. He also broke one of Babe Ruth's all-time marks by averaging one homer every 8.13 at-bats. (He bested Ruth's 1920 ratio in 1995 but didn't have enough plate appearances to set a record.)

Outfielder-DH Geronimo Berroa and catcher Terry Steinbach (since signed with Minnesota as a free agent) also had career years, both producing double-digit increases in their home run bests and huge

Team MVP

Mark McGwire: What could have been. Mark McGwire set an Oakland record and led the majors with 52 home runs in only 423 at-bats, with the 8.13 AB/HR ratio setting a major league record. His 488-foot blast into SkyDome's top deck was the majors' longest this season, and he led the majors in slugging and on-base averages, a rare feat. Plus, his .312 batting average was a career high. But how much more could he have done if not limited by injuries to 130 games?

increases in RBI as well. Two youngsters, third baseman Scott Brosius (.302, 22 HR, 71 RBI) and left fielder Jason Giambi (.291, 20 HR, 79 RBI), came into their own as major league hitters. Brosius, shortstop Mike Bordick and first baseman Mark McGwire were on the field for most of the A's club record (and major-league-leading) 195 double plays.

There were weaknesses in the offense. The most glaring was at the leadoff spot, where Oakland struggled until the final weeks of the season, when rookie second baseman Tony Batista took over. Several of the players who were expected to contribute didn't. Pedro Munoz and Brent Gates both missed most of the year with injuries, and backup catcher George Williams, a competent hitter in the minor leagues, never caught up to big league pitching.

Of the five men who started in the rotation for the A's in April, only Ariel Prieto is still there. Todd Van Poppel was released. Steve Wojciechowski, Carlos Reyes and Doug Johns were all bounced from the rotation, and John Wasdin, Don Wengert, Dave Telgheder and Willie Adams were starting at the end of the season. The bullpen, one of the club's strengths through July, blew up in August and September—so much so that the A's have to consider a remake of the pen for 1997.

1996 Athletics: Week-by-week notes

These notes were excerpted from the following issues of Baseball Weekly.

▶**April 3:** The A's are optimistic that first baseman Mark McGwire will be back in June or even May. McGwire injured the plantar fascia in his right foot three weeks ago. The A's lost an unusual opener in Las Vegas to Toronto, 9-6. The A's were displaced by ongoing renovations to Oakland Coliseum.

▶**April 24:** The A's lost to the White Sox 4-3 at the first game in new-look Oakland Coliseum on April 19. The late start to the home season might have affected the A's attendance. Compared with the first four games at home in 1995, home attendance is down 28%.

▶**May 1:** Mark McGwire homered in his first at-bat on April 27, a two-run shot that was his first hit since coming off the DL four days earlier.

▶**May 8:** Scott Brosius, who was beginning to blossom as a third baseman and as a hitter, will be lost for a minimum of five weeks. The loss of Brosius does solve one problem. Jason Giambi, the third baseman who played first while Mark McGwire was out, can now move back there from the outfield.

▶**May 15:** The bullpen is beginning to look as if it will be a source of strength. After some rocky moments early in the season, relievers are putting away opposing hitters with great consistency. In 13 games through May 11, relievers had a 1.43 ERA (six earned runs in 37⅔ innings) with four saves.

▶**May 22:** The A's reached the one-quarter mark with a record of 20-20, better than most experts had predicted. "When things look the darkest, that's when somebody steps up and gives us a big lift," manager Art Howe said.

▶**May 29:** Three of the four men who began the season in the A's rotation are no longer there. Opening Day starter Carlos Reyes was bounced from the rotation after going 3-7 in 10 starts. Game 2 starter Ariel Prieto is on the DL. And

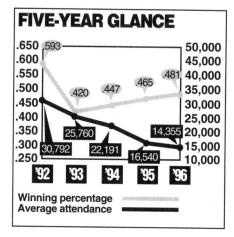

FIVE-YEAR GLANCE

Winning percentage
Average attendance

Game 3 starter Todd Van Poppel, like Reyes, is in the bullpen. Lefty Doug Johns is the only current starter who didn't begin the season at Class AAA.

▶**June 12:** The A's are trying not to get too emotional in the roller-coaster ride that comes with young starting pitching. Steve Wojciechowski won his first five decisions. Then he lost three in a row. Doug Johns dominated the opposition in his first two starts, but since then is just 2-7. John Wasdin made the jump from Class AAA and won his first three starts. Bobby Chouinard has only had two bad innings in his first three starts, but because of them he's 0-2.

▶**June 19:** Although Todd Van Poppel continues to struggle, he won't be going to the minor leagues any time soon. To get him to the minors, the A's would have to expose the faltering pitcher (0-4, 8.42) to waivers, and general manager Sandy Alderson is certain some other club would claim him.

▶**July 3:** The A's are on a record home-run pace. Through June 30, Oakland had a major league–leading 126 homers in 81 games, which projects to 252 for the season, 12 more than the 1961 Yankees. In four games from June 25 to June 29, the A's tied a record by hitting 18 homers.

▶**July 11:** The A's scored a team-record 13 runs in the first inning in a 16-8 win over California on July 5.

▶**July 31:** Mark McGwire's back spasms forced him to take last weekend off. McGwire had been having a productive week. He twice set the visitors' record at Comiskey Park for longest home runs, hitting one 452 feet, then another 470 feet the next day. Twenty-four hours later, he became the second player in SkyDome history to hit a home run into the fifth deck, setting a stadium record at 488 feet.

▶**Aug. 7:** Infielder Webster Garrison, who took waived Todd Van Poppel's position on the roster, made his long-overdue major league debut on Aug. 2. He's played 1,500 games in more than 13 years in the minor leagues.

▶**Aug. 14:** When rookie outfielder Jose Herrera went into an 0-for-25 tailspin, he was taken out of the lineup for the better part of a week and replaced in the leadoff spot by another rookie outfielder, Damon Mashore. Herrera was given a second chance starting on Aug. 6, and in six starts through Aug. 11, Herrera went 11-for-25 with a double and two home runs.

▶**Aug. 21:** Outfielder-DH Geronimo Berroa took over the spotlight. Starting with his second three-homer game of the season on Aug. 12, Berroa hit eight homers in six games, a span of just 25 at-bats.

▶**Aug. 28:** Mark McGwire, the cleanup hitter, is getting fewer and fewer good pitches to hit. He had 93 walks through Aug. 25, a direct result of his major-league-leading total of 44 homers.

▶**Sept. 4:** The A's spent their entire season waiting for pitching like this. Don Wengert, Dave Telgheder (with an inning of help from Buddy Groom) and Willie Adams gave the A's three straight shutouts for first time in 13 years.

▶**Sept. 11:** Second baseman Tony Batista isn't the 1,000th leadoff hitter the A's have used so far—it just seems like he is. Batista is hitting .291 overall, but as a leadoff hitter he's 24-for-65 (.369) in 15 games through Sept. 8.

▶**Sept. 18:** Mark McGwire hit his 50th home run of the season on Sept. 14 against Cleveland, making him the 13th 50-homer man in major league history.

▶**Sept. 25:** The A's pitchers set a club record for most runs allowed (866—the old record was 860 set by the 108-loss team of 1979) and extended their ongoing club record for home runs yielded (200—the old record was 177).

▶**Oct. 2:** The A's were picked by many to lose 100 games, but they were 60-60 on Aug. 12 and never dipped more than nine games under .500. En route, they set club offensive records for runs, home runs, hits, on-base average, total bases and doubles, and three players—Mark McGwire, Geronimo Berroa and catcher Terry Steinbach—had at least 30 home runs and 100 RBI each. On the downside, the A's set just about as many negative team pitching records, including having the first team ERA over 5.00. McGwire set a new Oakland and personal record with 52 homers, and he led the majors in homers, slugging percentage (.730) and on-base average (.467), becoming just the ninth player to lead the majors in all three categories.

Team directory

▶**Owners:** Steve Schott and Ken Hofman
▶**General manager:** Sandy Alderson
▶**Ballpark:**
Oakland Coliseum
Nimitz Freeway & Hegenberger Road
Oakland, Calif.
510-568-5600
Capacity 45,177
Public transportation available
Wheelchair sections and ramps, picnic areas
▶**Team publications:**
A's Magazine, media guide
510-638-4900, ext. 2328
▶**TV, radio broadcast stations:**
KFRC 610 AM, KRON Channel 4, SportsChannel
▶**Spring training:**
Phoenix Municipal Stadium
Phoenix, Ariz.
Capacity 8,500
602-392-0074

OAKLAND ATHLETICS 1996 final stats

BATTERS	BA	SLG	OB	G	AB	R	H	TB	2B	3B	HR	RBI	BB	SO	SB	CS	E
McGwire	.312	.730	.467	130	423	104	132	309	21	0	52	113	116	112	0	0	10
Spiezio	.310	.586	.394	9	29	6	9	17	2	0	2	8	4	4	0	1	2
Brosius	.304	.516	.393	114	428	73	130	221	25	0	22	71	59	85	7	2	10
Batista	.298	.433	.350	74	238	38	71	103	10	2	6	25	19	49	7	3	5
Giambi	.291	.481	.355	140	536	84	156	258	40	1	20	79	51	95	0	1	11
Berroa	.290	.532	.344	153	586	101	170	312	32	1	36	106	47	122	0	3	2
Stairs	.277	.547	.367	61	137	21	38	75	5	1	10	23	19	23	1	1	1
Steinbach	.272	.529	.342	145	514	79	140	272	25	1	35	100	49	115	0	1	7
Herrera	.269	.378	.318	108	320	44	86	121	15	1	6	30	20	59	8	2	6
Mashore	.267	.438	.366	50	105	20	28	46	7	1	3	12	16	31	4	0	1
Gates	.263	.381	.316	64	247	26	65	94	19	2	2	30	18	35	1	1	9
Munoz	.256	.446	.308	34	121	17	31	54	5	0	6	18	9	31	0	0	0
Young	.242	.424	.326	141	462	72	112	196	19	4	19	64	52	118	7	5	1
Bournigal	.242	.313	.290	88	252	33	61	79	14	2	0	18	16	19	4	3	2
Bordick	.240	.318	.307	155	525	46	126	167	18	4	5	54	52	59	5	6	16
Lesher	.232	.451	.281	26	82	11	19	37	3	0	5	16	5	17	0	0	1
Lovullo	.220	.378	.323	65	82	15	18	31	4	0	3	9	11	17	1	2	1
Plantier	.212	.346	.304	73	231	29	49	80	8	1	7	31	28	56	2	2	4
Molina	.200	.280	.231	14	25	0	5	7	2	0	0	1	1	3	0	0	0
Battle	.192	.238	.293	47	130	20	25	31	3	0	1	5	17	26	10	2	1
Williams	.152	.258	.311	56	132	17	20	34	5	0	3	10	28	32	0	0	3
Moore	.063	.125	.167	22	16	4	1	2	1	0	0	0	2	6	1	0	0
Garrison	.000	.000	.100	5	9	0	0	0	0	0	0	0	1	0	0	0	1

PITCHERS	W-L	ERA	G	GS	CG	GF	Sho	SV	IP	H	R	ER	HR	BB	SO
Mohler	6-3	3.67	72	0	0	30	0	7	81.0	79	36	33	9	41	64
Briscoe	0-1	3.76	17	0	0	8	0	1	26.1	18	11	11	2	24	14
Groom	5-0	3.84	72	1	0	16	0	2	77.1	85	37	33	8	34	57
Adams	3-4	4.01	12	12	1	0	1	0	76.1	76	39	34	11	23	68
Corsi	6-0	4.03	57	0	0	19	0	3	73.2	71	33	33	6	34	43
Prieto	6-7	4.15	21	21	2	0	0	0	125.2	130	66	58	9	54	75
Taylor	6-3	4.33	55	0	0	30	0	17	60.1	52	30	29	5	25	67
Telgheder	4-7	4.65	16	14	1	1	1	0	79.1	92	42	41	12	26	43
Reyes	7-10	4.78	46	10	0	14	0	0	122.1	134	71	65	19	61	78
Wengert	7-11	5.58	36	25	1	2	1	0	161.1	200	102	100	29	60	75
Wojciechowski	5-5	5.65	16	15	0	0	0	0	79.2	97	57	50	10	28	30
Wasdin	8-7	5.96	25	21	1	2	0	0	131.1	145	96	87	24	50	75
Johns	6-12	5.98	40	23	1	4	0	1	158.0	187	112	105	21	69	71
Chouinard	4-2	6.10	13	11	0	0	0	0	59.0	75	41	40	10	32	32
Acre	1-3	6.12	22	0	0	11	0	2	25.0	38	17	17	4	9	18
Witasick	1-1	6.23	12	0	0	6	0	0	13.0	12	9	9	5	5	12
Small	1-3	8.16	12	3	0	4	0	0	28.2	37	28	26	3	22	17
Montgomery	1-0	9.22	8	0	0	0	0	0	13.2	18	14	14	5	13	8
Fletcher	0-0	20.25	1	0	0	0	0	0	1.1	6	3	3	0	1	0

1997 preliminary roster

PITCHERS (21)
Mark Acre
Willie Adams
Bobby Chouinard
Carl Dale
Matt Dunbar
Buddy Groom
Doug Johns
Dane Johnson
Steve Karsay
Mike Mohler
Steve Montgomery
Wil Montoya

Ariel Prieto
Brad Rigby
Aaron Small
Billy Taylor
Dave Telgheder
Bret Wagner
John Wasdin
Don Wengert
Jay Witasick

CATCHERS (2)
Izzy Molina
George Williams

INFIELDERS (10)
Tony Batista
Rafael Bournigal
Scott Brosius
Frank Catalanotto
Steve Cox
Brent Gates
Jason Giambi
Jason McDonald
Mark McGwire
Scott Spiezio

OUTFIELDERS (6)
Allen Battle
Geronimo Berroa
Jose Herrera
Brian Lesher
Matt Stairs
Ernie Young

Games played by position

PLAYER	G	C	1B	2B	3B	SS	OF	DH
Batista	74	0	0	52	18	4	0	4
Battle	47	0	0	0	0	0	47	0
Berroa	153	0	0	0	0	0	61	91
Bordick	155	0	0	0	0	155	0	0
Bournigal	88	0	0	64	0	23	0	0
Brosius	114	0	10	0	109	0	4	0
Garrison	5	0	1	3	0	0	0	0
Gates	64	0	0	63	0	0	0	0
Giambi	140	0	45	0	39	0	45	12
Herrera	108	0	0	0	0	0	100	1
Lesher	26	0	1	0	0	0	25	0
Lovullo	65	0	42	2	11	1	1	4
Mashore	50	0	0	0	0	0	48	0
McGwire	130	0	109	0	0	0	0	18
Molina	14	12	0	0	0	0	0	1
Moore	22	0	0	0	0	0	18	2
Munoz	34	0	0	0	0	0	14	18
Plantier	73	0	0	0	0	0	68	1
Spiezio	9	0	0	0	5	0	0	4
Stairs	61	0	1	0	0	0	44	5
Steinbach	145	137	1	0	0	0	0	4
Williams	56	43	0	0	0	0	0	11
Young	141	0	0	0	0	0	140	0

Minor Leagues

Tops in the organization

BATTER	CLUB	AVG.	G	AB	R	H	HR	RBI
Mike Neill	Mod	.331	120	462	105	153	20	82
D.T. Cromer	Mod	.329	124	505	100	166	30	130
Ben Grieve	Hvl	.302	135	513	95	155	19	83
David Newhan	Mod	.301	117	455	96	137	25	75
Scott Sheldon	Edm	.300	98	350	61	105	10	60

HOME RUNS

D.T. Cromer	Mod	30
David Newhan	Mod	25
Several Players Tied At		20

WINS

Bill King	Mod	16
Todd Abbott	Wmi	11
Several Players Tied At		10

RBI

D.T. Cromer	Mod	130
Scott Spiezio	Edm	91
Jason Wood	Edm	84
Ben Grieve	Hvl	83
Several Players Tied At		82

SAVES

R. Kazmirski	Wmi	28
Steven Connelly	Mod	14
Scott Rose	Edm	10
Mike Maurer	Hvl	8
Mark Acre	Edm	8

STOLEN BASES

Kerwin Moore	Edm	38
Jason McDonald	Edm	33
Juan Dilone	Mod	31
Demond Smith	Edm	30
Mike Neill	Mod	28

STRIKEOUTS

Scott Rivette	Wmi	142
Chris Nelson	Mod	141
Kevin Mlodik	Wmi	135
Brad Rigby	Hvl	127
M. Rossiter	Hvl	116

PITCHER	CLUB	W-L	ERA	IP	H	BB	SO
Tim Kubinski	Edm	8-7	2.36	103	85	37	78
Kevin Mlodik	Wmi	8-6	2.77	136	118	53	135
Kevin Gunther	Wmi	5-5	2.92	96	83	25	90
Benito Baez	Wmi	8-4	3.47	130	123	52	92
Scott Rivette	Wmi	8-9	3.52	153	145	51	142

Sick call: 1996 DL report

PLAYER	Days on the DL
Scott Brosius	51
Jim Corsi	21
Brent Gates	106
Damon Mashore	48
Mark McGwire	22
Pedro Munoz	120
Ariel Prieto	70
Billy Taylor	28
Don Wengert	15

1996 salaries

	Bonuses	Total earned salary
Mark McGwire, 1b	$50,000	$7,050,000
Terry Steinbach, c		$4,200,000
Mike Bordick, ss	$150,000	$2,000,000
Geronimo Berroa, of		$1,150,000
Scott Brosius, 3b	$15,000	$970,000
Pedro Munoz, of		$595,000
Jim Corsi, p	$50,000	$450,000
Brent Gates, ss		$290,000
Buddy Groom, p		$195,000
Ariel Prieto, p	$56,000	$181,000
Carlos Reyes, p	$15,000	$170,000
Mike Mohler, p	$10,000	$155,000
Rafael Bournigal, ss	$5,000	$150,000
Dave Telgheder, p	$5,000	$147,500
Mark Acre, p		$140,000
Billy Taylor, p		$135,000
Matt Stairs, of		$130,000
Jason Giambi, 3b		$120,000
Don Wengert, p		$117,000
Doug Johns, p		$113,500
Jose Herrera, of		$112,000
Ernie Young, of		$112,000
John Wasdin, p		$111,000
Willie Adams, p		$109,000
Tony Batista, 2b		$109,000
Brian Lesher, of		$109,000
Damon Mashore, of		$109,000
Islay Molina, c		$109,000
Kerwin Moore, of		$109,000

Average 1996 salary: $670,620
Total 1996 team payroll: $19,448,000
Termination pay: $34,426

OAKLAND ATHLETICS / AL WEST

Oakland (1968-1996), incl. Philadelphia (1901-1952) and Kansas City (1953-1967)

Runs: Most, career

1169	R. HENDERSON, 1979-1995
997	Bob Johnson, 1933-1942
983	Bert Campaneris, 1964-1976
975	Jimmie Foxx, 1925-1935
969	Al Simmons, 1924-1944

Hits: Most, career

1882	Bert Campaneris, 1964-1976
1827	Al Simmons, 1924-1944
1705	Jimmy Dykes, 1918-1932
1640	R. HENDERSON, 1979-1995
1617	Bob Johnson, 1933-1942

2B: Most, career

365	Jimmy Dykes, 1918-1932
348	Al Simmons, 1924-1944
319	Harry Davis, 1901-1917
307	Bob Johnson, 1933-1942
292	Bing Miller, 1922-1934
273	RICKY HENDERSON, 1979-1995 (8)

3B: Most, career

102	Danny Murphy, 1902-1913
98	Al Simmons, 1924-1944
88	Frank Baker, 1908-1914
85	Eddie Collins, 1906-1930
82	Harry Davis, 1901-1917
70	Bert Campaneris, 1964-1976 (12)

HR: Most, career

329	MARK McGWIRE, 1986-1996
302	Jimmie Foxx, 1925-1935
269	Reggie Jackson, 1967-1987
252	Bob Johnson, 1933-1942
231	JOSE CANSECO, 1985-1992

RBI: Most, career

1178	Al Simmons, 1924-1944
1075	Jimmie Foxx, 1925-1935
1040	Bob Johnson, 1933-1942
860	MARK McGWIRE, 1986-1996
796	Sal Bando, 1966-1976

SB: Most, career

801	R. HENDERSON, 1979-1995
566	Bert Campaneris, 1964-1976
376	Eddie Collins, 1906-1930
232	Billy North, 1973-1978
223	Harry Davis, 1901-1917

BB: Most, career

1109	R. HENDERSON, 1979-1995
1043	Max Bishop, 1924-1933
853	Bob Johnson, 1933-1942
820	Elmer Valo, 1940-1956
792	Sal Bando, 1966-1976

BA: Highest, career

.356	Al Simmons, 1924-1944
.339	Jimmie Foxx, 1925-1935
.337	Eddie Collins, 1906-1930
.321	Mickey Cochrane, 1925-1933
.321	Frank Baker, 1908-1914
.293	RICKEY HENDERSON, 1979-1995 (17)

Slug avg: Highest, career

.640	Jimmie Foxx, 1925-1935
.584	Al Simmons, 1924-1944
.544	MARK McGWIRE, 1986-1996
.520	Bob Johnson, 1933-1942
.512	JOSE CANSECO, 1985-1992

On-base avg: Highest, career

.440	Jimmie Foxx, 1925-1935
.426	Ferris Fain, 1947-1952
.423	Eddie Collins, 1906-1930
.423	Max Bishop, 1924-1933
.412	R. HENDERSON, 1979-1995

Complete games: Most, career

362	Eddie Plank, 1901-1914
228	Chief Bender, 1903-1914
179	Lefty Grove, 1925-1933
168	Rube Waddell, 1902-1907
147	Eddie Rommel, 1920-1932
116	Catfish Hunter, 1965-1974 (8)

Saves: Most, career

320	D. ECKERSLEY, 1987-1995
136	Rollie Fingers, 1968-1976
73	John Wyatt, 1961-1969
61	Jay Howell, 1985-1987
58	Jack Aker, 1964-1968

Shutouts: Most, career

59	Eddie Plank, 1901-1914
37	Rube Waddell, 1902-1907
36	Chief Bender, 1903-1914
31	Catfish Hunter, 1965-1974
28	Vida Blue, 1969-1977
28	Jack Coombs, 1906-1914

Wins: Most, career

284	Eddie Plank, 1901-1914
195	Lefty Grove, 1925-1933
193	Chief Bender, 1903-1914
171	Eddie Rommel, 1920-1932
161	Catfish Hunter, 1965-1974

K: Most, career

1985	Eddie Plank, 1901-1914
1576	Rube Waddell, 1902-1907
1536	Chief Bender, 1903-1914
1523	Lefty Grove, 1925-1933
1520	Catfish Hunter, 1965-1974

Win pct: Highest, career

.712	Lefty Grove, 1925-1933
.654	Chief Bender, 1903-1914
.637	Eddie Plank, 1901-1914
.632	Jack Coombs, 1906-1914
.628	George Earnshaw, 1928-1933
.615	Bob Welch, 1988-1994 (6)

ERA: Lowest, career

1.97	Rube Waddell, 1902-1907
2.15	Cy Morgan, 1909-1912
2.32	Chief Bender, 1903-1914
2.39	Eddie Plank, 1901-1914
2.60	Jack Coombs, 1906-1914
2.91	Rollie Fingers, 1968-1976 (8)

Runs: Most, season

152	Al Simmons, 1930
151	Jimmie Foxx, 1932
145	Nap Lajoie, 1901
144	Al Simmons, 1932
137	Eddie Collins, 1912
123	Reggie Jackson, 1969 (10)

Hits: Most, season

253	Al Simmons, 1925
232	Nap Lajoie, 1901
216	Al Simmons, 1932
214	Doc Cramer, 1935
213	Jimmie Foxx, 1932
187	JOSE CANSECO, 1988 (*)

2B: Most, season

53	Al Simmons, 1926
48	Nap Lajoie, 1901
48	Wally Moses, 1937
47	Harry Davis, 1905
47	Eric McNair, 1932
40	JASON GIAMBI, 1996 (20)

3B: Most, season

21	Frank Baker, 1912
19	Frank Baker, 1909
18	Danny Murphy, 1910
17	Danny Murphy, 1904

16	Bing Miller, 1929	35	Chick Fraser, 1901	5	MIKE ALDRETE, 1993-1995	
16	Al Simmons, 1930	35	Eddie Plank, 1905			
16	Amos Strunk, 1915	28	Rick Langford, 1980 (14)			
12	Bert Campaneris, 1965 (*)					
12	Phil Garner, 1976 (*)					

Longest hitting streak

29	Billy Lamar, 1925
28	Bing Miller, 1929
27	Socks Seybold, 1901
27	Al Simmons, 1931
26	Bob Johnson, 1938
24	Carney Lansford, 1984

Saves: Most, season

51	DENNIS ECKERSLEY, 1992
48	DENNIS ECKERSLEY, 1990
45	DENNIS ECKERSLEY, 1988
43	DENNIS ECKERSLEY, 1991
36	Bill Caudill, 1984
36	DENNIS ECKERSLEY, 1993

HR: Most, season

58	Jimmie Foxx, 1932
52	MARK McGWIRE, 1996
49	MARK McGWIRE, 1987
48	Jimmie Foxx, 1933
47	Reggie Jackson, 1969

RBI: Most, season

169	Jimmie Foxx, 1932
165	Al Simmons, 1930
163	Jimmie Foxx, 1933
157	Al Simmons, 1929
156	Jimmie Foxx, 1930
124	JOSE CANSECO, 1988 (13)

Shutouts: Most, season

13	Jack Coombs, 1910
8	Vida Blue, 1971
8	Joe Bush, 1916
8	Eddie Plank, 1907
8	Rube Waddell, 1904
8	Rube Waddell, 1906

Most consecutive scoreless innings

53	Jack Coombs, 1910
43	Rube Waddell, 1905
37	Mike Torrez, 1976

No-hit games

Weldon Henley, Phi at StL AL, 6-0; July 22, 1905 (1st game).

Chief Bender, Phi vs Cle AL, 4-0; May 12, 1910.

Joe Bush, Phi vs Cle AL, 5-0; Aug. 26, 1916.

Dick Fowler, Phi vs StL AL, 1-0; Sept. 9, 1945 (2nd game).

Bill McCahan, Phi vs Was AL, 3-0; Sept. 3, 1947.

Catfish Hunter, Oak vs Min AL, 4-0; May 8, 1968 (perfect game).

Vida Blue, Oak vs Min AL, 6-0; Sept. 21, 1970.

Vida Blue (5 innings), Glenn Abbott (1 inning), Paul Lindblad (1 inning) and Rollie Fingers (2 innings), Oak vs Cal AL, 5-0; Sept. 28, 1975.

Mike Warren, Oak vs Chi AL, 3-0; Sept. 29, 1983.

Dave Stewart, Oak at Tor AL, 5-0; June 29, 1990.

Rube Waddell, five innings, rain, Phi vs StL AL, 2-0; Aug. 15, 1905.

Jimmy Dygert (3 innings) and Rube Waddell (2 innings), five innings, rain, Phi vs Chi AL, 4-3; Aug. 29, 1906. (Waddell allowed hit and two runs in 6th, but rain caused game to revert to 5 innings).

Rube Vickers, five perfect innings, darkness, Phi at Was AL, 4-0; Oct. 5, 1907 (2nd game).

ACTIVE PLAYERS in caps.

Leader from the franchise's current location is included. If not in the top five, leader's rank is listed in parenthesis; asterisk (*) indicates player is not in top 25.

Players' years of service are listed by the first and last years with this team and are not necessarily consecutive; all statistics record performances for this team only.

Wins: Most, season

31	Jack Coombs, 1910
31	Lefty Grove, 1931
28	Jack Coombs, 1911
28	Lefty Grove, 1930
27	Eddie Rommel, 1922
27	Rube Waddell, 1905
27	Bob Welch, 1990

SB: Most, season

130	RICKEY HENDERSON, 1982
108	RICKEY HENDERSON, 1983
100	RICKEY HENDERSON, 1980
81	Eddie Collins, 1910
75	Billy North, 1976

BB: Most, season

149	Eddie Joost, 1949
136	Ferris Fain, 1949
133	Ferris Fain, 1950
128	Max Bishop, 1929
128	Max Bishop, 1930
118	Sal Bando, 1970 (10)

K: Most, season

349	Rube Waddell, 1904
302	Rube Waddell, 1903
301	Vida Blue, 1971
287	Rube Waddell, 1905
232	Rube Waddell, 1907

BA: Highest, season

.426	Nap Lajoie, 1901
.390	Al Simmons, 1931
.387	Al Simmons, 1925
.381	Al Simmons, 1930
.365	Eddie Collins, 1911
.325	R. HENDERSON, 1990 (*)

Win pct: Highest, season

.886	Lefty Grove, 1931
.850	Chief Bender, 1914
.849	Lefty Grove, 1930
.821	Chief Bender, 1910
.818	Bob Welch, 1990

Slug avg: Highest, season

.749	Jimmie Foxx, 1932
.730	MARK McGWIRE, 1996
.708	Al Simmons, 1930
.703	Jimmie Foxx, 1933
.653	Jimmie Foxx, 1934

ERA: Lowest, season

1.30	Jack Coombs, 1910
1.39	Harry Krause, 1909
1.48	Rube Waddell, 1905
1.55	Cy Morgan, 1910
1.58	Chief Bender, 1910
1.82	Vida Blue, 1971 (10)

On-base avg: Highest, season

.469	Jimmie Foxx, 1932
.467	MARK McGWIRE, 1996
.463	Jimmie Foxx, 1929
.463	Nap Lajoie, 1901
.461	Jimmie Foxx, 1935

Most pinch-hit homers, season

4	Jeff Burroughs, 1982
3	Allie Clark, 1952
3	Kite Thomas, 1952
3	Bob Cerv, 1957
3	Frank Fernandez, 1970
3	Rich McKinney, 1977

Complete games: Most, season

39	Rube Waddell, 1904
37	Eddie Plank, 1904
35	Jack Coombs, 1910

Most pinch-hit homers, career

5	Gus Zernial, 1951-1957
5	Jeff Burroughs, 1982-1984

Anaheim Angels

Though beset by injuries, Jim Edmonds had the Angels' top batting and slugging averages.

By Neil Seiler, USA TODAY

1996 Angels: Turmoil wrecked the team

When the Angels offered free-agent infielder Randy Velarde a starting job and a three-year contract, he couldn't sign up fast enough. After eight seasons as a utility infielder with the Yankees, Velarde came west to play every day for a pennant contender. "To be in the playoffs last year, I said, that's what I want," Velarde said. "I wanted a chance to get back to the playoffs. In the nine years I've played, this is probably the most depressing one. I played on some bad teams in New York, but they were supposed to be bad. We were supposed to win, and we were last. How do you do that?" For the fourth time since their last division championship, in 1986, the Angels finished in last place. They were consensus favorites to win the AL West, but they did not spend a single day in first place and did not escape last place after July 4. How do you do that? In record-setting fashion, apparently. The Angels set a major league record by using 29 pitchers and a league record by hitting 82 batters. Many franchise records fell, almost all of them negative ones: most players used (52), most times using the disabled list (21), highest earned run average (5.30), most home runs hit (192) and most homers given up (219).

The Angels used three managers (Marcel Lachemann, John McNamara and Joe Maddon), went through nine coaches and used 116 different lineups.

Troy Percival survived an early-season controversy over closer Lee Smith's status and was a brilliant replacement for the veteran, with 36 saves and a 2.31 ERA. He made the All-Star team and anchored a pleasantly surprising bullpen that included Mike James, Chuck McElroy, Mike Holtz and Pep Harris. The Angels found one too many young outfielders in Tim Salmon, Jim Edmonds, Garret Anderson and Darin Erstad, so after the season they traded designated hitter Chili Davis, who was 36 years old in 1996, to make room in the lineup. They found possible catchers in Todd Greene and Jorge Fabregas but still don't know whether they've got

their third baseman of the future in George Arias. The Angels missed Tony Phillips a lot, but by the time the season ended, Erstad appeared ready to replace him as the leadoff hitter and Percival was taking charge as the clubhouse leader.

The team invested 40% of its player payroll in Chuck Finley, Mark Langston and Jim Abbott, so look no further than the starting pitchers to find the most significant reason for the Angels' fall. Finley (15-16) was adequate, but his record slipped from 15-12 in 1995. Langston had three trips to the disabled list this season after making only two in his first 12 seasons. Abbott (2-18) fell from ninth in the American League with a 3.70 ERA last season to off the charts this year (7.48), and he endured the first minor league appearances of his career after being demoted to Class AAA Vancouver in August.

It all happened in a season in which The Walt Disney Co. took over ownership. The Angels will begin 1997 with a new name (the Anaheim Angels), new uniforms, a remodeled stadium, and a new manager. He is Terry Collins, who was named after being deposed in Houston, where he finshed second last season.

1996 Angels: Week-by-week notes

These notes were excerpted from the following issues of Baseball Weekly.

▶**April 10:** The Walt Disney Co. and the city of Anaheim agreed on a $100 million plan to renovate Anaheim Stadium and keep the Angels there through 2019. The agreement clears the way for Disney to complete its purchase of a controlling interest in the franchise from owners Gene and Jackie Autry.

▶**April 17:** The Angels staff ERA was 6.05, third worst in baseball and particularly unacceptable for a team with 40% of its 25-man payroll invested in starters Chuck Finley, Mark Langston and Jim Abbott. Five one-run wins have kept the team afloat, at 5-6.

▶**April 24:** In their first appearance in Seattle since blowing an 11-game lead last season and losing a one-game playoff to the Mariners for the division championship, the Angels blew a 9-1 lead and lost 11-10.

▶**May 8:** While he waits to see whether the Angels can trade him, longtime closer Lee Smith now says he will pitch whenever asked. "If they ask me to set up, I'm going to do it," Smith said. "I'm not going to sit here and tell you I'm happy about it." When the Angels had decided they preferred Troy Percival as their closer, Smith met with club officials and said he would not set up. Smith said that general manager Bill Bavasi promised to try to trade him.

▶**May 22:** On its first day as operator of the franchise, the Walt Disney Co. fired 23 front office employees, according to outgoing president Richard Brown. However, Disney retained Bill Bavasi and his baseball-operations staff.

▶**May 29:** In the six games Chuck Finley did not pitch on a recent road trip, starters combined for a 9.67 ERA. In separate games, the Angels trailed 6-0, 8-1, 8-2 and 13-1, and that doesn't count the night the Red Sox scored 17.

▶**June 5:** When the Angels traded Lee Smith to Cincinnati, baseball's all-time save leader autographed his Angels jersey and handed it to the kid who took his

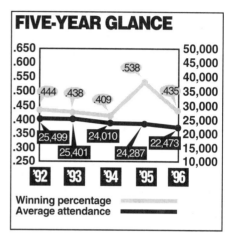

FIVE-YEAR GLANCE

Winning percentage
Average attendance

job. "There's not a man in here I respected more than him," Troy Percival said. "It'll be nice for me to have that on my wall." Could last month have been the finest of Chuck Finley's career? In May, Finley went 4-0 with a 0.79 ERA, and he carried a shutout into the seventh inning in each of his six starts.

▶**June 19:** The Angels lost All-Star center fielder Jim Edmonds for six to eight weeks with a partially torn ligament in his right thumb and then called up 1995 No. 1 draft pick Darin Erstad and installed him in center.

▶**June 26:** California finally lost patience with Jim Abbott (1-11, 7.92 ERA) and sent him to the bullpen after he walked six in his June 21 start.

▶**July 3:** Renovation work could restyle Anaheim from the biggest to the smallest stadium in the majors. Club president Tony Tavares said seating capacity next season could fall as low as 27,000, down from the current 64,593. As part of a $100 million reconstruction project that eventually will reduce capacity to about 45,000, almost all outfield seats will be demolished after this season.

▶**July 11:** After the Angels fell into last place with a 6-5 loss at Oakland on July 6, Marcel Lachemann held himself responsible for a defeat for the fourth time this season. Bill Bavasi said he would not discuss Lachemann's job security and said he did not see any purpose in issuing a public vote of confidence.

▶**Aug. 14:** The week that was: The manager was fired (or he resigned—reports differed) on Aug. 6 along with three coaches, the players bickered about whether there were any leaders before the interim manager designated two captains, the club president challenged the heart and commitment of the players and threatened an off-season shakeup, the team played 54 innings without having a lead, and the interim manager lost his first five games before managing the sixth by walkie-talkie from his office rather than hobbling to the dugout on crutches. After all that, the Angels asked pitcher Jim Abbott to accept an option to Vancouver.

▶**Aug. 28:** Interim manager John McNamara is expected to be released from a New York hospital this week after treatment to dissolve a blood clot in his right calf. Whether McNamara returns to his job is uncertain. Under coach Joe Maddon, the newest interim manager, the Angels were 4-1—including two shutouts—through Aug. 25.

▶**Sept. 4:** Former closer Bryan Harvey, disappointed by his inability to pitch this year, said he would consider working for minimum wage plus incentives in 1997 to repay the Angels for their investment in him. The Angels signed Harvey to a 1996 contract that guaranteed him $500,000 and the chance to earn another $1.7 million in incentives.

▶**Sept. 11:** In the wake of a shouting match and near-brawl between closer Troy Percival and the Yankees' Mariano Duncan, the Angels might have found the vocal clubhouse leader lacking since the departure of Tony Phillips in the off-season. After ripping the Yankees' attitude, Percival said he plans to adjust the Angels' attitude next spring. "When we come in here, there will not be the same aura in the locker room," he said.

▶**Oct. 2:** The Angels set a major league record by using 29 pitchers, set an AL record by hitting 82 batters and set franchise records for most players used (52), most times using the DL (21), highest

ERA (5.30), most home runs hit (192) and most home runs allowed (219). They used three managers (Marcel Lachemann, John McNamara and Joe Maddon), nine coaches and 116 lineups. Troy Percival emerged as an All-Star closer, anchoring a pleasantly surprising bullpen that included Mike James, Chuck McElroy, Mike Holtz and Pep Harris, but starters Chuck Finley, Mark Langston and Jim Abbott took 40% of the player payroll and the lion's share of the blame. Finley (15-16) made the All-Star team but said he didn't deserve to. Langston (6-5) made three trips to the DL after only two in his first 12 seasons. Abbott (2-18) fell from ninth in the AL in ERA last season to worst (if he had lasted long enough in his starts to qualify). And the team missed last year's leadoff man and clubhouse leader, Tony Phillips, more than they ever imagined.

Team directory

▶**Owner:** Gene Autry
▶**General manager:** Bill Bavasi
▶**Ballpark:**
Anaheim Stadium
2000 Gene Autry Way
Anaheim, Calif.
714-937-7200
Capacity 31,000 during renovations, 45,000 after renovations (1998)
Parking for 15,000 vehicles, $6; public transportation available; family and wheelchair sections, elevators, ramps, picnic section
▶**Team publications:**
Halo Insider Magazine, media guide, yearbook
714-937-6700, ext. 7281
▶**TV, radio broadcast stations:**
KMPC 710 AM, KCAL Channel 9, Fox Sports West
▶**Camps and/or clinics:**
Angels Clinic, on Saturdays during the season, 714-940-7204
▶**Spring training:**
Tempe Diablo Stadium
Tempe, Ariz.
Capacity 7,285 (9,785 including lawn)
602-438-4300

CALIFORNIA ANGELS 1996 final stats

BATTERS	BA	SLG	OB	G	AB	R	H	TB	2B	3B	HR	RBI	BB	SO	SB	CS	E
Turner	.333	.333	.400	4	3	1	1	1	0	0	0	1	1	0	0	0	0
Hudler	.311	.556	.337	92	302	60	94	168	20	3	16	40	9	54	14	5	6
Edmonds	.304	.571	.375	114	431	73	131	246	28	3	27	66	46	101	4	0	1
Davis	.292	.496	.387	145	530	73	155	263	24	0	28	95	86	99	5	2	0
Fabregas	.287	.335	.326	90	254	18	73	85	6	0	2	26	17	27	0	1	6
Palmeiro	.287	.379	.361	50	87	6	25	33	6	1	0	6	8	13	0	1	0
Salmon	.286	.501	.386	156	581	90	166	291	27	4	30	98	93	125	4	2	8
Anderson	.285	.405	.314	150	607	79	173	246	33	2	12	72	27	84	7	9	7
Velarde	.285	.426	.372	136	530	82	151	226	27	3	14	54	70	118	7	7	16
Erstad	.284	.375	.333	57	208	34	59	78	5	1	4	20	17	29	3	3	3
Howell	.270	.508	.324	66	126	20	34	64	4	1	8	21	10	30	0	1	9
Snow	.257	.384	.327	155	575	69	148	221	20	1	17	67	56	96	1	6	10
DiSarcina	.256	.347	.286	150	536	62	137	186	26	4	5	48	21	36	2	1	20
Schofield	.250	.250	.294	13	16	3	4	4	0	0	0	0	1	1	1	0	1
Arias	.238	.349	.284	84	252	19	60	88	8	1	6	28	16	50	2	0	10
Wallach	.237	.400	.306	57	190	23	45	76	7	0	8	20	18	47	1	0	8
Greene	.190	.278	.238	29	79	9	15	22	1	0	2	9	4	11	2	0	0
Eenhoorn	.172	.172	.212	18	29	3	5	5	0	0	0	2	2	5	0	2	0
Pritchett	.154	.154	.154	5	13	1	2	2	0	0	0	1	0	3	0	0	0

PITCHERS	W-L	ERA	G	GS	CG	GF	Sho	SV	IP	H	R	ER	HR	BB	SO
Ellis	0-0	0.00	3	0	0	3	0	0	5.0	0	0	0	0	4	5
VanRyn	0-0	0.00	1	0	0	1	0	0	1.0	1	0	0	0	1	0
Percival	0-2	2.31	62	0	0	52	0	36	74.0	38	20	19	8	31	100
Holtz	3-3	2.45	30	0	0	8	0	0	29.1	21	11	8	1	19	31
Smith	0-0	2.45	11	0	0	8	0	0	11.0	8	4	3	0	3	6
James	5-5	2.67	69	0	0	23	0	1	81.0	62	27	24	7	42	65
McElroy	5-1	2.95	40	0	0	11	0	0	36.2	32	12	12	2	13	32
Harris	2-0	3.90	11	3	0	0	0	0	32.1	31	16	14	4	17	20
Finley	15-16	4.16	35	35	4	0	1	0	238.0	241	124	110	27	94	215
Dickson	1-4	4.57	7	7	0	0	0	0	43.1	52	22	22	6	18	20
Langston	6-5	4.82	18	18	2	0	0	0	123.1	116	68	66	18	45	83
Eichhorn	1-2	5.04	24	0	0	6	0	0	30.1	36	17	17	3	11	24
Boskie	12-11	5.32	37	28	1	1	0	0	189.1	226	126	112	40	67	133
Springer	5-6	5.51	20	15	2	3	1	0	94.2	91	65	58	24	43	64
Monteleone	0-3	5.87	12	0	0	2	0	0	15.1	23	11	10	5	2	5
Pennington	0-2	6.20	22	0	0	8	0	0	20.1	11	15	14	2	31	20
Grimsley	5-7	6.84	35	20	2	4	1	0	130.1	150	110	99	14	74	82
Gohr	5-9	7.24	32	16	0	7	0	1	115.2	163	96	93	31	44	75
Leftwich	0-1	7.36	2	2	0	0	0	0	7.1	12	9	6	1	3	4
J. Abbott	2-18	7.48	27	23	1	2	0	0	142.0	171	128	118	23	78	58
Hancock	4-1	7.48	11	4	0	4	0	0	27.2	34	23	23	2	17	19
Sanderson	0-2	7.50	5	4	0	0	0	0	18.0	39	21	15	5	4	7
Schmidt	2-0	7.88	9	0	0	1	0	0	8.0	13	9	7	2	8	2
Holzemer	1-0	8.76	25	0	0	3	0	0	24.2	35	28	24	7	8	20
Williams	0-2	8.89	13	2	0	3	0	0	28.1	42	34	28	7	21	26
May	0-0	10.13	5	0	0	2	0	0	2.2	3	3	3	1	2	1
Edenfield	0-0	10.38	2	0	0	0	0	0	4.1	10	5	5	2	2	4
Frohwirth	0-0	11.12	4	0	0	2	0	0	5.2	10	11	7	1	4	1
K. Abbott	0-1	20.25	3	0	0	1	0	0	4.0	10	9	9	1	5	3

1997 preliminary roster

PITCHERS (23)
Jim Abbott
Jason Dickson
Geoff Edsell
Robert Ellis
Chuck Finley
Mike Freehill
Greg Gohr
Mark Gubicza
Pep Harris
Mike Holtz
Mike James

Pete Janicki
Mark Langston
Fausto Macey
Darrell May
Chuck McElroy
Troy Percival
Matt Perisho
Jeff Schmidt
Dennis Springer
Todd Van Poppel
Allen Watson
Shad Williams

CATCHERS (5)
Jorge Fabregas
Todd Greene
Bret Hemphill
Jim Leyritz
Chris Turner

INFIELDERS (8)
George Arias
Gary DiSarcina
Robert Eenhoorn
Craig Grebeck

Dave Hollins
Eddie Murray
Chris Pritchett
Randy Velarde

OUTFIELDERS (5)
Garret Anderson
Jim Edmonds
Darin Erstad
Orlando Palmeiro
Tim Salmon

Games played by position

PLAYER	G	C	1B	2B	3B	SS	OF	DH
Anderson	150	0	0	0	0	0	146	1
Arias	84	0	0	0	83	0	0	1
Davis	145	0	0	0	0	0	0	143
DiSarcina	150	0	0	0	0	150	0	0
Edmonds	114	0	0	0	0	0	111	1
Eenhoorn	18	0	0	12	2	4	0	0
Erstad	57	0	0	0	0	0	48	0
Fabregas	90	89	0	0	0	0	0	1
Greene	29	26	0	0	0	0	0	1
Howell	66	0	2	1	43	0	0	4
Hudler	92	0	7	53	0	0	21	8
Palmeiro	50	0	0	0	0	0	31	4
Pritchett	5	0	5	0	0	0	0	0
Salmon	156	0	0	0	0	0	153	0
Schofield	13	0	0	2	1	7	0	1
Snow	155	0	154	0	0	0	0	0
Turner	4	3	0	0	0	0	1	0
Velarde	136	0	0	114	28	7	0	0
Wallach	57	0	3	0	46	0	0	8

Sick call: 1996 DL report

PLAYER	Days on the DL
Damion Easley	39
Jim Edmonds	51*
Mark Eichhorn	103*
Tim Harkrider	182
Bryan Harvey	182
Mark Holzemer	83
Jack Howell	33
Mark Langston	93**
Chuck McElroy	17
Rich Monteleone	52
Steve Ontiveros	182
Brad Pennington	25
Scott Sanderson	28*
Dick Schofield	133
Don Slaught	15
Lee Smith	20

Indicates two separate terms on Disabled List.
**Indicates three separate terms on Disabled List.*

Minor Leagues
Tops in the organization

BATTER	CLUB	AVG.	G	AB	R	H	HR	RBI
Larry Barnes	Cr	.317	131	489	84	155	27	112
Greg Shockey	Mdl	.317	98	325	58	103	7	49
Eddie Christian	Mdl	.316	123	484	69	153	7	55
T. Takayoshi	Lke	.309	102	317	59	98	11	63
Matt Curtis	Boi	.305	75	305	57	93	12	62

HOME RUNS
Larry Barnes	Cr	27
Tony Moeder	Lke	19
J. Vandergriend	Cr	19
Bret Hemphill	Lke	17
Chris Pritchett	Van	16

WINS
Jason Dickson	Van	12
Pep Harris	Van	11
J. Washburn	Mdl	11
Several Players Tied At		10

RBI
Larry Barnes	Cr	112
Ryan Kane	Cr	75
Tony Moeder	Lke	73
Chris Pritchett	Van	73
Joe Urso	Lke	66

SAVES
Jeff Schmidt	Van	19
Mike Freehill	Mdl	17
Carlos Castillo	Mdl	14
Several Players Tied At		7

STOLEN BASES
J. Baughman	Cr	50
Trent Durrington	Cr	39
Jed Dalton	Lke	26
Nelson Castro	Ang	25
Several Players Tied At		24

STRIKEOUTS
J. Washburn	Mdl	156
Brian Cooper	Lke	155
Matt Perisho	Mdl	147
Matt Beaumont	Mdl	132
Jose Cintron	Cr	127

PITCHER	CLUB	W-L	ERA	IP	H	BB	SO
D. Springer	Van	10-3	2.72	109	89	36	78
Tommy Darrell	Boi	8-1	3.48	101	114	13	76
Jason Dickson	Van	12-13	3.73	186	189	50	110
Jose Cintron	Cr	10-8	3.88	179	192	41	127
Matt Perisho	Mdl	10-7	3.91	182	179	78	147

1996 salaries

	Bonuses	Total earned salary
Mark Langston, p		$5,000,000
Chili Davis, of		$3,800,000
Chuck Finley, p	$50,000	$3,050,000
Tim Salmon, of		$2,500,000
Jim Abbott		$2,200,000
Gary Disarcina, ss		$1,600,000
Chuck McElroy, p		$817,000
Randy Velarde, 2b		$800,000
J.T. Snow, 1b	$25,000	$725,000
Jim Edmonds, of	$75,000	$625,000
Bryan Harvey, p		$500,000
Shawn Boskie, p	$250,000	$450,000
Jason Grimsley, p		$425,000
Rex Hudler, of	$100,000	$400,000
Troy Percival, p	$25,000	$355,000
Jack Howell, 3b		$300,000
Garret Anderson, of		$250,000
Dick Schofield, ss		$250,000
Steve Ontiveros, p		$225,000
Greg Gohr, p	$15,000	$200,000
Jorge Fabregas, c		$175,000
Mark Eichhorn, p	$10,000	$170,000
Mike James, p		$150,000
Dennis Springer, p	$10,000	$150,000
Rich Monteleone, p		$135,000
Mark Holzemer, p		$117,500
Orlando Palmeiro, of		$113,500
George Arias, 3b		$109,000
Jason Dickson, p		$109,000
Todd Greene, c		$109,000
Tim Harkrider, ss		$109,000
Pep Harris, p		$109,000
Mike Holtz, p		$109,000

Average 1996 salary: $748,031
Total 1996 team payroll: $23,937,000
Termination pay: $1,203,142

California (1965-1996), includes Los Angeles (1961-1964)

Runs: Most, career

889	Brian Downing, 1978-1990
691	Jim Fregosi, 1961-1971
601	Bobby Grich, 1977-1986
520	CHILI DAVIS, 1988-1996
481	Don Baylor, 1977-1982

Hits: Most, career

1588	Brian Downing, 1978-1990
1408	Jim Fregosi, 1961-1971
1103	Bobby Grich, 1977-1986
973	CHILI DAVIS, 1988-1996
968	Rod Carew, 1979-1985

2B: Most, career

282	Brian Downing, 1978-1990
219	Jim Fregosi, 1961-1971
183	Bobby Grich, 1977-1986
170	WALLY JOYNER, 1986-1991
167	CHILI DAVIS, 1988-1996

3B: Most, career

70	Jim Fregosi, 1961-1971
32	Mickey Rivers, 1970-1975
27	LUIS POLONIA, 1990-1993
27	D. SCHOFIELD, 1983-1996
25	Bobby Knoop, 1964-1969

HR: Most, career

222	Brian Downing, 1978-1990
156	CHILI DAVIS, 1988-1996
154	Bobby Grich, 1977-1986
141	Don Baylor, 1977-1982
130	Doug DeCinces, 1982-1987

RBI: Most, career

846	Brian Downing, 1978-1990
618	CHILI DAVIS, 1988-1996
557	Bobby Grich, 1977-1986
546	Jim Fregosi, 1961-1971
523	Don Baylor, 1977-1982

SB: Most, career

186	Gary Pettis, 1982-1987
174	LUIS POLONIA, 1990-1993
139	Sandy Alomar, 1969-1974
126	Mickey Rivers, 1970-1975
123	DEVON WHITE, 1985-1990

BB: Most, career

866	Brian Downing, 1978-1990
630	Bobby Grich, 1977-1986
558	Jim Fregosi, 1961-1971
493	CHILI DAVIS, 1988-1996
405	Rod Carew, 1979-1985

BA: Highest, career

.314	Rod Carew, 1979-1985
.294	LUIS POLONIA, 1990-1993
.293	Juan Beniquez, 1981-1985
.293	TIM SALMON, 1992-1996
.288	WALLY JOYNER, 1986-1991

Slug avg: Highest, career

.530	TIM SALMON, 1992-1996
.464	CHILI DAVIS, 1988-1996
.463	Doug DeCinces, 1982-1987
.455	WALLY JOYNER, 1986-1991
.448	Don Baylor, 1977-1982

On-base avg: Highest, career

.393	Rod Carew, 1979-1985
.392	TIM SALMON, 1992-1996
.379	Albie Pearson, 1961-1966
.372	Brian Downing, 1978-1990
.370	Bobby Grich, 1977-1986

Complete games: Most, career

156	Nolan Ryan, 1972-1979
92	Frank Tanana, 1973-1980
70	Mike Witt, 1981-1990
52	CHUCK FINLEY, 1986-1996
51	Clyde Wright, 1966-1973

Saves: Most, career

126	Bryan Harvey, 1987-1992
65	Dave LaRoche, 1970-1980
61	Donnie Moore, 1985-1988
58	Bob Lee, 1964-1966
45	Joe Grahe, 1990-1994

Shutouts: Most, career

40	Nolan Ryan, 1972-1979
24	Frank Tanana, 1973-1980
21	Dean Chance, 1961-1966
14	George Brunet, 1964-1969
13	Geoff Zahn, 1981-1985

Wins: Most, career

138	Nolan Ryan, 1972-1979
129	CHUCK FINLEY, 1986-1996
109	Mike Witt, 1981-1990
102	Frank Tanana, 1973-1980
87	Clyde Wright, 1966-1973

K: Most, career

2416	Nolan Ryan, 1972-1979
1584	CHUCK FINLEY, 1986-1996
1283	Mike Witt, 1981-1990
1233	Frank Tanana, 1973-1980
1082	M. LANGSTON, 1990-1996

Win pct: Highest, career

.567	Frank Tanana, 1973-1980
.557	Andy Messersmith, 1968-1972
.553	Geoff Zahn, 1981-1985
.551	MARK LANGSTON, 1990-1996
.533	Nolan Ryan, 1972-1979

ERA: Lowest, career

2.78	Andy Messersmith, 1968-1972
2.83	Dean Chance, 1961-1966
3.07	Nolan Ryan, 1972-1979
3.08	Frank Tanana, 1973-1980
3.13	George Brunet, 1964-1969

Runs: Most, season

120	Don Baylor, 1979
120	JIM EDMONDS, 1995
119	TONY PHILLIPS, 1995
115	Albie Pearson, 1962
114	Carney Lansford, 1979

Hits: Most, season

202	Alex Johnson, 1970
188	Carney Lansford, 1979
186	Don Baylor, 1979
186	Billy Moran, 1962
184	Johnny Ray, 1988

2B: Most, season

42	Doug DeCinces, 1982
42	Johnny Ray, 1988
38	Fred Lynn, 1982
37	Brian Downing, 1982
35	TIM SALMON, 1993

3B: Most, season

13	Jim Fregosi, 1968
13	Mickey Rivers, 1975
13	DEVON WHITE, 1989
12	Jim Fregosi, 1963
11	Bobby Knoop, 1966
11	Mickey Rivers, 1974

HR: Most, season

39	Reggie Jackson, 1982
37	Bobby Bonds, 1977
37	Leon Wagner, 1962
36	Don Baylor, 1979
34	Don Baylor, 1978
34	WALLY JOYNER, 1987
34	TIM SALMON, 1995

RBI: Most, season

139	Don Baylor, 1979
117	WALLY JOYNER, 1987
115	Bobby Bonds, 1977
112	CHILI DAVIS, 1993
107	JIM EDMONDS, 1995
107	Leon Wagner, 1962

SB: Most, season

70	Mickey Rivers, 1975
56	Gary Pettis, 1985
55	LUIS POLONIA, 1993
51	LUIS POLONIA, 1992
50	Gary Pettis, 1986

BB: Most, season

113	TONY PHILLIPS, 1995
106	Brian Downing, 1987
96	Albie Pearson, 1961
95	Albie Pearson, 1962
93	Jim Fregosi, 1969
93	TIM SALMON, 1996

BA: Highest, season

.339	Rod Carew, 1983
.331	Rod Carew, 1980
.330	TIM SALMON, 1995
.329	Alex Johnson, 1970
.326	Brian Downing, 1979

Slug avg: Highest, season

.594	TIM SALMON, 1995
.561	CHILI DAVIS, 1994
.548	Doug DeCinces, 1982
.543	Bobby Grich, 1981
.537	Bobby Grich, 1979

On-base avg: Highest, season

.429	TIM SALMON, 1995
.429	CHILI DAVIS, 1995
.420	Albie Pearson, 1961
.418	Brian Downing, 1979
.410	CHILI DAVIS, 1994

Complete games: Most, season

26	Nolan Ryan, 1973
26	Nolan Ryan, 1974
23	Frank Tanana, 1976
22	Nolan Ryan, 1977
21	Nolan Ryan, 1976

Saves: Most, season

46	Bryan Harvey, 1991
37	LEE SMITH, 1995
36	TROY PERCIVAL, 1996
31	Donnie Moore, 1985
27	Minnie Rojas, 1967

Shutouts: Most, season

11	Dean Chance, 1964
9	Nolan Ryan, 1972

7	Nolan Ryan, 1976
7	Frank Tanana, 1977
6	Jim McGlothlin, 1967

Wins: Most, season

22	Nolan Ryan, 1974
22	Clyde Wright, 1970
21	Nolan Ryan, 1973
20	Dean Chance, 1964
20	Andy Messersmith, 1971
20	Bill Singer, 1973

K: Most, season

383	Nolan Ryan, 1973
367	Nolan Ryan, 1974
341	Nolan Ryan, 1977
329	Nolan Ryan, 1972
327	Nolan Ryan, 1976

Win pct: Highest, season

.773	Bert Blyleven, 1989
.704	MARK LANGSTON, 1991
.692	Geoff Zahn, 1982
.690	Dean Chance, 1964
.682	MARK LANGSTON, 1995

ERA: Lowest, season

1.65	Dean Chance, 1964
2.28	Nolan Ryan, 1972
2.40	CHUCK FINLEY, 1990
2.43	Frank Tanana, 1976
2.52	Andy Messersmith, 1969

Most pinch-hit homers, season

4	JACK HOWELL, 1996
3	Joe Adcock, 1966
3	George Hendrick, 1987

Most pinch-hit homers, career

4	Ruppert Jones, 1985-1987
4	George Hendrick, 1985-1988

Longest hitting streak

25	Rod Carew, 1982
23	JIM EDMONDS, 1995
22	Sandy Alomar, 1970
21	Bobby Grich, 1981
20	Bobby Grich, 1979

Most consecutive scoreless innings

36	Jim McGlothlin, 1967

No-hit games

Bo Belinsky, LA vs Bal AL, 2-0;
    May 5, 1962.
Clyde Wright, Cal vs Oak AL, 4-0;
    July 3, 1970.
Nolan Ryan, Cal at KC AL, 3-0;
    May 15, 1973.
Nolan Ryan, Cal at Det AL, 6-0;

July 15, 1973.
Nolan Ryan, Cal vs Min AL, 4-0;
    Sept. 28, 1974.
Nolan Ryan, Cal vs Bal AL, 1-0;
    June 1, 1975.
Mike Witt, Cal at Tex AL, 1-0;
    Sept. 30, 1984 (perfect game).
MARK LANGSTON (7 innings) and
    Mike Witt (2 innings), Cal vs Sea
    AL, 1-0; Apr. 11, 1990.

ACTIVE PLAYERS in caps.

Players' years of service are listed by the first and last years with this team and are not necessarily consecutive; all statistics record performances for this team only.

189

Atlanta Braves

By H. Darr Beiser, USA TODAY

Chipper Jones handled a difficult midseason conversion from third base to shortstop.

1996 Braves: Another year, another title

In many ways it was another exceptional regular season for the Braves. In other ways it wasn't. After all, this is a franchise that, no matter what kind of a positive spin management puts on the results, is satisfied with nothing less than a World Series championship. The loss to the New York Yankees, especially after winning the first two games on the road, was a bitter pill. "It's frustrating," said John Smoltz, one of eight Braves left from the 1991 team that went from worst to first. "We had a lot of opportunities to deliver, and we didn't come through. But I'd rather be the team that goes to the World Series every year and wins once than a team that wins one title and is never heard from again."

As everyone in the organization is quick to point out, 96 victories and another pennant means plenty of good things happened. First, there were Smoltz, infielder Chipper Jones and center fielder Marquis Grissom. Smoltz led the majors in wins with 24 and won the Cy Young Award, the fifth in the last six years for the Braves. Jones led the team's offense from the No. 3 hole even while making a difficult position change in August, and Grissom reached the 200-hit mark and led Atlanta with 28 steals.

This was the best Braves offensive team in more than a decade. Ryan Klesko emerged as a power hitter, leading the club with 34 home runs. First baseman Fred McGriff's 107 RBI were three behind club leader Jones, and catcher Javy Lopez had his best year yet.

Overall the starting pitching was excellent, with Tom Glavine and Greg Maddux backing Smoltz with 15 wins each. But for the third straight season, Steve Avery was a disappointment, going 7-9 with a 4.07 ERA and missing almost two months because of an injury. The trade for Denny Neagle also didn't have much of an impact before the postseason; the left-hander went 2-3 with the Braves and had a 5.59 ERA.

There were problems in the bullpen and the bench that were magnified in October. While closer Mark Wohlers finished

Team MVP

Chipper Jones: On a team with vaunted pitching and a strong, deep batting order, one of the younger members has become the most consistent component. Chipper Jones played both third base and shortstop, but what he did at the plate was his biggest addition to Atlanta's success. Stepping into the crucial third spot in the batting order, he hit 30 home runs and led the club with 110 RBI and a .309 batting average. His 87 walks, sixth in the National League, were also a factor in his top-10 ranking in runs scored.

with 39 saves, Brad Clontz had a team-high 5.74 ERA and Greg McMichael, since traded to the Mets, struggled down the stretch. The reserves were also unproductive, with outfielder Dwight Smith hitting .199 and infielder Mike Mordecai at .236. The experiment with outfield prospect Andruw Jones started strong, but the outfielder's average dropped to .217 by the end. His postseason performance reminded everyone that he was just 19 and there is no reason to doubt the predictions of stardom. What may have hurt the most was a season-ending injury to right fielder David Justice in May. Jermaine Dye filled in well at times but certainly wasn't the source of offense that Justice has been.

The Braves were so talented that it didn't matter. By the time they went into their first big slump of the season, which came in September, they were so far ahead that the closest Montreal could get was 4½ games back. "This organization has put us in position to win every year," said left-hander Glavine. "None of us have ever looked at this team as a dynasty. If people look at us that way years down the road, then fine. But that's not what motivates us. We want to be [in the postseason] every year."

1996 Braves: Week-by-week notes

These notes were excerpted from the following issues of Baseball Weekly.

192

▶**April 10:** A world championship has done little to put fans in the seats at Atlanta–Fulton County Stadium. The Braves announced their April 3 attendance as 28,728. With a season ticket base of 26,000, less than 3,000 single-game tickets were sold.

▶**April 17:** On April 11 in Montreal, Greg Maddux had his first road loss since June 27, 1994, a span of 20 games in which he was 18-0 and allowed 17 earned runs in 154⅔ innings.

▶**April 24:** Atlanta has as many players on the DL (Mike Mordecai, Jeff Blauser and Pedro Borbon) in April as it did all of last year. But John Smoltz just keeps rolling, following his near no-hitter with another dominating performance against the Padres on April 19. Hurling a three-hitter, Smoltz moved his record to 3-1.

▶**May 8:** Greg Maddux had faced 8,778 hitters covering 2,174⅔ innings before giving up his first regular-season grand slam, to Phillies catcher Benito Santiago on May 3. Tom Glavine, meanwhile, hasn't allowed a slam in 1,759 innings through May 5.

▶**May 15:** For the first time in 30 innings, on May 10 a Brave walked a hitter when John Smoltz gave Philadelphia's Lenny Dykstra a free pass with two out in the third. The streak lasted 114 hitters.

▶**May 22:** David Justice will not only miss the rest of this season, but rehabilitation from next week's right-shoulder surgery could take as long as a year. Justice, who is 30 and in the third season of a five-year deal, dislocated the shoulder while swinging at a pitch on May 14. Jermaine Dye will take over for Justice in right field, and the Braves will move Ryan Klesko into Justice's No. 5 spot while catcher Javy Lopez hits sixth.

▶**June 12:** Greg Maddux had his worst start in six years on June 7 in a 19-8 loss to the Rockies. At Coors Field, where the runs never seem to stop, Maddux lasted just 10 outs, allowing seven runs on 11 hits and watching his ERA balloon to 3.41. He was lucky not to get the loss, his record remaining at 5-4, as he left in the fourth with the score tied, 7-7.

▶**June 19:** The successful front office and managerial team of John Schuerholz and Bobby Cox will stay together at least through the rest of this century. The Braves last week gave Cox a contract extension through 1999, with a club option for 2000. General manager Schuerholz is signed through 1999. Cox, 55, with a 495-316 record for Atlanta, is the winningest manager in the major leagues since 1991.

▶**June 26:** The Braves put together back-to-back shutout victories against the Giants over the weekend. Tom Glavine allowed three hits in 7⅔ innings and Chipper Jones homered for the only run in a 1-0 victory on June 23. The day before, the Braves won 6-0 behind Greg Maddux.

▶**July 3:** Pitching coach Leo Mazzone spent June 27 studying videotape, trying to figure out what is wrong with left-hander Steve Avery, who was 0-3 in June and allowed 30 runs in five starts.

▶**July 11:** John Smoltz, whose string of 14 straight wins ended last month, was hit hard in his last three games, allowing 17 earned runs on 26 hits in 14⅓ innings. His ERA jumped from 2.26 to 3.16.

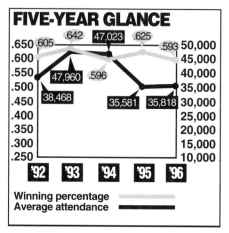

FIVE-YEAR GLANCE

Winning percentage
Average attendance

▶July 31: When Steve Avery went on the DL with a pulled muscle last week, he became the first of the top four to ever land there. Avery, Greg Maddux, John Smoltz and Tom Glavine had gone 7,058⅔ innings without going on the DL.

▶Aug. 14: The division race most likely will be over, but September could be a very interesting month for the Braves because minor league sensation Andruw Jones might be in Atlanta. He is hitting .338 in 112 games with 31 home runs, 85 RBI, 29 steals and 108 runs scored at Class A Durham, Class AA Greenville and Class AAA Richmond combined.

▶Aug. 21: Right-hander Mike Bielecki, the last pitcher to make the Braves out of spring training, pitched six shutout innings on Aug. 17 in a 7-1 victory against the Pirates before a sellout crowd of 49,024 in Atlanta–Fulton County Stadium.

▶Aug. 28: On Aug. 23, at 19 years, 3 months and 30 days, Andruw Jones became the youngest big leaguer to hit two homers in one game since the Cubs' Danny Murphy in 1961. Jones is the fourth-youngest player in the majors to perform the feat. Marquis Grissom went 0-for-4 on Aug. 25, ending his career-high hitting streak at 28 games, the longest streak in the majors since Jerome Walton hit in 30 consecutive games for the Cubs in 1989.

▶Sept. 4: Reliever Pedro Borbon could be out for two years after major reconstructive surgery on his left elbow. The Braves expect rookie Terrell Wade to replace Borbon in the bullpen, now that former Pirates ace Denny Neagle has joined the rotation.

▶Sept. 18: The Braves' biggest concern is their bullpen. Other than closer Mark Wohlers, manager Bobby Cox has no idea whom to turn to. For example, left-hander Steve Avery, pitching on Sept. 14 for the first time since July 11, threw five scoreless innings and left with a 5-0 lead. But the Braves' seven relievers blew the lead, and the Mets won 6-5 in 12 innings.

▶Oct. 2: John Smoltz, Chipper Jones and Marquis Grissom had tremendous years as the Braves became the second team to win five division titles in a row, after Oakland in 1971-75. Smoltz led the majors in wins with 24 and is favored to win the Cy Young Award; it would be the sixth in a row for the current Braves starters, counting the one that Greg Maddux got in 1992 with the Chicago Cubs. Jones had better overall numbers than anyone on the club despite shifting to a different position, shortstop, starting in mid-August. Grissom reached the 200-hit mark and won his fourth straight Gold Glove. But there were problems in the bullpen, and the bench was unproductive. While Mark Wohlers finished with 39 saves, Brad Clontz had a 5.69 ERA and Greg McMichael struggled down the stretch. A season-ending injury to David Justice in May caused a lot of lineup shuffling and hurt the team's depth.

Team directory

▶**Owner:** Ted Turner
▶**General manager:** John Schuerholz
▶**Ballpark:**
Turner Field
P.O. Box 4064
Atlanta, Ga. 30302
404-522-7630
Capacity 49,831
Parking for 3,500 cars; $5
Public transportation available by bus
Family and wheelchair sections,
no-alcohol section
▶**Team publications:**
Fan Magazine,
404-522-7630
Chop Talk
1-800-700-CHOP
▶**TV, radio broadcast stations:**
WSB 750 AM, WTBS Channel 17,
Sport South
▶**Spring training:**
Municipal Stadium
West Palm Beach, Fla.
Capacity 7,200
561-683-6100

ATLANTA BRAVES 1996 final stats

BATTERS	BA	SLG	OB	G	AB	R	H	TB	2B	3B	HR	RBI	BB	SO	SB	CS	E
Martinez	.500	.500	.500	4	2	1	1	1	0	0	0	0	0	0	0	1	0
Polonia	.419	.419	.424	22	31	3	13	13	0	0	0	2	1	3	1	1	1
Walton	.340	.511	.389	37	47	9	16	24	5	0	1	4	5	10	0	0	0
Justice	.321	.514	.409	40	140	23	45	72	9	0	6	25	21	22	1	1	0
C. Jones	.309	.530	.393	157	598	114	185	317	32	5	30	110	87	88	14	1	17
Grissom	.308	.489	.349	158	671	106	207	328	32	10	23	74	41	73	28	11	1
McGriff	.295	.494	.365	159	617	81	182	305	37	1	28	107	68	116	7	3	12
Lopez	.282	.466	.322	138	489	56	138	228	19	1	23	69	28	84	1	6	6
Klesko	.282	.530	.364	153	528	90	149	280	21	4	34	93	68	129	6	3	5
Dye	.281	.459	.304	98	292	32	82	134	16	0	12	37	8	67	1	4	8
Perez	.256	.404	.293	68	156	19	40	63	9	1	4	17	8	19	0	0	3
Lemke	.255	.319	.323	135	498	64	127	159	17	0	5	37	53	48	5	2	15
Blauser	.245	.419	.356	83	265	48	65	111	14	1	10	35	40	54	6	0	23
Whiten	.243	.408	.359	96	272	45	66	111	13	1	10	38	49	87	15	8	9
Mordecai	.241	.343	.297	66	108	12	26	37	5	0	2	8	9	24	1	0	2
Pendleton	.238	.345	.290	153	568	51	135	196	26	1	11	75	41	111	2	3	19
Giovanola	.232	.256	.304	43	82	10	19	21	2	0	0	7	8	13	1	0	1
A. Jones	.217	.443	.265	31	106	11	23	47	7	1	5	13	7	29	3	0	2
Smith	.203	.294	.285	101	153	16	31	45	5	0	3	16	17	42	1	3	2
Ayrault	.200	.200	.333	7	5	0	1	1	0	0	0	0	0	1	0	0	0
Graffanino	.174	.239	.250	22	46	7	8	11	1	1	0	2	4	13	0	0	2
Belliard	.169	.218	.179	87	142	9	24	31	7	0	0	3	2	22	3	1	5
Bautista	.150	.150	.261	17	20	1	3	3	0	0	0	1	2	5	0	0	0

PITCHERS	W-L	ERA	G	GS	CG	GF	Sho	SV	IP	H	R	ER	HR	BB	SO
Thobe	0-1	1.50	4	0	0	3	0	0	6.0	5	2	1	1	0	1
Bielecki	4-3	2.63	40	5	0	8	0	2	75.1	63	24	22	8	33	71
Schutz	0-0	2.70	3	0	0	1	0	0	3.1	3	1	1	0	2	5
Maddux	15-11	2.72	35	35	5	0	1	0	245.0	225	85	74	11	28	172
Borbon	3-0	2.75	43	0	0	19	0	1	36.0	26	12	11	1	7	31
Smoltz	24-8	2.94	35	35	6	0	2	0	253.2	199	93	83	19	55	276
Wade	5-0	2.97	44	8	0	13	0	1	69.2	57	28	23	9	47	79
Glavine	15-10	2.98	36	36	1	0	0	0	235.1	222	91	78	14	85	181
Wohlers	2-4	3.03	77	0	0	64	0	39	77.1	71	30	26	8	21	100
McMichael	5-3	3.22	73	0	0	14	0	2	86.2	84	37	31	4	27	78
Neagle	16-9	3.50	33	33	2	0	0	0	221.1	226	93	86	26	48	149
Avery	7-10	4.47	24	23	1	0	0	0	131.0	146	70	65	10	40	86
Hartgraves	1-0	4.78	39	0	0	9	0	0	37.2	34	21	20	4	23	30
Borowski	2-4	4.85	22	0	0	8	0	0	26.0	33	15	14	4	13	15
Lomon	0-0	4.91	6	0	0	1	0	0	7.1	7	4	4	0	3	1
Clontz	6-3	5.69	81	0	0	11	0	1	80.2	78	53	51	11	33	49
Woodall	2-2	7.32	8	3	0	2	0	0	19.2	28	19	16	4	4	20

1997 preliminary roster

PITCHERS (19)
Mike Bielecki
Pedro Borbon
Joe Borowski
Scott Brow
Paul Byrd
Brad Clontz
Tom Hartgraves
Dean Hartgraves
John LeRoy
Greg Maddux
Kevin Millwood

Denny Neagle
Yorkis Perez
Carl Schutz
John Smoltz
Terrell Wade
Jamie Walker
Mark Wohlers
Brad Woodall

CATCHERS (2)
Javy Lopez
Eddie Perez

INFIELDERS (11)
Rafael Belliard
Jeff Blauser
Ed Giovanola
Tony Graffanino
Chipper Jones
Mark Lemke
Marty Malloy
Fred McGriff
Mike Mordecai
Randall Simon
Robert Smith

OUTFIELDERS (9)
Danny Bautista
Jermaine Dye
Marquis Grissom
Damon Hollins
Andruw Jones
David Justice
Ryan Klesko
Marc Lewis
Wonderful Monds

Games played by position

PLAYER	G	C	1B	2B	3B	SS	OF
Ayrault	7	7	0	0	0	0	0
Bautista	17	0	0	0	0	0	14
Belliard	87	0	0	15	0	63	0
Blauser	83	0	0	0	0	79	0
Dye	98	0	0	0	0	0	92
Giovanola	43	0	0	5	6	25	0
Graffanino	22	0	0	18	0	0	0
Grissom	158	0	0	0	0	0	158
A. Jones	31	0	0	0	0	0	29
C. Jones	157	0	0	0	118	38	1
Justice	40	0	0	0	0	0	40
Klesko	153	0	2	0	0	0	144
Lemke	135	0	0	133	0	0	0
Lopez	138	135	0	0	0	0	0
Martinez	4	0	0	0	0	1	0
McGriff	159	0	158	0	0	0	0
Mordecai	66	0	1	20	10	6	0
Pendleton	153	0	0	0	149	0	0
Perez	68	54	7	0	0	0	0
Polonia	22	0	0	0	0	0	7
Smith	101	0	0	0	0	0	29
Walton	37	0	0	0	0	0	28
Whiten	96	0	0	0	0	0	80

Minor Leagues

Tops in the organization

BATTER	CLUB	AVG.	G	AB	R	H	HR	RBI
A. Jones	Rmd	.339	116	445	115	151	34	92
Raul Rodarte	Rmd	.322	129	438	69	141	15	80
A. Johnson	Eug	.314	76	318	58	100	7	56
Marc Lewis	Dur	.306	134	503	79	154	11	54
T. Pendergrass	Mac	.302	66	265	58	80	4	26

HOME RUNS

Andruw Jones	Rmd	34
Steve Hacker	Eug	21
Ron Wright	Dur	20
R. Brown	Mac	19
Gus Kennedy	Dur	19

WINS

Derrin Ebert	Dur	12
Mike Hostetler	Rmd	11
Damian Moss	Grv	11
Chris Brock	Rmd	10
Several Players Tied At		9

RBI

Andruw Jones	Rmd	92
R. Nunez	Dur	81
Raul Rodarte	Rmd	80
Randall Simon	Grv	77
Wes Helms	Grv	76

SAVES

Adam Butler	Grv	30
K. Ligtenberg	Dur	20
Rod Nichols	Rmd	20
R. Beasley	Eug	12
Jason Flach	Eug	11

STOLEN BASES

Marc Lewis	Dur	50
Joe Trippy	Dur	48
T. Pendergrass	Mac	45
Rob Sasser	Mac	38
Andruw Jones	Rmd	30

STRIKEOUTS

John Rocker	Dur	150
Kevin Millwood	Dur	139
Damian Moss	Grv	137
John Leroy	Grv	132
Raymond King	Dur	115

PITCHER	CLUB	W-L	ERA	IP	H	BB	SO
John Leroy	Grv	8-5	3.35	156	134	70	132
Damian Moss	Grv	11-6	3.36	142	109	75	137
Brad Woodall	Rmd	9-7	3.38	133	124	36	74
John Dettmer	Rmd	6-8	3.51	100	112	15	54
Mike Cather	Grv	3-4	3.70	88	89	29	61

Sick call: 1996 DL report

PLAYER	Days on the DL
Steve Avery	51
Danny Bautista	94
Jeff Blauser	67*
Pedro Borbon	56*
Lee Daniels	75
Chipper Jones	5
Dave Justice	137
Mark Lemke	17
Mike Mordecai	22
Eddie Perez	15
Jason Schmidt	46
Jerome Walton	123

Indicates two separate terms on Disabled List.

1996 Salaries

	Bonuses	Total earned salary
Greg Maddux, p	$175,000	$6,675,000
David Justice, of		$6,200,000
John Smoltz, p	$500,000	$6,000,000
Tom Glavine, p	$100,000	$5,350,000
Fred McGriff, of	$300,000	$5,050,000
Marquis Grissom, of	$50,000	$4,850,000
Steve Avery, p		$4,200,000
Jeff Blauser, ss		$3,500,000
Denny Neagle, p		$2,300,000
Terry Pendleton, 3b	$125,000	$1,625,000
Mark Lemke, 2b		$1,500,000
Mark Wohlers, p	$25,000	$1,425,000
Chipper Jones, 3b	$25,000	$775,000
Rafael Belliard, ss		$575,000
Jerome Walton, of		$500,000
Greg McMichael, p		$460,000
Dwight Smith, of	$50,000	$400,000
Ryan Klesko, of		$315,000
Javier Lopez, c		$290,000
Danny Bautista, of		$185,000
Pedro Borbon, of		$185,000
Brad Clontz, p		$137,500
Mike Mordecai, 2b		$135,000
Mike Bielecki, p		$125,000
Joe Borowski, p		$111,500
Eddie Perez, c		$111,500
Joe Aryault, c		$109,000
Lee Daniels, p		$109,000
Jermaine Dye, of		$109,000
Andruw Jones, of		$109,000
Luis Polonia, of		$109,000
Terrell Wade, p		$109,000

Average 1996 Salary: $1,625,288
Total 1996 team payroll: $53,634,500
Termination pay: None

right margin: MAJOR LEAGUE REPORT

ATLANTA BRAVES / NL EAST

Atlanta (1966-1996), incl. Boston (1876-1952) and Milwaukee (1953-1965)

Runs: Most, career

2107	Hank Aaron, 1954-1974
1452	Eddie Mathews, 1952-1966
1291	Herman Long, 1890-1902
1134	Fred Tenney, 1894-1911
1103	Dale Murphy, 1976-1990

Hits: Most, career

3600	Hank Aaron, 1954-1974
2201	Eddie Mathews, 1952-1966
1994	Fred Tenney, 1894-1911
1901	Dale Murphy, 1976-1990
1900	Herman Long, 1890-1902

2B: Most, career

600	Hank Aaron, 1954-1974
338	Eddie Mathews, 1952-1966
306	Dale Murphy, 1976-1990
295	Herman Long, 1890-1902
291	Tommy Holmes, 1942-1951

3B: Most, career

103	Rabbit Maranville, 1912-1935
96	Hank Aaron, 1954-1974
91	Herman Long, 1890-1902
80	John Morrill, 1876-1888
79	Bill Bruton, 1953-1960

HR: Most, career

733	Hank Aaron, 1954-1974
493	Eddie Mathews, 1952-1966
371	Dale Murphy, 1976-1990
239	Joe Adcock, 1953-1962
215	Bob Horner, 1978-1986

RBI: Most, career

2202	Hank Aaron, 1954-1974
1388	Eddie Mathews, 1952-1966
1143	Dale Murphy, 1976-1990
964	Herman Long, 1890-1902
927	Hugh Duffy, 1892-1900

SB: Most, career

431	Herman Long, 1890-1902
331	Hugh Duffy, 1892-1900
274	Billy Hamilton, 1896-1901
260	Bobby Lowe, 1890-1901
260	Fred Tenney, 1894-1911
240	Hank Aaron, 1954-1974 (6)

BB: Most, career

1376	Eddie Mathews, 1952-1966
1297	Hank Aaron, 1954-1974
912	Dale Murphy, 1976-1990
750	Fred Tenney, 1894-1911
598	Billy Nash, 1885-1895

BA: Highest, career

.338	Billy Hamilton, 1896-1901
.332	Hugh Duffy, 1892-1900
.327	Chick Stahl, 1897-1900
.317	Rico Carty, 1963-1972
.317	Ralph Garr, 1968-1975

Slug avg: Highest, career

.567	Hank Aaron, 1954-1974
.533	Wally Berger, 1930-1937
.517	Eddie Mathews, 1952-1966
.511	Joe Adcock, 1953-1962
.508	Bob Horner, 1978-1986

On-base avg: Highest, career

.456	Billy Hamilton, 1896-1901
.398	Bob Elliott, 1947-1951
.394	Hugh Duffy, 1892-1900
.388	Rico Carty, 1963-1972
.385	Chick Stahl, 1897-1900

Complete games: Most, career

475	Kid Nichols, 1890-1901
374	Warren Spahn, 1942-1964
268	Vic Willis, 1898-1905
242	Jim Whitney, 1881-1885
226	John Clarkson, 1888-1892
226	Phil Niekro, 1964-1987

Saves: Most, career

141	Gene Garber, 1978-1987
78	Cecil Upshaw, 1966-1973
71	M. WOHLERS, 1991-1996
57	Rick Camp, 1976-1985
55	MIKE STANTON, 1989-1995

Shutouts: Most, career

63	Warren Spahn, 1942-1964
44	Kid Nichols, 1890-1901
43	Phil Niekro, 1964-1987
30	Lew Burdette, 1951-1963
29	Tommy Bond, 1877-1881

Wins: Most, career

356	Warren Spahn, 1942-1964
329	Kid Nichols, 1890-1901
268	Phil Niekro, 1964-1987
179	Lew Burdette, 1951-1963
151	Vic Willis, 1898-1905

K: Most, career

2912	Phil Niekro, 1964-1987
2493	Warren Spahn, 1942-1964
1672	Kid Nichols, 1890-1901
1528	JOHN SMOLTZ, 1988-1996
1212	TOM GLAVINE, 1987-1996

Win pct: Highest, career

.707	GREG MADDUX, 1993-1996
.679	Fred Klobedanz, 1896-1902
.655	Harry Staley, 1891-1894
.645	John Clarkson, 1888-1892
.643	Kid Nichols, 1890-1901

ERA: Lowest, career

2.11	GREG MADDUX, 1993-1996
2.21	Tommy Bond, 1877-1881
2.49	Jim Whitney, 1881-1885
2.52	Art Nehf, 1915-1919
2.62	Dick Rudolph, 1913-1927

Runs: Most, season

160	Hugh Duffy, 1894
158	Bobby Lowe, 1894
152	Billy Hamilton, 1896
152	Billy Hamilton, 1897
149	Herman Long, 1893
131	Dale Murphy, 1983 (9)

Hits: Most, season

237	Hugh Duffy, 1894
224	Tommy Holmes, 1945
223	Hank Aaron, 1959
219	Ralph Garr, 1971
218	Felipe Alou, 1966

2B: Most, season

51	Hugh Duffy, 1894
47	Tommy Holmes, 1945
46	Hank Aaron, 1959
44	Wally Berger, 1931
44	Lee Maye, 1964
39	TERRY PENDLETON, 1992 (12)

3B: Most, season

20	Dick Johnston, 1887
20	Harry Stovey, 1891
19	Chick Stahl, 1899
18	Dick Johnston, 1888
18	Ray Powell, 1921
17	Ralph Garr, 1974 (6)

HR: Most, season

47	Hank Aaron, 1971
47	Eddie Mathews, 1953
46	Eddie Mathews, 1959
45	Hank Aaron, 1962
44	Hank Aaron, 1957
44	Hank Aaron, 1963
44	Hank Aaron, 1966
44	Hank Aaron, 1969
44	Dale Murphy, 1987

RBI: Most, season

145	Hugh Duffy, 1894	
135	Eddie Mathews, 1953	
132	Hank Aaron, 1957	
132	Jimmy Collins, 1897	
130	Hank Aaron, 1963	
130	Wally Berger, 1935	
127	Hank Aaron, 1966 (9)	

SB: Most, season

84	King Kelly, 1887	
83	Billy Hamilton, 1896	
72	OTIS NIXON, 1991	
68	King Kelly, 1889	
66	Billy Hamilton, 1897	

BB: Most, season

131	Bob Elliott, 1948	
127	Jim Wynn, 1976	
126	Darrell Evans, 1974	
124	Darrell Evans, 1973	
124	Eddie Mathews, 1963	

BA: Highest, season

.440	Hugh Duffy, 1894	
.387	Rogers Hornsby, 1928	
.373	Dan Brouthers, 1889	
.369	Billy Hamilton, 1898	
.366	Rico Carty, 1970	

Slug avg: Highest, season

.694	Hugh Duffy, 1894	
.669	Hank Aaron, 1971	
.636	Hank Aaron, 1959	
.632	Rogers Hornsby, 1928	
.627	Eddie Mathews, 1953	

On-base avg: Highest, season

.502	Hugh Duffy, 1894	
.498	Rogers Hornsby, 1928	
.480	Billy Hamilton, 1898	
.477	Billy Hamilton, 1896	
.462	Dan Brouthers, 1889	
.454	Rico Carty, 1970 (7)	

Complete games: Most, season

68	John Clarkson, 1889	
63	Charlie Buffinton, 1884	
59	Tommy Bond, 1879	
58	Tommy Bond, 1877	
57	Tommy Bond, 1878	
57	Charley Radbourn, 1886	
57	Jim Whitney, 1881	
23	Phil Niekro, 1979 (*)	

Saves: Most, season

39	MARK WOHLERS, 1996	
30	Gene Garber, 1982	
27	MIKE STANTON, 1993	
27	Cecil Upshaw, 1969	
25	Gene Garber, 1979	
25	MARK WOHLERS, 1995	

Shutouts: Most, season

11	Tommy Bond, 1879	
9	Tommy Bond, 1878	
8	Charlie Buffinton, 1884	
8	John Clarkson, 1889	
7	Kid Nichols, 1890	
7	Togie Pittinger, 1902	
7	Warren Spahn, 1947	
7	Warren Spahn, 1951	
7	Warren Spahn, 1963	
7	Irv Young, 1905	
6	Phil Niekro, 1974 (11)	

Wins: Most, season

49	John Clarkson, 1889	
48	Charlie Buffinton, 1884	
43	Tommy Bond, 1879	
40	Tommy Bond, 1877	
40	Tommy Bond, 1878	
24	JOHN SMOLTZ, 1996 (*)	

K: Most, season

417	Charlie Buffinton, 1884	
345	Jim Whitney, 1883	
284	John Clarkson, 1889	
276	JOHN SMOLTZ, 1996	
270	Jim Whitney, 1884	

Win pct: Highest, season

.905	GREG MADDUX, 1995	
.842	Tom Hughes, 1916	
.810	Phil Niekro, 1982	
.788	Fred Klobedanz, 1897	
.788	Bill James, 1914	

ERA: Lowest, season

1.56	GREG MADDUX, 1994	
1.63	GREG MADDUX, 1995	
1.87	Phil Niekro, 1967	
1.90	Bill James, 1914	
1.96	Tommy Bond, 1879	

Most pinch-hit homers, season

5	Butch Nieman, 1945	
4	Tommy Gregg, 1990	

Most pinch-hit homers, career

7	Joe Adcock, 1953-1962	
6	Tommy Gregg, 1988-1992	
6	Mike Lum, 1967-1981	

Longest hitting streak

37	Tommy Holmes, 1945	
31	Rico Carty, 1970	
29	Rowland Office, 1976	
28	MARQUIS GRISSOM, 1996	
26	Hugh Duffy, 1894	
26	Bill Sweeney, 1911	

Most consecutive scoreless innings

41	Art Nehf, 1917	
29	Phil Niekro, 1974	

No-hit games

Jack Stivetts, Bos vs Bro NL, 11-0; Aug. 6, 1892.

Frank (Jeff) Pfeffer, Bos vs Cin NL, 6-0; May 8, 1907.

George Davis, Bos vs Phi NL, 7-0; Sept. 9, 1914 (2nd game).

Tom L. Hughes, Bos vs Pit NL, 2-0; June 16, 1916.

Jim Tobin, Bos vs Bro NL, 2-0; Apr. 27, 1944.

Vern Bickford, Bos vs Bro NL, 7-0; Aug. 11, 1950.

Jim Wilson, Mil vs Phi NL, 2-0; June 12, 1954.

Lew Burdette, Mil vs Phi NL, 1-0; Aug. 18, 1960.

Warren Spahn, Mil vs Phi NL, 4-0; Sept. 16, 1960.

Warren Spahn, Mil vs SF NL, 1-0; Apr. 28, 1961.

Phil Niekro, Atl vs SD NL, 9-0; Aug. 5, 1973.

KENT MERCKER (6 innings), MARK WOHLERS (2 innings) and ALE-JANDRO PENA (1 inning), Atl at SD NL, 1-0; Sept. 11, 1991.

KENT MERCKER, Atl at LA NL, 6-0; Apr. 8, 1994.

Jack Stivetts, five innings, called so Boston could catch train to Cleveland for Temple Cub play-offs, Bos at Was NL, 6-0; Oct. 15, 1892 (2nd game).

Jim Tobin, five innings, darkness, Bos vs Phi NL, 7-0; June 22, 1944 (2nd game).

ACTIVE PLAYERS in caps.

Leader from the franchise's current location is included. If not in the top five, leader's rank is listed in parenthesis; asterisk (*) indicates player is not in top 25.

Players' years of service are listed by the first and last years with this team and are not necessarily consecutive; all statistics record performances for this team only.

Montreal Expos

By Eileen Blass, USA TODAY

Henry Rodriguez upped his homers from two to 36, and fans responded with candy.

1996 Expos: They contended to the wire

The Expos went down to the final weekend of the season with a chance in the National League wild-card race, though they had just lost the last four games of a five-game set in Atlanta against the National League East Division champions. It was just before the 161st game of the season that the Expos were eliminated with a San Diego Padres win over the Los Angeles Dodgers. "What makes it so tough is that after playing all those games that mean something, you come down to the 161st game and all of a sudden it's meaningless," said outfielder Moises Alou. "But we have to be proud of what we accomplished this year because nobody thought we'd come close."

Picked by many to finish near the bottom in the East, the Expos actually spent 46 days in first place. From the start of the year until Aug. 27, the Expos were either in first place or leading the wild card. On Aug. 8, they were a season-high four games ahead in the wild-card race. All this came despite injuries to center fielder Rondell White who missed 68 games with a bruised kidney and spleen; first baseman David Segui, who lost 41 with hand and wrist ailments; and left-hander Carlos Perez, who was out for the entire season with major shoulder surgery. One key performer was closer Mel Rojas, who converted 22 save opportunities in a row to break John Wetteland's club record. Rojas signed with the Cubs during the off-season.

The offense was much better than expected, as the Expos set a club record for home runs and grand slams, led by Henry Rodriguez's unexpected long-ball binge. His 36 homers set a team mark, and he also drove in 103 runs. "Henry Rodriguez's power wasn't only the biggest surprise on this team, it was one of the biggest surprises to the baseball world," said manager Felipe Alou. Shortstop Mark Grudzielanek and second baseman Mike Lansing were effective in the top two spots in the batting order, and Grudzielanek almost became the

Team MVP

Henry Rodriguez: The Expos again were considered overachievers, and the most surprising performance of all came from outfielder Henry Rodriguez. His 36 home runs were part of a club-record 148, and he added 42 doubles and a team-high 103 RBI. Five-year veteran Rodriguez had never hit more than eight home runs in a major league season. In fact, he had only once before played as many as half his team's games.

first Montreal player to get 200 hits and score 100 runs, missing by one run.

Other surprises? Ugueth Urbina made a relatively smooth transition to the bullpen, where he is clearly the organization's closer of the future. And outfielder F.P. Santangelo, who spent six years in the minor league system before getting a chance as a September callup in 1995, received support for NL Rookie of the Year last season.

Despite the club's overachieving ways, there were disappointments. The team ground to a halt offensively in September, as White and Moises Alou went into slumps. Alou, the son of the manager, was destined to go to Florida for 1997 as the Expos struggled with a $4 million–$5 million deficit. "I'm going to play this game like it's my last one as an Expo," said the younger Alou on the eve of the final game. And Jeff Fassero a 15-game winner who had 222 strikeouts, came up short in his final two starts against the Braves. He was traded to Seattle after the season.

After his team had been eliminated, Felipe Alou was asked if he felt that a lack of experience hurt his club down the stretch. "We won a lot of games with inexperience," he replied. "We went as far as we did with inexperience. So now that we're out of it, I can't start blaming that inexperience."

1996 Expos: Week-by-week notes

These notes were excerpted from the following issues of Baseball Weekly.

▶**April 17:** Shortstop Mark Grudzielanek and second baseman Mike Lansing, the Expos' No. 1 and 2 hitters, respectively, led the offense as the club came out of the blocks with a 7-3 start—its fastest since 1981's 8-2 opening. The leadoff hitter by default, Grudzielanek is hitting .340 but has walked only once through 10 games.

▶**May 15:** Left fielder Henry Rodriguez continued his power surge, with 15 home runs and 44 RBI in 129 at-bats, and right fielder Moises Alou drove in the winning run in the Expos' 10-9 victory over the Astros in the wee hours of May 12, the 61st birthday of his father, Expos manager Felipe Alou.

▶**May 22:** As of May 19, reliever Dave Veres had given up as many home runs (five) as he did in all of 1995, when he worked 103⅓ innings. He was also just six earned runs away from matching his season total in 1995.

▶**May 29:** Mark Grudzielanek was one of the early-season surprises in the majors. After 50 games, the leadoff hitter was batting .345 and had reached base in 46 of those games. He also had yet to miss a start.

▶**June 5:** Henry Rodriguez set an NL record for home runs by May 31 when he hit his 20th. The previous record was 19, set by Eric Davis in 1987 with the Reds.

▶**June 12:** There is a growing concern over Moises Alou's prolonged slump, one he called "the worst of my career." Alou's average fell as low as .249, and he has hit just one home run in 33 games.

▶**June 26:** Closer Mel Rojas has been the frequent target of Olympic Stadium boo-birds this season, but he hasn't let it bother him. "They booed me in '93, they booed me in '94, they booed me in '95, and they'll boo me in '97," he said. "John Wetteland used to ask me, 'Why are they booing you?' I said, 'I don't

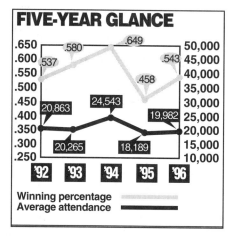

FIVE-YEAR GLANCE

Winning percentage
Average attendance

know. They're the ones who pay the money.'"

▶**July 3:** Henry Rodriguez, who had rocketed to the top of the NL home run derby, hit a 10-for-46 funk before snapping out of it at Coors Field, going 3-for-4 and hitting his 22nd homer. Four games later, he hit two more homers.

▶**July 17:** The Expos announced they will cut ticket prices for 1997, from $28 to $20; from $19 to $10; from $11 to $5 (another 5,656 will be cut from $11 to $10); and from $7 to $5. "We'll be the second-least-expensive ballpark in baseball, behind [Cincinnati's] Riverfront Stadium," said team president Claude Brochu.

▶**July 31:** Starter Ugueth Urbina doesn't pitch innings, according to pitching coach Joe Kerrigan. He pitches "rounds, because he's got a boxer's mentality," said Kerrigan. This approach to pitching has led to Urbina's being touted as the organization's closer of the future.

▶**Aug. 7:** The Expos sent right-handed reliever Tim Scott (3-5, 3.11 ERA) and lefty starter Kirk Rueter (5-6, 4.58) to the Giants for right-hander Mark Leiter. San Francisco picked up the balance of Leiter's $1.5 million contract. Leiter is leading the NL in homers and runs allowed, and in his first start with the Expos he left losing 7-6 after his new teammates had given him a 6-1 lead.

▶**Aug. 21:** One reason Moises Alou appealed a four-game suspension for his part in a brawl against the Astros on Aug. 12 is that he's on a roll, with 17 RBI during a 12-game hitting streak. "The way things are going right now, the last thing I want to do is miss playing time," he said. Alou was one of three Expos suspended after the fight. Henry Rodriguez served his four-game suspension on Aug. 16-19, while reliever Jeff Juden, like Alou, filed an appeal. Juden's four-game suspension was scheduled to begin on Aug. 20.

▶**Aug. 28:** Henry Rodriguez broke the Montreal home run record when he drilled his 33rd on Aug. 25, topping the mark set by Andre Dawson in 1983.

▶**Sept. 4:** Henry Rodriguez strikes out too often, though he says he doesn't pay attention to the numbers. Through Aug. 31 the number was 146, tops in the majors. The fans at Olympic Stadium have stopped throwing Oh Henry! bars and started booing him.

▶**Sept. 11:** Ugueth Urbina's addition to the bullpen has had a trickle-down effect. In the 38⅔ bullpen innings since Urbina made his first relief appearance, opposing teams had 21 hits and scored eight runs, only six earned.

▶**Sept. 18:** Mel Rojas has become money in the bank out of the bullpen. Rojas moved into a tie with John Wetteland for second on the Expos' all-time saves list on Sept. 14 with his 32nd of the season and 105th of his career. Jeff Reardon leads with 152. "He's zoned in right now," manager Alou said of Rojas, who was 32-for-36 in save opportunities; since the All-Star break, he's 2-1 with 20 saves and a 1.39 ERA.

▶**Sept. 25:** The Expos set a club record with 144 homers in a season on Sept. 21 when third baseman Shane Andrews homered off Atlanta's Denny Neagle. In Jeff Fassero and Pedro Martinez the Expos have two pitchers with 200-plus strikeouts in the same season for the first time in club history.

▶**Oct. 2:** The 1996 Expos were Nobody's Team. Nobody picked them to be even remotely in the wild-card race, and almost nobody came to see them at Olympic Stadium. Yet the Expos went into the final weekend of the season with a chance at the NL wild-card berth, even after losing the last four games of a five-game series in Atlanta. The Expos spent 46 days in first place in the NL East before falling out on May 19. From the start of the year until Aug. 27, the Expos were either in first or leading the wild-card. Henry Rodriguez set a club record for homers, and Mel Rojas converted 22 consecutive save opportunities to break John Wetteland's club record. There were also disappointments. The team ground to a halt offensively down the stretch as outfielders Rondell White and Moises Alou went into RBI funks. And 15-game winner Jeff Fassero, named NL Pitcher of the Month twice, came up short in his final two starts against the Braves.

Team directory

▶**Owner:** Montreal Baseball Club Inc., Claude R. Brochu (president and general partner)
▶**General manager:** Jim Beattie
▶**Ballpark:**
Olympic Stadium
4549 Avenue Pierre-de-Coubertin, Montreal, Quebec
514-253-3434
Capacity 46,500
Parking for 4,000 cars; $10
Public transportation available
Wheelchair sections, ramps, extensive food concessions, outfield bleachers
▶**Team publications:**
Media guide, *Expos Magazine*
P.O. Box 500, Station M, Montreal, Que., Canada H1V 3P2
▶**TV, radio broadcast stations:**
CIQC 600 AM, C-TV, TSN (English); CKAC 730 AM, FSRC-TV, RDS TQS (French)
▶**Spring training:**
Municipal Stadium
West Palm Beach, Fla.
Capacity 7,500
561-684-6801

MONTREAL EXPOS 1996 final stats

BATTERS	BA	SLG	OB	G	AB	R	H	TB	2B	3B	HR	RBI	BB	SO	SB	CS	E
Grudzielanek	.306	.397	.340	153	657	99	201	261	34	4	6	49	26	83	33	7	27
White	.293	.428	.340	88	334	35	98	143	19	4	6	41	22	53	14	6	2
Segui	.286	.442	.375	115	416	69	119	184	30	1	11	58	60	54	4	4	7
Stankiewicz	.286	.377	.356	64	77	12	22	29	5	1	0	9	6	12	1	0	3
Lansing	.285	.406	.341	159	641	99	183	260	40	2	11	53	44	85	23	8	11
Alou	.281	.457	.339	143	540	87	152	247	28	2	21	96	49	83	9	4	3
Santangelo	.277	.407	.369	152	393	54	109	160	20	5	7	56	49	61	5	2	6
Rodriguez	.276	.562	.325	145	532	81	147	299	42	1	36	103	37	160	2	0	11
Fletcher	.266	.414	.321	127	394	41	105	163	22	0	12	57	27	42	0	0	6
Obando	.247	.433	.332	89	178	30	44	77	9	0	8	22	22	48	2	0	3
Floyd	.242	.423	.340	117	227	29	55	96	15	4	6	26	30	52	7	1	5
Webster	.230	.322	.332	78	174	18	40	56	10	0	2	17	25	21	0	0	1
Andrews	.227	.429	.295	127	375	43	85	161	15	2	19	64	35	119	3	1	15
Silvestri	.204	.247	.340	86	162	16	33	40	4	0	1	17	34	41	2	1	10
Chavez	.200	.200	.333	4	5	1	1	1	0	0	0	0	1	1	1	0	0
Guerrero	.185	.296	.185	9	27	2	5	8	0	0	1	1	0	3	0	0	0
Benitez	.167	.167	.167	11	12	0	2	2	0	0	0	2	0	4	0	0	1
Spehr	.091	.182	.167	63	44	4	4	8	1	0	1	3	3	15	1	0	2
Barron	.000	.000	.000	1	1	0	0	0	0	0	0	0	0	1	0	0	0
Lukachyk	.000	.000	.000	2	2	0	0	0	0	0	0	0	0	1	0	0	0
Schu	.000	.000	.000	4	4	0	0	0	0	0	0	0	0	0	0	0	1

PITCHERS	W-L	ERA	G	GS	CG	GF	Sho	SV	IP	H	R	ER	HR	BB	SO
Alvarez	2-1	3.00	11	5	0	3	0	0	21.0	19	10	7	0	12	9
Rojas	7-4	3.22	74	0	0	64	0	36	81.0	56	30	29	5	28	92
Manuel	4-1	3.24	53	0	0	7	0	0	86.0	70	34	31	10	26	62
Juden	5-0	3.27	58	0	0	16	0	0	74.1	61	35	27	8	34	61
Fassero	15-11	3.30	34	34	5	0	1	0	231.2	217	95	85	20	55	222
Aucoin	0-1	3.38	2	0	0	0	0	0	2.2	3	1	1	0	1	1
Paniagua	2-4	3.53	13	11	0	0	0	0	51.0	55	24	20	7	23	27
Martinez	13-10	3.70	33	33	4	0	1	0	216.2	189	100	89	19	70	222
Urbina	10-5	3.71	33	17	0	2	0	0	114.0	102	54	47	18	44	108
Daal	4-5	4.02	64	6	0	9	0	0	87.1	74	40	39	10	37	82
Cormier	7-10	4.17	33	27	1	1	1	0	159.2	165	80	74	16	41	100
Veres	6-3	4.17	68	0	0	22	0	4	77.2	85	39	36	10	32	81
Dyer	5-5	4.40	70	1	0	20	0	2	75.2	79	40	37	7	34	51
Leiter	8-12	4.92	35	34	2	0	0	0	205.0	219	128	112	37	69	164
Leiper	2-1	7.20	33	0	0	8	0	0	25.0	40	21	20	4	9	13
Pacheco	0-0	11.12	5	0	0	2	0	0	5.2	8	7	7	2	1	7

1997 preliminary roster

PITCHERS (19)
Tavo Alvarez
Derek Aucoin
Jason Baker
Rheal Cormier
Omar Daal
Steve Falteisek
Jeff Juden
Barry Manuel
Pedro Martinez
Jose Paniagua
Carlos Perez

Tom Phelps
Everett Stull
Mike Thurman
Ugueth Urbina
Marc Valdes
Dave Veres
Matt Wagner
Neil Weber

CATCHERS (5)
Raul Chavez
Darrin Fletcher

Bob Henley
Tim Laker
Chris Widger

INFIELDERS (7)
Israel Alcantara
Shane Andrews
Orlando Cabrera
Mark Grudzielanek
Mike Lansing
Ryan McGuire
David Segui

OUTFIELDERS (8)
Yamil Benitez
Cliff Floyd
Vladimir Guerrero
Sherman Obando
Henry Rodriguez
F.P. Santangelo
Darond Stovall
Rondell White

Games played by position

PLAYER	G	C	1B	2B	3B	SS	OF
Alou	143	0	0	0	0	0	142
Andrews	127	0	0	0	123	0	0
Barron	1	0	0	0	0	0	0
Benitez	11	0	0	0	0	0	4
Chavez	4	3	0	0	0	0	0
Fletcher	127	112	0	0	0	0	0
Floyd	117	0	2	0	0	0	85
Grudzielanek	153	0	0	0	0	153	0
Guerrero	9	0	0	0	0	0	8
Lansing	159	0	0	159	0	2	0
Lukachyk	2	0	0	0	0	0	0
Obando	89	0	0	0	0	0	47
Rodriguez	145	0	51	0	0	0	89
Santangelo	152	0	0	5	23	1	124
Schu	1	0	0	0	1	0	0
Segui	115	0	113	0	0	0	0
Silvestri	86	0	1	1	47	10	2
Spehr	63	58	0	0	0	0	1
Stankiewicz	64	0	0	19	1	13	0
Webster	78	63	0	0	0	0	0
White	88	0	0	0	0	0	86

Minor Leagues

Tops in the organization

BATTER	CLUB	AVG.	G	AB	R	H	HR	RBI
V. Guerrero	Hrb	.360	138	497	100	179	24	96
H. Bocachica	WPb	.328	80	299	61	98	2	28
Jalal Leach	Ott	.325	120	369	50	120	9	57
Steve Bieser	Ott	.322	123	382	63	123	1	32
Tony Barron	Ott	.315	123	461	70	145	19	71

HOME RUNS
V. Guerrero	Hrb	24
Yamil Benitez	Ott	23
Tony Barron	Ott	19
Jose Vidro	Hrb	18
Several Players Tied At		14

WINS
Javier Vazquez	Del	14
Jose Paniagua	Ott	12
Tom Phelps	Hrb	12
Jeremy Powell	Del	12
Several Players Tied At		10

RBI
V. Guerrero	Hrb	96
Jose Vidro	Hrb	82
Yamil Benitez	Ott	81
Brad Fullmer	Hrb	77
Several Players Tied At		71

SAVES
Ben Fleetham	Hrb	31
Kirk Bullinger	Hrb	22
Tim Young	Vmt	18
Curt Schmidt	Ott	13
Several Players Tied At		12

STOLEN BASES
O. Cabrera	Del	51
Edward Bady	WPb	42
Jose Macias	Del	38
Jim Buccheri	Ott	33
Wes Denning	Del	31

STRIKEOUTS
Javier Vazquez	Del	173
Troy Mattes	Del	151
Everett Stull	Ott	150
Jason Baker	Del	147
Several Players Tied At		109

PITCHER	CLUB	W-L	ERA	IP	H	BB	SO
J. Paniagua	Ott	12-5	2.62	103	84	25	77
J. Vazquez	Del	14-3	2.68	164	138	57	173
Tom Phelps	Hrb	12-4	2.77	159	148	54	94
Jason Baker	Del	9-7	2.81	160	127	77	147
Troy Mattes	Del	10-9	2.86	173	142	50	151

Sick call: 1996 DL report

PLAYER	Days on the DL
Moises Alou	15
Tavo Alvarez	16
Rheal Cormier	18
Tim Laker	182
Sherman Obando	19
Jose Paniagua	21
Carlos Perez	182
Kirk Rueter	16
David Segui	43
Tim Spehr	19
Andy Stankiewicz	20
Rondell White	79

1996 salaries

	Bonuses	Total earned salary
Moises Alou, of	$50,000	$3,050,000
Jeff Fassero, p		$2,800,000
Mel Rojas, p		$2,025,000
Mark Leiter, p	$350,000	$1,850,000
David Segui, 1b		$1,550,000
Darrin Fletcher, c		$1,125,000
Rheal Cormier, p		$950,000
Mike Lansing, 2b		$315,000
Pedro Martinez, p		$315,000
Rondell White, of		$300,000
Henry Rodriguez, of	$10,000	$220,000
Dave Veres, p		$200,000
Lenny Webster, c	$30,000	$200,000
Andy Stankiewicz, ss		$190,000
Mike Dyer, p		$175,000
Sherman Obando, of		$165,000
Carlos Perez, p		$165,000
Omar Daal, p		$156,000
Cliff Floyd, of		$150,000
Tim Spehr, c		$150,000
Shane Andrews, 3b		$135,000
Mark Grudzielanek, ss		$135,000
Dave Silvestri, ss		$132,500
Tim Laker, c		$121,000
F.P. Santangelo, of		$121,000
Barry Manuel, p		$120,000
Jeff Juden, p	$4,000	$119,000
Ugueth Urbina, p		$112,000
Jose Paniagua, p		$109,000
Raul Chavez, c		$109,000

Average 1996 salary: $575,483
Total 1996 team payroll: $17,264,500
Termination pay: None

Montreal (1969-1996)

Runs: Most, career

934	TIM RAINES, 1979-1990
828	A. DAWSON, 1976-1986
737	TIM WALLACH, 1980-1992
707	Gary Carter, 1974-1992
446	Warren Cromartie, 1974-1983

Hits: Most, career

1694	TIM WALLACH, 1980-1992
1598	TIM RAINES, 1979-1990
1575	A. DAWSON, 1976-1986
1427	Gary Carter, 1974-1992
1063	Warren Cromartie, 1974-1983

2B: Most, career

360	TIM WALLACH, 1980-1992
295	ANDRE DAWSON, 1976-1986
274	Gary Carter, 1974-1992
273	TIM RAINES, 1979-1990
222	Warren Cromartie, 1974-1983

3B: Most, career

81	TIM RAINES, 1979-1990
67	ANDRE DAWSON, 1976-1986
31	TIM WALLACH, 1980-1992
30	Warren Cromartie, 1974-1983
25	DELINO DeSHIELDS, 1990-1993
25	Mitch Webster, 1985-1988

HR: Most, career

225	ANDRE DAWSON, 1976-1986
220	Gary Carter, 1974-1992
204	TIM WALLACH, 1980-1992
118	Bob Bailey, 1969-1975
106	ANDRES GALARRAGA, 1985-1991

RBI: Most, career

905	TIM WALLACH, 1980-1992
838	ANDRE DAWSON, 1976-1986
823	Gary Carter, 1974-1992
552	TIM RAINES, 1979-1990
466	Bob Bailey, 1969-1975

SB: Most, career

634	TIM RAINES, 1979-1990
266	MARQUIS GRISSOM, 1989-1994
253	ANDRE DAWSON, 1976-1986
187	DELINO DeSHIELDS, 1990-1993
139	Rodney Scott, 1976-1982

BB: Most, career

775	TIM RAINES, 1979-1990
582	Gary Carter, 1974-1992
514	TIM WALLACH, 1980-1992
502	Bob Bailey, 1969-1975
370	Ron Fairly, 1969-1974

BA: Highest, career

.301	TIM RAINES, 1979-1990
.294	Rusty Staub, 1969-1979
.292	MOISES ALOU, 1990-1996
.288	Ellis Valentine, 1975-1981
.282	LARRY WALKER, 1989-1994

Slug avg: Highest, career

.497	Rusty Staub, 1969-1979
.489	MOISES ALOU, 1990-1996
.483	LARRY WALKER, 1989-1994
.476	ANDRE DAWSON, 1976-1986
.476	Ellis Valentine, 1975-1981

On-base avg: Highest, career

.402	Rusty Staub, 1969-1979
.390	TIM RAINES, 1979-1990
.390	Ron Hunt, 1971-1974
.381	Ron Fairly, 1969-1974
.368	Bob Bailey, 1969-1975

Complete games: Most, career

129	Steve Rogers, 1973-1985
46	Bill Stoneman, 1969-1973
41	DENNIS MARTINEZ, 1986-1993
40	Steve Renko, 1969-1976
31	Bill Gullickson, 1979-1985

Saves: Most, career

152	Jeff Reardon, 1981-1986
109	MEL ROJAS, 1990-1996
105	J. WETTELAND, 1992-1994
101	Tim Burke, 1985-1991
75	Mike Marshall, 1970-1973

Shutouts: Most, career

37	Steve Rogers, 1973-1985
15	Bill Stoneman, 1969-1973
13	DENNIS MARTINEZ, 1986-1993
8	Woodie Fryman, 1975-1983
8	Charlie Lea, 1980-1987
8	SCOTT SANDERSON, 1978-1983
8	Bryn Smith, 1981-1989

Wins: Most, career

158	Steve Rogers, 1973-1985
100	D. MARTINEZ, 1986-1993
81	Bryn Smith, 1981-1989
72	Bill Gullickson, 1979-1985
68	Steve Renko, 1969-1976

K: Most, career

1621	Steve Rogers, 1973-1985
973	D. MARTINEZ, 1986-1993
838	Bryn Smith, 1981-1989
831	Bill Stoneman, 1969-1973
810	Steve Renko, 1969-1976

Win pct: Highest, career

.661	KEN HILL, 1992-1994
.623	Tim Burke, 1985-1991
.581	DENNIS MARTINEZ, 1986-1993
.573	Charlie Lea, 1980-1987
.556	Mike Torrez, 1971-1974

ERA: Lowest, career

3.06	DENNIS MARTINEZ, 1986-1993
3.17	Steve Rogers, 1973-1985
3.20	JEFF FASSERO, 1991-1996
3.28	Bryn Smith, 1981-1989
3.32	Charlie Lea, 1980-1987

Runs: Most, season

133	TIM RAINES, 1983
123	TIM RAINES, 1987
115	TIM RAINES, 1985
107	ANDRE DAWSON, 1982
106	TIM RAINES, 1984

Hits: Most, season

204	Al Oliver, 1982
201	M. GRUDZIELANEK, 1996
194	TIM RAINES, 1986
192	TIM RAINES, 1984
189	ANDRE DAWSON, 1983

2B: Most, season

46	Warren Cromartie, 1979
44	LARRY WALKER, 1994
43	Al Oliver, 1982
42	Dave Cash, 1977
42	ANDRES GALARRAGA, 1988
42	HENRY RODRIGUEZ, 1996
42	TIM WALLACH, 1987
42	TIM WALLACH, 1989

3B: Most, season

13	TIM RAINES, 1985
13	Rodney Scott, 1980
13	Mitch Webster, 1986
12	ANDRE DAWSON, 1979
11	Ron LeFlore, 1980

HR: Most, season

36   HENRY RODRIGUEZ, 1996
32   ANDRE DAWSON, 1983
31   Gary Carter, 1977
30   Larry Parrish, 1979
30   Rusty Staub, 1970

RBI: Most, season

123   TIM WALLACH, 1987
113   ANDRE DAWSON, 1983
109   Al Oliver, 1982
106   Gary Carter, 1984
103   HENRY RODRIGUEZ, 1996
103   Ken Singleton, 1973

SB: Most, season

97   Ron LeFlore, 1980
90   TIM RAINES, 1983
78   MARQUIS GRISSOM, 1992
78   TIM RAINES, 1982
76   MARQUIS GRISSOM, 1991

BB: Most, season

123   Ken Singleton, 1973
112   Rusty Staub, 1970
110   Rusty Staub, 1969
100   Bob Bailey, 1974
97   Bob Bailey, 1971
97   TIM RAINES, 1983

BA: Highest, season

.339   MOISES ALOU, 1994
.334   TIM RAINES, 1986
.331   Al Oliver, 1982
.330   TIM RAINES, 1987
.322   LARRY WALKER, 1994

Slug avg: Highest, season

.592   MOISES ALOU, 1994
.587   LARRY WALKER, 1994
.562   HENRY RODRIGUEZ, 1996
.553   ANDRE DAWSON, 1981
.551   Larry Parrish, 1979

On-base avg: Highest, season

.429   TIM RAINES, 1987
.426   Rusty Staub, 1969
.425   Ken Singleton, 1973
.422   Ron Fairly, 1973
.413   TIM RAINES, 1986

Complete games: Most, season

20   Bill Stoneman, 1971
19   Ross Grimsley, 1978
17   Steve Rogers, 1977
14   Steve Rogers, 1980
14   Steve Rogers, 1982

Saves: Most, season

43   JOHN WETTELAND, 1993
41   Jeff Reardon, 1985

---

37   JOHN WETTELAND, 1992
36   MEL ROJAS, 1996
35   Jeff Reardon, 1986

Shutouts: Most, season

5   DENNIS MARTINEZ, 1991
5   Steve Rogers, 1979
5   Steve Rogers, 1983
5   Bill Stoneman, 1969
4   MARK LANGSTON, 1989
4   Charlie Lea, 1983
4   Carl Morton, 1970
4   Steve Rogers, 1976
4   Steve Rogers, 1977
4   Steve Rogers, 1980
4   Steve Rogers, 1982
4   Bill Stoneman, 1972

Wins: Most, season

20   Ross Grimsley, 1978
19   Steve Rogers, 1982
18   Carl Morton, 1970
18   Bryn Smith, 1985
17   Bill Gullickson, 1983
17   Steve Rogers, 1977
17   Steve Rogers, 1983
17   Bill Stoneman, 1971

K: Most, season

251   Bill Stoneman, 1971
222   JEFF FASSERO, 1996
222   PEDRO MARTINEZ, 1996
206   Steve Rogers, 1977
202   Floyd Youmans, 1986

Win pct: Highest, season

.783   Bryn Smith, 1985
.762   KEN HILL, 1994
.704   Steve Rogers, 1982
.696   DENNIS MARTINEZ, 1989
.652   Mike Torrez, 1974
.652   Dale Murray, 1975

ERA: Lowest, season

2.39   DENNIS MARTINEZ, 1991
2.39   MARK LANGSTON, 1989
2.40   Steve Rogers, 1982
2.44   Pascual Perez, 1988
2.47   DENNIS MARTINEZ, 1992

Most pinch-hit homers, season

4   Hal Breeden, 1973
3   CLIFF FLOYD, 1996

Most pinch-hit homers, career

5   Jose Morales, 1973-1977
4   Hal Breeden, 1972-75
4   Jerry White, 1974-83

Longest hitting streak

21   DELINO DeSHIELDS, 1993
19   Warren Cromartie, 1979
19   ANDRE DAWSON, 1980
18   Pepe Mangual, 1975
18   Warren Cromartie, 1980
18   DAVID SEGUI, 1995

Most consecutive scoreless innings

32   Woodie Fryman, 1975

No-hit games

Bill Stoneman, Mon at Phi NL, 7-0; Apr. 17, 1969.
Bill Stoneman, Mon vs NY NL, 7-0; Oct. 2, 1972 (1st game).
Charlie Lea, Mon vs SF NL, 4-0; May 10, 1981 (2nd game).
MARK GARDNER, Mon at LA NL, 0-1; July 26, 1991 (9 innings, lost on 2 hits in 10th, relieved by JEFF FASSERO, who allowed 1 more hit).
DENNIS MARTINEZ, Mon at LA NL, 2-0; July 28, 1991 (perfect game).
PEDRO J. MARTINEZ (9 innings) and MEL ROJAS (1 inning), Mon at SD NL, 1-0; June 3,1995 (Martinez pitched 9 perfect innings, but allowed a hit in the 10th, Rojas relieved and finished the game).
David Palmer, five perfect innings, rain, Mon at StL NL, 4-0; Apr. 21, 1984 (2nd game).
Pascual Perez, five innings, rain, Mon at Phi NL, 1-0; Sept. 24, 1988.

ACTIVE PLAYERS in caps.

Players' years of service are listed by the first and last years with this team and are not necessarily consecutive; all statistics record performances for this team only.

Florida Marlins

Gary Sheffield was a one-man show for Florida and led the NL in on-base average.

By Porter Binks, USA TODAY

1996 Marlins: Arms, Sheffield not enough

The Marlins were underachievers for much of the season, but considering their troubles, they ended up with a surprisingly good record. Florida came within a last-game loss of its first .500 season. Right fielder Gary Sheffield, the team's star, put together what he rightfully classified as a "monster year," and the rest of the offense began to come together under the leadership of new manager John Boles after the All-Star break. Boles, who replaced the fired Rene Lachemann, had a 40-35 record but moved back to his former job as vice president of player development when the Marlins lured manager Jim Leyland from Pittsburgh after the season.

"I'll leave this season feeling good about what we've done as a team and a staff," said Boles, 48, who had never managed in the majors before. "I didn't want to be replaced because I couldn't do the job." General manager Dave Dombrowski gives Boles glowing reviews, and said if Leyland hadn't been hired, Boles would have been brought back to manage.

Throughout the season, right-hander Kevin Brown was brilliant on the mound, posting a 17-11 record that wasn't as indicative of his performance as was his major-league-leading 1.89 ERA. Brown had the worst run support among NL pitchers, as the Marlins scored only 11 runs in his 11 losses. Brown had 159 strikeouts and only 33 walks in 233 innings, and was the only starting pitcher in the majors to put on base less than a man per inning by hit or walk. "I've said all along that he is just as deserving of the Cy Young Award as anybody," said Atlanta's John Smoltz, whose 24-8 record made him the winner. "[Brown] has been flat-out outstanding." In addition, the Marlins got a career-best season from lefty Al Leiter, who was 16-12 and finished third in the league with a 2.93 ERA.

Sheffield hit .314 with 42 home runs and 120 RBI. His 142 walks indicated that he needed more protection in the batting order. In November the Marlins signed Bobby Bonilla, who hit 28 homers and

drove in 116 runs for Baltimore, to provide it.

First baseman Greg Colbrunn (16 HR, 69 RBI) and infielder Kurt Abbott (.253, 8 HR, 33 RBI) didn't perform to expectations, but the Marlins got major boosts from rookies Edgar Renteria (.309) and Luis Castillo (.262, 17 stolen bases in 41 games) in the middle of the infield. Renteria, called up from Class AAA in May, had the second-best fielding percentage among NL shortstops, and second baseman Castillo, called up from Class AA in August, has good speed and far better range than Quilvio Veras, who was demoted to the minors and then traded to the San Diego Padres after the season. Though he made a few uncharacteristic errors early, center fielder Devon White played well after the All-Star break; the former American Leaguer appeared to be more comfortable the second time through NL ballparks. Besides his numerous homer-saving catches, White had 49 RBI after Boles switched him to the fifth spot in the batting order.

Two things remained consistent under both Lachemann and Boles: The bullpen was inadequate apart from closer Robb Nen, who had 36 saves and a 1.95 ERA, and the Marlins had a terrible time on the road, tying the Colorado Rockies for the NL's worst with a 28-53 away record.

1996 Marlins: Week-by-week notes

These notes were excerpted from the following issues of Baseball Weekly.

▶**April 10:** Kevin Brown didn't get a victory in his first two starts, but he earned the confidence of his new teammates. He allowed just one earned run in 15 innings and has an 0-1 record to show for his efforts.

▶**April 17:** The Marlins are off to a disappointing 4-8 start, and it is easy to pinpoint the main problem: The team is averaging just 2.3 runs per game and was shut out in consecutive games at San Diego and Los Angeles last week.

▶**May 1:** Catcher Charles Johnson started out hot, going 10-for-30 (.333) in the first nine games, but was on a 4-for-23 (.174) downslide last week, with his average falling to .222.

▶**May 8:** Manager Rene Lachemann hopes the bottom was reached when the Marlins were humiliated by the Rockies in a 17-5 rout at Coors Field on May 4—Lachemann's 51st birthday. It was their sixth loss in seven games.

▶**May 15:** Center fielder Devon White, who had a dreadful first month with the Marlins, began hitting two weeks ago and had a 4-for-5 game against Colorado on May 9 that raised his average from .242 to .271.

▶**May 22:** It's been the streakiest of seasons for the Marlins, who followed a five-game losing skid with a franchise record nine-game winning streak that ended on May 15 against St. Louis.

▶**May 29:** Everybody knew Edgar Renteria was the Marlins' shortstop of the future. But few expected the future to arrive so soon. Impressed by Renteria's fill-in performance while Kurt Abbott was on the DL, the Marlins kept the Colombian youngster in the majors and optioned Abbott to Class AAA Charlotte on May 20. Renteria, 20, is the youngest player in the majors and is said to have been a year younger than advertised so that he could sign in 1992, when, his mother says, he was only 15.

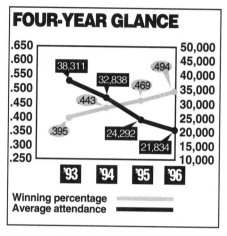

FOUR-YEAR GLANCE

38,311 · 494
.395 · .443 · 32,838 · .469
24,292 · 21,834

'93 '94 '95 '96

Winning percentage
Average attendance

▶**June 5:** Second baseman Quilvio Veras has not responded to treatment for an injured hamstring, so the Marlins are going with an all-rookie middle infield of Edgar Renteria and second baseman Ralph Milliard.

▶**June 12:** Kevin Brown has the best ERA (2.09) in the majors, and perhaps the worst luck. He had only a 4-4 record through June 10 because of poor run support, and he's battled leg injuries all season. He missed two starts after being struck in the lower right leg twice by line drives.

▶**June 26:** Closer Robb Nen called his June performance "an embarrassment" and "a joke." Through June 22, he had blown four saves in seven chances and allowed seven earned runs in 12⅓ innings in the month. In May, Nen converted all seven save opportunities and didn't allow an earned run in 14 innings.

▶**July 3:** Pitchers Kevin Brown and Al Leiter have more than lived up to advance billing, combining for 41% of Florida's victories through June and posting a 2.06 ERA between them. Brown (7-5, 1.89) had the majors' best ERA, and Leiter (9-6, 2.23) wasn't far behind.

▶**July 11:** Convinced that the 40-47 (as of July 7) Marlins were not doing what was necessary to turn the season around, GM Dave Dombrowski fired Rene Lachemann. Tapped as the new manager was John Boles, 47, who as the team's vice president of player development knows the young Marlins, current and incoming.

▶**July 17:** John Boles is stressing team unity. "I just asked for five things," Boles said of his first team meeting. "That we stretch together, take batting practice together, take infield together, stand together for the national anthem and play hard."

▶**July 31:** The honeymoon is wearing off quickly for John Boles, whose Marlins lost five of seven games through July 28 after winning seven of their first 10 under the new manager. The Marlins averaged 7.2 runs in their first 11 games under Boles and new hitting coach Jeff Pentland, then came back to reality, totaling only 10 runs over a five-game stretch.

▶**Aug. 7:** The Marlins made a team-record six errors on Aug. 1 and allowed a season-high five stolen bases before catcher Bob Natal was replaced by Joe Siddall. Any questions about how much the Marlins miss injured catcher Charles Johnson, on the DL since July 28, were answered. While the Marlins have floundered, outfielder Gary Sheffield has been putting together a great season. Through Aug. 4, Sheffield was batting .314 with 29 home runs, 80 RBI and a career-high 87 walks.

▶**Aug. 14:** Those wild-card playoff aspirations are officially dead for the Marlins. General manager Dave Dombrowski conceded that on Aug. 8, when he traded pitcher John Burkett to the Texas Rangers for prospects and demoted second baseman Quilvio Veras and reliever Yorkis Perez to the minors in order to get a good look at some prospects.

▶**Aug. 21:** Gary Sheffield may have sealed his fate with the Marlins when he launched into a 10-minute tirade against GM Dave Dombrowski on Aug. 16, telling reporters that Dombrowski has lied to him repeatedly during the past three years. Speculation is that Sheffield will get a first-hand look at Dombrowski's abilities when the slugger is traded before the end of his contract, which runs through 1997.

▶**Sept. 18:** One week ago the Marlins were excited. They had won 11 of 15 games and were talking about catching second-place Montreal. But Florida dropped five of seven through Sept. 15 and is struggling to stay ahead of the fourth-place Mets.

▶**Sept. 25:** The Marlins are considered the favorite to land soon-to-be ex-Pirates manager Jim Leyland, who wants to join a team that can spend the money to become a contender. John Boles is signed to manage through 1997 but said he would be pleased to move back to his former job if the Marlins can lure Leyland.

▶**Oct. 2:** For a team that went through two managers and was led by a hot-tempered star who publicly called the team's general manager a liar, the Marlins ended with a surprisingly good record. The fiery star, Gary Sheffield, had a .314 average and 42 homers, and the rest of the offense began to perform under John Boles after the All-Star break. Kevin Brown was an unrelenting force on the mound, with a major-league-leading 1.89 ERA to go with a hard-luck 17-11 record, and Al Leiter (16-12, 2.93 ERA) was also outstanding. The bullpen was shaky, however, and the team had a woeful 28-53 road record.

Team directory

▶**Owner:** H. Wayne Huizenga
▶**General manager:**
David Dombrowski
▶**Ballpark:**
Pro Player Stadium
2267 N.W. 199th St.
Miami, Fla.
305-626-7400
Capacity 41,855
Parking 24,137 cars; $5
Public transportation available
Wheelchair section, family section, alcohol-free section, ramps and elevators
▶**TV, radio broadcast stations:**
WQAM 560 AM (English), WCMQ 1210 AM (Spanish), WBFS Channel 33, Sunshine Network/Sports Channel
▶**Spring Training:**
Space Coast Stadium
Melbourne, Fla.
Capacity 7,200
407-633-9200

FLORIDA MARLINS 1996 final stats

BATTERS	BA	SLG	OB	G	AB	R	H	TB	2B	3B	HR	RBI	BB	SO	SB	CS	E
Booty	.500	.500	.500	2	2	1	1	1	0	0	0	0	0	0	0	0	0
Brooks	.400	.800	.571	8	5	2	2	4	0	1	0	3	1	1	0	0	1
Sheffield	.314	.624	.465	161	519	118	163	324	33	1	42	120	142	66	16	9	6
Renteria	.309	.399	.358	106	431	68	133	172	18	3	5	31	33	68	16	2	11
Conine	.293	.484	.360	157	597	84	175	289	32	2	26	95	62	121	1	4	8
Zaun	.290	.419	.353	10	31	4	9	13	1	0	1	2	3	5	1	0	0
Colbrunn	.286	.438	.333	141	511	60	146	224	26	2	16	69	25	76	4	5	6
Arias	.277	.384	.335	100	224	27	62	86	11	2	3	26	17	28	2	0	7
Dawson	.276	.414	.311	42	58	6	16	24	2	0	2	14	2	13	0	0	1
White	.274	.455	.325	146	552	77	151	251	37	6	17	84	38	99	22	6	4
Castillo	.262	.305	.320	41	164	26	43	50	2	1	1	8	14	46	17	4	3
Abbott	.253	.428	.307	109	320	37	81	137	18	7	8	33	22	99	3	3	12
Veras	.253	.340	.381	73	253	40	64	86	8	1	4	14	51	42	8	8	5
Orsulak	.221	.286	.274	120	217	23	48	62	6	1	2	19	16	38	1	1	4
Tavarez	.219	.246	.264	98	114	14	25	28	3	0	0	6	7	18	5	1	0
Johnson	.218	.358	.292	120	386	34	84	138	13	1	13	37	40	91	1	0	4
McMillon	.216	.216	.286	28	51	4	11	11	0	0	0	4	5	14	0	0	0
Grebeck	.211	.253	.245	50	95	8	20	24	1	0	1	9	4	14	0	0	2
Morman	.167	.333	.286	6	6	0	1	2	1	0	0	0	1	2	0	0	0
Milliard	.161	.194	.312	24	62	7	10	12	2	0	0	1	14	16	2	0	5
Siddall	.149	.170	.184	18	47	0	7	8	1	0	0	3	2	8	0	0	2
Natal	.133	.167	.257	44	90	4	12	15	1	1	0	2	15	31	0	1	5

PITCHERS	W-L	ERA	G	GS	CG	GF	Sho	SV	IP	H	R	ER	HR	BB	SO
Hernandez	0-0	0.00	1	0	0	0	0	0	3.0	3	0	0	0	2	2
Hurst	0-0	0.00	2	0	0	2	0	0	2.0	3	0	0	0	1	1
Larkin	0-0	1.80	1	1	0	0	0	0	5.0	3	1	1	0	4	2
Brown	17-11	1.89	32	32	5	0	3	0	233.0	187	60	49	8	33	159
Helling	2-1	1.95	5	4	0	0	0	0	27.2	14	6	6	2	7	26
Nen	5-1	1.95	75	0	0	66	0	35	83.0	67	21	18	2	21	92
Leiter	16-12	2.93	33	33	2	0	1	0	215.1	153	74	70	14	119	200
Hutton	5-1	3.67	13	9	0	0	0	0	56.1	47	23	23	6	18	31
F. Heredia	1-1	4.32	21	0	0	5	0	0	16.2	21	8	8	1	10	10
Burkett	6-10	4.32	24	24	1	0	0	0	154.0	154	84	74	15	42	108
Pena	0-1	4.50	4	0	0	3	0	0	4.0	4	5	2	2	1	5
Powell	4-3	4.54	67	0	0	16	0	2	71.1	71	41	36	5	36	52
Weathers	2-2	4.54	31	8	0	8	0	0	71.1	85	41	36	7	28	40
Valdes	1-3	4.81	11	8	0	0	0	0	48.2	63	32	26	5	23	13
Mathews	2-4	4.91	57	0	0	19	0	4	55.0	59	33	30	7	27	49
Rapp	8-16	5.10	30	29	0	1	0	0	162.1	184	95	92	12	91	86
Perez	3-4	5.29	64	0	0	15	0	0	47.2	51	28	28	2	31	47
Batista	0-0	5.56	9	0	0	4	0	0	11.1	9	8	7	0	7	6
Pall	1-1	5.79	12	0	0	2	0	0	18.2	16	15	12	3	9	9
Mantei	1-0	6.38	14	0	0	1	0	0	18.1	13	13	13	2	21	25
Hammond	5-8	6.56	38	9	0	5	0	0	81.0	104	65	59	14	27	50
Miller	1-3	6.80	26	5	0	6	0	0	46.1	57	41	35	5	33	30
Adamson	0-0	7.36	9	0	0	1	0	0	11.0	18	9	9	1	7	7

1997 preliminary roster

PITCHERS (22)
Antonio Alfonseca
Kevin Brown
Dennis Cook
Victor Darensbourg
Alex Fernandez
Rick Helling
Felix Heredia
Dustin Hermanson
Livan Hernandez
Bill Hurst
Mark Hutton
Andy Larkin

Al Leiter
Matt Mantei
Kurt Miller
Robb Nen
Jay Powell
Pat Rapp
Tony Saunders
Rob Stanifer
Bryan Ward
Matt Whisenant

CATCHERS (2)
Charles Johnson
Gregg Zaun

INFIELDERS (6)
Kurt Abbott
Alex Arias
Bobby Bonilla
Luis Castillo
Ralph Milliard
Edgar Renteria

OUTFIELDERS (9)
Moises Alou
John Cangelosi
Jeff Conine
Todd Dunwoody
Jim Eisenreich
Billy McMillon
Joe Orsulak
Gary Sheffield
Devon White

Games played by position

PLAYER	G	C	1B	2B	3B	SS	OF
Abbott	109	0	0	20	33	44	0
Arias	100	0	1	1	59	20	0
Booty	2	0	0	0	1	0	0
Brooks	8	0	1	0	0	0	2
Castillo	41	0	0	41	0	0	0
Colbrunn	141	0	134	0	0	0	0
Conine	157	0	48	0	0	0	128
Dawson	42	0	0	0	0	0	6
Grebeck	50	0	0	29	1	2	0
Johnson	120	120	0	0	0	0	0
McMillon	28	0	0	0	0	0	15
Milliard	24	0	0	24	0	0	0
Morman	6	0	2	0	0	0	0
Natal	44	43	0	0	0	0	0
Orsulak	120	0	2	0	0	0	59
Renteria	106	0	0	0	0	106	0
Sheffield	161	0	0	0	0	0	161
Siddall	18	18	0	0	0	0	0
Tavarez	98	0	0	0	0	0	65
Veras	73	0	0	67	0	0	0
White	146	0	0	0	0	0	139
Zaun	10	10	0	0	0	0	0

Minor Leagues

Tops in the organization

BATTER	CLUB	AVG.	G	AB	R	H	HR	RBI
Billy McMillon	Chr	.352	97	347	72	122	17	70
Russ Morman	Chr	.332	80	289	59	96	18	77
Jose Olmeda	Chr	.320	115	375	52	120	9	49
Kevin Millar	Prt	.318	130	472	69	150	18	86
Luis Castillo	Prt	.317	109	420	83	133	1	35

HOME RUNS

Jerry Brooks	Chr	34
T. Dunwoody	Prt	24
Tommy Gregg	Chr	22
Josh Booty	Knc	21
Several Players Tied At		18

WINS

Victor Hurtado	Knc	15
Tony Saunders	Prt	13
L. Hernandez	Prt	11
R. Mendoza	Chr	11
Several Players Tied At		10

RBI

Jerry Brooks	Chr	107
T. Dunwoody	Prt	93
Josh Booty	Knc	87
Kevin Millar	Prt	86
Tommy Gregg	Chr	80

SAVES

William Hurst	Prt	30
Donn Pall	Chr	17
Nigel Alejo	Bre	11
Gary Santoro	Knc	9
Gabe Gonzalez	Bre	9

STOLEN BASES

Luis Castillo	Prt	51
Amaury Garcia	Knc	37
Randy Winn	Knc	30
Matt Brunson	Bre	28
Julio Ramirez	Mrl	28

STRIKEOUTS

Tony Saunders	Prt	156
L. Hernandez	Prt	140
Victor Hurtado	Knc	126
Bryan Ward	Prt	124
Scott Dewitt	Knc	119

PITCHER	CLUB	W-L	ERA	IP	H	BB	SO
Travis Burgus	Knc	5-4	1.78	96	80	39	111
Tony Saunders	Prt	13-4	2.63	168	121	62	156
Gregg Press	Bre	9-9	2.75	150	134	37	90
Victor Hurtado	Knc	15-7	3.27	176	167	56	126
Daniel Vardijan	Knc	7-7	3.35	145	128	55	92

Sick call: 1996 DL report

PLAYER	Days on the DL
Kurt Abbott	38
Kevin Brown	15
Greg Colbrunn	15
Andre Dawson	79*
Craig Grebeck	40
Chris Hammond	35
Wilson Heredia	182
Charles Johnson	35
Andy Larkin	67
Matt Mantei	103
Terry Mathews	15
Alejandro Pena	169
Jay Powell	20
Edgar Renteria	17
Quilvio Veras	42

Indicates two separate terms on Disabled List.

1996 salaries

	Bonuses	Total earned salary
Gary Sheffield, of	$35,000	$6,135,000
Kevin Brown, p	$50,000	$3,375,000
Devon White, of		$3,000,000
Al Leiter, p	$50,000	$2,750,000
Jeff Conine, of		$1,800,000
Chris Hammond, p		$1,600,000
Greg Colbrunn, 1b		$1,200,000
Alejandro Pena, p		$750,000
Joe Orsulak, of		$625,000
Andre Dawson, of		$500,000
Alex Arias, 3b		$412,500
Craig Grebeck, ss		$400,000
Robb Nen, p		$340,000
Kurt Abbott, ss		$250,000
Charles Johnson, c		$220,000
Yorkis Perez, p		$187,500
Bob Natal, c		$165,000
Gregg Zaun, c		$140,000
Jesus Tavarez, of		$134,000
Matt Mantei, p		$130,000
Miguel Batista, p		$120,000
Mark Hutton, p		$119,000
Wilson Heredia, p		$118,000
Kurt Miller, p		$118,000
Jay Powell, p		$118,000
Marc Valdes, p		$118,000
Luis Castillo, 2b		$109,000
Felix Heredia, p		$109,000
Bill McMillon, of		$109,000
Edgar Renteria, ss		$109,000

Average 1996 salary: $842,033
Total 1996 team payroll: $25,261,000
Termination pay: $75,000

211

Florida (1993-1996)

Runs: Most, career

291	JEFF CONINE, 1993-1996
258	GARY SHEFFIELD, 1993-1996
190	CHUCK CARR, 1993-1995
147	GREG COLBRUNN, 1994-1996
138	KURT ABBOTT, 1994-1996

Hits: Most, career

639	JEFF CONINE, 1993-1996
390	GARY SHEFFIELD, 1993-1996
339	GREG COLBRUNN, 1994-1996
331	CHUCK CARR, 1993-1995
274	KURT ABBOTT, 1994-1996

2B: Most, career

109	JEFF CONINE, 1993-1996
65	GARY SHEFFIELD, 1993-1996
58	CHUCK CARR, 1993-1995
58	GREG COLBRUNN, 1994-1996
53	KURT ABBOTT, 1994-1996

3B: Most, career

17	KURT ABBOTT, 1994-1996
13	JEFF CONINE, 1993-1996
8	BENITO SANTIAGO, 1993-1994
8	QUILVIO VERAS, 1995-1996
6	DEVON WHITE, 1996

HR: Most, career

95	GARY SHEFFIELD, 1993-1996
81	JEFF CONINE, 1993-1996
45	GREG COLBRUNN, 1994-1996
34	KURT ABBOTT, 1994-1996
25	Orestes Destrade, 1993-1994
25	CHARLES JOHNSON, 1994-1996

RBI: Most, career

361	JEFF CONINE, 1993-1996
281	GARY SHEFFIELD, 1993-1996
189	GREG COLBRUNN, 1994-1996
136	TERRY PENDLETON, 1995-1996
126	KURT ABBOTT, 1994-1996

SB: Most, career

115	CHUCK CARR, 1993-1995
64	QUILVIO VERAS, 1995-1996
59	GARY SHEFFIELD, 1993-1996
22	DEVON WHITE, 1996
16	GREG COLBRUNN, 1994-1996
16	EDGAR RENTERIA, 1996

BB: Most, career

277	GARY SHEFFIELD, 1993-1996
220	JEFF CONINE, 1993-1996
131	QUILVIO VERAS, 1995-1996
117	CHUCK CARR, 1993-1995
87	CHARLES JOHNSON, 1994-1996

BA: Highest, career

.302	GARY SHEFFIELD, 1993-1996
.301	JEFF CONINE, 1993-1996
.289	BRET BARBERIE, 1993-1994
.284	GREG COLBRUNN, 1994-1996
.281	Jerry Browne, 1994-1995

Slug avg: Highest, career

.581	GARY SHEFFIELD, 1993-1996
.478	JEFF CONINE, 1993-1996
.451	GREG COLBRUNN, 1994-1996
.427	KURT ABBOTT, 1994-1996
.403	TERRY PENDLETON, 1995-1996

On-base avg: Highest, career

.430	GARY SHEFFIELD, 1993-1996
.383	QUILVIO VERAS, 1995-1996
.376	Jerry Browne, 1994-1995
.367	WALT WEISS, 1993
.365	JEFF CONINE, 1993-1996

Complete games: Most, career

6	PAT RAPP, 1993-1996
5	KEVIN BROWN, 1996
5	JOHN BURKETT, 1995-1996
5	CHRIS HAMMOND, 1993-1996
3	Ryan Bowen, 1993-1995

Saves: Most, career

73	ROBB NEN, 1993-1996
51	BRYAN HARVEY, 1993-1995
9	Jeremy Hernandez, 1994-1995
7	TERRY MATHEWS, 1994-1996
2	TREVOR HOFFMAN, 1993
2	JAY POWELL, 1995-1996

Shutouts: Most, career

3	KEVIN BROWN, 1996
3	CHRIS HAMMOND, 1993-1996
3	PAT RAPP, 1993-1996
1	Ryan Bowen, 1993-1995
1	MARK GARDNER, 1994-1995
1	Charlie Hough, 1993-1994
1	AL LEITER, 1996

Wins: Most, career

33	PAT RAPP, 1993-1996
29	CHRIS HAMMOND, 1993-1996
20	JOHN BURKETT, 1995-1996
17	KEVIN BROWN, 1996
16	AL LEITER, 1996
16	DAVE WEATHERS, 1993-1996

K: Most, career

324	CHRIS HAMMOND, 1993-1996
320	PAT RAPP, 1993-1996
247	ROBB NEN, 1993-1996
234	JOHN BURKETT, 1995-1996
206	DAVE WEATHERS, 1993-1996

Win pct: Highest, career

.607	KEVIN BROWN, 1996
.571	AL LEITER, 1996
.492	CHRIS HAMMOND, 1993-1996
.471	PAT RAPP, 1993-1996
.458	ROBB NEN, 1993-1996

ERA: Lowest, career

1.89	KEVIN BROWN, 1996
2.93	AL LEITER, 1996
3.26	ROBB NEN, 1993-1996
3.51	Luis Aquino, 1993-1994
3.84	TERRY MATHEWS, 1994-1996

Runs: Most, season

118	GARY SHEFFIELD, 1996
86	QUILVIO VERAS, 1995
84	JEFF CONINE, 1996

77 DEVON WHITE, 1996
75 CHUCK CARR, 1993
75 JEFF CONINE, 1993

Hits: Most, season

175 JEFF CONINE, 1996
174 JEFF CONINE, 1993
163 GARY SHEFFIELD, 1996
151 DEVON WHITE, 1996
149 TERRY PENDLETON, 1995

2B: Most, season

37 DEVON WHITE, 1996
33 GARY SHEFFIELD, 1996
32 JEFF CONINE, 1996
32 TERRY PENDLETON, 1995
27 JEFF CONINE, 1994

3B: Most, season

7 KURT ABBOTT, 1995
7 KURT ABBOTT, 1996
7 QUILVIO VERAS, 1995
6 JEFF CONINE, 1994
6 BENITO SANTIAGO, 1993
6 DEVON WHITE, 1996

HR: Most, season

42 GARY SHEFFIELD, 1996
27 GARY SHEFFIELD, 1994
26 JEFF CONINE, 1996
25 JEFF CONINE, 1995
23 GREG COLBRUNN, 1995

RBI: Most, season

120 GARY SHEFFIELD, 1996
105 JEFF CONINE, 1995
95 JEFF CONINE, 1996
89 GREG COLBRUNN, 1995
87 Orestes Destrade, 1993

SB: Most, season

58 CHUCK CARR, 1993
56 QUILVIO VERAS, 1995
32 CHUCK CARR, 1994
25 CHUCK CARR, 1995
22 DEVON WHITE, 1996

BB: Most, season

142 GARY SHEFFIELD, 1996
80 QUILVIO VERAS, 1995
79 WALT WEISS, 1993
66 JEFF CONINE, 1995
62 JEFF CONINE, 1996

BA: Highest, season

.319 JEFF CONINE, 1994
.314 GARY SHEFFIELD, 1996
.302 JEFF CONINE, 1995
.301 BRET BARBERIE, 1994
.295 Jerry Browne, 1994

Slug avg: Highest, season

.624 GARY SHEFFIELD, 1996
.526 JEFF CONINE, 1994
.520 JEFF CONINE, 1995
.484 JEFF CONINE, 1996
.455 DEVON WHITE, 1996

On-base avg: Highest, season

.465 GARY SHEFFIELD, 1996
.392 Jerry Browne, 1994
.384 QUILVIO VERAS, 1995
.379 JEFF CONINE, 1995
.373 JEFF CONINE, 1994

Complete games: Most, season

5 KEVIN BROWN, 1996
4 JOHN BURKETT, 1995
3 CHRIS HAMMOND, 1995
3 PAT RAPP, 1995
2 Ryan Bowen, 1993
2 AL LEITER, 1996
2 PAT RAPP, 1994

Saves: Most, season

45 BRYAN HARVEY, 1993
35 ROBB NEN, 1996
23 ROBB NEN, 1995
15 ROBB NEN, 1994
9 Jeremy Hernandez, 1994

Shutouts: Most, season

3 KEVIN BROWN, 1996
2 CHRIS HAMMOND, 1995
2 PAT RAPP, 1995
1 Ryan Bowen, 1993
1 MARK GARDNER, 1995
1 CHRIS HAMMOND, 1994
1 Charlie Hough, 1994
1 AL LEITER, 1996
1 PAT RAPP, 1994

Wins: Most, season

17 KEVIN BROWN, 1996
16 AL LEITER, 1996
14 JOHN BURKETT, 1995
14 PAT RAPP, 1995
11 CHRIS HAMMOND, 1993

K: Most, season

200 AL LEITER, 1996
159 KEVIN BROWN, 1996
126 JOHN BURKETT, 1995
126 CHRIS HAMMOND, 1995
126 Charlie Hough, 1993

Win pct: Highest, season

.667 PAT RAPP, 1995
.607 KEVIN BROWN, 1996
.571 AL LEITER, 1996
.500 JOHN BURKETT, 1995

ERA: Lowest, season

1.89 KEVIN BROWN, 1996
2.93 AL LEITER, 1996
3.44 PAT RAPP, 1995
3.80 CHRIS HAMMOND, 1995
4.27 Charlie Hough, 1993

Most pinch-hit homers, season

2 KURT ABBOTT, 1996
2 ANDRE DAWSON, 1996

Most pinch-hit homers, career

2 KURT ABBOTT, 1994-96
2 ANDRE DAWSON, 1995-96

Longest hitting streak

22 EDGAR RENTERIA, 1996
21 GREG COLBRUNN, 1996
17 GREG COLBRUNN, 1995
15 BRET BARBARIE, 1993
15 CHUCK CARR, 1993

Most consecutive scoreless innings

26.1 Luis Aquino, 1994
24 CHRIS HAMMOND, 1994

No-hit game

AL LEITER, Fla vs Col NL, 11-0;
May 11, 1996.

ACTIVE PLAYERS in caps.

Players' years of service are listed by the first and last years with this team and are not necessarily consecutive; all statistics record performances for this team only.

New York Mets

Lance Johnson brought needed speed to the Mets and led the NL with 227 hits.

By Eileen Blass, USA TODAY

1996 Mets: Great expectations, all unmet

They arrived in Port St. Lucie, Fla., with such high hopes. Yes, this was going to be the year the Mets finally turned the corner into contention. Instead, the 1996 season turned out to be just like all the rest of the recent ones for this struggling franchise. Despite having top seasons by John Franco, Bernard Gilkey, Todd Hundley and Lance Johnson, the Mets finished with their 16th 90-loss season in team history. And suddenly uncertainty has returned. It can soak promise and eat hype. It can render a franchise forgotten.

There was no uncertainty surrounding the Mets last year. They were a coming team then, one with three outstanding young pitchers for a foundation, one with an identity. Now Jason Isringhausen, Bill Pulsipher and Paul Wilson are recovering from surgery and are questionable for the start of next season. Now the Mets have a new manager, Bobby Valentine, their fifth of the decade. Now the team has more questions than fans who come watch them—and worse, they lack an identity.

There certainly was good news: Hundley emerged, breaking Roy Campanella's record for most homers by a catcher and solidifying his status as a rising star. His 41 home runs were fourth in the league. Center fielder Johnson became the first player to lead both leagues in hits and re-wrote many team offensive records. He finished at .333 and hit 21 triples, half again as many as the second-best figure in the majors, Twins second baseman Chuck Knoblauch's 14. Johnson's 227 hits also led the majors, as did his 75 multi-hit games. Left fielder Gilkey, who proved to be a steal from St. Louis, earned the four-year contract he got after the season. In addition to becoming a clubhouse leader, the left fielder ranked in the NL top 10 in batting, on-base average, slugging average, doubles, extra-base hits and RBI. And closer Franco notched his 300th save, the most by any left-hander in history, and had a 1.83 ERA.

Perhaps the only other positive performance was that turned in by Mark Clark,

who almost single-handedly salvaged some respect for the rotation. Picked up from Cleveland and expected to scrap for a spot as the fifth starter, the right-hander's 14 victories led the club, and his 3.43 ERA was easily the best among the starting pitchers. Bobby Jones was second on the team with 12 victories, but his ERA was a career-worst 4.42.

Overall, the bad news from the 1996 season was so overwhelming that it left a cloud over the Mets as they broke for winter. First baseman Rico Brogna hurt his shoulder, and Butch Huskey only infrequently delivered on the promise he showed in the spring. (Brogna was traded in the offseason to the Phillies for two relievers.) Rookie shortstop Rey Ordonez alternately dazzled and confounded at shortstop, but he declined at the plate as the year went on. The blockbuster midseason trade with Cleveland brought Carlos Baerga but precious few results, as he struggled with injuries and played only 26 games.

So, the unanswered questions are many, with most revolving around younger players. How will the starting pitchers rebound? Can Alex Ochoa or Carl Everett take over in right field? Will Baerga be able to bounce back? How much does Franco have left, and will the new relievers effectively share the bullpen load?

1996 Mets: Week-by-week notes

These notes were excerpted from the following issues of Baseball Weekly.

NEW YORK METS / NL EAST

1997 BASEBALL WEEKLY ALMANAC

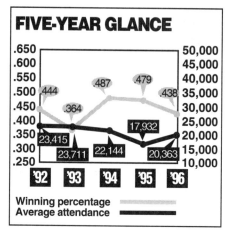

FIVE-YEAR GLANCE

Winning percentage
Average attendance

▶**April 3:** Outfielder Ryan Thompson was dealt—along with pitcher Reid Cornelius—to the Indians for pitcher Mark Clark. Although the Mets acquired an emergency starter in Clark, the 28-year-old Thompson was essentially dumped.

▶**April 10:** The Mets learned that lefty Bill Pulsipher, injured on March 18, will miss the season with a torn ligament in his pitching elbow. Team doctors deemed season-ending surgery the appropriate action, because it was Pulsipher's second elbow injury in less than a year.

▶**April 24:** After three starts, it's apparent that rookie starter Paul Wilson must go through some growing pains. In 12 innings, Wilson has given up 15 runs on 18 hits, and he has walked 12 but struck out only seven. Outfielders Bernard Gilkey and Lance Johnson have bolstered the Mets' offense, but Todd Hundley is the club's real power source. The Mets' catcher has homered seven times in the first 15 games, and has batted .377 with 16 RBI.

▶**May 1:** Lackluster pitching has been backed up by a suspect defense. The Mets led baseball with 28 errors in their first 22 games, including two four-error games.

▶**May 15:** How did the Chicago Cubs and the New York Mets honor John Franco, the all-time lefty save leader, on his "Appreciation Day" on May 11 at Shea Stadium? With a 16-minute brawl, of course. The fight led to the ejections of nine players, including Franco.

▶**May 22:** The Mets' slow start raised questions about the status of manager Dallas Green. But president of baseball operations Joe McIlvaine immediately offered his support. "Dallas is not the problem," he said. Entering a May 16 game against the Padres, Todd Hundley hadn't homered in 21 games, but the slump ended dramatically as he hit three homers in his next two games.

▶**May 29:** Through May 25, Bernard Gilkey was hitting .303 with 10 homers and 43 RBI. He had seven stolen bases and was tied with Houston's Derek Bell for the league lead in outfield assists, with seven.

▶**June 5:** Paul Wilson limited the Giants to three hits in eight innings in a 1-0 win on May 30. The club's other rookie, shortstop Rey Ordonez, continues to display his wizardry. He saved a 4-3 victory against the Dodgers on June 1 with a diving play on a grounder by Eric Karros with two on and nobody out in the eighth inning.

▶**June 19:** Robert Person, a 26-year-old righty, was recalled to replace tendinitis-plagued Paul Wilson in the rotation and made his first '96 start one to remember. Pitching in front of his hometown crowd at Busch Stadium on June 13, he shut out the Cards for seven innings to get the win.

▶**July 11:** Alex Ochoa, the ever-smiling rookie who the Mets said wasn't a savior, homered in the eighth inning of the 10-6 victory against the Phillies on July 3 to snap a 6-6 tie and become the third player to hit for the cycle in the majors this season. He added a double in the ninth and has hit .328 since his June 22 recall. For the team, the roller-coaster ride continues. After losing four in a row, including games to 1-6 Mike Williams and 1-6 Russ Springer of the Phillies, the Mets matched their season high with four consecutive wins, including three against the second-place Expos in Montreal.

▶**July 17:** Lance Johnson has proved to be

a delightful off-season signing. Through July 14, he led the league with 127 hits and a club-record 14 triples, was second with 31 steals and stood ninth with a .322 average.

▶**Aug. 7:** Carlos Baerga, recently acquired with Alvaro Espinoza in a trade for Jeff Kent and Jose Vizcaino, played second for the Indians but will play third for the Mets. Baerga was 4-for-15 in his first three games with the Mets, but then missed three games with a strained abdominal muscle.

▶**Aug. 21:** After falling behind 15-0 on the way to a 15-10 defeat in the opener of La Premier Serie in Monterrey, Mexico, against the Padres on Aug. 16, manager Dallas Green seemed embarrassed. "I don't think I've ever seen a worse game," he bristled. The Mets placed Jason Isringhausen on the disabled list with a strained rib cage. Isringhausen, who went 9-2 in his rookie season, is 5-13 with a 4.85 ERA in 24 starts in 1996.

▶**Aug. 28:** Dallas Green was blunt in an Aug. 19 statement: "These guys don't belong in the big leagues." That was his assessment of Jason Isringhausen and Paul Wilson, the supposed cornerstones of the pitching staff. The comment may have led to Green's firing on Aug. 26. Joe McIlvaine cited Green's inability to handle young players as the reason for the dismissal. He named Class AAA Norfolk manager Bobby Valentine as Green's replacement.

▶**Sept. 11:** Todd Hundley set a team record for home runs with his 40th on Sept. 8. Darryl Strawberry held the previous Mets mark with 39 homers in 1987 and '88.

▶**Sept. 18:** Todd Hundley caused the crowd at Shea Stadium to stand and cheer on Sept. 14 when he broke Roy Campanella's season record for homers by a catcher with his 41st, a three-run shot off the Braves' Greg McMichael.

▶**Sept. 25:** The Season to Forget for the Mets' young starting pitchers has become even more forgettable and worrisome. An examination of Jason Isringhausen's pitching arm last week revealed bone spurs in his elbow and a tear in the labrum in his shoulder. He soon will have two arthroscopic procedures after analysis of an MRI on his elbow. This means that both Isringhausen and Bill Pulsipher are questionable for 1997.

▶**Oct. 2:** Despite outstanding performances by Todd Hundley, Lance Johnson, Bernard Gilkey and John Franco, the Mets finished 71-91. The team was supposed to be on the rise, with a trio of outstanding young arms to build on. Now, Jason Isringhausen and Bill Pulsipher are recovering from major surgery, and Paul Wilson is coming off a disappointing rookie season (5-12, 5.38 ERA). Unheralded Mark Clark was the mainstay of the staff, with 14 wins and a 3.43 ERA. Hundley and Gilkey had career years, Johnson became the first player to lead both leagues in hits, and Franco became the first left-hander to notch his 300th save.

Team directory

▶**Owners:** Fred Wilpon (president and CEO) and Nelson Doubleday (chairman of the board)

▶**President of baseball operations:** Joseph McIlvaine

▶**Ballpark:**
William A. Shea Municipal Stadium
126th Street and Roosevelt Avenue
Flushing, N.Y.
718-507-METS
Capacity 55,777
Parking for 6,000 cars; $5
Public transportation available
Family and wheelchair sections, ramps, elevators

▶**Team publications:**
Yearbook, scorecard, press guide
919-688-0218

▶**TV, radio broadcast stations:**
WFAN 660 AM, WWOR Channel 9, SportsChannel

▶**Camps and/or clinics:**
Baseball Heaven, 800-898-METS

▶**Spring training:**
Thomas J. White Stadium
Port St. Lucie, Fla.
Capacity 7,347
407-871-2100

NEW YORK METS 1996 final stats

218

BATTERS	BA	SLG	OB	G	AB	R	H	TB	2B	3B	HR	RBI	BB	SO	SB	CS	E
Castillo	.364	.364	.364	6	11	1	4	4	0	0	0	0	0	4	0	0	0
Johnson	.333	.479	.362	160	682	117	227	327	31	21	9	69	33	40	50	12	12
Gilkey	.317	.562	.393	153	571	108	181	321	44	3	30	117	73	125	17	9	6
Espinoza	.306	.478	.324	48	134	19	41	64	7	2	4	16	4	19	0	2	8
Vizcaino	.303	.377	.356	96	363	47	110	137	12	6	1	33	28	58	9	5	6
Ochoa	.294	.426	.336	82	282	37	83	120	19	3	4	33	17	30	4	3	5
Kent	.290	.436	.331	89	335	45	97	146	20	1	9	39	21	56	4	3	21
Huskey	.278	.435	.319	118	414	43	115	180	16	2	15	60	27	77	1	2	15
Mayne	.263	.354	.342	70	99	9	26	35	6	0	1	6	12	22	0	1	0
Alfonzo	.261	.345	.304	123	368	36	96	127	15	2	4	40	25	56	2	0	11
Hundley	.259	.550	.356	153	540	85	140	297	32	1	41	112	79	146	1	3	8
Tomberlin	.258	.455	.355	63	66	12	17	30	4	0	3	10	9	27	0	0	0
Ordonez	.257	.303	.289	151	502	51	129	152	12	4	1	30	22	53	1	3	27
Brogna	.255	.431	.318	55	188	18	48	81	10	1	7	30	19	50	0	0	2
C. Jones	.242	.369	.307	89	149	22	36	55	7	0	4	18	12	42	1	0	3
Everett	.240	.307	.326	101	192	29	46	59	8	1	1	16	21	53	6	0	7
Petagine	.232	.384	.313	50	99	10	23	38	3	0	4	17	9	27	0	2	1
Roberson	.222	.500	.348	27	36	8	8	18	1	0	3	9	7	17	0	0	0
Bogar	.213	.258	.287	91	89	17	19	23	4	0	0	6	8	20	1	3	1
M. Franco	.194	.323	.235	14	31	3	6	10	1	0	1	2	1	5	0	0	3
Hardtke	.193	.281	.233	19	57	3	11	16	5	0	0	6	2	12	0	0	0
Baerga	.193	.301	.253	26	83	5	16	25	3	0	2	11	5	2	0	0	4
Greene	.000	.000	.000	2	1	0	0	0	0	0	0	0	0	0	0	0	0

PITCHERS	W-L	ERA	G	GS	CG	GF	Sho	SV	IP	H	R	ER	HR	BB	SO
J. Franco	4-3	1.83	51	0	0	44	0	28	54.0	54	15	11	2	21	48
Mlicki	6-7	3.30	51	2	0	16	0	1	90.0	95	46	33	9	33	83
Trlicek	0-1	3.38	5	0	0	2	0	0	5.1	3	2	2	0	3	3
Clark	14-11	3.43	32	32	2	0	0	0	212.1	217	98	81	20	48	142
Minor	0-0	3.51	17	0	0	4	0	0	25.2	23	11	10	4	6	20
Wallace	2-3	4.01	19	0	0	11	0	3	24.2	29	12	11	2	14	15
DiPoto	7-2	4.19	57	0	0	21	0	0	77.1	91	44	36	5	45	52
Harnisch	8-12	4.21	31	31	2	0	1	0	194.2	195	103	91	30	61	114
Byrd	1-2	4.24	38	0	0	14	0	0	46.2	48	22	22	7	21	31
MacDonald	0-2	4.26	20	0	0	6	0	0	19.0	16	10	9	2	9	12
B. Jones	12-8	4.42	31	31	3	0	1	0	195.2	219	102	96	26	46	116
Person	4-5	4.52	27	13	0	1	0	0	89.2	86	50	45	16	35	76
Henry	2-8	4.68	58	0	0	33	0	9	75.0	82	48	39	7	36	58
Isringhausen	6-14	4.77	27	27	2	0	1	0	171.2	190	103	91	13	73	114
Wilson	5-12	5.38	26	26	1	0	0	0	149.0	157	102	89	15	71	109
Fyhrie	0-1	15.43	2	0	0	0	0	0	2.1	4	4	4	0	3	0

1997 preliminary roster

PITCHERS (21)
Juan Acevedo
Jim Baron
Toby Borland
Mark Clark
Joe Crawford
Octvaio Dotel
John Franco
Pete Harnisch
Jason Isringhausen
Bobby Jones
Ricardo Jordan
Cory Lidle
Greg McMichael

Dave Mlicki
Bill Pulsipher
Hector Ramirez
Armando Reynoso
Jesus Sanchez
Derek Wallace
Mike Welch
Paul Wilson

CATCHERS (3)
Alberto Castillo
Charlie Greene
Todd Hundley

INFIELDERS (8)
Edgardo Alfonzo
Carlos Baerga
Tim Bogar
Alvaro Espinoza
Butch Huskey
John Olerud
Rey Ordonez
Roberto Petagine

OUTFIELDERS (7)
Carl Everett
Bernard Gilkey
Lance Johnson
Carlos Mendoza
Alex Ochoa
Jay Payton
Preston Wilson

Games played by position

PLAYER	G	C	1B	2B	3B	SS	OF
Alfonzo	123	0	0	66	36	15	0
Baerga	26	0	16	1	6	0	0
Bogar	91	0	32	8	25	19	0
Brogna	55	0	52	0	0	0	0
Castillo	6	6	0	0	0	0	0
Espinoza	48	0	1	2	38	7	0
Everett	101	0	0	0	0	0	55
M. Franco	14	0	2	0	8	0	0
Gilkey	153	0	0	0	0	0	151
Greene	2	1	0	0	0	0	0
Hardtke	19	0	0	18	0	0	0
Hundley	153	150	0	0	0	0	0
Huskey	118	0	75	0	6	0	40
Johnson	160	0	0	0	0	0	157
C. Jones	89	0	5	0	0	0	66
Kent	89	0	0	0	89	0	0
Mayne	70	21	0	0	0	0	0
Ochoa	82	0	0	0	0	0	76
Ordonez	151	0	0	0	0	150	0
Petagine	50	0	40	0	0	0	0
Roberson	27	0	0	0	0	0	10
Tomberlin	63	0	1	0	0	0	17
Vizcaino	96	0	0	93	0	0	0

Minor Leagues

Tops in the organization

BATTER	CLUB	AVG.	G	AB	R	H	HR	RBI
C. Mendoza	Clb	.337	85	300	61	101	0	37
Matt Franco	Nor	.323	133	508	74	164	7	81
P. Lopez	Ptf	.322	70	264	55	85	7	61
R. Petagine	Nor	.318	95	314	49	100	12	65
C. Saunders	Bng	.298	141	510	82	152	17	105

HOME RUNS

Brian Daubach	Bng	22
Chris Saunders	Bng	17
Fletcher Bates	Clb	15
Bryon Gainey	Clb	14
Several Players Tied At		12

WINS

Mike Fyhrie	Nor	15
N. Figueroa	Clb	14
Cory Lidle	Bng	14
Mike Gardiner	Nor	13
Arnold Gooch	Slu	12

RBI

Chris Saunders	Bng	105
Brian Daubach	Bng	82
Matt Franco	Nor	81
Terrence Long	Clb	78
Fletcher Bates	Clb	72

SAVES

Mike Welch	Nor	29
Derek Wallace	Nor	26
Rich Turrentine	Bng	24
Joseph Lisio	Clb	18
Several Players Tied At		10

STOLEN BASES

Scott Hunter	Slu	49
J. Simpson	Clb	32
Terrence Long	Clb	32
C. Mendoza	Clb	31
Several Players Tied At		30

STRIKEOUTS

N. Figueroa	Clb	200
Ethan McEntire	Clb	190
Octavio Dotel	Clb	142
Arnold Gooch	Slu	141
Cory Lidle	Bng	141

PITCHER	CLUB	W-L	ERA	IP	H	BB	SO
J. Sanchez	Slu	9-3	1.96	92	53	24	81
N. Figueroa	Clb	14-7	2.04	185	119	58	200
E. Mcentire	Clb	9-6	2.22	174	123	61	190
A. Trumpour	Clb	10-4	2.29	134	91	37	105
Corey Brittan	Ptf	8-3	2.30	98	74	20	84

Sick call: 1996 DL report

PLAYER	Days on the DL
Juan Acevedo	38
Rico Brogna	102
Paul Byrd	69
Carl Everett	15
Pete Harnisch	13
Butch Huskey	26
Jason Isringhausen	19
Bill Pulsipher	182
Paul Wilson	40

1996 salaries

	Bonuses	Total earned salary
Carlos Baerga, 2b		$4,791,667
Pete Harnisch, p	$225,000	$3,725,000
Bernard Gilkey, of		$2,787,500
Lance Johnson, of	$15,000	$2,715,000
John Franco, p	$200,000	$2,600,000
Todd Hundley, c		$1,837,500
Mark Clark, p	$200,000	$1,100,000
Doug Henry, p		$750,000
Brent Mayne, c		$725,000
Alvaro Espinoza, ss	$25,000	$425,000
Bobby Jones, p		$405,000
Chris Jones, of		$337,500
Rico Brogna, 1b		$325,000
Jerry Dipoto, p		$225,000
Tim Bogar, ss		$215,000
Dave Mlicki, p		$195,000
Edgardo Alfonzo, 2b		$180,000
Carl Everett, of		$178,000
Jason Isringhausen, p		$169,000
Bill Pulsipher, p		$155,000
Roberto Petagine, 1b		$135,000
Andy Tomberlin, of		$130,000
Paul Byrd, p		$123,000
Butch Huskey, 1b		$116,000
Alex Ochoa, of		$109,000
Rey Ordonez, ss		$109,000
Robert Person, p		$109,000
Derek Wallace, p		$109,000
Paul Wilson, p		$109,000

Average 1996 salary: $858,282
Total 1996 team payroll: $24,890,167
Termination pay: None

219

NEW YORK METS / NL EAST

New York (1962-1996)

Runs: Most, career

662	DARRYL STRAWBERRY, 1983-1990	
627	Howard Johnson, 1985-1993	
592	Mookie Wilson, 1980-1989	
563	Cleon Jones, 1963-1975	
536	Ed Kranepool, 1962-1979	

Hits: Most, career

1418	Ed Kranepool, 1962-1979
1188	Cleon Jones, 1963-1975
1112	Mookie Wilson, 1980-1989
1029	Bud Harrelson, 1965-1977
1025	DARRYL STRAWBERRY, 1983-1990

2B: Most, career

225	Ed Kranepool, 1962-1979
214	Howard Johnson, 1985-1993
187	DARRYL STRAWBERRY, 1983-1990
182	Cleon Jones, 1963-1975
170	Mookie Wilson, 1980-1989

3B: Most, career

62	Mookie Wilson, 1980-1989
45	Bud Harrelson, 1965-1977
33	Cleon Jones, 1963-1975
31	Steve Henderson, 1977-1980
30	DARRYL STRAWBERRY, 1983-1990

HR: Most, career

252	DARRYL STRAWBERRY, 1983-1990
192	Howard Johnson, 1985-1993
154	Dave Kingman, 1975-1983
122	Kevin McReynolds, 1987-1994
118	Ed Kranepool, 1962-1979

RBI: Most, career

733	DARRYL STRAWBERRY, 1983-1990
629	Howard Johnson, 1985-1993
614	Ed Kranepool, 1962-1979
521	Cleon Jones, 1963-1975
468	Keith Hernandez, 1983-1989

SB: Most, career

281	Mookie Wilson, 1980-1989
202	Howard Johnson, 1985-1993
191	DARRYL STRAWBERRY, 1983-1990
152	Lee Mazzilli, 1976-1989
116	LENNY DYKSTRA, 1985-1989

BB: Most, career

580	DARRYL STRAWBERRY, 1983-1990
573	Bud Harrelson, 1965-1977
556	Howard Johnson, 1985-1993
482	Wayne Garrett, 1969-1976
471	Keith Hernandez, 1983-1989

BA: Highest, career

.297	Keith Hernandez, 1983-1989
.292	DAVE MAGADAN, 1986-1992
.283	Wally Backman, 1980-1988
.281	Cleon Jones, 1963-1975
.278	LENNY DYKSTRA, 1985-1989

Slug avg: Highest, career

.520	DARRYL STRAWBERRY, 1983-1990
.460	Kevin McReynolds, 1987-1994
.459	Howard Johnson, 1985-1993
.453	Dave Kingman, 1975-1983
.429	Keith Hernandez, 1983-1989

On-base avg: Highest, career

.391	DAVE MAGADAN, 1986-1992
.387	Keith Hernandez, 1983-1989
.359	DARRYL STRAWBERRY, 1983-1990
.358	Rusty Staub, 1972-1985
.357	Lee Mazzilli, 1976-1989

Complete games: Most, career

171	Tom Seaver, 1967-1983
108	Jerry Koosman, 1967-1978
67	DWIGHT GOODEN, 1984-1994
65	Jon Matlack, 1971-1977
41	Al Jackson, 1962-1969

Saves: Most, career

175	JOHN FRANCO, 1990-1996
107	JESSE OROSCO, 1979-1987
86	Tug McGraw, 1965-1974
84	ROGER McDOWELL, 1985-1989
69	Neil Allen, 1979-1983

Shutouts: Most, career

44	Tom Seaver, 1967-1983
26	Jerry Koosman, 1967-1978
26	Jon Matlack, 1971-1977
23	DWIGHT GOODEN, 1984-1994
15	DAVID CONE, 1987-1992

Wins: Most, career

198	Tom Seaver, 1967-1983
157	DWIGHT GOODEN, 1984-1994
140	Jerry Koosman, 1967-1978
99	Ron Darling, 1983-1991
98	SID FERNANDEZ, 1984-1993

K: Most, career

2541	Tom Seaver, 1967-1983
1875	DWIGHT GOODEN, 1984-1994
1799	Jerry Koosman, 1967-1978
1449	SID FERNANDEZ, 1984-1993
1159	DAVID CONE, 1987-1992

Win pct: Highest, career

.649	DWIGHT GOODEN, 1984-1994
.625	DAVID CONE, 1987-1992
.615	Tom Seaver, 1967-1983
.586	Ron Darling, 1983-1991
.560	Bob Ojeda, 1986-1990

ERA: Lowest, career

2.57	Tom Seaver, 1967-1983
3.03	Jon Matlack, 1971-1977
3.08	DAVID CONE, 1987-1992
3.09	Jerry Koosman, 1967-1978
3.10	DWIGHT GOODEN, 1984-1994

Runs: Most, season

117	LANCE JOHNSON, 1996
108	BERNARD GILKEY, 1996
108	Howard Johnson, 1991
108	DARRYL STRAWBERRY, 1987
107	Tommie Agee, 1970

Hits: Most, season

227	LANCE JOHNSON, 1996
191	Felix Millan, 1975
185	Felix Millan, 1973
183	Keith Hernandez, 1985
182	Tommie Agee, 1970

2B: Most, season

44	BERNARD GILKEY, 1996
41	Howard Johnson, 1989
40	GREGG JEFFERIES, 1990
37	LENNY DYKSTRA, 1987
37	Howard Johnson, 1990
37	Felix Millan, 1975
37	EDDIE MURRAY, 1992
37	Joel Youngblood, 1979

3B: Most, season

21	LANCE JOHNSON, 1996
10	Mookie Wilson, 1984
9	Steve Henderson, 1978
9	Charlie Neal, 1962
9	Frank Taveras, 1979
9	Mookie Wilson, 1982

HR: Most, season

41	TODD HUNDLEY, 1996
39	DARRYL STRAWBERRY, 1987
39	DARRYL STRAWBERRY, 1988
38	Howard Johnson, 1991
37	Dave Kingman, 1976
37	Dave Kingman, 1982
37	DARRYL STRAWBERRY, 1990

RBI: Most, season

117	BERNARD GILKEY, 1996
117	Howard Johnson, 1991
112	TODD HUNDLEY, 1996
108	DARRYL STRAWBERRY, 1990
105	Gary Carter, 1986
105	Rusty Staub, 1975

SB: Most, season

58	Mookie Wilson, 1982
54	Mookie Wilson, 1983
50	LANCE JOHNSON, 1996
46	Mookie Wilson, 1984
42	Frank Taveras, 1979

BB: Most, season

97	Keith Hernandez, 1984
97	DARRYL STRAWBERRY, 1987
95	Bud Harrelson, 1970
94	Keith Hernandez, 1986
93	Lee Mazzilli, 1979

BA: Highest, season

.340	Cleon Jones, 1969
.333	LANCE JOHNSON, 1996
.328	DAVE MAGADAN, 1990
.319	Cleon Jones, 1971
.317	BERNARD GILKEY, 1996

Slug avg: Highest, season

.583	DARRYL STRAWBERRY, 1987
.562	BERNARD GILKEY, 1996
.559	Howard Johnson, 1989
.550	TODD HUNDLEY, 1996
.545	DARRYL STRAWBERRY, 1988

On-base avg: Highest, season

.422	Cleon Jones, 1969
.417	DAVE MAGADAN, 1990
.413	Keith Hernandez, 1986
.409	Keith Hernandez, 1984
.398	DARRYL STRAWBERRY, 1987

Complete games: Most, season

21	Tom Seaver, 1971
19	Tom Seaver, 1970
18	Tom Seaver, 1967
18	Tom Seaver, 1969
18	Tom Seaver, 1973

Saves: Most, season

33	JOHN FRANCO, 1990
31	JESSE OROSCO, 1984
30	JOHN FRANCO, 1991
30	JOHN FRANCO, 1994
29	JOHN FRANCO, 1995

Shutouts: Most, season

8	DWIGHT GOODEN, 1985
7	Jerry Koosman, 1968
7	Jon Matlack, 1974
6	Jerry Koosman, 1969
6	Jon Matlack, 1976

Wins: Most, season

25	Tom Seaver, 1969
24	DWIGHT GOODEN, 1985
22	Tom Seaver, 1975
21	Jerry Koosman, 1976
21	Tom Seaver, 1972

K: Most, season

289	Tom Seaver, 1971
283	Tom Seaver, 1970
276	DWIGHT GOODEN, 1984
268	DWIGHT GOODEN, 1985
251	Tom Seaver, 1973

Win pct: Highest, season

.870	DAVID CONE, 1988
.857	DWIGHT GOODEN, 1985
.783	Bob Ojeda, 1986
.781	Tom Seaver, 1969
.739	DWIGHT GOODEN, 1986

ERA: Lowest, season

1.53	DWIGHT GOODEN, 1985
1.76	Tom Seaver, 1971
2.08	Tom Seaver, 1973
2.08	Jerry Koosman, 1968
2.20	Tom Seaver, 1968

Most pinch-hit homers, season

4	Danny Heep, 1983
4	MARK CARREON, 1989

Most pinch-hit homers, career

8	MARK CARREON, 1987-1991
6	Ed Kranepool, 1962-1979
6	Rusty Staub, 1972-1985

Longest hitting streak

24	Hubie Brooks, 1984
23	Cleon Jones, 1970
23	Mike Vail, 1975
20	Tommie Agee, 1970
19	Felix Millan, 1975
19	Lee Mazzilli, 1979

Most consecutive scoreless innings

31	Jerry Koosman, 1973

No-hit games

None

ACTIVE PLAYERS in caps.

Players' years of service are listed by the first and last years with this team and are not necessarily consecutive; all statistics record performances for this team only.

Philadelphia Phillies

Curt Schilling bounced back from shoulder surgery to lead the Phillies' rotation.

By Eileen Blass, USA TODAY

1996 Phillies: Hardly anyone was healthy

A Phillies season filled with questions in April ended in late September with even more uncertainties. League and team records were set for frequency of personnel shifts: 54 different players appeared in games, which tied a National League record held by another bad team, the 1967 Mets; a total of 15 different pitchers started games, which tied a club record that was set in 1992; the disabled list was utilized 23 times, setting another team mark. With all that searching for players, however, there were few answers.

The season ended with a 67-95 record and was quickly followed by the firing of manager Jim Fregosi by GM Lee Thomas. Terry Francona was hired to replace him.

Even the team's best offensive performance was accompanied by a problem. Catcher Benito Santiago hit 30 homers and drove in 85 runs to lead the team in both categories. But his season concluded without a contract offer for next year from the Phils, and he signed with Toronto. Club president Bill Giles talked vaguely about signing free agents, but every indication is that the decision has been made to concede at least the next two years and take a look at kids. That means that Mike Lieberthal, the third pick overall in the 1990 draft, is likely to get his first chance to prove he's ready to be an everyday catcher. And it means that outfielder Wendell Magee Jr., who still has a long way to go at the plate, may do his learning at the big-league level.

There were, however, a few bright spots in 1996. Right-hander Curt Schilling came back from his August 1995 surgery to repair a torn labrum in his shoulder. Despite not making his first start until the middle of May, Schilling led the National League with eight complete games and ranked fifth with 8.9 strikeouts per nine innings. Ricky Bottalico blossomed in his first year as the closer, converting 34 of 38 save opportunities. Scott Rolen came up and, in 130 at-bats, showed the Phillies enough for them to pencil him in as their starting third baseman. He's an early

Rookie of the Year candidate. After a trip to the minors, shortstop Kevin Stocker turned his season around and played his way back into the team's plans.

But that wasn't nearly enough to overcome the problems, especially the string of injuries. The Phillies hope right-handers Tyler Green and Matt Beech will be able to return from surgery. Reports from the Florida Instructional League were encouraging. Coming off surgery to repair the torn anterior cruciate ligament in his right knee, Darren Daulton played only a handful of games the first week of the season before being forced to admit that he wasn't ready to play. Lenny Dykstra, coming off serious back problems, played brilliantly for three weeks before his back began bothering him again. He eventually required surgery. The careers of both players, who have been longtime mainstays of the Phillies' lineup, remain in doubt.

Just like the entire Philadelphia organization, come to think about it. A late-November trade with the Mets sent relievers Toby Borland and Ricardo Jordan to New York in exchange for first baseman Rico Brogna. What's the important thing to know about Brogna? He's coming off shoulder surgery and was sidelined for most of last season.

1996 Phillies: Week-by-week notes

These notes were excerpted from the following issues of Baseball Weekly.

▶**April 10:** Left fielder Darren Daulton, who had surgery to repair the torn anterior cruciate ligament in his right knee in September 1995, was placed on the 15-day DL. Meanwhile, the news got worse for Gregg Jefferies, who dived headfirst into third base on April 4 and tore the ligament in his left thumb. A hand specialist discovered that Jefferies had also fractured the little finger on his right hand, and he is expected to miss three months.

▶**April 17:** A hole in the middle: Through their first 10 games, Phillies cleanup hitters were a combined 3-for-31 (.097) with 12 strikeouts, no home runs and two RBI.

▶**April 24:** The Phillies lost back-to-back games after building early 5-0 leads, in St. Louis on April 14 and in Montreal on April 16. Then they lost consecutive 1-0 home games to the Cardinals, on April 19 and 20.

▶**May 8:** Who's on first? Nearly everyone—J.R. Phillips became the sixth player to start at first for the Phillies in their first 27 games, joining Gregg Jefferies, Gene Schall, Benito Santiago, Kevin Jordan and Jon Zuber.

▶**May 15:** Attendance is down sharply from last year, with three major factors cited—bad press, bad weather and the NHL's Flyers. "There was so much pre-season hype about us stinking," said shortstop Kevin Stocker.

▶**May 22:** So far, so good. On May 14, right-hander Curt Schilling made his first start since shoulder surgery last August—and threw seven shutout innings.

▶**June 12:** The offense perked up after Gregg Jefferies returned to the lineup, on June 4. In his first four games back, Jefferies went 8-for-19. In the 52 games he missed, the Phillies averaged 4.4 runs; in the seven he has played, 5.6.

▶**June 26:** Center fielder Lenny Dykstra will undergo season-ending surgery in

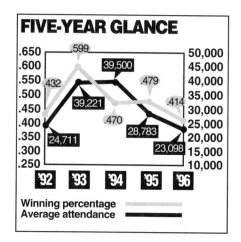

FIVE-YEAR GLANCE

.650	.599	50,000
.600	39,500	45,000
.550	432	.479	40,000
.500		35,000
.450	39,221	.414	30,000
.400	.470	25,000
.350	28,783	20,000
.300	24,711	23,098	15,000
.250		10,000

'92   '93   '94   '95   '96

Winning percentage
Average attendance

hopes of alleviating the spinal stenosis that has plagued him the last two seasons. He insisted he's not thinking about retirement. "That's why I'm getting it fixed—so I can play again," he said.

▶**July 3:** Nine of Curt Schilling's first 10 outings since coming back from shoulder surgery have been quality starts, but his record is just 2-3. The most recent tough loss came on June 29. Schilling pitched eight innings against Montreal, giving up one run on five hits and two walks, while striking out eight. He lost 1-0. The Phillies set a franchise record when they lost their 14th consecutive road game, on June 26 in Cincinnati.

▶**July 17:** The Phillies have confirmed that former All-Star catcher Darren Daulton and stellar rookie right-hander Mike Grace (7-2, 3.49 ERA) are through for the season, because of knee and shoulder problems, respectively.

▶**July 31:** Confronted with sagging attendance and dwindling radio and TV ratings, Phillies president Bill Giles has dropped hints that the team is willing to increase its payroll for 1997 to put a competitive team on the field. Phillies players were encouraged by the remarks, but cautious. "It's a start," said second baseman Mickey Morandini. "But it's one thing to say it. It's another thing to do it."

▶**Aug. 7:** On July 31 the Phillies traded veteran left-hander Terry Mulholland to

Seattle for 22-year-old shortstop Desi Relaford and triggered a massive upheaval of the team on the field. The next day, prized prospect Scott Rolen was called up from Class AAA Scranton/Wilkes-Barre and installed as the regular third baseman. That caused a ripple effect. Todd Zeile moved from third to first. Gregg Jefferies shifted from first to left. And with Relaford starting at short, the team had a radically different look.

▸**Aug. 14:** The Phillies announced on Aug. 8 that Scranton/Wilkes-Barre manager Butch Hobson had been released from his contract. Hobson, 44, had been on a leave of absence since being arrested in a Pawtucket, R.I., motel room for possession of cocaine. Club president Bill Giles had said a few days earlier that no decision on Hobson's status would be made until the end of the season. The dismissal apparently was made because of a signed statement made public by the *Pawtucket Times* in which Hobson admitted using cocaine with high school friend Jerry Poe and buying drugs from him on five occasions.

▸**Sept. 4:** After allowing one run in seven innings, giving up five hits and striking out 11 in a 1-0 loss to the Giants on Aug. 26, Curt Schilling made a plea for catcher Benito Santiago. "If [Santiago] is not back next year catching every day, we're not going to win a thing," Schilling said.

▸**Sept. 11:** The Phillies will wait until November to negotiate a contract extension for Curt Schilling. From the team's perspective, there is no sense of urgency. Schilling made his 22nd start on Sept. 5, which triggered a clause in his contract that guarantees his $3.5 million option year for 1997.

▸**Sept. 18:** Club president Bill Giles has directed GM Lee Thomas and manager Jim Fregosi to work out their differences. They once were best of friends, but another losing season has strained the relationship. Giles made it clear that if they can't make up, he might fire one of them—or both.

▸**Sept. 25:** Benito Santiago hit his 30th home run on Sept. 18, but there's no guarantee that the catcher will be back next year.

Santiago played for $1.1 million this year, and he's looking for a big raise and a long-term deal. The Phillies, who hope that their 1990 No. 1 draft choice Mike Lieberthal is nearly ready to be the regular catcher, are reluctant to make a commitment.

▸**Oct. 2:** A season that was loaded with questions in April finished the same way. In between, 54 players appeared, tying the NL record set by the 1967 Mets. Fifteen pitchers started games, tying a club record set in 1992. The DL was used 23 times, another team record. The season ended with the firing of manager Jim Fregosi, though GM Lee Thomas said that the friction between them was overstated. Jim Eisenreich hit .361, and Curt Schilling proved he was all the way back after 1995 surgery to repair a torn labrum in his shoulder, as he led the NL with eight complete games. But career-threatening injuries to Darren Daulton and Lenny Dykstra crippled the team's offense.

Team directory

▸**Owner:** Bill Giles
▸**General manager:** Lee Thomas
▸**Ballpark:**
Veterans Stadium
Broad Street & Pattison Avenue,
Philadelphia, Pa.
215-463-1000
Capacity 62,268
Parking for 10,000 cars; $5
Public transportation available
Wheelchair section and ramps, TDD
ticket information for hearing
impaired (215-463-2998)
▸**Team publications:**
Media guide, scorebook
▸**TV, radio broadcast stations:**
WPHL Channel 17, WPHT 1210 AM
SportsChannel, Prism Cable
▸**Spring training:**
Jack Russell Memorial Stadium
Clearwater, Fla.
Capacity 7,195
813-441-8638

PHILADELPHIA PHILLIES 1996 final stats

BATTERS	BA	SLG	OB	G	AB	R	H	TB	2B	3B	HR	RBI	BB	SO	SB	CS	E
Eisenreich	.361	.476	.413	113	338	45	122	161	24	3	3	41	31	32	11	1	4
Estalella	.353	.706	.389	7	17	5	6	12	0	0	2	4	1	6	1	0	0
Amaro	.316	.453	.380	61	117	14	37	53	10	0	2	15	9	18	0	0	0
Jefferies	.292	.401	.348	104	404	59	118	162	17	3	7	51	36	21	20	6	1
Sefcik	.284	.379	.341	44	116	10	33	44	5	3	0	9	9	16	3	0	7
K. Jordan	.282	.427	.309	43	131	15	37	56	10	0	3	12	5	20	2	1	0
Schall	.273	.470	.392	28	66	7	18	31	5	1	2	10	12	15	0	0	2
Otero	.273	.348	.330	104	411	54	112	143	11	7	2	32	34	30	16	10	4
Zeile	.268	.436	.353	134	500	61	134	218	24	0	20	80	67	88	1	1	14
Doster	.267	.371	.313	39	105	14	28	39	8	0	1	8	7	21	0	0	3
Santiago	.264	.503	.332	136	481	71	127	242	21	2	30	85	49	104	2	0	11
Dykstra	.261	.418	.387	40	134	21	35	56	6	3	3	13	26	25	3	1	0
Rolen	.254	.400	.322	37	130	10	33	52	7	0	4	18	13	27	0	2	4
Stocker	.254	.378	.336	119	394	46	100	149	22	6	5	41	43	89	6	4	13
Lieberthal	.253	.428	.297	50	166	21	42	71	8	0	7	23	10	30	0	0	3
Zuber	.253	.330	.296	30	91	7	23	30	4	0	1	10	6	11	1	0	2
Morandini	.250	.334	.321	140	539	64	135	180	24	6	3	32	49	87	26	5	12
Bennett	.250	.250	.333	6	16	0	4	4	0	0	0	1	2	6	0	0	0
Incaviglia	.234	.454	.318	99	269	33	63	122	7	2	16	42	30	82	2	0	3
Benjamin	.223	.408	.316	35	103	13	23	42	5	1	4	13	12	21	3	1	6
Martinez	.222	.333	.263	13	36	2	8	12	0	2	0	0	1	11	2	1	1
Magee	.204	.296	.252	38	142	9	29	42	7	0	2	14	9	33	0	0	2
Murray	.196	.289	.250	38	97	8	19	28	3	0	2	6	7	36	1	0	0
Relaford	.175	.225	.233	15	40	2	7	9	2	0	0	1	3	9	1	0	2
Daulton	.167	.167	.500	5	12	3	2	2	0	0	0	0	0	7	5	0	0
Phillips	.163	.413	.250	50	104	12	17	43	5	0	7	15	11	51	0	0	3
Tinsley	.135	.135	.196	31	52	1	7	7	0	0	0	2	4	22	2	4	1
Battle	.000	.000	.000	5	5	0	0	0	0	0	0	0	0	2	0	0	0

PITCHERS	W-L	ERA	G	GS	CG	GF	Sho	SV	IP	H	R	ER	HR	BB	SO
R. Jordan	2-2	1.80	26	0	0	2	0	0	25.0	18	6	5	0	12	17
Ryan	3-5	2.43	62	0	0	26	0	8	89.0	71	32	24	4	45	70
Schilling	9-10	3.19	26	26	8	0	2	0	183.1	149	69	65	16	50	182
Bottalico	4-5	3.19	61	0	0	56	0	34	67.2	47	24	24	6	23	74
Parrett	3-3	3.39	51	0	0	23	0	0	66.1	64	25	25	2	31	64
Fernandez	3-6	3.43	11	11	0	0	0	0	63.0	50	25	24	5	26	77
Grace	7-2	3.49	12	12	1	0	1	0	80.0	72	33	31	9	16	49
Maduro	0-1	3.52	4	2	0	0	0	0	15.1	13	6	6	1	3	11
Borland	7-3	4.07	69	0	0	11	0	0	90.2	83	51	41	9	43	76
Mitchell	0-0	4.50	7	0	0	2	0	0	12.0	14	6	6	1	5	7
Springer	3-10	4.66	51	7	0	12	0	0	96.2	106	60	50	12	38	94
Mulholland	8-7	4.66	21	21	3	0	0	0	133.1	157	74	69	17	21	52
Frey	0-1	4.72	31	0	0	12	0	0	34.1	38	19	18	4	18	12
West	2-2	4.76	7	6	0	0	0	0	28.1	31	17	15	0	11	22
Crawford	0-1	4.91	1	1	0	0	0	0	3.2	7	10	2	1	2	4
Williams	6-14	5.44	32	29	0	1	0	0	167.0	188	107	101	25	67	103
Mimbs	3-9	5.53	21	17	0	0	0	0	99.1	116	66	61	13	41	56
Blazier	3-1	5.87	27	0	0	9	0	0	38.1	49	30	25	6	10	25
Hunter	3-7	6.49	14	14	0	0	0	0	69.1	84	54	50	10	33	32
Heflin	0-0	6.75	3	0	0	2	0	0	6.2	11	7	5	1	3	4
Beech	1-4	6.97	8	8	0	0	0	0	41.1	49	32	32	8	11	33
Dishman	0-0	7.71	7	1	0	4	0	0	9.1	12	8	8	2	3	3
Munoz	0-3	7.82	6	6	0	0	0	0	25.1	42	28	22	5	7	8
Quirico	0-1	37.80	1	1	0	0	0	0	1.2	4	7	7	1	5	1

1997 preliminary roster

PITCHERS (19)
Matt Beech
Ron Blazier
Ricky Bottalico
Jason Boyd
Wayne Gomes
Mike Grace
Tyler Green
Rich Hunter
Mark Leiter
Calvin Maduro
Mike Mimbs
Larry Mitchell
Bobby Munoz
Ryan Nye
Mark Portugal
Edgar Ramos
Ken Ryan
Curt Schilling
Jerry Spradlin

CATCHERS (3)
Bobby Estalella
Mike Lieberthal
Mark Parent

INFIELDERS (9)
Rico Brogna
David Doster
Rex Hudler
Kevin Jordan
Mickey Morandini
Desi Relaford
Scott Rolen
Kevin Sefcik
Kevin Stocker

OUTFIELDERS (6)
Darren Daulton
Lenny Dykstra
Gregg Jefferies
Tony Longmire
Wendell Magee
Ricky Otero

Games played by position

PLAYER	G	C	1B	2B	3B	SS	OF
Amaro	61	0	1	0	0	0	35
Battle	5	0	0	0	1	0	0
Benjamin	35	0	0	1	0	31	0
Bennett	6	5	0	0	0	0	0
Daulton	5	0	0	0	0	0	5
Doster	39	0	0	24	1	0	0
Dykstra	40	0	0	0	0	0	39
Eisenreich	113	0	0	0	0	0	91
Estalella	7	4	0	0	0	0	0
Incaviglia	99	0	0	0	0	0	71
Jefferies	104	0	53	0	0	0	51
K. Jordan	43	0	30	7	1	0	0
Lieberthal	50	43	0	0	0	0	0
Magee	38	0	0	0	0	0	37
Martinez	13	0	0	0	0	0	11
Morandini	140	0	0	137	0	0	0
Murray	38	0	0	0	0	0	27
Otero	104	0	0	0	0	0	100
Phillips	50	0	21	0	0	0	15
Relaford	15	0	0	4	0	9	0
Rolen	37	0	0	0	37	0	0
Santiago	136	114	14	0	0	0	0
Schall	28	0	19	0	0	0	0
Sefcik	44	0	0	1	20	21	0
Stocker	119	0	0	0	0	119	0
Tinsley	31	0	0	0	0	0	22
Zeile	134	0	28	0	106	0	0
Zuber	30	0	22	0	0	0	0

Minor Leagues

Tops in the organization

BATTER	CLUB	AVG.	G	AB	R	H	HR	RBI
Scott Rolen	Swb	.324	106	398	67	129	11	61
Jon Zuber	Swb	.311	118	412	62	128	4	59
Mark Raynor	Pdt	.292	129	483	81	141	4	66
W. Magee	Swb	.289	115	425	69	123	16	62
Gene Schall	Swb	.288	104	371	66	107	17	67

HOME RUNS			WINS		
Bobby Estalella	Swb	26	Ryan Nye	Swb	13
Dan Held	Swb	26	Matt Beech	Swb	13
Jason Moler	Rea	18	Jason Boyd	Clw	11
Steve Carver	Clw	17	Jason Kershner	Pdt	11
Gene Schall	Swb	17	Randy Knoll	Clw	11

RBI			SAVES		
Dan Held	Swb	92	Brian Stumpf	Clw	26
Bobby Estalella	Swb	80	Wayne Gomes	Rea	24
Aaron Royster	Rea	80	Kyle Kawabata	Bat	20
Steve Carver	Clw	79	Pete Nyari	Pdt	18
Gene Schall	Swb	67	Bronson Heflin	Swb	13

STOLEN BASES			STRIKEOUTS		
Essex Burton	Rea	45	Rob Burger	Pdt	171
M. Anderson	Rea	43	Randy Knoll	Clw	163
Larry Huff	Clw	37	Jason Kershner	Pdt	156
Reggie Taylor	Pdt	36	Matt Beech	Swb	146
Jeremy Kendall	Clw	27	Ryan Nye	Swb	141

PITCHER	CLUB	W-L	ERA	IP	H	BB	SO
Randy Knoll	Clw	11-7	2.20	172	128	33	163
Matt Beech	Swb	13-6	3.09	148	117	33	146
Rob Burger	Pdt	10-12	3.38	160	129	61	171
Tony Fiore	Rea	9-6	3.40	159	134	74	99
Len Manning	Clw	3-7	3.69	102	94	63	77

Sick call: 1996 DL report

PLAYER	Days on the DL
Mike Benjamin	97*
Darren Daulton	176
Lenny Dykstra	134
Sid Fernandez	122*
Mike Grace	119
Tyler Green	182
Gregg Jefferies	60
Kevin Jordan	105
Mike Lieberthal	39
Tony Longmire	182
Mike Mimbs	26
Mickey Morandini	15
Bobby Munoz	159**
Glenn Murray	76*
Curt Schilling	43
Lee Tinsley	17
David West	141*

* Indicates two separate terms on Disabled List.
** Indicates three separate terms on Disabled List.

1996 salaries

	Bonuses	Total earned salary
Lenny Dykstra, of		$6,200,000
Gregg Jefferies, 1b		$5,500,000
Darren Daulton, c		$5,250,000
Curt Schilling, p	$1,400,000	$2,000,000
Mickey Morandini, 2b	$150,000	$1,900,000
Benito Santiago, c	$600,000	$1,700,000
Jim Eisenreich, of		$1,200,000
Sid Fernandez, p	$400,000	$650,000
David West, p	$150,000	$500,000
Mike Benjamin, ss		$325,000
Ken Ryan, p		$272,500
Kevin Stocker, ss		$265,000
Tony Longmire, of		$225,000
Mike Williams, p		$200,000
Ricky Bottalico, p		$185,000
Russ Springer, p		$185,000
Toby Borland, p		$175,000
Michael Mimbs, p		$160,000
Tyler Green, p		$155,000
Bobby Munoz, p	$5,000	$145,000
Jeff Parrett, p	$28,000	$137,000
Mike Lieberthal, c		$125,000
Ruben Amaro, of		$109,000
Matt Beech, p		$109,000
Gary Bennett, c		$109,000
Mike Grace, p		$109,000
Rich Hunter, p		$109,000
Kevin Jordan, 2b		$109,000
Ricardo Jordan, p		$109,000
Wendell Magee, of		$109,000
Larry Mitchell, p		$109,000
Glenn Murray, p		$109,000
Ricky Otero, of		$109,000
Scott Rolen, 3b		$109,000
Gene Schall, 1b		$109,000
Kevin Sefcik, ss		$109,000
Jon Zuber, 1b		$109,000

Average 1996 salary: $786,203
Total 1996 team payroll: $29,089,500
Termination pay: $1,313,958

Philadelphia (1883-1996)

Runs: Most, career

1506	Mike Schmidt, 1972-1989
1367	Ed Delahanty, 1888-1901
1114	Richie Ashburn, 1948-1959
963	Chuck Klein, 1928-1944
924	Sam Thompson, 1889-1898

Hits: Most, career

2234	Mike Schmidt, 1972-1989
2217	Richie Ashburn, 1948-1959
2213	Ed Delahanty, 1888-1901
1812	Del Ennis, 1946-1956
1798	Larry Bowa, 1970-1981

2B: Most, career

442	Ed Delahanty, 1888-1901
408	Mike Schmidt, 1972-1989
337	Sherry Magee, 1904-1914
336	Chuck Klein, 1928-1944
310	Del Ennis, 1946-1956

3B: Most, career

157	Ed Delahanty, 1888-1901
127	Sherry Magee, 1904-1914
106	Sam Thompson, 1889-1898
97	Richie Ashburn, 1948-1959
84	Johnny Callison, 1960-1969

HR: Most, career

548	Mike Schmidt, 1972-1989
259	Del Ennis, 1946-1956
243	Chuck Klein, 1928-1944
223	Greg Luzinski, 1970-1980
217	Cy Williams, 1918-1930

RBI: Most, career

1595	Mike Schmidt, 1972-1989
1286	Ed Delahanty, 1888-1901
1124	Del Ennis, 1946-1956
983	Chuck Klein, 1928-1944
957	Sam Thompson, 1889-1898

SB: Most, career

508	Billy Hamilton, 1890-1895
411	Ed Delahanty, 1888-1901
387	Sherry Magee, 1904-1914
289	Jim Fogarty, 1884-1889
288	Larry Bowa, 1970-1981

BB: Most, career

1507	Mike Schmidt, 1972-1989
946	Richie Ashburn, 1948-1959
946	Roy Thomas, 1899-1911
693	Willie Jones, 1947-1959
643	Ed Delahanty, 1888-1901

BA: Highest, career

.361	Billy Hamilton, 1890-1895
.348	Ed Delahanty, 1888-1901
.338	Elmer Flick, 1898-1901
.333	Sam Thompson, 1889-1898
.326	Chuck Klein, 1928-1944

Slug avg: Highest, career

.553	Chuck Klein, 1928-1944
.530	Dick Allen, 1963-1976
.527	Mike Schmidt, 1972-1989
.510	Dolph Camilli, 1934-1937
.508	Ed Delahanty, 1888-1901

On-base avg: Highest, career

.468	Billy Hamilton, 1890-1895
.421	Roy Thomas, 1899-1911
.419	Elmer Flick, 1898-1901
.415	Ed Delahanty, 1888-1901
.400	John Kruk, 1989-1994

Complete games: Most, career

272	Robin Roberts, 1948-1961
219	Pete Alexander, 1911-1930
185	Steve Carlton, 1972-1986
165	Charlie Ferguson, 1884-1887
156	Bill Duggleby, 1898-1907

Saves: Most, career

103	Steve Bedrosian, 1986-1989
102	Mitch Williams, 1991-1993
94	Tug McGraw, 1975-1984
90	Ron Reed, 1976-1983
65	Turk Farrell, 1956-1969

Shutouts: Most, career

61	Pete Alexander, 1911-1930
39	Steve Carlton, 1972-1986
35	Robin Roberts, 1948-1961
24	Chris Short, 1959-1972
23	Jim Bunning, 1964-1971

Wins: Most, career

241	Steve Carlton, 1972-1986
234	Robin Roberts, 1948-1961
190	Pete Alexander, 1911-1930
132	Chris Short, 1959-1972
115	Curt Simmons, 1947-1960

K: Most, career

3031	Steve Carlton, 1972-1986
1871	Robin Roberts, 1948-1961
1585	Chris Short, 1959-1972
1409	Pete Alexander, 1911-1930
1197	Jim Bunning, 1964-1971

Win pct: Highest, career

.676	Pete Alexander, 1911-1930
.642	Tom Seaton, 1912-1913
.607	Charlie Ferguson, 1884-1887
.606	Charlie Buffinton, 1887-1889
.600	Red Donahue, 1898-1901
.600	Ron Reed, 1976-1983

ERA: Lowest, career

1.79	George McQuillan, 1907-1916
2.18	Pete Alexander, 1911-1930
2.48	Tully Sparks, 1897-1910
2.61	Frank Corridon, 1904-1909
2.63	Earl Moore, 1908-1913

Runs: Most, season

192	Billy Hamilton, 1894
166	Billy Hamilton, 1895
158	Chuck Klein, 1930
152	Chuck Klein, 1932
152	Lefty O'Doul, 1929

Hits: Most, season

254	Lefty O'Doul, 1929
250	Chuck Klein, 1930
238	Ed Delahanty, 1899
226	Chuck Klein, 1932
223	Chuck Klein, 1933

2B: Most, season

59	Chuck Klein, 1930
55	Ed Delahanty, 1899
50	Chuck Klein, 1932
49	Ed Delahanty, 1895
48	Dick Bartell, 1932

3B: Most, season

27	Sam Thompson, 1894
23	Nap Lajoie, 1897
21	Ed Delahanty, 1892
21	Sam Thompson, 1895
19	JUAN SAMUEL, 1984
19	George Wood, 1887

HR: Most, season

48	Mike Schmidt, 1980
45	Mike Schmidt, 1979
43	Chuck Klein, 1929
41	Cy Williams, 1923
40	Dick Allen, 1966
40	Chuck Klein, 1930
40	Mike Schmidt, 1983

RBI: Most, season

170	Chuck Klein, 1930
165	Sam Thompson, 1895
146	Ed Delahanty, 1893
145	Chuck Klein, 1929
143	Don Hurst, 1932

SB: Most, season

111	Billy Hamilton, 1891
102	Jim Fogarty, 1887
102	Billy Hamilton, 1890
99	Jim Fogarty, 1889
98	Billy Hamilton, 1894

BB: Most, season

129	LENNY DYKSTRA, 1993
128	Mike Schmidt, 1983
126	Billy Hamilton, 1894
125	Richie Ashburn, 1954
121	Von Hayes, 1987

BA: Highest, season

.410	Ed Delahanty, 1899
.407	Ed Delahanty, 1894
.404	Billy Hamilton, 1894
.404	Ed Delahanty, 1895
.398	Lefty O'Doul, 1929

Slug avg: Highest, season

.687	Chuck Klein, 1930
.657	Chuck Klein, 1929
.654	Sam Thompson, 1895
.646	Chuck Klein, 1932
.644	Mike Schmidt, 1981

On-base avg: Highest, season

.523	Billy Hamilton, 1894
.500	Ed Delahanty, 1895
.490	Billy Hamilton, 1895
.478	Ed Delahanty, 1894
.472	Ed Delahanty, 1896

Complete games: Most, season

59	John Coleman, 1883
54	Kid Gleason, 1890
49	Ed Daily, 1885
46	Charlie Ferguson, 1884
46	Gus Weyhing, 1892

Saves: Most, season

43	Mitch Williams, 1993
40	Steve Bedrosian, 1987
34	RICKY BOTTALICO, 1996
32	HEATHCLIFF SLOCUMB, 1995
30	Mitch Williams, 1991

Shutouts: Most, season

16	Pete Alexander, 1916
12	Pete Alexander, 1915
9	Pete Alexander, 1913
8	Pete Alexander, 1917
8	Steve Carlton, 1972
8	Ben Sanders, 1888

Wins: Most, season

38	Kid Gleason, 1890
33	Pete Alexander, 1916
32	Gus Weyhing, 1892
31	Pete Alexander, 1915
30	Pete Alexander, 1917
30	Charlie Ferguson, 1886

K: Most, season

310	Steve Carlton, 1972
286	Steve Carlton, 1980
286	Steve Carlton, 1982
275	Steve Carlton, 1983
268	Jim Bunning, 1965

Win pct: Highest, season

.800	Tommy Greene, 1993
.800	Robin Roberts, 1952
.769	Charlie Ferguson, 1886
.760	Larry Christenson, 1977
.760	John Denny, 1983

ERA: Lowest, season

1.22	Pete Alexander, 1915
1.53	George McQuillan, 1908
1.55	Pete Alexander, 1916
1.83	Lew Richie, 1908
1.83	Pete Alexander, 1917

Most pinch-hit homers, season

5	Gene Freese, 1959
4	Rip Repulski, 1958
4	Del Unser, 1979

Most pinch-hit homers, career

9	Cy Williams, 1918-1930
6	Gavvy Cravath, 1912-1920
6	Rick Joseph, 1967-1970
6	Del Unser, 1973-1982

Longest hitting streak

36	Billy Hamilton, 1894
31	Ed Delahanty, 1899
26	Chuck Klein, 1930
26	Chuck Klein, 1930 (2nd streak)
24	Willie Montanez, 1974

Most consecutive scoreless innings

41	Grover Cleveland Alexander, 1911

No-hit games

Joe Borden, Phi vs Chi NA, 4-0; July 28, 1875.

Charlie Ferguson, Phi vs Pro NL, 1-0; Aug. 29, 1885.

Red Donahue, Phi vs Bos NL, 5-0; July 8, 1898.

Chick Fraser, Phi at Chi NL; 10-0; Sept. 18, 1903 (2nd game).

Johnny Lush, Phi at Bro NL, 6-0; May 1, 1906.

Jim Bunning, Phi at NY NL, 6-0; June 21, 1964 (1st game, perfect game).

Rick Wise, Phi at Cin NL, 4-0; June 23, 1971.

TERRY MULHOLLAND, Phi vs SF NL, 6-0; Aug. 15, 1990.

Tommy Greene, Phi at Mon NL, 2-0; May 23, 1991.

ACTIVE PLAYERS in caps.

Players' years of service are listed by the first and last years with this team and are not necessarily consecutive; all statistics record performances for this team only.

St. Louis Cardinals

By Anne Ryan, USA TODAY

Brian Jordan's bat, glove and leadership helped bring the Cards a division title.

1996 Cardinals: New Cards won the hand

The new owners of the St. Louis Cardinals bought the team in December 1995 and then went on a shopping spree. And like some children on Christmas morning, they saw their dreams come true. The Cardinals won the NL Central, and the expensive new "toys" (see page 235 for salary list) were big contributors. Ron Gant hit 30 homers and drove in 82 runs. Gary Gaetti added 80 RBI. Andy Benes overcame a 1-7 start to go 18-10, and Todd Stottlemyre added 14 victories. Closer Dennis Eckersley saved 30 games. New manager Tony La Russa, who was paid $1.5 million, won his sixth division championship. Willie McGee came back for a second term with the Cards and batted .307. A cheaper addition, rookie Alan Benes, won 13 games.

A couple of holdovers were important, too. Right fielder Brian Jordan came of age in the clubhouse and on the field. Catcher Tom Pagnozzi stayed healthy for the first time in four years and won La Russa's favor after he had fallen to third string at the start of the year.

Not much went wrong other than that the Cardinals were 0-6 at home against Atlanta during the regular season and blew a 3-1 lead to the Braves in the best-of-seven NLCS. The happiness over the team's division championship was tempered somewhat by the fact that it was the first time in franchise history that St. Louis had made the playoffs without advancing to the World Series.

The shortstop position, an uneasy topic for the first half of the season, settled itself as both newcomer Royce Clayton and legend Ozzie Smith had strong seasons. Clayton hit .277, and Smith was at .300 until going 1-for-18 in late September. Second base was a disaster for a long while as Luis Alicea had 22 errors by July 1, but he became a productive player in the second half. Mike Gallego filled in well defensively, making just one error in his first 44 games in the field. One of the surprises was that Gaetti, 38, played well defensively. Another was that McGee had the legs and

---

Team MVP

Brian Jordan: Brian Jordan's heroics in the Division Series against San Diego underlined what the Cardinals had already discovered: This guy can carry a team. In fact, veteran Ozzie Smith said Jordan had become the team's leader. The former football player had a breakthrough season, batting .310 with 104 RBI, 17 home runs, 22 stolen bases and often spectacular play in right field.

---

the bat speed at 37. And a third was that Eckersley wasn't washed up at 41.

They came from miles around to form the Cardinals' team this season, but Smith said that the leader of the club was already here. "Brian Jordan was our inspiration. He led the way more than anybody. Brian has made more strides than anybody on this team as far as leadership, ability and talent," Smith said.

Jordan, who led the Cards with 104 RBI, said, "It's the football in me. I'm very aggressive, and I want to take the role of being the leader. I want to get everybody fired up. I play the game hard, and hopefully people will follow."

Smith, who retired after the season, started instead of Clayton in the division-clinching game against the Pittsburgh Pirates and said of La Russa, with whom he had often disagreed during the season, "Tony knew how much I wanted to be out there. I thank Tony for giving me that opportunity."

The Cardinals' playoff hopes were tempered by the torn left rotator cuff suffered on Sept. 27 by center fielder Ray Lankford, who was hurt while diving for a ball. Lankford was in and out of the playoff lineup; he couldn't throw and didn't swing the bat with his usual gusto. His return to form will be a crucial element in the Cardinals' drive to repeat in 1997.

1996 Cardinals: Week-by-week notes

These notes were excerpted from the following issues of Baseball Weekly.

▶**April 3:** No winner emerged from the Cardinals' much-advertised shortstop competition. Ozzie Smith could have been the loser to Royce Clayton, who at 26 is 15 years his junior. But Smith, his arm rebounding to its strength level of two years ago, made all the plays this spring, and neither man really hit much.

▶**April 10:** When Royce Clayton beat out a bunt on Opening Day, it matched the Cardinals' bunt-hit total of last season. Geronimo Pena had the lone St. Louis bunt hit last year.

▶**April 24:** Alan Benes, junior member of the Benes firm, was 3-0 after a dazzling two-hit, no-run effort for eight innings in a 1-0 win at Philadelphia.

▶**May 8:** After 29 games, the Cardinals led the NL in home runs allowed (38) and errors (33). They yielded 71 runs on those 38 home runs and accounted for just 28 runs on their 21 homers.

▶**May 15:** Right-hander Andy Benes ran his losing streak to five with another lackluster performance. Signed to an $8.1 million contract in the Cardinals' off-season spending frenzy, Benes has yielded 30 runs (25 earned) and 41 hits in his last 26 innings.

▶**May 22:** Right-hander Todd Stottlemyre put together two consecutive games of double-figure strikeouts, including a 13-strikeout shutout at Florida. Stottlemyre is holding right-handed hitters to a .136 average this season.

▶**May 29:** The Cardinals, by sweeping Houston and winning the first game of a series in Florida, put together a five-game winning streak and moved within a game of first-place Houston.

▶**June 12:** The Cardinals' surge of 12 wins in 17 games corresponded to a resurgence by the starting pitching. In the 17 games, starters allowed just 48 earned runs in 123⅔ innings for an ERA of 3.49.

▶**June 19:** Alan Benes, who gave up 15 runs in 9⅓ innings in his first two starts

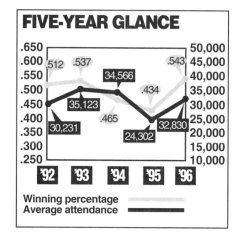

FIVE-YEAR GLANCE

Winning percentage
Average attendance

against the New York Mets, got his revenge on June 15, beating them 4-2. In that game Dennis Eckersley, 0-4 and just off the DL, recorded his ninth save, but his first since May 12.

▶**July 3:** Like Ozzie Smith, outfielder Willie McGee plans to retire after this season. "It's very, very, very doubtful that I'll be back," said McGee. "Except when I announce [my retirement], it'll be in spring training. They'll be saying, 'Where's Willie?' That's how I'm going to go out."

▶**July 11:** After a half-season of tinkering, the Cardinals lineup—at least at the top—has taken shape. Royce Clayton was 12-for-30 in his first seven games after being reinstalled as the leadoff hitter. At No. 2, center fielder Ray Lankford scored 11 runs in eight games, and No. 3 Ron Gant, the left fielder, had five homers in 13 games. Then there is cleanup hitter and right fielder Brian Jordan, who had 13 RBI in eight games, raising his average to .300.

▶**July 24:** Andy Benes, who beat the Reds 6-4 on July 17, has come back from 1-7 to even his record at 8-8.

▶**July 31:** Ozzie Smith has been brilliant for the most part since announcing his retirement in late June and then having a couple of days of crossfire with manager Tony La Russa. Smith, who had back-to-back three-hit games, said, "I think my announcement loosened everybody up.

There was a lot of tension because of the situation, but I've been able to get those things off my chest."

▶**Aug. 14:** Tony La Russa had to pull Dennis Eckersley from two consecutive save situations before Eckersley finally tied Rollie Fingers at 341 for third on the all-time list. Willie McGee got his 2,000th major-league hit on Aug. 8, joining teammate Ozzie Smith and only four other active NL players in that category.

▶**Aug. 21:** The Andy Benes Express was still on track. Benes ran off his 10th consecutive win when he beat Florida 5-2 on Aug. 16. Alan Benes also seems to be straightened out, pitching a complete-game, 6-1 win against Los Angeles on Aug. 14 for his 11th victory. He'd had four winless starts before beating the Dodgers.

▶**Sept. 4:** Mike Morgan, 4-8 with a 5.24 ERA and the loser of four in a row, was released to make room for Dmitri Young, a switch-hitting first baseman brought up from Louisville. John Mabry might move to third next year if Young, the fourth player taken in the 1991 draft, plays first.

▶**Sept. 11:** This year the Cards won 11 of 13 games against the Astros, their closest competitors. The season series was capped by a three-game blanking on Sept. 2-4, part of a season-high eight-game Cards winning streak. In one of the Houston games, Todd Stottlemyre's victory gave him and father Mel 259 wins (95 by Todd) for the father-son record, breaking the old mark set by Dizzy and Steve Trout.

▶**Sept. 18:** Richard Batchelor, a September call-up and childhood Dodgers fan, gained the first win of his career on Sept. 13 against Los Angeles. That victory was Tony La Russa's 1,400th, the most wins of any active manager.

▶**Sept. 25:** The Cards have had good balance this year: Four starters—Andy Benes, Alan Benes, Todd Stottlemyre and left-hander Donovan Osborne—have at least 13 wins. Offensively, the Cardinals have three players with 20 or more home runs and three with 20 or more steals for the first time in history. Third baseman Gary Gaetti, Ray Lankford and Ron Gant are in the 20-homer club. Lankford, Royce Clayton and Brian Jordan have at least 20 steals.

▶**Oct. 2:** The group of about a dozen owners who purchased the Cardinals in December 1995 were like kids in a candy shop. But their dream came true. The Cardinals won the NL Central title, and there was a variety of reasons why, especially the host of newcomers. Ron Gant ($4 million) hit 30 homers and drove in 82 runs despite missing five weeks with a hamstring strain. Andy Benes ($3.4 million) won 18 games, and Todd Stottlemyre ($4.2 million) won 14. Gary Gaetti ($2 million) had 80 RBI. Dennis Eckersley ($2.5 million) saved 30 games. Tony La Russa ($1.5 million) won his sixth division championship. Rookie Alan Benes won 13 games. The returning Willie McGee ($600,000) batted better than .300 and played four positions. Another newcomer, shortstop Royce Clayton, had the awkward task of sharing the position with retiring legend Ozzie Smith, but both men were effective. Perhaps the top Cardinal was Brian Jordan, who hit .310 and had his first 100-RBI season.

Team directory

▶**Owner:** St. Louis Cardinals LP
▶**General manager:** Walt Jocketty
▶**Ballpark:**
Busch Stadium
250 Stadium Plaza
St. Louis, Mo.
314-421-3060
Capacity 57,673 (includes 1,500 standing)
Parking for over 7,000 cars; $5
Public transportation available
Wheelchair section, ramps
▶**Team publications:**
Media guide,
The Cardinals Magazine
314-982-7336
▶**TV, radio broadcast stations:**
KMOX 1120 AM, KPLR Channel 11, Prime Sports
▶**Spring training:**
Al Lang Stadium
St. Petersburg, Fla.
Capacity 7,227
813-893-7490

ST. LOUIS CARDINALS 1996 final stats

BATTERS	BA	SLG	OB	G	AB	R	H	TB	2B	3B	HR	RBI	BB	SO	SB	CS	E
Bradshaw	.333	.381	.417	15	21	4	7	8	1	0	0	3	3	2	0	1	0
Borders	.319	.362	.329	26	69	3	22	25	3	0	0	4	1	14	0	1	3
Jordan	.310	.483	.349	140	513	82	159	248	36	1	17	104	29	84	22	5	2
McGee	.307	.417	.348	123	309	52	95	129	15	2	5	41	18	60	5	2	5
Mabry	.297	.431	.342	151	543	63	161	234	30	2	13	74	37	84	3	2	8
Difelice	.286	.429	.286	4	7	0	2	3	1	0	0	2	0	1	0	0	0
Smith	.282	.370	.358	82	227	36	64	84	10	2	2	18	25	9	7	5	8
Clayton	.277	.371	.321	129	491	64	136	182	20	4	6	35	33	89	33	15	15
Lankford	.275	.486	.366	149	545	100	150	265	36	8	21	86	79	133	35	7	1
Gaetti	.274	.473	.326	141	522	71	143	247	27	4	23	80	35	97	2	2	10
Pagnozzi	.270	.423	.311	119	407	48	110	172	23	0	13	55	24	78	4	1	8
Sweeney	.265	.371	.387	98	170	32	45	63	9	0	3	22	33	29	3	0	3
Alicea	.258	.382	.350	129	380	54	98	145	26	3	5	42	52	78	11	3	24
Gant	.246	.504	.359	122	419	74	103	211	14	2	30	82	73	98	13	4	5
Young	.241	.241	.353	16	29	3	7	7	0	0	0	2	4	5	0	1	1
Sheaffer	.227	.333	.271	79	198	10	45	66	9	3	2	20	9	25	3	3	6
Bell	.214	.276	.268	62	145	12	31	40	6	0	1	9	10	22	1	1	5
Gallego	.210	.224	.276	51	143	12	30	32	2	0	0	4	12	31	0	0	3
Mejia	.087	.087	.087	45	23	10	2	2	0	0	0	0	0	10	6	3	1
Holbert	.000	.000	.000	1	3	0	0	0	0	0	0	0	0	0	0	0	0

PITCHERS	W-L	ERA	G	GS	CG	GF	Sho	SV	IP	H	R	ER	HR	BB	SO
Batchelor	2-0	1.20	11	0	0	7	0	0	15.0	9	2	2	0	1	11
Fossas	0-4	2.68	65	0	0	11	0	2	47.0	43	19	14	7	21	36
Honeycutt	2-1	2.85	61	0	0	13	0	4	47.1	42	15	15	3	7	30
Bailey	5-2	3.00	51	0	0	12	0	0	57.0	57	21	19	1	30	38
Mathews	2-6	3.01	67	0	0	23	0	6	83.2	62	32	28	8	32	80
Loiselle	1-0	3.05	5	3	0	0	0	0	20.2	22	8	7	3	8	9
Eckersley	0-6	3.30	63	0	0	53	0	30	60.0	65	26	22	8	6	49
Osborne	13-9	3.53	30	30	2	0	1	0	198.2	191	87	78	22	57	134
Petkovsek	11-2	3.55	48	6	0	7	0	0	88.2	83	37	35	9	35	45
Andy Benes	18-10	3.83	36	34	3	1	1	1	230.1	215	107	98	28	77	160
Stottlemyre	14-11	3.87	34	33	5	0	2	0	223.1	191	100	96	30	93	194
Jackson	1-1	4.46	13	4	0	3	0	0	36.1	33	18	18	3	16	27
Alan Benes	13-10	4.90	34	32	3	1	1	0	191.0	192	120	104	27	87	131
Urbani	1-0	7.71	3	2	0	0	0	0	11.2	15	10	10	3	4	1
Ludwick	0-1	9.00	6	1	0	2	0	0	10.0	11	11	10	4	3	12
Barber	0-0	15.00	1	1	0	0	0	0	3.0	4	5	5	0	6	1
Busby	0-1	18.00	1	1	0	0	0	0	4.0	9	13	8	4	4	4

1997 preliminary roster

PITCHERS (20)
Manuel Aybar
Brian Barber
Rich Batchelor
Alan Benes
Andy Benes
Mike Busby
Dennis Eckersley
Tony Fossas
John Frascatore
Rick Honeycutt
Danny Jackson
Curtis King
Eric Ludwick

T.J. Mathews
Donovan Osborne
Lance Painter
Mark Petkovsek
Brady Raggio
Bill Stein
Todd Stottlemyre

CATCHERS (5)
Mike DeFelice
Tom Lampkin
Elieser Marrero
Tom Pagnozzi
Danny Sheaffer

INFIELDERS (9)
David Bell
Royce Clayton
Delino DeShields
Gary Gaetti
Mike Gulan
Aaron Holbert
Luis Ordaz
Mark Sweeney
Dmitri Young

OUTFIELDERS (7)
Terry Bradshaw
Ronnie Gant
Brian Jordan
Ray Lankford
John Mabry
Willie McGee
Miguel Mejia

Games played by position

PLAYER	G	C	1B	2B	3B	SS	OF
Alicea	129	0	0	125	0	0	0
Bell	62	0	0	20	45	1	0
Borders	26	17	1	0	0	0	0
Bradshaw	15	0	0	0	0	0	7
Clayton	129	0	0	0	0	113	0
Difelice	4	4	0	0	0	0	0
Gaetti	141	0	14	0	133	0	0
Gallego	51	0	0	43	7	1	0
Gant	122	0	0	0	0	0	116
Holbert	1	0	0	1	0	0	0
Jordan	140	0	1	0	0	0	136
Lankford	149	0	0	0	0	0	144
Mabry	151	0	146	0	0	0	14
McGee	123	0	6	0	0	0	83
Mejia	45	0	0	0	0	0	21
Pagnozzi	119	116	1	0	0	0	0
Sheaffer	79	47	6	0	17	0	3
Smith	82	0	0	0	0	52	0
Sweeney	98	0	15	0	0	0	43
Young	16	0	10	0	0	0	0

Minor Leagues

Tops in the organization

BATTER	CLUB	AVG.	G	AB	R	H	HR	RBI
K. Robinson	Peo	.359	123	440	98	158	2	47
Dmitri Young	Lou	.333	122	459	90	153	15	64
T. Bradshaw	Lou	.303	102	389	56	118	12	44
Brian Rupp	Ark	.303	114	353	46	107	4	41
Andy Hall	Peo	.300	128	446	80	134	4	68

HOME RUNS

Jose Oliva	Lou	31
Chris Fick	Ark	19
Elieser Marrero	Ark	19
Mike Gulan	Lou	17
Several Players Tied At		15

WINS

Blake Stein	Stp		16
Britt Reames	Peo		15
Cliff Politte	Peo		14
Several Players Tied At			12

RBI

Jose Oliva	Lou	86
Chris Richard	Stp	82
Shawn McNally	Peo	75
Chris Fick	Ark	74
Andy Hall	Peo	68

SAVES

Curtis King	Stp	31
Rich Batchelor	Lou	28
Matt Golden	Ark	25
Travis Welch	Peo	17
Jose DeLeon	Jcy	15

STOLEN BASES

Kerry Robinson	Peo	50
S. Green	Ark	34
Yudith Ozorio	Stp	30
Jason Woolf	Peo	28
Jeff Berblinger	Ark	23

STRIKEOUTS

Britt Reames	Peo	167
Blake Stein	Stp	159
Cliff Politte	Peo	151
Rigo Beltran	Lou	132
Several Players Tied At		129

PITCHER	CLUB	W-L	ERA	IP	H	BB	SO
Britt Reames	Peo	15-7	1.90	161	97	41	167
Blake Stein	Stp	16-5	2.15	172	122	54	159
Cliff Politte	Peo	14-6	2.59	150	108	47	151
M. Logan	Stp	7-7	2.91	133	125	49	99
Jose Jimenez	Peo	12-9	2.92	172	158	53	129

Sick call: 1996 DL report

PLAYER	Days on the DL
Dennis Eckersley	25
Gary Gaetti	16
Mike Gallego	102
Ron Gant	34
Danny Jackson	124
Brian Jordan	14
Miguel Mejia	30
Mike Morgan	47
Donovan Osborne	16
Tom Pagnozzi	14
Mark Petkovsek	18
Ozzie Smith	28

1996 salaries

	Bonuses	Total earned salary
Danny Jackson, p		$4,100,000
Ron Gant, of		$4,000,000
Todd Stottlemyre, p	$200,000	$4,000,000
Ozzie Smith, ss		$3,500,000
Andy Benes, p	$75,000	$3,325,000
Tom Pagnozzi, c		$2,675,000
Brian Jordan, of		$2,500,000
Ray Lankford, of		$2,416,666
Dennis Eckersley, p	$125,000	$2,375,000
Gary Gaetti, 3b		$2,000,000
Royce Clayton, ss		$1,600,000
Luis Alicea, 2b		$750,000
Donovan Osborne, p		$725,000
Tony Fossas, p		$650,000
Rick Honeycutt, p		$600,000
Willie McGee, of		$600,000
Danny Sheaffer, c		$335,000
Mike Gallego, ss		$300,000
John Mabry, of		$200,000
Mark Petkovsek, p		$150,000
T.J. Mathews, p		$130,000
Mark Sweeney, of		$125,000
Alan Benes, p		$112,000
Eric Ludwick, p		$109,000
Miguel Mejia, of		$109,000
Dmitri Young, 3b		$109,000

Average 1996 salary: $1,442,141
Total 1996 team payroll: $37,495,666
Termination pay: $1,175,000

St. Louis (1892-1996)

Runs: Most, career

1949	Stan Musial, 1941-1963	
1427	Lou Brock, 1964-1979	
1089	Rogers Hornsby, 1915-1933	
1071	Enos Slaughter, 1938-1953	
1025	R. Schoendienst, 1945-1963	

Hits: Most, career

3630	Stan Musial, 1941-1963
2713	Lou Brock, 1964-1979
2110	Rogers Hornsby, 1915-1933
2064	Enos Slaughter, 1938-1953
1980	Red Schoendienst, 1945-1963

2B: Most, career

725	Stan Musial, 1941-1963
434	Lou Brock, 1964-1979
377	Joe Medwick, 1932-1948
367	Rogers Hornsby, 1915-1933
366	Enos Slaughter, 1938-1953

3B: Most, career

177	Stan Musial, 1941-1963
143	Rogers Hornsby, 1915-1933
135	Enos Slaughter, 1938-1953
121	Lou Brock, 1964-1979
119	Jim Bottomley, 1922-1932

HR: Most, career

475	Stan Musial, 1941-1963
255	Ken Boyer, 1955-1965
193	Rogers Hornsby, 1915-1933
181	Jim Bottomley, 1922-1932
172	Ted Simmons, 1968-1980

RBI: Most, career

1951	Stan Musial, 1941-1963
1148	Enos Slaughter, 1938-1953
1105	Jim Bottomley, 1922-1932
1072	Rogers Hornsby, 1915-1933
1001	Ken Boyer, 1955-1965

SB: Most, career

888	Lou Brock, 1964-1979
549	VINCE COLEMAN, 1985-1990
433	OZZIE SMITH, 1982-1996
279	WILLIE McGEE, 1982-1996
203	Jack Smith, 1915-1926

BB: Most, career

1599	Stan Musial, 1941-1963
876	OZZIE SMITH, 1982-1996
838	Enos Slaughter, 1938-1953
681	Lou Brock, 1964-1979
660	Rogers Hornsby, 1915-1933

BA: Highest, career

.359	Rogers Hornsby, 1915-1933
.336	Johnny Mize, 1936-1941
.335	Joe Medwick, 1932-1948
.331	Stan Musial, 1941-1963
.326	Chick Hafey, 1924-1931

Slug avg: Highest, career

.600	Johnny Mize, 1936-1941
.568	Rogers Hornsby, 1915-1933
.568	Chick Hafey, 1924-1931
.559	Stan Musial, 1941-1963
.545	Joe Medwick, 1932-1948

On-base avg: Highest, career

.427	Rogers Hornsby, 1915-1933
.419	Johnny Mize, 1936-1941
.417	Stan Musial, 1941-1963
.413	Joe Cunningham, 1954-1961
.402	Miller Huggins, 1910-1916

Complete games: Most, career

255	Bob Gibson, 1959-1975
208	Jesse Haines, 1920-1937
196	Ted Breitenstein, 1892-1901
144	Bill Doak, 1913-1929
144	Bill Sherdel, 1918-1932

Saves: Most, career

160	LEE SMITH, 1990-1993
129	TODD WORRELL, 1985-1992
127	Bruce Sutter, 1981-1984
64	Lindy McDaniel, 1955-1962
60	Al Brazle, 1943-1954
60	Joe Hoerner, 1966-1969

Shutouts: Most, career

56	Bob Gibson, 1959-1975
30	Bill Doak, 1913-1929
28	Mort Cooper, 1938-1945
25	Harry Brecheen, 1940-1952
24	Jesse Haines, 1920-1937

Wins: Most, career

251	Bob Gibson, 1959-1975
210	Jesse Haines, 1920-1937
163	Bob Forsch, 1974-1988
153	Bill Sherdel, 1918-1932
144	Bill Doak, 1913-1929

K: Most, career

3117	Bob Gibson, 1959-1975
1095	Dizzy Dean, 1930-1937
1079	Bob Forsch, 1974-1988
979	Jesse Haines, 1920-1937
951	Steve Carlton, 1965-1971

Win pct: Highest, career

.718	Ted Wilks, 1944-1951
.705	John Tudor, 1985-1990
.677	Mort Cooper, 1938-1945
.667	Al Hrabosky, 1970-1977
.641	Dizzy Dean, 1930-1937

ERA: Lowest, career

2.52	John Tudor, 1985-1990
2.67	Slim Sallee, 1908-1916
2.67	Jack Taylor, 1904-1906
2.74	Johnny Lush, 1907-1910
2.74	Red Ames, 1915-1919

Runs: Most, season

142	Jesse Burkett, 1901
141	Rogers Hornsby, 1922
135	Stan Musial, 1948
133	Rogers Hornsby, 1925
132	Joe Medwick, 1935

Hits: Most, season

250	Rogers Hornsby, 1922
237	Joe Medwick, 1937
235	Rogers Hornsby, 1921
230	Stan Musial, 1948
230	Joe Torre, 1971

2B: Most, season

64	Joe Medwick, 1936
56	Joe Medwick, 1937
53	Stan Musial, 1953
52	Enos Slaughter, 1939
51	Stan Musial, 1944

3B: Most, season

29	Perry Werden, 1893
25	Roger Connor, 1894
25	Tom Long, 1915
20	Jim Bottomley, 1928
20	Duff Cooley, 1895
20	Rogers Hornsby, 1920
20	Stan Musial, 1943
20	Stan Musial, 1946

HR: Most, season

43	Johnny Mize, 1940
42	Rogers Hornsby, 1922
39	Rogers Hornsby, 1925
39	Stan Musial, 1948
36	Stan Musial, 1949

RBI: Most, season

154	Joe Medwick, 1937
152	Rogers Hornsby, 1922
143	Rogers Hornsby, 1925
138	Joe Medwick, 1936

137	Jim Bottomley, 1929
137	Johnny Mize, 1940
137	Joe Torre, 1971

SB: Most, season

118	Lou Brock, 1974
110	VINCE COLEMAN, 1985
109	VINCE COLEMAN, 1987
107	VINCE COLEMAN, 1986
81	VINCE COLEMAN, 1988

BB: Most, season

136	Jack Clark, 1987
136	Jack Crooks, 1892
121	Jack Crooks, 1893
116	Miller Huggins, 1910
107	Stan Musial, 1949

BA: Highest, season

.424	Rogers Hornsby, 1924
.403	Rogers Hornsby, 1925
.401	Rogers Hornsby, 1922
.397	Rogers Hornsby, 1921
.396	Jesse Burkett, 1899

Slug avg: Highest, season

.756	Rogers Hornsby, 1925
.722	Rogers Hornsby, 1922
.702	Stan Musial, 1948
.696	Rogers Hornsby, 1924
.652	Chick Hafey, 1930

On-base avg: Highest, season

.507	Rogers Hornsby, 1924
.489	Rogers Hornsby, 1925
.463	Jesse Burkett, 1899
.459	Jack Clark, 1987
.459	Rogers Hornsby, 1922

Complete games: Most, season

46	Ted Breitenstein, 1894
46	Ted Breitenstein, 1895
43	Kid Gleason, 1892
42	Jack Taylor, 1898
40	Jack Powell, 1899
40	Cy Young, 1899

Saves: Most, season

47	LEE SMITH, 1991
45	Bruce Sutter, 1984
43	LEE SMITH, 1992
43	LEE SMITH, 1993
36	Tom Henke, 1995
36	Bruce Sutter, 1982
36	TODD WORRELL, 1986

Shutouts: Most, season

13	Bob Gibson, 1968
10	Mort Cooper, 1942
10	John Tudor, 1985
7	Harry Brecheen, 1948
7	Mort Cooper, 1944
7	Dizzy Dean, 1934
7	Bill Doak, 1914

Wins: Most, season

30	Dizzy Dean, 1934
28	Dizzy Dean, 1935
27	Ted Breitenstein, 1894
26	Cy Young, 1899
24	Dizzy Dean, 1936
24	Jesse Haines, 1927

K: Most, season

274	Bob Gibson, 1970
270	Bob Gibson, 1965
269	Bob Gibson, 1969
268	Bob Gibson, 1968
245	Bob Gibson, 1964

Win pct: Highest, season

.811	Dizzy Dean, 1934
.810	Ted Wilks, 1944
.789	Harry Brecheen, 1945
.778	Johnny Beazley, 1942
.767	Bob Gibson, 1970

ERA: Lowest, season

1.12	Bob Gibson, 1968
1.72	Bill Doak, 1914
1.78	Mort Cooper, 1942
1.90	Max Lanier, 1943
1.93	John Tudor, 1985

Most pinch-hit homers, season

4	George Crowe, 1959
4	George Crowe, 1960
4	Carl Sawatski, 1961

Most pinch-hit homers, career

8	George Crowe, 1959-1961
6	Gerald Perry, 1991-1995
6	Carl Sawatski, 1960-1963

Longest hitting streak

33	Rogers Hornsby, 1922
30	Stan Musial, 1950
29	Harry Walker, 1943
29	Ken Boyer, 1959
28	Joe Medwick, 1935
28	Red Schoendienst, 1954

Most consecutive scoreless innings

| 47 | Bob Gibson, 1968 |
| 37 | George Bradley, 1876 |

No-hit games

George Bradley, StL vs Har NL, 2-0; July 15, 1876.

Jesse Haines, StL vs Bos NL, 5-0; July 17, 1924.

Paul Dean, StL at Bro NL, 3-0; Sept. 21, 1934 (2nd game).

Lon Warneke, StL at Cin NL, 2-0; Aug. 30, 1941.

Ray Washburn, StL at SF NL, 2-0; Sept. 18, 1968.

Bob Gibson, StL at Pit NL, 11-0; Aug. 14, 1971.

Bob Forsch, StL vs Phi NL, 5-0; Apr. 16, 1978.

Bob Forsch, StL vs Mon NL, 3-0; Sept. 26, 1983.

Stoney McGlynn, seven innings, agreement, StL at Bro NL, 1-1; Sept. 24, 1906 (2nd game).

Ed Karger, seven perfect innings, agreement, StL vs Bos NL, 4-0; Aug. 11, 1907 (2nd game).

Johnny Lush, six innings, rain, StL at Bro NL, 2-0; Aug. 6, 1908.

ACTIVE PLAYERS in caps.

Players' years of service are listed by the first and last years with this team and are not necessarily consecutive; all statistics record performances for this team only.

Houston
Astros

By Russell Beeker, USA TODAY

Jeff Bagwell was third in the NL in on-base average and sixth in slugging.

1996 Astros: That old September swoon

Doug Drabek stood by the locker in the Houston clubhouse that has been his for the last four years, quietly stuffing personal items into a duffel bag in between handshakes with teammates. In November of 1992 the Astros signed the righthander to a four-year, $23.5 million contract. A 38-42 record in the four years since persuaded management not to exercise the option year on Drabek. "Whatever happens, happens," said Drabek. What happened was a 7-9 record, just one of a number of disappointments in a season that started with high hopes. Projected to be the No. 1 starter during spring training, Drabek recorded his smallest number of victories since his rookie year of 1986 (7-8 with the Yankees).

Another starter, Greg Swindell, was released after winning just one game. Injuries limited Mike Hampton to 27 starts, but only 15 came when the lefthander was completely healthy. Shane Reynolds started 16-6 but did not register a win after Aug. 24. The fifth starter's spot was handled well early by Donne Wall, but the 29-year-old rookie faded after teams got a second look at his changeup.

No fewer than 13 pitchers were used out of the bullpen. Injuries took their toll on John Hudek and Todd Jones, and Billy Wagner's debut was accelerated because of the shortage of relievers.

Right fielder Derek Bell drove in a career-high 113 runs but hit just .238 in his last 23 games. His slide was only one factor that contributed to Houston's 7-18 September, which dropped the club behind St. Louis. "I don't want another one-year deal," the arbitration-eligible Bell said before being rewarded with a three-year contract. "I think I deserve a multi-year deal. I've had four years in the league and drove in over 100 runs, and I think I deserve it."

First baseman Jeff Bagwell had another fine season, leading the team with a .315 average, 31 homers and 120 RBI. Second baseman Craig Biggio, who slumped in September, hit .288 with 15 home runs and 113 runs scored. Those two, com-

Team MVP

Jeff Bagwell: Jeff Bagwell managed to stay healthy for the entire season, and it showed in his numbers. The 1994 league MVP led the team with a .315 average, 31 home runs and 120 RBI as Houston set a club record for runs in a season. He also led the National League with 48 doubles. There were no repeats of the broken hands that plagued him the previous two seasons, and Bagwell and teammate Craig Biggio were the only NL players who didn't miss a game.

bined with third baseman Sean Berry, who hit .279 with 17 homers and 94 RBI despite playing with an injured shoulder that required off-season surgery, were the major offensive bright spots on a team that set a club record for runs scored.

"We spent almost the whole year in first place only to collapse in September," manager Terry Collins said. "That has been extremely frustrating for myself and the players." It has also been trying for the front office. Collins was fired and replaced by former Astros pitcher Larry Dierker, who had been part of the club's broadcast crew.

"I've got a feeling you're going to see a lot of new faces in this clubhouse next year," Hudek said. "It's the economics thing again. We're close, but because we're a small market, we may not be able to get the guys we need to put us over the top." One long-term boost for the economic situation came on Election Day, when Harris County voters narrowly approved a $265 million, 42,000-seat, retractable-roof stadium to be located downtown. Commissioners would pay for the new stadium with a proposed tax on rental cars and downtown parking, state sales and liquor tax revenues, and $85 million in private funds.

1996 Astros: Week-by-week notes

These notes were excerpted from the following issues of Baseball Weekly.

▶**April 3:** A pulled muscle in his left leg kept Doug Drabek from starting on Opening Day. Manager Terry Collins said Drabek probably won't get his first start until April 10.

▶**April 10:** Owner Drayton McLane Jr. said he is optimistic that a plan for a new baseball stadium can be worked out in the coming weeks. "We need a much smaller venue for baseball, one that would [seat] about 42,000," McLane said.

▶**April 17:** Darryl Kile has a 10.57 ERA in two losing starts. In his last outing Kile gave up 10 runs and nine hits, including a grand slam, in 3⅔ innings.

▶**April 24:** After 17 games, first baseman Jeff Bagwell was hitting .383 with six homers and 17 RBI. In 1995 after 17 games, he was hitting .165 with two homers and nine RBI.

▶**May 8:** Todd Jones, forced into the closer's role during John Hudek's absence, has been inconsistent. He is 3-0 with five saves, but all three victories came after he blew save opportunities.

▶**May 15:** The Astros might be without two-fifths of their starting rotation for an indefinite period. Right-hander Doug Brocail left the May 10 game at Montreal after five innings because of a problem in his right shoulder. Lefty Mike Hampton departed the game on May 12 in the second inning because of a sore left shoulder.

▶**May 22:** General manager Gerry Hunsicker isn't happy with the Astros' play of late, even though the club has been in or near first place most of the season. "We're certainly a better team than we've shown recently," Hunsicker said.

▶**June 12:** John Hudek took the mound on June 9 in the Astrodome for the first time since June 22, 1995. Hudek, sidelined because of rib surgery, pitched six minutes of batting practice to first baseman Mike Simms and catcher Randy Knorr. The goal is to have Hudek back in action for the second half of the season.

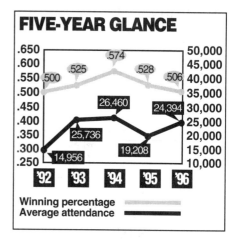

FIVE-YEAR GLANCE

Winning percentage
Average attendance

▶**June 26:** Rookie Billy Wagner's impressive performance since his call-up from Class AAA Tucson two weeks ago has stamped the left-hander as closer material. In 14⅔ innings, Wagner (1-0, one save, 1.84 ERA) has struck out 23 and walked seven.

▶**July 3:** The Astros passed the half-season point in the same position they spent most of the first 81 games: in first place but struggling to stay above .500. One big negative has been the performance of Doug Drabek, considered the ace of the staff in spring training, who is 3-6 with a 5.06 ERA.

▶**July 11:** The Braves beat Houston 4-2 on July 6, ending the Astros' seven-game winning streak. Houston's starters had pitched four complete games in their previous seven outings, helping the Astros put together their longest winning streak since 1991.

▶**July 24:** The Astros are averaging 23,716, which isn't keeping up with the 30,000 that Drayton McLane said he needed this year in order to keep the team in Houston. In the past 21 games, they have drawn an average of 27,017.

▶**July 31:** On July 24, GM Gerry Hunsicker picked up right-hander Danny Darwin from the Pirates for minor league right-hander Rich Loiselle, and Darwin quickly picked up two victories in relief, on July 26 and 28.

▶**Aug. 7:** The Astros were 15-12 in July despite sub-par performances from Jeff Bagwell (who hit .230 with two homers and eight RBI), right fielder Derek Bell (.250) and third baseman Sean Berry (.225). Quietly, right-handers Doug Drabek and Xavier Hernandez picked up the pace last month. Hernandez was 3-0 with a 2.57 ERA in July. Drabek is 2-0 in his last four starts with a 2.45 ERA. In his last 29⅓ innings, he has allowed only 22 hits.

▶**Aug. 14:** Right-hander Donne Wall was the toast of Houston's rotation after going 6-0 following his call-up from the minors. Houston was 10-0 in games that Wall had started. But lately, Wall has been toast. In seven starts since June 26, Wall is 0-4 with a 6.28 ERA. Manager Terry Collins decided it was time for a change, and Danny Darwin will take Wall's next turn in the rotation.

▶**Aug. 28:** The Astros lost left-hander Billy Wagner to the 15-day DL when he pulled his left groin muscle on Aug. 22. John Hudek, recalled to replace Wagner, got a standing ovation from the crowd of 35,544 the next night when he retired the side in order in the ninth inning of a 1-0 loss to the Cardinals. There were no cheers for the offense until catcher Tony Eusebio drove in Jeff Bagwell with a grounder to short during the fourth inning on Aug. 24, as the Astros had gone 22⅓ innings without scoring against St. Louis to that point.

▶**Sept. 11:** Jeff Bagwell had 294 total bases through Sept. 8 and needed seven to break the franchise record set by Cesar Cedeno in 1972 and matched by Bagwell in 1994.

▶**Sept. 18:** The Astros received good news on Sept. 14 when the city of Houston and Harris County officials agreed to terms with the team on a plan to build a $265 million, retractable-roof downtown stadium. Several steps remain for final approval, the last of which is a Nov. 5 referendum. On the field the Astros lost 10 of 14 as of Sept. 15 to fall 2½ games behind St. Louis. Second baseman Craig Biggio has been in a huge slump, having gone 5-for-45 in his last 12 games.

▶**Sept. 25:** The Astros' September swoon reached a low point in Florida on Sept. 21 when rookie Billy Wagner gave up homers on consecutive pitches to Jeff Conine and Devon White in the ninth to turn a 1-0 lead into a 2-1 loss. The team's record during the month stood at 4-15 after a 6-0 loss the next day.

▶**Oct. 2:** Doug Drabek's 7-9 season was but one of a number of disappointments in a season that had begun with much promise. Another starter, Greg Swindell, won just one game and was released. Shane Reynolds started 16-6 but did not win after Aug. 24. Jeff Bagwell led the team with a .315 average, 31 homers and 120 RBI. But Craig Biggio struggled in September and wound up hitting .288 with 15 homers and 75 RBI. Derek Bell drove in a career-high 113 runs but hit only .238 in his last 23 games. Houston's 7-18 September dropped the club into second place, six games behind the Cards.

Team directory

▶**Owner:** Drayton McLane Jr.
▶**General manager:** Gerry Hunsicker
▶**Ballpark:**
Houston Astrodome
8400 Kirby Dr.
Houston, Texas
713-799-9500
Capacity 54,350
Parking for 26,000 cars; $4 (subject to change)
Public transportation by bus
Wheelchair section and ramps
▶**Team publications:**
Astros Magazine, Astros Media Guide
713-799-9600
▶**TV, radio broadcast stations:**
KILT 610 AM, UPN Channel 20, Fox Sports Southwest
▶**Camps and/or clinics:**
Astros Youth Clinics, during the season, 713-799-9877
▶**Spring training:**
Osceola County Stadium
Kissimmee, Fla.
Capacity 5,130
407-933-6500

HOUSTON ASTROS 1996 final stats

BATTERS	BA	SLG	OB	G	AB	R	H	TB	2B	3B	HR	RBI	BB	SO	SB	CS	E
Goff	.500	1.250	.500	1	4	1	2	5	0	0	1	2	0	1	0	0	0
Bagwell	.315	.570	.451	162	568	111	179	324	48	2	31	120	135	114	21	7	16
Hajek	.300	.400	.417	8	10	3	3	4	1	0	0	0	2	0	0	0	0
Biggio	.288	.415	.386	162	605	113	174	251	24	4	15	75	75	72	25	7	10
Gutierrez	.284	.344	.359	89	218	28	62	75	8	1	1	15	23	42	6	1	12
Berry	.281	.492	.328	132	431	55	121	212	38	1	17	95	23	58	12	6	22
Hunter	.276	.363	.297	132	526	74	145	191	27	2	5	35	17	92	35	9	12
Eusebio	.270	.362	.343	58	152	15	41	55	7	2	1	19	18	20	0	1	1
Cangelosi	.263	.347	.378	108	262	49	69	91	11	4	1	16	44	41	17	9	3
Mouton	.263	.350	.343	122	300	40	79	105	15	1	3	34	38	55	21	9	5
Bell	.263	.418	.311	158	627	84	165	262	40	3	17	113	40	123	29	3	7
Miller	.256	.417	.291	139	468	43	120	195	26	2	15	58	14	116	3	7	21
Spiers	.252	.390	.320	122	218	27	55	85	10	1	6	26	20	34	7	0	5
May	.251	.378	.330	109	259	24	65	98	12	3	5	33	30	33	2	2	4
Cedeno	.231	.314	.284	52	156	11	36	49	2	1	3	18	11	33	3	2	10
Manwaring	.229	.282	.300	86	227	14	52	64	9	0	1	18	19	40	0	1	3
Abreu	.227	.273	.292	15	22	1	5	6	1	0	0	1	2	3	0	0	0
Montgomery	.214	.500	.267	12	14	4	3	7	1	0	1	4	1	5	0	0	0
Knorr	.195	.287	.245	37	87	7	17	25	5	0	1	7	5	18	0	1	0
Simms	.176	.279	.233	49	68	6	12	19	2	1	1	8	4	16	1	0	0

PITCHERS	W-L	ERA	G	GS	CG	GF	Sho	SV	IP	H	R	ER	HR	BB	SO
Wagner	2-2	2.44	37	0	0	20	0	9	51.2	28	16	14	6	30	67
Hudek	2-0	2.81	15	0	0	6	0	2	16.0	12	5	5	2	5	14
Hampton	10-10	3.59	27	27	2	0	1	0	160.1	175	79	64	12	49	101
Reynolds	16-10	3.65	35	35	4	0	1	0	239.0	227	103	97	20	44	204
Darwin	10-11	3.77	34	25	0	1	0	0	164.2	160	79	69	16	27	96
Kile	12-11	4.19	35	33	4	1	0	0	219.0	233	113	102	16	97	219
Jones	6-3	4.40	51	0	0	37	0	17	57.1	61	30	28	5	32	44
Wall	9-8	4.56	26	23	2	1	1	0	150.0	170	84	76	17	34	99
Drabek	7-9	4.57	30	30	1	0	0	0	175.1	208	102	89	21	60	137
Brocail	1-5	4.58	23	4	0	4	0	0	53.0	58	31	27	7	23	34
Young	3-3	4.59	28	0	0	10	0	0	33.1	36	18	17	4	22	19
Hernandez	5-5	4.62	61	0	0	27	0	6	78.0	77	45	40	13	28	81
Olson	1-0	4.82	9	0	0	2	0	0	9.1	12	5	5	1	7	8
Morman	4-1	4.93	53	0	0	9	0	0	42.0	43	24	23	8	24	31
Johnstone	1-0	5.54	9	0	0	6	0	0	13.0	17	8	8	2	5	5
Holt	0-1	5.79	4	0	0	3	0	0	4.2	5	3	3	0	3	0
Small	0-1	5.92	16	0	0	4	0	0	24.1	33	23	16	1	13	16
Tabaka	0-2	6.64	18	0	0	5	0	1	20.1	28	18	15	5	14	18
Swindell	0-3	7.83	8	4	0	3	0	0	23.0	35	25	20	5	11	15
Dougherty	0-2	9.00	12	0	0	2	0	0	13.0	14	14	13	2	11	6
Clark	0-2	11.37	5	0	0	3	0	0	6.1	16	10	8	1	2	5

1997 preliminary roster

PITCHERS (21)
Manuel Barrios
Ryan Creek
Sid Fernandez
Ramon Garcia
Mike Grzanich
Mike Hampton
Oscar Henriquez
Chris Holt
John Hudek
Darryl Kile
Jose Lima

Tom Martin
Trever Miller
Doug Mlicki
Alvin Morman
C.J. Nitkowski
Shane Reynolds
Mark Small
Billy Wagner
Donne Wall
Mike Walter

CATCHERS (2)
Brad Ausmus
Tony Eusebio

INFIELDERS (7)
Jeff Bagwell
Sean Berry
Craig Biggio
Andujar Cedeno
Ricky Gutierrez
Pat Listach
Bill Spiers

OUTFIELDERS (8)
Bobby Abreu
Derek Bell
Luis Gonzalez
Carlos Guillen
Richard Hidalgo
Thomas Howard
Ray Montgomery
James Mouton

Games played by position

PLAYER	G	C	1B	2B	3B	SS	OF
Abreu	15	0	0	0	0	0	7
Bagwell	162	0	162	0	0	0	0
Bell	158	0	0	0	0	0	157
Berry	132	0	0	0	110	0	0
Biggio	162	0	0	162	0	0	0
Cangelosi	108	0	0	0	0	0	78
Cedeno	52	0	0	0	3	49	0
Eusebio	58	47	0	0	0	0	0
Goff	1	1	0	0	0	0	0
Gutierrez	89	0	0	5	6	74	0
Hajek	8	0	0	2	3	0	0
Hunter	132	0	0	0	0	0	127
Knorr	37	33	0	0	0	0	0
Manwaring	86	86	0	0	0	0	0
May	109	0	0	0	0	0	71
Miller	139	0	0	0	29	117	0
Montgomery	12	0	0	0	0	0	6
Mouton	122	0	0	0	0	0	108
Simms	49	0	5	0	0	0	12
Spiers	122	0	4	7	77	4	2

Minor Leagues

Tops in the organization

BATTER	CLUB	AVG.	G	AB	R	H	HR	RBI
M. Meluskey	Jck	.326	112	365	47	119	1	52
Jeff Ball	Tcn	.324	116	429	64	139	19	73
Kary Bridges	Tcn	.322	129	478	75	154	5	54
Dave Hajek	Tcn	.317	121	508	81	161	4	64
R. Johnson	Jck	.310	132	496	86	154	15	74

HOME RUNS

Chris Hatcher	Tcn	31			
R. Montgomery	Tcn	22			
Jeff Ball	Tcn	19			
Russ Johnson	Jck	15			
Several Players Tied At		14			

WINS

Edgar Ramos	Jck	13
Scott Elarton	Kis	12
Paul O'Malley	Qc	11
Brian Sikorski	Qc	11
Doug Simons	Tcn	11

RBI

Chris Hatcher	Tcn	97
R. Hidalgo	Jck	78
R. Montgomery	Tcn	75
Russ Johnson	Jck	74
Jeff Ball	Tcn	73

SAVES

Manuel Barrios	Jck	23
Michael Walter	Qc	21
Chris McFerrin	Aub	20
O. Henriquez	Kis	15
Jason McCarter	Ast	8

STOLEN BASES

C. Hernandez	Qc	41
Pedro Santana	Ast	33
Bob Abreu	Tcn	24
Julio Lugo	Qc	24
Several Players Tied At		17

STRIKEOUTS

Brian Sikorski	Qc	150
Chris Holt	Tcn	137
Edgar Ramos	Jck	133
Scott Elarton	Kis	130
Ryan Creek	Jck	119

PITCHER	CLUB	W-L	ERA	IP	H	BB	SO
Tony Mounce	Kis	9-9	2.25	156	139	68	102
Luis Yanez	Aub	5-5	2.45	99	85	31	73
Jamie Walker	Jck	5-1	2.50	101	94	35	79
Scott Elarton	Kis	12-7	2.92	72	154	54	130
Edgar Ramos	Jck	13-5	3.06	144	114	44	133

Sick call: 1996 DL report

PLAYER	Days on the DL
Doug Brocail	96
Terry Clark	53
Doug Drabek	16
Tony Eusebio	86*
John Hudek	105
Todd Jones	49*
Brian Lee Hunter	28
Derrick May	15
Greg Swindell	32
Billy Wagner	15
Anthony Young	19

Indicates two separate terms on Disabled List.

1996 salaries

	Bonuses	Total earned salary
Doug Drabek, p		$5,050,000
Jeff Bagwell, 1b		$4,875,000
Derek Bell, of	$200,000	$2,800,000
Craig Biggio, 2b	$75,000	$2,075,000
Kirt Manwaring, c		$1,875,000
Sean Berry, 3b		$995,000
Darryl Kile, p		$750,000
Derrick May, of		$750,000
Danny Darwin, p	$300,000	$550,000
Gregg Olson, p		$400,000
Bill Spiers, 2b	$75,000	$400,000
Shane Reynolds, p		$330,000
Tony Eusebio, c		$300,000
Todd Jones, p		$300,000
John Cangelosi, of		$280,000
Randy Knorr, c		$280,000
Mike Hampton, p		$275,000
Ricky Gutierrez, ss		$235,000
Doug Brocail, p		$220,000
John Hudek, p		$210,000
Orlando Miller, ss		$205,000
James Mouton, of		$196,000
Terry Clark, p		$180,000
Brian Hunter, of		$180,000
Mike Simms, of		$160,000
Donne Wall, p		$115,000
Xavier Hernandez, p		$109,000
Alvin Morman, p		$109,000
Billy Wagner, p		$109,000

Average 1996 salary: $838,379
Total 1996 team payroll: $24,313,000
Termination pay: $4,800,000

Houston (1962-1996)

Runs: Most, career

890	Cesar Cedeno, 1970-1981
871	Jose Cruz, 1975-1987
829	Jim Wynn, 1963-1973
728	CRAIG BIGGIO, 1988-1996
676	Terry Puhl, 1977-1990

Hits: Most, career

1937	Jose Cruz, 1975-1987
1659	Cesar Cedeno, 1970-1981
1448	Bob Watson, 1966-1979
1357	Terry Puhl, 1977-1990
1291	Jim Wynn, 1963-1973

2B: Most, career

343	Cesar Cedeno, 1970-1981
335	Jose Cruz, 1975-1987
245	CRAIG BIGGIO, 1988-1996
241	Bob Watson, 1966-1979
228	Jim Wynn, 1963-1973

3B: Most, career

80	Jose Cruz, 1975-1987
63	Joe Morgan, 1963-1980
62	Roger Metzger, 1971-1978
56	Terry Puhl, 1977-1990
55	Cesar Cedeno, 1970-1981
55	Craig Reynolds, 1979-1989

HR: Most, career

223	Jim Wynn, 1963-1973
166	Glenn Davis, 1984-1990
163	Cesar Cedeno, 1970-1981
144	JEFF BAGWELL, 1991-1996
139	Bob Watson, 1966-1979

RBI: Most, career

942	Jose Cruz, 1975-1987
782	Bob Watson, 1966-1979
778	Cesar Cedeno, 1970-1981
719	Jim Wynn, 1963-1973
600	Doug Rader, 1967-1975

SB: Most, career

487	Cesar Cedeno, 1970-1981
288	Jose Cruz, 1975-1987
221	CRAIG BIGGIO, 1988-1996
219	Joe Morgan, 1963-1980
217	Terry Puhl, 1977-1990

BB: Most, career

847	Jim Wynn, 1963-1973
730	Jose Cruz, 1975-1987
678	Joe Morgan, 1963-1980
585	Bill Doran, 1982-1990
550	CRAIG BIGGIO, 1988-1996

BA: Highest, career

.307	JEFF BAGWELL, 1991-1996
.297	Bob Watson, 1966-1979
.292	Jose Cruz, 1975-1987
.289	Cesar Cedeno, 1970-1981
.285	CRAIG BIGGIO, 1988-1996

Slug avg: Highest, career

.525	JEFF BAGWELL, 1991-1996
.483	Glenn Davis, 1984-1990
.454	Cesar Cedeno, 1970-1981
.445	Jim Wynn, 1963-1973
.444	Bob Watson, 1966-1979

On-base avg: Highest, career

.406	JEFF BAGWELL, 1991-1996
.374	Joe Morgan, 1963-1980
.371	CRAIG BIGGIO, 1988-1996
.364	Bob Watson, 1966-1979
.362	Jim Wynn, 1963-1973

Complete games: Most, career

106	Larry Dierker, 1964-1976
82	Joe Niekro, 1975-1985
78	Don Wilson, 1966-1974
76	J.R. Richard, 1971-1980
42	Mike Scott, 1983-1991

Saves: Most, career

199	Dave Smith, 1980-1990
76	Fred Gladding, 1968-1973
72	Joe Sambito, 1976-1984
62	DOUG JONES, 1992-1993
50	Ken Forsch, 1970-1980

Shutouts: Most, career

25	Larry Dierker, 1964-1976
21	Joe Niekro, 1975-1985
21	Mike Scott, 1983-1991
20	Don Wilson, 1966-1974
19	J.R. Richard, 1971-1980

Wins: Most, career

144	Joe Niekro, 1975-1985
137	Larry Dierker, 1964-1976
110	Mike Scott, 1983-1991
107	J.R. Richard, 1971-1980
106	Nolan Ryan, 1980-1988

K: Most, career

1866	Nolan Ryan, 1980-1988
1493	J.R. Richard, 1971-1980
1487	Larry Dierker, 1964-1976
1318	Mike Scott, 1983-1991
1283	Don Wilson, 1966-1974

Win pct: Highest, career

.634	M. PORTUGAL, 1989-1993
.609	Jim Ray, 1965-1973
.601	J.R. Richard, 1971-1980
.577	PETE HARNISCH, 1991-1994
.576	Mike Scott, 1983-1991

ERA: Lowest, career

2.53	Dave Smith, 1980-1990
3.13	Nolan Ryan, 1980-1988
3.15	Don Wilson, 1966-1974
3.15	J.R. Richard, 1971-1980
3.18	Ken Forsch, 1970-1980

Runs: Most, season

123	CRAIG BIGGIO, 1995
117	Jim Wynn, 1972
113	CRAIG BIGGIO, 1996
113	Jim Wynn, 1969
111	JEFF BAGWELL, 1996

Hits: Most, season

195	Enos Cabell, 1978
189	Jose Cruz, 1983
187	Jose Cruz, 1984
185	Jose Cruz, 1980
185	Greg Gross, 1974

2B: Most, season

48	JEFF BAGWELL, 1996
44	CRAIG BIGGIO, 1994
44	Rusty Staub, 1967
41	CRAIG BIGGIO, 1993
40	DEREK BELL, 1996
40	Cesar Cedeno, 1971

3B: Most, season

14	Roger Metzger, 1973
13	Jose Cruz, 1984
13	STEVE FINLEY, 1992
13	STEVE FINLEY, 1993
12	Joe Morgan, 1965
12	Craig Reynolds, 1981

HR: Most, season

39	JEFF BAGWELL, 1994
37	Jim Wynn, 1967
34	Glenn Davis, 1989
33	Jim Wynn, 1969
31	JEFF BAGWELL, 1996
31	Glenn Davis, 1986

RBI: Most, season

120	JEFF BAGWELL, 1996
116	JEFF BAGWELL, 1994
113	DEREK BELL, 1996

| 110 | Bob Watson, 1977 |
| 107 | Jim Wynn, 1967 |

SB: Most, season

65	Gerald Young, 1988
64	Eric Yelding, 1990
61	Cesar Cedeno, 1977
58	Cesar Cedeno, 1976
57	Cesar Cedeno, 1974

BB: Most, season

148	Jim Wynn, 1969
135	JEFF BAGWELL, 1996
110	Joe Morgan, 1969
106	Jim Wynn, 1970
103	Jim Wynn, 1972

BA: Highest, season

.368	JEFF BAGWELL, 1994
.334	DEREK BELL, 1995
.333	Rusty Staub, 1967
.324	Bob Watson, 1975
.320	Cesar Cedeno, 1972

Slug avg: Highest, season

.750	JEFF BAGWELL, 1994
.570	JEFF BAGWELL, 1996
.537	Cesar Cedeno, 1973
.537	Cesar Cedeno, 1972
.516	JEFF BAGWELL, 1993

On-base avg: Highest, season

.451	JEFF BAGWELL, 1994
.451	JEFF BAGWELL, 1996
.436	Jim Wynn, 1969
.411	CRAIG BIGGIO, 1994
.410	Joe Morgan, 1966

Complete games: Most, season

20	Larry Dierker, 1969
19	J.R. Richard, 1979
18	Don Wilson, 1971
17	Larry Dierker, 1970
16	Mike Cuellar, 1967
16	Joe Niekro, 1982
16	J.R. Richard, 1978

Saves: Most, season

36	DOUG JONES, 1992
33	Dave Smith, 1986
29	Fred Gladding, 1969
27	Dave Smith, 1985
27	Dave Smith, 1988

Shutouts: Most, season

6	Dave Roberts, 1973
5	Larry Dierker, 1972
5	Bob Knepper, 1981
5	Bob Knepper, 1986
5	Joe Niekro, 1979
5	Joe Niekro, 1982

| 5 | Mike Scott, 1986 |
| 5 | Mike Scott, 1988 |

Wins: Most, season

21	Joe Niekro, 1979
20	Larry Dierker, 1969
20	Joe Niekro, 1980
20	J.R. Richard, 1976
20	Mike Scott, 1989

K: Most, season

313	J.R. Richard, 1979
306	Mike Scott, 1986
303	J.R. Richard, 1978
270	Nolan Ryan, 1987
245	Nolan Ryan, 1982

Win pct: Highest, season

.818	MARK PORTUGAL, 1993
.692	Mike Scott, 1985
.667	Mike Scott, 1989
.656	Joe Niekro, 1979
.652	DARRYL KILE, 1993
.652	Larry Dierker, 1972

ERA: Lowest, season

2.18	Bob Knepper, 1981
2.21	DANNY DARWIN, 1990
2.22	Mike Cuellar, 1966
2.22	Mike Scott, 1986
2.33	Larry Dierker, 1969

Most pinch-hit homers, season

| 5 | Cliff Johnson, 1974 |
| 3 | Joe Gaines, 1965 |

Most pinch-hit homers, career

| 8 | Cliff Johnson, 1972-1977 |
| 6 | Denny Walling, 1977-1992 |

Longest hitting streak

23	Art Howe, 1981
22	Cesar Cedeno, 1977
21	Lee May, 1973
21	Dickie Thon, 1982
20	Rusty Staub, 1967
20	Kevin Bass, 1986

Most consecutive
scoreless innings

| 31 | J.R. Richard, 1980 |

No-hit games

Don Nottebart, Hou vs Phi NL, 4-1;
   May 17, 1963.
Ken T. Johnson, Hou vs Cin NL, 0-1;
   Apr. 23, 1964 (lost the game).
Don Wilson, Hou vs Atl NL, 2-0;
   June 18, 1967.
Don Wilson, Hou at Cin NL, 4-0;
   May 1, 1969.

Larry Dierker, Hou vs Mon NL, 6-0;
   July 9, 1976.
Ken Forsch, Hou vs Atl NL, 6-0;
   Apr. 7, 1979.
Nolan Ryan, Hou vs LA NL, 5-0;
   Sept. 26, 1981.
Mike Scott, Hou vs SF NL, 2-0;
   Sept. 25, 1986.
DARRYL KILE, Hou vs NY NL, 7-1;
   Sept. 8, 1993.

ACTIVE PLAYERS in caps.

Players' years of service are listed by the first and last years with this team and are not necessarily consecutive; all statistics record performances for this team only.

Cincinnati Reds

By H. Darr Beiser, USA TODAY

Barry Larkin set career highs in homers, RBI, runs scored and slugging average.

1996 Reds: Injuries hurt the '95 champs

Pitching, or the lack of it, ruined what many thought would be a good season for the Cincinnati Reds. It began with the knowledge that No. 1 starter Jose Rijo wouldn't return from Tommy John elbow surgery performed the previous August. He tried to throw too soon in spring training, set himself back and was out for the season. Then, Pete Schourek, an 18-game winner in 1995, encountered elbow difficulties after throwing 137 pitches in his third start. Schourek was on the disabled list twice, finally undergoing surgery near the All-Star break that shelved him for the season. He was 1-4 in seven games after a 3-0 start.

A year of misery for right fielder Reggie Sanders added to the club's many woes. The man who batted .306 with 28 home runs and 99 RBI in '95 injured himself twice during spring training, and it continued throughout the season. He was on the disabled list three times for three different injuries, missed the final two weeks of the season and played only 81 games. He hit .251 with 14 homers, but had only 33 RBI and struck out 86 times in 287 at-bats.

Closer Jeff Brantley, who set a club record with 44 saves, was one of the team's bright lights. "How many guys have been released [by the Giants] and come back to set a team record in saves and win the Rolaids Award," Brantley said. "None. That's how many." After winning the NL MVP last year, Barry Larkin had an even better year, becoming the first shortstop in the 30-30 club, with team highs of 33 home runs and 36 stolen bases. Larkin also led the team with 89 RBI. After a slow start due to injuries, first baseman Hal Morris ended the season with a major-league-high 29-game hitting streak, the second longest on the Reds in this century to Pete Rose's 44. His .313 average led the club.

There were a few other pleasant surprises. Outfielder Eric Davis, out for nearly two seasons with a neck problem, signed with the Reds for a bargain-basement $500,000 and put together Comeback Player of the

Year numbers (.287, 26 HR, 83 RBI). Catcher Joe Oliver also was brought in on the cheap. Unhappily playing in a platoon situation, he still hit 11 homers and drove in 46 runs while starting 81 games to 76 for Eddie Taubensee, who had 48 RBI. The two also combined to hit 23 home runs.

The team's problems included second baseman Bret Boone, who struggled through a .233 year. Manager Ray Knight was never able to settle on a full-time solution at third base or in left field. He used six players at third, with Willie Greene finally making an impact by hitting 19 home runs. But he hit only .244 overall and showed no signs of being able to handle lefties. The left-field casting call included 11 names, with converted infielder Eric Owens's 52 games played being the team high for the position. Kevin Mitchell was reacquired from Boston late in the season and provided the most oomph, hitting .325 with six homers and 11 doubles in 37 games.

One player who won't be back is Lee Smith, baseball's all-time saves leader. Brought in at mid-season in a trade with California as a setup man for Brantley, Smith was not an integral piece of the puzzle. He said at season's end, "Cincinnati will be a quickly forgotten part of my career." The Reds will say the same thing of 1996 in their team history.

1996 Reds: Week-by-week notes

These notes were excerpted from the following issues of Baseball Weekly.

▶**April 3:** Eric Davis was so impressive that he is close to becoming the regular left fielder. Manager Ray Knight said if it becomes clear Davis is an every-day player, Knight might switch him back to his old position, center field.

▶**April 10:** In his first appearance after undergoing foot surgery on March 3, closer Jeff Brantley struck out the side in the ninth inning of an 8-4 victory against Philadelphia.

▶**April 24:** MVP shortstop Barry Larkin, who made only 11 errors last season, said nothing about his sore arm until he had four miscues after 13 games. "Tenderness in the biceps—no official diagnosis, but the pitchers tell me it's tendinitis," said Larkin.

▶**May 8:** Eric Davis had grand slams on May 4 and 5, becoming the 18th man in major league history to hit slams in consecutive games.

▶**May 15:** After a nine-game losing streak, the Reds reeled off seven consecutive victories as the starting pitching completely turned things around. The starters have put together a 2.66 ERA during May, allowing only 15 earned runs in 50⅔ innings.

▶**June 5:** Left-hander Pete Schourek tried skipping a couple of turns and tried extra rest, but it didn't help his aching elbow. So after a 9-1 loss to the Braves on May 31, Schourek was placed on the DL. He threw 137 pitches in his third start, and he hasn't been right since—1-4 in seven starts with a 7.51 ERA.

▶**June 12:** Mark Portugal, 0-4 in his first nine starts, beat Greg Maddux and the Atlanta Braves on June 1. He gave up two runs and six hits in seven innings for the 3-2 victory, his first in nearly 10 months.

▶**June 19:** With Marge Schott suspended, interim CEO John Allen is instituting major fan-friendly improvements and compiling a wish list from the players. On it is the repair of a clubhouse whirlpool

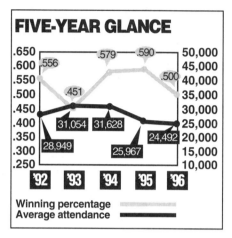

FIVE-YEAR GLANCE

Winning percentage
Average attendance

that hasn't worked in 2½ years.

▶**June 26:** After eight consecutive defeats in 1996 over 14 starts, Dave Burba won 5-3 on June 20 against the Mets. The long drought was not entirely Burba's fault. In his previous 10 starts, the Reds averaged only 1.3 runs. Outfielder Eric Davis continued his quest for the Comeback Player of the Year Award. Davis leads the team in homers (14), RBI (43), slugging percentage (.600) and walks (34).

▶**July 3:** For the first time last week, Ray Knight was able to put the team on the field that was projected during spring training, and things began dropping into place during a seven-game winning streak. Barry Larkin, second baseman Bret Boone, right fielder Reggie Sanders and Eric Davis all missed time, preventing them from being in the lineup at the same time.

▶**July 11:** Pete Schourek's season is over, and his career is in question. An 18-game winner and runner-up in Cy Young balloting last season, Schourek is expected to undergo exploratory surgery on his elbow by this week. The surgery will determine if Schourek needs ligament reconstruction, the same type of surgery that Jose Rijo has had. "That's $10 million worth of pitchers on the disabled list," said general manager Jim Bowden.

▶**July 24:** It looks as if the rehabilitating

Jose Rijo, who had ligament damage and surgery last August, won't return this year. If Rijo doesn't pitch, his $6 million-plus salary will be paid by insurance. If he throws even one pitch for the Reds this season, the club must pay his full salary.

▸**July 31:** Owner Marge Schott was allowed to return to her luxury box and to the field on July 28, but may not go to her executive office in the stadium. Schott was disciplined by Major League Baseball because of her insensitive comments about blacks, Jews and Asians. She also must give up day-to-day operation of the Reds through the 1998 season.

▸**Aug. 7:** With his 20th home run, off L.A.'s Chan Ho Park on Aug. 9, Barry Larkin tied the club record for shortstops set by Leo Cardenas in 1966. Pitchers are being extremely careful with the National League MVP. He is tied for fifth in the league with 63 walks.

▸**Aug. 14:** In the first two games that outfielder Kevin Mitchell started for the Reds after his acquisition from Boston, the Reds' offense exploded for 19 runs and 23 hits in wins over Houston and Montreal.

▸**Aug. 21:** Reggie Sanders was 3-for-36 with 18 strikeouts when he batted in the eighth inning of the second game of a doubleheader against the Rockies on Aug. 17. Catcher Eddie Taubensee had just homered to tie the game 4-4. Sanders also homered. After a single by Bret Boone, Jeff Branson and Barry Larkin slugged back-to-back homers, giving the Reds four in one inning en route to a 9-5 victory. The Reds hadn't homered in 196 plate appearances when Taubensee connected. Outfielder Thomas Howard went on a tear—22-for-39, including seven consecutive hits. Ray Knight played revolving outfielders to make certain Howard was in the lineup.

▸**Sept. 4:** In seven games at Coors Field, center fielder Eric Davis batted .478 (13-for-27) with five homers and 15 RBI. "Can I get traded here?" Davis asked.

▸**Sept. 11:** The Reds began putting together a 1997 pitching staff by signing three potential free agents to multiyear deals. Starter John Smiley, closer Jeff

Brantley and reliever Jeff Shaw agreed to terms.

▸**Sept. 25:** Jeff Brantley set a club record with his 40th save on Sept. 20 against St. Louis, eclipsing John Franco's 1988 record of 39.

▸**Oct. 2:** Lack of pitching ruined what many thought would be a decent season for the Reds. They began knowing No. 1 starter Jose Rijo wouldn't return soon from elbow surgery, and then Pete Schourek went on the DL twice, finally underwent surgery near the All-Star break and missed the rest of the season. Reggie Sanders was on the DL three times, playing only 81 games and hitting just .251 with 14 homers and 33 RBI. Closer Jeff Brantley was one of the team's bright lights, setting a club record with 44 saves. After being the NL MVP last year, Barry Larkin came back with a better year, hitting .298 with 33 homers and 36 steals. The most surprising Red was Eric Davis, who batted .287 and hit 26 homers after not playing since 1994.

Team directory

▸**Owners:** Marge Schott and a limited partnership
▸**General manager:** James G. Bowden
▸**Ballpark:**
Cinergy Stadium
Pete Rose Way
Cincinnati, Ohio
513-421-4510
Capacity 52,952
Parking for 5,022 cars; $3.50-$5
Wheelchair locations, ramps
▸**Team publications:**
Media guide, yearbook/program,
Reds Report, 513-421-4510
▸**TV, radio broadcast stations:**
WLW 700 AM, WSTR Channel 64,
SportsChannel-Ohio
▸**Spring training:**
Plant City Stadium
Plant City, Fla.
Capacity 6,700
813-752-1878

CINCINNATI REDS 1996 final stats

BATTERS	BA	SLG	OB	G	AB	R	H	TB	2B	3B	HR	RBI	BB	SO	SB	CS	E
Kev. Mitchell	.325	.579	.447	37	114	18	37	66	11	0	6	26	26	16	0	0	2
Morris	.313	.479	.374	142	528	82	165	253	32	4	16	80	50	76	7	5	8
Larkin	.298	.567	.410	152	517	117	154	293	32	4	33	89	96	52	36	10	17
Taubensee	.291	.462	.338	108	327	46	95	151	20	0	12	48	26	64	3	4	11
Davis	.287	.523	.394	129	415	81	119	217	20	0	26	83	70	121	23	9	3
Fordyce	.286	.429	.500	4	7	0	2	3	1	0	0	1	3	1	0	0	0
Harris	.285	.404	.330	125	302	33	86	122	17	2	5	32	21	31	14	6	6
Howard	.272	.431	.307	121	360	50	98	155	19	10	6	42	17	51	6	5	3
Kei. Mitchell	.267	.533	.313	11	15	2	4	8	1	0	1	3	1	3	0	0	1
Sabo	.256	.400	.354	54	125	15	32	50	7	1	3	16	18	27	2	0	4
Sanders	.251	.463	.353	81	287	49	72	133	17	1	14	33	44	86	24	8	2
Branson	.244	.408	.312	129	311	34	76	127	16	4	9	37	31	67	2	0	14
Greene	.244	.495	.327	115	287	48	70	142	5	5	19	63	36	88	0	1	16
Oliver	.242	.405	.311	106	289	31	70	117	12	1	11	46	28	54	2	0	5
Boone	.233	.354	.275	142	520	56	121	184	21	3	12	69	31	100	3	2	6
Goodwin	.228	.250	.323	49	136	20	31	34	3	0	0	5	19	34	15	6	2
Perez	.222	.472	.317	18	36	8	8	17	0	0	3	5	5	9	0	0	0
Mottola	.215	.367	.271	35	79	10	17	29	3	0	3	6	6	16	2	2	0
Belk	.200	.200	.250	7	15	2	3	3	0	0	0	0	1	2	0	0	0
Owens	.200	.229	.281	88	205	26	41	47	6	0	0	9	23	38	16	2	2
Kelly	.184	.327	.333	19	49	5	9	16	4	0	1	7	9	11	4	0	1
Coleman	.155	.226	.237	33	84	10	13	19	1	1	1	4	9	31	12	2	1
Gibralter	.000	.000	.000	2	2	0	0	0	0	0	0	0	0	2	0	0	1

PITCHERS	W-L	ERA	G	GS	CG	GF	Sho	SV	IP	H	R	ER	HR	BB	SO
Spradlin	0-0	0.00	1	0	0	1	0	0	0.1	0	0	0	0	0	0
Sullivan	0-0	2.25	7	0	0	4	0	0	8.0	7	2	2	0	5	3
Brantley	1-2	2.41	66	0	0	61	0	44	71.0	54	21	19	7	28	76
Shaw	8-6	2.49	78	0	0	24	0	4	104.2	99	34	29	8	29	69
Smiley	13-14	3.64	35	34	2	0	2	0	217.1	207	100	88	20	54	171
Carrasco	4-3	3.75	56	0	0	10	0	0	74.1	58	37	31	6	45	59
Burba	11-13	3.83	34	33	0	0	0	0	195.0	179	96	83	18	97	148
Service	1-0	3.94	34	1	0	5	0	0	48.0	51	21	21	7	18	46
Portugal	8-9	3.98	27	26	1	0	1	0	156.0	146	77	69	20	42	93
Smith	3-4	4.06	43	0	0	16	0	2	44.1	49	20	20	4	23	35
Lyons	2-0	4.50	3	3	0	0	0	0	16.0	17	8	8	1	7	14
Morgan	6-11	4.63	23	23	0	0	0	0	130.1	146	72	67	16	47	74
Salkeld	8-5	5.20	29	19	1	2	1	0	116.0	114	69	67	18	54	82
Ruffin	1-3	5.49	49	0	0	13	0	0	62.1	71	42	38	10	37	69
Remlinger	0-1	5.60	19	4	0	2	0	0	27.1	24	17	17	4	19	19
Moore	3-3	5.81	23	0	0	11	0	2	26.1	26	21	17	3	22	27
Carrara	1-0	5.87	8	5	0	1	0	0	23.0	31	17	15	6	13	13
Jarvis	8-9	5.98	24	20	2	2	1	0	120.1	152	93	80	17	43	63
Schourek	4-5	6.01	12	12	0	0	0	0	67.1	79	48	45	7	24	54
Martinez	0-0	6.30	9	0	0	0	0	0	10.0	13	9	7	2	8	9
McElroy	2-0	6.57	12	0	0	1	0	0	12.1	13	10	9	2	10	13
Lilliquist	0-0	7.36	5	0	0	3	0	0	3.2	5	3	3	1	0	1
Pugh	1-1	11.49	10	0	0	0	0	0	15.2	24	20	20	3	11	9

1997 preliminary roster

PITCHERS (18)
Ricky Bones
Jeff Brantley
Dave Burba
Hector Carrasco
Kevin Jarvis
Curt Lyons
Kent Mercker
Mike Morgan
Noe Najera
Mike Remlinger
Jose Rijo
Roger Salkeld

Pete Schourek
Scott Service
Jeff Shaw
John Smiley
Scott Sullivan
Gabe White

CATCHERS (4)
Paul Bako
Brook Fordyce
Eddie Taubensee
Justin Towle

INFIELDERS (10)
Aaron Boone
Bret Boone
Jeff Branson
Willie Greene
Lenny Harris
Barry Larkin
Hal Morris
Eric Owens
Eduardo Perez
Pokey Reese

OUTFIELDERS (8)
Steve Gibralter
Curtis Goodwin
Mike Kelly
Chad Mottola
Glenn Murray
Reggie Sanders
Ruben Sierra
Pat Watkins

Games played by position

PLAYER	G	C	1B	2B	3B	SS	OF
Belk	7	0	6	0	0	0	0
Boone	142	0	0	141	0	0	0
Branson	129	0	0	31	64	38	0
Coleman	33	0	0	0	0	0	20
Davis	129	0	1	0	0	0	126
Fordyce	4	4	0	0	0	0	0
Gibralter	2	0	0	0	0	0	2
Goodwin	49	0	0	0	0	0	42
Greene	115	0	2	0	74	1	10
Harris	125	0	16	8	24	0	37
Howard	121	0	0	0	0	0	103
Kelly	19	0	0	0	0	0	17
Larkin	152	0	0	0	0	151	0
Kei. Mitchell	11	0	0	0	0	0	5
Kev. Mitchell	37	0	3	0	0	0	31
Morris	142	0	140	0	0	0	0
Mottola	35	0	0	0	0	0	31
Oliver	106	97	3	0	0	0	3
Owens	88	0	0	6	5	0	52
Perez	18	0	8	0	3	0	0
Sabo	54	0	0	0	43	0	0
Sanders	81	0	0	0	0	0	80
Taubensee	108	94	0	0	0	0	0

Sick call: 1996 DL report

PLAYER	Days on the DL
Eric Anthony	44*
Bret Boone	15
Jeff Brantley	5
Eric Davis	15
Willie Greene	15
Thomas Howard	19
Chuck McElroy	27
Hal Morris	15
Mark Portugal	19
Pokey Reese	13
Jose Rijo	182
Chris Sabo	27
Reggie Sanders	60**
Pete Schourek	111*
Gabe White	13

Indicates two separate terms on Disabled List.
**Indicates three separate terms on Disabled List.*

Minor Leagues

Tops in the organization

BATTER	CLUB	AVG.	G	AB	R	H	HR	RBI
J. Parsons	W-S	.331	85	299	44	99	8	48
Ray Brown	Cng	.327	115	364	68	119	13	52
R. Santana	Ind	.300	104	360	51	108	8	58
Keith Mitchell	Ind	.300	112	357	60	107	16	66
Billy Hall	Cng	.295	117	461	80	136	2	43

HOME RUNS

Eduardo Perez	Ind	21
D. Conner	W-S	20
Darron Ingram	Bil	18
Nick Morrow	Cng	18
Several Players Tied At		17

WINS

Travis Buckley	Ind	14
Curt Lyons	Cng	13
Chris Reed	Cng	13
Clint Koppe	Cng	12
Brett Tomko	Cng	11

RBI

Aaron Boone	Cng	95
Eduardo Perez	Ind	84
Marlon Allen	W-S	82
Christian Rojas	Cwv	70
Mike Hampton	Cwv	68

SAVES

Domingo Jean	Cng	31
Scott Service	Ind	15
Adam Bryant	Cng	15
D. Cushman	Cwv	15
Jerry Spradlin	Ind	15

STOLEN BASES

Curtis Goodwin	Ind	40
S. Claybrook	Cwv	37
Billy Hall	Cng	34
D. Conner	W-S	33
C. Ladell	Cng	31

STRIKEOUTS

Curt Lyons	Cng	176
Brett Tomko	Cng	164
Ben Bailey	W-S	144
Chris Reed	Cng	135
Justin Atchley	W-S	128

PITCHER	CLUB	W-L	ERA	IP	H	BB	SO
Curt Lyons	Cng	13-4	2.41	142	113	52	176
Scott Sullivan	Ind	5-2	2.73	109	95	37	77
Eddy Garcia	Cwv	7-6	3.03	107	91	58	74
Ben Bailey	W-S	10-11	3.24	164	149	57	144
Jerry Spradlin	Ind	6-8	3.33	100	94	23	79

1996 salaries

	Bonuses	Total earned salary
Jose Rijo, p		$6,150,000
Barry Larkin, ss	$100,000	$5,700,000
John Smiley, p		$4,975,000
Mark Portugal, p		$4,333,334
Reggie Sanders, of		$3,575,000
Pete Schourek, p		$3,300,000
Lee Smith, p		$2,100,000
Jeff Brantley, p	$350,000	$1,850,000
Hal Morris, 1b		$1,600,000
Kevin Mitchell, of	$1,235,000	$1,485,000
Dave Burba, p	$25,000	$1,125,000
Eric Davis, of	$250,000	$750,000
Bret Boone, 2b		$725,000
Joe Oliver, c	$208,000	$708,000
Thomas Howard, of		$675,000
Eddie Taubensee, c		$625,000
Lenny Harris, 3b	$50,000	$550,000
Jeff Shaw, p	$100,000	$450,000
Jeff Branson, 3b		$425,000
Johnny Ruffin, p		$195,000
Hector Carrasco, p		$160,000
Curtis Goodwin, of		$145,000
Eduardo Perez, 3b		$140,000
Scott Service, p		$140,000
Willie Greene, 3b		$130,000
Mike Remlinger, p		$130,000
Giovanni Carrara, p		$115,000
Eric Owens, of		$109,000

Average 1996 salary: $1,513,048
Total 1996 team payroll: $42,365,334
Termination pay: $1,311,612

Cincinnati (1890-1996)

Runs: Most, career

1741	Pete Rose,	1963-1986
1091	Johnny Bench,	1967-1983
1043	Frank Robinson,	1956-1965
993	Dave Concepcion,	1970-1988
978	Vada Pinson,	1958-1968

Hits: Most, career

3358	Pete Rose,	1963-1986
2326	Dave Concepcion,	1970-1988
2048	Johnny Bench,	1967-1983
1934	Tony Perez,	1964-1986
1881	Vada Pinson,	1958-1968

2B: Most, career

601	Pete Rose,	1963-1986
389	Dave Concepcion,	1970-1988
381	Johnny Bench,	1967-1983
342	Vada Pinson,	1958-1968
339	Tony Perez,	1964-1986

3B: Most, career

152	Edd Roush,	1916-1931
115	Pete Rose,	1963-1986
112	Bid McPhee,	1890-1899
96	Vada Pinson,	1958-1968
94	Curt Walker,	1924-1930

HR: Most, career

389	Johnny Bench,	1967-1983
324	Frank Robinson,	1956-1965
287	Tony Perez,	1964-1986
251	Ted Kluszewski,	1947-1957
244	George Foster,	1971-1981

RBI: Most, career

1376	Johnny Bench,	1967-1983
1192	Tony Perez,	1964-1986
1036	Pete Rose,	1963-1986
1009	Frank Robinson,	1956-1965
950	Dave Concepcion,	1970-1988

SB: Most, career

406	Joe Morgan,	1972-1979
337	Arlie Latham,	1890-1895
321	Dave Concepcion,	1970-1988
320	Bob Bescher,	1908-1913
316	Bid McPhee,	1890-1899

BB: Most, career

1210	Pete Rose,	1963-1986
891	Johnny Bench,	1967-1983
881	Joe Morgan,	1972-1979
736	Dave Concepcion,	1970-1988
698	Frank Robinson,	1956-1965

BA: Highest, career

.332	Cy Seymour,	1902-1906
.331	Edd Roush,	1916-1931
.325	Jake Beckley,	1897-1903
.314	Bubbles Hargrave,	1921-1928
.311	Rube Bressler,	1917-1927

Slug avg: Highest, career

.554	Frank Robinson,	1956-1965
.514	George Foster,	1971-1981
.512	Ted Kluszewski,	1947-1957
.510	ERIC DAVIS,	1984-1996
.498	Wally Post,	1949-1963

On-base avg: Highest, career

.415	Joe Morgan,	1972-1979
.390	Dummy Hoy,	1894-1902
.389	Frank Robinson,	1956-1965
.379	Rube Bressler,	1917-1927
.379	Pete Rose,	1963-1986

Complete games: Most, career

209	Noodles Hahn,	1899-1905
195	Bucky Walters,	1938-1948
189	Paul Derringer,	1933-1942
188	Frank Dwyer,	1892-1899
184	Bob Ewing,	1902-1909

Saves: Most, career

148	JOHN FRANCO,	1984-1989
119	Clay Carroll,	1968-1975
88	Rob Dibble,	1988-1993
88	Tom Hume,	1977-1987
87	JEFF BRANTLEY,	1994-1996

Shutouts: Most, career

32	Bucky Walters,	1938-1948
30	Jim Maloney,	1960-1970
29	Johnny Vander Meer,	1937-1949
25	Ken Raffensberger,	1947-1954
24	Paul Derringer,	1933-1942
24	Noodles Hahn,	1899-1905
24	Dolf Luque,	1918-1929

Wins: Most, career

179	Eppa Rixey,	1921-1933
161	Paul Derringer,	1933-1942
160	Bucky Walters,	1938-1948
154	Dolf Luque,	1918-1929
134	Jim Maloney,	1960-1970

K: Most, career

1592	Jim Maloney,	1960-1970
1449	Mario Soto,	1977-1988
1289	Joe Nuxhall,	1944-1966
1251	Johnny Vander Meer,	1937-1949
1201	Jose Rijo,	1988-1995

Win pct: Highest, career

.674	Don Gullett,	1970-1976
.653	Pedro Borbon,	1970-1979
.623	Jim Maloney,	1960-1970
.623	Clay Carroll,	1968-1975
.621	Gary Nolan,	1967-1977

ERA: Lowest, career

2.18	Fred Toney,	1915-1918
2.37	Bob Ewing,	1902-1909
2.52	Noodles Hahn,	1899-1905
2.62	Hod Eller,	1917-1921
2.65	Pete Schneider,	1914-1918

Runs: Most, season

134	Frank Robinson,	1962
131	Vada Pinson,	1959
130	Pete Rose,	1976
129	Arlie Latham,	1894
126	Tommy Harper,	1965

Hits: Most, season

230	Pete Rose,	1973
219	Cy Seymour,	1905
218	Pete Rose,	1969
215	Pete Rose,	1976
210	Pete Rose,	1968
210	Pete Rose,	1975

2B: Most, season

51	Frank Robinson,	1962
51	Pete Rose,	1978
47	Vada Pinson,	1959
47	Pete Rose,	1975
45	George Kelly,	1929
45	Pete Rose,	1974

3B: Most, season

26	John Reilly,	1890
22	Sam Crawford,	1902
22	Jake Daubert,	1922
22	Bid McPhee,	1890
22	Mike Mitchell,	1911

HR: Most, season

52	George Foster,	1977
49	Ted Kluszewski,	1954
47	Ted Kluszewski,	1955
45	Johnny Bench,	1970
40	Johnny Bench,	1972
40	George Foster,	1978
40	Ted Kluszewski,	1953

40 Tony Perez, 1970
40 Wally Post, 1955

RBI: Most, season

149 George Foster, 1977
148 Johnny Bench, 1970
141 Ted Kluszewski, 1954
136 Frank Robinson, 1962
130 Deron Johnson, 1965

SB: Most, season

87 Arlie Latham, 1891
81 Bob Bescher, 1911
80 ERIC DAVIS, 1986
79 Dave Collins, 1980
76 Dusty Miller, 1896

BB: Most, season

132 Joe Morgan, 1975
120 Joe Morgan, 1974
117 Joe Morgan, 1977
115 Joe Morgan, 1972
114 Joe Morgan, 1976

BA: Highest, season

.377 Cy Seymour, 1905
.372 Bug Holliday, 1894
.351 Edd Roush, 1923
.351 Mike Donlin, 1903
.348 Edd Roush, 1924

Slug avg: Highest, season

.642 Ted Kluszewski, 1954
.631 George Foster, 1977
.624 Frank Robinson, 1962
.611 Frank Robinson, 1961
.595 Frank Robinson, 1960

On-base avg: Highest, season

.466 Joe Morgan, 1975
.449 Augie Galan, 1947
.444 Joe Morgan, 1976
.429 Cy Seymour, 1905
.428 Pete Rose, 1969

Complete games: Most, season

45 Billy Rhines, 1890
43 Elton Chamberlain, 1892
42 Tony Mullane, 1891
41 Noodles Hahn, 1901
40 Billy Rhines, 1891

Saves: Most, season

44 JEFF BRANTLEY, 1996
39 JOHN FRANCO, 1988
37 Clay Carroll, 1972
35 Wayne Granger, 1970
32 JOHN FRANCO, 1987
32 JOHN FRANCO, 1989

Shutouts: Most, season

7 Jack Billingham, 1973
7 Hod Eller, 1919
7 Fred Toney, 1917
6 Ewell Blackwell, 1947
6 Noodles Hahn, 1902
6 Jack Harper, 1904
6 DANNY JACKSON, 1988
6 Dolf Luque, 1923
6 Jim Maloney, 1963
6 Ken Raffensberger, 1952
6 Billy Rhines, 1890
6 Fred Toney, 1915
6 Johnny Vander Meer, 1941
6 Bucky Walters, 1944
6 Jake Weimer, 1906

Wins: Most, season

28 Billy Rhines, 1890
27 Pink Hawley, 1898
27 Dolf Luque, 1923
27 Bucky Walters, 1939
25 Paul Derringer, 1939
25 Eppa Rixey, 1922

K: Most, season

274 Mario Soto, 1982
265 Jim Maloney, 1963
244 Jim Maloney, 1965
242 Mario Soto, 1983
239 Noodles Hahn, 1901

Win pct: Highest, season

.826 Elmer Riddle, 1941
.821 Bob Purkey, 1962
.789 Don Gullett, 1975
.783 Tom Browning, 1988
.781 Paul Derringer, 1939

ERA: Lowest, season

1.58 Fred Toney, 1915
1.73 Bob Ewing, 1907
1.77 Noodles Hahn, 1902
1.82 Dutch Ruether, 1919
1.86 Andy Coakley, 1908

Most pinch-hit homers, season

5 Jerry Lynch, 1961
4 Bob Thurman, 1957

Most pinch-hit homers, career

13 Jerry Lynch, 1957-1963
7 Tony Perez, 1964-86

Longest hitting streak

44 Pete Rose, 1978
30 Elmer Smith, 1898
29 HAL MORRIS, 1996
27 Edd Roush, 1920
27 Edd Roush, 1924
27 Vada Pinson, 1965

Most consecutive scoreless innings

32 Jim Maloney, 1968-69
27 Tom Seaver, 1977

No-hit games

Bumpus Jones, Cin vs Pit NL, 7-1; Oct. 15, 1892 (first game in the major leagues).
Ted Breitenstein, Cin vs Pit NL, 11-0; Apr. 22, 1898.
Noodles Hahn, Cin vs Phi NL, 4-0; July 12, 1900.
Fred Toney, Cin at Chi NL, 1-0; May 2, 1917 (10 innings).
Hod Eller, Cin vs StL NL, 6-0; May 11, 1919.
Johnny Vander Meer, Cin vs Bos NL, 3-0; June 11, 1938
Johnny Vander Meer, Cin at Bro NL, 6-0; June 15, 1938 (next start after June 11)
Clyde Shoun, Cin vs Bos NL, 1-0; May 15, 1944.
Ewell Blackwell, Cin vs Bos NL, 6-0; June 18, 1947.
Johnny Klippstein (7 innings), Hershell Freeman (1 inning) and Joe Black (3 innings), Cin at Mil NL, 1-2; May 26, 1956 (lost on 3 hits in 11 innings after allowing the first hit in the 10th)
Jim Maloney, Cin vs NY NL, 0-1; June 14, 1965 (lost on 2 hits in 11 innings after pitching 10 hitless innings).
Jim Maloney, Cin at Chi NL, 1-0; Aug. 19, 1965 (1st game, 10 innings).
George Culver, Cin at Phi NL, 6-1; July 29, 1968 (2nd game).
Jim Maloney, Cin vs Hou NL, 10-0; Apr. 30, 1969.
Tom Seaver, Cin vs StL NL, 4-0; June 16, 1978.
Tom Browning, Cin vs LA NL, 1-0; Sept. 16, 1988 (perfect game).
Elton Chamberlain, seven innings, darkness, Cin vs Bos NL, 6-0; Sept. 23, 1893 (2nd game).
Jake Weimer, seven innings, agreement, Cin vs Bro NL, 1-0; Aug. 24, 1906 (2nd game).

ACTIVE PLAYERS in caps.

Players' years of service are listed by the first and last years with this team and are not necessarily consecutive; all statistics record performances for this team only.

Chicago Cubs

254

By Russell Becker, Baseball Weekly

Sammy Sosa was leading the NL with 40 homers when he was injured in August.

1996 Cubs: Wait till next year, part 88

It has always been easy to persuade Cubs fans to wait until next year, which has been their rallying cry for almost 90 years. So before the 1996 season, it was easy to claim that the Cubs would improve on a 73-71 record. But the reality of September ruined all that, with the team going 9-19 in the final month to finish a disappointing 76-86.

The ironic twist is that manager Jim Riggleman and GM Ed Lynch both received contract extensions during a stretch of 11 losses in 12 games. "It's been a disappointing year, but when we look back on it, it will look worse than it really was because of these final two weeks," said president Andy MacPhail, who handed out the extensions to show stability.

"We felt we made progress this year," Lynch said. "Our record won't indicate it, but we feel like we took a step in the right direction in terms of getting a better feel for who our players are." But there is no doubt the hierarchy is unhappy about the outcome of the season, in which Lynch refused to add any outside help even though his team was within striking distance of the NL Central lead for most of the second half. Contending was made possible by the mediocrity of the division, and the Cubs typified this, being stuck at .500 on 19 different occasions.

The pitching staff could have used help from Lynch. Except for All-Star Steve Trachsel and 15-game winner Jaime Navarro (signed by the White Sox during the offseason), the starting pitching was poor for much of the season. The other three in the spring rotation—Frank Castillo, Jim Bullinger and Kevin Foster—finished a combined 20-32, and only Castillo got his ERA under 6.00. The bullpen wasn't much better, as proved by the 34 one-run losses. No one had more than Turk Wendell's 18 saves, but Riggleman would never name him the replacement for the departed Randy Myers.

Offensively, the Cubs missed Sammy Sosa after he was injured, although their record was almost the same without him for a month. Sosa had a terrific year with

Team MVP

Sammy Sosa: The Cubs' offense suffered when Sammy Sosa was sidelined for the final six weeks of the season. No wonder. He was on a pace to hit more than 50 home runs. Sosa still finished tied for fifth in the NL with 40 dingers despite playing only 124 games. Ryne Sandberg with 25 was the only other Cub with more than 17 homers. Sosa also led the team with 100 RBI and showed improved defense, finishing third in the league with 15 outfield assists.

40 homers and 100 RBI in 124 games, but the next-highest production came from 36-year-old second baseman Ryne Sandberg, who came out of retirement to hit 25 homers and drive in 92 runs.

Sandberg, who re-signed in November, is one of the keys for next season. In fact, it is almost impossible to talk about this Cubs season without talking about the next one. First baseman Mark Grace, who led the team with a .331 average, and center fielder Brian McRae also re-signed with the club rather than become free agents, but left fielder Luis Gonzalez became one when the labor deal granted him enough service time to qualify.

It is clear that those players who have elected to stay need help. The 1997 season will most likely begin with more questions than answers, but MacPhail remains optimistic. "The parity in the league is such now that if a team adds a player or two, or keeps everyone healthy, or has a good performance out of a kid from the farm system, it can swing the balance as much as 20 games a year," he said during the offseason. "We have enough quality players, with the proper approach to the game, to be in a position to make that swing next season."

1996 Cubs: Week-by-week notes

These notes were excerpted from the following issues of Baseball Weekly.

▶**April 10:** The earliest Opening Day in Cubs history produced not only one of the colder weeks but also one of the more successful ones. It was so frigid for the third game against the Dodgers that ushers spread ice-melting salt on the aisles. The Cubs opened with a 4-2 homestand before beating the Rockies 9-6 in Denver.

▶**April 17:** General manager Ed Lynch has asked players not to carry cans of snuff in the back pockets of their uniforms. His letter was posted on the clubhouse bulletin board. "We do not want to encourage the use of these products by young baseball fans," Lynch wrote.

▶**May 1:** The statistics told the story of the Cubs' seven-game losing streak, which ended on April 27 in extra innings in Los Angeles: Hitters batted .218 and scored 22 runs, while striking out 57 times and grounding into 11 double plays.

▶**May 8:** Right fielder Sammy Sosa broke an 0-for-18 slump with a ninth-inning, game-winning three-run homer against Paul Wilson of the Mets. Sosa's hit came on May 3, just three days after rookie Robin Jennings pinch-hit a game-winning double in the ninth against the Cardinals' Dennis Eckersley.

▶**May 15:** The 16-minute brawl between the slumping Cubs and the Mets on May 11 was not surprising. "Some guys needed to let out some frustration," center fielder Brian McRae said. The game marked the Cubs' fifth consecutive loss.

▶**May 22:** On May 16, Sammy Sosa became the first Cub ever to homer twice in the same inning. A streak hitter, Sosa had six homers in six games.

▶**May 29:** Pitching problems: Starter Jaime Navarro threw a dugout tantrum after blowing a lead in Houston on May 25, and the bullpen got only six saves in its first 13 opportunities, with veteran closer Doug Jones blowing five saves and watching his ERA go to 5.32.

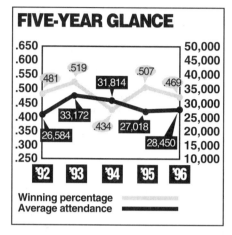

FIVE-YEAR GLANCE

Winning percentage
Average attendance

▶**June 5:** Manager Jim Riggleman dumped the set lineup that he used for the first 50 games. Second baseman Ryne Sandberg went from his familiar No. 2 spot to sixth, with left fielder Luis Gonzalez moving to second. First baseman Mark Grace and Sammy Sosa switched places, with Grace at cleanup and Sosa No. 3, and third baseman Dave Magadan made his Cubs debut at fifth. Sandberg was second on the team in home runs, but his on-base percentage had fallen below .300.

▶**June 12:** Through the first 60 games, the rotation had a 16-27 record and a 5.18 ERA. The only reliable starters were Steve Trachsel and Amaury Telemaco. The leading winner on the staff was new closer Turk Wendell, with four.

▶**June 19:** The Cubs placed their leading hitter, Mark Grace, on the DL with back spasms and released reliever Doug Jones, who had been signed to take the closer's role of departed Randy Myers.

▶**June 26:** The Cubs finally released the often-injured Jose Guzman in the last season of his four-year, $14 million contract. For that money the Cubs got a 14-12 record and a 4.78 ERA—or $1 million per victory.

▶**July 3:** The off-and-on starting pitching is mainly off again, most notably Frank Castillo, who could be demoted to bullpen duty after a weekend failure against the Reds dropped his record to 2-10. But not all starting pitchers have been struggling. With the second-best ERA in the majors (2.00 through June 30), starter Steve Trachsel was hoping to make the All-Star team.

▶July 11: Ryne Sandberg finally got hot before the break, hitting in eight consecutive games at one point (16-for-34) to raise his average above .240.

▶July 24: The Cubs had been playing so badly that Turk Wendell went nearly a month without a save, from June 20 to July 18. In fact, the Cubs' last previous save or save chance was on June 26. "It's like being a hitter and only getting to take batting practice," Wendell said.

▶July 31: As the trading deadline approached, the Cubs had a four-game winning streak in San Francisco and Colorado that left them within striking distance of first place—even though they were closer to last place. "All of a sudden it got interesting again," said GM Ed Lynch, who had been focusing more on building for the future.

▶Aug. 7: Jim Riggleman is taking a look at what it might take to win the Central. He thinks 86 victories will be enough, meaning his Cubs would have to win more than 60% of their remaining games. Hard-hitting Sammy Sosa will be critical to the Cubs' success. His average hovered near .300, and he continued to lead the league in home runs, total bases and outfield assists.

▶Aug. 21: Ed Lynch had a chance to make several trades, he said, but "either they wanted our entire minor league system or the middle of our order.... If a deal out there will help us, we'll make it."

▶Aug. 28: On the day Chicago's learned that Sammy Sosa had broken his right hand, they went over .500 for the first time since May 3. Three days later they were back under .500. Sosa had accounted for 28% of Chicago home runs, 18% of its RBI, 14% of its runs and 20% of its steals.

▶Sept. 4: Of the Cub's first 135 games, 67 were decided by one or two runs, including 29 one-run losses. The Cubs went 3-5 in eight consecutive one-run games, a string that ended on Aug. 31.

▶Sept. 18: The Cubs will finish the season with a winning record at Wrigley Field for the first time since 1993. Steve Trachsel, who won just two of 10 decisions at home in 1995, is now 9-5 with a 2.50 ERA in 16 starts at Wrigley this year.

▶Sept. 25: The Cubs saw their chances of playing .500 ball dwindle by matching a season-high eight-game losing streak.

▶Oct. 2: The Cubs went 9-19 in September to watch a .500 season slip away. Except for All-Star Steve Trachsel and Jaime Navarro, the rotation was in shambles much of the season. The bullpen wasn't much better, as the team had 34 one-run losses, second most in the NL, and only 34 saves, tied for last in the league. Offensively, the Cubs missed Sammy Sosa for the last six weeks. He had 40 homers and 100 RBI, but the next-highest production came from 36-year-old Ryne Sandberg, whose 92 RBI were 13 more than the third-ranked Cub.

Team directory

▶**Owner:** Tribune Company
▶**General manager:** Ed Lynch
▶**Ballpark:**
Wrigley Field
Clark and Addison Streets,
Chicago, Ill.
773-404-2827
Capacity 38,765
Parking for 900; $10 and $15 (private lots available)
Public transportation available
Family and wheelchair sections, ramps and elevators.
▶**Team publications:**
Vineline, Scorecard Magazine,
Cubs Quarterly
312-404-2827
▶**TV, radio broadcast stations:**
WGN 720 AM, WGN Channel 9
▶**Spring training:**
HoHoKam Park
Mesa, Ariz.
Capacity 12,500
602-644-2149

CHICAGO CUBS 1996 final stats

BATTERS	BA	SLG	OB	G	AB	R	H	TB	2B	3B	HR	RBI	BB	SO	SB	CS	E
Kieschnick	.345	.517	.406	25	29	6	10	15	2	0	1	6	3	8	0	0	1
Grace	.331	.455	.396	142	547	88	181	249	39	1	9	75	62	41	2	3	4
Houston	.317	.458	.358	79	142	21	45	65	9	1	3	27	9	27	3	2	3
Brown	.304	.536	.329	29	69	11	21	37	1	0	5	9	2	17	3	3	0
McRae	.276	.425	.360	157	624	111	172	265	32	5	17	66	73	84	37	9	5
Sosa	.273	.564	.323	124	498	84	136	281	21	2	40	100	34	134	18	5	10
Gonzalez	.271	.443	.354	146	483	70	131	214	30	4	15	79	61	49	9	6	3
Servais	.265	.384	.327	129	445	42	118	171	20	0	11	63	30	75	0	2	11
Magadan	.254	.367	.360	78	169	23	43	62	10	0	3	17	29	23	0	2	3
Sandberg	.244	.444	.316	150	554	85	135	246	28	4	25	92	54	116	12	8	6
Hernandez	.242	.381	.293	131	331	52	80	126	14	1	10	41	24	97	4	0	20
Glanville	.241	.361	.264	49	83	10	20	30	5	1	1	10	3	11	2	0	1
Gomez	.238	.431	.344	136	362	44	86	156	19	0	17	56	53	94	1	4	7
Shumpert	.226	.452	.286	27	31	5	7	14	1	0	2	6	2	11	0	1	1
Jennings	.224	.310	.274	31	58	7	13	18	5	0	0	4	3	9	1	0	0
Bullett	.212	.297	.256	109	165	26	35	49	5	0	3	16	10	54	7	3	1
Sanchez	.211	.253	.272	95	289	28	61	73	9	0	1	12	22	42	7	1	11
Timmons	.200	.379	.282	65	140	18	28	53	4	0	7	16	15	30	1	0	0
Haney	.134	.146	.200	49	82	11	11	12	1	0	0	3	7	15	1	0	3
Fermin	.125	.188	.222	11	16	4	2	3	1	0	0	1	2	0	0	0	1
Valdes	.125	.250	.222	9	8	2	1	2	1	0	0	1	1	5	0	0	0
Dorsett	.122	.195	.196	17	41	3	5	8	0	0	1	3	4	8	0	0	0
Hubbard	.105	.184	.103	21	38	1	4	7	0	0	1	4	0	15	0	0	0
Barberie	.034	.138	.176	15	29	4	1	4	0	0	1	2	5	11	0	1	0

PITCHERS	W-L	ERA	G	GS	CG	GF	Sho	SV	IP	H	R	ER	HR	BB	SO
Casian	1-1	1.88	35	0	0	4	0	0	24.0	14	5	5	2	11	15
Bottenfield	3-5	2.63	48	0	0	10	0	1	61.2	59	25	18	3	19	33
Wendell	4-5	2.84	70	0	0	49	0	18	79.1	58	26	25	8	44	75
Adams	3-6	2.94	69	0	0	22	0	4	101.0	84	36	33	6	49	78
Trachsel	13-9	3.03	31	31	3	0	2	0	205.0	181	82	69	30	62	132
Patterson	3-3	3.13	79	0	0	27	0	8	54.2	46	19	19	6	22	53
Navarro	15-12	3.92	35	35	4	0	1	0	236.2	244	116	103	25	72	158
Campbell	3-1	4.46	13	5	0	4	0	0	36.1	29	19	18	7	10	19
Perez	1-0	4.67	24	0	0	4	0	0	27.0	29	14	14	2	13	22
Myers	2-1	4.68	45	0	0	8	0	0	67.1	61	38	35	6	38	50
Jones	2-2	5.01	28	0	0	13	0	2	32.1	41	20	18	4	7	26
Castillo	7-16	5.28	33	33	1	0	1	0	182.1	209	112	107	28	46	139
Telemaco	5-7	5.46	25	17	0	2	0	0	97.1	108	67	59	20	31	64
Foster	7-6	6.21	17	16	1	0	0	0	87.0	98	63	60	16	35	53
Swartzbaugh	0-2	6.38	6	5	0	0	0	0	24.0	26	17	17	3	14	13
Bullinger	6-10	6.54	37	20	1	6	1	1	129.1	144	101	94	15	68	90
Sturtze	1-0	9.00	6	0	0	3	0	0	11.0	16	11	11	3	5	7

1997 preliminary roster

PITCHERS (20)
Terry Adams
Miguel Batista
Kent Bottenfield
Larry Casian
Frank Castillo
Kevin Foster
Jeremi Gonzalez
Terry Mulholland
Rod Myers
Bob Patterson
Marc Pisciotta
Steve Rain
Mel Rojas

Brian Stephenson
Dave Swartzbaugh
Kevin Tapani
Ramon Tatis
Amaury Telemaco
Steve Trachsel
Turk Wendell

CATCHERS (4)
Pat Cline
Tyler Houston
Mike Hubbard
Scott Servais

INFIELDERS (9)
Brant Brown
Miguel Cairo
Shawon Dunston
Mark Grace
Jose Hernandez
Jason Maxwell
Kevin Orie
Rey Sanchez
Ryne Sandberg

OUTFIELDERS (7)
Doug Glanville
Robin Jennings
Brooks Kieschnick
Brian McRae
Sammy Sosa
Ozzie Timmons
Pedro Valdes

Games played by position

PLAYER	G	C	1B	2B	3B	SS	OF
Barberie	15	0	0	6	2	1	0
Brown	29	0	18	0	0	0	0
Bullett	109	0	0	0	0	0	58
Dorsett	17	15	0	0	0	0	0
Fermin	11	0	0	6	0	2	0
Glanville	49	0	0	0	0	0	35
Gomez	136	0	8	0	124	1	0
Gonzalez	146	0	2	0	0	0	139
Grace	142	0	141	0	0	0	0
Haney	49	0	0	23	4	3	0
Hernandez	131	0	0	1	43	87	1
Houston	79	27	12	2	9	0	1
Hubbard	21	14	0	0	0	0	0
Jennings	31	0	0	0	0	0	11
Kieschnick	25	0	0	0	0	0	8
Magadan	78	0	10	0	51	0	0
McRae	157	0	0	0	0	0	155
Sanchez	95	0	0	0	0	92	0
Sandberg	150	0	0	146	0	0	0
Servais	129	128	1	0	0	0	0
Shumpert	27	0	0	4	10	1	0
Sosa	124	0	0	0	0	0	124
Timmons	65	0	0	0	0	0	47
Valdes	9	0	0	0	0	0	2

Sick call: 1996 DL report

PLAYER	Days on the DL
Scott Bullett	21
Mike Campbell	63
Mark Grace	17
Jose Guzman	84
Dave Magadan	61*
Rey Sanchez	66*
Terry Shumpert	15
Sammy Sosa	40
Amaury Telemaco	15

Indicates two separate terms on Disabled List.

1996 salaries

	Bonuses	Total earned salary
Sammy Sosa, of		$4,750,000
Mark Grace, 1b	$25,000	$4,175,000
Jaime Navarro, p	$200,000	$3,600,000
Brian McRae, of		$3,400,000
Ryne Sandberg, 2b	$800,000	$2,800,000
Frank Castillo, p		$1,600,000
Luis Gonzalez, of		$1,400,000
Rey Sanchez, ss		$1,200,000
Scott Servais, c		$822,500
Bob Patterson, p	$125,000	$675,000
Leo Gomez, 3b	$100,000	$550,000
Dave Magadan, 3b		$500,000
Jim Bullinger, p		$385,000
Larry Casian, p	$50,000	$275,000
Jose Hernandez, ss		$253,000
Kevin Foster, p		$230,000
Steve Trachsel, p		$220,000
Scott Bullett, of		$160,000
Turk Wendell, p		$160,000
Terry Shumpert, 2b		$150,000
Ozzie Timmons, of		$150,000
Todd Haney, 2b		$127,500
Mike Campbell, p		$125,000
Terry Adams, p		$113,000
Mike Hubbard, c		$112,000
Kent Bottenfield, p		$111,000
Tyler Houston, c		$109,000
Brooks Kieschnick, of		$109,000
Rodney Myers, p		$109,000
Amaury Telemaco, p		$109,000

Average 1996 salary: $949,333
Total 1996 team payroll: $28,480,000
Termination pay: $4,125,000

Minor Leagues

Tops in the organization

BATTER	CLUB	AVG.	G	AB	R	H	HR	RBI
Scott Vieira	Rkf	.324	134	442	81	143	8	81
Doug Glanville	Iwa	.308	90	373	53	115	3	34
Terry Joseph	Rkf	.305	128	449	98	137	9	94
Brant Brown	Iwa	.304	94	342	48	104	10	43
Ricky Freeman	Day	.304	127	477	70	145	13	64

HOME RUNS

Troy Hughes	Orl	18	
Robin Jennings	Iwa	18	
B. Kieschnick	Iwa	18	
Pat Cline	Day	17	
Ozzie Timmons	Iwa	17	

WINS

Jeff Yoder	Rkf	12	
C. Duncan	WPt	11	
Kerry Wood	Day	10	
Al Garcia	Orl	10	
Several Players Tied At			9

RBI

Terry Joseph	Rkf	94
Troy Hughes	Orl	93
Kevin Ellis	Day	89
Scott Vieira	Rkf	81
Marty Gazarek	Day	77

SAVES

B. Hammack	Day	29
Steve Rain	Iwa	20
Justin Speier	Orl	19
K. Bottenfield	Iwa	18
Skip Ames	Rkf	9

STOLEN BASES

Elinton Jasco	Rkf	48
Dennis Abreu	Cub	35
Bo Porter	Rkf	35
Franklin Font	Cub	31
Shawn Livsey	Orl	30

STRIKEOUTS

Kerry Wood	Day	136
Dennis Bair	Day	127
Jeff Yoder	Rkf	124
Wade Walker	Orl	117
B. Stephenson	Orl	106

PITCHER	CLUB	W-L	ERA	IP	H	BB	SO
M. Campbell	Iwa	8-2	2.73	96	75	23	87
Kerry Wood	Day	10-2	2.91	114	72	70	136
J. Montelongo	Day	6-6	3.10	102	84	36	77
Jairo Diaz	Day	7-4	3.14	115	111	40	102
Barry Markey	Rkf	6-2	3.15	97	97	16	39

Chicago (1876-1996)

Runs: Most, career

1719	Cap Anson, 1876-1897
1409	Jimmy Ryan, 1885-1900
1306	Billy Williams, 1959-1974
1305	Ernie Banks, 1953-1971
1262	RYNE SANDBERG, 1982-1996

Hits: Most, career

2995	Cap Anson, 1876-1897
2583	Ernie Banks, 1953-1971
2510	Billy Williams, 1959-1974
2267	RYNE SANDBERG, 1982-1996
2193	Stan Hack, 1932-1947

2B: Most, career

528	Cap Anson, 1876-1897
407	Ernie Banks, 1953-1971
402	Billy Williams, 1959-1974
391	Gabby Hartnett, 1922-1940
377	RYNE SANDBERG, 1982-1996

3B: Most, career

142	Jimmy Ryan, 1885-1900
124	Cap Anson, 1876-1897
117	Frank Schulte, 1904-1916
106	Bill Dahlen, 1891-1898
99	Phil Cavarretta, 1934-1953

HR: Most, career

512	Ernie Banks, 1953-1971
392	Billy Williams, 1959-1974
337	Ron Santo, 1960-1973
270	RYNE SANDBERG, 1982-1996
231	Gabby Hartnett, 1922-1940

RBI: Most, career

1879	Cap Anson, 1876-1897
1636	Ernie Banks, 1953-1971
1353	Billy Williams, 1959-1974
1290	Ron Santo, 1960-1973
1153	Gabby Hartnett, 1922-1940

SB: Most, career

400	Frank Chance, 1898-1912
399	Bill Lange, 1893-1899
369	Jimmy Ryan, 1885-1900
337	RYNE SANDBERG, 1982-1996
304	Joe Tinker, 1902-1916

BB: Most, career

1092	Stan Hack, 1932-1947
1071	Ron Santo, 1960-1973

952	Cap Anson, 1876-1897
911	Billy Williams, 1959-1974
794	Phil Cavarretta, 1934-1953

BA: Highest, career

.336	Riggs Stephenson, 1926-1934
.330	Bill Lange, 1893-1899
.329	Cap Anson, 1876-1897
.325	Kiki Cuyler, 1928-1935
.323	Bill Everitt, 1895-1900

Slug avg: Highest, career

.590	Hack Wilson, 1926-1931
.512	Hank Sauer, 1949-1955
.507	ANDRE DAWSON, 1987-1992
.506	SAMMY SOSA, 1992-1996
.503	Billy Williams, 1959-1974

On-base avg: Highest, career

.412	Hack Wilson, 1926-1931
.408	Riggs Stephenson, 1926-1934
.401	Bill Lange, 1893-1899
.395	Cap Anson, 1876-1897
.394	Stan Hack, 1932-1947

Complete games: Most, career

317	Bill Hutchison, 1889-1895
252	Larry Corcoran, 1880-1885
240	Clark Griffith, 1893-1900
206	Mordecai Brown, 1904-1916
188	Jack Taylor, 1898-1907

Saves: Most, career

180	LEE SMITH, 1980-1987
133	Bruce Sutter, 1976-1980
112	RANDY MYERS, 1993-1995
63	Don Elston, 1953-1964
60	Phil Regan, 1968-1972

Shutouts: Most, career

48	Mordecai Brown, 1904-1916
35	Hippo Vaughn, 1913-1921
31	Ed Reulbach, 1905-1913
29	Fergie Jenkins, 1966-1983
28	Orval Overall, 1906-1913

Wins: Most, career

201	Charlie Root, 1926-1941
188	Mordecai Brown, 1904-1916
181	Bill Hutchison, 1889-1895
175	Larry Corcoran, 1880-1885
167	Fergie Jenkins, 1966-1983

K: Most, career

2038	Fergie Jenkins, 1966-1983
1432	Charlie Root, 1926-1941
1367	Rick Reuschel, 1972-1984
1222	Bill Hutchison, 1889-1895
1138	Hippo Vaughn, 1913-1921

Win pct: Highest, career

.800	Al Spalding, 1876-1878
.773	Jim McCormick, 1885-1886
.706	John Clarkson, 1884-1887
.686	Mordecai Brown, 1904-1916
.677	Ed Reulbach, 1905-1913

ERA: Lowest, career

1.80	Mordecai Brown, 1904-1916
1.85	Jack Pfiester, 1906-1911
1.91	Orval Overall, 1906-1913
2.14	Jake Weimer, 1903-1905
2.24	Ed Reulbach, 1905-1913

Runs: Most, season

156	Rogers Hornsby, 1929
155	Kiki Cuyler, 1930
155	King Kelly, 1886
152	Woody English, 1930
150	George Gore, 1886

Hits: Most, season

229	Rogers Hornsby, 1929
228	Kiki Cuyler, 1930
227	Billy Herman, 1935
214	Woody English, 1930
212	Frank Demaree, 1936

2B: Most, season

57	Billy Herman, 1935
57	Billy Herman, 1936
51	MARK GRACE, 1995
50	Kiki Cuyler, 1930
49	Riggs Stephenson, 1932
49	Ned Williamson, 1883

3B: Most, season

21	Vic Saier, 1913
21	Frank Schulte, 1911
19	Bill Dahlen, 1892
19	Bill Dahlen, 1896
19	RYNE SANDBERG, 1984

HR: Most, season

56	Hack Wilson, 1930
49	ANDRE DAWSON, 1987
48	Dave Kingman, 1979
47	Ernie Banks, 1958
45	Ernie Banks, 1959

RBI: Most, season

190	Hack Wilson, 1930
159	Hack Wilson, 1929
149	Rogers Hornsby, 1929
147	Cap Anson, 1886
143	Ernie Banks, 1959

SB: Most, season

84	Bill Lange, 1896
76	Walt Wilmot, 1890
74	Walt Wilmot, 1894
73	Bill Lange, 1897
67	Frank Chance, 1903
67	Bill Lange, 1895

BB: Most, season

147	Jimmy Sheckard, 1911
122	Jimmy Sheckard, 1912
116	Richie Ashburn, 1960
113	Cap Anson, 1890
108	Johnny Evers, 1910

BA: Highest, season

.389	Bill Lange, 1895
.388	King Kelly, 1886
.380	Rogers Hornsby, 1929
.372	Heinie Zimmerman, 1912
.371	Cap Anson, 1886

Slug avg: Highest, season

.723	Hack Wilson, 1930
.679	Rogers Hornsby, 1929
.630	Gabby Hartnett, 1930
.618	Hack Wilson, 1929
.614	Ernie Banks, 1958

On-base avg: Highest, season

.483	King Kelly, 1886
.459	Rogers Hornsby, 1929
.456	Bill Lange, 1895
.454	Hack Wilson, 1930
.450	Frank Chance, 1905

Complete games: Most, season

68	John Clarkson, 1885
67	Bill Hutchison, 1892
65	Bill Hutchison, 1890
57	Larry Corcoran, 1880
57	Larry Corcoran, 1884
57	Terry Larkin, 1879

Saves: Most, season

53	RANDY MYERS, 1993
38	RANDY MYERS, 1995
37	Bruce Sutter, 1979
36	LEE SMITH, 1987
36	Mitch Williams, 1989

Shutouts: Most, season

10	John Clarkson, 1885
9	Pete Alexander, 1919

9	Mordecai Brown, 1906
9	Mordecai Brown, 1908
9	Bill Lee, 1938
9	Orval Overall, 1909

Wins: Most, season

53	John Clarkson, 1885
47	Al Spalding, 1876
44	Bill Hutchison, 1891
43	Larry Corcoran, 1880
42	Bill Hutchison, 1890

K: Most, season

313	John Clarkson, 1886
312	Bill Hutchison, 1892
308	John Clarkson, 1885
289	Bill Hutchison, 1890
274	Fergie Jenkins, 1970

Win pct: Highest, season

.941	Rick Sutcliffe, 1984
.875	Fred Goldsmith, 1880
.833	King Cole, 1910
.833	Jim McCormick, 1885
.826	Ed Reulbach, 1906

ERA: Lowest, season

1.04	Mordecai Brown, 1906
1.15	Jack Pfiester, 1907
1.17	Carl Lundgren, 1907
1.31	Mordecai Brown, 1909
1.33	Jack Taylor, 1902

Most pinch-hit homers, season

3	Chuck Tanner, 1958
3	Willie Smith, 1969
3	Thad Bosley, 1985
3	KEVIN ROBERSON, 1994

Most pinch-hit homers, career

6	Thad Bosley, 1983-1986
6	Kevin Roberson, 1993-1995

Longest hitting streak

42	Bill Dahlen, 1894
30	JEROME WALTON, 1989
28	Bill Dahlen, 1894 (2nd streak)
28	Ron Santo, 1966
27	Hack Wilson, 1929
27	Glenn Beckert, 1968

Most consecutive scoreless innings

50	Ed Reulbach, 1908-09
39	Mordecai Brown, 1908
38	Bill Lee, 1938
38	John Clarkson, 1885

No-hit games

Larry Corcoran, Chi vs Bos NL, 6-0; Aug. 19, 1880.

Larry Corcoran, Chi vs Wor NL, 5-0; Sept. 20, 1882.

Larry Corcoran, Chi vs Pro NL, 6-0; June 27, 1884.

John Clarkson, Chi at Pro NL, 4-0; July 27, 1885.

Walter Thornton, Chi vs Bro NL, 2-0; Aug. 21, 1898 (2nd game).

Bob Wicker, Chi at NY NL, 1-0; June 11, 1904 (won in 12 innings after allowing one hit in the 10th).

Jimmy Lavender, Chi at NY NL, 2-0; Aug. 31, 1915 (1st game).

Hippo Vaughn, Chi vs Cin NL, 0-1; May 2, 1917. (lost on two hits in the 10th, Toney pitched a no-hitter in this game).

Sam Jones, Chi vs Pit NL, 4-0; May 12, 1955.

Don Cardwell, Chi vs StL NL, 4-0; May 15, 1960 (2nd game).

Ken Holtzman, Chi vs Atl NL, 3-0; Aug. 19, 1969.

Ken Holtzman, Chi at Cin NL, 1-0; June 3, 1971.

Burt Hooton, Chi vs Phi NL, 4-0; Apr. 16, 1972.

Milt Pappas, Chi vs SD NL, 8-0; Sept. 2, 1972.

George Van Haltren, six innings, rain, Chi vs Pit NL, 1-0, June 21,1888.

King Cole, seven innings, called so Chicago could catch train, Chi at StL NL, 4-0; July 31, 1910 (2nd game).

ACTIVE PLAYERS in caps.

Players' years of service are listed by the first and last years with this team and are not necessarily consecutive; all statistics record performances for this team only.

Pittsburgh Pirates

Pittsburgh Pirates

By David Zalubowski, AP/World Wide Photos

Jeff King was the Pirates' main man, leading the team in RBI by 31.

1996 Pirates: Leyland's patience wore out

The unhappiness of the Pittsburgh Pirates' last-place finish was compounded by Jim Leyland's decision not to return as their manager. He moved on to skipper the Florida Marlins. Gene Lamont will manage the Pirates in 1997, and he inherits a young team probably destined to finish last again. In 1996, the Pirates went from a season-opening starting rotation of Paul Wagner, Denny Neagle, John Ericks, Zane Smith and Danny Darwin to a season-ending one featuring youngsters Jon Lieber, Rich Loiselle, Francisco Cordova, Esteban Loaiza and Jason Schmidt. The team went from a projected $23 million payroll for the 1997 season to a projected $18 million outlay.

There were some positive developments. Catcher Jason Kendall hit .300 and was third in the Rookie of the Year balloting, although his defensive skills—particularly his throwing—need vast improvement. Keith Osik proved a capable backup receiver. Jermaine Allensworth showed promise in center field. The young rotation pitched well enough in September that the Pirates were able to put together an 11-game winning streak, the longest in the major leagues all year.

"I think Cordova has pitched well," GM Cam Bonifay said. "I think he still has to get better and will get better, but he has shown he can throw solid innings as a starter. Schmidt has a fine arm, but I don't want people to forget that this young man has just completed his first half-season in the major leagues. I think if he goes out there every fifth day, he has a chance to be a very solid major league starter, but that might not be next year."

The Pirates contended for a while. On June 23, they were 1½ games out of first place in the Central, but they lost 46 of their next 70 games. Through it all, Al Martin, probably the cornerstone of next season's team, played well. The left fielder hit .300, scored 101 runs and drove in 72, and stole 38 bases, all career highs. Jeff King played all infield positions

except shortstop and was the team's only real power source, with 30 home runs and 111 RBI.

The 11-game winning streak was easily the highlight of the season, even though it came too late to make any difference. Except to Leyland. "The fact they didn't quit is the most important thing," he said. "They played it out like a true champion. Not that we're going to be champions, but they played hard. A manager appreciates that." Leyland's final home game as the Pirates' manager, on Sept. 25, attracted a paid crowd of 20,022—about 9,000 more than the advance sale through Sept. 24. The fans came to say good-bye to their manager. And they did it with standing ovations when he took out the lineup card before the game, made pitching changes, acknowledged an in-game video tribute and made several curtain calls after the game.

"We didn't need a stage to show the emotion out there tonight," Leyland said after the game as he fought back tears while flanked by his wife Katie in his crowded office. "Nobody could have planned a ceremony any better. That was unbelievable. In 1986, everybody said it was dead here. We created a hell of a lot of excitement over the next 10 years. They said it was pretty dark here in '86, but we turned it around—all of us. We just didn't have enough money to keep it that way."

1996 Pirates: Week-by-week notes

These notes were excerpted from the following issues of Baseball Weekly.

▶**April 10:** After two games, the Pirates were in first place in the NL Central—albeit at a modest 2-0. "Yeah," left fielder Al Martin mused, "but the other teams are still within reach of us. We'll just have to try to hold them off for the next, uh, 160 games."

▶**May 8:** On April 30, infielder Jeff King became the first player to hit two home runs in an inning in consecutive seasons, in a 10-7 victory at Cincinnati. The home runs lifted King's April total to nine—halfway to his career high of 18, which he set last season.

▶**May 15:** Dan Miceli was scheduled to be the Pirates' closer this season. The club hoped he could improve on the 21 saves he earned last year. But after one month—and only one save—they sent the right-hander to Class AA Carolina. Miceli had a 7.84 ERA in 11 games for Pittsburgh. He allowed 13 hits, including four home runs, and five walks in 10⅓ innings.

▶**May 29:** Danny Darwin had only two wins in his first nine starts despite having a 3.11 ERA. No Pirate starter has been more consistent than the 40-year-old. He allowed three earned runs or less in eight of his first nine starts, a huge improvement over last year, when Darwin was 3-10 with a 7.45 ERA for Toronto and Texas.

▶**June 5:** On May 29, the Pirates were just 4-for-18 with runners in scoring position in a 7-4 loss to Houston, the 17th defeat in a 22-game span.

▶**June 12:** Zane Smith has become a knuckleballer—sort of. The left-hander brought the dancer out of moth balls on June 2 to spice up an aging wardrobe. The result was his most effective start of the season and his first win since April 16, a 5-2 victory against Colorado.

▶**June 19:** The Pirates finished 7-1 on their first West Coast trip of the season. "We had a great trip," manager Jim Leyland said after the Pirates' 10th win in 12 games. "The pitching gave us a chance to win every game—and we almost did."

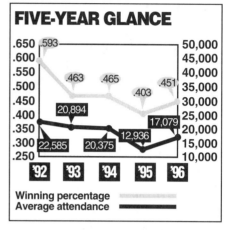

FIVE-YEAR GLANCE

Winning percentage ▨▨▨▨
Average attendance ▬▬▬▬

▶**July 3:** Danny Darwin's record is just 6-7, but his ERA is 2.64—fourth in the NL. And he's walked only 14 batters in 102⅓ innings.

▶**July 11:** Rookie catcher Jason Kendall was summoned to manager Jim Leyland's office on July 1. General manager Cam Bonifay sat near Leyland's desk and informed Kendall that he had been picked as a reserve on the NL All-Star team. "My mouth dropped," Kendall said. "I thought maybe it was a joke." On the day he was named an All-Star, Kendall had a .294 batting average, one home run and 26 RBI.

▶**July 24:** Staff ace Denny Neagle added a new role: He pinch-hit for the first time in his career on July 15 in Chicago and doubled off Frank Castillo.

▶**July 31:** The Pirates finished 7-13 in their run of 20 games against Central Division foes, falling from three games out to 10 back. In the 20-game stretch, during which relievers Dan Miceli and Jon Lieber moved into the rotation, starters pitched only 101⅔ innings and had a 6.55 ERA. On July 23 the Pirates lost two-fifths of their rotation: Danny Darwin was traded to Houston in return for right-hander Rich Loiselle, and Paul Wagner's season was ended by injury.

▶**Aug. 7:** Revolving doors: Dave Wainhouse became the 23rd pitcher used by the Pirates, on Aug. 1, to tie the club record set in 1990 and matched in 1993.

Right fielder Trey Beamon became the 42nd player on the Pirates' roster this season when he was called up on Aug. 2 to replace right fielder Orlando Merced, who went on the DL because of a strained right calf muscle.

▶**Aug. 21:** Chris Peters hit the trifecta Aug. 14, getting his first major league victory, hit and RBI as the Pirates beat San Francisco 4-3. The game was a big change from his previous two starts—8⅓ innings, 18 hits, 10 runs.

▶**Aug. 28:** Cam Bonifay learned only last week that his 1997 payroll would likely be $5 million less than anticipated. The salary slashing caught Bonifay and manager Jim Leyland by surprise. Until now, owner Kevin McClatchy had said the payroll would increase from $21 million this season to $23 million; instead, it might drop to $18 million, or only $1 million more than last season's. With $19.6 million already committed to 10 players next season, the Pirates have little choice but to make deals.

▶**Sept. 4:** Even after Denny Neagle was traded to Atlanta, Jim Leyland confirmed on Aug. 29 that he'll be Pittsburgh's manager through what promises to be tough times for most of the remaining four years of his contract. "I will be here," said Leyland. "I've made my decision."

▶**Sept. 11:** Since moving into the starting rotation on July 13, Jon Lieber is 5-3. Only twice in 11 starts has he allowed more than three earned runs. Amazingly, Lieber's 40 career starts is tops on the team.

▶**Sept. 18:** The Pirates can't be blamed if their enthusiasm has waned. "I remember how optimistic we were maybe 2½ months ago," reliever Dan Plesac said. "We thought we were going to be good again soon. You looked ahead to 1997 with Denny Neagle and maybe even Danny Darwin, and going out and getting another pitcher and developing Jon Lieber. But we've taken a turn in completely the opposite direction."

▶**Sept. 25:** Cam Bonifay won't rush to name a successor to Jim Leyland, who will step down as manager after the season. "I'm not going to name a manager

until Jim signs with somebody," Bonifay said. Gene Lamont, the Pirates' third base coach, will be considered.

▶**Oct. 2:** The Pirates' season was overshadowed by Jim Leyland's decision not to return as their manager next season. "I think it's the end of an era," shortstop Jay Bell said. The Pirates began the season with a veteran rotation, and ended it with a rotation of Jon Lieber, Rich Loiselle, Francisco Cordova, Esteban Loaiza and Jason Schmidt. The young rotation pitched well enough in September that the Pirates put together an 11-game win streak—the longest in the majors this season. Rookie catcher Jason Kendall made the All-Star team, and Jeff King hit his 30th home run on Sept. 24, becoming the first right-handed Pirate to hit that many since Dick Stuart hit 35 in 1961.

Team directory

▶**Owner:** Kevin McClatchy
▶**General manager:** Cam Bonifay
▶**Ballpark:**
Three Rivers Stadium
600 Stadium Circle
Pittsburgh, Pa.
412-323-5000
Capacity 47,972
Pay parking lot; $4
Public transportation available
Family and wheelchair sections, ramps, guest relations
▶**Team publications:**
Yearbook, scorecard,
Info Guide, On Deck
▶**TV, radio broadcast stations:**
KDKA 1020 AM, WPXI Channel 11,
TCI Cable, KBL Sports Network
▶**Camps and/or clinics:**
Youth Camps, 412-323-5098
Fantasy Camp for Adults, 412-323-5025
▶**Spring training:**
McKechnie Field
Bradenton, Fla.
Capacity 6,562
941-747-3031

PITTSBURGH PIRATES 1996 final stats

BATTERS	BA	SLG	OB	G	AB	R	H	TB	2B	3B	HR	RBI	BB	SO	SB	CS	E
Sveum	.353	.588	.450	12	34	9	12	20	5	0	1	5	6	6	0	0	2
Womack	.333	.500	.459	17	30	11	10	15	3	1	0	7	6	1	2	0	2
Encarnacion	.318	.409	.318	7	22	3	7	9	2	0	0	1	0	5	0	0	2
Martin	.300	.452	.354	155	630	101	189	285	40	1	18	72	54	116	38	12	8
Kendall	.300	.401	.372	130	414	54	124	166	23	5	3	42	35	30	5	2	18
Osik	.293	.429	.361	48	140	18	41	60	14	1	1	14	14	22	1	0	6
Merced	.287	.457	.357	120	453	69	130	207	24	1	17	80	51	74	8	4	3
Garcia	.285	.397	.329	101	390	66	111	155	18	4	6	44	23	58	16	6	11
Johnson	.274	.458	.361	127	343	55	94	157	24	0	13	47	44	64	6	4	6
King	.271	.497	.346	155	591	91	160	294	36	4	30	111	70	95	15	1	11
Liriano	.267	.392	.308	112	217	23	58	85	14	2	3	30	14	22	2	0	3
Allensworth	.262	.380	.337	61	229	32	60	87	9	3	4	31	23	50	11	6	3
Wehner	.259	.381	.299	86	139	19	36	53	9	1	2	13	8	22	1	5	2
Bell	.250	.391	.323	151	527	65	132	206	29	3	13	71	54	108	6	4	10
Aude	.250	.250	.250	7	16	0	4	4	0	0	0	1	0	8	0	0	1
Brumfield	.250	.438	.291	29	80	11	20	35	9	0	2	8	5	17	3	1	2
Hayes	.248	.368	.301	128	459	54	114	169	21	2	10	62	36	78	6	0	18
Kingery	.246	.337	.304	117	276	32	68	93	12	2	3	27	23	29	2	1	2
Cummings	.224	.388	.221	24	85	11	19	33	3	1	3	7	0	16	0	0	1
Beamon	.216	.255	.273	24	51	7	11	13	2	0	0	6	4	6	1	1	1

PITCHERS	W-L	ERA	G	GS	CG	GF	Sho	SV	IP	H	R	ER	HR	BB	SO
Loiselle	1-0	3.05	5	3	0	0	0	0	20.2	22	8	7	3	8	9
Wilkins	4-3	3.84	47	2	0	11	0	1	75.0	75	36	32	6	36	62
Lieber	9-5	3.99	51	15	0	6	0	1	142.0	156	70	63	19	28	94
Cordova	4-7	4.09	59	6	0	41	0	12	99.0	103	49	45	11	20	95
Plesac	6-5	4.09	73	0	0	30	0	11	70.1	67	35	32	4	24	76
Ruebel	1-1	4.60	26	7	0	3	0	1	58.2	64	38	30	7	25	22
Loaiza	2-3	4.96	10	10	1	0	1	0	52.2	65	32	29	11	19	32
Smith	4-6	5.08	16	16	1	0	1	0	83.1	104	53	47	7	21	47
Morel	2-1	5.36	29	0	0	4	0	0	42.0	57	27	25	4	19	22
Boever	0-2	5.40	13	0	0	9	0	2	15.0	17	11	9	2	6	6
Wagner	4-8	5.40	16	15	1	0	0	0	81.2	86	49	49	10	39	81
Peters	2-4	5.63	16	10	0	0	0	0	64.0	72	43	40	9	25	28
Schmidt	5-6	5.70	19	17	1	0	0	0	96.1	108	67	61	10	53	74
Wainhouse	1-0	5.70	17	0	0	6	0	0	23.2	22	16	15	3	10	16
Miceli	2-10	5.78	44	9	0	17	0	1	85.2	99	65	55	15	45	66
Ericks	4-5	5.79	28	4	0	13	0	8	46.2	56	35	30	11	19	46
Hancock	0-0	6.38	13	0	0	3	0	0	18.1	21	18	13	5	10	13
Christiansen	3-3	6.70	33	0	0	9	0	0	44.1	56	34	33	7	19	38
Hope	1-3	6.98	5	4	0	0	0	0	19.1	17	18	15	5	11	13
Parris	0-3	7.18	8	4	0	3	0	0	26.1	35	22	21	4	11	27
Cooke	0-0	7.56	3	0	0	1	0	0	8.1	11	7	7	1	5	7
Dessens	0-2	8.28	15	3	0	1	0	0	25.0	40	23	23	2	4	13
May	0-1	9.35	5	2	0	0	0	0	8.2	15	10	9	5	4	5

1997 preliminary roster

PITCHERS (21)
Jason Christiansen
Steve Cooke
Francisco Cordova
Kane Davis
Elmer Dessens
John Dillinger
John Ericks
Jeff Granger
Jeff Kelly
Jon Lieber
Esteban Loiaza
Rich Loiselle

Ramon Morel
Chris Peters
Jose Pett
Matt Ruebel
Jason Schmidt
Jose Silva
Clint Sodowsky
Paul Wagner
Marc Wilkens

CATCHERS (3)
Angelo Encarnacion
Jason Kendall
Keith Osik

INFIELDERS (7)
Lou Collier
Brandon Cromer
Kevin Elster
Freddy Garcia
Mark Johnson
Joe Randa
Tony Womack

OUTFIELDERS (10)
Jermaine Allensworth
Trey Beamon
Adrian Brown
Emil Brown
Midre Cummings
Jose Guillen
Mike Kingery
Al Martin
Charles Peterson
T.J. Staton

Games played by position

PLAYER	G	C	1B	2B	3B	SS	OF
Allensworth	61	0	0	0	0	0	61
Aude	7	0	4	0	0	0	0
Beamon	24	0	0	0	0	0	14
Bell	151	0	0	0	0	151	0
Brumfield	29	0	0	0	0	0	22
Cummings	24	0	0	0	0	0	21
Encarnacion	7	7	0	0	0	0	0
Garcia	101	0	0	77	14	19	0
Hayes	128	0	0	0	124	0	0
Johnson	127	0	100	0	0	0	1
Kendall	130	129	0	0	0	0	0
King	155	0	92	71	17	0	0
Kingery	117	0	0	0	0	0	83
Liriano	112	0	0	36	9	5	0
Martin	155	0	0	0	0	0	152
Merced	120	0	1	0	0	0	115
Osik	48	41	0	0	2	0	2
Sveum	12	0	0	0	10	0	0
Wehner	86	1	0	12	24	0	29
Womack	17	0	0	4	0	0	6

Minor Leagues

Tops in the organization

BATTER	CLUB	AVG.	G	AB	R	H	HR	RBI
J. Allensworth	Cgy	.330	95	352	77	116	8	43
Tim Marx	Cgy	.324	95	296	50	96	1	37
Jose Guillen	Lyn	.322	136	528	78	170	21	94
T.J. Staton	Car	.308	112	386	72	119	15	57
R. Martinez	Lyn	.307	91	306	58	94	1	30

HOME RUNS
C. Hermansen	Lyn	24
Dale Sveum	Cgy	23
Freddy Garcia	Lyn	21
Jose Guillen	Lyn	21
Several Players Tied At		17

WINS
E. Hernandez	Aug	17
J. Anderson	Car	13
Joe Boever	Cgy	12
Tom Bolton	Cgy	12
Several Players Tied At		11

RBI
Jose Guillen	Lyn	94
C. Hermansen	Lyn	87
Freddy Garcia	Lyn	86
Dale Sveum	Cgy	84
Rich Aude	Cgy	81

SAVES
D. Wainhouse	Car	25
Joe Maskivish	Aug	22
Matt Ryan	Cgy	20
Tim Collie	Lyn	13
David Daniels	Eri	10

STOLEN BASES
Adrian Brown	Car	45
Tony Womack	Cgy	37
Derek Swafford	Lyn	35
C. Peterson	Car	33
Several Players Tied At		29

STRIKEOUTS
E. Hernandez	Aug	171
Jason Phillips	Lyn	138
J. Anderson	Car	135
Jeff Kelly	Lyn	125
Blaine Beatty	Car	117

PITCHER	CLUB	W-L	ERA	IP	H	BB	SO
Chris Peters	Cgy	8-4	2.26	120	91	42	85
J. Anderson	Car	13-6	2.77	162	143	65	135
E. Hernandez	Aug	17-5	3.14	158	140	16	171
Blaine Beatty	Car	11-5	3.29	145	135	34	117
Jason Phillips	Lyn	10-10	3.37	163	161	64	138

Sick call: 1996 DL report

PLAYER	Days on the DL
Steve Cooke	79
Elmer Dessens	41
Carlos Garcia	51*
Orlando Merced	47**
Keith Osik	28
Steve Parris	124*
Zane Smith	15
Paul Wagner	97*

Indicates two separate terms on Disabled List.
**Indicates three separate terms on Disabled List.*

1996 salaries

	Bonuses	Total earned salary
Jay Bell, ss		$4,700,000
Orlando Merced, of		$2,700,000
Jeff King, 3b		$2,500,000
Carlos Garcia, 2b		$1,350,000
Dan Plesac, p	$200,000	$1,100,000
Mike Kingery, of		$750,000
Al Martin, of		$500,000
Nelson Liriano, 2b	$25,000	$350,000
Paul Wagner, p		$275,000
Dan Miceli, p		$220,000
John Wehner, 3b		$200,000
Jon Lieber, p		$150,000
Esteban Loaiza, p		$150,000
John Ericks, p		$135,000
Steve Parris, p		$135,000
Mark Johnson, 1b		$127,500
Jason Schmidt, p		$111,500
Ramon Morel, p		$110,000
Jermaine Allensworth, of		$109,000
Francisco Cordova, p		$109,000
Elmer Dessens, p		$109,000
Jason Kendall, c		$109,000
Keith Osik, c		$109,000
Chris Peters, p		$109,000
Matt Ruebel, p		$109,000
Dave Wainhouse, p		$109,000
Marc Wilkins, p		$109,000

Average 1996 salary: $612,778
Total 1996 team payroll: $16,545,000
Termination pay: $449,180

Pittsburgh (1887-1996)

Runs: Most, career

1521	Honus Wagner, 1900-1917
1493	Paul Waner, 1926-1940
1416	Roberto Clemente, 1955-1972
1414	Max Carey, 1910-1926
1195	Willie Stargell, 1962-1982

Hits: Most, career

3000	Roberto Clemente, 1955-1972
2967	Honus Wagner, 1900-1917
2868	Paul Waner, 1926-1940
2416	Max Carey, 1910-1926
2416	Pie Traynor, 1920-1937

2B: Most, career

558	Paul Waner, 1926-1940
551	Honus Wagner, 1900-1917
440	Roberto Clemente, 1955-1972
423	Willie Stargell, 1962-1982
375	Max Carey, 1910-1926

3B: Most, career

232	Honus Wagner, 1900-1917
187	Paul Waner, 1926-1940
166	Roberto Clemente, 1955-1972
164	Pie Traynor, 1920-1937
156	Fred Clarke, 1900-1915

HR: Most, career

475	Willie Stargell, 1962-1982
301	Ralph Kiner, 1946-1953
240	Roberto Clemente, 1955-1972
176	BARRY BONDS, 1986-1992
166	Dave Parker, 1973-1983

RBI: Most, career

1540	Willie Stargell, 1962-1982
1475	Honus Wagner, 1900-1917
1305	Roberto Clemente, 1955-1972
1273	Pie Traynor, 1920-1937
1177	Paul Waner, 1926-1940

SB: Most, career

688	Max Carey, 1910-1926
639	Honus Wagner, 1900-1917
412	Omar Moreno, 1975-1982
312	Patsy Donovan, 1892-1899
271	Tommy Leach, 1900-1918

BB: Most, career

937	Willie Stargell, 1962-1982
918	Max Carey, 1910-1926
909	Paul Waner, 1926-1940
877	Honus Wagner, 1900-1917
795	Ralph Kiner, 1946-1953

BA: Highest, career

.340	Paul Waner, 1926-1940
.336	Kiki Cuyler, 1921-1927
.328	Honus Wagner, 1900-1917
.327	Matty Alou, 1966-1970
.324	Arky Vaughan, 1932-1941
.324	Elmer Smith, 1892-1901

Slug avg: Highest, career

.567	Ralph Kiner, 1946-1953
.529	Willie Stargell, 1962-1982
.513	Kiki Cuyler, 1921-1927
.512	Dick Stuart, 1958-1962
.503	BARRY BONDS, 1986-1992

On-base avg: Highest, career

.415	Arky Vaughan, 1932-1941
.415	Elmer Smith, 1892-1901
.410	George Grantham, 1925-1931
.407	Paul Waner, 1926-1940
.405	Ralph Kiner, 1946-1953

Complete games: Most, career

263	Wilbur Cooper, 1912-1924
241	Sam Leever, 1898-1910
209	Deacon Phillippe, 1900-1911
206	Babe Adams, 1907-1926
167	Pud Galvin, 1887-1892

Saves: Most, career

188	Roy Face, 1953-1968
158	Kent Tekulve, 1974-1985
133	Dave Giusti, 1970-1976
61	STAN BELINDA, 1989-1993
59	Al McBean, 1961-1970

Shutouts: Most, career

44	Babe Adams, 1907-1926
39	Sam Leever, 1898-1910
35	Bob Friend, 1951-1965
33	Wilbur Cooper, 1912-1924
29	Lefty Leifield, 1905-1912

Wins: Most, career

202	Wilbur Cooper, 1912-1924
194	Babe Adams, 1907-1926
194	Sam Leever, 1898-1910
191	Bob Friend, 1951-1965
168	Deacon Phillippe, 1900-1911

K: Most, career

1682	Bob Friend, 1951-1965
1652	Bob Veale, 1962-1972
1191	Wilbur Cooper, 1912-1924
1159	John Candelaria, 1975-1993
1092	Vern Law, 1950-1967

Win pct: Highest, career

.683	Nick Maddox, 1907-1910
.667	Jesse Tannehill, 1897-1902
.660	Sam Leever, 1898-1910
.659	Vic Willis, 1906-1909
.656	Emil Yde, 1924-1927

ERA: Lowest, career

2.08	Vic Willis, 1906-1909
2.38	Lefty Leifield, 1905-1912
2.47	Sam Leever, 1898-1910
2.50	Deacon Phillippe, 1900-1911
2.60	Bob Harmon, 1914-1918

Runs: Most, season

148	Jake Stenzel, 1894
145	Patsy Donovan, 1894
144	Kiki Cuyler, 1925
142	Paul Waner, 1928
140	Max Carey, 1922

Hits: Most, season

237	Paul Waner, 1927
234	Lloyd Waner, 1929
231	Matty Alou, 1969
223	Lloyd Waner, 1927
223	Paul Waner, 1928

2B: Most, season

62	Paul Waner, 1932
53	Paul Waner, 1936
50	Paul Waner, 1928
47	Adam Comorosky, 1930
45	Dave Parker, 1979
45	Andy Van Slyke, 1992
45	Honus Wagner, 1900

3B: Most, season

36	Chief Wilson, 1912
28	Harry Davis, 1897
27	Jimmy Williams, 1899
26	Kiki Cuyler, 1925
23	Adam Comorosky, 1930
23	Elmer Smith, 1893

HR: Most, season

54	Ralph Kiner, 1949
51	Ralph Kiner, 1947
48	Willie Stargell, 1971
47	Ralph Kiner, 1950
44	Willie Stargell, 1973

RBI: Most, season

131	Paul Waner, 1927
127	Ralph Kiner, 1947
127	Ralph Kiner, 1949
126	Honus Wagner, 1901
125	Willie Stargell, 1971

SB: Most, season

96	Omar Moreno, 1980
77	Omar Moreno, 1979
71	Omar Moreno, 1978
71	Billy Sunday, 1888
70	Frank Taveras, 1977

BB: Most, season

137	Ralph Kiner, 1951
127	BARRY BONDS, 1992
122	Ralph Kiner, 1950
119	Elbie Fletcher, 1940
118	Elbie Fletcher, 1941
118	Arky Vaughan, 1936

BA: Highest, season

.385	Arky Vaughan, 1935
.381	Honus Wagner, 1900
.380	Paul Waner, 1927
.374	Jake Stenzel, 1895
.373	Paul Waner, 1936

Slug avg: Highest, season

.658	Ralph Kiner, 1949
.646	Willie Stargell, 1973
.639	Ralph Kiner, 1947
.628	Willie Stargell, 1971
.627	Ralph Kiner, 1951

On-base avg: Highest, season

.491	Arky Vaughan, 1935
.456	BARRY BONDS, 1992
.454	Elmer Smith, 1896
.453	Arky Vaughan, 1936
.452	Ralph Kiner, 1951

Complete games: Most, season

54	Ed Morris, 1888
49	Pud Galvin, 1888
48	Mark Baldwin, 1891
47	Pud Galvin, 1887
46	Harry Staley, 1889

Saves: Most, season

34	Jim Gott, 1988
31	Kent Tekulve, 1978
31	Kent Tekulve, 1979
30	Dave Giusti, 1971
28	Roy Face, 1962

Shutouts: Most, season

8	Babe Adams, 1920
8	Jack Chesbro, 1902
8	Lefty Leifield, 1906
8	Al Mamaux, 1915
7	Steve Blass, 1968
7	Wilbur Cooper, 1917
7	Sam Leever, 1903
7	Bob Veale, 1965
7	Vic Willis, 1908

Wins: Most, season

36	Frank Killen, 1893
31	Pink Hawley, 1895
30	Frank Killen, 1896
29	Ed Morris, 1888
28	Jack Chesbro, 1902
28	Pud Galvin, 1887

K: Most, season

276	Bob Veale, 1965
250	Bob Veale, 1964
229	Bob Veale, 1966
213	Bob Veale, 1969
199	Larry McWilliams, 1983

Win pct: Highest, season

.947	Roy Face, 1959
.842	Emil Yde, 1924
.824	Jack Chesbro, 1902
.806	Howie Camnitz, 1909
.800	John Candelaria, 1977
.800	Ed Doheny, 1902
.800	Sam Leever, 1905

ERA: Lowest, season

1.56	Howie Camnitz, 1908
1.62	Howie Camnitz, 1909
1.66	Sam Leever, 1907
1.73	Vic Willis, 1906
1.87	Lefty Leifield, 1906

Most pinch-hit homers, season

4	MARK JOHNSON, 1996
3	Ham Hyatt, 1913
3	Al Rubeling, 1944
3	Ed Stevens, 1948
3	Bob Skinner, 1956
3	Dick Stuart, 1959
3	Gene Freese, 1964
3	Jose Pagan, 1969
3	Willie Stargell, 1982

Most pinch-hit homers, career

8	Willie Stargell, 1962-1982
6	John Milner, 1978-1982
6	Dick Stuart, 1958-1962

Longest hitting streak

27	Jimmy Williams, 1899
26	Danny O'Connell, 1953
25	Charlie Grimm, 1923
25	Clyde Barnhart, 1925
25	Fred Lindstrom, 1933

Most consecutive scoreless innings

41	Jack Chesbro, 1902
36	Ed Morris, 1888

No-hit games

Nick Maddox, Pit vs Bro NL, 2-1; Sept. 20, 1907.

Cliff Chambers, Pit at Bos NL, 3-0; May 6, 1951 (2nd game).

Harvey Haddix, Pit at Mil NL, 0-1; May 26, 1959 (lost on 1 hit in 13 innings after pitching 12 perfect innings).

Bob Moose, Pit at NY NL, 4-0; Sept. 20, 1969.

Dock Ellis, Pit at SD NL, 2-0; June 12, 1970 (1st game).

John Candelaria, Pit vs LA NL, 2-0; Aug. 9, 1976.

Lefty Leifield, six innings, darkness, Pit at Phi NL, 8-0; Sept. 26, 1906 (2nd game).

Howie Camnitz, five innings, agreement, Pit at NY NL, 1-0; Aug. 23, 1907 (2nd game).

ACTIVE PLAYERS in caps.

Players' years of service are listed by the first and last years with this team and are not necessarily consecutive; all statistics record performances for this team only.

San Diego Padres

By Robert Hanashiro, USA TODAY

Ken Caminiti was only the fourth unanimous pick as the National League's MVP.

1996 Padres: Back to the playoffs, finally

Even if no one else did, the Padres thought all along they'd wind up playing baseball in October. It turns out they were right, and anyone who underestimated them was wrong. Those are probably the same people who had no idea that third baseman Ken Caminiti would take off for an MVP season, or that center fielder Steve Finley would hit 30 home runs. Or that the relief corps would lead all big league bullpens with a 3.30 ERA.

The Padres got their first postseason bid since 1984, and only the second in the 28-year history of the franchise, with a three-game season-ending road sweep of the Dodgers. The clincher came on a fitting play: Right fielder Tony Gwynn ripped a ball through the left side of the infield for a two-run single that put the Padres ahead for good. It had to be Gwynn. He's the only player linked to the '84 team that went to the World Series. Gwynn, who claimed his seventh NL batting title last season, termed that eighth-inning hit "as big a hit as I've gotten in my career."

The big hits mainly came from Caminiti and Finley, who both went well beyond the career years they'd posted in 1995, their first with the Padres after coming over from Houston in a landmark trade. Caminiti broke the club single-season records for home runs, with 40, and RBI, with 130, and the switch-hitting star broke his own major league mark with four games with homers from each side of the plate. Finley set team marks in runs scored (125), doubles (45), extra-base hits (84) and total bases (348), and he also won his second straight Gold Glove. Caminiti added a piece of baseball lore with an amazing game on Aug. 18 at Monterrey, Mexico. In the final game of the historic series against the Mets—the first series played outside the U.S. or Canada—Caminiti, who had been very ill the night before, got off the clubhouse floor, took two IVs, ate a candy bar and hit two home runs to lead the Padres to victory. That was one of many big games for Caminiti, who also

came up with innumerable highlight-reel plays on defense.

Throughout the season the Padres showed resilience. They bounced back from a stretch in June during which they lost 19 of 23 games, and they withstood a variety of significant injuries: Wally Joyner's fractured thumb, the nagging Achilles' tendon injury of Tony Gwynn and starter Andy Ashby's bad shoulder.

The starting pitching, led by Ashby, Joey Hamilton and veteran left-hander Fernando Valenzuela, held up thanks in part to Scott Sanders and Tim Worrell, who were effective both starting and relieving. Trevor Hoffman emerged as one of the league's dominant relievers, saving 42 games, holding opponents to a .161 batting average and striking out more than 11 batters per nine innings.

The June trade that brought catcher John Flaherty and shortstop Chris Gomez from Detroit solidified two key positions, but the Padres packed off several prospects to Milwaukee for slugging left fielder Greg Vaughn—only to have him struggle with NL pitching. Vaughn batted just .206 but did hit 10 homers in 43 games. Rickey Henderson, who scored 110 runs despite hitting .241, got most of the playing time in left down the stretch and in the three-game sweep by St. Louis against the Padres in the first round of the playoffs.

1996 Padres: Week-by-week notes

These notes were excerpted from the following issues of Baseball Weekly.

▶**April 10:** With runners on second and third in the 13th inning on April 6, Astros manager Terry Collins had right fielder Tony Gwynn intentionally walked. Third baseman Ken Caminiti then hit an Alvin Morman slider for a game-winning grand slam.

▶**April 17:** Adjusting to NL pitching obviously hasn't been much of a chore for Wally Joyner. After 10 years in the AL, the first baseman led his new league in hitting (.514), on-base percentage (.622) and doubles (five) through the first two weeks.

▶**May 8:** The way Ken Caminiti has performed this season, it's hard to believe he's been restricted by soreness in his left shoulder. Thirty games into the season, he had a .339 average and a team-high 19 RBI and 24 runs.

▶**May 15:** Amid the Padres' injuries, second baseman Jody Reed has emerged as the early-season iron man. He was the only player to start all of the club's first 37 games.

▶**May 29:** The bullpen continued its remarkable success with 3⅓ shutout innings against New York on May 25 to increase its streak to 30⅓ innings without allowing an earned run.

▶**June 5:** Wally Joyner, the team's second-leading hitter, most likely will be sidelined for at least six weeks after suffering a fractured left thumb.

▶**June 12:** No. 1 starter Andy Ashby, who's 7-2 with a 2.98 ERA, skipped a turn because of soreness in the back of his right shoulder.

▶**June 19:** The Padres lost 11 of 12 games, including a season-high eight in a row. The reason was simple: They couldn't hit, pitch or field well enough to win. "This has been a total team effort here," manager Bruce Bochy said.

▶**June 26:** The players and coaching staff were caught by surprise when their buses arrived at Jack Murphy Stadium from the airport at the end of a 1-6 road trip last

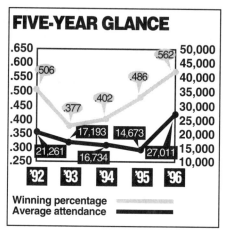

FIVE-YEAR GLANCE

Winning percentage
Average attendance

week. A throng of about 3,000 fans cheered the team as the Padres returned from a trip that extended their slump to 15 losses in 17 games. The worst slumper is Ken Caminiti, who is 3-for-43.

▶**July 3:** The Padres turned a 6-0 deficit into a 7-6 victory at San Francisco as center fielder Steve Finley hit two homers, including a two-run shot to tie the game in the eighth. Finley's team-high 15 homers are three more than his previous career high.

▶**July 11:** Tony Gwynn had a cast put on his right foot last week for a slightly torn right Achilles' tendon. With Gwynn on the DL, the Padres called up the anti-Gwynn—Rob Deer, the strikeout-prone slugger—from Class AAA Las Vegas.

▶**July 17:** On July 12, five Padres relievers helped the Rockies set a club record for most runs in an inning, when they allowed 11 runs in the seventh to turn a seven-run Padres lead into a four-run deficit. The Padres eventually lost 13-12.

▶**July 31:** Catcher John Flaherty's hitting streak was snapped on July 28 at 27 games. That was the second-longest by a catcher in major league history, next to the 34-gamer that Benito Santiago had as a rookie with the Padres in 1987.

▶**Aug. 7:** With general manager Kevin Towers' acquisition of outfielder Greg Vaughn (31 homers, 95 RBI) from Milwaukee, the Padres at last have their power hitter. Ken Caminiti was happy about it: He saw some juicy pitches as he smacked three homers in Vaughn's first two games.

▶**Aug. 14:** Tony Gwynn came off the DL, and the Padres' outfield suddenly has an overpopulation problem. But Bruce Bochy says he'll do what he can to make sure there's enough elbow room for the four veterans—Gwynn, Steve Finley, Greg Vaughn and Rickey Henderson. Of the four, Henderson shapes up as the odd man out.

▶**Aug. 21:** All the Padres and Mets had to adjust to the conditions for their series in Mexico. But probably no one had as much to adjust to as Greg Vaughn, who continues to struggle. Vaughn had hardly gotten used to National League pitchers before the Padres went south of the border. In the Aug. 17 game he had trouble finding fly balls in the dim Monterrey lights and went 0-for-5.

▶**Aug. 28:** Ken Caminiti's offensive explosion began the day he took two IVs of fluid, picked himself off the clubhouse floor in Monterrey and hit two home runs against the Mets. It didn't stop there. He hit a grand slam in his first at-bat back in San Diego and went on to have five homers and 14 RBI in the span of 14 at-bats. With 12 homers through the first three weeks of August, Caminiti set a franchise record for homers in a month.

▶**Sept. 4:** Initially, it looked as if Rickey Henderson might spend the most time on the bench when Tony Gwynn came off the DL. But Henderson has made it tough for Bruce Bochy by batting .351 (33-for-94) with a .500 on-base average in a 33-game stretch. His Aug. 31 home run gave him 100 runs scored.

▶**Sept. 11:** Greg Vaughn is at least temporarily in a reserve role. "I'm not happy about it, but I'm going to do whatever I can to help the team," Vaughn said. He started only four of the first 10 games on the 12-game road trip and went 2-for-14, to lower his NL average to .173.

▶**Sept. 18:** Ken Caminiti continued to show why he's a top candidate for MVP honors. In the series finale against the Pirates, Caminiti hit home runs from each side of the plate for a major-league-record fourth time this season.

▶**Sept. 25:** The crowds of 193,883 for the four-game series that the Padres split with the Dodgers set a franchise home attendance record for a four-game series.

▶**Oct. 2:** The Padres won the West by a game with a three-game sweep in Los Angeles on the season's last weekend. Ken Caminiti broke the club record for home runs with 40 and the RBI record with 130. Steve Finley set team single-season records in runs scored (126), doubles (45), extra-base hits (84) and total bases (348). The team showed resilience, bouncing back from a June swoon in which they lost 19 of 23 games and recovering from injuries to Wally Joyner, Tony Gwynn and Andy Ashby. The starters—led by Ashby, Joey Hamilton and resurgent lefty Fernando Valenzuela—held up, thanks in part to Scott Sanders and Tim Worrell, who straddled the line between the bullpen and the rotation.

Team directory

▶**Owner:** John Morris
▶**General manager:** Kevin Towers
▶**Ballpark:**
San Diego Jack Murphy Stadium
9449 Friars Rd.
San Diego, Calif.
619-283-4494
Capacity 57,750
Parking for 18,751 cars; $4
Public transportation available
Wheelchair sections, ramps, pre-registration for telephone paging, ATM machines
▶**Team publications:**
Padre Magazine
619-283-4494
▶**TV, radio broadcast stations:**
KFMB 760 AM, XEXX AM (Spanish), KFMB Channel 8, Prime Sports/Cox Communications
▶**Spring training:**
Peoria Sports Complex
Peoria, Ariz.
Capacity 10,000 with grass seating
602-878-4337

SAN DIEGO PADRES 1996 final stats

BATTERS	BA	SLG	OB	G	AB	R	H	TB	2B	3B	HR	RBI	BB	SO	SB	CS	E
T. Gwynn	.353	.441	.400	116	451	67	159	199	27	2	3	50	39	17	11	4	2
Caminiti	.326	.621	.408	146	546	109	178	339	37	2	40	130	78	99	11	5	20
Shipley	.315	.402	.337	33	92	13	29	37	5	0	1	7	2	15	7	0	1
Flaherty	.303	.451	.327	72	264	22	80	119	12	0	9	41	9	36	2	3	5
Finley	.298	.531	.354	161	655	126	195	348	45	9	30	95	56	88	22	8	7
Livingstone	.297	.366	.331	102	172	20	51	63	4	1	2	20	9	22	0	1	2
Cianfrocco	.281	.411	.315	79	192	21	54	79	13	3	2	32	8	56	1	0	3
Joyner	.277	.404	.377	121	433	59	120	175	29	1	8	65	69	71	5	3	3
Johnson	.272	.432	.290	82	243	18	66	105	13	1	8	35	4	36	0	0	5
Gomez	.262	.345	.349	89	328	32	86	113	16	1	3	29	39	64	2	2	13
Newfield	.251	.387	.311	84	191	27	48	74	11	0	5	26	16	44	1	1	3
Reed	.244	.297	.325	146	495	45	121	147	20	0	2	49	59	53	2	5	9
Henderson	.241	.344	.410	148	465	110	112	160	17	2	9	29	125	90	37	15	6
Thompson	.224	.429	.235	13	49	4	11	21	4	0	2	6	1	14	0	0	4
Vaughn	.206	.454	.329	43	141	20	29	64	3	1	10	22	24	31	4	1	2
Ausmus	.181	.228	.261	50	149	16	27	34	4	0	1	13	13	27	1	4	6
Deer	.180	.480	.359	25	50	9	9	24	3	0	4	9	14	30	0	0	0
Lopez	.180	.245	.233	63	139	10	25	34	3	0	2	11	9	35	0	0	4
C. Gwynn	.178	.256	.260	81	90	8	16	23	4	0	1	10	10	28	0	0	0
Dascenzo	.111	.111	.200	21	9	3	1	1	0	0	0	0	1	2	0	1	0
Mulligan	.000	.000	.000	2	1	0	0	0	0	0	0	0	0	0	0	0	0
Steverson	.000	.000	.000	1	1	0	0	0	0	0	0	0	0	1	0	0	0
Tatum	.000	.000	.000	5	3	0	0	0	0	0	0	0	0	1	0	0	0

PITCHERS	W-L	ERA	G	GS	CG	GF	Sho	SV	IP	H	R	ER	HR	BB	SO
Walker	0-0	0.00	1	0	0	0	0	0	0.2	0	0	0	0	3	1
Hoffman	9-5	2.25	70	0	0	62	0	42	88.0	50	23	22	6	31	111
Osuna	0-0	2.25	10	0	0	0	0	0	4.0	5	1	1	0	2	4
Oquist	0-0	2.35	8	0	0	3	0	0	7.2	6	2	2	0	4	4
Veras	3-1	2.79	23	0	0	6	0	0	29.0	24	10	9	3	10	23
Villone	1-1	2.95	21	0	0	9	0	0	18.1	17	6	6	2	7	19
Bochtler	2-4	3.02	63	0	0	17	0	3	65.2	45	25	22	6	39	68
Worrell	9-7	3.05	50	11	0	8	0	1	121.0	109	45	41	9	39	99
Ashby	9-5	3.23	24	24	1	0	0	0	150.2	147	60	54	17	34	85
Sanders	9-5	3.38	46	16	0	6	0	0	144.0	117	58	54	10	48	157
Valenzuela	13-8	3.62	33	31	0	0	0	0	171.2	177	78	69	17	67	95
Florie	2-2	4.01	39	0	0	11	0	0	49.1	45	24	22	1	27	51
Hamilton	15-9	4.17	34	33	3	0	1	0	211.2	206	100	98	19	83	184
Tewksbury	10-10	4.31	36	33	1	0	0	0	206.2	224	116	99	17	43	126
Bergman	6-8	4.37	41	14	0	11	0	0	113.1	119	63	55	14	33	85
Blair	2-6	4.60	60	0	0	17	0	1	88.0	80	52	45	13	29	67
Berumen	0-0	5.40	3	0	0	1	0	0	3.1	3	2	2	1	2	4
Hermanson	1-0	8.56	8	0	0	4	0	0	13.2	18	15	13	3	4	11

1997 preliminary roster

PITCHERS (18)
Andy Ashby
Sean Bergman
Andres Berumen
Doug Bochtler
Will Cunnane
Shane Dennis
Joey Eischen
Todd Erdos
Joey Hamilton
Sterling Hitchcock
Trevor Hoffman
Brad Kaufman
Marc Kroon
Joey Long
Heath Murray
Cam Smith
Dario Veras
Tim Worrell

CATCHERS (2)
John Flaherty
Sean Mulligan

INFIELDERS (15)
Homer Bush
Ken Caminiti
Archi Cianfrocco
Chris Gomez
Wally Joyner
Derrek Lee
Scott Livingstone
Luis Lopez
Juan Melo
Jody Reed
Craig Shipley
Jason Thompson
Jorge Velandia
Quilvio Veras

OUTFIELDERS (6)
Steve Finley
Tony Gwynn
Rickey Henderson
Earl Johnson
Chris Jones
Greg Vaughn

Games played by position

PLAYER	G	C	1B	2B	3B	SS	OF
Ausmus	50	46	0	0	0	0	0
Caminiti	146	0	0	0	145	0	0
Cianfrocco	79	1	33	6	11	10	8
Dascenzo	21	0	0	0	0	0	10
Deer	25	0	0	0	0	0	18
Finley	161	0	0	0	0	0	160
Flaherty	72	72	0	0	0	0	0
Gomez	89	0	0	0	0	89	0
T. Gwynn	116	0	0	0	0	0	111
C. Gwynn	81	0	1	0	0	0	29
Henderson	148	0	0	0	0	0	134
Johnson	82	66	1	0	1	0	0
Joyner	121	0	119	0	0	0	0
Livingstone	102	0	22	0	16	0	0
Lopez	63	0	0	22	2	35	0
Mulligan	2	0	0	0	0	0	0
Newfield	84	0	2	0	0	0	51
Reed	146	0	0	145	0	0	0
Shipley	33	0	0	17	4	7	3
Steverson	1	0	0	0	0	0	0
Tatum	5	0	0	0	1	0	0
Thompson	13	0	13	0	0	0	0
Vaughn	43	0	0	0	0	0	39

Minor Leagues

Tops in the organization

BATTER	CLUB	AVG.	G	AB	R	H	HR	RBI
B. Reynoso	Idf	.345	72	284	45	98	4	50
D. Rohrmeier	Mem	.344	134	471	98	162	28	95
D. Brinkley	Mem	.333	125	462	88	154	18	88
S. Chavez	Idf	.325	69	277	55	90	7	50
B. McClure	Idf	.321	72	308	62	99	6	45

HOME RUNS

Derrek Lee	Mem	34
D. Rohrmeier	Mem	28
Juan Espinal	Bak	26
J. Thompson	Lvg	21
Several Players Tied At		20

WINS

Brandon Kolb	Cln	16
Shane Dennis	Mem	13
Rob Mattson	Mem	13
Heath Murray	Mem	13
Several Players Tied At		12

RBI

Derrek Lee	Mem	104
Juan Espinal	Bak	98
Dan Rohrmeier	Mem	95
Dustin Allen	Rc	91
Darryl Brinkley	Mem	88

SAVES

Marc Kroon	Mem	22
D. Hermanson	Lvg	21
Todd Bussa	Cln	18
Todd Erdos	Rc	17
Todd Schmitt	Mem	15

STOLEN BASES

J. Johnson	Cln	44
Darryl Brinkley	Mem	31
Stoney Briggs	Mem	28
R. Lindsey	Idf	28
Mark Wulfert	Cln	26

STRIKEOUTS

Shane Dennis	Mem	185
Matt Clement	Rc	184
Brad Kaufman	Mem	163
F. Hernandez	Mem	161
Heath Murray	Mem	156

PITCHER	CLUB	W-L	ERA	IP	H	BB	SO
Shane Dennis	Mem	13-3	2.59	174	140	64	185
Mike Oquist	Lvg	9-4	2.89	140	136	44	110
Heath Murray	Mem	13-9	3.21	174	154	60	156
Hal Garrett	Rc	6-4	3.22	101	86	51	116
Brandon Kolb	Cln	16-9	3.42	181	170	76	138

Sick call: 1996 DL report

PLAYER	Days on the DL
Andy Ashby	68**
Homer Bush	133
Archi Cianfrocco	31*
Chris Gwynn	36*
Tony Gwynn	35
Wally Joyner	39
Scott Livingstone	20
Luis Lopez	49*
Craig Shipley	90*

Indicates two separate terms on Disabled List.
**Indicates three separate terms on Disabled List.*

1996 salaries

	Bonuses	Total earned salary
Greg Vaughn, of	$50,000	$5,825,000
Tony Gwynn, of	$300,000	$4,300,000
Rickey Henderson, of	$1,250,000	$3,250,000
Ken Caminiti, 3b	$75,000	$3,125,000
Steve Finley, of	$50,000	$2,850,000
Wally Joyner, 1b	$50,000	$2,550,000
Andy Ashby, p		$1,900,000
Bob Tewksbury, p		$1,500,000
Jody Reed, 2b	$250,000	$1,000,000
Fernando Valenzuela, p	$500,000	$1,000,000
Trevor Hoffman, p		$955,000
Willie Blair, p	$200,000	$750,000
Scott Livingstone, 3b		$550,000
Craig Shipley, ss		$500,000
Chris Gwynn, of	$75,000	$375,000
Joey Hamilton, p		$325,000
Scott Sanders, p	$75,000	$300,000
John Flaherty, c		$275,000
Chris Gomez, ss		$275,000
Archi Cianfrocco, 3b		$262,500
Tim Worrell, p	$65,000	$230,000
Sean Bergman, p		$205,000
Brian Johnson, c		$170,000
Luis Lopez, 2b		$155,000
Mike Oquist, p		$150,000
Doug Bochtler, p		$145,000
Homer Bush, ss		$109,000
Dario Veras, p		$109,000

Average 1996 salary: $1,183,589
Total 1996 team payroll: $33,140,500
Terminaton pay: None

San Diego (1969-1996)

Runs: Most, career

1140	TONY GWYNN, 1982-1996
599	Dave Winfield, 1973-1980
484	Gene Richards, 1977-1983
442	Nate Colbert, 1969-1974
430	Garry Templeton, 1982-1991

Hits: Most, career

2560	TONY GWYNN, 1982-1996
1135	Garry Templeton, 1982-1991
1134	Dave Winfield, 1973-1980
994	Gene Richards, 1977-1983
817	Terry Kennedy, 1981-1986

2B: Most, career

411	TONY GWYNN, 1982-1996
195	Garry Templeton, 1982-1991
179	Dave Winfield, 1973-1980
158	Terry Kennedy, 1981-1986
130	Nate Colbert, 1969-1974

3B: Most, career

82	TONY GWYNN, 1982-1996
63	Gene Richards, 1977-1983
39	Dave Winfield, 1973-1980
36	Garry Templeton, 1982-1991
29	Cito Gaston, 1969-1974

HR: Most, career

163	Nate Colbert, 1969-1974
154	Dave Winfield, 1973-1980
90	TONY GWYNN, 1982-1996
85	BENITO SANTIAGO, 1986-1992
84	FRED McGRIFF, 1991-1993

RBI: Most, career

854	TONY GWYNN, 1982-1996
626	Dave Winfield, 1973-1980
481	Nate Colbert, 1969-1974
427	Garry Templeton, 1982-1991
424	Terry Kennedy, 1981-1986

SB: Most, career

296	TONY GWYNN, 1982-1996
242	Gene Richards, 1977-1983
171	Alan Wiggins, 1981-1985
148	BIP ROBERTS, 1986-1995
147	OZZIE SMITH, 1978-1981

BB: Most, career

664	TONY GWYNN, 1982-1996
463	Dave Winfield, 1973-1980
423	Gene Tenace, 1977-1980
350	Nate Colbert, 1969-1974
338	Gene Richards, 1977-1983

BA: Highest, career

.337	TONY GWYNN, 1982-1996
.298	BIP ROBERTS, 1986-1995
.291	Gene Richards, 1977-1983
.286	Johnny Grubb, 1972-1976
.284	Dave Winfield, 1973-1980

Slug avg: Highest, career

.468	Nate Colbert, 1969-1974
.464	Dave Winfield, 1973-1980
.448	TONY GWYNN, 1982-1996
.422	Gene Tenace, 1977-1980
.409	Steve Garvey, 1983-1987

On-base avg: Highest, career

.403	Gene Tenace, 1977-1980
.389	TONY GWYNN, 1982-1996
.363	Johnny Grubb, 1972-1976
.361	BIP ROBERTS, 1986-1995
.357	Dave Winfield, 1973-1980

Complete games: Most, career

71	Randy Jones, 1973-1980
35	Eric Show, 1981-1990
34	Clay Kirby, 1969-1973
31	Steve Arlin, 1969-1974
29	Bruce Hurst, 1989-1993

Saves: Most, career

108	Rollie Fingers, 1977-1980
96	TREVOR HOFFMAN, 1993-1996
83	Rich Gossage, 1984-1987
78	Mark Davis, 1987-1994
64	Craig Lefferts, 1984-1992

Shutouts: Most, career

18	Randy Jones, 1973-1980
11	Steve Arlin, 1969-1974
11	Eric Show, 1981-1990
10	Bruce Hurst, 1989-1993
8	ANDY BENES, 1989-1995

Wins: Most, career

100	Eric Show, 1981-1990
92	Randy Jones, 1973-1980
77	Ed Whitson, 1983-1991
69	ANDY BENES, 1989-1995
60	Andy Hawkins, 1982-1988

K: Most, career

1036	ANDY BENES, 1989-1995
951	Eric Show, 1981-1990
802	Clay Kirby, 1969-1973
767	Ed Whitson, 1983-1991
677	Randy Jones, 1973-1980

Win pct: Highest, career

.591	Bruce Hurst, 1989-1993
.535	Eric Show, 1981-1990
.517	Ed Whitson, 1983-1991
.515	Dave Dravecky, 1982-1987
.512	Greg Harris, 1988-1993

ERA: Lowest, career

3.12	Dave Dravecky, 1982-1987
3.27	Bruce Hurst, 1989-1993
3.30	Randy Jones, 1973-1980
3.57	ANDY BENES, 1989-1995
3.59	Eric Show, 1981-1990

Runs: Most, season

126	STEVE FINLEY, 1996
119	TONY GWYNN, 1987
110	RICKEY HENDERSON, 1996
109	KEN CAMINITI, 1996
107	TONY GWYNN, 1986

Hits: Most, season

218	TONY GWYNN, 1987
213	TONY GWYNN, 1984
211	TONY GWYNN, 1986
203	TONY GWYNN, 1989
197	TONY GWYNN, 1985
197	TONY GWYNN, 1995

2B: Most, season

45	STEVE FINLEY, 1996
42	Terry Kennedy, 1982
41	TONY GWYNN, 1993
37	KEN CAMINITI, 1996
36	Johnny Grubb, 1975
36	TONY GWYNN, 1987
36	BIP ROBERTS, 1990

3B: Most, season

13	TONY GWYNN, 1987
12	Gene Richards, 1978
12	Gene Richards, 1981
11	Bill Almon, 1977
11	TONY GWYNN, 1991
11	Gene Richards, 1977

HR: Most, season

40	KEN CAMINITI, 1996
38	Nate Colbert, 1970
38	Nate Colbert, 1972
35	FRED McGRIFF, 1992
34	PHIL PLANTIER, 1993
34	Dave Winfield, 1979

RBI: Most, season

130	KEN CAMINITI, 1996
118	Dave Winfield, 1979
115	JOE CARTER, 1990
111	Nate Colbert, 1972
106	FRED McGRIFF, 1991

SB: Most, season

70	Alan Wiggins, 1984
66	Alan Wiggins, 1983
61	Gene Richards, 1980
57	OZZIE SMITH, 1980
56	TONY GWYNN, 1987
56	Gene Richards, 1977

BB: Most, season

132	Jack Clark, 1989
125	RICKEY HENDERSON, 1996
125	Gene Tenace, 1977
105	FRED McGRIFF, 1991
105	Gene Tenace, 1979

BA: Highest, season

.394	TONY GWYNN, 1994
.370	TONY GWYNN, 1987
.368	TONY GWYNN, 1995
.358	TONY GWYNN, 1993
.352	TONY GWYNN, 1984

Slug avg: Highest, season

.621	KEN CAMINITI, 1996
.580	GARY SHEFFIELD, 1992
.568	TONY GWYNN, 1994
.558	Dave Winfield, 1979
.556	FRED McGRIFF, 1992

On-base avg: Highest, season

.454	TONY GWYNN, 1994
.447	TONY GWYNN, 1987
.415	Gene Tenace, 1977
.410	RICKEY HENDERSON, 1996
.410	Jack Clark, 1989

Complete games: Most, season

25	Randy Jones, 1976
18	Randy Jones, 1975
14	Dave Roberts, 1971
13	Clay Kirby, 1971
13	Eric Show, 1988

Saves: Most, season

44	Mark Davis, 1989
42	TREVOR HOFFMAN, 1996
38	RANDY MYERS, 1992
37	Rollie Fingers, 1978
35	Rollie Fingers, 1977

Shutouts: Most, season

6	Randy Jones, 1975
6	Fred Norman, 1972
5	Randy Jones, 1976
4	Steve Arlin, 1971
4	Bruce Hurst, 1990
4	Bruce Hurst, 1992

Wins: Most, season

22	Randy Jones, 1976
21	Gaylord Perry, 1978
20	Randy Jones, 1975
18	Andy Hawkins, 1985
16	La Marr Hoyt, 1985
16	Tim Lollar, 1982
16	Eric Show, 1988
16	Ed Whitson, 1989

K: Most, season

231	Clay Kirby, 1971
189	ANDY BENES, 1994
185	Pat Dobson, 1970
184	JOEY HAMILTON, 1996
179	ANDY BENES, 1993
179	Bruce Hurst, 1989

Win pct: Highest, season

.778	Gaylord Perry, 1978
.692	Andy Hawkins, 1985
.667	La Marr Hoyt, 1985
.652	Bruce Hurst, 1991
.640	Tim Lollar, 1982

ERA: Lowest, season

2.10	Dave Roberts, 1971
2.24	Randy Jones, 1975
2.60	Ed Whitson, 1990
2.66	Ed Whitson, 1989
2.69	Bruce Hurst, 1989

Most pinch-hit homers, season

5	Jerry Turner, 1978
3	Luis Salazar, 1989
3	ARCHI CIANFROCCO, 1995

Most pinch-hit homers, career

9	Jerry Turner, 1974-1983

Longest hitting streak

34	BENITO SANTIAGO, 1987
27	JOHN FLAHERTY, 1996
25	TONY GWYNN, 1983
23	BIP ROBERTS, 1994
21	Bobby Brown, 1983
21	Steve Finley, 1996

Most consecutive scoreless innings

30	Randy Jones, 1980

No-hit games

None

ACTIVE PLAYERS in caps.

Players' years of service are listed by the first and last years with this team and are not necessarily consecutive; all statistics record performances for this team only.

Los Angeles Dodgers

Mike Piazza led the Dodgers to the playoffs and was second in the MVP voting.

1996 Dodgers: An emotional roller coaster

The Dodgers didn't have the celebration of a year ago, but after all of the emotional trauma and despair that they went through all season, they realized they at least owed it to themselves to celebrate reaching the playoffs for the second consecutive year. "I really can't recall a season when so many things have happened," said Fred Claire, the Dodgers' executive vice president, "when there have been so many difficult hurdles, so many obstacles. "Your manager [Tommy Lasorda] has a heart attack. Your center fielder [Brett Butler] has cancer. You lose your opening-day pitcher [Ramon Martinez] for six weeks. You lose your shortstop [Greg Gagne] for five weeks. You lose your third baseman [Mike Blowers] for the season. But the players never looked for excuses. They stayed focused and kept their competitiveness. It speaks volumes for their resiliency."

Butler said of the year, "It's as if all this devastation has brought us together." In a season when the Dodgers were presented with an inhuman amount of grief and heartache, they thrived on the adversity. But the nagging question that remained was whether all the trauma finally took its toll. The Dodgers streaked to the finish—almost. After a hot six weeks seemingly put them in command of the NL West, Los Angeles was swept at home in a season-ending home series with San Diego and finished a game behind the Padres. The Dodgers then were swept again, out of the first round of the playoffs in three games by the Atlanta Braves.

A team known for its pitching for decades, the Dodgers posted the lowest ERA in the majors for the first time since 1991. They won 90 games, drew their most fans in five years, had a reliever with a franchise-record 44 saves, had two players with more than 30 homers and 100 RBI, and had a pitcher throw a no-hitter against the Colorado Rockies in Coors Field. "We got into the playoffs," said catcher Mike Piazza, "so obviously we did something right. But we have shortcomings that need to be corrected."

Piazza led the offense with 36 home runs and 105 RBI but wilted at the finish.

Many of the shortcomings Piazza spoke of revolved around the rest of the offense. First baseman Eric Karros had a 34-homer, 111-RBI year, but the Dodgers still were among the three worst teams in the National League in 12 offensive categories. They had the worst slugging average (.384) and on-base average (.316) in the major leagues. Piazza's .422 on-base average not only led the team but was also more than 100 points higher than the average of the entire team. The hope is that young outfielders Raul Mondesi, Todd Hollandsworth (the National League Rookie of the Year, the fifth straight Dodger to win it) and Roger Cedeno improve, because the pitching is strong enough that Colorado-style offense isn't necessary.

Hideo Nomo led the club in victories with 16 and ERA at 3.19, capped by the no-hitter in Denver. Martinez came back from his injury to match Ismael Valdes at 15 wins. Pedro Astacio won only nine games, but his 3.44 ERA, while the highest among the top four starters, ranked 13th in the league. Closer Todd Worrell continued to pitch agelessly, tying Cincinnati's Jeff Brantley for the league lead in saves. The setup corps of Antonio Osuna, Mark Guthrie, Scott Radinsky and Chan Ho Park was the league's best by season's end.

1996 Dodgers: Week-by-week notes

These notes were excerpted from the following issues of Baseball Weekly.

▶**April 10:** Starter Ramon Martinez suffered a torn right groin muscle against the Cubs that is expected to sideline him for a minimum of four to six weeks. The Dodgers' ace, who had never been on the DL in his career, suffered the injury when he slipped running to first base at frigid Wrigley Field on April 6.

▶**April 17:** Putting on a pitching performance on April 13 that resurrected memories of Sandy Koufax, Hideo Nomo struck out a career-high 17 batters against the Marlins en route to his second consecutive three-hitter. Nomo came within one strikeout of tying the franchise record shared by Koufax (twice) and Ramon Martinez.

▶**April 24:** Catcher Mike Piazza went deep on April 20 to snap the longest homer drought of his career at 65 at-bats and 71 plate appearances.

▶**May 1:** The Dodgers set a bizarre record on April 27 when they played their 454th consecutive game without using a left-handed starting pitcher. It eclipses their own major league record, set from Oct. 2, 1902, to April 14, 1906.

▶**May 15:** The Dodgers were in a deep hitting slump. First baseman Eric Karros entered the week batting .188, third baseman Mike Blowers was at .200, and right fielder Raul Mondesi was struggling at .203. All three were hitting below their weight. Roger Cedeno will be the everyday center fielder in Brett Butler's absence. The diagnosis of cancer for Butler almost certainly means that he is out for the season.

▶**May 22:** The Dodgers entered the week with a 15-6 record and a 1.88 ERA at Dodger Stadium, yielding just 132 hits, including 14 homers, in 190 innings. On the road, the Dodgers pitching staff was 8-15 with a 3.71 ERA, giving up 214 hits, including 15 homers, in 199 innings.

▶**May 29:** The Dodgers, hearing that doctors are optimistic about Brett Butler's recovery from cancer surgery, hope that

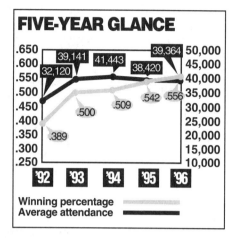

FIVE-YEAR GLANCE

Winning percentage
Average attendance

he'll be back in uniform in September. Butler, who will begin six weeks of radiation treatments on June 4, told manager Tommy Lasorda that he wants to return.

▶**June 12:** The Dodgers acknowledge that Hideo Nomo's fastball is down in velocity, between 83 and 86 mph. "I think he's a little out of whack mechanically," pitching coach Dave Wallace said, "but that will happen from time to time."

▶**June 19:** Eric Karros, hitting just .183 on May 12 and buried in an 0-for-27 slump, suddenly caught fire. He's batting .309 since then, with seven homers and 20 RBI in his last 29 games.

▶**June 26:** Todd Worrell saved all five victories during the Dodgers' 5-2 trip. During the last two trips, he has 10 of his league-leading 22 saves. Ramon Martinez, who spent five weeks on the DL, pitched a seven-hit shutout and is now 15-2 since last year's All-Star break.

▶**July 3:** Tommy Lasorda, hospitalized last week after a heart attack, said he has been overwhelmed with telephone calls, flowers and letters. "Maybe it takes something like this to realize how many people love you," he said.

▶**July 11:** Hard-hitting Mike Piazza leads the league with a .363 batting average and tops the Dodgers with 24 homers and 63 RBI. "It's to the point now when you see the ball go down the middle of the plate to him," reliever

Mark Guthrie said, "you flinch."

▶**July 24:** Mike Blowers is out for the season with a torn anterior cruciate ligament of the left knee. Blowers, who had never been on the disabled list, was on a hitting tear, with a .311 average since May 25.

▶**July 31:** Tommy Lasorda announced his retirement as Dodgers manager on July 29, citing his health concerns in ending his 20-year career. He had 1,613 wins, seven division titles, four NL pennants and two World Series championships with Los Angeles. Bill Russell, who filled in for Lasorda after his heart surgery, was named the new manager.

▶**Aug. 14:** Dodgers pitchers have the second-lowest earned run average in the National League, but the team is 12th in batting average and runs scored. "Until we get some more run production, we're putting a lot of pressure on our pitching staff," Russell said. "They're at the point of being afraid to make a bad pitch."

▶**Aug. 21:** Mike Piazza's season has been a trade-off between home runs hit and stolen bases allowed. After Montreal's game-tying double steal in the top of the ninth on Aug. 17, Piazza hit his 30th home run to give the Dodgers a 7-6 victory.

▶**Aug. 28:** The first six weeks of the season, when Eric Karros's batting average failed to top .200, have faded out of memory. Karros now leads the team with 88 RBI and has hit 28 homers.

▶**Sept. 4:** The first matchup of the Martinez brothers developed into a classic pitching duel. It ended with Ramon the victor in the Dodgers' 2-1 triumph against the Expos. Montreal starter Pedro, the younger brother, struck out a career-high 12, yielding only six hits and two runs in his complete-game performance. Ramon was even better. He permitted three infield hits and one run in eight innings before Todd Worrell closed out the ninth for his 36th save.

▶**Sept. 18:** "These five days, I'll never forget as long as I live," Brett Butler said of his comeback from a four-month bout with cancer and his brief return to the field before injuring his hand on Sept. 10. "So I don't want [the team] to get down about

it." Second baseman Delino DeShields has struggled since the All-Star break. He entered the week batting only .178 in the second half, with five extra-base hits and nine RBI. He was 1-for-29 through Sept. 14 and is batting .224 for the season.

▶**Sept. 25:** On Sept. 17, Hideo Nomo fired the first no-hitter in the history of Coors Field, a 9-0 win against the Rockies.

▶**Oct. 2:** The Dodgers didn't have the division title of a year ago, but after enduring emotional trauma all season, they deserved to celebrate reaching the playoffs for the second consecutive year. The Dodgers gained the wild card by winning 31 of their last 47 games. The team overcame Brett Butler's cancer and Tommy Lasorda's heart attack to advance, and the pitching staff had three 15-game winners and posted the lowest ERA in baseball for the first time since 1991. Mike Piazza led the offense, hitting .336 with 36 homers and 105 RBI.

Team directory

▶**Owner:** Peter O'Malley
▶**General manager:** Fred Claire
▶**Ballpark:**
Dodger Stadium
1000 Elysian Park Ave.
Los Angeles, Calif.
213-224-1400
Capacity 56,000
Parking for 16,000 cars; $4
Wheelchair section and ramps
▶**Team publications:**
Dodger Yearbook, Dodger On-Line (bi-monthly), *Dodger Magazine,* media guide
▶**TV, radio broadcast stations:**
KABC 790 AM, KWKW 1330 AM (Spanish), KTLA Channel 5, Fox Sports West
▶**Camps and/or clinics:**
Twenty clinics per year, 213-224-1435
▶**Spring training:**
Holman Stadium
Dodgertown
Vero Beach, Fla.
Capacity 7,000
407-569-4900

LOS ANGELES DODGERS 1996 final stats

BATTERS	BA	SLG	OB	G	AB	R	H	TB	2B	3B	HR	RBI	BB	SO	SB	CS	E
Marrero	.375	.500	.444	10	8	2	3	4	1	0	0	1	1	3	0	0	0
Piazza	.336	.563	.422	148	547	87	184	308	16	0	36	105	81	93	0	3	9
Prince	.297	.438	.365	40	64	6	19	28	6	0	1	11	6	15	0	0	1
Mondesi	.297	.495	.334	157	634	98	188	314	40	7	24	88	32	122	14	7	12
Hollandsworth	.291	.437	.348	149	478	64	139	209	26	4	12	59	41	93	21	6	5
Hernandez	.286	.286	.375	13	14	1	4	4	0	0	0	0	2	2	0	0	0
Parker	.286	.357	.333	16	14	2	4	5	1	0	0	1	0	2	1	0	0
Kirby	.271	.351	.333	65	188	23	51	66	10	1	1	11	17	17	4	2	3
Clark	.270	.447	.364	107	226	28	61	101	12	2	8	36	34	53	2	1	1
Butler	.267	.290	.313	34	131	22	35	38	1	1	0	8	9	22	8	3	1
Blowers	.265	.394	.341	92	317	31	84	125	19	2	6	38	37	77	0	0	9
Karros	.260	.479	.316	154	608	84	158	291	29	1	34	111	53	121	8	0	15
Gagne	.255	.364	.333	128	428	48	109	156	13	2	10	55	50	93	4	2	21
Cedeno	.246	.336	.326	86	211	26	52	71	11	1	2	18	24	47	5	1	2
Wallach	.228	.333	.286	45	162	14	37	54	3	1	4	22	12	32	0	1	3
DeShields	.224	.298	.288	154	581	75	130	173	12	8	5	41	53	124	48	11	17
Hansen	.221	.231	.293	80	104	7	23	24	1	0	0	6	11	22	0	0	1
Busch	.217	.410	.261	38	83	8	18	34	4	0	4	17	5	33	0	0	3
Curtis	.212	.317	.322	43	104	20	22	33	5	0	2	9	17	15	2	1	1
Fonville	.204	.234	.266	103	201	34	41	47	4	1	0	13	17	31	7	2	6
Ashley	.200	.482	.331	71	110	18	22	53	2	1	9	25	21	44	0	0	2
Castro	.197	.280	.254	70	132	16	26	37	5	3	0	5	10	27	1	0	3
Garcia	.000	.000	.000	1	1	0	0	0	0	0	0	0	0	1	0	0	0
Guerrero	.000	.000	.000	5	2	1	0	0	0	0	0	0	0	2	0	0	0

PITCHERS	W-L	ERA	G	GS	CG	GF	Sho	SV	IP	H	R	ER	HR	BB	SO
Guthrie	2-3	2.22	66	0	0	16	0	1	73.0	65	21	18	3	22	56
Radinsky	5-1	2.41	58	0	0	19	0	1	52.1	52	19	14	2	17	48
Osuna	9-6	3.00	73	0	0	21	0	4	84.0	65	33	28	6	32	85
Worrell	4-6	3.03	72	0	0	67	0	44	65.1	70	29	22	5	15	66
Nomo	16-11	3.19	33	33	3	0	2	0	228.1	180	93	81	23	85	234
Valdes	15-7	3.32	33	33	0	0	0	0	225.0	219	94	83	20	54	173
Martinez	15-6	3.42	28	27	2	1	2	0	168.2	153	76	64	12	86	134
Astacio	9-8	3.44	35	32	0	0	0	0	211.2	207	86	81	18	67	130
Park	5-5	3.64	48	10	0	7	0	0	108.2	82	48	44	7	71	119
Candiotti	9-11	4.49	28	27	1	0	0	0	152.1	172	91	76	18	43	79
Eischen	0-1	4.78	28	0	0	11	0	0	43.1	48	25	23	4	20	36
Dreifort	1-4	4.94	19	0	0	5	0	0	23.2	23	13	13	2	12	24
Bruske	0-0	5.68	11	0	0	5	0	0	12.2	17	8	8	2	3	12
Hall	0-2	6.00	9	0	0	3	0	0	12.0	13	9	8	2	5	12
Cummings	0-1	6.75	4	0	0	1	0	0	5.1	12	7	4	1	2	5

1997 preliminary roster

PITCHERS (18)
Pedro Astacio
Alvin Brown
Tom Candiotti
Darren Dreifort
Rick Gorecki
Mark Guthrie
Darren Hall
Matt Herges
Jesus Martinez
Ramon Martinez
Hideo Nomo
Antonio Osuna

Chan Ho Park
Scott Radinsky
Gary Rath
David Spykstra
Ismael Valdes
Todd Worrell

CATCHERS (4)
Henry Blanco
Ken Huckaby
Mike Piazza
Tom Prince

INFIELDERS (11)
Jeff Berblinger
Juan Castro
Chad Fonville
Greg Gagne
Wilton Guerrero
Chip Hale
Eric Karros
Nelson Liriano
Adam Riggs
John Wehner
Todd Zeile

OUTFIELDERS (7)
Billy Ashley
Brett Butler
Roger Cedeno
Karim Garcia
Todd Hollandsworth
Wayne Kirby
Raul Mondesi

Games played by position

PLAYER	G	C	1B	2B	3B	SS	OF
Ashley	71	0	0	0	0	0	38
Blowers	92	0	6	0	90	1	0
Busch	38	0	1	0	23	0	0
Butler	34	0	0	0	0	0	34
Castro	70	0	0	9	23	30	1
Cedeno	86	0	0	0	0	0	71
Clark	107	0	0	0	0	0	62
Curtis	43	0	0	0	0	0	40
DeShields	154	0	0	154	0	0	0
Fonville	103	0	0	23	2	20	35
Gagne	128	0	0	0	0	127	0
Garcia	1	0	0	0	0	0	0
Guerrero	5	0	0	0	0	0	0
Hansen	80	0	8	0	19	0	0
Hernandez	13	9	0	0	0	0	0
Hollandsworth	149	0	0	0	0	0	142
Karros	154	0	154	0	0	0	0
Kirby	65	0	0	0	0	0	53
Marrero	10	0	1	0	0	0	0
Mondesi	157	0	0	0	0	0	157
Parker	16	0	0	0	0	0	4
Piazza	148	146	0	0	0	0	0
Prince	40	35	0	0	0	0	0
Wallach	45	0	0	0	45	0	0

Minor Leagues

Tops in the organization

BATTER	CLUB	AVG.	G	AB	R	H	HR	RBI
W. Guerrero	Abq	.344	98	425	79	146	2	38
E. Wingate	Sbr	.324	115	383	60	124	12	55
J.P. Roberge	Abq	.310	127	432	53	134	11	50
S. Richardson	Sbr	.306	128	458	80	140	13	69
Paul Loduca	Vb	.305	124	439	54	134	3	66

HOME RUNS

Paul Konerko	Abq	30
Eddie Davis	Sbr	29
Adrian Beltre	Sbr	26
C. Townsend	Sbr	22
Billy Lott	Abq	19

WINS

Billy Neal	Vb	16
Nate Bland	Vb	11
Eddie Oropesa	Sbr	11
Dennis Reyes	Sbr	11
Eric Weaver	Abq	11

RBI

Adrian Beltre	Sbr	99
Eddie Davis	Sbr	89
Paul Konerko	Abq	88
Karim Garcia	Abq	80
Oreste Marrero	Abq	76

SAVES

Rich Linares	Sbr	33
Dan Ricabal	Sav	25
Jeff Kubenka	Yak	14
Mike Judd	Sav	13
Mike Harkey	Abq	13

STOLEN BASES

Kevin Gibbs	Vb	60
Jose Pimentel	Sav	50
E. Stcknschneidr	Sav	50
Juan Hernaiz	Sav	42
Ken Morimoto	Grf	41

STRIKEOUTS

Dennis Reyes	Sbr	176
Mark Mimbs	Abq	136
Dan Camacho	Sbr	133
Eddie Oropesa	Sbr	133
Eric Gagne	Sav	131

PITCHER	CLUB	W-L	ERA	IP	H	BB	SO
Billy Neal	Vb	16-6	2.28	111	94	39	75
Matt Herges	Abq	7-3	2.68	118	116	42	60
John Davis	Sav	9-5	2.74	112	72	58	123
Nate Bland	Vb	11-4	2.77	124	123	45	93
Eric Gagne	Sav	7-6	3.28	115	94	43	131

Sick call: 1996 DL report

PLAYER	Days on the DL
Billy Ashley	22
Mike Blowers	74
Mike Busch	34
Brett Butler	127
Tom Candiotti	24
Darren Dreifort	45
Greg Gagne	33
Rick Gorecki	182
Darren Hall	137
Carlos Hernandez	28
Garey Ingram	1
Ramon Martinez	37
Scott Radinsky	11

1996 salaries

	Bonuses	Total earned salary
Ramon Martinez, p		$4,800,000
Todd Worrell, p		$4,000,000
Eric Karros, 1b		$3,150,000
Tom Candiotti, p		$3,000,000
Delino DeShields, 2b		$3,000,000
Mike Piazza, c		$2,700,000
Greg Gagne, ss		$2,600,000
Mike Blowers, 3b		$2,300,000
Brett Butler, of		$2,000,000
Chad Curtis, of		$2,000,000
Pedro Astacio, p		$1,100,000
Raul Mondesi, of		$950,000
Mark Guthrie, p		$870,000
Dave Clark, of	$75,000	$800,000
Hideo Nomo, p		$600,000
Scott Radinsky, p		$600,000
Wayne Kirby, of		$437,500
Ismael Valdes, p		$425,000
Dave Hansen, 3b		$400,000
Tom Prince, c		$325,000
Billy Ashley, of		$195,000
Darren Hall, p		$175,000
Antonio Osuna, p		$150,000
Todd Hollandsworth, of		$136,000
Darren Dreifort, p		$134,000
Juan Castro, ss		$124,000
Chan Ho Park, p		$124,000
Rick Gorecki, p		$109,000
Tim Wallach, 3b		$109,000

Average 1996 salary: $1,286,672
Total 1996 team payroll: $37,313,500
Termination pay: None

Los Angeles (1958-1996), includes Brooklyn (1890-1957)

Runs: Most, career

1338	Pee Wee Reese, 1940-1958
1255	Zack Wheat, 1909-1926
1199	Duke Snider, 1947-1962
1163	Jim Gilliam, 1953-1966
1088	Gil Hodges, 1943-1961

Hits: Most, career

2804	Zack Wheat, 1909-1926
2170	Pee Wee Reese, 1940-1958
2091	Willie Davis, 1960-1973
1995	Duke Snider, 1947-1962
1968	Steve Garvey, 1969-1982

2B: Most, career

464	Zack Wheat, 1909-1926
343	Duke Snider, 1947-1962
333	Steve Garvey, 1969-1982
330	Pee Wee Reese, 1940-1958
324	Carl Furillo, 1946-1960

3B: Most, career

171	Zack Wheat, 1909-1926
110	Willie Davis, 1960-1973
97	Hy Myers, 1909-1922
87	Jake Daubert, 1910-1918
82	John Hummel, 1905-1915
82	Duke Snider, 1947-1962

HR: Most, career

389	Duke Snider, 1947-1962
361	Gil Hodges, 1943-1961
242	Roy Campanella, 1948-1957
228	Ron Cey, 1971-1982
211	Steve Garvey, 1969-1982

RBI: Most, career

1271	Duke Snider, 1947-1962
1254	Gil Hodges, 1943-1961
1210	Zack Wheat, 1909-1926
1058	Carl Furillo, 1946-1960
992	Steve Garvey, 1969-1982

SB: Most, career

490	Maury Wills, 1959-1972
418	Davey Lopes, 1972-1981
335	Willie Davis, 1960-1973
298	Tom Daly, 1890-1901
290	Steve Sax, 1981-1988

BB: Most, career

1210	Pee Wee Reese, 1940-1958
1036	Jim Gilliam, 1953-1966
925	Gil Hodges, 1943-1961
893	Duke Snider, 1947-1962
765	Ron Cey, 1971-1982

BA: Highest, career

.352	Willie Keeler, 1893-1902
.339	Babe Herman, 1926-1945
.337	Jack Fournier, 1923-1926
.326	MIKE PIAZZA, 1992-1996
.317	Zack Wheat, 1909-1926

Slug avg: Highest, career

.559	MIKE PIAZZA, 1992-1996
.557	Babe Herman, 1926-1945
.553	Duke Snider, 1947-1962
.552	Jack Fournier, 1923-1926
.528	Reggie Smith, 1976-1981

On-base avg: Highest, career

.421	Jack Fournier, 1923-1926
.416	Augie Galan, 1941-1946
.409	Jackie Robinson, 1947-1956
.405	Eddie Stanky, 1944-1947
.399	Mike Griffin, 1891-1898
.396	B. BUTLER, 1991-1996 (7)

Complete games: Most, career

279	B. Kennedy, 1892-1901
212	Dazzy Vance, 1922-1935
205	Burleigh Grimes, 1918-1926
186	Nap Rucker, 1907-1916
167	Don Drysdale, 1956-1969

Saves: Most, career

125	Jim Brewer, 1964-1975
101	Ron Perranoski, 1961-1972
92	TODD WORRELL, 1993-1996
85	Jay Howell, 1988-1992
83	Clem Labine, 1950-1960

Shutouts: Most, career

52	Don Sutton, 1966-1988
49	Don Drysdale, 1956-1969
40	Sandy Koufax, 1955-1966
38	Nap Rucker, 1907-1916
34	Claude Osteen, 1965-1973

Wins: Most, career

233	Don Sutton, 1966-1988
209	Don Drysdale, 1956-1969
190	Dazzy Vance, 1922-1935
177	B. Kennedy, 1892-1901
165	Sandy Koufax, 1955-1966

K: Most, career

2696	Don Sutton, 1966-1988
2486	Don Drysdale, 1956-1969
2396	Sandy Koufax, 1955-1966
1918	Dazzy Vance, 1922-1935
1759	F. VALENZUELA, 1980-1990

Win pct: Highest, career

.715	Preacher Roe, 1948-1954
.682	Jim Hughes, 1899-1902
.674	Tommy John, 1972-1978
.658	Billy Loes, 1950-1956
.655	Sandy Koufax, 1955-1966

ERA: Lowest, career

2.31	Jeff Pfeffer, 1913-1921
2.42	Nap Rucker, 1907-1916
2.56	Ron Perranoski, 1961-1972
2.58	Rube Marquard, 1915-1920
2.62	Jim Brewer, 1964-1975

Runs: Most, season

148	Hub Collins, 1890
143	Babe Herman, 1930
140	Mike Griffin, 1895
140	Willie Keeler, 1899
136	Mike Griffin, 1897
130	Maury Wills, 1962 (10)

Hits: Most, season

241	Babe Herman, 1930
230	Tommy Davis, 1962
221	Zack Wheat, 1925
219	Lefty O'Doul, 1932
217	Babe Herman, 1929

2B: Most, season

52	Johnny Frederick, 1929
48	Babe Herman, 1930
47	Wes Parker, 1970
44	Johnny Frederick, 1930
43	Augie Galan, 1944
43	Babe Herman, 1931
43	Steve Sax, 1986

3B: Most, season

26	George Treadway, 1894
22	Hy Myers, 1920
20	Dan Brouthers, 1892
20	Tommy Corcoran, 1894
19	Jimmy Sheckard, 1901
16	Willie Davis, 1970 (12)

HR: Most, season

43	Duke Snider, 1956
42	Gil Hodges, 1954
42	Duke Snider, 1953
42	Duke Snider, 1955
41	Roy Campanella, 1953
36	MIKE PIAZZA, 1996 (9)

RBI: Most, season

153	Tommy Davis, 1962
142	Roy Campanella, 1953
136	Duke Snider, 1955

130   Jack Fournier, 1925
130   Babe Herman, 1930
130   Gil Hodges, 1954
130   Duke Snider, 1954

SB: Most, season

104   Maury Wills, 1962
94   Maury Wills, 1965
88   John Ward, 1892
85   Hub Collins, 1890
77   Davey Lopes, 1975

BB: Most, season

148   Eddie Stanky, 1945
137   Eddie Stanky, 1946
119   Dolph Camilli, 1938
116   Pee Wee Reese, 1949
114   Augie Galan, 1945
110   Jim Wynn, 1975 (6)

BA: Highest, season

.393   Babe Herman, 1930
.381   Babe Herman, 1929
.379   Willie Keeler, 1899
.375   Zack Wheat, 1924
.368   Lefty O'Doul, 1932
.346   Tommy Davis, 1962 (16)

Slug avg: Highest, season

.678   Babe Herman, 1930
.647   Duke Snider, 1954
.628   Duke Snider, 1955
.627   Duke Snider, 1953
.612   Babe Herman, 1929
.606   MIKE PIAZZA, 1995 (7)

On-base avg: Highest, season

.467   Mike Griffin, 1894
.455   Babe Herman, 1930
.446   Jack Fournier, 1925
.444   Mike Griffin, 1895
.440   Jackie Robinson, 1952
.434   Wally Moon, 1961 (9)

Complete games: Most, season

40   Brickyard Kennedy, 1893
39   George Haddock, 1892
39   Tom Lovett, 1890
39   Tom Lovett, 1891
38   Oscar Jones, 1904
38   Brickyard Kennedy, 1898
38   Ed Stein, 1892
38   Adonis Terry, 1890
27   Sandy Koufax, 1965 (*)
27   Sandy Koufax, 1966 (*)

Saves: Most, season

44   TODD WORRELL, 1996
32   TODD WORRELL, 1995
28   Jay Howell, 1989
25   Jim Gott, 1993
24   Jim Brewer, 1970
24   Jim Hughes, 1954

Shutouts: Most, season

11   Sandy Koufax, 1963
9   Don Sutton, 1972
8   TIM BELCHER, 1989
8   Don Drysdale, 1968
8   OREL HERSHISER, 1988
8   Sandy Koufax, 1965
8   F. VALENZUELA, 1981

Wins: Most, season

30   Tom Lovett, 1890
29   George Haddock, 1892
28   Jim Hughes, 1899
28   Joe McGinnity, 1900
28   Dazzy Vance, 1924
27   Sandy Koufax, 1966 (6)

K: Most, season

382   Sandy Koufax, 1965
317   Sandy Koufax, 1966
306   Sandy Koufax, 1963
269   Sandy Koufax, 1961
262   Dazzy Vance, 1924

Win pct: Highest, season

.889   Freddie Fitzsimmons, 1940
.880   Preacher Roe, 1951
.864   OREL HERSHISER, 1985
.842   Ron Perranoski, 1963
.833   Sandy Koufax, 1963

ERA: Lowest, season

1.58   Rube Marquard, 1916
1.68   Ned Garvin, 1904
1.73   Sandy Koufax, 1966
1.74   Sandy Koufax, 1964
1.87   Kaiser Wilhelm, 1908

Most pinch-hit homers, season

6   Johnny Frederick, 1932
5   Lee Lacy, 1978
5   BILLY ASHLEY, 1996

Most pinch-hit homers, career

8   J. Frederick, 1929-1934
8   Lee Lacy, 1972-78
7   Duke Snider, 1947-62

Longest hitting streak

31   Willie Davis, 1969
29   Zach Wheat, 1916
27   Joe Medwick, 1942
27   Duke Snider, 1953
26   Willie Keeler, 1902
26   Zach Wheat, 1918

Most consecutive
scoreless innings

59   OREL HERSHISER, 1988
58   Don Drysdale, 1968
39   Don Newcombe, Bro-1956

No-hit games

Tom Lovett, Bro vs NY NL, 4-0; June 22, 1891.
Mal Eason, Bro at StL NL, 2-0; July 20, 1906.
Harry McIntyre, Bro vs Pit NL, 0-1; Aug. 1, 1906 (lost on 4 hits in 13 innings after allowing the first hit in the 11th).
Nap Rucker, Bro vs Bos NL, 6-0; Sept. 5, 1908 (2nd game).
Dazzy Vance, Bro vs Phi NL, 10-1; Sept. 13, 1925 (1st game).
Tex Carleton, Bro at Cin NL, 3-0; Apr. 30, 1940.
Ed Head, Bro vs Bos NL, 5-0; Apr. 23, 1946.
Rex Barney, Bro at NY NL, 2-0; Sept. 9, 1948.
Carl Erskine, Bro vs Chi NL, 5-0; June 19, 1952.
Carl Erskine, Bro vs NY NL, 3-0; May 12, 1956.
Sal Maglie, Bro vs Phi NL, 5-0; Sept. 25, 1956.
Sandy Koufax, LA vs NY NL, 5-0; June 30, 1962.
Sandy Koufax, LA vs SF NL, 8-0; May 11, 1963.
Sandy Koufax, LA at Phi NL, 3-0; June 4, 1964.
Sandy Koufax, LA vs Chi NL, 1-0; Sept. 9, 1965 (perfect game).
Bill Singer, LA vs Phi NL, 5-0; July 20, 1970.
Jerry Reuss, LA at SF NL, 8-0; June 27, 1980.
FERNANDO VALENZUELA, LA vs StL NL, 6-0; June 29, 1990.
KEVIN GROSS, LA vs SF NL, 2-0; Aug. 17, 1992.
RAMON MARTINEZ, LA vs Fla NL, 7-0; July 14, 1995.
HIDEO NOMO, LA at Col NL, 9-0; Sept. 17, 1996.
Ed Stein, six innings, rain, Bro vs Chi NL, 6-0; June 2, 1894.
Fred Frankhouse, seven and two-thirds innings, rain, Bro vs Cin NL, 5-0; Aug. 27, 1937.

ACTIVE PLAYERS in caps.

Leader from the franchise's current location is included. If not in the top five, leader's rank is listed in parenthesis; asterisk (*) indicates player is not in top 25.

Players' years of service are listed by the first and last years with this team and are not necessarily consecutive; all statistics record performances for this team only.

Colorado Rockies

Ellis Burks notched a healthy set of career highs in every offensive category last season.

1996 Rockies: They needed to stay at home

One day after watching San Francisco's Barry Bonds join the 40-40 club, left fielder Ellis Burks made some history of his own at Coors Field. With a home run off Dan Carlson in an 8-5 loss to the Giants on the next-to-last day of the season, Burks joined Hank Aaron as the second player in history to get 40 homers, 30 stolen bases and 200 hits in a season. Aaron accomplished the feat for the 1963 Milwaukee Braves. "I feel honored just to be there with him," Burks said. "He's a Hall of Famer. He hit 755 homers. But for one season, I can say I did the same things he did. I'm pretty proud of that."

With his 32nd stolen base, Burks also helped the Rockies make a little history. Colorado is the first team ever to hit 200 homers and steal 200 bases in a season. The threesome of Andres Galarraga (47), Burks (40) and Vinny Castilla (40) hit 127 home runs to break the National League record of 124 set by the 1973 Atlanta Braves' Davey Johnson, Darrell Evans and Aaron. It was another one of those seasons for the Rockies, with home runs regularly flying out of Coors Field. In fact, the Rockies became the first National League club to score 900 runs since the 1953 Brooklyn Dodgers, finishing with 961.

But unlike 1995's team, this version of the Rockies couldn't muster enough pitching or enough victories away from Denver to reach the playoffs. The Rockies' pitchers compiled a 5.59 ERA, nearly a run higher than the next-worst team in the NL. They gave up the most runs and walks and had the fewest strikeouts. Kevin Ritz was the most consistent member of the rotation, winning 17 games despite a 5.28 ERA, but the league batted .293 against Colorado starters. Colorado's 55 victories at Coors Field were only one short of Atlanta's major-league-leading total of home wins. But the Rockies went 28-53 on the road, tied with Florida for the league's worst away record.

The gaudy stats, compiled mostly at home, got the Rockies four games over .500 but still seven games short of a playoff berth. Nevertheless, the individual numbers of many players were impressive. Burks led the league in slugging average, runs scored and total bases, was second in hits and tied for second in doubles, and finished in the top 10 in almost every offensive category. First baseman Andres Galarraga was the NL home run and RBI (150) champ; he drove in more runs than any major leaguer since the Dodgers' Tommy Davis knocked in 153 in 1962. Second baseman Eric Young, the team's leadoff hitter, hit .324 and won the NL stolen base crown with 53. Right fielder Dante Bichette didn't hit for power in the first part of the season but still finished with 31 homers, 39 doubles, 141 RBI and a .313 average.

The offense could have been even better because center fielder Larry Walker was limited to 83 games by injury and hit only .276 with 18 home runs. Both Walker and Bichette will come into next season needing to prove their fitness after injury problems. The Rockies saw some good signs for the future, as Quinton McCracken hit .290 as a fill-in for Walker and young right-hander Jamey Wright joined the rotation in the second half and had a 4.93 ERA, better than any of the club's season-long starters.

Team MVP

Ellis Burks: It was supposed to be Ellis Burks's final year with the Rockies. But he started hitting at the beginning of the season and simply slugged his way into a new two-year contract. He led the league in slugging average, runs and total bases and finished in the top 10 in batting, home runs, RBI, hits, doubles, triples and on-base average. Burks joined Hank Aaron as the only players to get 200 hits, 40 home runs and 30 steals in the same season.

1996 Rockies: Week-by-week notes

These notes were excerpted from the following issues of Baseball Weekly.

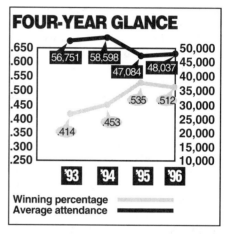

FOUR-YEAR GLANCE

Winning percentage
Average attendance

▶**April 3:** The Rockies were jolted when Bret Saberhagen and Bill Swift, their No. 1 and 2 starters, went on the disabled list during spring training. Now the two pitchers have been joined on the DL by catcher Jayhawk Owens, who injured his left thumb in the final week of spring training.

▶**April 10:** Third baseman Vinny Castilla is trying to convince skeptics about his ability to hit away from Coors Field. Castilla homered in a 6-4 loss in Montreal on April 5, then hit a first-inning grand slam in a 5-4 victory the next day. Last year he hit .383 with 23 homers at home but only .229 with nine homers on the road.

▶**May 1:** Manager Don Baylor has put his favorite batting order back in place. Baylor dropped shortstop Walt Weiss from leadoff to No. 8 on April 27 against Montreal and moved second baseman Eric Young from second to leadoff. Young responded with five hits in Colorado's 13-inning 6-5 victory.

▶**May 15:** After winning four in a row, the Rockies went to Fulton County Stadium and promptly were swept in a three-game series that raised Atlanta's all-time record against the Rockies to 33-6.

▶**May 29:** This year's Bret Saberhagen saga came to a disappointing conclusion when he decided to undergo reconstructive surgery on his right shoulder. Saberhagen will wear a sling for three weeks after the procedure, and it will probably be four months until he receives the go-ahead to pick up a baseball. Outfielder Larry Walker set an NL record with extra-base hits in six straight at-bats. He also set a club mark with 13 total bases in a game, with two home runs, a double and a triple in a 12-10 victory against Pittsburgh on May 21.

▶**June 12:** After a 10-game road trip, the Rockies returned home sporting a .221 team average away from home. They proceeded to score 32 runs in back-to-back victories over Atlanta. The offensive outburst raised Colorado's Coors Field batting average to .349. On June 9, though, they lost Larry Walker for at least eight weeks with a broken collarbone.

▶**June 19:** Bill Swift underwent arthroscopic surgery on his right shoulder on June 13 in Birmingham, Ala. "Hopefully I can come back and finish out the rest of this year—whether it's the end of August or September," Swift said. Until he returns, the Rockies will go with a rotation of Kevin Ritz, Armando Reynoso, Marvin Freeman, Mark Thompson and Bryan Rekar.

▶**June 26:** On June 22, Eric Young's 17-game hitting streak ended when he went hitless in five at-bats against the Phillies.

▶**July 3:** First baseman Andres Galarraga broke his own club record of seven RBI in a game when he drove in eight against the Dodgers on June 27.

▶**July 17:** The more the Rockies hit in Denver, the more their accomplishments (a league-best 31-15 record at home) are dismissed as altitude-enhanced. And the more they're criticized, the more they hit. Held to 10 runs in four games at Dodger Stadium a week after scoring 52 in four games with Los Angeles at Coors Field, the Rockies returned from the All-Star break to beat the Padres 8-5, 13-12, 11-6 and 8-4 at home.

▶**July 24:** As outfielder Ellis Burks enters the final two months of his three-year contract, the Rockies have an interesting choice ahead of them. After two injury-plagued seasons, Burks now ranks among the NL leaders in hitting, and he has a chance to finish with 30 homers and 30 stolen bases.

▶**Aug. 21:** Every day last week, it seemed, a new misadventure tested reliever Curtis Leskanic's will. In three appearances, Leskanic allowed a game-tying homer to Fred McGriff in Atlanta, a decisive solo homer to Joe Orsulak in a 2-1 loss at Florida, and the tying runs in a 7-6 loss to the Marlins. "It's like I'm living a nightmare," he said, "and I can't wake up."

▶**Aug. 28:** Mark Thompson pitched his third complete game of the year in a 9-3 victory against Pittsburgh on Aug. 24, his fourth win in five decisions. Meanwhile, Marvin Freeman was released to clear a spot for Bill Swift, returning from the disabled list. Freeman got a two-year, $4.4 million contract after going 10-2 in 1994. But he went 3-7 last season and was 7-9 with a 6.04 ERA this year.

▶**Sept. 11:** The Rockies called up David Nied, the No. 1 overall pick in the 1992 expansion draft. The Rockies had removed him from the 40-man roster after he went 3-8 with a 12.27 ERA for Colorado Springs. But his velocity gradually returned, and he earned the promotion after pitching well for Class A Salem. Andres Galarraga broke right fielder Dante Bichette's club records for homers and RBI with a three-run shot off Houston's Darryl Kile. The blast gave Galarraga 41 homers and 130 RBI.

▶**Sept. 18:** Ellis Burks and Dante Bichette joined the 1987 Mets' Howard Johnson and Darryl Strawberry in the teammates' 30-30 fraternity last week. Burks stole his 30th base in a 16-8 victory against Atlanta on Sept. 12. Bichette earned admission with a 448-foot homer the next night against Houston's Shane Reynolds.

▶**Sept. 25:** After starting for Colorado in Hideo Nomo's no-hit game, Bill Swift returned to the bullpen to end the season. David Nied took Swift's place in the rotation on Sept. 22 in San Francisco. "I'd just as soon finish the season healthy, then go get them in the spring," said Swift.

▶**Oct. 2:** Ellis Burks, with 40 homers and 32 steals, helped the Rockies make history in becoming the first team to hit 200 homers and steal 200 bases in a season. Andres Galarraga (47), Burks (40) and Vinny Castilla (40) combined for 127 home runs, breaking the league record of 124 set by the 1973 Braves threesome of Davey Johnson, Darrell Evans and Hank Aaron. "We put up some tremendous offensive numbers this year," Rockies manager Don Baylor said, "but the other part of the equation is our road record [28-53]." Aided by hit-happy Coors Field, where they were 55-26, the Rockies became the first NL club to score 900 runs since the 1953 Brooklyn Dodgers, but the staff allowed more than 900, too. Staff ace Kevin Ritz won a club-record 17 games but had a 5.28 ERA.

Team directory

▶**Owner:** Jerry McMorris (Colorado Baseball Partnership)
▶**General manager:** Bob Gebhard
▶**Ballpark:**
Coors Field
2001 Blake St., Denver, Colo.
303-762-5437
Capacity 50,200
Parking for 4,661 cars, 171 permanent handicapped spaces, 18,000 more spaces within a 15 minute walk
Public transportation available
Wheelchair section, family sections in all price ranges
▶**Team publications:**
Media guide, game program, yearbook
▶**TV, radio broadcast stations:**
KOA 850 AM, KWGN Channel 2
▶**Spring training:**
Hi Corbett Field
Tucson, Ariz.
Capacity 10,000
602-327-9467

COLORADO ROCKIES 1996 final stats

BATTERS	BA	SLG	OB	G	AB	R	H	TB	2B	3B	HR	RBI	BB	SO	SB	CS	E
Burks	.344	.639	.408	156	613	142	211	392	45	8	40	128	61	114	32	6	5
Young	.324	.421	.393	141	568	113	184	239	23	4	8	74	47	31	53	19	12
Bichette	.313	.531	.359	159	633	114	198	336	39	3	31	141	45	105	31	12	9
Castilla	.304	.548	.343	160	629	97	191	345	34	0	40	113	35	88	7	2	20
Galarraga	.304	.601	.357	159	626	119	190	376	39	3	47	150	40	157	18	8	14
Jones	.300	.300	.273	12	10	6	3	3	0	0	0	1	0	3	0	0	0
McCracken	.290	.410	.363	124	283	50	82	116	13	6	3	40	32	62	17	6	6
Echevarria	.286	.286	.346	26	21	2	6	6	0	0	0	6	2	5	0	0	0
J. Reed	.284	.419	.365	116	341	34	97	143	20	1	8	37	43	65	2	2	11
Weiss	.282	.375	.381	155	517	89	146	194	20	2	8	48	80	78	10	2	30
Walker	.276	.570	.342	83	272	58	75	155	18	4	18	58	20	58	18	2	1
Vander Wal	.252	.417	.335	104	151	20	38	63	6	2	5	31	19	38	2	2	1
Cockrell	.250	.375	.222	9	8	0	2	3	1	0	0	2	0	4	0	0	0
Decker	.245	.306	.323	67	147	24	36	45	3	0	2	20	18	29	1	0	0
Anthony	.243	.481	.353	79	185	32	45	89	8	0	12	22	32	56	0	2	2
Owens	.239	.367	.338	73	180	31	43	66	9	1	4	17	27	56	4	1	9
Bates	.206	.288	.312	88	160	19	33	46	8	1	1	9	23	34	2	1	7
Perez	.156	.200	.156	17	45	4	7	9	2	0	0	3	0	8	2	2	2
Pulliam	.133	.133	.235	10	15	2	2	2	0	0	0	0	2	6	0	0	0
Castellano	.118	.118	.286	13	17	1	2	2	0	0	0	2	3	6	0	0	0
Mi. Thompson	.106	.136	.192	62	66	3	7	9	2	0	0	3	7	13	1	1	0
Brito	.071	.071	.235	8	14	1	1	1	0	0	0	0	1	8	0	0	0

PITCHERS	W-L	ERA	G	GS	CG	GF	Sho	SV	IP	H	R	ER	HR	BB	SO
S. Reed	4-3	3.96	70	0	0	7	0	0	75.0	66	38	33	11	19	51
Holmes	5-4	3.97	62	0	0	21	0	1	77.0	78	41	34	8	28	73
Ruffin	7-5	4.00	71	0	0	56	0	24	69.2	55	35	31	5	29	74
Wright	4-4	4.93	16	15	0	0	0	0	91.1	105	60	50	8	41	45
Reynoso	8-9	4.96	30	30	0	0	0	0	168.2	195	97	93	27	49	88
Ritz	17-11	5.28	35	35	2	0	0	0	213.0	236	135	125	24	105	105
Ma. Thompson	9-11	5.30	34	28	3	2	1	0	169.2	189	109	100	25	74	99
Swift	1-1	5.40	7	3	0	2	0	2	18.1	23	12	11	1	5	5
Painter	4-2	5.86	34	1	0	4	0	0	50.2	56	37	33	12	25	48
Hawblitzel	0-1	6.00	8	0	0	3	0	0	15.0	18	12	10	2	6	7
Freeman	7-9	6.04	26	23	0	1	0	0	129.2	151	100	87	21	57	71
Leskanic	7-5	6.23	70	0	0	32	0	6	73.2	82	51	51	12	38	76
Bailey	2-3	6.24	24	11	0	4	0	1	83.2	94	64	58	7	52	45
Munoz	2-2	6.65	54	0	0	7	0	0	44.2	55	33	33	4	16	45
Habyan	1-1	7.13	19	0	0	5	0	0	24.0	34	19	19	4	14	25
Burke	2-1	7.47	11	0	0	3	0	0	15.2	21	13	13	3	7	19
Farmer	0-1	7.71	7	4	0	1	0	0	28.0	32	25	24	8	13	16
Rekar	2-4	8.95	14	11	0	0	0	0	58.1	87	61	58	11	26	25
Alston	1-0	9.00	6	0	0	4	0	0	6.0	9	6	6	1	3	5
Beckett	0-0	13.50	5	0	0	2	0	0	5.1	6	8	8	3	9	6
Nied	0-2	13.50	6	1	0	3	0	0	5.1	5	8	8	1	8	4

1997 preliminary roster

PITCHERS (19)
Garvin Alston
Roger Bailey
Robbie Beckett
John Burke
Mike DeJean
Jerry DiPoto
Luther Hackman
Darren Holmes
Bobby Jones
Curtis Leskanic
Mike Munoz
Steve Reed

Bryan Rekar
Kevin Ritz
Bruce Ruffin
Bill Swift
Mark Thompson
John Thomson
Jamey Wright

CATCHERS (4)
Steve Decker
Kurt Manwaring
Jayhawk Owens
Jeff Reed

INFIELDERS (8)
Jason Bates
Vinny Castilla
Craig Counsell
Andres Galarraga
Jeff Huson
Neifi Perez
Walt Weiss
Eric Young

OUTFIELDERS (9)
Dante Bichette
Ellis Burks

Angel Echevarria
Derrick Gibson
Terry Jones
Quinton McCracken
John VanderWal
Edgard Velazquez
Larry Walker

Games played by position

PLAYER	G	C	1B	2B	3B	SS	OF
Anthony	79	0	0	0	0	0	56
Bates	88	0	0	37	12	18	0
Bichette	159	0	0	0	0	0	156
Brito	8	8	0	0	0	0	0
Burks	156	0	0	0	0	0	152
Castellano	13	0	0	3	1	0	1
Castilla	160	0	0	0	160	0	0
Cockrell	9	0	0	0	0	0	1
Decker	67	40	3	0	2	0	0
Echevarria	26	0	0	0	0	0	11
Galarraga	159	0	159	0	1	0	0
Jones	12	0	0	0	0	0	4
McCracken	124	0	0	0	0	0	93
Owens	73	68	0	0	0	0	0
Perez	17	0	0	4	0	14	0
Pulliam	10	0	0	0	0	0	3
J. Reed	116	111	0	0	0	0	0
Mi. Thompson	62	0	0	0	0	0	18
Vander Wal	104	0	10	0	0	0	26
Walker	83	0	0	0	0	0	83
Weiss	155	0	0	0	0	155	0
Young	141	0	0	139	0	0	0

Minor Leagues

Tops in the organization

BATTER	CLUB	AVG.	G	AB	R	H	HR	RBI
A. Echevarria	Csp	.337	110	415	67	140	16	74
P. Castellano	Csp	.337	94	362	56	122	13	59
Todd Helton	Csp	.336	114	390	59	131	9	64
Neifi Perez	Csp	.316	133	570	77	180	7	72
G. Neubart	Sal	.300	95	367	76	110	0	28

HOME RUNS			WINS		
Tal Light	Sal	25	Scott Randall	Ash	14
John Giudice	Nhv	20	John Thomson	Csp	13
E. Velazquez	Nhv	19	Neil Garrett	Ash	12
Justin Drizos	Ash	18	Chandler Martin	Sal	12
Nate Holdren	Nhv	17	Several Players Tied At		10

RBI			SAVES		
Tal Light	Sal	87	Chris Macca	Nhv	30
John Giudice	Nhv	80	Heath Bost	Ash	15
Justin Drizos	Ash	76	Garvin Alston	Csp	14
A. Echevarria	Csp	74	L. Colmenares	Ash	12
Neifi Perez	Csp	72	Mike DeJean	Csp	12

STOLEN BASES			STRIKEOUTS		
Garrett Neubart	Sal	42	M. Brownson	Nhv	155
Elvis Pena	Sal	30	John Thomson	Csp	148
Terry Jones	Csp	26	Doug Million	Nhv	139
Gary Gordon	Sal	25	Chandler Martin	Sal	136
Chan Mayber	Sal	22	Scott Randall	Ash	136

PITCHER	CLUB	W-L	ERA	IP	H	BB	SO
Jamey Wright	Csp	9-3	1.90	104	80	34	94
Doug Million	Nhv	10-8	2.74	161	138	100	139
Scott Randall	Ash	14-4	2.74	154	121	50	136
Keith Barnes	Ash	5-5	2.99	105	93	33	85
Mike Saipe	Nhv	10-7	3.07	138	114	42	126

Sick call: 1996 DL report

PLAYER	Days on the DL
Roger Bailey	23
Jorge Brito	27
Curt Leskanic	29
Mike Munoz	19
Jayhawk Owens	24
Lance Painter	55
Harvey Pulliam	43
Bret Saberhagen	182
Bill Swift	147*
Larry Walker	66
Eric Young	21

Indicates two separate terms on Disabled List.

1996 salaries

	Bonuses	Total earned salary
Bret Saberhagen, p		$5,612,991
Andres Galarraga, 1b	$200,000	$4,700,000
Bill Swift, p		$4,608,333
Larry Walker, of		$4,375,000
Ellis Burks, of	$650,000	$3,650,000
Dante Bichette, of	$325,000	$3,591,666
Walt Weiss, ss	$150,000	$1,650,000
Vinny Castilla, ss	$200,000	$1,200,000
Darren Holmes, p	$25,000	$1,165,000
Eric Young, 2b	$75,000	$1,125,000
Eric Anthony, of	$25,000	$1,025,000
Bruce Ruffin, p		$1,000,000
Kevin Ritz, p	$90,000	$740,000
Jeff Reed, c	$100,000	$525,000
John Vander Wal, of	$20,000	$512,500
Steve Reed, p		$450,000
Armando Reynoso, p	$125,000	$440,000
Mike Munoz, p	$10,000	$290,000
Curtis Leskanic, p		$270,000
Jason Bates, ss		$181,500
Lance Painter, p		$167,000
Jayhawk Owens, c		$155,000
Roger Bailey, p		$150,000
Mark Thompson, p		$145,000
Quinton McCracken, of		$112,000
Neifi Perez, ss		$109,000
Jamey Wright, p		$109,000

Average 1996 salary: $1,409,592
Total 1996 team payroll: $38,058,990
Terminaton pay: $2,900,000

Colorado (1993-1996)

Runs: Most, career

383	DANTE BICHETTE, 1993-1996
356	ANDRES GALARRAGA, 1993-1996
300	ERIC YOUNG, 1993-1996
231	VINNY CASTILLA, 1993-1996
216	ELLIS BURKS, 1994-1996

Hits: Most, career

709	DANTE BICHETTE, 1993-1996
652	ANDRES GALARRAGA, 1993-1996
494	ERIC YOUNG, 1993-1996
483	VINNY CASTILLA, 1993-1996
363	WALT WEISS, 1994-1996

2B: Most, career

153	DANTE BICHETTE, 1993-1996
124	ANDRES GALARRAGA, 1993-1996
88	VINNY CASTILLA, 1993-1996
73	ERIC YOUNG, 1993-1996
68	CHARLIE HAYES, 1993-1994

3B: Most, career

22	ERIC YOUNG, 1993-1996
17	ELLIS BURKS, 1994-1996
12	DANTE BICHETTE, 1993-1996
12	MIKE KINGERY, 1994-1995
11	JOE GIRARDI, 1993-1995

HR: Most, career

131	ANDRES GALARRAGA, 1993-1996
119	DANTE BICHETTE, 1993-1996
84	VINNY CASTILLA, 1993-1996
67	ELLIS BURKS, 1994-1996
54	LARRY WALKER, 1995-1996

RBI: Most, career

453	DANTE BICHETTE, 1993-1996
439	ANDRES GALARRAGA, 1993-1996
251	VINNY CASTILLA, 1993-1996
201	ELLIS BURKS, 1994-1996
182	ERIC YOUNG, 1993-1996

SB: Most, career

148	ERIC YOUNG, 1993-1996
79	DANTE BICHETTE, 1993-1996
42	ELLIS BURKS, 1994-1996
40	ANDRES GALARRAGA, 1993-1996
37	WALT WEISS, 1994-1996

BB: Most, career

234	WALT WEISS, 1994-1996
197	ERIC YOUNG, 1993-1996
116	ELLIS BURKS, 1994-1996
115	ANDRES GALARRAGA, 1993-1996
114	DANTE BICHETTE, 1993-1996

BA: Highest, career

.320	ELLIS BURKS, 1994-1996
.317	DANTE BICHETTE, 1993-1996
.315	ANDRES GALARRAGA, 1993-1996
.306	MIKE KINGERY, 1994-1995
.299	ERIC YOUNG, 1993-1996

Slug avg: Highest, career

.607	ELLIS BURKS, 1994-1996
.594	LARRY WALKER, 1995-1996
.575	ANDRES GALARRAGA, 1993-1996
.556	DANTE BICHETTE, 1993-1996
.519	VINNY CASTILLA, 1993-1996

On-base avg: Highest, career

.392	ELLIS BURKS, 1994-1996
.382	ERIC YOUNG, 1993-1996
.375	WALT WEISS, 1994-1996
.375	MIKE KINGERY, 1994-1995
.367	LARRY WALKER, 1995-1996

Complete games: Most, career

5	ARMANDO REYNOSO, 1993-1996
3	DAVID NIED, 1993-1996
3	MARK THOMPSON, 1994-1996
2	KEVIN RITZ, 1994-1996
1	WILLIE BLAIR, 1993-1994
1	KENT BOTTENFIELD, 1993-1994
1	Greg Harris, 1993-1994
1	Butch Henry, 1993
1	LANCE PAINTER, 1993-1996
1	BRYAN REKAR, 1995-1996

Saves: Most, career

53	BRUCE RUFFIN, 1993-1996
43	DARREN HOLMES, 1993-1996
16	CURT LESKANIC, 1993-1996
9	STEVE REED, 1993-1996
3	WILLIE BLAIR, 1993-1994
3	MIKE MUNOZ, 1993-1996

Shutouts: Most, career

1	DAVID NIED, 1993-1996
1	MARK THOMPSON, 1994-1996

Wins: Most, career

33	KEVIN RITZ, 1994-1996
30	ARMANDO REYNOSO, 1993-1996
21	STEVE REED, 1993-1996
20	MARVIN FREEMAN, 1994-1996
17	BRUCE RUFFIN, 1993-1996

K: Most, career

288	BRUCE RUFFIN, 1993-1996
278	KEVIN RITZ, 1994-1996
270	ARMANDO REYNOSO, 1993-1996
232	STEVE REED, 1993-1996
230	CURT LESKANIC, 1993-1996

Win pct: Highest, career

.714	BILL SWIFT, 1995-1996
.636	STEVE REED, 1993-1996
.565	LANCE PAINTER, 1993-1996
.560	DARREN HOLMES, 1993-1996
.541	KEVIN RITZ, 1994-1996

ERA: Lowest, career

3.60	STEVE REED, 1993-1996
3.73	BRUCE RUFFIN, 1993-1996
4.07	DARREN HOLMES, 1993-1996
4.65	ARMANDO REYNOSO, 1993-1996
4.88	CURT LESKANIC, 1993-1996

Runs: Most, season

142	ELLIS BURKS, 1996
119	ANDRES GALARRAGA, 1996
114	DANTE BICHETTE, 1996
113	ERIC YOUNG, 1996
102	DANTE BICHETTE, 1995

Hits: Most, season

211 ELLIS BURKS, 1996
198 DANTE BICHETTE, 1996
197 DANTE BICHETTE, 1995
191 VINNY CASTILLA, 1996
190 ANDRES GALARRAGA, 1996

2B: Most, season

45 ELLIS BURKS, 1996
45 CHARLIE HAYES, 1993
43 DANTE BICHETTE, 1993
39 DANTE BICHETTE, 1996
39 ANDRES GALARRAGA, 1996

3B: Most, season

9 ERIC YOUNG, 1995
8 ELLIS BURKS, 1996
8 MIKE KINGERY, 1994
8 ERIC YOUNG, 1993
7 VINNY CASTILLA, 1993

HR: Most, season

47 ANDRES GALARRAGA, 1996
40 DANTE BICHETTE, 1995
40 ELLIS BURKS, 1996
40 VINNY CASTILLA, 1996
36 LARRY WALKER, 1995

RBI: Most, season

150 ANDRES GALARRAGA, 1996
141 DANTE BICHETTE, 1996
128 DANTE BICHETTE, 1995
128 ELLIS BURKS, 1996
113 VINNY CASTILLA, 1996

SB: Most, season

53 ERIC YOUNG, 1996
42 ERIC YOUNG, 1993
35 ERIC YOUNG, 1995
32 ELLIS BURKS, 1996
31 DANTE BICHETTE, 1996

BB: Most, season

98 WALT WEISS, 1995
80 WALT WEISS, 1996
63 ERIC YOUNG, 1993
61 ELLIS BURKS, 1996
56 WALT WEISS, 1994

BA: Highest, season

.370 ANDRES GALARRAGA, 1993
.344 ELLIS BURKS, 1996
.340 DANTE BICHETTE, 1995
.324 ERIC YOUNG, 1996
.319 ANDRES GALARRAGA, 1994

Slug avg: Highest, season

.639 ELLIS BURKS, 1996
.620 DANTE BICHETTE, 1995
.607 LARRY WALKER, 1995
.602 ANDRES GALARRAGA, 1993
.601 ANDRES GALARRAGA, 1996

On-base avg: Highest, season

.408 ELLIS BURKS, 1996
.403 ANDRES GALARRAGA, 1993
.403 WALT WEISS, 1995
.393 ERIC YOUNG, 1996
.381 WALT WEISS, 1996

Complete games: Most, season

4 ARMANDO REYNOSO, 1993
3 MARK THOMPSON, 1996
2 DAVID NIED, 1994
2 KEVIN RITZ, 1996
1 WILLIE BLAIR, 1993
1 KENT BOTTENFIELD, 1993
1 Greg Harris, 1994
1 Butch Henry, 1993
1 DAVID NIED, 1993
1 BRYAN REKAR, 1995
1 ARMANDO REYNOSO, 1994

Saves: Most, season

25 DARREN HOLMES, 1993
24 BRUCE RUFFIN, 1996
16 BRUCE RUFFIN, 1994
14 DARREN HOLMES, 1995
11 BRUCE RUFFIN, 1995

Shutouts: Most, season

1 DAVID NIED, 1994
1 MARK THOMPSON, 1996

Wins: Most, season

17 KEVIN RITZ, 1996
12 ARMANDO REYNOSO, 1993
11 KEVIN RITZ, 1995
10 MARVIN FREEMAN, 1994
9 DAVID NIED, 1994
9 STEVE REED, 1993
9 BILL SWIFT, 1995
9 MARK THOMPSON, 1996

K: Most, season

126 BRUCE RUFFIN, 1993
120 KEVIN RITZ, 1995
117 ARMANDO REYNOSO, 1993
107 CURT LESKANIC, 1995
105 KEVIN RITZ, 1996

Win pct: Highest, season

.833 MARVIN FREEMAN, 1994
.607 KEVIN RITZ, 1996
.522 ARMANDO REYNOSO, 1993

ERA: Lowest, season

4.00 ARMANDO REYNOSO, 1993
4.21 KEVIN RITZ, 1995
4.96 ARMANDO REYNOSO, 1996
5.28 KEVIN RITZ, 1996
5.30 MARK THOMPSON, 1996

Most pinch-hit homers, season

4 Howard Johnson, 1994
4 JOHN VANDER WAL, 1995

Most pinch-hit homers, career

8 JOHN VANDER WAL, 1994-1996
4 Howard Johnson, 1994

Longest hitting streak

23 DANTE BICHETTE, 1995
19 DANTE BICHETTE, 1995
19 ERIC YOUNG, 1995
16 DANTE BICHETTE, 1994
17 ERIC YOUNG, 1996

Most consecutive scoreless innings

16 BRUCE RUFFIN, 1993

No-hit games

None

ACTIVE PLAYERS in caps.

Players' years of service are listed by the first and last years with this team and are not necessarily consecutive; all statistics record performances for this team only.

Barry Bonds, almost alone among the Giants, could smile about his 1996 performance.

By Eileen Blass, USA TODAY

1996 Giants: Their stats fell

Without the magnificent performance of Barry Bonds this year, Giants fans would have had almost nothing to cheer for. What would it have been like without him? One hundred losses? Most likely. Dullsville? Without a doubt. In the final weeks of a very disappointing season, Bonds was the only reason to follow the last-place Giants. Bonds beat the odds—and many of his opponents—by playing in a lineup composed largely of minor leaguers yet posting perhaps his best overall season. Even better than his three MVP campaigns? "Barry never had a finer season," soon-to-be-replaced GM Bob Quinn said.

"Yeah," agreed Bonds. "As far as playing on a team with all the injuries, I feel it's the best season I've ever had, due to the circumstances." Bonds capped his year by becoming the second man in major league history to reach 40 homers and 40 steals, after Jose Canseco with the Oakland A's in 1988. Bonds's final stats included a .308 batting average, 42 home runs, 129 RBI and 122 runs scored. Through it all, Bonds was pitched with extreme care and set a National League record by drawing 151 walks.

Bonds was the only Giants regular to stick around all season, as injuries crippled the team. Sixteen players spent a total of 22 stints on the disabled list, breaking the previous franchise record for DL stays of 15. The Giants used their Opening Day lineup only three times, all in the first week. Stan Javier strained a hamstring in the season's fifth game, and the injuries became nonstop. Of the projected starters, Javier served 83 games on the DL, Robby Thompson 65, Shawon Dunston 65, Glenallen Hill 61, Matt Williams 53 and Kirt Manwaring 37. The other starter, first baseman Mark Carreon, was traded to Cleveland in July.

"[The injuries] were so frustrating because we left spring training healthy," manager Dusty Baker said. "I thought we did a great job getting everyone ready. But once the season started, it was one injury after another." That's part of the reason the Giants ranked among the worst in the

league in batting average and strikeouts. They were forced to rely on Class AAA players and were often overmatched late in the season. Among the young players, Bill Mueller hit .330 while filling in for Williams at third base. He'll probably take over at second next year.

The pitching staff stayed mostly healthy, but the Giants still had the worst ERA among NL teams that don't make Denver their home. The staff allowed a whopping 191 home runs, led by Mark Gardner (28), Allen Watson (28), Mark Leiter (25), Osvaldo Fernandez (20) and William VanLandingham (17). Closer Rod Beck had 35 saves but went 0-9 as the leader of an inconsistent bullpen.

The Giants were the only team in the NL West never to lead the division, but they were only 1½ games behind on June 20. They then lost 21 of their next 25 games and never recovered, going 32-61 from June 21 on.

In the end, there was only Bonds and his pursuit of the 40-40 milestone. "Finally, it's over with," he said after getting it. Bonds, who went into September with 35 home runs but only 25 stolen bases, swiped 10 bases in his final 12 games. "I think this is an inspiration for younger kids on our team to say, 'Hey, bar none, this man ain't quitting.'"

1996 Giants: Week-by-week notes

These notes were excerpted from the following issues of Baseball Weekly.

▶**April 3:** The Giants, finally having a ballpark measure approved after four defeats over the past nine years, will be allowed to bypass a neighborhood height limit at China Basin in downtown San Francisco. The club's ownership group must now devise a funding program to construct the $255 million, 42,000-seat waterfront facility.

▶**April 10:** Cuban defector Osvaldo Fernandez silenced critics with eight strong innings in his major league debut. He allowed one run and five hits in a 7-1 victory against Florida. His 112-pitch effort was unlike anything he had in spring training, when he posted a 9.45 ERA in six outings.

▶**April 17:** Since the day he signed with the Giants in January, shortstop Shawon Dunston dreamed about beating his old team, the Cubs. In the first Giants-Cubs series of the season, he made it happen with a pinch single in the 10th inning to secure a 3-2 victory.

▶**April 24:** The bullpen, the laughing-stock of the NL last year, has been surprisingly reliable. After allowing 25 runs in the first two games in Atlanta, the bullpen posted four victories and a 1.33 ERA over the next 15 games, allowing only six earned runs in 40⅓ innings.

▶**May 1:** In his first year with the Giants, Shawon Dunston tried to avoid the DL at all costs, but he finally was shelved on April 28 with a groin injury after missing 12 of 16 games.

▶**May 8:** In a 9-4 victory in San Diego on April 30, left fielder Barry Bonds homered twice—including his fourth career grand slam—to become the third player in 1996 to hit 11 April home runs and the sixth in major league history.

▶**May 22:** Right fielder Glenallen Hill was lost at the plate before manager Dusty Baker and hitting coach Bobby Bonds sat him down and gave him a piece of advice—stick to one batting

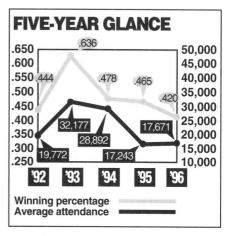

FIVE-YEAR GLANCE

Winning percentage
Average attendance

stance. Over the next nine games, he batted .417 (15-for-36) with four home runs, four doubles and eight RBI.

▶**May 29:** With his 3-2 victory against Philadelphia on May 25, Mark Gardner won his fourth consecutive decision and improved his record to 6-1. During the winning streak, he had a 1.33 ERA, 32 strikeouts and eight walks in 27 innings.

▶**June 5:** Shawon Dunston was critical of Barry Bonds in comments he made in the *New York Post.* "Andre Dawson, Mark Grace, Matt Williams—I wouldn't put Barry in their class." Bonds replied, "He doesn't know me well enough. He's the new guy here, not me."

▶**June 26:** Osvaldo Fernandez beat Florida 1-0 on June 17 for his first victory since April 21, allowing two hits in 7⅔ innings. In three starts against Florida, he has allowed four runs in 22⅔ innings for a 1.59 ERA. Against the rest of the league, his ERA is 7.58 ERA.

▶**July 3:** Through June 30 the Giants had lost 10 in a row to tie the San Francisco record. Closer Rod Beck was 0-3 with two blown saves and a 16.20 ERA in his last four outings.

▶**July 11:** The Giants were relieved to hear that Mark Gardner, who underwent a laproscopic appendectomy on July 5, is expected to spend only 15 days on the DL. Gardner is the Giants' winningest pitcher, at 8-3.

▶July 17: Left-hander Shawn Estes, the club's top pitching prospect, threw his first game of the season on July 13 for the Giants and pitched seven scoreless innings for his first major league win. He struck out 11, tying a Giants' season high. In one stretch, he fanned six in a row.

▶July 24: After the Giants lost for the 20th time in 24 games, Barry Bonds sounded off: "It's boring watching this. From the team's standpoint, from the fans' standpoint, from the players' standpoint. If I had to watch this, I'd be sick." After making his remarks, Bonds immediately broke out of his 1-for-13 slump. Over the next three games, he was 5-for-10 with three doubles and four RBI.

▶July 31: Giants players lost a popular teammate when the team traded catcher Kirt Manwaring to the Astros for another catcher, Rick Wilkins. The Astros also will receive an undisclosed amount of cash. "I'm disappointed," said Manwaring. "I don't want to leave."

▶Aug. 7: Matt Williams's sore right shoulder is getting worse. He can't lift his arm above his head, and his swing is out of whack. He has played first base instead of third in 12 of the last 15 games, so the Giants were considering moving Shawon Dunston to third, but on Aug. 4 Dunston suffered a head injury in a collision with Astros shortstop Ricky Gutierrez.

▶Aug. 14: Three tiny plates were placed around Shawon Dunston's left eye during his three-hour operation at Stanford Hospital. Dunston remained at the hospital overnight for observation and will be out for the season.

▶Aug. 21: After Matt Williams underwent shoulder surgery last weekend, Giants officials said they expect him back at third base by Opening Day 1997. Twice in a row last week, the Giants started their Firebird Infield, with all four starters—first baseman Desi Wilson, second baseman Jay Canizaro, shortstop Rich Aurilia and third baseman Bill Mueller—having opened the year with the Class AAA Phoenix Firebirds.

▶Sept. 4: Since coming off the DL on Aug. 5, Glenallen Hill hasn't stopped hitting—he's 37-for-104 (.356) with three home runs and 16 RBI.

▶Sept. 25: Injury-plagued second baseman Robby Thompson may have played his final Giants home game. He is not in the club's plans for 1997, and his contract will be bought out for $375,000.

▶Oct. 2: It's tough to imagine the Giants without Barry Bonds this season. Bonds capped his season on Sept. 27 by becoming the second man (after Jose Canseco) in major league history to reach 40 homers and 40 steals. Bonds's final stats: .308 average, 42 home runs, 129 RBI, 122 runs, and an NL-record 151 walks. Injuries took their toll, as 16 players spent a total of 22 stints on the disabled list. The pitching staff stayed healthy, so there was no excuse for its posting the second-worst ERA in the league.

Team directory

▶**Owner:** Peter Magowan (president and managing general partner)
▶**General manager:** Brian Sabean
▶**Ballpark:**
3Com Park
Jamestown Avenue and Harney Way
San Francisco, Calif.
415-468-3700
Capacity 63,000
Parking for 17,000 cars; $6
Public transportation available
Family and wheelchair sections, ramps, battery charger plug-ins for wheelchairs, designated handicapped pick-up and drop-off sights
▶**Team publications:**
Giants Magazine, Giants Info Guide
415-468-3700, ext. 478
▶**TV, radio broadcast stations:**
KNBR 680 AM, KTVU Channel 2, KIQI (Spanish), SportsChannel
▶**Camps and/or clinics:**
Rob Andrews Baseball, June and July, 510-935-3505
▶**Spring training:**
Scottsdale Stadium
Scottsdale, Ariz.
Capacity 7,500 (plus 2,500 on outfield grass)
602-990-7972

SAN FRANCISCO GIANTS 1996 final stats

BATTERS	BA	SLG	OB	G	AB	R	H	TB	2B	3B	HR	RBI	BB	SO	SB	CS	E
Delgado	.364	.364	.440	6	22	3	8	8	0	0	0	2	1	5	1	0	1
Mueller	.330	.415	.401	55	200	31	66	83	15	1	0	19	24	26	0	0	6
Bonds	.308	.615	.461	158	517	122	159	318	27	3	42	129	151	76	40	7	6
M. Williams	.302	.510	.367	105	404	69	122	206	16	1	22	85	39	91	1	2	14
Dunston	.300	.408	.331	82	287	27	86	117	12	2	5	25	13	40	8	0	15
Hill	.280	.499	.344	98	379	56	106	189	26	0	19	67	33	95	6	3	7
Wilson	.271	.339	.338	41	118	10	32	40	2	0	2	12	12	27	0	2	4
Javier	.270	.383	.336	71	274	44	74	105	25	0	2	22	25	51	14	2	3
Carreon	.260	.449	.317	81	292	40	76	131	22	3	9	51	22	33	2	3	8
Peltier	.254	.288	.328	31	59	3	15	17	2	0	0	9	7	9	0	0	0
K. Williams	.250	.250	.250	9	20	0	5	5	0	0	0	0	0	6	0	0	0
Benard	.248	.330	.333	135	488	89	121	161	17	4	5	27	59	84	25	11	5
Wilkins	.243	.399	.344	136	411	53	100	164	18	2	14	59	67	121	0	3	8
Aurilia	.239	.296	.295	105	318	27	76	94	7	1	3	26	25	52	4	1	10
Cruz	.234	.390	.352	33	77	10	18	30	3	0	3	10	12	24	0	1	1
Lampkin	.232	.379	.324	66	177	26	41	67	8	0	6	29	20	22	1	5	3
Mirabelli	.222	.278	.333	9	18	2	4	5	1	0	0	1	3	4	0	0	0
Scarsone	.219	.322	.286	105	283	28	62	91	12	1	5	23	25	91	2	3	11
McCarty	.217	.337	.294	91	175	16	38	59	3	0	6	24	18	43	2	1	3
Hubbard	.213	.382	.307	55	89	15	19	34	5	2	2	14	11	27	2	0	0
Thompson	.211	.335	.301	63	227	35	48	76	11	1	5	21	24	69	2	2	7
Jensen	.211	.263	.444	9	19	4	4	5	1	0	0	4	8	7	0	0	2
Batiste	.208	.323	.235	54	130	17	27	42	6	0	3	11	5	33	3	3	11
Canizaro	.200	.300	.260	43	120	11	24	36	4	1	2	8	9	38	0	2	6
Jones	.172	.293	.269	34	58	7	10	17	0	2	1	7	8	12	2	2	0
Hall	.120	.120	.148	25	25	3	3	3	0	0	0	5	1	4	0	0	0

PITCHERS	W-L	ERA	G	GS	CG	GF	Sho	SV	IP	H	R	ER	HR	BB	SO
Poole	2-1	2.66	35	0	0	5	0	0	23.2	15	7	7	2	13	19
Carlson	1-0	2.70	5	0	0	3	0	0	10.0	13	6	3	2	2	4
Beck	0-9	3.34	63	0	0	58	0	35	62.0	56	23	23	9	10	48
Bautista	3-4	3.36	37	1	0	12	0	0	69.2	66	32	26	10	15	28
Estes	3-5	3.60	11	11	0	0	0	0	70.0	63	30	28	3	39	60
Rueter	6-8	3.97	20	19	0	0	0	0	102.0	109	50	45	12	27	46
Dewey	6-3	4.21	78	0	0	19	0	0	83.1	79	40	39	9	41	57
Gardner	12-7	4.42	30	28	4	0	1	0	179.1	200	105	88	28	57	145
Watson	8-12	4.61	29	29	2	0	0	0	185.2	189	105	95	28	69	128
Fernandez	7-13	4.61	30	28	2	1	0	0	171.2	193	95	88	20	57	106
Scott	5-7	4.64	65	0	0	16	0	1	66.0	65	36	34	8	30	47
Soderstrom	2-0	5.27	3	3	0	0	0	0	13.2	16	11	8	1	6	9
VanLandingham	9-14	5.40	32	32	0	0	0	0	181.2	196	123	109	17	78	97
DeLucia	3-6	5.84	56	0	0	20	0	0	61.2	62	44	40	8	31	55
Bourgeois	1-3	6.30	15	5	0	4	0	0	40.0	60	35	28	4	21	17
Creek	0-2	6.52	63	0	0	15	0	0	48.1	45	41	35	11	32	38
Hook	0-1	7.43	10	0	0	3	0	0	13.1	16	13	11	3	14	4
Barton	0-0	9.72	7	0	0	2	0	0	8.1	19	12	9	2	1	3

1997 preliminary roster

PITCHERS (18)
Rod Beck
Steve Bourgeois
Dan Carlson
Doug Creek
Rich DeLucia
Shawn Estes
Osvaldo Fernandez
Keith Foulke
Chad Frontera
Mark Gardner
Jim Poole
Joe Roa

Kirk Rueter
Steve Soderstrom
Julian Tavarez
Carlos Valdez
William VanLandingham
Mike Villone

CATCHERS (3)
Marcus Jensen
Doug Mirabelli
Rick Wilkins

INFIELDERS (9)
Rich Aurilia
Jay Canizaro
Wilson Delgado
Jeff Kent
Mark Lewis
Bill Mueller
J.T. Snow
Jose Vizcaino
Desi Wilson

OUTFIELDERS (8)
Marvin Benard
Barry Bonds
Jacob Cruz
Glenallen Hill
Stan Javier
Dante Powell
Armando Rios
Chris Singleton

Games played by position

PLAYER	G	C	1B	2B	3B	SS	OF
Aurilia	105	0	0	11	0	93	0
Batiste	54	0	0	0	25	7	0
Benard	135	0	0	0	0	0	132
Bonds	158	0	0	0	0	0	152
Canizaro	43	0	0	35	0	7	0
Carreon	81	0	73	0	0	0	5
Cruz	33	0	0	0	0	0	23
Delgado	6	0	0	0	0	6	0
Dunston	82	0	0	0	0	78	0
Hall	25	0	0	0	0	0	4
Hill	98	0	0	0	0	0	98
Hubbard	55	0	0	0	0	0	28
Javier	71	0	0	0	0	0	71
Jensen	9	7	0	0	0	0	0
Jones	34	0	0	0	0	0	33
Lampkin	66	53	0	0	0	0	0
McCarty	91	0	51	0	0	0	20
Mirabelli	9	8	0	0	0	0	0
Mueller	55	0	0	8	45	0	0
Peltier	31	0	13	0	0	0	1
Scarsone	105	0	1	74	14	1	0
Thompson	63	0	0	62	0	0	0
Wilkins	136	124	7	0	0	0	0
K. Williams	9	0	0	0	0	0	4
M. Williams	105	0	13	0	92	1	0
Wilson	41	0	33	0	0	0	0

Minor Leagues

Tops in the organization

BATTER	CLUB	AVG.	G	AB	R	H	HR	RBI
Desi Wilson	Phx	.339	113	407	56	138	5	59
Craig Mayes	Sj	.334	124	512	61	171	3	71
Derek Reid	Shr	.318	118	468	87	149	18	76
Tim Garland	Sj	.311	132	550	96	171	5	61
Todd Wilson	Sj	.305	90	318	50	97	5	40

HOME RUNS			WINS		
Don Denbow	Sj	27	Darin Blood	Sj	17
Benji Simonton	Phx	24	Dan Carlson	Phx	13
Doug Mirabelli	Shr	21	L. Barcelo	Bur	12
Dante Powell	Phx	21	Keith Foulke	Shr	12
Derek Reid	Shr	18	Bobby Rector	Sj	12

RBI			SAVES		
Jesus Ibarra	Sj	95	Russ Ortiz	Shr	36
Don Denbow	Sj	81	S. Hernandez	Bur	35
Dante Powell	Phx	78	Steve Mintz	Phx	27
Benji Simonton	Phx	78	Shawn Purdy	Shr	16
Doug Mirabelli	Shr	77	Mick Pageler	Bel	12

STOLEN BASES			STRIKEOUTS		
Tim Garland	Sj	51	Darin Blood	Sj	193
Dante Powell	Phx	43	Bobby Rector	Sj	145
Jon Sbrocco	Shr	34	Jason Brester	Bur	143
C. Singleton	Phx	27	Mike Villano	Shr	140
Derek Reid	Shr	25	L. Barcelo	Bur	139

PITCHER	CLUB	W-L	ERA	IP	H	BB	SO
Darin Blood	Sj	17-6	2.65	170	140	71	193
Keith Foulke	Shr	12-7	2.76	183	149	35	129
C. Hartvigson	Sj	4-7	3.23	103	94	30	114
Shawn Estes	Phx	9-3	3.43	110	92	38	95
Dan Carlson	Phx	13-6	3.44	147	135	46	123

Sick call: 1996 DL report

PLAYER	Days on the DL
Rich Aurilia	6
Kim Batiste	15
Jose Bautista	17
Rich DeLucia	58*
Shawon Dunston	75*
Mark Gardner	18
Glenallen Hill	70
Trenidad Hubbard	17
Stan Javier	91*
Tom Lampkin	58*
Kirt Manwaring	43
Dave McCarty	21
Robby Thompson	84**
Sergio Valdez	182
Allen Watson	23
Matt Williams	56

Indicates two separate terms on Disabled List.

1996 salaries

	Bonuses	Total earned salary
Barry Bonds, of		$8,244,190
Matt Williams, 3b	$50,000	$6,600,000
Robby Thompson, 2b		$4,958,334
Rod Beck, p	$125,000	$2,907,463
Glenallen Hill, of		$1,700,000
Rick Wilkins, c		$1,550,000
Shawon Dunston, ss		$1,457,236
Stan Javier, of		$1,000,000
Jose Bautista, p	$30,000	$790,000
Tim Scott, p		$700,000
Osvaldo Fernandez, p		$633,333
Jim Poole, p	$100,000	$500,000
Rich DeLucia, p	$50,000	$475,000
Steve Scarsone, 2b	$25,000	$375,000
Allen Watson, p		$240,000
Tom Lampkin, c		$230,000
Mark Dewey, p	$50,000	$225,000
Mark Gardner, p	$25,000	$202,500
Sergio Valdez, p		$200,000
William VanLandingham, p	$17,500	$200,000
Dave McCarty, 1b		$150,000
Trenidad Hubbard, of		$127,500
Rich Aurilia, ss		$110,500
Marvin Benard, of		$110,500
Doug Creek, p		$110,500
Jay Canizaro, 2b		$109,000
Shawn Estes, p		$109,000
Dax Jones, of		$109,000
Doug Mirabelli, c		$109,000
Bill Mueller, 3b		$109,000
Desi Wilson, 1b		$109,000

Average 1996 salary: $1,111,324
Total 1996 team payroll: $34,451,056
Termination pay: $195,737

San Francisco (1958-1996), includes New York (1883-1957)

Runs: Most, career

2011	Willie Mays, 1951-1972
1859	Mel Ott, 1926-1947
1313	Mike Tiernan, 1887-1899
1120	Bill Terry, 1923-1936
1113	Willie McCovey, 1959-1980

Hits: Most, career

3187	Willie Mays, 1951-1972
2876	Mel Ott, 1926-1947
2193	Bill Terry, 1923-1936
1974	Willie McCovey, 1959-1980
1834	Mike Tiernan, 1887-1899

2B: Most, career

504	Willie Mays, 1951-1972
488	Mel Ott, 1926-1947
373	Bill Terry, 1923-1936
308	Willie McCovey, 1959-1980
291	Travis Jackson, 1922-1936

3B: Most, career

162	Mike Tiernan, 1887-1899
139	Willie Mays, 1951-1972
131	Roger Connor, 1883-1894
117	Larry Doyle, 1907-1920
112	Bill Terry, 1923-1936

HR: Most, career

646	Willie Mays, 1951-1972
511	Mel Ott, 1926-1947
469	Willie McCovey, 1959-1980
247	MATT WILLIAMS, 1987-1996
226	Orlando Cepeda, 1958-1966

RBI: Most, career

1860	Mel Ott, 1926-1947
1859	Willie Mays, 1951-1972
1388	Willie McCovey, 1959-1980
1078	Bill Terry, 1923-1936
929	Travis Jackson, 1922-1936

SB: Most, career

428	Mike Tiernan, 1887-1899
354	George Davis, 1893-1903
336	Willie Mays, 1951-1972
334	George Burns, 1911-1921
332	John Ward, 1883-1894

BB: Most, career

1708	Mel Ott, 1926-1947
1394	Willie Mays, 1951-1972
1168	Willie McCovey, 1959-1980
747	Mike Tiernan, 1887-1899
631	George Burns, 1911-1921

BA: Highest, career

.341	Bill Terry, 1923-1936
.332	George Davis, 1893-1903
.322	Ross Youngs, 1917-1926
.322	Frankie Frisch, 1919-1926
.321	G. Vanhaltren, 1894-1903
.313	B. BONDS, 1993-1996 (9)

Slug avg: Highest, career

.629	BARRY BONDS, 1993-1996
.564	Willie Mays, 1951-1972
.549	Johnny Mize, 1942-1949
.536	K. MITCHELL, 1987-1991
.535	Orlando Cepeda, 1958-1966

On-base avg: Highest, career

.446	BARRY BONDS, 1993-1996
.414	Mel Ott, 1926-1947
.403	Roger Bresnahan, 1902-1908
.402	Roger Connor, 1883-1894
.399	Ross Youngs, 1917-1926

Complete games: Most, career

433	C. Mathewson, 1900-1916
391	Mickey Welch, 1883-1892
372	Amos Rusie, 1890-1898
260	Carl Hubbell, 1928-1943
252	Tim Keefe, 1885-1891
244	Juan Marichal, 1960-1973 (6)

Saves: Most, career

162	ROD BECK, 1991-1996
127	Gary Lavelle, 1974-1984
125	Greg Minton, 1975-1987
83	Randy Moffitt, 1972-1981
78	Frank Linzy, 1963-1970

Shutouts: Most, career

79	C. Mathewson, 1900-1916
52	Juan Marichal, 1960-1973
36	Carl Hubbell, 1928-1943
29	Amos Rusie, 1890-1898
28	Mickey Welch, 1883-1892

Wins: Most, career

372	C. Mathewson, 1900-1916
253	Carl Hubbell, 1928-1943
238	Juan Marichal, 1960-1973
238	Mickey Welch, 1883-1892
234	Amos Rusie, 1890-1898

K: Most, career

2499	C. Mathewson, 1900-1916
2281	Juan Marichal, 1960-1973
1835	Amos Rusie, 1890-1898
1677	Carl Hubbell, 1928-1943
1606	Gaylord Perry, 1962-1971

Win pct: Highest, career

.693	Sal Maglie, 1945-1955
.680	Tim Keefe, 1885-1891
.664	C. Mathewson, 1900-1916
.656	Jesse Barnes, 1918-1923
.651	Doc Crandall, 1908-1913
.630	J. Marichal, 1960-1973 (11)

ERA: Lowest, career

2.12	C. Mathewson, 1900-1916
2.38	Joe McGinnity, 1902-1908
2.43	Jeff Tesreau, 1912-1918
2.45	Red Ames, 1903-1913
2.48	Hooks Wiltse, 1904-1914
2.82	Gary Lavelle, 1974-1984 (12)

Runs: Most, season

147	Mike Tiernan, 1889
139	Bill Terry, 1930
138	Mel Ott, 1929
137	Johnny Mize, 1947
136	George Vanhaltren, 1896
134	Bobby Bonds, 1970 (6)

Hits: Most, season

254	Bill Terry, 1930
231	Freddy Lindstrom, 1928
231	Freddy Lindstrom, 1930
226	Bill Terry, 1929
225	Bill Terry, 1932
208	Willie Mays, 1958 (13)

2B: Most, season

46	Jack Clark, 1978
43	Willie Mays, 1959
43	Bill Terry, 1931
42	George Kelly, 1921
42	Bill Terry, 1932

3B: Most, season

27	George Davis, 1893
25	Larry Doyle, 1911
22	Roger Connor, 1887
21	Mike Tiernan, 1890
21	Mike Tiernan, 1895
21	George Van Haltren, 1896
12	Willie Mays, 1960 (*)

HR: Most, season

52	Willie Mays, 1965
51	Willie Mays, 1955
51	Johnny Mize, 1947
49	Willie Mays, 1962
47	Willie Mays, 1964
47	KEVIN MITCHELL, 1989

RBI: Most, season

151	Mel Ott, 1929
142	Orlando Cepeda, 1961
141	Willie Mays, 1962
138	Johnny Mize, 1947
136	George Davis, 1897
136	George Kelly, 1924

SB: Most, season

111	John Ward, 1887
65	George Davis, 1897
62	George Burns, 1914
62	John Ward, 1889
61	Josh Devore, 1911
58	Billy North, 1979 (7)

BB: Most, season

151	BARRY BONDS, 1996
144	Eddie Stanky, 1950
137	Willie McCovey, 1970
127	Eddie Stanky, 1951
126	BARRY BONDS, 1993

BA: Highest, season

.401	Bill Terry, 1930
.379	Freddy Lindstrom, 1930
.372	Bill Terry, 1929
.371	Roger Connor, 1885
.369	Mike Tiernan, 1896
.347	Willie Mays, 1958 (23)

Slug avg: Highest, season

.677	BARRY BONDS, 1993
.667	Willie Mays, 1954
.659	Willie Mays, 1955
.656	Willie McCovey, 1969
.647	BARRY BONDS, 1994

On-base avg: Highest, season

.461	BARRY BONDS, 1996
.460	Eddie Stanky, 1950
.458	BARRY BONDS, 1993
.458	Mel Ott, 1930
.453	Willie McCovey, 1969

Complete games: Most, season

62	Tim Keefe, 1886
62	Mickey Welch, 1884
59	Amos Rusie, 1892
56	Amos Rusie, 1890
56	Mickey Welch, 1886
30	Juan Marichal, 1968 (*)

Saves: Most, season

48	ROD BECK, 1993
35	ROD BECK, 1996
33	ROD BECK, 1995
30	Greg Minton, 1982
28	ROD BECK, 1994

Shutouts: Most, season

11	Christy Mathewson, 1908

10	Carl Hubbell, 1933
10	Juan Marichal, 1965
9	Joe McGinnity, 1904
8	Tim Keefe, 1888
8	Juan Marichal, 1969
8	Christy Mathewson, 1902
8	Christy Mathewson, 1905
8	Christy Mathewson, 1907
8	Christy Mathewson, 1909
8	Jeff Tesreau, 1914
8	Jeff Tesreau, 1915

Wins: Most, season

44	Mickey Welch, 1885
42	Tim Keefe, 1886
39	Mickey Welch, 1884
37	Christy Mathewson, 1908
36	Amos Rusie, 1894
26	Juan Marichal, 1969 (25)

K: Most, season

345	Mickey Welch, 1884
341	Amos Rusie, 1890
337	Amos Rusie, 1891
335	Tim Keefe, 1888
304	Amos Rusie, 1892
248	Juan Marichal, 1963 (11)

Win pct: Highest, season

.833	Hoyt Wilhelm, 1952
.818	Sal Maglie, 1950
.814	Joe McGinnity, 1904
.813	Carl Hubbell, 1936
.810	Doc Crandall, 1910
.806	Juan Marichal, 1966 (7)

ERA: Lowest, season

1.14	Christy Mathewson, 1909
1.28	Christy Mathewson, 1905
1.43	Christy Mathewson, 1908
1.44	Fred Anderson, 1917
1.57	Tim Keefe, 1885
1.99	Bobby Bolin, 1968 (16)

Most pinch-hit homers, season

4	Ernie Lombardi, 1946
4	Bill Taylor, 1955
4	Mike Ivie, 1978
4	Candy Maldonado, 1986
4	Ernie Riles, 1990

Most pinch-hit homers, career

13	Willie McCovey, 1959-1980
9	Bobby Hofman, 1949-1957

Longest hitting streak

33	George Davis, 1893
27	Charlie Hickman, 1900
26	Jack Clark, 1978
24	Mike Donlin, 1908
24	Fred Lindstrom, 1930
24	Willie McCovey, 1963

Most consecutive scoreless innings

45	Carl Hubbell, 1933
45	Sal Maglie, 1950
40	Gaylord Perry, 1967
39	Christy Mathewson, 1901
39	Gaylord Perry, 1970

No-hit games

Amos Rusie, NY vs Bro NL, 6-0; July 31, 1891.

Christy Mathewson, NY at StL NL, 5-0; July 15, 1901.

Christy Mathewson, NY at Chi NL, 1-0; June 13, 1905.

Hooks Wiltse, NY vs Phi NL, 1-0; July 4, 1908 (1st game, 10 innings).

Red Ames, NY vs Bro NL. 0-3; Apr. 15, 1909 (lost on 7 hits in 13 innings after allowing the first hit in the 10th).

Jeff Tesreau, NY at Phi NL, 3-0; Sept. 6, 1912 (1st game).

Rube Marquard, NY vs Bro NL, 2-0; Apr. 15, 1915.

Jesse Barnes, NY vs Phi NL, 6-0; May 7, 1922.

Carl Hubbell, NY vs Pit NL, 11-0; May 8, 1929.

Juan Marichal, SF vs Hou NL, 1-0; June 15, 1963.

Gaylord Perry, SF vs StL NL, 1-0; Sept. 17, 1968.

Ed Halicki, SF vs NY NL, 6-0; Aug. 24, 1975 (2nd game).

John Montefusco, SF at Atl NL, 9-0; Sept. 29, 1976.

Ed Crane, seven innings, darkness, NY vs Was NL, 3-0; Sept. 27, 1888.

Red Ames, five innings, darkness, NY at StL NL, 5-0; Sept. 14, 1903 (2nd game, first game in the major leagues).

Mike McCormick, five innings, rain, SF at Phi NL, 3-0; June 12, 1959. (allowed hit in 6th, but rain caused game to revert to 5 innings).

Sam Jones, seven innings, rain, SF at StL NL, 4-0; Sept. 26, 1959.

ACTIVE PLAYERS in caps.

Leader from the franchise's current location is included. If not in the top five, leader's rank is listed in parenthesis; asterisk (*) indicates player is not in top 25.

Players' years of service are listed by the first and last years with this team and are not necessarily consecutive; all statistics record performances for this team only.

Final American League team statistics

BATTING	BA	SLG	OBA	AB	R	H	TB	2B	3B	HR	RBI	LOB	BB	SO	SB	CS	E
Baltimore	.274	.472	.350	5689	949	1557	2685	299	29	257	914	1154	645	915	76	40	97
Boston	.283	.457	.359	5756	928	1631	2628	308	31	209	882	1251	642	1020	91	44	135
California	.276	.431	.339	5686	762	1571	2451	256	24	192	727	1209	527	974	53	39	128
Chicago	.281	.447	.360	5644	898	1586	2521	284	33	195	860	1231	701	927	105	41	109
Cleveland	.293	.475	.369	5681	952	1665	2700	335	23	218	904	1224	671	844	160	50	124
Detroit	.256	.420	.323	5530	783	1413	2324	257	21	204	741	1040	546	1268	87	50	137
Kansas City	.267	.398	.332	5542	746	1477	2208	286	38	123	689	1117	529	943	195	85	111
Milwaukee	.279	.441	.353	5662	894	1578	2496	304	40	178	845	1198	624	986	101	48	134
Minnesota	.288	.425	.357	5673	877	1633	2413	332	47	118	812	1194	576	958	143	53	94
New York	.288	.436	.360	5628	871	1621	2456	293	28	162	830	1258	632	909	96	46	91
Oakland	.265	.452	.344	5630	861	1492	2546	283	21	243	823	1175	640	1114	58	35	103
Seattle	.287	.484	.366	5668	993	1625	2741	343	19	245	954	1238	670	1052	90	39	110
Texas	.284	.469	.358	5702	928	1622	2672	323	32	221	890	1253	660	1041	83	26	87
Toronto	.259	.420	.331	5599	766	1451	2354	302	35	177	712	1169	529	1105	116	38	110

			Starters							Relievers					Total
PITCHING	W-L	ERA	IP	CG	SHO	BB	SO	W-L	ERA	IP	SV	BB	SO	ERA
Baltimore	59-59	5.47	990.1	13	1	341	649	29-15	4.50	478.1	44	256	398	5.14
Boston	56-53	5.01	1003.1	17	3	438	804	29-24	4.99	454.2	37	284	361	4.98
California	46-72	5.57	961.0	12	3	413	651	24-19	4.78	478.0	38	249	401	5.30
Chicago	58-48	4.63	1000.0	7	1	376	716	27-29	4.31	461.0	43	240	323	4.52
Cleveland	69-42	4.59	985.1	13	3	301	631	30-20	3.82	467.0	46	183	402	4.34
Detroit	29-80	6.64	865.2	10	4	437	488	24-29	5.97	567.0	22	347	469	6.38
Kansas City	59-65	4.37	1022.2	17	5	291	647	16-21	4.97	427.1	35	169	279	4.55
Milwaukee	54-63	5.16	943.0	6	1	378	517	26-19	5.14	504.1	42	257	329	5.14
Minnesota	47-68	5.48	925.2	13	3	343	583	31-16	4.97	514.0	31	238	376	5.28
New York	67-49	4.96	921.2	6	2	388	632	25-21	4.10	518.1	52	222	507	4.65
Oakland	47-65	5.57	913.2	7	3	362	501	31-19	4.59	542.2	34	282	383	5.20
Seattle	56-52	5.70	864.2	4	2	344	524	29-24	4.46	567.0	34	261	476	5.21
Texas	75-47	4.79	1015.2	19	5	418	683	15-25	4.32	433.1	43	164	293	4.65
Toronto	58-65	4.76	1007.0	19	5	406	712	16-23	4.14	438.2	35	204	321	4.57

Final National League team statistics

BATTING	BA	SLG	OBA	AB	R	H	TB	2B	3B	HR	RBI	LOB	BB	SO	SB	CS	E
Atlanta	.270	.432	.333	5614	773	1514	2425	264	28	197	735	1154	530	1032	83	43	130
Chicago	.251	.401	.320	5531	772	1388	2218	267	19	175	725	1078	523	1090	108	50	104
Cincinnati	.256	.422	.331	5455	778	1398	2302	259	36	191	733	1116	604	1134	171	63	121
Colorado	.287	.472	.355	5590	961	1607	2641	297	37	221	909	1108	527	1108	201	66	149
Florida	.257	.393	.329	5498	688	1413	2163	240	30	150	650	1171	553	1122	99	46	111
Houston	.262	.397	.336	5508	753	1445	2187	297	29	129	703	1172	554	1057	180	63	138
Los Angeles	.252	.384	.316	5538	703	1396	2127	215	33	150	661	1113	516	1190	124	40	125
Montreal	.262	.406	.327	5505	741	1441	2236	297	27	148	696	1119	492	1077	108	34	126
New York	.270	.412	.324	5618	746	1515	2317	267	47	147	697	1124	445	1069	97	48	159
Philadelphia	.256	.387	.325	5499	650	1405	2128	249	39	132	604	1207	536	1092	117	41	116
Pittsburgh	.266	.407	.329	5665	776	1509	2308	319	33	138	738	1181	510	989	126	49	128
St. Louis	.267	.407	.330	5502	759	1468	2237	281	31	142	711	1087	495	1089	149	58	125
San Diego	.265	.402	.338	5655	771	1499	2273	285	24	147	718	1209	601	1014	109	55	118
San Francisco	.253	.388	.331	5533	752	1400	2146	245	21	153	707	1198	615	1189	113	53	136

			Starters							Relievers					Total
PITCHING	W-L	ERA	IP	CG	SHO	BB	SO	W-L	ERA	IP	SV	BB	SO	ERA
Atlanta	70-48	3.45	1026.2	14	3	292	851	26-18	3.72	442.1	46	159	394	3.52
Chicago	54-61	4.76	949.0	10	5	307	642	22-25	3.60	507.1	34	239	385	4.36
Cincinnati	55-58	4.55	922.2	6	5	340	658	26-23	3.96	520.1	52	251	431	4.32
Colorado	50-52	5.68	918.2	5	1	396	478	33-27	5.45	504.0	34	228	454	5.59
Florida	59-61	3.76	985.1	8	4	373	666	21-21	4.37	457.2	41	225	384	3.95
Houston	55-54	4.21	1004.1	13	3	305	797	27-26	4.76	442.2	35	234	366	4.37
Los Angeles	67-45	3.51	1020.1	6	4	357	788	23-27	3.41	446.0	50	177	424	3.46
Montreal	56-53	3.92	933.1	11	3	289	759	32-21	3.53	508.0	43	193	447	3.78
New York	49-63	4.38	1008.0	10	3	329	670	22-28	3.85	432.0	41	203	329	4.22
Philadelphia	44-71	4.79	934.0	12	3	304	643	23-24	3.90	489.1	42	206	401	4.48
Pittsburgh	48-58	4.58	910.0	5	2	272	608	25-31	4.74	543.1	37	207	436	4.61
St. Louis	66-50	4.20	1016.1	13	5	384	713	22-24	3.47	436.0	43	155	337	3.97
San Diego	61-48	3.95	976.1	5	1	299	697	30-23	3.30	512.2	47	207	497	3.72
San Francisco	46-66	4.70	981.2	9	1	371	685	22-28	4.77	460.2	35	199	312	4.71

League forecasts

▶1996 division-by-division wrap-ups

▶League batting and pitching leaders

▶1996 All-Star Game

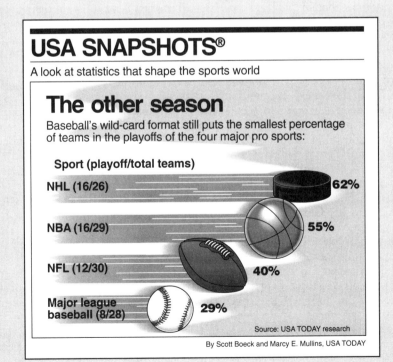

USA SNAPSHOTS®

A look at statistics that shape the sports world

The other season

Baseball's wild-card format still puts the smallest percentage of teams in the playoffs of the four major pro sports:

Sport (playoff/total teams)

NHL (16/26) — 62%

NBA (16/29) — 55%

NFL (12/30) — 40%

Major league baseball (8/28) — 29%

Source: USA TODAY research

By Scott Boeck and Marcy E. Mullins, USA TODAY

It's going to be an all-around power game

Let's see you do that again. That's the challenge for major league hitters in 1997. Will 1996 come to be seen as an aberration, or will it continue a trend that began in 1993? The theories about the increased offense range from smaller ballparks to shrinking strike zones, from expansion to stronger players, from juiced-up baseballs to the weather.

Whatever the cause, major league general managers apparently thought 1996's veritable home run derby was serious enough that they brought up the possibility of raising the mound in a bid to swing the balance of power toward the pitchers. Nothing that serious had been done since after the 1968 season, when the hurlers had become so dominant that lowering the mound was seen as a method of infusing offense and fan interest into the game.

The 83 players who hit 20 or more home runs was a major league record for a season, four more than in 1987. An astonishing 26 players topped their previous career best by 10 or more homers. The young talent in the game is tremendous. Seattle's 21-year-old shortstop, Alex Rodriguez, won a batting title and blasted 36 homers. The Mets' Todd Hundley, 27, set a major league record for catchers with 41 dingers. Take rising hitters like Tony Clark and Bobby Higginson in Detroit, Jim Thome in Cleveland, Bernie Williams with the World Series champion Yankees, Carlos Delgado in Toronto. Add them to the established players like Juan Gonzalez, Ken Griffey Jr., Gary Sheffield, Frank Thomas and Albert Belle, at 30 the oldest of this group. Don't expect the Year of the Pitcher anytime soon.

And don't expect any drastic changes in the game's power structure. The rich get richer, and the poor struggle. Even the new labor agreement complete with luxury taxes and revenue sharing won't reverse the trend overnight. When Chicago White Sox owner Jerry Reinsdorf can lead the battle against a free-wheeling free market economic system *and* claim

the system justifies his spending $55 million on Albert Belle, it's obvious that teams will remain in two leagues no matter what the fate of interleague play: the haves and the have-nots.

The winter before the 1996 season was marked by a high-stakes game of one-upmanship between New York Yankees owner George Steinbrenner and Baltimore Orioles owner Peter Angelos. A year later, Reinsdorf found his White Sox in a similar battle with the Cleveland Indians. Slugging third baseman Matt Williams was traded to the Indians and Belle went to the White Sox within weeks after the World Series.

But the White Sox, the Indians and others still have to catch the champion New York Yankees and the Atlanta Braves. And catching them certainly won't include outspending them. Clubs with less wherewithal can contend, as the chronically poor Montreal Expos did again in 1996, but they have to draw their talent from their farm systems and then often have to dump it as soon as it gets expensive. Teams like the Expos, the Milwaukee Brewers and the Kansas City Royals could make waves in the next few seasons, but they'll tend to rise and fall.

The Yankees and the Braves aren't going away. They have the farm system talent and available cash to fill any holes. Who can challenge them in 1997? In the AL, the White Sox, the Indians, the Orioles, the Texas Rangers and the Seattle Mariners have a chance, for sure, and maybe the Minnesota Twins, the Boston Red Sox and the Anaheim Angels. The San Diego Padres, the Los Angeles Dodgers and the St. Louis Cardinals could easily repeat as playoff teams in the National League, with the Houston Astros and the Florida Marlins as possible postseason visitors. Also keep an eye on the Colorado Rockies and the Cincinnati Reds.

Baseball 1997 will be a power game: the power of great sluggers, and the power of the sport's wealthiest franchises to buy championships.

AL East: Yanks' money vs. Orioles' power

The Yankees won it all last season with a major-league-record payroll of more than $60 million. Owner George Steinbrenner will spend again to fill in the holes when they appear, but he can count on several young Yankees to lead this year's drive to repeat. The shortstop is Derek Jeter, AL Rookie of the Year; the center fielder is Bernie Williams, the ALCS MVP; the ace lefty is Andy Pettitte, runner-up in the Cy Young voting; the incomparable setup man turned closer is Mariano Rivera, the team MVP. The oldest of them is 28.

Joining them is the usual array of high-priced veterans. In his first full season with the Yankees following the midseason trade with Detroit last year, Cecil "Big Daddy" Fielder must adjust to being a full-time DH. Tino Martinez, who replaced Don Mattingly and led the team with 117 RBI last season, returns as first baseman. Most of the rotation is back, led by Pettitte and David Cone, and filled out by Dwight Gooden, David Wells and Kenny Rogers, and Jimmy Key, who signed with Baltimore as a free agent, will be replaced by ex-Oriole David Wells. The bullpen should once again be strong, with Rivera, Mike Stanton and Jeff Nelson. World Series MVP John Wetteland was too expensive to fit into the Yankees' plan and signed with Texas.

Baltimore hit a record 257 homers last year, but a thin and erractic pitching staff is their primary concern. Staff ace Mike Mussina, Rocky Coppinger and Scott Erickson were solid, but the addition of Key only replaces Wells. With Brady Anderson (50 HR), Roberto Alomar (.328), Rafael Palmeiro (142 RBI), Cal Ripken, Chris Hoiles and B.J. Surhoff, the offense should again be formidable. The Orioles didn't bunt, didn't hit-and-run, didn't hit behind the runner—they just went deep. Johnson said of the '96 club, "That's who we are, that's what we do. We take pitchers' mistakes and hit them out of the park."

Boston tried to imitate that style of play, but it failed. Finishing third was a major achievement, but the Red Sox will be hard-pressed to repeat that feat. First baseman Mo Vaughn, who hit .326 and had 44 homers and 143 RBI, remains the franchise player, but almost everything else is unclear. Young shortstop Nomar Garciaparra appears to have forced out John Valentin, who may move to third base. Garciaparra's keystone partner will be Jeff Frye, who joined the club in midseason. Frye's return shifts Wil Codero to left field to replace departed free agent Mike Greenwell in front of the Green Monster. Another free agent, Roger Clemens, left for a lucrative deal with Toronto.

Toronto GM Gord Ash is committed to spending to build a winner in 1997. In November he traded six prospects to the Pirates for second baseman Carlos Garcia, outfielder Orlando Merced and reliever Dan Plesac. Slugger Carlos Delgado and shortstop Alex Gonzalez return, and the Jays signed catcher Benito Santiago. Veterans Joe Carter and Ed Sprague are solid, and the pitching is strong. Clemens joins AL Cy Young Award winner Pat Hentgen and ERA leader Juan Guzman to form an impressive threesome in the rotation, and closer Mike Timlim (31 saves) and Tim Crabtree (2.54 ERA) leads a confident young bullpen.

Improvement is almost certain for the 53-109 Detroit Tigers. Infielder Travis Fryman, who lead the team with 100 RBI, is only 28, and manager Buddy Bell was pleased with the development of youngsters Bobby Higginson, Tony Clark and Kimera Bartee. Another reason for optimism is left-hander Justin Thompson, who showed flashes of brilliance as a rookie, and there's hope for the farm system for the first time in years. "I don't think anybody likes being made fun of," said GM Randy Smith. "We have to stick to our plan. If we do our jobs right, we'll get the last laugh."

AL Central: Belle toils for Chicago now

With the loss of outfielder Albert Belle to the White Sox, do the Indians remain the team to beat? Cleveland GM John Hart added third baseman Matt Williams from San Francisco in exchange for infielders Jeff Kent and Jose Vizcaino and setup man Julian Tavarez. Williams was limited to 105 games by injury in 1996, but he still hit .302 with 22 home runs and 85 RBI. To make room for him, Cleveland will move third baseman Jim Thome to first base. The Indians need to replace starter Dennis Martinez and also hope to shore up their bullpen with increased productivity from young right-handers Danny Graves and Bartolo Colon. Jose Mesa fought through a slump in 1996, and the setup corps was also weaker than in '95. Kevin Seitzer was a valuable addition last August but is coming off arthroscopic surgery on his left knee. Shortstop Omar Vizquel had surgery on his right shoulder to repair a frayed labrum and to remove a bone spur from the shoulder socket.

Chicago's signing of Belle on Nov. 18 demonstrated their commitment to win in 1997 and beyond. White Sox owner Jerry Reinsdorf is paying $55 million to the slugger over the next five years, breaking almost all baseball-contract records. Based on performance in the past five years, Belle and first baseman Frank Thomas are arguably the best all-around offensive duo since a pair named Ruth and Gehrig. The combo should provide needed box office pull, too, as the Sox's attendance has fallen from 2.9 million in 1991 to 1.6 million last year. The White Sox re-signed manager Terry Bevington for two years, a move that was unpopular with fans and the media. Chicago has to beef up its setup roles (33 blown saves in '96). Catcher Ron Karkovice is coming off knee surgery and probably will play a platoon role.

The Milwaukee Brewers began retooling in the last two months of the '96 season. They brought in outfielder Marc Newfield and pitchers Ron Villone and Bryce Florie from San Diego for Greg Vaughn, and pitcher Bob Wickman and outfielder Gerald Williams from the Yankees for Graeme Lloyd and Ricky Bones. Newfield looks to have the inside track in left field, and Williams was brought in to handle center in case Chuckie Carr, who's rehabbing a knee injury, can't play. Florie, Villone and Wickman plug a big hole in middle relief. Ben McDonald, Scott Karl, Jeff D'Amico and Cal Eldred make up a pretty good starting rotation. Manager Phil Garner received a well-deserved two-year contract extension in November. The Brewers hoped to sign long-term deals with first baseman John Jaha, first baseman–DH Dave Nilsson and Eldred, who successfully bounced back from Tommy John surgery.

The Minnesota Twins enter the season looking for improvement on the mound and in the cleanup spot. The Twins' ERA has been over 5.00 for three consecutive years, but Brad Radke and Frank Rodriguez provide the solid nucleus of a young rotation. Rick Aguilera's role—starter or return to closer—was contingent on the Twins' off-season search for pitching help. Second baseman Chuck Knoblauch begins his five-year, $30 million contract, while ageless Paul Molitor returns on a two-year, $6.25 million deal. Left fielder Marty Cordova led the team with 16 home runs last year, making increased power a must.

The Royals hope Chili Davis, acquired from California for Mark Gubicza, and ex-Pirates Jeff King and Jay Bell will help them excape the cellar. Kansas City was last in the league in runs and home runs last year, as infielder-outfielder Craig Paquette led the team with 22 home runs and 67 RBI. Coming off surgery are closer Jeff Montgomery (shoulder), outfielder Michael Tucker (finger) and outfielder Tom Goodwin (shoulder). Bob Hamelin and Joe Vitiello, the DH platoon duo, have to bounce back from disappointing seasons. Jose Offerman is expected to be the full-time second baseman. Three promising young pitchers—Jim Pittsley, Brian Bevil and Glendon Rusch—will challenge for spots in the rotation.

AL West: It's home run derby again

The Texas Rangers didn't advance any further than the Division Series because they couldn't hold a lead. They solidified their chances of repeating as American League West champs by signing closer John Wetteland away from the New York Yankees.

Texas's 1996 transition from bashers to a complete lineup bodes well for AL co–Manager of the Year Johnny Oates. With catcher Ivan Rodriguez in the No. 2 spot and left fielder Rusty Greer as a good No. 3 hitter, the Rangers have the table-setters for the powerful middle of the order, led by resurgent league MVP Juan Gonzalez.

Despite Texas addressing its biggest need, the Seattle Mariners are gearing up to win their second divisional title in three years. Randy Johnson is expected to make a full recovery from back surgery. The Mariners added left-hander Jeff Fassero in a trade with Montreal and, with Sterling Hitchcock, will have at least three lefties in the rotation. If it can stay healthy, there's no doubt the Seattle attack will be loaded. Shortstop Alex Rodriguez, 21, became the third-youngest player in AL history to win a batting title, with a .358 average, and matched Ernie Banks' record of 379 total bases for a shortstop. On this team even superstar Ken Griffey Jr. occasionally is overlooked. He still had a club-record 49 homers and a club-record 140 RBI, and right fielder Jay Buhner added 44 homers and 138 RBI. Edgar Martinez, the DH, was chasing the major league record for doubles until he was injured in a rare defensive appearance at third base. Still, manager Lou Piniella knows that no matter how well his ballclub hits, it will need pitching to seriously contend.

The Oakland A's seem to be clones of Mariners. Like their homer-happy rivals to the north, the A's still resemble the "Bash Brothers" of old. That is, if they can keep their power-laden lineup together under the new labor agreement; Terry Steinbach (35 HR) went to Minnesota as a free agent.

If Oakland is going to compete against Texas and Seattle, it will also need to improve its pitching. The young starting rotation struggled, though it showed glimmers of success such as a streak of three straight shutouts in late August. For the first time in franchise history, no A's pitcher won nine games last season. The team's ERA (5.20) was the highest by an Athletics team since the 1955 Kansas City A's had a mark of 5.35. The pitching staff also set Oakland records for runs (900), hits (1,638) and home runs (205) allowed.

The Anaheim Angels, renamed by their new owners, could climb back into contention sooner then many expect. In the downturn of the last year and a half, it was forgotten that the Angels have the nucleus of a fine ballclub. Outfielders Tim Salmon and Jim Edmonds, shortstop Gary DiSarcina, and pitchers Mark Langston, Chuck Finley and Troy Percival are a good start to a contender. Terry Collins, who was fired by the Houston Astros, is the new Angels manager. The Angels job became open last Aug. 6, when Marcel Lachemann was fired after California went 52-59. John McNamara was named the interim manager, and the Angels went on to finish 19½ games behind Texas. Lachemann has since rejoined the club as the pitching coach.

The Angels' management, backed by new owners, the Disney Co., was won over by Collins's zeal. "We did a lot of work, talked to a lot of people," said GM Bill Bavasi, who added that Collins was particularly impressive when he was asked to spell out how he would run the Angels, starting with spring training and progressing through the season. "He's very organized," Bavasi said.

NL East: The Braves go for a six-pack

A large chunk of the Atlanta Braves' future was on display in the World Series when outfielders Jermaine Dye and Andruw Jones got the lion's share of the playing time. Dye hit .281 as a replacement for injured David Justice, and Jones, who hit two home runs in Game 1 against the Yankees, made the jump from Class A in less than two months, reaching the majors on Aug. 15.

On Nov. 20 the Braves signed Cy Young Award winner John Smoltz to a four-year, $31 million contract. The team's other Cy winners, Greg Maddux and Tom Glavine, can be free agents after next season. Atlanta wants to wrap them up to long-term deals, and they want to stay in Atlanta.

Despite a mere $16 million payroll, the Montreal Expos had a deficit close to $5 million last year. That reduced offseason shopping sprees to the Christmas season in the city's Underground. Does this sound familiar? Left-hander Jeff Fassero, who won 15 games and struck out 222 batters, was traded to Seattle for three prospects. Fassero signed a three-year, $13.5 million deal with the Mariners, something the Expos couldn't afford, and Moises Alou and Mel Rojas left as free agents.

Among those who are left, colorful left-hander Carlos Perez, who missed the 1996 season, will form a tough 1-2 starting punch with Pedro Martinez. The Expos need a reliable every-day catcher who can throw, and Chris Widger, who arrived from Seattle in the Fassero deal, will get a look. The Expos still have a decent bullpen with Dave Veres and Ugueth Urbina, and a solid infield with Shane Andrews, Mark Grudzielanek, Mike Lansing, and David Segui or Cliff Floyd at first. Left fielder Henry Rodriguez had 36 home runs and 103 RBI last year, and talented young outfielder Vladimir Guerrero will get a chance to play.

The Florida Marlins made the catch of the day when they landed Jim Leyland as their new manager, and they also signed Bobby Bonilla and Moises Alou, providing much needed protection for slugging right fielder Gary Sheffield, who drew 142 walks. Kevin Brown and Al Leiter, who had 33 of the Marlins' 80 victories last year, are joined by free-agent Alex Fernandez in the rotation, while late acquisitions Mark Hutton and Rick Helling looked strong down the stretch. The Marlins did a good job of addressing offseason priorities: a big-name power hitter to help the sagging offense and box office, a proven starter, and middle relievers to set up closer Robb Nen, who had a 1.95 ERA and 35 saves in 1996.

Catcher Todd Hundley, center fielder Lance Johnson and left fielder Bernard Gilkey anchor the New York Mets, but the three top pitching prospects all have to bounce back from surgery. Left-hander Bill Pulsipher missed the entire season after elbow surgery, right-hander Jason Isringhausen was 6-14 before arthroscopic shoulder and elbow surgery, and rookie Paul Wilson was 5-12 and then underwent arthroscopic shoulder surgery. First baseman Rico Brogna played just 55 games last year before shoulder surgery and was traded to Philadelphia, and second baseman Carlos Baerga still has to prove he's fit. Help is needed on offense for a team that was 10th in the league in scoring, and John Franco needs help in the bullpen—the Mets were 23-35 in one-run games.

The Philadelphia Phillies are off in search of the Fountain of Youth this season, committing themselves to young players such as third baseman Scott Rolen, outfielder Wendell Magee and catcher Mike Lieberthal. Rolen, who hit .254 in 130 at-bats last season, should be one of the league's top rookies. The Phillies hired new manager Terry Francona because of his ability to relate to younger players, among them pitchers Tyler Green, Matt Beech and Mike Grace, who are all returning from surgery. The futures of veterans Len Dykstra (back) and Darren Daulton (knee) remain in doubt.

NL Central: Cards hold a winning hand

The St. Louis Cardinals' postseason performance made it obvious that they're a force to be reckoned with in 1997. This is a team that improved as '96 wore on, and the pitching staff and the core regulars are back. Andy Benes leads a strong rotation, and outfielder Brian Jordan is the heart and soul of the team.

The legendary Ozzie Smith retired, leaving Royce Clayton as the full-time shortstop. Other than shoring up second base and the leadoff spot in the batting order by signing Delino DeShields, GM Walt Jocketty said backup players were what his club needed most. Veteran third baseman Gary Gaetti returns, buying at least one more year before the Cardinals have some position decisions to make. John Mabry is the first baseman, but power prospect Dmitri Young is nearly ready to play first, so third could eventually be an option for Mabry. The St. Louis starters—Andy Benes, Alan Benes, Todd Stottlemyre and Donovan Osborne—are either in their primes or are still improving. Relievers Dennis Eckersley and Rick Honeycutt are both are over 40, but T.J. Mathews looks like a closer in the making.

In the wake of a September fade, Houston Astros manager Terry Collins was canned and former Astros pitcher Larry Dierker was brought down from the broadcast booth. Unlike last winter, when the Astros were trying to come to terms with second baseman Craig Biggio, this time there were no free agents on the roster to worry about, so when Harris County voters gave the go-ahead for a new stadium, GM Gerry Hunsicker could begin to address the future. The immediate concern is the bullpen. Oft-injured John Hudek came on strong at season's end, and his return to form will enable Billy Wagner to move into the rotation to help aces Mike Hampton and Shane Reynolds.

Pitching depth was supposed to be Cincinnati's advantage in '96, but the Reds must put their rotation back together in front of closer Jeff Brantley. John Smiley

and Dave Burba will be back, Jose Rijo had surgery again in November and will probably not pitch this year, and left-hander Pete Schourek, an 18-game winner in '95 who underwent arthroscopic surgery on his elbow last year, needs to return to form. The club has solid offense, led by All-Star shortstop Barry Larkin, who last year became baseball's first 30-30 shortstop. But the Reds need a power hitter, though GM Jim Bowden hopes that reclamation project Ruben Sierra will be the guy.

Despite the loss of Jaime Navarro, the Cubs may have put together enough arms to be competitive with the signing of closer Mel Rojas and starter Kevin Tapani. With the re-signing of potential free agents Mark Grace and Brian McRae, plus the return of a healthy Sammy Sosa, the offensive core is intact. However, this still is a team that finished last in the league in batting average and next-to-last in on-base average. Team president Andy MacPhail promised to increase the team payroll of $32 million by as much as a third.

There won't be any payroll increases in Pittsburgh. "It's going to be a tough process," GM Cam Bonifay said, "but also very challenging and very rewarding." The financial rewards were immediate: On Nov. 15 the Pirates trimmed $6 million, as they sent veterans Orlando Merced, Carlos Garcia and Dan Plesac to Toronto in exchange for six prospects, then traded Jay Bell and Jeff King to Kansas City. The biggest change was the departure of manager Jim Leyland to Florida, with the challenges in Pittsburgh handed over to Gene Lamont. He'll be working primarily with homegrown Pirates. Shortstop Lou Collier, outfielder T.J. Staton and left-hander Jimmy Anderson could jump from Class AA Carolina to the majors next season to join talented youngsters like catcher Jason Kendall. "We're going to go through some growing pains we'll have to live with for a while," said Lamont.

NL West: Another Southern Cal showdown

Not even a week after the San Diego Padres' magical 1996 season came to a close, the first '97 problem popped up. Third baseman Ken Caminiti, the league MVP, had shoulder surgery four days after the Padres were swept by the Cardinals in the Division Series. He had two procedures, and the rehab time on his torn rotator cuff is estimated at five to nine months.

Other core players who contributed to the team's success in '96 are in relatively stable shape for next season. Steve Finley won his second consecutive Gold Glove and had a brilliant year at the plate. Tony Gwynn won his seventh NL batting title, but he needed medical attention for his ailing right heel. Closer Trevor Hoffman, who had 42 saves and a 2.25 ERA, signed a three-year contract extension in August. Starters Andy Ashby and Joey Hamilton hope to be healthier in '97. While Ashby was slated for surgery on his right shoulder, Hamilton will be able to avoid an operation after pitching through shoulder pain. One off-season addition was speedy second baseman Quilvio Veras, acquired from the Marlins.

The Los Angeles Dodgers won 90 games, led the National League in pitching, and had two players with more than 30 homers and 100 RBI, and executive vice president Fred Claire is trying to become the architect of the team that can also finally put an end to Atlanta's NL domination.

"[The Braves] have built it to a state of art," Claire said, "but we're not that far away." The Dodgers have relied on their pitching staff, but if they are to win, they must dramatically improve their offense. The Dodgers had the worst slugging percentage (.384) and on-base average (.316) in baseball. The team plans to keep Mike Piazza behind the plate for at least two more years, but the outfield could be a different story. They will give one last chance to Billy Ashley in left and move Rookie of the Year Todd Hollandsworth to center.

They also may give an opportunity to Roger Cedeno and rookie Karim Garcia. "We've taken tremendous strides this year," Claire said, "but there's work to be done."

The Colorado Rockies took a step back after their run to the playoffs in 1995. It doesn't take a master prognosticator to know they won't have trouble scoring runs in 1997, at least at Coors Field, but Colorado finished eight games out because of a 28-53 record on the road. One of GM Bob Gebhard's principal objectives this winter will be reshaping the team to make it more competitive on the road, though Gebhard doesn't have much wiggle room with Ellis Burks, Andres Galarraga, Dante Bichette, Larry Walker and Vinny Castilla under contract. Plus, ace Kevin Ritz and middle reliever Steve Reed were eligible for salary arbitration. Another potential problem is that Bichette is rehabbing his left knee. The two players closest to a major league breakthrough are shortstop Neifi Perez, who got a short look in 1996, and first baseman Todd Helton, Colorado's first draft pick in June 1995.

Catching up won't be easy for the San Francisco Giants. New GM Brian Sabean learned that quickly. One of his first moves was firing batting coach Bobby Bonds. The move prompted left fielder Barry Bonds to ask for a trade. Offers came quickly from several teams, but Sabean and Barry Bonds were able to patch things up. The three-time MVP was taken off the market, which led to the trade of Matt Williams to Cleveland. Infielders Jose Vizcaino and Jeff Kent came over in that trade, and young Bill Mueller could end up at second or third base. The Cleveland connection continues with ex-Indians Jim Poole and Julian Tavarez joining closer Rod Beck in the bullpen. The starting rotation comprises lefties Shawn Estes and Kirk Rueter, and righties Mark Gardner, Osvaldo Fernandez and William VanLandingham.

Final player statistics

American League
Designated hitters 312
Catchers 312
First basemen 313
Second basemen 313
Third basemen 314
Shortstops 314
Outfielders 315
Relief pitchers (batting) . . 316
Starting pitchers (batting) . 317
Relief pitchers 325
Starting pitchers 328

National League
Catchers 317
First basemen 317
Second basemen 318
Third basemen 319
Shortstops 319
Outfielders 320
Relief pitchers (batting) . . . 322
Starting pitchers (batting) . 323
Relief pitchers 329
Starting pitchers 332

Stats key for pitchers:

T–Throws right or left; W–Wins; L–Losses; ERA–Earned run average; G–Games; GS–Games started; CG–Complete games; SHO–Shutouts; GF–Games finished in relief; SV–Saves; IP–Innings pitched; H–Hits; R–Runs; ER–Earned runs; HR–Home runs; BB–Bases on balls; SO–Strikeouts; WP–Wild pitches; BA–Batting average against; RV–Rotisserie value.

Rotisserie values are provided by John Hunt. Dollar values are based on each player occupying a roster spot on a standard Rotisserie league team for an entire season. Players with dollar values less than $0 would have had a negative effect on a Rotisserie team in 1996. In a standard 12-team league only 276 players can be active at one time.

Stats key for batters:

B–Bats right, left, or both; BA–Batting average; G–Games; AB–At-bats; R–Runs; H–Hits; TB–Total Bases; 2B–Doubles; 3B–Triples; HR–Home runs; RBI–Runs batted in; SH–Sacrifice hits; SF–Sacrifice flies; BB–Bases on balls; SO–Strikeouts; SB–Stolen bases; CS–Caught stealing; SLG–Slugging average; OBA–On-base average; RV–Rotisserie value.

Players are listed alphabetically by position within each league. Each player is listed at the position where he played the most games in 1996; statistics are for all games played in 1996.

Statistics are provided by the Elias Sports Bureau.

American League designated hitters

Name/Team	B	BA	G	AB	R	H	TB	2B	3B	HR	RBI	SH	SF	BB	SO	SB	CS	SLG	OBA	RV
Aldrete, Mike, Cal.-NYA	L	.213	63	108	16	23	47	6	0	6	20	0	1	14	19	0	1	.435	.301	-6
Baines, Harold, ChiA	L	.311	143	495	80	154	249	29	0	22	95	0	3	73	62	3	1	.503	.399	18
Berroa, Geronimo, Oak.	R	.290	153	586	101	170	312	32	1	36	106	0	6	47	122	0	3	.532	.344	20
Canseco, Jose, Bos.	R	.289	96	360	68	104	212	22	1	28	82	0	3	63	82	3	1	.589	.400	15
Davis, Chili, Cal.	B	.292	145	530	73	155	263	24	0	28	95	1	6	86	99	5	2	.496	.387	19
Delgado, Carlos, Tor.	L	.270	138	488	68	132	239	28	2	25	92	0	8	58	139	0	0	.490	.353	12
Frazier, Lou, Tex.	B	.260	30	50	5	13	17	2	1	0	5	1	0	8	10	4	2	.340	.373	-2
Giles, Brian, Cle.	L	.355	51	121	26	43	74	14	1	5	27	0	3	19	13	3	0	.612	.434	4
Hamelin, Bob, K.C.	L	.255	89	239	31	61	104	14	1	9	40	0	4	54	58	5	2	.435	.391	5
Ibanez, Raul, Sea.	L	.000	4	5	0	0	0	0	0	0	0	0	0	0	1	0	0	.000	.167	-5
Jefferson, Reggie, Bos.	L	.347	122	386	67	134	229	30	4	19	74	0	4	25	89	0	0	.593	.388	15
Martinez, Edgar, Sea.	R	.327	139	499	121	163	297	52	2	26	103	0	4	123	84	3	3	.595	.464	22
Molitor, Paul, Min.	R	.341	161	660	99	225	309	41	8	9	113	0	9	56	72	18	6	.468	.390	31
Munoz, Pedro, Oak.	R	.256	34	121	17	31	54	5	0	6	18	0	0	9	31	0	0	.446	.308	-1
Murray, Eddie, Cle.-Bal.	B	.260	152	566	69	147	236	21	1	22	79	0	10	61	87	4	0	.417	.327	6
Ortiz, Luis, Tex.	R	.286	3	7	1	2	7	0	1	1	1	0	0	0	1	0	0	1.000	.286	-4
Penn, Shannon, Det.	B	.071	6	14	0	1	1	0	0	0	1	0	0	0	3	0	0	.071	.071	-5
Pirkl, Greg, Sea.-Bos.	R	.174	9	23	2	4	8	1	0	1	1	0	0	0	4	0	0	.348	.174	-10
Samuel, Juan, Tor.	R	.255	69	188	34	48	86	8	3	8	26	0	1	15	65	9	1	.457	.319	6
Seitzer, Kevin, Mil.-Cle.	R	.326	154	573	85	187	267	35	3	13	78	5	5	87	79	6	1	.466	.416	14
Sierra, Ruben, NYA-Det.	B	.247	142	518	61	128	194	26	2	12	72	0	9	60	83	4	4	.375	.320	3
Tettleton, Mickey, Tex.	B	.246	143	491	78	121	221	26	1	24	83	1	9	95	137	2	1	.450	.366	10
Vitiello, Joe, K.C.	R	.241	85	257	29	62	103	15	1	8	40	0	3	38	69	2	0	.401	.342	2
Williams, Eddie, Det.	R	.200	77	215	22	43	66	5	0	6	26	0	1	18	50	0	2	.307	.267	-3
Wilson, Nigel, Cle.	L	.250	10	12	2	3	9	0	0	2	5	0	0	1	6	0	0	.750	.308	-4

American League catchers

Name/Team	B	BA	G	AB	R	H	TB	2B	3B	HR	RBI	SH	SF	BB	SO	SB	CS	SLG	OBA	RV
Alomar, Sandy Jr., Cle.	R	.263	127	418	53	110	166	23	0	11	50	2	2	19	42	1	0	.397	.299	5
Ausmus, Brad, Det.	R	.248	75	226	30	56	80	12	0	4	22	5	2	26	45	3	4	.354	.328	0
Borders, Pat, Cal.-ChiA	R	.258	50	151	12	39	58	4	0	5	14	4	0	8	29	0	1	.384	.296	-4
Brown, Kevin, Tex.	R	.000	3	4	1	0	0	0	0	0	1	0	1	2	2	0	0	.000	.375	-5
Casanova, Raul, Det.	B	.188	25	85	6	16	29	1	0	4	9	0	0	6	18	0	0	.341	.242	-4
Delgado, Alex, Bos.	R	.250	26	20	5	5	5	0	0	0	1	1	0	3	3	0	0	.250	.348	-4
Devarez, Cesar, Bal.	R	.111	10	18	3	2	4	0	1	0	0	0	0	1	3	0	0	.222	.158	-5
Diaz, Einar, Cle.	R	.000	4	1	0	0	0	0	0	0	0	0	0	0	0	0	0	.000	.000	-5
Durant, Mike, Min.	R	.210	40	81	15	17	20	3	0	0	5	4	1	10	15	3	0	.247	.293	-3
Fabregas, Jorge, Cal.	L	.287	90	254	18	73	85	6	0	2	26	3	5	17	27	0	1	.335	.326	1
Fasano, Sal, K.C.	R	.203	51	143	20	29	49	2	0	6	19	1	0	14	25	1	1	.343	.283	-2
Flaherty, John, Det.	R	.250	47	152	18	38	62	12	0	4	23	3	1	8	25	1	0	.408	.290	-1
Girardi, Joe, NYA	R	.294	124	422	55	124	158	22	3	2	45	11	3	30	55	13	4	.374	.346	11
Greene, Todd, Cal.	R	.190	29	79	9	15	22	1	0	2	9	0	0	4	11	2	0	.278	.238	-3
Haselman, Bill, Bos.	R	.274	77	237	33	65	104	13	1	8	34	0	0	19	52	4	2	.439	.331	5
Hatteberg, Scott, Bos.	L	.182	10	11	3	2	3	1	0	0	0	0	0	3	2	0	0	.273	.357	-5
Hoiles, Chris, Bal.	R	.258	127	407	64	105	193	13	0	25	73	1	7	57	97	0	1	.474	.356	9
Karkovice, Ron, ChiA	R	.220	111	355	44	78	130	22	0	10	38	7	2	24	93	0	0	.366	.270	-1
Kreuter, Chad, ChiA	B	.219	46	114	14	25	42	8	0	3	18	2	1	13	29	0	0	.368	.308	-3
Levis, Jesse, Mil.	L	.236	104	233	27	55	66	6	1	1	21	1	0	38	15	0	0	.283	.348	-3
Leyritz, Jim, NYA	R	.264	88	265	23	70	101	10	0	7	40	2	3	30	68	2	0	.381	.355	3
Macfarlane, Mike, K.C.	R	.274	112	379	58	104	189	24	2	19	54	0	2	31	57	3	3	.499	.339	9
Machado, Robert, ChiA	R	.667	4	6	1	4	5	1	0	0	2	0	0	0	0	0	0	.833	.667	-3
Martinez, Sandy, Tor.	L	.227	76	229	17	52	76	9	3	3	18	1	1	16	58	0	0	.332	.288	-3
Marzano, John, Sea.	R	.245	41	106	8	26	32	6	0	0	6	3	0	7	15	0	0	.302	.316	-4
Matheny, Mike, Mil.	R	.204	106	313	31	64	107	15	2	8	46	7	4	14	80	3	2	.342	.243	0
McIntosh, Tim, Min.	R	.000	3	3	0	0	0	0	0	0	0	0	0	0	0	0	0	.000	.000	-5
Mercedes, Henry, K.C.	R	.250	4	4	1	1	1	0	0	0	0	0	0	0	1	0	0	.250	.250	-5
Molina, Izzy, Oak.	R	.200	14	25	0	5	7	2	0	0	1	0	0	1	3	0	0	.280	.231	-4
Mosquera, Julio, Tor.	R	.227	8	22	2	5	7	2	0	0	2	0	0	0	3	0	1	.318	.261	-5
Myers, Greg, Min.	L	.286	97	329	37	94	140	22	3	6	47	0	5	19	52	0	0	.426	.320	4
O'Brien, Charlie, Tor.	R	.238	109	324	33	77	133	17	0	13	44	3	2	29	68	0	1	.410	.331	2
Parent, Mark, Det.-Bal.	R	.226	56	137	17	31	65	7	0	9	23	1	1	5	37	0	0	.474	.252	-5
Pena, Tony, Cle.	R	.195	67	174	14	34	41	4	0	1	27	3	3	15	25	0	1	.236	.255	-4
Posada, Jorge, NYA	B	.071	8	14	1	1	1	0	0	0	0	0	0	1	6	0	0	.071	.133	-5
Rodriguez, Ivan, Tex.	R	.300	153	639	116	192	302	47	3	19	86	0	4	38	55	5	0	.473	.342	18
Slaught, Don, Cal.-ChiA	R	.313	76	243	25	76	104	10	0	6	36	1	2	15	22	0	0	.428	.355	4
Stanley, Mike, Bos.	R	.270	121	397	73	107	201	20	1	24	69	0	2	69	62	2	0	.506	.383	11
Steinbach, Terry, Oak.	R	.272	145	514	79	140	272	25	1	35	100	0	2	49	115	0	1	.529	.342	16
Stinnett, Kelly, Mil.	R	.077	14	26	1	2	2	0	0	0	0	0	0	2	11	0	0	.077	.172	-6

American League catchers

Name/Team	B	BA	G	AB	R	H	TB	2B	3B	HR	RBI	SH	SF	BB	SO	SB	CS	SLG	OBA	RV
Sweeney, Mike, K.C.	R	.279	50	165	23	46	68	10	0	4	24	0	3	18	21	1	2	.412	.358	1
Turner, Chris, Cal.	R	.333	4	3	1	1	1	0	0	0	1	0	1	1	0	0	0	.333	.400	-4
Valle, David, Tex.	R	.302	42	86	14	26	43	6	1	3	17	0	0	9	17	0	0	.500	.368	-1
Walbeck, Matt, Min.	B	.223	63	215	25	48	64	10	0	2	24	1	2	9	34	3	1	.298	.252	-2
Widger, Chris, Sea.	R	.182	8	11	1	2	2	0	0	0	0	0	0	0	5	0	0	.182	.250	-5
Williams, George, Oak.	B	.152	56	132	17	20	34	5	0	3	10	2	1	28	32	0	0	.258	.311	-6
Wilson, Dan, Sea.	R	.285	138	491	51	140	218	24	0	18	83	9	5	32	88	1	2	.444	.330	12
Zaun, Gregg, Bal.	B	.231	50	108	16	25	38	8	1	1	13	0	2	11	15	0	0	.352	.309	-4

American League first basemen

Name/Team	B	BA	G	AB	R	H	TB	2B	3B	HR	RBI	SH	SF	BB	SO	SB	CS	SLG	OBA	RV
Carreon, Mark, Cle.	R	.324	38	142	16	46	64	12	0	2	14	0	0	11	9	1	1	.451	.385	0
Clark, Phil, Bos.	R	.000	3	3	0	0	0	0	0	0	0	0	0	0	1	0	0	.000	.000	-5
Clark, Tony, Det.	B	.250	100	376	56	94	189	14	0	27	72	0	6	29	127	0	1	.503	.299	9
Clark, Will, Tex.	L	.284	117	436	69	124	190	25	1	13	72	0	7	64	67	2	1	.436	.377	10
Coomer, Ron, Min.	R	.296	95	233	34	69	119	12	1	12	41	0	3	17	24	3	0	.511	.340	6
Fielder, Cecil, Det. -NYA	R	.252	160	591	85	149	286	20	0	39	117	0	5	87	139	2	0	.484	.350	13
Franco, Julio, Cle.	R	.322	112	432	72	139	203	20	1	14	76	0	3	61	82	8	8	.470	.407	17
Giambi, Jason, Oak.	L	.291	140	536	84	156	258	40	1	20	79	1	5	51	95	0	1	.481	.355	13
Gonzales, Rene, Tex.	R	.217	51	92	19	20	30	4	0	2	5	0	2	10	11	0	0	.326	.288	-4
Hunter, Brian R., Sea.	R	.268	75	198	21	53	84	10	0	7	28	1	3	15	43	0	1	.424	.327	1
Hyers, Tim, Det.	L	.077	17	26	1	2	3	1	0	0	0	0	0	4	5	0	0	.115	.200	-6
Jaha, John, Mil.	R	.300	148	543	108	163	295	28	1	34	118	0	3	85	118	3	1	.543	.398	23
Jordan, Ricky, Sea.	R	.250	15	28	4	7	10	0	0	1	4	0	1	1	6	0	0	.357	.290	-4
Kent, Jeff, Cle.	R	.265	39	102	16	27	43	7	0	3	16	0	3	10	22	2	1	.422	.328	-1
Lovullo, Torey, Oak.	B	.220	65	82	15	18	31	4	0	3	9	3	1	11	17	1	2	.378	.323	-3
Martinez, Tino, NYA	L	.292	155	595	82	174	277	28	0	25	117	1	5	68	85	2	1	.466	.364	19
McGwire, Mark, Oak.	R	.312	130	423	104	132	309	21	0	52	113	0	1	116	112	0	0	.730	.467	25
Offerman, Jose, K.C.	B	.303	151	561	85	170	234	33	8	5	47	7	2	74	98	24	10	.417	.384	20
Olerud, John, Tor.	L	.274	125	398	59	109	188	25	0	18	61	0	1	60	37	1	0	.472	.382	8
Palmeiro, Rafael, Bal.	L	.289	162	626	110	181	342	40	2	39	142	0	8	95	96	8	0	.546	.381	28
Perry, Herbert, Cle.	R	.083	7	12	1	1	2	1	0	0	0	0	0	1	2	1	0	.167	.154	-4
Pritchett, Chris, Cal.	L	.154	5	13	1	2	2	0	0	0	1	0	0	0	3	0	0	.154	.154	-5
Robertson, Mike, ChiA	L	.143	6	7	0	1	2	1	0	0	0	0	0	0	1	0	0	.286	.143	-4
Snow, J.T., Cal.	L	.257	155	575	69	148	221	20	1	17	67	2	3	56	96	1	6	.384	.327	7
Sorrento, Paul, Sea.	L	.289	143	471	67	136	239	32	1	23	93	2	5	57	103	0	2	.507	.370	14
Stahoviak, Scott, Min.	L	.284	130	405	72	115	190	30	3	13	61	1	2	59	114	3	3	.469	.376	9
Stevens, Lee, Tex.	L	.231	27	78	6	18	35	2	3	3	12	0	1	6	22	0	0	.449	.291	-3
Thomas, Frank E., ChiA	R	.349	141	527	110	184	330	26	0	40	134	0	8	109	70	1	1	.626	.459	30
Unroe, Tim, Mil.	R	.188	14	16	5	3	3	0	0	0	0	0	0	4	5	0	1	.188	.350	-5
Vaughn, Mo, Bos.	L	.326	161	635	118	207	370	29	1	44	143	0	8	95	154	2	0	.583	.420	31
Young, Kevin, K.C.	R	.242	55	132	20	32	62	6	0	8	23	0	0	11	32	3	3	.470	.301	1

American League second basemen

Name/Team	B	BA	G	AB	R	H	TB	2B	3B	HR	RBI	SH	SF	BB	SO	SB	CS	SLG	OBA	RV
Alomar, Roberto, Bal.	B	.328	153	588	132	193	310	43	4	22	94	8	12	90	65	17	6	.527	.411	29
Baerga, Carlos, Cle.	B	.267	100	424	54	113	168	25	0	10	55	2	4	16	25	1	1	.396	.302	5
Batista, Tony, Oak.	R	.298	74	238	38	71	103	10	2	6	25	0	2	19	49	7	3	.433	.350	6
Bournigal, Rafael, Oak.	R	.242	88	252	33	61	79	14	2	0	18	8	0	16	19	4	3	.313	.290	-1
Brito, Tilson, Tor.	R	.238	26	80	10	19	29	7	0	1	7	2	0	10	18	1	1	.363	.344	-3
Cairo, Miguel, Tor.	R	.222	9	27	5	6	8	2	0	0	1	0	0	2	9	0	0	.296	.300	-5
Candaele, Casey, Cle.	B	.250	24	44	8	11	16	2	0	1	4	0	0	1	9	0	0	.364	.267	-4
Cedeno, D., Tor.-ChiA	B	.272	89	301	46	82	104	12	2	2	20	8	3	15	64	6	3	.346	.308	2
Cora, Joey, Sea.	B	.291	144	530	90	154	221	37	6	6	45	6	5	35	32	5	5	.417	.340	8
Cordero, Wil, Bos.	R	.288	59	198	29	57	80	14	0	3	37	1	1	11	31	2	1	.404	.330	2
Crespo, Felipe, Tor.	B	.184	22	49	6	9	13	4	0	0	4	0	0	12	13	1	0	.265	.375	-4
Cruz, Fausto, Det.	R	.237	14	38	5	9	11	2	0	0	1	0	1	1	11	0	0	.289	.256	-5
Duncan, Mariano, NYA	R	.340	109	400	62	136	200	34	3	8	56	2	5	9	77	4	3	.500	.352	13
Durham, Ray, ChiA	B	.275	156	557	79	153	226	33	5	10	65	7	7	58	95	30	4	.406	.350	23
Eenhoorn, R., NYA-Cal.	R	.172	18	29	3	5	5	0	0	0	2	1	2	2	5	0	0	.172	.212	-4
Fox, Andy, NYA	L	.196	113	189	26	37	50	4	0	3	13	9	0	20	28	11	3	.265	.276	1
Frye, Jeff, Bos.	R	.286	105	419	74	120	163	27	2	4	41	5	3	54	57	18	4	.389	.372	13
Garrison, Webster, Oak.	R	.000	5	9	0	0	0	0	0	0	0	0	0	1	0	0	0	.000	.100	-5
Gates, Brent, Oak.	B	.263	64	247	26	65	94	19	2	2	30	5	2	18	35	1	1	.381	.316	0
Hale, Chip, Min.	L	.276	85	87	8	24	32	5	0	1	16	0	1	10	6	0	0	.368	.347	-2
Howard, Matt, NYA	R	.204	35	54	9	11	15	1	0	1	9	2	1	2	8	1	0	.278	.228	-3

American League second basemen

Name/Team	B	BA	G	AB	R	H	TB	2B	3B	HR	RBI	SH	SF	BB	SO	SB	CS	SLG	OBA	RV
Hudler, Rex, Cal.	R	.311	92	302	60	94	168	20	3	16	40	2	1	9	54	14	5	.556	.337	15
Huson, Jeff, Bal.	L	.321	17	28	5	9	10	1	0	0	2	0	1	1	3	0	0	.357	.333	-4
Kelly, Pat, NYA	R	.143	13	21	4	3	3	0	0	0	2	0	0	2	9	0	1	.143	.217	-5
Knoblauch, Chuck, Min.	R	.341	153	578	140	197	299	35	14	13	72	0	6	98	74	45	14	.517	.448	41
Lewis, Mark, Det.	R	.270	145	545	69	147	216	30	3	11	55	4	3	42	109	6	1	.396	.326	9
Lockhart, Keith, K.C.	L	.273	138	433	49	118	178	33	3	7	55	1	5	30	40	11	6	.411	.319	10
Loretta, Mark, Mil.	R	.279	73	154	20	43	49	3	0	1	13	2	0	14	15	2	1	.318	.339	-1
McLemore, Mark, Tex.	B	.290	147	517	84	150	196	23	4	5	46	2	5	87	69	27	10	.379	.389	20
Munoz, Jose, ChiA	B	.259	17	27	7	7	7	0	0	0	1	0	0	4	1	0	0	.259	.355	-4
Perez, Tomas, Tor.	B	.251	91	295	24	74	98	13	4	1	19	6	1	25	29	1	2	.332	.311	-2
Pozo, Arquimedez, Bos.	R	.172	21	58	4	10	18	3	1	1	11	0	1	2	10	1	0	.310	.210	-4
Ripken, Billy, Bal.	R	.230	57	135	19	31	45	8	0	2	12	1	1	9	18	0	0	.333	.281	-4
Roberts, Bip, K.C.	B	.283	90	339	39	96	121	21	2	0	52	0	6	25	38	12	9	.357	.331	9
Selby, Bill, Bos.	L	.274	40	95	12	26	39	4	0	3	6	1	0	9	11	1	1	.411	.337	-2
Sojo, Luis, Sea.-NYA	R	.220	95	287	23	63	78	10	1	1	21	8	1	11	17	2	2	.272	.250	-3
Stillwell, Kurt, Tex.	B	.273	46	77	12	21	28	4	0	1	4	1	0	10	11	0	0	.364	.364	-4
Velarde, Randy, Cal.	R	.285	136	530	82	151	226	27	3	14	54	4	2	70	118	7	7	.426	.372	12
Vina, Fernando, Mil.	L	.283	140	554	94	157	217	19	10	7	46	6	4	38	35	16	7	.392	.342	14
Vizcaino, Jose, Cle.	B	.285	48	179	23	51	60	5	2	0	13	4	1	7	24	6	2	.335	.310	2

American League third basemen

Name/Team	B	BA	G	AB	R	H	TB	2B	3B	HR	RBI	SH	SF	BB	SO	SB	CS	SLG	OBA	RV
Arias, George, Cal.	R	.238	84	252	19	60	88	8	1	6	28	6	0	16	50	2	0	.349	.284	0
Beltre, Esteban, Bos.	R	.258	27	62	6	16	18	2	0	0	6	1	1	4	14	1	0	.290	.299	-3
Boggs, Wade, NYA	L	.311	132	501	80	156	195	29	2	2	41	1	5	67	32	1	2	.389	.389	7
Brosius, Scott, Oak.	R	.304	114	428	73	130	221	25	0	22	71	1	5	59	85	7	2	.516	.393	17
Cirillo, Jeff, Mil.	R	.325	158	566	101	184	285	46	5	15	83	6	6	58	69	4	9	.504	.391	18
Davis, Russ, Sea.	R	.234	51	167	24	39	63	9	0	5	18	4	0	17	50	2	0	.377	.312	-1
Espinoza, Alvaro, Cle.	R	.223	59	112	12	25	45	4	2	4	11	3	1	6	18	1	1	.402	.279	-3
Fryman, Travis, Det.	R	.268	157	616	90	165	269	32	3	22	100	1	10	57	118	4	3	.437	.329	15
Hayes, Charlie, NYA	R	.284	20	67	7	19	28	3	0	2	13	1	0	1	12	0	0	.418	.294	-2
Hiatt, Phil, Det.	R	.190	7	21	3	4	6	0	1	0	1	0	0	2	11	0	0	.286	.261	-5
Hollins, Dave, Min.-Sea.	B	.262	149	516	88	135	212	29	0	16	78	1	2	84	117	6	6	.411	.377	8
Howell, Jack, Cal.	L	.270	66	126	20	34	64	4	1	8	21	0	0	10	30	0	1	.508	.324	0
Leius, Scott, Cle.	R	.140	27	43	3	6	13	4	0	1	3	1	0	2	8	0	0	.302	.178	-5
Manto, Jeff, Bos.-Sea.-Bos.	R	.196	43	102	15	20	37	6	1	3	10	0	0	17	24	0	1	.363	.317	-4
Naehring, Tim, Bos.	R	.288	116	430	77	124	191	16	0	17	65	2	4	49	63	2	1	.444	.363	11
Nevin, Phil, Det.	R	.292	38	120	15	35	64	5	0	8	19	0	1	8	39	1	0	.533	.338	1
Palmer, Dean, Tex.	R	.280	154	582	98	163	307	26	2	38	107	0	6	59	145	2	0	.527	.348	20
Paquette, Craig, K.C.	R	.259	118	429	61	111	194	15	1	22	67	3	5	23	101	5	3	.452	.296	11
Pena, Geronimo, Cle.	B	.111	5	9	1	1	4	0	0	1	2	0	0	1	4	0	0	.444	.200	-4
Quinlan, Tom, Min.	R	.000	4	6	0	0	0	0	0	0	0	0	0	0	3	0	0	.000	.000	-5
Raabe, Brian, Min.	R	.222	7	9	0	2	2	0	0	0	1	1	0	1	0	1	0	.222	.200	-5
Randa, Joe, K.C.	R	.303	110	337	36	102	146	24	1	6	47	2	4	26	47	13	4	.433	.351	12
Sheets, Andy, Sea.	R	.191	47	110	18	21	29	8	0	0	9	2	1	10	41	2	0	.264	.262	-4
Snopek, Chris, ChiA	R	.260	46	104	18	27	53	6	1	6	18	1	1	6	16	0	1	.510	.304	-1
Spiezio, Scott, Oak.	B	.310	9	29	6	9	17	2	0	2	8	2	0	4	4	0	1	.586	.394	-3
Sprague, Ed Jr., Tor.	R	.247	159	591	88	146	293	35	2	36	101	0	7	60	146	0	0	.496	.325	13
Strange, Doug, Sea.	B	.235	88	183	19	43	61	7	1	3	23	0	2	14	31	1	0	.333	.290	-2
Surhoff, B.J., Bal.	L	.292	143	537	74	157	259	27	6	21	82	2	1	47	79	0	1	.482	.352	13
Tatum, Jim, Bos.	R	.125	2	8	1	1	1	0	0	0	0	0	0	0	2	0	0	.125	.125	-5
Thome, Jim, Cle.	L	.311	151	505	122	157	309	28	5	38	116	0	2	123	141	2	2	.612	.450	24
Ventura, Robin, ChiA	L	.287	158	586	96	168	305	31	2	34	105	0	8	78	81	1	3	.520	.368	19
Walker, Todd, Min.	L	.256	25	82	8	21	27	6	0	0	6	0	3	4	13	2	0	.329	.281	-3
Wallach, Tim, Cal.	R	.237	57	190	23	45	76	7	0	8	20	0	0	18	47	1	0	.400	.306	-1
Worthington, Craig, Tex.	R	.158	13	19	2	3	6	0	0	1	4	0	2	6	3	0	0	.316	.333	-4
Zeile, Todd, Bal.	R	.239	29	117	17	28	51	8	0	5	19	0	0	15	16	0	0	.436	.326	-2

American League shortstops

Name/Team	B	BA	G	AB	R	H	TB	2B	3B	HR	RBI	SH	SF	BB	SO	SB	CS	SLG	OBA	RV
Alexander, Manny, Bal.	R	.103	54	68	6	7	7	0	0	0	4	2	0	3	27	3	3	.103	.141	-5
Bordick, Mike, Oak.	R	.240	155	525	46	126	167	18	4	5	54	4	5	52	59	5	6	.318	.307	3
Cedeno, Andujar, Det.	R	.196	52	179	19	35	64	4	2	7	20	3	0	4	37	2	1	.358	.213	-2
DiSarcina, Gary, Cal.	R	.256	150	536	62	137	186	26	4	5	48	16	1	21	36	2	1	.347	.286	3
Easley, Damion, Cal.-Det.	R	.268	49	112	14	30	44	2	0	4	17	5	1	10	25	3	1	.393	.331	1
Elster, Kevin, Tex.	R	.252	157	515	79	130	238	32	2	24	99	16	11	52	138	4	1	.462	.317	13

American League shortstops

Name/Team	B	BA	G	AB	R	H	TB	2B	3B	HR	RBI	SH	SF	BB	SO	SB	CS	SLG	OBA	RV
Garciaparra, Nomar, Bos.	R	.241	24	87	11	21	41	2	3	4	16	1	1	4	14	5	0	.471	.272	1
Gil, Benji, Tex.	R	.400	5	5	0	2	2	0	0	0	1	1	0	1	1	0	1	.400	.500	-4
Gomez, Chris, Det.	R	.242	48	128	21	31	39	5	0	1	16	3	0	18	20	1	1	.305	.340	-3
Gonzalez, Alex, Tor.	R	.235	147	527	64	124	206	30	5	14	64	7	3	45	127	16	6	.391	.300	12
Guillen, Ozzie, ChiA	L	.263	150	499	62	131	183	24	8	4	45	12	7	10	27	6	5	.367	.273	5
Howard, David, K.C.	B	.219	143	420	51	92	128	14	5	4	48	17	4	40	74	5	6	.305	.291	1
Jackson, Damian, Cle.	R	.300	5	10	2	3	5	2	0	0	1	0	0	1	4	0	0	.500	.364	-4
Jeter, Derek, NYA	R	.314	157	582	104	183	250	25	6	10	78	6	9	48	102	14	7	.430	.370	21
Martin, Norberto, ChiA	R	.350	70	140	30	49	59	7	0	1	14	4	1	6	17	10	2	.421	.374	6
Meares, Pat, Min.	R	.267	152	517	66	138	202	26	7	8	67	4	7	17	90	9	4	.391	.298	10
Norton, Greg, ChiA	B	.217	11	23	4	5	11	0	0	2	3	0	0	4	6	0	1	.478	.333	-4
Reboulet, Jeff, Min.	R	.222	107	234	20	52	61	9	0	0	23	4	2	25	34	4	2	.261	.298	-2
Ripken, Cal, Bal.	R	.278	163	640	94	178	298	40	1	26	102	0	4	59	78	1	2	.466	.341	16
Rodriguez, Alex, Sea.	R	.358	146	601	141	215	379	54	1	36	123	6	7	59	104	15	4	.631	.414	38
Rodriguez, Tony, Bos.	R	.239	27	67	7	16	20	1	0	1	9	5	0	4	8	0	0	.299	.292	-4
Schofield, Dick C., Cal.	R	.250	13	16	3	4	4	0	0	0	0	0	0	1	1	1	0	.250	.294	-4
Trammell, Alan, Det.	R	.233	66	193	16	45	50	2	0	1	16	1	3	10	27	6	0	.259	.267	0
Valentin, John, Bos.	R	.296	131	527	84	156	230	29	3	13	59	2	7	63	59	9	10	.436	.374	14
Valentin, Jose, Mil.	B	.259	154	552	90	143	262	33	7	24	95	6	4	66	145	17	4	.475	.336	20
Vizquel, Omar, Cle.	B	.297	151	542	98	161	226	36	1	9	64	12	9	56	42	35	9	.417	.362	28

American League outfielders

Name/Team	B	BA	G	AB	R	H	TB	2B	3B	HR	RBI	SH	SF	BB	SO	SB	CS	SLG	OBA	RV
Amaral, Rich, Sea.	R	.292	118	312	69	91	111	11	3	1	29	4	1	47	55	25	6	.356	.392	15
Anderson, Brady, Bal.	L	.297	149	579	117	172	369	37	5	50	110	6	4	76	106	21	8	.637	.396	36
Anderson, Garret, Cal.	L	.285	150	607	79	173	246	33	2	12	72	5	3	27	84	7	9	.405	.314	13
Banks, Brian, Mil.	B	.571	4	7	2	4	9	2	0	1	2	0	0	1	2	0	0	1.286	.625	-4
Bartee, Kimera, Det.	R	.253	110	217	32	55	66	6	1	1	14	13	0	17	77	20	10	.304	.308	8
Battle, Allen, Oak.	R	.192	47	130	20	25	31	3	0	1	5	1	1	17	26	10	2	.238	.293	0
Bautista, Danny, Det.	R	.250	25	64	12	16	24	2	0	2	8	0	0	9	15	1	2	.375	.342	-3
Becker, Rich, Min.	L	.291	148	525	92	153	228	31	4	12	71	5	4	68	118	19	5	.434	.372	20
Belle, Albert, Cle.	R	.311	158	602	124	187	375	38	3	48	148	0	7	99	87	11	0	.623	.410	35
Bonilla, Bobby, Bal.	B	.287	159	595	107	171	292	27	5	28	116	0	17	75	85	1	3	.491	.363	19
Bowers, Brent, Bal.	L	.308	21	39	6	12	14	2	0	0	3	0	0	0	7	0	0	.359	.308	-4
Bragg, Darren, Sea.-Bos.	L	.261	127	417	74	109	169	26	2	10	47	2	7	69	74	14	9	.405	.366	7
Brede, Brent, Min.	L	.300	10	20	2	6	8	0	1	0	2	0	0	1	5	0	0	.400	.333	-4
Brumfield, Jacob, Tor.	R	.256	90	308	52	79	138	19	2	12	52	1	3	24	58	12	3	.448	.316	10
Buford, Damon, Tex.	R	.283	90	145	30	41	68	9	0	6	20	1	1	15	34	8	5	.469	.348	5
Buhner, Jay, Sea.	R	.271	150	564	107	153	314	29	0	44	138	0	10	84	159	0	1	.557	.369	22
Burnitz, Jeromy, Cle.-Mil.	L	.265	94	200	38	53	94	14	0	9	40	0	2	33	47	4	1	.470	.377	5
Cameron, Mike, ChiA	R	.091	11	11	1	1	1	0	0	0	0	0	0	1	3	0	1	.091	.167	-5
Carr, Chuck, Mil.	B	.274	27	106	18	29	40	6	1	1	11	0	1	6	21	5	4	.377	.310	0
Carter, Joe, Tor.	R	.253	157	625	84	158	297	35	7	30	107	0	6	44	106	7	6	.475	.306	17
Cole, Alex, Bos.	L	.222	24	72	13	16	23	5	1	0	7	2	1	8	11	5	3	.319	.296	-2
Cordova, Marty, Min.	R	.309	145	569	97	176	272	46	1	16	111	0	9	53	96	11	5	.478	.371	23
Curtis, Chad, Det.	R	.263	104	400	65	105	157	20	1	10	37	6	6	53	73	16	10	.393	.346	11
Cuyler, Milt, Bos.	B	.200	50	110	19	22	33	1	2	2	12	7	1	13	19	7	3	.300	.299	0
Damon, Johnny, K.C.	L	.271	145	517	61	140	190	22	5	6	50	10	5	31	64	25	5	.368	.313	17
Devereaux, Mike, Bal.	R	.229	127	323	49	74	113	11	2	8	34	2	2	34	53	8	2	.350	.305	4
Diaz, Alex, Sea.	B	.241	38	79	11	19	24	2	0	1	5	0	1	2	8	6	3	.304	.274	-1
Dunn, Todd, Mil.	R	.300	6	10	2	3	4	1	0	0	1	0	0	0	3	0	0	.400	.300	-4
Edmonds, Jim, Cal.	L	.304	114	431	73	131	246	28	3	27	66	0	2	46	101	4	0	.571	.375	16
Erstad, Darin, Cal.	L	.284	57	208	34	59	78	5	1	4	20	1	3	17	29	3	3	.375	.333	2
Faneyte, Rikkert, Tex.	R	.200	8	5	0	1	1	0	0	0	1	2	0	0	0	0	0	.200	.200	-5
Gonzalez, Juan, Tex.	R	.314	134	541	89	170	348	33	2	47	144	0	3	45	82	2	0	.643	.368	30
Goodwin, Tom, K.C.	L	.282	143	524	80	148	173	14	4	1	35	21	1	39	79	66	22	.330	.334	38
Green, Shawn, Tor.	L	.280	132	422	52	118	189	32	3	11	45	0	2	33	75	5	1	.448	.342	8
Greenwell, Mike, Bos.	L	.295	77	295	35	87	130	20	1	7	44	0	3	18	27	4	0	.441	.336	6
Greer, Rusty, Tex.	L	.332	139	542	96	180	287	41	6	18	100	0	10	62	86	9	0	.530	.397	24
Griffey, Ken Jr., Sea.	L	.303	140	545	125	165	342	26	2	49	140	1	7	78	104	16	1	.628	.392	36
Hamilton, Darryl, Tex.	L	.293	148	627	94	184	239	29	4	6	51	7	6	54	66	15	5	.381	.348	15
Hammonds, Jeffrey, Bal.	R	.226	71	248	38	56	95	10	1	9	27	6	1	23	53	3	3	.383	.301	1
Herrera, Jose, Oak.	L	.269	108	320	44	86	121	15	1	6	30	3	0	20	59	8	2	.378	.318	5
Higginson, Bobby, Det.	L	.320	130	440	75	141	254	35	0	26	81	3	6	65	66	6	3	.577	.404	20
Hocking, Denny, Min.	B	.197	49	127	16	25	34	6	0	1	10	1	1	8	24	3	3	.268	.243	-3
Hosey, Dwayne, Bos.	B	.218	28	78	13	17	26	2	2	1	3	2	0	7	17	6	3	.333	.282	-1
Huff, Michael, Tor.	R	.172	11	29	5	5	7	0	1	0	0	0	0	1	5	0	0	.241	.200	-5
Hulse, David, Mil.	L	.222	81	117	18	26	29	3	0	0	6	2	0	8	16	4	1	.248	.272	-3

American League outfielders

Name/Team	B	BA	G	AB	R	H	TB	2B	3B	HR	RBI	SH	SF	BB	SO	SB	CS	SLG	OBA	RV
Incaviglia, Pete, Bal.	R	.303	12	33	4	10	18	2	0	2	8	0	1	0	7	0	0	.545	.314	-3
James, Dion, NYA	L	.167	6	12	1	2	2	0	0	0	0	0	0	1	2	1	0	.167	.231	-4
Kelly, Roberto, Min.	R	.323	98	322	41	104	147	17	4	6	47	0	5	23	53	10	2	.457	.375	12
Kirby, Wayne, Cle.	L	.250	27	16	3	4	5	1	0	0	1	0	0	2	2	0	1	.313	.333	-4
Koslofski, Kevin, Mil.	L	.214	25	42	5	9	16	3	2	0	6	0	0	4	12	0	0	.381	.298	-4
Lawton, Matt, Min.	L	.258	79	252	34	65	92	7	1	6	42	0	2	28	28	4	4	.365	.339	4
Lennon, Patrick, K.C.	R	.233	14	30	5	7	10	3	0	0	1	0	0	7	10	0	0	.333	.378	-5
Lesher, Brian, Oak.	R	.232	26	82	11	19	37	3	0	5	16	1	1	5	17	0	0	.451	.281	-2
Lewis, Darren, ChiA	L	.228	141	337	55	77	105	12	2	4	53	15	5	45	40	21	5	.312	.321	11
Listach, Pat, Mil.-NYA	B	.240	87	317	51	76	99	16	2	1	33	6	2	36	51	25	5	.312	.317	11
Lofton, Kenny, Cle.	L	.317	154	662	132	210	295	35	4	14	67	7	6	61	82	75	17	.446	.372	55
Malave, Jose, Bos.	R	.235	41	102	12	24	39	3	0	4	17	0	0	2	25	0	0	.382	.257	-2
Martinez, Dave, ChiA	L	.318	146	440	85	140	206	20	8	10	53	2	1	52	52	15	7	.468	.393	18
Martinez, Manny, Sea.	R	.235	9	17	3	4	8	2	1	0	3	0	0	3	5	2	0	.471	.350	-3
Mashore, Damon, Oak.	R	.267	50	105	20	28	46	7	1	3	12	1	1	16	31	4	0	.438	.366	0
Mieske, Matt, Mil.	R	.278	127	374	46	104	176	24	3	14	64	1	6	26	76	1	5	.471	.324	8
Mitchell, Kevin, Bos.	R	.304	27	92	9	28	38	4	0	2	13	0	0	11	14	0	0	.413	.385	-2
Moore, Kerwin, Oak.	B	.063	22	16	4	1	2	1	0	0	0	0	0	2	6	1	0	.125	.167	-5
Mouton, Lyle, ChiA	R	.294	87	214	25	63	94	8	1	7	39	0	3	22	50	3	0	.439	.361	5
Myers, Rod, K.C.	L	.286	22	63	9	18	28	7	0	1	11	0	0	7	16	3	2	.444	.357	-5
Newfield, Marc, Mil.	R	.307	49	179	21	55	91	15	0	7	31	0	4	11	26	0	1	.508	.354	3
Newson, Warren, Tex.	L	.255	91	235	34	60	106	14	1	10	31	0	1	37	82	3	0	.451	.355	3
Nieves, Melvin, Det.	B	.246	120	431	71	106	209	23	4	24	60	0	3	44	158	1	2	.485	.322	7
Nilsson, Dave, Mil.	L	.331	123	453	81	150	238	33	2	17	84	0	3	57	68	2	3	.525	.407	17
Nixon, Otis, Tor.	B	.286	125	496	87	142	162	15	1	1	29	7	0	71	68	54	13	.327	.377	31
Nixon, Trot, Bos.	L	.500	2	4	2	2	3	1	0	0	0	0	0	0	1	1	0	.750	.500	-4
Norman, Les, K.C.	R	.122	54	49	9	6	6	0	0	0	0	0	0	6	14	1	1	.122	.232	-6
Nunnally, Jon, K.C.	L	.211	35	90	16	19	41	5	1	5	17	0	1	13	25	0	0	.456	.308	-2
O'Leary, Troy, Bos.	L	.260	149	497	68	129	212	28	5	15	81	1	3	47	80	3	2	.427	.327	9
O'Neill, Paul, NYA	L	.302	150	546	89	165	259	35	1	19	91	0	8	102	76	0	1	.474	.411	15
Palmeiro, Orlando, Cal.	L	.287	50	87	6	25	33	6	1	0	6	1	0	8	13	0	1	.379	.361	-3
Pemberton, Rudy, Bos.	R	.512	13	41	11	21	32	8	0	1	10	0	0	2	4	3	1	.780	.556	1
Perez, Danny, Mil.	R	.000	4	4	0	0	0	0	0	0	0	0	0	0	0	0	0	.000	.000	-5
Perez, Robert, Tor.	R	.327	86	202	30	66	82	10	0	2	21	4	1	8	17	3	0	.406	.354	3
Phillips, Tony, ChiA	B	.277	153	581	119	161	232	29	3	12	63	1	8	125	132	13	8	.399	.404	15
Plantier, Phil, Oak.	L	.212	73	231	29	49	80	8	1	7	31	0	1	28	56	2	2	.346	.304	-1
Polonia, Luis, Bal.	L	.240	58	175	25	42	54	4	1	2	14	1	0	10	20	8	6	.309	.285	1
Pride, Curtis, Det.	L	.300	95	267	52	80	137	17	5	10	31	3	0	31	63	11	6	.513	.372	10
Raines, Tim, NYA	B	.284	59	201	45	57	94	10	0	9	33	0	4	34	29	10	1	.468	.383	8
Ramirez, Manny, Cle.	R	.309	152	550	94	170	320	45	3	33	112	0	9	85	104	8	5	.582	.399	26
Rivera, Ruben, NYA	R	.284	46	88	17	25	39	6	1	2	16	1	2	13	26	6	2	.443	.381	2
Salmon, Tim, Cal.	R	.286	156	581	90	166	291	27	4	30	98	0	3	93	125	4	2	.501	.386	19
Singleton, Duane, Det.	L	.161	18	56	5	9	10	1	0	0	3	0	0	4	15	0	2	.179	.230	-6
Smith, Mark E., Bal.	R	.244	27	78	9	19	33	2	0	4	10	0	0	3	20	0	2	.423	.298	-3
Stairs, Matt, Oak.	L	.277	61	137	21	38	75	5	1	10	23	0	1	19	23	1	1	.547	.367	2
Stewart, Shannon, Tor.	R	.176	7	17	2	3	4	1	0	0	2	0	0	1	4	1	0	.235	.222	-4
Strawberry, Darryl, NYA	L	.262	63	202	35	53	99	13	0	11	36	0	3	31	55	6	5	.490	.359	6
Stynes, Chris, K.C.	R	.293	36	92	8	27	33	6	0	0	6	1	0	2	5	5	2	.359	.309	0
Tarasco, Tony, Bal.	L	.238	31	84	14	20	26	3	0	1	9	1	0	7	15	5	3	.310	.297	-1
Tartabull, Danny, ChiA	R	.254	132	472	58	120	230	23	3	27	101	0	5	64	128	1	2	.487	.340	13
Thompson, Ryan, Cle.	R	.318	8	22	2	7	10	0	0	1	5	0	0	1	6	0	0	.455	.348	-3
Tinsley, Lee, Bos.	B	.245	92	192	28	47	64	6	1	3	14	1	1	13	56	6	8	.333	.298	1
Tucker, Michael, K.C.	L	.260	108	339	55	88	150	18	4	12	53	3	4	40	69	10	4	.442	.346	10
Vaughn, Greg, Mil.	R	.280	102	375	78	105	214	16	0	31	95	0	5	58	99	5	2	.571	.378	17
Voigt, Jack, Tex.	R	.111	5	9	1	1	1	0	0	0	0	0	0	0	2	0	0	.111	.111	-5
Ward, Turner, Mil.	B	.179	43	67	7	12	22	2	1	2	10	1	1	13	17	3	0	.328	.309	-2
Whiten, Mark, Sea.	B	.300	40	140	31	42	85	7	0	12	33	0	0	21	40	2	1	.607	.399	4
Williams, Bernie, NYA	B	.305	143	551	108	168	295	26	7	29	102	1	7	82	72	17	4	.535	.391	28
Williams, Grld, NYA-Mil.	R	.252	125	325	43	82	124	19	4	5	34	3	5	19	57	10	9	.382	.299	2
Young, Ernie, Oak.	R	.242	141	462	72	112	196	19	4	19	64	3	4	52	118	7	5	.424	.326	9

American League relief pitchers (batting)

Name/Team	B	BA	G	AB	R	H	TB	2B	3B	HR	RBI	SH	SF	BB	SO	SB	CS	SLG	OBA
Hancock, Ryan, Cal.	R	1.000	11	1	1	1	1	0	0	0	0	0	0	0	0	0	0	1.000	1.000
Lewis, Richie, Det.	R	.000	72	1	0	0	0	0	0	0	0	0	0	0	0	0	0	.000	.000
Percival, Troy, Cal.	R	.000	62	1	0	0	0	0	0	0	0	0	0	0	1	0	0	.000	.000

American League starting pitchers (batting)

Name/Team	B	BA	G	AB	R	H	TB	2B	3B	HR	RBI	SH	SF	BB	SO	SB	CS	SLG	OBA
Clemens, Roger, Bos.	R	1.000	34	1	0	1	1	0	0	0	0	0	0	0	0	0	0	1.000	1.000

National League catchers

Name/Team	B	BA	G	AB	R	H	TB	2B	3B	HR	RBI	SH	SF	BB	SO	SB	CS	SLG	OBA	RV
Ausmus, Brad, S.D.	R	.181	50	149	16	27	34	4	0	1	13	1	0	13	27	1	4	.228	.261	-4
Ayrault, Joe, Atl.	R	.200	7	5	0	1	1	0	0	0	0	0	0	0	1	0	0	.200	.333	-4
Bennett, Gary, Phi.	R	.250	6	16	0	4	4	0	0	0	1	0	0	2	6	0	0	.250	.333	-4
Borders, Pat, St.L	R	.319	26	69	3	22	25	3	0	0	4	1	0	1	14	0	1	.362	.329	-2
Brito, Jorge, Col.	R	.071	8	14	1	1	1	0	0	0	0	1	0	1	8	0	0	.071	.235	-5
Castillo, Alberto, NYN	R	.364	6	11	1	4	4	0	0	0	0	0	0	0	4	0	0	.364	.364	-4
Chavez, Raul, Mon.	R	.200	4	5	1	1	1	0	0	0	0	0	0	1	1	1	0	.200	.333	-4
Decker, Steve, S.F.-Col.	R	.245	67	147	24	36	45	3	0	2	20	4	2	18	29	1	0	.306	.323	0
Difelice, Mike, St.L	R	.286	4	7	0	2	3	1	0	0	2	0	0	1	0	0	0	.429	.286	-4
Dorsett, Brian, ChiN	R	.122	17	41	3	5	8	0	0	1	3	0	1	4	8	0	0	.195	.196	-5
Encarnacion, Angelo, Pit.	R	.318	7	22	3	7	9	2	0	0	1	0	0	0	5	0	0	.409	.318	-4
Estalella, Bobby, Phi.	R	.353	7	17	5	6	12	0	0	2	4	0	0	1	6	1	0	.706	.389	-2
Eusebio, Tony, Hou.	R	.270	58	152	15	41	55	7	2	1	19	0	2	18	20	0	1	.362	.343	-1
Flaherty, John, S.D.	R	.303	72	264	22	80	119	12	0	9	41	1	3	9	36	2	3	.451	.327	8
Fletcher, Darrin, Mon.	L	.266	127	394	41	105	163	22	0	12	57	1	3	27	42	0	0	.414	.321	8
Fordyce, Brook, Cin.	R	.286	4	7	0	2	3	1	0	0	1	0	0	3	1	0	0	.429	.500	-4
Goff, Jerry, Hou.	L	.500	1	4	1	2	5	0	0	1	2	0	0	1	1	0	0	1.250	.500	-3
Greene, Charlie, NYN	R	.000	2	1	0	0	0	0	0	0	0	0	0	0	0	0	0	.000	.000	-4
Hernandez, Carlos, L.A.	R	.286	13	14	1	4	4	0	0	0	0	0	0	2	2	0	0	.286	.375	-4
Houston, Tyler, Atl.-ChiN	L	.317	79	142	21	45	65	9	1	3	27	0	0	9	27	3	2	.458	.358	5
Hubbard, Mike, ChiN	R	.105	21	38	1	4	7	0	0	1	4	0	1	0	15	0	0	.184	.103	-5
Hundley, Todd, NYN	B	.259	153	540	85	140	297	32	1	41	112	0	2	79	146	1	3	.550	.356	24
Jensen, Marcus, S.F.	B	.211	9	19	4	4	5	1	0	0	4	0	0	8	7	0	0	.263	.444	-4
Johnson, Brian D., S.D.	R	.272	82	243	18	66	105	13	1	8	35	2	4	4	36	0	0	.432	.290	4
Johnson, Charles, Fla.	R	.218	120	386	34	84	138	13	1	13	37	2	4	40	91	1	0	.358	.292	2
Kendall, Jason, Pit.	R	.300	130	414	54	124	166	23	5	3	42	3	4	35	30	5	2	.401	.372	9
Knorr, Randy, Hou.	R	.195	37	87	7	17	25	5	0	1	7	0	1	5	18	0	1	.287	.245	-4
Lampkin, Tom, S.F.	L	.232	66	177	26	41	67	8	0	6	29	0	2	20	22	1	5	.379	.324	1
Lieberthal, Mike, Phi.	R	.253	50	166	21	42	71	8	0	7	23	0	4	10	30	0	0	.428	.297	1
Lopez, Javier, Atl.	R	.282	138	489	56	138	228	19	1	23	69	1	5	28	84	1	6	.466	.322	16
Manwaring, Kirt, S.F.-Hou.	R	.229	86	227	14	52	64	9	0	1	18	2	2	19	40	0	1	.282	.300	-2
Mayne, Brent, NYN	L	.263	70	99	9	26	35	6	0	1	6	2	0	12	22	0	1	.354	.342	-3
Mirabelli, Doug, S.F.	R	.222	9	18	2	4	5	1	0	0	1	0	0	3	4	0	0	.278	.333	-4
Mulligan, Sean, S.D.	R	.000	2	1	0	0	0	0	0	0	0	0	0	0	0	0	0	.000	.000	-4
Natal, Bob, Fla.	R	.133	44	90	4	12	15	1	1	0	2	0	0	15	31	0	1	.167	.257	-6
Oliver, Joe, Cin.	R	.242	106	289	31	70	117	12	1	11	46	3	3	28	54	2	0	.405	.311	5
Osik, Keith, Pit.	R	.293	48	140	18	41	60	14	1	1	14	1	0	14	22	1	0	.429	.361	0
Owens, Jayhawk, Col.	R	.239	73	180	31	43	66	9	1	4	17	3	2	27	56	4	1	.367	.338	0
Pagnozzi, Tom, St.L	R	.270	119	407	48	110	172	23	0	13	55	3	4	24	78	4	1	.423	.311	10
Perez, Eddie, Atl.	R	.256	68	156	19	40	63	9	1	4	17	0	2	8	19	0	0	.404	.293	-1
Piazza, Mike, L.A.	R	.336	148	547	87	184	308	16	0	36	105	0	2	81	93	0	3	.563	.422	31
Prince, Tom, L.A.	R	.297	40	64	6	19	28	6	0	1	11	3	2	6	15	0	0	.438	.365	-2
Reed, Jeff, Col.	L	.284	116	341	34	97	143	20	1	8	37	6	3	43	65	2	2	.419	.365	6
Santiago, Benito, Phi.	R	.264	136	481	71	127	242	21	2	30	85	0	2	49	104	2	0	.503	.332	18
Servais, Scott, ChiN	R	.265	129	445	42	118	171	20	0	11	63	3	7	30	75	0	2	.384	.327	8
Sheaffer, Danny, St.L	R	.227	79	198	10	45	66	9	3	2	20	4	0	9	25	3	3	.333	.271	-1
Siddall, Joe, Fla.	L	.149	18	47	0	7	8	1	0	0	3	0	0	2	8	0	0	.170	.184	-5
Spehr, Tim, Mon.	R	.091	63	44	4	4	8	1	0	1	3	1	0	3	15	1	0	.182	.167	-5
Taubensee, Eddie, Cin.	L	.291	108	327	46	95	151	20	0	12	48	1	5	26	64	3	4	.462	.338	10
Webster, Lenny, Mon.	R	.230	78	174	18	40	56	10	0	2	17	1	1	25	21	0	0	.322	.332	-2
Wilkins, Rick, Hou.-S.F.	L	.243	136	411	53	100	164	18	2	14	59	0	10	67	121	0	3	.399	.344	7
Zaun, Gregg, Fla.	B	.290	10	31	4	9	13	1	0	1	2	1	0	3	5	1	0	.419	.353	-3

National League first basemen

Name/Team	B	BA	G	AB	R	H	TB	2B	3B	HR	RBI	SH	SF	BB	SO	SB	CS	SLG	OBA	RV
Aude, Rich, Pit.	R	.250	7	16	0	4	4	0	0	0	1	0	0	0	8	0	0	.250	.250	-4
Baerga, Carlos, NYN	B	.193	26	83	5	16	25	3	0	2	11	0	1	5	2	0	0	.301	.253	-3
Bagwell, Jeff, Hou.	R	.315	162	568	111	179	324	48	2	31	120	0	6	135	114	21	7	.570	.451	37
Belk, Tim, Cin.	R	.200	7	15	2	3	3	0	0	0	0	0	0	1	2	0	0	.200	.250	-4
Bogar, Tim, NYN	R	.213	91	89	17	19	23	4	0	0	6	3	2	8	20	1	3	.258	.287	-4
Brogna, Rico, NYN	L	.255	55	188	18	48	81	10	1	7	30	0	4	19	50	0	0	.431	.318	2
Brown, Brant, ChiN	L	.304	29	69	11	21	37	1	0	5	9	0	1	2	17	3	3	.536	.329	1

National League first basemen

Name/Team	B	BA	G	AB	R	H	TB	2B	3B	HR	RBI	SH	SF	BB	SO	SB	CS	SLG	OBA	RV
Carreon, Mark, S.F.	R	.260	81	292	40	76	131	22	3	9	51	0	2	22	33	2	3	.449	.317	6
Cianfrocco, Archi, S.D.	R	.281	79	192	21	54	79	13	3	2	32	0	1	8	56	1	0	.411	.315	2
Colbrunn, Greg, Fla.	R	.286	141	511	60	146	224	26	2	16	69	0	5	25	76	4	5	.438	.333	15
Galarraga, Andres, Col.	R	.304	159	626	119	190	376	39	3	47	150	0	8	40	157	18	8	.601	.357	44
Grace, Mark, ChiN	L	.331	142	547	88	181	249	39	1	9	75	0	6	62	41	2	3	.455	.396	19
Huskey, Butch, NYN	R	.278	118	414	43	115	180	16	2	15	60	0	4	27	77	1	2	.435	.319	11
Jefferies, Gregg, Phi.	B	.292	104	404	59	118	162	17	3	7	51	0	5	36	21	20	6	.401	.348	16
Johnson, Mark, Pit.	L	.274	127	343	55	94	157	24	0	13	47	0	4	44	64	6	4	.458	.361	10
Jordan, Kevin, Phi.	R	.282	43	131	15	37	56	10	0	3	12	3	2	5	20	2	1	.427	.309	0
Joyner, Wally, S.D.	L	.277	121	433	59	120	175	29	1	8	65	1	4	69	71	5	3	.404	.377	11
Karros, Eric, L.A.	R	.260	154	608	84	158	291	29	1	34	111	0	8	53	121	8	0	.479	.316	24
King, Jeff, Pit.	R	.271	155	591	91	160	294	36	4	30	111	1	8	70	95	15	1	.497	.346	27
Livingstone, Scott, S.D.	L	.297	102	172	20	51	63	4	1	2	20	0	0	9	22	0	1	.366	.331	1
Mabry, John, St.L	L	.297	151	543	63	161	234	30	2	13	74	3	5	37	84	3	2	.431	.342	16
Marrero, Oreste, L.A.	L	.375	10	8	2	3	4	1	0	0	1	0	0	1	3	0	0	.500	.444	-4
McCarty, David, S.F.	R	.217	91	175	16	38	59	3	0	6	24	0	2	18	43	2	1	.337	.294	0
McGriff, Fred, Atl.	L	.295	159	617	81	182	305	37	1	28	107	0	4	68	116	7	3	.494	.365	27
Morman, Russ, Fla.	R	.167	6	6	0	1	2	1	0	0	0	0	0	1	2	0	0	.333	.286	-4
Morris, Hal, Cin.	L	.313	142	528	82	165	253	32	4	16	80	5	6	50	76	7	5	.479	.374	21
Peltier, Dan, S.F.	L	.254	31	59	3	15	17	2	0	0	9	0	1	7	9	0	0	.288	.328	-3
Perez, Eduardo, Cin.	R	.222	18	36	8	8	17	0	0	3	5	0	0	5	9	0	0	.472	.317	-3
Petagine, Roberto, NYN	L	.232	50	99	10	23	38	3	0	4	17	1	1	9	27	0	2	.384	.313	-1
Phillips, J.R., S.F.-Phi.	L	.163	50	104	12	17	43	5	0	7	15	0	0	11	51	0	0	.413	.250	-1
Schall, Gene, Phi.	R	.273	28	66	7	18	31	5	1	2	10	0	0	12	15	0	0	.470	.392	-2
Segui, David, Mon.	B	.286	115	416	69	119	184	30	1	11	58	0	1	60	54	4	4	.442	.375	11
Thompson, Jason, S.D.	L	.224	13	49	4	11	21	4	0	2	6	0	1	1	14	0	0	.429	.235	-3
Wilson, Desi, S.F.	L	.271	41	118	10	32	40	2	0	2	12	0	0	12	27	0	2	.339	.338	-1
Young, Dmitri, St.L	B	.241	16	29	3	7	7	0	0	0	2	0	0	4	5	0	1	.241	.353	-4
Zuber, Jon, Phi.	L	.253	30	91	7	23	30	4	0	1	10	1	1	6	11	1	0	.330	.296	-2

National League second basemen

Name/Team	B	BA	G	AB	R	H	TB	2B	3B	HR	RBI	SH	SF	BB	SO	SB	CS	SLG	OBA	RV
Alfonzo, Edgardo, NYN	R	.261	123	368	36	96	127	15	2	4	40	9	5	25	56	2	0	.345	.304	4
Alicea, Luis, St.L	B	.258	129	380	54	98	145	26	3	5	42	4	6	52	78	11	3	.382	.350	8
Barberie, Bret, ChiN	B	.034	15	29	4	1	4	0	0	1	2	3	0	5	11	0	1	.138	.176	-5
Bates, Jason, Col.	B	.206	88	160	19	33	46	8	1	1	9	1	1	23	34	2	1	.287	.312	-4
Biggio, Craig, Hou.	R	.288	162	605	113	174	251	24	4	15	75	8	8	75	72	25	7	.415	.386	25
Boone, Bret, Cin.	R	.233	142	520	56	121	184	21	3	12	69	5	9	31	100	3	2	.354	.275	7
Canizaro, Jay, S.F.	R	.200	43	120	11	24	36	4	1	2	8	1	1	9	38	0	2	.300	.260	-4
Castellano, Pedro, Col.	R	.118	13	17	1	2	2	0	0	0	2	0	0	3	6	0	0	.118	.286	-4
Castillo, Luis, Fla.	R	.262	41	164	26	43	50	2	1	1	8	2	0	14	46	17	4	.305	.320	5
DeShields, Delino, L.A.	L	.224	154	581	75	130	173	12	8	5	41	2	5	53	124	48	11	.298	.287	18
Doster, David, Phi.	R	.267	39	105	14	28	39	8	0	1	8	1	0	7	21	0	0	.371	.313	-2
Fermin, Felix, ChiN	R	.125	11	16	4	2	3	1	0	0	1	1	0	2	0	0	0	.188	.222	-4
Fonville, Chad, L.A.	B	.204	103	201	34	41	47	4	1	0	13	3	0	17	31	7	2	.234	.266	-2
Gallego, Mike, St.L	R	.210	51	143	12	30	32	2	0	0	4	3	0	12	31	0	0	.224	.276	-5
Garcia, Carlos, Pit.	R	.285	101	390	66	111	155	18	4	6	44	3	2	23	58	16	6	.397	.329	13
Graffanino, Tony, Atl.	R	.174	22	46	7	8	11	1	1	0	2	0	1	4	13	0	0	.239	.250	-5
Grebeck, Craig, Fla.	R	.211	50	95	8	20	24	1	0	1	9	1	2	4	14	0	0	.253	.245	-4
Haney, Todd, ChiN	R	.134	49	82	11	11	12	1	0	0	3	2	1	7	15	1	0	.146	.200	-6
Hardtke, Jason, NYN	B	.193	19	57	3	11	16	5	0	0	6	0	0	2	12	0	0	.281	.233	-4
Holbert, Aaron, St.L	R	.000	1	3	0	0	0	0	0	0	0	0	0	0	0	0	0	.000	.000	-4
Lansing, Mike, Mon.	R	.285	159	641	99	183	260	40	2	11	53	9	1	44	85	23	8	.406	.341	21
Lemke, Mark, Atl.	B	.255	135	498	64	127	159	17	0	5	37	5	6	53	48	5	2	.319	.323	4
Liriano, Nelson, Pit.	B	.267	112	217	23	58	85	14	2	3	30	0	3	14	22	2	0	.392	.308	2
Milliard, Ralph, Fla.	R	.161	24	62	7	10	12	2	0	0	1	0	1	14	16	2	0	.194	.312	-4
Morandini, Mickey, Phi.	L	.250	140	539	64	135	180	24	6	3	32	5	4	49	87	26	5	.334	.321	11
Mordecai, Mike, Atl.	R	.241	66	108	12	26	37	5	0	2	8	4	1	9	24	1	0	.343	.297	-2
Reed, Jody, S.D.	R	.244	146	495	45	121	147	20	0	2	49	5	6	59	53	2	5	.297	.325	2
Sandberg, Ryne, ChiN	R	.244	150	554	85	135	246	28	4	25	92	1	5	54	116	12	8	.444	.316	19
Scarsone, Steve, S.F.	R	.219	105	283	28	62	91	12	1	5	23	8	1	25	91	2	3	.322	.286	-1
Shipley, Craig, S.D.	R	.315	33	92	13	29	37	5	0	1	7	1	2	2	15	7	0	.402	.337	1
Stankiewicz, Andy, Mon.	R	.286	64	77	12	22	29	5	1	0	9	1	1	6	12	1	0	.377	.356	-2
Thompson, Robby, S.F.	R	.211	63	227	35	48	76	11	1	5	21	3	0	24	69	2	2	.335	.301	-1
Veras, Quilvio, Fla.	B	.253	73	253	40	64	86	8	1	4	14	1	1	51	42	8	8	.340	.381	2
Vizcaino, Jose, NYN	B	.303	96	363	47	110	137	12	6	1	32	6	2	28	58	9	5	.377	.356	8
Young, Eric, Col.	R	.324	141	568	113	184	239	23	4	8	74	2	5	47	31	53	19	.421	.393	39

National League third basemen

Name/Team	B	BA	G	AB	R	H	TB	2B	3B	HR	RBI	SH	SF	BB	SO	SB	CS	SLG	OBA	RV
Andrews, Shane, Mon.	R	.227	127	375	43	85	161	15	2	19	64	0	2	35	119	3	1	.429	.295	9
Arias, Alex, Fla.	R	.277	100	224	27	62	86	11	2	3	26	1	1	17	28	2	0	.384	.335	2
Batiste, Kim, S.F.	R	.208	54	130	17	27	42	6	0	3	11	0	1	5	33	3	3	.323	.235	-2
Battle, Howard, Phi.	R	.000	5	5	0	0	0	0	0	0	0	0	0	0	2	0	0	.000	.000	-4
Bell, David, St.L	R	.214	62	145	12	31	40	6	0	1	9	0	1	10	22	1	1	.276	.268	-4
Berry, Sean, Hou.	R	.281	132	431	55	121	212	38	1	17	95	2	4	23	58	12	6	.492	.328	20
Blowers, Mike, L.A.	R	.265	92	317	31	84	125	19	2	6	38	0	3	37	77	0	0	.394	.341	3
Booty, Josh, Fla.	R	.500	2	2	1	1	1	0	0	0	0	0	0	0	0	0	0	.500	.500	-4
Branson, Jeff, Cin.	L	.244	129	311	34	76	127	16	4	9	37	7	3	31	67	2	0	.408	.312	3
Busch, Mike, L.A.	R	.217	38	83	8	18	34	4	0	4	17	0	0	5	33	0	0	.410	.261	-1
Caminiti, Ken, S.D.	B	.326	146	546	109	178	339	37	2	40	130	0	10	78	99	11	5	.621	.408	38
Castilla, Vinny, Col.	R	.304	160	629	97	191	345	34	0	40	113	0	4	35	88	7	2	.548	.343	33
Espinoza, Alvaro, NYN	R	.306	48	134	19	41	64	7	2	4	16	5	1	4	19	0	2	.478	.324	1
Franco, Matt, NYN	L	.194	14	31	3	6	10	1	0	1	2	0	1	1	5	0	0	.323	.235	-4
Gaetti, Gary, St.L	R	.274	141	522	71	143	247	27	4	23	80	4	5	35	97	2	2	.473	.326	16
Gomez, Leo, ChiN	R	.238	136	362	44	86	156	19	0	17	56	3	2	53	94	1	4	.431	.344	7
Greene, Willie, Cin.	L	.244	115	287	48	70	142	5	5	19	63	1	1	36	88	0	1	.495	.327	9
Hajek, Dave, Hou.	R	.300	8	10	3	3	4	1	0	0	0	0	0	2	0	0	0	.400	.417	-4
Hansen, Dave, L.A.	L	.221	80	104	7	23	24	1	0	0	6	0	1	11	22	0	0	.231	.293	-4
Harris, Lenny, Cin.	L	.285	125	302	33	86	122	17	2	5	32	6	3	21	31	14	6	.404	.330	10
Hayes, Charlie, Pit.	R	.248	128	459	51	114	169	21	2	10	62	2	3	36	78	6	0	.368	.301	8
Jones, Chipper, Atl.	B	.309	157	598	114	185	317	32	5	30	110	1	7	87	88	14	1	.530	.393	32
Kent, Jeff, NYN	R	.290	89	335	45	97	146	20	1	9	39	1	3	21	56	4	3	.436	.331	8
Magadan, Dave, ChiN	L	.254	78	169	23	43	62	10	0	3	17	1	2	29	23	0	2	.367	.360	-1
Mueller, Bill, S.F.	B	.330	55	200	31	66	83	15	1	0	19	1	2	24	26	0	0	.415	.401	2
Pendleton, Terry, Fla.-Atl.	B	.238	153	568	51	135	196	26	1	11	75	1	5	41	111	2	3	.345	.290	3
Rolen, Scott, Phi.	R	.254	37	130	10	33	52	7	0	4	18	0	2	13	27	0	2	.400	.322	-1
Sabo, Chris, Cin.	R	.254	54	125	15	32	50	7	1	3	16	1	0	18	27	2	0	.400	.354	0
Schu, Rick, Mon.	R	.000	1	4	0	0	0	0	0	0	0	0	0	0	0	0	0	.000	.000	-4
Shumpert, Terry, ChiN	R	.226	27	31	5	7	14	1	0	2	6	0	1	2	11	0	1	.452	.286	-3
Silvestri, Dave, Mon.	R	.204	86	162	16	33	40	4	0	1	17	3	1	34	41	2	1	.247	.340	-3
Spiers, Bill, Hou.	L	.252	122	218	27	55	85	10	1	6	26	1	1	20	34	7	0	.390	.320	4
Sveum, Dale, Pit.	R	.353	12	34	9	12	20	5	0	1	5	0	0	6	6	0	0	.588	.450	-2
Tatum, Jim, S.D.	R	.000	5	3	0	0	0	0	0	0	0	0	0	0	1	0	0	.000	.000	-4
Wallach, Tim, L.A.	R	.228	45	162	14	37	54	3	1	4	22	0	0	12	32	0	1	.333	.286	-1
Wehner, John, Pit.	R	.259	86	139	19	36	53	9	1	2	13	2	0	8	22	1	5	.381	.299	-1
Williams, Matt, S.F.	R	.302	105	404	69	122	206	16	1	22	85	0	6	39	91	1	2	.510	.367	18
Zeile, Todd, Phi.	R	.268	134	500	61	134	218	24	0	20	80	0	4	67	88	1	1	.436	.353	14

National League shortstops

Name/Team	B	BA	G	AB	R	H	TB	2B	3B	HR	RBI	SH	SF	BB	SO	SB	CS	SLG	OBA	RV
Abbott, Kurt, Fla.	R	.253	109	320	37	81	137	18	7	8	33	4	0	22	99	3	3	.428	.307	4
Aurilia, Rich, S.F.	R	.239	105	318	27	76	94	7	1	3	26	6	2	25	52	4	1	.296	.295	1
Bell, Jay, Pit.	R	.250	151	527	65	132	206	29	3	13	71	6	6	54	108	6	4	.391	.323	11
Belliard, Rafael, Atl.	R	.169	87	142	9	24	31	7	0	0	3	3	1	2	22	3	1	.218	.179	-5
Benjamin, Mike, Phi.	R	.223	35	103	13	23	42	5	1	4	13	1	0	12	21	3	1	.408	.316	-1
Blauser, Jeff, Atl.	R	.245	83	265	48	65	111	14	1	10	35	0	1	40	54	6	0	.419	.356	5
Castro, Juan, L.A.	R	.197	70	132	16	26	37	5	3	0	5	4	0	10	27	1	0	.280	.254	-5
Cedeno, Andjr, S.D.-Hou.	R	.231	52	156	11	36	49	2	1	3	18	0	1	11	33	3	2	.314	.284	1
Clayton, Royce, St.L	R	.277	129	491	64	136	182	20	4	6	35	2	4	33	89	33	15	.371	.321	19
Delgado, Wilson, S.F.	B	.364	6	22	3	8	8	0	0	0	2	0	0	1	5	1	0	.364	.440	-3
Dunston, Shawon, S.F.	R	.300	82	287	27	86	117	12	2	5	25	5	1	13	40	8	0	.408	.331	7
Gagne, Greg, L.A.	R	.255	128	428	48	109	156	13	2	10	55	4	3	50	93	4	2	.364	.333	8
Giovanola, Ed, Atl.	L	.232	43	82	10	19	21	2	0	0	7	2	1	8	13	1	0	.256	.304	-3
Gomez, Chris, S.D.	R	.262	89	328	32	86	113	16	1	3	29	3	2	39	64	2	2	.345	.349	2
Grudzielanek, Mark, Mon.	R	.306	153	657	99	201	261	34	4	6	49	1	3	26	83	33	7	.397	.340	26
Guerrero, Wilton, L.A.	R	.000	5	2	1	0	0	0	0	0	0	0	0	0	2	0	0	.000	.000	-4
Gutierrez, Ricky, Hou.	R	.284	89	218	28	62	75	8	1	1	15	4	1	23	42	6	1	.344	.359	2
Hernandez, Jose, ChiN	R	.242	131	331	52	80	126	14	1	10	41	5	2	24	97	4	0	.381	.293	5
Larkin, Barry, Cin.	R	.298	152	517	117	154	293	32	4	33	89	0	7	96	52	36	10	.567	.410	38
Lopez, Luis M., S.D.	B	.180	63	139	10	25	34	3	0	2	11	1	1	9	35	0	0	.245	.233	-4
Martinez, Pablo, Atl.	B	.500	4	2	1	1	1	0	0	0	0	1	0	0	0	0	1	.500	.500	-4
Miller, Orlando, Hou.	R	.256	139	468	43	120	195	26	2	15	58	1	3	14	116	3	7	.417	.291	9
Ordonez, Rey, NYN	R	.257	151	502	51	129	152	12	4	1	30	4	1	22	53	1	3	.303	.289	1
Perez, Neifi, Col.	B	.156	17	45	4	7	9	2	0	0	3	1	0	0	8	2	2	.200	.156	-4
Relaford, Desi, Phi.	B	.175	15	40	2	7	9	2	0	0	1	1	0	3	9	1	0	.225	.233	-4
Renteria, Edgar, Fla.	R	.309	106	431	68	133	172	18	3	5	31	2	3	33	68	16	2	.399	.358	14
Sanchez, Rey, ChiN	R	.211	95	289	28	61	73	9	0	1	12	8	2	22	42	7	1	.253	.272	-2

National League shortstops

Name/Team	B	BA	G	AB	R	H	TB	2B	3B	HR	RBI	SH	SF	BB	SO	SB	CS	SLG	OBA	RV
Sefcik, Kevin, Phi.	R	.284	44	116	10	33	44	5	3	0	9	1	2	9	16	3	0	.379	.341	-1
Smith, Ozzie, St.L	B	.282	82	227	36	64	84	10	2	2	18	7	0	25	9	7	5	.370	.358	3
Stocker, Kevin, Phi.	B	.254	119	394	46	100	149	22	6	5	41	3	4	43	89	6	4	.378	.336	5
Weiss, Walt, Col.	B	.282	155	517	89	146	194	20	2	8	48	14	6	80	78	10	2	.375	.381	12

National League outfielders

Name/Team	B	BA	G	AB	R	H	TB	2B	3B	HR	RBI	SH	SF	BB	SO	SB	CS	SLG	OBA	RV
Abreu, Bob, Hou.	L	.227	15	22	1	5	6	1	0	0	1	0	0	2	3	0	0	.273	.292	-4
Allensworth, J., Pit.	L	.262	61	229	32	60	87	9	3	4	31	2	2	23	50	11	6	.380	.337	6
Alou, Moises, Mon.	R	.281	143	540	87	152	247	28	2	21	96	0	7	49	83	9	4	.457	.339	21
Amaro, Ruben Jr., Phi.	B	.316	61	117	14	37	53	10	0	2	15	1	0	9	18	0	0	.453	.380	0
Anthony, Eric, Cin.-Col.	L	.243	79	185	32	45	89	8	0	12	22	0	1	32	56	0	2	.481	.353	3
Ashley, Billy, L.A.	R	.200	71	110	18	22	53	2	1	9	25	0	1	21	44	0	0	.482	.331	0
Barron, Tony, Mon.	R	.000	1	1	0	0	0	0	0	0	0	0	0	0	1	0	0	.000	.000	-4
Bautista, Danny, Atl.	R	.150	17	20	1	3	3	0	0	0	1	0	0	2	5	0	0	.150	.261	-4
Beamon, Trey, Pit.	L	.216	24	51	7	11	13	2	0	0	6	1	0	4	6	1	1	.255	.273	-3
Bell, Derek, Hou.	R	.263	158	627	84	165	262	40	3	17	113	0	9	40	123	29	3	.418	.311	28
Benard, Marvin, S.F.	L	.248	135	488	89	121	161	17	4	5	27	6	1	59	84	25	11	.330	.333	11
Benitez, Yamil, Mon.	R	.167	11	12	0	2	2	0	0	0	2	0	0	0	4	0	0	.167	.167	-4
Bichette, Dante, Col.	R	.313	159	633	114	198	336	39	3	31	141	0	10	45	105	31	12	.531	.359	44
Bonds, Barry, S.F.	L	.308	158	517	122	159	318	27	3	42	129	0	6	151	76	40	7	.615	.461	48
Bradshaw, Terry, St.L	L	.333	15	21	4	7	8	1	0	0	3	1	0	3	2	0	1	.381	.417	-3
Brooks, Jerry, Fla.	R	.400	8	5	2	2	4	0	1	0	3	0	0	1	1	0	0	.800	.571	-4
Brumfield, Jacob, Pit.	R	.250	29	80	11	20	35	9	0	2	8	0	1	5	17	3	1	.438	.291	-1
Bullett, Scott, ChiN	L	.212	109	165	26	35	49	5	0	3	16	1	1	10	54	7	3	.297	.256	0
Burks, Ellis, Col.	R	.344	156	613	142	211	392	45	8	40	128	3	2	61	114	32	6	.639	.408	51
Butler, Brett, L.A.	L	.267	34	131	22	35	38	1	1	0	8	1	3	9	22	8	3	.290	.313	1
Cangelosi, John, Hou.	B	.263	108	262	49	69	91	11	4	1	16	1	1	44	41	17	9	.347	.378	6
Cedeno, Roger, L.A.	B	.246	86	211	26	52	71	11	1	2	18	2	0	24	47	5	1	.336	.326	1
Clark, Dave, Pit.-L.A.	L	.270	107	226	28	61	101	12	2	8	36	0	1	34	53	2	1	.447	.364	7
Cockrell, Alan, Col.	R	.250	9	8	0	2	3	1	0	0	2	0	1	0	4	0	0	.375	.222	-4
Coleman, Vince, Cin.	B	.155	33	84	10	13	19	1	1	1	4	1	0	9	31	12	2	.226	.237	0
Conine, Jeff, Fla.	R	.293	157	597	84	175	289	32	2	26	95	0	7	62	121	1	4	.484	.360	22
Cruz, Jacob, S.F.	L	.234	33	77	10	18	30	3	0	3	10	1	0	12	24	0	1	.390	.352	-2
Cummings, Midre, Pit.	L	.224	24	85	11	19	33	3	1	3	7	1	1	0	16	0	0	.388	.221	-3
Curtis, Chad, L.A.	R	.212	43	104	20	22	33	5	0	2	9	0	0	17	15	2	1	.317	.322	-2
Dascenzo, Doug, S.D.	B	.111	21	9	3	1	1	0	0	0	0	0	0	1	2	0	1	.111	.200	-4
Daulton, Darren, Phi.	L	.167	5	12	3	2	2	0	0	0	0	0	0	7	5	0	0	.167	.500	-4
Davis, Eric, Cin.	R	.287	129	415	81	119	217	20	0	26	83	1	4	70	121	23	9	.523	.394	27
Dawson, Andre, Fla.	R	.276	42	58	6	16	24	2	0	2	14	0	0	2	13	0	0	.414	.311	-1
Deer, Rob, S.D.	R	.180	25	50	9	9	24	3	0	4	9	0	0	14	30	0	0	.480	.359	-3
Dye, Jermaine, Atl.	R	.281	98	292	32	82	134	16	0	12	37	0	3	8	67	1	4	.459	.304	7
Dykstra, Lenny, Phi.	L	.261	40	134	21	35	56	6	3	3	13	1	1	26	25	3	1	.418	.387	0
Echevarria, Angel, Col.	R	.286	26	21	2	6	6	0	0	0	6	0	2	2	5	0	0	.286	.346	-3
Eisenreich, Jim, Phi.	L	.361	113	338	45	122	161	24	3	3	41	0	3	31	32	11	1	.476	.413	15
Everett, Carl, NYN	B	.240	101	192	29	46	59	8	1	1	16	1	1	21	53	6	0	.307	.326	0
Finley, Steve, S.D.	L	.298	161	655	126	195	348	45	9	30	95	1	5	56	87	22	8	.531	.354	33
Floyd, Cliff, Mon.	L	.242	117	227	29	55	96	15	4	6	26	1	3	30	52	7	1	.423	.340	3
Gant, Ron, St.L	R	.246	122	419	74	103	211	14	2	30	82	1	4	73	98	13	4	.504	.359	20
Garcia, Karim, L.A.	L	.000	1	1	0	0	0	0	0	0	0	0	0	0	1	0	0	.000	.000	-4
Gibralter, Steve, Cin.	R	.000	2	2	0	0	0	0	0	0	0	0	0	0	2	0	0	.000	.000	-4
Gilkey, Bernard, NYN	R	.317	153	571	108	181	321	44	3	30	117	0	8	73	125	17	9	.562	.393	35
Glanville, Doug, ChiN	R	.241	49	83	10	20	30	5	1	1	10	2	1	3	11	2	0	.361	.264	-2
Gonzalez, Luis, ChiN	L	.271	146	483	70	131	214	30	4	15	79	1	6	61	49	9	6	.443	.354	16
Goodwin, Curtis, Cin.	L	.228	49	136	20	31	34	3	0	0	5	1	0	19	34	15	6	.250	.323	2
Grissom, Marquis, Atl.	R	.308	158	671	106	207	328	32	10	23	74	4	4	41	73	28	11	.489	.349	33
Guerrero, Vladimir, Mon.	R	.185	9	27	2	5	8	0	0	1	1	0	0	0	3	0	0	.296	.185	-4
Gwynn, Chris, S.D.	L	.178	81	90	8	16	23	4	0	1	10	0	0	10	28	0	0	.256	.260	-4
Gwynn, Tony, S.D.	L	.353	116	451	67	159	199	27	2	3	50	1	6	39	17	11	4	.441	.400	18
Hall, Mel, S.F.	L	.120	25	25	3	3	3	0	0	0	5	0	1	1	4	0	0	.120	.148	-6
Henderson, Rickey, S.D.	R	.241	148	465	110	112	160	17	2	9	29	0	2	125	90	37	15	.344	.410	17
Hill, Glenallen, S.F.	R	.280	98	379	56	106	189	26	0	19	67	0	3	33	95	6	3	.499	.344	15
Hollandsworth, Todd, L.A.	L	.291	149	478	64	139	209	26	4	12	59	3	2	41	93	21	6	.437	.348	20
Howard, Thomas, Cin.	L	.272	121	360	50	98	155	19	10	6	42	2	4	17	51	6	5	.431	.307	7
Hubbard, Trenidad, Col.-S.F.	R	.213	55	89	15	19	34	5	2	2	14	0	0	11	27	2	0	.382	.307	-1
Hunter, Brian L., Hou.	R	.276	132	526	74	145	191	27	2	5	35	1	7	17	92	35	9	.363	.297	19
Incaviglia, Pete, Phi.	R	.234	99	269	33	63	122	7	2	16	42	0	0	30	82	2	0	.454	.318	6
Javier, Stan, S.F.	B	.270	71	274	44	74	105	25	0	2	22	5	0	25	51	14	2	.383	.336	6

National League outfielders

Name/Team	B	BA	G	AB	R	H	TB	2B	3B	HR	RBI	SH	SF	BB	SO	SB	CS	SLG	OBA	RV
Jennings, Robin, ChiN	L	.224	31	58	7	13	18	5	0	0	4	0	0	3	9	1	0	.310	.274	-4
Johnson, Lance, NYN	L	.333	160	682	117	227	327	31	21	9	69	3	5	33	40	50	12	.479	.362	41
Jones, Andruw, Atl.	R	.217	31	106	11	23	47	7	1	5	13	0	0	7	29	3	0	.443	.265	0
Jones, Chris C., NYN	R	.242	89	149	22	36	55	7	0	4	18	0	0	12	42	1	0	.369	.307	-1
Jones, Dax, S.F.	R	.172	34	58	7	10	17	0	2	1	7	0	1	8	12	2	2	.293	.269	-3
Jones, Terry, Col.	B	.300	12	10	6	3	3	0	0	0	1	0	1	0	3	0	0	.300	.273	-4
Jordan, Brian, St.L	R	.310	140	513	82	159	248	36	1	17	104	2	9	29	84	22	5	.483	.349	30
Justice, David, Atl.	L	.321	40	140	23	45	72	9	0	6	25	0	2	21	22	1	1	.514	.409	4
Kelly, Mike, Cin.	R	.184	19	49	5	9	16	4	0	1	7	0	0	9	11	4	0	.327	.333	-2
Kieschnick, Brooks, ChiNL	.345	25	29	6	10	15	2	0	1	6	0	0	3	8	0	0	.517	.406	-2
Kingery, Mike, Pit.	L	.246	117	276	32	68	93	12	2	3	27	1	3	23	29	2	1	.337	.304	1
Kirby, Wayne, L.A.	L	.271	65	188	23	51	66	10	1	1	11	1	1	17	17	4	2	.351	.333	0
Klesko, Ryan, Atl.	L	.282	153	528	90	149	280	21	4	34	93	0	4	68	129	6	3	.530	.364	24
Lankford, Ray, St.L	L	.275	149	545	100	150	265	36	8	21	86	1	7	79	133	35	7	.486	.366	30
Lukachyk, Rob, Mon.	L	.000	2	2	0	0	0	0	0	0	0	0	0	0	1	0	0	.000	.000	-4
Magee, Wendell, Phi.	R	.204	38	142	9	29	42	7	0	2	14	0	0	9	33	0	0	.296	.252	-3
Martin, Al, Pit.	L	.300	155	630	101	189	285	40	1	18	72	1	7	54	116	38	12	.452	.354	33
Martinez, Manny, Phi.	R	.222	13	36	2	8	12	0	2	0	0	1	0	1	11	2	1	.333	.263	-3
May, Derrick, Hou.	L	.251	109	259	24	65	98	12	3	5	33	0	3	30	33	2	2	.378	.330	2
McCracken, Quinton, Col.	B	.290	124	283	50	82	116	13	6	3	40	12	1	32	62	17	6	.410	.363	11
McGee, Willie, St.L	B	.307	123	309	52	95	129	15	2	5	41	1	1	18	60	5	2	.417	.348	9
McMillon, Billy, Fla.	L	.216	28	51	4	11	11	0	0	0	4	0	0	5	14	0	0	.216	.286	-4
McRae, Brian, ChiN	B	.276	157	624	111	172	265	32	5	17	66	2	5	73	84	37	9	.425	.360	28
Mejia, Miguel, St.L	R	.087	45	23	10	2	2	0	0	0	0	0	0	0	10	6	3	.087	.087	-2
Merced, Orlando, Pit.	L	.287	120	453	69	130	207	24	1	17	80	0	3	51	74	8	4	.457	.357	18
Mitchell, Keith, Cin.	R	.267	11	15	2	4	8	1	0	1	3	0	0	1	3	0	0	.533	.313	-3
Mitchell, Kevin, Cin.	R	.325	37	114	18	37	66	11	0	6	26	0	1	26	16	0	0	.579	.447	3
Mondesi, Raul, L.A.	R	.297	157	634	98	188	314	40	7	24	88	0	2	32	122	14	7	.495	.334	27
Montgomery, Ray, Hou.	R	.214	12	14	4	3	7	1	0	1	4	0	0	1	5	0	0	.500	.267	-3
Mottola, Chad, Cin.	R	.215	35	79	10	17	29	3	0	3	6	0	0	6	16	2	2	.367	.271	-2
Mouton, James, Hou.	R	.263	122	300	40	79	105	15	1	3	34	2	3	38	55	21	9	.350	.343	10
Murray, Glenn, Phi.	R	.196	38	97	8	19	28	3	0	2	6	0	0	7	36	1	1	.289	.250	-4
Newfield, Marc, S.D.	R	.251	84	191	27	48	74	11	0	5	26	0	3	16	44	1	1	.387	.311	1
Obando, Sherman, Mon.	R	.247	89	178	30	44	77	9	0	8	22	0	1	22	48	2	0	.433	.332	2
Ochoa, Alex, NYN	R	.294	82	282	37	83	120	19	3	4	33	0	3	17	30	4	3	.426	.336	6
Orsulak, Joe, Fla.	L	.221	120	217	23	48	62	6	1	2	19	0	1	16	38	1	1	.286	.274	-2
Otero, Ricky, Phi.	B	.273	104	411	54	112	143	11	7	2	32	0	2	34	30	16	10	.348	.330	9
Owens, Eric, Cin.	R	.200	88	205	26	41	47	6	0	0	9	1	2	23	38	16	2	.229	.281	1
Parker, Rick, L.A.	R	.286	16	14	2	4	5	1	0	0	1	0	0	0	2	1	0	.357	.333	-3
Polonia, Luis, Atl.	L	.419	22	31	3	13	13	0	0	0	2	0	1	1	3	1	1	.419	.424	-2
Pulliam, Harvey, Col.	R	.133	10	15	2	2	2	0	0	0	0	0	0	2	6	0	0	.133	.235	-4
Roberson, Kevin, NYN	B	.222	27	36	8	8	18	1	0	3	9	0	2	7	17	0	0	.500	.348	-2
Rodriguez, Henry, Mon.	L	.276	145	532	81	147	299	42	1	36	103	0	4	37	160	2	0	.562	.325	24
Sanders, Reggie, Cin.	R	.251	81	287	49	72	133	17	1	14	33	0	1	44	86	24	8	.463	.353	14
Santangelo, F.P., Mon.	B	.277	152	393	54	109	160	20	5	7	56	9	5	49	61	5	2	.407	.369	9
Sheffield, Gary, Fla.	R	.314	161	519	118	163	324	33	1	42	120	0	6	142	66	16	9	.624	.465	38
Simms, Mike, Hou.	R	.176	49	68	6	12	19	2	1	1	8	0	0	4	16	1	0	.279	.233	-4
Smith, Dwight, Atl.	L	.203	101	153	16	31	45	5	0	3	16	0	1	17	42	1	3	.294	.285	-3
Sosa, Sammy, ChiN	R	.273	124	498	84	136	281	21	2	40	100	0	4	34	134	18	5	.564	.323	31
Steverson, Todd, S.D.	R	.000	1	1	0	0	0	0	0	0	0	0	0	0	1	0	0	.000	.000	-4
Sweeney, Mark, St.L	L	.265	98	170	32	45	63	9	0	3	22	5	0	33	29	3	0	.371	.387	1
Tavarez, Jesus, Fla.	B	.219	98	114	14	25	28	3	0	0	6	3	0	7	18	5	1	.246	.264	-2
Thompson, Milt, L.A.-Col.	L	.106	62	66	3	7	9	2	0	0	3	0	0	7	13	1	1	.136	.192	-4
Timmons, Ozzie, ChiN	R	.200	65	140	18	28	53	4	0	7	16	1	0	15	30	1	0	.379	.282	-1
Tinsley, Lee, Phi.	B	.135	31	52	1	7	7	0	0	0	2	1	0	4	22	2	4	.135	.196	-4
Tomberlin, Andy, NYN	L	.258	63	66	12	17	30	4	0	3	10	0	0	9	27	0	0	.455	.355	-2
Valdes, Pedro, ChiN	L	.125	9	8	2	1	2	1	0	0	1	0	0	1	5	0	0	.250	.222	-4
Vander Wal, John, Col.	L	.252	104	151	20	38	63	6	2	5	31	0	2	19	38	2	2	.417	.335	2
Vaughn, Greg, S.D.	R	.206	43	141	20	29	64	3	1	10	22	0	0	24	31	4	1	.454	.329	2
Walker, Larry, Col.	L	.276	83	272	58	75	155	18	4	18	58	0	3	20	58	18	2	.570	.342	18
Walton, Jerome, Atl.	R	.340	37	47	9	16	24	5	0	1	4	1	2	5	10	0	0	.511	.389	-2
White, Devon, Fla.	B	.274	146	552	77	151	251	37	6	17	84	4	9	38	99	22	6	.455	.325	23
White, Rondell, Mon.	R	.293	88	334	35	98	143	19	4	6	41	0	1	22	53	14	6	.428	.340	12
Whiten, Mark, Phi.-Atl.	B	.243	96	272	45	66	111	13	1	10	38	0	1	49	87	15	8	.408	.359	5
Williams, Keith, S.F.	R	.250	9	20	0	5	5	0	0	0	0	0	0	0	6	0	0	.250	.250	-4
Womack, Tony, Pit.	L	.333	17	30	11	10	15	3	1	0	7	3	0	6	1	2	0	.500	.459	-2

321

National League relief pitchers (batting)

Name/Team	B	BA	G	AB	R	H	TB	2B	3B	HR	RBI	SH	SF	BB	SO	SB	CS	SLG	OBA
Adams, Terry, ChiN	R	.000	69	6	0	0	0	0	0	0	0	0	0	1	3	0	0	.000	.143
Alston, Garvin, Col.	R	.000	6	1	0	0	0	0	0	0	0	0	0	0	0	0	0	.000	.000
Alvarez, Tavo, Mon.	R	.500	11	4	0	2	2	0	0	0	0	1	0	1	0	0	0	.500	.500
Bailey, Cory, St.L	R	.000	51	1	2	0	0	0	0	0	0	1	0	2	0	0	0	.000	.667
Bailey, Roger, Col.	R	.263	24	19	4	5	10	0	1	1	5	3	0	3	4	0	0	.526	.364
Batchelor, Rich, St.L	R	.000	11	1	0	0	0	0	0	0	0	0	0	0	1	0	0	.000	.000
Bautista, Jose, S.F.	R	.111	37	9	1	1	1	0	0	0	0	1	0	0	4	0	0	.111	.111
Beck, Rod, S.F.	R	.333	63	3	0	1	1	0	0	0	1	0	0	0	2	0	0	.333	.333
Bergman, Sean, S.D.	R	.100	43	30	1	3	6	0	0	1	5	0	0	0	9	0	0	.200	.100
Bielecki, Mike, Atl.	R	.100	40	10	1	1	1	0	0	0	1	0	0	2	5	0	0	.100	.250
Blair, Willie, S.D.	R	.000	60	3	0	0	0	0	0	0	0	0	0	0	1	0	0	.000	.000
Blazier, Ron, Phi.	R	1.000	27	1	0	1	1	0	0	0	0	0	0	0	0	0	0	1.000	1.000
Boever, Joe, Pit.	R	.000	13	1	0	0	0	0	0	0	0	0	0	0	1	0	0	.000	.000
Borbon, Pedro Jr., Atl.	R	1.000	43	1	0	1	1	0	0	0	0	0	0	0	0	0	0	1.000	1.000
Borland, Toby, Phi.	R	.000	69	4	0	0	0	0	0	0	0	0	0	0	2	0	0	.000	.000
Borowski, Joe, Atl.	R	.000	22	2	0	0	0	0	0	0	0	1	0	0	2	0	0	.000	.000
Bottalico, Ricky, Phi.	L	.333	61	3	0	1	2	1	0	0	0	0	0	0	2	0	0	.667	.333
Bottenfield, Kent, ChiN	R	.500	48	2	0	1	1	0	0	0	0	1	0	0	1	0	0	.500	.500
Bourgeois, Steve, S.F.	R	.273	15	11	1	3	5	2	0	0	1	1	0	2	2	0	0	.455	.385
Brantley, Jeff, Cin.	R	.000	66	1	0	0	0	0	0	0	0	1	0	0	0	0	0	.000	.000
Brocail, Doug, Hou.	L	.000	25	11	0	0	0	0	0	0	0	0	0	0	4	0	0	.000	.000
Burke, John, Col.	B	.500	11	2	0	1	1	0	0	0	1	0	0	0	0	0	0	.500	.500
Byrd, Paul, NYN	R	.000	38	2	0	0	0	0	0	0	0	0	0	0	0	0	0	.000	.000
Campbell, Mike, ChiN	R	.364	13	11	2	4	6	2	0	0	1	1	0	0	5	0	0	.545	.364
Carlson, Dan, S.F.	R	.000	5	1	0	0	0	0	0	0	0	0	0	0	0	0	0	.000	.000
Carrasco, Hector, Cin.	R	.200	56	5	0	1	1	0	0	0	0	0	0	0	4	0	0	.200	.200
Christiansen, Jason, Pit.	R	.000	33	4	0	0	0	0	0	0	0	1	0	0	4	0	0	.000	.000
Clontz, Brad, Atl.	R	.000	81	2	1	0	0	0	0	0	0	1	0	2	2	0	0	.000	.500
Cooke, Steve, Pit.	R	.000	3	1	0	0	0	0	0	0	0	0	0	0	0	0	0	.000	.000
Cordova, Francisco, Pit.	R	.125	59	16	1	2	2	0	0	0	2	2	0	0	7	0	0	.125	.125
Creek, Doug, S.F.	L	.000	63	1	0	0	0	0	0	0	0	1	0	0	1	0	0	.000	.000
Daal, Omar, Mon.	L	.000	64	11	0	0	0	0	0	0	0	0	0	0	5	0	0	.000	.000
DeLucia, Rich, S.F.	R	.250	56	4	1	1	1	0	0	0	0	0	0	1	0	0	0	.250	.400
Dessens, Elmer, Pit.	R	.400	15	5	1	2	2	0	0	0	2	0	0	0	0	0	0	.400	.400
Dewey, Mark, S.F.	R	.000	78	7	0	0	0	0	0	0	0	0	0	1	3	0	0	.000	.125
DiPoto, Jerry, NYN	R	.000	57	1	0	0	0	0	0	0	0	0	0	0	1	0	0	.000	.000
Dishman, Glnn, S.D.-Phi.	R	---	7	0	0	0	0	0	0	0	0	2	0	0	0	0	0	---	---
Dreifort, Darren, L.A.	R	.000	20	3	0	0	0	0	0	0	0	0	0	0	2	0	0	.000	.000
Dyer, Mike, Mon.	R	.000	70	7	0	0	0	0	0	0	0	0	0	0	4	0	0	.000	.000
Eckersley, Dennis, St.L	R	.000	63	1	0	0	0	0	0	0	0	0	0	0	0	0	0	.000	.000
Eischen, Joey, L.A.	L	.000	28	6	0	0	0	0	0	0	0	0	0	0	2	0	0	.000	.000
Ericks, John, Pit.	R	.000	28	5	0	0	0	0	0	0	0	0	0	0	1	0	0	.000	.000
Florie, Bryce, S.D.	R	.000	39	3	0	0	0	0	0	0	0	0	0	0	1	0	0	.000	.000
Fossas, Tony, St.L	L	.000	65	1	0	0	0	0	0	0	0	0	0	0	0	0	0	.000	.000
Franco, John, NYN	L	.000	51	1	0	0	0	0	0	0	0	0	0	1	0	0	0	.000	.000
Guthrie, Mark, L.A.	B	.000	66	3	0	0	0	0	0	0	0	0	0	0	0	0	0	.000	.000
Habyan, John, Col.	R	.000	19	3	0	0	0	0	0	0	0	0	0	1	1	0	0	.000	.250
Hammond, Chris, Fla.	L	.067	38	15	1	1	1	0	0	0	0	2	0	1	7	0	0	.067	.125
Hartgraves, D., Hou.-Atl.	R	.000	39	1	0	0	0	0	0	0	0	1	0	0	0	0	0	.000	.000
Hawblitzel, Ryan, Col.	R	.000	8	1	0	0	0	0	0	0	0	0	0	0	0	0	0	.000	.000
Henry, Doug, NY-N	R	.000	58	5	0	0	0	0	0	0	0	0	0	0	0	0	0	.000	.000
Hernandez, Livan, Fla.	R	1.000	1	1	1	1	1	0	0	0	0	0	0	0	0	0	0	1.000	1.000
Hernandez, X., Cin.-Hou.	L	.000	61	2	0	0	0	0	0	0	0	1	0	0	1	0	0	.000	.000
Hoffman, Trevor, S.D.	R	.000	70	8	0	0	0	0	0	0	0	1	0	0	4	0	0	.000	.000
Holmes, Darren, Col.	R	.000	62	2	0	0	0	0	0	0	0	0	0	1	1	0	0	.000	.333
Holt, Chris, Hou.	R	.000	4	1	0	0	0	0	0	0	0	0	0	0	0	0	0	.000	.000
Honeycutt, Rick, St.L	L	.000	61	1	0	0	0	0	0	0	0	1	0	2	1	0	0	.000	.667
Hook, Chris, S.F.	R	.500	10	2	0	1	1	0	0	0	1	0	0	0	1	0	0	.500	.500
Jackson, Danny, St.L	R	.333	13	9	1	3	5	2	0	0	4	1	0	0	1	0	0	.556	.333
Jones, Todd, Hou.	L	.000	51	1	0	0	0	0	0	0	0	0	0	0	0	0	0	.000	.000
Jordan, Ricardo, Phi.	L	.000	26	1	0	0	0	0	0	0	0	0	0	0	0	0	0	.000	.000
Juden, Jeff, S.F.-Mon.	R	.000	58	3	0	0	0	0	0	0	0	1	0	0	2	0	0	.000	.000
Leskanic, Curtis, Col.	R	.333	70	3	0	1	2	1	0	0	1	1	0	0	2	0	0	.667	.333
Lieber, Jon, Pit.	L	.194	51	36	4	7	10	3	0	0	3	3	0	3	11	0	0	.278	.256
Ludwick, Eric, St.L	R	.000	6	2	0	0	0	0	0	0	0	0	0	0	1	0	0	.000	.000
Maduro, Calvin, Phi.	R	.000	4	4	0	0	0	0	0	0	0	0	0	0	2	0	0	.000	.000
Mantei, Matt, Fla.	R	.000	14	1	0	0	0	0	0	0	0	0	0	0	1	0	0	.000	.000
Manuel, Barry, Mon.	R	.000	53	7	0	0	0	0	0	0	0	1	0	1	3	0	0	.000	.125
Mathews, Terry, Fla.	L	.000	57	4	0	0	0	0	0	0	0	0	0	0	2	0	0	.000	.000
Mathews, T.J., St.L	R	.000	67	4	0	0	0	0	0	0	0	0	0	0	3	0	0	.000	.000

National League relief pitchers (batting)

Name/Team	B	BA	G	AB	R	H	TB	2B	3B	HR	RBI	SH	SF	BB	SO	SB	CS	SLG	OBA
May, Darrell, Pit.	L	.333	5	3	1	1	1	0	0	0	0	0	0	0	1	0	0	.333	.333
McElroy, Chuck, Cin.	L	.000	12	2	0	0	0	0	0	0	0	0	0	0	0	0	0	.000	.000
Miceli, Dan, Pit.	R	.000	44	13	0	0	0	0	0	0	0	0	0	0	4	0	0	.000	.000
Miller, Kurt, Fla.	R	.375	26	8	0	3	3	0	0	0	2	1	0	0	0	0	0	.375	.375
Minor, Blas, NYN	R	.000	17	1	0	0	0	0	0	0	0	0	0	0	0	0	0	.000	.000
Mitchell, Larry, Phi.	R	.000	7	2	0	0	0	0	0	0	0	0	0	0	1	0	0	.000	.000
Mlicki, Dave, NYN	R	.100	51	10	0	1	1	0	0	0	0	0	0	1	3	0	0	.100	.182
Moore, Marcus, Cin.	B	.333	23	3	0	1	2	1	0	0	0	0	0	0	2	0	0	.667	.333
Morel, Ramon, Pit.	R	.000	29	4	0	0	0	0	0	0	0	1	0	0	2	0	0	.000	.000
Munoz, Mike, Col.	L	.000	54	1	0	0	0	0	0	0	0	0	0	0	1	0	0	.000	.000
Myers, Rodney, ChiN	R	.000	45	5	0	0	0	0	0	0	0	0	0	0	4	0	0	.000	.000
Nen, Robb, Fla.	R	.000	75	2	0	0	0	0	0	0	0	0	0	0	0	0	0	.000	.000
Nied, David, Col.	R	.000	6	1	0	0	0	0	0	0	0	0	0	0	1	0	0	.000	.000
Osuna, Al, S.D.	R	.000	10	1	0	0	0	0	0	0	0	0	0	0	0	0	0	.000	.000
Osuna, Antonio, L.A.	R	.000	73	1	0	0	0	0	0	0	0	1	0	1	1	0	0	.000	.333
Painter, Lance, Col.	L	.133	35	15	1	2	2	0	0	0	2	0	0	0	8	0	0	.133	.133
Pall, Donn, Fla.	R	.000	12	2	0	0	0	0	0	0	0	0	0	1	0	0	0	.000	.333
Park, Chan Ho, L.A.	R	.053	48	19	0	1	1	0	0	0	2	3	0	1	9	0	0	.053	.100
Parrett, Jeff, St.L-Phi.	R	.000	51	2	1	0	0	0	0	0	0	0	0	1	1	0	0	.000	.333
Parris, Steve, Pit.	R	.167	8	6	1	1	1	0	0	0	0	2	0	1	1	0	0	.167	.286
Patterson, Bob, ChiN	R	.333	79	3	0	1	1	0	0	0	0	0	0	0	2	0	0	.333	.333
Perez, Mike, ChiN	R	.000	24	1	0	0	0	0	0	0	0	0	0	0	1	0	0	.000	.000
Perez, Yorkis, Fla.	B	.000	64	1	0	0	0	0	0	0	0	0	0	0	1	0	0	.000	.000
Person, Robert, NYN	R	.143	29	21	1	3	4	1	0	0	5	0	0	12	0	0	.190	.143
Petkovsek, Mark, St.L	R	.188	48	16	1	3	3	0	0	0	0	0	0	0	3	0	0	.188	.235
Plesac, Dan, Pit.	L	.000	73	5	0	0	0	0	0	0	0	0	0	0	2	0	0	.000	.000
Poole, Jim Ri., S.F.	L	.000	35	2	0	0	0	0	0	0	0	0	0	0	1	0	0	.000	.000
Powell, Jay, Fla.	R	.000	67	5	0	0	0	0	0	0	0	1	0	0	4	0	0	.000	.000
Pugh, Tim, Cin.	R	---	10	0	0	0	0	0	0	0	0	1	0	0	0	0	0	---	---
Radinsky, Scott, L.A.	L	.000	58	1	0	0	0	0	0	0	0	0	0	0	0	0	0	.000	.000
Reed, Steve, Col.	R	.333	70	3	0	1	1	0	0	0	0	0	0	0	1	0	0	.333	.333
Remlinger, Mike, Cin.	L	.143	19	7	0	1	1	0	0	0	0	0	0	1	3	0	0	.143	.250
Rojas, Mel, Mon.	R	.375	74	8	0	3	4	1	0	0	3	0	0	0	2	0	0	.500	.375
Ruebel, Matt, Pit.	L	.231	26	13	0	3	3	0	0	0	0	2	0	1	4	0	0	.231	.286
Ruffin, Bruce, Col.	B	.000	71	1	0	0	0	0	0	0	0	0	0	1	1	0	0	.000	.500
Ruffin, Johnny, Cin.	R	.500	49	4	0	2	2	0	0	0	0	0	0	1	1	0	0	.500	.500
Ryan, Ken, Phi.	R	.143	62	7	0	1	1	0	0	0	0	1	0	0	4	0	0	.143	.143
Sanders, Scott, S.D.	R	.194	46	36	2	7	10	3	0	0	1	4	0	1	11	0	0	.278	.216
Scott, Tim, Mon.-S.F.	R	.000	65	5	0	0	0	0	0	0	0	0	0	0	4	0	0	.000	.000
Service, Scott, Cin.	R	.000	34	5	0	0	0	0	0	0	0	0	0	0	2	0	0	.000	.000
Shaw, Jeff, Cin.	R	.000	78	5	0	0	0	0	0	0	0	0	0	1	3	0	0	.000	.167
Small, Mark, Hou.	R	.000	16	1	0	0	0	0	0	0	0	0	0	0	1	0	0	.000	.000
Springer, Russ, Phi.	R	.059	51	17	1	1	1	0	0	0	0	2	0	0	12	0	0	.059	.059
Sturtze, Tanyon, ChiN	R	.000	6	1	0	0	0	0	0	0	0	0	1	0	0	0	0	.000	.000
Sullivan, Scott, Cin.	R	.000	7	1	0	0	0	0	0	0	0	1	0	0	0	0	0	.000	.000
Swift, Bill C., Col.	R	.333	7	6	0	2	2	0	0	0	0	0	0	0	1	0	0	.333	.333
Swindell, Greg, Hou.	R	.333	8	6	0	2	3	1	0	0	0	0	0	0	1	0	0	.500	.333
Tabaka, Jeff, Hou.	R	.000	18	1	0	0	0	0	0	0	0	0	0	0	1	0	0	.000	.000
Thobe, Tom, Atl.	L	.000	4	1	0	0	0	0	0	0	0	0	0	0	0	0	0	.000	.000
Veres, Dave, Mon.	R	.375	68	8	1	3	4	1	0	0	1	0	0	0	4	0	0	.500	.375
Wade, Terrell, Atl.	L	.154	44	13	0	2	2	0	0	0	1	2	0	1	7	0	0	.154	.214
Wagner, Billy, Hou.	L	.000	37	5	0	0	0	0	0	0	0	0	0	0	2	0	0	.000	.000
Wainhouse, Dave, Pit.	L	.000	17	1	0	0	0	0	0	0	0	0	0	0	0	0	0	.000	.000
Weathers, David, Fla.	R	.158	32	19	1	3	6	0	0	1	2	0	0	0	13	0	0	.316	.200
Wendell, Turk, ChiN	L	.500	70	2	0	1	1	0	0	0	0	1	0	1	0	0	0	.500	.667
Wilkins, Marc, Pit.	R	.222	47	9	1	2	2	0	0	0	1	0	0	1	6	0	0	.222	.300
Wohlers, Mark, Atl.	R	.000	77	3	0	0	0	0	0	0	0	0	0	0	3	0	0	.000	.000
Woodall, Brad, Atl.	B	.200	8	5	0	1	1	0	0	0	0	0	0	1	2	0	0	.200	.333
Worrell, Tim, S.D.	R	.150	50	20	1	3	3	0	0	0	2	6	0	1	10	0	0	.150	.190
Young, Anthony, Hou.	R	.000	28	2	0	0	0	0	0	0	0	0	0	0	2	0	0	.000	.000

National League starting pitchers (batting)

Name/Team	B	BA	G	AB	R	H	TB	2B	3B	HR	RBI	SH	SF	BB	SO	SB	CS	SLG	OBA
Ashby, Andy, S.D.	R	.244	25	45	6	11	16	5	0	0	5	9	1	0	13	0	0	.356	.239
Astacio, Pedro, L.A.	R	.088	35	68	1	6	6	0	0	0	3	8	0	1	28	0	0	.088	.101
Avery, Steve, Atl.	L	.239	24	46	5	11	23	4	1	2	11	1	2	1	12	0	0	.500	.245
Beech, Matt, Phi.	L	.071	8	14	1	1	1	0	0	0	1	0	0	0	4	0	0	.071	.071
Benes, Alan, St.L	R	.148	34	61	4	9	12	3	0	0	5	7	0	2	25	0	0	.197	.175

National League starting pitchers (batting)

Name/Team	B	BA	G	AB	R	H	TB	2B	3B	HR	RBI	SH	SF	BB	SO	SB	CS	SLG	OBA
Benes, Andy, St.L	R	.151	36	73	5	11	15	4	0	0	6	9	2	1	37	0	0	.205	.158
Brown, Kevin, Fla.	R	.120	34	75	1	9	10	1	0	0	3	4	0	6	28	0	0	.133	.185
Bullinger, Jim, ChiN	R	.250	38	32	8	8	17	3	0	2	6	3	0	5	11	0	0	.531	.368
Burba, Dave, Cin.	R	.104	34	67	3	7	13	0	0	2	5	3	0	3	26	0	0	.194	.143
Burkett, John, Fla.	R	.173	24	52	2	9	11	2	0	0	1	3	0	0	17	0	0	.212	.173
Busby, Mike, St.L	R	.500	1	2	0	1	1	0	0	0	0	0	0	0	1	0	0	.500	.500
Candiotti, Tom, L.A.	R	.089	28	45	3	4	4	0	0	0	2	9	1	0	14	0	0	.089	.106
Carrara, Giovanni, Cin.	R	.000	8	7	1	0	0	0	0	0	0	0	0	0	1	0	0	.000	.000
Castillo, Frank, ChiN	R	.088	33	57	1	5	5	0	0	0	2	4	0	2	21	0	0	.088	.119
Clark, Mark, NYN	R	.043	32	69	3	3	4	1	0	0	2	10	1	1	26	0	0	.058	.056
Cormier, Rheal, Mon.	L	.186	33	43	2	8	10	0	1	0	4	11	0	2	12	0	0	.233	.222
Crawford, Carlos, Phi.	R	.000	1	1	0	0	0	0	0	0	0	0	0	0	0	0	0	.000	.000
Darwin, Danny, Pit.-Hou.	R	.184	34	49	2	9	16	4	0	1	3	7	0	0	27	1	0	.327	.184
Drabek, Doug, Hou.	R	.179	32	56	5	10	11	1	0	0	3	7	0	0	12	0	0	.196	.179
Estes, Shawn, S.F.	R	.158	15	19	3	3	3	0	0	0	1	6	0	1	8	0	0	.158	.200
Farmer, Mike, Col.	R	.400	7	10	1	4	4	0	0	0	0	0	0	0	0	0	0	.400	.400
Fassero, Jeff, Mon.	L	.094	34	64	5	6	6	0	0	0	4	14	1	8	32	1	0	.094	.192
Fernandez, Osvaldo, S.F.	R	.088	33	57	0	5	5	0	0	0	1	5	0	0	25	0	0	.088	.088
Fernandez, Sid, Phi.	L	.105	11	19	0	2	3	1	0	0	2	2	1	3	10	0	0	.158	.217
Foster, Kevin, ChiN	R	.296	19	27	3	8	14	4	1	0	6	3	0	4	11	0	0	.519	.406
Freeman, Marvin, Col.	R	.122	26	41	3	5	5	0	0	0	0	4	0	2	21	0	0	.122	.163
Gardner, Mark, S.F.	R	.162	33	68	6	11	12	1	0	0	4	8	0	2	26	0	0	.176	.197
Glavine, Tom, Atl.	L	.289	39	76	8	22	26	4	0	0	3	15	0	5	17	0	0	.342	.333
Grace, Mike, Phi.	R	.138	12	29	1	4	4	0	0	0	0	1	0	2	11	0	0	.138	.219
Hamilton, Joey, S.D.	R	.162	34	68	7	11	16	2	0	1	4	11	0	2	32	0	0	.235	.186
Hampton, Mike, Hou.	R	.238	29	42	9	10	11	1	0	0	3	7	0	4	11	0	0	.262	.319
Harnisch, Pete, NYN	R	.091	32	55	3	5	6	1	0	0	1	10	1	2	18	0	0	.109	.121
Helling, Rick, Fla.	R	.111	5	9	1	1	1	0	0	0	0	0	0	0	3	0	0	.111	.111
Hope, John, Pit.	R	.200	5	5	0	1	1	0	0	0	0	1	0	0	0	1	0	.200	.200
Hunter, Rich, Phi.	R	.167	15	18	2	3	4	1	0	0	0	4	0	1	5	0	0	.222	.211
Hutton, Mark, Fla.	R	.316	13	19	2	6	9	0	0	1	1	1	0	0	6	0	0	.474	.316
Isringhausen, J., NYN	R	.255	27	51	5	13	21	2	0	2	9	2	1	3	15	0	0	.412	.291
Jarvis, Kevin, Cin.	L	.167	24	36	2	6	7	1	0	0	1	8	0	0	12	0	0	.194	.167
Jones, Bobby J., NYN	R	.117	31	60	6	7	9	2	0	0	2	9	0	3	20	0	0	.150	.159
Kile, Darryl, Hou.	R	.137	37	73	3	10	14	4	0	0	5	7	1	3	34	0	0	.192	.169
Larkin, Andy, Fla.	R	.000	1	2	0	0	0	0	0	0	0	0	0	0	1	0	0	.000	.000
Leiter, Al, Fla.	L	.100	33	70	3	7	7	0	0	0	1	7	0	4	45	0	0	.100	.149
Leiter, Mark, S.F.-Mon.	R	.119	35	67	4	8	9	1	0	0	5	9	0	3	35	0	0	.134	.157
Loaiza, Esteban, Pit.	R	.118	11	17	1	2	2	0	0	0	1	5	0	0	2	0	0	.118	.118
Loiselle, Rich, Pit.	R	.250	5	8	0	2	3	1	0	0	2	0	0	0	3	0	0	.375	.250
Lyons, Curt, Cin.	R	.000	3	5	0	0	0	0	0	0	0	0	0	1	0	0	0	.000	.000
Maddux, Greg, Atl.	R	.147	35	68	6	10	12	2	0	0	2	11	0	3	12	0	0	.176	.183
Martinez, Pedro J., Mon.	R	.094	33	64	5	6	7	1	0	0	4	16	0	4	29	0	0	.109	.159
Martinez, Ramon, L.A.	R	.119	30	59	3	7	7	0	0	0	2	8	0	2	22	0	0	.119	.148
Mimbs, Michael, Phi.	L	.121	21	33	0	4	4	0	0	0	0	2	0	0	12	0	0	.121	.121
Morgan, Mike, St.L-Cin.	R	.050	23	40	1	2	2	0	0	0	0	11	0	0	17	0	0	.050	.050
Mulholland, Terry, Phi.	R	.178	21	45	2	8	12	1	0	1	2	4	0	0	20	0	0	.267	.178
Munoz, Bobby, Phi.	R	.143	6	7	1	1	2	1	0	0	0	1	0	0	3	0	0	.286	.143
Navarro, Jaime, ChiN	R	.130	35	77	1	10	11	1	0	0	3	8	0	0	26	0	0	.143	.141
Neagle, Denny, Pit.-Atl.	L	.174	36	69	3	12	13	1	0	0	4	16	1	2	18	0	0	.188	.194
Nomo, Hideo, L.A.	R	.133	33	75	1	10	14	4	0	0	3	10	0	2	38	0	0	.187	.156
Osborne, Donovan, St.L	L	.220	30	59	6	13	20	4	0	1	10	10	0	3	24	0	1	.339	.258
Paniagua, Jose, Mon.	R	.000	13	11	1	0	0	0	0	0	0	1	0	2	7	0	0	.000	.154
Peters, Chris, Pit.	L	.211	16	19	2	4	5	1	0	0	1	1	0	0	8	0	0	.263	.211
Portugal, Mark, Cin.	R	.167	28	48	4	8	9	1	0	0	1	7	0	1	11	0	0	.188	.184
Rapp, Pat, Fla.	R	.121	30	58	2	7	8	1	0	0	2	0	0	0	21	0	0	.138	.121
Rekar, Bryan, Col.	R	.267	14	15	2	4	5	1	0	0	0	1	0	1	5	0	0	.333	.313
Reynolds, Shane, Hou.	R	.184	35	76	6	14	22	0	0	2	3	14	0	3	28	0	0	.289	.215
Reynoso, Armando, Col.	R	.173	30	52	4	9	10	1	0	0	2	7	0	5	25	0	0	.192	.246
Ritz, Kevin, Col.	R	.231	35	65	7	15	20	2	0	1	5	11	0	7	28	0	0	.308	.306
Rueter, Kirk, Mon.-S.F.	L	.125	20	32	2	4	4	0	0	0	3	2	1	2	5	0	0	.125	.171
Salkeld, Roger, Cin.	R	.031	29	32	1	1	1	0	0	0	0	4	0	1	21	0	0	.031	.061
Schilling, Curt, Phi.	R	.175	28	63	1	11	12	1	0	0	4	7	0	1	24	0	0	.190	.188
Schmidt, Jason, Atl.-Pit.	R	.032	19	31	1	1	1	0	0	0	3	2	0	2	15	0	0	.032	.091
Schourek, Pete, Cin.	L	.263	13	19	1	5	5	0	0	0	2	5	0	1	5	0	0	.263	.300
Smiley, John, Cin.	L	.191	35	68	1	13	15	2	0	0	6	4	0	4	22	0	0	.221	.236
Smith, Zane, Pit.	L	.154	16	26	2	4	4	0	0	0	3	2	0	0	6	0	0	.154	.154
Smoltz, John, Atl.	R	.218	35	78	3	17	23	3	0	1	12	15	1	3	26	0	0	.295	.253
Soderstrom, Steve, S.F.	R	.000	3	5	0	0	0	0	0	0	0	0	0	0	3	0	0	.000	.000
Stottlemyre, Todd, St.L	L	.227	34	66	8	15	15	0	0	0	2	9	0	7	27	1	1	.227	.301

National League starting pitchers (batting)

Name/Team	B	BA	G	AB	R	H	TB	2B	3B	HR	RBI	SH	SF	BB	SO	SB	CS	SLG	OBA
Swartzbaugh, D., ChiN	R	.000	6	6	0	0	0	0	0	0	0	0	0	1	3	0	0	.000	.143
Telemaco, Amaury, ChiN	R	.103	25	29	1	3	3	0	0	0	1	4	0	1	15	0	0	.103	.133
Tewksbury, Bob, S.D.	R	.031	36	65	1	2	3	1	0	0	2	8	0	3	27	0	0	.046	.074
Thompson, Mark, Col.	R	.138	34	58	3	8	11	3	0	0	2	5	0	1	21	0	0	.190	.153
Trachsel, Steve, ChiN	R	.106	31	66	3	7	12	2	0	1	5	6	0	1	20	0	0	.182	.119
Urbani, Tom, St.L	L	.167	5	6	0	1	1	0	0	0	0	0	0	0	1	0	0	.167	.167
Urbina, Ugueth, Mon.	R	.103	33	29	3	3	3	0	0	0	1	3	0	2	17	0	0	.103	.161
Valdes, Ismael, L.A.	R	.143	33	70	6	10	11	1	0	0	2	13	0	1	25	0	0	.157	.155
Valdes, Marc, Fla.	R	.000	11	14	0	0	0	0	0	0	0	0	0	1	2	0	0	.000	.067
Valenzuela, F., S.D.	L	.143	36	63	4	9	11	2	0	0	2	3	0	0	15	0	0	.175	.143
VanLandingham, W., S.F.	R	.131	32	61	3	8	9	1	0	0	2	6	1	2	31	0	0	.148	.156
Wagner, Paul, Pit.	R	.040	17	25	1	1	1	0	0	0	2	3	0	2	8	0	1	.040	.111
Wall, Donne, Hou.	R	.205	26	44	5	9	10	1	0	0	1	8	0	2	11	0	0	.227	.239
Watson, Allen, S.F.	L	.231	32	65	5	15	18	3	0	0	7	2	0	5	8	0	0	.277	.286
West, David, Phi.	L	.286	7	7	0	2	2	0	0	0	0	2	0	2	2	0	0	.286	.444
Williams, Mike, Phi.	R	.157	33	51	4	8	8	0	0	0	1	6	0	2	11	1	0	.157	.189
Wilson, Paul, NYN	R	.080	26	50	3	4	7	0	0	1	4	4	0	1	32	0	0	.140	.115
Wright, Jamey, Col.	R	.077	16	26	3	2	4	2	0	0	0	5	0	2	13	0	0	.154	.143

American League relief pitchers

Name/Team	T	W	L	ERA	G	GS	CG	SHO	GF	SV	IP	H	R	ER	HR	BB	SO	WP	BA	RV
Abbott, Kyle, Cal.	L	0	1	20.25	3	0	0	0	1	0	4.0	10	9	9	1	5	3	1	.500	-4
Acre, Mark, Oak.	R	1	3	6.12	22	0	0	0	11	2	25.0	38	17	17	4	9	18	0	.339	0
Alberro, Jose, Tex.	R	0	1	5.79	5	1	0	0	1	0	9.1	14	6	6	1	7	2	0	.368	-2
Assenmacher, Paul, Cle.	L	4	2	3.09	63	0	0	0	25	1	46.2	46	18	16	1	14	44	2	.260	7
Ayala, Bobby, Sea.	R	6	3	5.88	50	0	0	0	26	3	67.1	65	45	44	10	25	61	2	.256	7
Belinda, Stan, Bos.	R	2	1	6.59	31	0	0	0	10	2	28.2	31	22	21	3	20	18	2	.272	4
Benitez, Armando, Bal.	R	1	0	3.77	18	0	0	0	8	4	14.1	7	6	6	2	6	20	1	.143	4
Bennett, Erik, Min.	R	2	0	7.90	24	0	0	0	10	1	27.1	33	24	24	7	16	13	1	.306	-1
Bertotti, Mike, ChiA	L	2	0	5.14	15	2	0	0	4	0	28.0	28	18	16	5	20	19	4	.257	1
Bevil, Brian, K.C.	R	1	0	5.73	3	1	0	0	1	0	11.0	9	7	7	2	5	7	0	.237	0
Bluma, Jaime, K.C.	R	0	0	3.60	17	0	0	0	10	5	20.0	18	9	8	2	4	14	1	.247	4
Boehringer, Brian, NYA	R	2	4	5.44	15	3	0	0	1	0	46.1	46	28	28	6	21	37	1	.260	2
Bohanon, Brian, Tor.	L	0	1	7.77	20	0	0	0	6	1	22.0	27	19	19	4	19	17	2	.303	-2
Bosio, Chris, Sea.	R	4	4	5.93	18	9	0	0	4	0	60.2	72	44	40	8	24	39	1	.299	3
Boze, Marshall, Mil.	R	0	2	7.79	25	0	0	0	8	1	32.1	47	29	28	5	25	19	3	.362	-3
Brandenbrg, M., Tex.-Bos.	R	5	5	3.43	55	0	0	0	13	0	76.0	76	35	29	8	33	66	0	.258	7
Brewer, Billy, NYA	L	1	0	9.53	4	0	0	0	1	0	5.2	7	6	6	0	8	8	0	.292	-2
Briscoe, John, Oak.	R	0	1	3.76	17	0	0	0	8	1	26.1	18	11	11	2	24	14	3	.205	1
Brow, Scott, Tor.	R	1	0	5.59	18	1	0	0	9	0	38.2	45	25	24	5	25	23	2	.294	-1
Burrows, Terry, Mil.	L	2	0	2.84	8	0	0	0	4	0	12.2	12	4	4	2	10	5	0	.261	1
Carmona, Rafael, Sea.	R	8	3	4.28	53	1	0	0	15	1	90.1	95	47	43	11	55	62	4	.273	9
Carpenter, Cris, Mil.	R	0	0	7.56	8	0	0	0	2	0	8.1	12	8	7	1	2	2	0	.333	-2
Carrara, Giovanni, Tor.	R	0	1	11.40	11	0	0	0	3	0	15.0	23	19	19	5	12	10	1	.359	-4
Castillo, T. J., Tor.-ChiA	L	5	4	3.60	55	0	0	0	13	2	95.0	95	45	38	10	24	57	3	.262	10
Charlton, Norm, Sea.	L	4	7	4.04	70	0	0	0	50	20	75.2	68	37	34	7	38	73	9	.244	21
Christopher, Mike, Det.	R	1	1	9.30	13	0	0	0	3	0	30.0	47	36	31	12	11	19	1	.351	-4
Clark, Terry, K.C.	R	1	1	7.79	12	0	0	0	5	0	17.1	28	15	15	3	7	12	3	.350	-2
Cook, Dennis, Tex.	L	5	2	4.09	60	0	0	0	9	0	70.1	53	34	32	2	35	64	0	.214	8
Corbin, Archie, Bal.	R	2	0	2.30	18	0	0	0	5	0	27.1	22	7	7	2	22	20	2	.222	3
Corsi, Jim, Oak.	R	6	0	4.03	57	0	0	0	19	3	73.2	71	33	33	6	34	43	1	.270	10
Crabtree, Tim, Tor.	R	5	3	2.54	53	0	0	0	21	1	67.1	59	26	19	4	22	57	3	.231	10
Cummings, John, Det.	L	3	3	5.12	21	0	0	0	7	0	31.2	36	20	18	3	20	24	1	.283	1
Darwin, Jeff, ChiA	R	0	1	2.93	22	0	0	0	9	0	30.2	26	10	10	5	9	15	0	.232	2
Davis, Tim, Sea.	L	2	2	4.01	40	0	0	0	4	0	42.2	43	21	19	4	17	34	0	.259	3
Davison, Scott, Sea.	R	0	0	9.00	5	0	0	0	3	0	9.0	11	9	9	6	3	9	0	.297	-2
Doherty, John, Bos.	R	0	0	5.68	3	0	0	0	1	0	6.1	8	10	4	1	4	3	0	.276	-2
Edenfield, Ken, Cal.	R	0	0	10.38	2	0	0	0	0	0	4.1	10	5	5	2	2	4	0	.435	-2
Eichhorn, Mark, Cal.	R	1	2	5.04	24	0	0	0	6	0	30.1	36	17	17	3	11	24	0	.308	0
Eischen, Joey, Det.	L	1	1	3.24	24	0	0	0	3	0	25.0	27	11	9	3	14	15	3	.284	1
Ellis, Robert, Cal.	R	0	0	0.00	3	0	0	0	3	0	5.0	0	0	0	0	4	5	1	.000	-1
Embree, Alan, Cle.	L	1	1	6.39	24	0	0	0	2	0	31.0	30	26	22	10	21	33	3	.259	-1
Eshelman, Vaughn, Bos.	L	6	3	7.08	39	10	0	0	1	0	87.2	112	79	69	13	58	59	4	.311	0
Fetters, Mike, Mil.	R	3	3	3.38	61	0	0	0	55	32	61.1	65	28	23	4	26	53	5	.274	29
Fletcher, Paul, Oak.	R	0	0	20.25	1	0	0	0	0	0	1.1	6	3	3	0	1	0	0	.667	-2
Florie, Bryce, Mil.	R	0	1	6.63	15	0	0	0	5	0	19.0	20	16	14	3	13	12	3	.270	-2
Frohwirth, Todd, Cal.	R	0	0	11.12	4	0	0	0	2	0	5.2	10	11	7	1	4	1	1	.370	-3
Garces, Rich, Bos.	R	3	2	4.91	37	0	0	0	9	0	44.0	42	26	24	5	33	55	0	.251	2

American League relief pitchers

Name/Team	T	W	L	ERA	G	GS	CG	SHO	GF	SV	IP	H	R	ER	HR	BB	SO	WP	BA	RV
Garcia, Ramon, Mil.	R	4	4	6.66	37	2	0	0	14	4	75.2	84	58	56	17	21	40	2	.287	5
Gibson, Paul, NYA	L	0	0	6.23	4	0	0	0	2	0	4.1	6	3	3	1	0	3	0	.316	-2
Gohr, Greg, Det.-Cal.	R	5	9	7.24	32	16	0	0	7	1	115.2	163	96	93	31	44	75	6	.330	-2
Granger, Jeff, K.C.	L	0	0	6.61	15	0	0	0	5	0	16.1	21	13	12	3	10	11	2	.313	-2
Graves, Danny, Cle.	R	2	0	4.55	15	0	0	0	5	0	29.2	29	18	15	2	10	22	1	.246	2
Groom, Buddy, Oak.	L	5	0	3.84	72	1	0	0	16	2	77.1	85	37	33	8	34	57	5	.281	8
Grundt, Ken, Bos.	L	0	0	27.00	1	0	0	0	0	0	0.1	1	1	1	0	0	0	0	.500	-2
Guardado, Eddie, Min.	L	6	5	5.25	83	0	0	0	17	4	73.2	61	45	43	12	33	74	3	.228	9
Guetterman, Lee, Sea.	L	0	2	4.09	17	0	0	0	1	0	11.0	11	8	5	0	10	6	0	.275	-1
Gunderson, Eric, Bos.	L	0	1	8.31	28	0	0	0	2	0	17.1	21	17	16	5	8	7	3	.300	-3
Hancock, Ryan, Cal.	R	4	1	7.48	11	4	0	0	4	0	27.2	34	23	23	2	17	19	2	.306	0
Hansell, Greg, Min.	R	3	0	5.69	50	0	0	0	23	3	74.1	83	48	47	14	31	46	9	.285	5
Harris, Pep, Cal.	R	2	0	3.90	11	3	0	0	0	0	32.1	31	16	14	4	17	20	4	.254	2
Harris, Reggie, Bos.	R	0	0	12.46	4	0	0	0	1	0	4.1	7	6	6	2	5	4	0	.389	-3
Haynes, Jimmy, Bal.	R	3	6	8.29	26	11	0	0	8	1	89.0	122	84	82	14	58	65	5	.333	-5
Helling, Rick, Tex.	R	1	2	7.52	6	2	0	0	2	0	20.1	23	17	17	7	9	16	1	.280	-1
Henneman, Mike, Tex.	R	0	7	5.79	49	0	0	0	45	31	42.0	41	28	27	6	17	34	4	.258	22
Heredia, Gil, Tex.	R	2	5	5.89	44	0	0	0	21	1	73.1	91	50	48	12	14	43	2	.301	3
Hernandez, Roberto, ChiA	R	6	5	1.91	72	0	0	0	61	38	84.2	65	21	18	2	38	85	6	.208	41
Holtz, Mike, Cal.	L	3	3	2.45	30	0	0	0	8	0	29.1	21	11	8	1	19	31	1	.204	4
Holzemer, Mark, Cal.	L	1	0	8.76	25	0	0	0	3	0	24.2	35	28	24	7	8	20	0	.327	-2
Howe, Steve, NYA	L	0	1	6.35	25	0	0	0	4	1	17.0	19	12	12	1	6	5	2	.284	-1
Hudson, Joe, Bos.	R	3	5	5.40	36	0	0	0	16	1	45.0	57	35	27	4	32	19	0	.318	2
Huisman, Rick, K.C.	R	2	1	4.60	22	0	0	0	5	1	29.1	25	15	15	4	18	23	0	.231	2
Hurtado, Edwin, Sea.	R	2	5	7.74	16	4	0	0	6	2	47.2	61	42	41	10	30	36	2	.324	-1
Hutton, Mark, NYA	R	0	2	5.04	12	2	0	0	5	0	30.1	32	19	17	3	18	25	0	.269	-1
Jackson, Mike R., Sea.	R	1	1	3.63	73	0	0	0	23	6	72.0	61	32	29	11	24	70	2	.225	10
Jacome, Jason, K.C.	L	0	4	4.72	49	2	0	0	21	1	47.2	67	27	25	5	22	32	1	.337	0
James, Mike, Cal.	R	5	5	2.67	69	0	0	0	23	1	81.0	62	27	24	7	42	65	5	.214	11
Johnson, Dane, Tor.	R	0	0	3.00	10	0	0	0	2	0	9.0	5	3	3	0	5	7	0	.161	-1
Jones, Doug, Mil.	R	5	0	3.41	24	0	0	0	8	1	31.2	31	13	12	3	13	34	1	.254	6
Jones, Stacy, ChiA	R	0	0	0.00	2	0	0	0	1	0	2.0	0	0	0	0	1	1	0	.000	-1
Karchner, Matt, ChiA	R	7	4	5.76	50	0	0	0	13	1	59.1	61	42	38	10	41	46	4	.268	5
Keagle, Greg, Det.	R	3	6	7.39	26	6	0	0	5	0	87.2	104	76	72	13	68	70	2	.298	-3
Keyser, Brian, ChiA	R	1	2	4.98	28	0	0	0	10	1	59.2	78	35	33	3	28	19	2	.328	1
Kiefer, Mark, Mil.	R	0	0	8.10	7	0	0	0	2	0	10.0	15	9	9	1	5	5	1	.366	-2
Klingenbeck, Scott, Min.	R	1	1	7.85	10	3	0	0	2	0	28.2	42	28	25	5	10	15	1	.339	-2
Klink, Joe, Sea.	L	0	0	3.86	3	0	0	0	1	0	2.1	3	1	1	1	1	2	0	.300	-2
Knackert, Brent, Bos.	R	0	1	9.00	8	0	0	0	2	0	10.0	16	12	10	1	7	5	1	.356	-3
Krivda, Rick, Bal.	L	3	5	4.96	22	11	0	0	4	0	81.2	89	48	45	14	39	54	3	.283	4
Lacy, Kerry, Bos.	R	2	0	3.38	11	0	0	0	3	0	10.2	15	5	4	2	8	9	0	.333	0
Levine, Alan, ChiA	R	0	1	5.40	16	0	0	0	5	0	18.1	22	14	11	1	7	12	0	.289	-2
Lewis, Richie, Det.	R	4	6	4.18	72	0	0	0	19	2	90.1	78	45	42	9	65	78	14	.238	8
Lima, Jose, Det.	R	5	6	5.70	39	4	0	0	15	3	72.2	87	48	46	13	22	59	3	.296	6
Lloyd, Graeme, Mil.-NYA	L	2	6	4.29	65	0	0	0	15	0	56.2	61	30	27	4	22	30	4	.276	2
Maddux, Mike, Bos.	R	3	2	4.48	23	7	0	0	2	0	64.1	76	37	32	12	27	32	1	.295	4
Magnante, Mike, K.C.	L	2	2	5.67	38	0	0	0	9	0	54.0	58	38	34	5	24	32	3	.282	1
Magrane, Joe, ChiA	L	1	3	6.88	19	8	0	0	3	0	53.2	70	45	41	10	25	21	3	.318	-2
Mahomes, Pat, Min.-Bos.	R	3	4	6.91	31	5	0	0	10	2	57.1	72	46	44	13	33	36	2	.308	-1
Mathews, Terry, Bal.	R	2	2	3.38	14	0	0	0	5	0	18.2	20	7	7	3	7	13	0	.282	2
Maxcy, Brian, Det.	R	0	0	13.50	2	0	0	0	0	0	3.1	8	5	5	2	2	1	0	.471	-3
May, Darrell, Cal.	L	0	0	10.13	5	0	0	0	2	0	2.2	3	3	3	1	2	1	0	.333	-2
McCarthy, Greg, Sea.	L	0	0	1.86	10	0	0	0	1	0	9.2	8	2	2	0	4	7	0	.229	0
McCaskill, Kirk, ChiA	R	5	5	6.97	29	4	0	0	13	0	51.2	72	41	40	6	31	28	1	.344	0
McCurry, Jeff, Det.	R	0	0	24.30	2	0	0	0	1	0	3.1	9	9	9	3	2	0	0	.474	-3
McDowell, Roger, Bal.	R	1	1	4.25	41	0	0	0	11	4	59.1	69	32	28	7	23	20	0	.296	5
McElroy, Chuck, Cal.	L	5	1	2.95	40	0	0	0	11	0	36.2	32	12	12	2	13	32	1	.239	6
Meacham, Rusty, Sea.	R	1	1	5.74	15	5	0	0	3	1	42.1	57	28	27	9	13	25	1	.328	1
Mecir, Jim, NYA	R	1	1	5.13	26	0	0	0	10	0	40.1	42	24	23	6	23	38	6	.275	0
Mercedes, Jose, Mil.	R	0	2	9.18	11	0	0	0	4	0	16.2	20	18	17	6	5	6	2	.294	-3
Mercker, Kent, Bal.-Cle.	L	4	4	6.98	24	12	0	0	2	0	69.2	83	60	54	13	38	29	3	.297	-2
Mesa, Jose, Cle.	R	2	7	3.73	69	0	0	0	60	39	72.1	69	32	30	6	28	64	4	.257	34
Milchin, Mike, Min.-Bal.	L	3	1	7.44	39	0	0	0	7	0	32.2	44	28	27	6	17	29	1	.336	-1
Mills, Alan, Bal.	R	3	2	4.28	49	0	0	0	23	3	54.2	40	26	26	10	35	50	6	.208	6
Minor, Blas, Sea.	R	0	1	4.97	11	0	0	0	6	0	25.1	27	14	14	6	11	14	2	.276	-1
Miranda, Angel, Mil.	L	7	6	4.94	46	12	0	0	5	1	109.1	116	68	60	12	69	78	10	.277	8
Mohler, Mike, Oak.	L	6	3	3.67	72	0	0	0	30	7	81.0	79	36	33	9	41	64	9	.263	14
Monteleone, Rich, Cal.	R	0	3	5.87	12	0	0	0	2	0	15.1	23	11	10	5	2	5	0	.348	-1
Montgomery, Jeff, K.C.	R	4	6	4.26	48	0	0	0	41	24	63.1	59	31	30	14	19	45	0	.251	24
Montgomery, Steve, Oak.	R	1	0	9.22	8	0	0	0	0	0	13.2	18	14	14	5	13	8	3	.310	-2

American League relief pitchers

Name/Team	T	W	L	ERA	G	GS	CG	SHO	GF	SV	IP	H	R	ER	HR	BB	SO	WP	BA	RV
Myers, Jimmy, Bal.	R	0	0	7.07	11	0	0	0	5	0	14.0	18	13	11	4	3	6	1	.305	-2
Myers, Mike, Det.	L	1	5	5.01	83	0	0	0	25	6	64.2	70	41	36	6	34	69	2	.272	6
Myers, Randy, Bal.	L	4	4	3.53	62	0	0	0	50	31	58.2	60	24	23	7	29	74	3	.265	28
Naulty, Dan, Min.	R	3	2	3.79	49	0	0	0	15	4	57.0	43	26	24	5	35	56	2	.207	8
Nelson, Jeff, NYA	R	4	4	4.36	73	0	0	0	27	2	74.1	75	38	36	6	36	91	4	.262	7
Olson, Gregg, Det.	R	3	0	5.02	43	0	0	0	28	8	43.0	43	25	24	6	28	29	5	.259	8
Orosco, Jesse, Bal.	L	3	1	3.40	66	0	0	0	10	0	55.2	42	22	21	5	28	52	2	.207	6
Parra, Jose, Min.	R	5	5	6.04	27	5	0	0	7	0	70.0	88	48	47	15	27	50	4	.308	3
Patterson, Danny, Tex.	R	0	0	0.00	7	0	0	0	5	0	8.2	10	4	0	0	3	5	0	.286	0
Pavlas, Dave, NYA	R	0	0	2.35	16	0	0	0	8	1	23.0	23	7	6	0	7	18	3	.264	2
Pennington, B., Bos.-Cal.	L	0	2	6.20	22	0	0	0	8	0	20.1	11	15	14	2	31	20	2	.157	-3
Percival, Troy, Cal.	R	0	2	2.31	62	0	0	0	52	36	74.0	38	20	19	8	31	100	2	.149	35
Pichardo, Hipolito, K.C.	R	3	5	5.43	57	0	0	0	28	3	68.0	74	41	41	5	26	43	4	.284	6
Plunk, Eric, Cle.	R	3	2	2.43	56	0	0	0	12	2	77.2	56	21	21	6	34	85	4	.203	11
Polley, Dale, NYA	L	1	3	7.89	32	0	0	0	9	0	21.2	23	20	19	5	11	14	0	.264	-2
Poole, Jim Ri., Cle.	L	4	0	3.04	32	0	0	0	8	0	26.2	29	15	9	3	14	19	2	.274	4
Potts, Mike, Mil.	L	1	2	7.15	24	0	0	0	7	1	45.1	58	39	36	7	30	21	3	.319	-2
Pugh, Tim, K.C.	R	0	1	5.45	19	1	0	0	8	0	36.1	42	24	22	9	12	27	2	.282	0
Reyes, Al, Mil.	R	1	0	7.94	5	0	0	0	2	0	5.2	8	5	5	1	2	2	2	.320	-1
Reyes, Carlos, Oak.	R	7	10	4.78	46	10	0	0	14	0	122.1	134	71	65	19	61	78	2	.282	8
Rhodes, Arthur, Bal.	L	9	1	4.08	28	2	0	0	5	1	53.0	48	28	24	6	23	62	0	.241	11
Risley, Bill, Tor.	R	0	1	3.89	25	0	0	0	11	0	41.2	33	20	18	7	25	29	1	.221	2
Rivera, Mariano, NYA	R	8	3	2.09	61	0	0	0	14	5	107.2	73	25	25	1	34	130	1	.189	24
Roa, Joe, Cle.	R	0	0	10.80	1	0	0	0	0	0	1.2	4	2	2	0	3	0	0	.500	-2
Robinson, Ken, K.C.	R	1	0	6.00	5	0	0	0	2	0	6.0	9	4	4	0	3	5	1	.346	-1
Rodriguez, Nerio, Bal.	R	0	1	4.32	8	1	0	0	2	0	16.2	18	11	8	2	7	12	0	.265	-1
Ruffcorn, Scott, ChiA	R	0	1	11.37	3	1	0	0	1	0	6.1	10	8	8	1	6	3	2	.370	-3
Russell, Jeff, Tex.	R	3	3	3.38	55	0	0	0	11	3	56.0	58	22	21	5	22	23	3	.269	7
Sackinsky, Brian, Bal.	R	0	0	3.86	3	0	0	0	2	0	4.2	6	2	2	1	3	2	0	.316	-2
Sager, A.J., Det.	R	4	5	5.01	22	9	0	0	1	0	79.0	91	46	44	10	29	52	1	.294	5
Sauveur, Rich, ChiA	L	0	0	15.00	3	0	0	0	0	0	3.0	3	5	5	1	5	1	0	.333	-2
Scanlan, Bob, Det.-K.C.	R	0	1	6.85	17	0	0	0	4	0	22.1	29	19	17	2	12	6	1	.322	-3
Schmidt, Jeff, Cal.	R	2	0	7.88	9	0	0	0	1	0	8.0	13	9	7	2	8	2	1	.394	-1
Shepherd, Keith, Bal.	R	0	1	8.71	13	0	0	0	6	0	20.2	31	27	20	6	18	17	0	.341	-4
Shuey, Paul, Cle.	R	5	2	2.85	42	0	0	0	18	4	53.2	45	19	17	6	26	44	3	.231	10
Silva, Jose, Tor.	R	0	0	13.50	2	0	0	0	0	0	2.0	5	3	3	1	0	0	0	.455	-2
Simas, Bill, ChiA	R	2	8	4.58	64	0	0	0	16	2	72.2	75	39	37	5	39	65	0	.265	5
Sirotka, Mike, ChiA	L	1	2	7.18	15	4	0	0	2	0	26.1	34	27	21	3	12	11	1	.315	-1
Slocumb, Heathcliff, Bos.	R	5	5	3.02	75	0	0	0	60	31	83.1	68	31	28	2	55	88	10	.222	32
Small, Aaron, Oak.	R	1	3	8.16	12	3	0	0	4	0	28.2	37	28	26	3	22	17	2	.308	-3
Smith, Lee, Cal.	R	0	0	2.45	11	0	0	0	8	0	11.0	8	4	3	0	3	6	1	.205	0
Spoljaric, Paul, Tor.	L	2	2	3.08	28	0	0	0	12	1	38.0	30	17	13	6	19	38	0	.214	5
Stanton, Mike, Bos.-Tex.	L	4	4	3.66	81	0	0	0	28	1	78.2	78	32	32	11	27	60	3	.265	7
Stephenson, Garrett, Bal.	R	0	1	12.79	3	0	0	0	2	0	6.1	13	9	9	1	3	3	0	.433	-3
Stevens, Dave, Min.	R	3	3	4.66	49	0	0	0	38	11	58.0	58	31	30	12	25	29	1	.264	12
Suppan, Jeff, Bos.	R	1	1	7.54	8	4	0	0	2	0	22.2	29	19	19	3	13	13	3	.330	-2
Suzuki, Mac, Sea.	R	0	0	20.25	1	0	0	0	0	0	1.1	2	3	3	0	2	1	0	.333	-2
Swindell, Greg, Cle.	L	1	1	6.59	13	2	0	0	1	0	28.2	31	21	21	8	8	21	0	.279	0
Tavarez, Julian, Cle.	R	4	7	5.36	51	0	0	0	13	0	80.2	101	49	48	9	22	46	1	.315	4
Taylor, Bill, Oak.	R	6	3	4.33	55	0	0	0	30	17	60.1	52	30	29	5	25	67	1	.231	20
Thomas, Larry, ChiA	L	2	3	3.23	57	0	0	0	11	0	30.2	32	11	11	1	14	20	1	.281	2
Timlin, Mike, Tor.	R	1	6	3.65	59	0	0	0	56	31	56.2	47	25	23	4	18	52	3	.229	27
Trombley, Mike, Min.	R	5	1	3.01	43	0	0	0	19	6	68.2	61	24	23	2	25	57	4	.236	13
Urbani, Tom, Det.	L	2	2	8.37	16	2	0	0	3	0	23.2	31	22	22	8	14	20	3	.310	-2
Valera, Julio, K.C.	R	3	2	6.46	31	2	0	0	7	1	61.1	75	44	44	7	27	31	1	.307	1
Van Poppel, T., Oak.-Det.	R	3	9	9.06	37	15	1	1	8	1	99.1	139	107	100	24	62	53	7	.335	-7
VanRyn, Ben, Cal.	L	0	0	9.00	1	0	0	0	1	0	1.0	1	1	1	0	1	0	0	.250	-2
Veres, Randy, Det.	R	0	4	8.31	25	0	0	0	11	0	30.1	38	29	28	6	23	28	2	.306	-4
Villone, Ron, Mil.	L	0	0	3.28	23	0	0	0	10	2	24.2	14	9	9	4	18	19	2	.175	2
Vosberg, Ed, Tex.	L	1	1	3.27	52	0	0	0	21	8	44.0	51	17	16	4	21	32	1	.298	8
Walker, Mike C., Det.	R	0	0	8.46	20	0	0	0	12	1	27.2	40	26	26	10	17	13	2	.351	-3
Ware, Jeff, Tor.	R	1	5	9.09	13	4	0	0	6	0	32.2	35	34	33	6	31	11	6	.271	-4
Weathers, David, NYA	R	0	2	9.35	11	4	0	0	1	0	17.1	23	19	18	1	14	13	1	.315	-4
Wells, Bob, Sea.	R	12	7	5.30	36	16	1	1	6	0	130.2	141	78	77	25	46	94	0	.274	12
Wetteland, John, NYA	R	2	3	2.83	62	0	0	0	58	43	63.2	54	23	20	9	21	69	1	.224	38
Whiteside, Matt, Tex.	R	0	1	6.68	14	0	0	0	7	0	32.1	43	24	24	8	11	15	1	.321	-1
Wickander, Kevin, Mil.	L	2	0	4.97	21	0	0	0	6	0	25.1	26	16	14	2	17	19	2	.265	1
Wickman, Bob, NYA-Mil.	R	7	1	4.42	70	0	0	0	18	0	95.2	106	50	47	10	44	75	4	.283	7
Williams, Brian, Det.	R	3	10	6.77	40	17	2	1	17	2	121.0	145	107	91	21	85	72	8	.304	-1
Williams, Shad, Cal.	R	0	2	8.89	13	2	0	0	3	0	28.1	42	34	28	7	21	26	2	.341	-5

American League relief pitchers

Name/Team	T	W	L	ERA	G	GS	CG	SHO	GF	SV	IP	H	R	ER	HR	BB	SO	WP	BA	RV
Witasick, Jay, Oak.	R	1	1	6.23	12	0	0	0	6	0	13.0	12	9	9	5	5	12	2	.245	0
Yan, Esteban, Bal.	R	0	0	5.79	4	0	0	0	2	0	9.1	13	7	6	3	3	7	0	.333	-2

American League starting pitchers

Name/Team	T	W	L	ERA	G	GS	CG	SHO	GF	SV	IP	H	R	ER	HR	BB	SO	WP	BA	RV
Abbott, Jim, Cal.	L	2	18	7.48	27	23	1	0	2	0	142.0	171	128	118	23	78	58	13	.306	-5
Adams, Willie, Oak.	R	3	4	4.01	12	12	1	1	0	0	76.1	76	39	34	11	23	68	2	.257	6
Aguilera, Rick, Min.	R	8	6	5.42	19	19	2	0	0	0	111.1	124	69	67	20	27	83	6	.276	9
Aldred, Scott, Det.-Min.	L	6	9	6.21	36	25	0	0	0	0	165.1	194	125	114	29	68	111	10	.294	3
Alvarez, Wilson, ChiA	L	15	10	4.22	35	35	0	0	0	0	217.1	216	106	102	21	97	181	2	.258	23
Anderson, Brian, Cle.	L	3	1	4.91	10	9	0	0	0	0	51.1	58	29	28	9	14	21	2	.296	3
Andujar, Luis, ChiA-Tor.	R	1	3	6.99	8	7	0	0	0	0	37.1	46	30	29	8	16	11	1	.311	-2
Appier, Kevin, K.C.	R	14	11	3.62	32	32	5	1	0	0	211.1	192	87	85	17	75	207	10	.245	27
Baldwin, James, ChiA	R	11	6	4.42	28	28	0	0	0	0	169.0	168	88	83	24	57	127	12	.257	17
Belcher, Tim, K.C.	R	15	11	3.92	35	35	4	1	0	0	238.2	262	117	104	28	68	113	7	.281	27
Bere, Jason, ChiA	R	0	1	10.26	5	5	0	0	0	0	16.2	26	19	19	3	18	19	2	.356	-4
Bones, Ricky, Mil.-NYA	R	7	14	6.22	36	24	0	0	2	0	152.0	184	115	105	30	68	63	2	.301	2
Boskie, Shawn, Cal.	R	12	11	5.32	37	28	1	0	1	0	189.1	226	126	112	40	67	133	10	.294	13
Burkett, John, Tex.	R	5	2	4.06	10	10	1	1	0	0	68.2	75	33	31	4	16	47	0	.280	7
Chouinard, Bobby, Oak.	R	4	2	6.10	13	11	0	0	0	0	59.0	75	41	40	10	32	32	0	.316	1
Clemens, Roger, Bos.	R	10	13	3.63	34	34	6	2	0	0	242.2	216	106	98	19	106	257	8	.237	25
Cone, David, NYA	R	7	2	2.88	11	11	1	0	0	0	72.0	50	25	23	3	34	71	4	.198	11
Coppinger, Rocky, Bal.	R	10	6	5.18	23	22	0	0	1	0	125.0	126	76	72	25	60	104	4	.263	11
D'Amico, Jeff, Mil.	R	6	6	5.44	17	17	0	0	0	0	86.0	88	53	52	21	31	53	1	.267	6
Dickson, Jason, Cal.	R	1	4	4.57	7	7	0	0	0	0	43.1	52	22	22	6	18	20	1	.306	1
Eldred, Cal, Mil.	R	4	4	4.46	15	15	0	0	0	0	84.2	82	43	42	8	38	50	1	.259	6
Erickson, Scott, Bal.	R	13	12	5.02	34	34	6	0	0	0	222.1	262	137	124	21	66	100	1	.297	17
Farrell, John E., Det.	R	0	2	14.21	2	2	0	0	0	0	6.1	11	10	10	2	5	0	1	.407	-3
Fernandez, Alex, ChiA	R	16	10	3.45	35	35	6	1	0	0	258.0	248	110	99	34	72	200	5	.253	34
Finley, Chuck, Cal.	L	15	16	4.16	35	35	4	1	0	0	238.0	241	124	110	27	94	215	17	.263	25
Flener, Huck, Tor.	L	3	2	4.58	15	11	0	0	0	0	70.2	68	40	36	9	33	44	1	.251	4
Freeman, Marvin, ChiA	R	0	0	13.50	1	1	0	0	0	0	2.0	4	3	3	0	1	1	0	.364	-2
Givens, Brian, Mil.	L	1	3	12.86	4	4	0	0	0	0	14.0	32	22	20	3	7	10	0	.438	-4
Gooden, Dwight, NYA	R	11	7	5.01	29	29	1	1	0	0	170.2	169	101	95	19	88	126	9	.259	13
Gordon, Tom, Bos.	R	12	9	5.59	34	34	4	1	0	0	215.2	249	143	134	28	105	171	6	.284	11
Grimsley, Jason, Cal.	R	5	7	6.84	35	20	2	1	4	0	130.1	150	110	99	14	74	82	11	.286	0
Gross, Kevin, Tex.	R	11	8	5.22	28	19	1	0	4	0	129.1	151	78	75	19	50	78	4	.293	11
Gubicza, Mark, K.C.	R	4	12	5.13	19	19	2	1	0	0	119.1	132	70	68	22	34	55	5	.284	7
Guzman, Juan, Tor.	R	11	8	2.93	27	27	4	1	0	0	187.2	158	68	61	20	53	165	7	.228	27
Haney, Chris, K.C.	L	10	14	4.70	35	35	4	1	0	0	228.0	267	136	119	29	51	115	8	.291	18
Hanson, Erik, Tor.	R	13	17	5.41	35	35	4	1	0	0	214.2	243	143	129	26	102	156	13	.289	13
Harikkala, Tim, Sea.	R	0	1	12.46	1	1	0	0	0	0	4.1	6	6	6	1	2	1	0	.250	-2
Hawkins, LaTroy, Min.	R	1	1	8.20	7	6	0	0	1	0	26.1	42	24	24	8	9	24	1	.372	-3
Hentgen, Pat, Tor.	R	20	10	3.22	35	35	10	3	0	0	265.2	238	105	95	20	94	177	8	.241	39
Hershiser, Orel, Cle.	R	15	9	4.24	33	33	1	0	0	0	206.0	238	115	97	21	58	125	11	.287	22
Hill, Ken, Tex.	R	16	10	3.63	35	35	7	3	0	0	250.2	250	110	101	19	95	170	5	.263	30
Hitchcock, Sterling, Sea.	L	13	9	5.35	35	35	0	0	0	0	196.2	245	131	117	27	73	132	4	.309	13
Janzen, Marty, Tor.	R	4	6	7.33	15	11	0	0	3	0	73.2	95	65	60	16	38	47	7	.318	-1
Johns, Doug, Oak.	L	6	12	5.98	40	23	1	0	4	1	158.0	187	112	105	21	69	71	9	.297	5
Johnson, Randy, Sea.	L	5	0	3.67	14	8	0	0	2	1	61.1	48	27	25	8	25	85	3	.211	8
Kamieniecki, Scott, NYA	R	1	2	11.12	7	5	0	0	0	0	22.2	36	30	28	6	19	15	1	.364	-5
Karl, Scott, Mil.	L	13	9	4.86	32	32	3	1	0	0	207.1	220	124	112	29	72	121	5	.271	18
Key, Jimmy, NYA	L	12	11	4.68	30	30	0	0	0	0	169.1	171	93	88	21	58	116	2	.266	17
Langston, Mark, Cal.	L	6	5	4.82	18	18	2	0	0	0	123.1	116	68	66	18	45	83	4	.247	10
Leftwich, Phil, Cal.	R	0	1	7.36	2	2	0	0	0	0	7.1	12	9	6	1	3	4	0	.375	-2
Linton, Doug, K.C.	R	7	9	5.02	21	18	0	0	0	0	104.0	111	65	58	13	26	87	3	.271	9
Lira, Felipe, Det.	R	6	14	5.22	32	32	3	2	0	0	194.2	204	123	113	30	66	113	7	.269	11
Lopez, Albie, Cle.	R	5	4	6.39	13	10	0	0	0	0	62.0	80	47	44	14	22	45	2	.311	2
Martinez, Dennis, Cle.	R	9	6	4.50	20	20	1	1	0	0	112.0	122	63	56	12	37	48	0	.278	12
McDonald, Ben, Mil.	R	12	10	3.90	35	35	2	0	0	0	221.1	228	104	96	25	67	146	4	.264	24
McDowell, Jack, Cle.	R	13	9	5.11	30	30	5	1	0	0	192.0	214	119	109	22	67	141	5	.282	16
Mendoza, Ramiro, NYA	R	4	5	6.79	12	11	0	0	0	0	53.0	80	43	40	5	10	34	2	.343	1
Menhart, Paul, Sea.	R	2	2	7.29	11	6	0	0	4	0	42.0	55	36	34	9	25	18	1	.327	-2
Milacki, Bob, Sea.	R	1	4	6.86	7	4	0	0	1	0	21.0	30	20	16	3	15	13	0	.330	-2
Miller, Travis, Min.	L	1	2	9.23	7	7	0	0	0	0	26.1	45	29	27	7	9	15	0	.388	-3
Miller, Trever, Det.	L	0	4	9.18	5	4	0	0	0	0	16.2	28	17	17	3	9	8	0	.384	-4
Minchey, Nate, Bos.	R	0	2	15.00	2	2	0	0	0	0	6.0	16	11	10	1	5	4	1	.533	-4

1997 BASEBALL WEEKLY ALMANAC

American League starting pitchers

Name/Team	T	W	L	ERA	G	GS	CG	SHO	GF	SV	IP	H	R	ER	HR	BB	SO	WP	BA	RV
Moehler, Brian, Det.	R	0	1	4.35	2	2	0	0	0	0	10.1	11	10	5	1	8	2	1	.262	-1
Moyer, Jamie, Bos.-Sea.	L	13	3	3.98	34	21	0	0	1	0	160.2	177	86	71	23	46	79	3	.276	18
Mulholland, Terry, Sea.	L	5	4	4.67	12	12	0	0	0	0	69.1	75	38	36	5	28	34	1	.286	6
Mussina, Mike, Bal.	R	19	11	4.81	36	36	4	1	0	0	243.1	264	137	130	31	69	204	3	.275	26
Nagy, Charles, Cle.	R	17	5	3.41	32	32	5	0	0	0	222.0	217	89	84	21	61	167	7	.255	31
Nitkowski, C.J., Det.	L	2	3	8.08	11	8	0	0	0	0	45.2	62	44	41	7	38	36	2	.332	-4
Ogea, Chad, Cle.	R	10	6	4.79	29	21	1	1	2	0	146.2	151	82	78	22	42	101	2	.266	14
Olivares, Omar, Det.	R	7	11	4.89	25	25	4	0	0	0	160.0	169	90	87	16	75	81	4	.275	10
Oliver, Darren, Tex.	L	14	6	4.66	30	30	1	1	0	0	173.2	190	97	90	20	76	112	5	.279	17
Pavlik, Roger, Tex.	R	15	8	5.19	34	34	7	0	0	0	201.0	216	120	116	28	81	127	8	.276	17
Pettitte, Andy, NYA	L	21	8	3.87	35	34	2	0	1	0	221.0	229	105	95	23	72	162	6	.271	30
Prieto, Ariel, Oak.	R	6	7	4.15	21	21	2	0	0	0	125.2	130	66	58	9	54	75	6	.273	10
Quantrill, Paul, Tor.	R	5	14	5.43	38	20	0	0	7	0	134.1	172	90	81	27	51	86	1	.317	5
Radke, Brad, Min.	R	11	16	4.46	35	35	3	0	0	0	232.0	231	125	115	40	57	148	1	.256	23
Robertson, Rich, Min.	L	7	17	5.12	36	31	5	3	1	0	186.1	197	113	106	22	116	114	7	.273	8
Rodriguez, Frankie, Min.	R	13	14	5.05	38	33	3	0	4	2	206.2	218	129	116	27	78	110	2	.272	19
Rogers, Kenny, NYA	L	12	8	4.68	30	30	2	1	0	0	179.0	179	97	93	16	83	92	5	.261	16
Rosado, Jose, K.C.	L	8	6	3.21	16	16	2	1	0	0	106.2	101	39	38	7	26	64	5	.249	15
Sanderson, Scott, Cal.	R	0	2	7.50	5	4	0	0	0	0	18.0	39	21	15	5	4	7	0	.433	-3
Sele, Aaron, Bos.	R	7	11	5.32	29	29	1	0	0	0	157.1	192	110	93	14	67	137	2	.303	7
Serafini, Dan, Min.	L	0	1	10.38	1	1	0	0	0	0	4.1	7	5	5	1	2	1	0	.368	-2
Sodowsky, Clint, Det.	R	1	3	11.84	7	7	0	0	0	0	24.1	40	34	32	5	20	9	3	.370	-5
Sparks, Steve, Mil.	R	4	7	6.60	20	13	1	0	2	0	88.2	103	66	65	19	52	21	6	.297	0
Springer, Dennis, Cal.	R	5	6	5.51	20	15	2	1	3	0	94.2	91	65	58	24	43	64	1	.251	5
Tapani, Kevin, ChiA	R	13	10	4.59	34	34	1	0	0	0	225.1	236	123	115	34	76	150	13	.268	21
Telgheder, Dave, Oak.	R	4	7	4.65	16	14	1	1	1	0	79.1	92	42	41	12	26	43	2	.292	6
Thompson, Justin, Det.	L	1	6	4.58	11	11	0	0	0	0	59.0	62	35	30	7	31	44	1	.267	2
Torres, Salomon, Sea.	R	3	3	4.59	10	7	1	1	1	0	49.0	44	27	25	5	23	36	1	.242	4
VanEgmond, Tim, Mil.	R	3	5	5.27	12	9	0	0	1	0	54.2	58	35	32	6	23	33	0	.274	3
Viola, Frank, Tor.	L	1	3	7.71	6	6	0	0	0	0	30.1	43	28	26	6	21	18	1	.350	-3
Wagner, Matt, Sea.	R	3	5	6.86	15	14	1	0	0	0	80.0	91	62	61	15	38	41	0	.285	0
Wakefield, Tim, Bos.	R	14	13	5.14	32	32	6	0	0	0	211.2	238	151	121	38	90	140	4	.280	16
Wasdin, John, Oak.	R	8	7	5.96	25	21	1	0	2	0	131.1	145	96	87	24	50	75	2	.283	7
Wells, David, Bal.	L	11	14	5.14	34	34	3	0	0	0	224.1	247	132	128	32	51	130	4	.285	18
Wengert, Don, Oak.	R	7	11	5.58	36	25	1	1	2	0	161.1	200	102	100	29	60	75	4	.307	7
Whitehurst, Wally, NYA	R	1	1	6.75	2	2	0	0	0	0	8.0	11	6	6	1	2	1	0	.324	-1
Williams, Woody, Tor.	R	4	5	4.73	12	10	1	0	0	0	59.0	64	33	31	8	21	43	2	.278	5
Witt, Bobby, Tex.	R	16	12	5.41	33	32	2	0	1	0	199.2	235	129	120	28	96	157	4	.295	15
Wojciechowski, S., Oak.	L	5	5	5.65	16	15	0	0	0	0	79.2	97	57	50	10	28	30	3	.300	4
Wolcott, Bob, Sea.	R	7	10	5.73	30	28	1	0	0	0	149.1	179	101	95	26	54	78	3	.297	7

National League relief pitchers

Name/Team	T	W	L	ERA	G	GS	CG	SHO	GF	SV	IP	H	R	ER	HR	BB	SO	WP	BA	RV
Adams, Terry, ChiN	R	3	6	2.94	69	0	0	0	22	4	101.0	84	36	33	6	49	78	5	.231	11
Adamson, Joel, Fla.	L	0	0	7.36	9	0	0	0	1	0	11.0	18	9	9	1	7	7	0	.400	-3
Alston, Garvin, Col.	R	1	0	9.00	6	0	0	0	4	0	6.0	9	6	6	1	3	5	1	.375	-1
Alvarez, Tavo, Mon.	R	2	1	3.00	11	5	0	0	3	0	21.0	19	10	7	0	12	9	0	.235	1
Aucoin, Derek, Mon.	R	0	1	3.38	2	0	0	0	0	0	2.2	3	1	1	0	1	1	0	.300	-1
Bailey, Cory, St.L	R	5	2	3.00	51	0	0	0	12	0	57.0	57	21	19	1	30	38	3	.263	5
Bailey, Roger, Col.	R	2	3	6.24	24	11	0	0	4	1	83.2	94	64	58	7	52	45	3	.288	-3
Barton, Shawn, S.F.	L	0	0	9.72	7	0	0	0	2	0	8.1	19	12	9	2	1	3	1	.442	-3
Batchelor, Rich, St.L	R	2	0	1.20	11	0	0	0	7	0	15.0	9	2	2	0	1	11	0	.173	3
Batista, Miguel, Fla.	R	0	0	5.56	9	0	0	0	4	0	11.1	9	8	7	0	7	6	1	.231	-1
Bautista, Jose, S.F.	R	3	4	3.36	37	1	0	0	12	0	69.2	66	32	26	10	15	28	0	.249	6
Beck, Rod, S.F.	R	0	9	3.34	63	0	0	0	58	35	62.0	56	23	23	9	10	48	1	.238	28
Beckett, Robbie, Col.	L	0	0	13.50	5	0	0	0	2	0	5.1	6	8	8	3	9	6	1	.286	-1
Bergman, Sean, S.D.	R	6	8	4.37	41	14	0	0	11	0	113.1	119	63	55	14	33	85	7	.274	7
Berumen, Andres, S.D.	R	0	0	5.40	3	0	0	0	1	0	3.1	3	2	2	1	2	4	0	.231	-1
Bielecki, Mike, Atl.	R	4	3	2.63	40	5	0	0	8	2	75.1	63	24	22	8	33	71	2	.224	9
Blair, Willie, S.D.	R	2	6	4.60	60	0	0	0	17	1	88.0	80	52	45	13	29	67	2	.240	4
Blazier, Ron, Phi.	R	3	1	5.87	27	0	0	0	9	0	38.1	49	30	25	6	10	25	3	.310	0
Bochtler, Doug, S.D.	R	2	4	3.02	63	0	0	0	17	3	65.2	45	25	22	6	39	68	8	.195	7
Boever, Joe, Pit.	R	0	2	5.40	13	0	0	0	9	2	15.0	17	11	9	2	6	6	3	.288	0
Borbon, Pedro Jr., Atl.	L	3	0	2.75	43	0	0	0	19	1	36.0	26	12	11	1	7	31	0	.203	6
Borland, Toby, Phi.	R	7	3	4.07	69	0	0	0	11	0	90.2	83	51	41	9	43	76	10	.239	7
Borowski, Joe, Atl.	R	2	4	4.85	22	0	0	0	8	0	26.0	33	15	14	4	13	15	1	.324	0
Bottalico, Ricky, Phi.	R	4	5	3.19	61	0	0	0	56	34	67.2	47	24	24	6	23	74	3	.197	30
Bottenfield, Kent, ChiN	R	3	5	2.63	48	0	0	0	10	1	61.2	59	25	18	3	19	33	2	.255	7

National League relief pitchers

Name/Team	T	W	L	ERA	G	GS	CG	SHO	GF	SV	IP	H	R	ER	HR	BB	SO	WP	BA	RV
Bourgeois, Steve, S.F.	R	1	3	6.30	15	5	0	0	4	0	40.0	60	35	28	4	21	17	4	.355	-3
Brantley, Jeff, Cin.	R	1	2	2.41	66	0	0	0	61	44	71.0	54	21	19	7	28	76	2	.215	36
Brocail, Doug, Hou.	R	1	5	4.58	23	4	0	0	4	0	53.0	58	31	27	7	23	34	0	.289	0
Bruske, Jim, L.A.	R	0	0	5.68	11	0	0	0	5	0	12.2	17	8	8	2	3	12	1	.315	-2
Burke, John, Col.	R	2	1	7.47	11	0	0	0	3	0	15.2	21	13	13	3	7	19	1	.318	-1
Byrd, Paul, NYN	R	1	2	4.24	38	0	0	0	14	0	46.2	48	22	22	7	21	31	3	.265	1
Campbell, Mike, ChiN	R	3	1	4.46	13	5	0	0	4	0	36.1	29	19	18	7	10	19	0	.216	3
Carlson, Dan, S.F.	R	1	0	2.70	5	0	0	0	3	0	10.0	13	6	3	2	2	4	0	.310	0
Carrasco, Hector, Cin.	R	4	3	3.75	56	0	0	0	10	0	74.1	58	37	31	6	45	59	8	.214	5
Casian, Larry, ChiN	L	1	1	1.88	35	0	0	0	4	0	24.0	14	5	5	2	11	15	1	.187	2
Christiansen, Jason, Pit.	L	3	3	6.70	33	0	0	0	9	0	44.1	56	34	33	7	19	38	4	.311	-2
Clark, Terry, Hou.	R	0	2	11.37	5	0	0	0	3	0	6.1	16	10	8	1	2	5	1	.471	-3
Clontz, Brad, Atl.	R	6	3	5.69	81	0	0	0	11	1	80.2	78	53	51	11	33	49	0	.255	4
Cooke, Steve, Pit.	L	0	0	7.56	3	0	0	0	1	0	8.1	11	7	7	1	5	7	1	.314	-2
Cordova, Francisco, Pit.	R	4	7	4.09	59	6	0	0	41	12	99.0	103	49	45	11	20	95	2	.263	15
Creek, Doug, S.F.	L	0	2	6.52	63	0	0	0	15	0	48.1	45	41	35	11	32	38	2	.243	-3
Cummings, John, L.A.	L	0	1	6.75	4	0	0	0	1	0	5.1	12	7	4	1	2	5	0	.462	-2
Daal, Omar, Mon.	L	4	5	4.02	64	6	0	0	9	0	87.1	74	40	39	10	37	82	1	.228	6
DeLucia, Rich, S.F.	R	3	6	5.84	56	0	0	0	20	0	61.2	62	44	40	8	31	55	7	.259	0
Dessens, Elmer, Pit.	R	0	2	8.28	15	3	0	0	1	0	25.0	40	23	23	2	4	13	0	.385	-4
Dewey, Mark, S.F.	R	6	3	4.21	78	0	0	0	19	0	83.1	79	40	39	9	41	57	4	.257	5
DiPoto, Jerry, NYN	R	7	2	4.19	57	0	0	0	21	0	77.1	91	44	36	5	45	52	3	.298	4
Dishman, Glenn, S.D.-Phi.	L	0	0	7.71	7	1	0	0	4	0	9.1	12	8	8	2	3	3	1	.316	-4
Dougherty, Jim, Hou.	R	0	2	9.00	12	0	0	0	2	0	13.0	14	14	13	2	11	6	0	.280	-3
Dreifort, Darren, L.A.	R	1	4	4.94	19	0	0	0	5	0	23.2	23	13	13	2	12	24	2	.256	0
Dyer, Mike, Mon.	R	5	5	4.40	70	1	0	0	20	2	75.2	79	40	37	7	34	51	4	.277	5
Eckersley, Dennis, St.L	R	0	6	3.30	63	0	0	0	53	30	60.0	65	26	22	8	6	49	0	.274	24
Eischen, Joey, L.A.	L	0	1	4.78	28	0	0	0	11	0	43.1	48	25	23	4	20	36	1	.282	-1
Ericks, John, Pit.	R	4	5	5.79	28	4	0	0	13	8	46.2	56	35	30	11	19	46	2	.292	6
Florie, Bryce, S.D.	R	2	2	4.01	39	0	0	0	11	0	49.1	45	24	22	1	27	51	3	.239	2
Fossas, Tony, St.L	L	0	4	2.68	65	0	0	0	11	2	47.0	43	19	14	7	21	36	3	.231	4
Franco, John, NYN	L	4	3	1.83	51	0	0	0	44	28	54.0	54	15	11	2	21	48	2	.260	25
Frey, Steve, Phi.	L	0	1	4.72	31	0	0	0	12	0	34.1	38	19	18	4	18	12	0	.295	-1
Fyhrie, Mike, NYN	R	0	1	15.43	2	0	0	0	0	0	2.1	4	4	4	0	3	0	0	.364	-2
Guthrie, Mark, L.A.	L	2	3	3.22	66	0	0	0	16	1	73.0	65	21	18	3	22	56	1	.240	8
Habyan, John, Col.	R	1	1	7.13	19	0	0	0	5	0	24.0	34	19	19	4	14	25	5	.347	-3
Hall, Darren, L.A.	R	0	2	6.00	9	0	0	0	3	0	12.0	13	9	8	2	5	12	0	.271	-2
Hammond, Chris, Fla.	L	5	8	6.56	38	9	0	0	5	0	81.0	104	65	59	14	27	50	1	.315	-1
Hancock, Lee, Pit.	L	0	0	6.38	13	0	0	0	3	0	18.1	21	18	13	5	10	13	1	.276	-2
Hartgraves, D., Hou.-Atl.	L	1	0	4.78	39	0	0	0	9	0	37.2	34	21	20	4	23	30	2	.245	-2
Hawblitzel, Ryan, Col.	R	0	1	6.00	8	0	0	0	3	0	15.0	18	12	10	2	6	7	1	.290	-2
Heflin, Bronson, Phi.	R	0	0	6.75	3	0	0	0	2	0	6.2	11	7	5	1	3	4	0	.367	-2
Henry, Doug, NYN	R	2	8	4.68	58	0	0	0	33	9	75.0	82	48	39	7	36	58	6	.273	7
Heredia, Felix, Fla.	L	1	1	4.32	21	0	0	0	5	0	16.2	21	8	8	1	10	10	2	.313	-1
Hermanson, Dustin, S.D.	R	1	0	8.56	8	0	0	0	4	0	13.2	18	15	13	3	4	11	0	.340	-2
Hernandez, Livan, Fla.	R	0	0	0.00	1	0	0	0	0	0	3.0	3	0	0	0	2	2	0	.273	-1
Hernandez, X., Cin.-Hou.	R	5	5	4.62	61	0	0	0	27	6	78.0	77	45	40	13	28	81	9	.258	8
Hoffman, Trevor, S.D.	R	9	5	2.25	70	0	0	0	62	42	88.0	50	23	22	6	31	111	2	.161	44
Holmes, Darren, Col.	R	5	4	3.97	62	0	0	0	21	1	77.0	78	41	34	8	28	73	2	.260	6
Holt, Chris, Hou.	R	0	1	5.79	4	0	0	0	3	0	4.2	5	3	3	0	3	0	1	.263	-2
Honeycutt, Rick, St.L	L	2	1	2.85	61	0	0	0	13	4	47.1	42	15	15	3	7	30	1	.240	7
Hook, Chris, S.F.	R	0	1	7.43	10	0	0	0	3	0	13.1	16	13	11	3	14	4	1	.308	-3
Hudek, John, Hou.	R	2	0	2.81	15	0	0	0	6	2	16.0	12	5	5	2	5	14	1	.207	3
Hurst, Bill, Fla.	R	0	0	0.00	2	0	0	0	2	0	2.0	3	0	0	0	1	1	1	.333	-1
Jackson, Danny, St.L	L	1	1	4.46	13	4	0	0	3	0	36.1	33	18	18	3	16	27	0	.243	1
Johnstone, John, Hou.	R	1	0	5.54	9	0	0	0	6	0	13.0	17	8	8	2	5	5	0	.321	-1
Jones, Doug, ChiN	R	2	2	5.01	28	0	0	0	13	2	32.1	41	20	18	4	7	26	0	.306	2
Jones, Todd, Hou.	R	6	3	4.40	51	0	0	0	37	17	57.1	61	30	28	5	32	44	3	.274	15
Jordan, Ricardo, Phi.	L	2	2	1.80	26	0	0	0	9	0	25.0	18	6	5	0	12	17	1	.202	3
Juden, Jeff, S.F.-Mon.	R	5	0	3.27	58	0	0	0	16	0	74.1	61	35	27	8	34	61	5	.223	6
Leiper, Dave, Phi.-Mon.	L	2	1	7.20	33	0	0	0	8	0	25.0	40	21	20	4	9	13	2	.370	-3
Leskanic, Curtis, Col.	R	7	5	6.23	70	0	0	0	32	6	73.2	82	51	51	12	38	76	6	.285	5
Lieber, Jon, Pit.	R	9	5	3.99	51	15	0	0	6	1	142.0	156	70	63	19	28	94	0	.279	13
Lilliquist, Derek, Cin.	L	0	0	7.36	5	0	0	0	3	0	3.2	5	3	3	1	0	1	0	.357	-2
Lomon, Kevin, Atl.	R	0	0	4.91	6	0	0	0	1	0	7.1	7	4	4	0	3	1	0	.259	-1
Ludwick, Eric, St.L	R	0	1	9.00	6	1	0	0	2	0	10.0	11	11	10	4	3	12	0	.275	-2
MacDonald, Bob, NYN	L	0	2	4.26	20	0	0	0	5	0	19.0	16	10	9	2	9	12	1	.235	-1
Maduro, Calvin, Phi.	R	0	1	3.52	4	2	0	0	0	0	15.1	13	6	6	1	3	11	1	.232	0
Mantei, Matt, Fla.	R	1	0	6.38	14	0	0	0	1	0	18.1	13	13	13	2	21	25	2	.197	-2
Manuel, Barry, Mon.	R	4	1	3.24	53	0	0	0	7	0	86.0	70	34	31	10	26	62	4	.220	9

330

National League relief pitchers

Name/Team	T	W	L	ERA	G	GS	CG	SHO	GF	SV	IP	H	R	ER	HR	BB	SO	WP	BA	RV
Martinez, P. A., NYN-Cin.	L	0	0	6.30	9	0	0	0	0	0	10.0	13	9	7	2	8	9	0	.317	-3
Mathews, Terry, Fla.	R	2	4	4.91	57	0	0	0	19	4	55.0	59	33	30	7	27	49	0	.273	3
Mathews, T.J., St.L	R	2	6	3.01	67	0	0	0	23	6	83.2	62	32	28	8	32	80	1	.203	12
May, Darrell, Pit.	L	0	1	9.35	5	2	0	0	0	0	8.2	15	10	9	5	4	5	0	.357	-3
McElroy, Chuck, Cin.	L	2	0	6.57	12	0	0	0	1	0	12.1	13	10	9	2	10	13	0	.265	-1
McMichael, Greg, Atl.	R	5	3	3.22	73	0	0	0	14	2	86.2	84	37	31	4	27	78	4	.253	10
Miceli, Dan, Pit.	R	2	10	5.78	44	9	0	0	17	1	85.2	99	65	55	15	45	66	9	.291	-2
Miller, Kurt, Fla.	R	1	3	6.80	26	5	0	0	6	0	46.1	57	41	35	5	33	30	1	.313	-4
Minor, Blas, NYN	R	0	0	3.51	17	0	0	0	4	0	25.2	23	11	10	4	6	20	1	.237	1
Mitchell, Larry, Phi.	R	0	0	4.50	7	0	0	0	2	0	12.0	14	6	6	1	5	7	0	.311	-1
Mlicki, Dave, NYN	R	6	7	3.30	51	2	0	0	16	1	90.0	95	46	33	9	33	83	7	.277	9
Moore, Marcus, Cin.	R	3	3	5.81	23	0	0	0	11	2	26.1	26	21	17	3	22	27	1	.263	1
Morel, Ramon, Pit.	R	2	1	5.36	29	0	0	0	4	0	42.0	57	27	25	4	19	22	1	.324	-1
Morman, Alvin, Hou.	L	4	1	4.93	53	0	0	0	9	0	42.0	43	24	23	8	24	31	3	.261	1
Munoz, Mike, Col.	L	2	2	6.65	54	0	0	0	7	0	44.2	55	33	33	4	16	45	0	.302	-2
Myers, Rodney, ChiN	R	2	1	4.68	45	0	0	0	8	0	67.1	61	38	35	6	38	50	4	.243	1
Nen, Robb, Fla.	R	5	1	1.95	75	0	0	0	66	35	83.0	67	21	18	2	21	92	4	.225	36
Nied, David, Col.	R	0	2	13.50	6	1	0	0	3	0	5.1	5	8	8	1	8	4	0	.250	-3
Olson, Gregg, Hou.	R	1	0	4.82	9	0	0	0	2	0	9.1	12	5	5	1	7	8	1	.308	-1
Oquist, Mike, S.D.	R	0	0	2.35	8	0	0	0	3	0	7.2	6	2	2	0	4	4	1	.231	-1
Osuna, Al, S.D.	L	0	0	2.25	10	0	0	0	0	0	4.0	5	1	1	0	2	4	1	.313	-1
Osuna, Antonio, L.A.	R	9	6	3.00	73	0	0	0	21	4	84.0	65	33	28	6	32	85	3	.220	15
Pacheco, Alex, Mon.	R	0	0	11.12	5	0	0	0	2	0	5.2	8	7	7	2	1	7	0	.320	-2
Painter, Lance, Col.	L	4	2	5.86	34	1	0	0	4	0	50.2	56	37	33	12	25	48	1	.280	0
Pall, Donn, Fla.	R	1	1	5.79	12	0	0	0	2	0	18.2	16	15	12	3	9	9	1	.232	-1
Park, Chan Ho, L.A.	R	5	5	3.64	48	10	0	0	7	0	108.2	82	48	44	7	71	119	4	.209	7
Parrett, Jeff, St.L-Phi.	R	3	3	3.39	51	0	0	0	23	0	66.1	64	25	25	2	31	64	10	.254	2
Parris, Steve, Pit.	R	0	3	7.18	8	4	0	0	3	0	26.1	35	22	21	4	11	27	2	.321	-3
Patterson, Bob, ChiN	L	3	3	3.13	79	0	0	0	27	8	54.2	46	19	19	6	22	53	1	.229	10
Pena, Alejandro, Fla.	R	0	1	4.50	4	0	0	0	3	0	4.0	4	5	2	2	1	5	0	.235	-1
Perez, Mike, ChiN	R	1	0	4.67	24	0	0	0	4	0	27.0	29	14	14	2	13	22	1	.264	0
Perez, Yorkis, Fla.	L	3	4	5.29	64	0	0	0	15	0	47.2	51	28	28	2	31	47	2	.274	0
Person, Robert, NYN	R	4	5	4.52	27	13	0	0	1	0	89.2	86	50	45	16	35	76	3	.247	4
Petkovsek, Mark, St.L	R	11	2	3.55	48	6	0	0	7	0	88.2	83	37	35	9	35	45	2	.251	12
Plesac, Dan, Pit.	L	6	5	4.09	73	0	0	0	30	11	70.1	67	35	32	4	24	76	4	.247	14
Poole, Jim Ri., S.F.	L	2	1	2.66	35	0	0	0	5	0	23.2	15	7	7	2	13	19	1	.188	2
Powell, Jay, Fla.	R	4	3	4.54	67	0	0	0	16	2	71.1	71	41	36	5	36	52	3	.255	4
Pugh, Tim, Cin.	R	1	1	11.49	10	0	0	0	0	0	15.2	24	20	20	3	11	9	1	.353	-4
Radinsky, Scott, L.A.	L	5	1	2.41	58	0	0	0	19	1	52.1	52	19	14	2	17	48	0	.264	7
Reed, Steve, Col.	R	4	3	3.96	70	0	0	0	7	0	75.0	66	38	33	11	19	51	1	.239	6
Remlinger, Mike, Cin.	L	0	1	5.60	19	4	0	0	2	0	27.1	24	17	17	4	19	19	2	.245	-2
Rojas, Mel, Mon.	R	7	4	3.22	74	0	0	0	64	36	81.0	56	30	29	5	28	92	3	.193	35
Ruebel, Matt, Pit.	L	1	1	4.60	26	7	0	0	3	1	58.2	64	38	30	7	25	22	2	.277	1
Ruffin, Bruce, Col.	L	7	5	4.00	71	0	0	0	56	24	69.2	55	35	31	5	29	74	10	.212	24
Ruffin, Johnny, Cin.	R	1	3	5.49	49	0	0	0	13	0	62.1	71	42	38	10	37	69	8	.292	-2
Ryan, Ken, Phi.	R	3	5	2.43	62	0	0	0	26	8	89.0	71	32	24	4	45	70	4	.223	14
Sanders, Scott, S.D.	R	9	5	3.38	46	16	0	0	6	0	144.0	117	58	54	10	48	157	7	.221	16
Schutz, Carl, Atl.	L	0	0	2.70	3	0	0	0	1	0	3.1	3	1	1	0	2	5	0	.273	-1
Scott, Tim, Mon.-S.F.	R	5	7	4.64	65	0	0	0	16	1	66.0	65	36	34	8	30	47	3	.262	3
Service, Scott, Cin.	R	1	0	3.94	34	1	0	0	5	0	48.0	51	21	21	7	18	46	5	.277	1
Shaw, Jeff, Cin.	R	8	6	2.49	78	0	0	0	24	4	104.2	99	34	29	8	29	69	0	.252	17
Small, Mark, Hou.	R	0	1	5.92	16	0	0	0	4	0	24.1	33	23	16	1	13	16	1	.308	-3
Smith, Lee, Cin.	R	3	4	4.06	43	0	0	0	16	2	44.1	49	20	20	4	23	35	2	.277	3
Spradlin, Jerry, Cin.	R	0	0	0.00	1	0	0	0	1	0	0.1	0	0	0	0	0	0	1	.000	-1
Springer, Russ, Phi.	R	3	10	4.66	51	7	0	0	12	0	96.2	106	60	50	12	38	94	5	.272	4
Sturtze, Tanyon, ChiN	R	1	0	9.00	6	0	0	0	3	0	11.0	16	11	11	3	5	7	0	.348	-2
Sullivan, Scott, Cin.	R	0	0	2.25	7	0	0	0	4	0	8.0	7	2	2	0	5	3	1	.250	-1
Swift, Bill C., Col.	R	1	1	5.40	7	3	0	0	2	2	18.1	23	12	11	1	5	5	0	.307	1
Swindell, Greg, Hou.	L	0	3	7.83	8	4	0	0	3	0	23.0	35	25	20	5	11	15	0	.340	-4
Tabaka, Jeff, Hou.	L	0	2	6.64	18	0	0	0	5	1	20.1	28	18	15	5	14	18	3	.322	-2
Thobe, Tom, Atl.	L	0	1	1.50	4	0	0	0	3	0	6.0	5	2	1	0	1	0	0	.217	0
Trlicek, Rick, NYN	R	0	1	3.38	5	0	0	0	2	0	5.1	3	2	2	0	3	3	0	.214	-1
Veras, Dario, S.D.	R	3	1	2.79	23	0	0	0	6	0	29.0	24	10	9	3	10	23	1	.231	3
Veres, Dave, Mon.	R	6	3	4.17	68	0	0	0	22	4	77.2	85	39	36	10	32	81	3	.277	8
Villone, Ron, S.D.	L	1	1	2.95	21	0	0	0	9	0	18.1	17	6	6	2	7	19	0	.243	1
Wade, Terrell, Atl.	L	5	0	2.97	44	8	0	0	13	1	69.2	57	28	23	9	47	79	2	.227	7
Wagner, Billy, Hou.	L	2	2	2.44	37	0	0	0	20	9	51.2	28	16	14	6	30	67	1	.165	11
Wainhouse, Dave, Pit.	R	1	0	5.70	17	0	0	0	6	0	23.2	22	16	15	3	10	16	2	.250	-1
Walker, Pete, S.D.	R	0	0	0.00	1	0	0	0	0	0	0.2	0	0	0	0	3	1	0	.000	-2
Wallace, Derek, NYN	R	2	3	4.01	19	0	0	0	11	3	24.2	29	12	11	2	14	15	2	.290	2

National League relief pitchers

Name/Team	T	W	L	ERA	G	GS	CG	SHO	GF	SV	IP	H	R	ER	HR	BB	SO	WP	BA	RV
Weathers, David, Fla.	R	2	2	4.54	31	8	0	0	8	0	71.1	85	41	36	7	28	40	2	.302	1
Wendell, Turk, ChiN	R	4	5	2.84	70	0	0	0	49	18	79.1	58	26	25	8	44	75	3	.201	20
Wilkins, Marc, Pit.	R	4	3	3.84	47	2	0	0	11	1	75.0	75	36	32	6	36	62	5	.266	5
Wohlers, Mark, Atl.	R	2	4	3.03	77	0	0	0	64	39	77.1	71	30	26	8	21	100	10	.240	33
Woodall, Brad, Atl.	L	2	2	7.32	8	3	0	0	2	0	19.2	28	19	16	4	4	20	1	.333	-1
Worrell, Tim, S.D.	R	9	7	3.05	50	11	0	0	8	1	121.0	109	45	41	9	39	99	0	.236	15
Worrell, Todd, L.A.	R	4	6	3.03	72	0	0	0	67	44	65.1	70	29	22	5	15	66	4	.265	36
Young, Anthony, Hou.	R	3	3	4.59	28	0	0	0	10	0	33.1	36	18	17	4	22	19	2	.279	1

National League starting pitchers

Name/Team	T	W	L	ERA	G	GS	CG	SHO	GF	SV	IP	H	R	ER	HR	BB	SO	WP	BA	RV
Ashby, Andy, S.D.	R	9	5	3.23	24	24	1	0	0	0	150.2	147	60	54	17	34	85	3	.259	17
Astacio, Pedro, L.A.	R	9	8	3.44	35	32	0	0	0	0	211.2	207	86	81	18	67	130	6	.261	18
Avery, Steve, Atl.	L	7	10	4.47	24	23	1	0	0	0	131.0	146	70	65	10	40	86	5	.285	7
Barber, Brian, St.L	R	0	0	15.00	1	1	0	0	0	0	3.0	4	5	5	0	6	1	0	.364	-3
Beech, Matt, Phi.	L	1	4	6.97	8	8	0	0	0	0	41.1	49	32	32	8	11	33	0	.306	-2
Benes, Alan, St.L	R	13	10	4.90	34	32	3	1	1	0	191.0	192	120	104	27	87	131	5	.266	10
Benes, Andy, St.L	R	18	10	3.83	36	34	3	1	1	1	230.1	215	107	98	28	77	160	6	.247	25
Brown, Kevin, Fla.	R	17	11	1.89	32	32	5	3	0	0	233.0	187	60	49	8	33	159	6	.220	41
Bullinger, Jim, ChiN	R	6	10	6.54	37	20	1	1	6	1	129.1	144	101	94	15	68	90	7	.283	-2
Burba, Dave, Cin.	R	11	13	3.83	34	33	0	0	0	0	195.0	179	96	83	18	97	148	9	.244	15
Burkett, John, Fla.	R	6	10	4.32	24	24	1	0	0	0	154.0	154	84	74	15	42	108	0	.263	10
Busby, Mike, St.L	R	0	1	18.00	1	1	0	0	0	0	4.0	9	13	8	4	4	4	0	.409	-3
Candiotti, Tom, L.A.	R	9	11	4.49	28	27	1	0	0	0	152.1	172	91	76	18	43	79	3	.288	9
Carrara, Giovanni, Cin.	R	1	0	5.87	8	5	0	0	1	0	23.0	31	17	15	6	13	13	0	.323	-2
Castillo, Frank, ChiN	R	7	16	5.28	33	33	1	1	0	0	182.1	209	112	107	28	46	139	2	.288	5
Clark, Mark, NYN	R	14	11	3.43	32	32	2	0	0	0	212.1	217	98	81	20	48	142	6	.265	23
Cormier, Rheal, Mon.	L	7	10	4.17	33	27	1	1	1	0	159.2	165	80	74	16	41	100	8	.270	11
Crawford, Carlos, Phi.	R	0	1	4.91	1	1	0	0	0	0	3.2	7	10	2	1	2	4	0	.389	-2
Darwin, Danny, Pit.-Hou.	R	10	11	3.77	34	25	0	0	1	0	164.2	160	79	69	16	27	96	3	.257	16
Drabek, Doug, Hou.	R	7	9	4.57	30	30	1	0	0	0	175.1	208	102	89	21	60	137	9	.298	6
Estes, Shawn, S.F.	L	3	5	3.60	11	11	0	0	0	0	70.0	63	30	28	3	39	60	4	.243	4
Farmer, Mike, Col.	L	0	1	7.71	7	4	0	0	1	0	28.0	32	25	24	8	13	16	1	.286	-3
Fassero, Jeff, Mon.	L	15	11	3.30	34	34	5	1	0	0	231.2	217	95	85	20	55	222	5	.244	27
Fernandez, Osvaldo, S.F.	R	7	13	4.61	30	28	2	0	1	0	171.2	193	95	88	20	57	106	6	.286	7
Fernandez, Sid, Phi.	R	3	6	3.43	11	11	0	0	0	0	63.0	50	25	24	5	26	77	1	.215	5
Foster, Kevin, ChiN	R	7	6	6.21	17	16	1	0	0	0	87.0	98	63	60	16	35	53	2	.288	1
Freeman, Marvin, Col.	R	7	9	6.04	26	23	0	0	1	0	129.2	151	100	87	21	57	71	13	.294	0
Gardner, Mark, S.F.	R	12	7	4.42	30	28	4	1	0	0	179.1	200	105	88	28	57	145	2	.283	12
Glavine, Tom, Atl.	L	15	10	2.98	36	36	1	0	0	0	235.1	222	91	78	14	85	181	4	.249	27
Grace, Mike, Phi.	R	7	2	3.49	12	12	1	1	0	0	80.0	72	33	31	9	16	49	0	.238	10
Hamilton, Joey, S.D.	R	15	9	4.17	34	33	3	1	0	0	211.2	206	100	98	19	83	184	14	.256	17
Hampton, Mike, Hou.	L	10	10	3.59	27	27	2	1	0	0	160.1	175	79	64	12	49	101	7	.280	14
Harnisch, Pete, NYN	R	8	12	4.21	31	31	2	1	0	0	194.2	195	103	91	30	61	114	7	.260	13
Helling, Rick, Fla.	R	2	1	1.95	5	4	0	0	0	0	27.2	14	6	6	2	7	26	0	.143	4
Hope, John, Pit.	R	1	3	6.98	5	4	0	0	0	0	19.1	17	18	15	5	11	13	2	.246	-1
Hunter, Rich, Phi.	R	3	7	6.49	14	14	0	0	0	0	69.1	84	54	50	10	33	32	4	.304	-1
Hutton, Mark, Fla.	R	5	1	3.67	13	9	0	0	0	0	56.1	47	23	23	6	18	31	2	.222	6
Isringhausen, J., NYN	R	6	14	4.77	27	27	2	1	0	0	171.2	190	103	91	13	73	114	14	.284	5
Jarvis, Kevin, Cin.	R	8	9	5.98	24	20	2	1	2	0	120.1	152	93	80	17	43	63	3	.305	1
Jones, Bobby J., NYN	R	12	8	4.42	31	31	3	1	0	0	195.2	219	102	96	26	46	116	2	.288	14
Kile, Darryl, Hou.	R	12	11	4.19	35	33	4	0	1	0	219.0	233	113	102	16	97	219	13	.276	13
Larkin, Andy, Fla.	R	0	0	1.80	1	1	0	0	0	0	5.0	3	1	1	0	4	2	0	.176	-1
Leiter, Al, Fla.	L	16	12	2.93	33	33	2	1	0	0	215.1	153	74	70	14	119	200	5	.202	27
Leiter, Mark, S.F.-Mon.	R	8	12	4.92	35	34	2	0	0	0	205.0	219	128	112	37	69	164	6	.273	6
Loaiza, Esteban, Pit.	R	2	3	4.96	10	10	1	1	0	0	52.2	65	32	29	11	19	32	0	.308	-2
Loiselle, Rich, Pit.	R	1	0	3.05	5	3	0	0	0	0	20.2	22	8	7	3	8	9	3	.268	0
Lyons, Curt, Cin.	R	2	0	4.50	3	3	0	0	0	0	16.0	17	8	8	1	7	14	0	.274	0
Maddux, Greg, Atl.	R	15	11	2.72	35	35	5	1	0	0	245.0	225	85	74	11	28	172	4	.241	35
Martinez, Pedro J., Mon.	R	13	10	3.70	33	33	4	1	0	0	216.2	189	100	89	19	70	222	6	.232	22
Martinez, Ramon, L.A.	R	15	6	3.42	28	27	2	2	1	0	168.2	153	76	64	12	86	133	2	.245	18
Mimbs, Michael, Phi.	L	3	9	5.53	17	17	0	0	0	0	99.1	116	66	61	13	41	56	7	.294	0
Morgan, Mike, St.L-Cin.	R	6	11	4.63	23	23	0	0	0	0	130.1	146	72	67	16	47	74	2	.289	4
Mulholland, Terry, Phi.	L	8	7	4.66	21	21	3	0	0	0	133.1	157	74	69	17	21	52	5	.293	8
Munoz, Bobby, Phi.	R	0	3	7.82	6	6	0	0	0	0	25.1	42	28	22	5	7	8	0	.375	-4
Navarro, Jaime, ChiN	R	15	12	3.92	35	35	4	1	0	0	236.2	244	116	103	25	72	158	10	.269	21
Neagle, Denny, Pit.-Atl.	L	16	9	3.50	33	33	2	0	0	0	221.1	226	93	86	26	48	149	3	.267	23
Nomo, Hideo, L.A.	R	16	11	3.19	33	33	3	2	0	0	228.1	180	93	81	23	85	234	11	.218	28

National League starting pitchers

Name/Team	T	W	L	ERA	G	GS	CG	SHO	GF	SV	IP	H	R	ER	HR	BB	SO	WP	BA	RV
Osborne, Donovan, St.L	L	13	9	3.53	30	30	2	1	0	0	198.2	191	87	78	22	57	134	6	.254	21
Paniagua, Jose, Mon.	R	2	4	3.53	13	11	0	0	0	0	51.0	55	24	20	7	23	27	2	.282	2
Peters, Chris, Pit.	L	2	4	5.63	16	10	0	0	0	0	64.0	72	43	40	9	25	28	4	.287	-1
Portugal, Mark, Cin.	R	8	9	3.98	27	26	1	1	0	0	156.0	146	77	69	20	42	93	6	.248	13
Quirico, Rafael, Phi.	L	0	1	37.80	1	1	0	0	0	0	1.2	4	7	7	1	5	1	0	.444	-3
Rapp, Pat, Fla.	R	8	16	5.10	30	29	0	0	1	0	162.1	184	95	92	12	91	86	13	.301	2
Rekar, Bryan, Col.	R	2	4	8.95	14	11	0	0	0	0	58.1	87	61	58	11	26	25	4	.345	-7
Reynolds, Shane, Hou.	R	16	10	3.65	35	35	4	1	0	0	239.0	227	103	97	20	44	204	5	.249	27
Reynoso, Armando, Col.	R	8	9	4.96	30	30	0	0	0	0	168.2	195	97	93	27	49	88	4	.291	6
Ritz, Kevin, Col.	R	17	11	5.28	35	35	2	0	0	0	213.0	236	135	125	24	105	105	10	.282	9
Rueter, Kirk, Mon.-S.F.	L	6	8	3.97	20	19	0	0	0	0	102.0	109	50	45	12	27	46	2	.275	6
Salkeld, Roger, Cin.	R	8	5	5.20	29	19	1	1	2	0	116.0	114	69	67	18	54	82	7	.261	5
Schilling, Curt, Phi.	R	9	10	3.19	26	26	8	2	0	0	183.1	149	69	65	16	50	182	5	.223	21
Schmidt, Jason, Atl.-Pit.	R	5	6	5.70	19	17	1	0	0	0	96.1	108	67	61	10	53	74	8	.286	-2
Schourek, Pete, Cin.	L	4	5	6.01	12	12	0	0	0	0	67.1	79	48	45	7	24	54	3	.293	0
Smiley, John, Cin.	L	13	14	3.64	35	34	2	2	0	0	217.1	207	100	88	20	54	171	7	.256	22
Smith, Zane, Pit.	L	4	6	5.08	16	16	1	1	0	0	83.1	104	53	47	7	21	47	0	.309	2
Smoltz, John, Atl.	R	24	8	2.94	35	35	6	2	0	0	253.2	199	93	83	19	55	276	10	.216	41
Soderstrom, Steve, S.F.	R	2	0	5.27	3	3	0	0	0	0	13.2	16	11	8	1	6	9	0	.302	0
Stottlemyre, Todd, St.L	R	14	11	3.87	34	33	5	2	0	0	223.1	191	100	96	30	93	194	8	.231	21
Swartzbaugh, Dave, ChiN	R	0	2	6.38	6	5	0	0	0	0	24.0	26	17	17	3	14	13	2	.277	-2
Telemaco, Amaury, ChiN	R	5	7	5.46	25	17	0	0	2	0	97.1	108	67	59	20	31	64	3	.281	2
Tewksbury, Bob, S.D.	R	10	10	4.31	36	33	1	0	0	0	206.2	224	116	99	17	43	126	2	.275	14
Thompson, Mark, Col.	R	9	11	5.30	34	28	3	1	2	0	169.2	189	109	100	25	74	99	1	.285	4
Trachsel, Steve, ChiN	R	13	9	3.03	31	31	3	2	0	0	205.0	181	82	69	30	62	132	5	.235	25
Urbani, Tom, St.L	L	1	0	7.71	3	2	0	0	0	0	11.2	15	10	10	3	4	1	0	.319	-2
Urbina, Ugueth, Mon.	R	10	5	3.71	33	17	0	0	2	0	114.0	102	54	47	18	44	108	3	.234	12
Valdes, Ismael, L.A.	R	15	7	3.32	33	33	0	0	0	0	225.0	219	94	83	20	54	173	1	.251	26
Valdes, Marc, Fla.	R	1	3	4.81	11	8	0	0	0	0	48.2	63	32	26	5	23	13	3	.315	-1
Valenzuela, Frnando, S.D.	L	13	8	3.62	33	31	0	0	0	0	171.2	177	78	69	17	67	95	7	.269	16
VanLandingham, W., S.F.	R	9	14	5.40	32	32	0	0	0	0	181.2	196	123	109	17	78	97	7	.276	4
Wagner, Paul, Pit.	R	4	8	5.40	16	15	1	0	0	0	81.2	86	49	49	10	39	81	7	.275	1
Wall, Donne, Hou.	R	9	8	4.56	26	23	2	1	1	0	150.0	170	84	76	17	34	99	3	.286	10
Watson, Allen, S.F.	L	8	12	4.61	29	29	2	0	0	0	185.2	189	105	95	28	69	128	9	.273	9
West, David, Phi.	L	2	2	4.76	7	6	0	0	0	0	28.1	31	17	15	0	11	22	1	.272	0
Williams, Mike, Phi.	R	6	14	5.44	32	29	0	0	1	0	167.0	188	107	101	25	67	103	16	.290	2
Wilson, Paul, NYN	R	5	12	5.38	26	26	1	0	0	0	149.0	157	102	89	15	71	109	3	.268	2
Wright, Jamey, Col.	R	4	4	4.93	16	15	0	0	0	0	91.1	105	60	50	8	41	45	1	.298	1

Minor league report

▶Player of the year and manager of the year

▶Hot prospects and other highlights

▶1996 league wrap-ups

▶Final AAA and AA player stats

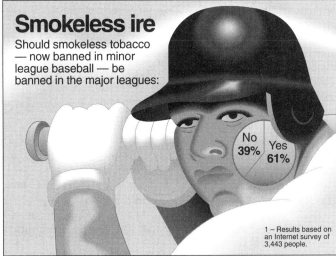

USA SNAPSHOTS®

A look at statistics that shape the sports world

Smokeless ire

Should smokeless tobacco — now banned in minor league baseball — be banned in the major leagues:

No 39%

Yes 61%

1 – Results based on an Internet survey of 3,443 people.

Source: ESPNET SportsZone

By Scott Boeck and Bob Laird, USA TODAY

1996 wrap-up: Keeping up with Jones

Think of a firecracker's swift ascent and the noisy explosion of color. Or picture a time-lapsed sequence of a flower erupting into bloom. That pretty much sums up the meteoric career of Andruw Jones, *Baseball Weekly*'s 1996 Minor League Player of the Year.

"I've likened him to a comet streaking across the baseball sky," says John Schuerholz, general manager of the Atlanta Braves. "That's how fast he went this year."

The 19-year-old began the season at Class A Durham and finished as a record-setting World Series star for the Braves. At his three stops in the minors—Durham, Class AA Greenville and Class AAA Richmond—he hit .339 with 34 homers, 92 RBI and 30 steals in just 116 games, with his average rising at each new level.

Jones hits for average, adds explosive power, shows speed on the bases, fields his outfield position with grace and has an arm like a rocket launcher. Hailing from the Dutch-governed island of Curaçao, he signed with the Braves a few months after his 16th birthday, in July 1993.

After making an impressive pro debut in 1994, he emerged as perhaps the top talent in the minors in 1995 with Class A Macon. There, at 18, he hit .277 with 25 homers, 100 RBI and 56 steals.

Last October he became the youngest player to homer in the World Series, replacing Yankees immortal Mickey Mantle, and only the second, after Oakland's Gene Tenace, to hit home runs in his first two Series at-bats. After hitting .400 overall against the Yankees, Jones, who had 106 major league at-bats last season, will still be eligible for a new award in 1997: National League Rookie of the Year.

Manager of the Year

Brian Graham, a 36-year-old who looks even younger, is *Baseball Weekly*'s 1996 Minor League Manager of the Year. Since his first managerial job in the Cleveland Indians system in 1989, Graham has taken teams to the playoffs seven years in a row, posted the best record in his league three times and set franchise records for victories another three times.

This past season Graham's Class AAA Buffalo Bisons served as the often-raided taxi squad for Cleveland. "Brian Graham has contributed championship-caliber players to our big-league club, and he's still managed to maintain a winning club and a positive environment down there in Triple A," says Mark Shapiro, the Indians' director of minor league operations. One week into 1996, Graham lost his starting rotation to Cleveland. Within a two-week period after the All-Star break, two of his top hitters were recalled to Cleveland to stay. Yet Graham and company still had an American Association–best 84-60 record before falling in five games to Indianapolis in the Eastern Division playoffs.

Graham may still look like a fresh-faced player, but there is no mistaking his achievements as a skipper: Overall Graham has amassed a 622-434 record, for a .589 winning percentage. "My desire to win," Graham says, "has always been an overriding factor in everything I do."

Perhaps the biggest reason for Graham's success is his honesty. Says Shapiro, "He gives players the feedback they need, he's honest with them about their situation and where they stand, and that gives them a more comfortable environment in which to succeed."

1996 hot prospects of the week

The following players were chosen by *Baseball Weekly* as minor leaguers to look out for in 1996. Here is how they did for the season:

▸**Derrick Gibson**, OF, Class AA New Haven Ravens (Colorado Rockies): Hit .256 with 15 homers, 62 RBI and 21 doubles.

▸**Andruw Jones**, OF, Class A Durham Bulls (Atlanta Braves): *Baseball Weekly*'s

1996 Minor League Player of the Year; also hit .217 with five homers and 13 RBI for Atlanta.

▶**Russell Branyan**, 3B, Class A Columbus RedStixx (Cleveland Indians): Second in the minors with 40 homers. Hit .268 with 106 RBI. South Atlantic League MVP.

▶**Rob Burger**, P, Class A Piedmont Boll Weevils (Philadelphia Phillies): 10-12, 3.38 ERA and .219 average against. Threw first no-hitter of the minor league season.

▶**Karim Garcia**, OF, Class AAA Albuquerque Dukes (Los Angeles Dodgers): Hit .297 with 13 homers, 10 triples, 17 doubles and 58 RBI.

▶**Jose Cepeda**, 3B, Class A Lansing Lugnuts (Kansas City Royals): 28-game hitting streak was best in the minors. Led Midwest League in hits (161).

▶**Richie Sexson**, 1B, Class AA Canton-Akron Indians (Cleveland): Hit .276 with 16 homers, 33 doubles and 76 RBI.

▶**Nelson Figueroa**, P, Class A Capital City Bombers (New York Mets): 14-7, 2.04 ERA, plus minor-league-best 200 strikeouts. Eight complete games, four shutouts, .181 batting average against. South Atlantic League's Most Outstanding Pitcher.

▶**Vladimir Guerrero**, OF, Class AA Harrisburg Senators (Montreal Expos): Eastern League MVP, won batting crown, hitting .360 with 19 homers, eight triples, 32 doubles, 78 RBI, .438 on-base average and .612 slugging average.

▶**Mike Cameron**, OF, Class AA Birmingham Barons (Chicago White Sox): Hit .300 with 28 homers, 77 RBI and 39 steals. Led Southern League in stolen bases, slugging average (.600) and runs (120).

▶**Don Denbow**, 1B, Class A Burlington Bees (San Francisco Giants): Led organization with 27 homers, 80 RBI, .440 on-base average and .556 slugging average.

▶**Darryl Brinkley**, OF, Class A Rancho Cucamonga Quakes (San Diego Padres): Hit .325 with 15 homers, 83 RBI and 30 steals between Rancho Cucamonga and Class AA Memphis.

▶**Bubba Trammell**, OF, Class AA Jacksonville Suns (Detroit Tigers), and **Bubba Smith**, 1B, Class AA Tulsa Drillers (Texas Rangers): Trammell hit .320 with 33 homers and 99 RBI between Jacksonville and Class AAA Toledo. Smith, the Texas League MVP, led league with 32 homers and 94 RBI, hit .292 with 150 hits, .534 slugging average and 82 runs.

▶**Todd Walker**, 3B, Class AAA Salt Lake City Buzz (Minnesota Twins): Hit .339 and led PCL with 28 homers and 111 RBI. Had 187 hits, 41 doubles, .400 on-base average and .599 slugging average. Also hit .256 with Minnesota.

▶**Dmitri Young**, 1B, Class AAA Louisville Redbirds (St. Louis Cardinals): Won American Association batting crown, hitting .333 with 15 homers and 64 RBI. Had 153 hits, eight triples and .534 slugging average; led league with 90 runs. Also hit .241 with St. Louis.

▶**Billy McMillon**, OF, Class AAA Charlotte Knights (Florida Marlins): Won International League batting crown, hitting .352 with 17 homers and 70 RBI. Had 32 doubles, .418 on-base average and .602 slugging average. Also hit .216 with Florida.

▶**Britt Reames**, P, Class A Peoria Chiefs (St. Louis): 15-7, 1.90 ERA and .170 batting average against. Midwest League Prospect of the Year. Led league in ERA and strikeouts, and tied for second in wins.

▶**Adam Butler**, P, Class AA Greenville Braves (Atlanta): Led Braves system with 30 total saves at Class A Macon, Class A Durham and Greenville.

▶**Ricky Ledee**, OF, Class AAA Columbus Clippers (New York Yankees): Hit .282 and slugged .553 with 21 homers, 64 RBI and 22 doubles in 96 games at Columbus. Hit .365 for Class AA Norwich before promotion.

▶**Wes Helms**, 3B, and **Ron Wright**, 1B, Class AA Greenville Braves (Atlanta): Helms hit .255 with four homers and 22 RBI for Greenville after promotion from Class A Durham. Wright was third in Carolina League with 20 homers before promotion, then traded to Pittsburgh in Denny Neagle deal. Hit .248 with 16 homers and 52 RBI in the Southern League at Greenville and Pirates' Carolina Mudcats.

▶**Derrek Lee**, 1B, Class AA Memphis Chicks (San Diego): Southern League MVP, hit .280 and led league with 34 homers and 104 RBI. Had 39 doubles, .570 slugging average, 98 runs, 140 hits.

Overall leaders

When Todd Greene hit 40 homers at Class AA Midland and Class AAA Vancouver in 1995, he was the first player in 10 years to hit 40 or more homers in the minors. But in 1996, two more players reached that plateau—Toledo Mud Hens veteran third baseman **Phil Hiatt**, with 42, and Columbus (Ga.) Redstixx third baseman **Russell Branyan**, with 40. Each was the MVP in his league. Among the other individual achievements of the 1996 season were these overall minor league leaders: Harrisburg Senators outfielder **Vladimir Guerrero** led the minors in batting with a .360 mark, trailed closely by Peoria Chiefs outfielder **Kerry Robinson**, at .359.

Salt Lake Buzz third baseman **Todd Walker** had a minor-league-best 187 hits, while the High Desert Mavericks' **Chris Kirgan** edged fellow California League slugging first baseman **D.T. Cromer** of Modesto in the minors' RBI race, 131 to 130.

Also lighting it up in the California League was Lake Elsinore second baseman **Joe Urso**, who led all minor leaguers with 47 doubles. Tucson Toros outfielder **Bob Abreu** led the minors in triples for the third time in four years, tying with Cedar Rapids Kernels outfielder **Norm Hutchins** at 16 each.

Visalia Oaks outfielder **David Roberts**, a Tigers farmhand, stole 65 bases to lead the minors, while Birmingham Barons outfielder **Mike Cameron** was tops with 120 runs scored. Atlanta Braves sensation **Andruw Jones** had a minors-high .652 slugging average, while High Desert's third baseman **Mike Berry** led the minors with a .471 on-base average.

Among pitchers, Peoria's **Britt Reames** had a minors-low 1.90 ERA and also led with his .170 batting average against, while the Columbia Bombers' **Nelson Figueroa** set the pace with 200 strike-outs. **Sean Maloney** of the El Paso Diablos had 38 saves, while three pitchers—**Ted Silva** of the Tulsa Drillers, **Elvin Hernandez** of the Augusta Greenjackets and **Darin Blood** of the San Jose Giants—shared the minor league high of 17 wins.

Great performances

▶**Neifi Perez**, the Colorado Springs shortstop prospect known for his dazzling defense, posted a seven-hit game that included hitting for the cycle in a 13-inning contest against Salt Lake on Aug. 25. It was the first seven-hit game since Lee Tinsley did it for Calgary in 1991. Three players had six-hit games—**Mike Berry** of High Desert, **Chris Stowers** of Vermont and **Bob Mummau** of Knoxville.

▶**Mark Kotsay**, the Marlins' first-round draft pick in 1996, made a splash in his debut season as he became the only player in the minors to score six runs in a game—the Kane County outfielder did it on the final day of the season, Sept. 2, against Wisconsin.

▶Twenty-one players posted three-homer games, with one—veteran player-coach Ty Van Burkleo of Lake Elsinore—doing it twice, on April 14 and May 17. The three-homer game of Pawtucket's Dwayne Hosey, on Aug. 10, included two homers in the same inning; he was one of eight players to do that. Toledo's **Phil Hiatt** had a streak in which he went deep six games in a row. Huntsville's **Demond Smith**, known more for his speed than his power, had two grand slams in a game on June 28. Three players—**Tal Light** of Asheville, **Mike Whitlock** of Hagerstown and **Freddy Diaz** of Vancouver—had nine-RBI games. Along with Smith, six other players, including Hosey, had eight-RBI games.

▶Speedy Braves prospect **Tyrone Pendergrass** of Danville had three triples in a July 4 game, while Bakersfield's **Kyle Towner** swiped six bases on July 30.

▶**Eddy Diaz** of Tacoma, **Calvin Murray** of Phoenix, **Brian Blair** of Tulsa and **Todd Walker** of Salt Lake each had a four-double game.

▶**Keith Luuloa** of Midland had the longest streak without striking out, 75 at-bats.

▶**Bobby Rodgers** of Lowell had a 16-strikeout game, the highest total in the minors, while **Jeriome Robertson** of the Gulf Coast League's Astros and **Joe Mays** of Everett each fanned 15 in only six innings, and **Steve Hoff** of the Arizona League's Padres also had a 15-strikeout game.

▶**Matt Clement** of High Desert struck out 12 in a row over two games to end his season, so his streak is still alive.

▶**Nate Minchey** completed five games in a row for Pawtucket.

▶The minors' longest hitting streak, 28 games, was by Lansing's **Jose Cepeda**, Orlando's nephew. **Jesus Hernaiz** of Savannah and **Mike Rennhack** of Stockton each had 26-game streaks.

▶**Jeff Ferguson** of New Britain had a 25-game streak alive through the end of the season, while Williamsport pitcher **Courtney Duncan**'s 11-game winning streak was also still going when the season ended.

▶A Braves farmhand, reliever **Adam Butler,** had a 36-inning scoreless streak among three teams, Macon, Durham and Greenville, from April 15 to July 13. **Brett Herbison** of Kingsport had a 42-inning streak without allowing an earned run.

▶There were 25 no-hitters thrown in the minors in 1996. The first was on April 30 by Piedmont's **Rob Burger,** a 1-0 win against Augusta. The last was on Sept. 3 when **Dennis Martinez Jr.** combined with three relievers for a 3-0 win by Watertown.

In between, the more notable no-nos: **Scott Randall** of Asheville threw one on July 17, beating Fayetteville 4-0, and then threw no-hit ball for 11 innings on Aug. 14 in a game his team eventually won, 2-1, in 19 innings, the longest game in the minors.

Kerry Wood of Daytona started a pair of no-hitters, combining with two relievers on July 28 for a 5-1 win against Tampa, and two relievers on Aug. 24 for a 3-0 win against Vero Beach; Wood went eight innings in the first, seven in the second.

Rick Helling of Oklahoma City pitched the lone perfect game of the year, a 4-0 gem on Aug. 13 against Nashville.

▶Perhaps the best single minor league season of 1996 was that enjoyed by **Kevin Sweeney**, in his pro debut with Lethbridge, the short-season Pioneer League farm team of the expansion Arizona Diamondbacks. Sweeney, the league MVP, hit .424 for the season, the first time in eight years that a player had hit over .400 in a National Association league. He also had a .734 slugging average and a .552 on-base average. Imagine how Ogden's **Gerald Parent** must have felt—Parent hit .385 in the Pioneer League and didn't even win the batting crown!

▶Not all the notable on-field accomplishments were positive ones, however: The Bakersfield Blaze finished the season with a 22-game losing streak, a California League record that they will lug into 1997. However, don't look for the streak to last too long into the new season—the Blaze was a co-op team that had been stripped of most of its players, while the 1997 club will be a San Francisco farm team.

Attendance

Minor league baseball still proved to be a box-office smash as the turnstiles rotated to the tune of 33,289,278 fans, the third year in a row that the National Association topped the 33-million mark and the second-highest total since the record year of 1949, when 59 leagues and 448 teams hosted 39,782,717 fans.

With 171 teams in 16 leagues that charge admission (neither of the spring-training-complex leagues, the Gulf Coast and the Arizona, is counted), attendance was up 162,344 over 1995. It was actually 65,921 fewer than in 1994, when the major league strike helped bring in 33,355,199 fans to the minors.

—*by Lisa Winston*

Class AAA WRAP-UPS

Final AAA and AA Player Stats

American Association

Two teams weakened by major league call-ups nonetheless made it to the American Association finals. The Oklahoma City 89ers won the league title three games to one over the Indianapolis Indians, taking the clincher 4-2. Indianapolis had to use six players from Class A and two from Class AA after their parent club, the Cincinnati Reds, brought eight Indians up to the majors. Despite the drastic changes, Indianapolis beat the heavily favored Buffalo Bisons in a five-game semifinal. Meanwhile, Oklahoma City, although missing league MVP first baseman Lee Stevens, who was called up by the Texas Rangers, won two extra-inning games in its four-game triumph over the Omaha Royals.

League leaders: BA: Dmitri Young, Louisville, .333. HR: Lee Stevens, Oklahoma City, 32. RBI: Nigel Wilson, Buffalo, 95. SB: Curtis Goodwin, Indianapolis, 40. ERA: Rick Helling, Oklahoma City, 2.96. W: Scott Ruffcorn, Nashville, 13. S: Richard Batchelor, Louisville, 28. SO: Helling, 157.

AMERICAN ASSOCIATION (AAA)
Eastern Division

	W	L	Pct.	GB
Buffalo	84	60	.583	—
Indianapolis	78	66	.542	6
Nashville	77	67	.535	7
Louisville	60	84	.417	24

Western Division

	W	L	Pct.	GB
Omaha	79	65	.549	—
Oklahoma City	74	70	.514	5
Iowa	64	78	.451	14
New Orleans	58	84	.408	20

Semifinals: Oklahoma City 3, Omaha 1; Indianapolis 3, Buffalo 2. **Finals:** Oklahoma City 3, Indianapolis 1.
Switch-hitter
* Left-handed

American Association

Buffalo Bisons (Indians) AAA

BATTING	AVG	AB	R	H	2B	3B	HR	RBI	SB
Aven, Bruce, OF	.667	9	5	6	0	0	1	2	0
Bryant, Pat, OF	.172	64	6	11	1	0	0	0	0
#Candaele, Casey, 2B	.311	392	66	122	22	2	6	37	3
Costo, Tim, 1B	.214	252	25	54	12	0	8	28	1
*Dunn, Steve, 1B	.290	300	35	87	20	1	12	48	2
Faries, Paul, 2B	.247	397	45	98	14	4	3	31	10
*Giles, Brian, OF	.314	318	65	100	17	6	20	64	1
*Helfand, Eric, C	.209	258	31	54	10	0	5	22	0
Jackson, Damian, SS	.257	452	77	116	15	1	12	49	24
Leius, Scott, 1B	.268	123	22	33	3	1	4	17	0
Lis, Joe, 2B	.233	146	21	34	8	0	6	22	0
Marsh, Tom, OF	.235	395	45	93	16	1	10	49	9
#Pena, Geronimo, 2B	.313	195	32	61	15	3	10	35	0
Perry, Herb, 1B	.338	151	21	51	7	1	5	30	4
Sparks, Don, 3B	.295	511	69	151	32	5	8	68	2
Thompson, Ryan, OF	.259	540	79	140	26	4	21	83	12
#Wilson, Enrique, 3B	.500	8	1	4	1	0	0	0	0
*Wilson, Nigel, OF	.299	482	88	144	23	6	30	95	4
Wilson, Tom, C	.269	208	28	56	14	2	9	30	0

PITCHING	W	L	ERA	G	SV	IP	H	BB	SO
*Anderson, Brian	11	5	3.59	19	0	128.0	125	28	85
Butcher, Mike	1	2	8.18	12	0	22.0	31	13	21
*Cadaret, Greg	1	5	3.66	32	2	64.0	59	29	44
Colon, Bart	0	0	6.00	8	0	15.0	16	8	19
Cornelius, Reid	5	7	5.60	20	0	90.0	101	49	62
*Embree, Alan	4	1	3.93	20	5	34.1	26	14	46
Farrell, John	3	0	3.67	4	0	27.0	20	7	14
Graves, Danny	4	3	1.48	43	19	79.0	57	24	46
Grigsby, Benji	0	0	5.40	8	0	13.1	18	4	3
Lewis, James	9	6	5.01	21	0	120.1	134	49	71
Lopez, Albie	10	2	3.87	17	0	104.2	90	40	89
*Mercker, Kent	0	2	3.94	3	0	16.0	11	9	11
Ogea, Chad	0	1	5.26	5	0	25.2	27	6	20
*Plantenberg, Erik	2	2	3.74	17	1	33.2	35	14	29
Roa, Joe	11	8	3.27	26	0	165.1	161	36	82
Scott, Darryl	3	5	2.89	50	9	81.0	61	24	73
Shuey, Paul	3	2	0.81	19	4	33.1	14	9	57
Tavarez, Julian	1	0	1.29	2	0	14.0	10	3	10
Wertz, Bill	1	2	4.71	17	0	28.2	32	19	22
*Whitten, Casey	3	4	8.04	12	0	43.2	54	24	35
*Williams, Jimmy	12	3	4.04	35	0	113.2	116	45	96

Indianapolis Indians (Reds) AAA

BATTING	AVG	AB	R	H	2B	3B	HR	RBI	SB
Anthony, Eric, DH	.238	21	4	5	1	0	2	7	0
#Arias, Amador, SS	.000	3	0	0	0	0	0	0	0
Belk, Tim, 1B	.287	436	63	125	27	3	15	63	5
#Coleman, Vince, OF	.077	26	2	2	0	0	0	1	0
Fordyce, Brook, C	.275	374	48	103	20	3	16	64	2
Garcia, Guillermo, C	.255	47	4	12	2	0	0	0	0
Gibralter, Steve, OF	.255	447	58	114	29	2	11	54	2
*Goodwin, Curtis, OF	.261	337	57	88	19	4	2	30	40
#Howard, Tom, OF	.400	5	2	2	0	0	1	2	0
*Howitt, Dann, OF	.266	297	38	79	12	2	8	40	4
Kelly, Mike, OF	.209	292	43	61	10	1	8	30	13
Kmak, Joe, C	.280	143	20	40	3	0	2	19	3
Kremblas, Frank, 2B	.198	91	14	18	5	0	0	8	3
Ladell, Cleveland, PH	.000	7	0	0	0	0	0	0	0
Mejia, Roberto, 2B	.291	374	55	109	24	9	13	58	13
Mitchell, Keith, OF	.300	357	60	107	21	3	16	66	9
*Morris, Hal, 1B	.500	4	1	2	1	0	1	1	0
Mottola, Chad, OF	.262	362	45	95	24	3	9	47	9
Owens, Eric, SS	.320	128	24	41	8	2	4	14	6
Perez, Eduardo, 3B	.293	451	84	132	29	5	21	84	11

1997 BASEBALL WEEKLY ALMANAC

BATTING	AVG	AB	R	H	2B	3B	HR	RBI	SB
Reese, Pokey, SS	.232	280	26	65	16	0	1	23	5
Sabo, Chris, 3B	.290	31	0	9	1	0	0	1	0
*Sanchez, Yuri, SS	.000	4	0	0	0	0	0	0	0
Sanders, Reggie, OF	.417	12	3	5	2	0	0	1	0
Santana, Ruben, 3B	.118	17	4	2	1	0	0	2	0
#Valdez, Trovin, PH	.000	1	0	0	0	0	0	0	0
Wilson, Brandon, SS	.233	305	48	71	7	3	4	31	10

PITCHING	W	L	ERA	G	SV	IP	H	BB	SO
*Buckley, Travis	11	7	4.50	22	0	122.0	126	32	58
Carrara, Giovanni	4	0	0.76	9	1	47.2	25	9	45
Carrasco, Hector	0	1	2.14	13	0	21.0	18	13	17
*Doyle, Tom	0	1	3.86	1	0	2.1	2	1	1
Drahman, Brian	0	0	7.20	3	0	5.0	7	4	1
*Fortugno, Tim	5	5	3.41	41	2	58.0	55	25	46
Frazier, Ron	0	1	11.05	2	0	7.1	8	3	4
Jarvis, Kevin	4	3	5.06	8	0	42.2	45	12	32
Jean, Domingo	1	1	8.68	7	0	9.1	13	8	5
*Lilliquist, Derek	4	1	2.60	47	1	52.0	47	7	51
Luebbers, Larry	5	4	3.91	14	0	71.1	76	23	35
*McElroy, Chuck	1	1	2.70	5	0	13.1	11	4	10
Moore, Marcus	4	7	3.45	15	0	88.2	72	38	70
*Ojala, Kirt	7	7	3.77	22	0	133.2	143	31	92
Olson, Gregg	0	0	4.26	7	4	6.1	6	6	4
*Powell, Ross	6	3	5.56	17	0	68.0	82	28	61
Pugh, Tim	2	1	2.45	4	0	25.2	19	4	18
*Remlinger, Mike	4	3	2.52	28	0	89.1	64	44	97
Service, Scott	1	4	3.00	35	15	48.0	34	10	58
Spradlin, Jerry	6	8	3.33	49	15	100.0	94	23	79
Sullivan, Scott	5	2	2.73	53	1	108.2	95	37	77
Warren, Brian	2	3	3.90	50	0	64.2	68	25	40
*White, Gabe	6	3	2.77	11	0	68.1	69	9	51

Iowa Cubs (Cubs) AAA

BATTING	AVG	AB	R	H	2B	3B	HR	RBI	SB
#Barberie, Bret, 3B	.233	210	26	49	8	0	5	24	3
*Brown, Brant, 1B	.304	342	48	104	25	3	10	43	6
Campos, Miguel, C	.250	4	0	1	0	0	0	0	0
Carter, Mike, OF	.266	384	41	102	13	1	2	18	4
Cholowsky, Dan, OF	.176	108	13	19	7	0	3	11	1
Dorsett, Brian, C	.207	29	2	6	2	0	1	2	0
Erdman, Brad, C	.175	171	18	30	6	0	2	16	1
Fermin, Felix, SS	.286	119	8	34	4	1	0	8	1
Finn, John, 3B	.273	55	10	15	1	0	1	5	1
Glanville, Doug, OF	.308	373	53	115	23	3	3	34	15
Haney, Todd, 2B	.246	240	20	59	13	0	2	19	3
Hubbard, Mike, C	.293	232	38	68	12	0	7	33	2
*Jennings, Robin, OF	.284	331	53	94	15	6	18	56	2
#Kessinger, Keith, SS	.239	184	19	44	8	0	4	26	0
*Kieschnick, Brooks, 1B	.259	441	47	114	20	1	18	64	0
*Kosco, Bryn, 3B	.253	79	8	20	2	0	2	7	0
*Magadan, Dave, 3B	.222	9	0	2	1	0	0	1	0
*Merullo, Matt, DH	.236	89	8	21	8	0	1	10	1
Orie, Kevin, 3B	.208	48	5	10	1	0	2	6	0
Ortiz, Hector, C	.241	79	6	19	2	0	0	3	0
Petersen, Chris, SS	.247	194	12	48	6	3	2	23	1
Sanchez, Rey, SS	.167	12	2	2	0	0	0	1	2
Shumpert, Terry, 2B	.276	246	45	68	13	4	5	32	13
Timmons, Ozzie, OF	.249	213	32	53	7	0	17	40	1
*Valdes, Pedro, OF	.295	397	61	117	23	0	15	60	2
Woodson, Tracy, 3B	.184	38	2	7	3	0	2	8	0

PITCHING	W	L	ERA	G	SV	IP	H	BB	SO
Bottenfield, Kent	1	2	2.19	28	18	24.2	19	8	14
Burlingame, Ben	5	6	4.30	27	0	98.1	104	20	66
Campbell, Mike	8	2	2.73	16	0	95.2	75	23	87
*Casian, Larry	3	2	1.71	24	1	47.1	37	11	32
*Dabney, Fred	2	3	4.34	33	0	64.1	76	24	33
Foster, Kevin	7	6	4.30	18	0	115.0	106	46	87
Guzman, Jose	1	6	8.45	8	0	38.1	51	19	24
Moten, Scott	1	2	9.21	21	0	42.0	55	18	18
Perez, Mike	0	4	6.53	23	0	30.1	42	15	19
*Pulido, Carlos	2	8	5.31	28	0	101.2	133	36	48
Rain, Steve	2	1	3.12	26	10	26.0	17	8	23
Ratliff, Jon	4	8	5.28	32	1	93.2	107	31	59
Renko, Steve	2	0	2.57	3	0	21.0	16	5	11
*Rivera, Roberto	1	0	2.70	35	2	33.1	26	8	18

Class AAA WRAP-UPS

International League

The Columbus Clippers sailed through the postseason without losing a game, winning the Governors' Cup with a three-game sweep of the Rochester Red Wings for their seventh title in 18 seasons in the International League. Columbus overwhelmed the Red Wings, outscoring them 19-6 in the series. Columbus had earlier swept the Norfolk Tides, whom they also topped in winning the Western Division in the regular season, while Rochester advanced by beating Pawtucket in four games, dropping their first contest but winning the next three. The PawSox set a league record by hitting 209 homers in winning the Eastern Division in the regular season.

League leaders: BA: Billy McMillon, Charlotte, .352. HR: Phil Hiatt, Toledo, 42. RBI: Hiatt, 119. SB: Shannon Stewart, Syracuse, 35. ERA: Mike Fyhrie, Norfolk, 3.04. W: Fyhrie, 15. S: Derek Wallace, Norfolk, 26. SO: Jeff Suppan, Pawtucket, 142.

INTERNATIONAL LEAGUE (AAA)

Eastern Division

	W	L	Pct.	GB
Pawtucket	78	64	.549	—
Rochester	72	69	.511	5½
Scranton	70	72	.493	8
Syracuse	67	75	.472	11
Ottawa	60	82	.423	18

Western Division

	W	L	Pct.	GB
Columbus	85	57	.599	—
Norfolk	82	59	.582	2½
Toledo	70	72	.493	15
Richmond	62	79	.440	22½
Charlotte	62	79	.440	22½

Semifinals: Rochester 3, Pawtucket 1; Columbus 3, Norfolk 0.
Finals: Columbus 3, Rochester 0.
Switch-hitter
* Left-handed

Class AAA WRAP-UPS

Pacific Coast League

The Edmonton Trappers rallied for three wins in a row against the Phoenix Firebirds to claim the Pacific Coast League crown. Edmonton became the first club from the Northern Division to not only win both halves of the league's split-season format, but also to post the best record in the league and win the championship. Among the Trappers' heroes were 13-year minor leaguer Webster Garrison, who hit .344 in the playoffs, and Scott Spiezio, who belted six homers in the postseason, which Edmonton started with a four-game win over the Salt Lake Buzz in the semifinals.

League leaders: BA: **Brian Raabe**, Salt Lake, .351. HR: **Todd Walker**, Salt Lake, 28. RBI: **Walker**, 111. SB: **Kerwin Moore**, Edmonton, 38. ERA: **Bob Milacki**, Tacoma, 2.74. W: **Dan Carlson**, Phoenix, and **Milacki**, 13. S: **Steve Mintz**, Phoenix, 27. SO: **Travis Miller**, Salt Lake, 143.

PACIFIC COAST LEAGUE (AAA)
Northern Division

	W	L	Pct.	GB
Edmonton	84	58	.592	—
Salt Lake	78	66	.542	7
Calgary	74	68	.521	10
Vancouver	68	70	.493	14
Tacoma	69	73	.486	15

Southern Division

	W	L	Pct.	GB
Las Vegas	73	67	.521	—
Tucson	70	74	.486	5
Phoenix	69	75	.479	6
Albuquerque	67	76	.469	7½
Colo. Springs	58	83	.411	15½

Semifinals: Edmonton 3, Salt Lake 1; Phoenix 3, Las Vegas 0; **Finals:** Edmonton 3, Phoenix 1.

Switch-hitter
* Left-handed

PITCHING	W	L	ERA	G	SV	IP	H	BB	SO
Steenstra, Kennie	8	12	5.01	26	0	158.0	170	47	101
Sturtze, Tanyon	6	4	4.85	51	4	72.1	80	33	51
Swartzbaugh, Dave	8	11	3.88	44	0	118.1	106	33	103
Telemaco, Amaury	3	1	3.06	8	0	50.0	38	18	42

Louisville Redbirds (Cardinals) AAA

BATTING	AVG	AB	R	H	2B	3B	HR	RBI	SB
Bell, David, 2B	.176	136	9	24	5	1	0	7	1
*Bradshaw, Terry, OF	.303	389	56	118	23	1	12	44	21
Correia, Rod, OF	.159	113	7	18	3	0	2	8	1
Cromer, Tripp, SS	.225	244	28	55	4	4	4	25	3
#Deak, Darrel, DH	.232	164	19	38	4	0	8	18	2
Difelice, Mike, C	.285	246	25	70	13	0	9	33	0
#Diggs, Tony, OF	.205	308	35	63	14	2	7	23	5
#Franklin, Micah, OF	.232	289	43	67	18	3	15	53	2
Gulan, Mike, 3B	.255	419	47	107	27	4	17	55	7
*Hare, Shawn, OF	.163	49	3	8	1	0	1	1	1
Hemond, Scott, C	.260	150	15	39	10	1	3	15	1
Holbert, Aaron, 2B	.264	436	54	115	16	6	4	32	20
McNeely, Jeff, OF	.125	8	0	1	0	0	0	1	0
Oliva, Jose, DH	.242	413	53	100	13	0	31	86	3
Pagnozzi, Tom, C	.154	26	5	4	0	0	2	3	0
Stefanski, Mike, C	.206	126	11	26	7	1	2	9	1
Torres, Paul, 1B	.500	2	0	1	0	0	0	0	0
Wimmer, Chris, OF	.249	345	40	86	11	2	2	23	11
#Young, Dmitri, 1B	.333	459	90	153	31	8	15	64	16

PITCHING	W	L	ERA	G	SV	IP	H	BB	SO
Arrandale, Matt	5	4	4.78	63	3	79.0	83	33	38
Aybar, Manuel	2	2	3.23	5	0	30.2	26	7	25
Badorek, Mike	0	4	5.29	20	0	49.1	52	18	22
Bailey, Cory	2	4	5.82	22	1	34.0	29	20	27
Barber, Brian	0	6	5.62	11	0	49.2	49	26	33
Batchelor, Rich	5	2	4.12	51	28	54.2	59	19	57
*Beltran, Rigo	8	6	4.35	38	0	130.1	132	24	132
Busby, Mike	2	5	6.38	14	0	72.0	89	44	53
*Dixon, Steve	0	0	10.38	5	0	4.1	4	3	2
Eiland, Dave	0	1	5.55	8	0	24.1	27	8	17
Frascatore, John	6	13	5.18	36	0	156.1	180	42	95
*Jackson, Danny	0	0	3.46	8	0	13.0	14	5	10
Lowe, Sean	8	9	4.70	25	0	115.0	127	51	76
Ludwick, Eric	3	4	2.83	11	0	60.1	55	24	73
Maxcy, Brian	4	2	4.79	36	1	62.0	63	32	52
Morgan, Mike	1	3	7.04	4	0	23.0	29	11	10
Morris, Matt	0	1	3.38	1	0	8.0	8	1	9
*Mutis, Jeff	2	3	5.87	32	1	38.1	44	19	21
*Osborne, Donovan	1	0	2.57	1	0	7.0	6	2	3
Petkovsek, Mark	0	1	9.00	2	0	3.0	5	1	4
*Simmons, Scott	5	6	4.15	30	1	99.2	98	35	58
*Urbani, Tom	2	2	3.27	7	0	44.0	40	12	26
VanRyn, Ben	4	6	4.88	19	1	66.1	69	27	42

Nashville Sounds (White Sox) AAA

BATTING	AVG	AB	R	H	2B	3B	HR	RBI	SB
Abbott, Jeff, OF	.325	440	64	143	27	1	14	60	12
#Brady, Doug, 2B	.241	427	59	103	18	7	6	42	20
*Cappuccio, C'm'ne, OF	.273	407	55	111	22	3	10	61	1
*Disarcina, Glenn, SS	.237	97	8	23	9	0	0	11	1
*Hall, Mel, DH	.267	15	1	4	0	0	1	1	0
Hurst, Jimmy, OF	.333	6	2	2	1	0	1	2	0
#Martin, Norberto, 2B	.206	68	9	14	3	0	2	8	1
#Munoz, Jose, DH	.234	295	30	69	17	1	6	34	8
#Norton, Greg, SS	.287	164	28	47	14	2	7	26	2
Ramsey, Fernando, OF	.218	395	42	86	3	0	7	24	12
*Robertson, Mike, 1B	.258	450	64	116	16	4	21	74	1
Robledo, Nilson, 1B	.100	10	0	1	0	0	0	0	0
Saenz, Olmedo, 3B	.261	476	86	124	29	1	18	63	4
Snopek, Chris, SS	.248	153	18	38	8	0	2	12	2
Tremie, Chris, C	.219	215	17	47	10	1	0	26	2
Valrie, Kerry, OF	.273	498	59	136	32	5	13	66	10
Vinas, Julio, C	.237	338	48	80	18	2	11	52	1
Wilson, Craig, SS	.179	123	13	22	4	1	1	6	0

PITCHING	W	L	ERA	G	SV	IP	H	BB	SO
Andujar, Luis	1	4	5.92	8	0	38.0	50	8	24
Baldwin, James	1	1	0.64	2	0	14.0	5	4	15

PITCHING	W	L	ERA	G	SV	IP	H	BB	SO
Bere, Jason	0	0	1.42	3	0	12.2	9	4	15
*Bertotti, Mike	5	3	4.37	28	1	82.1	80	42	73
Darwin, Jeff	5	2	3.55	25	3	63.1	52	17	33
Ellis, Robert	3	8	6.01	19	0	70.1	78	45	35
*Fordham, Tom	10	8	3.45	22	0	140.2	117	69	118
Gajkowski, Steve	5	6	3.94	49	2	107.1	113	41	47
Johnson, Barry	7	2	2.80	38	0	103.0	93	39	68
Jones, Stacy	3	1	3.15	28	12	34.1	35	13	28
Keyser, Brian	3	3	2.01	6	0	44.2	38	13	22
Levine, Alan	4	5	3.65	43	12	61.2	58	24	45
*Magrane, Joe	1	1	5.47	21	1	26.1	29	8	26
Ruffcorn, Scott	13	4	3.87	24	0	149.0	142	61	129
*Sauveur, Rich	4	3	3.70	61	8	73.0	63	28	69
Schrenk, Steve	4	10	4.42	16	0	95.2	93	29	58
*Sirotka, Mike	7	5	3.60	15	0	90.0	90	24	58
Thigpen, Bobby	0	1	7.11	4	0	6.1	8	2	6
*Worrell, Steve	1	1	3.15	11	0	20.0	19	5	11
Zappelli, Mark	0	0	0.68	9	1	13.1	11	2	9

New Orleans Zephyrs (Brewers) AAA

BATTING	AVG	AB	R	H	2B	3B	HR	RBI	SB
#Banks, Brian, OF	.271	487	71	132	29	7	16	64	17
#Caceres, Edgar, SS	.270	397	40	107	10	2	4	29	8
#Carr, Chuck, OF	.385	13	2	5	1	0	0	1	2
Faries, Paul, 3B	.227	110	7	25	1	1	1	8	1
Felder, Ken, OF	.216	430	55	93	20	1	17	45	2
Felix, Lauro, SS	.000	4	0	0	0	0	0	0	0
*Harris, Mike, OF	.193	150	17	29	2	1	2	11	1
Hughes, Bobby, C	.200	125	11	25	5	0	4	15	1
*Hulse, David, OF	.276	29	2	8	2	0	0	1	0
*James, Dion, OF	.290	31	0	9	0	0	0	3	0
Jenkins, Brett, DH	.225	71	9	16	3	0	6	11	0
*Koslofski, Kevin, OF	.231	238	39	55	8	3	4	25	5
Landry, Todd, 1B	.240	391	41	94	19	2	5	44	14
Lopez, Pedro, C	.218	87	7	19	4	0	0	3	0
#Lopez, Roberto, 2B	.233	438	50	102	20	3	7	39	8
Loretta, Mark, SS	.254	71	10	18	5	1	0	11	1
*Maas, Kevin, DH	.256	117	18	30	8	0	8	22	0
Matheny, Mike, C	.227	66	3	15	4	0	1	6	1
*Nilsson, Dave, DH	.269	26	3	7	1	0	1	2	0
Ortega, Hector, 3B	.556	18	2	10	0	1	0	2	0
Perez, Danny, OF	.187	198	25	37	5	0	2	15	4
Stinnett, Kelly, C	.287	334	63	96	21	1	27	70	3
Talanoa, Scott, DH	.188	80	9	15	1	0	2	11	2
Unroe, Tim, 3B	.270	404	72	109	26	4	25	67	8
#Ward, Turner, DH	.348	23	4	8	1	0	1	1	0
Weger, Wes, 2B	.210	210	23	44	11	0	4	23	0
*Williamson, Antone, 1B	.261	199	23	52	10	1	5	23	1

PITCHING	W	L	ERA	G	SV	IP	H	BB	SO
Archer, Kurt	1	3	5.46	23	0	31.1	39	9	15
Bowen, Ryan	2	2	4.94	6	0	27.1	27	19	23
Boze, Marshall	4	3	4.89	25	3	38.2	35	29	32
Browne, Byron	3	9	6.20	23	0	107.1	104	73	80
*Burrows, Terry	3	0	2.51	18	6	28.2	19	8	17
Carpenter, Cris	1	0	2.52	40	8	50.0	46	7	41
*Eddy, Chris	0	0	9.72	12	0	8.1	13	11	11
Eldred, Cal	2	2	3.34	6	0	32.1	24	17	30
*Farrell, Mike	5	3	4.20	29	2	64.1	72	13	39
Ganote, Joe	6	11	5.19	41	0	109.1	121	44	65
Garcia, Ramon	2	1	1.88	11	0	38.1	31	12	32
*Givens, Brian	10	9	3.02	29	1	137.0	124	57	117
Jones, Doug	0	3	3.75	13	6	24.0	28	6	17
Mercedes, Jose	3	7	3.56	25	1	101.0	109	28	47
Misuraca, Mike	2	7	4.13	23	2	80.2	93	31	57
*Montoya, Norm	0	0	8.53	11	2	12.2	15	5	8
Phillips, Tony	2	1	2.92	20	0	52.1	51	7	32
*Potts, Mike	0	1	6.75	11	0	16.0	23	11	8
*Roberson, Sid	0	1	4.91	2	0	11.0	10	9	3
Rodriguez, Frankie	0	2	6.75	13	0	18.2	24	11	16
Slusarski, Joseph	2	4	4.95	40	1	60.0	70	24	36
Sparks, Steve	2	6	4.99	11	0	57.2	64	35	27
Talanoa, Scott	0	0	16.20	2	0	3.1	8	3	0
VanEgmond, Tim	5	1	1.50	7	0	48.0	28	11	32
*Wickander, Kevin	0	1	12.79	8	0	6.1	9	5	9

Class AA WRAP-UPS

Eastern League

The Harrisburg Senators became the first team in the Eastern League in almost 10 years to perform a worst-to-best act, rebounding from a 61-80 record in 1995 to win the Eastern League title. Led by league MVP Vladimir Guerrero, the Senators beat the Portland Sea Dogs three games to one for the title. Though Guerrero was just 1-for-12 in the four-game semifinal upset win against the regular-season Southern Division champion Trenton Thunder, he came on in the finals with a fourth-inning grand slam in the 15-3 opener and then had an RBI double and a two-run homer in the 6-1 clincher. In the other semifinal, regular-season Northern Division champ Portland edged Binghamton in five games.

League leaders: BA: **Vladimir Guerrero,** Harrisburg, .360. HR: **Shane Spencer,** Norwich, 29. RBI: **Chris Saunders,** Binghamton, 105. SB: **Luis Castillo,** Portland, 51. ERA: **Carl Pavano,** Trenton, and **Tony Saunders,** Portland, 2.63. W: **Pavano,** 16. S: **William Hurst,** Portland, 30. SO: **Saunders,** 156.

EASTERN LEAGUE (AA)
Northern Division

	W	L	Pct.	GB
Portland	83	58	.589	—
Binghamton	76	66	.535	7½
Norwich	71	70	.504	12
New Haven	66	75	.468	17
New Britain	61	81	.430	22½

Southern Division

	W	L	Pct.	GB
Trenton	86	56	.606	—
Harrisburg	74	68	.521	12
Canton-Akron	71	71	.500	15
Reading	66	75	.468	19½
Bowie	54	88	.380	32

Semifinals: Portland 3, Binghamton 2; Harrisburg 3, Trenton 1. ***Finals:*** Harrisburg 3, Portland 1.
Switch-hitter
* *Left-handed*

Class AA WRAP-UPS

Southern League

The Jacksonville Suns barely made the Southern League finals after winning both halves of the Eastern Division title. It took them the full five games of the semifinals to knock off the pesky Carolina Mudcats, and in the end, it was Jacksonville's day in the sun as the Detroit farm team rallied from an opening-game loss in the finals to sweep the next three from Chattanooga. The Suns beat the Lookouts 4-0 in the clincher as ace Brian Moehler, the league's top regular-season winner, pitched a four-hit shutout. Chattanooga, the second-half regular-season winner in the Western Division, had beaten the first-half champion Memphis Chicks in four games to win the Western playoff title.

League leaders: BA: **Dan Rohrmeier**, Memphis, .344. HR: **Derrek Lee**, Memphis, 34. RBI: **Lee**, 104. SB: **Mike Cameron**, Birmingham, 39. ERA: **Shane Dennis**, Memphis, 2.27. W: **Brian Moehler**, Jacksonville, 15. S: **Domingo Jean**, Chattanooga, 31. SO: **Curt Lyons**, Chattanooga, 176.

SOUTHERN LEAGUE (AA)
Eastern Division

	W	L	Pct.	GB
Jacksonville	75	63	.543	—
Carolina	70	69	.504	5½
Orlando	60	78	.439	15
Greenville	58	82	.414	18
Port City	58	84	.400	19

Western Division

	W	L	Pct.	GB
Memphis	81	58	.583	—
Chattanooga	81	59	.579	½
Knoxville	75	65	.536	6½
Birmingham	74	65	.532	7
Huntsville	66	74	.471	15½

Semifinals: Jacksonville 3, Carolina 2; Chattanooga 3, Memphis 1.

Finals: Jacksonville 3, Chattanooga 1.

Oklahoma City 89ers (Rangers) AAA

BATTING	AVG	AB	R	H	2B	3B	HR	RBI	SB
Bryant, Scott, OF	.268	41	4	11	3	0	0	3	0
Cardenas, Johnny, C	.169	77	8	13	5	0	0	2	0
Charles, Frank, C	.186	113	10	21	7	2	1	8	0
Estrada, Osmani, 3B	.262	130	15	34	6	1	1	13	3
Faneyte, Rikkert, OF	.236	364	53	86	15	0	11	44	14
#Frazier, Lou, OF	.245	208	28	51	8	3	3	16	13
Frye, Jeff, 2B	.238	181	25	43	10	0	1	18	10
Gil, Benji, SS	.223	292	32	65	15	1	6	28	4
Gonzales, Rene, SS	.260	154	21	40	8	2	3	13	1
Kennedy, Darryl, C	.286	7	0	2	0	0	0	0	0
*Lee, Derek, OF	.301	409	59	123	32	2	13	62	6
*McFarlin, Jason, DH	.167	12	0	2	1	0	0	1	0
Ortiz, Luis, 1B	.317	501	70	159	25	0	14	73	0
#Owen, Spike, SS	.000	4	0	0	0	0	0	0	0
Pappas, Erik, C	.206	330	38	68	15	0	5	36	3
Pemberton, Rudy, OF	.254	71	6	18	3	0	2	11	1
*Sagmoen, Marc, OF	.293	116	16	34	6	0	5	16	1
Shave, Jon, 2B	.266	414	54	110	20	2	7	41	8
Smith, Alex, 2B	.225	200	22	45	12	0	6	20	4
*Stevens, Lee, DH	.325	431	84	140	37	2	32	94	3
#Stillwell, Kurt, 2B	.235	17	1	4	0	0	0	1	0
#Tatis, Fernando, 3B	.500	4	0	2	1	0	0	0	0
*Thomas, Brian, OF	.263	247	30	65	14	4	7	36	1
Voigt, Jack, OF	.297	445	77	132	26	1	21	80	5
Worthington, Craig, 3B	.264	53	5	14	2	0	1	4	0

PITCHING	W	L	ERA	G	SV	IP	H	BB	SO
Alberro, Jose	9	9	3.47	29	0	171.0	154	57	140
Anderson, Mike	3	4	6.34	11	0	32.2	45	11	21
Curtis, Chris	2	5	5.11	41	1	75.2	91	34	38
Davis, Clint	0	0	3.46	8	0	13.0	14	6	16
Dreyer, Steve	6	8	3.89	29	2	118.0	130	31	79
Estrada, Osmani	0	0	0.00	2	0	2.0	2	1	0
*Eversgerd, Bryan	3	3	2.74	38	4	65.2	57	14	60
Gross, Kevin	0	0	6.75	1	0	4.0	6	2	3
Helling, Rick	12	4	2.96	23	0	140.0	124	38	157
Heredia, Gil	0	0	1.86	6	0	9.2	11	0	4
Johnson, Jonathan	1	0	0.00	1	0	9.0	2	1	6
Lacy, Kerry	3	3	2.89	37	6	56.0	48	15	31
Manning, David	0	0	5.40	1	0	5.0	6	2	1
Mauser, Tim	1	1	2.16	8	0	8.1	8	2	11
Nichting, Chris	1	0	1.00	4	0	9.0	9	3	7
Patterson, Danny	6	2	1.68	44	10	80.1	79	15	53
Russell, Jeff	1	0	1.04	5	2	8.2	8	1	5
Sanford, Mo	6	10	3.97	30	0	143.0	155	49	130
Santana, Julio	11	12	4.02	29	0	185.2	171	66	113
*Smith, Dan	0	2	9.00	5	0	15.0	27	7	12
*Vierra, Joey	0	1	9.64	4	0	4.2	7	2	4
Whiteside, Matt	9	6	3.45	36	0	94.0	95	24	52

Omaha Royals (Royals) AAA

BATTING	AVG	AB	R	H	2B	3B	HR	RBI	SB
#Burton, Darren, OF	.270	463	75	125	28	5	15	67	7
Diaz, Lino, 3B	.271	266	32	72	13	2	3	28	0
Fasano, Sal, C	.231	104	12	24	4	0	4	15	0
*Grotewold, Jeff, DH	.278	338	63	94	20	0	10	51	1
Halter, Shane, OF	.258	299	43	77	24	0	3	33	7
*Hamelin, Bob, 1B	.313	16	4	5	1	1	0	0	1
Hansen, Jed, 2B	.232	99	14	23	4	0	3	9	2
#Martinez, Felix, SS	.235	395	54	93	13	3	5	35	18
Martinez, Ramon, 2B	.253	320	35	81	12	3	6	41	3
Mercedes, Henry, C	.215	223	28	48	9	1	8	35	0
#Merchant, Mark, DH	.245	249	39	61	13	0	8	36	2
#Mota, Jose, 3B	.245	229	24	56	5	2	3	20	7
*Myers, Rod, OF	.292	411	68	120	27	1	16	54	37
Norman, Les, OF	.260	77	8	20	6	0	1	13	0
*Nunnally, Jon, OF	.281	345	76	97	21	4	25	77	10
Paquette, Craig, DH	.333	63	9	21	3	0	4	13	1
Randa, Joe, 3B	.111	9	1	1	0	1	0	0	0
Stewart, Andy, 1B	.215	181	23	39	10	2	2	13	0
Stynes, Chris, OF	.356	284	50	101	22	2	10	40	7
Sweeney, Mike, C	.257	101	14	26	9	0	3	16	0
Tucker, Scooter, C	.162	74	5	12	2	0	1	4	0
Vitiello, Joe, 1B	.280	132	26	37	7	0	9	31	1

BATTING	AVG	AB	R	H	2B	3B	HR	RBI	SB
Young, Kevin, 1B	.306	186	29	57	11	1	13	46	3
Zupcic, Bob, OF	.143	7	1	1	0	0	0	1	0

PITCHING	W	L	ERA	G	SV	IP	H	BB	SO
Bevil, Brian	7	5	4.12	12	0	67.2	62	19	73
Bluma, Jaime	1	2	3.12	52	25	57.2	57	20	40
Bunch, Mel	8	9	6.08	33	0	146.2	181	59	94
Clark, Terry	3	1	2.56	16	2	45.2	42	13	36
*Granger, Jeff	5	3	2.34	45	4	77.0	65	29	68
Huisman, Rick	2	4	4.87	27	0	57.1	54	24	50
Kiefer, Mark	6	8	4.56	30	0	118.1	109	42	99
Linton, Doug	1	1	4.76	4	0	22.2	26	7	14
*Magnante, Mike	1	0	0.00	1	0	3.0	3	0	6
Meacham, Rusty	3	3	4.82	23	2	52.1	56	18	39
Olsen, Steve	7	4	5.07	24	0	65.2	70	23	41
*Patterson, Ken	0	1	1.80	16	1	20.0	16	4	13
Pittsley, Jim	7	1	3.97	13	0	70.1	74	39	53
Ralston, Kris	0	0	3.00	1	0	3.0	3	0	1
Robinson, Ken	2	0	0.79	6	0	11.1	7	4	9
*Rodriguez, Rich	2	3	3.99	47	3	70.0	75	20	68
*Rosado, Jose	8	3	3.17	15	0	96.2	80	38	82
*Rusch, Glendon	11	9	3.98	28	0	169.2	177	40	117
Scanlan, Bob	0	0	0.73	12	5	12.1	10	3	9
Torres, Dilson	4	7	4.60	16	0	86.0	102	19	36
Toth, Robert	3	3	7.04	11	0	46.0	63	17	20
Valera, Julio	1	3	5.17	6	0	15.2	22	5	9

International League

Charlotte Knights (Marlins) AAA

BATTING	AVG	AB	R	H	2B	3B	HR	RBI	SB
Abbott, Kurt, SS	.377	69	20	26	10	1	5	11	2
Brooks, Jerry, OF	.288	466	72	134	29	2	34	107	5
#Clapinski, Chris, SS	.285	362	74	103	20	1	10	39	13
Fagley, Dan, C	.000	1	1	0	0	0	0	0	0
*Gregg, Tommy, 1B	.286	405	69	116	24	0	22	80	10
Halter, Shane, OF	.293	41	3	12	1	0	0	4	0
Johnson, Erik, 2B	.178	185	19	33	6	0	0	10	0
Lucca, Lou, 3B	.260	273	26	71	14	1	7	35	0
*McMillon, Billy, OF	.352	347	72	122	32	2	17	70	5
Milliard, Ralph, 2B	.276	250	47	69	15	2	6	26	8
Morman, Russ, 1B	.332	289	59	96	18	1	18	77	2
#Olmeda, Jose, 3B	.320	375	52	120	26	1	9	49	7
Renteria, Edgar, SS	.280	132	17	37	8	0	2	16	10
Riley, Marquis, OF	.227	300	43	68	10	0	0	13	16
*Robertson, Jason, OF	.040	25	2	1	0	0	1	2	0
*Ronan, Marc, C	.305	220	23	67	10	0	4	20	3
Sheff, Chris, OF	.264	284	41	75	15	1	12	49	7
*Siddall, Joe, C	.280	189	22	53	13	1	3	20	1
Torres, Tomas, PH	.250	4	0	1	0	0	0	1	0
#Veras, Quilvio, 2B	.327	104	22	34	5	2	2	8	8
*Whitmore, Darrell, OF	.304	204	27	62	13	0	11	36	2

PITCHING	W	L	ERA	G	SV	IP	H	BB	SO
Adamson, Joel	6	6	3.78	44	3	97.2	108	28	84
Alfonseca, Antonio	4	4	5.53	14	1	71.2	86	22	51
Batista, Miguel	4	3	5.38	47	4	77.0	93	39	56
Brito, Mario	1	0	1.80	6	4	5.0	3	2	10
Chergey, Dan	0	1	6.21	45	1	75.1	86	28	43
Clapinski, Chris	0	0	4.50	1	0	2.0	1	0	2
*Darensbourg, Vic	1	5	3.69	47	7	63.1	61	32	66
*Gonzalez, Gabe	0	0	3.00	2	0	3.0	4	2	3
*Hammond, Chris	1	0	7.20	1	0	5.0	5	0	3
Harris, Doug	2	3	3.92	10	0	20.2	25	6	5
Hernandez, Livan	2	4	5.14	10	0	49.0	61	34	45
Juelsgaard, Jarod	4	2	3.48	26	1	44.0	43	21	29
Mantei, Matt	0	2	4.70	7	2	7.2	6	7	8
Mendoza, Reynol	7	4	5.64	15	0	91.0	112	33	41
Miller, Kurt	3	5	4.66	12	0	65.2	77	26	38
Mix, Greg	1	3	6.87	4	0	18.1	27	7	9
Olmeda, Jose	0	0	31.50	2	0	2.0	11	0	0
Pall, Donn	3	3	2.96	38	17	51.2	42	12	53
*Perez, Yorkis	3	0	4.22	9	0	10.2	6	3	13
Rapp, Pat	1	1	8.18	2	0	11.0	18	4	9

Class AA WRAP-UPS

Texas League

The 1996 championship series marked the arrival of new blood, as the Shreveport Captains, the defending league champions, were absent from postseason play for the first time in 10 years. The Jackson Generals, first-half Eastern Division winners but last in the regular season's second half, routed the Wichita Wranglers. After winning three consecutive games at home, Jackson rallied from a 3-1 deficit to score five in the fourth and never looked back, winning 7-3 for a four-game sweep. Kary Bridges, Nate Peterson and Tim Forkner all hit over .400 in the playoffs for Jackson, which had advanced to the finals by beating the Tulsa Drillers, tops in the Eastern Division's second half, three games to one. In the other semifinal, Wichita, the Western first-half champ, upset the second-half winners, the El Paso Diablos, also in four games.

League leaders: BA: **Todd Dunn**, El Paso, .340. HR: **Bubba Smith**, Tulsa, 32. RBI: **Jonas Hamlin**, El Paso, and Smith, 94. SB: **Dante Powell**, Shreveport, 43. ERA: **Keith Foulke**, Shreveport, 2.76. W: **Jonathan Johnson**, Tulsa, 13. S: **Sean Maloney**, El Paso, 38. SO: **Matt Beaumont**, Midland, 132.

TEXAS LEAGUE (AA)

Eastern Division

	W	L	Pct.	GB
Tulsa	75	64	.540	--
Shreveport	73	66	.525	2
Jackson	70	70	.500	5½
Arkansas	67	73	.479	8½

Western Division

	W	L	Pct.	GB
El Paso	76	63	.547	--
Wichita	70	70	.500	6½
San Antonio	69	70	.496	7
Midland	58	82	.414	18½

Semifinals: Jackson 3, Tulsa 1; Wichita 3, El Paso 1. **Finals:** Jackson 4, Wichita 0.
Switch-hitter
* Left-handed

Class A WRAP-UPS

California League

The Lake Elsinore Storm, a wild-card entry in the playoffs, won the title with its five-game series triumph against San Jose, the second-half Northern Division winner. In the clincher, a 7-2 Storm win, Kyle Sebach limited the Giants to four hits over eight innings as Bret Hemphill drove in four runs with a pair of home runs. Lake Elsinore had beaten Rancho Cucamonga, the Southern Division first-half champ, two games to one in the opening round before sweeping Southern second-half winner High Desert in three games in the semifinals. San Jose had a bye to the semifinals and then beat Stockton in four games.

League leaders: BA: **Mike Berry**, High Desert, .359. HR: **Chris Kirgan**, High Desert, 34. RBI: **Chris Kirgan**, High Desert, 131. SB: **David Roberts**, Visalia, 65. ERA: **Darin Blood**, San Jose, 2.65. W: **Blood**, 17. S: **Rich Linares**, San Bernardino, 33. SO: **Blood**, 193.

CALIFORNIA LEAGUE (A):
Northern Division

	W	L	Pct.	GB
San Jose	89	51	.636	—
Modesto	82	58	.586	7
Stockton	79	61	.584	10
Visalia	50	90	.357	39
Bakersfield	39	101	.279	50

Southern Division:

	W	L	Pct.	GB
High Desert	76	64	.543	—
Lake Elsinore	75	65	.507	1
Lancaster	71	69	.507	5
S. Bernardino	70	70	.500	6
Rancho Cuca.	69	71	.493	7

First round: Stockton 2, Modesto 0; Lake Elsinore 2, Rancho Cucamonga 1.
Semifinals: San Jose 3, Stockton 1; Lake Elsinore 3, High Desert 0.
Finals: Lake Elsinore 3, San Jose 2.

PITCHING	W	L	ERA	G	SV	IP	H	BB	SO
Rojas, Euclides	0	0	6.00	6	0	9.0	12	3	8
Seelbach, Chris	6	13	7.35	25	0	138.1	167	76	98
Valdes, Marc	2	4	5.12	8	0	51.0	66	15	24
Weston, Mickey	5	9	5.78	31	1	104.1	131	39	47
*Whisenant, Matt	8	10	6.92	28	0	121.0	149	101	97

Columbus Clippers (Yankees) AAA

BATTING	AVG	AB	R	H	2B	3B	HR	RBI	SB
Barker, Tim, 2B	.266	402	71	107	27	8	2	45	24
Benavides, Freddie, SS	.000	4	0	0	0	0	0	1	0
*Carpenter, Bubba, OF	.245	466	55	114	23	3	7	48	10
*Cruz, Ivan, 1B	.258	446	84	115	26	0	28	96	2
Dalesandro, Mark, 3B	.282	255	34	72	29	4	2	38	2
*Delvecchio, Nick, DH	.000	1	0	1	0	0	0	0	0
Duncan, Mariano, 2B	.200	5	0	1	0	0	0	2	0
Eenhoorn, Robert, SS	.337	172	28	58	14	1	1	16	7
Fermin, Felix, 2B	.211	19	3	4	0	0	0	3	0
Figga, Mike, C	.273	11	3	3	1	0	0	0	0
Hinds, Rob, 2B	.087	23	4	2	0	0	0	1	1
Howard, Matt, SS	.347	202	36	70	12	2	2	16	9
Katzaroff, Robbie, OF	.444	9	0	4	0	0	0	0	0
Kelly, Pat, 2B	.378	37	6	14	1	1	2	7	3
*Ledee, Ricky, OF	.282	358	79	101	22	6	21	64	6
#Long, R.D., 2B	.226	124	18	28	3	2	0	9	5
*Luke, Matt, OF	.280	264	46	74	14	2	19	70	1
*Marini, Marc, OF	.267	135	23	36	11	0	2	23	1
Martindale, Ryan, C	.263	19	3	5	2	1	0	3	0
McIntosh, Tim, C	.277	206	30	57	11	1	10	28	0
Motuzas, Jeff, C	.250	12	1	3	0	1	0	1	0
Northrup, Kevin, OF	.286	168	22	48	13	1	4	20	4
#Posada, Jorge, C	.271	354	76	96	22	6	11	62	3
#Raines, Tim, OF	.250	12	3	3	1	0	0	0	1
Rivera, Ruben, OF	.235	362	59	85	20	4	10	46	15
Romano, Scott, 2B	.150	40	5	6	2	0	0	4	1
Spencer, Shane, OF	.355	31	7	11	4	0	3	6	0
*Strawberry, Darryl, DH	.375	8	3	3	0	0	3	5	0
Torres, Jaime, C	.270	37	5	10	3	0	1	7	1
Wilson, Tom, DH	.000	1	0	0	0	0	0	0	0
Woodson, Tracy, 3B	.288	420	53	121	34	3	21	81	4

PITCHING	W	L	ERA	G	SV	IP	H	BB	SO
Boehringer, Brian	11	7	4.00	25	0	153.0	155	56	132
*Brewer, Billy	0	2	7.20	13	0	25.0	27	19	27
*Burrows, Terry	1	0	5.96	23	0	22.2	24	11	20
Carper, Mark	1	2	6.62	15	0	35.1	43	16	16
Croghan, Andy	2	0	8.46	14	0	22.1	27	13	21
*Cumberland, Chris	2	7	6.52	12	0	58.0	86	23	35
DeJesus, Jose	0	0	14.40	3	0	5.0	9	1	6
Drews, Matt	0	4	8.41	7	0	20.1	18	27	7
*Dunbar, Matt	2	0	1.74	14	0	20.2	12	13	16
Edenfield, Ken	4	1	2.34	33	3	42.1	32	15	28
Eiland, Dave	8	4	2.92	15	0	92.1	77	13	76
*Gibson, Paul	1	0	7.04	9	0	7.2	8	9	4
*Hines, Rich	6	3	5.16	32	0	66.1	70	37	48
Hutton, Mark	0	0	0.00	2	0	2.0	0	2	3
Kamieniecki, Scott	2	1	5.64	5	0	30.1	33	8	27
*Kotarski, Mike	0	0	6.75	1	0	4.0	3	2	5
Mecir, Jim	3	3	2.27	33	7	47.2	37	15	52
Melendez, Jose	1	0	6.52	8	0	9.2	9	2	7
Mendoza, Ramiro	6	2	2.51	15	0	97.0	96	19	61
Monteleone, Rich	4	3	3.60	21	0	35.0	42	7	21
Pavlas, Dave	8	2	1.99	57	26	77.0	64	13	65
*Polley, Dale	2	2	3.13	31	1	31.2	29	9	29
Ricken, Ray	4	5	4.76	20	1	68.0	62	37	58
Rios, Dan	4	1	1.95	24	0	27.2	22	6	22
*Rumer, Tim	3	1	2.72	12	0	49.2	39	14	35
Wallace, Kent	4	2	4.68	13	0	67.1	69	15	34
Weathers, David	0	2	5.68	4	0	19.0	25	8	7
Whitehurst, Wally	8	7	3.08	28	3	108.0	101	25	83

Norfolk Tides (Mets) AAA

BATTING	AVG	AB	R	H	2B	3B	HR	RBI	SB
Agbayani, Benny, OF	.278	331	43	92	13	9	7	56	14
Castillo, Alberto, C	.208	341	34	71	12	1	11	39	2
Chimelis, Joel, SS	.382	76	9	29	6	0	0	4	1

BATTING	AVG	AB	R	H	2B	3B	HR	RBI	SB
*Daubach, Brian, 1B	.204	54	7	11	2	0	0	6	1
Flora, Kevin, OF	.222	135	20	30	8	1	3	15	9
*Franco, Matt, 3B	.323	508	74	164	40	2	7	81	5
Gilbert, Shawn, 3B	.256	493	76	126	28	1	9	50	17
#Hardtke, Jason, 2B	.300	257	49	77	17	2	9	35	4
Howard, Chris, C	.160	119	8	19	6	0	2	15	0
Lowery, Terrell, OF	.233	193	25	45	7	2	4	21	6
Mahalik, John, PH	.235	17	1	4	0	0	0	0	0
McCoy, Trey, PH	.191	47	2	9	1	0	1	7	0
Morgan, Kevin, 2B	.134	82	7	11	3	0	0	3	3
Ochoa, Alex, OF	.339	233	45	79	12	4	8	39	5
Payton, Jay, DH	.307	153	30	47	6	3	6	26	10
*Petagine, Roberto, 1B	.318	314	49	100	24	3	12	65	4
Rivera, Luis, SS	.225	356	34	80	23	3	6	39	1
#Roberson, Kevin, OF	.265	215	26	57	13	3	7	33	0
Thurman, Gary, OF	.267	449	81	120	24	6	9	39	25
*Tomberlin, Andy, OF	.326	129	17	42	6	1	8	18	1

PITCHING	W	L	ERA	G	SV	IP	H	BB	SO
Acevedo, Juan	4	8	5.96	19	0	102.2	116	53	83
Ahearne, Pat	1	2	4.62	5	0	25.1	26	9	14
Ausanio, Joe	3	3	5.86	35	4	43.0	38	29	40
*Bark, Brian	1	0	4.63	12	0	11.2	9	6	13
Bullard, Jason	0	3	4.89	24	0	38.2	45	16	24
Byrd, Paul	2	0	3.52	5	1	7.2	4	4	8
*Crawford, Joe	6	5	3.44	20	0	96.2	98	20	68
Fyhrie, Mike	15	6	3.04	27	0	169.0	150	33	103
Gardiner, Mike	13	3	3.21	24	0	146.0	125	38	125
Larson, Toby	1	0	4.76	1	0	5.2	6	1	1
*MacDonald, Bob	4	1	3.13	27	0	31.2	27	12	36
*Martinez, Pedro	4	4	3.02	34	2	56.2	45	20	37
McCready, Jim	0	0	4.15	6	0	8.2	11	0	1
Person, Robert	5	0	3.35	8	0	43.0	33	21	32
Ramirez, Hector	1	0	3.38	3	0	10.2	13	3	8
Reed, Rick	8	10	3.16	28	0	182.0	164	33	128
Rogers, Bryan	0	2	3.38	20	0	24.0	20	11	23
Trlicek, Rick	4	5	1.87	62	10	77.0	52	16	54
Wallace, Derek	5	2	1.72	49	26	57.2	37	17	52
Welch, Mike	0	1	4.15	10	2	8.2	8	2	6
Withem, Shannon	3	3	4.64	8	0	42.2	56	6	30

Ottawa Lynx (Expos) AAA

BATTING	AVG	AB	R	H	2B	3B	HR	RBI	SB
Barron, Tony, OF	.320	394	58	126	29	2	14	59	9
Benitez, Yamil, OF	.278	439	56	122	20	2	23	81	11
#Bieser, Steve, OF	.322	382	63	123	24	4	1	32	27
Buccheri, Jim, OF	.257	206	40	53	3	4	1	12	33
*Castleberry, Kevin, 2B	.280	193	27	54	8	3	3	22	9
Chavez, Raul, C	.247	198	15	49	10	0	2	24	0
Coolbaugh, Scott, 3B	.208	173	20	36	12	1	3	22	2
*Floyd, Cliff, OF	.303	76	7	23	3	1	1	8	2
*Heffernan, Bert, C	.303	198	20	60	8	1	1	27	1
*Leach, Jalal, OF	.317	101	12	32	4	0	3	9	0
*Lukachyk, Rob, OF	.264	246	38	65	15	4	9	39	10
Martin, Chris, SS	.264	451	68	119	30	1	8	54	25
Matos, Francisco, 2B	.238	307	30	73	15	3	2	23	4
*McDavid, Ray, OF	.155	58	7	9	1	0	0	2	6
*McGuire, Ryan, 1B	.257	451	62	116	21	2	12	60	11
Montoyo, Charlie, SS	.351	57	10	20	5	1	0	5	0
Reyes, Gilberto, C	.182	44	5	8	3	0	3	5	0
Schu, Rick, 3B	.271	395	48	107	24	3	12	54	9
Yan, Julian, 1B	.184	136	17	25	3	1	4	21	0

PITCHING	W	L	ERA	G	SV	IP	H	BB	SO
Alvarez, Tavo	4	9	4.70	20	0	113.0	128	25	86
Aucoin, Derek	3	5	3.96	52	3	75.0	74	53	69
*Baxter, Bob	3	3	5.51	54	3	81.2	104	23	60
*Boucher, Denis	3	7	9.30	17	0	61.0	90	40	24
Buccheri, Jim	0	0	0.00	1	0	2.0	2	0	0
Bullinger, Kirk	2	1	3.52	10	0	15.1	10	9	9
Dorlarque, Aaron	1	1	13.27	14	0	19.2	39	11	13
Falteisek, Steve	2	5	6.36	12	0	58.0	75	25	26
*Gray, Dennis	0	1	6.75	3	0	5.1	9	5	3
Habyan, John	0	1	2.45	7	1	7.1	7	2	8
Henderson, Rod	4	11	5.19	25	0	121.1	117	52	83
*Leiper, Dave	3	1	1.93	25	6	32.2	29	6	26
Montoyo, Charlie	0	0	0.00	1	0	2.0	0	0	0

Class A WRAP-UPS

Carolina League

The Carolina League finals pitted a rematch of last year's two divisional winners: the Wilmington Blue Rocks and the defending champion Kinston Indians. This year, however, the final result was reversed as the Blue Rocks beat Kinston three games to one for the title. Wilmington had given up only two runs in each of the first three games, winning the first two before losing a chance for a sweep by allowing a two-run ninth-inning rally in the 2-1 third game. In the hurricane-postponed semifinals, second-half Southern Division winner Kinston beat the first-half champion Durham Bulls in three games, while Northern champ Wilmington had a bye (and a long wait) after winning both halves of the split season.

League leaders: BA: Sean Casey, Kinston, .331. HR: Freddy Garcia and Jose Guillen, Lynchburg, 21. RBI: Johnny Isom, Frederick, 104. SB: Sergio Nunez, Wilmington, 44. ERA: Noe Najera, Kinston, 2.70. W: David Caldwell, Kinston, 13. S: Steve Prihoda, Wilmington, 25. SO: Russ Herbert, Prince William, 148.

CAROLINA LEAGUE (A):
Northern Division

	W	L	Pct.	GB
Wilmington	80	60	.571	—
Frederick	67	72	.482	12½
Lynchburg	65	74	.468	14½
Prince William	58	80	.420	21

Southern Division

	W	L	Pct.	GB
Kinston	76	62	.551	—
Winston-Salem	74	65	.532	2½
Durham	73	66	.525	3½
Salem	62	76	.449	14

Semifinals: Wilmington bye; Kinston 2, Durham 1.
Finals: Wilmington 3, Kinston 1.

Class A WRAP-UPS

Florida State League

The St. Lucie Mets rallied to win three in a row to beat the Clearwater Phillies for the league championship. The Mets, second-half East Division winners, made the postseason on the last day and then swept the first-half champion Vero Beach Dodgers in the semifinals to earn a meeting with first-half West winner Clearwater, which won two straight over the Tampa Yankees, second-half West champs. The Phillies scored four runs in the first to win the finals opener, but St. Lucie won the next three. The 8-5 second game was won with a five-run eighth-inning rally, and the last two were one-run games won by reliever Barry Short.

League leaders: BA: **Mike Murphy**, Charlotte, .332. HR: **John Curt**, Dunedin, 18. RBI: **Kevin Ellis**, Daytona, 89. SB: **Kevin Gibbs**, Vero Beach, 60. ERA: **Blake Stein**, St. Petersburg, 2.15. W: **Stein** and **Billy Neal**, Vero Beach, 16. S: **Jay Tessmer**, Tampa, 35. SO: **Stein**, 159.

FLORIDA STATE LEAGUE (A):

Eastern Division

	W	L	Pct.	GB
St. Lucie	71	62	.534	—
Daytona	71	66	.518	2
W. Palm Bch	68	67	.504	4
Vero Beach	65	66	.496	5
Kissimmee	60	75	.444	12
Brevard	47	92	.338	27

Western Division

	W	L	Pct.	GB
Tampa	84	50	.627	—
Fort Myers	79	58	.577	6½
Clearwater	75	62	.547	10½
St. Petersburg	75	63	.543	11
Sarasota	67	69	.493	18
Dunedin	67	70	.489	18½
Charlotte	63	76	.453	23½
Lakeland	61	77	.442	25

Semifinals: St. Lucie 2, Vero Beach 0; Clearwater 2, Tampa 0.
Finals: St. Lucie 3, Clearwater 1.

PITCHING	W	L	ERA	G	SV	IP	H	BB	SO
Pacheco, Alex	2	2	6.48	33	6	41.2	47	18	34
Paniagua, Jose	9	5	3.18	15	0	85.0	72	23	61
Rivera, Ben	4	9	6.46	31	1	100.1	112	47	87
*Rueter, Kirk	1	2	4.20	3	0	15.0	21	3	3
Schmidt, Curt	1	5	2.43	54	13	70.1	60	22	45
Stull, Everett	2	6	6.33	13	0	69.2	87	39	69
Telford, Anthony	7	2	4.11	30	0	118.1	128	34	69
Urbina, Ugueth	2	0	2.66	5	0	23.2	17	6	28

Pawtucket Red Sox (Red Sox) AAA

BATTING	AVG	AB	R	H	2B	3B	HR	RBI	SB
#Bell, Juan, 2B	.248	210	28	52	13	2	5	23	2
Brown, Randy, SS	.167	6	0	1	0	0	0	1	0
Canseco, Jose, DH	.200	5	0	1	0	0	0	0	0
Clark, Phil, 3B	.325	369	57	120	36	2	12	69	3
*Cole, Alex, OF	.296	304	57	90	14	8	4	39	11
Cordero, Wil, 2B	.300	10	2	3	1	0	1	2	0
Delgado, Alex, C	.216	88	15	19	3	0	1	6	0
*Dodson, Bo, 1B	.344	276	37	95	20	0	11	43	4
#Fuller, Aaron, OF	.500	2	0	1	0	0	0	0	0
Garciaparra, Nomar, SS	.343	172	40	59	15	2	16	46	3
*Greenwell, Mike, OF	.273	11	3	3	0	0	2	2	0
*Hatteberg, Scott, C	.268	287	52	77	16	0	12	49	1
*Holifield, Rick, OF	.069	29	1	2	1	0	0	1	1
#Hosey, Dwayne, OF	.297	367	77	109	25	4	14	53	20
Jackson, Gavin, SS	.250	44	5	11	2	0	0	1	0
Levangie, Dana, C	.250	4	1	1	0	0	0	1	0
Lewis, T.R., OF	.314	274	55	86	23	1	14	52	2
Malave, Jose, OF	.271	155	30	42	6	0	8	29	2
Manto, Jeff, 3B	.244	45	6	11	5	0	2	6	1
Mejia, Roberto, 2B	.257	74	9	19	4	0	0	4	4
Merloni, Lou, 3B	.252	115	19	29	6	0	1	12	0
Mitchell, Kevin, DH	.125	16	1	2	0	0	0	0	0
Pemberton, Rudy, OF	.326	396	77	129	28	3	27	92	16
Pough, Pork Chop, 3B	.236	242	43	57	17	2	12	40	2
Pozo, Arquimedez, 3B	.243	37	6	9	1	0	1	3	0
Rodriguez, Tony, SS	.245	265	37	65	14	1	3	28	3
*Selby, Bill, 2B	.254	260	39	66	14	5	11	47	0
Tatum, Jim, 3B	.273	66	11	18	2	0	5	16	2
Zambrano, Eduardo, OF	.111	9	0	1	0	0	0	1	0
#Zinter, Alan, 1B	.269	357	78	96	19	5	26	69	5

PITCHING	W	L	ERA	G	SV	IP	H	BB	SO
Austin, Jim	0	1	9.00	10	0	14.0	15	9	7
Belinda, Stan	1	0	0.00	6	0	7.2	2	2	7
Cain, Tim	1	0	1.86	11	0	19.1	15	6	10
Cederblad, Brett	0	0	3.60	10	0	20.0	26	4	19
DeSilva, John	4	3	5.21	16	0	84.2	99	27	68
Doherty, John	1	4	6.62	19	1	50.1	79	8	13
*Eshelman, Vaughn	1	2	4.33	7	0	43.2	40	19	28
Finnvold, Gar	3	2	6.62	8	0	35.1	50	11	35
Garces, Rich	4	0	2.30	10	0	15.2	10	5	13
*Grundt, Ken	9	4	4.20	44	2	64.1	72	16	46
*Gunderson, Eric	2	1	3.48	26	2	33.2	38	9	34
Hansen, Brent	1	0	6.23	2	0	8.2	8	8	3
Hudson, Joe	1	1	3.51	25	5	33.1	29	21	18
Knackert, Brent	2	3	5.17	19	2	47.0	48	26	34
Lacy, Kerry	0	0	0.00	7	4	8.0	1	2	8
*Looney, Brian	5	6	4.81	27	1	82.1	78	27	78
Maddux, Mike	2	0	3.21	3	0	14.0	13	2	9
Minchey, Nate	7	4	2.96	14	0	97.1	89	21	61
*Orellano, Rafael	4	11	7.88	22	0	99.1	124	62	66
Pierce, Jeff	2	1	4.94	12	0	31.0	37	8	22
Ricci, Chuck	8	4	3.01	60	13	80.2	56	32	79
Schullstrom, Erik	1	4	5.01	15	0	55.2	57	28	62
Sele, Aaron	0	0	6.00	1	0	3.0	3	1	4
Suppan, Jeff	10	6	3.22	22	0	145.1	130	25	142
*Tomlin, Randy	0	2	8.31	5	1	13.0	17	5	5
VanEgmond, Tim	5	3	4.38	11	0	61.2	66	24	46

Richmond Braves (Braves) AAA

BATTING	AVG	AB	R	H	2B	3B	HR	RBI	SB
Ayrault, Joe, C	.229	314	23	72	15	0	5	34	1
Beltre, Esteban, SS	.209	43	4	9	3	0	0	1	0

BATTING	AVG	AB	R	H	2B	3B	HR	RBI	SB
Benbow, Lou, 3B	.232	250	21	58	8	0	1	23	3
Cox, Darron, C	.238	168	19	40	9	0	3	20	1
Dye, Jermaine, OF	.232	142	25	33	7	1	6	19	3
Garcia, Omar, 1B	.264	311	36	82	15	1	4	35	4
*Giovanola, Ed, SS	.295	210	29	62	15	1	3	16	2
Graffanino, Tony, 2B	.283	353	57	100	29	2	7	33	11
*Grijak, Kevin, 1B	.367	30	3	11	3	0	1	8	0
Hollins, Damon, OF	.199	146	16	29	9	0	0	8	2
Jones, Andruw, OF	.378	45	11	17	3	1	5	12	2
*Malloy, Marty, 2B	.203	64	7	13	2	1	0	8	3
#Martinez, Pablo, SS	.270	263	29	71	12	3	1	18	14
Moore, Bobby, OF	.270	200	29	54	10	0	3	14	9
Mordecai, Mike, SS	.182	11	2	2	0	0	1	2	0
Pecorilli, Aldo, 1B	.290	403	61	117	27	0	15	62	5
Pegues, Steve, OF	.341	167	31	57	10	1	7	30	0
Rodarte, Raul, OF	.338	219	30	74	12	2	9	46	4
Smith, Robert, 3B	.256	445	49	114	27	0	8	58	15
*Swann, Pedro, OF	.250	296	42	74	11	4	4	35	7
Walton, Jerome, OF	.444	18	3	8	2	1	1	5	0
*Warner, Mike, OF	.207	29	4	6	1	0	0	1	1
*Williams, Juan, OF	.272	357	55	97	22	2	15	52	5

PITCHING	W	L	ERA	G	SV	IP	H	BB	SO
Borowski, Joe	1	5	3.71	34	7	53.1	42	30	40
Brock, Chris	10	11	4.67	26	0	150.1	137	61	112
Dettmer, John	3	5	3.92	19	0	59.2	69	9	26
Fox, Chad	3	10	4.73	18	0	93.1	91	49	87
Harrison, Tommy	0	0	5.21	10	0	19.0	16	12	12
*Hartgraves, Dean	0	0	2.08	4	0	8.2	4	2	8
Hostetler, Mike	11	9	4.38	27	0	148.0	168	41	81
*Lee, Mark	4	5	2.69	53	1	67.0	69	17	71
Lomon, Kevin	9	8	4.33	26	0	141.1	151	44	102
Murray, Matt	2	10	7.38	18	0	68.1	75	63	43
Nichols, Rod	3	3	1.99	57	20	72.1	54	20	64
Schmidt, Jason	3	0	2.56	7	0	45.2	36	19	41
*Schutz, Carl	4	3	5.30	41	3	69.2	86	26	52
Steph, Rod	2	3	3.84	38	1	79.2	75	17	41
*Thobe, Tom	1	8	6.13	31	3	72.0	89	37	40
*Woodall, Brad	9	7	3.38	21	0	133.1	124	36	74

Rochester Red Wings (Orioles) AAA

BATTING	AVG	AB	R	H	2B	3B	HR	RBI	SB
Avila, Rolo, OF	.298	47	7	14	2	1	0	6	2
Bellinger, Clay, SS	.301	459	68	138	34	4	15	78	8
*Blosser, Greg, OF	.235	115	11	27	6	1	2	12	2
*Bowers, Brent, OF	.325	206	40	67	8	4	4	19	9
Brown, Jarvis, OF	.211	204	28	43	6	6	4	19	9
Cookson, Brent, OF	.269	368	73	99	20	1	25	71	4
Denson, Drew, DH	.350	60	14	21	7	1	2	10	0
Devarez, Cesar, C	.287	223	24	64	9	1	4	27	5
Figueroa, Bien, 2B	.312	154	25	48	7	0	1	16	3
Gordon, Keith, OF	.250	104	15	26	4	1	5	19	0
Hall, Joe, OF	.288	479	96	138	26	10	19	95	15
Hammonds, Jeffrey, OF	.272	125	24	34	4	2	3	19	3
*Huson, Jeff, OF	.250	8	0	2	0	0	0	1	0
Martinez, Domingo, 1B	.362	116	18	42	7	0	7	38	0
McClain, Scott, 3B	.281	463	76	130	23	4	17	69	8
#Owens, Billy, OF	.254	201	19	51	14	0	5	30	2
*Polonia, Luis, OF	.240	50	9	12	2	0	0	3	5
#Rosario, Mel, C	.000	2	0	0	0	0	0	0	0
Smith, Mark, OF	.348	132	24	46	14	1	8	32	10
*Tarasco, Tony, DH	.262	103	18	27	6	0	2	9	4
*Tyler, Brad, 2B	.270	382	68	103	18	10	13	52	19
Waszgis, B.J., C	.266	304	37	81	16	0	11	48	2
*Wawruck, Jim, OF	.284	204	31	58	14	6	0	15	4
#Zaun, Greg, C	.319	47	11	15	2	0	0	4	0
Zosky, Eddie, SS	.256	340	42	87	22	4	3	34	5

PITCHING	W	L	ERA	G	SV	IP	H	BB	SO
Benitez, Armando	0	0	2.25	2	0	4.0	3	1	5
Coppinger, Rocky	6	4	4.19	12	0	73.0	65	39	81
Corbin, Archie	0	2	4.74	20	1	43.2	44	25	47
Dedrick, Jim	6	3	6.51	39	4	66.1	88	41	37
*Dixon, Steve	0	2	3.41	32	2	34.1	27	23	32
Edens, Tom	4	6	5.19	20	0	67.2	73	23	36
*Florence, Don	4	4	6.14	36	0	85.0	111	30	53

Class A WRAP-UPS

Midwest League

The West Michigan Whitecaps sailed to the league title in a three-games-to-one series win in the finals against the Wisconsin Timber Rattlers. The Whitecaps swept the Rockford Cubbies in two games in the semis. In the first round, West Michigan beat Lansing two games to one. Each of Wisconsin's first two series went the distance, as they edged Quad City in the semis after beating the Peoria Chiefs. Quad City had beaten the Cedar Rapids Kernels in the first round.

League leaders: BA: **Kerry Robinson**, Peoria, .359. HR: **Larry Barnes**, Cedar Rapids, 27. RBI: **Barnes**, 112. SB: **Robinson** and **Justin Baughman**, Cedar Rapids, 50. ERA: **Britt Reames**, Peoria, 1.90. W: **Brandon Kolb**, Clinton, 16. S: **Santos Hernandez**, Burlington, 35. SO: **Reames**, 167.

MIDWEST LEAGUE (A):
Eastern Division

	W	L	Pct.	GB
West Michigan	77	61	.558	—
Fort Wayne	69	67	.507	7
Lansing	68	71	.489	9½
Michigan	60	78	.435	17
South Bend	54	82	.397	22

Central Division

	W	L	Pct.	GB
Peoria	79	57	.581	—
Wisconsin	77	58	.570	1½
Rockford	70	65	.519	8½
Beloit	69	67	.507	10
Kane County	65	68	.489	12½

Western Division

	W	L	Pct.	GB
Quad City	70	61	.534	—
Clinton	64	70	.478	7½
Burlington	65	73	.471	8½
Cedar Rapids	63	72	.467	9

First round: West Michigan 2, Lansing 1; Wisconsin 2, Peoria 1; Quad City 2, Cedar Rapids 1; Rockford 2, Beloit 1.
Semifinals: West Michigan 2, Rockford 0; Wisconsin 2, Quad City 1.
Finals: West Michigan 3, Wisconsin 1.

Class A WRAP-UPS

South Atlantic League

The Savannah Sand Gnats swept a doubleheader from the Delmarva Shorebirds to wrap up the league championship, winning 3-1 in 13 innings in the opener and 4-1 in the nightcap. Dan Ricabal came on in the sixth inning of the first game and pitched eight shutout innings for the win. In the first game of the series, Savannah edged Delmarva 3-2, but the Shorebirds rallied to win the second game 5-4.

League leaders: BA: **Carlos Mendoza**, Capital City, .336. HR: **Russell Branyan**, Columbus, 40. RBI: **Branyan,** 106. SB: **Rod Smith**, Greensboro, and **Ramon Gomez**, Hickory, 57. ERA: **Nelson Figueroa**, Capital City, 2.04. W: **Elvin Hernandez**, Augusta, 17. S: **Bryan Corey**, Fayetteville, 34. SO: **Figueroa**, 200.

SOUTH ATLANTIC LEAGUE (A)

Northern Division

	W	L	Pct.	GB
Delmarva	83	59	.585	—
Fayetteville	76	63	.547	5½
Hagerstown	70	71	.496	12½
Charleston, WV	58	84	.408	25

Central Division

	W	L	Pct.	GB
Asheville	84	52	.618	—
Columbia	82	57	.590	3½
Piedmont	72	66	.522	13
Charleston, SC	63	78	.447	23½
Greensboro	56	86	.394	31
Hickory	55	85	.393	31

Southern Division

	W	L	Pct.	GB
Columbus	79	63	.556	—
Savannah	72	69	.511	6½
Augusta	71	70	.504	7½
Macon	61	79	.436	17

First round: Delmarva 2, Fayetteville 0; Asheville 2, Columbia 0; Columbus 2, Augusta 1; Savannah 2, Piedmont 0.
Semifinals: Savannah 2, Columbus 0; Delmarva 2, Asheville 1.
Finals: Savannah 3, Delmarva 2.

PITCHING	W	L	ERA	G	SV	IP	H	BB	SO
*Flynt, Will	1	1	8.27	4	0	16.1	26	13	9
Frohwirth, Todd	0	2	4.50	9	0	16.0	11	5	16
*Grott, Matt	1	3	4.78	32	0	96.0	105	29	68
Haynes, Jimmy	1	1	5.65	5	0	28.2	31	18	24
*Krivda, Rick	3	1	4.30	8	0	44.0	51	15	34
*Lane, Aaron	1	0	5.64	9	1	22.1	31	8	13
Maduro, Calvin	3	5	4.74	8	0	43.2	49	18	40
Munoz, Oscar	6	7	4.23	21	0	112.2	100	37	85
Myers, Jimmy	7	5	2.89	39	12	53.0	53	12	21
*Powell, Dennis	0	0	1.35	5	1	6.2	4	1	4
Revenig, Todd	2	0	7.50	3	0	6.0	8	0	4
Rodriguez, Nerio	1	0	1.80	2	0	15.0	10	2	6
Sackinsky, Brian	7	3	3.46	14	0	67.2	75	15	38
Shepherd, Keith	4	7	4.01	27	9	94.1	91	37	98
*Shouse, Brian	1	2	4.50	32	2	50.0	53	16	45
Stephenson, Garrett	7	6	4.81	23	0	121.2	123	44	86
Williams, Jeff	1	1	1.13	8	0	8.0	11	4	4
Yan, Esteban	5	4	4.27	22	1	71.2	75	18	61

Scranton/WB Red Barons (Phillies) AAA

BATTING	AVG	AB	R	H	2B	3B	HR	RBI	SB
#Amaro, Ruben, OF	.270	230	36	62	11	3	2	24	13
Battle, Howard, 3B	.228	391	37	89	24	1	8	44	3
Benjamin, Mike, SS	.385	13	2	5	2	0	0	4	0
Bennett, Gary, C	.248	286	37	71	15	1	8	37	1
Burton, Essex, 2B	.172	58	4	10	3	0	0	1	5
*Butler, Robert, OF	.255	298	39	76	15	8	4	34	3
Diaz, Mario, 2B	.274	241	29	66	9	0	5	33	0
Doster, David, 2B	.258	322	37	83	20	0	7	48	7
Estalella, Bobby, C	.250	36	7	9	3	0	3	8	0
Fisher, David, SS	.156	64	6	10	1	0	1	3	1
Flores, Jose, 2B	.257	70	10	18	1	0	0	3	0
Held, Dan, 1B	.000	14	1	0	0	0	0	0	0
#Jefferies, Gregg, 1B	.118	17	1	2	0	1	0	0	0
Magee, Wendell, OF	.284	155	31	44	9	2	10	32	3
Manahan, Anthony, SS	.105	38	3	4	2	0	0	0	0
Martinez, Manuel, OF	.209	67	8	14	1	1	0	5	3
McNair, Fred, PH	.160	25	3	4	0	0	0	3	0
Murray, Glenn, OF	.366	142	31	52	10	2	7	22	7
#Otero, Ricky, OF	.299	177	38	53	9	8	1	9	15
*Phillips, J.R., OF	.285	200	33	57	14	2	13	42	2
#Relaford, Desi, SS	.235	85	12	20	4	1	1	11	7
Rolen, Scott, 3B	.274	168	23	46	17	0	2	19	4
Schall, Gene, 1B	.288	371	66	107	16	5	17	67	1
Sefcik, Kevin, SS	.333	180	34	60	7	5	0	19	11
#Stocker, Kevin, SS	.227	44	5	10	3	0	2	6	1
*Tokheim, David, OF	.212	255	35	54	10	4	1	21	5
Wrona, Rick, C	.229	175	10	40	8	0	5	20	1
*Zuber, Jon, 1B	.311	412	62	128	22	5	4	59	4
Zupcic, Bob, OF	.235	119	12	28	5	0	2	16	1

PITCHING	W	L	ERA	G	SV	IP	H	BB	SO
Bakkum, Scott	5	7	6.08	44	6	93.1	119	28	50
*Beech, Matt	2	0	2.40	2	0	15.0	9	1	14
Blazier, Ron	4	0	2.57	33	12	42.0	33	9	38
Brumley, Duff	2	1	5.85	20	0	20.0	19	22	15
Crawford, Carlos	9	10	4.54	28	1	158.2	169	63	89
*Dodd, Robert	0	0	8.10	8	0	20.0	32	9	12
Doolan, Blake	1	1	6.50	18	1	18.0	26	7	8
Elliott, Donnie	5	11	4.79	21	0	103.1	105	59	93
*Frey, Steve	2	2	5.40	10	0	13.1	11	8	9
Greene, Tommy	2	0	3.77	5	0	31.0	31	7	26
Heflin, Bronson	4	0	2.61	30	12	38.0	25	3	23
Holman, Craig	3	2	5.89	36	0	62.2	77	34	36
Hunter, Rich	2	4	6.69	8	0	40.1	39	22	22
*Ilsley, Blaise	6	4	5.43	25	0	61.1	73	19	31
*Jordan, Ricardo	3	3	5.26	32	1	39.1	40	22	40
*Karp, Ryan	1	1	3.07	7	0	41.0	35	14	30
*Mimbs, Mike	2	1	2.48	7	0	29.0	27	5	20
Mitchell, Larry	1	1	2.55	11	1	24.2	19	10	24
Munoz, Bobby	4	2	3.91	8	0	50.2	50	7	34
Nye, Ryan	5	2	5.02	14	0	80.2	97	30	51
*Quirico, Rafael	4	4	3.32	13	0	65.0	48	26	51
Schilling, Curt	1	0	1.38	2	0	13.0	9	5	10
Troutman, Keith	1	1	5.14	8	0	14.0	19	5	9
*West, Dave	1	0	5.25	2	0	12.0	14	2	12

PITCHING	W	L	ERA	G	SV	IP	H	BB	SO
*Wiegandt, Scott	5	6	2.71	46	2	63.0	63	33	46
*Williams, Mitch	2	2	10.20	9	0	15.0	25	11	15

Syracuse Chiefs (Blue Jays) AAA

BATTING	AVG	AB	R	H	2B	3B	HR	RBI	SB
Adriana, Sharnol, 3B	.281	292	48	82	12	5	10	37	18
*Boston, D.J., 1B	.247	85	12	21	7	0	4	12	0
Brito, Tilson, SS	.278	400	63	111	22	8	10	54	11
Cairo, Miguel, 2B	.277	465	71	129	14	4	3	48	27
Chamberlain, Wes, DH	.344	131	20	45	5	0	10	37	2
Cradle, Rickey, OF	.200	130	22	26	5	3	8	22	1
#Crespo, Felipe, 2B	.282	355	53	100	25	0	8	58	10
*Dismuke, Jamie, 1B	.167	42	3	7	1	0	0	5	1
Huff, Mike, OF	.290	248	40	72	20	3	8	42	8
#Jose, Felix, DH	.253	359	50	91	17	2	18	66	3
Knorr, Randy, C	.278	36	1	10	5	0	0	5	0
*Kowitz, Brian, OF	.222	176	23	39	11	3	1	22	4
McGriff, Terry, C	.186	59	7	11	1	0	1	6	0
Mosquera, Julio, C	.250	72	6	18	1	0	0	5	0
Mummau, Bob, PR	.000	3	1	0	0	0	0	0	0
Perez, Tomas, SS	.276	123	15	34	10	1	1	13	8
*Pose, Scott, OF	.272	419	71	114	11	6	0	39	30
Ramos, John, 1B	.243	317	38	77	16	0	8	42	1
Rowland, Rich, C	.226	288	43	65	24	2	8	45	1
Stewart, Shannon, OF	.298	420	77	125	26	8	6	42	35
Turang, Brian, 3B	.172	93	13	16	2	1	1	8	3
*Weinke, Chris, 1B	.186	161	21	30	8	1	3	18	0

PITCHING	W	L	ERA	G	SV	IP	H	BB	SO
Andujar, Luis	0	0	2.25	2	0	12.0	17	2	10
*Baptist, Travis	7	6	5.43	30	0	141.0	187	48	77
*Bohanon, Brian	4	3	3.86	31	0	58.1	56	17	38
Brandow, Derek	8	7	4.28	24	0	124.0	118	57	103
Brow, Scott	5	4	4.93	18	0	76.2	84	26	52
Carrara, Giovanni	4	4	3.58	9	0	37.2	37	12	28
Czajkowski, Jim	6	4	3.83	48	1	89.1	85	37	71
*Flener, Huck	7	3	2.28	14	0	86.2	73	23	62
*Horsman, Vince	0	3	5.40	29	0	35.0	37	11	21
Janzen, Marty	3	4	7.76	10	0	55.2	74	24	34
Johnson, Dane	3	2	2.45	43	22	51.1	37	17	51
*Pace, Scotty	3	3	5.05	20	0	51.2	53	27	35
Pett, Jose	2	9	5.83	20	0	109.2	134	42	50
Pose, Scott	0	0	13.50	2	0	2.0	4	2	3
Robinson, Ken	3	7	4.64	47	1	64.0	52	39	78
Rogers, Jimmy	1	3	6.04	8	0	22.1	28	7	15
Sievert, Mark	2	5	5.93	10	0	54.2	62	33	46
*Spoljaric, Paul	3	0	3.27	17	4	22.0	20	6	24
Ware, Jeff	3	7	5.68	13	0	77.2	83	32	59
Williams, Woody	3	1	1.41	7	0	32.0	22	7	33

Toledo Mud Hens (Tigers) AAA

BATTING	AVG	AB	R	H	2B	3B	HR	RBI	SB
Baez, Kevin, SS	.245	302	34	74	12	3	11	44	3
Barker, Glen, OF	.250	80	13	20	2	1	0	2	6
Casanova, Raul, C	.273	161	23	44	11	0	8	28	0
#Clark, Tony, 1B	.299	194	42	58	7	1	14	36	1
*Cotton, John, OF	.187	171	14	32	7	1	4	19	4
Cruz, Fausto, SS	.250	384	49	96	18	2	12	59	11
#Franklin, Micah, OF	.246	179	32	44	10	1	7	21	3
Hansen, Terrel, OF	.125	16	2	2	0	0	1	1	1
Hiatt, Phil, 3B	.261	555	99	145	27	3	42	119	17
*Higginson, Bob, OF	.308	13	4	4	0	1	0	1	0
*Hyers, Tim, 1B	.259	437	55	113	17	6	7	59	7
#Mitchell, Tony, OF	.278	288	45	80	10	4	12	43	3
#Penn, Shannon, OF	.287	356	65	102	12	4	6	42	22
*Pride, Curtis, DH	.231	26	4	6	1	0	1	2	4
Rodriguez, Steve, 2B	.285	333	49	95	18	2	4	30	18
*Singleton, Duane, OF	.221	294	42	65	15	6	8	30	17
Tackett, Jeff, C	.237	283	41	67	10	3	7	49	4
Trammell, Bubba, OF	.294	180	32	53	14	1	6	24	5
*Ward, Daryle, 1B	.174	23	1	4	0	0	0	1	0
Wedge, Eric, DH	.235	332	61	78	25	0	15	57	2

PITCHING	W	L	ERA	G	SV	IP	H	BB	SO
Barnes, Brian	6	6	3.99	14	0	88.0	85	29	70
Blomdahl, Ben	2	6	6.22	53	2	59.1	77	18	34

Class A WRAP-UPS

New York–Penn League (SS)

The Vermont Expos gave Burlington its fourth championship in nine seasons, rallying from losing their first game to sweep the last two from the St. Catharines Stompers. In the clincher, a 4-3 win, Jamey Carroll went 3-for-4. In the opener, Josh Bradford made his only appearance of the postseason, tossing a one-hit shutout for a 2-0 win. The second game was a 6-5 win for the Expos. In the semifinals, both teams had advanced with two-game sweeps, St. Catharines over Watertown, and Vermont against Pittsfield.

League leaders: BA: Joe Freitas, New Jersey, .344. HR: Will Skett, St. Catharines, 15. RBI: Kevin Burns, Auburn, 55. SB: Donzell McDonald, Oneonta, 54. ERA: Ken Raines, Hudson Valley, 1.07. W: Courtney Duncan, Williamsport, 11. S: Chris McFerrin, Auburn, and Kyle Kawabata, Batavia, 20. SO: Bobby Rodgers, Lowell, 108.

NEW YORK–PENN LEAGUE (SS-A)

McNamara Division

	W	L	Pct.	GB
Vermont	48	26	.649	—
Pittsfield	46	29	.613	2½
Lowell	33	41	.446	15
Hudson Valley	32	44	.421	17
New Jersey	28	47	.373	20½

Pinckney Division

	W	L	Pct.	GB
Watertown	45	30	.600	—
Williamsport	43	32	.573	2
Auburn	37	39	.487	8½
Oneonta	31	45	.408	14½
Utica	29	47	.382	16½

Stedler Division

	W	L	Pct.	GB
St. Catharines	44	32	.579	—
Batavia	42	33	.560	1½
Jamestown	39	36	.520	4½
Erie	30	46	.395	14

Semifinals: Vermont 2, Pittsfield 0; St. Catharines 2, Watertown 0. *Finals:* Vermont 2, St. Catharines 1.

Class A WRAP-UPS

Northwest League (SS)

The eight-team league dispensed with such formalities as semifinals and cut right to the chase with a best-of-three final series. The Yakima Bears pitching staff dominated, sweeping the Eugene Ems, 2-1 and 9-2, while holding league home run leader Steve Hacker hitless. In the opener, Theodore Lilly tossed 6⅔ innings of two-hit ball, striking out eight. In the clincher, Kevin Culmo (five innings) and Blake Mayo (four hitless innings) combined on the six-hitter—fittingly, since the two finished the season holding the top two slots in the league in ERA. Tony Mota was 4-for-4 with a triple and Brian Sankey was 3-for-5 with a double and an RBI for the Bears, while leadoff hitter Peter Bergeron added two hits and two RBI.

League leaders: BA: **Adam Johnson**, Eugene, .314. HR: **Steve Hacker**, Eugene, 21. RBI: **Kit Fallow**, Spokane, 66. SB: **Trent Durrington**, Boise, and **Michael Caruso**, Bellingham, 24. ERA: **Blake Mayo**, Yakima, 1.20. W: **Tommy Darrell**, Boise, 8. S: **Jeff Kubenka**, Yakima, 14. SO: **Brandon Leese**, Bellingham, 90.

NORTHWEST LEAGUE (SS-A)

Northern Division

	W	L	Pct.	GB
Yakima	40	36	.526	—
Bellingham	39	36	.520	½
Spokane	37	39	.487	3
Everett	33	42	.440	6½

Southern Division

	W	L	Pct.	GB
Eugene	49	27	.645	—
Boise	43	33	.566	6
Portland	33	43	.434	16
South. Oregon	29	47	.382	20

Finals: Yakima 2, Eugene 0.

PITCHING	W	L	ERA	G	SV	IP	H	BB	SO
Christopher, Mike	4	1	3.92	39	22	39.0	50	5	40
Farrell, John	2	4	8.10	6	0	30.0	38	9	21
Gallaher, Kevin	0	0	21.00	2	0	3.0	9	4	4
Gohr, Greg	0	0	7.50	2	0	12.0	17	5	15
*Guilfoyle, Michael	5	5	5.14	54	1	49.0	59	31	42
Henry, Dwayne	1	0	7.23	18	1	18.2	21	12	23
Keagle, Greg	2	3	10.00	6	0	27.0	42	11	24
Lewis, Richie	0	0	2.25	2	0	4.0	1	1	4
Lima, Jose	5	4	6.78	12	0	69.0	93	12	57
*Marshall, Randy	3	5	4.15	29	0	95.1	97	25	60
Maxcy, Brian	3	1	3.97	15	0	22.2	24	9	8
McCurry, Jeff	1	4	4.76	39	2	58.2	66	26	56
*Miller, Trever	13	6	4.90	27	0	165.1	167	65	115
*Nitkowski, C.J.	4	6	4.46	19	0	111.0	104	53	103
Olivares, Omar	1	0	8.44	1	0	5.1	4	3	5
Sager, A.J.	1	0	2.63	18	0	37.2	38	3	24
Scanlan, Bob	1	3	7.50	14	0	36.0	46	15	18
Sodowsky, Clint	6	8	3.94	19	0	118.2	128	51	59
*Thompson, Justin	6	3	3.42	13	0	84.1	74	26	69
*Urbani, Thomas	0	3	6.43	4	0	14.0	18	7	10
Walker, Mike	3	2	3.83	28	6	44.2	37	27	37
Williams, Brian	1	2	5.49	3	0	19.2	22	9	21

Pacific Coast League

Albuquerque Dukes (Dodgers) AAA

BATTING	AVG	AB	R	H	2B	3B	HR	RBI	SB
*Anderson, Cliff, SS	.269	186	19	50	9	2	4	17	3
Ashley, Billy, OF	.348	23	6	8	1	0	1	9	2
Blanco, Henry, C	.167	6	1	1	0	0	0	0	0
Busch, Mike, 1B	.303	142	30	43	6	1	12	36	0
Castro, Juan, 3B	.375	56	12	21	4	2	1	8	1
#Cedeno, Roger, OF	.224	125	16	28	2	3	1	10	6
Dandridge, Brad, OF	.263	80	14	21	4	0	2	7	0
*Demetral, Chris, 2B	.263	209	30	55	8	0	4	26	4
#Fonville, Chad, SS	.240	96	17	23	1	0	0	5	7
#Fox, Eric, OF	.330	91	8	30	6	1	0	2	1
Gagne, Greg, SS	.273	11	1	3	1	0	0	1	0
*Garcia, Karim, OF	.297	327	54	97	17	10	13	58	6
Guerrero, Wilton, 2B	.344	425	79	146	17	12	2	38	26
Hernandez, Carlos, C	.240	233	19	56	11	0	5	30	5
Huckaby, Ken, C	.276	286	37	79	16	2	3	41	0
Ingram, Garey, PH	.100	10	1	1	0	0	0	0	0
Johnson, Keith, SS	.250	16	2	4	1	0	0	2	0
*Kirkpatrick, Jay, 1B	.243	107	12	26	5	0	0	9	0
Konerko, Paul, 1B	.429	14	2	6	0	0	1	2	0
Lott, Billy, OF	.266	418	67	111	20	1	19	66	6
Luzinski, Ryan, PH	.143	14	0	2	0	0	0	1	0
*Marrero, Oreste, 1B	.283	441	50	125	29	1	13	76	2
Maurer, Ron, SS	.275	222	32	61	14	1	5	30	2
*Melendez, Dan, 1B	.152	46	5	7	2	0	0	2	0
Parker, Rick, OF	.303	175	26	53	7	3	0	23	7
Prince, Tom, C	.411	95	24	39	5	1	7	22	0
Richardson, Brian, 3B	.245	355	52	87	17	2	9	43	4
Rios, Eduardo, 2B	.069	29	3	2	0	0	0	1	1
Roberge, J.P., OF	.321	156	17	50	6	1	4	17	3
Romero, Willie, OF	.385	13	1	5	0	0	1	3	1
#Williams, Reggie, OF	.287	352	60	101	25	2	6	42	17

PITCHING	W	L	ERA	G	SV	IP	H	BB	SO
*Brewer, Billy	2	2	3.13	31	2	31.2	28	22	33
*Brunson, William	3	4	4.47	9	0	54.1	53	23	47
Bruske, Jim	5	2	4.06	36	4	62.0	63	21	51
Correa, Ramser	0	3	5.75	23	1	36.0	44	22	30
*Cummings, John	2	6	4.14	27	2	78.1	91	28	49
Dreifort, Darren	5	6	4.17	18	0	86.1	88	52	75
*Elvira, Narciso	1	1	4.76	3	0	17.0	19	9	14
Garcia, Jose	6	1	4.71	44	0	78.1	97	40	34
Harkey, Mike	7	11	5.38	49	13	118.2	146	39	90
Henderson, Ryan	0	0	7.94	3	0	5.2	5	6	7
Herges, Matt	4	1	2.60	10	0	34.2	33	14	15
Hubbs, Dan	7	1	4.76	49	2	75.2	89	47	82
Jones, Calvin	0	0	4.50	10	0	12.0	11	12	15
Lagarde, Joe	0	0	5.25	10	0	12.0	14	9	11

PITCHING	W	L	ERA	G	SV	IP	H	BB	SO
*Mimbs, Mark	8	8	4.59	34	0	151.0	165	43	136
*Pyc, Dave	2	3	9.17	13	0	35.1	53	19	27
*Rath, Gary	10	11	4.19	30	0	180.1	177	89	125
Rodriguez, Felix	3	9	5.53	27	0	107.1	111	60	65
Seanez, Rudy	0	2	6.52	20	6	19.1	27	11	20
Treadwell, Jody	1	1	7.85	5	0	18.1	30	10	16
Weaver, Eric	1	4	5.40	13	0	46.2	63	22	38

Calgary Cannons (Pirates) AAA

BATTING	AVG	AB	R	H	2B	3B	HR	RBI	SB
Allensworth, J'rm'ne, OF	.330	352	77	116	23	6	8	43	25
Aude, Rich, 1B	.292	394	69	115	29	0	17	81	4
*Beamon, Trey, OF	.288	378	62	109	15	3	5	52	16
Clark, Jerald, OF	.266	248	33	66	20	1	8	45	0
*Cummings, Midre, OF	.304	368	60	112	24	3	8	55	6
Edge, Tim, C	.333	36	6	12	3	0	2	11	0
Encarnacion, Angelo, C	.319	263	38	84	18	0	4	31	6
Espinosa, Ramon, OF	.282	245	37	69	8	8	0	25	2
#Felder, Mike, OF	.284	81	14	23	3	0	1	5	0
Finn, John, 2B	.255	192	24	49	13	1	0	32	2
Garcia, Carlos, 2B	.333	6	0	2	0	1	0	0	0
Marx, Tim, C	.324	296	50	96	20	1	1	37	6
Millette, Joe, PH	.213	108	7	23	8	0	0	7	0
Polcovich, Kevin, SS	.274	336	53	92	21	3	1	46	7
Ratliff, Darryl, OF	.336	131	19	44	3	0	0	12	4
*Secrist, Reed, 3B	.307	420	68	129	30	0	17	66	2
#Sveum, Dale, 3B	.300	343	62	103	28	2	23	84	2
*Womack, Tony, SS	.300	506	75	152	19	11	1	47	37

PITCHING	W	L	ERA	G	SV	IP	H	BB	SO
Agosto, Juan	2	3	3.67	24	0	27.0	28	12	10
Backlund, Brett	3	2	6.00	7	0	39.0	47	16	16
Boever, Joe	12	1	2.15	44	4	83.2	78	19	66
*Bolton, Tom	12	5	4.02	40	2	116.1	121	47	92
*Cadaret, Greg	0	3	6.57	9	0	12.1	19	12	10
*Christiansen, Jason	1	0	3.27	2	0	11.0	9	1	10
Dessens, Elmer	2	2	3.15	6	0	34.1	40	15	15
Ericks, John	1	2	4.20	14	1	30.0	31	15	40
Greer, Ken	5	4	3.97	46	3	68.0	74	17	36
Hope, John	4	7	4.82	23	0	125.0	147	49	71
Konuszewski, Dennis	0	0	24.30	3	0	3.1	13	5	0
Loaiza, Esteban	3	4	4.02	12	0	69.1	61	25	38
Loiselle, Rich	4	4	3.43	13	0	84.0	92	27	72
*May, Darrell	7	6	4.10	23	0	131.2	146	36	75
*Peters, Chris	1	1	0.98	4	0	27.2	18	8	16
Phoenix, Steve	1	1	1.69	10	0	16.0	16	5	9
Pisciotta, Marc	2	7	4.11	57	1	65.2	71	46	46
*Ruebel, Matt	5	3	4.60	13	0	76.1	89	28	48
Ryan, Matt	2	6	5.30	51	20	52.2	70	28	35
Rychel, Kevin	2	0	8.18	11	0	11.0	15	8	5
*Shouse, Brian	1	0	10.66	12	0	12.2	22	4	12
Wilson, Gary	6	9	5.08	27	0	161.1	209	44	88

Colo. Springs Sky Sox (Rockies) AAA

BATTING	AVG	AB	R	H	2B	3B	HR	RBI	SB
Brito, Jorge, C	.340	159	32	54	17	0	7	31	0
#Carter, Jeff, 2B	.255	161	19	41	9	0	1	12	3
Castellano, Pedro, 3B	.337	362	56	122	30	3	13	59	0
Cockrell, Alan, OF	.300	357	55	107	25	3	14	60	1
*Counsell, Craig, 2B	.240	75	17	18	3	0	2	10	4
Decker, Steve, C	.400	25	4	10	1	0	0	3	0
Echevarria, Angel, OF	.337	415	67	140	19	2	16	74	4
Figueroa, Bien, 3B	.207	29	2	6	2	0	0	6	0
*Gainer, Jay, 1B	.234	333	51	78	16	0	14	49	6
*Giannelli, Ray, 3B	.230	148	16	34	9	0	2	17	1
Gonzalez, Pedro, C	.174	86	10	15	7	0	2	13	1
*Helton, Todd, 1B	.352	71	13	25	4	1	2	13	0
Hubbard, Trent, OF	.314	188	41	59	15	5	6	16	6
*Huson, Jeff, 2B	.295	61	10	18	4	0	0	8	6
#Jones, Terry, OF	.288	497	75	143	7	4	0	33	26
Kennedy, David, 1B	.255	333	46	85	27	0	11	50	1
List, Lou, PH	.083	12	1	1	0	0	0	1	0
Miller, Roger, C	.000	2	0	0	0	0	0	0	0
Owens, Jayhawk, C	.227	22	6	5	3	0	0	6	0
#Perez, Neifi, SS	.316	570	77	180	28	12	7	72	16

Rookie League WRAP-UPS

Appalachian League

The matchup of Bluefield and Kingsport in the finals was a repeat of 1995. In '95, while Bluefield brought in the better record, Kingsport won the title. This year, the situation was reversed, with the North Division champion Orioles winning the series two games to one. Bluefield's victory was led by first baseman Calvin Pickering, who hit a bases-loaded double in the 8-5 opening win and scored twice in the clincher. The Kingsport Mets won only the second game of the play-offs, behind the arm of Andy Zwirchitz, who fanned eight in a 9-0 win. Along with Pickering, Bluefield was paced during the season by all-star second baseman Carlos Casimiro, an 18-year-old who hit .276 with 16 doubles, 10 homers and 22 steals.

League leaders: BA: **Rodger Harris**, Johnson City, .369. HR: **Calvin Pickering**, Bluefield, 18. RBI: **Pickering**, 66. SB: **Tyrone Pendergrass**, Danville, 40. ERA: **Kevin McGlinchy**, Danville, 1.13. W: **Grant Roberts**, Kingsport, 9. S: Jose DeLeon, Johnson City, 15. SO: **Roberts**, 92.

APPALACHIAN LEAGUE (Rookie)

North Division

	W	L	Pct.	GB
Bluefield	42	26	.618	—
Danville	37	29	.561	4
Burlington	29	38	.433	12½
Princeton	28	40	.412	14
Martinsville	20	47	.299	21½

South Division

	W	L	Pct.	GB
Kingsport	48	19	.716	—
Johnson City	42	26	.618	6½
Elizabethton	40	27	.597	8
Bristol	17	51	.250	31½

Finals: Bluefield 2, Kingsport 1

Rookie League WRAP-UPS

Pioneer League

Both expansion-team entries, the Lethbridge Black Diamonds (Diamondbacks) and the Butte Copper Kings (Devil Rays), won their divisions in the second half to advance to the playoff semifinals, but the finals pitted two Milwaukee teams against each other, with the Helena Brewers beating the Ogden Raptors in a two-game sweep. In the North Division semifinal, Lethbridge won the opener 13-0 behind triple-crown-winning pitcher Vladimir Nunez, before Helena rallied for a pair of wins. In the South Division, Ogden won the opener and the finale, while the Copper Kings sneaked in a thrilling 12-11 win in 16 innings in the middle.

League leaders: BA: **Kevin Sweeney**, Lethbridge, .424. HR: **Darron Ingram**, Billings; **Miguel Rodriguez**, Ogden; and **David Hayman**, Lethbridge, 17. RBI: **Sweeney** and **Ronald Hartman**, Lethbridge, 72. SB: **Randy Albaral**, Medicine Hat, and **Marcus McCain**, Butte, 33. ERA: **Vladimir Nunez**, Lethbridge, 2.22. W: **Nunez**, 10. S: **David Bleazard**, Medicine Hat, 10. SO: **Nunez**, 93.

PIONEER LEAGUE (Rookie)

Northern Division

	W	L	Pct.	GB
Lethbridge	50	22	.694	—
Helena	43	29	.597	7
Great Falls	33	39	.458	17
Medicine Hat	22	50	.306	28

Southern Division

	W	L	Pct.	GB
Ogden	42	30	.583	—
Idaho Falls	38	34	.528	4
Butte	37	35	.514	5
Billings	23	49	.319	19

Semifinals: Helena 2, Lethbridge 1; Ogden 2, Butte 1.
Finals: Helena 2, Ogden 0

BATTING	AVG	AB	R	H	2B	3B	HR	RBI	SB
Pozo, Yohel, C	.277	47	8	13	2	0	1	5	0
Pulliam, Harvey, OF	.276	283	46	78	13	1	10	58	2
Strittmatter, Mark, C	.233	159	21	37	8	1	2	18	2
*Walker, Larry, OF	.364	11	2	4	0	0	2	8	0
White, Billy, 2B	.243	284	24	69	11	2	3	26	2
Young, Eric, 2B	.261	23	4	6	1	1	0	3	0

PITCHING	W	L	ERA	G	SV	IP	H	BB	SO
Alston, Garvin	1	4	5.77	35	14	34.1	47	27	36
Ausanio, Joe	1	1	4.34	13	0	18.2	18	10	18
Bailey, Roger	4	4	6.29	9	0	48.2	60	20	27
*Beckett, Robbie	0	2	2.19	12	1	12.1	6	11	15
Burke, John	2	4	5.94	24	1	63.2	75	28	54
Bustillos, Albert	6	10	5.23	33	1	144.2	167	44	95
DeJean, Mike	0	2	5.13	30	1	40.1	52	21	31
*Farmer, Mike	3	3	3.30	9	0	57.1	51	25	28
Fredrickson, Scott	2	2	6.64	55	2	63.2	71	40	66
Habyan, John	0	0	4.50	1	0	4.0	2	1	4
Hawblitzel, Ryan	7	6	5.00	26	1	117.0	131	27	75
Henry, Dwayne	1	4	7.71	28	0	39.2	43	30	33
*Jones, Bobby	2	8	4.97	57	3	88.2	88	63	78
Kramer, Tom	8	4	5.37	41	4	112.1	129	47	79
Leskanic, Curt	0	0	3.00	3	0	3.0	5	1	2
*Munoz, Mike	1	1	2.03	10	3	13.1	8	6	13
Nied, David	3	8	12.27	16	0	62.1	116	32	53
Pedraza, Rod	1	1	8.36	6	0	28.0	39	4	13
Rekar, Bryan	8	8	4.46	19	0	123.0	138	36	75
Thomson, John	4	7	5.04	11	0	69.2	76	26	62
Viano, Jake	0	2	10.89	7	0	20.2	33	13	12
Wright, Jamey	4	2	2.72	9	0	59.2	53	22	40

Edmonton Trappers (Athletics) AAA

BATTING	AVG	AB	R	H	2B	3B	HR	RBI	SB
Batista, Tony, SS	.322	205	33	66	17	4	8	40	2
Battle, Allen, OF	.304	224	53	68	12	4	3	33	9
Brosius, Scott, 3B	.625	8	5	5	1	0	0	0	0
Correia, Rod, SS	.087	23	1	2	0	0	0	0	1
Garrison, Webster, 1B	.303	294	56	89	18	0	10	49	2
Gubanich, Creighton, C	.248	117	14	29	7	1	4	19	3
*Horne, Tyrone, OF	.230	204	28	47	7	2	4	16	5
*Lee, Derek, OF	.200	25	3	5	1	0	0	1	0
Lennon, Patrick, OF	.327	251	37	82	16	2	12	42	3
Lesher, Brian, 1B	.287	414	57	119	29	2	18	75	6
#Lovullo, Torey, 1B	.280	93	18	26	4	0	4	19	0
Mashore, Damon, OF	.268	183	32	49	9	1	8	29	6
#McDonald, Jason, 2B	.238	479	71	114	7	5	8	46	33
Molina, Izzy, C	.263	342	45	90	12	3	12	56	2
#Moore, Kerwin, OF	.230	452	90	104	12	11	2	32	38
*Neill, Mike, OF	.150	20	4	3	1	0	1	4	0
*Plantier, Phil, OF	.352	122	25	43	7	1	9	45	1
Poe, Charles, OF	.200	15	2	3	0	0	0	0	0
Sheldon, Scott, SS	.300	350	61	105	27	3	10	60	5
#Smith, Demond, OF	.333	3	0	1	0	0	0	0	0
#Spiezio, Scott, 3B	.262	523	87	137	30	4	20	91	6
*Stairs, Matt, DH	.344	180	35	62	16	1	8	41	0
*Tomberlin, Andy, OF	.283	60	12	17	2	1	0	5	1
Ventura, Wilfredo, C	.250	4	1	1	0	0	0	0	0
Walters, Dan, C	.250	64	5	16	5	0	1	8	0
#Williams, George, C	.404	57	10	23	5	0	5	18	0
Wood, Jason, 1B	.000	12	0	0	0	0	0	0	0

PITCHING	W	L	ERA	G	SV	IP	H	BB	SO
Acre, Mark	6	2	2.09	39	8	43.0	33	16	50
Adams, Willie	10	4	3.78	19	0	112.0	95	39	80
Briscoe, John	5	2	4.77	30	1	54.2	69	23	62
Chouinard, Bobby	10	2	2.77	15	0	84.1	70	24	45
Daspit, Jamie	4	5	4.12	33	0	89.2	96	29	76
Dressendorfer, Kirk	0	1	5.54	10	0	13.0	23	3	10
Fletcher, Paul	4	6	2.70	38	1	83.1	66	41	76
Grigsby, Benji	0	3	7.25	11	0	22.1	29	7	15
*Lorraine, Andrew	8	10	5.68	30	0	141.0	181	46	73
Lovullo, Torey	0	0	4.50	2	0	4.0	3	3	0
Montgomery, Steve	2	0	2.89	36	1	56.0	51	12	40
Prieto, Ariel	3	0	0.57	3	0	15.2	11	6	18
Rose, Scott	4	4	2.91	50	10	55.2	57	16	20
*Shaw, Curtis	0	0	18.00	1	0	3.0	6	2	1
Small, Aaron	8	6	4.29	25	1	119.2	111	28	83

PITCHING	W	L	ERA	G	SV	IP	H	BB	SO
Taylor, Billy	0	0	0.79	7	4	11.1	10	3	13
Telgheder, Dave	8	6	4.17	17	0	101.1	102	23	59
Wasdin, John	2	1	4.14	9	0	50.0	52	17	30
Williams, Todd	5	3	5.50	35	0	91.2	125	37	33
Witasick, Jay	0	0	4.15	6	2	8.2	9	6	9
*Wojciechowski, Steve	4	3	3.73	11	0	60.1	56	21	46
Wood, Jason	0	0	0.00	1	0	2.0	1	3	1

Las Vegas Stars (Padres) AAA

BATTING	AVG	AB	R	H	2B	3B	HR	RBI	SB
Barry, Jeff, OF	.083	12	1	1	0	0	0	0	0
Bruno, Julio, 2B	.273	297	36	81	16	1	2	30	6
Bush, Homer, 2B	.362	116	24	42	11	1	2	3	3
Colbert, Craig, C	.250	200	18	50	8	0	5	19	3
#Dascenzo, Doug, OF	.284	320	48	91	17	3	0	20	15
Deer, Rob, OF	.224	259	43	58	14	2	20	47	5
Ingram, Riccardo, OF	.249	409	54	102	21	1	8	51	6
#Lopez, Luis, 2B	.206	68	4	14	3	0	1	12	0
Mulligan, Sean, C	.288	358	55	103	24	3	19	75	1
*Prieto, Chris, OF	.000	7	1	0	0	0	0	0	0
Ready, Randy, DH	.324	105	19	34	7	0	3	11	0
Rossy, Rico, SS	.252	413	56	104	21	2	4	35	6
Russo, Paul, 3B	.252	226	16	57	15	2	4	33	2
Schwenke, Matt, PH	.250	16	0	4	0	0	0	2	0
Scott, Gary, 3B	.272	217	24	59	16	2	2	27	0
Sharperson, Mike, 3B	.304	112	17	34	8	0	1	21	1
Shipley, Craig, SS	.000	2	1	0	0	0	0	0	0
Smith, Ira, OF	.242	252	37	61	16	1	5	25	3
Steverson, Todd, OF	.239	301	42	72	16	3	12	50	6
Tatum, Jimmy, OF	.343	233	40	80	20	1	12	56	4
*Thompson, Jason, 1B	.300	387	80	116	27	0	21	57	7
#Tredaway, Chad, 2B	.224	196	26	44	10	2	5	19	4

PITCHING	W	L	ERA	G	SV	IP	H	BB	SO
Abbott, Paul	4	2	4.18	28	7	28.0	27	12	37
Berumen, Andres	4	7	6.11	50	1	70.2	73	58	59
*Dishman, Glenn	6	8	5.57	26	0	155.0	177	43	115
Drahman, Brian	1	0	1.00	9	0	9.0	4	4	10
Freitas, Mike	0	1	3.18	3	0	5.2	8	1	1
Harriger, Denny	10	7	4.22	26	0	164.1	183	51	102
Harris, Greg W.	0	1	18.00	1	0	4.0	11	3	2
Hermanson, Dustin	1	4	3.13	42	21	46.0	41	27	54
Lewis, Scott	3	9	5.34	29	0	150.0	174	36	109
*Long, Joey	3	3	4.24	32	1	34.0	39	23	23
Oquist, Mike	9	4	2.89	27	1	140.1	136	44	110
*Osuna, Al	1	0	2.30	11	0	15.2	9	5	17
Schmitt, Todd	0	0	4.50	4	0	4.0	2	6	6
Smith, Pete	11	9	4.95	26	0	169.0	192	42	95
*Swan, Russ	5	6	5.08	25	0	125.2	148	47	71
Veras, Dario	6	2	2.90	19	1	40.1	41	6	30
*Villone, Ron	2	1	1.64	23	3	22.0	13	9	29
Walker, Pete	5	1	6.83	26	0	27.2	37	14	23
Weber, Weston	2	1	6.30	7	0	10.0	12	8	4

Phoenix Firebirds (Giants) AAA

BATTING	AVG	AB	R	H	2B	3B	HR	RBI	SB
Aurilia, Rich, SS	.433	30	9	13	7	0	0	4	1
Batiste, Kim, 3B	.297	165	32	49	8	3	14	44	1
*Benard, Marvin, OF	.368	19	2	7	0	0	0	4	1
Canizaro, Jay, 2B	.262	363	50	95	21	2	7	64	14
*Cruz, Jacob, OF	.285	435	60	124	26	4	7	75	5
#Delgado, Wilson, SS	.140	43	1	6	0	1	0	1	0
DeLeon, Roberto, 3B	.194	36	1	7	2	0	0	2	0
#Duncan, Andres, SS	.226	106	11	24	7	2	1	12	2
Ehmann, Kurt, SS	.201	134	14	27	6	2	0	12	0
Florez, Tim, 2B	.290	366	42	106	31	3	4	39	0
Glenn, Darrin, PH	.056	18	3	1	0	0	0	1	0
Hill, Glenallen, OF	.353	17	4	6	1	0	2	2	1
#Jensen, Marcus, C	.264	405	41	107	22	4	5	53	1
Jones, Dax, OF	.309	298	52	92	20	6	6	41	13
Kennedy, Darryl, C	.307	192	27	59	11	3	2	24	2
Manwaring, Kirt, C	.182	11	1	2	0	0	0	1	0
McCarty, Dave, OF	.400	25	4	10	1	1	1	7	0
Mirabelli, Doug, C	.298	47	10	14	7	0	0	7	0
#Mueller, Bill, 3B	.302	440	73	133	14	6	4	36	2

Rookie League WRAP-UPS

Arizona League

Mirroring the success of their parent club, the Padres won the Arizona League title, going 36-20 to edge the second-place Athletics by three games. Finishing last in the six-team league were the debuting Diamondbacks (20-37), but most of their top prospects were sent to the Pioneer League, where they helped lead the Lethbridge Black Diamonds to the playoffs. Leading the Padres were Brandon Pernell, who finished second in the league in batting at .333, and Shane Cronin, who led the loop with nine homers and 54 RBI while hitting .327. Jacob Ruotsinoja (.297, 6 HR, 40 RBI) also excelled. Three Padres pitchers were in the top 10 in ERA— Josef Thompson (2.65), Steve Hoff (2.85) and Damond Nash (3.05), while Thompson and Hoff tied for the league lead in wins with eight apiece. Hoff also led the loop with 104 strikeouts in 85 innings. Although they finished fourth at 26-30, the Rockies boasted both the league's batting champion (Brad Schwartzbauer, .344) and its ERA leader (Shawn Chacon, 1.60). Nelson Castro of the Angels led the league in steals with 25, while three pitchers had a league-leading six saves: Greg Winkleman (A's), Jeromy Palki (Mariners) and Justin Sellers (Padres).

ARIZONA LEAGUE (Rookie)

Padres	36	20	.643	—
Athletics	33	23	.589	3
Mariners	29	27	.518	7
Rockies	26	30	.464	10
Angels	24	32	.429	12
Diamondbacks	20	36	.357	16

No league playoffs.

Rookie League WRAP-UPS

Gulf Coast League

The Yankees won the Northern Division and then upset the favored Eastern champ Expos in the one-game semifinal, 4-0. Meanwhile, the Rangers, tops in the Northwest, beat the Southwest-winning Cubs 5-3 to set up the finals. The league batting champ, catcher Donny Leon, provided the clout, going 2-for-4 with a home run.

League leaders: BA: Donny Leon, Yankees, .361. HR: Derrick Bly, Cubs, 13. RBI: Leon, 46. SB: Dennis Abreu, Cubs, and Luis Rivas, Twins, 35. ERA: Jeriome Robertson, Astros, and Antonio Gholar, Twins, 1.72. W: Jonathan Widersk, Marlins, 8. S: Bobby Styles, Rangers, 13. SO: Robertson, 98.

GULF COAST LEAGUE (Rookie)

Eastern Division

	W	L	Pct.	GB
Expos	41	18	.695	—
Marlins	34	25	.576	7
Mets	29	30	.492	12
Braves	14	45	.237	27

Northwest Division

	W	L	Pct.	GB
Rangers	37	23	.617	—
Orioles	36	24	.600	1
Pirates	28	31	.475	8½
White Sox	20	40	.333	17

Northern Division

	W	L	Pct.	GB
Yankees	37	21	.638	—
Astros	31	28	.525	6½
Tigers	26	34	.433	12
Devil Rays	24	35	.407	13½

Southwest Division

	W	L	Pct.	GB
Cubs	34	26	.567	—
Royals	30	29	.508	3.5
Twins	30	30	.500	4
Red Sox	24	36	.400	10

Semifinals: Yankees 1, Expos 0; Rangers 1, Cubs 0.
Finals: Yankees 2, Rangers 0

1997 BASEBALL WEEKLY ALMANAC

BATTING	AVG	AB	R	H	2B	3B	HR	RBI	SB
Murray, Calvin, OF	.244	311	50	76	16	6	3	28	12
*Peltier, Dan, 1B	.285	267	40	76	8	3	0	27	0
Powell, Dante, OF	.250	8	0	2	0	1	0	0	0
Simonton, Benji, 1B	.750	4	1	3	0	0	1	2	0
*Singleton, Chrstphr, OF	.125	32	3	4	0	0	0	0	0
Williams, Keith, OF	.274	398	63	109	25	3	13	63	2
*Wilson, Desi, 1B	.339	407	56	138	26	7	5	59	15
Woods, Ken, OF	.279	208	32	58	12	1	2	13	3

PITCHING	W	L	ERA	G	SV	IP	H	BB	SO
*Barton, Shawn	4	4	4.74	44	2	49.1	52	19	27
Bautista, Jose	2	2	4.35	6	0	39.1	41	5	18
Bourgeois, Steve	8	6	3.62	20	0	97.0	112	42	65
Brewington, Jamie	6	9	7.02	35	1	110.1	130	72	75
Carlson, Dan	13	6	3.44	33	1	146.2	135	46	123
*Carter, Andy	1	5	5.54	37	0	79.2	98	36	50
*Estes, Shawn	9	3	3.43	18	0	110.1	92	38	95
*Hancock, Lee	0	2	3.58	26	0	50.1	51	17	28
Heredia, Julian	0	5	4.91	52	4	69.2	71	23	59
Hook, Chris	7	10	4.78	32	0	128.0	139	51	70
Mintz, Steve	3	5	5.37	59	27	57.0	63	25	35
*Pickett, Ricky	0	3	8.64	8	0	8.1	12	5	7
*Rueter, Kirk	1	2	3.51	5	0	25.2	25	12	15
Soderstrom, Steve	7	8	4.41	29	0	171.1	178	58	80
Valdez, Carlos	4	3	4.98	44	5	59.2	63	34	38
Vanderweele, Doug	4	2	5.36	41	0	89.0	101	35	42

Salt Lake Buzz (Twins) AAA

BATTING	AVG	AB	R	H	2B	3B	HR	RBI	SB
Brede, Brent, OF	.348	483	102	168	38	8	11	86	14
Durant, Mike, C	.287	101	21	29	7	0	1	12	7
Hazlett, Steve, OF	.203	301	44	61	14	4	10	41	7
#Hocking, Denny, SS	.277	130	18	36	6	2	3	22	2
Horn, Jeff, C	.337	83	14	28	5	0	3	13	0
Johnson, J.J., OF	.339	56	8	19	3	1	1	13	0
#Latham, Chris, OF	.274	376	59	103	16	6	9	50	26
*Lawton, Matt, OF	.297	212	40	63	16	1	7	33	2
*Leonard, Mark, DH	.250	192	25	48	6	2	5	27	0
Lopez, Rene, C	.241	58	5	14	4	0	0	14	1
Miller, Damian, C	.286	385	54	110	27	1	7	55	1
*Ogden, Jamie, 1B	.263	448	80	118	22	2	18	74	17
Quinlan, Tom, 3B	.283	491	81	139	38	1	15	81	4
Raabe, Brian, 2B	.351	482	103	169	39	4	18	69	8
Simons, Mitch, SS	.264	512	76	135	27	8	5	59	35
*Walker, Todd, 3B	.339	551	94	187	41	9	28	111	13

PITCHING	W	L	ERA	G	SV	IP	H	BB	SO
Barcelo, Marc	2	2	6.52	12	0	59.1	82	17	34
Bennett, Erik	3	1	6.38	17	0	24.0	27	14	10
Hawkins, Latroy	9	8	3.92	20	0	137.2	138	31	99
Klingenbeck, Scott	9	3	3.11	22	0	150.2	159	41	100
*Konieczki, Dom	0	0	18.00	4	0	3.0	8	5	2
Legault, Kevin	5	4	5.36	50	0	80.2	100	24	57
Mahomes, Pat	3	1	3.74	22	7	33.2	32	12	41
*Milchin, Mike	0	0	3.68	19	2	22.0	21	11	18
*Miller, Travis	8	10	4.83	27	0	160.1	187	57	143
Misuraca, Mike	1	2	6.27	18	1	37.1	50	16	25
Norris, Joe	1	1	5.79	21	2	37.1	48	17	38
Parra, Jose	5	3	5.11	23	8	44.0	51	13	26
*Redman, Mark	0	0	9.00	1	0	4.0	7	2	4
Ritchie, Todd	0	4	5.47	16	0	24.2	27	11	19
Roberts, Brett	9	7	5.40	31	0	168.1	211	71	86
*Serafini, Dan	7	7	5.58	25	0	130.2	164	58	109
Stidham, Phil	10	5	6.78	33	0	78.1	100	40	54
Trombley, Mike	2	2	2.45	24	10	36.2	24	10	38
*Watkins, Scott	4	6	7.69	47	1	50.1	60	34	43

Tacoma Rainiers (Mariners) AAA

BATTING	AVG	AB	R	H	2B	3B	HR	RBI	SB
Bonnici, James, 1B	.292	497	76	145	25	0	26	74	1
*Bragg, Darren, OF	.282	71	17	20	8	0	3	8	1
Bryant, Scott, OF	.266	214	21	57	10	3	2	19	0
#Cruz, Jose, OF	.237	76	15	18	1	2	6	15	1
#Diaz, Alex, OF	.244	176	19	43	5	0	0	7	5
Diaz, Eddy, SS	.280	422	63	118	28	4	13	58	3
Drinkwater, Sean, 3B	.258	31	2	8	1	0	0	1	0

BATTING	AVG	AB	R	H	2B	3B	HR	RBI	SB
*Friedman, Jason, DH	.164	73	9	12	6	1	1	4	0
Hunter, Brian, OF	.348	92	19	32	6	1	7	24	1
*Ibanez, Raul, OF	.284	405	59	115	20	3	11	47	7
Jordan, Ricky, DH	.200	50	3	10	0	0	2	7	0
Knapp, Mike, C	.190	184	12	35	10	1	3	18	1
Martinez, Manny, OF	.314	277	54	87	15	1	4	24	14
#Peguero, Julio, OF	.280	328	41	92	15	1	1	21	7
Pirkl, Greg, 1B	.302	348	50	105	22	2	21	75	1
Pozo, Arquimedez, 3B	.279	365	55	102	12	5	15	64	3
*Reimer, Kevin, OF	.283	286	38	81	12	0	13	44	4
#Relaford, Desi, 2B	.205	317	27	65	12	0	4	32	10
Rodriguez, Alex, SS	.200	5	0	1	0	0	0	0	0
Saunders, Doug, 3B	.252	131	16	33	6	0	3	13	1
Sheets, Andy, SS	.358	232	44	83	16	5	5	33	6
*Vazquez, Ramon, 2B	.224	49	7	11	2	1	0	4	0
Wakamatsu, Don, C	.000	3	0	0	0	0	0	0	0
Widger, Chris, C	.304	352	42	107	20	2	13	48	7
Yelding, Eric, 2B	.267	60	5	16	2	1	0	5	3

PITCHING	W	L	ERA	G	SV	IP	H	BB	SO
Bosio, Chris	0	0	0.00	2	0	4.0	2	0	3
*Brosnan, Jason	3	1	2.84	12	1	31.2	19	15	26
Butcher, Mike	1	4	11.79	14	0	42.0	70	27	42
Carmona, Rafael	0	0	1.42	4	0	6.1	5	5	9
*Davis, Tim	0	1	5.29	8	0	17.0	19	10	19
Davison, Scott	1	1	0.39	17	9	23.0	13	6	23
*Fernandez, Osvaldo	0	0	5.40	1	0	3.1	4	0	4
Gould, Clint	0	1	4.50	1	0	4.0	4	2	2
*Guetterman, Lee	2	2	3.77	25	0	28.2	27	10	28
Guzman, Jose	0	1	3.52	5	0	15.1	14	6	11
Harikkala, Tim	8	12	4.83	27	0	158.1	204	48	115
Hurtado, Edwin	1	2	3.73	5	0	31.1	23	12	26
*Klink, Joe	1	0	4.05	7	0	6.2	9	3	4
Lowe, Derek	6	9	4.54	17	0	105.0	118	37	54
*McCarthy, Greg	4	2	3.29	39	4	68.1	58	53	90
Meacham, Rusty	2	1	2.29	7	2	19.2	13	5	20
Menhart, Paul	0	3	11.08	6	0	26.0	53	16	12
Milacki, Bob	13	3	2.74	23	0	164.1	131	39	117
Minor, Blas	1	2	8.38	7	1	9.2	15	3	8
Phillips, Tony	1	3	6.40	21	1	52.0	70	9	24
Pirkl, Greg	0	0	0.00	2	0	5.2	1	0	2
Suzuki, Mac	0	3	7.25	13	0	22.1	31	12	14
Torres, Salomon	7	10	5.29	22	0	134.1	150	52	121
*Urso, Sal	6	2	2.35	46	3	72.2	69	32	45
Wagner, Matt	9	2	2.41	15	0	93.1	89	30	82
Wertz, Bill	0	3	5.01	16	0	32.1	46	23	25
Witte, Trey	2	2	2.15	35	7	46.0	47	13	22
Wolcott, Bob	0	2	7.30	3	0	12.1	17	3	16
Zimmerman, Mike	1	1	9.17	13	0	17.2	23	13	13

Tucson Toros (Astros) AAA

BATTING	AVG	AB	R	H	2B	3B	HR	RBI	SB
Abreu, Bob, OF	.283	484	86	137	14	16	13	68	24
Ball, Jeff, 1B	.324	429	64	139	31	2	19	73	10
*Bridges, Kary, 2B	.314	140	24	44	9	1	1	21	1
#Brumley, Mike, SS	.234	278	40	65	11	7	4	28	9
Christopherson, Eric, C	.287	223	31	64	15	3	6	36	2
*Davis, Jay, OF	.337	101	18	34	7	1	1	17	4
Eusebio, Tony, C	.415	53	8	22	4	0	0	14	0
*Goff, Jerry, C	.236	275	39	65	14	2	9	52	1
Groppuso, Mike, 3B	.255	145	15	37	3	1	5	18	2
Hajek, Dave, 2B	.317	508	81	161	31	5	4	64	9
Hatcher, Chris, OF	.302	348	53	105	21	4	18	61	10
Holbert, Ray, SS	.247	97	13	24	3	2	0	10	4
Hunter, Brian, OF	.357	14	3	5	0	1	0	1	3
#Kellner, Frank, SS	.272	254	37	69	12	5	1	31	3
Luce, Roger, C	.300	50	8	15	2	1	2	8	0
Montgomery, Ray, OF	.306	359	70	110	20	0	22	75	7
Mora, Melvin, 3B	.281	228	35	64	11	2	3	26	3
Mouton, James, OF	.250	4	1	1	0	0	0	0	0
Probst, Alan, C	.286	7	0	2	1	0	0	1	0
Pye, Eddie, 2B	.258	275	39	71	15	6	2	25	5
*Ramos, Ken, OF	.270	385	54	104	22	3	4	34	6
Simms, Mike, 1B	.297	64	11	19	3	0	7	19	0
*Trammell, Gary, OF	.400	10	3	4	0	0	1	2	0

Class AAA Directory

American Association

Buffalo Bisons (Indians)
NorthAmeriCare Park
(capacity 20,900)
Indianapolis Indians (Reds)
Victory Field (15,400)
Iowa Cubs (Cubs)
Sec Taylor Stadium (10,500)
Louisville Redbirds
(Cardinals)
Cardinal Stadium (33,500)
Nashville Sounds
(White Sox)
Herschel Greer Stadium
(17,000)
New Orleans Zephyrs
(Astros)
Jefferson Ballpark (10,000)
Oklahoma City 89ers
(Rangers)
All-Sports Stadium (15,000)
Omaha Royals (Royals)
Rosenblatt Stadium (19,500)

Switch-hitter
* Left-handed

Class AAA Directory

International League

Charlotte Knights
(Marlins)
Knights Castle (10,917)
Columbus Clippers
(Yankees)
Harold Cooper Stadium
(15,000)
Norfolk Tides (Mets)
Harbor Park (12,000)
Ottawa Lynx (Expos)
Rec Complex (10,000)
Pawtucket Red Sox
(Red Sox)
McCoy Stadium (6,010)
Richmond Braves (Braves)
The Diamond (12,500)
Rochester Red Wings (Orioles)
Frontier Field (10,000)
Scranton/Wilkes-Barre Red
Barons (Phillies)
Lackawanna County Stadium
(10,800)
Syracuse Sky Chiefs (Blue Jays)
P & C Stadium (11,400)
Toledo Mud Hens (Tigers)
Ned Skeldon Stadium (10,025)

Switch-hitter
* Left-handed

PITCHING	W	L	ERA	G	SV	IP	H	BB	SO
Bell, Eric	4	14	5.65	30	0	127.1	177	48	58
Brocail, Doug	0	1	7.36	5	0	7.1	12	1	4
Dault, Donnie	0	0	9.00	1	0	2.0	4	0	2
Dougherty, Jim	4	3	3.50	46	1	61.2	65	27	53
Evans, Dave	6	12	5.24	43	1	111.2	120	47	80
Gallaher, Kevin	4	2	4.66	35	1	87.0	88	45	81
*Hartgraves, Dean	2	1	1.89	18	4	19.0	17	8	13
Holt, Chris	9	6	3.72	28	0	186.1	209	38	137
Hudek, John	1	0	3.10	17	4	20.1	17	8	26
Humphrey, Rich	1	1	10.80	10	0	13.1	23	7	8
Johnstone, John	3	3	3.42	45	5	55.1	59	22	70
Jones, Todd	0	0	0.00	1	0	2.0	1	2	0
*Martin, Tom	0	0	0.00	5	0	6.0	6	2	1
Mlicki, Doug	5	11	4.72	26	0	137.1	171	41	98
Patrick, Bronswell	7	3	3.51	33	1	118.0	137	33	82
*Simons, Doug	3	4	5.40	8	0	41.2	53	15	27
Small, Mark	3	3	2.08	32	7	39.0	32	18	36
*Tabaka, Jeff	6	2	2.93	41	4	43.0	40	21	51
*Wagner, Billy	6	2	3.28	12	0	74.0	62	33	86
Wall, Donne	3	3	4.13	8	0	52.1	67	6	36
Young, Anthony	1	0	3.86	4	0	4.2	3	5	3

Vancouver Canadians (Angels) AAA

BATTING	AVG	AB	R	H	2B	3B	HR	RBI	SB
Arias, George, 3B	.337	243	49	82	24	0	9	55	2
Burke, Jamie, 3B	.250	156	12	39	5	0	1	14	2
#Carvajal, Jovino, OF	.239	272	29	65	6	2	4	31	17
#Coleman, Vince, OF	.207	87	9	18	2	1	0	5	4
#Diaz, Freddy, 3B	.260	123	19	32	9	2	3	23	0
Easley, Damion, SS	.313	48	13	15	2	1	2	8	4
*Erstad, Darin, OF	.305	351	63	107	22	5	6	41	11
*Fabregas, Jorge, DH	.297	37	4	11	3	0	0	5	0
Forbes, P.J., 2B	.274	409	58	112	24	2	0	46	4
Grebeck, Brian, 3B	.232	237	25	55	10	3	1	27	1
Greene, Todd, C	.305	223	27	68	18	0	5	33	0
Ledesma, Aaron, SS	.305	440	60	134	27	4	1	51	2
Martinez, Ray, SS	.253	87	8	22	5	2	0	10	1
Orton, John, C	.056	18	0	1	0	0	0	0	0
*Palmeiro, Orlando, OF	.306	245	40	75	13	4	0	33	7
Pennyfeather, Wm., OF	.283	413	56	117	36	3	5	63	19
*Pritchett, Chris, 1B	.295	485	78	143	39	1	16	73	5
Riley, Marquis, OF	.234	47	8	11	2	0	0	0	3
*Takayoshi, Todd, C	.286	7	1	2	0	0	0	2	0
Tejero, Fausto, C	.200	155	21	31	4	1	1	12	0
Turner, Chris, C	.256	390	51	100	19	1	2	47	1
Wolff, Mike, OF	.250	256	46	64	15	3	10	38	6

PITCHING	W	L	ERA	G	SV	IP	H	BB	SO
*Abbott, Jim	0	2	3.41	4	0	29.0	16	20	20
Dickson, Jason	7	11	3.80	18	0	130.1	134	40	70
Edenfield, Ken	2	4	2.81	19	0	32.0	26	20	18
Edsell, Geoff	4	6	3.43	15	0	105.0	93	45	48
Ellis, Robert	2	3	3.25	7	0	44.1	30	28	29
Freehill, Mike	1	1	9.90	7	0	10.0	16	8	5
Frohwirth, Todd	0	1	3.21	9	2	14.0	11	3	13
Grimsley, Jason	2	0	1.20	2	0	15.0	8	3	11
Hancock, Ryan	4	6	3.70	19	0	80.1	69	38	65
Harris, Pep	9	3	4.56	18	0	118.1	135	46	61
Holdridge, David	2	1	4.63	29	1	35.0	39	23	26
Janicki, Pete	2	9	6.75	31	1	104.0	135	37	86
Leftwich, Phil	6	6	5.15	19	0	110.0	113	41	87
*Novoa, Rafael	1	1	7.11	13	1	12.2	19	5	10
*Pennington, Brad	3	0	4.23	11	1	27.2	20	22	43
*Rosselli, Joe	2	3	2.91	47	3	58.2	53	26	37
Schmidt, Jeff	0	1	2.87	35	19	37.2	29	25	19
Springer, Dennis	10	3	2.72	16	0	109.1	89	36	78
Swingle, Paul	2	2	3.00	15	1	24.0	20	11	24
*VanRyn, Ben	3	3	3.89	18	0	34.2	35	13	28
*Washburn, Jarrod	0	2	10.80	2	0	8.1	12	12	5
Williams, Shad	6	2	3.96	15	0	75.0	73	28	57

Eastern League

Binghamton Mets (Mets) AA

BATTING	AVG	AB	R	H	2B	3B	HR	RBI	SB
Agbayani, Benny, OF	.170	53	7	9	1	0	2	8	1
Azuaje, Jesus, 2B	.237	249	36	59	16	0	2	26	5
*Daubach, Brian, 1B	.296	436	80	129	24	1	22	76	7
*Geisler, Phil, OF	.251	355	47	89	17	2	11	59	5
Greene, Charlie, C	.244	336	35	82	17	0	2	27	2
Grifol, Pedro, C	.238	202	22	48	3	0	7	28	0
#Hardtke, Jason, 2B	.263	137	23	36	11	0	3	16	0
*Horne, Tyrone, OF	.272	125	17	34	10	0	3	19	3
*Leiper, Tim, PH	.167	6	0	1	0	0	0	0	0
Lowery, Terrell, OF	.275	211	34	58	13	4	7	32	5
Mahalik, John, 2B	.241	216	37	52	11	2	3	22	6
Maness, Dwight, OF	.243	399	65	97	14	7	6	47	25
Morgan, Kevin, SS	.252	409	61	103	11	2	6	35	13
#Pagano, Scott, OF	.259	464	63	120	15	3	1	46	26
Payton, Jay, DH	.200	10	0	2	0	0	0	2	0
Saunders, Chris, 3B	.298	510	82	152	27	3	17	105	5
White, Don, OF	.192	219	29	42	6	1	6	22	5

PITCHING	W	L	ERA	G	SV	IP	H	BB	SO
Carter, John	9	3	4.23	19	0	110.2	120	54	48
*Crawford, Joe	5	1	1.45	7	0	49.2	34	9	34
*Dixon, Steve	0	1	5.40	5	0	8.1	10	8	11
Edmondson, Brian	6	6	4.25	39	0	114.1	130	38	83
Fuller, Mark	5	4	4.18	51	1	75.1	86	22	43
Guerra, Mark	7	6	3.53	27	0	140.1	143	34	84
Larson, Toby	2	4	6.00	11	0	48.0	57	14	25
Lidle, Cory	14	10	3.31	27	0	190.1	186	49	141
*Pierson, Jason	5	3	3.38	34	1	53.1	56	15	42
Ramirez, Hector	1	5	5.14	38	6	56.0	51	23	49
*Roberts, Chris	2	7	7.24	9	0	46.0	55	37	30
*Roque, Rafael	0	4	7.27	13	0	60.2	71	39	46
*Sauerbeck, Scott	3	3	3.47	8	0	46.2	48	12	30
Tam, Jeff	6	2	2.44	49	2	62.2	51	16	48
Turrentine, Rich	1	1	2.89	8	3	9.1	12	5	10
Welch, Mike	4	2	4.59	46	27	51.0	55	10	53
Wilson, Paul	0	1	7.20	1	0	5.0	6	5	5
Withem, Shannon	6	3	3.24	12	0	86.0	86	17	59

Bowie Baysox (Orioles) AA

BATTING	AVG	AB	R	H	2B	3B	HR	RBI	SB
Avila, Rolo, OF	.266	233	31	62	12	1	2	17	8
Bautista, Juan, SS	.234	441	35	103	18	3	3	33	15
Berrios, Harry, OF	.187	123	19	23	4	0	6	17	7
Berry, Mike, DH	.143	7	1	1	0	0	0	2	0
*Bowers, Brent, OF	.311	228	37	71	11	1	9	25	10
*Castaneda, Hector, C	.216	51	6	11	1	0	1	5	2
*Clark, Howie, 2B	.272	449	55	122	29	3	4	52	2
Clyburn, Danny, OF	.252	365	51	92	14	5	18	55	4
Curtis, Kevin, OF	.246	460	69	113	21	2	18	58	2
Davis, Tommy, 1B	.261	524	75	137	32	2	14	54	5
*Dellucci, David, OF	.291	251	27	73	14	1	2	33	2
Foster, Jim, C	.303	33	7	10	0	1	2	9	0
Gordon, Keith, OF	.261	306	38	80	13	2	5	28	13
Gresham, Kris, C	.202	129	12	26	7	0	0	6	1
*Huson, Jeff, OF	.385	13	3	5	2	0	0	0	0
Millares, Jose, 2B	.186	70	3	13	3	0	0	1	1
O'Toole, Bobby, C	.000	10	0	0	0	0	0	0	0
Otanez, Willis, 3B	.265	506	60	134	27	2	24	75	3
Raleigh, Matt, 1B	.250	8	0	2	1	0	0	2	0
#Rice, Lance, C	.213	164	8	35	4	0	2	17	0
#Rosario, Melvin, C	.210	162	14	34	10	0	2	17	3
Smith, Mark, DH	.091	22	1	2	0	0	1	2	0
*Thompson, Fltchr, SS	.256	172	30	44	4	1	1	19	8

PITCHING	W	L	ERA	G	SV	IP	H	BB	SO
Benitez, Armando	0	0	4.50	4	0	6.0	7	0	8
Bennett, Joel	3	3	3.66	13	0	59.0	39	19	56
*Brewer, Brian	2	4	4.89	11	0	57.0	61	27	35
Cafaro, Rocco	4	8	4.96	27	0	103.1	130	36	55
Chavez, Carlos	4	6	4.34	56	7	83.0	69	52	80
Clayton, Royal	0	1	10.80	3	0	8.1	12	4	5
Conner, Scott	1	5	5.05	21	0	82.0	86	36	59

Class AAA Directory

Pacific Coast League

Albuquerque Dukes (Dodgers) Albuquerque Sports Stadium (10,510)
Calgary Cannons (Pirates) Foothills Stadium (7,500)
Colorado Springs Sky Sox (Rockies) Sky Sox Stadium (6,130)
Edmonton Trappers (Athletics) Telus Field (10,000)
Las Vegas Stars (Padres) Cashman Field (9,370)
Phoenix Firebirds (Giants) Scottsdale Stadium (10,000)
Salt Lake Buzz (Twins) Franklin Quest Field (15,000)
Tacoma Rainiers (Mariners) Cheney Stadium (8,002)
Tucson Toros (Brewers) Hi Corbett Field (9,500)
Vancouver Canadians (Angels) Nat Bailey Stadium (6,500)

Switch-hitter
* Left-handed

359

Class AA Directory

Eastern League

Binghamton Mets (Mets)
Municipal Stadium (6,064)
Bowie Baysox (Orioles)
Prince Georges County
Stadium (10,000)
Akron Aeros (Indians)
Canal Park (10,000)
Harrisburg Senators (Expos)
Riverside Stadium (5,600)
New Britain Rock Cats (Twins)
Beehive Field (4,700)
New Haven Ravens (Rockies)
Yale Field (6,200)
Norwich Navigators (Yankees)
Dodd Stadium (6,000)
Portland Sea Dogs (Marlins)
Hadlock Field (6,000)
Reading Phillies (Phillies)
Municipal Stadium (7,500)
Trenton Thunder (Red Sox)
Waterfront Park (6,200)

Switch-hitter
* Left-handed

PITCHING	W	L	ERA	G	SV	IP	H	BB	SO
*Courtright, John	1	1	6.56	23	0	48.0	61	24	22
Dean, Greg	0	3	8.53	3	0	12.2	21	13	4
Dedrick, Jim	1	1	3.38	13	0	26.2	28	14	21
*Grott, Matt	2	1	4.98	9	0	21.2	26	5	15
*Hale, Shane	5	13	5.00	24	0	135.0	146	51	86
Hill, Milt	5	7	6.67	25	1	87.2	126	18	66
Hostetler, Marcus	3	0	3.32	32	1	57.0	51	22	44
*Jarvis, Matt	1	3	7.45	6	0	19.1	31	7	13
*Lane, Aaron	3	5	4.59	13	2	51.0	44	24	35
Lemp, Chris	1	3	4.72	27	1	47.2	53	24	35
Maduro, Calvin	9	7	3.26	19	0	124.1	116	36	87
Maine, Dalton	0	1	5.06	11	0	21.1	24	11	18
*O'Donoghue, John	1	3	4.38	7	0	37.0	42	16	26
Plaster, Allen	0	0	13.50	1	0	2.0	5	1	3
Revenig, Todd	3	4	2.63	38	7	61.2	42	18	39
Rhodes, Joey	2	1	1.50	4	0	12.0	6	5	9
Ryan, Kevin	0	1	9.00	2	0	3.0	7	1	2
*Schuermann, Lance	0	0	3.18	6	0	5.2	7	2	6
Strange, Don	2	1	2.45	12	3	14.2	11	5	10
*Tranbarger, Mark	3	3	5.40	40	3	55.0	67	35	45
Yan, Esteban	0	2	5.63	9	0	16.0	18	8	16

Canton-Akron Indians (Indians) AA

BATTING	AVG	AB	R	H	2B	3B	HR	RBI	SB
Aven, Bruce, OF	.297	481	91	143	31	4	23	79	22
*Betts, Todd, 3B	.252	238	35	60	13	0	1	26	0
Betzsold, James, OF	.239	268	35	64	11	5	3	35	4
Bryant, Pat, OF	.193	109	13	21	2	1	3	17	8
Diaz, Einar, C	.281	395	47	111	26	2	3	35	3
Gutierrez, Ricky, 2B	.252	484	69	122	11	3	7	55	18
*Harvey, Ray, OF	.353	17	3	6	3	0	0	0	0
*McCall, Rod, DH	.300	440	80	132	29	2	27	85	2
Neal, Mike, 2B	.224	254	42	57	9	3	4	32	2
Ramirez, Alex, OF	.329	513	79	169	28	12	14	85	18
Raven, Luis, 3B	.302	268	57	81	17	0	21	64	0
Sexson, Richie, 1B	.276	518	85	143	33	3	16	76	2
Soliz, Steve, C	.259	143	18	37	4	2	2	15	1
*Thomas, Greg, OF	.279	301	44	84	14	4	13	55	2
#Wilson, Enrique, SS	.304	484	70	147	17	5	5	50	23

PITCHING	W	L	ERA	G	SV	IP	H	BB	SO
Brown, Dickie	0	2	8.03	6	0	12.1	13	9	11
Bullard, Jason	1	1	2.57	17	0	21.0	18	11	22
Cabrera, Jose	4	3	5.63	15	0	62.1	78	17	40
Colon, Bartolo	2	2	1.74	13	0	62.0	44	25	56
De La Maza, Roland	9	7	4.38	40	1	139.2	122	49	132
De La Rosa, Maximo	11	5	3.91	40	3	119.2	104	81	109
Dougherty, Anthony	0	0	9.00	3	0	5.0	3	8	6
Driskill, Travis	13	7	3.61	29	0	172.0	169	63	148
Grigsby, Benji	1	2	1.26	16	2	28.2	22	11	21
*Kline, Steven	8	12	5.46	25	0	146.2	168	55	107
Martinez, Johnny	0	1	5.40	5	0	8.1	9	4	3
*Matthews, Mike	9	11	4.66	27	0	162.1	178	74	112
Montoya, Wilmer	2	5	3.38	43	23	50.2	41	28	42
*Plantenberg, Erik	0	0	3.00	19	0	21.0	21	2	26
Sexton, Jeff	2	4	5.11	9	0	49.1	45	23	34
*Tolar, Kevin	1	3	2.62	50	1	44.2	42	26	39
Vaught, Jay	5	4	4.77	51	3	94.1	101	35	78
*Whitten, Casey	3	1	1.67	8	0	37.2	23	13	44

Harrisburg Senators (Expos) AA

BATTING	AVG	AB	R	H	2B	3B	HR	RBI	SB
Alcantara, Israel, 3B	.211	218	26	46	5	0	8	19	1
Barron, Tony, OF	.284	67	12	19	3	1	5	12	1
#Blum, Geoffrey, 2B	.240	396	47	95	22	2	1	41	6
Cabrera, Jolbert, SS	.240	354	40	85	18	2	3	29	10
Campos, Jesus, OF	.260	208	15	54	4	0	0	17	5
Carvajal, Jhonny, 2B	.300	60	7	18	3	2	0	4	1
*Crosby, Mike, C	.202	99	3	20	4	0	1	6	0
*Fullmer, Brad, OF	.276	98	11	27	4	1	4	14	0
Guerrero, Vladimir, OF	.360	417	84	150	32	8	19	78	17
Henley, Bob, C	.228	289	33	66	12	1	3	27	1
Koeyers, Ramsey, C	.208	77	6	16	3	0	1	9	0
*Leach, Jalal, OF	.328	268	38	88	22	3	6	48	3
*Lukachyk, Rob, 1B	.326	92	22	30	6	0	5	24	4

BATTING	AVG	AB	R	H	2B	3B	HR	RBI	SB
*Masteller, Dan, 1B	.328	128	21	42	11	0	2	21	0
Montoyo, Charlie, 1B	.224	183	21	41	3	1	0	18	1
*Rendina, Mike, 1B	.143	42	4	6	2	0	0	0	0
Renteria, Dave, SS	.236	72	7	17	6	0	0	4	0
*Saffer, Jon, OF	.300	487	96	146	26	4	10	52	8
#Stovall, Darond, OF	.221	272	38	60	7	1	10	36	10
Talanoa, Scott, 1B	.210	138	20	29	5	0	11	23	0
*Thoutsis, Paul, 1B	.200	20	1	4	3	0	0	3	0
#Vidro, Jose, 3B	.259	452	57	117	25	3	18	82	3
White, Rondell, OF	.350	20	5	7	1	0	3	6	1

PITCHING	W	L	ERA	G	SV	IP	H	BB	SO
Bennett, Shayne	8	8	2.53	53	12	92.2	83	35	89
*Benz, Jake	1	4	5.97	34	4	37.2	42	27	25
*Boucher, Denis	1	0	1.50	1	0	6.0	2	2	6
Bullinger, Kirk	3	4	1.97	47	22	45.2	46	18	29
*DeHart, Rick	1	2	2.68	30	1	43.2	46	19	30
Dorlarque, Aaron	1	0	6.00	13	0	24.0	32	7	14
Falteisek, Steve	6	5	3.81	17	0	115.2	111	48	62
Fleetham, Ben	0	0	0.00	4	1	6.0	2	5	6
*Forster, Scott	10	7	3.78	28	0	176.1	164	67	97
Gentile, Scott	2	2	2.63	15	1	24.0	14	14	23
*Gray, Dennis	0	0	7.59	9	0	10.2	12	14	10
*Hmielewski, Chris	1	2	12.00	3	0	3.0	4	3	2
Kendrena, Ken	1	0	4.63	7	0	11.2	10	2	4
*Martinez, Ramiro	0	4	4.50	8	0	24.0	23	15	10
McCommon, Jason	10	10	3.94	30	1	153.0	169	44	92
Pacheco, Alexander	5	2	2.73	18	0	26.1	26	12	27
Paniagua, Jose	3	0	0.00	3	0	18.0	12	2	16
*Phelps, Tom	2	2	2.47	8	0	47.1	43	19	23
Pisciotta, Scott	2	1	5.50	27	1	36.0	35	27	18
Pote, Lou	1	7	5.07	25	1	104.2	114	48	61
Stull, Everett	6	3	3.15	14	0	80.0	64	52	81
Thurman, Mike	3	1	5.11	4	0	24.2	25	5	14
*Weber, Neil	7	4	3.03	18	0	107.0	90	44	74

New Britain Rock Cats (Twins) AA

BATTING	AVG	AB	R	H	2B	3B	HR	RBI	SB
Byrd, Anthony, OF	.247	194	23	48	8	1	1	10	11
Caraballo, Gary, 3B	.240	292	32	70	16	0	7	32	1
Ferguson, Jeff, 2B	.285	284	46	81	16	2	5	20	5
*Hilt, Scott, C	.194	180	19	35	5	1	2	19	3
Horn, Jeff, C	.267	45	4	12	2	0	0	3	0
Hunter, Torii, OF	.263	342	49	90	20	3	7	33	7
Johnson, J.J., OF	.273	440	62	120	23	3	16	59	10
Lane, Ryan, SS	.222	117	13	26	5	1	2	12	3
*Lewis, Anthony, DH	.253	458	58	116	15	2	24	95	6
Lopez, Rene, C	.233	180	23	42	9	0	3	16	0
Nevers, Tom, SS	.264	459	65	121	27	7	7	44	3
*Radmanovich, Ryan, OF	.280	453	77	127	31	2	25	86	4
Roper, Chad, 3B	.251	466	59	117	18	2	10	48	4
Rupp, Chad, 1B	.252	278	38	70	14	0	18	48	3
*Turner, Brian, 1B	.228	241	27	55	13	2	8	30	6
#Valentin, Jose, C	.236	165	22	39	8	0	3	14	0
Valette, Ramon, SS	.239	71	7	17	2	2	1	6	6
#Walbeck, Matt, DH	.208	24	1	5	0	0	0	0	0

PITCHING	W	L	ERA	G	SV	IP	H	BB	SO
Barcelo, Marc	3	8	5.06	14	0	80.0	98	38	59
Bell, Jason	2	6	4.40	16	0	94.0	93	38	94
Bowers, Shane	6	8	4.19	27	0	131.0	134	42	96
Caridad, Ron	0	2	5.01	20	0	32.1	29	24	21
*Carrasco, Troy	6	9	5.07	34	0	110.0	113	66	69
Gavaghan, Sean	2	2	6.46	28	6	39.0	42	29	44
*Konieczki, Dom	1	3	4.98	28	2	34.1	32	23	23
*Lewis, Anthony	0	0	13.50	2	0	2.0	1	2	0
Linebarger, Keith	7	5	3.27	42	4	99.0	98	32	69
Morse, Paul	6	4	5.34	35	4	55.2	55	26	48
*Ohme, Kevin	5	6	4.33	51	3	81.0	83	33	42
*Redman, Mark	7	7	3.81	16	0	106.1	101	50	96
Ritchie, Todd	3	7	5.44	29	4	82.2	101	30	53
*Sampson, Benj	5	7	5.73	16	0	75.1	108	25	51
Stidham, Phil	1	0	2.63	12	1	13.2	11	8	16
Trinidad, Hector	6	6	3.84	25	0	138.1	137	31	93

Class AA Directory

Southern League

Birmingham Barons (White Sox)
Hoover Met (10,000)
Carolina Mudcats (Pirates)
Five County Stadium (6,000)
Chattanooga Lookouts (Reds)
Engel Stadium (7,500)
Greenville Braves (Braves)
Municipal Stadium (7,027)
Huntsville Stars (Athletics)
Joe W. Davis Stadium (10,200)
Jacksonville Suns (Tigers)
Wolfson Park (8,200)
Knoxville Smokies (Blue Jays)
Bill Meyer Stadium (6,412)
Memphis Chicks (Mariners)
Tim McCarver Stadium (10,000)
Mobile Bay Bears (Padres)
Hank Aaron Stadium (6,000)
Orlando Cubs (Cubs)
Tinker Field (6,000)

361

Switch-hitter
* Left-handed

Class AA Directory

Texas League

Arkansas Travelers
(Cardinals)
Ray Winder Field (6,083)
El Paso Diablos
(Brewers)
Cohen Stadium (10,000)
Jackson Generals (Astros)
Smith-Wills Stadium (5,200)
Midland Angels (Angels)
Christensen Stadium (4,000)
San Antonio Missions
(Dodgers)
Missions Stadium (6,500)
Shreveport Captains
(Giants)
Fairgrounds Field (6,200)
Tulsa Drillers (Rangers)
Drillers Stadium (10,500)
Wichita Wranglers
(Royals)
Lawrence-Dumont Stadium
(7,488)

Switch-hitter
* Left-handed

New Haven Ravens (Rockies) AA

BATTING	AVG	AB	R	H	2B	3B	HR	RBI	SB
Bernhardt, Steve, 3B	.286	84	5	24	3	0	0	10	0
Garcia, Vicente, 2B	.214	295	32	63	10	1	3	18	1
Gibson, Derrick, OF	.256	449	58	115	21	4	15	62	3
Giudice, John, OF	.254	118	13	30	4	1	4	13	2
*Goligoski, Jason, 2B	.172	64	6	11	0	1	0	3	0
Gonzalez, Pete, C	.185	119	9	22	1	0	2	8	1
#Grunewald, Keith, 3B	.227	352	27	80	13	2	3	28	2
*Helton, Todd, 1B	.332	319	46	106	24	2	7	51	2
Higgins, Mike, C	.181	72	6	13	2	1	0	5	1
Holdren, Nate, 1B	.167	36	3	6	1	0	1	6	1
#Jarrett, Link, 2B	.195	164	18	32	6	0	1	9	1
Miller, Roger, C	.242	256	23	62	8	1	3	29	0
Myrow, John, OF	.251	406	46	102	11	3	4	36	11
Scalzitti, Will, C	.231	26	1	6	2	0	0	1	0
Sexton, Chris, SS	.216	444	50	96	12	2	0	28	8
*Taylor, Jamie, 3B	.243	362	46	88	20	1	8	37	1
Velazquez, Edgard, OF	.290	486	72	141	29	4	19	62	6
*Wells, Forry, OF	.230	304	44	70	19	1	7	43	1
Young, Eric, 2B	.067	15	0	1	0	0	0	0	0

PITCHING	W	L	ERA	G	SV	IP	H	BB	SO
*Beckett, Robbie	7	3	5.11	33	0	61.2	55	59	62
Bost, Heath	1	0	1.50	4	0	6.0	5	2	7
Brownson, Mark	8	13	3.50	37	3	144.0	141	43	155
Cimorelli, Frank	0	1	5.00	5	0	9.0	10	1	8
Crowther, Brent	3	7	6.20	25	1	85.2	109	30	54
Dejean, Mike	0	0	3.22	16	11	22.1	20	8	12
*Eden, Bill	1	1	5.23	29	0	41.1	48	24	41
*Kusiewicz, Mike	2	4	3.30	14	0	76.1	83	27	64
Macca, Chris	3	1	1.30	28	15	34.2	18	18	34
Martin, Chandler	1	0	7.20	1	0	5.0	6	3	4
*Million, Doug	3	3	3.15	10	0	54.1	54	40	40
Moore, Joel	0	5	4.60	6	0	31.1	35	5	15
Neier, Chris	1	7	4.98	55	2	81.1	99	44	54
Pedraza, Rodney	7	3	2.95	19	0	122.0	115	21	74
Pool, Matt	0	1	2.70	4	0	6.2	9	1	7
Saipe, Mike	10	7	3.07	32	3	138.0	114	42	126
Sobkoviak, Jeff	0	1	5.40	4	0	6.2	7	5	4
Thomson, John	9	4	2.86	16	0	97.2	82	27	86
Viano, Jake	4	3	4.84	23	0	44.2	39	24	32
Voisard, Mark	0	2	9.35	8	0	8.2	10	5	7
Wright, Jamey	5	1	0.81	7	0	44.2	27	12	54
Zolecki, Mike	2	8	5.46	47	2	90.2	82	68	83

Norwich Navigators (Yankees) AA

BATTING	AVG	AB	R	H	2B	3B	HR	RBI	SB
Delafield, Wil, OF	.196	46	3	9	1	0	0	3	1
*Delvecchio, Nick, DH	.278	36	7	10	3	0	2	7	1
*DeBerry, Joe, 1B	.154	26	1	4	0	0	0	6	0
*Donato, Daniel, 3B	.285	459	47	131	27	1	2	48	5
Fithian, Grant, C	.197	178	19	35	7	1	5	26	1
#Fleming, Carlton, 2B	.321	28	4	9	0	0	0	1	0
Hinds, Rob, 2B	.228	180	25	41	3	1	2	15	9
Imrisek, Jason, C	.333	6	2	2	1	0	0	2	0
Katzaroff, Robbie, OF	.274	84	11	23	4	0	0	5	0
Kelly, Pat, 2B	.294	17	3	5	2	1	0	0	1
Knowles, Eric, SS	.245	396	56	97	23	1	7	42	9
*Ledee, Ricky, OF	.365	137	27	50	11	1	8	37	2
#Long, R.D., 3B	.300	10	4	3	0	0	0	3	0
McNair, Fred, 1B	.276	246	31	68	10	1	7	43	2
Motuzas, Jeff, C	.333	9	1	3	0	0	0	2	0
Northrup, Kevin, OF	.243	235	36	57	10	2	7	37	3
Norton, Chris, C	.279	172	24	48	12	1	7	28	3
#Pichardo, Sandy, SS	.353	17	3	6	1	0	1	3	1
*Pledger, Kinnis, OF	.265	445	80	118	27	6	19	67	20
#Raines, Tim, OF	.185	27	8	5	1	0	1	1	2
*Riggs, Kevin, 2B	.290	403	75	117	24	1	2	37	9
Romano, Scott, 3B	.283	113	14	32	4	0	3	8	2
*Seefried, Tate, 1B	.208	361	52	75	17	0	14	47	2
#Smith, Sloan, OF	.218	202	27	44	10	2	2	20	4
Spencer, Shane, OF	.253	450	70	114	19	0	29	89	4
Torres, Jaime, C	.251	334	42	84	19	2	6	40	1
Troilo, Jason, C	.500	8	3	4	0	0	2	2	0

1997 BASEBALL WEEKLY ALMANAC

PITCHING	W	L	ERA	G	SV	IP	H	BB	SO
Beverlin, Jason	0	3	8.44	8	0	16.0	25	6	17
Brock, Russ	0	1	8.18	4	0	11.0	14	5	14
Brown, Charlie	0	0	0.00	1	0	2.1	1	1	1
Buddie, Mike	7	12	4.45	29	0	159.2	176	71	103
Cone, David	0	0	0.90	2	0	10.0	9	1	13
Croghan, Andy	9	5	3.07	35	4	41.0	41	16	49
*Cumberland, Chris	5	7	5.27	16	0	95.2	112	37	44
Drews, Matt	1	3	4.50	9	0	46.0	40	33	37
*Dunbar, Matt	4	2	1.78	33	1	70.2	59	28	59
Henthorne, Kevin	5	3	2.26	12	0	59.2	50	22	47
*Hubbard, Mark	2	0	5.49	4	0	19.2	19	10	14
Jerzembeck, Mike	3	6	4.52	14	0	69.2	74	26	65
*Kotarski, Mike	1	2	4.35	42	3	72.1	73	29	66
Lankford, Frank	7	8	2.66	61	4	88.0	82	40	61
Maeda, Katsuhiro	3	2	4.05	9	0	53.1	49	21	30
Medina, Rafael	5	8	3.06	19	0	103.0	78	55	112
*Meyer, David	0	0	4.71	19	1	21.0	20	11	13
Motuzas, Jeff	0	0	0.00	1	0	2.0	2	1	0
Musselwhite, Jim	2	1	2.25	5	0	36.0	28	10	25
Perez, Melido	1	0	0.00	1	0	8.0	4	1	7
*Quirico, Rafael	2	0	2.21	9	0	36.2	27	14	32
Resz, Greg	1	1	2.54	19	2	39.0	38	18	37
Ricken, Ray	5	2	4.47	8	0	46.1	42	20	42
Rios, Dan	3	1	2.09	38	17	43.0	34	21	38
*Rumer, Tim	3	1	2.25	8	0	40.0	32	18	44
Sutherland, John	3	2	2.74	26	1	42.2	37	19	31
Wallace, Kent	0	0	6.00	1	0	6.0	10	0	1

Portland Sea Dogs (Marlins) AA

BATTING	AVG	AB	R	H	2B	3B	HR	RBI	SB
#Aversa, Joe, 3B	.234	167	25	39	8	0	0	22	2
Berg, David, SS	.302	414	64	125	28	5	9	73	17
Brown, Ron, OF	.100	10	1	1	0	1	0	1	0
#Castillo, Luis, 2B	.317	420	83	133	15	7	1	35	51
#Clapinski, Chris, SS	.260	73	15	19	7	0	3	11	3
Cook, Hayward, OF	.304	46	7	14	3	0	0	2	2
*Dunwoody, Todd, OF	.277	552	88	153	30	6	24	93	24
Gonzalez, Alex, SS	.235	34	4	8	0	1	0	1	0
Hastings, Lionel, 3B	.232	293	30	68	12	1	6	44	5
*Mack, Quinn, OF	.216	111	12	24	5	0	3	19	3
Millar, Kevin, 1B	.318	472	69	150	32	0	18	86	6
Milliard, Ralph, 2B	.200	20	2	4	0	1	0	2	1
O'Neill, Doug, OF	.257	241	39	62	10	2	7	26	8
Redmond, Mike, C	.287	394	43	113	22	0	4	44	3
*Robertson, Jason, OF	.272	338	65	92	17	3	12	48	12
Rodriguez, Maximo, C	.176	17	1	3	0	0	0	1	0
Roskos, John, 1B	.275	396	53	109	26	3	9	58	3
Sheff, Chris, OF	.295	105	16	31	12	2	2	17	3
Torres, Tony, 2B	.270	126	21	34	11	0	1	13	3
*Wilson, Pookie, OF	.256	375	46	96	16	5	6	35	7

PITCHING	W	L	ERA	G	SV	IP	H	BB	SO
*Alkire, Jeff	0	2	6.41	11	0	19.2	26	7	24
Chergey, Dan	0	2	4.00	13	2	18.0	18	6	16
Cunnane, Will	10	12	3.74	25	0	151.2	156	30	101
Harris, Doug	6	5	5.59	23	1	48.1	50	21	31
*Heredia, Felix	8	1	1.50	55	5	60.0	48	15	42
Hernandez, Livan	9	2	4.34	15	0	93.1	81	34	95
Hurst, William	2	3	2.20	45	30	49.0	45	31	46
Larkin, Andy	4	1	3.10	8	0	49.1	45	10	40
Meadows, Brian	0	1	4.33	4	0	27.0	26	4	13
Mendoza, Reynol	4	2	3.43	10	0	63.0	60	14	41
Mix, Greg	3	0	4.52	25	1	65.2	80	19	57
Nunez, Clemente	2	7	5.47	32	0	97.0	119	31	52
*Saunders, Tony	13	4	2.63	26	0	167.2	121	62	156
Stanifer, Robby	3	1	1.57	18	2	34.1	27	9	33
Thornton, Paul	3	6	4.17	52	4	77.2	74	44	64
Valdes, Marc	6	2	2.66	10	0	64.1	60	12	49
*Ward, Bryan	9	9	4.91	28	0	146.2	170	32	124

Reading Phillies (Phillies) AA

BATTING	AVG	AB	R	H	2B	3B	HR	RBI	SB
#Amador, Manuel, PH	.278	18	5	5	2	0	1	3	0
*Anderson, Marlon, 2B	.274	314	38	86	14	3	3	28	17
Angeli, Doug, SS	.235	187	24	44	9	0	8	29	3

Class A Directory (full season)

California League

Bakersfield Blaze (Giants)
Sam Lynn Ballpark (3,200)
High Desert Mavericks (Diamondbacks)
Maverick Stadium (3,500)
Lake Elsinore Storm (Angels)
Lake Elsinore Diamond (6,000)
Lancaster Jethawks (Mariners)
The Hangar Stadium (7,000)
Modesto A's (Athletics)
Thurman Field (2,500)
Rancho Cucamonga Quakes (Padres)
The Epicenter (4,600)
San Bernardino Stampede (Dodgers)
The Ranch Stadium (5,000)
San Jose Giants (Giants)
Municipal Stadium (4,500)
Stockton Ports (Brewers)
Billy Hebert Field (3,500)
Visalia Oaks (Athletics)
Recreation Park (2,000)

 # Switch-hitter
** Left-handed*

Class A Directory
(full season)
Carolina League

Durham Bulls (Braves)
Athletic Park (6,400)
Frederick Keys (Orioles)
Harry Grove Stadium (5,200)
Kinston Indians (Indians)
Grainger Stadium (4,100)
Lynchburg Hillcats (Pirates)
City Stadium (4,200)
Prince William Cannons
(Cardinals)
Pfitzner Memorial Stadium
(6,000)
Salem Avalanche
(Rockies)
Salem Memorial Field (6,000)
Wilmington Blue Rocks (Royals)
Legends Stadium (5,500)
Winston-Salem Warthogs
(White Sox)
Ernie Shore Field (6,280)

BATTING	AVG	AB	R	H	2B	3B	HR	RBI	SB
Burton, Essex, 2B	.304	381	66	116	19	5	1	30	40
Dawkins, Walt, OF	.268	254	40	68	16	3	4	28	4
Estalella, Bobby, C	.244	365	48	89	14	2	23	72	2
Fisher, David, 3B	.269	171	21	46	9	0	4	24	5
Guiliano, Matt, SS	.200	220	19	44	9	3	0	19	0
Gyselman, Jeff, C	.172	128	9	22	2	0	0	12	0
*Haws, Scott, DH	.000	1	0	1	0	0	0	0	0
Held, Dan, 1B	.243	497	77	121	17	5	26	92	3
Kendall, Jeremey, OF	.168	131	23	22	5	1	1	10	5
Magee, Wendell, OF	.293	270	38	79	15	5	6	30	10
McConnell, Chad, OF	.247	385	70	95	18	1	12	50	6
Moler, Jason, 3B	.246	374	59	92	22	0	18	59	4
Rolen, Scott, 3B	.361	230	44	83	22	2	9	42	8
Royster, Aaron, OF	.257	230	42	59	11	0	4	20	4
Shores, Scott, OF	.229	398	52	91	19	8	11	51	19

PITCHING	W	L	ERA	G	SV	IP	H	BB	SO
*Beech, Matt	11	6	3.17	21	0	133.1	108	32	132
Costa, Tony	5	13	4.81	27	0	153.1	150	92	112
*Dodd, Robert	2	3	3.56	18	0	43.0	41	24	35
*Estavil, Mauricio	0	3	11.57	20	0	18.2	30	22	19
Fiore, Tony	1	2	4.35	5	0	31.0	32	18	19
*Foster, Mark	4	5	5.80	50	0	76.0	84	45	56
Gomes, Wayne	0	4	4.48	67	24	64.1	53	48	79
Heflin, Bronson	2	2	5.22	25	1	29.1	37	15	27
*Herrmann, Gary	1	5	4.99	23	0	39.2	43	27	31
Holman, Craig	6	1	3.50	8	0	46.1	42	13	34
Hunter, Rich	4	3	3.17	10	0	71.0	69	12	40
*Juhl, Mike	1	1	2.79	9	0	9.2	8	5	4
Loewer, Carlton	7	10	5.26	27	0	171.0	191	57	119
Metheney, Nelson	0	2	5.59	26	0	38.2	50	19	17
Mitchell, Larry	3	6	5.21	34	0	57.0	55	44	71
Munoz, Bobby	0	1	2.93	4	0	27.2	24	8	29
Nye, Ryan	8	2	3.84	14	0	86.2	76	30	90
Troutman, Keith	6	3	3.31	52	1	73.1	62	40	73
Westbrook, Destry	4	3	3.97	25	0	34.0	40	14	15

Trenton Thunder (Red Sox) AA

BATTING	AVG	AB	R	H	2B	3B	HR	RBI	SB
*Abad, Andy, 1B	.277	213	33	59	22	1	4	39	5
Allison, Chris, 2B	.230	357	49	82	7	1	0	22	14
Borrero, Richie, C	.310	71	12	22	5	2	3	26	2
Brown, Randy, SS	.298	245	46	73	15	2	11	38	9
*Carey, Todd, 3B	.250	440	78	110	34	3	20	78	4
Collier, Dan, DH	.213	94	12	20	3	0	4	9	2
*Coughlin, Kevin, 1B	.271	170	24	46	2	1	0	18	5
Delgado, Alex, C	.222	81	7	18	4	0	3	14	1
*Holifield, Rick, OF	.267	375	73	100	20	4	10	38	35
Hyzdu, Adam, OF	.337	374	71	126	24	3	25	80	1
Jackson, Gavin, SS	.250	20	2	5	2	0	0	3	0
Levangie, Dana, C	.218	55	5	12	3	0	2	7	2
Manto, Jeff, 3B	.286	21	3	6	0	0	0	5	0
McKeel, Walt, C	.302	464	86	140	19	1	16	78	2
Merloni, Lou, 3B	.232	95	11	22	6	1	3	16	0
Naehring, Tim, 3B	.222	9	2	2	1	0	1	2	0
*Nixon, Trot, OF	.251	438	55	110	11	4	11	63	7
Ortiz, Nick, 2B	.223	130	20	29	4	0	3	13	2
Patton, Greg, 3B	.188	16	3	3	1	0	0	1	0
*Rappoli, Paul, OF	.212	193	16	41	8	0	3	22	4
Sadler, Donnie, SS	.267	454	68	121	20	8	6	46	34
Woods, Tyrone, DH	.312	356	75	111	16	2	25	71	5

PITCHING	W	L	ERA	G	SV	IP	H	BB	SO
*Barkley, Brian	8	8	5.72	22	0	119.2	126	56	89
*Betti, Rick	9	1	3.67	31	1	81.0	70	44	65
Blais, Mike	10	3	3.94	53	5	77.2	74	23	52
Cederblad, Brett	1	3	3.72	27	2	58.0	59	16	49
Doherty, John	1	1	1.85	4	0	24.1	20	2	14
*Emerson, Scott	1	0	5.85	19	0	32.1	34	26	23
*Eversgerd, Bryan	1	0	2.57	4	0	7.0	6	4	2
Fernandez, Jared	9	9	5.08	30	0	179.0	185	83	94
*Grundt, Ken	1	0	0.00	12	0	12.2	6	6	13
Harris, Reggie	2	1	1.46	33	17	37.0	17	19	43
Hecker, Doug	0	1	2.25	13	2	20.0	18	5	12
Knackert, Brent	0	0	1.38	11	10	13.0	6	6	21
*Mahay, Ron	0	1	29.45	1	0	3.2	12	6	0

Switch-hitter
* Left-handed

PITCHING	W	L	ERA	G	SV	IP	H	BB	SO
*McGraw, Tom	3	4	3.18	30	1	34.0	34	19	32
*Merrill, Ethan	3	6	7.05	13	0	60.0	71	26	42
Pavano, Carl	16	5	2.63	27	0	185.0	154	47	146
Pierce, Jeff	0	0	1.00	4	0	9.0	6	4	5
Rose, Brian	12	7	4.01	27	0	163.2	157	45	115
Schullstrom, Erik	3	0	2.54	19	1	28.1	23	13	22
*Senior, Shawn	5	6	4.72	16	0	82.0	89	42	49

Southern League

Birmingham Barons (White Sox) AA

BATTING	AVG	AB	R	H	2B	3B	HR	RBI	SB
Cameron, Mike, OF	.300	473	120	142	34	12	28	77	39
*Disarcina, Glenn, 3B	.366	175	25	64	10	3	7	36	4
*Duross, Gabe, 1B	.202	198	16	40	3	1	0	21	1
Hurst, Jimmy, OF	.265	472	62	125	23	1	18	88	19
Larregui, Ed, OF	.245	282	38	69	14	1	1	19	1
Machado, Robert, C	.239	309	35	74	16	0	6	28	1
Menechino, Frank, 2B	.292	415	77	121	25	3	12	62	7
#Norton, Greg, SS	.282	287	40	81	14	3	8	44	5
Ordonez, Magglio, OF	.263	479	66	126	41	0	18	67	9
*Pearson, Eddie, 1B	.223	323	38	72	20	0	8	40	2
#Polidor, Wil, SS	.235	81	7	19	3	0	0	6	0
Robledo, Nilson, 1B	.231	26	3	6	1	0	1	6	0
*Rose, Pete, 3B	.243	399	40	97	13	1	3	44	1
#Sawkiw, Warren, SS	.232	56	7	13	2	0	0	5	2
*Valdez, Mario, 1B	.274	168	22	46	10	2	3	28	0
Vollmer, Scott, C	.260	361	41	94	21	0	4	31	0
Wilson, Craig, SS	.282	202	36	57	9	0	3	26	1

PITCHING	W	L	ERA	G	SV	IP	H	BB	SO
Bere, Jason	0	0	4.15	1	0	4.1	4	4	5
Clemons, Chris	5	2	3.15	19	0	94.1	91	40	69
Cruz, Nelson	6	6	3.20	37	1	149.0	150	41	142
Ellis, Robert	0	1	11.05	2	0	7.1	6	8	8
*Eyre, Scott	12	7	4.38	27	0	158.1	170	79	137
*Fordham, Tom	2	1	2.65	6	0	37.1	26	14	37
Heathcott, Mike	11	8	4.02	23	0	147.2	138	55	108
Johnson, Barry	0	0	0.00	9	4	10.2	2	1	15
Jones, Stacy	1	1	2.57	27	14	28.0	25	6	31
Moore, Tim	1	4	8.54	9	0	26.1	43	6	23
Perschke, Greg	2	1	2.25	9	0	12.0	12	3	12
Place, Mike	2	3	7.09	22	1	33.0	43	18	20
*Pratt, Rich	13	9	3.86	27	0	177.1	180	40	122
*Rizzo, Todd	4	4	2.75	46	10	68.2	61	40	48
Smith, Chuck	2	1	2.64	7	1	30.2	25	15	30
Snyder, John	3	5	4.83	9	0	54.0	59	16	58
Vazquez, Archie	0	6	6.61	31	1	65.1	68	48	51
Woods, Brian	5	5	3.76	53	5	67.0	59	38	46
*Worrell, Steve	5	1	2.12	35	3	51.0	28	21	55

Carolina Mudcats (Pirates) AA

BATTING	AVG	AB	R	H	2B	3B	HR	RBI	SB
Beasley, Tony, OF	.312	269	40	84	17	5	4	30	10
*Bonifay, Ken, 3B	.243	272	33	66	18	2	6	42	4
*Boston, D.J., 1B	.280	321	47	90	16	4	8	48	5
#Brown, Adrian, OF	.296	341	48	101	11	3	3	25	27
Collier, Lou, SS	.280	443	76	124	20	3	3	49	29
*Conger, Jeff, OF	.230	178	19	41	7	1	3	17	12
Cranford, Jay, 3B	.269	268	34	72	15	2	2	37	6
Edge, Tim, C	.242	153	18	37	10	0	4	21	1
Farrell, Jon, OF	.216	51	6	11	3	0	0	3	0
Hanel, Marcus, C	.178	332	22	59	19	1	5	36	2
*Leary, Rob, 1B	.183	109	13	20	4	1	4	12	2
Munoz, Omer, SS	.000	1	0	1	0	0	0	0	0
Peterson, Charles, OF	.275	462	71	127	24	2	7	63	33
Ratliff, Darryl, OF	.274	270	39	74	11	0	0	36	13
#Reynolds, Chance, C	.167	6	0	1	0	0	0	1	0
*Sanford, Chance, 2B	.245	470	62	115	16	13	4	56	11
*Staton, T.J., OF	.308	386	72	119	24	3	15	57	17
*Sweet, Jon, C	.100	40	2	4	2	0	0	1	0
Wright, Ron, 1B	.248	246	40	61	11	1	16	52	1

Class A Directory (full season)

Florida State League

Brevard County Manatees (Marlins)
Space Coast Stadium (7,200)
Charlotte Rangers (Rangers)
Charlotte County Stadium (6,026)
Clearwater Phillies (Phillies)
Jack Russell Stadium (7,385)
Daytona Cubs (Cubs)
Jackie Robinson Ballpark (4,900)
Dunedin Blue Jays (Blue Jays)
Grant Field (6,218)
Fort Myers Miracle (Twins)
Lee County Complex (7,500)
Kissimmee Cobras (Astros)
Osceola County Stadium (5,100)
Lakeland Tigers (Tigers)
Joker Marchant Stadium (7,000)
Port St. Lucie Mets (Mets)
White Stadium (7,400)
St. Petersburg Devil Rays (Devil Rays)
Al Lang Stadium (7,004)
Sarasota Red Sox (Red Sox)
Ed Smith Stadium (7,500)
Tampa Yankees (Yankees)
Legends Field (10,000)
Vero Beach Dodgers (Dodgers)
Holman Stadium (6,500)
West Palm Beach Expos (Expos)
Municipal Stadium (4,400)

Class A Directory
(full season)

Midwest League

Michigan Battle Cats (Red Sox)
Brown Stadium (6,200)
Beloit Snappers (Brewers)
Pohlman Field (3,500)
Burlington Bees (Reds)
Community Field (3,500)
Cedar Rapids Kernels (Angels)
Veterans Memorial Ballpark (6,000)
Clinton Lumber Kings (Padres)
Riverview Stadium (3,400)
Fort Wayne Wizards (Twins)
Memorial Stadium (6,000)
Kane County Cougars (Marlins)
Elfstrom Stadium (4,800)
Lansing Lugnuts (Royals)
Oldsmobile Park (10,000)
Peoria Chiefs (Cardinals)
Pete Vonachen Stadium (6,200)
Quad City River Bandits (Astros)
John O'Donnell Stadium (5,500)
Rockford Cubbies (Cubs)
Marinelli Field (4,300)
South Bend Silver Hawks (Diamondbacks)
Coveleski Stadium (5,000)
West Michigan Whitecaps (Tigers)
Old Kent Park (5,500)
Wisconsin Timber Rattlers (Mariners)
Goodland Field (4,300)

PITCHING	W	L	ERA	G	SV	IP	H	BB	SO
Anderson, Jimmy	8	3	3.34	17	0	97.0	92	44	79
Backlund, Brett	4	6	5.13	26	0	80.2	77	28	84
Beasley, Tony	1	0	0.00	2	0	2.1	1	0	1
*Beatty, Blaine	11	5	3.29	23	0	145.0	135	34	117
Chaves, Rafael	1	2	1.37	19	0	26.1	21	8	15
*Cooke, Steve	1	5	4.53	12	0	53.2	56	26	45
Delossantos, Mariano	3	5	3.53	52	1	66.1	67	23	79
Dessens, Elmer	0	1	5.40	5	0	11.2	15	4	7
*Farson, Bryan	0	0	16.20	4	0	5.0	9	4	3
Harris, Gene	0	2	16.20	4	0	3.1	6	3	7
Holman, Shawn	1	0	3.12	5	0	8.2	11	6	6
Konuszewski, Dennis	2	8	6.30	32	0	80.0	103	36	59
*Lawrence, Sean	3	5	3.95	37	2	82.0	80	36	81
Miceli, Danny	1	0	1.00	3	1	9.0	4	1	17
Morel, Ramon	2	5	5.09	11	0	63.2	75	16	44
Parris, Steve	2	0	3.04	5	0	26.2	24	6	22
*Peters, Chris	7	3	2.64	14	0	92.0	73	34	69
Phoenix, Steve	2	2	4.98	20	5	21.2	31	6	16
*Pontbriant, Matt	2	2	5.95	45	0	56.0	73	25	36
Rychel, Kevin	1	1	4.46	26	1	36.1	32	11	21
Taylor, Scott	11	7	4.61	29	0	158.0	170	62	100
Wainhouse, Dave	5	3	3.16	45	25	51.1	43	31	34
White, Rick	0	1	11.37	2	0	6.1	9	1	7
Wilkins, Marc	2	3	4.01	11	0	24.2	19	11	19

Chattanooga Lookouts (Reds) AA

BATTING	AVG	AB	R	H	2B	3B	HR	RBI	SB
Arias, Amador, 2B	.000	1	0	0	0	0	0	0	0
*Bako, Paul, C	.294	360	53	106	27	0	8	48	1
Boone, Aaron, 3B	.288	548	86	158	44	7	17	95	21
Broach, Donald, OF	.261	349	58	91	10	2	6	37	20
*Brown, Ray, 1B	.327	364	68	119	26	5	13	52	2
Garcia, Guillermo, C	.315	203	25	64	12	0	6	36	3
#Hall, Billy, 2B	.295	461	80	136	24	3	2	43	34
#Howard, Tom, OF	.333	30	4	10	1	0	1	2	1
King, Andre, OF	.070	43	1	3	0	1	0	3	0
Ladell, Cleveland, OF	.252	405	59	102	15	7	4	41	31
Magdaleno, Ricky, SS	.222	424	60	94	21	1	17	63	2
Meggers, Mike, OF	.198	111	13	22	6	0	5	18	1
Morrow, Nick, OF	.000	1	1	1	0	0	0	0	0
Rumfield, Toby, 1B	.280	364	49	102	25	1	9	53	2
Santana, Ruben, OF	.309	343	47	106	21	2	8	56	5
#Thomas, Keith, OF	.095	21	3	2	1	0	0	3	0
Watkins, Pat, OF	.276	492	63	136	31	2	8	59	15
*White, Jimmy, PH	.132	38	5	5	1	1	0	2	0
PITCHING	**W**	**L**	**ERA**	**G**	**SV**	**IP**	**H**	**BB**	**SO**
*Allen, Cedric	1	2	6.51	12	0	27.2	31	11	12
Beltran, Alonso	0	1	8.10	3	0	13.1	18	6	10
Buckley, Travis	3	4	4.86	8	0	53.2	57	13	41
*Courtright, John	8	0	2.39	9	0	60.1	52	11	36
Donnelly, Brendan	1	2	5.52	22	0	29.1	27	17	22
*Doyle, Tom	4	2	4.80	53	0	54.1	54	39	32
*Fortugno, Tim	2	0	0.00	11	6	11.1	4	4	10
Frazier, Ron	2	5	5.83	31	0	71.0	91	25	54
Giron, Emiliano	0	0	2.25	4	0	8.0	5	5	8
Jean, Domingo	2	3	4.08	39	31	39.2	34	17	33
Koppe, Clint	4	2	3.49	10	1	56.2	54	18	30
*Lister, Martin	0	1	5.31	19	0	20.1	25	11	10
Luebbers, Larry	3	5	3.63	11	0	69.1	64	26	38
Lyons, Curt	13	4	2.41	24	0	141.2	113	52	176
McKenzie, Scott	2	4	3.40	27	0	47.2	51	23	28
Nix, Jim	7	2	3.34	62	11	89.0	80	46	93
Reed, Chris	13	10	4.09	28	1	176.0	157	91	135
Robbins, Jason	5	3	4.72	25	1	76.1	81	43	72
Roper, John	0	2	9.75	3	0	12.0	19	7	6
Sparks, Jeff	0	0	4.50	3	0	2.0	5	1	2
Tomko, Brett	11	7	3.88	27	0	157.2	131	54	164

Greenville Braves (Braves) AA

BATTING	AVG	AB	R	H	2B	3B	HR	RBI	SB
#Brito, Luis, SS	.116	43	4	5	0	0	0	4	1
#Correa, Miguel, OF	.222	225	20	50	13	2	5	25	2
Helms, Wes, 3B	.255	231	24	59	13	2	4	22	2
Hicks, Jamie, C	.167	6	0	1	0	0	0	0	0

BATTING	AVG	AB	R	H	2B	3B	HR	RBI	SB
Jimenez, Manny, SS	.274	474	68	130	21	2	3	57	12
Jones, Andruw, OF	.369	157	39	58	10	1	12	37	12
*Malloy, Marty, 2B	.312	429	82	134	27	2	4	36	11
#Martinez, Pablo, SS	.324	37	7	12	2	2	1	11	3
McBride, Charles, OF	.268	291	38	78	17	5	4	50	4
*McFarlin, Jason, OF	.230	244	40	56	14	0	4	21	6
Monds, Wonderful, OF	.300	110	17	33	9	1	2	14	7
Newell, Brett, SS	.219	297	23	65	5	0	1	21	0
Nunez, Raymond, 3B	.201	169	15	34	6	0	4	26	1
Ripplemeyer, Brad, PH	.067	15	2	1	0	0	0	1	0
Rodarte, Raul, 3B	.306	219	39	67	12	0	6	34	2
*Simon, Randall, 1B	.279	498	74	139	26	2	18	77	4
*Stricklin, Scott, C	.145	131	14	19	4	0	0	11	1
*Swann, Pedro, OF	.310	129	15	40	5	0	3	20	4
Toth, David, C	.266	376	63	100	31	1	10	55	2
Walton, Jerome, OF	.200	5	0	1	0	1	0	0	0
*Warner, Mike, OF	.259	205	39	53	19	2	6	33	10

PITCHING	W	L	ERA	G	SV	IP	H	BB	SO
Arnold, Jamie	7	7	4.92	23	0	128.0	149	44	64
Bock, Jeff	6	5	5.35	20	0	106.0	136	41	51
*Butler, Adam	1	4	5.09	38	17	35.1	36	16	31
Byrd, Matt	4	9	6.97	51	2	90.1	108	40	66
Carper, Mark	0	0	0.00	4	0	6.1	4	5	1
Cather, Mike	3	4	3.70	53	5	87.2	89	29	61
Daniels, Lee	2	0	2.65	16	9	17.0	10	14	23
Dettmer, John	3	3	2.88	26	0	40.2	43	6	28
Duncan, Chip	0	2	11.48	8	0	13.1	23	11	10
*Etheridge, Roger	4	2	6.89	49	2	66.2	71	55	43
*Gray, Dennis	3	2	6.99	28	0	46.1	45	51	37
Harrison, Tommy	8	4	4.71	20	0	99.1	88	34	82
Hollinger, Adrian	2	1	5.46	20	0	29.2	30	17	24
*Jacobs, Ryan	3	9	6.68	21	0	99.2	127	57	64
Koller, Jerry	2	10	5.50	14	0	73.2	83	27	45
LeRoy, John	1	1	2.98	8	0	45.1	43	18	38
*Moss, Damian	2	5	4.97	11	0	58.0	57	35	48
Schmidt, Jason	0	0	9.00	1	0	2.0	4	0	2
Steed, Rick	6	9	3.92	33	0	101.0	100	44	70
Steph, Rod	0	0	0.00	2	0	3.1	1	0	3
*Stewart, Rachaad	3	5	6.06	24	0	71.1	89	48	74

Huntsville Stars (Athletics) AA

BATTING	AVG	AB	R	H	2B	3B	HR	RBI	SB
#Bellhorn, Mark, 2B	.250	468	84	117	24	5	10	71	19
*Bowles, Justin, OF	.333	12	1	4	0	0	0	2	0
Correia, Rod, SS	.253	241	38	61	9	1	2	30	11
*Cox, Steve, 1B	.281	381	59	107	21	1	12	61	2
Deboer, Rob, C	.279	122	24	34	6	0	5	21	1
Francisco, David, OF	.259	386	59	100	12	1	3	28	13
Garrison, Webster, 2B	.281	178	28	50	12	2	7	31	1
*Grieve, Ben, OF	.237	232	34	55	8	1	8	32	0
Gubanich, Creighton, C	.276	217	40	60	19	0	9	43	1
*Herrera, Jose, OF	.286	84	18	24	4	0	1	7	3
Hust, Gary, OF	.223	197	22	44	11	0	3	26	3
Martins, Eric, 3B	.255	388	61	99	23	2	1	34	7
Morales, William, C	.292	377	54	110	24	0	18	73	0
Poe, Charles, OF	.264	416	74	110	18	3	12	68	5
#Smith, Demond, OF	.260	447	75	116	17	14	9	62	30
Wood, Jason, 3B	.261	491	77	128	21	1	20	84	2

PITCHING	W	L	ERA	G	SV	IP	H	BB	SO
Bennett, Bob	5	3	5.27	38	0	83.2	92	36	83
Dressendorfer, Kirk	4	4	4.99	30	2	52.1	54	21	43
Gogolin, Al	0	0	0.00	5	0	6.0	3	2	4
Haught, Gary	3	2	3.90	45	4	67.0	67	24	52
Hollins, Stacy	9	9	5.11	28	0	141.0	149	56	102
Jimenez, Miguel	0	4	8.84	19	0	37.2	43	27	28
*Kubinski, Tim	8	7	2.38	43	3	102.0	84	36	78
*Manning, Derek	0	4	6.75	18	1	72.0	96	22	51
Martins, Eric	1	0	3.86	2	0	2.1	4	3	2
Maurer, Mike	4	6	3.76	52	8	64.2	67	35	46
*Michalak, Chris	4	0	7.71	21	0	23.1	32	26	15
Rigby, Brad	9	12	3.95	26	0	159.1	161	59	127
Rossiter, Michael	8	9	4.84	27	0	145.0	167	44	116
Silva, Luis	0	0	13.50	1	0	2.2	5	2	2
*Wagner, Bret	8	8	4.23	27	0	134.0	125	77	98

Class A Directory

(full season)

South Atlantic League

Asheville Tourists
(Rockies)
McCormick Field (4,000)

Augusta Greenjackets (Pirates)
Greenjacket Stadium (4,000)

Capital City Bombers (Mets)
Capital City Stadium (6,100)

Charleston (S.C.)
River Dogs (Devil Rays)
College Park (4,300)

Charleston (W.Va.)
Alley Cats (Reds)
Watt Powell Park (6,000)

Columbus Redstixx
(Indians)
Golden Park (5,500)

Delmarva Shorebirds
(Orioles)
Perdue Stadium (5,200)

Fayetteville Generals (Expos)
J.P. Riddle Stadium (3,200)

Greensboro Bats
(Yankees)
War Memorial Stadium
(7,500)

Hagerstown Suns
(Blue Jays)
Municipal Stadium (4,500)

Hickory Crawdads
(White Sox)
L.P. Frans Stadium (4,500)

Macon Braves (Braves)
Luther Williams Field (3,500)

Piedmont Boll Weevils
(Phillies)
Fieldcrest Cannon Stadium
(4,600)

Savannah Sand Gnats
(Dodgers)
Grayson Stadium (8,000)

MINOR LEAGUE REPORT

367

PITCHING	W	L	ERA	G	SV	IP	H	BB	SO
Witasick, Jay	0	3	2.30	25	4	66.2	47	26	63
Wood, Jason	0	0	.00	2	0	2.1	0	3	3
*Zancanaro, Dave	3	3	5.61	10	0	43.1	54	26	36

Batting leaders across all leagues

BATTING AVERAGE
(minimum 383 TPA)

Player	Club	Lg.	BA
T Guerrero, V.	Hrb	East	.360
*Robinson, K.	Peo	Mid	.359
T Berry, Mike	HD	Cal	.354
*McMillon, Billy	Chr	Int	.352
Raabe, Brian	SLk	PCL	.351
*Brede, Brent	SLk	PCL	.348
Rohrmeier, Dan	Mem	Sou	.344
Guerrero, W.	Abq	PCL	.344
Dunn, Todd	EIP	Tex	.340
*Walker, Todd	SLk	PCL	.339
*Wilson, Desi	Phx	PCL	.339
T Jones, A.	Rmd	Int	.339
Castellano, P.	CSp	PCL	.337
Hyzdu, Adam	Tre	East	.337
Echevarria, A.	CSp	PCL	.337

SLUGGING PERCENTAGE

Player	Club	Lg.	SLUG
T Jones, A.	Rmd	Int	.652
*Stevens, Lee	OkC	AmA	.643
*Cromer, D.T.	Mod	Cal	.626
T Guerrero, V.	Hrb	East	.618
Hyzdu, Adam	Tre	East	.618
T Trammell, B.	Tol	Int	.605
*McMillon, Billy	Chr	Int	.602
Cameron, Mike	Bir	Sou	.600
*Walker, Todd	SLk	PCL	.599
Dunn, Todd	EIP	Tex	.593
Rohrmeier, Dan	Mem	Sou	.592
T Denbow, Don	SJ	Cal	.591
*Nunnally, Jon	Oma	AmA	.583
T Pemberton, R.	Paw	Int	.580
Woods, Tyrone	Tre	East	.579

Jacksonville Suns (Tigers) AA

BATTING	AVG	AB	R	H	2B	3B	HR	RBI	SB
Barker, Glen, OF	.158	120	9	19	2	1	0	8	6
#Bream, Scott, OF	.241	108	18	26	3	1	3	12	2
*Brock, Tarrik, OF	.127	102	14	13	2	0	0	6	3
Casanova, Papo, C	.333	30	5	10	2	0	4	9	0
*Catalanotto, Frank, 2B	.298	497	105	148	34	6	17	67	15
*Cotton, John, OF	.240	217	34	52	7	4	13	39	15
*Dismuke, Jamie, DH	.266	79	7	21	4	1	4	12	0
*Freeman, Sean, 1B	.267	412	72	110	18	1	25	74	3
Garcia, Luis, SS	.245	522	68	128	22	4	9	46	15
Hansen, Terrel, OF	.264	367	49	97	18	2	25	66	5
Kimsey, Keith, OF	.179	106	8	19	0	1	2	6	2
Lidle, Kevin, 3B	.250	8	2	2	0	0	1	2	1
Makarewicz, Scott, C	.314	258	42	81	16	1	14	49	4
Mashore, Justin, OF	.285	453	67	129	27	8	7	50	17
#Mitchell, Tony, OF	.312	173	30	54	13	0	11	41	1
Nevin, Phil, C	.294	344	77	101	18	1	24	69	6
Pough, Pork Chop, 3B	.500	4	1	2	0	0	0	0	0
*Roberts, David, OF	.222	9	0	2	0	0	0	0	0
Schmidt, Tom, 3B	.221	385	45	85	24	2	11	45	4
Thompson, Billy, C	.232	112	9	26	5	0	3	10	1
Trammell, Bubba, OF	.328	311	63	102	23	2	27	75	3

PITCHING	W	L	ERA	G	SV	IP	H	BB	SO
*Barnes, Brian	4	6	3.74	13	0	74.2	74	25	74
Carlyle, Ken	8	5	4.05	27	0	155.2	167	51	89
Cedeno, Blas	0	0	5.40	26	0	46.2	63	26	30
Drews, Matt	0	4	4.35	6	0	31.0	26	19	40
Drumright, Mike	6	4	3.97	18	0	99.2	80	48	109
Fermin, Ramon	6	6	4.50	46	3	84.0	82	46	48
Gaillard, Eddie	9	6	3.38	56	1	88.0	82	50	76
Greene, Rick	2	7	4.98	57	30	56.0	67	39	42
Gutierrez, Jim	8	6	3.76	51	1	105.1	98	54	71
Kelly, John	2	2	4.58	9	0	55.0	54	35	29
Moehler, Brian	15	6	3.48	28	0	173.1	186	50	120
Norman, Scott	6	5	4.82	27	0	97.0	122	37	30
Reed, Brandon	1	0	2.08	7	1	26.0	18	3	18
*Rosengren, John	5	1	4.55	60	1	55.1	48	37	47
*Salazar, Michael	2	5	4.30	16	0	29.1	34	14	19
Skrmetta, Matt	0	0	4.50	4	0	6.0	4	5	7
*Whiteside, Sean	1	0	5.84	8	0	12.1	11	9	9

Knoxville Smokies (Blue Jays) AA

BATTING	AVG	AB	R	H	2B	3B	HR	RBI	SB
*Candelaria, Ben, OF	.278	162	16	45	11	2	3	14	3
Cradle, Rickey, OF	.282	333	59	94	23	2	12	47	15
*Cromer, Brandon, SS	.277	318	56	88	15	8	7	32	3
de la Cruz, Lorenzo, OF	.247	441	60	109	24	4	18	79	8
Evans, Tom, 3B	.282	394	87	111	27	1	17	65	4
*Harmes, Kris, C	.213	122	16	26	8	1	2	8	1
Henry, Santiago, SS	.270	371	37	100	15	7	3	32	11
Jones, Ryan, 1B	.271	506	70	137	26	3	20	97	2
*Martinez, Angel, C	.188	16	2	3	0	0	0	0	0
#Melhuse, Adam, C	.213	94	13	20	3	0	1	6	0
Mosquera, Julio, C	.230	318	36	73	17	0	2	31	6
Mummau, Bob, 3B	.279	154	23	43	11	0	2	22	1
#Patzke, Jeff, 2B	.303	429	70	130	31	4	4	66	6
Ramirez, Angel, OF	.281	392	64	110	25	7	5	54	16
#Roberts, Lonell, OF	.291	237	35	69	1	0	1	12	24
Sanders, Anthony, OF	.271	133	16	36	8	0	1	18	1
*Weinke, Chris, DH	.264	265	48	70	18	2	15	55	2

PITCHING	W	L	ERA	G	SV	IP	H	BB	SO
Almanzar, Carlos	7	8	4.85	54	9	94.2	106	33	105
*Bogott, Kurtiss	2	2	5.33	33	3	54.0	64	29	56
Brandow, Derek	1	2	7.71	5	2	11.2	11	5	6
*Brown, Chad	2	4	4.06	46	7	64.1	72	23	63
Carpenter, Chris	7	9	3.94	28	0	171.1	161	91	150
Doman, Roger	1	1	5.49	17	0	39.1	51	14	30
*Duran, Roberto	4	6	5.13	19	0	80.2	72	61	74

Switch-hitter
* Left-handed
T Player has been with more than one team; listed with last team.
(Players in major leagues are listed with last minor league club.)

PITCHING	W	L	ERA	G	SV	IP	H	BB	SO
Escobar, Kelvim	3	4	5.33	10	0	54.0	61	24	44
Freeman, Chris	6	1	3.35	26	0	45.2	45	23	54
*Halperin, Mike	13	7	3.48	28	0	155.0	156	71	112
Harmes, Kris	0	0	3.38	1	0	2.2	3	2	1
*Pace, Scotty	2	0	3.00	4	0	12.0	8	6	5
Pett, Jose	4	2	4.09	7	0	44.0	37	10	38
Rhine, Kendall	0	0	5.84	11	2	12.1	12	11	9
Romano, Michael	9	9	4.98	34	1	130.0	148	72	92
Sievert, Mark	9	2	2.58	17	0	101.1	79	51	75
Silva, Jose	2	3	4.91	22	0	44.0	45	22	26
Smith, Brian	3	5	3.81	54	16	75.2	76	31	58
*Viola, Frank	0	0	1.64	4	0	22.0	16	3	15

Memphis Chicks (Padres) AA

BATTING	AVG	AB	R	H	2B	3B	HR	RBI	SB
Alvarez, Gabe, 3B	.247	368	58	91	23	1	8	40	2
#Barry, Jeff, 3B	.243	226	29	55	7	0	3	25	3
Briggs, Stoney, OF	.274	452	72	124	24	6	12	80	28
Brinkley, Darryl, OF	.296	203	36	60	9	0	9	29	13
Bruno, Julio, 2B	.238	84	11	20	8	1	0	9	1
#Johnson, Earl, OF	.252	337	50	85	10	6	2	33	15
Keefe, Jamie, 2B	.176	17	2	3	0	0	0	0	0
*Killeen, Tim, C	.259	224	44	58	10	6	11	51	0
LaRocca, Greg, 2B	.274	445	66	122	22	5	6	42	5
Lee, Derrek, 1B	.280	500	98	140	39	2	34	104	13
Massarelli, John, OF	.263	205	26	54	16	3	2	15	9
*Moore, Vince, OF	.206	141	24	29	11	2	1	11	7
*Prieto, Chris, OF	.333	12	1	4	0	1	0	0	2
Rohrmeier, Dan, DH	.344	471	98	162	29	2	28	95	2
#Romero, Mandy, C	.269	297	40	80	15	0	10	46	3
Velandia, Jorge, SS	.240	392	42	94	19	0	9	48	3
*Woodridge, Dickie, 2B	.154	65	10	10	0	0	0	11	1

PITCHING	W	L	ERA	G	SV	IP	H	BB	SO
Clark, Dera	4	3	3.13	9	0	46.0	47	13	42
Clayton, Craig	0	0	5.59	5	0	9.2	14	5	9
Cole, Victor	1	0	1.20	8	1	15.0	11	8	13
*Dennis, Shane	9	1	2.27	19	0	115.0	83	45	131
*Dixon, Bubba	2	3	4.12	42	3	63.1	53	28	77
*Fesh, Sean	1	1	5.63	7	0	8.0	7	7	5
Freitas, Mike	3	0	5.11	44	0	68.2	78	26	36
Hernandez, Fernando	11	10	4.64	27	0	147.1	128	85	161
Kaufman, Brad	12	10	3.63	29	0	178.1	161	83	163
*Kilgo, Rusty	1	4	3.65	48	2	74.0	80	18	58
Kroon, Marc	2	4	2.89	44	22	46.2	33	28	56
*Long, Joey	2	0	2.00	10	0	18.0	16	11	14
Mattson, Rob	13	8	4.33	27	0	164.1	172	54	88
*Murray, Heath	13	9	3.21	27	0	174.0	154	60	156
Schmitt, Todd	4	4	3.43	38	11	39.1	39	21	47
Veras, Dario	3	1	2.32	29	1	42.2	38	9	47
Yoda, Tsuyoshi	0	0	11.74	9	0	7.2	9	8	3

Orlando Cubs (Cubs) AA

BATTING	AVG	AB	R	H	2B	3B	HR	RBI	SB
*Bullett, Scott, OF	.182	11	2	2	0	0	0	0	2
Cholowsky, Dan, 3B	.238	143	21	34	4	0	4	14	2
Dowler, Dee, OF	.278	352	59	98	15	6	6	47	25
Forkerway, Trey, SS	.242	161	22	39	9	1	3	20	0
*Fryman, Troy, OF	.225	249	35	56	18	1	2	28	2
#Hightower, Vee, OF	.067	75	2	5	0	0	0	4	3
Hughes, Troy, OF	.273	450	75	123	26	3	18	93	3
#Kingston, Mark, 3B	.205	122	21	25	9	0	3	17	1
#Livsey, Shawn, 2B	.257	257	36	66	15	2	2	33	13
Maxwell, Jason, SS	.266	433	64	115	20	1	9	45	19
*Morris, Bobby, 1B	.262	465	72	122	29	3	8	62	12
Orie, Kevin, 3B	.314	296	42	93	25	0	8	58	2
Ortiz, Hector, C	.218	216	16	47	8	0	0	15	1
Perez, Richard, 1B	.167	18	0	3	0	0	0	1	0
Petersen, Chris, 2B	.296	152	21	45	3	4	2	12	3
*Samuels, Scott, OF	.260	342	62	89	19	5	2	33	21
Thurston, Jerrey, C	.209	177	16	37	6	1	3	23	0
#Walker, Steve, OF	.254	224	31	57	7	4	4	21	6
*Williams, Harold, DH	.266	301	36	80	10	0	10	40	2

Batting leaders across all leagues

(Cont'd from previous page)

ON-BASE AVERAGE

Player	Club	Lg.	OBA
T Berry, Mike	HD	Cal	.471
Evans, Tom	Knx	Sou	.452
Vieira, Scott	Rkf	Mid	.451
*Brede, Brent	SLk	PCL	.446
T Denbow, Don	SJ	Cal	.446
T*Valdez, Mario	Bir	Sou	.443
T*Takayoshi, T.	LkE	Cal	.442
T Deboer, Rob	Hvl	Sou	.437
Rohrmeier, Dan	Mem	Sou	.435
T Guerrero, V.	Hrb	East	.431
T*Helton, Todd	CSp	PCL	.427
Stcknschndr, E.	Sav	SAL	.424
Hyzdu, Adam	Tre	East	.424
T*Neill, Mike	Mod	Cal	.422
*Robinson, K.	Peo	Mid	.422

HOME RUNS

Player	Club	Lg.	HR
Hiatt, Phil	Tol	Int	42
*Branyan, R.	Clm	SAL	40
T Wright, Ron	Car	Sou	36
*Kirgan, Chris	HD	Cal	35
Brooks, Jerry	Chr	Int	34
T Jones, A.	Rmd	Int	34
Lee, Derrek	Mem	Sou	34
T Trammell, B.	Tol	Int	33
Smith, Bubba	Tul	Tex	32
T Spencer, S.	Col	Int	32
*Stevens, Lee	OkC	AmA	32
T Hatcher, C.	Tcn	PCL	31
Oliva, Jose	Lou	AmA	31
SEVERAL TIED AT 30			

Switch-hitter
* Left-handed
T Player has been with more than one team; listed with last team.
(Players in major leagues are listed with last minor league club.)

Batting leaders across all leagues

(Cont'd from previous page)

RUNS BATTED IN

Player	Club	Lg.	RBI
*Kirgan, Chris	HD	Cal	131
*Cromer, D.T.	Mod	Cal	130
Hiatt, Phil	Tol	Int	119
T Berry, Mike	HD	Cal	116
T Wright, Ron	Car	Sou	114
*Barnes, Larry	CR	Mid	112
*Walker, Todd	SLk	PCL	111
Brooks, Jerry	Chr	Int	107
*Branyan, R.	Clm	SAL	106
*Marquez, J.	LNC	Cal	106
Saunders, Chris	BNG	East	105
Isom, Johnny	Fre	Car	104
Lee, Derrek	Mem	Sou	104
T Pemberton, R.	Paw	Int	103
#Rennhack, M.	Stk	Cal	103

STOLEN BASES

Player	Club	Lg.	SB
T*Roberts, D.	Jax	Sou	65
#Gibbs, Kevin	VB	FSL	60
Gomez, Ramon	Hck	SAL	57
#Smith, Rod	Gbo	SAL	57
Almanzar, R.	Lak	FSL	53
#Nunez, Juan	CSC	SAL	53
#Towner, Kyle	Bak	Cal	53
Cabrera, O.	Del	SAL	51
#Castillo, Luis	Prt	East	51
Garland, Tim	SJ	Cal	51
Baughman, J.	CR	Mid	50
T Lewis, Marc	Dur	Car	50
Pimentel, Jose	Sav	SAL	50
*Robinson, K.	Peo	Mid	50
Stcknschndr, E.	Sav	SAL	50

Arkansas Travelers... (continued on the right)

Switch-hitter
* Left-handed
T Player has been with more than one team; listed with last team.
(Players in major leagues are listed with last minor league club.)

PITCHING	W	L	ERA	G	SV	IP	H	BB	SO
Bogle, Sean	0	0	0.00	4	0	5.2	2	6	6
Burlingame, Ben	1	1	3.71	11	0	17.0	21	10	16
*Byrne, Earl	1	2	5.59	11	0	37.0	36	26	30
Connolly, Matt	7	3	3.31	31	2	87.0	79	35	80
*Dabney, Fred	0	0	2.57	12	0	14.0	15	5	16
Gambs, Chris	0	0	5.40	2	0	5.0	3	5	3
Garcia, Al	6	7	4.85	23	0	118.2	149	32	66
Gonzalez, Jeremi	6	3	3.34	17	0	97.0	95	28	85
*Graves, Ryan	0	2	12.00	4	1	9.0	16	9	3
Hart, Jason	3	5	3.21	51	4	73.0	59	28	78
Hutcheson, David	4	3	3.51	19	0	84.2	82	28	60
Moten, Scott	2	6	5.63	18	1	54.1	59	31	35
*Pulido, Carlos	2	2	7.45	6	0	9.2	17	3	12
Rain, Steve	1	0	2.56	35	10	38.2	32	12	48
*Rivera, Roberto	1	2	6.35	9	1	17.0	20	8	14
Ryan, Jay	2	5	5.71	7	0	34.2	39	24	25
Speier, Justin	4	1	2.05	24	6	26.1	23	5	14
Stephenson, Brian	5	13	4.69	32	1	128.2	130	61	106
Thomas, Royal	3	2	6.35	10	0	45.1	57	18	20
Trachsel, Steve	0	1	2.77	2	0	13.0	11	0	12
*Twiggs, Greg	4	2	3.95	44	1	54.2	53	33	40
Walker, Wade	8	14	4.41	29	0	187.2	205	76	117
*Williams, Gregory	0	0	4.26	12	0	19.0	21	13	11
Winslett, Dax	1	3	7.84	4	0	20.2	31	7	13

Port City Roosters (Mariners) AA

BATTING	AVG	AB	R	H	2B	3B	HR	RBI	SB
Barger, Mike, OF	.205	366	45	75	17	4	0	26	19
Cardenas, John, C	.189	74	4	14	0	0	1	6	1
#Cruz, Jose, OF	.282	181	39	51	10	2	3	31	5
Drinkwater, Sean, 3B	.267	101	10	27	9	0	1	13	1
*Friedman, Jason, DH	.188	133	7	25	5	3	1	11	0
Gipson, Charles, OF	.268	407	54	109	12	3	1	30	26
Griffey, Craig, OF	.222	396	43	88	14	7	2	35	20
#Guevara, Giomar, SS	.266	414	60	110	18	2	2	41	21
#Hickey, Mike, 2B	.255	247	35	63	14	3	1	23	9
*Ibanez, Raul, OF	.368	76	12	28	8	1	1	13	3
*Jorgensen, Randy, 1B	.280	460	61	129	32	1	8	81	2
Ladjevich, Rick, 3B	.283	414	44	117	23	1	7	48	1
*Patel, Manny, 2B	.220	369	48	81	9	1	1	32	12
*Rackley, Keifer, OF	.158	19	0	3	1	0	0	1	0
Ramirez, Roberto, OF	.225	182	19	41	12	1	3	19	1
Sealy, Scot, DH	.085	59	2	5	1	0	0	1	0
*Sturdivant, Marcus, OF	.284	243	34	69	11	4	2	23	13
#Varitek, Jason, C	.262	503	63	132	34	1	12	67	7
Wakamatsu, Don, C	.314	70	10	22	4	0	2	9	1

PITCHING	W	L	ERA	G	SV	IP	H	BB	SO
Apana, Matt	3	8	5.33	18	0	96.1	86	69	55
*Brosnan, Jason	5	6	3.62	30	1	77.0	71	32	76
Brumley, Duff	0	1	3.86	6	0	28.0	27	21	17
Crow, Dean	2	3	3.18	60	26	68.0	64	20	43
Franklin, Ryan	6	12	4.01	28	0	182.0	186	37	127
Gipson, Charles	0	1	1.93	4	0	4.2	3	4	3
Gould, Clint	0	1	3.38	11	0	21.1	17	6	9
Hanson, Craig	0	0	3.86	5	0	9.1	5	6	9
Lowe, Derek	5	3	3.05	10	0	65.0	56	17	33
Montane, Ivan	3	8	5.20	18	0	100.1	96	75	81
*Moore, Trey	1	6	7.71	11	0	53.2	73	33	42
*Newton, Geronimo	4	1	2.76	33	0	45.2	45	22	25
Russell, Lagrande	7	7	4.34	42	2	118.1	127	50	89
*Simmons, Scott	1	1	3.79	11	0	19.0	19	6	12
Smith, Ryan	6	9	3.13	50	2	97.2	92	37	65
Suzuki, Mac	3	6	4.72	16	0	74.1	69	32	66
Wertz, Bill	2	2	2.57	6	0	28.0	28	9	26
Worley, Robert	2	5	3.93	35	0	66.1	66	39	40
Zimmerman, Mike	4	4	6.94	14	0	48.0	56	33	25

Texas League

Arkansas Travelers (Cardinals) AA

BATTING	AVG	AB	R	H	2B	3B	HR	RBI	SB
*Anderson, Charlie, PH	.000	1	0	0	0	0	0	0	0

BATTING	AVG	AB	R	H	2B	3B	HR	RBI	SB
Berblinger, Jeff, 2B	.288	500	78	144	32	7	11	53	23
Dalton, Dee, 3B	.238	345	38	82	17	2	6	42	4
#Diggs, Tony, OF	.304	138	23	42	7	3	3	22	7
*Ellis, Paul, C	.255	157	16	40	5	0	3	26	0
*Fick, Chris, OF	.257	448	64	115	25	2	19	74	2
Green, Scarborough, OF	.199	301	45	60	6	3	3	24	21
Johns, Keith, SS	.246	447	52	110	17	1	1	40	8
Marrero, Elieser, C	.270	374	65	101	17	3	19	65	9
McEwing, Joe, OF	.208	216	27	45	7	3	2	14	2
#Murphy, Jeffrey, C	.571	7	3	4	1	0	0	1	0
Pages, Javier, PH	.261	46	3	12	2	0	1	7	0
Rupp, Brian, 1B	.303	353	46	107	17	2	4	41	5
Santucci, Steve, OF	.150	20	2	3	0	0	0	0	0
Torres, Paul, OF	.262	309	38	81	16	0	11	44	1
#Velez, Jose, OF	.273	264	36	72	11	2	2	32	8
Warner, Ron, 3B	.300	233	36	70	22	4	6	39	5
Wolfe, Joel, 1B	.215	200	29	43	11	2	4	26	11

PITCHING	W	L	ERA	G	SV	IP	H	BB	SO
Aybar, Manuel	8	6	3.05	20	0	121.0	120	34	83
Carpenter, Brian	1	2	3.16	37	0	74.0	63	26	53
Croushore, Rick	5	10	4.92	34	3	108.0	113	51	85
Davis, Ray	0	1	5.16	12	0	22.2	25	10	15
*Detmers, Kris	12	8	3.35	27	0	163.2	154	70	97
Garcia, Frank	0	0	3.72	11	0	19.1	20	7	12
Golden, Matt	3	4	4.14	52	18	63.0	74	26	43
Hiljus, Erik	3	5	6.11	10	0	45.2	62	30	21
King, Curtis	0	1	19.80	5	1	5.0	15	6	5
*Lovingier, Kevin	2	3	4.10	60	1	63.2	60	48	73
Lowe, Sean	2	3	6.00	6	0	33.0	32	15	25
Matranga, Jeff	6	5	2.15	62	4	79.2	56	30	82
Matulevich, Jeff	4	3	3.64	41	1	59.1	48	29	51
Morris, Matt	12	12	3.88	27	0	167.0	178	48	120
Raggio, Brady	9	10	3.22	26	0	162.1	160	40	123

El Paso Diablos (Brewers) AA

BATTING	AVG	AB	R	H	2B	3B	HR	RBI	SB
Belliard, Ronnie, 2B	.279	416	73	116	20	8	3	57	26
Dobrolsky, Bill, C	.282	202	26	57	11	1	2	21	1
Dunn, Todd, OF	.340	359	72	122	24	5	19	78	13
Felix, Lauro, SS	.269	301	71	81	15	2	10	59	11
Hamlin, Jonas, 1B	.283	515	81	146	35	8	21	94	9
*Harris, Mike, OF	.308	260	47	80	15	5	7	35	5
Hughes, Bobby, C	.304	237	43	72	18	1	15	39	3
*Jenkins, Geoff, DH	.286	77	17	22	5	4	1	11	1
Krause, Scott, OF	.318	85	16	27	5	2	3	11	2
Lopez, Pedro, C	.306	144	22	44	10	1	2	20	2
#Martinez, Gabby, SS	.251	338	44	85	11	8	0	37	8
#Martinez, Greg, OF	.313	166	27	52	2	2	1	21	14
Nicholas, Darrell, OF	.274	237	46	65	12	4	2	24	7
Ortega, Hector, 3B	.242	351	52	85	12	4	7	53	11
Perez, Danny, OF	.351	154	31	54	16	6	2	19	5
Rodriques, Cecil, OF	.283	389	63	110	23	6	5	50	5
Seitzer, Brad, 3B	.319	433	78	138	31	1	17	87	6

PITCHING	W	L	ERA	G	SV	IP	H	BB	SO
D'Amico, Jeff	5	4	3.19	13	0	96.0	89	13	76
*Farrell, Mike	1	0	0.66	11	1	13.2	6	2	13
Ganote, Joe	0	0	5.79	1	0	4.2	9	1	5
Gavaghan, Sean	4	1	5.11	24	0	37.0	48	15	24
Kloek, Kevin	3	1	4.02	9	0	53.2	58	18	46
Kramer, Jeff	3	4	6.34	21	1	59.2	76	29	36
Maloney, Sean	3	2	1.43	51	38	56.2	49	12	57
*Montoya, Norm	9	8	4.67	24	1	125.1	153	28	73
*Mullins, Greg	1	5	7.07	23	2	28.0	30	17	28
Paul, Andy	5	6	4.72	38	3	95.1	105	43	72
Rodriguez, Frank	3	4	6.62	16	0	35.1	45	24	40
Sadler, Aldren	3	3	4.71	26	1	42.0	39	40	31
Salazar, Luis	1	0	11.81	3	0	5.1	14	1	2
*Santos, Henry	7	7	6.16	35	0	99.1	126	50	73
Smith, Travis	7	4	4.18	17	0	107.2	119	39	68
Taylor, Tommy	2	1	4.67	14	0	17.1	24	6	20
Tollberg, Brian	7	5	4.90	26	0	154.1	183	23	109
Webb, Doug	1	0	6.75	10	0	8.0	4	10	3
*Whitaker, Steve	11	7	4.58	25	0	145.1	157	87	85
Wilstead, Judd	0	1	8.47	7	0	17.0	19	7	11

Batting leaders across all leagues

(Cont'd from previous page)

HITS

Player	Club	Lg.	H
*Walker, Todd	SLk	PCL	187
#Perez, Neifi	CSp	PCL	180
T Guerrero, V.	Hrb	East	179
T Avila, Rolo	Roc	Int	174
Garland, Tim	SJ	Cal	171
T*Mayes, Craig	SJ	Cal	171
T#Brown, A.	Car	Sou	170
Guillen, Jose	Lyn	Car	170
T Berry, Mike	HD	Cal	169
Raabe, Brian	SLk	PCL	169
T Ramirez, Alex	Can	East	169
*Brede, Brent	SLk	PCL	168
*Cromer, D.T.	Mod	Cal	166
*Franco, Matt	Nor	Int	164
*Monahan, S.	Lnc	Cal	164

DOUBLES

Player	Club	Lg.	2B
Urso, Joe	LkE	Cal	47
Kapler, Gabriel	Fay	SAL	45
T Berry, Mike	HD	Cal	44
Boone, Aaron	Cng	Sou	44
T Stone, Craig	Dun	FSL	42
Ordonez, M.	Bir	Sou	41
*Walker, Todd	SLk	PCL	41
*Cromer, D.T.	Mod	Cal	40
*Franco, Matt	Nor	Int	40
T Guerrero, V.	Hrb	East	40
Garcia, Freddy	Lyn	Car	39
Lee, Derrek	Mem	Sou	39
*Pritchett, Chris	Van	PCL	39
Raabe, Brian	SLk	PCL	39
T Rolen, Scott	SWB	Int	39

Switch-hitter
* Left-handed
T Player has been with more than one team; listed with last team.
(Players in major leagues are listed with last minor league club.)

Batting leaders across all leagues

(Cont'd from previous page)

TRIPLES

Player	Club	Lg.	3B
*Abreu, Bob	Tcn	PCL	16
#Hutchins, N.	CR	Mid	16
*Robinson, K.	Peo	Mid	14
T#Smith, D.	Edm	PCL	14
#Bates, Fletcher	Clb	SAL	13
*Sanford, C.	Car	Sou	13
Cameron, Mike	Bir	Sou	12
#Frias, Hanley	Tul	Tex	12
Guerrero, Wilton	Abq	PCL	12
*Monahan, S.	Lnc	Cal	12
#Perez, Neifi	CSp	PCL	12
T Ramirez, Alex	Can	East	12
SEVERAL TIED AT 11			

EXTRA BASE HITS

Player	Club	Lg.	EBH
*Cromer, D.T.	Mod	Cal	80
*Walker, Todd	SLk	PCL	78
Lee, Derrek	Mem	Sou	75
Cameron, Mike	Bir	Sou	74
T Trammell, B.	Tol	Int	73
T Guerrero, V.	Hrb	East	72
Hiatt, Phil	Tol	Int	72
Kapler, Gabriel	Fay	SAL	71
*Stevens, Lee	OkC	AmA	71
T*Ledee, Ricky	Col	Int	69
*Barnes, Larry	CR	Mid	68
Boone, Aaron	Cng	Sou	68
T Hatcher, Chris	Tcn	PCL	66
T Jones, A.	Rmd	Int	66
SEVERAL TIED AT 65			

Jackson Generals (Astros) AA

BATTING	AVG	AB	R	H	2B	3B	HR	RBI	SB
*Bridges, Kary, 2B	.325	338	51	110	12	2	4	33	4
*Colon, Dennis, 1B	.280	432	49	121	23	1	12	58	0
*Forkner, Tim, 3B	.293	379	55	111	20	3	7	46	0
Gonzalez, Jimmy, C	.200	5	1	1	0	0	0	0	0
Groppuso, Mike, 3B	.252	111	17	28	0	2	3	12	1
Hatcher, Chris, OF	.308	156	29	48	9	1	13	36	2
Hidalgo, Richard, OF	.294	513	66	151	34	2	14	78	11
Johnson, Russ, SS	.310	496	86	154	24	5	15	74	9
Luce, Roger, C	.255	243	29	62	11	4	8	36	0
Magallanes, Bobby, 2B	.268	41	7	11	2	0	2	4	0
*McNabb, Buck, OF	.301	279	38	84	15	5	0	26	10
#Meluskey, Mitch, C	.313	134	18	42	11	0	0	21	0
*Mitchell, Donovan, 2B	.252	408	57	103	22	2	3	32	11
Mora, Melvin, OF	.286	255	36	73	6	1	5	23	4
Mota, Gary, OF	.240	25	3	6	0	0	0	0	0
*Peterson, Nate, OF	.278	324	36	90	19	0	2	34	1
Probst, Alan, C	.244	180	20	44	9	1	7	33	1
Ross, Tony, OF	.175	80	13	14	0	1	0	3	2
Sanchez, Victor, 1B	.219	210	30	46	9	0	13	34	4

PITCHING	W	L	ERA	G	SV	IP	H	BB	SO
Barrios, Manuel	6	4	2.37	60	23	68.1	60	29	69
Brocail, Doug	0	0	0.00	2	0	4.0	1	1	5
Creek, Ryan	7	15	5.26	27	0	142.0	139	121	119
*Dace, Derek	0	0	2.25	1	0	4.0	5	5	0
Dault, Donnie	0	0	0.00	1	0	2.0	2	2	1
Grzanich, Mike	5	4	3.98	57	6	72.1	60	43	80
*Halama, John	9	10	3.21	27	0	162.2	151	59	110
Humphrey, Rich	4	2	2.51	43	1	64.2	53	15	37
Kester, Tim	2	4	3.73	48	1	103.2	105	16	55
Loiselle, Rich	7	4	3.47	16	0	98.2	107	27	65
*Martin, Tom	6	2	3.24	57	3	75.0	71	42	58
Narcisse, Tyrone	7	12	5.54	27	0	126.2	151	55	88
Ramos, Edgar	4	5	4.88	12	0	66.1	63	29	52
*Simons, Doug	8	7	3.48	20	0	126.2	132	30	75
*Walker, Jamie	5	1	2.50	45	2	101.0	94	35	79

Midland Angels (Angels) AA

BATTING	AVG	AB	R	H	2B	3B	HR	RBI	SB
Alfonzo, Edgar, 3B	.274	310	37	85	22	1	4	40	1
Betten, Randy, 3B	.171	82	5	14	2	0	0	5	3
Boykin, Tyrone, 1B	.252	127	27	32	10	1	6	30	0
*Bryant, Ralph, DH	.208	216	33	45	16	0	9	26	1
Burke, Jamie, 3B	.319	144	24	46	8	2	2	16	1
#Carvajal, Jovino, OF	.269	160	20	43	5	2	2	22	7
#Christian, Eddie, OF	.305	426	59	130	30	5	5	46	7
Davalillo, David, SS	.171	82	6	14	1	0	0	5	2
#Diaz, Freddy, SS	.199	156	23	31	7	2	3	18	1
Doty, Derrin, OF	.272	158	32	43	10	3	5	25	3
Easley, Damion, 3B	.429	14	1	6	2	0	0	2	1
*Glenn, Leon, 1B	.213	319	30	68	14	2	10	53	8
*Guiel, Aaron, 3B	.269	439	72	118	29	7	10	48	11
Luuloa, Keith, 2B	.260	531	80	138	24	4	7	44	4
McNeely, Jeff, OF	.240	125	16	30	8	1	0	18	2
Moeder, Tony, 1B	.224	85	19	19	3	1	5	7	0
Molina, Ben, C	.274	365	45	100	21	2	8	54	0
Monzon, Jose, C	.279	140	15	39	4	0	3	22	1
Ortiz, Bo, OF	.296	507	73	150	32	5	11	64	12
*Shockey, Greg, OF	.317	325	58	103	26	6	7	49	2

PITCHING	W	L	ERA	G	SV	IP	H	BB	SO
*Abbott, Kyle	3	5	4.50	15	0	88.0	93	34	48
*Beaumont, Matt	7	16	5.85	28	0	161.2	198	71	132
Bonanno, Rob	1	2	5.32	23	2	64.1	79	23	52
Brown, Willard	0	6	11.61	9	0	33.1	58	9	16
Castillo, Carlos	2	3	4.26	25	1	38.0	37	21	15
Chavez, Tony	2	4	4.21	31	1	72.2	81	24	55
*DeClue, Jon	6	9	5.32	32	0	111.2	137	51	76
Diaz, Freddy	0	0	0.00	2	0	2.1	1	0	1
Dickson, Jason	5	2	3.58	8	0	55.1	55	10	40
Doorneweerd, Dave	1	2	5.79	9	0	18.2	25	12	20
Edsell, Geoff	5	5	4.70	14	0	88.0	84	47	60
Freehill, Mike	7	6	3.42	47	17	50.0	49	21	48
Goedhart, Darrell	0	1	3.86	3	0	14.0	15	4	5

Switch-hitter
* Left-handed
T Player has been with more than one team; listed with last team.
(Players in major leagues are listed with last minor league club.)

PITCHING	W	L	ERA	G	SV	IP	H	BB	SO
Harris, Pep	2	2	5.31	6	0	39.0	47	9	28
Hollinger, Adrian	1	1	4.32	13	2	16.2	18	11	8
*Holtz, Mike	1	2	4.17	33	2	41.0	52	9	41
Ingram, Todd	0	1	7.94	15	0	22.2	25	21	11
Janicki, Pete	1	3	6.39	5	0	31.0	37	10	17
Keling, Korey	0	1	6.90	17	1	30.0	42	14	13
Leftwich, Phil	4	2	2.90	6	0	40.1	33	4	33
*Novoa, Rafael	0	1	6.66	19	2	24.1	28	12	16
*Perisho, Matt	3	2	3.21	8	0	53.1	48	20	50
Sebach, Kyle	2	0	7.59	4	0	21.1	31	15	11
*Washburn, Jarrod	5	6	4.40	13	0	88.0	77	25	58

San Antonio Missions (Dodgers) AA

BATTING	AVG	AB	R	H	2B	3B	HR	RBI	SB
*Anderson, Cliff, SS	.231	26	2	6	0	1	0	2	0
Blanco, Henry, C	.267	307	39	82	14	1	5	40	2
Dandridge, Brad, OF	.282	177	22	50	7	0	3	25	4
*Durkin, Chris, OF	.300	30	6	9	2	0	1	3	0
*Garcia, Karim, OF	.248	129	21	32	6	1	5	22	1
Johnson, Keith, SS	.274	521	74	143	28	6	10	57	15
*Kirkpatrick, Jay, DH	.242	91	6	22	4	0	3	10	1
Konerko, Paul, 1B	.300	470	78	141	23	2	29	86	1
Luzinski, Ryan, C	.291	103	12	30	6	0	0	10	2
*Martin, Jim, OF	.211	114	9	24	6	1	1	8	2
Maurer, Ron, C	.263	19	3	5	0	0	0	0	0
*Melendez, Dan, DH	.238	189	19	45	10	0	1	29	0
Moore, Mike, OF	.240	200	21	48	10	4	2	21	8
Richardson, Brian, 3B	.323	62	10	20	1	1	0	7	0
Riggs, Adam, 2B	.283	506	68	143	31	6	14	66	16
Rios, Eddie, 3B	.277	242	29	67	11	2	5	37	2
Roberge, J.P., 3B	.293	232	28	68	14	2	6	27	9
Romero, Willie, OF	.295	444	66	131	36	6	6	48	21
*Spearman, Vernon, OF	.257	471	66	121	15	9	1	30	26
Stare, Lonny, OF	.224	67	7	15	2	0	0	4	2
Steed, Dave, C	.118	17	0	2	1	0	0	2	0
*Yard, Bruce, SS	.314	153	25	48	15	1	1	13	0

PITCHING	W	L	ERA	G	SV	IP	H	BB	SO
Ahearne, Pat	2	4	5.76	8	0	45.1	59	18	21
*Brunson, William	3	1	2.14	11	0	42.0	32	15	38
Camacho, Dan	1	1	2.70	4	0	16.2	11	17	11
Colon, Julio	2	3	4.46	6	0	36.1	35	17	14
Correa, Ramser	4	1	2.88	31	9	34.1	26	16	29
Garcia, Jose	2	0	0.00	8	2	11.1	4	0	8
Henderson, Ryan	3	3	3.82	39	6	63.2	59	29	46
Herges, Matt	3	2	2.71	30	3	83.0	83	28	45
Hollis, Ron	0	3	3.43	25	1	39.1	38	19	36
Jacobsen, Joe	1	4	4.19	38	5	58.0	62	24	39
LaGarde, Joseph	3	1	1.74	24	9	31.0	28	10	22
*Martinez, Jesus	10	13	4.40	27	0	161.2	157	92	124
Martinez, Ramon	0	0	0.00	1	0	2.2	0	3	1
Pincavitch, Kevin	0	0	5.63	11	0	16.0	26	10	11
Prado, Jose	2	1	5.01	18	1	32.1	32	24	20
*Price, Tom	0	4	9.36	7	0	25.0	50	3	11
*Pyc, Dave	7	5	2.98	14	0	96.2	106	24	62
*Roach, Petie	6	3	3.82	13	0	75.1	81	34	40
*Watts, Brandon	6	10	4.50	22	0	126.0	136	70	79
Weaver, Eric	10	5	3.30	18	0	122.2	106	44	69
*Zerbe, Chad	4	6	4.50	17	1	86.0	98	37	38

Shreveport Captains (Giants) AA

BATTING	AVG	AB	R	H	2B	3B	HR	RBI	SB
*Alguacil, Jose, 2B	.208	24	2	5	0	0	0	0	0
#Bess, Johnny, C	.246	175	25	43	10	3	7	30	1
DeLeon, Roberto, 2B	.236	263	30	62	11	4	4	34	0
#Duncan, Andres, 2B	.264	193	33	51	6	2	2	10	8
Florez, Tim, 2B	.273	66	9	18	1	0	2	8	2
Glenn, Darrin, C	.182	11	1	2	0	0	1	4	0
King, Brett, SS	.233	460	61	107	23	4	7	48	19
*Mayes, Craig, C	.400	40	5	16	2	0	0	3	0
Mirabelli, Doug, C	.295	380	60	112	23	0	21	70	0
Murray, Calvin, OF	.260	169	32	44	7	0	7	24	6
Phillips, Gary, 3B	.246	337	37	83	18	4	2	43	1
Powell, Dante, OF	.280	508	92	142	27	2	21	78	43
Ramirez, Hiram, C	.000	3	2	3	1	0	0	4	0

Batting leaders across all leagues

(Cont'd from previous page)

RUNS

Player	Club	Lg.	R
Cameron, Mike	Bir	Sou	120
T Jones, A.	Rmd	Int	115
T Berry, Mike	HD	Cal	112
T*Roberts, D.	Jax	Sou	112
Stcknschndr, E.	Sav	SAL	111
Davis, Eddie	SBr	Cal	107
*Monahan, S.	Lnc	Cal	107
*Catalanotto, F.	Jax	Sou	105
T*Ledee, Ricky	Col	Int	106
Urso, Joe	LkE	Cal	106
Kinkade, Mike	BLT	Mid	105
T*Neill, Mike	Mod	Cal	105
Raabe, Brian	SLk	PCL	103
*Branyan, R.	Clm	SAL	102
*Brede, Brent	SLk	PCL	102

WALKS

Player	Club	Lg.	BB
Evans, Tom	Knx	Sou	115
*Walker, Dane	WMi	Mid	112
Stcknschndr, E.	Sav	SAL	111
*Whitlock, Mike	Hag	SAL	108
T Allen, Dustin	RC	Cal	105
T Berry, Mike	HD	Cal	103
T Simonton, B.	Phx	PCL	102
T Deboer, Rob	Hvl	Sou	99
T*Roberts, D.	Jax	Sou	99
T Denbow, Don	SJ	Cal	98
#Moore, Kerwin	Edm	PCL	95
Goodhart, S.	CWV	SAL	94
Towle, Justin	W-S	Car	93
T Felix, Lauro	EIP	Tex	92
SEVERAL TIED AT 89			

Switch-hitter

* Left-handed

T Player has been with more than one team; listed with last team.

(Players in major leagues are listed with last minor league club.)

Batting leaders across all leagues

(Cont'd from previous page)

TOTAL BASES

Player	Club	Lg.	TB
*Walker, Todd	SLk	PCL	330
*Cromer, D.T.	Mod	Cal	316
T Guerrero, V.	Hrb	East	307
Hiatt, Phil	Tol	Int	304
T Trammell, B.	Tol	Int	297
T Jones, A.	Rmd	Int	290
*Kirgan, Chris	HD	Cal	287
T Hatcher, Chris	Tcn	PCL	286
T*Ledee, Ricky	Col	Int	285
Lee, Derrek	Mem	Sou	285
Cameron, Mike	Bir	Sou	284
*Barnes, Larry	CR	Mid	282
Kapler, Gabriel	Fay	SAL	280
Rohrmeier, Dan	Mem	Sou	279
SEVERAL TIED AT 277			

STRIKEOUTS

Player	Club	Lg.	K
Booty, Josh	KnC	Mid	195
T Kimsey, Keith	Jax	Sou	190
Hiatt, Phil	Tol	Int	180
Lee, Derrek	Mem	Sou	170
*Rolison, Nate	KnC	Mid	170
*Gainey, Bryon	Clb	SAL	169
*Haas, Chris	Peo	Mid	169
*Branyan, R.	Clm	SAL	166
Samuel, Cody	Gbo	SAL	165
#Bates, Fletcher	Clb	SAL	162
*Kirgan, Chris	HD	Cal	162
Scott, Thomas	CWV	SAL	156
T#Smith, Sloan	Tam	FSL	156
T Denbow, Don	SJ	Cal	153
T Wright, Ron	Car	Sou	151

BATTING	AVG	AB	R	H	2B	3B	HR	RBI	SB
Reid, Derek, OF	.246	118	16	29	4	0	4	18	2
*Rios, Armando, OF	.283	329	62	93	22	2	12	49	9
*Sbrocco, Jon, 2B	.244	82	16	20	2	1	1	5	5
Schneider, Dan, C	.238	21	3	5	1	0	2	6	0
Simonton, Benji, 1B	.249	469	86	117	25	1	23	76	6
*Singleton, Chris, OF	.298	500	68	149	31	9	5	72	27
Weaver, Terry, 3B	.125	8	1	1	0	0	0	1	0
Woods, Kenny, 3B	.279	287	36	80	17	1	1	29	14

PITCHING	W	L	ERA	G	SV	IP	H	BB	SO
*Brohawn, Troy	9	10	4.60	28	0	156.2	163	49	82
Castillo, Marino	5	5	3.58	38	3	50.1	48	14	53
Corps, Edwin	2	3	4.48	38	1	70.1	74	26	39
Foulke, Keith	12	7	2.76	27	0	182.2	149	35	129
Howry, Bobby	10	8	4.65	27	0	156.2	163	56	57
Hyde, Rich	1	2	5.94	19	1	33.1	36	12	25
Macey, Fausto	10	7	4.30	27	0	157.0	165	47	62
Ortiz, Russ	1	2	4.05	26	13	26.2	22	21	29
*Peterson, Mark	5	3	3.21	41	2	56.0	58	8	32
Phillips, Randy	1	4	3.23	35	4	69.2	77	21	31
*Pickett, Ricky	4	1	2.77	29	2	48.2	35	35	51
Purdy, Shawn	5	4	3.10	54	16	52.1	46	16	23
Taulbee, Andy	6	10	5.00	27	1	138.2	169	47	55
Villano, Mike	2	0	3.00	2	0	12.0	6	8	7

Tulsa Drillers (Rangers) AA

BATTING	AVG	AB	R	H	2B	3B	HR	RBI	SB
Arnold, Ken, 2B	.138	58	9	8	1	0	0	7	0
Bell, Mike, 3B	.267	484	62	129	31	3	16	59	3
*Blair, Brian, OF	.245	379	47	93	28	3	3	29	7
Brown, Kevin, C	.263	460	77	121	27	1	26	86	0
Charles, Frank, DH	.265	147	18	39	6	0	5	15	2
*Clark, Will, 1B	.222	9	3	2	0	0	0	0	0
Coolbaugh, Mike, 2B	.348	23	6	8	3	0	2	9	1
Cossins, Tim, C	.500	4	0	2	0	0	0	1	0
Diaz, Edwin, 2B	.264	500	70	132	33	6	16	65	8
Estrada, Osmani, 3B	.259	85	12	22	4	0	2	16	1
#Frias, Hanley, SS	.287	505	73	145	24	12	3	41	9
Kennedy, Darryl, C	.302	43	11	13	3	1	1	10	0
Little, Mark, OF	.291	409	69	119	24	2	13	50	22
*McFarlin, Jason, DH	.273	11	1	3	1	0	0	2	0
Murphy, Mike, OF	.231	121	22	28	7	2	4	16	1
O'Neill, Doug, OF	.307	75	8	23	3	0	5	15	1
*Sagmoen, Marc, OF	.282	387	58	109	21	6	10	62	5
*Sanders, Tracy, DH	.232	168	31	39	10	0	7	20	2
Smith, Bubba, 1B	.292	513	82	150	28	0	32	94	0
Texidor, Jose, OF	.256	301	34	77	15	0	11	37	2
*Thomas, Brian, OF	.222	9	0	2	0	0	0	0	0
*Unrat, Chris, C	.182	55	6	10	2	0	1	7	0

PITCHING	W	L	ERA	G	SV	IP	H	BB	SO
Brower, Jim	3	2	3.78	5	0	33.1	35	10	16
Castillo, Juan	6	6	5.04	19	0	89.1	94	49	37
Davis, Clint	3	3	1.88	32	10	48.0	31	12	40
Davis, Jeff	7	2	4.59	16	0	98.0	110	20	51
Geeve, Dave	7	6	5.55	18	0	82.2	105	23	60
Johnson, Jonathan	13	10	3.56	26	0	174.1	176	41	97
Keusch, Joe	0	0	17.18	8	0	11.0	25	5	8
Kolb, Danny	1	0	0.77	2	0	11.2	5	8	7
Lacy, Kerry	0	0	0.00	2	2	4.0	3	0	1
Manning, David	6	5	3.26	39	3	91.0	89	45	48
Martin, Jerry	5	4	4.94	36	5	85.2	98	42	49
*Martinez, Ramiro	0	2	8.56	11	0	13.2	23	5	7
Moody, Eric	8	4	3.57	44	16	95.2	92	23	80
Morvay, Joe	2	6	6.26	24	2	46.0	55	20	27
*O'Donoghue, John	2	4	4.18	27	0	79.2	89	23	46
Powell, John	3	8	4.89	39	4	114.0	121	31	79
Russell, Jeff	0	0	0.00	2	0	5.0	0	1	4
Sanders, Tracy	0	0	0.00	2	0	2.0	2	0	1
*Shea, John	0	1	13.97	9	0	9.2	23	5	4
Silva, Ted	7	2	2.99	11	0	75.1	72	16	27
*Smith, Dan	2	3	4.29	9	0	50.1	53	21	29
Texidor, Jose	0	0	13.50	2	0	2.0	3	3	3

Switch-hitter
* Left-handed
T Player has been with more than
one team; listed with last team.
(Players in major leagues are listed
with last minor league club.)

Wichita Wranglers (Royals) AA

BATTING	AVG	AB	R	H	2B	3B	HR	RBI	SB
Cameron, Stanton, OF	.143	7	0	1	0	0	0	2	0
Carr, Jeremy, OF	.260	453	69	118	23	2	6	40	41
Delaney, Sean, C	.208	48	5	10	3	0	2	5	2
Diaz, Lino, 3B	.252	159	18	40	8	1	3	19	2
Gonzalez, Raul, OF	.286	84	17	24	5	1	1	9	1
Hansen, Jed, 2B	.286	405	60	116	27	4	12	50	14
*Long, Kevin, OF	.273	436	62	119	31	3	3	48	9
Long, Ryan, OF	.283	442	64	125	29	1	20	78	6
Lopez, Mendy, 3B	.281	327	47	92	20	5	6	32	14
Martinez, Ramon, 2B	.344	93	16	32	4	1	1	8	4
Medrano, Anthony, SS	.274	474	59	130	26	1	8	55	10
#Morillo, Cesar, SS	.235	119	8	28	3	1	2	7	3
*Rodriguez, Boi, PH	.063	32	0	2	1	0	0	1	0
Sheppard, Don, OF	.216	97	12	21	2	0	3	12	3
Sisco, Steve, OF	.297	462	80	137	24	1	13	74	4
Stewart, Andy, C	.302	202	28	61	17	3	3	32	3
Strickland, Chad, C	.226	239	35	54	15	2	5	34	1
*Sutton, Larry, 1B	.296	463	84	137	22	2	22	84	4
Sweeney, Mike, DH	.319	235	45	75	18	1	14	51	3
*Tucker, Michael, OF	.450	20	4	9	1	3	0	7	0

PITCHING	W	L	ERA	G	SV	IP	H	BB	SO
Bevil, Brian	9	2	2.02	13	0	75.2	56	26	74
Bovee, Mike	10	11	4.84	27	0	176.2	223	46	102
*Byrdak, Tim	5	7	6.91	15	0	84.2	112	44	47
*Eddy, Chris	0	0	2.97	30	0	30.1	33	18	22
Evans, Bart	1	2	11.84	9	0	24.1	31	36	16
Gamboa, Javier	5	5	5.93	15	0	91.0	118	33	39
Grundy, Phillip	1	0	1.29	1	0	7.0	4	2	0
Harrison, Brian	9	2	3.66	49	6	118.0	118	14	80
*McDill, Allen	1	5	5.54	54	11	65.0	79	21	62
Morones, Geno	1	5	6.93	13	0	37.2	50	19	24
Olsen, Steve	6	0	2.77	15	1	55.1	40	14	39
Pittsley, Jim	3	0	0.41	3	0	22.0	9	5	7
*Rawitzer, Kevin	0	6	4.74	42	3	68.1	77	39	48
Ray, Ken	4	12	6.12	22	0	120.2	151	57	79
*Rosado, Jose	2	0	0.00	2	0	13.0	10	1	12
Smith, Toby	4	2	4.13	42	8	52.1	46	19	44
Telgheder, Jim	0	2	3.43	13	0	21.0	23	6	11
Torres, Dilson	5	3	3.88	9	1	55.2	62	13	27
Toth, Robert	4	6	3.78	19	4	104.2	100	24	51

Batting leaders across all leagues

(Cont'd from previous page)

SACRIFICE HITS

Player	Club	Lg.	SH
#Bieser, Steve	Ott	Int	23
Garcia, Jesse	HD	Cal	20
T Martinez, R.	Wch	Tex	20
T#Lopez, M.	Stk	Cal	19
King, Brett	Shr	Tex	17
T Burton, Essex	Rea	East	16
Baughman, J.	CR	Mid	15
Freel, Ryan	Dun	FSL	14
Garcia, Ossie	Peo	Mid	14
Gilbert, Shawn	Nor	Int	14
T#Martinez, G.	ElP	Tex	14
#Mercedes, G.	Kin	Car	14
T Morgan, Kevin	Bng	East	14
*Womack, Tony	Cgy	PCL	14
SEVERAL TIED AT 13			

SACRIFICE FLIES

Player	Club	Lg.	SF
#Durkac, Bo	VIS	Cal	16
T Allen, Marlon	W-S	Car	12
Garcia, Freddy	Lyn	Car	12
Sparks, Don	Buf	AmA	12
T Woodson, T.	Col	Int	12
Bellinger, Clay	Roc	Int	11
*Cruz, Jacob	Phx	PCL	11
Lee, Carlos	Hck	SAL	11
McNally, Shawn	Peo	Mid	11
Saunders, Chris	Bng	East	11
T Wood, Jason	Edm	PCL	11
Vessel, Andrew	Chl	FSL	11
SEVERAL TIED AT 10			

375

Switch-hitter
* Left-handed
T Player has been with more than one team; listed with last team.
(Players in major leagues are listed with last minor league club.)

Batting leaders across all leagues

(Cont'd from previous page)

HIT-BY-PITCH

Player	Club	Lg.	HBP
Kinkade, Mike	Blt	Mid	32
T Kendall, J.	Clw	FSL	30
T Hansen, T.	Jax	Sou	27
Schreimann, E.	Pdt	SAL	26
Vieira, Scott	Rkf	Mid	26
Joseph, Terry	Rkf	Mid	25
T Held, Dan	SWB	Int	23
McConnell, C.	REA	East	19
T Aven, Bruce	Buf	AmA	18
Eaglin, Mike	Dur	Car	18
Tinoco, Luis	Wsc	Mid	18
T Krause, Scott	Stk	Cal	17
T Amado, Jose	Lan	Mid	16
Cook, Jason	Lnc	Cal	16
Northeimer, J.	Clw	FSL	16

CAUGHT STEALING

Player	Club	Lg.	CS
#Castillo, Luis	Prt	East	28
*Robinson, K.	Peo	Mid	26
Solano, Fausto	Hag	SAL	25
T Powell, Dante	Phx	PCL	24
Davis, Eddie	SBr	Cal	23
T*Roberts, D.	Jax	Sou	22
T*Trippy, Joe	Dur	Car	22
T#Brown, A.	Car	Sou	20
T*Simpson, J.	Clb	SAL	20
*Weaver, Scott	Fay	SAL	20
SEVERAL TIED AT 19			

TOUGHEST TO STRIKE OUT

Player	Club	Lg.	TPA/SO
Raabe, Brian	SLk	PCL	28.37
T*Bridges, Kary	Tcn	PCL	24.23
Diaz, Einar	Can	East	19.00
Polanco, Placido	StP	FSL	17.12
Molina, Ben	Mdl	Tex	16.20
Hajek, Dave	Tcn	PCL	14.97
Ortiz, Luis	OkC	AmA	14.81
Cepeda, Jose	Lan	Mid	14.18
Medrano, A.	Wch	Tex	13.97
*Robles, Oscar	Kis	FSL	13.97
*Long, Kevin	Wch	Tex	13.89
Fortin, Troy	FtM	FSL	13.83
*Spearman, Vrnn	SAn	Tex	13.71
T Amado, Jose	Lan	Mid	13.65
LoDuca, Paul	VB	FSL	13.55

| *Switch-hitter*

* *Left-handed*

T *Player has been with more than one team; listed with last team.*
(Players in major leagues are listed with last minor league club)

Batting leaders across all leagues

SWITCH HITTERS

Player	Club	Lg.	BA
#Young, Dmitri	Lou	AmA	.333
T#Meluskey, M.	Jck	Tex	.326
#Bieser, Steve	Ott	Int	.322
#Olmeda, Jose	Chr	Int	.320
#Rennhack, M.	Stk	Cal	.320
#Castillo, Luis	Prt	East	.317
#Perez, Neifi	CSp	PCL	.316
T#Christian, E.	Mdl	Tex	.316
#Candaele, C.	Buf	AmA	.311
T#Wilson, E.	Buf	AmA	.307
T#Brown, Adrian	Car	Sou	.306
#Melo, Juan	RC	Cal	.304
#Patzke, Jeff	Knx	Sou	.303
#Mueller, Bill	Phx	PCL	.302
SEVERAL TIED AT .300			

Pitching leaders across all leagues

ERA (MINIMUM 112 IP)

Player	Club	Lg.	ERA
Reames, Britt	Peo	Mid	1.90
Figueroa, N.	Clb	SAL	2.04
Stein, Blake	StP	FSL	2.15
T Knoll, Randy	Clw	FSL	2.20
T Rodriguez, N.	Roc	Int	2.21
*McEntire, E.	Clb	SAL	2.22
*Mounce, Tony	Kis	FSL	2.25
T*Peters, Chris	Cgy	PCL	2.26
Trumpour, A.	Clb	SAL	2.29
Lyons, Curt	Cng	Sou	2.41
T Henthorne, K.	Tam	FSL	2.47
Sanders, F.	Clm	SAL	2.52
T Johnson, B.	Nvl	AmA	2.53
Gooch, Arnold	SLu	FSL	2.58
SEVERAL TIED AT 2.59			

WINS

Player	Club	Lg.	W
Blood, Darin	SJ	Cal	17
Hernandez, E.	Aug	SAL	17
T Silva, Ted	Tul	Tex	17
T Bevil, Brian	Oma	AmA	16
King, Bill	Mod	Cal	16
Kolb, Brandon	Cln	Mid	16
Neal, Billy	VB	FSL	16
Pavano, Carl	Tre	East	16
Stein, Blake	StP	FSL	16
SEVERAL TIED AT 15			

Pitching leaders across all leagues

COMPLETE GAMES

Player	Club	Lg.	CG
T Dickson, J.	Van	PCL	10
T Castillo, C.	PrW	Car	9
Figueroa, N.	Clb	SAL	8
T Johnson, J.	Tul	Tex	7
Suppan, Jeff	Paw	Int	7
Lidle, Cory	Bng	East	6
Minchey, Nate	Paw	Int	6
Pavano, Carl	Tre	East	6
T Silva, Ted	Tul	Tex	6
Springer, Dennis	Van	PCL	6
SEVERAL TIED AT 5			

SHUTOUTS

Player	Club	Lg.	SO
Figueroa, N.	Clb	SAL	4
T Morris, Matt	Lou	AmA	4
Coggin, David	Pdt	SAL	3
Johnson, Mike	Hag	SAL	3
T*Kell, Rob	Tul	Tex	3
T Knoll, Randy	Clw	FSL	3
T Maduro, C.	Roc	Int	3
Mattes, Troy	Del	SAL	3
T*Phelps, Tom	Hrb	East	3
SEVERAL TIED AT 2			

SAVES

Player	Club	Lg.	SV
Maloney, Sean	EIP	Tex	38
T Ortiz, Russ	Shr	Tex	36
Hernandez, S.	Bur	Mid	35
Tessmer, Jay	Tam	FSL	35
Corey, Bryan	Fay	SAL	34
Linares, Rich	SBr	Cal	33
T Fleetham, Ben	Hrb	East	31
T Jean, D.	Cng	Sou	31
T King, Curtis	StP	FSL	31
T*Butler, Adam	Grv	Sou	30
Greene, Rick	Jax	Sou	30
Hurst, William	Prt	East	30
T Macca, Chris	NHv	East	30

GAMES

Player	Club	Lg.	G
Tessmer, Jay	Tam	FSL	68
Gomes, Wayne	Rea	East	67
Arrandale, Matt	Lou	AmA	63
T*Martin, Tom	Jck	Tex	62
T Maskivish, J.	Aug	SAL	62
Matranga, Jeff	Ark	Tex	62
Nix, Jim	Cng	Sou	62
T Rios, Dan	Col	Int	62
Trlicek, Rick	Nor	Int	62
Hernandez, S.	Bur	Mid	61
Lankford, Frank	Nrw	East	61
T Rain, Steve	Iwa	AmA	61
*Sauveur, Rich	Nvl	AmA	61

Pitching leaders across all leagues

Pitching leaders across all leagues

Batting leaders by position

INNINGS PITCHED

Player	Club	Lg.	IP
T Edsell, Geoff	Van	PCL	193.0
T*Redman, M.	SLk	PCL	193.0
Lidle, Cory	Bng	East	190.1
T*Washburn, J.	Mdl	Tex	189.0
T Silva, Ted	Tul	Tex	188.2
Pena, Juan	Mch	Mid	187.2
Walker, Wade	Orl	Sou	187.2
Holt, Chris	Tcn	PCL	186.1
T Dickson, J.	Van	PCL	185.2
Santana, Julio	OkC	AmA	185.2

STRIKEOUTS

Player	Club	Lg.	SO
Figueroa, N.	Clb	SAL	200
T Young, Joe	Dun	FSL	193
Blood, Darin	SJ	Cal	193
*McEntire, E.	Clb	SAL	190
T*Dennis, S.	Mem	Sou	185
T Clement, M.	RC	Cal	184
T Bell, Jason	NBr	East	177
Lyons, Curt	Cng	Sou	176
*Reyes, Dennis	SBr	Cal	176
T*Redman, M.	SLk	PCL	175
Vazquez, Javier	Del	SAL	173
Burger, Rob	Pdt	SAL	171
Hernandez, E.	Aug	SAL	171
Santana, M.	Lnc	Cal	167
Reames, Britt	Peo	Mid	167

SO/9 IP RATIO (STARTERS)

Player	Club	Lg.	SO/9IP
Lyons, Curt	Cng	Sou	11.18
T Young, Joe	Dun	FSL	11.16
T Clement, M.	RC	Cal	10.85
Wood, Kerry	Day	FSL	10.71
Gagne, Eric	Sav	SAL	10.22
Blood, Darin	SJ	Cal	10.22
Helling, Rick	OkC	AmA	10.09
Hernandez, F.	Mem	Sou	9.83
*McEntire, Ethan	Clb	SAL	9.83
Hernandez, Elvn	Aug	SAL	9.76
Figueroa, Nlson	Clb	SAL	9.71
Burger, Rob	Pdt	SAL	9.62
T*Dennis, Shane	Mem	Sou	9.57
Santana, Marino	LNC	Cal	9.55
*Reyes, Dennis	SBr	Cal	9.54

AVERAGE AGAINST (STARTERS)

Player	Club	Lg.	BA
Reames, Britt	Peo	Mid	.170
Wood, Kerry	Day	FSL	.179
Figueroa, Nlson	Clb	SAL	.181
T Kolb, Danny	Tul	Tex	.197
*McEntire, Ethan	Clb	SAL	.198
Politte, Cliff	Peo	Mid	.199
Stein, Blake	StP	FSL	.203
*Saunders, Tony	Prt	East	.203
T Knoll, Randy	Clw	FSL	.206
T*Beech, Matt	SWB	Int	.209
Bruner, Clayton	Fay	SAL	.213
Gooch, Arnold	SLu	FSL	.213
T Quirico, Rafael	Nrw	East	.214
T*Moss, Dmn	Grv	Sou	.215
SEVERAL TIED AT .216			

SO/9 IP RATIO (RELIEVERS)

Player	Club	Lg.	SO/9IP
T Fleetham, Ben	Hrb	East	14.06
T Ortiz, Russ	Shr	Tex	13.07
T Giard, Ken	Dur	Car	12.46
Walter, Michael	QC	Mid	12.41
*Lowe, Ben	Hag	SAL	12.20
T Bussa, Todd	Cln	Mid	12.10
T Ricabal, Dan	Sav	SAL	12.02
T Bost, Heath	Ash	SAL	11.96
Scheffer, Aaron	Wsc	Mid	11.84
T Rath, Fred	FtM	FSL	11.72
Snyder, Matt	HD	Cal	11.63
T Hammack, B.	Day	FSL	11.57
T*Brooks, Antne	Dur	Car	11.56
Nyari, Pete	Pdt	SAL	11.52
Ligtenberg, Krry	Dur	Car	11.46

AVERAGE AGAINST (RELIEVERS)

Player	Club	Lg.	BA
T Fleetham, Ben	Hrb	East	.137
T Ricabal, Dan	Sav	SAL	.154
T Macca, Chris	NHv	East	.157
Hernandez, S.	Bur	Mid	.169
Walter, Michael	QC	Mid	.170
T Ortiz, Russ	Shr	Tex	.171
T Bost, Heath	Ash	SAL	.173
Corey, Bryan	Fay	SAL	.174
*Lowe, Ben	Hag	SAL	.176
*Prihoda, Stphn	Wil	Car	.177
Wallace, Derek	Nor	Int	.180
*Worrell, Steve	Nvl	AmA	.182
Brown, Alvin	SBr	Cal	.182
Dinyar, Eric	Lak	FSL	.188
SEVERAL TIED AT .189			

CATCHER

Player	Club	Lg.	BA
T*Mayes, Craig	SJ	Cal	.334
T#Meluskey, M.	Jck	Tex	.326
*Newstrom, D.	HD	Cal	.313
LoDuca, Paul	VB	FSL	.305
Widger, Chris	Tac	PCL	.304
McKeel, Walt	Tre	East	.302
T Sweeney, M.	Oma	AmA	.301
T Mirabelli, D.	Shr	Tex	.295
*Bako, Paul	Cng	Sou	.294
Nevin, Phil	Jax	Sou	.294
Morales, William	Hvl	Sou	.292
Thompson, K.	Wsc	Mid	.292
Mulligan, Sean	LVg	PCL	.288
Redmond, Mike	Prt	East	.287
Miller, Damian	SLk	PCL	.286

FIRST BASE

Player	Club	Lg.	BA
*Wilson, Desi	Phx	PCL	.339
T*Helton, Todd	CSp	PCL	.336
#Young, Dmitri	Lou	AmA	.333
*Casey, Sean	Kin	Car	.331
T*Valdez, Mario	Bir	Sou	.330
*Cromer, D.T.	Mod	Cal	.329
*Brown, Ray	Cng	Sou	.327
Vieira, Scott	Rkf	Mid	.324
Ball, Jeff	Tcn	PCL	.324
Wingate, Ervan	SBr	Cal	.324
*Arias, David	Wsc	Mid	.320
Millar, Kevin	Prt	East	.318
Ortiz, Luis	OkC	AmA	.317
*Barnes, Larry	CR	Mid	.317
*Zuber, Jon	SWB	Int	.311

SECOND BASE

Player	Club	Lg.	BA
Raabe, Brian	SLk	PCL	.351
Guerrero, Wilton	Abq	PCL	.344
T*Bridges, Kary	Tcn	PCL	.322
Hajek, Dave	Tcn	PCL	.317
#Castillo, Luis	Prt	East	.317
#Candaele, C.	Buf	AmA	.311
Almanzar, R.	Lak	FSL	.306
#Patzke, Jeff	Knx	Sou	.303
#Hall, Andy	Peo	Mid	.300
*Catalanotto, F.	Jax	Sou	.298
T*Malloy, Marty	Grv	Sou	.298
T*Sbrocco, Jon	Shr	Tex	.298
Febles, Carlos	Lan	Mid	.295
#Hall, Billy	Cng	Sou	.295
Jasco, Elinton	Rkf	Mid	.293

 # Switch-hitter

* Left-handed

T Player has been with more than one team; listed with last team.
(Players in major leagues are listed with last minor league club

Batting leaders
by position

THIRD BASE

Player	Club	Lg.	BA
T Berry, Mike	HD	Cal	.354
*Walker, Todd	SLk	PCL	.339
Castellano, P.	CSp	PCL	.337
Clark, Phil	Paw	Int	.325
T Rolen, Scott	SWB	Int	.324
*Franco, Matt	Nor	Int	.323
#Olmeda, Jose	Chr	Int	.320
Seitzer, Brad	EIP	Tex	.319
T Amado, Jose	Lan	Mid	.318
Lee, Carlos	Hck	SAL	.313
Short, Rick	Fre	Car	.312
Fernandez, A.	RC	Cal	.308
T#Wilson, E.	Buf	AmA	.307
*Secrist, Reed	Cgy	PCL	.307
Garcia, Freddy	Lyn	Car	.306

SHORTSTOP

Player	Club	Lg.	BA
#Perez, Neifi	CSp	PCL	.316
Johnson, Russ	Jck	Tex	.310
Ledesma, A.	Van	PCL	.305
#Melo, Juan	RC	Cal	.304
Berg, David	Prt	East	.302
Bellinger, Clay	Roc	Int	.301
Sheldon, Scott	Edm	PCL	.300
*Womack, Tony	Cgy	PCL	.300
Lugo, Julio	QC	Mid	.295
Cruz, Deivi	Bur	Mid	.294
T Raynor, Mark	Pdt	SAL	.292
#Frias, Hanley	Tul	Tex	.287
T*Yard, Bruce	SAn	Tex	.287
T#Norton, Greg	Nvl	AmA	.284
#Prieto, A.	Wil	Car	.284

OUTFIELD

Player	Club	Lg.	BA
T Guerrero, V.	Hrb	East	.360
*Robinson, K.	Peo	Mid	.359
*McMillon, Billy	Chr	Int	.352
*Brede, Brent	SLk	PCL	.348
Dunn, Todd	EIP	Tex	.340
T Jones, A.	Rmd	Int	.339
Hyzdu, Adam	Tre	East	.337
Echevarria, A.	CSp	PCL	.337
T Brinkley, D.	Mem	Sou	.333
T*Neill, Mike	Mod	Cal	.331
Allensworth, J.	Cgy	PCL	.330
T Ramirez, Alex	Can	East	.329
Abbott, Jeff	Nvl	AmA	.325
T*Leach, Jalal	Ott	Int	.325
SEVERAL TIED AT .322			

Youth leagues

▶Practice makes perfect for Little League champs
▶Championship scores

▶A baseball magazine for kids
▶How to find a team
▶*and more...*

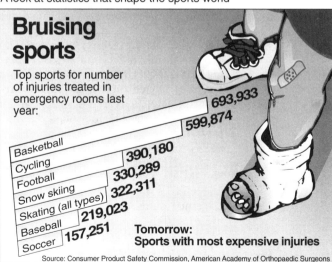

USA SNAPSHOTS®

A look at statistics that shape the sports world

Bruising sports

Top sports for number of injuries treated in emergency rooms last year:

Sport	Injuries
Basketball	693,933
Cycling	599,874
Football	390,180
Snow skiing	330,289
Skating (all types)	322,311
Baseball	219,023
Soccer	157,251

Tomorrow: Sports with most expensive injuries

Source: Consumer Product Safety Commission, American Academy of Orthopaedic Surgeons

By Scott Boeck and Web Bryant, USA TODAY

PONY championship scores

▶**Mustang (9-10):** Tamiami (Fla.) 9, Humble (Texas) 2

▶**Bronco (11-12):** Anaheim 6, Seoul (South Korea) 1

▶**Pony (13-14):** Kao-Hsiung (Taiwan) 4, Evansville (Ind.) 0

▶**Colt (15-16):** Corona (Ill.) 10, Will County (Ill.) 0

▶**Palomino (17-18):** Suffolk (Va.) 5, Long Island (N.Y.) 2

Little League championship: Practice makes perfect

It was over early. Real early. At about 6:45 a.m. on Saturday, as the first 15 of 35,000 fans staked their claim to prime positions on the two steep hills beyond Lamade Stadium's outfield wall, manager Ho Tung-Yu and his Little Leaguers from Kao-Hsiung, Chinese Taipei, were quietly marching, two abreast, toward the place where every World Series championship is won—practice.

While 12-year-old Cranston, R.I., pitcher Tom Michael and his upstart teammates slept in anticipation of the big day, Hsieh Chin-Hsiung—a 4-foot-11, 95-pounder who says he'd like to join his hero, Ken Griffey Jr., in a Seattle Mariners uniform one day—was all business during a 2½-hour sunrise session in the batting cages. Wanna guess who won?

Actually, Kao-Hsiung's 13-3, five-inning triumph, its nation's 17th in 21 trips to Williamsport, was as unusual as this team from the southwest coast of Taiwan itself. Tossing aside the stoicism of their predecessors, the wide-eyed, fun-seeking bunch from Fu-Hsing Elementary School delighted in joining locals sliding down the hills on cardboard flats. Their coaches sneaked pictures of each other sliding into second base after games. By week's end, Ho's players were dancing (in a perfect line, of course) to the Macarena as if their batting averages depended on it—even in the middle of the third inning, as a nervous 4-2 lead against Cranston seemed anything but secure.

But before play comes work. You'll never hear a quieter practice, or see a more efficient one. Equipment bags were placed neatly alongside each other. Players enthusiastically did 15 minutes of running and stretching drills, then 50 jumping jacks. Caps were removed and eyes riveted on Ho as the 28-year-old gardener-turned-coach delivered a short game-day message. Then 14 players rotated around the four batting cages for two hours without missing a beat. Or a pitch.

"Discipline is an important part of baseball training everywhere in Taiwan," said team interpreter Chang Shih-Ming, a 45-year-old college professor who lives 250 miles from Kao-Hsiung, Taiwan's leading port. "The first thing Americans notice is that we look like a machine, but they're still kids. It's just that during lessons, they are concentrating."

The smallest team in the eight-team tournament despite the imposing presence of 5-foot-9 pitcher Yang Chia-Chen, Kao-Hsiung "wasn't supposed to be one of the best teams" in its country, Chang said. Nor was Cranston, which upset Panama City, Fla., 6-3 in the semifinals after going 1-2 in pool play.

"It's been a great experience for the whole team and the coaches just to be here," Ho told the media as his team laughed its way to the final, outscoring its opponents 49-6. But privately he confided that his team would "not lose to an American team if we play fundamentally and nothing extraordinary happens." When a third-inning double by Wu Chao-Kuan turned into a 7-6-2-5 double play that left the bases empty, Ho's words seemed to be coming back to haunt him.

Michael and catcher Craig Stinson had homered to chase starter Cheng Chi-Hung in the first, and now Cranston was thinking upset. But Ho knew what to say: Go have fun. And it was Macarena to the rescue. "I thought it would be a good opportunity for the kids to dance, have a good time and relax," Ho said after the game. "I think that helped a lot."

Kao-Hsiung then erupted for nine runs in the fourth and fifth innings. Hsieh blasted a three-run homer, his seventh of the week and a Series record. Chiu Chi-Pen allowed only one run and three hits, striking out nine, after relieving Cheng with the score tied 2-2.

When it was over, the boys from Kao-Hsiung showed their appreciation—and their arms—by lobbing balls into the outfield crowd. With them went a lot of myths about the kids from Taiwan.

—by Donnie Wilkie

New magazine geared to youth

He looked on newsstands. He went to the library and dug through mounds of microfilm. He wrote letters. Yet publisher Dave Destler couldn't come up with an answer for his 7-year-old son, Dusty, who kept asking, "Daddy, why are there no baseball magazines for kids?"

Destler, 41, and his wife, Dayna, 39, think that they've answered their son with the launching of *Junior League Baseball*, whose colorful, slick debut issue ran 44 pages and covered everything from "Little League elbow" to how bats are made to former Los Angeles Dodgers manager Tommy Lasorda lecturing kids—and their parents.

"We did a lot of research after my son asked me that question, and were amazed that no one has done this," Destler says. "It took us four years to get this off the ground ... and the entire time, we were holding our breath, hoping that Time [Inc.] or some other big corporation wasn't doing the exact same thing."

The Destlers, who live in West Hills, Calif., had published *British Cars* magazine since 1985, but decided to sell it and start anew. "We were sucked up by the

NABF championship scores

▸**Freshman (11-12):** Columbus (Ohio) 6, Nashville 4

▸**Sophomore (13-14):** Norman (Okla.) 13, Miamisburg (Ohio) 8

▸**Junior (15-16):** Bayside (N.Y.) 9, Mobile (Ala.) 5

▸**Senior (17-18):** Jackson (Miss.) 6, New Lenox (Ill.) 2

▸**High school:** Indianapolis 4, Apopka (Fla.) 0

American Legion World Series scores

Yardley (Pa.) 6, Gonzales (La.) 3

Babe Ruth championship scores

▶**Bambino (11-12):** Oakland 6, Henderson (Ky.) 0

▶**13 year olds:** Nederland (Texas) 5, Lompoc (Calif.) 4

▶**13-15 year olds:** Vancouver (Wash.) 8, Brazoswood (Texas) 3

▶**16 year olds:** W. Torrance (Calif.) 5, Nashville 3

▶**16-18 year olds:** Nashville 3, Alacosta (Calif.) 2

AABC championship scores

▶**Roberto Clemente (8 and under):** Puerto Rico 19, Dallas 5

▶**Willie Mays (10 and under):** Houston 6, Montebello (Calif.) 5

▶**Pee Wee Reese (12 and under):** Houston 16, Adefaico (P.R.) 4

▶**Sandy Koufax (14 and under):** Houston 9, Michigan 8

▶**Mickey Mantle (16 and under):** Encinitas (Calif.) 14, Dallas 5

▶**Connie Mack (18 and under):** Dallas 23, Memphis 5

whole youth-baseball thing," Destler says, laughing. "I had gotten involved in coaching teams, and my wife was a team mom and scorekeeper. Once you're in it, it sort of drives your agenda. But we also realized there were others all around us who were just as enthusiastic as we were, just as involved." So as Dusty reached his 10th birthday (he's now 11) and was playing second base for the national AAU champion Valley Vipers, *Junior League Baseball* was nearing its start-up with a full-time staff of five. The first issue, with Dusty on the cover ("publisher's prerogative," says the proud father), came out in August 1996. The magazine will be coming out monthly.

"We worked our hardest to come up with a reason not to do it," Destler says of his four years of research and planning. "If you can't, then at some point you give it the green light and just go for it."

Destler visited the Easton sports-equipment factory in Van Nuys, Calif., for the feature on the production and testing of bats. And he sat down for an interview with Dodgers rookie outfielder Todd Hollandsworth, who says that even at the major league level, the game is "kids playing baseball, it's kids having fun."

Junior League Baseball is about kids—no matter what page you turn to. "The Rookie Club" is written at a second-grade reading level; "Coach Don Sez" targets the fifth-grade-and-up group; and "All-Star Clinic" addresses seventh-graders. (Coach Don, by the way, is Don Marsh, author of *101 Things You Can Teach Your Kids About Baseball*.) Issues and subjects that the magazine plans to address include children's health, safety, fitness and nutrition; how to deal with tough coaches; practice time versus homework; and how youngsters can improve their skills.

But the Destlers don't want to forget Mom and Dad. "They're the ones who sign up the kids, drive them to practices and games—and, in many cases, are the ones who really need this kind of information," he says. "We want the kids and parents to fight over every issue."

—*by Donnie Wilkie*

Wisconsin family plays game with relish

Baseball and the Kaebisch family of Milwaukee go together like hot dogs and mustard. The folks at French's Mustard thought so, too, and made them the Youth Baseball Family of the Year. In the Kaebisches' decade of involvement, parents Terry and Kathy have built and maintained ball fields, coached teams, ordered uniforms, headed up everything from concession stands to boards of directors—and raised more than $100,000 for the Germantown, Wis., Little League.

"They started when I was about 7," says Ben, now 17 and pitching for his high school team, "and about three years in, I think they really started going at it.... They put forth the most effort compared to the other parents I see. They really love baseball."

They were just the type of people that French's was looking for when it began a two-year program in cooperation with USA Baseball, the national governing body of amateur baseball in the United States. "Families have been an important part of French's Mustard for more than 90 years," said Sherri Kantor, a spokeswoman for the company. "There is no better way to celebrate our association ... than to honor the Kaebisches. They have truly enriched the game of baseball in their communities." The Kaebisches, picked from among a group of 40 state winners, were rewarded with a trip to the Summer Olympics in Atlanta.

Terry, 44, manages a lawn and garden center. Kathy, 43, is a speech therapist in the Germantown school district. Ben is a talented left-handed pitcher with an 85-mph fastball and two no-hitters as a high school junior; Chris, 14, is already a nine-year Little League veteran; and Mollie, 9, is one of only two girls playing baseball in the Germantown league.

"We're thankful that someone recognizes us the way French's has, but the work we've done has been for the kids," Terry Kaebisch said. "In Little League, everything is about volunteering. It's what Little League parents do. But there are so many other people everywhere who give up their time, too."

The family was nominated for the award by Dan Krueger, a second-grade teacher in Germantown. "I did it as a way of saying, 'What you're doing is great for Germantown,' " Krueger said. "Positive recognition is important for anyone who donates their time, but with the Kaebisches, we're talking about thousands and thousands of hours."

Terry, the first coach to take a Germantown All-Star team to the state tournament (he did it twice), juggles his work with coaching two teams, but he concedes that his wife, thanks to her job, knows the players as well as he does—or better. She acts as a scout, checking with physical education teachers about the kids before her husband drafts the players.

"We just do it," Kathy said. "It's the one thing we all do as a family. To get an award for this is like wanting to be a ballplayer your whole life and then having someone pay you to do it."

—by Donnie Wilkie

Dixie championship scores

▸**Youth (11-12):** Philadelphia (Miss.) 13, Decatur (Ala.) 3

▸**Dixie Boys (13-14):** Valdosta (Ga.) 8, Florence (S.C.) 1

▸**Pre-majors (15-16):** Auburn-Montgomery (Ala.) 10, Vinton (Va.) 0

▸**Majors (15-18):** Columbia County (Ga.) 2, Lufkin (Texas) 0

CABA championship scores

▶**9 and under:** Honolulu 12, Marysville (Ohio) 6

▶**10 and under:** Columbus (Ohio) 3, Houston 2

▶**11 and under:** Germantown (Tenn.) 5, Denver 2

▶**12 and under:** Carolina (P.R.) 10, Atlanta 1

▶**13 and under:** Dallas 25, Greenwood (Ill.) 5

▶**14 and under:** Encinitas (Calif.) 3, Baltimore 2

▶**15 and under:** Hawaii 6, Crystal Lake (Ill.) 3

▶**16 and under:** Paramount (Calif.) 17, Kansas City (Mo.) 13

▶**High school:** Brooklyn, (N.Y.) 8, Honolulu 6

▶**18 and under:** Wisconsin 10, Lombard (Ill.) 2

Who's playing the field

▶**American Amateur Baseball Congress:** Founded in 1935. 12,895 teams, 257,900 players. Ages: 8-up.

▶**American Legion Baseball:** Founded in 1925. 4,680 teams, 84,000 players. Ages: 16-18.

▶**Babe Ruth League Inc.:** Founded in 1951. 5,800 leagues, 41,000 teams, 815,000 players in baseball; 3,500 teams, 70,000 participants in softball. Ages: 5-18.

▶**Continental Amateur Baseball Association:** Founded in 1984. 1,379 leagues, 8,274 teams, approximately 124,110 players. Ages: 9-18.

▶**Dixie Baseball Inc. (includes Dixie Softball):** Founded in 1956. 24,241 baseball teams, 363,615 players; 4,369 softball teams, 65,535 players (total 429,150 players, 11 states). Ages: 4-18.

▶**Little League Baseball Inc.:** Founded in 1939. 196,000 teams, 2.7 million participants in the USA, 3 million worldwide. Ages: 5-18.

▶**National Amateur Baseball Federation:** Founded in 1914. 5,000 teams, 110,000 players (who advance into tournament competition). Ages: 12-up (including 30-and-over leagues).

▶**National Police Athletic League Baseball:** Founded in 1960. 200,000 players in regional and national tournaments. Ages: 14-16.

▶**PONY Baseball/Softball Inc.:** Founded in 1951. 28,500 teams, nearly 400,000 athletes in 45 states and 12 foreign countries. 2,000 softball teams. Ages: 5-18.

How to find a team

To find a team in your area, contact the national headquarters listed below for a regional reference.

▶**American Amateur Baseball Congress:** 118-19 Redfield Plaza, P.O. Box 467, Marshall, MI 49068; (616) 781-2002.

▶**American Legion:** P.O. Box 1055, Indianapolis, IN 46206; (317) 630-1213.

▶**Babe Ruth League:** 1771 Brunswick Ave., P.O. Box 5000, Trenton, NJ; (609) 695-1434.

▶**Continental Amateur Baseball Association:** 82 University St., Westerville, OH 43081; (614) 899-2103.

▶**Dixie Baseball:** P.O. Box 222, Lookout Mountain, TN 37350; (615) 821-6811.

▶**Little League:** P.O. Box 3485, Williamsport, PA 17701; (717) 326-1921.

▶**National Amateur Baseball Federation:** P.O. Box 705, Bowie, MD 20718; (301) 262-5005.

▶**National Police Athletic League:** 614 U.S. Hwy. 1, Ste. 20, North Palm Beach, FL 33408; (407) 844-1823.

▶**PONY Baseball/Softball:** P.O. Box 225, Washington, PA 15301-0225; (412) 225-1060.

High school/ college/Olympics

- ▸**1996 Super 25 high schools**
- ▸**All-USA high school teams**
- ▸**1996 Olympics**

- ▸**1996 Top 25 college coaches' poll**
- ▸**1997 college preview**
- ▸**1996 College World Series**
- ▸*and more ...*

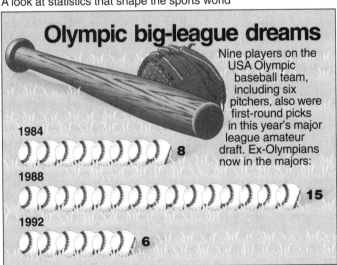

USA SNAPSHOTS®

A look at statistics that shape the sports world

Olympic big-league dreams

Nine players on the USA Olympic baseball team, including six pitchers, also were first-round picks in this year's major league amateur draft. Ex-Olympians now in the majors:

1984 8

1988 15

1992 6

Source: *Baseball America*

By Scott Boeck and Marcy E. Mullins, USA TODAY

USA TODAY Super 25: Final 1996 high school rankings

▶1. **Westminster Christian, Miami (36-0-1)** Season recap: Won Class 2A state title, Dole National Classic and second USA TODAY national title. Junior Manny Crespo batted .468 with 10 HR, 45 runs and 32 RBI. K.O. Wiegandt (13-0, 1.03 ERA) tied school record for wins.

▶2. **Kennedy, Granada Hills, Calif. (31-3)** Season recap: Won second consecutive Los Angeles Class 4A city title. Derek Morse was 15-0 with a 1.62 ERA, striking out 119 in 99⅓ innings. Junior Jon Garland was 11-1 with 1.77 ERA and batted .303 with seven HR and 28 RBI.

▶3. **Key West, Fla. (31-5)** Season recap: Won second consecutive Class 4A state title and a Florida-record ninth overall title. Team hit .322. Craig Lariz batted .482 with eight HR and a school-record 54 RBI. Junior Randy Sterling was 8-2 with a 1.65 ERA.

▶4. **Monterey, Lubbock, Texas (36-3)** Season recap: Won fourth Class 5A state title. Mark Martinez was 17-0 with a 1.55 ERA, striking out 177 in 103⅔ innings. Dusty Hart batted .444 with 32 runs and 54 RBI.

▶5. **Horizon, Scottsdale, Ariz. (32-2)** Season recap: Won second consecutive Class 5A state title, setting a 5A record with 32 wins. Also set school records with 387 hits and 290 runs. Jared Berkowitz was 16-0 with a 1.42 ERA. Russ Jacobson batted .459 with seven HR and 36 RBI.

▶6. **Bishop Amat, La Puente, Calif. (24-6)** Season recap: Won first Southern Section Division I title, setting school records with 351 hits and 290 runs, averaging 9.7 runs a game. Steve Wood batted .462 with 32 runs and 38 RBI. Eric Valentine was 9-1 with a 1.34 ERA. Joe Hurka batted .461 with 39 RBI.

▶7. **Mission Bay, San Diego (29-5)** Season recap: Won second consecutive San Diego Section Division II title. Catcher Josh Glassey batted .314 with eight HR, 41 RBI and just two errors. Kevin Reese was 11-0 with a 1.86 ERA and batted .414 with six HR and 39 RBI.

▶8. **Cherry Creek, Englewood, Colo. (22-0)** Season recap: Won fourth Class 5A state title with second unbeaten season. Set school records with .450 team batting average, 43 HR and 258 RBI. Junior Darnell McDonald batted .581 with a school-record 15 HR and 48 RBI. Catcher Josh Bard batted .519 with nine HR and 36 RBI and threw out 15 of 16 base stealers.

▶9. **Glen Oak, Canton, Ohio (24-2)** Season recap: First public school in state with back-to-back Division I state titles. Set school records with 24 HR and a .956 fielding percentage. Mike Muzi was 8-0 (25-0 career) with a 1.62 ERA and batted .435 with seven HR and 42 RBI. Greg McClellan batted .388 with five HR and 29 RBI.

▶10. **Tottenville, Staten Island, N.Y. (33-1)** Season recap: Won fifth PSAL Class A title. Jason Marquis was 14-1 with three saves and an 0.71 ERA, striking out 136 and walking 22 in 82 innings. He batted .468 with 11 HR and 45 RBI. Greg Belson was 10-0 with an 0.88 ERA.

▶11. **North Allegheny, Wexford, Pa. (24-2)** Season recap: Won first Class 3A state title after finishing second in 1991, '93 and '94. John Korn set school records with 10 victories (1 loss) and 102 strikeouts. Jeremy Purcell batted .323 with 21 RBI and a school-record 13 doubles.

▶12. **New Hope, Columbus, Miss. (43-0)** Season recap: Won Class 4A state title with state-record 43 victories. Junior Robert Shelton batted .431 with eight HR, 53 RBI and a school-record 57 runs. Leslie West batted .386 with 30 walks and 43 runs and also was 7-0 with a 2.38 ERA. Buddy Wyers was 10-0 with a 1.88 ERA.

▶**13. Tahlequah, Okla. (29-2)** Season recap: Class 6A state champion. Set 18 school records, including team batting average (.327) and ERA (1.27). Matt Hendrix batted .473 with nine HR and 45 RBI. Chad Cole batted .408 with 11 HR, 43 RBI and a school-record 45 runs. Sophomore Jason Akin hit a school-record 12 HR.

▶**14. Lee County, Sanford, N.C. (26-2)** Season recap: Won first Class 4A state title, setting school records for team batting average (.332), ERA (1.90) and victories (26). Mark Osborne batted .469 with 31 RBI and was 3-0 with seven saves. Junior Danny Borrell batted .420 with 41 RBI and was 12-0 with a 1.70 ERA.

▶**15. South Kitsap, Port Orchard, Wash. (23-0)** Season recap: Won second Class 3A state title with first undefeated season. Willie Bloomquist batted .463 with 35 runs, 25 RBI and a school-record 20 stolen bases. Jason Ellison batted .384 with 26 RBI and 20 runs and was 10-0 (20-0 career) with an 0.89 ERA and 124 strikeouts in 70⅔ innings.

▶**16. Frank W. Cox, Virginia Beach, Va. (27-1)** Season recap: Won first Class 3A state title and had team batting average of .383. Junior Jason DuBois was 10-0 with a 1.23 ERA, batting .482 with seven HR and 41 RBI. Tim LaVigne batted .454 with eight HR and 36 RBI.

▶**17. Columbus, Ga. (30-4)** Season recap: Won third consecutive Class 3A state title. Mike VanBiber batted .402 with 24 RBI. Brent Schoening was 12-2 with four saves and an 0.87 ERA, striking out 137 in 88⅔ innings.

▶**18. Tampa Jesuit (32-4)** Season recap: Eliminated in Class 4A state semifinals. Ronnie Merrill batted .415 with 39 runs and 25 RBI. Sam Marsonek was 12-1 with an 0.98 ERA, striking out 153 in 93 innings. Nick Stocks was 13-1 with a 1.02 ERA.

▶**19. Fontana, Calif. (25-2)** Season recap: Eliminated in Southern Section Division I quarterfinals. Kris Stevens was 12-1 with four shutouts and a 1.14 ERA, striking out 115 in 80 innings. He set school career records with 30 victories (4 losses), 299 strikeouts and a 1.03

ERA. Junior Robert Womack batted .527 with school records for hits (49), runs (40) and doubles (9).

▶**20. Gloucester (N.J.) Catholic (29-2-1)** Season recap: Won eighth Parochial B state title. Sophomore Pat Sperone was 8-0 with a 1.40 ERA, a no-hitter and two two-hitters. Junior Brian Ward batted .481 with 48 RBI.

▶**21. Wootton, Rockville, Md. (16-3)** Season recap: Won first Class 4A state title. Junior Brian Link batted .446 with 31 runs and 14 RBI. Sophomore Joey Popovich was 8-1 with a 1.22 ERA, striking out 105 in 69 innings.

▶**22. Mater Dei, Santa Ana, Calif. (24-4)** Season recap: Eliminated in Southern Section Division I semifinals. Mike Hessman was 9-0 with a 2.10 ERA and batted .413 with 11 HR and 30 RBI, setting career school record with 25 HR. Junior Mike Kolbach was 10-1 with a 2.27 ERA and led team with .443 batting average and 38 RBI.

▶**23. Ralston, Neb. (26-1)** Season recap: Won sixth Class A state title in last 11 years with a school-record 26 victories. The team batted .343 and had an ERA of 1.88. Junior Jeremy Clark batted .467 with 13 doubles and 31 RBI. Brian Doerr was 10-0, tying school record for victories.

▶**24. Mount Pleasant, Mich. (31-4)** Season recap: Won Class A state title. Junior Jeff Dzingle was 12-2 with five saves and a 1.10 ERA, striking out 143 in 108 innings. Jake Fuller batted .473 with 32 runs and 22 RBI.

▶**25. Glenwood, Chatham, Ill. (31-6)** Season recap: Won first Class 2A state title. Junior Jason Werth batted .463 with five HR, 51 runs and 36 RBI. Junior Matt Whalen batted .418 with 41 RBI. Junior Jay Crawford was 12-1 with a 1.75 ERA. Adam Feld was 12-0, setting school records with 100 strikeouts and 34 career victories (1 loss).

—ranked by Dave Krider,
USA TODAY

1996 USA TODAY All-USA high school team

Player of the year:
Pitcher Matt White

School: Waynesboro (Pa.)
Ht.: 6-5 / **Wt.:** 230 / **Class:** Senior / **Position:** RHP / **B-T:** R-R
1996 statistics: W-L: 10-1. ERA: 0.66. IP: 74⅓. BB: 16. SO: 131.
Quick facts: Set school career records with 29 victories (4 losses), 401 strikeouts and an 0.79 ERA. Set single-season record with 0.66 ERA and single-game record with 20 strikeouts. Had three no-hitters as senior.
Drafted by: San Francisco Giants (No. 7 in first round), became free agent.

First team

▸John Patterson
School: West Orange Stark (Orange, Texas)
Ht.: 6-6 / **Wt.:** 187 / **Class:** Senior / **Position:** RHP / **B-T:** R-R
1996 Statistics: W-L: 7-2. ERA: 0.77. IP: 72⅓. BB: 36. SO: 142.
Drafted by: Montreal Expos (No. 5 in first round), became free agent, signed with Arizona Diamondbacks.

▸Eric Munson
School: Mount Carmel (San Diego)
Ht.: 6-3 / **Wt.:** 210 / **Class:** Senior / **Position:** C / **B-T:** L-R
1996 Statistics: BA: .432. Hits: 38. 2B: 6. HR: 10. RBI: 30. R: 29. SB: 18. BB: 22.
Drafted by: Atlanta Braves, did not sign; signed with University of Southern California.

▸Brent Abernathy
School: Lovett (Atlanta)
Ht.: 6-0 / **Wt.:** 185 / **Class:** Senior / **Position:** SS / **B-T:** R-R
1996 Statistics: BA: .635. OBA: .706. SA: 1.190. Hits: 80. 2B: 23. 3B: 4. HR: 13. RBI: 50.
Signed by: Toronto Blue Jays.

▸Eric Chavez
School: Mount Carmel (San Diego)
Ht.: 6-1 / **Wt.:** 190 / **Class:** Senior / **Position:** SS / **B-T:** L-R
1996 Statistics: BA: .458. Hits: 44. 2B: 8. 3B: 3. HR: 11. RBI: 24. R: 37. SB: 33.
Drafted by: Oakland A's (No. 10 in first round), signed.

▸Joe Lawrence
School: Barbe (Lake Charles, La.)
Ht.: 6-2 / **Wt.:** 190 / **Class:** Senior / **Position:** SS / **B-T:** L-R
1996 Statistics: BA: .449. OBA: .590. SA: .955. Hits: 40. 2B: 8. 3B: 5. HR: 9. RBI: 38.

Drafted by: Toronto Blue Jays (No. 16 in first round), signed.

▸Jimmy Rollins
School: Encinal (Alameda, Calif.)
Ht.: 5-8 / **Wt.:** 165 / **Class:** Senior / **Position:** SS / **B-T:** B-R
1996 Statistics: BA: .510. OBA: .670. SA: .924. Hits: 54. 2B: 16. 3B: 3. HR: 6. RBI: 39.
Drafted by: Philadelphia Phillies, signed.

▸Dermal Brown
School: Central (Marlboro, N.Y.)
Ht.: 6-1 / **Wt.:** 210 / **Class:** Senior / **Position:** CF / **B-T:** L-R
1996 Statistics: BA: .450. Hits: 27. 2B: 4. 3B: 1. HR: 9. RBI: 36. R: 36. SB: 20. BB: 31.
Drafted by: Kansas City Royals (No. 14 in first round), signed.

▸Darnell McDonald
School: Cherry Creek (Englewood, Colo.)
Ht.: 5-11 / **Wt.:** 190 / **Class:** Junior / **Position:** CF / **B-T:** R-R
1996 Statistics: BA: .581. OBA: 656. SA: 1.392. Hits: 43. 2B: 11. 3B: 2. HR: 15. RBI: 48.

▸John Oliver
School: Lake-Lehman (Lehman, Pa.)
Ht.: 6-3 / **Wt.:** 185 / **Class:** Senior / **Position:** CF / **B-T:** R-R
1996 Statistics: BA: .604. OBA: .654. SA: 1.055. Hits: 55. 2B: 12. 3B: 3. HR: 11. RBI: 43.
Drafted by: Cincinnati Reds (No. 25 in first round), signed.

Coach of the year:
Rich Hofman

School: Westminster Christian (Miami).
Age: 51 **Family:** Wife, Jo; children, James (30), Laura (26), David (22), Chip (21) and Chris (20).
College: Calvin (graduated in 1966), Western Michigan (master's degree in 1968).
1996 record: 36-0-1 (Class 2A state champion; No. 1 in USA TODAY Super 25 rankings).
Career record and titles: 667-178 in 28 years. Won six state titles and two national titles (also USA TODAY champion in 1992). Also national coach of year in 1988 (American Baseball Coaches Association) and 1992 (USA TODAY and National High School Baseball Coaches Association).

Olympics: USA fails under pressure, settles for bronze

After failing to win a medal in the Barcelona Olympics in '92, USA Baseball made an ambitious plan for Atlanta in '96. More than $5 million was spent on the team in the past two summers. Twelve players on the 20-man Olympic roster played both years, and U.S. coach Skip Bertman often recounted how everything went exactly as planned.

However, one thing might have been overlooked in the entire process: Through the round-robin stage of the Olympics, the U.S. team never had to play a must-win game. Then came the Olympic semifinal, and the USA got hammered 11-2 by Japan. "We played poorly, [and] we weren't able to beat a team that played well," said Bertman.

The following day, the team won the bronze medal, defeating Nicaragua 10-3 as Seth Greisinger retired 19 of the final 21 hitters he faced. But all that time and money were supposed to lead to gold. "To put two years of effort into it and end up like this, it's like taking a dream away," said catcher A.J. Hinch.

In the world of international baseball, Cuba always comes through in the must-win games. After dispatching Nicaragua 8-1 in the other semifinal, the Cubans won their second consecutive gold with a wild 13-9 victory against Japan.

The U.S. players, of course, denied they were looking past Japan to a gold-medal rematch with Cuba, which beat the USA 10-8 in a July 28 preliminary game. But if they were, they could almost be forgiven: In two games during the pre-Olympic tour, the USA hammered Japan 15-4 and 10-5. Then in Atlanta, the USA hit seven homers to beat Japan 15-5 in a round-robin game on July 25.

Things were different, though, in the semifinal, mostly because of a familiar nemesis of the U.S. team: veteran pitcher Masanori Sugiura, who allowed the USA only one homer and six hits in 5⅔ innings. Sugiura, 28, had appeared in Atlanta just twice in short stints because of a groin pull. But in the 1992 Olympics, Sugiura didn't allow a run in two appearances against the USA, covering 9⅓ innings, and at the 1994 World Championships, he struck out 17 U.S. hitters in a 6-0 blanking. "He carved us up," Hinch said of Sugiura's Atlanta work.

Still, with the No. 1 major league draft pick on the mound for the USA, the team had to like its chances. Instead, Kris Benson gave up three homers in his four-plus innings of work and left with the USA down 6-0. Benson had been literally unbeatable all year—except in must-win games. But he lost his only two starts in the College World Series as well as the Japan game. "If I had the chance to turn in all 21 wins I had this year for this one, I guess I would," Benson said.

Without the expected USA-Cuba matchup, the gold-medal game lost some of its luster. Things still got interesting: With Cuba up 6-2 in the fifth, third baseman Omar Linares failed to tag a runner heading to third base with two out. When Japan's Nobuhiko Matsunaka followed with a grand slam to tie the score, it looked like a potentially crucial misplay, but Linares atoned, hitting three homers on the night. Cuba hit eight in all in a victory that gave the Cubans a 50-game winning streak in official world tournaments.

Amateur play in baseball probably died with this summer's Olympics. On Sept. 21, in Lausanne, Switzerland, the International Baseball Association voted to make future competitions open, paving the way for "dream teams." The expectation of International Olympic Committee president Juan Antonio Samaranch is that major leaguers will be playing in Sydney in 2000, but the timing of those games (late September) makes that unlikely. That's too bad: A dream-team baseball tournament would be much more competitive than the ones in basketball have been.

—by Rick Lawes

1996 *Baseball Weekly*/ABCA Top 25 coaches' poll (college baseball)

▶1. **Louisiana State (52-15)** Poll points: 822 (32 No. 1 votes). Won College World Series 9-8 against Miami after winning South II Regional.

▶2. **Miami (Fla.) (50-14)** Poll points: 787. Lost in CWS final after winning Central I Regional.

▶3. **Florida (50-18)** Poll points: 736. Tied for third in CWS after winning East Regional.

▶4. **Clemson (51-17)** Poll points: 722. Tied for third in CWS after winning Atlantic Regional.

▶5. **Florida State (52-17)** Poll points: 676. Tied for fifth in CWS after winning East Regional.

▶6. **Alabama (50-19)** Poll points: 669. Tied for fifth in CWS after winning South I Regional.

▶7. **Wichita State (54-11)** Poll points: 643. Tied for seventh in CWS after winning Midwest Regional.

▶8. **Oklahoma State (45-21)** Poll points: 567. Tied for seventh in CWS after winning Central II Regional.

▶9. **Southern California (44-16)** Poll points: 552. Second place, Central II Regional.

▶10. **Cal State Northridge (52-18)** Poll points: 463. Second place, West Regional.

▶11. **Cal State Fullerton (45-16)** Poll points: 443. Third place, Midwest Regional.

▶12. **Texas Tech (49-15)** Poll points: 427. Third place, Central II Regional.

▶13. **Tennessee (43-20)** Poll points: 409. Second place, Atlantic Regional.

▶14. **Stanford (41-19)** Poll points: 366. Third place, West Regional.

▶15. **Rice (42-23)** Poll points: 298. Second place, Midwest Regional.

▶16. **UCLA (38-28)** Poll points: 277. Second place, Central I Regional.

▶17. **Virginia (44-21)** Poll points: 272. Second place, South I Regional.

▶18. **South Florida (47-19)** Poll points: 222. Third place, East Regional.

▶19. **Texas (39-24)** Poll points: 204. Tied for fourth, Central I Regional.

▶20. **Georgia Tech (40-24)** Poll points: 192. Second place, South II Regional.

▶21. **Georgia Southern (46-14)** Poll points: 158. Fourth place, Atlantic Regional.

▶22. **Nevada-Las Vegas (43-17)** Poll points: 127. Tied for fifth, South II Regional.

▶23. **Massachusetts (40-13)** Poll points: 121. Second place, East Regional.

▶24. **Mississippi State (38-24)** Poll points: 79. Tied for third, West Regional.

▶25. **South Alabama (42-17)** Poll points: 62. Tied for fifth, South I Regional.

CWS All-Stars

Miami lost in the finals of the 1996 College World Series but placed five players on the all-tournament team:

C	Tim Lanier, LSU
1B	Chris Moller, Alabama
2B	Rudy Gomez, Miami
3B	Pat Burrell, Miami
SS	Alex Cora, Miami
OF	Justin Bowles, LSU
OF	Michael DeCelle, Miami
OF	Brad Wilkerson, Florida
DH	Chuck Hazzard, Florida
P	J.D. Arteaga, Miami
P	Eddie Yarnall, LSU

Most Outstanding Player:
  Pat Burrell, Miami

College World Series wrap-up: Might of Morris pains the 'Canes

OK, so the best team at this year's College World Series probably didn't win. But the Louisiana State Tigers showed what a little belief, a little fight and, above all, a whole lot of luck can do for a team not playing its best.

When Warren Morris came to the plate at 3:29 p.m. on June 8 with two outs in the ninth, one man on, and his LSU team down a run, there was no reason to expect what was going to happen next. But somehow Morris, a left-handed batter who was still recovering from wrist surgery, turned on a curveball from Miami freshman Robbie Morrison. He jerked it about two rows deep into the right-field bleachers, just inside the foul pole. The final score read: LSU 9, Miami 8. In the 50-year history of the College World Series, it was the first time that the final game ended on a home run, let alone one that turned defeat into victory. "I think I only hit it about two-thirds of the way, and the guys on the bench blew it the rest of the way," Morris said.

That LSU won had to be a surprise to even the most ardent Tigers supporter. LSU committed 12 errors in four games and ended with one of the worst fielding percentages ever for a national champion. And the so-called Bayou Bombers had been anything but that during the series. The heart of the LSU lineup—SEC player of the year Eddy Furniss, third baseman Nathan Dunn and DH Brad Wilson—finished with just 11 hits and no homers in 50 at-bats. The Tigers had 125 homers in 63 games coming into the series, but hit just six in four CWS games in what is normally a hitter's park.

To make the final, LSU had to squeak past Florida 2-1, the first time all season the Tigers had won with less than three runs. It was also the first time they'd ever won in Omaha with less than five runs.

Morris is a walk-on, one of those rare college players who does not have a baseball scholarship. A zoology major, he carries a 3.73 grade-point average and plans to attend medical school when his baseball-playing days are over. But for a player who had to look to an equipment manager to find someone smaller than himself when he was a freshman, no one in College World Series history has ever come up with a bigger hit.

—by Rick Lawes

Clemson's Benson is nation's top player

Not only did Clemson junior fireballer Kris Benson receive the American Baseball Coaches Association's Howser Trophy for the top collegiate baseball player, but the Pittsburgh Pirates also made Benson the top pick during the June 4-6 draft.

Benson had been solid his first two years, going 7-3 and 8-3. But then the Kennesaw, Ga., native showed extra muscle and carried a 14-0 record into the College World Series before losing his first game of the year, 7-3 to Miami. More impressive was the kind of pitcher he had become. He struck out 193 batters in 149 innings (including 15 in that loss to Miami, the 10th time he hit double digits) while walking just 26. "In my 20 years of coaching he's far superior mentally to anyone I've ever had at 21 years of age," Clemson coach Jack Leggett said.

Back in June 1995, Benson had been among the final cuts from the U.S. national team formed to prepare for the Atlanta Olympics. In December, however, his improved command and increased bulk helped him make the team at the Olympic trials in Homestead, Fla. Though his Olympic performance was disappointing (17 IP, 11 ER), next spring he will start his pro journey. "I'm hoping to get up [to the majors] in three years, maybe late 1998," Benson said.

—by Rick Lawes

1997 college preview: Top contenders

▶**Louisiana State** (52-15 in 1996): With their third national championship in six seasons, the Tigers have become the pre-eminent college program. Coach Skip Bertman has some rebuilding to do, but a huge cornerstone is already in place: 6-foot-4 first baseman Eddy Furniss, who led the nation in homers (26) and RBI (103) last year. Sophomore southpaw Chris Demouy (10-3) leads the pitching staff.

▶**Florida** (50-18): The Gators were the surprise of college baseball, advancing to the College World Series in coach Andy Lopez's second year in Gainesville. Brad Wilkerson leads the Gators both at the plate (.407, 9 HR, 68 RBI) and on the mound (5-2, 2.97 ERA, 5 saves). But he won't be alone: DH Chuck Hazzard (18 HR) and third baseman Mark Ellis (.351) are also back.

▶**Stanford** (41-19): The Cardinal has a pitching staff to drool over. Coach Mark Marquess has the entire rotation back from '96: Junior Kyle Peterson (9-5, 3.69 ERA) and sophomores Chad Hutchinson (7-1, 3.30 ERA) and Jeff Austin (6-3, 3.63). There's also plenty of pop in the lineup, led by first baseman Jon Schaeffer (11 HR, 43 RBI) and center fielder Jody Gerut (.314, 5 HR, 42 RBI).

▶**Miami (Fla.)** (50-14): After last year's tough loss in the final, coach Jim Morris has the horses to get Miami back to Omaha for the third time in four years. Third baseman Pat Burrell (.484, 23 HR) and DH Rick Saggese (.339, 14 HR) will provide offense, while sophomore closer Robbie Morrison had 14 saves and a 1.68 ERA in '96.

▶**Florida State** (52-17): Coach Mike Martin's Seminoles reached Omaha for the seventh time in 10 years, and last year's young lineup has another year of maturity. Center fielder J.D. Drew (.386, 21 HR, 94 RBI) is an early candidate for player of the year, and he'll be joined by shortstop Brooks Badeaux (.355).

▶**Texas** (39-24): Augie Garrido takes over from Cliff Gustafson, who left Austin as Division I's all-time winningest coach, to become just the Longhorns' third skipper since 1940. Garrido will rely heavily on shortstop Kip Harkrider (.381, 43 RBI), who was one of the few sophomores on the U.S. Olympic team.

▶**Mississippi State** (38-24): Coach Ron Polk's veterans could get the Bulldogs back to Omaha for the first time since 1990. Left-hander Eric DuBose (10-4, 3.11 ERA), a late cut from the Olympic team, will lead a staff that includes Van Johnson (6-1, 3.09 ERA) and Scott Polk (3-5, 2.62 ERA, 3 saves). Infielder Rob Hauswald (.354, 16 HR, 63 RBI) also returns.

▶**Arizona State** (34-21): The Sun Devils were left out of the dance for the second consecutive year in '96, but Pat Murphy could make his first head-coaching trip to Omaha. Juniors Dan McKinley (.386, 9 HR, 57 RBI) and Mikel Moreno (.378, 11 HR) will lead ASU's offense, and the pitching is also stacked, led by closer Ryan Bradley and highly touted Ryan Mills.

▶**Cal State Fullerton** (45-16): Coach Augie Garrido moved to Texas, but with former associate coach George Horton taking over, the Titans shouldn't miss a beat. Outfielders Mark Kotsay and Jeremy Giambi are gone, but the pitching staff is strong with juniors Brent Billingsley (11-1, 2.76) and Scott Hild (8-3, 4.57). First baseman C.J. Ankrum (.304) leads the offense.

▶**Wichita State** (54-11): The winningest team in college baseball last year, the Shockers crashed and burned in Omaha. In '97 coach Gene Stephenson has an all-sophomore double-play combination of Kevin Hooper (.321) and Zach Sorensen (.307), plus 11-game winner Steve Foral.

—by Rick Lawes

Nostalgia

▶ **100 years of baseball at Tiger Stadium**
▶ **Charlie Metro's managerial tricks**

▶ **Orlando Cepeda's comeback**
▶ **The Yanks' forgotten shortstop**

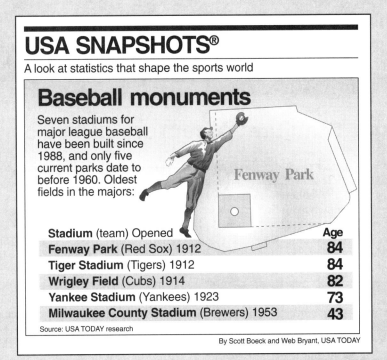

USA SNAPSHOTS®

A look at statistics that shape the sports world

Baseball monuments

Seven stadiums for major league baseball have been built since 1988, and only five current parks date to before 1960. Oldest fields in the majors:

Fenway Park

Stadium (team) Opened	Age
Fenway Park (Red Sox) 1912	**84**
Tiger Stadium (Tigers) 1912	**84**
Wrigley Field (Cubs) 1914	**82**
Yankee Stadium (Yankees) 1923	**73**
Milwaukee County Stadium (Brewers) 1953	**43**

Source: USA TODAY research

By Scott Boeck and Web Bryant, USA TODAY

Crowds have gathered to watch baseball at Michigan and Trumbull for 101 seasons.

Tiger Stadium: A century at the corner

In the first inning of the first game at Michigan and Trumbull, Dick Butler, center fielder for the Columbus Senators, was chasing a long fly ball hit by Detroit's player-manager George Stallings when Butler collided with a spectator who was crossing the field. While Butler lay stunned, Stallings circled the bases. Detroit ended up routing the visitors 17-2. It was Tuesday, April 28, 1896, and the unusual play was a fitting beginning to a century of intense fan involvement at the oldest continuously used address in U.S. professional team sports.

The Tigers of the Western League on that day had been christening Bennett Park before an overflow crowd of 8,000 fans. After the 1911 season, Bennett Park was torn down and replaced by Navin Field, the forerunner of Tiger Stadium. No other professional baseball team has played 100 years at the same site, but neither the Tigers nor Major League Baseball celebrated the centennial.

The club is busy laying plans for a new stadium—trying to raise $140 million from private investors—and in August finally defeated a legal challenge by the Tiger Stadium Fan Club over a $55 million state subsidy. The fate of the old stadium is not clear, but demolition is the most likely scenario if the Tigers build a new ballpark.

The site was once a peach and apple orchard, then a wooded picnic grounds, and finally a haymarket and lumberyard before George Arthur van der Beck acquired the land. The Tigers owner invested $10,000 to build a new park for his struggling club, which had been playing in tiny Boulevard Park on the east side of town.

In 1896, Detroit was a sleepy stove-making city of 250,000 in which Henry Ford was still an unknown inventor tinkering with engines. On a cool, clear morning, the Tigers and the Senators boarded brightly festooned trolley cars and led a throng of civic dignitaries and fans through the streets to the new ballpark.

The hastily-built park seated 5,000 fans, but an overflow crowd stood behind ropes around the outfield. At 3:30, cannons boomed as Wayne County treasurer Alex McLeod threw out the ceremonial first pitch. The wheelchair-bound catcher was Charlie Bennett, hero of the city's 1887 National League champions. He had lost his legs in a train accident in 1894. The park was named after him, and Bennett would catch the Opening Day first pitch every year until his death in 1927.

The original 1912 single-deck grandstand behind home plate is still a part of Tiger Stadium. A second deck was added to Navin Field in 1923, positioned directly above the lower deck to create what are widely acknowledged as baseball's best seats. In *Why Time Begins on Opening Day,* Thomas Boswell called this perch, a bare 90 feet away from home plate, "the best spot I've found to grasp the central aspect of the sport, the tense business being conducted between the pitcher and the hitter. It was here that I suddenly said to myself, 'So that's changing speeds.'"

After the Tigers won their first World Series, in 1935, owner Walter Briggs plowed his profits into an ambitious expansion, creating the first completely enclosed double-decked park in the majors. Briggs, an owner of several automotive parts plants, wanted to maximize affordable seating for his workers and their families and so created 25,000 out-field seats, including 11,000 in the bleachers. To squeeze in more in right field, he placed the upper deck 10 feet closer to home plate than the lower, creating the famous overhang, a home-run porch friendly to lefty sluggers such as Norm Cash and Darrell Evans. Tiger Stadium, as it was renamed in 1961, has seats that are, on average, the closest to the field in the majors, making it the premier fan-friendly ballpark.

The tradition of fans' being a part of the game has continued for the 100 years since Butler and the spectator collided on that first Opening Day. Notorious instances include a 1915 Yankees-Tigers brawl in which hundreds of fans joined the melee, and the 1934 World Series incident in which bleacher patrons, angry at the Cardinals' Ducky Medwick for spiking Tigers third baseman Marv Owen, forced Medwick off the field by pelting him with produce and garbage. In 1976, Tigers fans fell in love with Mark "The Bird" Fidrych, perhaps because they were seated close enough to see his heartfelt emotional expressions.

In a century of baseball, Michigan and Trumbull has hosted more pro baseball games than any other place on earth—at least 6,600 of them. More than 100 million spectators have seen more than 10,000 home runs, six World Series and three All-Star games. The National Football League's Detroit Lions also played there from 1938 through 1974.

The Tigers project that a new stadium, a mile from Michigan and Trumbull, will open in mid-1998. With the defeat of the Fan Club's lawsuit, the old stadium's future is precarious. Without the fame of Fenway Park or Wrigley Field, but their equal in tradition and accessibility, Tiger Stadium remains one of baseball's best-kept secrets, a no-frills park where the action on the field retains center stage.

—by Michael Betzold, co-author of Queen of Diamonds: The Tiger Stadium Story; *an updated edition is being produced by Northmont Publishing*

Charlie Metro's tricks of the trade

You've heard fielders time and again during a game. A pop fly goes up and someone yells, "I've got it." A base stealer takes off: "There he goes." Common enough shouts in a game, right? But what if the command is coming from an opposing coach? Just a little interactive bench jockeying, huh? But what if the base coach is a ventriloquist and the phantom voice is coming out of nowhere? And can a manager rest easy knowing his counterpart is studying up on handwriting analysis in the opposing dugout? Yet another mystery of the game or an invasion of the occult?

In the early 1960s, when I was at the helm of the Chicago Cubs, I tried to use ventriloquism and graphology to snatch whatever wins I could for the club. Major league managers will try a lot of things to win.

Now some managers use computers to predict tendencies. Sign stealing, lineup shuffling, baiting umpires, reverse psychology, disguised moves and decoying are all part of the weave of the game. But I am the first and only skipper to try to throw a voice on the field and collect other managers' autographs for something more than souvenirs.

In 1962, I got my first opportunity to manage in the major leagues when the Cubs hired me as one of their "college of coaches." The Cubs had used a rotating-managers system in 1961. But when it came to my turn in 1962, owner Phil Wrigley let me manage the Cubs the rest of the way.

I got the idea of learning ventriloquism probably as early as 1946, in the minors. Sacramento's third baseman, Steve Mesner, had a high-pitched voice. He could disrupt plays occasionally. I thought if only I could throw my voice on the field, I could manipulate plays our way.

There was a husband-and-wife ventriloquism act playing down on State Street in Chicago. I attended their performance and became friends with them. They

agreed to teach me the skill. But I just couldn't get the hang of it; I didn't have the right voice box or something. One time, however, when I was coaching first base against the Giants, I succeeded in distracting their first baseman, Orlando Cepeda, from catching a foul pop. I thought he was angry enough to pinch my head off.

Voice-throwing didn't pan out, but graphology did. I had read that during World War II, General Eisenhower had selected his officers partly on the basis of their handwriting. I wanted to get a bead on the other managers. I had played for Casey Stengel at Oakland in 1946 and managed against Freddie Hutchinson in the Coast League, but I didn't know much about the others. Their handwriting could be some sort of giveaway about their styles. I mentioned this to a friend, who knew of a famous handwriting expert in California. I got each of the managers to sign a scorecard and signed it myself. With the help of a go-between, I had the graphologist analyze the autographs.

I found out that in most cases, the profile was right on target. For example, Walt Alston of the Dodgers managed his club just as the expert diagnosed: "Friendly, obliging and good-natured. Appeals to the players' sportsmanship, fun, gamesmanship. Not critical or carping. Warm, genuine reassurance; emphasizes courage and unselfishness. Good strategist. Plans far ahead, figures the whole season. Impulsive and instinctive, responds with intuition and repetition. Not very profound or scientific; often inaccurate. Look for errors in judgment due to too casual an attitude. Be opportunistic with this man.... Favors long hitting or throwing. Overly optimistic. Loves the game."

Danny Murtaugh of the Pirates was indeed "a good and dangerous manager of baseball.... executive, persistent and brilliant."

1997 BASEBALL WEEKLY ALMANAC

The scoop on the Phillies' Gene Mauch read: "Conducts his team like an orchestra leader. Coordinates, harmonizes. Thinks quickly, reacts smartly with certainty of aim. Diagnoses situations like a doctor."

The Cardinals' Johnny Keane was "demanding, exact, persistent, insistent and resistant. His ideal [was] beauty, aesthetic precision. His taste [was] Renaissance, mental and physical symmetry."

Hutchinson, who had won the pennant with the Reds the previous year, was "persevering, industrious" and had "power of will," but he would "scheme up plays that are overcomplicated" with "confusing results not justifying the energy expended."

The portrait of Casey Stengel was quite provocative: "A pioneer, explorer, discoverer type. Goes into things with great verve and enthusiasm. Assumes responsibility in a paternal manner. Outspoken and unambiguous. Mentally objective, emotionally subjective. Rational, ethical, spiritually sincere. A real sales manager, wins through conviction, not persuasion. He is modest in ego, noble and grand in conception, demanding more and expecting more from his men after he shows them how to do it, using his great originality which always appears at the end of the game. His script shows that he has really studied the history of the game. He acts like a psychiatrist to his boys—open, receptive, giving standards that are capable of flexibility only when necessary. He loves to excel, loves to surprise you at the finish, loves the new."

And Charlie Metro of the Cubs? Here's how the graphologist characterized me: "Objective, matter-of-fact, efficient. Knows and likes his material, and is master of it. Purposive, pursues goal without interruption. Steady, quiet, strong effective personality. No showmanship. Not decorative except order and arrangement. Inclined to be serious. Conservative. Is exact. Likes simplicity. Needs enthusiasm and persuasiveness. Appeals too much to the player's reason, should appeal more to their values and ideals. Very observant. Conservative, dislikes

change. Possibly narrow-minded but very good insight. A good leader in times of peace but not in times of war. He is sane and sober-minded. Best balance of all the managers."

I disagreed only a bit. I thought I was a better manager in the clutch—"in times of war"—but I took some of the criticism to heart and worked to improve myself as a manager. The Cubs had a rough season that year. We finished ninth, ahead of only the Mets. We had some great players on the team, including future Hall of Famers Ernie Banks, Lou Brock and Billy Williams, but we were a little thin at catching, and our pitching staff had a combined ERA of about 4.50. But I've always wondered, if we'd had the pitching and catching talent to match up with the other clubs, how many games those graphology studies might have helped win. I even thought of getting the players' signatures, too.

I had always been something of an innovator. In high school back in Pennsylvania, I invented the batting tee, and later I introduced batting cages to warm up pinch hitters, the manager's dugout lineup card and some new scouting techniques. If only I had been able to throw my voice. We would have won the pennant, for sure. The Series? Well, maybe.

So, the next time you're playing or managing at Coors Field and you hear a strange voice shout, "It's all mine," or a man with a pixie grin asks for your autograph, don't look at me. I'm just sitting up behind the third base dugout with my hands in my pockets.

—*by Charlie Metro and Tim Altherr*

Orlando Cepeda is happier now than he was when he missed making the Hall of Fame in 1994.

'Cha Cha' Finds a Different Rhythm

"*Good morning*!" The booming voice splits the crisp morning air and echoes past the sleepy suburban tract homes of the Suisun City, Calif., neighborhood. A dark-skinned, youthful face—the product of a Puerto Rican heritage and many hours in the sun—breaks slowly into an awkward smile, challenging the brilliance of the morning sun.

His powerful frame fills the space in the doorway as he opens his home and his heart. At 58 years old and 21 years into retirement, Orlando Cepeda still looks like he could hit one out of the ballpark.

He has been called "Cha Cha" because of his love of Latin jazz. He was the first to bring a tape player into the clubhouse, long before it became fashionable, and the first to be banned from doing so. Most fondly, he is known as "Baby Bull," after his father, Perucho, "The Bull."

His middle-class home is adjacent to a field running up to the mountains near California's wine country. The site was carefully selected by one whose previous imprisonment has instilled an uncommon love of freedom. The walls of this modest home, where he lives with his wife, Mirian, and their 19-year-old son, Ali, are lined with photographs. Each room is adorned by trophies and awards. A

Buddhist altar reflects the faith at the center of his life for the past 10 years. "We chant first," he says purposefully.

Cepeda is comfortable with himself. His manner reveals nothing of the racism he has endured. When he was in San Francisco, he heard people question Latin players' willingness to work. A former manager, Alvin Dark, forbade Latin players from speaking Spanish on the team bus and was quoted as saying black and Latin players lacked mental alertness and pride. By the end of his 17-year major league career, Cepeda had erased any doubts about his ability to play through the insults and the injuries. Afterward, however, a conviction for smuggling marijuana led to 10 months in a Puerto Rican jail in 1975 and financially ruined him. It probably also killed his chance of being elected to the Hall of Fame by the writers.

"All my life, whatever I get, I have to work very, very hard. Nothing comes easy for me," Cepeda says, relaxing in the living room. He never wanted to be anything but a baseball player. "I grew up in baseball. It comes with the package," he says with a shrug of his massive shoulders. Growing up in the shadow of "The Bull" in Puerto Rico, Cepeda was told he would never be as good as his father. The elder Cepeda, a victim of baseball's color barrier, never made the majors but was known as "the Babe Ruth of the Caribbean."

Orlando's career in the USA began in 1955 when he signed a contract with the Giants for $500. He immediately was forced to use the money to bury his father. Depressed, Cepeda didn't want to return to the USA, but his mother reminded him of his father's dream for him. Surrounded by poverty and "too many brothers ... I did it to make money. I don't know if we would have survived in Puerto Rico," Cepeda says. He went on to become the National League Rookie of the Year in 1958.

Cepeda powered 379 career home runs, had nine seasons of 95-plus RBI and a .297 career batting average. He played in six All-Star Games and three World Series. In 1993, the same people who once scorned and ostracized him because of his drug involvement chose him for the Puerto Rican Hall of Fame. "They really went to bat for me, 100 percent," he says, putting his hands on his heart. "The support of my own people, that's the best."

Cepeda rubs the knee of one leg. Both knees have been replaced in the past two years. He has no bitterness. "I got into a problem with the law. There's always an excuse to put you up or put you down ... lots of reasons. I'm going forward," he says with a broad smile. "It's a matter of karma. It means, by your own actions you got yourself into this situation, and by your own actions you can turn it around." With his hands placed together as if in prayer, Cepeda says, "Buddhism is life."

Two years ago, in his final year on the Hall of Fame ballot, when he learned he again had fallen short Cepeda declared to the media, "It's a victory." He says he was shocked for about 10 minutes after hearing the results but then determined, "It's happening. I have to go forward ... be positive and keep going." Leaning forward, very animated, he says, "Even though I didn't get in, I won—big time. Over myself, over a lot of people. I'm just trying to clean up my life, be a better per-

son. There's a reason; Buddhism *is* reason. I will deal with it because it's there."

As baseball was Perucho Cepeda's dream for his son, Orlando holds the same aspirations for his own sons. "Whatever you do, you like for your sons to follow in your footsteps." Unlike his father, however, Cepeda says he only talks to his sons about baseball—he doesn't push. Ali plays right field for his high school team, and Malcolm signed a minor league contract to play first base in the Giants system.

When asked if he would have done anything differently, Cepeda says without hesitation, "Start chanting right away. I chant every day. Right now, I'm living my best life."

—*Jacquelyn A. Estrella, a freelance writer in San Francisco*

Stirnweiss was top AL weapon in war

Not many fans would put George Stirnweiss on the list of distinguished New York Yankees second basemen, a list with such stars as Tony Lazzeri and Joe Gordon. Yet in 1945, Stirnweiss won the only batting championship by a Yankees second baseman.

True, there was a war on, and Joe DiMaggio, Ted Williams and Hank Greenberg, among others, were in the service. Nevertheless, there remained behind many excellent players who, for a variety of reasons, were not in the service— Stirnweiss was 4-F because of ulcers.

In 1944 Stirnweiss was arguably the best every-day player in the American League, and in 1945 he proved he was the best. Among the players active in one or both seasons were Cleveland's Lou Boudreau, St. Louis's Vern Stephens, Boston's Bobby Doerr and Detroit's Rudy York.

The 5-foot-8 Stirnweiss was a native New Yorker whose nickname, "Snuffy," came from either a comic book character, Snuffy Smith, or a vaudeville character, Snuffy the Cabman.

A star college running back at North

Carolina, he was drafted by the NFL's Chicago Cardinals in 1940, but he turned down the $4,000 salary offer and signed with the New York Yankees instead. After three years in the minors, the Yankees brought him to the big leagues in 1943. He batted .219 that year in 83 games for the world champions, after replacing Frank Crosetti at shortstop in midseason. In 1944, when Joe Gordon went into the Army, Stirnweiss moved to second base.

Like all big-league teams during the war, the Yankees played a patchwork lineup of old-timers, kids, 4-Fs and an occasional major-league-caliber player. In 1944 Stirnweiss was their best player. He batted .319 and played all 154 games. He led the league in hits with 205, and his 16 triples tied teammate Johnny Lindell for the league high. His 296 total bases were just one behind the leader. But the best was yet to come.

In 1945 Stirnweiss, again playing in each of the Yankees' games, led the AL in seven offensive departments, some by a wide margin. Still, Hal Newhouser of the Tigers, who led the league with 25 wins and a 1.81 ERA, deservedly won his second consecutive MVP award.

Newhouser's teammate, second baseman Eddie Mayo on the pennant-winning Tigers, finished second, just ahead of Stirnweiss, but the numbers don't justify the outcome: Although Mayo's fielding percentage was higher, he had 106 fewer putouts, 99 fewer assists, participated in 28 fewer double plays and batted only .285.

Newsweek columnist John Lardner wrote, "It is possible to imagine putting Stirnweiss on an all-star team in any year, so skillful and valuable has this young reformed football player become," and no less an authority than Babe Ruth claimed, "That sawed-off runt playing second base is the only ballplayer who could've gotten a uniform when the Yankees really had a ball club."

On Sept. 30, the final day of the 1945 season, Stirnweiss trailed Chicago's Tony Cuccinello in the batting race, .308 to .306. The Yanks were at home against Boston, while Chicago had a doubleheader with Cleveland. Rain, however, canceled the games in Chicago.

In New York, Stirnweiss doubled in the first and singled in the third. He was still trailing Cuccinello, .30745 to .30846, as he took his last at bat in the eighth. He came through with a single to right to raise his average to .30854.

Stirnweiss is the only major leaguer to win a batting title without ever having led at any time during the season. The .309 was the lowest to lead the AL since 1905.

With the war over, Joe Gordon returned to the Yankees in 1946, and Stirnweiss split the season playing second and third. When New York traded Gordon to Cleveland, Stirnweiss was the team's regular second baseman for 1947 and '48. He lost the job in 1949 to Jerry Coleman, and a year later the Yankees sent him to the St. Louis Browns as part of an eight-player trade. He finished his playing career in Cleveland and then managed at Binghamton and Schenectady in the Yankee farm system before leaving baseball.

Stirnweiss was working in financial management and was director of the *New York Journal-American* sandlot baseball program when he died in a New York commuter-train accident on Sept. 15, 1958. He was only 39 years old and left a wife and six children.

—by Lyle Spatz, chairman of the records committee of the Society for American Baseball Research